CARRIAGE OF GOODS BY SEA

CARRIAGE OF GOODS BY SEA

STEPHEN GIRVIN

OXFORD

UNIVERSITY PRESS

OXFORD

UNIVERSITY PRESS

Great Clarendon Street, Oxford OX2 6DP

Oxford University Press is a department of the University of Oxford.
It furthers the University's objective of excellence in research, scholarship,
and education by publishing worldwide in

Oxford New York

Auckland Cape Town Dar es Salaam Hong Kong Karachi
Kuala Lumpur Madrid Melbourne Mexico City Nairobi
New Delhi Shanghai Taipei Toronto

With offices in

Argentina Austria Brazil Chile Czech Republic France Greece
Guatemala Hungary Italy Japan Poland Portugal Singapore
South Korea Switzerland Thailand Turkey Ukraine Vietnam

Oxford is a registered trade mark of Oxford University Press
in the UK and in certain other countries

Published in the United States
by Oxford University Press Inc., New York

British Library Cataloguing in Publication Data
Data available

Library of Congress Cataloging in Publication Data
Data available

Typeset by Cepha Imaging Private Ltd, Bangalore, India
Printed in Great Britain
on acid-free paper by
Biddles Ltd, King's Lynn

ISBN 978–0–19–876458–8

1 3 5 7 9 10 8 6 4 2

PREFACE

My principal aim in writing this book on the Carriage of Goods by Sea has been to add to the rather small store of one-volume texts covering the whole subject, by way of counterpoint to increased specialization within this field of the law. My conviction is that there is a place for a one-volume text which provides an overview of the subject in its entirety.

I have, I believe, tried to take a fresh look at the subject, given the broad canvas of the undertaking. The reader opening this book for the first time will find that the subject matter is discussed within eight broad themes. Part I contains a single chapter which is designed to introduce the major actors and contracts and the underlying commercial basis for the subject as a whole. I felt strongly that there should be some attempt to provide this framework at the outset.

Part II is devoted to bills of lading and other documents of carriage. Here I have tried to follow a broadly temporal treatment of bills of lading and other documents, starting with those documents which are typically issued before shipment and introducing next the many types of bills of lading which are likely to be encountered in practice. I consider also other documents of carriage which are encountered to a greater or lesser degree, namely sea waybills and ship's delivery orders. I then consider the issue and transfer of bills of lading. This is followed by chapters which are linked to the traditional functions of the bill of lading as a receipt, as the contract of carriage, and as a document of title. I then consider the position of third parties and bill of lading terms. This necessarily includes discussion of such matters as bailment and the use of Himalaya clauses. The next three chapters are devoted to the carrier's delivery obligation, the possible alteration of these obligations, and the sometimes complex interrelationship between charterparties and bills of lading. There is, finally, some consideration of paperless alternatives to the bill of lading.

Part III examines domestic and international regulation in the carriage of goods by sea. There are chapters on early domestic legislation and then a consideration of international movements towards uniform cargo liability regimes. Inevitably, the focus here is on the Hague Rules and later modifications of those Rules in the Visby and SDR Protocols. This is followed by a consideration of the movement to the Hamburg Rules and subsequent developments. Part III then shifts to consider the legal effect and scope of application of the Hague and Hague–Visby Rules.

Part IV of the book is concerned with the shipper's responsibilities. There are three principal chapters and these consist of a discussion of the shipper's responsibilities at common law, his obligation to pay freight, and his obligations under the Hague and Hague–Visby Rules.

Part V switches to a consideration of the carrier's responsibilities. The chapters in this part are therefore devoted to the carrier's obligation to provide a seaworthy ship, not to deviate, and to proceed with utmost despatch. Finally, there is an analysis of these (and other) obligations under the Hague and Hague–Visby Rules.

Part VI is concerned with the carrier's rights and immunities. This part includes an analysis of the carrier's right of lien, both at common law and contractually, his right to rely on exception clauses and, perhaps most important of all, his right to limit his liability. The limitation of liability chapter includes coverage of the carrier's right to limit his liability 'per package or unit' and globally under the 1976 LLMC and the 1996 Protocol.

Part VII is concerned with the subject of charterparties. There are two chapters which deal with voyage charterparties, one on general issues as to responsibilities connected with loading and discharge and the provision of cargo, and a subsequent chapter on the crucially important topic of laytime and demurrage. There is a single chapter on time charterparties, which, though covering most of the traditional topics, also considers the mechanism for the settlement of claims in the Interclub Agreement.

Part VIII of the book is concerned with cargo claims and grouped here are three chapters, one on frustration of the contract of carriage, one on limitation of time (or prescription), and a final chapter which examines admiralty claims. I felt that there should be a chapter on admiralty claims, because it seemed to me that one could not write about the substantive law and ignore one of the main vehicles for the enforcement of claims.

The appendices contain the most important statutes, a selection of standard forms representing the areas covered in the book, and a list of the signatories to the Hague Rules, the Visby and SDR Protocols, and the Hamburg Rules.

Inevitably, there are omissions. Although there is a broad coverage of most of the main topics in the carriage of goods by sea, I elected to omit coverage of two significant areas, namely conflict of laws issues, and damages. Both are, in themselves, substantial and complex areas of the law well covered in other accounts. Likewise, the section on cargo claims might have benefited from coverage of maritime arbitration, but this was omitted for similar reasons.

Originally, I had hoped to write a book which would incorporate all the main legal developments in leading commonwealth countries in a systematic way. I soon realized, however, that I faced an impossible task. It was difficult enough to keep pace with developments in the United Kingdom, let alone in a host of other commonwealth countries. Thus, while many commonwealth developments are indeed referred to, I do not claim that these references are systematic and comprehensive.

A further decision which confronted me in the writing of this book was what to do about what is now known as the 'Draft Convention on Carriage [wholly] or [partly by] Sea'. At an earlier point, I was becoming convinced that it would be impossible to write a book on the carriage of goods by sea in the first decade of the twenty-first century without trying to interweave some of the proposed changes into the fabric of the book. In the end, however, I elected not to do so, principally because the Draft has undergone continuous change and review. More importantly, the real risk of never finishing this book forced me to abandon any hope of trying to make sense of what is now an enormously complex and comprehensive Draft. No doubt the time will come when many books will have to be devoted to it.

This project has had a protracted genesis and work on it atrophied at points as my life straddled three continents. Inevitably, it is not possible to complete a big project such as this without the support of a large number of individuals who have, either knowingly or unwittingly, contributed to its eventual completion. I thought it right that I should name those who have assisted me.

I must record my thanks to the School of Law at the University of Nottingham for giving me the opportunity to develop my interest in this subject and in the field of maritime law generally. Respective Heads of School there were especially supportive and I want to thank Michael Bridge (now at UCL) and Geoffrey Morse (now a colleague in Birmingham) for early encouragement and support. Additionally, I should like to thank Howard Bennett and James Fawcett for their encouragement in matters maritime.

I also thank the Faculty of Law at the National University of Singapore (NUS), where a substantial part of the writing was undertaken. To the Dean, Tan Cheng Han, and most especially the then Vice-Dean, Bob Beckman, and the helpful staff of the CJ Koh Law Library, I record my gratitude. I should also like to thank my NUS colleague, Yeo Hwee Ying, for taking me under her wing throughout my time in Singapore. She and her family showed me great generosity and hospitality. Outside the Faculty, I would like to thank Leonard Chia, the Legal Committee of the Singapore Shipping Association (SSA), and the members of the Committee of the Singapore Maritime Law Association, for their friendship and the opportunity to work on a range of maritime law matters.

I have had the good fortune to work with two distinguished maritime lawyers. I would like to thank John Hare of the University of Cape Town, who on three occasions invited me to co-teach his graduate students in the Shipping Law Unit at the Faculty of Law. I learned much from him (and from them). I owe a great debt of gratitude to Neale Gregson, my good friend and co-teacher on maritime courses at the National University of Singapore. I cannot imagine a more pleasant or knowledgeable colleague to have had the pleasure of working with and I learnt much from his great experience as a practising maritime lawyer.

When work commitments and the demands of writing this book seemed overwhelming, I have been fortunate to count on professional colleagues and friends in the law who have supported me in ways too numerous to mention. I would like to single out Neil Boister, Simone Degeling, Paolo Galizzi, Paul Myburgh, Ian MacDuff, Tom Poole, and Keith Wotherspoon.

No less important, however, have been my many friends outside the law who have provided welcome distraction and companionship. Here I would like to express my thanks to Michael and Jenny Davidson, Suzanne Innes-Kent, Mark Hacking and Elizabeth Johnson, and my goddaughter, Charlotte Hacking, Edem (Joe) Kuenyehia, and Philip Rushforth. In particular, I should like to thank Joe, who stepped in at the eleventh hour to help with last minute proof-reading and checking.

Students stand out as well. Over the years, many provided willing research assistance and helped me through their questions. At the risk of forgetfulness, I thank Colin Chow, Marco Crusafio, Chinyere Ezeoke, Clara Feng, Charmaine Fu, Niels Friborg, Craig Johnson, Thulasi Kamalanathan, Rikke Laursen, Shaun Lee, Karin Lehmann, Alberto Lopez, Darrell Low, Jason Mantovan, Maureen Poh, Ooi Zhao Rong, Anton Roets, Christos Roussos, Daniel Teo, Marius van Niekerk, and Zhou Ping.

Finally, no project such as this one could possibly be completed without the love and support of those closest to me. I single out here my most supportive and loving family. My parents, my late father, Brian, and my mother, May, and my two brothers, Craig and Andrew and their families, have stood behind me every step of the way. In the last few years, Henry Fong has been a tower of strength to me, both in Singapore and on my return to the UK. To each and every one of these, my gratitude knows no bounds.

My publishers, Oxford University Press, have waited an inordinately long time for this book. I am grateful to them for their indulgence. In particular, I wish to thank Rachel Mullaly and Wendy Lynch who in the past few years have had to bear the brunt of my dilatoriness. Finally, I thank Darcy Ahl and Rob Dickinson for their kind assistance and attention to fine detail in turning the manuscript into the final published work. Any remaining omissions or errors rest with me.

The law is stated as I believe it to be on 30 April 2006, although some later changes have been incorporated, where possible.

Stephen Girvin
Birmingham
St Alban's Day
2006

ACKNOWLEDGEMENTS

The publishers and author wish to acknowledge with thanks the permission given by the following bodies to reprint material from the copyright sources indicated:

The Baltic and International Maritime Council (BIMCO)
<www.bimco.dk>
Conlinebill and Congenbill
Gencon 1994 charterparty
NYPE 93 charterparty

The International Group of P & I Clubs
<www.igpandi.org>
The NYPE Inter-Club Agreement 1996

The Office of Public Sector Information
Carriage of Goods by Sea Act 1971
Carriage of Goods by Sea Act 1992

CONTENTS—SUMMARY

IV THE RESPONSIBILITIES OF THE SHIPPER

V THE OBLIGATIONS OF THE CARRIER

VI THE RIGHTS AND IMMUNITIES OF THE CARRIER

VII CHARTERPARTIES

VIII CARGO CLAIMS

CONTENTS

I INTRODUCTION

1. The Business of Carriage of Goods

II BILLS OF LADING AND OTHER DOCUMENTS OF CARRIAGE

2. Shipping Documents Issued before Shipment

3. Types of Bills of Lading

4. Other Documents of Carriage

III INTERNATIONAL AND DOMESTIC REGULATION

Contents

V THE OBLIGATIONS OF THE CARRIER

VIII CARGO CLAIMS

TABLES OF CASES

AUSTRALIA

CANADA

FRANCE

HONG KONG

PAKISTAN

SINGAPORE

London Arbitration

UNITED STATES OF AMERICA

TABLE OF LEGISLATION

BIBLIOGRAPHY

Abbott (1984) — see Aspinall and Moore (1984)

Ashburner, Walter, (ed), *The Rhodian Sea-Law* (1909)

Aspinall, JP, & Moore, HS, *Abbott's Treatise of the Law Relative to Merchant Ships and Seamen* 14th edn (Abingdon, Professional Books reprint, 1984)

Benjamin (2002) — See Guest (2002)

Bennett, Howard, *Law of Marine Insurance* 2nd edn (Oxford, Oxford University Press, 2006)

Bennett, WP, *The History and Present Position of the Bill of Lading as a Document of Title to Goods* (Cambridge, Cambridge University Press, 1914)

Berlingieri, Francesco, *Berlingieri on Arrest of Ships* 3rd edn (London, LLP, 2000)

Berlingieri, Francesco, (ed), *The Travaux Préparatoires of the Hague Rules and of the Hague–Visby Rules* (Antwerp, CMI, 1997)

Berman, Harold J, *Law and Revolution: The Formation of the Western Legal Tradition* (Harvard, Harvard University Press,1983)

Boisson, Philippe, *Safety at Sea: Policies, Regulations and International Law* (Paris, Bureau Veritas, 1999)

Bourguignon, Henry J, *Sir William Scott, Lord Stowell, Judge of the High Court of Admiralty 1798-1828* (Cambridge, Cambridge University Press, 1987)

Boyd, SC, Burrows, AS, and Foxton, D, *Scrutton on Charterparties* 20th edn (London, Sweet & Maxwell, 1996)

Branch, Alan E, *Elements of Shipping* 7th edn (London, Chapman & Hall, 1996)

Bridge, Michael, *International Sale of Goods: Law and Practice* (Oxford, Clarendon Press, 1999)

Bridge, Michael, *Personal Property Law* 3rd edn (Oxford, Clarendon Press, 2002)

Brodie, Peter, *Commercial Shipping Handbook* 2nd edn (London, Informa, 2006)

Brodie, Peter, *Dictionary of Shipping Terms* (London, LLP, 2003)

Bugden, Paul, *Freight Forwarding and Goods in Transit* (London, Sweet & Maxwell, 1999)

Carver (2005) — see Treitel & Reynolds (2005)

Clarke, MA, *Aspects of the Hague Rules* (The Hague, Martinus Nijhoff, 1976)

Cole, Sanford D, *The Hague Rules Explained* (London, Effingham Wilson, 1924)

Cooke, Julian, Young, Timothy, Taylor, Andrew, Kimball, John D, Martowski, David, and Lambert, LeRoy, *Voyage Charters* 2nd edn (London, LLP, 2001)

Coote, Brian, *Exception Clauses* (London, Sweet & Maxwell, 1964)

Davies, Donald, *Commencement of Laytime* 4th edn (London, Informa, 2006)

Davies, Martin, & Dickey, Anthony, *Shipping Law* 3rd edn (Pyrmont, Law Book Co, 2004)

Davis, Mark, *Bareboat Charters* 2nd edn (London, LLP, 2005)

Debattista, Charles, *The Sale of Goods Carried by Sea* 2nd edn (London, Butterworths, 1998)

de la Rue, Colin, and Anderson, Charles B, *Shipping and the Environment* (London, LLP, 1998)

Dor, Stephane, *Bills of Lading Clauses and the Brussels International Convention of 1924* 2nd edn (London, Witherby & Co Ltd, 1960)

Faber, Diana, *Multimodal Transport: Avoiding Legal Problems* (London, LLP, 1997)

Farthing, Bruce, and Brownrigg, Mark, *Farthing on International Shipping* 3rd edn
  (London, LLP, 1997)

Fisher, Christopher, and Lux, Jonathan, *Bunkers: An Analysis of the Practical, Technical
  and Legal Issues* 2nd edn (London, LLP, 1994)

Gardiner, Robert (ed), *The Shipping Revolution: The Modern Merchant Ship*
  (London, Conway Maritime Press, 1992)

Gardiner, Robert (ed), *The Golden Age of Shipping: The Classic Merchant Ship 1900–1960*
  (London, Conway Maritime Press, 1994)

Gaskell, Nicholas (ed), *Limitation of Shipowners Liability: The New Law*
  (London, Sweet & Maxwell, 1986)

Gaskell, Nicholas, Asariotis, Regina, and Baatz, Yvonne, *Bills of Lading: Law and
  Contracts* (London, LLP, 2000)

Gilmore, Grant, and Black, Charles L Jr, *The Law of Admiralty* 2nd edn
  (Mineola, The Foundation Press, 1975)

Glass, David, *Freight Forwarding and Multimodal Transport Contracts*
  (London, LLP, 2004)

Gold, Edgar, Chircop, Aldo, and Kindred, Hugh, *Maritime Law* (Toronto,
  Irwin Law, 2003)

Griggs, Patrick, Williams, Richard, and Farr, Jeremy, *Limitation of Liability for Maritime
  Claims* 4th edn (London, LLP, 2005)

Grönfors, Kurt (ed), *Damage from goods* (Göteborg, 1978)

Guest, AG (ed), *Benjamin's Sale of Goods* 6th edn (London, Sweet & Maxwell, 2002)

Hare, John, *Shipping Law & Admiralty Jurisdiction in South Africa* (Kenwyn, Juta & Co
  Ltd, 1999)

Hayuth, Yehuda, *Intermodality: Concept and Practice* (Colchester, LLP, 1987)

Hazelwood, Stephen J, *P & I Clubs: Law and Practice* 3rd edn (London, LLP, 2000)

Hill, Christopher, Robertson, Bill, and Hazelwood, Steven, *An Introduction to P & I* 2nd
  edn (London, LLP, 1996)

Hill, DJ, *Freight Forwarders* (London, Stevens & Sons, 1972)

Holmes, OW, *The Common Law* (Boston, Little Brown, 1881)

Honka, Hannu (ed), *New Carriage of Goods by Sea: The Nordic Approach* (Åbo, Åbo
  Akademis tryckeri, 1997)

Hooke, Norman, *Maritime Casualties 1963–1996* 2nd edn (London, LLP, 1997)

Hutchison, Geoffrey, *Roscoe's Admiralty Jurisdiction and Practice* 5th edn (Abingdon,
  Professional Books Reprint, 1987)

Huybrechts, Marc, *International Encyclopaedia of Laws: Transport Law* vols 1–3
  (The Hague, Kluwer, 2002)

Ibbetson, David, *A Historical Introduction to the Law of Obligations* (Oxford, Oxford
  University Press, 1999)

Jack, Raymond, Malek, Ali, and Quest, David, *Documentary Credits: the law and practice
  of documentary credits including standby credits and demand guarantees* 3rd edn
  (London, Butterworths, 2001)

Jackson, DC, *Enforcement of Maritime Claims* 4th edn (London, LLP, 2005)

Kegels, Tony (ed), *The Hamburg Rules: A Choice for the EEC* (Antwerp, Maklu
  Uitgevers, 1994)

Kendall, Lane C, and Buckley, James J, *The Business of Shipping* 7th edn (Centreville, Cornell Maritime Press, 2001)

Kindred, Hugh, and Brooks, Mary, *Multimodal Transport Rules* (The Hague, Kluwer, 1997)

Kiralfy, AKR, *Potter's Historical Introduction to English Law* (London, Sweet & Maxwell, 1958)

Knauth, Arnold W, *The American Law of Ocean Bills of Lading* 4th edn (Baltimore, American Maritime Cases, 1953)

Lloyd's Survey Handbook 7th edn (London, LLP, 1999)

Lüddeke, Christof, *Marine Claims* 2nd edn (London, LLP, 1996)

Mankabady, Samir (ed), *The Hamburg Rules on the Carriage of Goods by Sea* (Leiden, AW Sijthoff, 1978)

Markesinis, BS, *Butterworth Lectures 1990–1991* (London, Butterworths, 1992)

Marsden, Reginald G (ed), *Select Pleas in the Court of Admiralty* (Vol 1: 1390–1545) (London, Selden Society Vol VI, 1894)

Marsden, Reginald G, (ed), *Select Pleas in the Court of Admiralty* (Vol 2: 1547–1602) (London, Selden Society Vol XI, 1897)

McGregor, Harvey, *McGregor on Damages* 13th edn (London, Sweet & Maxwell, 2003)

Meeson, Nigel, *Admiralty Jurisdiction and Practice* 3rd edn (London, LLP, 2003)

Mitchelhill, Alan, *Bills of Lading: Law and Practice* (London, Chapman and Hall, 1982)

Myburgh, Paul, 'New Zealand' in M Huybrechts (ed), *International Encyclopaedia of Laws: Transport* (The Hague, Kluwer, 2002)

Packard, William V, *Voyage Estimating* 2nd edn (London, Fairplay, 1981)

Packard, William V, *Sea-trading* vol 2 (London, Fairplay, 1996)

Palmer, NE, *Bailment* 2nd edn (Sydney, Law Book Co, 1991)

Palmer, NE, and McKendrick, E, *Interests in Goods* (London, LLP, 1998)

Pritchard, MJ, and Yale, DEC (eds), *Hale and Fleetwood on Admiralty Jurisdiction* (London, Selden Society, 1993)

Richardson, John, *A Guide to the Hague and Hague–Visby Rules* 3rd edn (London, LLP, 1994)

Richardson, John, *The Merchants Guide* (London, P & O Nedlloyd, 2003)

Rogers, Philip, Strange, John, and Studd, Brian, *Coal: Carriage by Sea* 2nd edn (London, LLP, 1997)

Rose, FD, *General Average: Law and Practice* 2nd edn (London, LLP, 2005)

Rose, Francis D (ed), *Lex Mercatoria: Essays on International Commercial Law in Honour of Francis Reynolds* (London, LLP, 2000)

Sanborn, FR, *Origins of the Early English Maritime and Commercial Law* (New York, The Century Co, 1930)

Schoenbaum, Thomas J, *Admiralty and Maritime Law* 4th edn (St Paul, Thomson/West, 2004)

Schofield, John, *Laytime and Demurrage* 5th edn (London, LLP, 2005)

Scrutton (1996) — See Boyd, Burrows and Foxton (1996)

Sewell, Tom, *Grain: Carriage by Sea* (London, LLP, 1999)

Sotiropoulos, Panayotis (ed), *Demetrios Markianos: In Memoriam* (Athens, Greek Maritime Law Association, 1988)

Stopford, Martin, *Maritime Economics* 2nd edn (London, Routledge, 1997)

Sturley, Michael F, *The Legislative History of the Carriage of Goods by Sea Act and the Travaux Préparatoires of the Hague Rules* (Littleton, Fred B Rothman & Co, 1990), 3 Vols

Tan, Lee Meng, *The Law in Singapore on Carriage of Goods by Sea* 2nd edn (Singapore, Butterworths Asia, 1994)

Temperley, Robert, and Vaughan, Francis, *Carriage of Goods by Sea Act 1924* 4th edn (London, Stevens and Sons, 1932)

Tetley, William, *Marine Cargo Claims* 3rd edn (Montreal, Les Editions Yvon Blais, 1988)

Thomas, Michael, and Steel, David, *The Merchant Shipping Acts* 7th edn (London, Stevens & Sons, 1976)

Tiberg, Hugo, *Law of Demurrage* 4th edn (London, Sweet & Maxwell, 1995)

Todd, Paul, *Bills of Lading and Bankers Documentary Credits* 3rd edn (London, LLP, 1998)

Todd, Paul, *Maritime Fraud* (London, LLP, 2003)

Treitel, Sir Guenter, *Some landmarks of twentieth century contract law* (London, Sweet & Maxwell, 2002)

Treitel, Sir Guenter, *The Law of Contract* 11th edn (London, Sweet & Maxwell, 2003)

Treitel, Sir Guenter, *Frustration and Force Majeure* 2nd edn (London, Sweet & Maxwell, 2004)

Treitel, Sir Guenter, and Reynolds, FMB, *Carver on Bills of Lading* 2nd edn (London, Sweet & Maxwell, 2005)

Ullmann, Gerald H, *The Ocean Freight Forwarder, The Exporter and the Law* (Cambridge, Cornell Maritime Press Inc, 1967)

Ventris, FM, *Tanker Voyage Charter Parties* (The Hague, Kluwer, 1986)

von Ziegler, A, and Burckhardt, T, (eds.), *Internationales Recht auf see und Binnengewässern —Festschrift für Walter Müller* (Zürich, Schulthess Polygraphischer Verlag, 1993)

White, MWD (ed), *Australian Maritime Law* 2nd edn (Annandale, Federation Press, 2000)

Wilford, Michael, *Time Charters* 5th edn (London, LLP, 2003)

Williams, Harvey, *Chartering Documents* 4th edn (London, LLP, 1999)

Wiswall, Frank L Jr, *The Development of Admiralty Jurisdiction and Practice since 1800* (Cambridge, Cambridge University Press, 1970)

Wiswall, Frank L Jr, *Comité Maritime International* (Antwerp, CMI, 1997)

Yiannopoulos, Athanassios N, *Negligence Clauses in Ocean Bills of Lading* (Baton Rouge, Louisiana State University Press, 1962)

Yiannopoulos, AN (ed), *Ocean Bills of Lading: Traditional Forms, Substitutes, and EDI Systems* (The Hague, Kluwer, 1995)

Zimmermann, Reinhard, *The Law of Obligations: Roman Foundations of the Civilian Tradition* (Kenwyn, Juta & Co, 1990)

LIST OF ABBREVIATIONS

BC	British Columbia
BFL	Bombay Floating Light
BIFA	British International Freight Association
BIFFEX	Baltic Exchange Freight Futures Market
BIMCO	The Baltic and International Maritime Council
BL	bill of lading
BOLERO	Bills of Lading for Europe
c. & f./CFR	cost and freight
c.i.f.	cost, insurance, freight
CISG	The Vienna Convention on the International Sale of Goods 1980
CLC	Civil Liability Convention 1969 and 1992
CMI	Comité Maritime International
CMR	Convention on the Contract for International Carriage of Goods by Road 1956
COA	contract of affreightment
COGSA	US Carriage of Goods by Sea Act 1936
Congenbill	charterparty bill of lading
Conlinebill 2000	liner bill of trading
CPR	Civil Procedure Rules
CSP	Commercial Sea Port
DOC	Document of Compliance
dwt	deadweight tonnage
ECOSOC	The Economic and Social Council of the UN
EDI	Electronic Data Interchange
ERL	expected ready to load
FCL	full container load
FIATA	International Federation of Freight Forwarders Associations
FIO	free in and out
FIOS	free in and out, stowed
FIOST	free in and out, stowed and trimmed
f.o.b	free on board
FONASBA	Federation of National Associations of Ship Brokers and Agents
FOSFA	The Federation of Oils, Seeds and Fats Associations
GAFTA	The Grain and Feed Trade Association
HNS Convention	Hazardous and Noxious Substances Convention 1996
IACS	International Association of Classification Societies
ICC	International Chamber of Commerce
ICS	International Chamber of Shipping
ILA	International Law Association
IMCO	Intergovernmental Maritime Consultative Organisation
IMDG Code	International Maritime Dangerous Goods Code
IMF	International Monetary Fund
IMO	International Maritime Organisation
INCOTERMS	International Commercial Terms

IOPC Funds	International Oil Pollution Compensation Funds
ISM Code	International Safety Management Code
LLMC	International Convention on Limitation of Liability for Maritime Claims 1976
LLMC Protocol	Protocol of 1996 to Amend the International Convention on Limitation of Liability for Maritime Claims
LOF	Lloyds Open Form
LOI	letter of indemnity
lo-lo	lift on, lift off
LOOP	Louisiana Offshore Oil Port
LOU	letter of undertaking
LR	Lloyd's Register
MARPOL	International Convention for the Prevention of Pollution from Ships
MSC	Mediterranean Shipping Company
MT contract	Multimodal Transport Contract
MTO	Multimodal Transport Operator
NOR	notice of readiness
NVOC	non vessel operating carrier
NVOCC	non vessel owning common carrier
NYPE	New York Produce Exchange
OBO	Ore, Bulk and Oil
OCL	Overseas Containers Limited
OPA 1990	Oil Pollution Act 1990
P & I	Protection and Indemnity
ro-ro	roll on, roll off
SDR	Special Drawing Right
SGA 1979	Sale of Goods Act 1979
SG Policy	Ship and Goods Policy
SMC	Safety Management Certificate
SMS	Safety Management System
TCM	Transport Combiné de Merchandises (Draft Convention of the Combined Transport of Goods)
TEUs	Twenty Foot Equivalent Units
UCP 500	Uniform Customs and Practice
UCTA	Unfair Contract Terms Act 1977
ULCC	Ultra Large Crude Carrier
UNCITRAL	United Nations Commission on International Trade Law
UNCTAD	United Nations Conference on Trade and Development
UNIDROIT	International Institute for the Unification of Private Law
VLCC	Very Large Crude Carrier
Voylayrules 93	*Voyage Charterparty Laytime Interpretation Rules 1993*
WIBON	whether in berth or not
WIPON	whether in port or not

LAW JOURNALS

ABLR	Australian Business Law Review
AJCL	American Journal of Comparative Law

Alberta LR	Alberta Law Review
American JLH	American Journal of Legal History
American LR	American Law Review
Anglo-American LR	Anglo-American Law Review
Auckland ULR	Auckland University Law Review
AYIL	Australian Yearbook of International Law
Canadian BLJ	Canadian Business Law Journal
Canadian BR	Canadian Bar Review
CLJ	Cambridge Law Journal
CLP	Current Legal Problems
ETL	European Transport Law
HKLJ	Hong Kong Law Journal
Houston JIL	Houston Journal of International Law
ICLQ	International & Comparative Law Quarterly
IJOSL	International Journal of Shipping Law
IML	International Maritime Law
JBL	Journal of Business Law
JCL	Journal of Contract Law
JCLIL	Journal of Comparative Legislation & International Law
JENRL	Journal of Energy & Natural Resources Law
JILE	Journal of International Law & Economics
JILI	Journal of Indian Law Institute
JILT	Journal of Information, Law and Technology
JIML	Journal of International Maritime Law
JMLC	Journal of Maritime Law & Commerce
LMCLQ	Lloyd's Maritime & Commercial Law Quarterly
LQR	Law Quarterly Review
McGill LJ	McGill Law Journal
Michigan LR	Michigan Law Review
MLR	Modern Law Review
Monash LR	Monash Law Review
NYULQ	New York University Law Quarterly
OGLTR	Oil & Gas Law & Taxation Review
OJLS	Oxford Journal of Legal Studies
Sydney LR	Sydney Law Review
Temple ICLJ	Temple International & Comparative Law Journal
Texas ILJ	Texas International Law Journal
Transnational LJ	Transnational Law Journal
Transportation LJ	Transportation Law Journal
Tulane LR	Tulane Law Review
Tulane MLJ	Tulane Maritime Law Journal
UMLR	University of Miami Law Review
Uniform LR	Uniform Law Review
USFMLJ	University of San Francisco Maritime Law Journal
Victoria UWLR	Victoria University of Wellington Law Review
Virginia JIL	Virginia Journal of International Law
Western Ontario LR	Western Ontario Law Review
Yale LJ	Yale Law Journal

LAW REPORTS

AC	Appeal Cases
ALR	Australian Law Reports
AMC	American Maritime Cases
App Cas	Appeal Cases
CA	Court of Appeal
CLR	Commonwealth Law Reports
Com Cas	Commercial Cases (1896–1941)
ER	English Reports Reprint (1378-1865)
FR	Federal Reports (Australia)
HL	House of Lords
KB	King's Bench
Ll LR	Lloyd's List Law Reports (1919–1950)
Lloyd's Rep	Lloyd's Reports (1951–)
LMLN	Lloyd's Maritime Law Newsletter
MLJ	Malayan Law Journal
NSWLR	New South Wales Law Reports
NZLR	New Zealand Law Reports
PC	Privy Council
QBD	Queen's Bench Division
SC	Session Cases
SLR	Singapore Law Reports
VR	Victorian Reports
WLR	Weekly Law Reports

PART I

INTRODUCTION

1

THE BUSINESS OF CARRIAGE OF GOODS

A. Introduction

Overview   The concern of this book is the law relating to the carriage of goods by sea.   **1.01**
Its main focus therefore is the legal relationships which follow from carriage by sea. This
chapter considers, in outline, the nature of the business which underpins the legal relationships entered into. It also introduces the *dramatis personae* to the various contracts.

B. Cargoes

Introduction   In the 2004 trading year, 6,758 million tonnes of cargo were transported   **1.02**
by sea. This was almost 60 per cent more than in 1990[1] and reflects a continuing growth in
the transport of cargoes to all four corners of the globe. The cargo transported is extremely
varied. There are raw materials, such as oil, coal, and iron ore, agricultural commodities,
such as grain, sugar, and refrigerated food, industrial materials such as rubber, cement, fertilizers, fibres, and chemicals, and manufactured goods, which can include anything from
motor cars to machinery and consumer goods.[2] In this part of the book we look in more
detail at some of these cargoes, as a vehicle for an understanding of the legal issues which
are discussed subsequently.

Nature and size   When goods are carried by sea from one place to another in the course   **1.03**
of international trade, it is their nature and size which ultimately influences the contractual
relationships which the parties enter into. As we have seen, the goods shipped by sea comprise

---

[1] *Review of Maritime Transport* (UNCTAD, 2005), 5.
[2] See Stopford (1997), 11.

3

an almost infinite variety. Thus, bulk goods are invariably treated differently from general cargoes,[3] containerized cargoes, and refrigerated cargoes. Bulk cargoes are usually shipped aboard vessels which are tramps or general ships, in the sense that they do not operate on a fixed schedule, but respond to the market and are chartered either on a time basis or a voyage basis. General cargoes, on the other hand, are usually shipped on a liner basis. A definition of a liner service is that it is

> a fleet of ships, with a common ownership or management, which provide a fixed service, at regular intervals, between named ports, and offer transport to any goods in the catchment area served by those ports and ready for transit by their sailing dates. A fixed itinerary, inclusion in a regular service, and the obligation to accept cargo from all comers and to sail, whether filled or not, on the date fixed by a published schedule are what distinguish the liner from the tramp.[4]

1.04 Dry bulk cargoes Economists typically divide dry bulk cargoes into two main categories, the major bulks (grain, iron ore, coal, bauxite, phosphate) and minor bulks (lumber, paper, steel ingots, bagged fertilizers).[5] Each cargo type has different properties and stowage requirements which have to be considered when being carried. By way of illustration, among the major bulks, grain, whether for human or animal consumption, requires a high standard of hold cleanliness, is susceptible to water damage, and can carry infestation.[6] Another example, coal,[7] may emit flammable gases, depending on methane content, is liable to spontaneous combustion,[8] and can exacerbate the corrosion of the steel hull of the vessel owing to the presence of sulphur.[9]

1.05 Illustration: grain carriage Among the major bulks, grain may be taken as illustrative.[10] This major agricultural commodity is seasonal in its trade and is irregular both as to route and potential volume in a given year. Within the category of 'grain', wheat tends to account for about half the annual trade and is destined for human consumption. The rest consists of maize, barley, and oilseeds, mostly used for feeding animals.[11] A typical contract of carriage might involve the processing of Canadian wheat into consumer products, such as flour or starch. Spring-sown wheat harvested in the Canadian Prairies, such as Saskatchewan, Manitoba, or Alberta, will be shifted by truck from the production field to a local storage elevator and then fed by either the Canadian National Railway or Canadian Pacific Railway, across the Rockies to Vancouver or Prince Rupert or eastwards to Thunder Bay on the St Lawrence. At the designated port, the wheat will be transferred to a quayside

---

[3] ie those cargoes which are too small for bulk shipment and which do not warrant the use of the entire ship space. Also known sometimes as 'break-bulk'.
[4] Stopford (1997), 343.
[5] One of the five major dry bulk goods: see Stopford (1997), 294.
[6] cf *Effort Shipping Co Ltd v Linden Management SA (The Giannis NK)* [1998] AC 605, which arose out of an infestation of Khapra beetle in a cargo of groundnuts. See also para 22.13.
[7] See the *Code of Safe Practice for Solid Bulk Cargoes* (IMO, 2001), Appendix B, 69–74.
[8] See, eg, *The Athanasia Comninos & Georges Chr Lemos* [1990] 1 Lloyd's Rep 277. See also para 20.19.
[9] See *Lloyd's Survey Handbook* (1999), 104; Rogers (1997), ch 7.
[10] On the carriage of grain generally, see Sewell (1999).
[11] In 2003, 250 million tonnes of grain were shipped, with a more or less equal split between wheat and so-called 'coarse grains' (i.e. maize, barley, soybeans, sorghum, oats, and rye): *Review of Maritime Transport* (2005), 13.

elevator while awaiting transfer to a ship. It will be necessary for the shipper, who will commonly be the seller of the goods, to transport such large quantities of grain by using the entire carrying capacity of a ship, probably a bulk carrier.

Minor bulk cargoes   A much bigger range of cargoes falls into the category of minor bulk **1.06** cargoes. This can include anything from steel products to forest products, cement, sugar, non-ferrous metals, fertilizers, scrap, salt, and rice. Although sometimes shipped solely on bulk carriers, one of the features of these cargoes is that they sometimes lend themselves to shipment either in bulk or by liner. Examples of this variability in shipment methods include cement, fertilizers, and sugar, each of which can be shipped in bulk or bags. As was noted in relation to the major bulk cargoes, each of the main minor bulk cargoes also have unique properties which will have to be taken into account for shipment purposes. Fertilizers, however, require very special handling being classed within the IMDG Code.[12]

Illustration: sugar   A good example of a minor bulk cargo is sugar. Much of it comes from **1.07** various developing countries, such as Cuba, Brazil, and the Dominican Republic, and South Africa and Australia. Trade in sugar is actually divisible into three trades: raw sugar, which is shipped in bulk, refined sugar, which is shipped in bags, and molasses, a by-product, which is shipped in tankers. Sugar also needs to be carefully treated when shipped.[13] Thus, it is liable to set hard if it becomes overheated, while if kept too cold the sugar content will diminish. As is the case with many cargoes, it is particularly susceptible to water damage from fresh or salt water.

Liquid bulk cargoes   A no less important type of bulk cargo transported is the general class **1.08** known as liquid bulks. This consists principally of crude oil and its associated products, liquefied gas and liquid chemicals, and vegetable oils. By far the most important among these is crude oil and oil products.[14] Although in earlier times trade in crude oil was somewhat predictable, this changed dramatically by the end of the late 1980s and is now recognized as a volatile and risky business.[15] Oil cargoes typically originate in defined areas, with the greatest source being the Middle East. Saudi Arabia is still the world's largest producer.

Illustration: oil   A typical consignment of oil cargo, such as that destined for shipment **1.09** from Ras Tanura, the main export terminal in Saudi Arabia, will be transported from the oil field to the port by pipeline where it will be stored in large terminal areas with storage tanks. It is pumped on board tankers directly, at Ras Tanura from a series of off-shore jetties. At the discharge port, which may be a deep water harbour or an offshore facility, such as the LOOP[16] facility off New Orleans or the much smaller single buoy mooring off Durban in South Africa, the oil will be discharged into a local oil terminal and then pumped to a refinery by pipeline or direct to a shoreside refinery.

---

[12] ie the International Maritime Dangerous Goods Code.

[13] *Lloyd's Survey Handbook,* 252

[14] In 2004, 2,316 million tonnes of liquid cargoes were shipped in tankers, just more than three-quarters of which was crude oil: see *Review of Maritime Transport* (UNCTAD, 2005), 8.

[15] See Stopford (1997), 306.

[16] 'Louisiana Offshore Oil Port'. Around 12% of all US oil imports arrive via this particular facility. See Kendall & Buckley (2001), 156–158.

1.10 **Break bulk cargoes** As we have seen, there are many types of cargoes which do not need to be shipped in bulk, mainly because the quantities involved are unlikely to require the use of the entire carrying capacity of a vessel. Such cargoes may be loose individual items, boxes, cartons, crates, bags, or bales and must be handled and stowed separately. The effect of such carriage requires the use of dunnage[17] to keep in place the various individual items to limit damage by sweat, breakage, chafing, crushing, or contact with the hold. Increasingly, however, there has been a trend for loose cargo to be unitized,[18] either as containerized cargo, or onto pallets[19] which can easily be stacked and handled. These innovations have cut down on the movement of individual items of cargo from ship to shore and reverse.

1.11 **Containerized cargoes** The movement of goods in a single container by means of more than one mode of transport has led to a revolutionary development in international and domestic trade.[20] Indeed, the packing[21] of a cargo or a series of different cargoes into a single modular box — a container[22] — which can form a single lorry load, railway wagon load, or be transported by ship or aircraft has dramatic economic consequences, including increasing the speed of transit, reducing handling costs, and giving increased protection to the goods being transported since, in theory at least, the container can be transferred between different modes of transport in a single operation. In just a few decades, containers have become the principal form of general cargo transport and in the 2004 trading year some 1.94 billion tonnes of cargo were shipped in containers.[23]

C. Vessels

1.12 **Introduction** As important as the cargoes carried are the ships which are used to carry them. In this section we look briefly at some of the main vessel[24] types and their characteristics, as a vehicle for an understanding of the kinds of cargo disputes which may arise.

1.13 **Traditional multi-purpose cargo vessels**[25] Traditionally, at least until the 1970s, most general cargo was shipped aboard multi-purpose cargo vessels. Such vessels were attractive because they were able to accommodate a wide range of cargoes. Although displaced in some trades, because many general cargoes are containerized, general cargo vessels still have a place in carrying goods. Typically, such a vessel would include 'tween decks,[26] dividing

---

[17] ie pieces of wood, burlap (coarse canvas), or matting.

[18] Unitization is said to increase the rate of loading and discharging of the ship and help contain costs.

[19] ie flat trays which can be moved by fork-lift truck, on which single or multiple units can be packed for easy handling.

[20] See Kendall and Buckley (1994), 171.

[21] Or 'stuffing', to use the trade jargon.

[22] For illustrations of the different container types, see Branch (1996), 378; Lüddeke (1996), 128.

[23] *Review of Maritime Transport* (2005), 15.

[24] The terms 'vessel' and 'ship' are used interchangeably. For statutory definitions of 'ship', see the Merchant Shipping Act 1985, s 313(1): ' "ship" includes every description of vessel used in navigation'. The phrase 'used in navigation' has sometimes caused difficulty: see *Steedman v Scofield* [1992] 2 Lloyd's Rep 163 and the discussion in para 35.44.

[25] See Stopford (1997), 398. See, eg, *Transgrain Shipping BV v Global Transporte Oceanico SA (The Mexico I)* [1990] 1 Lloyd's Rep 507 (CA), discussed at para 31.31.

[26] See Brodie (2003), 241.

each hold of the vessel into lower and upper portions, for the carriage of mixed general cargo, and helping to avoid problems caused by compression of overstowed cargo. Apart from holds for various types of general cargo, such multi-purpose cargo vessels also generally had tanks for carrying liquid cargoes and, usually, some refrigerated cargo as well. A further feature of such vessels is that they may have their own cargo handling gear, or derricks,[27] with heavy lift ability. The numbers of older type general cargo vessels of this sort have gradually diminished.[28] Although very effective in being able to load a wide range of cargo types, a major drawback is the amount of time and labour which must be applied to load and discharge cargoes. A more modern solution has been to commission the building of general cargo vessels which are lo-lo[29] vessels, having traditional holds and 'tween-decks, but are also designed to hold containers[30] as well as general cargo.[31]

Container vessels[32]   In the nineteenth century the most important change in the ship-   **1.14**
ping industry was the gradual move from sail to steam in the 1860s and 1870s. In the 1960s and 1970s, approximately a century later, there was a similar significant technological advance: from general cargo vessels carrying all kinds of cargoes to container vessels carrying containers which consolidate cargo. The movement of goods in a single container by means of more than one mode of transport has led to a revolutionary development in international and domestic trade. Although this was a US invention, in the sense that the first two recorded voyages were an experimental journey by the *Ideal X* from New York on 26 April 1956 and the inaugural sailing from San Francisco of the *Hawaiian Merchant*, a converted C-3 freighter, on 31 August 1958,[33] it was introduced into British shipping by four leading British shipowners and then took off in a big way in continental Europe and in Japan. Container ships, or cellular container ships as they are sometimes known, are today very much part of the commercial shipping scene and, in particular, the liner trades and comprise just over 10 per cent of the total world fleet.[34] Most importantly, containers, although of many different types, come in two standard dimensions, 20ft × 8ft × 8ft 6in units and 40ft × 8ft × 8ft 6in, which in the industry are measured as TEUs.[35] The size and capacity of these ships has shown a tendency to grow; thus, by 2005, the average has risen to 2,235 TEUs and vessels over 4,000 TEUs made up some 74 per cent of the total deliveries of new container vessels.[36] The larger vessels tend to spend longer at sea,[37] while smaller and medium sized vessels tend to concentrate regionally. Container vessels tend now to be categorized as either Sub-Panamax[38] (2,000–3,000 TEUs), Panamax (3,000–4,000 TEUs),

---

[27] Brodie (2003), 84.
[28] Many excellent examples from former times are to be found in Gardiner (1994), ch 2.
[29] ie 'lift on, lift off'.
[30] For container ships generally, see para. 1.14.
[31] See Branch (1996), 58; Gardiner (1992), 32.
[32] See Stopford (1997), 394; Gardiner (1992), ch 3; Lüddeke (1996), ch 8.
[33] See Hayuth (1987), 1; Kendall and Buckley (2001), ch 16.
[34] *Review of Maritime Transport* (2005), 21.
[35] ie 'Twenty Foot Equivalent Units'.
[36] *Review of Maritime Transport* (2005), 19.
[37] The largest container ships are currently the *MSC Pamela* and the *MSC Susanna,* of 9,200 TEUs.
[38] A Panamax ship, in general terms, is one whose dimensions enable it to transit the Panama Canal. See Brodie (2003), 175.

and post-Panamax (over 4,000 TEUs). The last named class of container ship is too large to transit the Panama Canal.

1.15 **Refrigerated ships** Refrigerated vessels (or reefers) are vessels which are equipped to carry cargoes, such as fruit, vegetables, meat, and fish, which must be refrigerated to preserve them. In many respects, these ships resemble normal cargo ships, with the principal exception that the main cargo spaces are refrigerated. Statistical data on these types of vessels usually places them in the class of general cargo ships.

1.16 **Bulk carriers**[39] A significant proportion of the world fleet falls into the general category of bulk carriers.[40] As the type suggests, they are manufactured for the carriage of specific bulk cargoes. As a class, bulk carriers are categorized as Handy bulk carriers (10,000–29,999 dwt), Handymax bulk carriers (30,000–49,999 dwt), Panamax (50,000–79,999 dwt), and Capesize (over 80,000 dwt) and are designed to carry a range of bulk cargoes, including grain, iron ore, logs, and coal.[41] A major factor in the design of such vessels is flexibility, particularly in the case of vessels of smaller size, which carry minor bulk cargoes and smaller parcels of major bulk cargoes. However, equally important factors are cheapness and simplicity. For the operator of such a ship, questions of cubic capacity, ease of access to the holds, and cargo handling gear are important considerations. The design of the holds of such vessels is a major safety consideration as bulk cargoes can shift easily and, if unchecked, can cause the vessel to capsize. A further point of difficulty has sometimes been associated with steel hatch covers. There were many well-publicized examples of this in the 1990s,[42] and this eventually led to the adoption by the IMO of a new chapter into SOLAS 1974, Chapter XII, Additional Safety Measures for Bulk Carriers, which entered into force on 1 July 1999 and has since been amended in 2002 and 2004. Many modern bulk carriers now have self-trimming holds which are sloped in such a way that cargoes can be loaded by gravity without having to trim the cargo.

1.17 **Ro-ro ships**[43] 'Roll on, roll off' ships were first developed from tank-landing craft used during World War II. They come in two principal versions, the better-known passenger version (or ro-ro ferry),[44] and the version for cargo. The main distinguishing feature of such vessels is a hinged ramp, typically offset at the stern, which allows motor vehicles (including passenger cars, trucks, trailers, bulldozers and farm tractors) to drive on and off the vessel. The passenger version often permits access through a bow door and this allows vehicles to be stored on the car deck below the passenger accommodation areas. A number of disasters[45] focused attention on this type and were one of the factors which led to the promulgation

---

[39] See *Transpacific Discovery SA v Cargill International SA (The Elpa)* [2001] 1 Lloyd's Rep 596, a case involving the NYPE Inter-Club Agreement, para 32.102.

[40] In 2005, this type made up 35.8% of the total world fleet. See *Review of Maritime Transport* (2005), 21.

[41] See Brodie (1999), 67.

[42] Eg *The Derbyshire*, which was lost with all hands off Japan on or about 9 September 1980. See <www.mv-derbyshire.org.uk/> and for litigation involving the vessel, *Coltman v Bibby Tankers Ltd (The Derbyshire)* [1988] AC 276 (the Employer's Liability (Defective Equipment) Act 1969). See too Stephen E Roberts and Peter B Marlow, 'Casualties in dry bulk shipping (1963–1990)' (2002) 26 Marine Policy 437.

[43] See *Tor Line AB v Alltrans Group of Canada Ltd (The TFL Prosperity)* [1982] 1 Lloyd's Rep 617.

[44] Such ferries are commonly used in short sea transportation.

[45] In particular the *Herald of Free Enterprise* disaster off Zeebrugge on 6 March 1987 and the *Estonia* disaster on 28 September 1994. See Hooke (1997), 272; Boisson (1999), 218.

of the International Safety Management Code (the ISM Code) as part of the SOLAS 1974 Convention.[46] The cargo version has not attracted such adverse attention. One of the principal attractions of such vessels is that they permit relatively fast cargo handling while also allowing greater cargo flexibility. The price of this flexibility is that such ro-ro vessels do require particularly careful stowage planning. Originating in the 1960s, such vessels became attractive in those trades with cargoes which could not readily be containerized. Thus, such vessels are particularly useful for the carriage of general cargo which can be handled by a fork-lift truck, including palletized cargo, bales, and packaged timber. An important sub-type is the car ferry, a specialized ro-ro vessel which is designed to carry newly manufactured cars.

Ore, Bulk, and Oil (OBO) carriers   OBO carriers, or combined carriers, are essentially   **1.18** dry bulk carriers which are designed also to carry oil. The principal advantage of such ships is that shipowners are in a position to switch between the tanker and dry bulk markets and to reduce the amount of time spent in ballast by carrying dry and liquid cargoes on alternate legs. Up until the 1970s such vessels made substantial profits, particularly in the periods of tanker boom, but in subsequent years there has been a fall in such capacity and this class of vessels is now relatively unimportant compared with tonnage and number of vessels of other types.

Crude oil tankers   A significant proportion of the world's energy needs comes from crude   **1.19** oil and vessels for the transportation of this particular commodity form a significant part of the total world fleet.[47] Oil tankers now vary enormously in size.[48] The smallest sized tankers, known as Handysized[49] tankers, are those with a deadweight tonnage[50] of less than 50,000 tonnes. In tonnage terms, the next class is Panamax tankers, which are capable of transiting the Panama Canal, and can be up to 70,000 tonnes. Aframax tankers can be up to 120,000 tonnes. However, a number of factors have latterly promoted the building of even larger tankers, particularly after the 1970s. The first of these was pure economics; an increase in physical size could be matched by an increase in the earning power of the ship, although this has to be set beside countervailing demands, such as investment in port infrastructure, primarily for the purpose of enlarging and deepening facilities for accommodating such large vessels. Political factors, such as war, have also played a role in the increased size of oil tankers.[51] Suezmax tankers, those which are capable of transiting the Suez Canal,[52] may be up to 200,000 tonnes. The biggest class of tankers are VLCCs,[53] which carry up to 299,000 tonnes of oil, and ULCCs,[54] which can carry over 300,000 tonnes of oil. A notorious feature of the tanker trade was encapsulated in 1967 when the *Torrey Canyon* struck

---

[46] See Chapter IX.
[47] In 2005 some 37.5% of the total world fleet comprised tankers for the carriage of crude oil. See *Review of Maritime Transport* (2005), 21.
[48] See Gardiner (1992), ch 4.
[49] This term can also be applied to bulk carriers of 10,000–35,000 dwt. See Brodie (2003), 120.
[50] ie the carrying capacity of a tanker when loaded to her summer loadline.
[51] See Stopford (1997), 64.
[52] The Canal permits the transit of 150,000 dwt vessels.
[53] 'Very Large Crude Carrier'.
[54] 'Ultra Large Crude Carrier'.

Pollard's Rock in the Seven Stones reef between the Scilly Isles and Land's End, discharging much of her oil cargo into the sea. The resultant outcry was the catalyst for work on liability and compensation within the IMO, directed by that organization's newly-established Legal Committee.[55] Later disasters, such as that involving the *Amoco Cadiz*,[56] which ran aground off the rocks at Porsall in Brittany in 1978, and the *Exxon Valdez*, which grounded in Prince William Sound in Alaska in 1989, have led to a raft of measures which have sought to address safety problems with tankers, including issues relating to structural weakness, lack of manoeuvrability, low buoyancy margins, and anchoring and towing difficulties.[57] Particular responses have included the Convention for the Prevention of Pollution from Ships (MARPOL) of 1973, and, in the years following the *Exxon Valdez* incident, tough domestic legislation in the United States[58] and a particular focus on single hulls. Most tankers had single hulls only until well into the 1990s, but in 1992 an important amendment was made to MARPOL, which enacted a new Regulation 13F which requires tankers built after July 1993 to have a double hull.[59] Provision was also made, in Regulation 13G, for the phasing-out of the existing fleet of single hulled tankers. Following the *Erika* incident in 1999, when a tanker carrying 30,000 tonnes of heavy fuel oil broke up in heavy seas off the coast of Brittany (France),[60] and the *Prestige* incident in November 2002, when a tanker laden with 77,000 tonnes of heavy fuel oil broke in two off the coast of Galicia (Spain),[61] the timetable for phasing out has picked up speed and further amendments have been made to Regulation 13G, advancing the phase out of single hulls with effect from 5 April 2005.[62] The *Erika* and *Prestige* incidents have also led to similar moves within the European Union.

1.20 **Products tankers** Products tankers, as the name suggests, carry oil products, ranging from crude oil to so-called 'clean' and 'dirty' petroleum products being carried from refineries to consumers. However, such vessels also carry acids, vegetable oils, molasses, caustic soda, and other chemicals. Global trade in such products has increased significantly[63] but still the fleet is considerably smaller than the equivalent fleet of crude oil tankers. Indeed, it constitutes a mere fraction of the total world fleet.[64] A particular feature of this class of vessel is its ability to carry many different types of cargoes as parcels within the ship, hence the further name, 'parcels tanker', which is sometimes used. As some chemical cargoes react violently to others, or through exposure to the atmosphere, or are flammable, explosive, or give off noxious vapours, safety is an important consideration. Accordingly, the carriage of chemicals is regulated internationally by the IMO Convention on the Carriage of Dangerous Chemicals by Sea.

---

[55] In particular, the Civil Liability Convention (CLC) 1969. See now the CLC 1992.

[56] See, eg, *The Amoco Cadiz* [1984] 2 Lloyd's Rep 304.

[57] See Boisson (1999), ch 13.

[58] See the Oil Pollution Act (OPA) 1990, discussed in de la Rue and Anderson (1998), 58–69. See also Steven R Swanson, 'OPA 90 + 10: The Oil Pollution Act of 1990 After Ten Years' (2001) 32 JMLC 135.

[59] See Reg 13F(3).

[60] See *IOPC Funds: Annual Report 2004* (IOPC 2004), 74.

[61] *IOPC Funds: Annual Report 2004*, 92.

[62] See Reg 13G (as amended in 2003).

[63] *Review of Maritime Transport* (2005), 11.

[64] Just 0.1%. See *Review of Maritime Transport* (2005), 21.

Liquid gas carriers[65]   While not as important in deadweight terms as most other major   **1.21**
classes of vessels discussed here, liquid gas carriers have emerged as an important, though
niche sector, in the last thirty years or so. There are two main types: liquid natural gas
(LNG) carriers and liquid petroleum gas (LPG) carriers. The former type carries natural
gas, or methane, and is notable for special domed or cylindrical tanks which protrude above
the deck. Such LNG carriers are invariably purpose-built for particular routes. The latter
type carries liquid petroleum gas, such as butane or propane, which is housed in special
tanks capable of freezing the gas to very low temperatures. Given the highly volatile nature
of such cargoes, the manufacture of such ships and the carriage of their cargoes is subject
to strict regulatory control in such conventions as the IMDG Code and MARPOL.

D. Parties

Sellers and buyers   Most contracts for the carriage of goods are ancillary to other contrac-   **1.22**
tual arrangements, such as contracts of sale and financing, between parties in different
countries. Of especial importance here are contracts for the sale of goods, which involve a
seller in one country, and a buyer in a different country. The responsibilities of sellers and
buyers under their contracts of sale will depend upon the type of sale contract entered into.
The underlying principles governing such sales may be the common law, where English law
is stated to apply,[66] or INCOTERMS 2000, to the extent incorporated by the parties in
their contracts.[67] The Vienna Convention on the International Sale of Goods (CISG) may
also be relevant,[68] where not excluded.[69] In the case of an f.o.b[70] sales contract, the seller's
principal obligation is to perform his duty to load the cargo, although under certain types
of f.o.b. sale he may have documentary obligations.[71] Thus, under the 'classic' type, he must
'procure a bill of lading in terms usual in the trade'.[72] Under a c.i.f.[73] contract, the seller
must ship the goods to a named destination, take out insurance on the terms usual in the
trade while the goods are in transit,[74] and, within a reasonable time after shipment,[75]

---

[65] See *Golar Gas Transport Inc v The Liquefied Gas Shipping Co Ltd (The Hilli, Khannur & Gimi)* [1979]
1 Lloyd's Rep 153.

[66] As it often is, particularly in the case of commodity contracts. See, eg GAFTA 100, cl 26; FOSFA 53, cl 27.

[67] As they commonly are in oil transactions, but not dry commodities, where they are often excluded,
e.g. GAFTA 100, cl 28(d). See Bridge (1999), para 1.17; Benjamin (2002), para 18-002.

[68] The United Kingdom is not a party although many countries in other parts of the Commonwealth are,
including Australia and Singapore.

[69] For more detailed discussion, see JD Feltham, 'C.I.F. and F.O.B. Contracts and the Vienna Convention
on Contracts for the International Sale of Goods' [1991] JBL 413.

[70] ie 'free on board'. See INCOTERMS 2000, Group F, p 49. See Benjamin (2002), ch 20; Bridge
(1999), ch 4.

[71] This will depend upon how the respective obligations of the seller and buyer are expressed. See the
various explanations of the three main types in *Pyrene Co Ltd v Scindia Navigation Co Ltd* [1954] 2 QB 402.

[72] At 424.

[73] ie 'cost, insurance, freight'. See INCOTERMS 2000, Group C, p 65. See also Bridge (1999), ch 5;
Benjamin (2002), ch 19.

[74] Another variant of c.i.f. is c. & f. (i.e. 'cost and freight') — CFR under INCOTERMS — which does
not oblige the seller to take out insurance.

[75] See *Groom Ltd v Barber* [1915] 1 KB 316, 324 (Atkin J).

tender the shipping documents to the purchaser.[76] The seller's obligation is to enter into a 'proper' contract of carriage[77] which would cover the whole transit of the goods from the port of shipment to the port of discharge, breach of which would entitle the buyer to reject the bill of lading. Thus, in many cases, the seller of the goods is also the shipper of the goods and named as such on the face of the bill of lading.

1.23 **Agents: forwarding agents** It would be an onerous responsibility for the parties to carriage contracts to make their own arrangements for shipment. Accordingly, most parties make use of various types of specialist agents for this purpose. In the case of a straightforward port-to-port shipment the seller (or shipper) will make use of the services of a forwarding agent, or freight forwarder to arrange all the formalities relating to shipment of the cargo.[78] Traditionally, these duties would include booking space on a ship, preparing in advance a bill of lading, sending a draft to the loading brokers, or agents for the shipowner, arranging for the goods to be brought alongside, arranging customs clearance, and collecting the signed bill of lading after shipment.[79] In addition to these traditional duties, forwarders, when acting as agents, may also undertake further responsibilities, which may extend to the packaging, warehousing, lighterage, and insurance of the goods. Some forwarders may also carry out functions as consolidators or groupage operators who group together several compatible consignments into a full container load. In such a case the forwarder will issue a house bill of lading[80] for the particular shipper's consignment. The forwarder will receive from the shipowner a groupage bill of lading, covering all the consignments. One point of difficulty which arises is whether the forwarder is, in fact, acting as an agent or whether he is acting as principal.[81]

1.24 **Agents: loading brokers** Loading brokers are agents who act for shipowners, usually at the port of loading. Among their principal functions are advertising sailings by the shipping line and obtaining cargoes for carriage.[82] They will sign bills of lading on behalf of the master, receive payment of freight[83] on the shipowners' behalf, and will be paid commission on the freight engaged. Brokers have a lien on the bill of lading, and thus indirectly on the goods, for these commission charges.[84]

1.25 **Shipowners** The ownership of ships is an expensive and risky business. This is one of the reasons why, historically, limitation of liability was permitted.[85] Shipowning companies are therefore often structured in a way which exposes the shipowner to the least risk. Thus, there may be a beneficial owner, who is the ultimate controlling owner who benefits from

---

[76] ie a bill of lading, a policy of insurance, and an invoice. See *Ireland v Livingston* (1872) LR 5 HL 395, 406 (Blackburn J).
[77] As to which, see eg *Plaimar Ltd v Waters Trading Co Ltd* (1945) 72 CLR 305, 316.
[78] For extended treatment, see Hill (1972); Glass (2004). For an American perspective, see Ullmann (1967).
[79] See *Heskell v Continental Express* (1950) 83 Ll LR 438, 449 (Devlin J); *In re Black & Geddes Inc* 35 BR 830, 832 (Bkrtcy, SDNY 1984). See Bugden (1999), ch 1.
[80] See para 3.19. The BIFA (British International Freight Association) house bill of lading is an example. See <www.bifa.org>.
[81] Discussed at para 3.20.
[82] See *Heskell v Continental Express* (1950) 83 Ll LR 438, 449 (Devlin J).
[83] See ch 21.
[84] See *Edwards v Southgate* (1862) 10 WR 528.
[85] See ch 29.

the profits made but is not the registered shipowner. Often beneficial ownership is associated with one-ship companies,[86] or companies which are incorporated with just one ship and no other assets, which protects the beneficial owner from claims.[87] Another device for owning ships is to form a holding company, the sole assets of which are the shares in each one-ship company. Day to day running of the ships owned by the holding company may be vested in a management company, formed specially for this purpose. A disponent owner, on the other hand, is a person who is not the shipowner but who charters the ship and controls its commercial operations, usually under a time charterparty. The disponent owner may sub-charter the vessel under the time charterparty.[88]

Carriers A carrier is a person who enters into a contract of carriage with a charterer or shipper.[89] His identity will depend upon the particular contract of affreightment[90] which is entered into. In the most straightforward scenario, the contract will be embodied in a liner bill of lading with a shipper. If however, the vessel is under charter, the charterer may be the carrier, if the contract is on his standard form. The charterer may seek to restrict his liability under the bill of lading by inserting in it a demise clause or identity of carrier clause[91] which identifies the shipowner as the carrier. A further scenario is the case where the shipper enters into a contract with a combined transport operator or multimodal transport operator. Such would be the case where the contract of carriage involves at least two legs, usually including one at sea. In such a contract the carrier will usually be responsible for the carriage of goods from the time of shipment until they are received by the consignee at the destination.[92] A non vessel owning common carrier (NVOCC) or non vessel operating carrier (NVOC) is any person who does not actually operate the carrying ship. In many cases such a person would be a freight forwarder who is combining the shipments of many small shippers who are too small to deal directly with a shipping line. Thus, the NVOCC or NVOC will often contract not only for a sea leg, but also the carriage of the cargo to an inland destination. In such circumstances, whether he is the carrier for the purpose of suit will depend upon a construction of the contract. **1.26**

Charterers Few large shipping companies necessarily have available the tonnage which may be needed to respond to the demands of the freight market at any one time, whether there is an oversupply or shortage of particular types of vessels. For this reason, much of the world fleet is on charter at any one time. The shipowner will place his ship on the market for hire and, when this is agreed, it is said that the ship has been fixed. The hirer may, depending on the contract, be a time charterer, a voyage charterer, or a demise charterer. **1.27**

The master Of all the shipboard personnel, it is the master or captain who is the most important, as he is in command of the ship. To reach this position he will have progressed **1.28**

---

[86] See, eg, *The Evpo Agnic* [1988] 1 WLR 1090, 1097 (Donaldson MR); *The Skaw Prince* [1994] 2 SLR 379, 386.
[87] Such structures avoid the possibility of an arrest of a sister ship. See para 35.46.
[88] See, eg, NYPE 93, cl 18; NYPE 1946, line 16.
[89] See Hague–Visby Rules, art I(a); Hamburg Rules, art 1(1).
[90] See para 1.32.
[91] See para 12.11.
[92] See, eg, Multidoc 95, cl 10(a).

through the deck officer positions, from third mate to second mate to first mate and will have served in these capacities in a number of different ships. His principal responsibility is the safety and welfare of everybody who sails on the vessel, the vessel itself, and its cargo. Other tasks for which he is commonly responsible include: planning of the ship's route; ensuring that all maritime laws, rules, and regulations are followed; ensuring that the speed, position, and course of the ship are correct; ensuring that a log is kept of events, weather conditions, and the ship's position; ensuring that repairs, fuel, and supplies for the ship are arranged; ensuring that the vessel is maintained; ensuring that the loading, unloading, and stowing of cargo is supervised; overseeing any harbour pilot when entering and leaving ports. Some of these basic functions may vary considerably, depending upon the type of company and the type of contract under which the master is engaged. So far as the shipowner is concerned, the master is his agent and the scope of his authority as such will be defined in his contract of employment. In relation to contracts of carriage, the master must sign bills of lading 'as presented',[93] but may not vary the contract. If he signs bills of lading for goods which are not actually shipped, the carrier will be bound by his signature.[94] He is not bound to sign bills of lading which contain some discrepancy, such as a false statement,[95] and must note on the face of the bill of lading any qualification to the statement that the goods are shipped in 'apparent good order and condition'.[96]

1.29 Consignees The consignee is the person named in the bill of lading to whom the goods have been consigned.[97] His name will be stated in the appropriate box on the face of the bill of lading.[98] The consignor, on the other hand, is the person who places the goods in the charge of the carrier. He may be (and often is) named as the shipper in the bill of lading. If the bills of lading name the consignee and are to order, they are said to be made out to the order of a named consignee.[99]

1.30 Tally clerks A tally clerk is an individual who is employed by a shipping company, a shipper, a receiver, or a stevedoring company, to carry out a physical count of the cargo which is being loaded or discharged from a vessel. Entries as to this cargo are recorded in a tally sheet or tally book and the information recorded relates to the number of pieces, their description, and also any distinctive marks[100] on the goods or packaging, for the purpose of identification.

1.31 Stevedores Stevedores or longshoremen,[101] or dockers, are individuals (or more likely a company) providing the service of loading, stowage, and unloading of ships. Stevedores are

---

[93] See, eg, NYPE 93, cl 30(a).

[94] But cf *Grant v Norway* (1851) 10 CB 665 (CP); 138 ER 263, now rendered obsolete by the Carriage of Goods by Sea Act 1992, s 4 and art III, r 4 of the Hague and Hague–Visby Rules. See para 6.06.

[95] See *Rudolf A Oetker v IFA Internationale Frachagentur AG (The Almak)* [1985] 1 Lloyd's Rep 557.

[96] For the extent to which he may do so, see now *The David Agmashenebeli* [2002] EWHC 104; [2003] 1 Lloyd's Rep 92; para 6.36.

[97] See, eg, Hamburg Rules, art 1(4).

[98] See, eg, Conlinebill 2000 (liner bill of lading); Congenbill (charterparty bill of lading).

[99] See para 5.13.

[100] Sometimes known as shipping or loading marks.

[101] This tends to be the term used in the United States. See, eg, the treatment of the subject in Schoenbaum (2004), ch 7.

invariably independent contractors and shipowners will not be vicariously liable in tort for damage caused in the course of their work.[102] Charterparties often make provision for the payment of stevedores[103] and also the question of liability for damage.[104] In such a case the question may also arise as to whether the stevedore is the servant of the owners or charterers, but it is probably true to say that no principle can be laid down. A further point is whether or not stevedores might rely on the terms of a Himalaya clause.[105] It is now apparent that an appropriately worded clause may indeed extend the terms of contractual clauses to stevedores.[106]

E. Contracts

Contracts of affreightment Although also used in a technical sense,[107] the term contract of affreightment is also a generic term for all contracts of carriage by sea.[108] Thus whenever a shipowner, or some other person, agrees to carry goods by sea in return for the payment of freight[109] or hire,[110] such a contract is a contract of affreightment.[111] In this part of the chapter, we look further at each of the main types which will be encountered in this book.

1.32

Destination Considerations of quantity and destination are among the principal factors which determine the form that a contract of affreightment will take. If the contract is for a sea voyage only, or port-to-port, the contract of affreightment will reflect this by being in an appropriate form.[112] On the other hand, if the contract is intended to be door-to-door, or from the shipper's inland destination to the buyer's inland destination, the contract of affreightment may reflect the fact that it is for through transport to the destination. A contract which involves two or more modes of transport is known as a through contract or a multimodal contract.

1.33

Nature and size The nature of the goods and their size are two further factors which will affect the contract of affreightment entered into. In the case of the bulk cargoes discussed earlier in this chapter, it is likely that the shipper will need the entire carrying capacity of the ship. In such a case, he will charter a whole ship, or part of a ship, either on time charter, or voyage charter or, if he intends to contract on the basis of long term contract lifting the same cargoes, on a contract of affreightment or volume contract. It would not, however,

1.34

---

[102] A remedy lies against the stevedore: see *Murray v Currie* (1870) LR 6 CP 24.

[103] See, eg, *Blaikie v Stembridge* (1860) 6 CB (NS) 894; 144 ER 703; *Brys & Gylsen v Drysdale* (1920) 4 Ll LR 24; *The Helene* (1865) B & L 415; 167 ER 426; *Steinmen v Angier* [1891] 1 QB 619; *Harris v Best* (1892) 7 Asp MLC 272.

[104] NYPE 93, cl 35; Gencon 1994, cl 5(c). See too the NYPE Inter-Club Agreement 1996, cl 8 (discussed further at para 32.100).

[105] See para 9.21.

[106] See *New Zealand Shipping Line v Satterthwaite (The Eurymedon)* [1975] AC154 (PC); *Port Jackson Stevedoring Pty Ltd v Salmond & Spraggon (Australia) Pty Ltd (The New York Star)* [1981] 1 WLR 138 (PC).

[107] Discussed at para 1.39.

[108] See para 1.39.

[109] Discussed in detail in ch 21.

[110] Hire is payable in the case of a time charterparty, not freight. See para 32.47.

[111] See too *Hansson v Hamel & Horley Ltd* (1921) 6 Ll LR 432 (CA), 433 (Barkes LJ).

[112] Some bills of lading are in 'hybrid' form, permitting their use port-to-port or door-to-door (see eg P & O Nedlloyd bill of lading). The practice was disapproved of in *JI MacWilliam Co Inc v Mediterranean Shipping Co SA (The Rafaela S)* [2003] EWCA Civ 556; [2004] QB 702, 752 (Rix LJ).

be necessary to charter the entire carrying capacity of a vessel for the carriage of most goods, apart from bulk goods, and the contract of affreightment in such a case would be a bill of lading. If the bill of lading is issued in a liner trade, it will be a liner bill of lading. However, the bill of lading may be a charterparty bill of lading if it is issued pursuant to a charterparty. Finally, as we have previously noted, bills of lading can also be issued by freight forwarders — so-called house or groupage bills of lading — and, in the case of contracts which are door-to-door, through transport bills of lading and multimodal bills of lading. Where the parties have no need for a bill of lading, particularly in the case of short sea shipments and where goods are moved between the constituent companies in a corporate group, a sea waybill[113] may be issued.[114]

1.35 **Charterparties: in general** Most charterparties, which are in effect leases of ships,[115] are tramps,[116] which is to say they are fixed where and when particular cargoes are available. The charter market for ships is highly competitive and the costs of chartering can fluctuate significantly, depending upon market conditions.[117] Information on the state of the market is readily available from larger firms of specialized shipbrokers,[118] but also published in print form daily in *Lloyd's List*,[119] and weekly in *Fairplay* magazine.[120] Most charterparties are fixed on published forms and it would today be quite rare to have an oral charterparty, although such is legally possible. One of the positive aspects of having a printed standard form is that it should make the negotiation of the final contract much easier. The negative side of this practice lies in the fact that the contracting parties do not apply their minds to the terms as printed or that rider terms are introduced to reflect the parties' particular requirements, sometimes without consideration of the existing printed terms.

1.36 **Time charterparties**[121] For a shipowner, the main advantage of fixing a ship on time charter is that he has the security of an assured income throughout the period of the charter. Large vessels, in particular, are usually heavily mortgaged and the financial risk in not having the vessel earning is usually a powerful incentive to time charter. This is also assisted by the fact that, with some types of cargoes, supply and demand is relatively well known and this also lends itself to time charters. However, where the market is rising, it is less attractive to time charter, simply because the shipowner will lose out on the better rates available in a bullish market. The basic principle of time chartering is that the shipowner provides the charterer

---

[113] Sometimes just referred to as a 'waybill', although this may sometimes cause confusion with similar documents which are well known in air transport, viz air waybills.

[114] For detailed discussion, see para 4.02.

[115] This term comes from *carta partita*, a medieval term used to indicate an instrument written in duplicate on a single piece of parchment and subsequently divided, so that each part fitted together. See further CL Trowbridge, 'The History, Development and Characteristics of the Charter Concept' (1975) 49 Tulane LR 743; *Leighton v Green & Garrett* (1613) Godb 204; 78 ER 124.

[116] For detailed explanation of the business, see Kendall & Buckley (2001), ch 3.

[117] For a classic statement of the nature of this market, see *Federal Commerce and Navigation Co Ltd v Tradax Export SA (The Maratha Envoy)* [1978] AC 1, 7 (Lord Diplock).

[118] See, eg Clarksons <www.clarksons.co.uk>.

[119] See <www.lloydslist.com>.

[120] See <www.fairplay.co.uk>.

[121] Discussed in detail at ch 32. For specialist treatment, see Wilford (2003); Williams (1999), ch 3; Gorton (2004), ch 13.

with the services of the ship and its crew for the stated period of time. The shipowner runs the ship, takes out hull and machinery insurance and P & I insurance,[122] is responsible for the hiring and remuneration of the master and crew, but is not responsible for finding commercial employment for the ship. The charterer has to find employment for the ship and must pay hire to the shipowner throughout the period of the charterparty.[123] There are a range of standard forms in use in the industry. Pre-eminent among the general forms are the New York Produce Exchange Form, NYPE 93,[124] and its predecessor NYPE (1946), which are widely used in the market.[125] Another equally well known general form is Baltime 1939.[126] There are specialised time charterparty forms for the carriage of oil, most of them associated with the major oil companies. These include Shelltime [127] and Beepeetime.

Voyage charterparties[128]   A shipowner who fixes his vessel for a voyage is better placed to respond quickly to a rising market. On the other hand, he can also be adversely affected when freight rates are in a trough. It is often a question of luck or good judgement in estimating when freight rates will stop rising and how long they will remain depressed. Seasonal commodities, such as grain,[129] are particularly well suited to voyage chartering. However, whether a commodity is shipped on a voyage or time basis will ultimately depend on the particular preferences of shipowners and charterers. A voyage charterparty, contrasted with a time charterparty, involves the chartering of a ship for a single voyage from the port of loading to an agreed delivery port or range. The shipowner is responsible for payment for virtually everything, with the exception of delays at the loading and discharge ports, which are paid for by the charterer in his freight payment and in agreed days or hours for loading and discharge, called laytime. If the charterer then exceeds the agreed days or hours, he is liable to pay demurrage at an agreed rate.[130] As with time charterparties, so with voyage charterparties are there a full range of standard forms available. The most widely used general form is Gencon (1994).[131] A successor to this, Multiform 1982, has not generated nearly as much interest as was hoped.[132] Among the forms for specialized commodities may be mentioned the following: Amwelsh 93, for coal, is one of the oldest. Centrocon is a well known form used for grain carriage from South America, while Synacomex, also for grain, is issued by French charterers. Two of the best known North American grain forms are Norgrain 89 and Baltimore Form C. Among other commodities, may be noted Nubaltwood (1964), for timber, Sugar (1977), for sugar. As with time charters, there are **1.37**

---

122 As to this, see Hazelwood (2000).

123 See *Care Shipping Corporation v Itex Itagrani Export SA (The Cebu (No 2))* [1993] QB 1, 11–12 (Steyn J); *Torvald Klaveness A/S v Arni Maritime Corp (The Gregos)* [1995] 1 Lloyd's Rep 1 (HL), 4 (Lord Mustill); *Whistler International Ltd v Kawasaki Kisen Kaisha Ltd (The Hill Harmony)* [2001] 1 AC 638, 641 (Lord Bingham).

124 An intermediate version produced in 1981, Asbatime, has been little used.

125 The 1946 form is also still used extensively, often with many rider clauses.

126 The most recent revision was undertaken in 2001.

127 Revised most recently in 2003.

128 Discussed in detail at ch 30. For specialist treatment, see Cooke (2001); Williams (1999), ch 1; Gorton (2004), ch 12.

129 See the discussion above, at para 1.05.

130 See ch 31.

131 Its predecessor form, Gencon (1976), is also still used.

132 Despite a revision in 1986.

a number of well known forms for oil, the best known of which is Asbatankvoy. Other important forms are connected with oil companies, and include Shellvoy 5, and Beepeevoy. For other oils, such as vegetable oils and fats, Biscoilvoy is widely known and used.

1.38 **Time trip charterparties**   The time trip charterparty, or trip charterparty, is a hybrid form type of charterparty, usually on one of the well known time standard forms.[133] The difference with most time charters, however, is that a trip charterparty is for a single trip or voyage only, defined more precisely or (more commonly) quite loosely.

1.39 **Contracts of affreightment or volume contracts**[134]   In some cases, it may be necessary for a shipper to transport large quantities of a particular commodity which far exceeds the carrying capacity of a particular ship. It would, therefore, be necessary to use the carrying capacity of many ships. Such a contract is known as a contract of affreightment (or COA), used here in its more precise technical sense. Such contracts are sometimes simply known as 'volume' contracts. They share many of the characteristics of voyage charterparties. For this reason, the parties often choose simply to use one of the well known voyage forms, modified for a succession of contracts. Alternatively, they may use one of the specialized standard form contracts which are available, such as Volcoa, for dry cargoes, or Intercoa 80, for oil.

1.40 **Slot charterparties**   Slot charterparties are a relative newcomer to the chartering scene. A slot charter is, in effect, the charter of a part of a ship. This type of charter is quite common in the chemical parcels trade[135] but may also be found in trading in container vessels.[136] Slot charterparties are basically voyage charterparties.

1.41 **Demise (bareboat) charterparties**[137]   Demise or bareboat charterparties[138] are quite different, in several respects, to all the other types we have encountered so far. The fundamental difference lies in the fact that, in the case of a demise charterparty, possession and control of the vessel passes to the charterers, which vessel is supplied 'bare' to them. As confirmed by Evans LJ in *The Guiseppe di Vittorio*:

> [The hallmarks of the demise charter] . . . are that the legal owner gives the charterer sufficient of the rights of possession and control which enable the transaction to be regarded as a letting — a lease, or demise, in real property terms — of the ship. Closely allied to this is the fact that the charterer becomes the employer of the master and crew. Both aspects are combined in the common description of a 'bareboat' lease or hire arrangement.[139]

Whether or not a charterparty amounts to a demise of the vessel will depend upon construing its terms, looking at those terms as a whole:

> . . . [t]he question depends, where other things are not in the way, upon this: whether the owner has by the charter, where there is a charter, parted with the whole possession and

---

[133] See *Care Shipping Corporation v Itex Itagrani Export SA (The Cebu (No 2))* [1993] QB 1, 12 (Steyn J); *Chiswell Shipping Ltd & Liberian Jaguar Transports Inc v National Iranian Tanker Co (The World Symphony & World Renown)* [1991] 2 Lloyd's Rep 251, 257 (Hobhouse J).

[134] See Williams (1999), ch 5; Gorton (2004), ch 14.

[135] See above, para 1.20. See also *The Tychy* [1999] 2 Lloyd's Rep 11 (CA), 21 (Clarke LJ).

[136] See, eg, *Coli Shipping (UK) Ltd v Andrea Merzario Ltd* [2002] 1 Lloyd's Rep 608.

[137] For specialist treatment, see Davis (2005); Williams (1999), ch 4.

[138] The terms are used interchangeably.

[139] [1998] 1 Lloyd's Rep 136 (CA), 156.

control of the ship, and to this extent, that he has given to the charterer a power and right independent of him and without reference to him to do what he pleases with regard to the captain, the crew, and the management and employment of the ship. That has been called a letting or a demise of the ship. The right expression is that it is a parting with the whole possession and control of the ship; and in such case the captain is not the captain of the owner, and if so he has no authority to bind the owner by any bill of lading or by any contract.[140]

Demise charterparties are not uncommon and are used mainly for those periods of time when the charterer wishes to hire a vessel, with full operational control, or by way of a long-term lease of the vessel, for its entire commercial life. In the former case, it is not unusual to find such demise chartering in the case of passenger ferries, cruise ships, and yachts. Charterers in such cases are usually permitted to change the vessel's name, to use their own markings on the vessel's funnel, and to fly their chosen flag. In return for this, the charterer is responsible for the costs of repair and maintenance and also for insurance. In the case of a long-term lease, the scenario is that of a finance charter or lease, with the lessor as financier and holding title, but with all operational responsibilities on the lessee. This is a popular form of ship finance, usually because of the tax incentives offered by flag states. The capital cost of the vessel may be offset against the taxable profits on the vessel. As with most other types of charterparties, there are a relatively small number of standard forms in use, by far the most popular of which is the Barecon (2001) form.[141]

---

[140] *Baumwoll Manufactur von Scheibler v Gilchrist & Co* [1892] 1 QB 253 (CA), 259 (Lord Esher MR); *Australasian United Steam Navigation Co Ltd v The Shipping Control Board* (1945) 71 CLR 508, 521 (Latham CJ).
[141] Previously Barecon 89.

PART II

BILLS OF LADING AND OTHER DOCUMENTS OF CARRIAGE

2

SHIPPING DOCUMENTS ISSUED BEFORE SHIPMENT

A. Introduction

Overview This chapter focuses on a variety of shipping documents which are in com- **2.01** mon use before and at the time of shipment, including booking notes, tally clerk's receipts, and mate's receipts.[1] The issue of these documents anticipates the subsequent issue and release of bills of lading, which are the subject of the forthcoming chapters.

B. Liner Booking Notes

Context It is customary in the carriage of goods by sea for contractual negotiations to **2.02** take place in advance of shipment and well before the goods carried are brought alongside the designated vessel for shipment or stuffed in a container at an inland destination. In the case of liner shipments[2] of break-bulk goods or container shipments with shipping lines,[3] the goods will customarily have been booked in advance with a line for carriage as failure to do so will involve the shipper in potential additional expense in container yard storage,[4] while awaiting shipment, or the likelihood of the goods being shut out when presented at

---

[1] For other shipping documents which may be used in place of a bill of lading, see ch 4.

[2] As to liner shipments generally, see para 3.06.

[3] This is much the more common nowadays and the volume of traffic continues to increase annually. Thus, in 2004, the total seaborne carrying capacity rose to 9.4 million TEUs (an 8.5% increase of 2003). See *Review of Maritime Transport* (UNCTAD, 2005), 60.

[4] In some cases this could, depending on the contractual arrangements, lead to container demurrage charges. See, eg, *Evergreen Marine Corporation v Aldgate Warehouse (Wholesale) Ltd* [2003] EWHC 667 (Comm); [2003] 2 Lloyd's Rep 597.

the ship's side.[5] In the case of bulk goods, which are often carried in accordance with sales contracts negotiated between buyers and sellers for carriage in a chartered or sub-chartered ship,[6] contractual arrangements will also be well in hand to bring the goods to the quayside or to storage facilities at the port where they can be made available for loading once the carrying ship reaches port. Failure to do so where the ship is on voyage charter might lead to legal difficulties for the charterer, both in respect of his absolute duty to provide cargo and his liability in demurrage once the laydays have been exceeded. If the ship is on time charter, any delay in having cargo available will have a knock-on effect for the time charterers' voyage planning.

2.03 **Status** Liner booking notes are ordinary documents which are not, in law, generally regarded as being documents of title.[7] There has, to date, been no authority which has suggested that there is any custom[8] to the contrary.[9] Liner booking notes are also not within the terms of the Carriage of Goods by Sea Act 1992.[10] Accordingly, the regime of that Act for the acquisition of rights and liabilities[11] is not open to someone holding a mate's receipt.[12]

2.04 **Form and content** Most shipping lines have their own standard booking forms which can be issued in conjunction with their own bills of lading. The 'Conlinebooking 2000' liner booking note[13] is a standard example as it is intended for use with Conlinebill 2000,[14] its associated liner bill of lading. Given the symbiosis between the two documents, it may be noted that, in many respects, Conlinebooking 2000 closely resembles the format and style of a modern liner bill of lading. Thus, the form is in contemporary 'box' format, with page one (the face) containing a number of boxes for filling in and page two (the reverse) containing the 'full terms of the carrier's bill of lading form', the latter being identical to those in Conlinebill.

2.05 **Information** As the form is intended for use for the purpose of booking space, certain of the boxes on the face are worth noting simply because they do not appear in the bill of lading form. Of central importance under the form are the following boxes: (i) 'Agents'; (ii) 'Carrier'; (iii) 'Merchant'; (iv) 'Merchant's representatives at loading port'; and (v) 'Time for shipment (about)'. The face also contains standard boxes for information about the cargo intended for carriage and also a box for 'special terms, if agreed'. It does not contain a 'shipped' statement as it is intended that the document will be superseded[15] by a bill of lading once the cargo is shipped on board.

---

[5] See, eg *Scancarriers A/S v Aotearoa International Ltd (The Barranduna and Torrago)* [1985] 2 Lloyd's Rep 419 (PC) (goods shut out following a telex quotation).

[6] Note that the term 'booking note' is also sometimes used to confirm that a booking has been made for the charter of a vessel: see *Alpine Bulk Transport Co Inc v Saudi Eagle Shipping Co Inc (The Saudi Eagle)* [1986] 2 Lloyd's Rep 221 (CA); *A Meredith Jones & Co Ltd v Vangemar Shipping Co Ltd (The Apostolis) (No 2)* [2000] 2 Lloyd's Rep 337 (CA).

[7] ie, unlike bills of lading (potentially) can be. See para 8.02.

[8] Generally, as to proof of custom, see Treitel (2003), 198–199, 213–214; Scrutton (1996), 16–21.

[9] Unlike for mate's receipts. See para 2.19.

[10] See s 1.

[11] ie, in ss, 2 and 3 of the Act.

[12] See para 8.15.

[13] A BIMCO approved form.

[14] See para 3.07. See <www.bimco.dk>.

[15] See para 4.13.

Contractual obligations   The underlying basis on which liner booking notes are made is   **2.06**
the general law of contract and, in this respect, booking notes are no different from the other
shipping documents in common use. Thus, with respect to formation, it is clear law that
binding contractual obligations will be effected where shipping space is offered and accepted
by the parties to the booking note and embodied in the terms on the reverse of the booking
note.[16] Furthermore, there must be an unconditional acceptance of the terms contained in
the booking note.[17]

Contracting parties   The general rule in contract is that only those who are party to a con-   **2.07**
tract can be bound by or enforce its terms. In many instances, however, the booking of space
for shipment will not be carried out by the actual parties who intend to be bound by the terms
of the subsequently issued bill of lading, but through agents acting on their behalf.[18] In certain circumstances this may mean that the agents become bound by its terms[19] or that the parties to the booking note become embroiled in difficulties which subsequently arise in
identifying the carrier in the bill of lading.[20]

Liability of the agent   As booking notes are commonly made by agents, acting on behalf   **2.08**
of the parties, a question which sometimes arises is the liability of the agent. Such liabilities
arise on general agency principles. Thus, in *Anglo Overseas Transport Co Ltd v Titan Industrial
Corp (UK) Ltd*,[21] the issue was whether a forwarding company, which had booked space with
a line, was liable in freight and dead freight[22] to the shipowner. The court confirmed that it
was, as such was (then) the custom on the London freight market.[23] It is not clear whether this
is still the custom, particularly as freight forwarding companies have become ever more
important in multimodal transport agreements.[24] In another case, *ED & F Man (Sugar) Ltd
v Evalend Shipping Co SA*,[25] the court, in agreeing to an application for the lifting of a mareva
injunction,[26] held that the first defendants were not parties to the booking note, as they had
never authorized or instructed brokers either directly or indirectly to contract on their behalf.

Who is the carrier?   Other cases where such questions as to the contracting parties can   **2.09**
arise is in the context of whether it is the charterer or the shipowner who is the 'carrier' when
the bills of lading are eventually issued.[27] Thus, in the Canadian case of *Canficorp (Overseas
Projects) Ltd v Cormorant Bulk-Carriers Inc*,[28] a booking note was issued by a charterer stating

---

[16] See, eg, *Anglo Overseas Transport Co Ltd v Titan Industrial Corp (UK) Ltd* [1959] 2 Lloyd's Rep 152.

[17] See *CPC Consolidated Pool Carriers GmbH v CTM Cia Transmediterranea SA (The CPC Gallia)* [1994]
1 Lloyd's Rep 68, 75 (Potter J): no binding agreement because of the use of the words 'subject details'.

[18] This is clear from the box on the face of Conlinebooking 2000.

[19] See para 2.08.

[20] See para 2.09.

[21] [1959] 2 Lloyd's Rep 152.

[22] As to these concepts, see para 21.32.

[23] [1959] 2 Lloyd's Rep 152, 160 (Barry J). See too *Cory Brothers Shipping Ltd v Baldan Ltd* [1997] 2
Lloyd's Rep 58.

[24] See para 3.22.

[25] [1989] 2 Lloyd's Rep 192.

[26] As such applications were then known, now 'freezing injunctions'. See CPR Pt 25 and the associated
'Practice Direction—Interim Injunctions'.

[27] See, further, para 12.07.

[28] 1985 AMC 1444 (Can Fed Ct of Appeal).

that Cormorant was the 'carrier' and containing the full terms of the carrier's bill of lading form. When issued, the liner bills of lading similarly referred to Cormorant as carrier but there was no reference anywhere on the bill of lading to the name of the shipowners of the vessel, the *Acmi*, on which it was intended to carry a quantity of asbestos from Montreal to Kuwait. During the subsequent outbreak of hostilities between Iran and Iraq,[29] the shipper gave instructions for Cormorant to prepare bills of lading showing that the asbestos was intended for Iraq, but they refused. The shipper agreed to indemnify Cormorant for the costs of transit and, when the vessel was delayed at Kuwait, Cormorant claimed against the shippers under the indemnity. The shippers, however, denied that there was privity between them and Cormorant, on the basis that Cormorant was only the time charterer of the *Acmi*. The Federal Court of Appeal of Canada confirmed that, as the action was between the shipper and the carrier, recourse could be had to both the booking note and the bill of lading[30] and these established that Cormorant was the contracting carrier.[31]

2.10 **Contractual terms**   The contractual terms on which the booking note are made are customarily to be found on the reverse and should mirror those which will appear on the reverse of the bill of lading, once issued. However, there is the possibility that recourse may be had to prior negotiations between the parties. This was the case in *Electrosteel Castings Ltd v Scan-Trans Shipping & Chartering Sdn Bhd*,[32] which arose pursuant to proceedings under the Arbitration Act 1996.[33] In issue was the question whether a booking note drawn up between the parties was a binding contract or whether reference could be made to a recap telex sent two days previously. The court concluded that it could and should have regard to the latter, when construing the former,[34] whether or not the booking note was intended to supersede the prior contract, although cautioning against encouraging trawling through pre-contractual negotiations.[35]

2.11 **Terms not carried over to the bill of lading**   The case of *Nelson Pine Industries Ltd v Seatrans New Zealand Ltd (The Pembroke)*[36] highlighted a potential problem which may occur once the booking note is replaced by a bill of lading, viz that endorsements in the booking note may not be carried over to the face of the bills.[37] In this case a clause in a booking note provided that the goods were to be carried below deck, but the bill of lading did not state that the goods were to be so carried.[38] Leaving aside the outcome of the case on

---

[29] As to some of the issues arising, see also BJ Hibbits, 'The Impact of the Iran–Iraq Cases on the Law of Frustration of Charterparties' (1985) 16 JMLC 441.

[30] [1985] AMC 1444, 1455 (Stone J).

[31] See too *Ngo Chew Hong Edible Oil Pte Ltd v Scindia Steam Navigation Co Ltd (The Jalamohan)* [1988] 1 Lloyd's Rep 443 (where a fixture note between parties other than shipper and carrier was held not to be the contract).

[32] [2002] EWHC 1993 (Comm); [2003] 1 Lloyd's Rep 190.

[33] c 23.

[34] Drawing, inter alia, on dicta of Rix LJ in *HIH Casualty and General Insurance Ltd v New Hampshire Insurance Co* [2001] EWCA Civ 735; [2001] 2 Lloyd's Rep 161 (CA), at [83]–[84].

[35] [2002] EWHC 1993 (Comm), at [28].

[36] [1995] 2 Lloyd's Rep 290 (HC of NZ).

[37] Similar problems may occur when endorsements in mate's receipts are not carried through to the bills of lading: cf *The David Agmashenebeli* [2002] EWHC 104; [2003] 1 Lloyd's Rep 92.

[38] The case held that, following *The Chanda* [1989] 2 Lloyd's Rep 494, the carrier could not rely on a package limitation clause in the Hague–Visby Rules but the reasoning in that case was firmly overruled in *Daewoo Heavy Industries Ltd v Klipriver Shipping Ltd (The Kapitan Petko Voivoda)* [2003] EWCA Civ 451; [2003] 2 Lloyd's Rep 1. See too *The Tasman Pioneer* [2003] 2 Lloyd's Rep 713, at [45].

limitation, which is thought to be wrongly decided and has not been followed,[39] the court held that the obligation to ship under deck survived the issue of the bills of lading and were not superseded by its issue.[40]

Termination of contract   It is clear that booking notes are subject to termination by one **2.12** or other of the parties. This may be illustrated by *MSC Mediterranean Shipping Co SA v BRE-Metro Ltd*,[41] where a contract of affreightment contained in a liner booking note provided for the carriage by the plaintiffs of 1,240 rail wagons from 'London River or Hull' to Mombasa. In an action for wrongful repudiation against the defendants, the court found, on the facts, that the repudiation had been accepted by the plaintiffs who had given no clear and unequivocal representation that their claim would be abandoned.

Supersession   Liner booking notes commonly provide that they are intended to be replaced **2.13** or superseded[42] following the issue of a bill of lading.[43] In contractual terms this would probably amount to a novation or variation.[44] Conlinebooking 2000 provides explicitly that the terms contained in it are to 'be superseded (except as to dead freight) by the terms of the Bill of Lading' and, in such circumstances, it would be difficult to argue that any oral terms ought to prevail.

C. Tally Clerk's Receipts

Introduction   Once the goods arrive at the ship's side, various contracting parties, such as **2.14** the carrier, the shipper, the receiver, or stevedoring company, will arrange to have employees on hand to verify the loading and unloading of cargo to and from the ship's side.[45] The function of the verification process is the tallying, or physical counting, of the cargo as it is loaded or discharged from the ship.[46] During and as a result of the loading and discharging the tallies taken are recorded in tally sheets (or books) and tally clerk's[47] receipts completed.[48] As these receipts will likely be used in combination with other records of what has been loaded or discharged there is potential for contradiction, particularly when cargoes are overlanded or shortlanded on discharge.[49]

Forms   Unlike many other types of shipping documents, there are no standard approved **2.15** forms in circulation.[50]

---

[39] For further discussion on limitation of liability under the Hague–Visby Rules, see para 29.06.
[40] [1995] 2 Lloyd's Rep 290, 292 (Ellis J).
[41] [1985] 2 Lloyd's Rep 239.
[42] As to supersession clauses in bills of lading, see para 12.05.
[43] See, eg, *Ceval International Ltd v Cefetra BV* [1996] 1 Lloyd's Rep 464 (CA).
[44] As to which, see Treitel (2003), 189–190, 701–702.
[45] See *Munton & Baker Ltd v Berggren, Nomico & Co* (1922) 12 Ll LR 340.
[46] See Brodie (2006), 281–282.
[47] See *United Baltic Corp Ltd v Dundee, Perth & London Shipping Co Ltd* (1928) 32 Ll LR 272, where the evidence of a tally clerk was heard (at 273).
[48] See *The Thomaseverett* [1992] 2 SLR 1068, 1074–1076.
[49] See, eg, *San Carlos Milling Inc v Mainsail Navigation Corp (The MAS Venture)*, unreported, 8 November 2000.
[50] Unlike, eg, that approved by BIMCO, the 'Standard Statement of Facts (Short Form)', for use with voyage charterparties.

2.16 **Status**   Tally clerk's receipts, like booking notes, are not documents of title and do not fall within the class of documents covered by the Carriage of Goods by Sea Act 1992.

2.17 **Clausing**   An area of dispute concerning tally clerk's receipts, as it is with mate's receipts[51] and bills of lading,[52] is the extent to which such receipts should be claused to reflect any imperfections as to the condition, weight, or number of the goods loaded. Many standard form time charterparties, such as NYPE93, provide that the master, being under the employment and agency of the charterer, is inter alia to sign the bills of lading 'as presented in conformity with . . . tally clerk's receipts'.[53] As will be emphasized elsewhere, the clausing of receipts, if carried forward to the bills of lading will have the effect, in many cases, of rendering the bills worthless and so the master of the vessel will be put under considerable pressure not to do so.

2.18 **Tallying costs**   An issue which may arise is the question of the costs of tallying. This issue invariably surfaces in the context of charterparties and certain standard form charterparties make express provision for such responsibilities. In the most recent revisions of certain well-known time charterparty standard forms, this usually appears in the context of the obligation as to employment and agency.[54] Thus, the NYPE93 form provides that the time charterer 'shall perform' any tallying operations 'at their risk and expense'.[55] Older versions of standard forms still in current use, such as NYPE (1946), do not make such provision[56] and it was held in one reported London arbitration that there was no implied obligation on charterers to appoint tallymen.[57] In the case of voyage charterparties, this is not explicitly dealt with in most standard forms, but there is authority for the proposition that the task of tallying is an integral part of the loading operation and so should be for the charterers' account.[58]

D. Mate's Receipts

2.19 **Introduction**   A mate's[59] receipt is an acknowledgement that the ship has taken delivery of the goods[60] and will customarily be issued before the eventual issue of a bill of lading.

2.20 **Forms**   As is the case also with tally receipts, there are no standard form mate's receipts in circulation.[61] Typically, however, the mate's receipt will contain information as to the cargo which has been loaded, stating the quantity and type of goods which have been received and usually the name of the shipper of the goods.

---

[51] See para 2.22.

[52] See paras 6.10; 6.19.

[53] Cl 30(a), ll 308–309.

[54] See para 32.81.

[55] At ll 103–105. See too Gentime cl 13(d), ll 331–334.

[56] See NYPE (1946), cl 8, ll 76–79.

[57] London Arbitration 21/91, LMLN 313, 2 November 1991.

[58] London Arbitration 1/83, LMLN 85, 3 February 1983. But cf also London Arbitration 13/02, LMLN 594.

[59] So called because it is customarily issued by the ship's employee known as the 'mate', ie the officer next below that of the master.

[60] *AR Brown, McFarlane & Co v C Shaw Lovell & Sons* (1921) 7 Ll LR 36, 37 (Rowlatt J); *Kum v Wah Tat Bank Ltd* [1971] 1 Lloyd's Rep 439, 442 (Lord Devlin).

[61] Although, for an old example, see Mitchelhill (1982), 121.

Entitlement to the bills of lading   The normal rule, in the absence of provision to the   **2.21**
contrary, is that the person in possession of the mate's receipt is the person entitled to the
bills of lading.[62] On presentation of the mate's receipts to the shipowner or his agent, they
will be exchanged for bills of lading.[63]

Not a document of title at common law   It has been clearly established in a succession of   **2.22**
cases that a mate's receipt is not a document of title[64] at common law.[65] Notwithstanding
this basic principle, it is established that custom may be proved to the contrary. In
Hathesing v Laing, however, Bacon V-C was not satisfied that a custom was proved; the evidence, in his view, merely showed possibly 'a pernicious and loose habit'.[66] The leading case
of *Kum v Wah Tat Bank Ltd*[67] involved a common problem usually encountered with bills
of lading, namely the delivery up of goods without the presentation of the bills.[68] In this
case the bank claimed for conversion of the goods, contending that the mate's receipts were
equivalent to bills of lading because these were so treated in trades between Singapore and
Sarawak. The claim was dismissed in the Singapore High Court and successfully taken to
the Malaysia Court of Appeal.[69] However, the Privy Council, though agreeing that the custom alleged was neither uncertain nor unreasonable,[70] concluded that it was inconsistent
with the words on the mate's receipt, 'not negotiable', which could not be ignored.[71]

Document of title under the Factors Acts   Although it has been settled that mate's receipts   **2.23**
are not documents of title at common law, it may be possible for the receipts to function as a
document of title under section 1(4) of the Factors Act 1889.[72] This provides that

> 'document of title' includes any bill of lading, dock warrant, warehouse-keeper's certificate,
> and warrant or order for the delivery of goods, and any other document used in the ordinary
> course of business as proof of the possession or control of goods, or authorising or purport-
> ing to authorise, either by endorsement or by delivery, the possessor of the document to
> transfer or receive goods thereby represented.

The issue of a mate's receipt being such a document of title would arise in those situations
where it is 'proof of the possession or control of goods'. There are authorities, most of them
relatively old, which show that mate's receipts can be used as a form of security for the price
under contracts which provide for payment against mate's receipts[73] although it seems not
to have been argued before that such usage would constitute the mate's receipts documents

---

[62] *Nippon Yusen Kaisha v Ramjiban Serowgee* [1938] AC 429 (PC), 445 (Lord Wright).
[63] See, eg, *Ben Line Steamers Ltd v Joseph Heureux (London) Ltd* (1935) 52 Ll LR 27, 29 (Greer LJ).
[64] See para 8.02.
[65] See *Hathesing v Laing* (1873) LR 17 Eq 92; *FE Napier v Dexters Ltd* (1926) 26 Ll LR 184 (CA), 189
(Scrutton LJ); *Nippon Yusen Kaisha v Ramjiban Serowgee* [1938] AC 429 (PC), 445 (Lord Wright).
[66] (1873) LR 17 Eq 92, 104.
[67] [1971] 1 Lloyd's Rep 439 (PC); [1971] 1 MLJ 177.
[68] As to which, see para 10.05.
[69] [1967] 2 Lloyd's Rep 437.
[70] [1971] 1 Lloyd's Rep 439, 444.
[71] The bank nevertheless succeeded on the argument that shipment of the goods was a delivery to the ship
as bailee for the bank and that thereby the pledge was completed and the bank given the possessory title on
which it relied.
[72] 52 & 53 Vict, c 45.
[73] See especially *AR Brown, McFarlane & Co v C Shaw Lovell & Sons* (1921) 7 Ll LR 36; *FE Napier v Dexters
Ltd* (1926) 26 Ll LR 184 (CA); *Nippon Yusen Kaisha v Ramjiban Serowgee* [1938] AC 429 (PC).

of title under statute, possibly because it is almost always the case that a bill of lading is subsequently issued.

2.24 **Status as a receipt**   As suggested above, a mate's receipt is a simple receipt, albeit prima facie evidence of receipt of the goods. It is usual for the receipt to also be evidence of receipt in good order and condition[74] and so if the receipt is signed without qualification this may create difficulties for the owner.[75] In one case, which involved the shipment of 225 bundles of galvanized sheets, the annotation 'several bundles dirty before shipment' in the mate's receipts was not carried forward to the bills of lading which stated that the goods were 'shipped in good order and condition'.[76] The goods were, in fact, wet-stained before shipment and the court held that the defendant merchants were not liable under the agreement which they had signed to indemnify the shipowner against the latter's liability for signing clean bills of lading.[77] In another leading case, a 'ship's receipt' was marked 'many bags [of sugar] stained, torn and resewn' but the bills of lading stated that they were 'received in apparent good order and condition'. The latter also contained the endorsement 'signed under guarantee to produce ship's clean receipt', and the Privy Council concluded that the language of the bill of lading, read fairly, and as a whole, was not such as to found an estoppel against the shipowner.[78]

2.25 **No liability where shipper knows the truth**   It would seem that if the shipper were to put pressure on the master to release clean receipts, knowing full well that the goods were not shipped in apparent good order and condition, then the shipowner will not be liable for breach of contract.[79] Nor, for that matter, would liability attach to the shipowner where a charter (or a sub-charterer acting as his agent) persuaded the master to do so.

2.26 **Liability in tort[80]**   It is accepted that when the master or the first officer signs mate's receipts, he does so on behalf of his employer and must record the apparent condition accurately. He must likewise do so with respect to third parties as any representation which is made in the subsequent bill of lading can give rise to claims in tort.[81]

2.27 **Mate's receipts and time charterparties**   As was noted in relation to tally clerk's receipts, many standard form time charterparties, such as NYPE 93, provide that the master, being under the employment and agency of the charterer, is inter alia to sign the bills of lading 'as presented in conformity with . . . mate's receipts'.[82] In the leading case,[83] a quantity of salt

---

[74] *Naviera Mogor SA v Société Metallurgique de Normandie (The Nogar Marin)* [1988] 1 Lloyd's Rep 412 (CA), 420 (Mustill LJ).
[75] ibid. See too *Hunter Grain Pty Ltd v Hyundai Merchant Marine Co Ltd* (1993) 117 ALR 507.
[76] *Ben Line Steamers Ltd v Joseph Heureux (London) Ltd* (1935) 52 Ll LR 27 (CA).
[77] Although they would have been liable under the indemnity had the goods been 'dirty'. See too *United Baltic Corporation Ltd v Dundee, Perth & London Shipping Co Ltd* (1928) 32 Ll LR 272.
[78] *Canada & Dominion Sugar Co Ltd v Canadian National (West Indies) Steamships Ltd* [1947] AC 46 (PC). As to estoppel, see the speech of Lord Wright (at 56) and also paras 6.05;6.19.
[79] See *Trade Star Line Corp v Mitsui & Co Ltd (The Arctic Trader)* [1996] 2 Lloyd's Rep 449 (CA), 458–459 (Evans LJ).
[80] As suggested in *Naviera Mogor SA v Société Metallurgique de Normandie (The Nogar Marin)* [1988] 1 Lloyd's Rep 412 (CA), 422 (Mustill LJ).
[81] At 456.
[82] Cl 30(a), ll 308–309.
[83] *Trade Star Line Corp v Mitsui & Co Ltd (The Arctic Trader)* [1996] 2 Lloyd's Rep 449 (CA).

discharged was found to be contaminated and time charterers sought damages on the ground that the master had failed to clause the mate's receipts. Arbitrators found that the master had been prevailed upon not to do so and found for the charterers. On appeal, the issue was that the master was under an implied duty to the charterers to clause the mate's receipts, but this was rejected by Tuckey J, who allowed the appeal. The Court of Appeal agreed: the charterers' losses flowed from the issue of clean bills of lading, which ought to have been claused and under the charterparty this was their responsibility.[84]

Clausing and delay   It may happen that the decision by the master to clause the mate's **2.28** receipts results in delay, particularly where this comes to light after loading. In circumstances where this is problematic for the shipper (or charterer),[85] the question may arise whether the charterers have to pay hire for any period of delay owing to a delay by the master in signalling his intention to clause the receipts. In a reported arbitration on this point, the tribunal concluded (by a majority) that, given that the loss which occurred to them flowed directly from a breach by the master of his contractual obligations, the charterers should be entitled to damages in the form of hire for the relevant period or, alternatively, should be entitled to treat the ship as off-hire.[86]

Mate's receipts and voyage charterparties   Voyage charterparties do not commonly con- **2.29** tain clauses similar to clause 8 of the NYPE form,[87] simply because of the nature of such charterparties. The leading case involving mate's receipts under such charterparties is *Naviera Mogor SA v Société Metallurgique de Normandie (The Nogar Marin)*.[88] Here mate's receipts were signed by the master, but with no reference to the condition of wire rods which were rusty on delivery. After settling a claim against them, the owners sought to recover this from the charterers, inter alia on the basis the charterers were in breach of the charterparty by tendering a clean mate's receipt. The Court of Appeal refused to so hold;[89] there was no implied term of the charter that the bills of lading as presented should correctly state the apparent condition of the cargo.

Mate's receipts and contract   In the case of *Hathesing v Laing* it was suggested by Bacon **2.30** V-C that a mate's receipt was a chose in action[90] although it is evident that this does not mean that it is the contract of carriage.[91] It has been suggested, nevertheless, that, although it is not the contract of carriage, it is the 'best evidence' of it until the issue of the bills of lading,[92] apparently recognizing that the contract of carriage is always concluded before the

---

[84] At 459. See, further, in the context of a claim under the Inter-Club Agreement, *Oceanfocus Shipping Ltd v Hyundai Merchant Marine Co Ltd (The Hawk)* [1999] 1 Lloyd's Rep 176 and para 32.100.

[85] ie because they require the subsequent issue of clean bills of lading.

[86] London Arbitration 67/00, LMLN 547, 26 October 2000. See too London Arbitration 15/2002, LMLN 598, 17 October 2002.

[87] Although cf Gencon (1976), cl 9 (ll 114–119) (and cl 10 of Gencon 1994).

[88] [1988] 1 Lloyd's Rep 412 (CA).

[89] At 420.

[90] (1873) LR 17 Eq 92, 103. Generally as to choses in action, see Bridge (2002) 4–9.

[91] 'The mate's receipt, although it shows the person who is likely to get the contract of affreightment, and the person whom the shipowner regards as the owner of the goods, still is not a contract of affreightment': *AR Brown, McFarlane & Co v C Shaw Lovell & Sons* (1921) 7 Ll LR 36, 37 (Rowlatt J).

[92] See *Sunrise Maritime Inc v Uvisco Ltd (The Hector)* [1998] 2 Lloyd's Rep 287, 299 (Rix J).

bill of lading, which evidences its terms, is actually issued.[93] The same would likely apply to the booking note which is issued even earlier than the mate's receipt.

2.31 **Not within the Carriage of Goods by Sea Act 1992**   Mate's receipts are not within the documents to which the 1992 Act applies.[94] Accordingly, the regime of the Act for the acquisition of rights and liabilities is not open to someone holding a mate's receipt.

2.32 **Mate's receipts and seller's retention of property**   A final point for consideration concerns the ability of the mate's receipt to enable the seller of the goods to retain the property in the goods until the price has been paid.[95] Although this is a point more properly within the sale contract, this depends not so much whether the mate's receipt is a document of title, but rather whether it is the seller's intention to reserve his right of disposal of the goods.[96] There appear to be three potential cases: (i) where a mate's receipt is issued in the seller's name and retained by the seller;[97] (ii) where a mate's receipt is issued in the buyer's name and sent to the buyer;[98] (iii) where a mate's receipt is issued in the buyer's name yet retained by the seller.[99]

---

[93] *Pyrene Co Ltd v Scindia Navigation Co Ltd* [1954] 2 QB 402, 419 (Devlin J).
[94] By s 1(1), the Act applies to '(a) any bill of lading; (b) any sea waybill; and (c) any ship's delivery order'.
[95] Generally as to this, see Benjamin (2002), paras 18–179.
[96] See Carver (2005), para 6-044.
[97] See, eg, *Falk v Fletcher* (1865) 18 CB (NS) 403; 141 ER 501.
[98] As was the case in *FE Napier v Dexters Ltd* (1926) 26 Ll LR 184 (CA).
[99] See *Nippon Yusen Kaisha v Ramjiban Serowgee* [1938] AC 429 (PC).

3

TYPES OF BILLS OF LADING

A. Introduction

Overview Having in the previous chapter considered various shipping documents which **3.01** may be issued prior to the receipt of the goods for shipment, we turn our attention now to the bill of lading and the various types which may be encountered in practice.[1] We begin by looking briefly at the historical background to bills of lading, before moving to a consideration of liner bills of lading, straight bills of lading, charterparty bills of lading, freight forwarders' bills of lading, combined transport bills of lading, and multimodal bills of lading.

B. Historical Background

Origins: no written document[2] The precise early history of the bill of lading is shrouded in **3.02** some mystery but can be traced to the early middle ages,[3] when many of the basic institutions and concepts of modern mercantile law were being developed.[4] The origins probably lie with the register book[5] which ships' clerks were obliged to maintain. Before the invention of any written document embodying the contract, the owner of the goods would have sailed with the ship.

---

[1] See too Gaskell (1999), para 1C.

[2] See Daniel E Murray, 'History and Development of the Bill of Lading' (1983) 37 UMLR 689; Boris Kozolchyk, 'Evolution and Present State of the Ocean Bill of Lading from a Banking Law Perspective' (1992) 23 JMLC 161; Bools (1997), ch 1.

[3] One assertion that such documents were in use in Roman times seems erroneous. See Chester B McLaughlin, 'The Evolution of the Ocean Bill of Lading' (1925–1926) 35 Yale LJ 548, 550.

[4] See, eg, Berman (1983), ch 11.

[5] See Bennett (1914), 4; *Consolato del Mare* (c 1340), ch 55.

3.03   **Need for a written document**   At some point, however, the practice of merely keeping an 'on board' record of the goods handed over for carriage changed, perhaps predictably when trading practices began to change and goods' owners were no longer able to travel with the goods to their destination. From this point in time, historical records of actual bills of lading become verifiable, initially issued as a receipt by the shipowner to the merchant for the goods received. Such bills of lading were originally used for goods shipped from Spain. Thus, a bill of lading issued in Cadiz in 1544 stated that the master of *The Andrewe* had received '112 bags of allam' to be delivered

> well condyshioned in the ryver of Themys as nyghe London as she may convenyentlye come to her right discharge to William Clyfton merchaunte or to his assignes payinge for the freyghte of every tonne 30 shillyngs sterling and average accustomed.[6]

By 1549, statements of the condition of the shipped goods were becoming more specific. Thus, a bill of lading issued in Bordeaux by the master of the *White Angle* acknowledged

> receipt of the numbre and quantetie of one hundred and fyftie tonnes of wyne full and ullagid, which wynes the sayede maister confessyth to have receyved for the sayede Naudyn Revell [merchaunt of Roon in Normandye].[7]

3.04   **Terms**   Since disputes quickly arose between shipper or cargo owner and the carrier, it became appropriate for the terms of the contract to be incorporated into the bill of lading.[8] It was only later that the terms were placed on the reverse of the bill of lading (and invariably in small print). Older forms of bills of lading traditionally contained all the relevant terms on one side only, with spaces for the commercial details agreed between the shipper and carrier.[9] This practice changed over time to that which is common today, that is the commercial and business details on the front or 'face' of the bill of lading, and the contractual terms on the reverse.[10]

3.05   **Title**   With the increasing availability of methods of international transport by the eighteenth century and the availability of good roads in Europe during the first half of the nineteenth century, merchants were encouraged to sell their goods while they were still on the high seas. But in such circumstances physical delivery of the goods, ordinarily associated with any sale of goods, was not possible and so some method of facilitating such sales had to be devised. This occurred in the case of *Lickbarrow v Mason*[11] when the court recognized a custom of merchants that a bill of lading in which goods were stated to have been 'shipped by any person or persons to be delivered to order or assigns' enabled the holder to transfer the property in the goods to the transferee.

---

6 Marsden (1894),126–127.

7 Marsden (1897), 59–60.

8 See *Crooks v Allen* (1879) 5 QBD 38, 40 (Lush LJ).

9 See, eg, the bill of lading reproduced in Abbott (1827), 214.

10 See, eg, *The Berkshire* [1974] 1 Lloyd's Rep 185, 187 (Brandon J); *Homburg Houtimport BV v Agrosin Private Ltd (The Starsin)* [2003] UKHL 12; [2004] 1 AC 715, at [3] (Lord Bingham).

11 (1794) 5 TR 683; 101 ER 380. For a full account, see Bools (1997), 8. See too the discussion at para 8.05.

C. Liner Bills of Lading

Functions   Bills of lading of various types constitute the main contract of carriage for **3.06** many commercial parties engaged in the shipment of their goods from one country to another. In the case of cargoes shipped with a line, the bill of lading issued for carriage will be a liner bill of lading, which is usually issued in the case of goods carried port-to-port.[12] The owner or operator of such a vessel will not undertake carriage to a large number of ports at once but instead sends his ships on advertised routes, stopping at the same ports in the same order. The service offered is called a liner service.[13]

Characteristics   A common feature of such liner bills of lading is that the face of the doc- **3.07** ument contains various boxes and, on the reverse, the detailed terms of carriage.[14] A well-known example of a liner bill of lading is Conlinebill 2000, which is an approved BIMCO[15] form. There are, however, countless other such forms, as most lines have their own standard forms.[16] The boxes on the front include one for the name of the shipper, who may be the seller of the goods, as he will often be the party who has prepared the bill of lading or, at least, is the person who has supplied the information which is contained in it. The box for the consignee is intended for the name of the person to whom the goods are to be delivered at the discharge port. The consignee may be named, and may also be 'to bearer' or 'holder', or simply left blank. The words used in this box will affect the transferability of the bill of lading and,[17] in effect, also control over the delivery of the goods. The box for the notify party is intended for the name and address of the person to whom notice should be given once the goods arrive at their destination.[18] Often this person will be the consignee or his agent, or possibly also a bank. It is important also to indicate in the relevant box the name of the vessel.

D. Straight Bills of Lading

Introduction   A straight,[19] or non-negotiable, bill of lading is one made out to a named con- **3.08** signee which omits the words 'negotiable', or 'to order', or 'order or assigns'[20] on its face.[21] Alternatively, in place of the non-inclusion of these words, there may appear words which

---

¹² Sometimes also referred to as a 'marine bill of lading' or 'ocean bill of lading'.

¹³ Usually organized into conferences and now increasingly subject to regulation, because of their anti-competitive tendencies, for example by the European Union.

¹⁴ Unless a short-form bill of lading is issued, in which case the terms will not appear on the reverse, but are obtainable from the office of the shipowners.

¹⁵ See <www.bimco.dk>.

¹⁶ See some of the forms referred to in Gaskell (1999). A particularly well-known example is that issued by P & O Nedlloyd: see Richardson (2003).

¹⁷ As to which, see para 5.11.

¹⁸ See *E Clemens Horst Co v Norfolk & North Western American Steam Navigation Co Ltd* (1906) 11 Com Cas 141.

¹⁹ Known as 'recta' bills of lading in continental countries. See Hugo Tiberg, 'Legal Qualities of Transport Documents' (1998–99) Tulane MLJ 1, 23.

²⁰ *CP Henderson & Co v The Comptoir d'Escompte de Paris* (1873) LR 5 PC 253, 259–260 (Sir Robert Collier).

²¹ For detailed consideration, see Stephen Girvin, 'Straight bills of lading in international trade: principles and practice' [2006] JBL 86.

negative transferability, such as 'non transferable' or 'not negotiable'.[22] In practice, many standard form bills of lading are hybrids permitting their issue in either form.[23] The effect of these words is to make impossible to transfer such bills of lading by endorsement, if required, and delivery.

3.09 **Background** The appearance, on the commercial scene, of straight bills of lading is shrouded in some uncertainty. Although it seems that straight bills of lading were not wholly disregarded by the drafters of the Hague Rules in 1924,[24] there are also other indications that, although not very common at this time,[25] they were certainly not unknown.[26]

3.10 **Issue** Today, such bills of lading are issued in those trades where a negotiable bill of lading is not required, particularly where it is envisaged that the bill of lading will not need to pass down a chain of buyers. Examples include: (i) the sale of goods to a consignee who does not wish to resell the goods; (ii) in-house transfers within large multinational companies; (iii) the issue of house bills by NVOCCs[27] or freight forwarders; (iv) regular sales between companies well known to each other.[28]

E. Charterparty Bills of Lading

3.11 **Functions** As we have seen, in many instances goods will be transported on a ship which is under charter. In the case where the shipper of the goods is the charterer, the terms of the contract of carriage will be contained in the charterparty and not in any bill of lading issued in respect of the goods.[29] In such an instance, a charterparty bill of lading, rather than a liner bill of lading, will often be issued. Depending on the needs of the charterer, this bill of lading may be issued in negotiable or non-negotiable form. Where a charterparty bill of lading is issued and consigned to a third party or an endorsee, the bill of lading will constitute the contract of carriage and the shipowner will wish to ensure that his rights against the charterer are carried forward to the bill of lading terms.[30]

---

[22] As they were in *Mobil Shipping & Transportation Co v Shell Eastern Petroleum plc (The Mobil Courage)* [1987] 2 Lloyd's Rep 655, 658, (AW Hamilton QC).

[23] This was the case with the bill of lading in *JI MacWilliam Co Inc v Mediterranean Shipping Co SA (The Rafaela S)* [2005] UKHL 11; [2005] 2 AC 423. But cf *The Chitral* [2000] 1 Lloyd's Rep 529.

[24] On the contrary, the effect of such bills of lading, in the light of Art I(b) was actively considered by those attending the diplomatic conferences in 1922: see Berlingieri (1997), 109.

[25] See, eg *Thrige v United Shipping Co Ltd* (1924) 18 Ll LR 6, where Scrutton LJ referred to the bills of lading as being in a 'very odd and unusual form . . .' (at 8).

[26] See *CP Henderson & Co v Comptoir d'Escompte de Paris* (1873) LR 5 PC 253, 259–260.

[27] ie 'Non-Vessel Owning Common Carrier', defined in the US Shipping Act 1984, s 3(17)(B), as a 'common carrier that does not operate the vessels by which the ocean transportation is provided, and is a shipper in its relationship with an ocean common carrier' (see 46 App USC §1702 (2002).

[28] See, eg, Gaskell (1999), para 1.47; *The use of transport documents in international trade* (UNCTAD, 2003) 23.

[29] *Sewell v Burdick* (1884) 10 App Cas 74, 105 (Lord Bramwell); *Radocanachi v Milburn* (1886) 18 QBD 67, 75–76 (Lord Esher MR); *Leduc v Ward* (1888) 20 QBD 475, 479 (Lord Esher MR); *President of India v Metcalfe Shipping Co (The Dunelmia)* [1970] 1 QB 289 (CA), 305 (Lord Denning MR); *The Al Battani* [1993] 2 Lloyd's Rep 219, 222 (Sheen J).

[30] See *Welex AG v Rosa Maritime Ltd (The Epsilon Rosa)* [2003] EWCA Civ 938; [2003] 2 Lloyd's Rep 509, at [25] (Tuckey LJ).

Characteristics   The main formal difference between a charterparty bill of lading and a liner   **3.12**
bill of lading consists in the terms on the reverse. In place of the long list of clauses found in a
liner bill of lading,[31] a charterparty bill of lading contains a much smaller number of clauses.
The most important of these is an incorporation clause, which incorporates into the bill of lading the terms of the charterparty. A typical example states that 'All terms and conditions, liberties and exceptions of the Charter Party, dated as overleaf, including the Law and Arbitration
Clause, are herewith incorporated'.[32] Other clauses in the Congenbill form include a general
paramount clause,[33] a clause relating to the adjustment of general average under the
York–Antwerp Rules 1994,[34] the New Jason clause,[35] and a both-to-blame collision clause.[36]

F. Freight Forwarders' Bills of Lading

Introduction: As we have already noted, the task of arranging and consolidating shipments   **3.13**
for export is often delegated to freight forwarders.[37] When acting in their traditional role,
which is as agent for the cargo owner or shipper,[38] freight forwarders are said to be willing to
'forward goods for you or to book you to the uttermost ends of the earth' and '. . . do not undertake to carry, and they are not undertaking to do it either themselves or by their agent. They are
simply undertaking to get somebody to do the work . . .'.[39] Hill defined the freight forwarder as

> any person which holds itself out to the general public to . . . provide and arrange transporta-
> tion of property, for compensation, and which may assemble and consolidate shipments of
> such property, and performs or provides for the performance of break bulk and distributing
> operations with respect to such consolidated shipments and assumes responsibility for the
> transportation of such property from point of receipt to point of destination and utilises for
> the whole or any part of the transportation of such shipments, the services of a carrier or
> carriers by sea, land, or air, or any combination thereof.[40]

Modern role: exporting goods   In tandem with the now widespread use of containers for   **3.14**
the transportation of goods,[41] other than bulk goods, it has become increasingly common
in modern trading conditions for the freight forwarder to perform a much wider role, particularly when arranging through and multimodal carriage.[42] In relation to exports, freight
forwarders may provide all or some of the following services:

(a) *Transport distribution analysis* — an examination of the options available to the shipper
to distribute the goods; (b) *Transportation arrangements* — a major function involving the

---

[31] Eg, Conlinebill 2000, where there are eighteen numbered clauses. See above, para, 3.07.
[32] Congenbill, cl 1. For full discussion of incorporation clauses, see para 12.14.
[33] Clause 2. See para 19.51.
[34] Clause 3. As to general average, see Rose (2005).
[35] Clause 4. Named after *The Jason* (1912) 225 US 32.This clause is included to deal with certain problems which arise under US law concerning general average and salvage and is usually to be found in most bills
of lading and charterparties. See, eg, Gilmore and Black (1975), §5–13.
[36] Clause 5. This clause is also introduced to deal with US law.
[37] See para 1.23. See too Jan Ramberg, 'Freight forwarders' in Faber (1997), ch 2.
[38] See *Jones v European & General Express Co Ltd* (1920) 25 Com Cas 296, 298.
[39] *C A Pisani & Co Ltd v Brown, Jenkinson & Co Ltd* (1939) 64 Ll LR 340, 342 (Goddard J).
[40] Hill (1972), para 22. This definition was adapted from the US Interstate Commerce Act 1887.
[41] See para 1.11.
[42] ie carriage door-to-door.

booking and despatch of the goods between the consignor's and consignee's premises or other specified points; (c) *Documentation* — provision of all the prescribed documentation for the goods having regard to all the statutory requirements and terms of the export sales contract; (d) *Customs* — all the customs clearance arrangements including documentation and entry requirements at the time of exportation and importation; (e) *Payment of freight and other charges* — payment of freight to the prescribed carrier, including handling charges raised by the airport, seaport or elsewhere during the transit; (f) *Packaging and warehousing* — packing of goods for transit and warehousing provision; (g) *Cargo insurance* — the process of insuring goods during the transit; (h) *Consolidation, groupage and special services* — many forwarders specialize in consolidation offering major benefits to the shipper.[43]

3.15 **Modern role: importing goods** Freight forwarders also play an important role when goods are imported. In this context, they may provide all or some of the following services:

(a) *Notification of arrival* — the process of informing the importer of the date and location of the goods' arrival and the requisite documents required for customs clearance . . .; (b) *Customs clearance* — presentation and clearance of the cargo through customs . . .; (c) *Payment of VAT, duty, freight and other charges* — the forwarder will co-ordinate and effect payment of all such payments on behalf of his principal at the time of importation . . .; (d) *Delivery to the importer* — the process of delivering the goods to the importer's premises following customs clearance; (e) *Breaking bulk and distribution* — the agent may be an umbrella agent whereby he consolidates not only his own client's merchandise, but also those of other agents with whom he has a contractual arrangement. On arrival of the goods in the destination country, the cargo is handed over to the respective agents to process through customs and distribute.[44]

3.16 **Legal role** The legal role played by the freight forwarder has not comfortably kept pace with developments in commercial practice. Freight forwarders continue to act in an agency capacity only but, increasingly, such forwarders act as the principal to the contract,[45] particularly when they issue through transport bills of lading,[46] or multimodal transport bills of lading.[47] Determining the capacity in which the freight forwarder acts has often proved to be an elusive problem for those courts faced with contracts negotiated by forwarders, but a number of principles may be deduced from the cases.

3.17 **General considerations** The exact status of any document of carriage issued by a forwarder will be determined by a number of factors.[48] It should be noted, however, that the fact that a forwarder is described in the document of carriage as an agent will not, as a matter of law, prevent him from being regarded as the principal party to the contract.[49] Putting this another way, mere description as 'freight forwarder',[50] 'principal', 'agent', or 'forwarding

---

[43] See Branch (1996), 323–324.
[44] ibid.
[45] In which case he is sometimes known as a multimodal transport operator (MTO).
[46] See para 3.21 below.
[47] Discussed at para 3.22 below.
[48] See Shane Nossal, 'The legal status of freight forwarders' bills of lading' (1995) 25 HKLJ 78; Ian C Holloway, 'Troubled Waters: The Liability of the Freight Forwarder as a Principal Under Anglo-Canadian Law' (1986) 17 JMLC 243.
[49] See, eg, *Elektronska Industrija Oour TVA v Transped Oour Kintinentalna Spedicna* [1986] 1 Lloyd's Rep 49, 52, (Hobhouse J).
[50] See, eg, *Tetroc v Cross-Con (International) Ltd* [1981] 1 Lloyd's Rep 192, 196 (His Honour Judge Martin)— under the CMR.

agent', is not determinative; it is the substance of the obligation undertaken which is often pivotal in answering the question. The court's principal task is to construe the contract made with the shipper and it will have regard to the surrounding circumstances in determining this question.[51] Thus, each case invariably turns on its own facts.[52]

Factors In determining the question whether the forwarder is the agent or principal, the **3.18** courts will be guided by considerations such as whether the forwarder has held himself out as a carrier[53] and whether the forwarder has arranged 'to collect' rather than to 'arrange for the collection of the goods' or whether he has agreed 'to carry' rather than 'to arrange for the carriage of the goods'. The remuneration agreed with the forwarder may also assist the court. Thus, the fact that the remuneration is derived from a commission based on the actual cost of the transportation may point towards an agency role,[54] while a lump sum freight charged to the shipper will indicate the forwarder's role as carrier.[55] Other factors may include whether there is a lien over the goods in favour of the forwarder,[56] whether the cargo owner is to be informed of the arrangements made as to the carriage,[57] and whether the freight forwarder issues its own bill of lading while receiving a bill of lading from the actual carrier naming it as the shipper.[58] Inevitably, there have also been cases where forwarders have been held to have acted in a hybrid capacity.[59] In the case of *Aqualon (UK) Ltd v Vallana Shipping Corp*,[60] Mance J provided the following guidance as to the factors which throw light on the role undertaken by the freight forwarder:

a. the terms of the particular contract including the nature of the instructions given, for example whether they were to carry or for carriage or were to arrange carriage . . .; in this connection the nature and terms of any governing conditions also arise for consideration;

b. any description used or adopted by the parties in relation to the contracting party's role;

c. the course of any dealings, including the manner of performance — at least in so far as it throws light on the way in which the parties understood their relationship; thus whether or not the contracting party informed the goodsowner of or identified the actual arrangements made for carriage may be one factor in determining the former's role;

---

51 See *Marston Excelsior Ltd v Arbuckle Smith & Co* [1971] 2 Lloyd's Rep 306 (CA), 309 (Denning MR); *Elektronska Industrija Oour TVA v Transped Oour Kintinentalna Spedicna* [1986] 1 Lloyd's Rep 49, 51 (Hobhouse J).

52 *EMI (New Zealand) Ltd v William Holyman & Sons Pty Ltd* [1976] 2 NZLR 566 (HC).

53 See *Marston Excelsior Ltd v Arbuckle Smith & Co* [1971] 2 Lloyd's Rep 306 (CA), 311 (forwarders were agents); *Elektronska Industrija Oour TVA v Transped Oour Kintinentalna Spedicna* [1986] 1 Lloyd's Rep 49, 52 (forwarders were carriers); *Harlow & Jones Ltd v PJ Walker Shipping & Transport Ltd* [1986] 2 Lloyd's Rep 141, 144 (forwarders were agents); *Blue Nile Co Ltd v Emery Customs Brokers (S) Pte Ltd* [1992] 1 SLR 296, 310–311 (forwarders were carriers).

54 *Marston Excelsior Ltd v Arbuckle Smith & Co* [1971] 2 Lloyd's Rep 306 (CA), 310–311, (Denning MR).

55 *Elektronska Industrija Oour TVA v Transped Oour Kintinentalna Spedicna* [1986] 1 Lloyd's Rep 49, 53 (Hobhouse J).

56 See *Langley, Beldon & Gaunt Ltd v Morley* [1965] 1 Lloyd's Rep 297.

57 *Blue Nile Co Ltd v Emery Customs Brokers (S) Pte Ltd* [1992] 1 SLR 296, 311.

58 See *Platzhoff v Lebean* (1865) 4 F & F 545; 176 ER 684 (forwarder an agent).

59 See, eg, *Lee Cooper Ltd v CH Jeakins & Sons* [1967] 2 QB 1; *The Maheno* [1977] 1 Lloyd's Rep 81, 88 (Beattie J); *Carrington Slipways Pty Ltd v Patrick Operations Pty Ltd* (1991) 24 NSWLR 745.

60 [1994] 1 Lloyd's Rep 669, 674, cited with approval in *Lukoil-Kalingradmorneft Plc v Tata Ltd (No 2)* [1999] 2 Lloyd's Rep 129, 137.

    d. the nature and basis of charging (in particular whether an all-in fee was charged, leaving the contracting party to make such profit as he could from the margin between it and costs incurred);

    e. the nature and terms of any [document] issued.[61]

3.19   **Freight forwarder's house bills of lading**   Although, as we have seen, it is always a matter of construction, house bills of lading are not, technically speaking, bills of lading. This is because, in issuing such a bill of lading, the freight forwarder may be acting in his capacity as the agent of the shipper. In these circumstances, the bill of lading which is issued will be no more than a receipt for the goods;[62] further, the forwarder will not even be regarded as the bailee of the goods.[63] It follows also from this that such a house bill of lading cannot be regarded as a document of title.[64]

3.20   **Freight forwarder as principal**   As we have seen, it is a question of construction as to whether or not a forwarding agent is acting as agent or as principal. If acting as principal, the forwarding agent will usually be regarded as having the right to employ subcontracting carriers to carry out all, or part of, the carriage. This right to subcontract the actual carriage may be implied by custom, in the absence of express provision, but is usually spelt out in more detail in the terms of carriage.

G. Through (Combined Transport) Bills of Lading

3.21   **Introduction**   The distinction between through (combined transport) bills of lading and multimodal transport bills of lading is notoriously difficult to pin down, mainly because the terms tend to be used interchangeably and very imprecisely. As with multimodal transport bills of lading, the term tends to be used for carriage of goods which involves more than one leg. It is sometimes said that a through bill of lading is issued when at least one of the stages is by sea.[65] Most of the problems that arise from the use of through bills of lading arise with multimodal bills of lading and this is dealt with in the next section.

H. Multimodal Transport and Bills of Lading

3.22   **Liability**   The main difficulty which is likely to be encountered by the parties to a multimodal contract will arise from the potentially wide disparity of terms and conditions in operation in the various unimodal forms of transport. There are a series of mandatory unimodal transport conventions which impose different liability regimes on the operators of the various modes of transport. As we shall see in due course, attempts to achieve a uniform scheme of liability internationally has been fraught with difficulty. There are strong views

---

[61] See also *Coli Shipping (UK) Ltd v Andrea Merzario Ltd* [2002] 1 Lloyd's Rep 608.

[62] See *Emilio Clot & Co v Compagnie Commerciale du Nord SA* (1921) 8 Ll LR 380.

[63] *A Gagniere & Co v Eastern Co of Warehouses Insurance and Transport of Goods with Advances Ltd* (1921) 7 Ll LR 188, 189.

[64] See para 8.02.

[65] As, eg, in the important US case of *Norfolk Southern Railway Co v James N Kirby Pty Ltd* 2004 AMC 2705.

as to the scheme of liability which should be adopted. While proponents of the 'uniform' approach advocate a single uniform regime of liability for the contract from the point of despatch until its arrival at its destination, proponents of the 'network' system argue that, where it can be established at which stage of transit particular loss or damage occurred, the liability of the carrier should be regulated by the appropriate convention or national law which is applicable to that mode of transport.

The International Chamber of Commerce (ICC) Uniform Rules (1975)   The ICC has **3.23** played an important role in the publication of rules for documents used in combined transport. The first such attempt was its document, Uniform Rules for a Combined Transport Document (1975),[66] which proposed the adoption of a single combined transport document for the transportation of goods by means of two or more modes of transport. The issue of such a document would avoid the need to issue a series of separate transport documents for each stage of the transport. It based itself very heavily on the TCM Convention and its underlying basis was 'network liability', viz, that, if the stage where the loss or damage occurred could be localized, the relevant international convention which governed that particular mode of transport would apply. The ICC Rules are designed to be incorporated into a combined transport document by private contract. The precise extent to which they are successful depends on how readily they are utilized in commerce. In practice, however, the Rules have had quite a widespread influence, although it has been rare for them to be incorporated in full into carriage documents. The usual practice has been a partial incorporation of the ICC Rules with the addition of other clauses and variations peculiar to particular carriers. But there are two significant exceptions, where the Rules have been incorporated in full: the FIATA FBL combined transport bill of lading (1978) and the COMBIDOC bill published under the auspices of BIMCO (1977).

Background to the Multimodal Convention   Work on a liability regime for multimodal **3.24** transport began as early as the 1950s by the International Institute for the Unification of Private Law (UNIDROIT) which took as its point of departure the Convention on the Contract for International Carriage of Goods by Road (CMR)(1956). This work was also taken up by the Comité Maritime International (CMI). A particular concern was the difficulty of damage which could not be accurately located either in time or in place. The CMI produced a draft set of rules in Tokyo in 1969 ('The Tokyo Convention on Combined Transports'), known as the Tokyo Rules. A modified draft convention, which became known as the TCM (*Transport Combiné de Marchandises* — 'Draft Convention of the Combined Transport of Goods'), was produced in 1971.

UNCTAD   At about the same time as the emergence of the TCM, preparations were well **3.25** under way for a UN Conference on Containerisation at Geneva, sponsored by the UN and IMCO. When it met in 1972, it recommended that further studies be carried out on aspects of multimodal transport, including the basic economic implications, with special attention to be given to developing countries. ECOSOC (the Economic and Social Council of the UN) endorsed the recommendations of the UN/IMCO Conference and in its Resolution 1734 (LIV) requested that UNCTAD create an Intergovernmental

---

[66] Brochure No 298.

Preparatory Group (known as the IPG)[67] to prepare a draft convention on international multimodal transport. This was agreed to by the Trade and Development Board of UNCTAD in May 1973. The main point of interest here is that UNCTAD has neither a technical nor a legal orientation. Its primary focus is on economic issues in a political context and this can be seen from its statement of principle, enunciated at its first session in 1964:

> All countries should cooperate in devising measures to help developing countries to build up maritime and other means of transport for their economic development, to ensure the unhindered use of international transport facilities, the improvement of terms of freight and insurance for the developing countries, and to promote tourism in these countries in order to increase their earnings and reduce their expenditures on invisible trade.

The IPG, consisting of representatives of fifty member countries of the UN as well as other intergovernmental groups, was formed and met on six occasions between 1973 and 1979 under the chairmanship of Professor Erling Selvig.

3.26 **Diplomatic conference**[68] A diplomatic conference of plenipotentiaries convened at Geneva in 1979 and in May 1980. There were eight outstanding issues: the liability regime; mandatory application and invalid clauses; documentation; the air-leg problem and pick-up and delivery; scope of application and entry into force; the recognition and enforcement of judgments; relation to other conventions; issues relating to customs. Certain of these issues were dealt with easily and real confrontation then surfaced only in relation to the question of the liability regime to be adopted and the relation of the Convention to the other conventions. The developed nations were the only ones to insist on the 'network' scheme of liability but this was forcefully opposed by each of the other groups. In the end the Group B countries gave up this entrenched position in return for the Group of 77's compromise on other issues.

3.27 **Convention** At the conclusion of its deliberations on 24 May 1980, the delegates to the Conference adopted, by consensus, the Convention on International Multimodal Transport of Goods.[69] It remained open for signature until 31 August 1981 and provided that it was to come into force twelve months after the ratifications of thirty states.[70] The Convention comprises a preamble, followed by forty articles and an annex containing provisions on customs matters. The preamble contains agreement to a number of principles, especially 'that a fair balance of interests between developed and developing countries should be established and an equitable distribution of activities between these groups of countries should be attained in international multimodal transport'.

---

[67] For a detailed analysis, see William J Driscoll, 'The Convention on International Multimodal Transport: A Status Report' (1978) 8 JMLC 441.

[68] See Wei Jia Ju, 'UN Multimodal Transport Convention' (1981) 15 Journal of World Trade Law 285.

[69] See Erik Chrispeels, 'The United Nations Convention on International Multimodal Transport of Goods: A background note' (1980) 15 ETL 355; Samir Mankabady, 'The multimodal transport of goods convention: A challenge to unimodal transport conventions' (1983) 32 ICLQ 120; Kurosh Nasseri, 'The Multimodal Convention' (1988) 19 JMLC 231; Anthony Diamond, 'The United Nations Convention on International Multimodal Transport of Goods' in Faber (1997), ch 5.

[70] Article 36.

Problems   One of the remaining issues for the delegates to the Multimodal Conference   **3.28**
was whether the Convention's entry into force should be relatively easy to accomplish or
whether it should depend upon adoption by a substantial number of states having a substantial amount of trade. The former was favoured by the Group of 77 while the latter was
endorsed by the Group B countries. Eventually the Group B countries accepted the proposal of the Group of 77 for entry into force based on the number of ratifying states but the
Group of 77 were forced to concede a substantially higher number of states. Thus article
36(1) of the Convention provided that it was to come into force 12 months after the governments of 30 states have become parties to it.

Failure   The prospects for the coming into force of this Convention are poor in view of   **3.29**
the very slow rate of ratification thus far.[71] The underlying philosophy of the Convention
is so strongly linked to the Hamburg Rules that it is hardly surprising that the Convention
has not attracted the signatures of any developed country or, indeed, any country with a
substantial fleet.[72]

The UNCTAD/ICC Rules for Multimodal Transport Documents 1992   Following the   **3.30**
adoption of the Multimodal Convention in Geneva in 1980, UNCTAD, its sponsor, mon-
itored very carefully its progress. When in 1986 it became clear that it was likely to take several years before the required number of ratifications could be achieved and, bearing in
mind that the Convention had not provided for any model form of transport document,
the UNCTAD secretariat set out to produce one which might encourage eventual commercial adoption of the Convention. The UNCTAD secretariat established a joint working group with the ICC with the intention to elaborate provisions for multimodal
transport documents based on the Hague Rules and Hague–Visby Rules as well as existing
transport documents. The result of the joint deliberations of UNCTAD and the ICC is the
UNCTAD/ICC Rules for Multimodal Transport Documents,[73] adopted in 1991 and
brought into effect on 1 January 1992. The new Rules therefore replace the 1975 ICC
Uniform Rules and hence the reason for a more detailed consideration of the new regime.[74]

Application   Rule 1.1 provides that the Rules apply when they are incorporated (howso-   **3.31**
ever this is done) into a contract of carriage and irrespective of whether there is a unimodal
or MT contract involving one or several modes of transport or whether such a document
has been issued or not. Where the Rules are so made applicable to the contract in this way,
Rule 1.2 provides that the parties are to agree that the Rules are to supersede any additional
terms of the MT contract which conflict with the Rules 'except insofar as they increase the
responsibility or obligations of the MTO'.

Definitions   On the whole the definitions in the Rules are simpler than those in the   **3.32**
Multimodal Convention. Thus, a multimodal contract 'means a single contract for the

---

[71] The ten countries which have ratified the Convention are: Chile, Georgia, Lebanon, Liberia,
Malawi, Mexico, Morocco, Rwanda, Senegal, and Zambia. Source: <www.untreaty.un.org> (UN Treaty
Collection).
[72] See ch 16.
[73] Brochure No 481.
[74] See particularly Kindred and Brooks (1997).

carriage of goods by at least two different modes of transport' (Rule 2.1). A 'carrier' is 'the person who actually performs or undertakes to perform the carriage, or part thereof, whether he is identical with the multimodal transport operator or not'. The definition of 'MT document' is intended to include negotiable and non-negotiable transport documents as well as the case where the paper document has been replaced by electronic data interchange messages (Rule 2.6).

3.33 **Evidentiary effect** Rule 3 provides that the MT document 'shall be *prima facie* evidence of the taking in charge by the MTO of the goods as described by such information unless a contrary indication . . . has been made in the printed text or superimposed on the document'. But proof to the contrary is not admissible when the MT document has been 'transferred . . . by the consignee who in good faith has relied and acted thereon'. It may be noted that the MT document under the Rules does not require any particular information to be included.[75]

3.34 **Responsibilities of the MTO** These are set out in Rule 4. Thus Rule 4.1 simply provides that the period of responsibility is 'from the time the MTO has taken the goods in his charge to the time of delivery'. This may be compared with the more complex regulation set out in the Convention in article 14. Rule 4.2 ('the liability of the MTO for his servants, agents and other persons') corresponds to article 15 of the Convention and Rule 4.3 which sets out to whom the MTO should deliver is in roughly the same terms as articles 6 and 7 of the Convention.

3.35 **The liability of the MTO** Rule 13 of the Rules provides that they 'shall only take effect to the extent that they are not contrary to the mandatory provisions of international conventions or national law applicable to the MT contract'. In view of this, the liability scheme proposed by the Rules is rather more simplified than the scheme in the Convention. The basic liability in Rule 5.1 is similar to article 16 of the Convention in the sense the presumption of fault of the MTO is the general principle of liability: it provides that the MTO is 'liable for loss of or damage to the goods, as well as for delay in delivery, if the occurrence which caused the loss, damage or delay in delivery took place while the goods were in his charge . . .' There is no distinction between 'concealed' or 'localized' loss.

3.36 **Sea carriage** Rule 5.4 provides that if the goods are carried by sea or inland waterway then the MTO can rely on the Hague–Visby defences of act, neglect, or default in the navigation or management of the ship and fire without actual fault or privity unless there has been a failure to exercise due diligence to make the vessel seaworthy. This marks out an important distinction between the Convention and the Rules and is intended to reflect commercial reality.

3.37 **Limitation of liability of the MTO** This is specified in Rule 6 and has been based on the Hague–Visby Rules. Thus the MTO's liability is not to exceed 'the equivalent of 666.67 SDR per package or unit or 2 SDR per kilogramme of gross weight of the goods lost or damaged, whichever is the higher'. There is also a container formula in Rule 6.2 whereby

---

[75] cf art 8 of the Convention.

the claimant can use the units inside the container for limitation purposes provided they have been mentioned in the transport document. Much like article 18(3) of the Convention, Rule 6.3 provides that, if the multimodal contract does not include a sea leg, the liability of the MTO is to be limited to 'an amount not exceeding 8.33 SDR per kilogramme of gross weight of the goods lost or damaged'. Rule 6.4 provides that, where the loss of or damage to the goods occurred during one particular stage of the multimodal transport where an applicable international convention or mandatory national law would have provided another limit of liability if a separate contract of carriage had been made for that particular stage of transport, then the limit of the MTO's liability for such loss or damage is to be determined by reference to the provisions of that convention or mandatory national law. Thus, another monetary limit may be applicable when loss or damage can be localized to a particular stage of transport: both parties to the MT contract can then have access to such higher or lower limit of liability as they would have had if they had concluded a contract of carriage for the relevant segment of the transport. Where the MTO is liable for loss following from delay in delivery or consequential loss or damage other than loss of or damage to the goods then Rule 6.5 goes on to say that the liability of the MTO is to be limited to 'an amount not exceeding the equivalent of the freight under the MT contract . . .'. As it should not be possible for the claimant to get the freight limitation in addition to the unit and per kilogramme limitation, Rule 6.6 provides for an aggregation of the limits so that they may never exceed the limit of liability for a total loss of the goods.

Remaining provisions   So far as the liability of the consignor is concerned, this is set out **3.38** in Rule 8. Again the provision is more limited than the equivalent provision in the Multimodal Convention.[76] Rule 9 provides for notice of loss or damage to be given at the time of delivery in the case of apparent damage and this is analogous to article 24(1) of the Convention which refers to the working day after the day the goods were delivered to the consignee. In the case of non-apparent loss, the requirement of six days' notice in Rule 9.2 is the same as in article 24(2) of the MT Convention. So far as any time bar is concerned this is specified in Rule 10 as '9 months after the delivery of the goods, or the date when the goods should have been delivered, or the date when, in accordance with Rule 5.3, failure to deliver the goods would give the consignee the right to treat the goods as lost'. This is in respect of claims against the MTO and may be compared with the period of two years allowed under article 25(1) of the Convention.

Assessment   In an effort to move the debate forward both UNCTAD and the ICC have **3.39** co-operated in a venture in which the former has effectively backtracked on its support for the 1980 Convention. As the use of the new Rules is not mandatory in contracts, the success of the initiative will depend heavily on the acceptability of the new Rules to the major participants. The inclusion of consequential loss in the Rules acknowledges strongly that this form of loss is a very real concern. However, the potential impact of this innovation is somewhat diminished because the limits of liability for this kind of loss are tied to the value of the freight and also curtailed by the strictures on the aggregate limit set out in Rule 6.6. So far as the liability of the MTO is concerned, the Rules may be regarded by cargo

---

[76] See arts 12, 22, 23.

interests as a step back from the Convention because of the inclusion of the exceptions from liability in the case of a sea leg. But the new Rules are likely to be more favourably received by shipowners, given that the basic scheme is based on the Hague and Hague–Visby Rules rather than the Hamburg Rules. Further, given that shippers commonly defer to the rules imprinted by the MTO on the back of his contractual documents, the shipper may ultimately have little choice over their use.

4

OTHER DOCUMENTS OF CARRIAGE

A. Introduction

Overview   In this chapter we consider other documents of carriage which are sometimes   **4.01**
encountered, often in place of the use of the bill of lading, or in conjunction with it. In particular, we concentrate on two documents of some significance, sea waybills (or waybills), and ship's delivery orders.

B. Sea Waybills

Importance   Sea waybills,[1] once described as the 'modern contract of carriage of goods by   **4.02**
sea',[2] are very much part of the commercial shipping scene today.[3] Judith Prakash J
provided the following succinct summary of their main features in the Singapore case of
Voss Peer v APL Co Pte Ltd:

> A sea waybill is the maritime version of a document that has long been in use in the context
> of land and air carriage. It operates as a receipt for goods received for shipment and evidences
> the contract of carriage. One significant difference between it and a bill of lading is that it is
> never ever a negotiable instrument and is therefore usually used on short sea routes and where
> neither the shipper nor the cargo receiver needs to pledge shipping documents in order to
> raise finance. It is not issued in sets and the receiver is able to take delivery of the goods merely

---

[1] See Richard Williams, 'Waybills and Short Form Documents: A lawyer's view' [1979] LMCLQ 297;
John F Wilson, 'Legal problems at common law associated with the use of the sea waybill' (1989) 91 II Diritto
Marittimo 115; Charles Debattista, 'Waybills: conclusive evidence with respect to details of the cargo' (1989)
91 II Diritto Marittimo 127; Gordon Humphreys & Andrew Higgs, 'Waybills: A Case of Common Law
Laissez Faire in European Commerce' [1992] JBL 453; Carver (2005), para 8-001.

[2] William Tetley (1983) 14 JMLC 465; (1984) 15 JMLC 41.

[3] Although they are nothing like as widely used as negotiable bills of lading. In one survey, 51% of
users indicated that they issued sea waybills, although only 23% of this total indicated that they were used
in a majority of transactions: see *The use of transport documents in international trade* (UNCTAD, 2003),
para 47.

by establishing his identity. The original sea waybill need not be produced. Further, since it is not a bill of lading the Hague Rules and the Hague–Visby Rules do not apply to it.[4]

This summary highlights a number of important points which we shall look at.

4.03 **Usage** Where goods are carried by sea it is not uncommon to find that the shipper and receiver of the goods do not require a negotiable document of title. Thus, for example, if an importer and exporter of goods have a long-standing commercial relationship, the exporter may be prepared to send goods to the importer on credit trusting the importer to pay when the exporter sends his account. Alternatively, the importer may pay in advance, trusting the exporter to send the goods. In such a case the parties will not have any need for a bill of lading to secure the payment of the purchase price and may therefore choose instead to use a sea waybill. Another example involves multinational groups of companies. Where, for example, the national subsidiary of a multinational company in one country sends goods to another subsidiary in a different country it would be possible for payment to be made in-house, through group accounting, or through the transfer of credit from the one subsidiary to the other.[5] Finally, in some trades it will be the custom of the trade for sea way-bills to be issued, although whether that is so will be a matter for actual agreement between the shipper and the carrier. Recent research has indicated that such documents are primarily used in liner trades to and from North America and the Far East, as well as intra-European routes.[6] They are particularly attractive in trades involving short sea voyages, such as the cross-channel ferry trade, where it is likely that the goods will reach the receiver before any bills of lading could.

4.04 **Advantages** Unlike a bill of lading, the sea waybill does not change hands because it is not usually used for the purpose of payment for the goods. The clear advantage of this is that the shipper can vary his delivery instructions to the carrier at any time during transit. Furthermore, commercial documents (such as invoices and certificates of origin) can be sent to the buyer earlier than otherwise because there is no waiting period for the waybill to be produced, as there is with a bill of lading. There is no problem with the ship arriving ahead of the documents and so the ship can discharge at once. This means that the goods can be cleared faster, that there are lower inventory costs, and an overall faster shipping process. UNCTAD has recommended waybills to the market as one of the main instruments against documentary fraud.[7]

4.05 **Functions of a sea waybill** As we have already noted,[8] a sea waybill performs two of the three functions that a traditional bill of lading performs. In the first place, the sea waybill acts as a receipt for the goods shipped.[9] Secondly, the sea waybill evidences the contract of carriage between the shipper and the carrier.[10] A sea waybill is not a document of title at

---

[4] [2002] 3 SLR 176, 186.
[5] See Richardson (2003), 39.
[6] *The use of transport documents in international trade* (UNCTAD, 2003) para 67. See too Debattista (1998), para 2-22.
[7] See Debattista (1998), para 2-22.
[8] See para 4.02.
[9] See ch 6.
[10] See ch 7.

common law[11] and hence <u>ownership in the goods</u> represented in the sea waybill <u>will pass by reason of the underlying transaction.</u>

Same as a straight bill of lading?   A question which arises is whether a sea waybill is the   **4.06** same as a straight bill of lading.[12] <u>Several authorities have, in the past, suggested that they are one and the same thing</u>[13] and <u>empirical research has revealed a great deal of uncertainty</u> on the matter among users.[14] The authorities will now have to be read in the light of two recent cases which have concluded differently. The first is <u>V*oss Peer v APL Co Pte Ltd*</u>,[15] a decision at first instance of the Singapore High Court, subsequently affirmed by the Singapore Court of Appeal.[16] At first instance Judith Prakash J <u>clearly differentiated between the two transport documents</u>:

> A shipper who . . . asks for the issue of a <u>straight bill</u> of lading even though the alternative of a sea waybill is available to him, wants to <u>retain some degree of control over the delivery of the goods</u>. The shipowner is aware of this. If he is not prepared to accept the restriction on delivery rights that a bill of lading imposes he can insist on issuing a waybill instead.[17]

Although this statement went to the question of <u>whether a straight bill of lading needed to be presented in order to obtain delivery of the goods</u>,[18] the Court of Appeal subsequently took a firmer view:

> The entire argument of the appellants is that a straight BL is the same as a sea waybill. While it is true that a BL, devoid of the characteristic of negotiability, is substantially similar in effect to that of a sea waybill, that is not to say that they are the same. If the parties had intended to create a sea waybill they would have done so.[19]

This issue was then taken up by the English courts and, in particular, Rix LJ confirmed in *J I MacWilliam Co Inc v Mediterranean Shipping Co SA (The Rafaela S)* that '<u>carriers should not use bill of lading forms if what they invite shippers to do is to enter into sea waybill type contracts</u>'.[20] In the House of Lords Lord Steyn warned that when the carrier tried to equate the function of a straight bill of lading, this was 'plainly unrealistic':

> <u>In the hands of the named consignee the straight bill of lading is *his* document of title. On the other hand, a sea waybill is never a document of title.</u> No trader, insurer or banker would assimilate the two. The differences between the documents include the fact that a straight bill of lading contains the standard terms of the carrier on the reverse side of the document but a sea waybill is blank and straight bills of lading are invariably issued in sets of three and waybills not. Except for the fact that <u>a straight bill of lading is only transferable to a named</u>

---

[11] Although it could become a document of title if there was a proof of custom to this effect. This seems unlikely.

[12] As to straight bills of lading, see para 3.08.

[13] See, eg, *Rights of Suit in Respect of Carriage of Goods by Sea*, Law Com No 196 (Scot Law Com No 130), para 5.6; Debattista (1998), para 2-32; Gaskell (1999), para 1.49.

[14] *The use of transport documents in international trade* (UNCTAD, 2003), 11.

[15] [2002] 3 SLR 176.

[16] [2002] 2 Lloyd's Rep 707.

[17] [2002] 3 SLR 176, at [33].

[18] See para 10.12.

[19] [2002] 2 Lloyd's Rep 707, at [48].

[20] [2003] EWCA Civ 556; [2004] QB 702, at [146].

consignee and not generally, a straight bill of lading shares all the principal characteristics of a bill of lading as already described.[21]

4.07 **Format**   Sea waybills bear a striking resemblance to bills of lading, at least superficially. There are a number of well-known private forms, such as P & O Nedlloyd,[22] and equally certain forms which are endorsed by BIMCO, the most well known of which is Genwaybill.[23] The face of the sea waybill contains a number of boxes which will be filled in by the contracting parties. Thus, these include such matters as the name of the shipper, the consignee, the name and address of the notify party, the name of the vessel, the port of discharge, and the port of loading. There is also space for the description of the cargo. The conditions of carriage are contained on the reverse of the waybill and may include a paramount clause,[24] making the Hague or Hague–Visby Rules applicable to the waybill as a matter of contract.[25]

4.08 **Presentation**   The receiver of the cargo under a sea waybill does not need to present the original in order to obtain delivery. This is because the sea waybill simply names the receiver in the box marked 'consignee' and the carrier may deliver the goods to the receiver once he identifies himself as the named consignee. This is provided for in the Overseas Containers Limited (OCL) non-negotiable waybill:

> Delivery will be made to the consignee named or his authorised agent, on production of proof of identity at the place of delivery. Should the consignee require delivery elsewhere than at the place of delivery as shown below then written instructions must be given by the consignee to the carrier or his agent. Should delivery be required to be made to a party other than that named as consignee, authorisation must be given in writing by the shipper to the carrier or his agent.[26]

4.09 **Carriage of Goods by Sea Act 1992**   Hitherto, one of the main difficulties with sea waybills was that it was unclear whether a consignee could sue under the contract of carriage. Sea waybills were not documents to which the Bills of Lading Act 1855 applied.[27] This potential difficulty has been much ameliorated by the Carriage of Goods by Sea Act 1992, which applies to sea waybills[28] and defines a sea waybill in section 1(3) as a document which is not a bill of lading but

> (a) is such a receipt for goods as contains or evidences a contract for the carriage of goods by sea; and
> (b) identifies the person to whom delivery of the goods is to be made by the carrier in accordance with that contract.

The Law Commission saw the advantage of including sea waybills in the following terms:

> Reform would be for the benefit of cargo and ship alike. For cargo interests, because it is unsatisfactory that the only person who has suffered loss (the consignee) cannot sue, even

---

[21] [2005] UKHL 11; [2005] 2 AC 423, at [46].
[22] See Richardson (2003), 38.
[23] See <www.bimco.dk>.
[24] As to paramount clauses generally, see para 19.51.
[25] See too the Carriage of Goods by Sea Act 1971, s 1(6)(b), which can have the effect of giving the Hague–Visby Rules the 'force of law'. See para 18.08.
[26] See the similar wording in Genwaybill.
[27] The Act only applied to bills of lading: see para 8.12.
[28] Section 1(1)(b).

though the contract was made for his benefit, whereas the only person who has a contractual right of action (the shipper) may have no incentive to sue where he has suffered no loss, and may in any event be unable to recover substantial damages. For shipowners, because any actions brought against them will be on the terms of the contract of carriage. Such liability is clearly preferable to the potentially greater and more indeterminate liability in tort.[29]

Transfer of rights   For the purposes of the Act, section 2(1)(b) provides that the holder of   **4.10**
a sea waybill has transferred and vested in him 'all rights of suit under the contract of carriage as if he had been a party to that contract'. Thus the Act gives the holder of a sea waybill contractual rights of suit in return for the liabilities under section 3.[30]

Change in the name of the consignee   Section 5(3) of the Act provides that: **4.11**

> References in this Act to a person's being identified in a document include references to his being identified by a description which allows for the identity of the person in question to be varied, in accordance with the terms of the document, after its issue; and the reference in section 1(3)(b) of this Act to a document's identifying a person shall be construed accordingly.

This provision makes it clear that, in the case of a sea waybill, the person entitled to rights of suit under the Act includes a person not originally named as the consignee who subsequently becomes that person. This confirms that the shipper would be able to vary his instructions to the carrier so that the latter is required to deliver to someone other than the original consignee.

CMI Rules   In June 1990 the Comité Maritime International (CMI) produced the CMI   **4.12**
Uniform Rules for Sea Waybills.[31] The Rules were the product of an International Sub-Committee chaired by Sir Anthony Lloyd.[32] Rule 1(ii) provides that:

> They shall apply when adopted by a contract of carriage which is not covered by a bill of lading or similar document of title, whether the contract be in writing or not.

This makes it clear that the Rules are not mandatory and will apply only when specifically incorporated into the contract of carriage.[33] Other provisions of the Rules address rights and responsibilities (Rule 4), the description of the goods (Rule 5), rights of control (Rule 6), and delivery (Rule 7). The terms of carriage are specified to be the carrier's standard terms, 'unless otherwise agreed by the parties'.[34] However, this provision is subject to the compulsory application of any international convention or national law.[35]

C. Ship's Delivery Orders

Meaning   At common law, ship's delivery orders[36] are documents either issued by a carrier,   **4.13**
or by a seller, followed by an attornment by the carrier,[37] and contain an undertaking by the

---

29 *Rights of Suit in Respect of Carriage of Goods by Sea*, Law Com No 196 (Scot Law Com No 130), para 5.11.
30 See para 8.22.
31 See <www.comitemaritime.org/cmidocs/> where the Rules are reproduced.
32 See Sir Anthony Lloyd, 'The bill of lading: do we really need it?' [1989] LMCLQ 47.
33 As they are to Genwaybill.
34 Rule 4(ii)(b).
35 Rule 4(i).
36 See Nigel Teare, 'Ship's Delivery Orders' [1976] LMCLQ 154; Carver (2005), para 8-027.
37 See *Laurie & Morewood v Dudin & Sons* [1926] 1 KB 223 (CA), 236–238 (Scrutton LJ).

carrier to a person identified in the document to deliver the goods to which the document relates to that person. No rights are conferred against the carrier until the carrier has attorned to the person to whom delivery is due.

4.14 **Commercial need** The commercial need for such documents derives from the marked importance of the shipment of bulk cargoes by sea.[38] [The seller of bulk cargo may wish to sell parts of the bulk cargo to a number of different buyers while the goods are at sea. Where there is a single bill of lading covering the whole consignment, the seller cannot give the bill of lading to each of the buyers. Accordingly, he can stipulate for the right to tender a ship's delivery order in respect of each of the small parcels.] Standard form c.i.f. contracts, such as GAFTA 100, permit the seller to tender a ship's delivery order as one of the ship's documents.[39] The Law Commission referred to ship's delivery orders in the following terms:

> A ship's delivery order is really designed to act like a 'mini' bill of lading, the main difference being that a ship's delivery order is issued after shipment and is usually issued in respect of a smaller cargo. It is sometimes possible to arrange for the ship's agent at the port of discharge to accept a surrender of the original bill and re-issue a number of fresh bills. However, this practice has been judicially disapproved, and the use of ship's delivery orders commended as the only legitimate way of splitting a bulk cargo, on the ground that bills of lading have to be issued on shipment or, if later, without undue delay and within the ordinary course of business. Thus, a ship's delivery order may look like a bill of lading and would be one but for the fact that it was not issued on shipment.[40]

4.15 **Not a document of title** At common law a ship's delivery order is not a transferable document of title.[41]

4.16 **Rights of suit** As we have already noted, the Bills of Lading Act 1855 was of limited scope and did not apply to documents other than bills of lading. Accordingly, the holder of a ship's delivery order did not have any rights of suit under the Act. At common law it was possible for an implied contract[42] to arise provided that the holder, when presenting the delivery order, furnished some consideration for the ship's attornment or issue of the delivery warrant. Thus in *Cremer v General Carriers SA (The Dona Mari)*[43] the holder of a ship's delivery order, which incorporated by reference the terms of the bill of lading, presented it to the ship and paid the freight on the portion of the goods covered by the order.

4.17 **Carriage of Goods by Sea Act 1992** The Law Commission recommended that ship's delivery orders be included in the reforms because failure to do so would weaken the position of the buyer of part of the bulk cargo.[44] Accordingly, ship's delivery orders, like sea waybills, are now covered by the Carriage of Goods by Sea Act 1992[45] and such an order is defined in section 1(4) as an undertaking which

---

[38] See para 1.04 (dry bulk cargoes); para 1.08 (liquid bulk cargoes).
[39] See cl 11(b).
[40] *Rights of Suit in Respect of Carriage of Goods by Sea*, Law Com No 196 (Scot Law Com No 130), para 5.29.
[41] See, in relation to sea waybills, para 4.05. For bills of lading, see para 8.02.
[42] For implied contracts generally, see para 9.02.
[43] [1974] 1 WLR 341.
[44] *Rights of Suit in Respect of Carriage of Goods by Sea*, Law Com No 196 (Scot Law Com No 130), para 5.30.
[45] Section 1(1)(c).

(a) is given under or for the purposes of a contract for the carriage by sea of the goods to which the document relates, or of goods which include those goods; and

(b) is an undertaking by the carrier to a person identified in the document to deliver the goods to which the document relates to that person.

Presentation   The person identified as the party entitled to delivery in the ship's delivery   **4.18** order will now have a contractual right against the carrier to take delivery of the goods.[46] It seems that he need only prove his identity before claiming delivery.

Rights   Section 2(1)(c) gives to the person to whom delivery of the goods to which a ship's   **4.19** delivery order relates 'all rights of suit under the contract of carriage'. However, this does not mean that the proprietary effect (as opposed to the contractual effect) of a transfer of a ship's delivery order has been altered. For a ship's delivery order to become a document of title at common law would require proof of a custom of merchants to that effect.

---

[46] At common law, an attornment from the carrier would have been required. See *Laurie & Morewood v Dudin & Sons* [1926] 1 KB 223 (CA), 236–238 (Scrutton LJ).

5

ISSUE AND TRANSFER OF BILLS OF LADING

A. Introduction

Overview In this chapter we consider the processes leading to the issue of bills of lading, **5.01** including the practice of issuing bills of lading in sets. We look finally at the different ways of negotiating bills of lading.

B. Issue of Bills of Lading

Introduction As we have already noted, not all carriage by sea warrants the issue of a bill **5.02** of lading.[1] Other documents are in common usage, particularly when bills of lading are not required, such as where there are short journeys involved and where a document of title is not required. Where bills of lading are issued, it is important to establish when they are issued and by whom.

Need for a bill of lading In many instances, unless otherwise specified, a bill of lading **5.03** will be required for shipment. Usually, such bills of lading are issued following the issue of a mate's receipt[2] and are exchanged for it. The shipper of the goods will invariably require the issue of a bill of lading where this is needed pursuant to an underlying contract of sale.[3] If no bill of lading is tendered to the master of the vessel on whose ship the goods have been loaded, then it would be prudent for him to make enquiries with the shipper as to what document of carriage is intended to be tendered. As much as anything else, there would be strong practical reasons for requiring that a bill of lading be issued in the absence of any other document of carriage. This is for the reason that this would at least indicate to whom

---

[1] See paras 1.33; 1.34.
[2] See para 2.19.
[3] In many instances the shipper of the goods will be the seller of them.

the goods are to be delivered at the discharge port. In some countries, it might also be impermissible for the ship to leave port unless a bill of lading has been issued.

5.04 **Preparation of a bill of lading** Traditionally, the bill of lading will be prepared by agents representing the shipper. In many instances this will be a freight forwarding company who the shipper has also engaged to perform all his shipping requirements.[4] However, if not making use of such agency services, the bill of lading will be prepared by the shipper. It would be very unusual for the bill of lading to be prepared by the shipowner or his agents. The shipper should present the bills of lading in a reasonable time after loading of the cargo.[5] Once presented, the bill of lading will be signed by the carrier or his agent[6] and delivered to the shipper or his agent. It should be noted at this point that it is most important that the bill of lading is only issued and dated once all the cargo covered by the bill of lading has actually been loaded.[7]

5.05 **Modern practice: a note** Whereas in the past it would have been quite usual for shipping agents to keep copies of many standard forms in their offices, this has become less necessary as more and more carriers have computerized their forms.

5.06 **Bills of lading in sets** It is standard practice for bills of lading to be issued in sets, usually of three originals (although there may be more). The practice was explained by Gerard Maylnes in his *Consuetudo vel Lex Mercatoria* in 1686:

> Of the Bills of Lading there is commonly Three Bills of one tenor. One of them is enclosed in the letters written by the same Ship; another Bill is sent overland to the Factor or Party to whom the goods are consigned; the third remaineth with the Merchant, for his testimony against the Master, if there were any occasion of loose dealing.[8]

There are no signs of any change to this long-standing practice, notwithstanding cogent criticism of the practice by Lord Blackburn in 1882:

> I have never been able to learn why merchants and shipowners continue the practice of making out a bill of lading in parts. I should have thought that, at least since the introduction of quick and regular communication by steamers, and still more since the establishment of the electric telegraph, every purpose would be answered by making one bill of lading only which should be the sole document of title, and taking as many copies, certified by the master to be true copies, as it is thought convenient; those copies would suffice for every legitimate purpose for which the other parts of the bill can now be applied, but could not be used for the purpose of pretending to be the holder of a bill of lading already parted with. However, whether because there is some practical benefit of which I am not aware, or because, as I suspect, merchants dislike to depart from an old custom for fear that the novelty may produce some unforeseen effect, bills of lading are still made out in parts, and probably will continue to be so made out.[9]

---

4 See *Heskell v Continental Express* (1950) 83 Ll LR 438, 449.
5 *Oriental Steamship Co v Tylor* [1893] 2 QB 518 (CA).
6 Within a reasonable time. See *Halcyon Steamship Co v Continental Grain Co* [1943] KB 355.
7 See, eg, *Mendala III Transport v Total Transport Corp (The Wilomi Tanana)* [1993] 2 Lloyd's Rep 41.
8 (1686) 97.
9 *Glyn, Mills & Co v East & West India Dock Co* (1882) 7 App Cas 591, 605. Cf *Sanders v Maclean* (1883) 11 QBD 327 (CA), 342: 'If it survives it is probably that the commercial world still finds it more convenient or less troublesome to preserve it than to change it' (Bowen LJ).

Bill of lading accomplished One of the potential difficulties associated with the issue **5.07** of bills of lading in sets is fraud. For this reason a standard clause in all bills of lading provides that:

> IN WITNESS whereof the Carrier, Master or their Agent has signed the number of original Bills of Lading stated below, all of this tenor and date, one of which being accomplished, the others stand void.[10]

In *Glyn, Mills & Co v East & West India Dock Co* Lord Cairns explained that the effect of this statement was

> that if upon one of them the shipowner acts in good faith he will have 'accomplished' his contract, will have fulfilled it, and will not be liable or answerable upon any of the others. If one is produced to him in good faith he is to act upon that and not to embarrass himself by considering what has become of the other bills of lading.[11]

The problem of delivery against part of a set The problem of double presentation was **5.08** highlighted in the case of *Glyn, Mills & Co v East & West India Dock Co*. In this case goods were deliverable to 'Cottam and Co, or assigns'. Cottam deposited one bill of the set with the plaintiffs (a bank) as security for a loan. He then obtained delivery at the port of discharge of twenty hogsheads of sugar on presentation of the second, unendorsed, bill of the set. When the plaintiffs then sued the dock company for wrongful delivery, the court held that delivery had been made bona fide and in ignorance of the bank's claim and that no liability arose. The company was entitled to make delivery on presentation of a bill of lading as they had not had notice of the assignment to the bank. Lord Blackburn made the point thus:

> But I think that when the master has not notice or knowledge of anything but that there are other parts of the bill of lading, one of which it is possible may have been assigned, he is justified or excused in delivering according to his contract to the person appearing to be the assign of the bill of lading which is produced to him.[12]

The difficulty faced by the bank here could be avoided by the bank simply requiring that the full set of bills of lading is given to it. In the absence of this, the bank might also protect its rights by giving notice to the carrier of its rights as pledgee of part of the set.

Competing pledges of originals It would be possible for several parts of the set to be **5.09** pledged to a number of individuals for more than the value of the goods. In such a case, the general rule is that as laid down in the leading case of *Barber v Meyerstein*,[13] namely that successive pledges would rank according to the order of their pledges.[14]

Tender of less than a full set It might be thought that it would be prudent for the shipper **5.10** or the buyer of the goods to object to the tender of less than a full set of the bills of lading. Banks would certainly be advised to do so, for some of the reasons already noted. However, this issue was dealt with in the leading case of *Sanders Bros v Maclean & Co*[15] where the

---

[10] See, eg, Conlinebill 2000.
[11] (1882) 7 App Cas 591.
[12] At 614.
[13] (1870) LR 4 HL 317.
[14] See also the discussion of this case at para 8.26.
[15] (1883) 11 QBD 327(CA).

Court of Appeal held that tender did not have to be made of the full set. To require otherwise, said Bowen LJ, would 'deal a fatal blow at this established custom of merchants, according to which, time out of mind, bills of lading are drawn in sets, and one of the set is habitually dealt with as representing the cargo independently of the rest'.[16] Accordingly, this case is authority for the proposition that any subsequent dealing with the other parts of a bill of lading could not be objected to, unless, again in the words of Bowen LJ, 'the absent original had been misused so as to defeat the title of the indorsees of the tendered residue of the set, [then] the tender would have been bad'.[17]

C. Transfer of Bills of Lading

5.11 **Introduction**   One of the most important characteristics of the bill of lading is as follows. If drawn in the appropriate form, the bill of lading is a symbol of the goods. Transfer of the bill of lading gives constructive possessive of the goods to the holder. In this part of this chapter we examine how this transfer must be effected.

5.12 **'Negotiation' of bills of lading**   It is not disputed that bills of lading in 'negotiable'[18] form pre-dated the emergence of straight (or non-negotiable) bills of lading. It must first be noted that the idea that a bill of lading is 'negotiable', at least in the strict sense of the term,[19] is a misnomer. As Lord Devlin explained in *Kum v Wah Tat Bank*, negotiable in this context means no more than that the bill of lading is 'simply transferable . . . and cannot . . . give to the transferee a better title than the transferor has got, but it can by endorsement and delivery give as good a title'.[20] Thus, a negotiable bill of lading does not give the transferee a better title than the transferor.

5.13 **Bills of lading to 'order'**   It is settled law that, for a bill of lading to function as a document of title, it must state that it is to 'order'.[21] Determining whether this is the case requires an examination of the face of the bill of lading and, absent those words, as in *Henderson v The Comptoir d'Escompte de Paris*,[22] there can be no argument that the bill of lading is transferable.[23] In the case of a bill of lading which gives the name of the consignee and provides that it is

---

[16] At 342.

[17] At 343.

[18] Described by Devlin J as being used in its 'popular sense': see *Heskell v Continental Express Ltd* (1950) 83 Ll LR 438, 453. See too para 8.02.

[19] For example, when used in the context of truly negotiable instruments, such as bills and cheques.

[20] [1971] 1 Lloyd's Rep 439 (PC), 446. See also *Gurney v Behrend* (1854) 3 El & Bl 622, 633–634; 118 ER 1275, 1279; *JI MacWilliam Co Inc v Mediterranean Shipping Co SA (The Rafaela S)* [2005] UKHL 11; [2005] 2 AC 423, at [37].

[21] Generally as to this characteristic of bills of lading, see para 8.07.

[22] (1873) LR 5 PC 253, 259–260.

[23] Similarly, in *The Chitral* [2000] 1 Lloyd's Rep 529, where the bills of lading provided that 'delivery is to be unto the above-mentioned consignee or to his or their assigns' that did not have the effect of making the bills of lading transferable. See too *JI MacWilliam Co Inc v Mediterranean Shipping Co SA (The Rafaela S)* [2003] EWCA Civ 556; 2004 QB 702, where the bills of lading did not contain the vital words 'order of': at [12] (Rix LJ).

'to order', transfer is effected by delivery of the bill of lading.[24] If the transferee wishes to endorse the bill of lading to a subsequent named endorsee, he may do so by writing on the reverse 'deliver to B or order' and adding his signature.[25] He must also deliver the bill of lading to B. Subsequent transfers, for example from B to C, would require a further endorsement by the original transferee. However, if the bill of lading is endorsed in blank, ie with the signature of the transferor on the reverse, then only delivery is required for future transfers.[26] In the case of bills of lading which are to the order of the shipper, ie which state that they are 'to order (or assigns)', transfer is effected by delivery and should be endorsed on the reverse with the transferor's signature.[27]

Bills of lading made out to a name left blank   Bills of lading need not specify the name   **5.14** of the consignee. In such a case they are 'in blank' and transfer is effected by the signature of the transferor on the reverse and delivery to the transferee.[28]

Bills of lading made out to bearer   Bills of lading may also be made out to 'bearer'.[29] Such   **5.15** bills of lading are still transferable and, indeed, transfer is effected by delivery. Bearer bills of lading are expressly stated to fall within the documents covered by the Carriage of Goods by Sea Act 1992.[30]

---

[24] Such bills of lading need not be endorsed, but in practice sometimes are: see *East West Corp v DKBS 1912 and AKTS Svendborg* [2002] EWHC 83 (Comm); [2002] 2 Lloyd's Rep 182, 185 (Thomas J).

[25] This is called a 'special' endorsement or 'endorsement in full'.

[26] See Benjamin (2002), para 18-012.

[27] ie an endorsement 'in blank'. Subsequent transfers are effected by delivery.

[28] Such bills of lading may also be transferred by simple delivery.

[29] ie whoever has the possession of the bill itself.

[30] See s 1(2)(a); s 5(2)(b).

6

THE BILL OF LADING AS A RECEIPT FOR THE GOODS SHIPPED

A. Introduction

Overview   We have previously noted that, at common law, the original function per-   **6.01**
formed by the bill of lading was that it was a receipt for the goods[1] and contained statements as to quantity, a description of the goods, and the condition in which they were
received by the carrier. These facets of the bill of lading came to have important commercial consequences and, in practice, this often forms an area where disputes arise. In this
chapter we consider these aspects from the standpoint of the common law.[2]

B. Statements on the Face of the Bill of Lading

General importance   The face of the bill of lading contains a great deal of important   **6.02**
information.[3] This includes information as to the loading port and date of shipment, the
discharge port, and the name of the ship. However, more significantly, the face contains
information as to the description of the goods, the quantity (or weight) shipped, and
the condition of those goods. This information is intended to inform subsequent holders

---

[1] See para 3.03.
[2] See, generally, Carver (2005), ch 2; Gaskell (2000), ch 7; Scrutton (1996), arts 54–65.
[3] See, eg, the information which will be filled in on the Conlinebill 2000 form. See Appendix II.

of the facts represented, for those facts are likely to be relevant to their exercise of contractual rights against sellers of the goods or, indeed, the carriers themselves.[4] Thus, it could be said that it is in the interest of the carrier for the bill of lading to say as little as possible about the goods shipped.

6.03 **Guarantee of particulars**   Statements on the face of the bill of lading as to quantity and weight, any leading marks, and the apparent order and condition of the goods, are effectively statements made by the shipper and accepted by the carrier, usually on his behalf by the master. The tender to the master of a bill of lading is, in effect, an invitation to the carrier to express his acknowledgement of the truth of the statements in the bill of lading.[5] Thus, the current version of Conlinebill provides that 'particulars declared by the shipper but not acknowledged by the carrier'.[6] Such statements do not constitute a promise or undertaking and it has been said that the words are 'at most an affirmation of fact or a representation'.[7] However, as we shall see in due course, the words do also have important consequences for third parties who, in reliance on these statements, pay bill of lading freight and take delivery of the goods represented by the bills of lading.

C. Quantity or Weight

6.04 **Evidential value**   Statements as to the quantity of goods shipped or the weight of goods shipped in a bill of lading have an evidential function in the sense that they provide strong prima facie evidence of the weight or quantity of goods shipped.[8] If accepted by the carrier, the burden will fall on him to prove the contrary. This principle may be illustrated by *Henry Smith & Co v Bedouin Steam Navigation Co Ltd*.[9] Here a cargo of jute was shipped from Calcutta to Dundee on the *Emir*, but on arrival 12 bales were missing from the 1,000 stated to have been shipped. The shipowners argued that the tallymen at Calcutta, who were locally employed labour, probably made a mistake because there was no way that the bales, which each weighed 400 lbs, could have been removed from the ship after loading. In concluding that the shipowners had not done enough to defeat the inference from the bill of lading, Lord Shand indicated that in order to succeed

> it will not be sufficient to show that fraud may have been committed, or to suggest that the tallymen may have made errors or mistakes, in order to meet a case of positive proof on the other side. It must be shown that there was in point of fact a short shipment — that is, the evidence must be sufficient to lead to the inference not merely that the goods may possibly not have been shipped, but that in point of fact they were not shipped. Any proposition short of this would appear to me to give less effect to the evidence of the shippers than that

---

[4] See *The David Agmashenebeli* [2002] EWHC 104; [2003] 1 Lloyd's Rep 92, 103 (Colman J).

[5] Ibid.

[6] The earlier version of Conlinebill just says 'Particulars furnished by the Merchant'. The P & O Nedlloyd bill of lading says: 'Above particulars as declared by Shipper, but not acknowledged by the Carrier (see clause 11)'. See Richardson (2003), 49.

[7] *V/O Rasnoimport v Guthrie* [1966] 1 Lloyd's Rep 1, 7 (Mocatta J).

[8] ie 'evidence which raises a rebuttable presumption of fact; it stands until rebutted; it therefore cannot establish more than a probability, but a probability which may be displaced by evidence': *The Draupner* [1910] AC 450, 451 (Lord Loreburn LC).

[9] [1896] AC 70.

evidence ought to have, and unwarrantably to diminish the onus which that evidence has thrown on the shipowner.[10]

Thus the carrier needs to show more than mere inference that the bill of lading figure is wrong, perhaps by proving that the missing goods could not have been stolen while they were in the custody of the carrier. Evidence in rebuttal might include conclusive evidence that after receipt by the shipowner none of the goods were lost or stolen and that everything received has been delivered.[11] Alternatively, evidence may be adduced of disputed tallies and reference might be made to the mate's receipts or even to the ship's loaded draught.[12]

Estoppel and third parties   So far as third parties are concerned, it may be possible to **6.05** show that the requirements of estoppel are satisfied. If this is the case, it will enable a third party claimant to make a claim under the bill of lading for short delivery. The essential requirements are that (i) the statement must embody a statement of fact; (ii) the maker intended that the representation should be relied upon; and (iii) the party arguing the estoppel should in fact have relied upon the representation to his detriment.[13]

False statements: goods not shipped   The leading authority on this point is *Grant v* **6.06** *Norway*.[14] Here the master of the *Belle* signed a bill of lading which acknowledged that twelve bales of silk had been shipped at Calcutta for delivery in London. The bill of lading was endorsed to the plaintiffs as security for a bill of exchange. However, the goods were never shipped and the statement in the bill of lading was accordingly untrue. Jervis CJ, in the course of his judgment, took the view that it was not usual for the master to give a bill of lading for goods not put on board the ship; all concerned had 'a right to assume that an agent has authority to do all which is usual.'[15] More problematically, he went on to say that:

> It is not contended that the captain had any real authority to sign bills of lading, unless the goods had been shipped: nor can we discover any ground upon which a party taking a bill of lading by endorsement, would be justified in assuming that he had authority to sign such bills, whether the goods were on board or not . . . [16]

It was clear therefore that this decision was based upon the proposition that the master had no actual or ostensible authority to sign bills of lading. However, this reasoning is clearly outdated, if not erroneous: masters of vessels commonly have authority to sign bills of lading in general and normally only the master would be in a position to know whether the goods were shipped.[17]

Grant v Norway limited   Ever since the decision in *Grant v Norway*, courts throughout **6.07** the common law world have been at pains to distinguish it.[18] One trenchant view held that it was 'extremely doubtful whether *Grant v Norway* can be held, or has ever been held,

---

[10] At 79.
[11] See *Sanday & Co v Strath Steamship Co Ltd* (1920) 26 Com Cas 277 (CA), 279.
[12] eg, *Hine Bros v Free, Rodwell & Co Ltd* (1897) 2 Com Cas 149, 152.
[13] See *Silver v Ocean Steamship Co* [1930] 1 KB 416 (CA), 433 (Greer, LJ).
[14] (1851) 10 CB 665 (CP); 138 ER 263.
[15] At 688; 138 ER 272.
[16] ibid.
[17] See FMB Reynolds, 'Warranty of Authority' (1967) 88 LQR 189, 193.
[18] It was followed by the High Court of Australia in the case of *Rosenfeld Hillas & Co Pty Ltd v The Ship Fort Laramie* (1923) 32 CLR 25.

to represent the general law . . . '.[19] Thus in *Lloyd v Grace, Smith & Co*,[20] a firm of solicitors was held liable for the conduct of a clerk, employed to conduct conveyancing transactions, who defrauded a client. This was because the clerk had general authority to undertake conveyancing even though he did not have specific authority to act wrongfully. In the carriage context, two decisions have sought to limit the scope of *Grant v Norway*. In *The Nea Tyhi*, Sheen J stated that, though he was bound by a decision which had 'survived for 130 years', he confessed that he found it impossible to reconcile and could only conclude that it was 'to be regarded as an exception and not as laying down a general principle'.[21] In this case, bills of lading issued by the charterer's agents were claused 'shipped under deck' for plywood which was shipped above deck. The plywood was damaged by rainwater. The shipowner argued that the charterers' agents had no authority to issue the bill of lading so claused. However, Sheen J limited *Grant v Norway* to the situation where the goods were not loaded on board at all and refused to extend it to the case of under-deck statements for goods shipped on deck. In *The Saudi Crown*[22] Sheen J, though again indicating that he did not like *Grant v Norway*, accepted that he was bound by it and refused to extend it to those cases where the master had authority to issue falsely dated bills of lading.[23]

6.08 **Survival of *Grant* v *Norway*?**   At least at common law, *Grant v Norway* appears to be limited to statements as to quantity, including the situation where some goods are left behind but the bill of lading says that all goods were shipped.[24] It has been suggested that in order to displace the effect of the representation in the bill of lading, which is prima facie evidence, the carrier must establish beyond reasonable doubt that the goods were never shipped and 'the evidence of exoneration must be clear and distinct and convincing'.[25]

6.09 **Statutory response: 1855 Act**   A possible recourse for consignees was heralded in section 3 of the Bills of Lading Act 1855,[26] which sought to overrule *Grant* v *Norway*. It provided that

> Every bill of lading in the hands of a consignee or endorsee for valuable consideration representing goods to have been shipped on a vessel shall be conclusive evidence of such shipment as against the master or other persons signing the same, notwithstanding that such goods or some part thereof may not have been shipped, unless such holder of the bill of lading shall have had actual notice at the time of receiving the same that the goods had not been in fact laden on board.

> Provided that the master or other person so signing may exonerate himself in respect of such misrepresentation by showing that it was caused without any default on his part, and wholly by the fraud of the shipper, or of the holder, or some person under whom the holder claims.

---

[19] *George Whitechurch Ltd v Cavanagh* [1902] AC 117, 137 (Lord Robertson).
[20] [1912] AC 716.
[21] [1982] 1 Lloyd's Rep 606, 610.
[22] [1986] 1 Lloyd's Rep 261.
[23] At 265. See also *Blue Nile Co Ltd v Emery Customs Brokers (S) Pte Ltd* [1992] 1 SLR 296.
[24] See *V/O Rasnoimport v Guthrie & Co* [1966] 1 Lloyd's Rep 1.
[25] *Rosenfeld Hillas & Co Pty Ltd v The Ship Fort Laramie* (1923) 32 CLR 25, 33 (Isaacs J).
[26] Now repealed by s 6 of the Carriage of Goods by Sea Act 1992.

The remedy provided was ultimately illusory because it operated only against the 'master or other persons signing the same' and did not create a cause of action in favour of the party holding the bill of lading. In *V/O Rasnoimport v Guthrie & Co*[27] defendant loading brokers for the *Demodocus* signed a bill of lading stating that 225 bales of rubber had been shipped, whereas only 90 had been shipped. The plaintiffs were the endorsees for value of the bill of lading and claimed damages for breach of warranty of authority under section 3 of the Bills of Lading Act 1855. Mocatta J described the section as being enacted in order to lessen the stringency of *Grant v Norway* 'in favour of endorsees of bills of lading who could not by reason of it recover against the shipowner, notwithstanding that his master or agent had signed a bill of lading, purporting to act on his behalf, for goods not on board'.[28] He was persuaded by the argument of counsel that:

> It was right to stretch the words 'other persons signing the same' to cover the owners in this case, even if the defendants had their actual authority. To apply the section to the present assumed facts would, in my view, exceed the meaning of the words of the statute on any canon of construction and go far beyond any reported case.[29]

In this case, the endorsee succeeded independently of section 3 against the loading broker on the basis of the latter's breach of warranty of authority which was said to operate independently of section 3 because it did not depend on evidence of shipment. It is clear, however, that this was intended to avoid the unsatisfactory results of section 3. Thus only where the consignee (or holder for value) had an independent cause of action against the master or other party signing the bill, could use be made of the statutory estoppel in section 3.

Contracting out: generally   At common law, it is possible for the shipowner to contract   **6.10** out of any prima facie representations on the face of the bill of lading. Often the decision whether to do so will vest in his agent, the master, and, as he may not have precise knowledge of the actual weight or quantity loaded, it would be advisable for representations as to these matters to be qualified. Some standard form bills of lading, such as Conlinebill 2000, state expressly 'weight unknown'.[30] The effect of such a qualification (or endorsement as it is sometimes known) is that the bill of lading would not constitute prima facie evidence of the matter excluded.

Contracting out: 'said to be' or 'weight and quantity unknown'   Various types of   **6.11** qualifying statements might be made. In *New Chinese Antimony Co Ltd v Ocean Steamship Co Ltd*[31] a bill of lading for antimony oxide ore stated that 937 tons had been shipped on board the *Tientsin*. The margin of the bill contained the words 'a quantity said to be 937 tons' while a clause in the bill itself said 'weight, measurement contents and value (except for the purpose of estimating freight) unknown'. The *Tientsin* carried the ore from Hankow to Shanghai and it was then transhipped and taken to London and Newcastle. The ore on arrival only weighed 861 tons. It was held that the bill of lading was not prima facie evidence of the quantity of ore shipped and that in an action against the shipowners

---

[27] [1966] 1 Lloyd's Rep 1.
[28] At 18.
[29] ibid.
[30] Conlinebill 2000 actually says '. . . weight, measure, marks, numbers, quality, contents and value unknown . . .'.
[31] [1917] 2 KB 664 (CA).

for short delivery the onus was on the plaintiff of proving that 937 tons had in fact been shipped:

> Where in a bill of lading, which is prepared by the shippers for acceptance by the defendants' agent, the agent accepts in the margin a quantity 'said to be 937 tons', and in the body of the bill of lading there is a clause 'weight &c unknown', there is no prima facie evidence that 937 tons have been shipped. I think that the true effect of this bill of lading is that the words 'weight unknown' have the effect of a statement by the shipowners' agent that he has received a quantity of ore which the shippers' representative says weighs 937 tons but which he does not accept as being of that weight, the weight being unknown to him, and that he does not accept the weight of 937 tons except for the purpose of calculating freight and for that purpose only . . .[32]

The Court of Appeal, who overturned the decision of Sankey J, held that the defendant shipowners were not responsible for any of the loss.

6.12 **Contracting out: 'said to contain'** Another commonly used qualification of quantity is 'said to contain' or 'STC' and, where this appears before the quantity of goods listed, it will also have the effect that the representation does not constitute prima facie evidence of quantity.[33]

6.13 **Contracting out: 'FCL/FCL'** The annotation 'FCL/FCL', which is shorthand for 'full container load', is used in the context of containerized goods and is inserted to indicate that the container has been packed by the shipper, such that the carrier will not have the opportunity of checking the contents. By themselves, it is not clear whether these words would have the effect of qualifying any representations as to quantity. In the case of *Ace Imports Pty Ltd v Companhia De Navegacao Lloyd Brasileiro* these words were used together with the words 'said to contain—packed by shippers' and the Supreme Court of New South Wales held that this did not constitute a representation by the carrier as to the accuracy of the statement on the face of the bill of lading as to the contents of the container.[34] Thus, where such phrases are used, the representation in the bill of lading has no real effect, and the claimant in any action for short delivery must adduce evidence of the quantity or weight of the goods on shipment.

6.14 **Precise words** The words of qualification which are used must be precise. Thus in an appeal from the Supreme Court of Ceylon to the Privy Council in *Attorney-General of Ceylon v Scindia Steam Navigation Co Ltd*[35] bills of lading for rice, shipped from Rangoon to Colombo,[36] stated that a total of 100,652 bags had been shipped in apparent good order and condition, 'weight, contents and value when shipped unknown'. The appellants claimed short delivery of 235 bags of rice. Lord Morris of Borth-y-Gest stated that:

> Their Lordships consider that, though these statements in the bills of lading as to the number of bags shipped do not constitute conclusive evidence as against the shipowner, they

---

[32] At 669. See also *Rosenfeld Hillas & Co Pty Ltd v The Ship Fort Laramie* (1923) 32 CLR 25.

[33] See, eg, *Rosenfeld Hillas & Co Pty Ltd v The Ship Fort Laramie* (1923) 32 CLR 25, 38; *Ace Imports Pty Ltd v Companhia De Navegacao Lloyd Brasileiro* (1987) 10 NSWLR 32; *Marbig Rexel Pty Ltd v ABC Container Line NV (The TNT Express)* [1992] 2 Lloyd's Rep 636.

[34] (1987) 10 NSWLR 32, 37.

[35] [1962] AC 60 (PC).

[36] These were subject to the Indian Carriage of Goods by Sea Act 1925, No 26 of 1925 (which gave effect to the Hague Rules).

form strong *prima facie* evidence that the stated numbers of bags were shipped unless it be that there is some provision in the bills of lading which precludes this result. . . . Their Lordships cannot agree with the view. . . that the conditions in the bills of lading disentitled the plaintiff from relying upon the admissions that bags to the numbers stated in the bills of lading were taken on board.[37]

Thus, as the qualifying words did not relate to the number of bags shipped, the Privy Council confirmed that evidence as to the contents of the bags had to be proved independently of the bill.

D. Condition

External condition   The second type of representation by the shipowner concerns the   **6.15** condition of the goods shipped. Typically, the bill of lading will state that the goods have been shipped on board 'in apparent good order and condition'.[38] This refers to their external and apparent condition[39] or, as Sir Robert Phillimore put it in *The Peter der Grosse*, '. . . apparently, and so far as met the eye, and externally, they were placed in good order on board this ship'.[40] Thus, a representation as to the condition of the goods is not one as to the internal condition (or quality) of the goods, since this cannot be verified by the carrier. As stated by Channel J in *Compania Naviera Vascongada v Churchill & Sim*:[41]

> I think that 'condition' refers to external and apparent condition, and 'quality' to something which is usually not apparent, at all events to an unskilled person. I think a captain is expected to notice the apparent condition of the goods, though not the quality. It is probably unnecessary for him to protect himself as regards quality, which it is not his business to know anything about, except perhaps when the description of the goods set out in the bill of lading contains words importing a statement as to the quality.[42]

The master cannot be expected to be aware of 'the particular mercantile quality of the goods before they are put on board'[43] but has a duty to 'make an accurate statement in the circumstances of the case'.[44]

Reasonable inspection   The representation as to condition only applies to a reasonable   **6.16** appraisal of the condition of the goods. Here the leading case is *Silver v Ocean Steamship Co Ltd*.[45] Damage was done to a large shipment of Chinese eggs in transit from China to London. The transit was from the shippers' warehouse in Shanghai to cold stores in London and the defendants' ship was only responsible from delivery on board in Shanghai

---

[37] At 74.

[38] See, eg, Conlinebill 2000, which then goes on to state '(unless otherwise stated herein)'.

[39] *Compania Naviera Vascongada v Churchill & Sim* [1906] 1 KB 237, 245.

[40] (1875) 1 PD 414, 420.

[41] [1906] 1 KB 237.

[42] At 245.

[43] *Cox, Patterson & Co v Bruce & Co* (1886) 18 QBD 147, 152 (Lord Esher MR).

[44] See *Trade Star Line Corp v Mitsui & Co Ltd (The Arctic Trader)* [1996] 2 Lloyd's Rep 449 (CA), 458 (Evans LJ). Cf, however, *The David Agmashenebeli* [2003] 1 Lloyd's Rep 92, where Colman J suggested that the master need not exercise more than 'his own [honest] judgment on the appearance of the cargo being loaded' (at 105).

[45] [1930] 1 KB 416 (CA).

to delivery overside in London. The liquid content of the eggs was contained in rectangular metal cases which were not covered in any way. The contents were frozen and the cases carried in refrigerated holds. Considerable damage was caused to the cases. The carrier was estopped by the Court of Appeal from invoking the exception of 'insufficiency of packing' against a consignee who had relied in good faith on the clean bill of lading which provided that the goods were 'shipped in apparent good order and condition'.

6.17 Evidential value Representations in the bills of lading as to the condition of the goods are prima facie evidence in favour of the shipper of the goods, but conclusive evidence once in the hands of a bona fide purchaser for value. Thus, in *Compania Naviera Vascongada v Churchill & Sim*[46] certain timber, although stained with petroleum, was stated in the bill of lading to be 'shipped in good order and condition'. The court held that the endorsees of the bill of lading could sue the shipowner for damages and that the shipowner was estopped from denying that the timber was shipped in good condition. The endorsees had relied, to their detriment, on the statement by the shipowners.[47]

6.18 Condition: containerized goods This will be difficult when containers are used because it will not be readily apparent what the condition of the goods is. In practice, the carrier would have to rely on its agents to note defects and record them in a received for shipment bill of lading. The difficulty for the carrier is compounded because containers are often sealed from the time they leave the shipper's warehouse, often at an inland depot, until they arrive at the place of inland delivery. The seals on the container will be regulated by the local customs authorities and the carrier will often have no means of knowing what is inside, particularly when, as is the usual case, he has not stuffed the container himself. Thus, where containers are loaded, the carrier would normally be entitled to say that, if the container appeared sound from the outside, the apparent good order and condition statement in the bill gives no evidence at all about what is inside the container. If the cargo owner (or endorsee) wished to prove that damage occurred while the goods were in the care of the carrier it would have to lead independent evidence to that effect. This would usually consist of evidence from the person who stuffed the container and any independent pre-shipment survey report. Where similar goods have been stuffed in a number of different containers, it may be possible to draw inferences from what happened to the other containers. In the case of wet damage, often the biggest source of damage, it may be possible with the aid of expert evidence to indicate whether the damage was from fresh water or from salt water. The former would indicate that rain water entered while the container was ashore, while the latter would indicate the ingress of sea water from stowage on deck. Thus, in the case of *Marbig Rexel Pty Ltd v ABC Container Line NV (The TNT Express)*[48] goods containerized at Jakarta and bound for Sydney were, on arrival, found to be damaged by water. The receipt clause on the face of the bill of lading stated that the container was received by the carriers in apparent good order and condition. Accordingly, the endorsee of the bill of lading argued that the

---

[46] [1906] 1 KB 237.
[47] See too *Brandt v Liverpool, Brazil & River Plate SN Co* [1924] 1 KB 575 (CA).
[48] [1992] 2 Lloyd's Rep 636.

shipowner was estopped from denying that the goods were in apparent good order and condition. This was rejected by the Supreme Court of New South Wales who referred to the words in the bill of lading stating that 'shipper's load stow and count' and the abbreviation 'STC' before the description of the goods. Carruthers J concluded that

> It is, in my view, apparent from the wording of the receipt clause and the notation inserted in the box beneath that clause that the defendant is merely acknowledging the receipt of the 20′ container in apparent good order and condition. The acknowledgment could not possibly extend to the apparent good order and condition of the contents of the sealed container which had been consolidated by the shipper.[49]

Contracting out: 'condition unknown' It would be possible to contract out of the representation as to condition, in much the same way as this is possible in relation to the representations in the bill of lading as to quantity or weight. A typical phrase which might be used is 'condition unknown'. However, if these words are inserted into the bill of lading, they are taken to refer to the internal condition of the goods, rather than their externally observable condition.[50] Clearly, if the goods are damaged on shipment, the shipowner would be wise to qualify his representation as to the condition of the goods by accurately listing the damage on the bill of lading. In *Canada & Dominion Sugar Co Ltd v Canadian National (West Indies) Steamships Ltd*[51] a received for shipment bill of lading relating to the shipment of sugar from Demerara to Montreal aboard the *Colborne* contained the qualifying words, 'signed under guarantee to produce ship's clean receipt'. However the ship's receipt[52] contained the statement that 'many bags stained, torn and re-sewn'. The only basis on which the consignee of the bill of lading could rely on estoppel as against the shipowner was if the statement as to condition was unambiguous and unqualified. As this was not so, the Privy Council held that the assignee could not rely on the estoppel, for the reason that '. . . the language of the bill of lading, read fairly, and as a whole, is not . . . such as to found an estoppel'.[53]

6.19

E. Leading Marks

Introduction We come finally to the legal position relating to the way in which the goods are marked. Most goods intended for shipment by sea are marked in some way. Our concern here is the marks which identify the shipment for the convenience of all those who will be handling the goods until delivery, rather than any marks of identity of the commercial character of the goods.

6.20

Identification Any identification or quality marks on the goods shipped are normally recorded in the bill of lading. The shipowner will not be estopped at common law from denying that the goods were shipped under the marks as described in the bill unless such

6.21

---

49 At 642.
50 *The Tromp* [1921] P 337.
51 [1947] AC 46 (PC).
52 This was provided by the chief tally clerk.
53 At 55 (Lord Wright).

marks are essential to their identity or description. In *Parsons v New Zealand Shipping Co*, Collins LJ stated that:

> It is obvious that, where marks have no market meaning and indicate nothing whatever to a buyer as to the nature, quality, or quantity of the goods which he is buying, it is absolutely immaterial to him whether the goods bear one mark or another . . . Now, the goods which the bill of lading represents as shipped continue to be the same goods, whichever out of any number of merely arbitrary marks are put on them, and will remain the same whether the marks were on them before shipment or are rubbed off or changed after shipment. In other words, they go to the identification only, and not the identity. The goods represented by the bill of lading to have been shipped have been shipped, and a mistaken statement as to marks of this class merely makes identification more difficult; it does not affect the existence or identity of the goods. It seems to me that . . . the plaintiff has failed to bring his case within the estoppel which it creates.[54]

6.22 **Description**   The leading marks may refer to the identity or description of the goods. In such a case, the marks recorded in the bill follow the normal common law rule in providing prima facie evidence against the carrier and conclusive evidence when the bill is in the hands of a bona fide endorsee for value.

F. Receipt and the Carriage of Goods by Sea Act 1992

6.23 **Introduction**   As we shall see in due course, the Carriage of Goods by Sea Act 1992 was passed primarily with the intention of addressing a number of acute problems concerning rights of suit until then encountered under the Bills of Lading Act 1855. However, the opportunity was also taken to address other matters, in particular those relating to representations in bills of lading.

6.24 **Representations: section 4**   In those situations where the Carriage of Goods by Sea Act 1992 applies, section 4 provides that a bill of lading, signed by the master or by someone having express, implied, or apparent authority of the carriers, and which represents goods to have been shipped or received for shipment, and in the hands of the lawful holder (who is acting in good faith), is conclusive evidence against the carrier of such shipment or receipt. Section 4 is therefore intended to dispose of *Grant v Norway* and, at first sight, also follows the equivalent provision in the Hague and Hague–Visby Rules.

6.25 **Interface with the Hague–Visby Rules**   Section 5(5) of the Act provides that it has effect without prejudice to the application of the Hague–Visby Rules. Thus, where the Hague–Visby Rules apply, whether mandatorily or otherwise,[55] section 4 will be of limited ambit because the representation provisions of those rules, article III, rule 4, will be the governing provision.

6.26 **Other transport documents**   There are some important differences between article III, rule 4 of the Hague–Visby Rules and section 4 of the Carriage of Goods by Sea Act 1992. The most significant of these is that, unlike article III, rule 4, section 4 only applies to bills of lading and not the other transport documents within its ambit.

---

[54] [1901] 1 KB 548 (CA), 564–565.
[55] As to this, see para 18.06.

G. Endorsements and Indemnities

Avoidance of endorsements   Most shippers will wish to avoid any endorsements on the   **6.27**
bill of lading reflecting that the goods are damaged in some way. This is particularly so
when the underlying sale contract is financed by a documentary credit from a bank.
Documentary credits routinely require bills of lading which are 'clean' and state that the
goods are shipped 'in good order and condition'. Thus, under article 32 of the UCP 500,
a 'clean' transport document is one which bears no clause or notation which expressly
declares a defective condition of the goods and/or the packaging.[56] As Coleman J explained
in *The David Agmashenebeli*:

> Clean bills of lading are essential documents for the purpose of triggering the right to receive
> payment under documentary credits issued in respect of contracts for the international
> sale of goods. If claused bills of lading are presented under such documentary credits they
> will ordinarily be rejected [by banks]. Indeed, the inability of sellers to present clean bills
> of lading may operate as a repudiatory breach of the sale contract.[57]

Inducement to ignore defects   Sometimes the master of the vessel may be placed under   **6.28**
considerable commercial pressure to ignore defects in the condition of the goods and to sign
the bills of lading. Obviously, he should not do so, because if he does he will expose the
shipowner to a claim for damaged goods and himself to a claim for fraud. Ultimately whether
to give in to such pressure is a decision which will be made by the shipowner, who may choose
to accept a letter of indemnity (LOI)[58] to cover loss from any action subsequently brought by
a receiver of the goods. Any decision whether to do so would be well advised to bear in mind
the following advice laid down in a decision of the Federal Court of Australia:

> ... Honesty and integrity in relation to the signing of receipts for goods the subject of bills of
> lading is essential if persons engaged in international trade are to have any confidence in doc-
> uments which play such a vital role in relation to the authorisation of the payment of money.
> If receipts are signed dishonestly or in bad faith, the confidence of the international trading
> community is undermined and a whole system that was designed to work for the benefit and
> protection of both parties to a transaction such as this will be called into question.[59]

Indemnities: generally   On one view the issue of an indemnity is a practical solution   **6.29**
to a common legal problem[60] and possibly also an expedient method of avoiding delay
and overcoming a difficulty out of proportion to its importance.[61] However, in law
such an indemnity provides a rather illusory protection for the shipowner. In itself the
indemnity is ineffective as a defence to any claim brought by a third party on the clean
bill. More seriously, however, the indemnity may be unenforceable against the shipper
on the ground that its object is to defraud the consignee or his bank.

---

[56] See also art 31(ii). See now *Sea Success Maritime Inc v African Maritime Carriers Ltd* [2005] EWHC 1542 (Comm); [2005] 2 Lloyd's Rep 692.
[57] [2002] EWHC 104; [2003] 1 Lloyd's Rep 92, 94. See too *Standard Chartered Bank v Pakistan National Shipping Corp (No 2)* [2000] 1 Lloyds' Rep 218 (CA), 221 (Evans LJ).
[58] Also sometimes known as 'letters of undertaking' (LOUs) or 'back letters'.
[59] *Hunter Grain Pty Ltd v Hyundai Merchant Marine Co Ltd* (1993) 117 ALR 507, 518 (Sheppard J).
[60] Such indemnities are also commonly offered when the bills of lading are not available at the discharge port. See para 10.19.
[61] See eg *Malayan Motor & General Underwriters (Pte) Ltd v Abdul Karim* [1980–1981] SLR 86 (CA), 90–91.

6.30 **Indemnities: fraud**   The leading case on the unenforceability of indemnities — at least where there is an intention to defraud — is *Brown, Jenkinson & Co Ltd v Percy Dalton (London) Ltd.*[62] In this case, the defendants sold 100 barrels of orange juice to a company in Rotterdam, who in turn resold them to a purchaser in Hamburg. The claimants were loading brokers for the *MV Titania*, the vessel on which the orange juice was to be shipped. They informed the defendants that the barrels were old, frail, and leaky and that a 'claused' bill of lading was appropriate. However, at the request of the defendants and on promise of an indemnity, the claimants signed a clean bill of lading on behalf of the master, stating that the barrels were 'shipped in apparent good order and condition'. On delivery in Hamburg, the barrels were indeed found to be leaking and the shipowners had to make good the loss. The claimants sued the defendants under the indemnity agreement, the benefit of which had been assigned to them by the shipowners. The majority of the Court of Appeal held that the shipowners, by making in the bill of lading a representation of fact that they knew to be false with intent that it should be acted upon, were committing the tort of deceit. Accordingly, the defendants' promise to indemnify the shipowners against loss resulting from the making of that representation was unenforceable. As Morris LJ stated

> the position was that . . . the plaintiffs made a representation which they knew to be false and which they intended should be relied upon by persons who received the bill of lading, including any banker who might be concerned. In these circumstances, all the elements of the tort of deceit were present. Someone who could prove that he suffered damage by relying on the representation could sue for damages. I feel impelled to the conclusion that a promise to indemnify the plaintiffs against any loss resulting to them from making the representation is unenforceable. The claim cannot be put forward without basing it upon an unlawful transaction.[63]

6.31 **Indemnities: no fraud?**   There remains a question as to whether an indemnity might be enforceable if no fraud is involved. Although an indemnity might superficially be seen as a practical solution to the difficulties arising from issuing a qualified bill of lading, it must be borne in mind that the risk of doing so ultimately lies on the shipowner.

6.32 **Indemnities and P & I cover**   A more serious potential difficulty for the shipowner is the effect on his P & I insurance cover.[64] Most P & I Clubs will not indemnify their members against the consequences of issuing clean bills of lading in circumstances where they should have been claused.[65]

H. The Master's Role in Clausing the Bills of Lading

6.33 **Master's role: generally**   Although the ordinary authority of the master may be said to have been reduced, compared to what it was in earlier times, his role is still a fundamental one. Indeed, he is usually the central figure in determining whether a clean or a qualified (claused) bill of lading should be issued. It is clear law that the master should not sign a bill of lading which he knows to be untrue, or which he believes may be untrue, or

---

[62] [1957] 2 QB 621 (CA).
[63] At 632. See also *Hunter Grain Pty Ltd v Hyundai Merchant Marine Co Ltd* (1993) 117 ALR 507.
[64] See Hazelwood (2000), 178.
[65] See, eg, Britannia Club, Rule 19(17)(iii)(g); Gard Club, Rule 34.1(ix); Standard Club, Rule 20.21(v)(e).

where he has not given careful thought to the facts enumerated therein.[66] If he does so, apart from constituting a fraud, he might hold himself open to liability in negligence. Although initially dismissed as a possibility, in a case involving a loading broker,[67] this has been opened up following the later decision of *Hedley Byrne & Co Ltd v Heller & Partners Ltd*,[68] although subject to satisfying the requirements of negligence.

Master's role: detailed   The master's principal responsibility in relation to the bill of lading **6.34** is to ensure that the information listed on the face of the bill of lading corresponds to that which appears on the mate's receipt. In the case where the bill of lading is subject to a charter-party there will be additional considerations.[69] At its most basic, the master must ensure that each of the boxes on the face of the bill of lading have been filled in accurately.[70] Of critical importance, however, are those boxes which relate to the description of the cargo. As the master will not know all those facts about the cargo that appear on the bill of lading that he is asked to sign, these will require his specific attention. In practice this usually comes down to consideration of two of the matters that we have looked at in this chapter, namely quantity and condition. Thus, in relation to quantity, if the master is not appraised of the quantity or weight loaded, he should qualify the bills of lading with the words 'weight and quantity unknown'. Similarly, if the tally conducted on board differs from that represented on the bill of lading, this should be indicated also by the words 'weight and quantity unknown'.[71] In relation to condition, the master should, as we have seen, only indicate what he knows as to the apparent external condition of the cargo. If there is nothing apparently wrong, then he should be happy to verify that the cargo has been received 'in apparent good order and condition'.[72]

Defective goods   We turn now to the question of what the master should do when the **6.35** goods are defective or sub-standard in some way. The difficulty here is that the master is obliged to take a view on a cargo with which he may have considerable professional familiarity or none. The principal difficulties he may face are when the goods appear to be dirty or where they are mixed in with foreign particles or debris,[73] or where they are discoloured in some way, or giving off an abnormal odour. The master may be fortunate to be assisted by a surveyor appointed by the shipowner, his P & I Club, or the shipper, but often he will have to make the decision on his own.

Reasonable basis for clausing   An earlier authority had suggested that the master's duty **6.36** was to make an accurate statement in the circumstances of the case.[74] However, the leading case

---

[66] See *Derry v Peek* (1889) 14 App Cas 337.
[67] ie *Heskell v Continental Express Ltd* (1950) 83 Ll LR 438.
[68] [1964] AC 465.
[69] See para 32.93.
[70] Including the boxes as to 'shipper', 'consignee', 'notify address', 'vessel', 'port of loading', and 'port of discharge'. See, eg, Conlinebill 2000.
[71] See *Boukadoura Maritime Corp v Marocaine de l'Industrie et du Raffinage SA (The Boukadoura)* [1989] 1 Lloyd's Rep 393, 399, (Evans J).
[72] See para 6.15. cf al. *Sea Success Maritime Inc v African Maritime Carriers Ltd* [2005] EWHC 1542 (Comm); [2005].
[73] As in *The David Agmashenebeli* [2003] 1 Lloyd's Rep 92. See Benjamin Parker, 'Liability for incorrectly clausing bills of lading' [2003] LMCLQ 201; Paul Todd, 'Representations in bills of lading' [2003] JBL 160.
[74] See *Trade Star Line Corp v Mitsui & Co Ltd (The Arctic Trader)* [1996] 2 Lloyd's Rep 449 (CA), 458, (Evans LJ).

on reasonably qualifying the bills of lading is now *The David Agmashenebeli*.[75] Claimant cargo owners brought an action against the shipowners, claiming damages for breach of the duty to issue a bill of lading accurately describing the cargo's apparent condition. The cargo had been sold on, with payment by letter of credit upon presentation of a clean bill of lading. The circumstances were that, shortly after loading commenced, the master had expressed his concern at the cargo's condition. This led to a mate's certificate being issued which stated 'cargo discoloured also foreign materials eg plastic, rust, rubber, stone, black particles found in cargo'. Bills of lading, claused using the same wording, were eventually signed, but were rejected by the end buyer. Delivery was eventually taken on reduction of the price. On inspection, the cargo's condition was found to be normal with minor stains, contamination, and discolouration. The main point in the case was the allegation by the claimants that the master had claused the bills of lading when he had no basis for doing so. They argued that it was not sufficient for the bills of lading to show the apparent order and condition which the master or other agent of the carrier honestly believed the cargo to be in if that description did not accurately describe the actual apparent order and condition of the cargo. Alternatively, the claimants submitted that there was an implied term of the contract of carriage by which the shipowners were under a duty to the shippers to ensure that the master would only sign bills of lading which accurately described the actual apparent order and condition of the goods, the specific duty of the master being to exercise the judgement of a responsible and reasonable ship's officer. The judge found that though the master was entitled to clause the mate's receipt to refer to the fact that a small proportion of the cargo was discoloured, he was not entitled to use words which conveyed the meaning that the whole or a substantial part of the cargo was so affected. Accordingly, he was not entitled to clause the mate's receipt or bills of lading to suggest that the presence of a minuscule quantity of contaminants rendered the cargo otherwise than in good order and condition. The master who honestly took an eccentric view of the apparent condition of the cargo which would not be shared by any other reasonably observant master would not be justified in issuing bills of lading which were qualified to reflect his view.[76]

6.37   **Refusal to sign**   We have so far seen the extent of the master's duties in relation to clausing of the bills of lading. We now consider in more detail those circumstances when he should refuse to sign the bills of lading. If the master believes that he is entitled to refuse to sign because the goods do not meet with their contractual description, it would be prudent for him to seek guidance from the shipowner or from the ship's P & I Club. Such advice is usually forthcoming and P & I Clubs have correspondents in most world ports who are on hand to give this. Any decision to clause the mate's receipts or bills of lading must be exercised with care by the master and he should give adequate warning to the shipper's representatives that he proposes to do so. The master should refuse to sign where he is placed under commercial pressure to sign the bills of lading; as we have seen, it is for the shipowner to make such decisions. So as to avoid delays it may be recommended that the master signs a bill of lading which he considers to be accurate and this can be left with the ship's agent.

---

[75] [2003] 1 Lloyd's Rep 92.
[76] At 105.

7

THE BILL OF LADING AS EVIDENCE
OF THE CONTRACT OF CARRIAGE

A. Introduction

Overview   As a rule, most bills of lading, particularly those which are issued on liner   **7.01**
terms[1] and also those which are for multimodal carriage, contain detailed contractual terms
on the reverse. In *Crooks v Allen*, Lush LJ stated that:

> . . . [A] shipper has a right to suppose that his goods are received on the usual terms, and to
> require a bill of lading which shall express those terms.[2]

In this chapter we consider whether these terms constitute the contract of carriage, to what
extent they are binding on the shipper, and whether there is a separate rule when the bills
of lading are passed to third parties.[3]

B. Bills of Lading between Shippers and Shipowners

No need for writing   Contracts for the carriage of goods share certain basic characteristics   **7.02**
of general contract law, in particular that they are bilateral contracts which are validly
concluded when there has been an exchange of mutual promises. These promises need
not be embodied in a written record and this possibility of informality means, as Devlin J
put it, that 'the issue of the bill of lading does not necessarily mark any stage in the
development of the contract'.[4]

---

[1] eg, Conlinebill 2000.
[2] (1879) 5 QBD 38 (CA), 40.
[3] See, generally, Carver (2005), ch 3; Gaskell (2000), ch 21; Scrutton (1996), arts 33–43.
[4] See *Pyrene Co Ltd v Scindia Navigation Co Ltd* [1954] 2 QB 402, 419.

7.03 **No contract in the bill of lading?** The Bills of Lading Act 1855 spoke in section 1[5] of the bill of lading as 'representing the contract of carriage'. However, this was criticized by Lord Bramwell in the case of *Sewell v Burdick*, as follows:

> [The statute] speaks of the contract contained in the bill of lading. To my mind there is no contract in it. It is a receipt for the goods, stating the terms on which they were delivered to and received by the ship, and therefore excellent evidence of those terms, but it is not a contract. That has been made before the bill of lading was given.[6]

7.04 **Significance** Accordingly, the view, at least since the latter part of the nineteenth century, has been that the terms on the reverse of the bill of lading do not constitute the contract itself, but merely provide evidence of it.[7] Thus, where the contract of carriage is concluded before the bill of lading is issued, it is not open to the shipowner to unilaterally alter the terms of the contract by introducing contradictory written terms in the bill of lading. The significance of this fundamental point of principle may be illustrated by the leading modern case, *SS Ardennes (Cargo Owners) v SS Ardennes (Owners)*.[8] The exporter, who was the claimant in this case, shipped 3,000 cases of mandarin oranges on the *Ardennes* at Cartagena in Spain. The carrier had orally agreed to carry the vessel direct to London. However, the ship called first at Antwerp. On arrival at the Port of London the import tax payable on mandarin oranges had risen, as it did each year on 1 December, and the market price had fallen because four other cargoes of mandarin oranges had already arrived at the port. The bill of lading, issued after the cargo had been loaded, contained a liberty clause to the effect that the *Ardennes* could call at intermediate ports, could proceed by any route directly or indirectly, and could tranship the goods.[9] The claimant sued for breach of contract and the shipowner raised the liberty clause by way of defence to the claim. The question for the court was whether oral evidence was admissible to establish the original terms of the contract. Lord Goddard CJ held that such evidence was admissible. He said:

> It is, I think, well settled that a bill of lading is not in itself the contract between the shipowner and the shipper of goods, though it has been said to be excellent evidence of its terms . . . The contract has come into existence before the bill of lading is signed; the latter is signed by one party only, and handed to him by the shipper usually after the goods have been put on board. No doubt if the shipper finds that the bill contains terms with which he is not content, or does not contain some term for which he has stipulated, he might, if there was time, demand his goods back; but he is not, in my opinion, for that reason, prevented from giving evidence that there was in fact a contract entered into before the bill of lading or containing some additional term. He is no party to the preparation of the bill of lading; nor does he sign it. It is unnecessary to cite authority further than the two

---

[5] Since repealed by the Carriage of Goods by Sea Act 1992, s 6(2).

[6] (1884) 10 App Cas 74, 105; *Peninsula & Oriental Steam Navigation Co Ltd v Rambler Cycle Co Ltd* [1964] MLJ 443, 447.

[7] See also *Crooks v Allen* (1879) 5 QBD 38 (CA), 40; *Moss Steamship Co v Whinney* [1912] AC 254, 264.

[8] [1951] 1 QB 55.

[9] Clause 2 (in full) provided that: 'The owners are to be at liberty to carry the said goods to their port of destination by the above or other steamer or steamers, ship or ships, or railway ... proceeding by any route and whether directly or indirectly to such port, and in doing so to carry the goods beyond their port of destination, and so tranship or land and store the goods either on shore or afloat and reship and forward the same at the owners' expense but at merchant's risk . . .'.

cases already mentioned for the proposition that the bill of lading is not itself the contract; therefore in my opinion evidence as to the true contract is admissible.[10]

Contract made when?   It is clear then that the above case is premised on the fact that the   **7.05** bill of lading is issued after shipment, even after the ship has sailed, and there may already have been a contract in existence before this. The contract may have been made by telephone, by letter, by e-mail, by fax, or by a liner booking note. The difficulty is in establishing at what point the contract is made,[11] given that it is clear that a contract of carriage can come into effect at some point in time before the actual issue of the bill of lading, even on the basis that the parties have previously done business together.[12] There is authority to the effect that a fixture note is the contract[13] and it has been held that the bill of lading evidences a contract even though the goods have actually been discharged before the bill of lading is issued.[14]

Contractual obligation to pay freight   One issue which has arisen is whether the   **7.06** insertion of the words 'freight prepaid' could negative a pre-existing contractual liability to pay freight. In *Cho Yang Shipping Co Ltd v Coral (UK) Ltd*[15] the Court of Appeal had to determine whether the defendants, Coral, were liable to the shipowners for freight under three bills of lading issued in Hamburg by their agents. The bills of lading named Coral as the shippers and provided that 'freight prepaid' and 'clean on board'. In his judgment, Hobhouse LJ stated that:

> merely to look at the bill of lading may not in all cases suffice. It remains necessary to look at and take into account the other evidence bearing upon the relationship between the shipper and the carrier and the terms of the contract between them . . . The terms upon which the goods have been shipped may not be in all respects the same as those actually set out in the bill of lading. It does not necessarily follow in any given case that the named shipper is to be under a personal liability for the payment of freight.[16]

Hallgarten QC had held that Coral was liable for the bill of lading freight. Allowing the appeal, Hobhouse LJ concluded that:

> . . . in the present case, the mere inclusion of those words in the bill of lading does not preclude a liability of Coral for the freight but it is part of the evidence to be taken into account when considering whether or not Coral were under a contractual liability to the plaintiffs for the freight.[17]

If the judge had asked whether, having regard to the facts of this particular shipment, it was to be inferred that Coral were undertaking to the plaintiffs that they would pay freight to them,[18] it would have been clear that there was no agreement by Coral to pay freight to the plaintiffs.

---

[10] At 59–60.
[11] See, eg, *Heskell v Continental Express Ltd* (1950) 83 Ll LR 438, 448–449 (Devlin J).
[12] *Hanjin Shipping v Procter & Gamble (Philippines) Inc* [1997] 2 Lloyd's Rep 341, 342.
[13] *Ngo Chew Hong Edible Oil Pte Ltd v Scindia Steam Navigation Co Ltd (The Jalamohan)* [1988] 1 Lloyd's Rep 443.
[14] *Golodetz & Co Inc v Czarnikow-Rionda Co Inc (The Galatia)* [1979] 2 Lloyd's Rep 450.
[15] [1997] 2 Lloyd's Rep 641.
[16] At 643.
[17] ibid.
[18] At 645.

7.07 **Conclusion: terms excellent evidence** At most then, it seems that one should regard the written statements on the reverse of the bill of lading as excellent evidence of the terms of the contract.[19] The party who wishes to challenge the accuracy of the terms will have to prove that the terms are inconsistent with those previously agreed. It will not be easy for someone challenging the accuracy of a statement in the bill of lading to discharge the onus of proof which falls on him.[20]

C. Where a Charterer Holds a Bill of Lading

7.08 **General rule** The normal rule as to the terms of the contract differs when there is a charterparty relationship between a charterer and a shipowner. In such a case the terms of the legal relationship will be embodied in the charterparty.

7.09 **Bill of lading merely a receipt** Where the charterer also holds a bill of lading as the shipper of the goods, the bill of lading is merely a receipt for the goods because all terms of carriage are in the charterparty.[21] The purpose of releasing a bill of lading in these circumstances is so as to enable the charterer to deal with the goods while they are in the course of transit.[22]

7.10 **Bill of lading transferred to the charterer** The next question for consideration is whether this rule is altered when the bill of lading is transferred to the charterer. The answer is the same; the charterer's contract is still embodied in the terms of the charterparty.[23] However, when the bill of lading is endorsed to a third party, the bill of lading must be considered the contract because the shipowner has given it so that the charterer can pass it on as the contract of carriage in respect of the goods.[24]

D. The Position of a Transferee

7.11 **The general principle** That the bill of lading will be conclusive evidence as to the terms of the contract once it is endorsed to a third party was established in the case of *Leduc v Ward*.[25] In this case the claimants were the endorsees of a bill of lading for goods shipped on the *Austria*. The bill of lading stated that the ship was:

> now lying in the port of Fiume (Yugoslavia), and bound for Dunkirk, with liberty to call at any ports in any order, and to deviate for the purpose of saving life or property.

---

[19] See, eg, *National Jaya (Pte) Ltd v Hong Tat Marine Shipping Pte Ltd* [1979] 2 MLJ 6.
[20] See, eg, *Playing Cards (M) Sdn Bhd v China Mutual Navigation Co Ltd* [1980] 2 MLJ 182, where such an attempt failed.
[21] *Rodocanachi v Milburn* (1886) 18 QBD 67 (CA), 75 (Esler MR); *Leduc v Ward* (1888) 20 QBD 475 (CA), 479 (Esler MR); *Wagstaff v Anderson* (1880) 5 CPD 171 (CA), 177 (Bramwell LJ).
[22] *The Al Battani* [1993] 2 Lloyd's Rep, 219, 222 (Sheen J).
[23] See *President of India v Metcalfe Shipping Co Ltd (The Dunelmia)* [1970] 1 QB 289 (CA).
[24] *The Al Battani* [1993] 2 Lloyd's Rep 219, 222 (Sheen J).
[25] (1888) 20 QBD 475 (CA).

However, instead of proceeding directly to Dunkirk, the *Austria* sailed for Glasgow. Both the ship and cargo were lost near Ailsa Craig, off the mouth of the River Clyde. The carrier argued that the goods were lost through perils of the sea and that the bill of lading exempted such liability. The endorsee argued that the carrier had lost the protection of such bill of lading exemptions because of the deviation to Glasgow. Counsel for the carrier argued that the bill of lading was not the contract of carriage and that his client could therefore avoid liability. The Court of Appeal held that the bill of lading provided conclusive evidence of the terms of the contract in the hands of an endorsee.

Basis   The outcome in *Leduc v Ward* is now so well established that it is difficult to question. On one view, the decision in *Leduc v Ward* was based on the Bills of Lading Act 1855, section 1, which provides that an endorsee of a bill 'shall have transferred to, and vested in, him all rights of suit, and be subject to the same liability in respect of such goods, as if the contract contained in the bill of lading had been made with himself'. The difficulty, in the case of an endorsement from a charterer-shipper is, as we have seen, that the bill of lading does not contain the contract as between him and the shipowner. Thus, how could it be said that the transfer passes something which does not exist? The response of Fry LJ in *Leduc v Ward* was: **7.12**

> It seems to me impossible . . . now to contend that there is no contract contained in the bill of lading, whatever may have been the case before the [Bills of Lading Act 1855] . . . the provision of the statute, making the contract contained in the bill of lading assignable, is inconsistent with the idea that anything which took place between the shipper and shipowner and not embodied in the bill of lading, could affect the contract.[26]

In the view of Lord Esher MR

> it may be true that the contract of carriage is made before [the bill] is given because it would generally be made before the goods are sent down to the ship; but when the goods are put on board the captain has authority to reduce that contract into writing; and then the general doctrine of law is applicable by which, where the contract has been reduced into writing, which is intended to constitute the contract, parol evidence to alter or qualify the effect of such writing is not admissible, and the writing is the only evidence of the contract.[27]

This reasoning seems to cast some doubt on the equally widely held view that the bill of lading is no more than excellent evidence of the terms of the contract.[28] Nevertheless, it is better, if for nothing else than commercial certainty, to assume that the line of cases, which established that the bill of lading is excellent evidence of its terms and conclusive evidence when in the hands of a third party, is correct. So far as third parties are concerned, the matter is clarified somewhat by the provision in section 2(1) of the Carriage of Goods by Sea Act 1992 which provides that the lawful holder has all the rights of suit under the bill of lading 'as if he had been a party to that contract'. One suggestion is that this means that the lawful holder has vested in him all rights of suit 'as if there had been a contract in the terms contained in the bill of lading and he had been a party to that contract'.[29]

---

[26] At 483–484.

[27] At 479.

[28] See, eg, Charles Debattista, 'The Bill of Lading as the Contract of Carriage —A Reassessment of *Leduc v Ward*' (1982) 45 MLR 652.

[29] Scrutton (1996), 75.

8

THE BILL OF LADING AS A DOCUMENT OF TITLE

A. Introduction

Overview   We turn in this chapter to a consideration of one of the most unique features   **8.01**
of the bill of lading, namely the possibility that, in an appropriate form, the bill of lading
can function as a document of title. We consider first the significance of the bill of lading as
a document of title and then move on to a consideration of some of the problems associated with the transfer of rights of suit and the solutions provided by the Carriage of Goods
by Sea Act 1992.[1] We consider finally the position of spent bills of lading.

B. Common Law Principles

Meaning of document of title   A bill of lading can function as a negotiable[2] document of title   **8.02**
at common law, provided that it is in an appropriate form. Although it is generally recognized
that there is no widely accepted definition of the term 'document of title at common law', the
essentials are that bills of lading in the correct form can, by endorsement and delivery,[3]

---

[1] See, generally, Carver (2005), chs 5 & 6; Scrutton (1996), arts 94–104. See also Sarah Dromgoole and
Yvonne Baatz, 'The Bill of Lading as a Document of Title' in Palmer & McKendrick (1998), ch 22.

[2] As to the meaning of this, see para 8.03.

[3] See *Sanders Bros v Maclean & Co* (1883) 11 QBD 327; *Barber v Meyerstein* (1870) LR 4 HL 317; *Biddell
Bros v E Clemens Horst Co* [1911] 1 KB 934 (CA), 957 (Kennedy LJ); *The Future Express* [1992] 2 Lloyd's Rep
79, 100 (Judge Diamond QC); *Hispanica de Petroleos SA v Vencedora Oceanica Navegacion SA (The Kapetan
Markos NL) (No 2)* [1987] 2 Lloyd's Rep 321, 340, (Dillon LJ).

transfer constructive possession[4] in the goods to the holder.[5] The effect of the transfer of constructive possession is that the holder of the bill of lading is entitled to delivery of the goods at the port of destination[6] and the bill can be used as security for a debt.[7]

8.03 **Negotiability** It is not disputed that bills of lading in 'negotiable' form pre-dated the emergence of straight (or non-negotiable) bills of lading.[8] However, negotiability in this context does not mean that the bill of lading is 'negotiable' in the normal strict legal sense of that term and indeed negotiable simply means 'transferable' in this context.[9] Thus, a negotiable bill of lading does not give the transferee a better title than the transferor.[10] In practice, a substantial number of carriers issue negotiable bills of lading,[11] principally because these are required as security under a letter of credit (or other financing arrangement). Such bills of lading are also often requested or suggested by the seller or shipper because it is intended that the goods should be sold during transit.

8.04 **Symbol of the goods** In *Sanders v Maclean*, Bowen LJ said that the transfer and delivery of a bill of lading operates 'as a symbolical delivery of the cargo'.[12] Thus, the bill of lading represents the goods and possession of the bill of lading is treated as equivalent to possession of the goods covered by it.[13] Bowen LJ went on to say that:

> A cargo at sea while in the hands of the carrier is necessarily incapable of physical delivery. During this period of transit and voyage the bill of lading by the law merchant is universally recognised as its symbol . . . [It] remains in force as a symbol, and carries with it not only the full ownership of the goods, but also all rights created by the contract of carriage between the shipper and the shipowner. It is the key which in the hands of the rightful owner is intended to unlock the door of the warehouse, floating or fixed, in which the goods may chance to be.[14]

---

[4] See too *Enichem Anic SpA v Ampelos Shipping Co Ltd (The Delfini)* [1990] 1 Lloyd's Rep 252 (CA), 268 (Mustill LJ).

[5] As to the meaning of 'holder', see now the Carriage of Goods by Sea Act 1992, s 2(1), discussed at para 8.17.

[6] See para 10.02.

[7] As to which, see para 8.06.

[8] See Raymond Negus, 'The negotiability of bills of lading' (1921) 37 LQR 442.

[9] In *Heskell v Continental Express Ltd* (1950) 83 Ll LR 438, Devlin J described the use of negotiable in this context as being used in its 'popular sense' (at 453). In *The Future Express* [1993] 2 Lloyd's Rep 542 (CA), 547, Lloyd LJ stated that '[A bill of lading] is a document which is transferable by delivery'. See the further consideration of this case at para 8.30.

[10] See *Thompson v Dominy* (1845) 14 M&W 403, 408; 153 ER 532, 534 (Alderson B); *Gurney v Behrend* (1854) 3 El&Bl 622, 633–634; 118 ER 1275, 1279 (Lord Campbell CJ); *Kum v Wah Tat Bank* [1971] 1 Lloyd's Rep 439 (PC), 446 (Lord Devlin); *JI MacWilliam Co Inc v Mediterranean Shipping Co SA (The Rafaela S)* [2005] UKHL 11; [2005] 2 AC 423, at [37] (Lord Steyn).

[11] An UNCTAD survey in 2003 indicated that 88% of respondents issued negotiable bills of lading and, of this number, a further 70% mainly or exclusively used such bills: see *The use of transport documents in international trade* (UNCTAD, 2003), 42.

[12] *Sanders Bros v Maclean & Co* (1883) 11 QBD 327, 341 (Bowen LJ).

[13] Said to be 'an application of the principles of bailment and attornment': see *Borealis AB v Stargas Ltd (The Berge Sisar)* [2002] 2 AC 205, at [18] (Lord Hobhouse). For the problem of fraud, see *Lloyds Bank Ltd v Bank of America National Trust & Savings Association* [1938] 2 KB 147 (CA).

[14] (1883) 11 QBD 327 (CA), 341.

Transfer of property   The transfer of the bill of lading also transfers such rights of property[15]   **8.05**
in the goods[16] as it is the transferor's intention to transfer.[17] This point arose as a matter of
mercantile custom in the case of *Lickbarrow v Mason*.[18] In that case, the jury recognized a
custom of merchants that a bill of lading by which goods were stated to have been 'shipped
by any person or persons to be deliverable to the order or assigns' enabled the holder, by
transferring the bill, to transfer the property in the goods to the transferee:

> . . . [B]y the custom of merchants, bills of lading, expressing goods or merchandise to have
> been shipped by any person or persons to be delivered to order or assigns, have been, and are,
> at any time after such goods have been shipped, negotiable and transferable by the shipper or
> shippers of such goods to any other person or persons, by such shipper or shippers endorsing
> such bills of lading with his, her, or their name or names, and delivering or transmitting the
> same so endorsed, or causing the same to be so delivered or transmitted to such other person
> or persons; and that by such endorsement and delivery, or transmission, the property in such
> goods hath been, and is transferred and passed to such other person or persons. And that, by
> the custom of merchants, endorsements of bills of lading in blank, that is to say, by the ship-
> per or shippers with their names only, have been, and are, and may be, filled up by the person
> or persons to whom they are so delivered or transmitted as aforesaid, with words ordering the
> delivery of the goods or contents of such bills of lading to be made to such person or
> persons: and, according to the practice of merchants, the same, when filled up, have the same
> operation and effect, as if the same had been made or done by such shipper or shippers when
> he, she, or they endorsed the same bills of lading, with their names as aforesaid.[19]

If there is no intention to transfer the property in the goods to the transferee, then no such
property passes.[20]

Pledge of the goods   A bill of lading can also be pledged[21] so as to give the endorsee security   **8.06**
over the goods.[22] Where the bill of lading operates in this way,[23] the pledgee has the power
to obtain delivery of the goods on arrival at the discharge port and, if necessary, may realize
them for the purpose of the security. However, at common law, the mere endorsement and
delivery of a bill of lading by way of pledge does not pass the property in the goods to the
endorsee, such that the liabilities are transferred to him.[24] Thus, in *Sewell v Burdick*[25] the
endorsees were held not liable in an action by the shipowner for freight. If the goods are not

---

[15] ie rights of general property (or title to the goods): see *Borealis AB v Stargas Ltd (The Berge Sisar)* [2002]
2 AC 205, at [22] (Lord Hobhouse).

[16] Strictly speaking, 'property does not pass by indorsement of the bill of lading, but by the contract in
pursuance of which the indorsement is made': *Sewell v Burdick* (1884) 10 App Cas 74, 105 (Lord Bramwell).

[17] *Sanders Bros v Maclean & Co* (1883) 11 QBD 327, 341 (Bowen LJ).

[18] (1794) 5 TR 683; 101 ER 382, later described by Diplock LJ as having 'laid the foundation for the
financing of overseas trade and the growth of commodity markets in the 19th century': *Barclays Bank v
Customs and Excise* [1963] 1 Lloyd's Rep 81 (CA), 88.

[19] At 685–686; 101 ER 382.

[20] See, eg, *East West Corp v DKBS 1912 AF A/S* [2003] EWCA Civ 83; [2003] QB 1509, at [3], (Mance LJ).

[21] The pledge nevertheless preserves the right of the pledgor to bring an action for damage to the goods:
see *Owners of the SS Glamorganshire v Owners of the Clarissa B Carver (The Clarissa B Carver)* (1888) 13 App
Cas 454 (PC).

[22] *Sewell v Burdick* (1884) 10 App Cas 74; *Barclays Bank Ltd v Commissioners of Customs & Excise* [1963] 1
Lloyd's Rep 81.

[23] No such intention was demonstrated in *The Future Express* [1993] 2 Lloyd's Rep 542 (CA).

[24] cf the Carriage of Goods by Sea Act 1992, discussed at para 8.16.

[25] *Sewell v Burdick* (1884) 10 App Cas 74.

delivered to the pledgee when he demands them, he may bring an action for wrongful interference with them, unless this was before he acquired his title to the goods.[26]

8.07 **Form of the bill of lading** In order to qualify as a document of title, the bill of lading must be made out to 'order', that is, it must be in a form in which the carrier agrees to deliver the goods at their destination to a named consignee or to his 'order or assigns'.[27] Alternatively, the bill of lading may be made out to 'bearer'.[28] Further, the bill of lading must state that the goods have been 'shipped', as it is well established that a 'received for shipment' (or 'on board') bill of lading is not a document of title at common law.[29] Provided these two main requirements are fulfilled, the shipper may direct the carrier to deliver the goods to another person,[30] 'at any rate before the delivery of the goods themselves or of the bill of lading to the party named in it'.[31] Under the Carriage of Goods by Sea Act 1992,[32] the shipper's right to redirect the goods will be lost once the consignee acquires rights under the bill of lading.[33]

C. Documents of Title under Statute

8.08 **Limited sense at common law** We have now looked at the main principles underlying the status of the bill of lading as a document of title at common law.[34]

8.09 **Statutory meaning** There is, however, another sense in which bills of lading are considered documents of title. This arises under the Factors Act 1889.[35] Section 1(4) provides that 'the expression "document of title" shall include any bill of lading' and is incorporated, by reference, in section 61(1) of the Sale of Goods Act 1979.[36] Section 1(4) also provides that certain other documents are documents of title for the purposes of the Act. However, it is clear that these will not be documents of title in the common law sense unless a custom is proved to this effect. The effect of the Act is that a statutory transfer of title may be effected to the transferee, even though the transferor was not the owner, by way of an exception to the *nemo dat* principle.

D. Transfer of Bills of Lading and Earlier Statutory Remedies

8.10 **Property not contract** We have seen that it is possible, at common law, to transfer the property in the goods by transferring the bill of lading. However, the transfer could not effect a

---

[26] As in *Glyn, Mills & Co v East & West India Dock Co* (1882) 7 App Cas 591. See the discussion of this case at para 10.03.
[27] See *Lickbarrow v Mason* (1794) 5 TR 683; 101 ER 380 and the discussion at para 5.13.
[28] See the discussion at para 5.15.
[29] See *Diamond Alkali Export Corp v Fl Bourgeois* [1921] 3 KB 443.
[30] See *Elder Dempster Lines v Zaki Ishag (The Lycaon)* [1983] 2 Lloyd's Rep 548.
[31] *Mitchell v Ede* (1840) 11 Ad & El 888, 903; 113 ER 651, 657 (Lord Denman CJ). See Benjamin (2002), para 18-015.
[32] See para 8.16.
[33] See s 2(5).
[34] See para 8.02.
[35] 52 & 53 Vict, c 45.
[36] c 54.

transfer of the rights and obligations in the contract of carriage. This was expressed by Parke B in the case of *Thompson v Dominy*:

> I have never heard it argued that a contract was transferable, except by the law merchant, and there is nothing to show that a bill of lading is transferable under any custom of merchants. It transfers no more than the property in the goods; it does not transfer the contract.[37]

Privity of contract   At common law, the doctrine of privity of contract opposed the trans-   **8.11**
fer of the rights and obligations arising under the contract of carriage.[38] Only the original parties to the contract can sue and be sued on it. The Bills of Lading Act 1855 was passed to remedy some of the difficulties, but, as we shall shortly see, it did so unsuccessfully. The preamble stated why it had been passed:

> Whereas by the custom of merchants a bill of lading of goods being transferable by endorsement the property in the goods may thereby pass to the endorsee, but nevertheless all rights in respect of the contract contained in the bill of lading continue in the original shipper or owner, and it is expedient that such rights should pass with the property. . .

Section 1 of the 1855 Act   Section 1 of the 1855 Act provided that: **8.12**

> Every consignee of goods named in a bill of lading and every endorsee of a bill of lading to whom the property in the goods therein mentioned shall pass upon or by reason of such consignment or endorsement shall have transferred to and vested in him all rights of suit, and be subject to the same liabilities in respect of such goods as if the contract contained in the bill of lading had been made with himself.

This provision provided a claimant with a statutory form of assignment, by linking the transfer of rights and liabilities with the passing of property (or title) in the goods, requiring property to pass 'upon or by reason of consignment or endorsement'. In effect, what was transferred to a consignee or endorsee with the property in the goods was not only the right to sue but also the burden of the contract. The transferee of the bill of lading did not take the same contract as the consignor but a new contract on the basis of what appeared on the face and reverse of the bill of lading. Even at an early stage, it was recognized that there were a number of problems with the particular formula adopted in the 1855 Act.[39]

Problem areas   The difficulties with the drafting of the 1855 Act became particularly notice-   **8.13**
able with changed trading conditions in the latter half of the twentieth century. Some examples may be given.[40] In the case of a bill of lading endorsed by way of a pledge, for example to a bank, the endorsee acquired no rights under the carriage contract because there was no intention that such endorsement should transfer to him the property in the goods covered by the bill.[41]

---

[37] (1845) 14 M & W 403, 407; 153 ER 532, 534. See also *Sewell v Burdick* (1884) 10 App Cas 74, 83 (Lord Selborne LC); *The Jag Shakti* [1986] AC 337 (PC), 345 (Lord Brandon).

[38] In 1915 Viscount Haldane LC expressly stated that '[in] the law of England certain principles are fundamental. Our law knows nothing of a *jus quaesitum tertio* arising by way of contract': *Dunlop Pneumatic Tyre Co Ltd v Selfridge & Co Ltd* [1915] AC 847, 853.

[39] See TG Carver, 'On some defects in the Bills of Lading Act 1855' (1890) 6 LQR 289, 292: 'Perhaps the time has arrived when fresh legislation on the subject may be attempted with advantage.'

[40] These are developed further in the Law Commission's Report, *Rights of Suit in Respect of Carriage of Goods by Sea*, Law Com No 196 (Scot Law Com No 130), para 2.2.

[41] *Sewell v Burdick* (1884) 10 App Cas 74 (HL). See the discussion at para 8.06.

Where goods were carried in bulk and lost in transit, an endorsee of the bill of lading was faced with the problem that, in the case of bulk cargoes, section 16 of the Sale of Goods Act 1979 required goods to be ascertained before the property in those goods can pass.[42] In the carriage context, the endorsee had no remedy under the contract of carriage because he could not claim to have acquired property to the goods 'upon or by reason of such . . . endorsement'.[43] The requirements of section 1 were also not met where bulk cargo was covered by a single bill of lading and portions of the cargo were sold and delivered against shipper's delivery orders.[44] Nor would the section apply where, on late arrival of the bill of lading, delivery of the cargo was made against a letter of indemnity. This latter problem arose in *Enichem Anic SpA v Ampelos Shipping Co Ltd (The Delfini)*.[45]

8.14 *The Delfini* *Enichem Anic SpA v Ampelos Shipping Co Ltd (The Delfini)*[46] concerned a chain of oil contracts, with provision for delivery against letters of indemnity, in the event that the bills of lading were unavailable at the time of discharge.[47] The contract of sale was for 100,000 tonnes of Algerian condensate (oil). On the arrival of the ship at Gela, the original purchasers had not received the bills of lading. However, they had sold between 20,000 and 25,000 tonnes of the oil c.i.f. to subsequent purchasers who, in turn, sold an identical cargo to the claimants. On the day after the *Delfini's* arrival, a letter of indemnity was issued to the shipowners, signed by Chase Manhattan Bank. The shipowners delivered against the letter of indemnity. The claimants alleged a short delivery of 275.789 tonnes of oil. At first instance, Phillips J held that, once the cargo had been discharged, the bill of lading ceased to be effective as a transferable document of title and hence no contractual rights were acquired by the transferees under the 1855 Act.[48] The Court of Appeal held that the plaintiffs did not have any rights of suit under the Act because the subsequent endorsement of the bills of lading had not played an essential causal part in the passing of property which had occurred when the invoice price was paid. Mustill LJ stated that

> section 1 presents two alternative situations in which the contract is transferred to the endorsee. The first is where the property passes 'upon' the endorsement (and delivery of the document). This means that the passing of property is simultaneous with the endorsement, and the endorsement is the act which brings it about. . . The second is where the property passes 'by reason of' the endorsement. This must signify something different, since the expression is 'upon or by reason of' not 'upon and by reason of'. In my judgment it means that although the endorsement of the bill is not the immediate occasion of the passing of property, nevertheless it plays an essential causal part in it. . . I do not think it legitimate to

---

[42] See now s 20A of the Act, as inserted by the Sale of Goods (Amendment) Act 1995. The Act was the result of *Sale of Goods Forming Part of a Bulk*, Law Com No 215 (Scots Law Com No 145) (1993). See Janet Ulph, 'The Sale of Goods (Amendment) Act 1995: co-ownership and the rogue seller' [1996] LMCLQ 93 and Tom Burns, 'Better Late than Never: The Reform of the Law on the Sale of Goods Forming Part of a Bulk' (1996) 59 MLR 260.

[43] See *The Owners of Cargo Lately Laden on Board the Ship Aramis v Aramis Maritime Corp (The Aramis)* [1989] 1 Lloyd's Rep 213 (CA).

[44] As to delivery orders, see para 4.13.

[45] [1990] 1 Lloyd's Rep 252 (CA). See GH Treitel, 'Passing of property under c.i.f. contracts and the Bills of Lading Act 1855' [1990] LMCLQ 1.

[46] ibid.

[47] A not uncommon problem in oil contracts. See para 10.19 and see RM Wiseman, 'Transaction Chains in North Sea Oil Cargoes' (1984) 2 JENRL 134.

[48] [1988] 2 Lloyd's Rep 599, 609.

read the Act so as to enable a transferee to sue on a bill of lading, even if the property did not pass either 'upon', or 'by reason of', the transfer.[49]

The outcome of this case was clearly unsatisfactory: the final buyer, who had borne the risk and suffered the loss, could not assert any contractual rights against the shipowner, even though he had, in due course, received bills of lading. Thus, the requirement under section 1 that the buyer could only sue the shipowner if there was a causal link between endorsement and the passing of property effectively defeated the expectations of the contracting parties.

Reform As we have seen, almost from the time of the enactment of the 1855 Act there were **8.15** calls for its amendment but it was not until a century later that there were concerted attempts to bring this about. This followed representations to the Law Commission in the aftermath of *The Gosforth*, a case decided by the Commercial Court in Rotterdam according to English law.[50] The Law Commission of England and Wales was prompted to look into the question, inter alia by representatives of Gafta.[51] After the issue of questionnaires to interested parties in 1987,[52] the Law Commission (and by now also the Scottish Law Commission) published a Working Paper on *Rights to Goods in Bulk*[53] in June 1989. Two seminars, attended by leading academics, practitioners, and judges were held and this led to a joint final Report of the two Law Commissions.[54] The latter included a draft Bill, which was enacted virtually unaltered in 1992.[55] The Act repeals the 1855 Act.[56] A number of other jurisdictions have since drafted similar legislation.[57]

E. The Carriage of Goods by Sea Act 1992

Documents The Act[58] is principally concerned with the acquisition of rights and liabilities **8.16** by those holding bills of lading, sea waybills, and ship's delivery orders.[59] Though the bill of lading is nowhere defined in the Act, the Act does provide that what is not included is a

---

[49] [1990] I Lloyd's Rep 252 (CA), 274.

[50] S en S 1985 Nr 91; BJ Davenport, 'Ownership of Bulk Cargoes: *The Gosforth*' [1986] LMCLQ 4. See too Tim Howard, 'The Carriage of Goods by Sea Act 1992' (1993) 24 JMLC 181.

[51] The Grain and Free Trade Association, <www.gafta.com>.

[52] Appendix, Working Paper No 112.

[53] Working Paper No 112.

[54] *Rights of Suit in Respect of Carriage of Goods by Sea*, Law Com No 196 (Scot Law Com No 130). The Scottish Law Commissioner, Dr EM Clive, recorded a note of partial dissent: at 41–44.

[55] The draft Bill was introduced in the House of Lords by Lord Goff: *Hansard*, HL, vol 538, cols 73–79. The only difference between the draft Bill and the Act is s 6(4) which extends its ambit to Northern Ireland.

[56] Section 6(2).

[57] See Stephen D Girvin, 'Carriage by Sea: The Sea Transport Documents Act 2000 in Historical and Comparative Perspective' (2002) 119 SALJ 317, where some of these developments are considered, from the perspective of the South African Sea Transport Documents Act 2000, No 65.

[58] See, generally, Scrutton (1996), art 35; Carver (2005), para 5-012. For discussion of the Act, see J Beatson and JJ Cooper, 'Rights of suit in respect of carriage of goods by sea' [1990] LMCLQ 196; Robert Bradgate and Fidelma White, 'The Carriage of Goods by Sea Act 1992' (1993) 56 MLR 188; G Humphreys and A Higgs, 'An Overview of the Implications of the Carriage of Goods by Sea Act 1992' [1993] JBL 61; FMB Reynolds, 'The Carriage of Goods by Sea Act 1992' [1993] LMCLQ 436; Tim Howard, 'The Carriage of Goods by Sea Act 1992' (1993) 24 JMLC 181; Barney Reynolds, 'Further Thoughts on The Carriage of Goods by Sea Act 1992 (UK)' (1994) 25 JMLC 143.

[59] Section 1(1).

document which is incapable of transfer by endorsement or, as a bearer bill, by delivery without endorsement.[60] Subject to this, a 'received for shipment' bill of lading is included.[61] The Law Commission thought that too elaborate a definition of the bill of lading could ultimately be counter-productive.[62] Sea waybills and ship's delivery orders are defined in the Act[63] and cautious provision is made for EDI.[64] The Law Commission took the view that there were 'formidable technical and legal problems' to be overcome before paperless transactions became the norm[65] and that provision should be made for this possibility to the extent that the Secretary of State should be able to make regulations modifying the Act as necessary and containing supplemental, incidental, consequential, and transitional provisions.[66]

8.17 **Rights** The core of the Act is section 2(1) which provides that the 'holder'[67] of a designated shipping document will have transferred to and vested in him all rights of suit under the contract of carriage as if he had been a party to that contract. This section of the Act implements one of the Law Commission's principal recommendations, namely that the lawful holder of a bill of lading should be entitled to assert contractual rights against the carrier, irrespective of the passing of property in the goods.[68] Thus, the Act provides that the 'lawful' holder of a bill of lading has these rights,[69] as does the holder of a sea waybill[70] and a ship's delivery order.[71] The Singapore Court of Appeal has recently stated that, in relation to section 2(1):

> One must bear in mind the object behind s 2(1) of the Act which is to transfer the right to sue the shipper (who is the original party to the contract of carriage as reflected in the B/L) to those categories of persons set out therein. It is to promote international trade and to facilitate the enforcement of rights by third parties against the carrier.[72]

8.18 **Contractual rights extinguished** Section 2(5) contains two provisions of importance:

> Where rights are transferred by virtue of the operation of subsection (1) above in relation to any document, the transfer for which that subsection provides shall extinguish any entitlement to those rights which derives—
>
> (a) where that document is a bill of lading, from a person's having been an original party to the contract of carriage; or
> (b) in the case of any document to which this Act applies, from the previous operation of that subsection in relation to that document;

---

[60] Section 1(2). As to this, see *UCO Bank v Golden Shore Transportation Pte Ltd* [2005] SGCA 42; [2006] 1 SLR 1.

[61] Thereby resolving some of the difficulties produced, inter alia, by *The Marlborough Hill v Alex Cowan & Sons Ltd* [1921] 1 AC 444 (PC); *Elder Dempster Lines v Zaki Ishag (The Lycaon)* [1983] 2 Lloyd's Rep 548.

[62] Law Commission Report, para 2.50.

[63] Section 1(2) and (3).

[64] See now also the Electronic Communications Act 2000, c 7. See also ch 13.

[65] Law Commission Report, para 6.3.

[66] Section 1(5) and (6).

[67] For a case where the original shippers remained as 'holder' under wrongly dated bills of lading, see *Mendala III Transport v Total Transport Corp (The Wilomi Tanana)* [1993] 2 Lloyd's Rep 41.

[68] Law Commission Report, para 2.22.

[69] Section 2(1)(a).

[70] Section 2(1)(b).

[71] Section 2(1)(c).

[72] *UCO Bank v Golden Shore Transportation Pte Ltd* [2005] SGCA 42; [2006] 1 SLR 1, at [40] (Chao Hick Tin JA).

but the operation of that subsection shall be without prejudice to any rights which derive from a person's having been an original party to the contract contained in, or evidenced by, a sea waybill, in relation to a ship's delivery order, shall be without prejudice to any rights deriving otherwise than from the previous operation of that subsection in relation to that order.

Thus, under section 2(5)(a), the shipper under a bill of lading ceases to have contractual rights when someone else becomes the lawful holder. Further, under section 2(5)(b) the intermediate holder of the bill of lading also ceases to have contractual rights once someone else becomes the lawful holder.

Holder It is critical to read section 2(1) with section 5(2), which provides as follows: **8.19**

References in this Act to the holder of a bill of lading are references to any of the following persons, that is to say—

(a) a person with possession of the bill who, by virtue of being the person identified in the bill, is the consignee of the goods to which the bill relates;

(b) a person with possession of the bill as a result of the completion, by delivery of the bill, of any indorsement of the bill or, in the case of a bearer bill, of any other transfer of the bill;

(c) a person with possession of the bill as a result of any transaction by virtue of which he would have become a holder falling within paragraph (a) or (b) above had not the transaction been effected at a time when possession of the bill no longer gave a right (as against the carrier) to possession of the goods to which the bill relates;

and a person shall be regarded for the purposes of this Act as having become the lawful holder of a bill of lading wherever he has become the holder of the bill in good faith.

Each of these provisions has been considered in cases on the Act. We shall now examine each provision in turn by reference to the decided cases.

'A person with possession . . . identified in the bill' Under s 5(2)(a) a person is a holder who **8.20** is identified in the bill of lading as the consignee. This definition has been considered in two cases. *East West Corp v DKBS 1912 & AKTS Svendborg*[73] involved an action by the sellers for damages for delivery of their cargoes shipped from Hong Kong to Chile, without presentation of the bills of lading.[74] The bills of lading were consigned to the order of certain named Chilean banks and, in due course, were endorsed by the sellers and sent to their correspondent banks in Chile for payment. The goods were carried to Chile by Maersk and P & O whose containers were placed by their respective agents in different customs warehouses at San Antonio. Following payment of customs duty, the goods were released, without presentation of the original bills of lading. No payment was made by the buyers. It was argued that the sellers had no title to sue. Thomas J[75] concluded that it was clear that the Chilean banks were lawful holders of the bills of lading, within the meaning of the Carriage of Goods by Sea Act 1992, section 5(2)(a), and the sellers did not have rights of suit as holders of the bills of lading.[76] In response

---

[73] [2003] EWCA Civ 83; [2003] QB 1509 (CA).

[74] As to this point generally, see ch 10.

[75] [2002] EWHC 83 (Comm); [2002] 2 Lloyd's Rep 182.

[76] However, in respect of one of the bills of lading, where the words 'or order' were omitted, this was a 'straight' or non-negotiable bill and so the sellers were entitled to maintain their claim in respect of this bill of lading, as shippers.

to the argument advanced by the sellers, Thomas J held that they were not undisclosed princi-
pals of the Chilean bank. This reasoning was upheld by the Court of Appeal,[77] who concluded
that the express consignment of the bills of lading to the Chilean banks meant that, pursuant
to section 5(2)(a) of the 1992 Act, they were the holders of the bills of lading.[78] Accordingly,
the sellers did not have rights of suit under the 1992 Act.[79] There was nothing in the Act which
supported the idea that, after a statutory transfer of contractual rights by a principal to its agent,
the principal could still sue in contract in its own name.[80] A subsequent case from Singapore,
UCO Bank v Golden Shore Transportation Pte Ltd,[81] has considered the scope of section 5(2)(a)
of the equivalent Singaporean legislation.[82] This time the context was suit by a bank against a
carrier. UCO Bank sued the carrier for wrongful delivery of a cargo of Sarawak round logs,
which were discharged in India without the bills of lading. The seller of the goods had
presented the bills of lading to another bank, HSBC, who negotiated them and paid the seller.
HSBC then presented the bills of lading to UCO Bank, as issuing bank, for reimbursement
and UCO paid HSBC. However, the buyer did not reimburse UCO. At first instance,[83] the
court held that, as there had been no endorsement of the bills of lading to UCO, any rights of
action under the bills of lading remained with the seller. UCO was not the holder for the purpose of section 5(2)(a) (or section 5(2)(b)). This decision was reversed by the Court of Appeal
which held that UCO had become the holder because it satisfied the requirements which
were specified in section 5(2)(a), namely (i) it was in possession of the bills of lading; (ii) it was
the named consignee on the bills of lading; (iii) it was in possession of the bills of lading in
good faith.[84]

8.21 **'A person with possession . . . by indorsement'** A person is also a holder if they have
'possession of the bill as a result of the completion, by delivery of the bill, of any indorsement of the bill or, in the case of a bearer bill, of any other transfer of the bill'. This was
considered in the case of *Aegean Sea Traders Corporation v Repsol Petroleo SA (The Aegean
Sea)*.[85] The owners of a tanker chartered her for the carriage of crude oil to. . . one or two safe
port(s) EUROPEAN MEDITERRANEAN . . .' and bills of lading for the cargo specified
discharge as 'port of Spain'. After leaving Sullom Voe, the *Aegean Sea* was ordered to La
Coruña to discharge her cargo. On being given orders to berth in the early hours of
3 December the *Aegean Sea* grounded on the Torre de Hercules rocks, breaking in two and
subsequently exploding. The vessel and most of her cargo were lost and there was large-
scale oil pollution of the environment and damage to private property. The cargo was the

---

[77] [2003] EWCA Civ 83; [2003] QB 1509 (CA).
[78] Although the Chilean banks had physical possession of the bills of lading, it was doubted that they had
acquired at common law sufficient possessory title to sue in tort for loss or damage to the goods.
[79] We shall see, in due course, that although the sellers were not successful under the Act they were at first
instance held to have a claim in tort and, on appeal, in bailment. For discussion of these arguments, see para 9.22.
[80] [2003] EWCA Civ 83; [2003] QB 1509 (CA), at [18] (Mance LJ).
[81] [2005] SGCA 42; [2006] 1 SLR 1.
[82] More appropriately named as the Bill of Lading Act 1992, cap 384.
[83] [2005] 2 SLR 735.
[84] See as to this requirement, para 8.23.
[85] [1998] 2 Lloyd's Rep 39. See Nicholas Gaskell, 'Pollution, Limitation and Carriage in *The Aegean Sea*'
in Rose (2000), ch 5.

subject of a chain of contracts and the litigation arose when the shipowners sought to recover amounts for which claims were brought against them, the bunkers on board, and freight; in all $65 million. Following the incident, an intermediate buyer of the cargo had endorsed the bills of lading to the end purchaser, but sent the bills of lading to another intermediate buyer, an associate company of the end purchaser in Liechtenstein. The associate company sent the bills of lading to the end purchaser, which was when the mistaken endorsement was discovered. The court had to consider whether the end purchasers were 'holders' of the bills of lading. Under section 5(2)(b) the end purchasers were the holder if they had possession of the bills of lading as the result of completion of any endorsement by delivery. The owners tried to argue that, once the bill of lading was endorsed and put in the post to them, that was sufficient for the purposes of section 5(2)(b). Thomas J did not accept this; a person did not satisfy the requirements of section 5(2)(b) if he obtained the bill of lading merely in consequence of someone endorsing it and sending it to him:

> The section requires him to have possession as a result of the completion of an endorsement by delivery. Although the sending and receipt of a document through the post often constitutes service of a document, the sending of a bill of lading through the post does not without more constitute delivery; the person receiving it has to receive it into his possession and accept the delivery before he becomes the holder.[86]

The Singapore Court of Appeal in *Keppel Tatlee Bank Ltd v Bandung Shipping Pte Ltd*[87] has also considered section 5(2)(b). This case arose when a receiver of a cargo of crude palm oil obtained the cargo without the bills of lading and then absconded without paying the bill of lading freight. The bills of lading, which were in blank, were delivered to Keppel without filling in any name onto the endorsement made in blank by the seller. Keppel filled in the name of the 'State Bank' onto the endorsement and these were forwarded to it. The State Bank returned the bills of lading without any further endorsement and Keppel then stamped 'cancelled' over the endorsement on the bill of lading. The question for the court was whether Keppel had rights of suit in the bills of lading. The Court of Appeal held that Keppel had not acquired rights of suit, because by inserting the name of the State Bank onto the original blank endorsement, the State Bank had acquired the rights of suit under section 5(2)(b). The mere fact of physical possession of the bills of lading did constitute the holder the lawful holder for the purpose of suit under the Act.[88]

'A person with possession . . . by virtue of which he would have become a holder . . .' **8.22**
Section 5(2)(c) provides that a person is a holder if he has possession of the bill 'as a result of any transaction by virtue of which he would have become a holder falling within paragraph (a) or (b) above had not the transaction been effected at a time when possession of the bill no longer gave a right (as against the carrier) to possession of the goods to which the bill relates'. This was considered in *Borealis AB v Stargas Ltd (The Berge Sisar)*.[89] Borealis contracted to buy

---

[86] At 59–60.
[87] [2003] 1 Lloyd's Rep 619, sub nom *Bandung Shipping Pte Ltd v Keppel Tatlee Bank Ltd* [2003] 1 SLR 295.
[88] [2003] 1 Lloyd's Rep 619, at [28]. But it would seem that if an agent is in possession of the bills of lading the claimant would be regarded as being the holder: see *The Cherry* [2002] 3 SLR 431. In such a case, there was no justification for confining possession to physical possession: at [21] (Kan Ting Chiu J).
[89] [2002] 2 AC 205.

43,000 mt of Field Grade refrigerated propane on CFR terms.[90] The contract of sale expressly stated that this cargo should not obtain corrosive compounds producing an adverse result when tested. The propane was carried aboard the *Berge Sisar*, a vessel chartered to the seller and five bills of lading were issued. The cargo failed a sampling test on arrival at the discharge berth and the buyer refused to take it, selling the cargo on to a subsequent buyer, but at a much reduced price.[91] The buyers issued a writ against the sellers claiming damages for breach of contract. Borealis issued a third party notice against the shipowners, who claimed that, as holders of the bills of lading who had demanded or requested delivery of the cargo, Borealis were liable for corrosion damage to the vessel by virtue of section 3 of the Carriage of Goods by Sea Act 1992.[92] As a preliminary point, however, it had to be established whether rights of suit lay against Borealis or the subsequent buyer. The House of Lords concluded that they were successive holders of the bills of lading under section 5(2)(c).[93] The case of *Primetrade AG v Ythan Ltd (The Ythan)*[94] required further and more detailed consideration of section 5(2)(c). This arose when cargo, described as 'Metallic HBI Fines', was fixed for carriage from Venezuela to China aboard the *Ythan*. However, an explosion while the *Ythan* was off the coast of Colombia caused the death of the master and five crew and the total loss of the vessel and the cargo. Bills of lading stated that the shipper was the seller, although there was a sub-sale of almost the same quantity to an Australian company. The bills of lading were held by the seller's bank and, after the loss of the *Ythan*, the buyer, acting with the agreement of its insurers, instructed its bank to pay the sums due under the bills of lading in order to obtain all the necessary documents needed to make a claim under its insurance. Upon receipt of the bills of lading, the buyer's bank transferred them to the buyer's insurance brokers. The insurers succeeded in obtaining a letter of undertaking from the shipowners' P & I club covering the losses arising from the lost cargo. In arbitration proceedings, the shipowners successfully claimed for their loss against the buyers. The buyers then applied under section 67 of the Arbitration Act 1996 to challenge the jurisdiction of the tribunal and raised several arguments as to why it was not the 'lawful holder' of the bills of lading. The central plank of this argument was that where the goods had been destroyed the relevant section to consider was section 5(2)(c) of the 1992 Act, which related to the situation where a transaction was 'effected at a time when possession of the bill no longer gave a right (as against the carrier) to possession of the goods to which the bill relates'. It was argued that in order for a person to become a 'holder' the transaction had to be inter alia one which would have come within section 5(2)(b) 'by virtue' of any transaction if the transaction had occurred before the goods were lost. The question for the court was whether the buyer had indeed become the lawful holder of the bills of lading.[95] It found that it had not become the holder of the bills of lading because the conditions in section 5(2)(c), which was the relevant section of the Act where goods had been destroyed, were not met. The transaction by which the

---

90 ie 'Cost and freight' terms.
91 [2002] 2 AC 205, at [8].
92 We return to this point again at para 8.24.
93 [2002] 2 AC 205, at [30], (Lord Hobhouse).
94 [2005] EWHC 2399; [2006] 1 Lloyd's Rep 457.
95 There was also an issue as to whether the buyers had made a claim in accordance with s 3(1)(b) of the 1992 Act. As to this, see para 8.25.

insurance broker came to possess the bills of lading, on the buyer's behalf, was effected so that the underwriters could fulfil their obligation under the actual or proposed settlement agreement. But for this, the buyers would never have had possession of the bills and they would have remained with the bank until they had been paid for by the final purchasers of the goods. Such a transaction had nothing to do with the normal course of trading and was not one falling within section 5(2)(b) and, accordingly, the buyer would not have become 'holder' of the bills of lading 'by virtue of' such a transaction had it occurred at a time when possession of the bills gave a right (as against the carrier) to possession of the goods to which the bills related.

'Holder in good faith' An additional requirement is specified in section 5(2) for becoming **8.23** a 'holder'; this is that the person becoming the holder must do so 'in good faith'.[96] In *Aegean Sea Traders Corporation v Repsol Petroleo SA (The Aegean Sea)*[97] Thomas J noted that 'good faith' was not defined in the Act, but took the view that as used it denoted 'honest conduct'[98] and not a broader concept of good faith such as 'the observance of reasonable commercial standards of fair dealing in the conclusion and performance of the transaction concerned'.[99]

Obligations The Law Commission was much exercised by the question concerning the **8.24** extent to which the holder should become liable for the burdens of the contract.[100] It was decided that contractual liabilities should not be automatically imposed on every holder of a bill of lading, but only where the holder purported to enforce any rights conferred on him. Thus section 3(1) of the Act provides that where a holder of a bill of lading takes or demands delivery from the carrier of any of the goods to which the document relates, makes a claim under the contract of carriage against the carrier in respect of any of those goods, or is a person who, at a time before those rights were vested in him, took or demanded delivery from the carrier of any of those goods,[101] then that person will be subject to the same liabilities as if he had been party to that contract. As Lord Hobhouse explained in *Borealis AB v Stargas Ltd (The Berge Sisar)*:[102]

> The second principle [under the Act] is that of mutuality (or, if preferred, reciprocity or fairness). I have already quoted passages from the [Law Commission] report demonstrating that this was the guiding principle in arriving at the recommendations which have led to section 3(1). Section 3(1) is drafted following this principle because it makes it fundamental that, for a person to be caught by section 3(1), he must be the person in whom the rights of suit under the contract of carriage are vested pursuant to section 2(1). The liability is dependent upon the possession of the rights.[103]

---

96 The Singapore Court of Appeal, in *UCO Bank v Golden Shore Transportation Pte Ltd* [2005] SGCA 42; [2006] 1 SLR 1, interpreted the requirement as to 'lawful' in s 2(1)(a) as meaning no more than that prescribed in s 5(2), namely that a person became a lawful holder if he had become the holder in good faith: at [40].

97 [1998] 2 Lloyd's Rep 39. See para 8.21.

98 By analogy, inter alia, with s 62(2) of the SGA 1979. See too *UCO Bank v Golden Shore Transportation Pte Ltd* [2005] SGCA 42; [2006] 1 SLR 1, at [39] (Chao Hick Tin JA).

99 [1998] 2 Lloyd's Rep 39, 60.

100 Law Commission Report, para 3.1.

101 This provision accordingly takes care of the problem in *Enichem Anic SpA v Ampelos Shipping Co Ltd (The Delfini)* [1990] 1 Lloyd's Rep 252 (CA), where the bills of lading in respect of the goods were endorsed eleven days after delivery of the cargo.

102 [2002] 2 AC 205.

103 At [45].

8.25 **Scope of the obligation**   The scope of the obligation has been considered in two cases. In *Aegean Sea Traders Corporation v Repsol Petroleo SA (The Aegean Sea)*[104] one of the questions which had to be considered, assuming that the end purchaser was the 'lawful holder', was whether it had become subject to the liabilities under the bill of lading by virtue of section 3(1)(a) and section 3(1)(c). Thomas J held, however, that it had not 'demanded' delivery because a letter of indemnity was not a demand for delivery.[105] The next question was whether it had 'taken' delivery for the purposes of the section. The shipowners argued that 5,475 tonnes of the crude oil retrieved by the salvors had been received into the end purchaser's refinery. This was not accepted by the judge because the taking of delivery under section 3 involved

> delivery under the bill of lading of the cargo to which the bill of lading relates from the carrier itself (or from someone who holds them for the carrier such as a warehouseman or a person whom the carrier has entrusted them for delivery) after discharge at the port of destination.[106]

In *Borealis AB v Stargas Ltd (The Berge Sisar)*[107] the principal question was the extent of the liability, if any, of the intermediate purchaser of the propane.[108] It will be recalled that Borealis had requested delivery but rejected the cargo after taking samples. It was therefore argued that, by virtue of section 3, Borealis had become subject to the same liabilities under the bills of lading as if they had originally been party to those contracts and the shipper of the cargo. It was accepted that though Borealis was not the 'holder' when delivery of the cargo was sought, that nevertheless it was for a period of 24 hours 'liable' under section 3(1)(c) of the 1992 Act. Borealis argued that its liability ceased when the bills were endorsed to the end purchaser and accordingly that no claim lay against it. In the Court of Appeal, a majority concluded that an intermediate holder, such as Borealis, was discharged from liability because such liability did not remain irrevocably with the holder of the bill. The House of Lords agreed and held that taking delivery pursuant to section 3(1) meant the voluntary transfer of possession from one person to another. This meant more than co-operating in the discharge of the cargo from the vessel. Delivery for the purposes of section 3 involved a full transfer of the possession of the relevant goods by the carrier to the holder of the bill of lading. The mere surrender of the relevant bill of lading to the carrier or his agent before delivery would ordinarily be an incident of such delivery but the taking of routine samples from the cargo tanks before clearing the vessel for discharge into the terminal could not be treated as a demand to deliver. Accordingly, given that there was no demand by Borealis, there was no liability. Indeed, it was fundamental that for a person to be caught by section 3(1) he must be the person in whom the rights of suit under the contract of carriage were vested pursuant to section 2(1).[109]

---

104 [1998] 2 Lloyd's Rep 39. See the earlier discussion of this case at para 8.21.

105 At 61–62. The judge also concluded that, because the crude oil was received into the refinery before the bill of lading was received by the end purchaser, the shipowners had no claim under s 3(1)(a) but would have had to succeed under s 3(1)(c).

106 At 62.

107 [2002] 2 AC 205. See GH Treitel, 'Bills of Lading: Liabilities of Transferee' [2001] LMCLQ 344; Natalie Campbell, 'Defining the frontiers of the bill of lading holder's liability—*The Berge Sisar* and *The Aegean Sea*' [2000] JBL 196. The facts of the case were thought to be 'unusual' and not within the contemplation of the drafters of the 1992 Act: [1999] QB 863 (CA), 880 (Sir Brian Neill).

108 See the earlier discussion of the case at para 8.22.

109 See *Primetrade AG v Ythan Ltd (The Ythan)* [2005] EWHC 2399; [2006] 1 Lloyd's Rep 457 where the failure to establish that the buyer was a holder precluded any consideration of its liabilities under s 3(1). See the discussion of the case at para 8.22.

Liabilities of the original party   Although there was some argument as to whether the holder   **8.26**
should only become liable for post-shipment liabilities and not pre-shipment liabilities,[110]
the Law Commission took the view that no satisfactory line could be drawn between the
two. The Act therefore provides expressly that, in so far as liabilities are imposed on any
holder, this is without prejudice to the liabilities under the contract of any person as an
original party to the contract.[111]

Recovery by those not suffering loss   At common law it is not usually possible for substan-   **8.27**
tial damages to be recovered by a claimant who has not suffered any loss. This rule was affirmed
by the House of Lords in *Albacruz (Cargo Owners) v Albazero (Owners)(The Albazero)*[112] and
has been followed in other jurisdictions.[113] The 1992 Act now provides, however, that, where
someone suffers loss or damage but does not have rights of suit, the person with rights of suit
can exercise those rights for the benefit of the person who has suffered the loss or damage.[114]

F. Spent Bills of Lading

Meaning   Where possession of the bill of lading no longer gives any right to possession of   **8.28**
the goods — for example, where delivery has already been made to someone with the right
to claim the goods — the bill of lading is no longer an effective document of title[115] and the
other originals in the set[116] become spent.[117] Moreover, once the carrier parts with possession of the goods the bill of lading can no longer transfer constructive possession of the
goods.[118] However, whether the bill of lading is in fact exhausted will depend upon whether
delivery has been made to the person entitled to receive the goods.[119] The underlying principle was explained by Lord Hatherley in *Barber v Meyerstein*:

> When [goods] have arrived . . . , until they are delivered to some person who has the right to
> hold them the bill of lading still remains the only symbol that can be dealt with by way of assign-
> ment, or mortgage, or otherwise. As soon as delivery is made, or a warrant for delivery has been
> issued, or an order for delivery accepted . . . then those symbols replace the symbol which before

---

[110] Such as the shipper's breach of warranty in shipping dangerous goods. See Stephen D Girvin, 'Shipper's liability for the carriage of dangerous cargoes by sea' [1996] LMCLQ 487; Francis Rose, 'Cargo risks: "dangerous"
goods' (1996) 55 CLJ 601.

[111] Section 3(3). This preserves the position at common law and also under the 1855 Act: see *Fox v Nott*
(1861) 6 H & N 630; 158 ER 260; *The Athanasia Comninos & George Chr Lemos* [1990] 1 Lloyd's Rep 277,
281 (Mustill J); *Effort Shipping Co Ltd v Linden Management SA (The Giannis NK)* [1998] AC 605, 618
(Lord Lloyd).

[112] [1977] AC 774. cf *National Mineral Development Corp Ltd v Obestain Inc (The Sanix Ace)* [1987] 1
Lloyd's Rep 465.

[113] See, for example, *EMI (NZ) Ltd v Wm Holyman & Sons Pty Ltd* [1976] 2 NZLR 566.

[114] Section 2(4). See too the Law Commission Report, para 2.27. The Singapore Court of Appeal, in *UCO
Bank v Golden Shore Transportation Pte Ltd* [2005] SGCA 42; [2006] 1 SLR 1, held, on the facts, that s 2(4)
was inapplicable, notwithstanding arguments by counsel for the respondents: at [45].

[115] *Short v Simpson* (1866) LR 1 CP 248.

[116] As to bills of lading in sets, see para 5.06.

[117] The bills of lading are 'accomplished'. Conlinebill 2000 states 'all other Bills of Lading to be void'.

[118] Although cf *The Future Express* [1992] 2 Lloyd's Rep 79, 99 (Judge Diamond QC). See too para 8.02.

[119] *Barclays Bank Ltd v Commissioners of Customs and Excise* [1963] 1 Lloyd's Rep 81, 88–89 (Diplock J);
Enichem Anic SpA v Ampelos Shipping Co Ltd (The Delfini) [1990] 1 Lloyd's Rep 252 (CA), 269 (Mustill LJ).

existed. Until that time bills of lading are effective representations of the ownership of the goods, and their force does not become extinguished until possession, or what is equivalent in law to possession, has been taken on the part of the person having a right to demand it.... [T]he bills of lading cannot be considered as having been fully spent or exhausted ...[120]

In this case the issue was whether a holder of the bill of lading could pledge the bills of lading while the goods were still in the carrier's warehouse.[121] The House of Lords held that the bill of lading remained in force so long as complete delivery of possession had been made to some person having the right to claim under it.[122]

8.29   **Whether a document of title**   One of the issues which arises is whether a spent bill of lading can still be a document of title.[123] One view is that a bill of lading can still be a document of title whether or not the carrier's contractual duty to deliver the goods is legally enforceable by the holder of the bill of lading.[124]

8.30   **Spent bills of lading and letters of indemnity**   If the carrier delivers as against a letter of indemnity, do the bills of lading become spent? This was considered in *The Future Express*.[125] The shipowners had delivered cargo to a c. & f. buyer, without production of the bills of lading, after being given an indemnity by the seller. About a year after shipment, the bills were eventually presented to a bank, under a letter of credit under an arrangement where the buyer had instructed the bank to extend the date by which the documents had to be negotiated. The buyer had agreed with the seller that the bills should be withheld from the banking chain in order to delay the time for payment. On paying under the credit, the bank knew that the goods had been delivered and dispersed. The bank claimed against the shipowners in conversion. The bank, although named as consignee, was never a party to the original contract of carriage, nor did it have title under the Bills of Lading Act 1855, section 1.[126] The main issue was whether the bank had title to sue for non-delivery. Judge Diamond QC held that the bank never became a pledgee and there was no intention to pass constructive possession of the goods.[127] On the spent bill of lading point, Judge Diamond QC doubted whether the bill of lading became spent when the carrier delivered goods against an indemnity:

> [T]here is a more fundamental reason why it is not relevant that the primary obligations of the owners as carriers under the contract of carriage may have come to an end at that stage. It would completely destroy the value of bills of lading as documents of title to hold that, even where delivery is made to a person having no right under the bills to call for possession of the goods, the bills cease to operate as documents of title at the stage where the primary obligations of the carrier under the contract of carriage come to an end. Nor is there any support in the authorities for such a view.[128]

---

[120] (1870) LR 4 HL 317, 329–330.

[121] They had been placed there because of the carrier's claim for freight and were subject to a stop order.

[122] (1870) LR 4 HL 317, 329. The House of Lords upheld the decision of Willes J in the Court of Common Pleas: see (1866) LR 2 CP 38, 53.

[123] See the earlier discussion of this at para 8.02.

[124] See Carver (2005), para 6-031.

[125] [1992] 2 Lloyd's Rep 76, affirmed by the Court of Appeal: [1993] 2 Lloyd's Rep 542 (CA). See too Fidelma White and Robert Bradgate, 'No protection for banks against fraud and folly' [1994] LMCLQ 350.

[126] At this time the Carriage of Goods by Sea Act 1992 did not apply as it was not in force then.

[127] He also concluded that it was not possible for the bank to establish that it had title to sue in bailment.

[128] [1992] 2 Lloyd's Rep 76.

Spent bills of lading and misdelivery   In the case of a misdelivery of the goods, it has been   **8.31**
held that the bill of lading will remain in force and will not be spent. In *East West Corp v*
DKBS 1912 and AKTS Svendborg Utaniko Ltd, Thomas J stated that:

> It is clear . . . that a bill of lading remains in force even if the goods are misdelivered to a person
> not entitled to them. The reason is clear. At or after the time of misdelivery to a person not
> entitled, the bill of lading may be being negotiated between banks on the basis that it is still a
> valid document of title. In short haul bulk trades, it is not uncommon that the cargo arrives at
> the port of destination while the documents are still being negotiated. Until the goods are
> delivered to the person actually entitled, the bill of lading must remain the document of title
> to the goods. Although there may be a debate as to whether a bill is or is not spent when the
> goods are delivered against an indemnity to a person entitled to them . . . there can be no doubt
> that they are not spent when the goods are delivered to a person not entitled.[129]

The Carriage of Goods by Sea Act   The principles just noted as to spent bills of lading   **8.32**
can be particularly harsh for those receiving a bill of lading perhaps as much as a year after
the goods are physically discharged. The Law Commission recognized that by extending
rights of suit to those acquiring the bill of lading after delivery

> there arises the possibility that bills of lading could be negotiated for cash on the open mar-
> ket, without any dealings in the goods: in other words, trafficking in bills of lading simply as
> pieces of paper which gives causes of action against sea carriers.[130]

The 1992 Act thus provides that though, ordinarily, the holder would not have any rights of
suit transferred to him once the bills are 'spent', the same does not hold true where he becomes
the holder by virtue of a transaction effected in pursuance of any contractual (or other) arrangements made before the time when such a right to possession ceased to attach to the possession
of the bill.[131] Equally the basic position would not hold where a person becomes the holder of
the bill of lading as a result of the rejection to that person by another person of goods or documents delivered to the other person in pursuance of any such arrangements.[132] The Act also
provides that where rights are transferred to a holder, this extinguishes any entitlement to those
rights deriving from a person having been an original party to the contract of carriage.[133]

Sales contract

---

[129] [2002] EWHC 83 (Comm); [2002] 2 Lloyd's Rep 182, at [39]. Note that this point was not considered in the appeal: see [2003] EWCA Civ 83; [2003] QB 1509 (CA), at [19] (Mance LJ).
[130] *Rights of Suit in Respect of Carriage of Goods by Sea*, Law Com No 196 (Scot Law Com No 130),
para 2.43.
[131] Section 2(2)(a).
[132] Section 2(2)(b).
[133] Section 2(5).

9

THIRD PARTIES AND BILL OF LADING TERMS

A. Introduction

Overview   A fundamental rule of English law, now ameliorated to some extent by statute,[1]   **9.01**
is that only the parties to contracts are bound by their terms. During the time when the Bills
of Lading Act 1855 was in force and because of the difficulties which we have noted,[2] a number of creative solutions were devised by the courts,[3] some of them of continuing utility.[4]
In this chapter, we will examine each of these solutions in turn, before turning to consider
the impact of the Contracts (Rights of Third Parties) Act 1999.

B. Implied Contracts

Generally   One solution, where section 1 of the 1855 Act was inapplicable as between the   **9.02**
original contracting parties and third party consignees or endorsees, was a degree of willingness on the part of the courts to imply a contract[5] between consignee or endorsee and the carrier. This contract was a separate contract from the original contract between shipper and

---

[1] In the Contracts (Rights of Third Parties) Act 1999. See para 9.31.
[2] See, eg, *Mitsui & Co Ltd v Novorossiysk Shipping Co (The Gudermes)* [1993] 1 Lloyd's Rep 311 (CA), 314 (Staughton LJ).
[3] On one view these solutions were 'highly technical': see John F Wilson, 'A flexible contract of carriage —
the third dimension?' [1996] LMCLQ 187.
[4] See, generally, Carver (2005), ch 7.
[5] See GH Treitel, 'Bills of lading and third parties' [1986] LMCLQ 294; J Browne, 'The rise and demise
of the *Brandt v Liverpool* contract' (2005) 11 JIML 221.

carrier and the terms were those of the bill of lading against which delivery had been obtained. The problem of consideration could be met, inter alia, by the carrier paying any freight charges or other charges, such as demurrage, and the holder taking delivery of the goods on presentation of the bill of lading.

9.03 *Brandt v Liverpool* The implied contract became known as a *Brandt v Liverpool* contract after the case of *Brandt v Liverpool, Brazil & River Plate SN Co*,[6] although it was not the first case in which such contracts became known.[7] In this case zinc ashes were intended to be shipped from Buenos Aires to Liverpool aboard the *Bernini*. The shipment was damaged before shipment[8] but the shipowner nevertheless issued a bill of lading stating that they were shipped in apparent good order and condition. Subsequently, the master unloaded the cargo and had it reconditioned at a cost of £748. The cargo was loaded aboard another vessel, the *Cavour*, and arrived late to its destination. The bill of lading was endorsed in favour of the claimants (a bank) who had advanced money on it in good faith. When the *Cavour* arrived at its destination, the endorsees presented the bill of lading, paid the freight, and, under protest, the sum of £748 as demanded by the shipowner and took delivery of the cargo. They then sued the shipowner for damages due to delay and for repayment of the £748. As pledgees, the bank had no action based on the Bills of Lading Act 1855, but the Court of Appeal nevertheless found in their favour. By presenting the bill of lading, paying the freight, and having the cargo delivered to them, a contract was implied between the endorsees and shipowner on the terms of the bill of lading. This was expressed as follows by Scrutton LJ:

> But when one comes to consider the contract to be inferred from the fact of taking delivery and the promise by the person who takes delivery to perform the terms of the bill of lading, and one asks what was the consideration moving from the shipowner for that promise, one sees it was to deliver the goods on the terms of the bill of lading. That document contains the terms on both sides which were implied from presenting the bill of lading and taking delivery under it.

> When a holder of a bill of lading, who has some property in the goods, presents the bill of lading and accepts the goods, can there be inferred a contract on each side to perform the terms of the bill of lading? The view that Greer J has taken is that such a contract can and ought to be implied in this case, and I take the same view. It follows, therefore, that Brandt & Co may enforce the terms of the bill of lading.[9]

9.04 **Criteria** The limits of the *Brandt v Liverpool* doctrine were initially not so clearly defined other than that the decision whether or not the courts would imply a contract would be one of fact and not of law. Thus, in *Ilyssia Compania Naviera SA v Ahmed Bamaodah (The Elli 2)*[10] Ackner LJ said that:

> It is common ground that the implication of such a contract is a matter of fact to be decided in the circumstances of each case . . . although one usually finds that freight has been paid, this is not essential . . . Presenting a bill of lading and supplying a guarantee that it will be

---

6 [1924] 1 KB 575 (CA). The Court of Appeal in this consisted of Bankes, Scrutton and Atkin LJJ, widely recognized as being an exceptionally strong bench in the inter-war period.

7 See the earlier cases of *Cock v Taylor* (1811) 13 East 399; 104 ER 424; *Stindt v Roberts* (1848) 17 LJ QB 166; *White & Co v Furness, Withy & Co Ltd* [1895] AC 40.

8 Some of the bags had been wetted by rain before shipment and the upper layers of bags in one of the holds became heated.

9 [1924] 1 KB 575 (CA), 595–596.

10 [1985] 1 Lloyd's Rep 107 (CA).

presented on arrival can both equally tend to the inference that the delivery and acceptance of the goods was on the terms of the bill of lading produced, or to be produced, as far as they were applicable at the port of discharge.[11]

May LJ said that:

> No such contract should be implied on the facts of any given case unless it is necessary to do so: necessary, that is to say, in order to give business reality to a transaction and to create enforceable obligations between parties who are dealing with one another in circumstances in which one would expect that business reality and those enforceable obligations to exist.[12]

In *The Aramis*[13] Bingham LJ suggested that there were two questions which might be asked: (1) Whether the conduct of the bill of lading holder in presenting the bill of lading would be reasonably understood as an offer to enter into a contract on the bill of lading terms; and (2) Whether the conduct of the ship's agent in accepting the bill or the conduct of the master in agreeing to give delivery or in giving delivery would be reasonably understood by the bill of lading holder as an acceptance of his offer.[14]

Mutual co-operation   Where there has been a degree of mutual co-operation between   **9.05** carrier and receiver of cargo, there is authority to the effect that the courts would be prepared to imply a contract to give 'business reality' to the transaction. This was the case in *Compania Portorafti Commerciale SA v Ultramar Panama Inc (The Captain Gregos No 2)*.[15] Amoco sold 800,000 barrels of Gulf of Suez crude to Ultramar Panama Inc who sold the cargo on to PEAG and subsequently BP. The cargo was stated to be shipped 'in apparent good order and condition' and the bills of lading provided that the consignee was Ultramar Panama Inc or order on payment of freight at the rate of 'freight payable as agreed'. PEAG undertook to provide BP with a letter of indemnity if full shipping documentation was not available to BP prior to discharge. On discharge of the goods at Rotterdam, a complaint was made to the shipowners for short delivery, but the claim was not then pursued until after the one year time limit under article III, rule 6 of the Hague–Visby Rules had elapsed. As neither PEAG nor BP were named as the consignees in the bill of lading, property in the cargo did not pass to either of them upon or by reason of the endorsement of the bills to them.[16] The bills were endorsed and transferred to PEAG after completion of discharge and were never endorsed to BP. Was a contract incorporating the bill of lading terms to be implied between the shipowners and BP? On the facts of the case, Bingham LJ (as he then was) held that there were 'very powerful grounds' for concluding that it is necessary to imply a contract between BP and the shipowners to give business reality to the transaction between them and create the obligations which both parties believed to exist.[17] However, as BP were bound by the bill of lading terms, their claim was time barred.

---

[11] At 111.

[12] At 115.

[13] [1989] 1 Lloyd's Rep 213 (CA).

[14] At 224. See also the judgment of Stuart-Smith LJ (at 230) and *Ilyssia Compania Naviera SA v Ahmed Bamaodah (The Elli 2)* [1985] 1 Lloyd's Rep 107 (CA), 111 (Ackner LJ); 115 (May LJ).

[15] [1990] 2 Lloyd's Rep 395. See MA Clarke, 'The consignee's right of action against the carrier of goods by sea' [1991] LMCLQ 5.

[16] ie under the Bills of Lading Act 1855, s 1. For discussion, see para 8.12.

[17] [1990] 2 Lloyd's Rep 395, 403. It was not thought necessary to imply a contract on the bill of lading terms between PEAG and the shipowners.

9.06 **Other limitations** Two further cases put a brake on the scope of *Brandt v Liverpool* contracts. In *The Aramis*[18] the carrier failed to deliver any cargo at all and the plaintiffs claimed damages for non-delivery and short delivery. A quantity of goods covered by several bills of lading had been shipped in bulk and, by the time that the final bill was presented at the port of discharge, the supply of cargo had been exhausted. Bingham LJ found that it was impossible to imply a contract on the facts of the case for the business relationship between the shipowners and bill of lading holders 'was entirely efficacious without the implication of any contract between them'.[19] A mere presentation of a bill of lading without a corresponding response from the carrier could not be interpreted as an 'acceptance' of the plaintiff's 'offer'. As Stuart-Smith LJ put it:

> In this case presentation of bill of lading 6 coupled with part delivery is entirely consistent with the performance of obligations and rights of the parties under their existing contractual arrangements with others. There is no evidence of the performance of any act which is explicable only on the basis that the terms of the bill of lading govern their relationship inter se.[20]

Significantly, Bingham LJ felt some hesitation in reversing the judgment of Evans J at first instance[21] because he fully recognized 'the good sense and commercial convenience underlying [that] decision . . . but . . . [this did not] entitle one to cast principle aside and simply opt for a commercially convenient solution'.[22] Thus, he emphasized that whether 'a contract may be implied must be considered in the light of ordinary contractual principles'.[23]

9.07 *The Gudermes* The Court of Appeal was even less accommodating in *Mitsui & Co Ltd v Novorossiysk Shipping Co (The Gudermes)*.[24] Here a quantity of Straight Run Atmospheric fuel oil was shipped aboard the *Gudermes* from Aden to Ravenna. However, the vessel had no operative heating coils so that the cargo was carried unheated on the voyage. The claimants' sub-purchasers refused delivery on the basis that they feared that it might clog their underwater sealine at which the vessel was directed to discharge. The claimants then procured and paid for the transhipment of the cargo onto the *Sea Oath* off Malta, had it reheated on board and thereafter delivered at Ravenna. They argued that, as a result of the dealings between themselves and the carrier in respect of the transhipment, there was to be implied a *Brandt v Liverpool* contract on the terms of the bill of lading which had expressly incorporated the Hague–Visby Rules. The Court of Appeal refused to accede. In particular, Staughton LJ said that:

> . . . we do not find that there must have been a contract, express or implied, from those facts alone. All that happened was that both parties were prepared to co-operate in finding a solution to the problem that had arisen . . . Seeing that the implication must be one of fact . . . we cannot accept that there was an implied contract between Mitsui and the owners to

---

[18] [1989] 1 Lloyd's Rep 213 (CA). See GH Treitel, 'Bills of lading and implied contracts' [1989] LMCLQ 162.
[19] ibid.
[20] At 230.
[21] [1987] 2 Lloyd's Rep 58.
[22] [1989] 1 Lloyd's Rep 213 (CA), 225.
[23] By which he was referring to offer, acceptance, and consideration: at 224. For criticism of this aspect of the case, see Treitel [1990] LMCLQ 162, 170.
[24] [1993] 1 Lloyd's Rep 311 (CA). For criticism, see Fidelma White and Robert Bradgate, 'The survival of the *Brandt v Liverpool* contract' [1993] LMCLQ 483. See also Simon Baughen, 'Contract and Co-operation: *The Gudermes*' [1991] LMCLQ 459, commenting on the decision of Evans J at first instance ([1991] 1 Lloyd's Rep 456).

deliver the cargo at Ravenna; nor a contract to be responsible for having failed to deliver the cargo at Ravenna; nor for having failed to deliver the cargo at the same temperature as when loaded, or at the temperature required by Mitsui . . . We conclude that Mitsui have no contractual remedy against the owners.[25]

Commentary   Whatever misgivings one might feel about the outcome of these last two   **9.08**
cases, this has to be tempered by an equal recognition that whatever defects there might have been in the 1855 Act ought to be remedied by legislative reform.[26] That reform has now taken place in the Carriage of Goods by Sea Act 1992 and accordingly one must ask whether there is still any scope for implying contracts or whether they have been consigned to history. The answer to this is that the 1992 Act does not expressly affect the law relating to such contracts. Accordingly, one could assume that it will be used in situations to which the Act does not extend, few as they may now be. It is possible that implied contract arguments could be used in cases of delivery against letters of indemnity,[27] merchants' delivery orders, or multimodal transport documents, none of which fall within the category of shipping documents to which the Act will apply. There has so far been no indication of any rush to do so.

C. Tort

Negligence   An alternative basis for a claim, particularly where the Bills of Lading Act 1855   **9.09**
precluded a claim, lay potentially with an action in the tort of negligence. Some restrictions on this were, however, laid down by the court in *Margarine Union GmbH v Cambay Prince SS Co Ltd (The Wear Breeze)*.[28] In this case Roskill J held that an action for negligence would not succeed unless the claimant was, at the time of the commission of the tort, the owner of the goods in question or the person entitled to immediate possession of them. In this case a cargo of copra, shipped in bulk, was seriously damaged by giant cockroaches as the result of the negligence of the shipowner in failing to have the holds of his ship fumigated before the commencement of the voyage. The claimant was the holder of a delivery order for part of the cargo, issued by the seller under a c.i.f. contract. As he did not become owner of the goods in question until they had been ascertained on discharge, Roskill J held that an action in negligence would not lie.

The Aliakmon   The approach in *The Wear Breeze* was endorsed by the House of Lords in   **9.10**
Leigh & Sullivan Ltd v Aliakmon Shipping Co (The Aliakmon).[29] In this case a cargo of steel suffered damage in transit due inter alia to negligent stowage at a time when the risk in the goods — but not the property in the goods — had passed to a c.i.f. buyer. The House of Lords denied the buyer a remedy in negligence on the basis that he was not the owner of the steel at the time that the damage was inflicted. The House took the view that there was no lacuna in the law relating to carrier liability which would require them to extend the range

---

[25] At 323.
[26] The latter being the gist of the argument advanced by Bingham LJ in *The Aramis*.
[27] As was the case in *The Captain Gregos (No 2)* [1990] 2 Lloyd's Rep 395, discussed at para 9.05.
[28] [1969] 1 QB 219.
[29] [1986] AC 785.

of the duty of care in negligence. Unless a claimant had a proprietary right in the property damaged, he could not recover in tort for economic loss arising therefrom.

9.11 **The Carriage of Goods by Sea Act 1992** Actions in tort are not expressly excluded by the Carriage of Goods by Sea Act[30] and consequently, subject to the earlier authorities, might be available to the claimant in an appropriate case.

D. The Special Contract

9.12 *Dunlop v Lambert* An old Scots case, *Dunlop v Lambert,*[31] is authority for the view that the court might treat the consignor as having made a 'special contract' with the shipowner for the benefit of the consignee and this would be enforceable by the consignor even after property in the goods had passed to the consignee.

9.13 *The Albazero* This remedy was, however, rejected by the House of Lords in *Albacruz (Cargo Owners) v Albazero (Owners)(The Albazero).*[32] Here the plaintiffs (time charterers) had shipped a cargo of crude oil from Venezuela under bills of lading nominating the charterers as consignees. During the course of the voyage to Antwerp, the bills were endorsed to f.o.b. buyers (Raffinerie Belge de Petroles SA). The cargo subsequently became a total loss because the *Albacruz* sank owing to a breach of the charterparty by the shipowners. This occurred after the property in the oil had passed to the f.o.b. purchasers. The cargo owners failed to institute proceedings against the carrier within the 12-month period required by the Hague Rules.[33]

E. Bailment

9.14 **The principle** Bailment[34] involves the delivery of possession of goods by one person (the bailor) to another person (the bailee), for some purpose, express or implied, and may be enforced against strangers by the bailee utilizing the possessory remedies. Although bailment is frequently founded upon contract, contract is not essential for bailment[35] and so the bailee may incur liability in tort to the bailor. Similarly, obligations under a bailment are independent of liability in tort, although it not infrequently happens that liability under the two heads overlaps.

---

[30] See *Rights of Suit in Respect of Carriage of Goods by Sea*, Law Com No 196 (Scot Law Com No 130), para 2.45, where the Law Commission stated that: 'We do not recommend that rights of action in tort should be explicitly excluded from implementing legislation'.

[31] (1839) 6 Cl&F 600; 7 ER 825.

[32] [1977] AC 774. Followed also in *Homburg Houtimport BV v Agrosin Private Ltd (The Starsin)* [2003] UKHL 12; [2004] 1 AC 715. See Stephen Girvin, 'Contracting carriers, Himalaya clauses and Tort in the House of Lords' [2003] LMCLQ 311.

[33] Article III, r 6.

[34] From the French *bailler*, 'to deliver'. For a historical analysis of the basis of bailment, see Alice Erh-Soon Tay, 'The Essence of a Bailment: Contract, Agreement or Possession?' (1966) 5 Sydney LR 239.

[35] See *Morris v CW Martin & Sons Ltd* [1966] 1 QB 716 (CA), 731; (Diplock LJ); *Compania Portorafti Commerciale SA v Ultramar Panama Inc (The Captain Gregos)(No 2)* [1990] 2 Lloyd's Rep 395 (CA), 405 (Bingham LJ).

Coggs v Bernard   In one of the earliest authorities on bailment,[36] *Coggs v Bernard*,[37] Lord   **9.15**
Chief Justice Holt identified 'six sorts of bailments',[38] including 'where there is a delivery of
goods or chattels to somebody, who is to carry them, or do something about them *gratis*,
without any reward for such his work or carriage . . .'.[39]

The carriage context   In *Barclays Bank Ltd v Commissioners of Customs and Excise*   **9.16**
Diplock LJ explained that:

> The contract for the carriage of goods by sea, which is evidenced by a bill of lading, is a com-
> bined contract of bailment and transportation under which the shipowner undertakes to
> accept possession of the goods from the shipper, to carry them to their contractual destina-
> tion and there to surrender possession of them to the person who, under the terms of the
> contract, is entitled to obtain possession of them from the shipowners.[40]

Thus, in the carriage context there may be a bailment relationship in the charterparty
context, in the sense that the owner of the ship (A) is the bailor, the charterer (B) is the
bailee, and the consignee of the cargo (C) is a sub-bailee. Another scenario, not involving
a charterparty, is where A (the bailor) is the owner of the goods, B (the bailee) is the carrier,
and C (the sub-bailee) is an independent contractor (such as a stevedore).

Elder, Dempster   Bailment reasoning has often arisen in the context of exemption clauses.   **9.17**
One of the earliest cases to consider such clauses in this context was the decision of the
House of Lords in *Elder, Dempster & Co Ltd v Paterson, Zachonis & Co Ltd*,[41] a case which
commentators have professed themselves unable to understand.[42] Here A was the owner of
a steamship, the *Grelwen*, that he time chartered to B. B carried a cargo of palm oil belonging
to C and issued to him a bill of lading. C's cargo was damaged. The main question was
whether this damage was classified as damage arising from unseaworthiness of the ship due
to the absence of 'tween decks, or as damage arising from bad stowage. If it was the latter, the
charterer was exempted because 'bad stowage' was an excepted peril in the bill of lading.
C sued both B and A. Once the House had classified the cause of the damage as 'bad
stowage',[43] the charterer (B) could rely on the excepted peril in the bill of lading, because
the bill of lading was issued by him to C. But could A, the owner, avoid being sued in tort
and rely on the exception clause contained in the contract between B and C? The House of
Lords unanimously found in A's favour, in effect recognizing an exception (or at least a

---

[36] Though it is not the first. See eg *Southcote's* case (1601) 4 Co Rep 83b; 76 ER 1061.
[37] (1703) 2 Ld Raym 909; 92 ER 107.
[38] Holt CJ borrowed extensively from Roman law in identifying these categories, his chief sources being
Justinian and Bracton. See Zimmermann (1990), 203.
[39] (1703) 2 Ld Raym 909, 913; 92 ER 109. The bailment in this case did not involve carriage by sea, but
concerned the carriage of several hogsheads of brandy from one cellar to another.
[40] [1963] 1 Lloyd's Rep 81 (CA), 88; *Borealis AB v Stargas Ltd (The Berge Sisar)* [2002] 2 AC 205, at [18]
(Lord Hobhouse). See too *Bryans v Nix* (1839) 4 M & W 775; 150 ER 1634; *Evans v Nichol* (1841) 3 M & G
614; 133 ER 1286.
[41] [1924] AC 522.
[42] Carver referred to the case as a 'mystery' (at 529) while Scrutton (1996) contends that no general principle is to be extracted from the case: 251, n 36. Others have argued that the case is 'now ripe for resuscitation':
FMB Reynolds (1995) 111 LQR 8, 9.
[43] On this point the House of Lords differed from the majority of the Court of Appeal and agreed with
Scrutton LJ (dissenting): [1923] 1 KB 420 (CA).

modification) to the privity doctrine. In the Court of Appeal, Scrutton LJ[44] (dissenting) had given as his reason for the same finding that A took C's goods on behalf of and as agents for B and could therefore rely on the same protection as B, via the so-called doctrine of vicarious immunity. According to this, an agent who performs a contract may benefit from any immunity from liability which his principal would have had. Applying this reasoning to the facts of the case, although A was not privy to the contract between B and C, A took possession of the goods on behalf of and as agents for B and so could claim the same protection as B. Scrutton LJ's reasoning received some support in the House of Lords in the speech of Viscount Cave[45] with whom Lord Carson agreed.[46] However another reason given, this time in the speech of Lord Sumner,[47] was that there was an implied contract[48] between A and C, incorporating the terms of the bill of lading, including the exceptions. This implied contract arose as a result of a 'bailment upon terms, which include the exceptions and limitations stipulated in the known and contemplated form of bill of lading' between A, as bailee and C as bailor.[49]

9.18 *Elder Dempster* **limited** The reasoning in the *Elder Dempster* case was, however, severely limited by the majority of the House of Lords in *Scruttons Ltd v Midland Silicones Ltd*.[50] Viscount Simonds borrowed freely from the judgment of Fullagar J in the Australian case of *Wilson v Darling Island Stevedoring & Lighterage Co Ltd*,[51] making much of the great difficulty in determining the ratio of *Elder Dempster*. In particular, Viscount Simonds cited the following *ipsissima verba* of Fullagar J:

> . . . what the *Elder Dempster* case decided, and all that it decided, is that in such a case, the master having signed the bill of lading, the proper inference is that the shipowner, when he receives the goods into his possession, receives them on the terms of the bill of lading. The same inference might perhaps be drawn in some cases even if the charterer himself signed the bill of lading, but it is unnecessary to consider any such question.[52]

In his speech, Lord Reid dismissed *Elder Dempster* 'as an anomalous and unexplained exception to the general principle that a stranger cannot rely for his protection on provisions in a contract to which he is not a party'[53] and distinguished the case on its facts. Lord Denning, in his dissenting speech, took an entirely different view. He expressly supported the dissenting judgment of Scrutton LJ in the Court of Appeal in *Elder Dempster* arguing

---

[44] [1923] 1 KB 420 (CA), 441. See also *Mersey Shipping & Transport Co Ltd v Rea Ltd* (1925) 21 Ll LR 375, 378 (Scrutton LJ).

[45] [1924] AC 522, 534. Lord Cave also suggested that A could rely on the terms in the contract between B and C because B was A's agent.

[46] It was accepted by Devlin J in *Pyrene Co Ltd v Scindia Steam Navigation Co Ltd* [1954] 2 QB 402, 421.

[47] [1924] AC 522, 564. This was also supported by Lords Dunedin and Carson, though not with further reasoning of their own.

[48] See above, para 9.02.

[49] [1924] AC 522, 564. This reasoning was later described by Bingham LJ as 'a pragmatic legal recognition of commercial reality . . .': *Dresser UK Ltd and others v Falcongate Freight Management Ltd (The Duke of Yare)* [1992] 1 QB 502 (CA), 511. More recently, it seems to have been accepted as the fundamental point in the case: see *The Mahkutai* [1996] 3 WLR 1 (PC), 6–7 (Lord Goff).

[50] [1962] AC 446.

[51] Fullagar J had there condemned 'a curious, and seemingly irresistible, anxiety to save grossly negligent people from the normal consequences of their negligence': (1955–56) 95 CLR 43, 71.

[52] (1955-56) 95 CLR 43, 78.

[53] [1962] AC 446, 479.

that one could not understand that case without some knowledge of the previous law. However, he also suggested that, if the owner of the goods could, by suing the stevedore, escape the exceptions in the contract of carriage and the limitations in the Hague Rules, 'it would expose a serious gap in our commercial law'.[54] Speaking for himself he

> would not allow this gap to be driven in our commercial law. I would not give the 'fundamental principle' of the nineteenth century a free rein. It should not have unbridled scope to defeat the intentions of business men. I would stand by the proposition stated by Scrutton LJ and affirmed, as I believe, by this House 37 years ago.[55]

Bailment on terms　The notion of a 'bailment on terms', floated in the *Elder Dempster* case **9.19** in 1924, was explored further in *Morris v CW Martin*,[56] which was not a shipping case,[57] but is widely regarded as the most important case on bailment in English law this century.[58] Quoting expressly from Pollock and Wright's treatise on *Possession in the Common Law*, Lord Denning, now Master of the Rolls, noted that:

> If the bailee of a thing sub-bails it by authority . . . and there is no direct privity of contract between the third person and the owner . . . it would seem that both the owner and the first bailee have concurrently the rights of a bailor against the third person according to the nature of the sub-bailment.[59]

Denning MR stressed that the owner of the goods, the bailor, would be bound by the conditions in the contract if he had expressly or impliedly consented to the bailee making a sub-bailment containing those conditions, but not otherwise.[60] In the context of carriage of goods by sea, Denning MR continued, obiter, that if the carrier accepted goods for carriage on a bill of lading containing exempting conditions (a 'bailment upon terms'), the owner of the goods, although not a party to the contract, was bound by those conditions if he expressly or impliedly consented to them.[61]

Gilchrist　This reasoning was accepted as authoritative by the Privy Council in *Gilchrist Watt* **9.20** *& Sanderson Pty Ltd v York Products Pty Ltd*,[62] where plaintiff cargo owners sought to hold stevedores liable in bailment as bailees of the goods. Lord Pearson asserted that the stevedores had taken 'upon themselves an obligation to the plaintiffs to exercise due care for the safety of the goods, although there was no contractual relation . . . between the defendants and the plaintiffs'.[63] The notion of a bailment (or sub-bailment) on terms was taken further by Donaldson J

---

[54] At 491.

[55] At 492.

[56] [1966] 1 QB 716 (CA).

[57] The case concerned the theft of a mink stole which had been subcontracted for cleaning to a third party and which was stolen by an employee.

[58] See Palmer (1990), 1295. Probably this would now have to be joined by *The Pioneer Container* [1994] 2 AC 324 (PC).

[59] [1966] 1 QB 716 (CA), 729.

[60] ibid.

[61] At 730, citing the words of Lord Sumner in *Elder Dempster*. Diplock LJ expressed no view on this (see 731) and Salmon LJ, although 'strongly attracted' to Denning LJ's stance, expressed no concluded view (see 741).

[62] [1970] 1 WLR 1262 (PC).

[63] At 1267. See also *Singer Co (UK) Ltd v Tees & Hartlepool Port Authority* [1988] 2 Lloyd's Rep 164, noted NE Palmer, 'Sub-bailment on terms' [1988] LMCLQ 466 and A Phang, 'Exception Clauses and Negligence — the Influence of Contract in Bailment and Tort' (1989) 9 OJLS 418.

(as he then was) in *Johnson Matthey & Co Ltd v Constantine Terminals Ltd*.[64] He held that the sub-bailee could rely on the terms of the sub-bailment as against the bailor regardless of whether the bailor consented to them; consent was only relevant between the bailor and the bailee.[65]

9.21   *The Pioneer Container*   The leading recent case on such issues is now *The Pioneer Container*,[66] a decision of the Privy Council on appeal from the Court of Appeal of Hong Kong.[67] The issue in the case was whether certain words used in 'feeder' bills of lading from the contracting carrier (the bailee) to the actual carrier (the sub-bailee) were sufficiently wide to authorize consent to the application of an exclusive jurisdiction clause to the sub-bailment. Lord Goff regarded the reasoning in the earlier cases of *Gilchrist* and *Morris* as 'authoritative':[68]

> ... if the effect of the sub-bailment is that the sub-bailee voluntarily receives into his custody the goods of the owner and so assumes towards the owner the responsibility of a bailee, then to the extent that the terms of the sub-bailment are consented to by the owner, it can properly be said that the owner has authorised the bailee so to regulate the duties of the sub-bailee in respect of the goods entrusted to him, not only towards the bailee but also towards the owner.[69]

Such a conclusion, he said, produced a result 'which in their [Lordships'] opinion is both principled and just'.[70] He expressly overruled the reasoning of Donaldson J in *Johnson Matthey* on this point.[71] On the question whether the words used in the 'feeder' bills of lading were wide enough to authorize consent to the application of an exclusive jurisdiction clause to the sub-bailment,[72] Lord Goff concluded that this would be in accordance with the reasonable commercial expectations of those who engaged in such trades.[73] This important case confirms a line of reasoning already well established in English law and gives some considerable prominence to the policy of producing a result which is in tune with commercial expectations and practice. It also circumvents certain of the more deleterious consequences of too rigid an adherence to contract doctrine, itself out of tune with more modern commercial arrangements. Bailment arguments have, consequently, been most useful for third party claimants in the shipping context.[74]

---

[64] [1976] 2 Lloyd's Rep 215. Donaldson J described the reasoning in *Elder Dempster* as 'something of a judicial nightmare' (at 219). See J Beatson, 'Bailment—vicarious immunity' (1977) 55 Canadian BR 746.

[65] At 222. cf *Singer Co (UK) Ltd v Tees & Hartlepool Port Authority* [1988] 2 Lloyd's Rep 164, *Compania Portorafti Commerciale SA v Ultramar Panama Inc (The Captain Gregos)(No 2)* [1990] 2 Lloyd's Rep 395 (CA).

[66] [1994] 2 AC 324 (PC). See Martin Davies, 'Sub-bailment on Terms: A Case Note on *The KH Enterprise* (aka *The Pioneer Container*)' (1994) 10 Maritime Law Association of Australia and New Zealand J 51; AP Bell, 'Sub-bailment on terms: a new landmark' [1995] LMCLQ 177; Andrew Phang, 'Sub-Bailments and Consent' (1995) 58 MLR 422; Peter Devonshire, 'Sub-bailment on Terms and the Efficacy of Contractual Defences against a Non-Contractual Bailor' [1996] JBL 329.

[67] Unreported, but noted by WJ Swadling, 'Sub-bailment on terms' [1993] LMCLQ 10.

[68] [1994] 2 AC 324 (PC), 336.

[69] At 339 and 341.

[70] At 342.

[71] At 340–341.

[72] This aspect of the Privy Council's judgment is discussed by Toh Kian Sing 'Jurisdiction clauses in bill of lading — the cargo claimant's perspective' [1995] LMCLQ 183.

[73] [1994] 2 AC 324 (PC), 347.

[74] But they do not always work. See, for example, *The Mahkutai* [1996] AC 650 where Lord Goff held that there was an 'insuperable objection' to bailment arguments, namely that the bill of lading contained a Himalaya clause whereby the shipowners, as subcontractors, were entitled to the benefit of certain terms in the bill of lading, though not the exclusive jurisdiction clause. To hold that there was a bailment, said Lord Goff, would 'be inconsistent with the express terms of the bill of lading': at 668.

Continuing vitality of bailment Further cases have shown that bailment arguments can be **9.22** useful to a potential claimant, especially where other rights of recourse are not available.[75] Thus, in *East West Corp v DKBS 1912 & AKTS Svendborg*,[76] where it was established that a claimant did not have rights of suit under the Carriage of Goods by Sea Act 1992, because these vested in certain Chilean banks, the Court of Appeal held that the carriers were in breach of duty in bailment, or on a basis analogous to bailment, by virtue of their failure either to deliver up the goods to a person entitled to them on presentation of an original bill of lading, or when they parted with possession of the goods to third parties. Further, the Court of Appeal held that the doctrine of bailment on terms afforded the carriers the benefit of any relevant exemption or protective conditions in the terms of their bills of lading. However, on a true construction of the bills of lading there were no relevant exemptions or protective conditions.[77]

F. Himalaya Clauses

Background In *Adler v Dickson*,[78] a passenger aboard the P & O liner *The Himalaya* **9.23** brought an action in tort against the ship's master and boatswain following a fall of 16 feet from an improperly secured gangway. The defendants sought to rely upon the exemption clause in the ticket issued to the plaintiff, although they were not themselves parties to it. The exemption clause provided that 'the company' would not be liable for 'any damage or injury whatsoever' and the Court of Appeal was forced to hold that this did not extend to their servants or agents. Mrs Adler was thus able to pursue her claim in negligence against the master and boatswain. The exemption clause in *Adler* encouraged the drafting of so-called Himalaya clauses,[79] framed to extend the defences of the carrier to servants, agents, and independent contractors engaged in the loading and unloading process.

The Eurymedon One of the first cases to consider the efficacy of such clauses was the appeal **9.24** to the Privy Council from the New Zealand Court of Appeal[80] in *New Zealand Shipping Co Ltd v AM Satterthwaite & Co Ltd (The Eurymedon)*.[81] An expensive drilling machine, en route from Liverpool to Wellington, was damaged on arrival at Wellington owing to the negligence of the stevedores during unloading. The bill of lading for the carriage incorporated the Hague Rules. When the consignees sued the stevedores for their negligence, the stevedores sought to rely on the time limitation clause in the bill of lading to the effect that the carrier and the ship

---

[75] For criticism, see G McMeel, 'The redundancy of bailment' [2003] LMCLQ 169. But cf *Homburg Houtimport BV v Agrosin Private Ltd (The Starsin)* [2003] UKHL 12; [2004] 1 AC 715, at [132] (Lord Hobhouse). For discussion of this case in relation to Himalaya clauses, see para 9.29.

[76] [2003] EWCA Civ 83; [2003] QB 1509 (CA).

[77] At [24]–[30].

[78] [1955] 1 QB 158 (CA).

[79] See William Tetley QC, 'Himalaya clauses — revisited' (2003) 9 JIML 40.

[80] [1973] 1 NZLR 174.

[81] [1975] AC 154 (PC). See Norman Palmer, 'The Stevedore's Dilemma: Exemption Clauses and Third Parties' [1974] JBL 101; FMB Reynolds, 'Himalaya Clause Resurgent' (1974) 90 LQR 301; F Dawson, 'Himalaya Clauses, Consideration and Privity of Contract' (1975) 6 NZULR 161; Norman Palmer and PJ Davies, '*The Eurymedon* Five Years On' [1979] JBL 337.

would be discharged from all liability in respect of the drill unless suit was brought against them within one year after delivery.[82] Clause 1 of the bill of lading inter alia stated that:

> It is hereby expressly agreed that no servant or agent of the carrier (including every independent contractor from time to time employed by the carrier) shall in any circumstances whatsoever be under any liability whatsoever to the shipper, consignee or owner of the goods or to any holder of this bill of lading for any loss or damage or delay of whatsoever kind arising or resulting directly or indirectly from any act neglect or default on his part while acting in the course of or in connection with his employment and, without prejudice to the generality of the foregoing provisions in this clause, every exemption, limitation, condition and liberty herein contained and every right, exemption from liability, defence and immunity of whatsoever nature applicable to the carrier or to which the carrier is entitled hereunder shall also be available and shall extend to protect every such servant or agent of the carrier acting as aforesaid and for the purpose of all the foregoing provisions of this clause the carrier is or shall be deemed to be acting as agent or trustee on behalf of and for the benefit of all persons who are or might be his servants or agents from time to time (including independent contractors as aforesaid) and all such persons shall to this extent be or be deemed to be parties to the contract in or evidenced by this bill of lading.

Was this clause as drafted effective in favour of the stevedores? The Privy Council, by a majority of three to two,[83] thought so, reversing the New Zealand Court of Appeal[84] and restoring the finding of Beattie J,[85] the judge of first instance. Lord Wilberforce, who delivered the judgment of the majority, reasoned that to give the stevedores the benefit of the exemptions and limitations contained in the bill of lading was 'to give effect to the clear intentions of a commercial document . . .'.[86] A finding the other way would, he said, encourage actions against servants, agents, and independent contractors in order to get around exempting clauses.[87] His starting point was the speech of Lord Reid in *Midland Silicones*.[88] Did the bill of lading in question satisfy the four conditions spelt out by Lord Reid?[89] In particular, had the stevedores met the difficulty suggested by Lord Reid that there would have to be consideration? On the face of the clause it would be difficult to perceive how the stevedores might answer this point. However, Lord Wilberforce's response was that the bill of lading brought into existence a bargain initially unilateral but capable of becoming mutual between the shipper and the stevedores, made through the carrier as agent. This became a full contract when the stevedore discharged the goods. The performance of these services for the benefit of the shipper was the consideration for the agreement by the shipper that the stevedore should have the benefit of the exemptions and limitations contained in the bill of lading.[90] His emphasis was that

> the whole contract is of a commercial character, involving service on one side, rates of payment on the other, and qualifying stipulations as to both. The relations of all parties to each other are commercial relations entered into for business reasons of ultimate profit. To describe one set of

---

[82] Article III, r 6 of the Hague (and Hague–Visby) Rules.
[83] Lords Wilberforce, Hodson, and Salmon; Viscount Dilhorne and Lord Simon of Glaisdale dissenting.
[84] [1973] 1 NZLR 174.
[85] [1972] NZLR 385.
[86] [1975] AC 154 (PC), 169.
[87] ibid.
[88] [1962] AC 446.
[89] At 474.
[90] [1975] AC 154 (PC), 167–168. This reasoning was directly applied by the Supreme Court of Canada in *ITO — International Terminal Operators Ltd v Miida Electronics Inc; Miida Electronics Inc v Mitsui OSK Lines Ltd* (1986) 28 DLR (4th) 641, 671 (McIntyre J).

promises, in this context, as gratuitous . . . seems paradoxical and is *prima facie* implausible. It is only the precise analysis of this complex of relations into the classical offer and acceptance, with identifiable consideration, that seems to present difficulty, but this same difficulty exists in many situations of daily life . . . English law, having committed itself to a rather technical and schematic doctrine of contract, in application takes a practical approach, often at the cost of forcing the facts to fit uneasily into the marked slots of offer, acceptance and consideration.[91]

Criticism   Desirable as the commercial consequences might be, Lord Wilberforce's reasoning, **9.25** analysed from the standpoint of contract doctrine, has been much criticized by commentators.[92] Thus it is argued that the reasoning is artificial because the actual wording of the clause appears to create an immediate bilateral contract between the agent and the consignor and not an offer of a unilateral contract by the consignor. It was hoped that legislative reform might answer these criticisms of Lord Wilberforce's judgment but the opportunity was lost in the Visby Protocol to the Hague Rules.[93]

The New York Star   Notwithstanding the criticisms of *The Eurymedon*, the majority view **9.26** was endorsed, once again by the Privy Council, in *Port Jackson Stevedoring Pty Ltd v Salmond & Spraggon (Australia) Pty Ltd (The New York Star)*.[94] A cargo of razor blades shipped from Canada to Australia under a bill of lading which contained a Himalaya clause was discharged from the *New York Star* by stevedores but then negligently delivered by their servant to thieves without production of a bill of lading. After a lapse of a year the lawful consignees sued the stevedores in negligence, and the stevedores sought to rely on clause 17 of the bill of lading which provided that suit had to be brought within a year. The case came on appeal from the High Court of Australia, where the majority judges,[95] Barwick CJ dissenting, found against the stevedores[96] on the basis that they were no longer acting on behalf of the carrier under the bill of lading. The majority judges had also advanced the reason that a country, such as Australia, which depended upon foreign carriers for the movement of goods, would be prejudiced if carriers were allowed to exclude liability as against shippers of goods, not only for themselves, but also for others performing services on their behalf, especially where shippers were not necessarily able to influence the terms of shipment or the performance of the contract.[97] Barwick CJ, however, had had no difficulty in finding

---

[91] At 167.

[92] See Francis Rose, 'Return to *Elder Dempster*?' (1975) 4 Anglo-American LR 7; William Tetley, 'The Himalaya clause — heresy or genius?' (1977–78) 9 JMLC 111. Cf the comments of McIntyre J in *ITO — International Terminal Operators Ltd v Miida Electronics Inc; Miida Electronics Inc v Mitsui OSK Lines Ltd* (1986) 28 DLR (4th) 641, 667: '. . . conceptual difficulties of this nature are not a novel feature of the common law. In fact it may be said that one of the virtues of the common law is that it has never really let pure logic get in the way of common sense and practical necessity when a desirable result is sought to be achieved.'

[93] Article IV bis 1 and 2 of the Hague–Visby Rules provide that a servant or agent of the carrier 'such servant or agent not being an independent carrier' may rely on the defences and limits of liability which may be invoked under the Rules in an action in tort or contract against him. This specifically excludes independent contractors, which would in most cases be stevedores. See Kurt Grönfors, 'Why not Independent Contractors?' [1964] JBL 25.

[94] [1981] 1 WLR 138 (PC). See FMB Reynolds, 'The Negligent Stevedore Yet Again' (1980) 96 LQR 506, 508; Brian Coote, 'Pity the Poor Stevedore!' [1981] CLJ 13; and Malcolm Clarke, 'Transport-Riding Someone Else's Contract' [1981] CLJ 17.

[95] Stephen J and Murphy J. See FMB Reynolds, 'Again the Negligent Stevedore' (1979) 95 LQR 183.

[96] [1979] 1 Lloyd's Rep 298. The appeal to the High Court was from the Court of Appeal of New South Wales: see [1977] Lloyd's Rep 445.

[97] Stephen J at 312; Murphy J at 325.

that the carrier acted as agent for the stevedores in making an arrangement with the consignor for the protection of the stevedores. In accepting the bill of lading, the consignee became a party to that arrangement. This reasoning was expressly accepted by Lord Wilberforce for the Privy Council:

> [The *Eurymedon*] was a decision, in principle, that the Himalaya clause is capable of conferring on a third person falling within the description 'servant or agent of the Carrier (including every independent contractor from time to time employed by the Carrier)' defences and immunities conferred by the bill of lading on the Carrier as if such persons were parties to the contract contained in or evidenced by the bill of lading . . . Their Lordships would not encourage a search for fine distinctions which would diminish the general applicability in the light of established commercial practice, of the principle.[98]

9.27 Himalaya clauses in other jurisdictions Since these two landmark cases, both of them incidentally Privy Council appeals from Australia, Himalaya clauses have been upheld in most commonwealth jurisdictions, including Australia,[99] Canada,[100] and South Africa.[101]

9.28 Limitations: *The Mahkutai* One of the last appeals from the Hong Kong Court of Appeal[102] to the Privy Council was heard in *The Mahkutai*.[103] The case involved a time charter and a voyage sub-charter for a voyage charter between Jakarta and Shantou. The bill of lading stated that the carrier was the disponent owner who could subcontract to stevedores 'all exceptions, limitations, provisions, conditions and liberties herein benefiting the carrier as if such provisions were expressly made for their benefit'.[104] There was also a jurisdiction and choice of law clause to the effect that the contract evidenced by the bill of lading should be governed by the law of Indonesia and any dispute was to be determined by the Indonesian courts.[105] When the cargo of plywood was discovered to have been damaged by sea water, the ship was arrested at the behest of the cargo owners in Hong Kong. To this the shipowners issued a stay of jurisdiction. Lord Goff gave the judgment of the Committee and reviewed the 'pendulum of judicial opinion'[106] on the shipowners' alternative submissions, namely that they were entitled to relief either under a Himalaya clause or on the principle of bailment on terms.[107] Lord Goff noted that in the instant case the owners were not seeking

---

[98] [1981] 1 WLR 138 (PC), 143–144. See FD Rose, 'Return to the Antipodes' (1981) 44 MLR 336.

[99] See *Celthene Pty Ltd v WJK Hauliers Pty Ltd* [1981] 1 NSWLR 606; *Life Savers (Aust) Pty Ltd v Frigmobile Pty Ltd* [1983] 1 NSWLR 431; *Godina v Patrick Operations Pty Ltd* [1984] 1 Lloyd's Rep 333; *Carrington Slipways Pty Ltd v Patrick Operations Pty Ltd (The Cape Comorin)* (1991) 24 NSWLR 745; *Glebe Island Terminals Pty Ltd v Continental Seagram Pty Ltd (The Antwerpen)* [1994] 1 Lloyd's Rep 213.

[100] *ITO — International Terminal Operators Ltd v Miida Electronics Inc; Miida Electronics Inc v Mitsui OSK Lines Ltd* (1986) 28 (DLR) 4th 641. See Linda C Reif, 'A comment on *ITO Ltd v Miida Electronics Inc* — The Supreme Court of Canada, Privity of Contract and the Himalaya Clause' (1987–1988) 26 Alberta LR 372.

[101] See *Santam Insurance Co Ltd v SA Stevedores Ltd (The Sanko Vega)* (1989) 1 SA 182 (D); *Bouygues Offshore v Owner of the MT Tigr* 1995 (4) SA 49 (C). See too Hilton Staniland, 'The Himalaya clause in South Africa' [1992] LMCLQ 317.

[102] [1994] 1 HKLR 212.

[103] [1996] AC 650 (PC). See Andrew Phang and Toh Kian Sing 'On Himalaya Clauses, Bailments, Choice of Law and Jurisdiction — Recent Privy Council Perspectives from *The Mahkutai*' (1996) 10 JCL 212.

[104] Clause 4.

[105] Clause 19.

[106] [1996] AC 650 (PC), 658.

[107] At 659.

to invoke an exception or limitation in the ordinary sense of those words, but the benefit of an exclusive jurisdiction clause which 'would involve a significantly wider application of the relevant principles . . .'[108]

On the question whether the exclusive jurisdiction clause fell within the scope of clause 4, Lord Goff concluded that such a clause could not be an 'exception, limitation, condition or liberty' and neither could 'provision . . . extend to include a mutual agreement, such as an exclusive jurisdiction clause, which is not of that character'.[109] He drew support for this from the function of the Himalaya clause, which was 'to prevent cargo owners from avoiding the effect of contractual defences available to the carrier (typically the exceptions and limitations in the Hague–Visby Rules) by suing in tort persons who perform the contractual services on the carrier's behalf'.[110]

The Starsin   In *The Starsin*[111] various cargoes of timber and timber products were loaded **9.29** at Malaysian ports. Although some of the cargo was wetted by rain before shipment, clean bills of lading were issued. Subsequently, the cargo was also improperly stowed and seventeen consignments were out-turned seriously damaged by water. The claimants in the proceedings were the notify parties of the cargo[112] to whom the relevant bills of lading had been endorsed. The Himalaya clause[113] provided, in the first part, that 'no servant or agent of the carrier including every independent contractor . . . shall in any circumstances whatsoever be under any liability whatsoever . . .'. The second part, which was 'without prejudice to the generality' of the terms of the bill, was essentially on the Conlinebill form,[114] to the effect that 'every exemption, limitation, condition and liberty herein contained and every right exemption from liability, defence and immunity whatsoever . . . applicable to the carrier' was also to be available to 'every such servant or agent of the carrier'. The main issue for their Lordships was the interpretation of the clause to determine whether its terms could include the shipowners. The answer to this turned on the phrase '. . . servant or agent of the carrier . . . including every independent contractor'. A majority of their Lordships agreed with the view taken by Colman J and the Court of Appeal that the shipowner was an independent contractor.[115]

Himalaya clauses and statute   It is an open question whether parties will continue to rely **9.30** on contractual Himalaya clauses or whether the possibility of statutory reliance will now be open following the Contracts (Rights of Third Parties) Act 1999. This is discussed below.[116]

---

[108] At 658. He recognized that the time might be coming for the recognition of a fully-fledged exception to the privity rule, as had been done 'head-on' by the Court of Appeal of British Columbia (*London Drugs Ltd v Kuehne & Nagel International Ltd* (1992) 97 DLR (4th) 261) and by the Australian High Court (*Trident General Insurance Co Ltd v McNeice Bros Pty Ltd* (1988) 165 CLR 107), although neither of these cases were shipping cases.

[109] [1996] AC 650 (PC), 666.

[110] ibid.

[111] *Homburg Houtimport BV v Agrosin Private Ltd (The Starsin)* [2003] UKHL 12; [2004] 1 AC 715.

[112] Makros Hout BV, Homburg Houtimport BV, Fetim BV, and Hunter Timber Ltd.

[113] Reproduced by Lord Bingham: [2003] UKHL 12, at [20].

[114] See cl 15(b) of Conlinebill 2000.

[115] See Lord Bingham at [28]; Lord Steyn at [55]; Lord Hoffmann at [95].

[116] See para 9.36.

G. The Contracts (Rights of Third Parties) Act 1999

9.31 Background More than seventy years ago the (then) Law Revision Committee recommended that the privity rule ought to be revised[117] but this was achieved only in the last decade, following work by the Law Commission of England and Wales, first in a Consultation Paper[118] and subsequently in a Report.[119] In its Report, the Law Commission proposed draft legislation, which became the Contracts (Rights of Third Parties) Act 1999,[120] intended to ease the plight of third parties seeking to rely on the terms of a contract to which they were not privy.[121] The underlying aim of the reform was that 'it should be straightforwardly possible for contracting parties to confer on third parties the right to enforce the contract'.[122] The Law Commission did not, however, seek to alter the existing rule that obligations may not be imposed upon a third party by the contracting parties.[123]

9.32 Main provisions Section 1 of the Act provides that, in general, a third party should have the right to enforce a contractual provision where in an express term of the contract[124] he is identified by name, class, or description.[125] Alternatively, a third party will have such a right where the provision purports to confer a benefit,[126] but subject to the proviso that there shall be no such right where, on a proper construction of the contract, it appears that the contracting parties did not in fact intend the third party to have that right.[127]

9.33 Carriage by sea So far as contracts for the carriage of goods by sea are concerned, however, the above principles must be read with section 6(5) which provides that section 1 will not confer any rights on a third party in the case of a contract of carriage of goods by sea, 'except that a third party may by virtue of that section avail himself of an exclusion or limitation of liability in such a contract'. The reason given for this is that, were third parties entitled to claim under the Act, this would contradict the policy underlying the Carriage of Goods by Sea Act 1992 and 'cause unacceptable commercial uncertainty'.[128] Provided the third party can bring himself within the category of persons protected by the Act he will, as a matter of statute, be able to rely on the exclusion clause.

---

[117] Sixth Interim Report, *Statute of Frauds and the Doctrine of Consideration*, (1937) Cmd 5449, para 48.
[118] *Privity of Contract: Contracts for the Benefit of Third Parties*: LCCP No 121 (1991). See J Beatson, 'Reforming the Law of Contracts for the Benefit of Third Parties: A Second Bite at the Cherry' (1992) 45 CLP 1. For criticism of the Consultation Paper, see S Degeling, 'A Consideration of the UK [sic] Law Commission's Consultation Paper, "Privity of Contract" ' (1993) 6 JCL 177.
[119] *Privity of Contract: Contracts for the Benefit of Third Parties*: Law Com No 242, Cm 3329 (1996). See Andrew Burrows, 'Reforming privity of contract: Law Commission Report No 242' [1996] LMCLQ 467; Andrew Tettenborn, 'Third Party Contracts — Pragmatism from the Law Commission' [1996] JBL 602; FMB Reynolds, 'Privity of Contract' (1997) 113 LQR 53.
[120] c 31.
[121] Other common law jurisdictions have also enacted legislation which has opened up the doctrine. The most notable example is the New Zealand Contracts (Privity) Act 1982. See RH Newman, 'The Doctrine of Privity of Contract: The Common Law and the Contracts (Privity) Act 1982' (1983) 4 Auckland ULR 339.
[122] Cmd 3329 (1996), para 3.28.
[123] Paragraphs 2.1. and 10.24–10.32.
[124] section 1(1)(a).
[125] section 1(3).
[126] section 1(1)(b).
[127] section 1(2).
[128] Cmd 3329 (1996), para 12.6.

Reliance on the Act: shipbrokers   There have been two important cases on the Act, in the   **9.34**
shipping context. In the first, *Nisshin Shipping Co Ltd v Cleaves & Co Ltd*,[129] the court had
to consider whether a firm of shipbrokers were entitled to their commission. The arbitration clause in each of the charterparties contained wording which referred to disputes
between the 'parties' to the charterparty. The shipbrokers referred the dispute over the commission to arbitration, though it was not a party to any of the arbitration agreements. The
arbitrators concluded that they did have jurisdiction to determine claims for commission
said to be due. The court agreed that although the parties to the charterparties clearly
expressed their mutual intention that their disputes should be arbitrated, that mutual
intention was entirely consistent with a mutual intention that the brokers should be
obliged to recover their commission by court arbitration. The shipbrokers were entitled to
enforce the commission clause in their own right by reason of section 1 of the 1999 Act.

Reliance on the Act: enforcement of a letter of indemnity   The second case was *Laemthong*   **9.35**
International Lines Ltd v Artis (The Laemthong Glory)(No 2).[130] The buyer of a consignment
of sugar asked the charterer to issue a letter of indemnity to the shipowner requesting the latter to instruct the master/ship's agents to allow the vessel to commence discharge and deliver
the cargo without production of the bills of lading. This was repeated to the charterer and a
letter of indemnity was issued in its favour against the consequences of releasing the cargo
without presentation of the bills of lading.[131] In due course, the cargo was so discharged and
the ship arrested by a third party, claiming wrongful delivery. The court was now asked to
address the validity of the relevant LOIs, each of which was in substantially the same terms:

> In consideration of your complying with our above request we hereby agree as follows:
>
> (1) To indemnify you, your servants and agents and to hold all of you harmless in
>   respect of any liability, loss, damage or expense of whatsoever nature which you may
>   sustain by reason of delivering the cargo in accordance with our request.
>
> (3) If in connection with delivery of the cargo as aforesaid the ship or any other ship . . . in
>   the same or associated ownership . . . should be arrested or detained . . . to provide on
>   demand such bail or other security as may be required to prevent such arrest or deten-
>   tion or to secure the release of the ship . . . and to indemnify you in respect of any liabil-
>   ity, loss, damage or expense caused by such arrest or detention . . . whether or not such
>   arrest or detention or threatened arrest or detention or interference may be justified.

The shipowner also sought to enforce the consignee's LOI against them by relying on the
Contracts (Rights of Third Parties) Act 1999. The consignee contended that they were not
entitled to do so. At first instance Cooke J[132] held that the LOI was enforceable against the
consignee at the suit of the shipowner, and that the shipowner was entitled to an order that
both the charterer and consignee provide bail or other security required to secure the release
of the vessel from arrest. The Court of Appeal confirmed that the term of the consignee's

---

[129] [2003] EWHC 2602; [2004] 1 Lloyd's Rep 38. See Benjamin Parker, 'Shipbrokers' commission and
arbitration clauses: the Contracts (Rights of Third Parties) Act 1999 has its first outing to court' [2004]
LMCLQ 445.
[130] [2005] EWCA Civ 519; [2005] 1 Lloyd's Rep 688.
[131] At [45].
[132] [2004] EWHC 2738 (Comm); [2005] 1 Lloyd's Rep 632.

LOI relied upon by the shipowner purported to confer a benefit upon *Laemthong International* within the meaning of section 1(1)(b) of the 1999 Act. In particular, it held that the use of the word 'you' in clause 1 of the LOI had to be construed in the context of the LOI as a whole and viewed against its surrounding circumstances or factual matrix. There was no evidence, on a proper construction of the contract, that it appeared that the parties did not intend the term to be enforceable by them.

9.36 **Himalaya clauses and the Act** The extension of protection to stevedores was in the contemplation of the Law Commission both in its Consultation Paper and in its Report.[133] Indeed, the latter recognized that the (then) proposed draft Bill would 'bring about at a stroke what Lord Goff [in *The Mahkutai*] regarded as a desirable development in that it would sweep away the technicalities applying to the enforcement by expressly designated third parties of exclusion clauses'.[134] Under the terms of the Act, stevedores would be directly protected under a Himalaya clause, falling within the class of persons identified by 'name, as a member of a class or as answering a particular description' in section 1(3). This would seem to be a prudent recognition of the long line of decisions which have recognized the efficacy of Himalaya clauses. Such a step is also in line with two of the principal arguments for reform advanced by the Law Commission, namely, that as things stand the intentions of the original contracting parties may be thwarted[135] and the third party rule does cause difficulties in commercial life.[136]

---

[133] *Privity of Contract: Contracts for the Benefit of Third Parties*: Law Com No 242, Cm 3329 (1996), para 4.10.
[134] At para 2.35.
[135] See para 3.1.
[136] At para 3.9.

10

THE CARRIERS' DELIVERY
OBLIGATION

A. Introduction

Overview   Following on from the recognition that the bill of lading is a document of title   **10.01**
at common law, a further principle has evolved which requires the master only to part with
the goods on presentation of the bill of lading[1] by the holder.[2] In this chapter we examine
the fundamental principles, both for bills of lading and other documents. We consider also
where delivery shall be made against letter of indemnity and what happens when the consignee fails to take delivery. We conclude by examining the consequences of a breach on the
part of the carrier.

---

[1] See *Barclays Bank Ltd v Commissioners of Customs and Excise* [1963] 1 Lloyd's Rep 81, 88–89 (Diplock LJ);
Kuwait Petroleum Corporation v I & D Oil Carriers Ltd (The Houda) [1994] 2 Lloyd's Rep 541 (CA), 550
(Neill LJ). For further discussion of the position in the Far East, see Caslav Pejovic, 'Delivery of goods with-
out a bill of lading: revival of an old problem in the Far East' (2003) 9 JIML 448.

[2] See now the definition of 'holder' in the Carriage of Goods by Sea Act 1992, s 5(2); para 8.19.

B. The General Principles

10.02 **Main propositions** Two general propositions may be stated. The first is that the holder of a bill of lading who, within a reasonable time, presents[3] it to the master is, in the absence of any custom to the contrary, entitled to have the goods delivered to him.[4] The second is that the master may give up the goods to the first person who presents him with a bill of lading, provided (i) that he has no notice of other claimants to the goods and (ii) in the absence of any circumstances which might raise a reasonable suspicion that the holder is not entitled to the goods.[5] The master may also give up the goods without the bills of lading if it is proved to his reasonable satisfaction both that the person seeking the goods is entitled to possession of them and that there is some reasonable explanation of what has become of the bills of lading.[6]

10.03 **Delivery without notice** In *Glyn, Mills & Co v East & West India Dock Co*[7] a cargo of sugar was handed over to the holder of a bill of lading although the holder had, unbeknown to the master, deposited one of the set with the plaintiff bank as security for a loan. Lord Blackburn held that

> . . . when the master has not notice or knowledge of anything but that there are other parts of the bill of lading, one of which it is possible may have been assigned, he is justified or excused in delivering according to his contract to the person appearing to be the assign of the bill of lading which is produced to him.[8]

Once the master makes delivery against a bill of lading validly presented to him, he is secure in the knowledge that 'one . . . being accomplished, the others stand void'.[9] Once, however, the master does have knowledge or notice of other claimants, he delivers 'at his peril'.[10]

10.04 **Interpleading** Where the master is faced with more than one bill of lading, presented by different parties, then he would be wise to interplead[11] the claims, declining to make delivery until the rival claimants have had their competing claims settled by a court of law.

---

[3] Of course the reality, in practice, is that it is rarely the holder who presents the bill of lading in person. In practice, on discharge of the goods from the ship they are normally in the hands of agents or contractors rather than the shipowner or holder. In these circumstances, delivery actually occurs when the goods are placed in the hands of an agent: see, for example, *The Jaederen* [1892] P 351.

[4] See *Enrichsen v Barkworth* (1858) 3 H & N 601, 616; 157 ER 608, 615 (Bramwell B).

[5] See the Scottish case of *Carlberg v Wemyss* 1915 SC 616, 624 (Lord Johnson).

[6] See *SA Sucre Export v Northern River Shipping Ltd (The Sormovskiy 3068)* [1994] 2 Lloyd's Rep 266, 272 (Clarke J). But note the contrary view taken by Rix J in *Motis Exports Ltd v Dampskibsselskabet AF 1912, A/S* [1999] 1 Lloyd's Rep 837, 841 (but not canvassed by the Court of Appeal in the same case).

[7] (1882) 7 App Cas 591.

[8] At 614.

[9] This statement appears in many standard form bills of lading (see, eg, Conlinebill 2000). See too *Glyn, Mills & Co v East & West India Dock Co* (1882) 7 App Cas 591, 599 (Earl Cairns).

[10] *Sze Hai Tong Bank Ltd v Rambler Cycle Co Ltd* [1959] AC 576 (PC), 586 (Lord Denning).

[11] The process whereby a person in possession of property claimed by two or more persons is relieved from liability by compelling them to bring their claims to court (at their expense). The shipowner (or his agent, the master) will then have the protection of a court order when he disposes of the property. See RSC Ord. 17, discussed in Lord Justice May (gen ed), *Civil Procedure* (London, Sweet & Maxwell, 2002), vol 1, 1415–1427.

Delivery without the bills of lading Where the master is asked to deliver without the **10.05**
bills of lading, the law is clear. In the words of Butt J in *The Stettin*:

> . . . A shipowner is not entitled to deliver goods to the consignee without the production of
> the bill of lading. . . . The shipowner must take the consequences of having delivered these
> goods to the consignee without the production of either of the two parts of which the bill of
> lading consisted.[12]

Thus, if the master does deliver without a bill of lading, he takes a considerable risk that
the consignee is not, in fact, entitled to the goods; indeed, it has been said that he does so
'at his peril'.[13]

No obligation to deliver without the bills of lading There is no obligation on the mas- **10.06**
ter to deliver the goods to a consignee without the bills of lading[14] and nor could he ordinarily be ordered to make such delivery under a voyage or time charterparty.[15] In the event
that the master does make delivery pursuant to directions from the time charterer, the
shipowner will be entitled, at least at common law,[16] to be indemnified by the time charterers against his subsequent liability to the holders of the bills of lading.[17]

C. Delivery and Forged Bills of Lading

Generally The leading case on delivery as against forged[18] bills of lading is *Motis Exports* **10.07**
Ltd v Dampskibsselskabet AF 1912, A/S.[19] The case was brought by the claimants, who were
the shippers of various consignments of goods between ports in Hong Kong and China to
West African ports. The vessels carrying the goods were operated by the defendants who
ran a liner service. The bills of lading for the cargoes stated that the consignees purported
to absolve the shipowner from 'liability whatsoever for any loss or damage to the goods
while in its actual or constructive possession before loading or after discharge over ships
rail, or if applicable, on the ships ramp, however caused'. The question for the court was
whether the defendants were liable for the loss of the goods after discharge, where the cause
of the loss was the use of forged bills of lading to obtain delivery orders and thus delivery of
the goods at the discharge ports. At first instance, Rix J noted that in general the law did not

---

[12] (1889) 14 PD 142, 147. See too *London Joint Stock Bank v Amsterdam Co* (1910) 16 Com Cas 102; *SA Sucre Export v Northern River Shipping Ltd (The Sormovskiy 3068)* [1994] 2 Lloyd's Rep 266; *MB Pyramid Sound NV v Briese Schiffahrts GmbH & Co KG (The Ines)* [1995] 2 Lloyd's Rep 144; *The Taveechai Marine* [1995] 1 MLJ 413.

[13] *Skibsaktieselskapet Thor v Tyrer* (1929) 35 Ll LR 163, 170 (Wright J); *Sze Hai Tong Bank v Rambler Cycle Co* [1959] AC 576 (PC), 586 (Lord Denning).

[14] *Gatoil International Inc v Tradax Petroleum Ltd (The Rio Sun)* [1985] 1 Lloyd's Rep 350, 361 (Bingham J).

[15] *Kuwait Petroleum Corporation v I & D Oil Carriers Ltd (The Houda)* [1994] 2 Lloyd's Rep 541 (CA), 558 (Millett LJ).

[16] See *Strathlorne Steamship Co v Andrew Weir & Co* (1934) 50 Ll LR 185 (CA), 193 (Lord Hanworth MR); *A/S Hansen-Tengens Rederi III v Total Transport Corporation (The Sagona)* [1984] 1 Lloyd's Rep 194, 206 (Staughton J).

[17] Although there might be a question whether, under a specific time charter form, such an obligation to indemnify is express or may be implied.

[18] Generally on fraud in the maritime context, see Todd (2003).

[19] [1999] 1 Lloyd's Rep 837. See Stephen Girvin, 'Forged Bills of Lading' [2000] JBL 81.

protect persons who acted on forgeries,[20] being concerned to protect those whose true title was assailed by the forgery. He concluded that a shipowner was not free to release goods on the basis of a forged bill of lading because the integrity of the bill of lading as the key to the floating warehouse would be lost. He also reasoned that the shipowner (through the master) controlled the form, signature, and issue of bills of lading and that, if an innocent party had to suffer through the fraud of a third party, it was better that the loss fell on the shipowner, who had the responsibility to look to the integrity of his bills of lading and to care for the cargo in his possession, as well as to deliver it aright.[21] Although the case went on appeal,[22] this centred on the question whether the shipowner was entitled to rely on the exception clause as a defence. The decision of the court below on the forgery issue was not challenged except that the court agreed that a forged bill of lading was a nullity: it was simply a piece of paper with writing on it, which had no effect whatsoever.[23]

D. Delivery and Express Terms

10.08 **Express clauses**   It may sometimes be the case that an express clause in a bill of lading seeks to absolve the shipowner from the consequences of releasing the goods without the bill. Such was the case in a case decided by the Privy Council on appeal from the Singapore High Court, *Sze Hai Tong Bank Ltd v Rambler Cycle Co Ltd*.[24] Clause 2(c) of the bill of lading provided that the 'responsibility of the carrier . . . shall be deemed . . . to cease absolutely after the goods are discharged from the ship'.[25] The Privy Council adopted the approach which has regularly been applied to exempting clauses of such width,[26] as explained by Lord Denning:

> If such an extreme width were given to the exemption clause, it would run counter to the main object and intent of the contract. For the contract, as it seems to their Lordships, has, as one of its main objects, the proper delivery of the goods by the shipping company, 'unto order or his or their assigns', against production of the bill of lading. It would defeat this object entirely if the shipping company was at liberty, at its own will and pleasure, to deliver the goods to somebody else, to someone not entitled at all, without being liable for the consequences. The clause must therefore be limited and modified to the extent necessary to enable effect to be given to the main object and intent of the contract . . .[27]

10.09 **Approach confirmed**   More recently, the English Court of Appeal in *Motis Exports Ltd v Dampskibsselskabet AF 1912, A/S*[28] adopted a similar approach in respect of a clause which provided that 'the Carrier shall have no liability whatsoever for any loss or damage to the

---

[20] By analogy with the law on cheques, to the effect that a paying bank debiting its customer on a forged cheque had to repay its customer, and on forged share certificates: *Ruben v Great Fingall Consolidated* [1906] AC 439, 444 (Lord Macnaghten); *Sheffield Corp v Barclay* [1905] AC 392.

[21] [1999] 1 Lloyd's Rep 837, 842–843.

[22] [2000] 1 Lloyd's Rep 211 (CA), criticized by Brian Davenport QC in 'Misdelivery: a fundamental breach?' [2000] LMCLQ 455.

[23] At 216 (Stuart-Smith LJ).

[24] [1959] AC 577 (PC).

[25] See *Motis Exports Ltd v Dampskibsselskabet AF 1912, A/S* [2000] 1 Lloyd's Rep 211 (CA).

[26] On the general contractual approach to exemption clauses, see Treitel (2003), ch 7.

[27] [1959] AC 577 (PC), 587.

[28] [2000] 1 Lloyd's Rep 211 (CA).

goods while in its actual or constructive possession before loading or after discharge over ship's rail, or if applicable, on the ship's ramp, however caused'.[29] In the words of Mance LJ:

> The natural subject-matter of [the clause] consists in loss or damage caused to the goods while in the carrier's custody, but not deliberate delivery up of the goods, whether without any bill of lading or against a forged and therefore null document believed to be a bill of lading.[30]

It would seem, nevertheless, that it would be possible for the carrier to protect himself by an appropriately drawn exclusion clause[31] although it is clear from the above cases that a generally worded clause would not apply to a misdelivery.[32]

E. Delivery: Modified by Custom?

The Sormovskiy   On at least two occasions the court has had to consider whether the **10.10** custom of a particular port might dispense with the general rule. Such a case was *SA Sucre Export* v *Northern River Shipping Ltd (The Sormovskiy 3068)*.[33] In this case the Russian consignees of a cargo of sugar entered into a contract with the Commercial Seaport of Vyborg (CSP) for the discharge of the goods. Some time after this it was agreed between all the parties that St Petersburg be substituted as the port of discharge. However, the vessel in fact commenced discharge at Vyborg, without the bills of lading. In response to a claim for loss as a result of the delivery of a quantity of sugar without the bills, the shipowners sought to argue that they had complied with their obligations by delivering in accordance with the practice and custom and law of the port of Vyborg.[34] After reviewing the evidence given by various Russian witnesses, Clarke J concluded that:

> . . . If there were a custom of the port of Vyborg that cargo was always delivered to the CSP as the agent of the person entitled to possession without the production of an original bill of lading, delivery to the CSP would probably amount to performance of the defendants' obligations under the contract of carriage. However custom in this context means custom in its strict sense; that is it must be reasonable, certain, consistent with the contract, universally acquiesced in and not contrary to law: see *Scrutton on Charterparties*[35] at pp. 14–16.[36]

Approach confirmed   A more recent case is *East West Corp v DKBS 1912 and AKTS* **10.11** *Svendborg*.[37] Here there was an action by certain claimant sellers against DKBS, for damages for delivery of their cargoes shipped from Hong Kong to Chile, without presentation of the bills of lading. The sellers had sold the goods to a regular client in Chile and, in due

---

[29] Clause 5(b) of the bill of lading.

[30] [2000] 1 Lloyd's Rep 211 (CA), 217. See also *East West Corp v DKBS 1912 and AKTS Svendborg* [2003] 1 Lloyd's Rep 239 (CA).

[31] See *Nissho Iwai (Australia) Ltd v Malaysian International Shipping Corp Berhad* (1989) 167 CLR 219.

[32] See also *Glebe Island Terminals Pty Ltd v Continental Seagram Pty Ltd (The Antwerpen)* [1994] 1 Lloyd's Rep 213, 245; *Kamil Export (Aust) Pty Ltd v NPL (Aust) Pty Ltd* [1996] 1 VR 538.

[33] [1994] 2 Lloyd's Rep 266.

[34] An alternative argument that they were not prohibited under English law from delivering without production of the original bills of lading received short shrift from Clarke J: [1994] 2 Lloyd's Rep 266, 274.

[35] Note that this is a reference to the 19th edn (London, Sweet & Maxwell, 1984).

[36] [1994] 2 Lloyd's Rep 266, 275, cited with approval in *Olivine Electronics Pte Ltd v Seabridge Transport Pte Ltd* [1995] 3 SLR 143, 149.

[37] [2002] 2 Lloyd's Rep 182.

course, the bills of lading were endorsed by the sellers to their correspondent banks in Chile for payment. The cargoes were placed by the agents in different customs warehouses at San Antonio and, following payment of duty, released, without presentation of the original bills of lading. The shipowners raised a number of defences, inter alia that, under the law of Chile, they were obliged to deliver the goods to a licensed customs warehouse and that, further, they were not negligent in delivering the goods without production of the bills of lading. After hearing the expert evidence, the judge, Thomas J, concluded that delivery by a shipowner to the customs warehouse was not a delivery to customs and was accordingly not a delivery of the goods in the sense that this relinquished the shipowner's control over them. The shipowner should have ensured that he could discharge his obligation to deliver only on presentation of a bill of lading, by an appropriate contract with the customs warehouse operators and container operators.[38]

F. Delivery: Straight Bills of Lading

10.12   **Introduction**   We have now seen that, at least for bills of lading to order, there is uncontroversial authority that the bills of lading must be presented in order to obtain delivery. For long, it has been unsettled whether there is a similar rule with respect to straight bills of lading,[39] although a number of academic writers have suggested that there is no need for this to be the case.[40]

10.13   **Older English authorities**   Until recently the point has not received express consideration in English law. No distinction appears to have been made in the short judgment in *The Stettin*,[41] although, like many of the authorities on the point, this was a case concerned with order bills of lading. The subsequent authorities have not been entirely uniform. Those in favour include *Evans & Reid v Cornouaille*,[42] where Hill J suggested, obiter, that it was not open to the carrier to deliver without the bills of lading even if the bills of lading had been made out to a named consignee.[43] Some years later, in *Barclays Bank v Commissioners of Customs & Excise*, Diplock LJ confirmed that the presentation rule was applicable in the case of a person 'whether named as consignee or not'.[44] In *East West Corp v DKBS 1912 & AKTS Svendborg*[45] Thomas J seemed to suggest, in relation to one set of bills of lading which were straight,[46] that the carrier was bound to deliver to the consignee against presentation of the bill.[47] However, against these authorities is *Thrige v United Shipping Co Ltd*,[48] where Scrutton

---

[38] This aspect of the case did not go to the Court of Appeal: see [2003] 1 Lloyd's Rep 239 (CA).

[39] See, eg, Felix WH Chan, 'A Plea for Certainty: Legal and Practical Problems in the Presentation of Non-negotiable Bills of Lading' (1999) 29 HKLJ 44.

[40] See Gaskell (1990), para 14.25; Benjamin (2002), para 18-017; Carver (2005), para 6-017.

[41] (1889) 14 PD 142.

[42] (1921) 8 Ll LR 76.

[43] At 77.

[44] [1963] 1 Lloyd's Rep 81, 89. See also *The Sormovskiy 3068* [1994] 2 Lloyd's Rep 266, 274; *The Houda* [1994] 2 Lloyd's Rep 541 (Clarke J); *The Ines* [1995] 2 Lloyd's Rep 144.

[45] [2002] EWHC 83 (Comm); [2002] 2 Lloyd's Rep 182.

[46] ie the 'Maersk bill of lading No 4'.

[47] [2002] EWHC 83 (Comm); [2002] 2 Lloyd's Rep 182, at [24].

[48] (1924) 18 Ll LR 6.

LJ indicated that, though it was not necessary to decide the point, if *The Stettin*[49] had decided that there was such a duty, 'it may require consideration'.[50]

Other jurisdictions   A number of common law jurisdictions have considered the question of   **10.14**
presentation and straight bills of lading. In the Hong Kong SAR, the leading case is *The Brij*,[51]
which involved the shipment of garments subsequently released under straight bills. The shipper sued for misdelivery of the goods but Waung J held that the contractual mandate under the bills of lading was to 'deliver to named consignee without the production of the original document'.[52] In Singapore, an earlier case, *Olivine Electronics Pte Ltd v Seabridge Transport Pte Ltd*[53]
involved the shipment of goods on straight bills of lading stating that 'if required by the carrier one (1) original bill of lading must be surrendered duly endorsed in exchange for the goods or delivery order'. The carrier delivered the goods to the buyer without the presentation of the bills of lading and the seller sought damages in conversion. Goh Joon Seng J ruled that it was a term of the bill of lading that delivery must be made against the bill of lading.[54] Other than this, the rule on presentation for straight bills of lading was still 'somewhat open'.[55]

Voss Peer   The leading case in Singapore is now *Voss Peer v APL Co Pte Ltd*.[56] This arose out   **10.15**
of the carriage of a Mercedes Benz convertible from Hamburg to Busan on the *Hyundai General*. At Busan, the car was discharged into the custody of APL's Korean office and later released to an individual who inter alia presented a commercial invoice from the seller. On a claim for alleged misdelivery, the carrier argued that it was entitled to make delivery to a named consignee without production of the original bill of lading. In finding against the carrier, Judith Prakash J stated that:

> Once [the shipowner] issues a bill of lading . . ., whether it is an order bill or a straight bill, he must not deliver the cargo except against its production. The contrary view had much less support and most of it was recent and cursory.[57]

This reasoning was upheld by the Singapore Court of Appeal. Chao Hick Tin JA (delivering the judgment of the court) held that

> . . . looking at the matter from the perspective of the market place, there is much to commend the rule that even in respect of a straight bill presentation of it is a pre-requisite to obtaining delivery. If nothing else, the advantage of this rule is that it is simple to apply. It is certain. It would prevent confusion and avoid the shipowners and/or their agents having to decide whether a bill is a straight bill or an order bill . . . and run the risk attendant thereto if the determination they make on that point should turn out to be erroneous. The rule would obviate such wholly unnecessary litigation.[58]

In reaching this conclusion both the Singapore High Court and Court of Appeal were heavily influenced by certain dicta of Clarke J in *The Sormovskiy 3068*,[59] although that case

---

49 (1889) 14 PD 142.
50 At 9. See too *The River Ngada* [2001] LMLN 570.
51 [2001] 1 Lloyd's Rep 431.
52 At 434. cf. *Carewins Development (China) Ltd v Bright Fortune Shipping Ltd*, unrep, 27 July 2006.
53 [1995] 3 SLR 143. See Toh Kian Sing, 'Of straight and switch bills of lading' [1996] LMCLQ 416.
54 At 148.
55 At 149.
56 [2002] 2 Lloyd's Rep 707.
57 [2002] 3 SLR 176, 189.
58 [2002] 2 Lloyd's Rep 707, at [51].
59 [1994] 2 Lloyd's Rep 266, 274.

in fact concerned order bills of lading. Thus, at least for Singapore law, the law is now clear and will have to be followed. Regardless of whether the bill of lading is to order or is to a named consignee, the bill of lading must be presented in order to obtain delivery of the goods. It now remains to be seen whether other Asian common law jurisdictions will follow suit.

10.16 *The Rafaela S* We turn now to *The Rafaela S*.[60] The issue as to presentation was strictly obiter, as this was not the essential point for consideration. The relevant MSC bills of lading provided that:

> IN WITNESS whereof the number of Original Bills of Lading stated above all of this tenor and date, has been signed, one of which being accomplished, the others to stand void.[61] *One of the Bills of Lading must be surrendered duly endorsed in exchange for the goods or delivery order.*[62]

At first instance, Langley J agreed with the arbitrators that, though a point of 'some nicety', delivery against the bill of lading was not necessary because the printed words referred to above appeared in a document which could be used either as a straight bill of lading or as a transferable bill of lading.[63] In the Court of Appeal, Rix LJ considered that it was

> undesirable to have a different rule for different kinds of bills of lading . . . It is true . . . that in the case of a negotiable bill the carrier needs to have the bill produced in order to be able to police the question of who is entitled to delivery. Yet an analogous problem arises with a straight bill. A shipper needs the carrier to assist him in policing his security in the retention of the bill. He is entitled to redirect the consignment on notice to the carrier, and, although notice is required, a rule of production of the bill is the only safe way, for the carrier as well as the shipper, to police such new instructions. In any event, if proof of identity is necessary, as in practice it is, what is wrong with the bill itself as a leading form of proof?[64]

In the House of Lords, Lord Bingham agreed with Rix LJ: he would 'if necessary' hold that the production of a straight bill of lading was a necessary precondition of requiring delivery, even where there was no express provision in the bill of lading to that effect.[65] Lord Steyn expressed no direct view, although it may be implied that he agreed with these views, as he found the analysis of Rix LJ 'entirely convincing'[66] and joined with the opinions of Lord Bingham and Lord Rodger.[67] Similarly, Lord Rodger,[68] Lord Brown of Eaton-under-Heywood,[69] and Lord Nicholls[70] did not touch upon the point, but expressed themselves to be in agreement with the opinions of the other law lords.

---

[60] *JI MacWilliam Co Inc v Mediterranean Shipping Co SA (The Rafaela S)* [2005] UKHL 11; [2005] 2 AC 423.

[61] This first of these sentences follows what has been termed 'the time honoured form': *The Marlborough Hill v Alex Cowan & Sons Ltd* [1921] 1 AC 444, 453 (Lord Phillimore).

[62] Emphasis supplied. This is a standard clause in MSC bills of lading: see also *El Greco (Australia) Pty Ltd v Mediterranean Shipping Co SA* [2004] FCAFC 448; [2004] 2 Lloyd's Rep 537.

[63] [2002] 2 Lloyd's Rep 403, 407.

[64] [2003] EWCA Civ 556; [2004] QB 702, at [145]. See too Jacob J, at [150].

[65] [2005] UKHL 11; [2005] 2 AC 423, at [20]. See also Carewins Development (China) Ltd v Bright Fortune Shipping Ltd, unrep, 27 July 2006, at [117]-[118] (Stone J).

[66] At [51].

[67] At [52].

[68] At [78].

[69] At [79].

[70] At [26].

Settled issues While it is undoubtedly the case that recent decisions clarify the law arising **10.17** out of the use of straight bills of lading, new issues are likely to arise as a result of these decisions. A measure of uniformity has also been achieved with respect to the rule requiring presentation of the bills of lading, although this is not too remarkable given the general principle that the courts will seek to give effect to the contract agreed between the parties.[71] Thus, it is confirmed that if there is an appropriate clause in the bill of lading — such as 'one of the bills of lading must be surrendered duly endorsed in exchange for the goods or delivery order' — a straight bill of lading will be treated in the same way as an order bill of lading and must be presented in order to obtain delivery of the goods. Singapore law would go further than this and holds that, regardless of whether there is an express statement, both straight and order bills of lading must be presented in order to obtain delivery of the cargo. There is obiter support for this proposition in English law and elsewhere in Asia. It remains to be seen whether there will be fresh consideration of this at first instance in the light of developments elsewhere. While it is clear that the parties may specify that the bills of lading must be presented,[72] it is still unclear in many jurisdictions whether the general rule will apply where the straight bill of lading is silent. As we have seen, the law in Singapore and Hong Kong is now clear that the bills of lading must be presented and there is obiter support too in the House of Lords. However, it is a moot point whether there should be a rule requiring presentation in the absence of an express clause to this effect. An issue which also needs further clarification is the effect of a clause which specifies that the straight bill of lading should not be presented in order to obtain delivery. While such a clause would be contractually valid, the presence of such a clause might also have the (perhaps unintended) consequence of affecting the status of the bill of lading as a document of title, although that question also awaits further consideration.

G. Delivery: Sea Waybills

Generally A sea waybill[73] performs two of the three functions that a traditional bill of **10.18** lading performs: it is a receipt for the goods shipped and it is also evidence of the contract of carriage between the shipper and the carrier.[74] But it is not a document of title. Accordingly, the receiver of the cargo under a sea waybill does not need to present the original in order to obtain delivery. This is because the sea waybill simply names the receiver in the box marked 'consignee' and the carrier may deliver the goods to the receiver once he identifies himself as the named consignee. An example is the Overseas Containers Limited (OCL) non-negotiable waybill:

> Delivery will be made to the consignee named or his authorised agent, on production of proof of identity at the place of delivery. Should the consignee require delivery elsewhere

---

[71] See, eg, *Homburg Houtimport BV v Agrosin Private Ltd (The Starsin)* [2003] UKHL 12; [2004] 1 AC 715, at [9].

[72] As they did in *The Rafaela S* [2005] UKHL 11; [2005] 2 AC 423.

[73] See, generally, Benjamin (2002), para 18-124.

[74] See para 4.02.

than at the place of delivery as shown below then written instructions must be given by the consignee to the carrier or his agent. Should delivery be required to be made to a party other than that named as consignee, authorisation must be given in writing by the shipper to the carrier or his agent.[75]

H. Delivery against Letters of Indemnity

10.19 **The background**   The principles so far examined were settled relatively early in the development of the common law and, as we have seen, have lost none of their legal force. Such principles must also operate in the context in which trade is conducted in modern times. International trade in bulk commodities, particularly crude oil cargoes, has since the turmoil in these markets in the 1970s[76] led to the business practice whereby a single cargo might be sold more than 150 times,[77] both before and after loading.[78] Cargoes often arrive at the discharge port well before the arrival of the bill of lading, either because the voyage is short[79] or, more commonly, simply because the bill of lading is held up in the banking chain.[80]

10.20 **Commercial response**   One commercial response to this practical problem has been for the shipowner to make delivery as against a letter of indemnity,[81] usually countersigned by a bank, offered by the consignee. The difficulty with letters of indemnity,[82] however, is that they are only as good as the financial standing of the guarantor because, as we have seen, delivery without presentation of the bills of lading can lead to extensive liabilities for the shipowner. As was pointed out by Leggatt LJ in *Kuwait Petrolum Corporation v I & D Oil Carriers Ltd (The Houda)*:

> In default of production of the bill of lading an indemnity is afforded to the shipowner not on account of the lawfulness of the order to deliver but so as to protect him if he does what he is *not* contractually obliged to do.[83]

The courts have, on occasion, accepted that the issue of such letters of indemnity has become almost a matter of routine commercial life. Thus, in the case of *Pacific Carriers Ltd v BNP Paribas*,[84] the High Court of Australia held that, in light of the surrounding circumstances known to the carrier and to the bank, the purpose and object of the transaction, and the market in which the parties were operating, a reasonable reader in the postion of the

---

[75] See also Genwaybill.

[76] For a readable account of this period, see Stopford (1997), 304.

[77] See Williams (1999), 112.

[78] See *Voest Alpine Intertrading GmbH v Chevron International Oil Co Ltd* [1987] 2 Lloyd's Rep 547, 550 (Hirst J); Bridge (1999), 30.

[79] Voyages from the North Sea oilfields (eg from Sullom Voe) to North Western Europe are relatively short. See RM Wiseman, 'Transaction Chains in North Sea Oil Cargoes' (1984) 2 JENRL 134.

[80] At one time this also created difficulties relating to title to sue, because of the terms of the Bills of Lading Act 1855.

[81] There may be difficulties if the indemnity also purports to be fraudulent: see *Brown, Jenkinson & Co Ltd v Percy Dalton (London) Ltd* [1957] 2 QB 621 (CA) and *Hunter Grain Pty Ltd v Hyundai Merchant Marine Co Ltd* (1993) 117 ALR 507.

[82] They have the status in law of an independent binding agreement: see *The Stone Gemini* [1999] 2 Lloyd's Rep 255.

[83] [1994] 2 Lloyd's Rep 541 (CA), 553.

[84] [2004] HCA 35; (2004) 208 ALR 203.

carrier would have understood the letters of indemnity to give rise to a liability on the part of the bank as an indemnifying party in support of a similar undertaking by the seller of the cargo. Accordingly, it held that it would be unjust to permit the bank to depart from the carrier's assumption that the letters of credit had been executed with the bank's authority in circumstances where the bank had placed the officer who dealt with requests for letters of indemnity in a position to sign and stamp them.

No obligation to accept an indemnity It is clearly established that the shipowner cannot be placed under an obligation to accept an indemnity.[85] However, this might sometimes be modified by the terms of a particular contract, as was the case in *The Nordic Freedom*[86] where a clause provided that: **10.21**

> Should the bill of lading not arrive at discharge port and also not available on board vessel prior to scheduled discharge, owners shall discharge entire cargo per charterer, telex instructions against letter of indemnity.

Choo Han Teck JC held that:

> I am of the view that cl. 23 directs the master to deliver the cargo against a letter of indemnity should the bill of lading be unavailable. That letter of indemnity serves as his comfort against any claim. It does not relieve the master of his obligations under the contract of carriage. This is how admiralty courts and the shipping industry understand the practice of releasing cargo against a letter of indemnity *in lieu* of the bill of lading.[87]

P & I cover Shipowners' mutual Protection and Indemnity Associations (P & I Clubs)[88] which otherwise cover liability risks arising from the carriage of cargoes[89] usually expressly exclude cover[90] for the liabilities, costs, and expenses arising out of delivery without production of a bill of lading.[91] Notwithstanding the rule against cover, most clubs will give advice as to how to secure against the potential risks, such as using one of the International Group's standard forms.[92] **10.22**

I. Failure to Take Delivery

Generally It hardly needs saying that time is money. In the light of the preceding rules, what can the master do if no consignee (or his agent) appears at the port of discharge to take **10.23**

---

[85] See *Kuwait Petrolum Corporation v I & D Oil Carriers Ltd (The Houda)* [1994] 2 Lloyd's Rep 541 (CA), 558 (Millett LJ), cited in *The Cherry* [2003] 3 SLR 431 (CA).
[86] [2001] 1 SLR 232.
[87] At 237.
[88] See, generally, Hazelwood (2000), 182.
[89] Other cover typically provided includes: oil pollution liability; liability for loss of life and injury to crew members, passengers, and others, such as stevedores; damage to fixed and floating objects and property; that part of collision damage which is not covered under the shipowners' hull policy; wreck removal.
[90] This is because it is contrary to the principles of mutuality to permit one member to follow a practice which is for his sole economic benefit and involve the other members who do not engage in such commercial practices: See Hill, Robertson & Hazelwood (1996), 91.
[91] See, for example, the Britannia P & I Club, Rule 19(iii)(c); Gard Club, Rule 34.1(i) Standard Club, Rule 20.20 (and 20.21)(v.c).
[92] See, eg, the 'P & I Standard Form Letter of Indemnity to be given in return for Delivering Cargo without Production of the Original Bill of Lading' [Int Group A].

delivery of the cargo? In the absence of statutory provisions, or particular customs at the port of discharge, the common law rule is that the master must allow the consignee of the cargo a reasonable time in which to receive the goods and cannot discharge his responsibility by simply landing them immediately on the ship's arrival.[93] If the consignee or holder of the bill of lading does not appear to take delivery of the cargo within a reasonable time, then the master may land and warehouse the cargo at the expense of the cargo owner. In this way any delay to the ship is prevented. Some countries make provision in statute law enabling the shipowner to land and warehouse the goods immediately. Thus, in Singapore,[94] section 126 of the Merchant Shipping Act 1995[95] provides that

> ... in case the owner of the goods is not ready or does not offer to land or take delivery under such arrangement as soon as the ship is ready to unload, a shipowner may land or unship the goods imported in any ship into Singapore at any time after the arrival of the ship.[96]

10.24   **Bill of lading clauses**   More common than this, however, are bill of lading clauses which seek to regulate the rights and liabilities of the parties in relation to the delivery of goods. An example is clause 9(e) of Conlinebill 2000:[97]

> The Merchant or his Agent shall take delivery of the cargo as fast as the Vessel can discharge including, if required by the Carrier, outside ordinary working hours notwithstanding any custom of the port. If the Merchant or his Agent fails to take delivery of the cargo the Carrier's discharging of the cargo shall be deemed fulfilment of the contract of carriage. Should the cargo not be applied for within a reasonable time, the Carrier may sell the same privately or by auction. If the Merchant or his Agent fails to take delivery of the cargo as fast as the Vessel can discharge, the Merchant shall be liable to the Carrier for any overtime charges, losses, costs and expenses incurred by the Carrier.[98]

There is relatively little authority on the effect of such clauses, but a number of Australian authorities[99] suggest that clauses of this type provide for an agreed method of delivery and that, provided the agreed method is followed, the carriage of goods comes to an end.[100]

---

[93] See *Bourne v Gatliff* (1844) 11 Cl & Fin 45; 8 ER 1019; *Proctor, Garratt, Marston v Oakwin Steamship Co* [1926] 1 KB 244; *Turner, Nott & Co v Lord Mayor of Bristol* (1928) 31 Ll LR 359.

[94] This section was based on the UK Merchant Shipping Act 1894, 57 & 58 Vict, c 60, s 493, now repealed (see Statute Law (Repeals) Act 1993, c 50: Schedule I, Part XV).

[95] cap 179.

[96] Section 126(1). Section 126(2) goes on to say that: '(a) if any wharf or warehouse is named in the charter-party, bill of lading or agreement, as the wharf or warehouse where the goods are to be placed and if they can be conveniently there received, on that wharf or in that warehouse; and (b) in any other case, on some wharf or in some warehouse on or in which goods of a like nature are usually placed'.

[97] The older (1978) version provided (at cl 8) that: 'The Merchant or his Assign shall take delivery of the goods and continue to receive the goods as fast as the vessel can deliver and — but only if required by the Carrier — also outside ordinary working hours notwithstanding any custom of the port. Otherwise the Carrier shall be at liberty to discharge the goods and any discharge to be deemed a true fulfillment of the contract ... '.

[98] See, for other examples, cl 20 of the P & O Nedlloyd Bill of Lading. For other clauses, see Gaskell (2000), 436–444.

[99] See also *Center Optical (Hong Kong) Ltd v Jardine Transport Services (China) Ltd* [2001] 2 Lloyd's Rep 678 (Hong Kong High Court).

[100] See *Australasian United Steam Navigation Co v Hiskens* (1914) 18 CLR 646; *Keane v Australian Steamships* (1929) 41 CLR 484. The correctness of these decisions has, however, been doubted. See Cooke (2001), para 10.24.

J. Consequences of Wrongful Delivery

Generally   We come finally to the consequences for wrongful delivery. These are twofold. **10.25**
As explained by Lord Denning in *Sze Hai Tong Bank Ltd v Rambler Cycle Co Ltd*[101] these
consist of (i) liability for breach of contract[102] and (ii) liability in the tort of conversion to
the person entitled to delivery.

Breach of contract   Liability for breach of contract might arise, for example, even where **10.26**
the shipowner delivers the goods to their lawful owner.[103] The normal contractual measure
of damages for non-delivery is the market value[104] of the goods at the time and place at
which they should have been delivered less the amount it would have cost to get them to
the place of delivery.[105]

Conversion   Liability for misdelivery generally arises, however, under the tort[106] of con- **10.27**
version.[107] The measure of damages in conversion[108] was explained in the following terms
by Lord Brandon in *Chabbra Corp Pte Ltd v Jag Shakti (The Jag Shakti)*:

> It has further . . . been established, by authority of long standing, that where one person, A, who
> has or is entitled to have the possession of goods, is deprived of such possession by the tortious
> conduct of another person, B, whether such conduct consists in conversion or negligence, the
> proper measure in law of the damages recoverable by A from B is the full market value of the
> goods at the time when and the place where possession of them should have been given.[109]

---

[101] [1959] AC 576 (PC), 586.

[102] See *Glyn, Mills & Co v East & West India Dock Co* (1882) 7 App Cas 591, 610 (Lord Blackburn); *MB Pyramid Sound NV v Briese Schiffahrts GmbH & Co KG (The Ines)* [1995] 2 Lloyd's Rep 144, 151 (Clarke J).

[103] See *Kuwait Petrolum Corporation v I & D Oil Carriers Ltd (The Houda)* [1994] 2 Lloyd's Rep 541 (CA), 552 (Neill LJ) where it was noted that the damages for such a breach would normally be nil.

[104] If there is no available market then it is also possible that consequential losses will arise. See, generally, McGregor (2003), 902.

[105] See the leading case of *Rodocanachi v Milburn* (1886) 18 QBD 67 (CA), 78 (Lindley LJ), endorsed in *Attorney General of the Republic of Ghana v Texaco Overseas Tankships Ltd (The Texaco Melbourne)* [1994] 1 Lloyd's Rep 473 (HL).

[106] The standard definition of conversion is provided in *Lancashire and Yorkshire Railway Co v MacNicoll* (1918) 88 LJ KB 601, 605: 'It appears to me plain that dealing with goods in a manner inconsistent with the right of the true owner amounts to a conversion, provided that it is also established that there is also an intention on the part of the defendant in so doing to deny the owner's right or to assert a right which is inconsistent with the owner's right' (Atkin J). See Bridge (2002) 52.

[107] See *Chabbra Corp Pte Ltd v Jag Shakti (The Jag Shakti)* [1986] AC 337 (PC); *Bristol and West of England Bank v Midland Railway Co* [1891] 2 QB 653 (CA); *London Joint Stock Bank Ltd v British Amsterdam Maritime Agency Ltd* (1910) 16 Com Cas 102; *APL Co Pte Ltd v Voss Peer* [2002] 2 Lloyd's Rep 707, 716.

[108] McGregor (2003), 1072.

[109] [1986] AC 337 (PC), 345.

11

ALTERATIONS OF DELIVERY OBLIGATIONS AND OTHER PROBLEMS

A. Introduction

Overview   In this chapter we consider the effect of certain ancillary matters, in particular, the   **11.01**
legal consequences attaching to alterations of the carrier's delivery obligations. We look, in
particular, at alterations of the bill of lading and the problem of antedating, alterations of the
named parties, and the common practice, in some jurisdictions, of issuing switch bills of lading.

B. Problems Associated with the Commencement of Carriage

Correction of mistakes   There may sometimes be an issue as to whether mistakes in the bills   **11.02**
of lading can be corrected at the time when they are presented for signature by the master.
In essence, the rule here is that the master should indicate when the bill of lading misrepresents
information as to the condition, quantity, or nature of the cargo. Other situations arise where
the bill of lading is subject to a charterparty. Thus, it is clear that the master is only bound to
sign a bill of lading which is in the ordinary form for that trade.[1] If the bill of lading contains
incorrect information which is unverifiable it would be prudent not to sign the bills of lading
as presented, at least until the information has been altered. These situations might include
where the bill of lading provides for a destination which is outside the limits prescribed in the
charterparty,[2] or does not include terms which the charterparty requires to be incorporated.

---

[1] See *Boukadoura Maritime Corp v Marocaine de l'Industrie et du Raffinage SA (The Boukadoura)* [1989] 1
Lloyd's Rep 393.
[2] But cf *SIAT di del Ferro v Tradax Overseas SA* [1980] 1 Lloyd's Rep 53, where a buyer rejected a bill of lading
where the destination had been altered by the master in an attempt to make it conform to the destination in
the sale contract.

Also of particular importance is a bill of lading which provides (or requires) that the cargo should be stowed below deck, when it is, in fact, loaded on the deck.

11.03 **Fraudulent alterations/antedating** Particular problems are associated with wrongly dated bills of lading. In the earlier case of *Kwei Teck Chao v British Traders & Shippers*, Devlin J said, in response to such an issue that the

> true view is that one must examine the nature of the alteration and see whether it goes to the whole or to the essence of the instrument or not. If it does, and if the forgery corrupts the whole of the instrument or its heart, then the instrument is destroyed; but if it corrupts merely a limb, the instrument remains alive, though no doubt defective.[3]

More recently, however, the following statement was endorsed by Evans LJ in the case of *Standard Chartered Bank v Pakistan National Shipping Corp (No 2)*:

> Antedated and false bills of lading are a cancer in international trade. A bill of lading is issued in international trade with the purpose that it should be relied upon by those into whose hands it properly comes — consignees, bankers and endorsees. A bank, which receives a bill of lading signed by or on behalf of a shipowner (as one of the documents presented under a letter of credit), relies upon the veracity and authenticity of the bill. Honest commerce requires that those who put bills of lading into circulation do so only where the bill of lading, as far as they know, represents the true facts.[4]

The significance of the dating of the bill of lading relates to the value of the cargo. The price to be paid — and also the underlying sale transaction[5] — will be determined by the date of issue of the bill of lading.[6] Thus, it is essential that a shipped bill of lading actually shows the date on which completion of loading occurred in respect of the cargo covered by the bill of lading.[7]

11.04 **Master not required to sign wrongly dated bills of lading** It is clear law that the master cannot be obliged to sign bills of lading which are wrongly dated. In *Rudolf A Oetker v IFA Internationale Frachagentur AG (The Almak)* Mustill J stated that:

> The obligation to sign bills of lading as presented could not of course ever require the master to sign bills which stated a falsehood. He would always be entitled to refuse if he noticed the discrepancy. If he did notice it and nevertheless chose to sign, it might be that the shipowner would lose his right of indemnity, on the grounds that:— (i) the decision to sign incorrect bills with knowledge of the true facts broke the causal connection between the request to sign and the subsequent loss, or (ii) the act of signing was 'manifestly unlawful in itself', so as to take the case outside the charterer's implied right of indemnity at common law.[8]

11.05 **Consequences of wrongful signature** Where the bills of lading are wrongly dated and signed by the master and these are intended to be relied upon as being accurate, then the law is clear, particularly following the leading case of *Standard Chartered Bank v Pakistan National Shipping Corp*.[9] This case arose following an agreement for the shipment of a

3 [1954] 2 QB 459, 476.
4 [2000] 1 Lloyd's Rep 218 (CA), 221.
5 Timely shipment is of the essence of the contract in c.i.f. contracts: see, eg, *Bowes v Shand* (1877) 2 App Cas 455 and the discussion in Bridge (1999), 180.
6 See, eg, *Novorossisk Shipping Co of the USSR v Neopetro Co Ltd (The Ulyanovsk)* [1990] 1 Lloyds Rep 425.
7 See *Mendala III Transport v Total Transport Corp (The Wilomi Tanana)* [1993] 2 Lloyd's Rep 41.
8 [1985] 1 Lloyd's Rep 557, 561.
9 [2002] UKHL 43; [2003] 1 AC 959.

cargo of bitumen to a Vietnamese buyer, with payment against a letter of credit stipulating for shipment no later than 25 October 1993. The cargo was not shipped by this date but the seller's agent and the shipowners agreed with the seller's managing director to issue a bill of lading which was falsely dated so as to appear to comply with the letter of credit. In due course, these documents were presented to Standard Chartered and, although after the expiry date of the credit, it waived this and authorized payment. Standard Chartered then wrote to the issuing bank in Vietnam, stating that the documents had been presented before the expiry date and seeking reimbursement. The Vietnamese bank refused and Standard Chartered claimed damages for deceit and conspiracy against the shipowner and the managing director of the sellers for the antedated bills of lading. The judge at first instance[10] held that Standard Chartered had established a good cause of action against both the shipowner and the managing director. On appeal, the managing director was successful on the basis that that he had acted throughout as the representative for his company and was not personally liable.[11] The decision at first instance was restored by the House of Lords on the basis that, although the managing director's fraudulent misrepresentation was attributable to his company, it had been relied upon by the Bank, based on his knowledge. Accordingly, it was not possible for him to escape personal liability on the ground that he was committing the fraud on behalf of his employer. He was therefore personally liable for the loss caused to Standard Chartered.[12]

Indemnities   The person seeking to have the bills of lading antedated may seek to per-   **11.06**
suade the master to do so on the basis of a letter of indemnity. However, this should always be refused, simply on the basis that it will be unenforceable as being designed to defraud a third party, such as a bank, which relies on it.[13]

P & I consequences   A potentially serious difficulty for shipowners lies also with the   **11.07**
P & I Clubs. Thus, most clubs expressly decline to cover

> liabilities, costs and expenses arising out of the issue of an ante-dated or post-dated Bill of Lading, waybill or other document containing or evidencing the contract of carriage, that is to say a Bill of Lading, waybill or other document recording the loading or shipment or receipt for shipment on a date prior or subsequent to the date on which the cargo was in fact loaded, shipped or received as the case may be.[14]

C. Correction or Amendment of the Bills of Lading after Signature

Generally   An issue which sometimes arises is whether mistakes may be amended after the   **11.08**
bills of lading have been signed. The answer to this is that this may be possible, but it would not be wise of the shipowner to accede to later corrections unless all the bills of lading in the

---

[10] [1998] 1 Lloyd's Rep 684.
[11] [2000] 1 Lloyd's Rep 218 (CA), 221 (Evans LJ).
[12] [2002] UKHL 43; [2003] 1 AC 959, at [20] (Lord Hoffmann).
[13] See the earlier discussion on indemnities, in the context of indemnities issued in return for delivery of the cargo without the bills of lading: para 6.27.
[14] Britannia P & I Club, Rule 19(17)(iii)(f); Gard Club, Rule 34(1)(vii); Standard Club, Rule 20.20 (and 20.21)(v)(d).

set are present. The master would not, of his own volition, have authority to sign a second bill of lading for goods where bills of lading have originally been signed.[15]

11.09 **Bill of lading lost or destroyed** It may happen that a master is approached by someone who claims to be entitled to possession of the bills of lading, or to have been in possession of them, and alleges that the originals have been lost or destroyed. If approached to issue new bills of lading in substitution for those allegedly lost or destroyed, the master should not agree to do so, even if an indemnity is offered in return.

11.10 **Alteration of the named consignee** It may sometimes be problematic for a master when a shipper decides that it wishes to alter the name of the consignee. It is established that the shipper may direct the carrier to deliver the goods to another person,[16] 'at any rate before the delivery of the goods themselves or of the bill of lading to the party named in it'.[17] Thus, under the Carriage of Goods by Sea Act 1992, the shipper's right to redirect the goods will be lost once the consignee acquires rights under the bill of lading.[18] In *Elder Dempster Lines v Zaki Ishag (The Lycaon)*,[19] a set of received for shipment bills of lading named a particular party as consignee but the bills of lading were pledged to a bank which insisted that the consignee should be named as notify party only. When the bank demanded shipped bills of lading these were issued to the shipper. In due course there were problems as to which party delivery should be made to and the goods were shipped back from Douala and stored at a warehouse in Hamburg. The court held that the shipper was entitled to change the name of the consignee.[20]

D. Switch Bills of Lading

11.11 **Introduction** In some parts of the world, notably in Asia, it is not at all uncommon to meet the situation where a request is made for the issue of fresh bills of lading, usually at some time after the originals have been signed. When such bills of lading are issued, they are usually known as 'switch'[21] bills of lading.[22]

11.12 **Reasons for issue** Switch bills of lading are usually issued when there is a desire to conceal the name of a supplier or to avoid export duties or embargoes. The issued bills of lading will be surrendered to the carrier (or his agents) in exchange for another set of bills in which some details, such as the name and address of the shipper, the port of shipment,[23] or their date of issue, might be altered. The 'switch' bills, as they are now termed, will be transferred down the chain of buyers in the customary way. There have been very few cases on

---

[15] For this proposition, see the old case of *Hubbersty v Ward* (1853) 8 Ex 330; 155 ER 1374.

[16] See *Elder Dempster Lines v Zaki Ishag (The Lycaon)* [1983] 2 Lloyd's Rep 548.

[17] *Mitchell v Ede* (1840) 11 Ad & El 888, 903; 113 ER 651, 657. See Benjamin (2002), para 18-015.

[18] See s 2(5).

[19] [1983] 2 Lloyd's Rep 548.

[20] At 555.

[21] Sometimes known as 'split' or 'global' bills of lading.

[22] See Toh Kian Sing, 'Of straight and switch bills of lading' [1996] LMCLQ 416.

[23] See, eg, *Noble Resources Ltd v Cavalier Shipping Corporation (The Atlas)* [1996] 1 Lloyd's Rep 642.

such bills of lading (we shall shortly refer to one of them), but they have been acknowledged by the High Court of Singapore in *Samsung Corp v Devon Industries Sdn Bhd*.[24] In that case Selvam J stated that:

> The practice of cutting and releasing 'global bills of lading' is perfectly in order provided the authentic [ie original] bills of lading issued to the real shippers, the true owners of the cargo at that stage, have been accomplished, that is that they have been received lawfully by the [buyers] duly endorsed and surrendered to the shipowners or their agents. In other words, shipowners may issue 'global bills of lading' in exchange for the first set of bills of lading issued to the shippers.[25]

Risks   There is clearly little difficulty where the switched bills of lading are the only bills **11.13** in circulation. If, however, there is fraud or negligence, such that both the originals and the switch bills are in circulation, the shipowners would potentially be exposing themselves to liability were different endorsees to compete for delivery. Thus in the *Samsung* case shipping agents had combined with the defendants in unlawfully issuing the second set of bills of lading. These were unlawfully negotiated by the defendants and they lost substantial sums of money as a result.

Contractual terms   The case of *Noble Resources Ltd v Cavalier Shipping Corporation (The* **11.14** *Atlas)*[26] was unusual in that the bills of lading provided that:

> If required by Charterers, Owners agree to issue 2nd set of freight prepaid Bill(s) of Lading in Hong Kong marked different Shippers/Receivers, notify party than those of the 1st set of Bills of Lading and marked cargo description as steel billets, after receiving 100% of freight and against Charterers' Letter of Indemnity only. Charterers will return 1st set of original Bills of Lading to Owners once same in their hands.

> In the absence of original Bills of Lading at discharge port Receivers to submit a Letter of Indemnity in accordance with Owners' P & I Club's form. Charterers should advise full details of 2nd set Bills of Lading upon completion of loading.

Although not the material point in the case,[27] Longmore J noted that

> No doubt this provision for a second set of bills of lading to come into existence was agreed for not unreasonable commercial motives but it is a practice fraught with danger; not only does it give rise to obvious opportunities for fraud (which is not suggested in this case) but also, if it is intended that the bills of lading should constitute contracts of carriage with the actual owner of the ship (as opposed to any disponent owner), the greatest care has to be taken to ensure that the practice has the shipowner's authority.[28]

Conclusion   In view of the caution directed against the issue of 'switch' bills of lading, it **11.15** would be prudent for a master, faced with a request for such bills, not to issue them. If he is minded to do so, he should act only in concurrence with the shipowner and only release the 'switch' bills when in possession of the full set of the original bills.

---

[24] [1996] 1 SLR 469.
[25] At 473. See also *Swiss Singapore Overseas Enterprise Pte Ltd v Navalmar UK Ltd (No 2)* [2003] 1 SLR 688.
[26] [1996] 1 Lloyd's Rep 642.
[27] As to this, see para 26.13.
[28] [1996] 1 Lloyd's Rep 642, 644.

12

CHARTERPARTIES AND THEIR
RELATIONSHIP WITH BILLS OF LADING

A. Introduction

Overview   In this chapter we consider the relationship of charterparties and bills of lading.   **12.01**
We look first at the background to trading in charterparties and bills of lading before examining the effect of bills of lading in the hands of the charterer. We then look at a prominent issue which faces a cargo claimant, namely, whether to sue the shipowner or the charterer. We consider finally some of the problems associated with the incorporation of charterparties into bills of lading and the consequences of the transfer of the bill of lading to a third party.

B. Background

Changed shipping business   Principles of law governing the issue of bills of lading were   **12.02**
worked out in the days of sailing ships, when the master was effectively the co-owner of the ship and signed the bills of lading personally. The shipping business is today very much more complex, largely because of the advent of container ships and also the increasing use of very large vessels to transport bulk goods, both wet and dry. It is relatively unusual to find a shipping line which actually owns the ships on which it carries cargoes. There is much competition between operators and, sometimes, collaboration in the form of price-fixing cartels known as liner conferences, in which the operators on a designated route agree the tariffs for carriage on that route. Conference members often issue bills of lading for carriage on one another's ships; a ship time chartered to one conference member may actually be carrying cargoes under bills of lading issued by a whole range of different shipping lines.

137

Further, the shipping line that charters the ship may sub-charter parts of the ship's carrying capacity to other Conference members under contracts known as slot charters, or it may allow them to issue bills of lading for carriage on its ship in return for reciprocal rights over their ships.

C. Bills of Lading in the Hands of the Charterer

12.03 **Not the charterer's contract**   A bill of lading issued by the shipowner to the charterer performs two of the functions of a normal bill of lading, namely it operates as a receipt for the goods shipped and as a potential document of title which may, provided it is made out in the appropriate form, be endorsed to a third party.[1] The bill of lading in such a case is not evidence of the contract of carriage because the relationship between shipowner and charterer is governed by the terms of the charterparty. The bill of lading does not operate either as a new contract between the charterer and shipowner[2] and does not modify the charterparty contract[3] unless the charterparty contains a provision to the effect that its terms may be varied by a subsequent bill of lading.

12.04 **Bill of lading endorsed to the charterer**   The position is similar when a bill of lading, initially issued to a third party, is later endorsed to the charterer. The classic example of this situation is where the charterer agrees to purchase goods f.o.b. and a charterparty bill of lading (such as Congenbill) is issued to the seller, who is then named as shipper and endorses the bill of lading to the charterer as part of the sale contract. In *The President of India v Metcalfe Shipping Co (The Dunelmia)*[4] the government of India bought 8,000 tons of urea (for fertilizer) f.o.b. from certain sellers in Italy (ANIC) and chartered *The Dunelmia* to carry the cargo from Ravenna and Ancona to Madras. The sellers loaded the fertilizer and received a bill of lading to order which they then endorsed in blank. The Indian government paid the purchase price, took the bill of lading and obtained delivery of the goods. Clause 17 of the charterparty with Metcalfe provided that:

> Any dispute arising under this charter shall be settled in accordance with the provisions of the Arbitration Act 1950 in London.

The Indian government made a claim for short delivery and, as charterers of the *Dunelmia*, wished to refer the dispute to arbitration. The shipowners refused because they said that the carriage was governed by the bill of lading which did not contain an arbitration clause. Which was the governing contract? Upholding the judgment of Megaw J, the Court of Appeal held the charterparty regulated the relationship between the parties. Lord Denning MR stated that:

> After full consideration, I am prepared to hold that in a case such as this the relations between shipowner and charterer are governed by the charterparty. Even though the charterer is not the shipper and takes as endorsee of a bill of lading, nevertheless their relations are governed

---

[1] See para 5.12.
[2] *Rodocanachi v Milburn* (1886) 18 QBD 67 (CA); *The Al Battani* [1993] 2 Lloyd's Rep 219, 222 (Sheen, J).
[3] *Temperley Steam Shipping Co Ltd v Smyth & Co* [1905] 2 KB 791.
[4] [1970] 1 QB 289 (CA).

by the charter, at any rate when the master is authorised to sign bills of lading without prejudice to the charter.[5]

Supersession clauses   A voyage charterparty for the carriage of dry goods may contain a   **12.05**
superseding clause to the following effect:

> This contract shall be completed and superseded by the signing of bills of lading in the form
> customary for such voyages for grain cargoes, which bills of lading shall contain the following
> clauses . . .

In *Oriental Maritime Pte Ltd v The Peoples' Republic of Bangladesh (The Silva Plana)*,[6] the
Ministry of Food of Bangladesh bought three lots of wheat from Cargill Commodities
Trading Pte Ltd chartering *Silva Plana* to carry two lots of cargo from the USA. The
Bahamastars and *Magic Sky* were to carry the remainder. All the charterparties were in the
Baltimore Form C Berth Grain form. The ships were in fact sub-chartered by the Ministry
of Food from the disponent owners, Oriental Maritime Pte Ltd. Clause 42 of the charter-
parties provided that:

> It is also mutually agreed that this contract shall be completed and superseded by the signing
> of Bills of Lading which shall be deemed to incorporate the above clauses as well as contain-
> ing the following additional clauses(s)

A further clause (clause 49) provided that 90 per cent of the freight was payable within
10 clear days of signing and releasing bills of lading and 10 per cent was payable on completion of discharge. Bills of lading issued in respect of the cargoes stated that:

> All terms, conditions and exceptions of the governing charterparty and any addendums
> thereto shall be considered as embodied in this bill of lading. In the event of any conflict
> between this bill of lading and the charterparty, the latter shall control.

Finally, there were separate arbitration agreements governing the charterparties and the bill of
lading contracts and the arbitration agreements had to be invoked separately. Disputes arose
between the parties and arbitrators were in due course appointed under the charterparty provisions. The principal claim by the disponent owners was for the 10 per cent balance of
freight. The arbitrators appointed to adjudicate the claim stated that as they had been
appointed under the charterparties and that these had been superseded by the bills of lading
by virtue of clause 42, they had no jurisdiction over the bills of lading. Steyn J stated that:

> The charterparties were made between the disponent owners and the sub-charterers. On the
> other hand, it is clear (and not disputed) that the bills of lading were owners' bills of lading.
> In other words, insofar as those bills of lading contained or evidence contracts, the contracts
> were not between disponent owners and sub-charterers (the Government of Bangladesh) but
> between head or registered owners and the holders of the bills of lading (the Government of
> Bangladesh).[7]

Had supersession taken place under clause 42? Steyn J concluded that:

> Concentrating in the first place on the words of cl 42, it seems to me that the very concept of
> 'completion' of a contract, or its 'supersession', by the conclusion of a further contract,

---

[5] At 308. See also *Gardner Smith Pty Ltd v The Ship Tomoe 8* (1990) NSWLR 588.
[6] [1989] 2 Lloyd's Rep 371.
[7] At 374.

carries with it the clearest indication, absent other *indicia*, that the contracts in question would be between the same parties.

> ...[M]y firm view is that the language of cl 42 (which, as always, must be the starting point), and the commercial reality that businessmen do not abandon valuable enforceable legal rights for mere speculative expectations, compellingly indicate that, on a proper construction of cl 42, there has been no supersession of the charterparty. Accordingly, the arbitrators had jurisdiction to entertain the claims ...[8]

He reached this conclusion on the basis that it was unlikely, as a matter of interpretation, that the disponent owner had intended to give up valuable rights of freight against the sub-charterer without receiving in turn any enforceable rights against the sub-charterer.

12.06 **Time charterers' contracts** If a time charterer enters into a voyage sub-charterparty and the shipowner issues a bill of lading to the sub-charterer on shipment of the goods, the bill of lading will act as evidence of a contract of carriage between the shipowner and the voyage sub-charterer. But if the time charterer were to issue a bill of lading in its own name to the voyage sub-charterer, that bill of lading would not be evidence of a contract of carriage between the time charterer and the voyage sub-charterer, because the contract of carriage between these two parties would be the voyage sub-charterparty.

12.07 **Voyage charterer as consignee** Where the voyage charterer is the consignee or endorsee of the bill of lading, transfer of the bill of lading to the charterer-receiver does not affect the contractual relationship between shipowner and charterer, which continues to be governed by the charterparty. The agent of the shipowner would not usually have the authority to vary the terms of the contract between its principal and the charterer, and so any bills of lading issued by the carrier's agent in terms different from the charterparty do not bind either party to the charterparty. This is usually confirmed by express provision in the charterparty to the effect that:

> All bills of lading or waybills shall be without prejudice to this Charter Party and the Charterers shall indemnify the Owners against all consequences or liabilities which may arise from any inconsistency between this Charter Party and any bills of lading or waybills signed by the Charterers or by the Master at their request.[9]

D. Who Is the Carrier?

12.08 **Introduction** A shipper who ships his goods on a chartered vessel will face two problems in the event of the cargo being lost or damaged: he will have to identify the carrier against whom the cargo claim can be pursued and he will have to establish the precise terms of the contract of carriage. The first of these is a major difficulty for a third party shipper because the bill of lading may well be issued in the name of the shipowner, the charterer, a sub-charterer or the agent of any one of them. An additional complication is that the bill will often be signed by or on behalf of the ship's master as agent of the shipowner. It will be important for the shipper to make the correct choice of person to sue[10] as the rule of English law is that only one party

---

[8] At 374–375.

[9] NYPE 93, cl 30(b), lines 311–314; Shelltime 4, cl 13(a), line 228.

[10] See David Chong Gek Sian, 'Unravelling the identity of the carrier' (1994) 6 SAcLJ 182; Debattista (1998), ch 8.

may be liable as carrier under any individual contract of carriage. If the contract is governed by the Hague–Visby Rules, by article III, rule 6 any cargo claim will be time barred unless it is brought within the prescribed 12-month period.[11]

General rule   The general rule is that the shipowner is the carrier as he remains responsible   **12.09** for the management of the ship and the master customarily signs bills of lading as his agent. This was stated to be the case by Channell J in *Wehner v Dene Steamship Co*:

> In ordinary cases, where the charterparty does not amount to a demise of the ship, and where possession of the ship is not given up to the charterer, the rule is that the contract contained in the bill of lading is made, not with the charterer, but with the owner, and that will, I think, explain away and accounts for all the difficulties which would otherwise arise as to the existence of the shipowners' lien. When there is a sub-charterparty there is no direct contract between the sub-charterer and the owner, and if the contract in the bill of lading were made, not with the owner, but with the sub-charterer, how is the shipowners' lien to be accounted for as against the holder of the bill of lading? It would be very difficult to deal with the question upon any logical or intelligible footing unless one starts with the proposition that the bill of lading contract is made, as it appears upon its face to be made, with the shipowner.[12]

However, because it is the charterer who deals with third parties shipping goods aboard the ship, it is the charterer who prepares and issues bills of lading in accordance with the particulars provided by third party shippers. Once the bills of lading have been drawn up, the charterer either presents them to the master for signature, or signs them himself on behalf of the master if he has been authorized to do so under the terms of the charterparty. The right of the charterer to issue such bills will be dependant on an express clause in the charterparty, for example, that provided for in clause 30(a) of the NYPE 93 charterparty:

30. <u>Bills of Lading</u>

(a) The Master shall sign the bills of lading or waybills for cargo as presented in conformity with mates or tally clerk's receipts. However, the Charterers may sign bills of lading or waybills on behalf of the Master, with the Owner's prior written authority, always in conformity with mates or tally clerk's receipts.[13]

This clause makes it clear that the master cannot refuse to sign the bills of lading presented by the charterer unless they are manifestly inconsistent with the charterparty. For this reason, an indemnity will be implied, assuming that the charterparty does not expressly provide an indemnity. Clause 30(b) of the NYPE 93 charterparty does so expressly:

(b) All bills of lading or waybills shall be without prejudice to this Charter Party and the Charterers shall indemnify the Owners against all consequences or liabilities which may arise from any inconsistency between this Charter Party and any bills of lading or waybills signed by the Charterers or by the Master at their request.[14]

If there is any inconsistency between the terms of the bill of lading presented by the charterer and signed by the master, and the terms agreed by the shipowner under the charterparty, the charterer must indemnify the shipowner for any loss it suffers as a result.

---

[11] As to this time bar, see para 34.03.
[12] [1905] 2 KB 92, 98.
[13] Lines 307–310.
[14] Lines 311–314. Clauses 30(a) and 30(b) also correspond to the terms of clause 8 of the NYPE 1946 charterparty. See further as to indemnities, para 32.86.

Bills of lading presented by the charterer and signed by the master under a clause such as clause 30 of NYPE 93, will be binding on the shipowner. Equally, the shipowner will be bound where the bills of lading are signed by the charterer himself, provided that he indicates on the bill that he is signing on behalf of the master and owners.

12.10   **Authority to bind the shipowner**   Are there any limits on the authority of the charterer to bind the shipowner? In *Gulf Steel Co Ltd v Al Khalifa Shipping Co Ltd (The Anwar Al Sabar)*[15] the owners let the *Anwar Al Sabar* to the charterers for the carriage of cargo from Sharjah in the United Arab Emirates to Alexandria. The charter provided that the owners were to have a lien on the cargo for freight, dead freight and demurrage and the charterers were to remain responsible for dead freight and demurrage incurred at the port of loading.[16] Clause 9 provided that:

> The Captain to sign Bills of Lading at such rate of freight as presented without prejudice to this Charter-party.

On completion of loading at Sharjah, four mate's receipts were issued covering the quantities of cargo shipped. The charterers presented to the agents of the vessel, in London, bills of lading in conformity with the mate's receipts. However, the owners took the view that their lien on the cargo created by the draft bills of lading presented by the charterers might not be effective at Alexandria. They declined to present the bills tendered unless a clause was added to the effect that:

> Demurrage and dead-freight are claimed by carriers who may exercise their right to lien the cargo under clause 8 of the charterparty.

The charterers objected to the inclusion of the clause because it would seriously affect the negotiability of the documents under the letter of credit which they had opened and applied for a mandatory injunction requiring the owners to issue bills of lading without the extra clause. Mustill J assumed for the purpose of argument that if the bill of lading had differed from the charterparty in any relevant respect the owner would not have been obliged to sign it.[17] He held that:

> I feel at liberty to read cl 9 in the sense which appears appropriate, namely that is for the charterer, not the owner, to decide on the form of bill of lading, always provided that the bill of lading does not encroach on the rights conferred on the owner by the charterparty . . . I consider that [the owners'] insistence on inserting this clause is ill-founded and . . . hold that the plaintiffs are entitled to the relief for which they ask.[18]

It would appear that there are few occasions when the master could refuse to sign bills presented by the charterer although there is authority for the view that he might do so where the terms of the bill are 'manifestly inconsistent with the charterparty'.[19] There have been cases where shipowners have been unable to resist the inclusion in a bill of a demise clause or a jurisdiction clause differing from its counterpart in the charterparty.

---

[15] [1980] 2 Lloyd's Rep 261.
[16] Clause 8.
[17] [1980] 2 Lloyd's Rep 261, 263.
[18] At 265.
[19] *Kruger v Moel Tryvan Ship Co* [1907] AC 272, 278 (Earl of Halsbury).

Charterer as carrier   Thus far we have seen what the position is where the shipowner is the   **12.11**
carrier. What about where the charterer is the carrier? Where the contract of carriage is governed by the Hague–Visby Rules, it is possible under article I(a) for the carrier to be either
the shipowner or the charterer.[20] The charterparty might itself provide that the master is
authorized to sign bills 'as agent on behalf of the charterers' and here the charterers would
be bound. The charterer may also be regarded as the carrier where he contracts as principal,
negotiating the contract of carriage in his own name and issuing his own bills of lading.
He may also be bound where he signs the bill of lading without indicating that he is acting
as the agent of the master and owners. The crucial thing is always the terms of the bill of lading and the construction of the documents as a whole. In *The Rewia*[21] a cargo of nutmegs
and mace was loaded aboard the *Rewia* for carriage from St George's, Granada to Felixstowe,
Rotterdam, and Hamburg. The owners (third defendants) of the vessel had time chartered
her to the fourth defendants who had in turn sub-chartered her to the first defendants. The
time charter made in Hamburg in 1988 was on the NYPE form and stated that:

> 8.   The Captain is to sign Bills of Lading for cargo as presented in conformity with Mates' or
>   Tally Clerks' receipts.

Clause 53 provided that:

> It is understood that the Master will authorize Charterers, or their Agents, to sign Bills of
> Lading on his behalf provided the Bills are made up in accordance with Mate's and Tally
> Clerk's receipts.

The bills of lading were liner bills of lading on the sub-charterers' standard form and signed
by the second defendants (as managers). One of the issues in the case was whether the third
defendants (the owners) were parties to the bills of lading. The plaintiffs argued that the
bills of lading were charterer's bills since they had been issued by or in the name of the
sub-charterers and there was nothing in the bills to limit or qualify an assumption of personal liability on the part of the sub-charterers. The bills of lading contained no clause identifying any person other than the sub-charterers as 'carriers'. Leggatt LJ held that:

> . . . in the present case the master was required to sign bills of lading as presented, and the
> understanding was that with his authority the charterers or their agents would sign them on
> his behalf. In any event, even had there been no prior authorisation, since with knowledge of
> the bills of lading the master proceeded to carry the goods, there was the plainest possible case
> of ratification.

> . . . [A] bill of lading signed for the master cannot be a charterers' bill unless the contract was
> made with the charterers alone, and the person signing has authority to sign, and does sign,
> on behalf of the charterers and not the owners. Accordingly, the bills of lading in this case
> were owners' bills. The plaintiffs have no claim against the first defendants.[22]

In *MB Pyramid Sound NV v Briese Schiffahrts GmbH & Co and Latvian Shipping
Association Ltd (The Ines)*[23] the second defendants, the charterers (Maras Linja), operated a
liner service from Belgium and Holland to Russian ports. Eimskip Rotterdam NV were

---

[20] See para 19.17.
[21] [1991] 2 Lloyd's Rep 325 (CA).
[22] At 333.
[23] [1995] 2 Lloyd's Rep 144.

their agents in Holland. They time chartered the *Ines* from the first defendants. Clause 9 of the charterparty provided that:

> . . . The Charterers to indemnify the Owners against all consequences or liabilities arising from the Master, Officers or Agents signing Bills of Lading . . . or otherwise complying with such orders.

The plaintiffs bought telephones in Hong Kong and these were then shipped to Antwerp before shipment to St Petersburg. The plaintiffs instructed Meyer & Co of Antwerp to arrange carriage to St Petersburg. Although the telephones were in due course shipped to St Petersburg, the plaintiffs were not paid and retained the original bills of lading. Shipped bills of lading bearing the date 14.10.91 had been issued and the signature box at the bottom right hand corner of the printed form contained the words: 'Signed as agents for carrier Maras Linja, pp EIMSKIP-Rotterdam as agents only'. Discharge of the cargo was carried out by stevedores employed by the Commercial Sea Port (CSP) at St Petersburg. It was the charterers' responsibility to provide and pay for the discharge of the cargo. CSP subsequently released the containers to the notify party specified in the bills of lading (Rusworld) without presentation of bills of lading. The plaintiffs argued that there was misdelivery in breach of contract. The owners sought to deny liability, contending that the charterers were the contractual carriers. Clarke J accepted the plaintiffs' submission that:

> in order to ascertain who the true contracting parties were it is necessary to examine the whole document and indeed to consider the whole context in which it came into existence.[24]

He concluded that:

> Although the signature box itself is ambiguous, a consideration of the other clauses and the document as a whole leads in my judgment to the conclusion that the parties intended that the contracts should be between the shippers and the shipowners. It follows that I have reached the conclusion that the parties to the contract of carriage contained in or evidenced by the bills of lading were the plaintiffs on the one hand and the owners on the other.[25]

Following the established lines of authority on delivery of goods without presentation of bills of lading, Clarke J concluded that the shipowners were liable to the plaintiffs for damages for breach of contract by reason of the delivery of the goods by CSP to Rusworld.[26]

12.12 **Demise clauses** Where the charterer is a party to the bill of lading, he may seek to transfer contractual liability to the shipowner by means of a demise clause[27] in the bill of lading. A typical example provides that:

> If the ship is not owned or chartered by demise to the company or line by whom the bill of lading is issued (as may be the case notwithstanding anything which appears to the contrary) this Bill of Lading shall take effect as a contract with the Owner or demise charterer, as the case may be, as principal made through the agency of the said company or line who acts as agents only and shall be under no personal liability whatsoever in respect thereof.

If such a clause appears in the bill of lading, the holder will be left in some doubt as to the identity of the party with whom he is contracting. It has been argued that this kind of

---

[24] At 149.
[25] At 150.
[26] At 154.
[27] On the history of such clauses, see Lord Roskill, 'The Demise Clause' (1990) 106 LQR 403.

ambiguity is undesirable when a contracting party only has 12 months under the Hague–Visby Rules in which to institute his action. Some jurisdictions refuse to give effect to such clauses, while others construe them strictly. However its validity was recognized in this country in *The Berkshire*.[28] The shippers consigned 528 compressed bales of cotton from New York to the second plaintiffs in Massawa, Ethiopia, aboard the *Lancashire*, a vessel operating under a time charter. The bills of lading issued by the charterers contained a demise clause. On the charterer's instructions, the cargo was discharged at Jeddah and transhipped on another vessel (which was not owned by the shipowners). On arrival in Massawa the cargo was found to have been damaged by sea water. When the receivers in Massawa claimed damages for £5119.56, the shipowners denied liability. Brandon J held that the contract evidenced by the bill of lading was one between the shippers and shipowners, and not one between the shippers and the charterers. He went on to say that:

> All the demise clause does is to spell out in unequivocal terms that the bill of lading is intended to be a shipowners' bill of lading. The charterparty entitled the charterers to present to the master for signature by him on the shipowners' behalf, or to sign themselves on the same behalf, bills of lading of that kind . . . In my view [the demise clause] . . . is an entirely usual and ordinary one.[29]

A demise clause does not offend against article III, rule 8 of the Hague–Visby Rules[30] as it does not seek to exclude liability. Its aim is merely to identify the party liable under the Rules. As an alternative to a demise clause,[31] the charterer might avoid liability by inserting an 'Identity of Carrier' clause in the bill of lading. This clearly designates the shipowner as carrier and is regarded by some as being more acceptable than a demise clause. A number of cases in recent years have sought to rationalize these clauses, but they have, on the whole, produced rather contradictory results.[32] The matter has, however, been authoritatively settled by the House of Lords in *Homburg Houtimport BV v Agrosin Private Ltd (The Starsin)*,[33] a decision to which we now return.[34]

The Starsin   The *Starsin*, a vessel of about 27,000 tonnes, was demise chartered by her   **12.13** registered owners and the demise charterer fixed the *Starsin* on NYPE terms to Continental Pacific Shipping Ltd (CPS). Various cargoes of timber and timber products were loaded at Malaysian ports and, although some of the cargo was wetted by rain before shipment, clean bills of lading were issued. The cargo was also improperly stowed and seventeen consignments

---

[28] [1974] 1 Lloyd's Rep 185.

[29] At 188.

[30] See para 19.39.

[31] Such clauses have been heavily criticized, but this was rejected by Hirst J in *Ngo Chew Hong Edible Oil Pty Ltd v Scindia Steam Navigation Co Ltd (The Jalamohan)* [1988] 1 Lloyd's Rep 443, 450. See William Tetley, 'The Demise of the Demise clause?' (1999) 44 McGill LJ 807.

[32] See *The Berkshire* [1974] 1 Lloyd's Rep 185; *The Venezuela* [1980] 1 Lloyd's Rep 393; *The Rewia* [1991] 2 Lloyd's Rep 325; *MB Pyramid Sound NV v Briese Schiffahrts GmbH & Co KG MS Sina (The Ines) (No 2)* [1995] 2 Lloyd's Rep 144; *Sunrise Maritime Inc v Uvisco Ltd (The Hector)* [1998] 2 Lloyd's Rep 287; *Fetim BV v Oceanspeed Shipping Ltd (The Flecha)* [1999] 1 Lloyd's Rep 612.

[33] [2003] UKHL 12; [2004] 1 AC 715. See Stephen Girvin, 'Contracting carriers, Himalaya clauses, and Tort in the House of Lords: *The Starsin*' [2003] LMCLQ 311; Edwin Peel, 'Actual carriers and the Hague Rules' (2004) 120 LQR 11.

[34] See the earlier discussion in the context of Himalaya clauses: para 9.29.

were out-turned seriously damaged by water. The claimants in the proceedings were the 'notify parties' of the cargo[35] to whom the relevant bills of lading had been endorsed. They were endorsees of the bills of lading and hence had rights of suit under the Carriage of Goods by Sea Act 1992.[36] All the bills of lading were on liner bill of lading forms clearly marked with CPS's logo. The signature box on the face contained the words 'As Agent for Continental Pacific Shipping (The Carrier)' and below this was a rubber stamp containing the words 'United Pansar Sdn Bhd', being the company which acted as CPS's port agent in Malaysia. The reverse of the bills contained three pertinent clauses: (i) clause 1(c), which provided that 'carrier' meant the party on whose behalf the bill of lading had been signed; (ii) clause 33, which was an identity of carrier clause;[37] (iii) clause 35, which was a demise clause providing that the bill of lading would only take effect as a contract of carriage 'with the owner or demise chartered'. By the time of the present proceedings CPS was insolvent, which doubtless accounted for the willingness of the cargo claimants to pursue the shipowner in contract and, failing that, in tort. In earlier proceedings, Colman J concluded that the bills of lading were charterers' bills[38] and although this was upheld by Rix LJ in the Court of Appeal,[39] the majority, in a much criticized judgment,[40] concluded that the printed clauses on the reverse should be given greater weight. The House of Lords unanimously overturned the majority approach in the Court of Appeal, overruling *The Flecha*,[41] and preferring to take what Lord Steyn described as 'the mercantile view'.[42] This view was developed at greater length by Lord Bingham who restated the importance of construing legal documents commercially[43] and of reading documents in a 'business sense'[44] so as not to frustrate the reasonable expectations of businessmen.[45] This view of the issues underpinned all the speeches by their Lordships, as did their recourse to the provisions of the UCP 500,[46] in particular articles 23(a) and 23(v),[47] which their Lordships saw as confirming that one should look for the identity of the carrier on the face of the bill rather than the clauses on the reverse.[48] Lord Hoffmann thought the majority of the Court of Appeal were wrong in seeking to construe the bill of lading as a whole; on the facts, reading the terms on the reverse was not something that the 'reasonable reader of the bill of lading' did.[49] Given the conflict between the signature on the face and the terms on the reverse, Lord Millett

---

[35] Makros Hout BV, Homburg Houtimport BV, Fetim BV, and Hunter Timber Ltd.

[36] See s 2(1) and s 5(2)(b). See para 8.17 and 8.19.

[37] 'The Contract evidenced by this Bill of Lading is between the Merchant and the Owner of the vessel named herein . . . and it is therefore agreed that said Shipowner only shall be liable for any damage or loss. . .'.

[38] [2000] 1 Lloyd's Rep 85, 93.

[39] [2001] EWCA Civ 56; [2001] 1 Lloyd's Rep 437.

[40] See Charles Debattista, 'Is the end in sight for chartering demise clauses?', *Lloyd's List*, 21 February 2001; Steven Gee, 'Interpretation of commercial contracts' (2001) 117 LQR 358.

[41] *Fetim BV v Oceanspeed Shipping Ltd (The Flecha)* [1999] 1 Lloyd's Rep 612. See [2003] UKHL 12; [2004] 1 AC 715, at [48] (Lord Steyn); [83] (Lord Hoffmann). cf also *The Arktis Sky* [2000] 1 SLR 57.

[42] [2003] UKHL 12; [2004] 1 AC 715, at [46].

[43] See Scrutton (1996), arts 9 & 12.

[44] [2003] UKHL 12; [2004] 1 AC 715, at [10]. See also Lord Millett at [188].

[45] At [12].

[46] The Uniform Customs and Practice for Documentary Credits, 1993 Revision (ICC No 500).

[47] See Jack, Malek & Quest (2001), 215.

[48] [2003] UKHL 12; [2004] 1 AC 715, at [126]. See Lord Bingham at [16]; Lord Steyn at [47]; Lord Hoffmann at [77]–[80]; Lord Millett at [188].

[49] At [82]. See Lord Bingham at [15].

simply stated that it was not appropriate to embark on the unrewarding task of 'attempting to reconcile the irreconcilable'.[50] In his view, the identity of the contracting parties was not something which was capable of variation by the detailed terms and conditions of the contract.[51] Some of their Lordships were also clearly influenced by the fact that bills of lading were addressed not only to the shipper or consignee named on the bill but also to a potentially wider class of third parties.[52] It may be noted that their Lordships refused to countenance an interesting argument that both CPS and the owners were the contractual carriers, a suggestion raised by Rix LJ in the Court of Appeal.[53] The House unanimously held that the language of the bill itself did not support it. The result on this point has been welcomed[54] and indeed the case seems to have produced a strongly commercially outcome. It is a strong endorsement of arguments that it should be possible to identify the contracting parties to the bill of lading with some degree of certainty. Demise clauses, which hitherto provided much fuel for litigation, are now anomalous, both where the bill of lading is on the charterer's standard form and the owner's form. More precise drafting of the definition of 'carrier' and other terms on the reverse of bills of lading[55] should now be a priority.

Circular indemnity clauses Charterers' bills of lading sometimes contain a clause known **12.14** as a 'circular indemnity clause', which seeks to bring about precisely the opposite effect. In such a clause, the party who issues the bill of lading (such as a time charterer) undertakes that it and it only is the contracting carrier and, in return, the shipper undertakes not to sue anyone other than that party, and to indemnify that party against any loss it may suffer as a result of any holder of the bill of lading suing anyone other than it. Such provisions have proved to be of particular importance to carriers operating in consortia and in modern combined transport bills of lading such terms are to be found in the same clause as Himalaya provisions. The clause has been upheld on a number of occasions.[56] Thus, where the bill of lading contains such a clause, the party identified as the contracting carrier may obtain a permanent stay of proceedings brought by a holder of the bill of lading against another party if there is a real possibility that, if the claim is allowed to proceed, the contracting carrier may suffer financial loss by reason of that other party seeking an indemnity from it. Such clauses, like demise clauses, are not caught by article III, rule 8 of the Hague or Hague–Visby Rules — in the event of those rules being applicable — because, although the shipowner is the 'carrier', it is not the 'carrier' of the goods for the purposes of the Hague or Hague–Visby Rules, as it is not a party to the contract of carriage evidenced by the bill of lading.[57]

---

[50] At [182].

[51] At [187].

[52] At [74] (Lord Hoffmann).

[53] [2001] 1 Lloyd's Rep 437 (CA), at [70]–[76]. See William Tetley, 'The House of Lords decision in *The Starsin*' (2004) 25 JMLC 121.

[54] See N Miller, '*Starsin* ruling on carrier identity puts small print in its place', *Lloyd's List*, 19 March 2003.

[55] See Lord Hoffmann's remarks on this point: [2003] UKHL 12; [2004] 1 AC 715, at [71].

[56] See *Nippon Yusen Kaisha v International Import and Export Co Ltd (The Elbe Maru)* [1978] 1 Lloyd's Rep 606; *Broken Hill Co Pty Ltd v Hapag-Lloyd Aktiengesellschaft* [1980] 2 NSWLR 572; *Sidney Cooke Ltd v Hapag-Lloyd Aktiengesellschaft* [1980] 2 NZWLR 587.

[57] *Sidney Cooke Ltd v Hapag-Lloyd Aktiengesellschaft* [1980] 2 NZWLR 587, 594–595 (Yeldham J).

E. Incorporation of Charterparty Terms

12.15 **Introduction** In the case of goods shipped by a third party, the bill of lading will provide prima facie evidence of the terms of the contract of carriage. This may be rebutted by proof of other terms specifically agreed by shipper and carrier. In general, the commercial face of bills of lading are broadly similar. But in the case of a liner bill of lading, such as Conlinebill, the reverse of the bill of lading will contain many typed clauses. A charterparty bill of lading, such as Congenbill,[58] may only have a small number of clauses. The reason for this difference is that it is common, particularly in the case of bulk trades, for bills of lading to be issued which incorporate the terms of the charterparty. But not all bulk cargoes are carried under such bills of lading, especially in the case of highly specialized trades for the carriage of cement or coal. The difficulty comes when construing the terms of an incorporation clause in a general charterparty bill of lading, such as Congenbill. The main difficulty for the bill of lading holder is knowing which charter it is sought to incorporate, because the details may not be identified on the face of the bill of lading, where only the date of issue is recorded. Problems for the bill of lading holder can be especially acute where many of the clauses in the printed form of charterparty have been deleted or there are many added clauses. Even if he has a copy of the charterparty, the bill of lading holder is not likely to have the specialized knowledge of those in the tramp (charterparty) market and so may find that he has incurred onerous liabilities, perhaps for freight or even demurrage. Demurrage liability could equal a high proportion of the value of the cargo. For this reason, most banks opening documentary credits are entitled to reject bills of lading which are subject to charterparties.[59] If the documentary credit does call for the issue of a charterparty bill of lading, then it will, in terms of the UCP 500, be required to conform to the requirements of article 25.

12.16 **Conflicting terms** Generally speaking, the third party will not be bound by any terms of the charterparty which conflict with the terms of the bill of lading or the Hague–Visby Rules, where they are applicable. However, most shipowners will insist on the inclusion, in bills of lading issued to third parties, of a clause incorporating the terms of the charterparty. This clause will be effective so long as steps have been taken to bring it reasonably to the notice of the shipper before or at the time that he enters into the contract of carriage. This was neatly explained by Bingham LJ in *Federal Bulk Carriers Inc v C Itoh & Co Ltd (The Federal Bulker)*:

> Generally speaking, the English law of contract has taken a benevolent view of the use of general words to incorporate by reference standard terms to be found elsewhere. But in the present field a different, and stricter, rule has developed, especially where the incorporation of arbitration clauses is concerned. The reason no doubt is that a bill of lading is a negotiable commercial instrument and may come into the hands of a foreign party with no knowledge and no ready means of knowledge of the terms of the charterparty. The cases show that a strict test of incorporation having, for better or worse, been laid down, the courts have in general defended this rule with some tenacity in the interests of commercial certainty. If commercial parties do not like the English rule, they can meet the difficulty by spelling

---

[58] See Appendix II.
[59] UCP 500, article 23(a)(vi).

out the arbitration provision in the bill of lading and not relying on general words to achieve incorporation.[60]

Effective words of incorporation   The traditional first requirement is that effective words **12.17** of incorporation must be found in the bill of lading itself, without reference to the provisions of the charterparty. This is because so far as the shipper or holder is concerned, his contract is to be found exclusively in the bill of lading. A general reference in the bill of lading to the incorporation of charterparty terms will not enable the court to peruse the provisions of the charterparty in order to discover which precise clauses were intended to be incorporated. In *Skips A/S Nordheim v Syrian Petroleum Co (The Varenna)*,[61] Donaldson MR said that:

> What the shipowners agreed with the charterers, whether in the charterparty or otherwise, is wholly irrelevant, save in so far as the whole or part of any such agreement has become part of the bill of lading contract. Such an incorporation cannot be achieved by agreement between the owners and charterers. It can only be achieved by the agreement of the parties to the bill of lading contract and thus the operative words of incorporation must be found in the bill of lading itself.[62]

In *The Annefield*[63] Brandon J stated that:

> . . . [I]n order to decide whether a clause under a bill of lading incorporates [a] . . . clause in a charterparty it is necessary to look at both the precise words in the bill of lading alleged to do the incorporating, and also the precise terms of the . . . clause in the charterparty alleged to be incorporated.[64]

Lord Denning MR stated that:

> In this case we should read the documents together. I would take the clauses in the charterparty and apply them to the bill of lading in so far as they are reasonably applicable to it: and I would reject the others . . . I would say that a clause which is directly germane to the subject-matter of the bill of lading (that is, to the shipment, carriage and delivery of goods)[65] can and should be incorporated into the bill of lading contract, even though it may involve a degree of manipulation of the words in order to fit exactly the bill of lading. But if the clause is one which is not thus directly germane, it should not be incorporated into the bill of lading contract unless it is done explicitly in clear words either in the bill of lading or in the charterparty.[66]

Problems of identification   Particular difficulties of identification can arise when the bill **12.18** of lading does not make it clear which of a number of charterparties in a string is to apply. The general rule is that any charter under which the goods are carried will be incorporated. Thus, in *Pacific Molasses Co & United Molasses Trading Co Ltd v Entre Rios Compania Naviera SA (The San Nicholas)* Lord Denning MR stated that:

> . . . It seems to me plain that the shipment was carried under and pursuant to the terms of the head charter . . . the head charter was the only charter to which the shipowners were parties: and

---

[60] [1989] 1 Lloyd's Rep 103 (CA), 105.
[61] [1984] 1 QB 599 (CA).
[62] At 615–616.
[63] [1971] P 168 (CA).
[64] At 173.
[65] Or the payment of freight. See *TW Thomas & Co Ltd v Portsea Steamship Co Ltd* [1912] AC 1, 6 (Lord Atkinson).
[66] [1971] P 168 (CA), 184. Adapting the test as laid down in *The Merak* [1965] P 223 (CA), 260 (Russell LJ).

they must, in the bill of lading, be taken to be referring to that head charter. I find myself in agreement with the statement in *Scrutton on Charterparties* (18th ed (1974)), at p 63:

> A general reference will normally be construed as relating to the head charter, since this is the contract to which the shipowner, who issues the bill of lading, is a party . . .[67]

This principle may, however, give way to a sub-charter, especially where the charterer issues the bill of lading.[68] Some of these difficulties arose before Judge Diamond QC in *The Heidberg*.[69] The *Heidberg*, loaded with a cargo of bulk maize shipped c.i.f. at Bordeaux for carriage to New Holland (on the River Humber), collided with a Shell jetty at Bordeaux. Some of the cargo sustained water damage and the balance was transhipped and on-carried to New Holland. The cargo on board the *Heidberg* gave rise, in Judge Diamond QC's words, 'to a tangled web of legal proceedings both in France and England'.[70] The basis of the c.i.f. contract was a contract of affreightment between UNCAC (the first defendants) and another company (Peter Dohle), on the Synacomex form, in terms of which a minimum of six and a maximum of 12 voyages were to be performed, carrying 2,500 tons of bulk maize from France to New Holland. The charterparty contained an arbitration clause which provided for arbitration in Paris. Negotiations for the fixture of the *Heidberg* between a firm of English shipbrokers acting for Peter Dohle and the managers acting for the owners of the *Heidberg* were conducted by telephone on the basis of previous dealings between the parties under a charterparty which had provided for arbitration in London according to English law:

> Centrocon Arbitration Clause (with three months limitation amended to twelve months), in London according to English law.

The English shipbrokers subsequently sent a so-called 'recap telex' to the ship managers referring to the Synacomex form (with Paris arbitration) instead of the earlier charterparty.[71] There was no other written evidence as to the fixture of the *Heidberg* at the time of shipment. When the relevant bill of lading was issued to Grosvenor, an English company, it provided for the arbitration clause of an unidentified charterparty to be incorporated:

> . . . [A]ll the terms, conditions and exceptions of which Charter Party, including the Arbitration clause, are incorporated herewith.

At this time the only charterparty which could be referred to (the Synacomex contract of affreightment) provided for arbitration in Paris. There was merely an oral contract for the charter of the *Heidberg* on the basis of an earlier charterparty; the only written evidence was the recap telex. Grosvenor paid for the cargo and recovered for its loss at Bordeaux from its insurers. Leaving aside the private international law issues in the case, Judge Diamond QC also had to consider whether the Centrocon clause had been incorporated into the bill of lading. There were two questions: first, whether the bill of lading was capable of incorporating a charterparty whose terms had not been reduced to writing by the time the bill of lading was issued and, second, whether the bill of lading incorporated the terms of the

---

[67] [1976] 1 Lloyd's Rep 8 (CA), 11. Cited with approval in *K/S A/S Seateam & Co v Iraq National Oil Co (The Sevonia Team)* [1983] 1 Lloyd's Rep 640, 644 (Lloyd J).

[68] See *Lignell v Samuelson & Co Ltd* (1921) 9 Ll LR 361.

[69] *Partenreederei M/S Heidberg & Vega Reederei Friederich Dauber v Grosvenor Grain & Feed Co Ltd, Union Nationale des Cooperatives Agricoles de Cereales & Assurances Mutuelles Agricoles* [1994] 2 Lloyd's Rep 287.

[70] At 289.

[71] At 293.

earlier charterparty or the contract of affreightment, or neither contract. On the first issue, the judge concluded that:

> I . . . consider that, as a matter of the construction of the bill of lading, it does not incorporate the terms of a charter-party which, at the date the bill of lading is issued, has not been reduced to writing. . . . [A]n oral contract, evidenced only by a recap telex, does not seem to me to qualify for this purpose. I should add moreover that, if I am wrong on this, I would still conclude that the bill of lading does not on its true construction incorporate an oral agreement for arbitration in London which, at the date of the bill of lading, was not evidenced by any document at all. It follows that [the earlier] charterparty fixture . . . was not incorporated in the bill of lading and that, if I am wrong on this, still no clause providing for arbitration in London was incorporated.[72]

On the second issue, he said that:

> In the end I would give weight to two factors; first that the words set out in the bill of lading are more apt to refer to an instrument in writing than to an oral contract evidenced by a recap telex; second, that the parties in my view are more likely to have intended the freight referred to in the bill of lading to be that defined in the contract of affreightment . . . than that defined in the voyage charter. I therefore consider, if it be material and on the assumption set out earlier, that the terms of the contract of affreightment . . . are incorporated in the bill of lading and that those of the [earlier] voyage charter . . . are not.[73]

Description   A related requirement, sometimes called the 'description issue', is that the   **12.19**
words of incorporation must be apt to describe the charterparty clause sought to be incorporated. Thus a whole range of charterparty provisions have been held enforceable against the bill of lading holder, including claims for freight, for dead freight, and demurrage.[74]

'All terms, conditions, and exceptions. . .'   A reference to 'all terms, conditions, and   **12.20**
exceptions to be as per charterparty' would normally be given a limited meaning and taken to refer only to those terms, conditions, and exceptions in the charterparty relating to the main undertakings in the bill of lading agreement. In *TW Thomas & Co Ltd v Portsea Steamship Co Ltd*, Lord Atkinson stated that:

> I think it would be a sound rule of construction to adopt that when it is sought to introduce into a document like a bill of lading — a negotiable instrument — a clause such as this arbitration clause, not germane to the receipt, carriage, or delivery of the cargo or the payment of the freight — the proper subject matters with which the bill of lading is conversant — this should be done by distinct and specific words, and not by such general words as those written in the margin of the bill of lading in this case.[75]

Arbitration clauses not incorporated   In *Skips A/S Nordheim v Syrian Petroleum Co Ltd*   **12.21**
(The Varenna)[76] the incorporation clause stated that:

> All conditions and exceptions of [the] charterparty including the negligence clause are deemed to be incorporated in bill of lading.

---

[72] At 311.

[73] At 312–313. See too *Welex AG v Rosa Maritime Ltd (The Epsilon Rosa)(No 2)* [2003] EWCA Civ 938; [2003] 2 Lloyd's Rep 509 where the Court of Appeal found that the charterparty to be incorporated was readily ascertainable.

[74] But cf *Miramar Maritime Corp v Holborn Oil Trading Ltd (The Miramar)* [1984] 1 AC 676, discussed at para 12.24.

[75] [1912] AC 1, 6.

[76] [1984] 1 QB 599 (CA).

The Court of Appeal held that the phrase 'all conditions and exceptions' was inadequate to describe an arbitration clause since the phrase meant

> such conditions and exceptions as are appropriate to the carriage and delivery of goods and do not, as a matter of ordinary construction, extend to collateral terms such as an arbitration clause even if that clause is expressed . . . in terms which are capable, without modification, of referring to the bill of lading contract.[77]

In *Federal Bulk Carriers Inc v C Itoh & Co Ltd (The Federal Bulker)*[78] a clause provided that:

> All terms conditions and exceptions as per charter-party dated January 20, 1986 and any addenda thereto to be considered as fully incorporated herein as if fully written.

The dispute here arose out of bills of lading on the Baltimore Form C Berth Grain Bill of Lading form, which recorded the shipment, in good order and condition, of quantities of soya beans. The bills of lading were negotiated to nine cargo receivers, who took delivery of the goods but complained that the goods had been delivered in a damaged condition. They and the charterers of the *Federal Bulker* commenced arbitration proceedings against the owners but the owners challenged the arbitrators' jurisdiction. Had there been an effective incorporation of the charterparty arbitration clause? Noting the earlier House of Lords authority of *TW Thomas & Co Ltd v Portsea Steamship Co Ltd*,[79] Bingham LJ said that:

> I do not think that this authority can be distinguished on grounds that the words in question were used in a different context nor on the ground that arbitration clauses were in 1911 viewed with less favour than they are today. It seems to me that this is clear authority, binding on us, that general language of the kind used here is not sufficient to incorporate an arbitration clause.[80]

He noted that in *Skips A/S Nordheim v Syrian Petroleum Co Ltd (The Varenna)*[81] the bill of lading had made reference to conditions and not terms. If the expression 'terms' had been used, he thought that Donaldson MR would have been bound to have reached the same conclusion.

12.22 Arbitration clauses incorporated The older case law on the incorporation of arbitration clauses is notable in highlighting a lack of certainty in the terms of the incorporation clause. This changed, however, in *Daval Aciers D'Unisor et de Sacilor v Armare SRL (The Nerano)*.[82] Here a consignment of 248 cylinder steel coils were shipped aboard the *Nerano* at Fos (in France) for carriage to Masra el Brega in Libya. The bill of lading for the goods was signed by Cargill International SA but contained an identity of carrier clause, the effect of which was that the contract of carriage was initially between DAU (the first plaintiffs) as shippers and the shipowners (the defendants). On the face of the bill of lading appeared the following clause:

> The conditions as per relevant charterparty dated 02.07.1990 are incorporated in this bill of lading and have precedence if there is a conflict. English Law and Jurisdiction applied.

Clause 1 of the conditions on the reverse provided

> All terms and conditions liberties exceptions and arbitration clause of the Charterparty, dated as overleaf, are herewith incorporated.

[77] At 619.
[78] [1989] 1 Lloyd's Rep 103 (CA).
[79] [1912] AC 1.
[80] [1989] 1 Lloyd's Rep 103 (CA), 107. See also Butler-Sloss LJ at 109.
[81] [1984] 1 QB 599 (CA).
[82] [1996] 1 Lloyd's Rep 1 (CA).

The reference to a charterparty was to a voyage charter, on the Gencon 1976 form, between Cargill as owners and the charterers (the fourth plaintiffs). The plaintiffs claimed damages in respect of alleged sea water damage and rusting to 71 of the coils and served a writ on the defendant shipowners. They contended that the arbitration clause had not been incorporated. The shipowners, however, contended that the contract of carriage contained in or evidenced by the bill of lading contained an arbitration clause and that they were entitled to a stay of action under section 1 of the then Arbitration Act 1975 (as amended).[83] Saville LJ confirmed that it was necessary to read the provisions on the front and on the back of the bill of lading.[84] In doing so he concluded that:

> In the present case the parties have not merely used general words of incorporation. They have expressly identified and specified the charter-party arbitration clause as something to be incorporated into their contract. Such a clause does not impose unusual burdens on the parties: it is a common agreement in contracts of all kinds for the carriage of goods by sea. On the contrary, by identifying and specifying the charter-party arbitration clause it seems to me to be clear that the parties to the bill of lading contract did intend and agree to arbitration, so that to give force to that intention and agreement the words in the clause must be read and construed as applying to those parties. Indeed it seems to me that it would be an extraordinary result if English law reached a different conclusion.[85]

In *The Delos*[86] the claimants were the lawful holders of bills of lading relating to various cargoes carried aboard the *Delos* from Brazil to India during 1998. The charterparty for the *Delos* provided that disputes were to be settled by arbitration in London. The bills of lading were in two forms: (1) bills for soya bean oil, on the Congenbill form, providing for the incorporation of the charterparty law and arbitration clause; (2) bills for other cargoes, providing that 'all the terms whatsoever of the said charter . . . apply to and govern the rights of the parties'. The claimants alleged that the cargoes were delivered underweight, that one was short delivered and contaminated with sea water. The shipowner sought to stay the action under section 9 of the Arbitration Act 1996, on the basis that the bills of lading incorporated the arbitration clause. The court granted the stay in respect of the Congenbill bills but not the ocean bills because they did not make any express reference to an arbitration clause and nor did the arbitration clauses in the charterparty refer to the bills. The court confirmed that arbitration clauses were not directly germane to the carriage nor were collateral to it. While the word 'whatsoever' was a word of considerable width, its interpretation in other contexts was of assistance in the present context where the need for express incorporation has been long established by authority.

Exclusive jurisdiction clauses   The courts have adopted a similar interpretation to the attempt to incorporate exclusive jurisdiction clauses. In *Siboti K/S v BP France SA*[87] a charterparty clause stated that: **12.23**

> (a) This Charter Party shall be construed and interpreted in accordance with, and governed by, the laws of England.

---

[83] See now s 9 of the Arbitration Act 1996.
[84] [1996] 1 Lloyd's Rep 1 (CA), 4.
[85] ibid.
[86] [2001] 1 Lloyd's Rep 703.
[87] [2003] EWHC 1278 (Comm); [2003] 2 Lloyd's Rep 364.

(b) ... any dispute of whatsoever nature arising under this Charter Party shall be determined by the English [Court] ... and the parties hereby expressly submit to the exclusive jurisdiction of the English ... Courts ...

(e) All bills of lading under this Charter Party shall incorporate this exclusive dispute resolution clause. . .

Bills of lading issued for a cargo shipped at Malta acknowledged shipment in apparent good order and condition. The bills of lading provided that:

> This shipment is carried under and pursuant to the terms of the charter dated ... between ... and all the terms whatsoever of the said charter apply to and govern the rights of the parties concerned in this shipment.

The cargo was discharged at Sete into shoretanks for the the ultimate purchaser of the cargo. As the charterer failed to pay any of the freight or loadport demurrage which was alleged to be due in respect of the carriage of the cargo from India, the shipowner asserted a lien over the cargo and obtained from the French court two *saisies conservatoire* to secure its claim to the freight and demurrage. In the current proceedings, the shipowner sought to recover from the defendant (the ultimate purchaser of the cargo) the amounts allegedly outstanding for the freight and demurrage. The shipowner alleged that, as endorsee of the bills of lading, the final purchaser was the holder pursuant to section 2(1) of the Carriage of Goods by Sea Act, and so was subject to the outstanding liabilities pursuant to section 3(1) of that Act, which included freight and demurrage. The defendant inter alia contended that the exclusive jurisdiction clause in the charterparty had not been validly incorporated into the bill of lading and that the claim should be set aside. The court held that, on the authorities, general wording such as 'all terms' was insufficient to incorporate an ancillary charterparty arbitration clause and that the same result must follow with regard to the charterparty jurisdiction clauses. With or without the word 'whatsoever', the incorporation wording in the bill of lading was general wording and not sufficient to incorporate the exclusive jurisdiction clause into the bill of lading. Had the original parties to the bill of lading intended to do so, they could have put the matter beyond argument by adding to the language of incorporation in the bill of lading the words 'including the dispute resolution clause'.

12.24 **Consistency**   The third requirement (sometimes called the 'consistency issue') is that the charterparty clause, when incorporated, must be consistent with the remaining terms of the bill of lading. If there is a conflict, the terms of the bill of lading will prevail over those in the charterparty. In *Miramar Maritime Corp v Holborn Oil Trading Ltd (The Miramar)*,[88] the shipowner on the insolvency of the charterer sought to invoke an incorporation clause in order to recover demurrage due under the charterparty from a bill of lading holder. Although the incorporation clause was broadly drafted to incorporate the charterparty provisions verbatim, the provisions of Exxonvoy 1969, clause 8 explicitly stated that 'charterer shall pay demurrage'. The House of Lords held that only the charterer was liable for demurrage. Lord Diplock outlined the practical effect of any other construction:

> [The suggested verbal manipulation would have the effect that] every consignee to whom a bill of lading covering any part of the cargo is negotiated, is not only accepting personal liability to pay the owner's freight, as stated in the bill of lading, but is also accepting

---

[88] [1984] 1 AC 676.

blindfold a potential liability to pay an unknown and wholly unpredictable sum for demurrage which may, unknown to him, already have accrued or may subsequently accrue without any ability on his own part to prevent it, even though that sum may actually exceed the delivered value of the goods to which the bill of lading gives title.

My Lords, I venture to assert that no business man who had not taken leave of his senses would intentionally enter into a contract which exposed him to a potential liability of this kind; and this, in itself, I find to be an overwhelming reason for not indulging in verbal manipulation of the actual contractual words used in the charterparty so as to give them this effect when they are treated as incorporated in the bill of lading.

. . . [T]his House should take this opportunity of stating unequivocally that, where in a bill of lading there is included a clause which purports to incorporate the terms of a specified charterparty, there is not any rule of construction that clauses in that charterparty which are directly germane to the shipment, carriage or delivery of goods and impose obligations upon the 'charterer' under that designation, are presumed to be incorporated in the bill of lading with the substitution of (where there is a cesser clause), or inclusion in (where there is no cesser clause), the designation 'charterer', the designation 'consignee of the cargo' or 'bill of lading holder'.[89]

Avoidance of difficulties   The criticism of incorporation clauses, when they are invoked **12.25** against the endorsee of a bill of lading or where there are a series of sub-charters which refer to a charterparty but do not specify which one, is well made. One way to avoid any difficulties would be to require that a copy of the relevant charterparty be attached to the bill.

F. Bills of Lading Transferred to a Third Party

Generally   When a bill of lading is endorsed by a charterer to a third party bona fide pur- **12.26** chaser, the terms of the bill of lading will supplant the charterparty and become conclusive evidence of the contract of carriage. A difficulty is that the Carriage of Goods by Sea Act 1992, section 2(1) (and its predecessor, section 1 of the Bills of Lading Act 1855) vests in the lawful holder of a bill of lading, by virtue of becoming holder, 'all rights of suit under the contract of carriage as if he had been a party to that contract'.[90] Prior to endorsement of the bill of lading the terms of the contract would be found in the charterparty and the bill of lading would be a mere receipt in the hands of the charterer. It has been suggested that, in such cases, the view of Lord Atkin in *Tate and Lyle Ltd v Hain Steamship Co Ltd* should be followed, namely that, on endorsement of the bill by the charterer,

the consignee has not assigned to him the obligations under the charterparty, nor in fact any obligation of the charterer under the bill of lading, for *ex hypothesi* there is none. A new contract appears to spring up between the ship and the consignee on the terms of the bill of lading.[91]

If the Hague–Visby Rules apply, then the bill of lading 'regulates the relations between . . . carrier and holder' (Article I(b)).

---

[89] At 684–685; 688.
[90] See para 8.17.
[91] (1936) 55 Ll LR 159 (HL), 174.

12.27   **The shipowner's recourse against charterer**   The liability of the shipowner could be considerable where the charterer has the right to issue bills of lading. This is particularly so when the provisions of the Hague–Visby Rules become applicable after the bill of lading has been endorsed to a third party. However, where there are clauses which require the master to sign bills presented by the charterer, these will usually be coupled with provisions requiring the charterer to indemnify the shipowner for any resulting increase in cargo liability.[92] Even if there is not such an express clause, there is authority for the view that there is

> an implied term in the charterparty to the effect that, in case the charterers should present — or cause to be presented — bills of lading imposing a greater liability on the shipowners than that contained in the charterparty, the charterers would indemnify the shipowners in respect of that greater liability.[93]

---

[92] See Baltime 1939, cl 9.
[93] *Coast Lines Ltd v Hudig & Veder Chartering NV* [1972] 2 QB 34, 42–43 (Lord Denning MR).

13

PAPERLESS TRADING

A. Introduction

Overview   Having in the previous chapters considered all the traditional topics con-   **13.01**
cerned with paper bills of lading, we now move on to a consideration of the impact of the
development of paperless alternatives.

B. Background

Terminology   Electronic Data Interchange (EDI)[1] is the computer-to-computer trans-   **13.02**
mission of standard business documents. It must be understood that such transmissions
can cover the whole gamut of dealings between businessmen in their interactions with each
other across the globe. There is, for example, already a system called SWIFT,[2] which is in
common use by the banking industry for the communication of commercial letters of
credit among banks worldwide. It is said that computers are used 'to communicate with
those outside the firm: suppliers, customers, transporters, financiers, banks, and insurers in
inter-firm communications'.[3]

---

[1] Generally, see Todd (1998) and the articles in *Electronic Data Interchange*, (1997) 32 ETL 643. For an
earlier attempt to map EDI, see Diana Faber, 'Electronic bills of lading' [1996] LMCLQ 232.

[2] The Society for Worldwide Inter-Bank Financial Telecommunications was established in 1972 to 'facilitate the transmission of bank-to-bank financial transaction messages'. More than a million messages per day
are transmitted on the SWIFT network (including letters of credit and bank guarantees). It is based in
Belgium and has 3,000 member banks worldwide. It is reckoned that over 800 million messages were carried
by SWIFT in 1997. The average daily value of payment messages is estimated to be above US$2 trillion.

[3] See Amelia H Boss 'The emerging law of international electronic commerce' (1992) 6 Temple ICLJ 293, 294.

13.03 **Paper bills of lading** In the context of the carriage of goods by sea, the paper bill of lading is traditionally perceived to have the following advantages: rights represented by the bill of lading can be transferred by endorsement and delivery; it is reliable collateral for the financing of international trade; it is possible to determine title to goods by means of a visual inspection of the bill of lading; the terms and conditions of the contract of carriage are contained in the bill of lading itself. There are, however, a number of equally serious disadvantages, such as delayed arrival at the destination port because of a detour to a bank for the purpose of securing a documentary credit;[4] the high cost of issuing and processing the documents;[5] problems of fraud; problems of inaccurate or insufficient information.

13.04 **Technological advances** Technological advances in the field of maritime commerce, including faster ships and containerized cargo processing, have provided an impetus for the revision of current transport documentation procedures, the adoption of electronic bills of lading, and the increased use of sea waybills. As the result of technological advances, goods arrive at the port of destination much quicker than formerly. It is possible for containerized cargo to be loaded and unloaded more quickly and, with multimodal transport, the goods can remain on the same vehicle or in the same container, which is then moved from one form of transport to the next. Yet the traditional bill of lading still moves at the same slow pace. The use of electronic bills of lading would help to solve the problems caused by delayed arrival of the bill of lading (congestion, delayed delivery of the goods, and also possible demurrage costs). There are few practical difficulties associated with EDI systems and non-negotiable bills of lading. The same is not, however, true of negotiable bills of lading. As we have already noted, negotiable bills are needed when ownership of the goods is to be transferred while the goods are in transit (frequently the case with commodities), or when the seller requires a document of title as security for payment, or when payment is made by documentary credit. There are also practical problems because many Customs and Excise authorities require paper bills of lading. There are also parts of the world which simply do not have the requisite technology. Finally, there is a lack of compatibility between computer systems.

13.05 **Legal problems** A number of legal problems arise. Among the more significant of these is whether an electronic signature is to be treated as the equivalent of a manual one and whether an electronic message can be treated as a 'document'. In respect of the latter point, the United Kingdom Interpretation Act 1978 defines writing to include 'typing, printing, lithography, photography and other modes of representing or reproducing words in a visible form . . .'.[6] This would not appear, in principle, to include an electronic message, which is not, of itself, visible but this has been modified by the Electronic Communications Act 2000.[6A] A final legal point is whether electronic messages could be documents of title. In this respect provision is made for regulations to be made pursuant to the Carriage of Goods

---

   [4] See the description of the so-called paper trail in shipping transactions: Richard Brett Kelly, 'The CMI Charts a Course on the Sea of Electronic Data Interchange: Rules for Electronic Bills of Lading' (1992) 16 Tulane MLJ 349, 353.

   [5] In 1989 a report of the Commission of the European Communities estimated that 'in the transport industry, the cost of raising conventional documents and the attendant delays involved in their issuance and verification constitute 10 to 15% of total transportation costs': cited in Yiannopoulos (1995) 18.

   [6] c 30, Schedule I.

   [6A] See particularly Part II of the Act.

by Sea Act 1992 to extend its provisions to cases where telecommunications systems (such as EDI) are used.[7] Even if such regulations were enacted, it is questionable whether banks would accept electronic messages as security and also whether it would be possible to pass property in the goods using an electronic bill.

C. Seadocs

Introduction   The first attempt at an electronic bill of lading system was through SeaDocs **13.06**
Registry Limited (SeaDocs),[8] a joint project of Chase Manhattan Bank and INTERTANKO.[9]
The initiative resulted from the fundamental changes in the oil markets in the period since 1973 and, in particular, following a rapid growth in trading.[10] During the 1970s and early 1980s a bill of lading could very easily represent a single cargo worth anything up to US$40million. Shipowners were constantly faced with the problem of arriving at the destination and having to discharge cargo without having original bills of lading presented to them. One of the reasons why the SeaDocs project was started was because it is rather common in the oil trading business for cargoes of crude oil or petroleum products to be sold and resold numerous times.[11] This situation resulted in a network of letters of indemnity issued to cover the financial and discharging risks.[12] The SeaDocs project, which started in 1986, ultimately lasted less than a year. It was intended for the electronic negotiation of bills of lading issued for oil shipments, specifically for North Sea crude oils.

Method   SeaDocs was set up to act as a depository and custodian of the paper based origi- **13.07**
nal bill of lading as well as a registry of bill of lading negotiations. It acted as agent for all the parties in the transaction, with authority to endorse the bill of lading and effect transfers of ownership during transit. In addition it had authority to deliver the original paper bill of lading to the final consignee. Under the system set up under SeaDocs, a bill of lading was issued by the carrier in the traditional paper form, but then taken out of circulation and sent to SeaDocs by courier for safekeeping. Upon delivery of the original to SeaDocs, the shipper was given a code or test key (akin to a bank PIN number). When the bill was negotiated the shipper/seller would notify SeaDocs by computer of the buyer's (or endorsee's) name and also provide the endorsee with a portion of the shipper's test key. The seller's message was to be tested by SeaDocs before it accepted the communication from the endorsee buyer. Likewise, the endorsee buyer's message was also tested and accepted if it contained the portion of the original seller's test key. After this process was completed, the name of the new buyer was recorded in the registry and also entered on the documentary bill of lading in SeaDocs' vault. When the goods arrived at the port of discharge, SeaDocs was to have

---

[7] Section 1(5)l(6).
[8] See Boris Kozolchyk, 'Evolution and Present State of the Ocean Bill of Lading from a Banking Law Perspective' (1992) 23 JMLC 161, 227.
[9] The International Association of Independent Tanker Owners. See their website, <www.intertanko.com>.
[10] See Stopford (1997), 303.
[11] See FL de May, 'News' [1985/86] 8 OGLTR D93–D94; 'A Registry for Bills of Lading' [1986/87] 3 OGLTR 65–69.
[12] See RM Wiseman, 'Transaction Chains in North Sea Oil Cargoes' (1984) 2 JENRL 134.

transmitted an identifying code number to the ship's master. A similar identifying code number was to be sent to the last endorsee or owner of record of the original bill of lading. Use of the codes allowed the last endorsee to claim the goods. SeaDocs did not entirely eliminate paper documents owing to the apparent legal difficulties of doing so.

13.08 **Reasons for failure** Although the system and process were well received by those in the oil trade, the concept never really took off because of the following practical reasons:[13] there was no sector of the industry that perceived a clear benefit from the Registry; the legal complexity of the bill of lading — because it performed so many functions for so many people it was impossible to devise a simple system which could satisfy all interested parties and escape potential conflicts of interest; insurance costs were formidable (assuming insurance was available) — said to be a risk of $20 million for one error in 10,000 — and the P & I Clubs were not supportive; the cost of the central registry — which carriers were not interested in paying for and which traders did not wish to pay a fee of $500 or more for using (per transfer); the major traders were wary about having all of their trades recorded in a central location and hence readily available to unscrupulous competitors or intrusive governments; reticence by the ultimate buyers of spot crude oil to acquire bills of lading from an entity designed to service intermediaries and speculators; the banks' discomfort at the exclusive control of the registry business by one of their competitors; the banks' discomfort that they were bound by all their strict obligations under letters of credit but were deprived of the opportunity to inspect the documents themselves. Nevertheless, notwithstanding its demise, SeaDocs proved that it was possible for an international, centralized (and largely electronic) bill of lading system to work reliably on a worldwide basis.

D. The CMI Rules for Electronic Bills of Lading

13.09 **Introduction** The Comité Maritime International (CMI) on 29 June 1990 adopted its Rules for Electronic Bills of Lading.[14] Efforts to produce these Rules had begun in the early 1980s and came to fruition following the appointment of a CMI International Sub-Committee.[15]

13.10 **Voluntariness** The CMI Rules are entirely voluntary — they do not have the force of law and are effective only when contracted for between the parties.[16]

13.11 **Definitions** Various definitions are provided in Rule 2. Thus, Rule 2(b) provides that:

> 'EDI' means Electronic Data Interchange, i.e. the interchange of trade data effected by teletransmission.

The contract of carriage for the purpose of the Rules is set out in Rule 2(a):

> 'Contract of Carriage' means any agreement to carry goods wholly or partly by sea.

---

[13] See Kathy Love, 'SeaDocs: The Lessons Learned' (1992) 2 OGLTR 53.
[14] See Richard Brett Kelly, 'The CMI Charts a Course on the Sea of Electronic Data Interchange: Rules for Electronic Bills of Lading' (1992) 16 Tulane MLJ 349; Todd (1998), 158.
[15] See George F Chandler III, 'The Electronic Transmission of Bills of Lading' (1989) 20 JMLC 571.
[16] Rule 1.

The Rules therefore provide for carriage of goods which travel only partly by sea. Presumably this would include multimodal contracts of carriage, even where there was only a short sea leg. The Rules then go on to provide that the Uniform Rules of Conduct for Interchange of Trade Data by Teletransmission (UNCID) of 1987[17] will apply to the extent that they are not in conflict with the Rules. Further, the Rules provide that the contract of carriage will be subject to any international convention or national law which would have been compulsorily applicable if a paper bill of lading had been issued.[18] Although the suggested computer format for transmission is UN/EDIFACT, a United Nations standard commercial format, other standards may be adopted if so desired.[19] One of the unique EDI requirements in the Rules is that all transmissions must be confirmed before they are acted upon.[20]

Method   The essence of the CMI system is set out in Rule 4. This provides for an electronic **13.12** document containing information similar to that on a paper bill of lading to be sent by the carrier to an electronic address specified by the shipper. Thus, in addition to information such as the name of the shipper, the description of the goods, the date and place of the receipt of the goods, and reference to the carrier's terms and conditions of carriage, a 'private key' must be sent to the shipper to be used in subsequent transactions.[21] This private key is described as unique to each successive holder and is not transferable by the holder.[22] The private key issued by the carrier to the shipper is known only by the shipper and the carrier. The code used must be 'separate and distinct' from any other security passwords or system access codes.[23] The carrier is only obliged to send a confirmation of an electronic message to the last holder to whom it issued a private key when such a holder secured the transmission containing such an electronic message by the use the private key.[24] The shipper is required to confirm the receipt message to the carrier, whereupon the shipper becomes the 'holder'.[25] The holder, as he now is, can subsequently demand that the receipt message be updated with the date and place of shipment as soon as the goods have been loaded on board.[26] The shipper (and any subsequent holder) can transfer the so-called 'right of control and transfer' in the private key to a subsequent holder by Rule 7(b):

A transfer of the Right of Control and Transfer shall be effected:

(i)   by notification of the current Holder to the carrier of its intention to transfer its Right of Control and Transfer to a proposed new Holder, and

(ii) confirmation by the carrier of such notification message, whereupon

---

[17] ICC Publication No 452.

[18] Rule 6.

[19] Rule 3(b).

[20] Rule 3(d).

[21] Rule 4(b). Such information is stated to 'have the same force and effect as if the receipt message were contained in a paper bill of lading': Rule 4(d).

[22] Rule 8(a).

[23] Rule 8(c).

[24] Rule 8(b).

[25] Rule 4(b). See also Rule 7(a) — which provides that the holder is 'the only party' who can claim delivery of the goods, nominate the consignee, transfer rights of control and transfer to another party, and instruct the carrier on any other subject concerning the goods.

[26] Rule 4(c).

(iii)   the carrier shall transmit the information as referred to in Article 4 (except for the Private Key) to the proposed new Holder, whereafter

(iv)   the proposed new Holder shall advise the carrier of its acceptance of the Right of Control and Transfer, whereupon

(v)   the carrier shall cancel the current Private Key and issue a new Private Key to the new Holder.

Rule 7(c) allows the proposed new holder to advise the carrier that he refuses to accept the transfer, and requires the carrier to assume this unless the new holder accepts within a reasonable time. In this event, the carrier advises the current holder and the current private key retains its validity. The effect of the transfer of the right of control and transfer is the same as a transfer of such rights under a paper bill of lading.[27] It is important to note that any transfers of rights to the goods in question are confidential and 'shall not be released to any outside party not connected to the transport or clearance of the goods'.[28]

13.13   Delivery   The carrier is required to notify the holder of the place and date of intended delivery of the goods. The holder on notification must then nominate a consignee and give adequate delivery instructions to the carrier with verification by the private key. In the absence of such notification, the holder will be deemed to be the consignee.[29] The carrier must then deliver the goods to the consignee upon production of 'proper' identification.[30] The carrier will not be liable for misdelivery if he can prove that he has exercised reasonable care in ascertaining that the party who claimed to be the consignee was in fact that person.[31]

13.14   Paper   The Rules provide that the holder has the option at any time prior to the delivery of the goods to demand from the carrier a paper bill of lading.[32] In such an event, however, the carrier will not be responsible for delays in delivering the goods resulting from the holder exercising this option.[33] The carrier also has the option at any time prior to delivery to issue a paper bill of lading, unless such issue would result in undue delay or disrupt the delivery of the goods.[34] If either of these options is selected the private key would be cancelled and the procedures for EDI under the Rules would be terminated.[35]

13.15   Problems   The CMI Rules appear to be very promising, at least at a first glance. However, there are a number of potential disadvantages of the scheme. First, there is no provision for the transfer of contractual rights and liabilities along with the documentation. Thus if the carrier were to refuse to deliver to the eventual holder, he would be in breach of contract, but only the original holder would be able to sue him. It may be that section 2(4) of the Carriage of Goods by Sea Act 1992 would be of assistance.[36] A second potential problem is that it is not self-evident what would happen should a holder, who has accepted the right of control and transfer, not pay for the goods. Here the seller might be advised to require

---

[27] Rule 7(d).
[28] Rule 3(f).
[29] Rule 9(a).
[30] Rule 9(b).
[31] Rule 9(c).
[32] Rule 10(a).
[33] ibid.
[34] Rule 10(b).
[35] Rule 10(d).
[36] See para 8.27.

payment by what would amount to an electronic equivalent of a documentary credit and only to transfer any right of control and transfer to a reputable bank against payment. A third difficulty with the Rules is that no provision is made for the passing of property (ie title) in the goods. This difficulty may of course also be encountered in the paper equivalent. It would be necessary for the parties to make appropriate provision for the passing of property in the contract of sale. The chief criticism of the Rules has come from the banking community which is uneasy about the switch to EDI and the lack of any specified security. Notwithstanding the extensive use of SWIFT, the switch to EDI for most banks is a significant, even dangerous, change. Should the banks accept the CMI Rules, they would have to interface with networks which are not subject to their security. In the United States, for example, bankers object to the CMI Rules because of their endorsement of UN/EDIFACT standards, when US Banks use the ASNI X12 system.[37]

E. The UNCITRAL Model Law on Electronic Commerce

Introduction The Secretariat of UNCITRAL recommended that a Working Group **13.16** investigate this area in 1991.[38] The Working Group's preliminary recommendations were accepted in 1992 and it was then charged with developing laws to facilitate EDI. A draft Model Law was produced in 1995 and adopted by UNCITRAL on 12 June 1996.[39] It is important to note that the Model Law is intended to apply to any kind of information which is transferred in the form of a data message used in commercial activities. Bills of lading therefore constitute but one of the documents which come within the scope of the Model Law. It was recognized during the Working Group's activities that a study on the negotiability and transferability of EDI transport documents could not be avoided. This was brought to prominence following a proposal by the United Kingdom.[40] UNCITRAL then requested the assistance of the CMI and an ad hoc group of experts was formed and met in London during 1995. They proceeded to draft an article concerning maritime transport, which was termed article 'X'. This draft article eventually became Articles 16 and 17 of the Model Law.

Purpose The purpose of the Model Law is to provide national legislators with a set of inter- **13.17** nationally acceptable rules which states could enact in a single statute. The Model Law does not seek to prescribe which technical methods must be used as substitutes for conventional documents — nor does it seek to change or extend definitions of such words as 'writing', 'signature', and 'original', stretching their ordinary and expected meanings to cover computer techniques. The Model Law takes what is termed as a 'functional equivalent' approach. The essence of this approach entails identifying the essential purpose and function of a

---

[37] See Boris Kozolchyk, 'Evolution and Present State of the Ocean Bill of Lading from a Banking Law Perspective' (1992) 23 JMLC 161, 237–240.

[38] For discussion see George F Chandler III, 'Maritime Electronic Commerce for the Twenty-First Century' (1998) 22 Tulane MLJ 463, 488; John Livermore & Krailerk Euarjai, 'Electronic Bills of Lading and Functional Equivalence' (1998) 2 JILT 4; RIL Howland, 'UNCITRAL Model Law on Electronic Commerce' (1997) 32 ETL 703.

[39] See *UNCITRAL Model Law on Electronic Commerce with Guide to Enactment 1996* (UN, May 1997).

[40] See UN Doc A/CN.9/WG.IV/WP.66 (1995).

traditional method and deriving from that the criteria which must be met by electronic messages or records, if they are to be as legally recognized as the corresponding paper documents performing the same function.[41]

13.18 **Provisions** The first fifteen articles of the Model Law have no direct application to maritime commerce, though they are essential if maritime commerce is to be performed in an electronic environment. Chapter I of the Model Law contains general provisions concerned with Law's sphere of application (Article 1), definitions (Article 2), interpretation (Article 3), and variation by agreement (Article 4). Chapter II is concerned with the application of legal requirements to data messages — thus there are provisions concerning writing (Article 6), signatures (Article 7), and originals (Article 8).

13.19 **Carriage of goods** Part Two of the Model Law is concerned with electronic commerce in specific areas, the first being carriage of goods. Article 16 ('Actions related to contracts of carriage of goods') is concerned with various actions that would have been recorded on separate pieces of paper as the goods were processed for transport. It provides that:

> Without derogating from the provisions of part one of this Law, this chapter applies to any action in connection with, or in pursuance of, a contract of carriage of goods, including but not limited to:
> (a) (i)   furnishing the marks, number, quantity or weight of goods;
>   (ii) stating or declaring the nature or value of goods;
>   (iii) issuing a receipt for goods;
>   (iv) confirming that goods have been loaded;
> (b) (i)   notifying a person of terms and conditions of the contract;
>   (ii) giving instructions to a carrier;
> (c) (i)   claiming delivery of goods;
>   (ii) authorising release of goods;
>   (iii) giving notice of loss of, or damage to, goods;
> (d) giving any other notice or statement in connection with the performance of the contract;
> (e) undertaking to deliver goods to a named person or a person authorised to claim delivery;
> (f) granting, acquiring, renouncing, surrendering, transferring or negotiating rights in goods;
> (g) acquiring or transferring rights and obligations under the contract.

Article 17 ('Transport documents') provides that:

> (1) Subject to paragraph (3), where the law requires that any action referred to in article 16 be carried out in writing or by using a paper document, that requirement is met if the action is carried out by using one or more data messages.
> (2) Paragraph (1) applies whether the requirement therein is in the form of an obligation or whether the law simply provides consequences for failing either to carry out the action in writing or to use a paper document.
> (3) If a right is to be granted to, or an obligation is to be acquired by, one person and no other person, and if the law requires that, in order to effect this, the right or obligation must be

---

[41] See especially Livermore and Euarjai, 'Electronic Bills of Lading and Functional Equivalence' (1998) 2 JILT 4.

conveyed to that person by the transfer, or use of, a paper document, that requirement is met if the right or obligation is conveyed by using one or more data messages, provided that a reliable method is used to render such data message or messages unique.

(4) For the purposes of paragraph (3), the standard of reliability required shall be assessed in the light of the purpose for which the right or obligation was conveyed and in the light of all the circumstances, including any relevant agreement.

(5) Where one or more data messages are used to effect any action in subparagraphs (f) and (g) of article 16, no paper document used to effect any such action is valid unless the use of data messages has been terminated and replaced by the use of paper documents.

A paper document issued in these circumstances shall contain a statement of such termination. The replacement of data messages by paper documents shall not affect the rights or obligations of the parties involved.

(6) If a rule of law is compulsorily applicable to a contract of carriage of goods which is in, or is evidenced by, a paper document, that rule shall not be inapplicable to such a contract of carriage of goods which is evidenced by one or more data messages by reason of the fact that the contract is evidenced by such data message or messages instead of by a paper document.

(7) The provisions of this article do not apply to the following: [. . .].

F. The Bolero project

Introduction The most successful project on electronic bills of lading is called BOLERO ('Bills of Lading for Europe'),[42] which started in April 1994. Various trials were carried out over a number of years by users based in the United Kingdom, the Netherlands, Sweden, Hong Kong, and the USA.[43] The project is operated by a business consortium of shipping companies, banks, and telecommunications companies with the aim of replacing paper-based shipping documents with an online computerized registry. The London headquarters of Bolero Operations Ltd is owned through a joint venture of the Through Transport (TT) Club, the London-based P & I Club, and SWIFT, which have pledged about US$30million to develop Bolero. Clearly, to guarantee global success, not only large numbers of shippers, carriers, and consignees will have to be committed to it, but so too will banks. Indeed, the banks have been involved in the project right from the very beginning.   **13.20**

Launch Bolero was launched with tests by a selected group of users in 13 countries.[44] The launch programme[45] tested the service and its operational procedures, as well as the *Bolero Rulebook*. The commodity sectors involved in the launch programme included bulk agricultural commodities, chemicals, crude oil, computer products, and processed foodstuffs. The names of the companies involved in the launch programme were announced in a press release on 11 September 1998. Companies in the programme began using Bolero software in December 1998 and the system operated alongside paper-based processes during the first part of 1999. The full commercial launch took place in the second quarter of 1999.   **13.21**

---

[42] See the Bolero website: (<www.bolero.net>).

[43] See, eg, *Mitsui & Co Ltd Commercial Assessment*, July 1997.

[44] Belgium, Brazil, Japan, France, Germany, China (Hong Kong), Italy, Norway, Singapore, Spain, Taiwan, the UK, and the USA.

[45] See *Bolero Launch Programme*, 13 February 1998.

13.22 **Features** The Bolero project[46] seeks to address those legal issues which have been thrown up by the work of the CMI and UNCITRAL in the past. In particular, the initial focus has had to be the use of EDI systems as negotiable bills of lading. The electronic processes used in the project are partially based on the CMI Rules. Thus parties who accede to Bolero agree that their legal relationship will be governed by the *Rulebook* which is binding on all trading parties in the system. The *Rulebook* is concerned with standardization of messages, evidentiary provisions, and further contractual duties of the parties. It also contains clauses on dispute resolution and a choice of law in favour of English law. The Bolero electronic bill of lading is defined as follows:

> An instrument, created and evidenced by the transmission into the System of Messages, which operates as a receipt for a consignment of goods shipped and/or received for shipment by the Carrier and as evidence of a negotiable contract of carriage, which instrument has the legal effect described in these Rules.[47]

All parties agree to be satisfied with the issue of an electronic bill of lading or the use of a digital signature whenever international or national law requires a bill to be in writing or to be signed.[48] Rule 8.2 of the *Rulebook* then provides that the holder of an electronic bill of lading has the same rights and privileges under and in relation to the contract of carriage evidenced by the electronic bill, and in respect of the goods to which the electronic bill of lading relates, as he would have enjoyed had he been the holder of a tangible bill of lading. The Bolero services are based on the exchange of EDI messages between a central service (the 'central registry') and users. The users — ie carriers, shippers, freight forwarders, and banks — send and receive messages from this central registry by means of a computer workstation. Thus, were a seller to conclude a contract of carriage, the Bolero system allows him to electronically book the space needed on a particular sailing. The shipper will electronically instruct the carrier on the specifics of the goods concerned. The carrier will issue the electronic bill of lading and deposit it at the central registry. The registry stores details of the shipping documents in what is known as a 'consignment record'. Users having the appropriate authority can access this record, either to read it or even alter it (depending upon whether they have the authority to do so). The registry will validate and authenticate messages and will, if appropriate, generate messages and send them to other users involved in the transaction. There are strong security controls and procedures to protect the integrity and authenticity of the electronic messages. It is particularly important that banks can view consignment records electronically and check whether or not the bill of lading tendered by the seller corresponds to the instructions of the buyer.

13.23 **Success?** It remains to be seen whether the project will remain successful. In particular, a continuing difficulty will be whether the legal difficulties associated with the bill of lading as a document of title will be overcome to the satisfaction of users, such that a much greater number will be encouraged to embrace some of the benefits of paperless trading.

---

[46] For discussion, see Willem H van Boom, 'Certain legal aspects of electronic bills of lading' (1997) 32 ETL 9, 11–13.

[47] *Rulebook*, p 8.

[48] Rule 7.

Part III

INTERNATIONAL AND DOMESTIC REGULATION

14

DOMESTIC LEGISLATION ON CARGO LIABILITY

A. Introduction

Overview The modern law relating to contracts of carriage by sea has evolved as a response to **14.01** what has traditionally been characterized as an acute imbalance of bargaining power between shipowners and cargo owners.[1] Accordingly, in this chapter we turn to consider the domestic legislation on carrier liability which was to provide the template for international developments and, in particular, the eventual enactment of the Hague Rules. Before considering these initiatives, however, we consider first basic liability of the carrier from a historical viewpoint.

B. The Basic Liability of the Carrier

Earliest principles Until at least the latter part of the nineteenth century, the general **14.02** principle in English law was that the carrier was liable as an 'insurer' of the goods.[2] This is to say that he was absolutely responsible for delivering in like order and condition at the destination the goods bailed to him for carriage.[3] Putting this another way, the carrier had the same strict liability as a bailee for reward, at least when he was acting in his capacity as

---

[1] See especially Michael Sturley, 'The History of COGSA and the Hague Rules' (1991) 22 JMLC 1; 'The development of cargo liability regimes' in Hugo Tiberg (ed), *Cargo Liability in Future Maritime Carriage* (Svenska Sjörättsföreningen Skrifter 73, 1998), 10.

[2] *Forward v Pittard* (1785) 1 TR 27, 33; 99 ER 953, 956 (Lord Mansfield).

[3] See *Paterson Steamships Ltd v Canadian Co-operative Wheat Producers Ltd* [1934] AC 538 (PC), 544–545; Joseph H Beale, 'The carrier's liability: its history' (1897–1898) Harvard LR 158; Clarke (1976), 118.

a common carrier.[4] Holt CJ put this in the following way in the famous case of *Coggs v Bernard*:

> The law charges this person, thus entrusted, to carry goods against all events, but acts of God, and of the enemies of the king. For though the force be never so great, as if an irresistible multitude of people should rob him, nevertheless he is chargeable. And this is a politick establishment, contrived by the policy of the law, for the safety of all persons, the necessity of whose affairs oblige them to trust these sorts of persons, that they may be safe in their ways of dealing; for else these carriers might have an opportunity of undoing all persons that had any dealings with them, by combining with thieves . . . and yet doing it in such a clandestine manner, as would not be possible to be discovered. And this is the reason the law is founded upon in that point.[5]

Thus, the carrier was liable for cargo damage, unless it could be proved that his negligence had not contributed to the loss suffered or if the loss fell within the recognized exemptions. Later the scheme of exemptions developed further.[6] Apart from acts of God[7] and acts of public enemies,[8] case law has come to recognize three other principal exceptions. These are where the loss is caused by inherent defect or vice in the cargo,[9] where goods are damaged because they have been insufficiently packaged by the shipper,[10] and where the goods are lost or damaged by jettison or other general average sacrifice.[11]

14.03 **Later nineteenth century** In the nineteenth century the dominating credo of the common law courts in their approach to matters of contract, of which the carriage of goods by sea is a part, was laissez-faire or 'freedom of contract'.[12] Taken together with the substantial negotiating strength of liner shipping companies, in particular following the move from sail to steam, it became possible for shipowners to impose virtually any terms on shippers,[13] who were obliged to negotiate contracts for the carriage of their goods by sea on the terms as presented by the shipowners.[14] Shippers found themselves with little in the way of rights against shipowners for loss of or damage to cargo. In effect, the only 'freedom of contract' was the freedom either to ship on terms dictated by the sea carrier or not to ship at all. One of the main criticisms levelled by shippers related to the insertion of clauses exempting shipowners from negligence caused by their servants and agents. Other criticisms concerned

---

[4] In traditional terms, a carrier would not be a 'common carrier' when operating his vessel under charter. See, generally, Yung F Chiang, 'Characterization of a Vessel As a Common or Private Carrier' (1973–1974) 48 Tulane LR 299.

[5] (1703) 2 Ld Raym 909, 918; 92 ER 107, 112. See also *Riley v Horne* (1828) 5 Bing 217, 220; 130 ER 1044, 1045 (Best CJ).

[6] Indeed, many of these exemptions remain in the Hague and Hague–Visby Rules. See ch 28.

[7] See art IV, r 2(d) of the Hague and Hague–Visby Rules; para 28.23.

[8] Article IV, r 2(f). See para 28.26.

[9] Article IV, r 2(m). See para 28.39.

[10] Article IV, r 2(n). See para 28.40.

[11] There is no equivalent in the Hague or Hague–Visby Rules.

[12] See particularly, Ibbetson (1999), ch 12; *Printing & Numerical Registering Co v Sampson* (1875) LR 19 Eq 462, 465 (Jessel MR).

[13] Temperley & Vaughan (1932) state that 'the liner companies . . . were for all practical purposes in the position of monopolists, and therefore able to dictate the terms of their bills of lading' (at 2). See too *Australasian United Steam Navigation Co Ltd v Hiskens* (1914) 18 CLR 646, 671.

[14] For a particularly strong instance, where negligence was also excluded, see *Re Missouri Steamship Co* (1889) LR 42 Ch D 321 (CA).

terms which required claims to be presented within impossibly short periods, immunity from theft, a system of proof rendering any claim impossible, and too frequent and unjustified exercise of the right of lien over cargo.[15] In 1890, the Glasgow Corn Trade Association complained that the so-called 'negligence clauses' had 'surpassed all bounds of reason and fairness'[16] and that bills of lading were 'so unreasonable and unjust in their terms as to exempt [the carriers] from almost every conceivable risk and responsibility'.[17] The position of shipowners was further strengthened by the Merchant Shipping Act 1894[18] which conferred a range of rights and immunities on shipowners. It is therefore true to say that by the end of the nineteenth century ocean carriers had strengthened their position to such an extent that the position for shippers and consignees had become almost impossible.

Early reforms   In response to the trend towards the issuing of bills of lading excluding virtu- **14.04**
ally everything, model bills of lading were promoted at liner shipping conferences and sought to achieve a fairer balance between the interests of carriers and shippers. The then Association for the Reform and Codification of the Law of Nations[19] turned its attention to the subject of bills of lading at its Liverpool Conference in 1882.[20] The Conference adopted the Conference Form Model Bill of Lading[21] which inter alia introduced the notion of 'due diligence' on part of the carrier to make the vessel seaworthy,[22] 'unit limitation' whereby the maximum liability of the shipowner 'per package' (boxes, barrels, bales, bags, drums) would be £100. Shipowners' obligations were further modified with the provision of a long list of causes for which the shipowner would not be liable. Although not widely adopted,[23] the Conference Form was influential in that some of its innovations appeared in the Hague Rules. More immediately, the Conference Model was taken over and amended by the New York Produce Exchange,[24] but the form was never comprehensively adopted by any of the major shipping countries.

C. The Harter Act

Background   Notwithstanding constant complaints from traders, we have thus far seen **14.05**
that there was insufficient impetus internationally for an international solution. As a result several countries went ahead and enacted domestic legislation, with the United States in the lead.[25] The reason for this may be found in the fact that shipowning activities in the

---

[15] See Dor (1960), 16.

[16] Knauth (1953), 120.

[17] Sturley (1998), 16–17. See also *The Delaware* (1896) 161 US 459, 472.

[18] 57 & 58 Vict, c 60. This Act has since been superseded by the Merchant Shipping Act 1995, c 21.

[19] This later became the International Law Association. In 1877 the Association was responsible for drafting the York–Antwerp Rules on general average.

[20] For the Reports of the Proceedings, see Sturley (1990), vol 2, 1.

[21] For the text, see Sturley (1990), vol 2, 61.

[22] See now the Hague (and Hague–Visby) Rules, art III, r 1.

[23] WR Bisschop suggested that: 'This want of success was doubtless owing in some measure to the fact that the conditions and requirements of different trades are too various to be covered by one form of words. Had the Conference of 1882, instead of formulating a complete bill of lading, laid down certain fundamental rules of affreightment which might have been imported into any bill of lading by agreement, its labours would probably have been more productive' (Berlingieri (1997) 16).

[24] The New York Produce Bill of Lading: Knauth (1953), 119. See also the General Produce, Mediterranean, Black Sea, and Baltic Steamer Bill of Lading 1885.

[25] Followed at a later stage by various commonwealth countries.

United States were at a low ebb following the devastation of the American flag merchant fleet during the Civil War of 1861–1865 and because of the failure of American owners to invest in modern steam-driven iron ships.[26] Accordingly, the export trade from the United States was largely in the hands of some twenty British liner companies who enjoyed a virtual monopoly of carriage to the United Kingdom.[27] Unlike in most other places, cargo interests were sufficiently powerful to get the notice of a leading congressman and led eventually to the passage of the Harter Act. The judge in *Charles Pfizer & Co v Convoy SS Co Ltd (The Willdomino)*, Morris DJ, put the situation as follows:

> A carrier of goods by water, like a carrier by land, is an insurer and, although no actual blame is imputable to it, is absolutely liable, in the absence of a special contract or statute limiting its liability, for all damage sustained by the goods intrusted to its care, unless the damage is occasioned by the act of God, the public enemy, the public authority, the fault of the shipper, or the inherent nature of the thing shipped. *Clark* v *Barnwell* 12 How 272, 279. The law however, recognized the right of the carrier to limit in many particulars its common-law liability by special agreement or stipulations in the bill of lading. But in America it was established that a common carrier by sea could not so exempt itself from liability to the owner of cargo for damage arising from the negligence of the master or crew of the vessel. *The Jason* 225 US 32, 49. To meet the ever increasing attempts further to limit the liability of the vessel and her owners by inserting in bills of lading stipulations against losses arising from unseaworthiness, bad stowage, negligence, and other causes of liability by which the common-law responsibility of carriers by sea was being frittered away the Harter Act . . . was passed. It was designed to fix the relations between the cargo and the vessel and to prohibit contracts restricting the liability of the vessel in certain particulars. *The Delaware* 161 US 459.[28]

14.06   **The Harter Act initiative**   In 1892 a congressman from Ohio, Michael Harter, introduced the Bill which later carried his name.[29] His principal argument went as follows:

> [The Bill] is a measure which deprives nobody of any right, but which will by its operation deprive some foreign steamship companies of certain privileges which for many years they have exercised, to the great disadvantage of American commerce. That is all there is in it.[30]

After extensive amendment in the Senate Commerce Committee, the Bill passed the Senate and the House of Representatives, without dissent, and was signed by the President on 13 February 1893 and took effect on 1 July 1893.[31]

14.07   **The Act in outline**   The statute is short.[32] It applies 'from or between ports of the United States of America, and foreign ports' and places certain minimum (mandatory) liabilities on carriers in order to afford shippers and consignees some protection. Thus, owners, masters, agents, or managers are not permitted to insert terms which 'lessen, weaken, or avoid'

---

[26] See Joseph Sweeney, 'The Prism of COGSA' (1999) 30 JMLC 543, 551.

[27] Knauth (1953), 120.

[28] 300 F 5, 9–10 (3d Cir, 1924).

[29] See especially, on the interpretation of the Act, Joseph C Sweeney, 'Happy Birthday, Harter: A Reappraisal of the Harter Act on its 100th Anniversary' (1993) 24 JMLC 1.

[30] See Sturley (1998), 18.

[31] Section 8. See 46 USC §§190–196. For the background, see Knauth (1953), 120; Sweeney (1993), 9–14; Sturley (1998), 17–20.

[32] See Frederick Green, 'The Harter Act' (1902–1903) 16 Harvard LR 157; Knauth (1953), 163; *C Itoh & Co (America) Inc v M/V Hans Leonhardt* (1989) 719 F Supp 479, 501.

the obligation to exercise 'due diligence to properly equip, man, provision, and outfit [the] vessel . . .'.[33] Section 3, which applies 'to or from any port in the United States',[34] states that, if due diligence is exercised, a number of exceptions apply: these include so-called nautical fault,[35] acts of God, or public enemies, and various other defences.[36] In effect, this section sets out the bargain between shippers and carriers. Section 4 of the Act deals with the carrier's obligation to issue a bill of lading or shipping document, the mandatory contents of the bill, and the legal consequences of issue. Section 5 provides for criminal liability for failure to issue the bill of lading on demand and also creates a statutory maritime lien on the vessel. Section 6 preserves the Fire Statute of 1851 and, in particular, preserves the owner's right to limit his liability.[37] Finally, section 7 excludes the transport of live animals from the prohibition of those clauses which relieve the carrier from negligence liability and the obligation to issue bills of lading containing certain information.

Critique   On one view the Harter Act was an important step in the eventual move towards   **14.08** promulgating the Hague Rules and in addressing the difficulties then facing American cargo interests. It did not, however, address all the difficulties then being faced. It did not, for example, address the problem of low limitation clauses or time for suit clauses. Within its provisions it did also not address the question of the burden of proof when the carrier brought the loss within one of the exempting clauses. Thus, as one commentator has remarked, the Harter Act 'though an important step in the development of the law of maritime carriage . . . was, at best, a partial, and, at worst, an unsatisfactory solution'.[38]

The Act and COGSA   There have been a number of problems of interpretation of the   **14.09** Harter Act. Nevertheless, despite this, the Act has not been amended or repealed and, to this day, continues in full force and effect. The passage of the US Carriage of Goods by Sea Act in 1936, which gives effect to the Hague Rules, has not altered the status of the Harter Act.[39] It continues in full effect and applies, in particular, to contracts of carriage between ports in the United States and inland water carriage under bills of lading.[40] The Act will also apply to the period, even in foreign trade, when the carrier retains custody of the goods before they are loaded on the ship and after unloading. It has been noted that the Harter Act and the Carriage of Goods by Sea Act are functionally the same,[41] except that the Harter Act does not permit exoneration for nautical fault if there has been any failure to exercise due diligence to provide a seaworthy vessel, even if this is not the cause of the loss.

---

[33] Section 2.

[34] Compared with s 2 which applies 'from or between ports of the United States of America'.

[35] ie no responsibility 'for damage or loss resulting from faults or errors in navigation, or in the management of the vessel' (s 3). Cf art IV, r 2(a) of the Hague (and Hague–Visby) Rules.

[36] Described as the 'most enigmatic' of the provisions of the Act: Sweeney (1993), 3.

[37] See Joel M Bassoff, 'Fire Losses and the Statutory Fire Exceptions' (1981) 12 JMLC 507.

[38] Benjamin W Yancey, 'The Carriage of Goods: Hague, COGSA, Visby, and Hamburg' (1982–1983) 57 Tulane LR 1238, 1241.

[39] Indeed, it expressly preserves the status quo as to the Harter Act (see 46 USCA §1311). See, generally, Gilmore & Black (1975), §3-25; Schoenbaum (2004), §10-15.

[40] The Carriage of Goods by Sea Act also provides that bills of lading may validly stipulate that that Act is to apply, rather than the Harter Act, to domestic voyages: 46 USCA §1312.

[41] Schoenbaum (2004), 653.

Other major differences include the fact that the Harter Act does not contain any limitation provisions.

D. Legislation in Other Countries

14.10 **Background** The passage of the Harter Act in 1893 provided important impetus to other shipping nations. In this section we consider the legislation passed in these countries and the effect of that legislation on later international developments.

14.11 **New Zealand** New Zealand was the earliest of the commonwealth countries to enact legislation duplicating the Harter Act.[42] This was achieved in the Shipping & Seaman Act 1903.[43] The relevant provisions of this Act and its successor in 1908 were in many ways identical to the Harter Act,[44] except that the New Zealand legislation permitted a court to uphold an exemption clause if the court 'adjudge[d] the [clause] to be just and reasonable'.[45]

14.12 **Australia** Australia followed hot on the heels of New Zealand in enacting legislation along the lines of the Harter Act. Thus, in 1904, the Commonwealth of Australia Parliament passed the Sea-Carriage of Goods Act,[46] mainly in response to pressure exerted by fruit growers from Tasmania and also other shippers of perishable cargoes.[47] The intention behind the Act was expressly to improve on the Harter Act by being more generous to the interests of cargo. Thus, the obligation to provide a ship which was seaworthy was initially made an absolute one, rather than (as in the Harter Act) an obligation to exercise due diligence to provide such a seaworthy vessel.[48]

14.13 **Canada** The next country to pass legislation protecting cargo interests was Canada,[49] which enacted the Water Carriage of Goods Act in 1910.[50] This Act went further than the Harter Act, notwithstanding some arguments that it should follow the Harter Act closely. The most significant provision was one that provided that the 'ship, the owner, charterer, master or agent' would not be liable for cargo loss or damage for 'a greater amount than one hundred dollars per package, unless a higher value is stated in the bill of lading'.[51] This Act later proved to be pivotal in providing the model for the Hague Rules and in form and style and content is much closer to those Rules than the Harter Act of 1893.

---

[42] See Sturley (1998), 20.

[43] Act No 96. See too *The Tasman Discoverer* [2001] 2 Lloyd's Rep 665 (NZ HC), 667. This Act was repealed and re-enacted, in virtually identical terms, in 1908: The Shipping and Seamen Act 1908, No 178 (Part XI). For the text of this Act, see, eg, TE Scrutton and FD Mackinnon, *The Contract of Affreightment as expressed in Charterparties and Bills of Lading* (London, Sweet & Maxwell, 1921), 472.

[44] See particularly ss 293 and 300.

[45] Section 300.

[46] Act No 14. The Act commenced on 1 January 1905: see s 2.

[47] Sturley (1998), 20.

[48] Although the Act as passed reflected the due diligence standard: see s 5.

[49] Sturley (1998), 21.

[50] 9–10 Edw 7, c 61. See Cole (1924), 131.

[51] Section 8.

Other countries It was thought that other countries were becoming interested in enacting **14.14** similar legislation, particularly other countries in the common law world. However, when, in 1913, there was a proposal for similar reforms in France, they were not even discussed.[52]

Future developments: World War I Any future developments on the domestic front and **14.15** internationally were largely abandoned because of the cataclysmic impact of World War I. It was only after the armistice in 1918 that most countries were once again in a position to consider the regulation of private trade. And, as we shall see in the next chapter, the time had come (finally) for an international instrument.

---

[52] See Clarke (1976), 4.

15

THE RISE OF INTERNATIONAL REGULATION

A. Introduction

Overview In the preceding chapter our focus was various developments at the domestic **15.01** level which sought to address the perceived imbalance between shipowning and cargo interests. In this chapter we consider in more detail the major international developments, beginning first with attempts in the late nineteenth century and early part of the twentieth century.

B. Early Developments

The International Law Association (ILA) As we have already seen,[1] the earliest efforts at **15.02** international uniformity were promoted by the International Law Association (ILA),[2] earlier known as the Association for the Reform and Codification of the Law of Nations. Although the Association abandoned the Conference Form developed in Liverpool, it did so in favour of a set of rules, known as the 'Hamburg Rules of Affreightment', which were developed in 1885 and were intended to be incorporated into bills of lading by reference.[3] These Rules were rescinded in 1887 at the Association's London Conference, when the Conference Form was reaffirmed.[4] Nevertheless, the principle of seeking to achieve uniformity

---

[1] See para 14.04.
[2] For a contemporary history, see James Crawford, 'The International Law Association from 1873 to the Present' (1997) 2 Uniform LR 68.
[3] For the proceedings, see Sturley (1990), vol 2, 65; for discussion, see Sturley (1998), 15.
[4] After this point the Association moved away from private law subjects.

through the development of uniform rules had been established. As Dr F Sieveking put it, in answering his own question whether the Harter Act and bills of lading should be dropped by the ILA altogether:

> I think not . . . It is impossible to draft a bill of lading which suits all interests concerned, and is adapted to all the ever-changing requirements of maritime commerce. It is not impossible, however, that abuses may arise which show the necessity of legislation.[5]

15.03 **The Comité Maritime International (CMI)**   The CMI,[6] a transnational association of national maritime law associations, was founded by the eminent Belgian lawyer, Louis Franck, in 1897. Its objects were

> to give to the sea, which is the natural tie between the nations, the benefit of a uniform law, which will be rational, deliberated, equitable in its inception and practical in its text. We have considered that in our work, the shipowner, the merchant, the underwriter, the average adjuster, the banker, the parties directly interested should have the leading part: that the task of the lawyer was to discern what in this maritime community was the general feeling, which, among these divergent interests, is common to all; to discern also which of the various solutions is the best; to contribute to the common work his science and his experience, but that ultimately the lawyer should hold the pen and that the man of practice should dictate the solutions.[7]

Although initially involved in other projects, such as collisions at sea,[8] private law concerns surfaced at the first Diplomatic Conference on Maritime Law, which was sponsored by the Belgian government and held in Brussels in 1905.

C. Hague Rules

15.04 **Incentive for change**   Following the end of the First World War, British shipowning interests were in a much weakened financial state. These conditions paved the way for international support for a series of discussions among the representatives of leading shipowners, underwriters, shippers, and bankers which would lead to uniform rules relating to bills of lading. Sir Norman Hill, the representative of the Liverpool Steamship Owners Association at the Hague Conference of 1921, explained this volte-face in the respective positions of shippers and carriers:

> It may be argued that bills of lading are not contracts that are entered into freely and voluntarily — that they are forced by the all-powerful shipowners upon the helpless cargo

---

[5] 'The Harter Act and bills of lading legislation' (1906–1907) Yale LJ 25, 39.

[6] For the history of the CMI, see Leslie Scott and Cyril Miller, 'The Unification of Maritime and Commercial Law through the Comité Maritime International' (1947) 1 International LQ 482; AN Yiannopolous, 'The Unification of Private Maritime Law by International Conventions' (1965) 30 Law & Contemporary Problems 370; Francesco Berlingieri, 'The Work of the Comité Maritime International: Past, Present, and Future' (1983) 57 Tulane LR 1260; Francesco Berlingieri, 'The Role of the CMI for the International Unification of Maritime Law' in Von Ziegler and Burckhardt (1993), 167; Wiswall (1997).

[7] The words of Louis Franck, one of the CMI's founders, cited by William Birch Reynardson, 'Unification of International Maritime Law: The Work of the Comité Maritime International' in Sotiropoulos (1988), 318.

[8] See, eg, Louis Franck, 'Collisions at Sea in Relation to International Maritime Law' (1896) 12 LQR 260; James Whiteley, 'A reform in maritime law' (1903) 37 American LR 863.

owners, bankers, and underwriters. . . . But what is the position at the moment: the all-powerful shipowners are at their wits end to secure freights to cover their working expenses. Voyage after voyage is being made at a dead loss. Vessels by the hundreds are lying idle in port. At the moment any cargo owner could secure any conditions of carriage he required provided he would only offer a freight that could square the yards.[9]

The Imperial Shipping Committee   The initial impetus after World War I came from the overseas dominions of the British Empire. As we have already seen, the cargo owning interests in New Zealand, Australia, and Canada[10] had already successfully lobbied their parliaments for shipping legislation along the lines of the Harter Act. However, this legislation only applied to cargoes shipped outward from these countries and accordingly importers of goods were often faced with bills of lading which were on much less favourable terms. In 1917 a Dominions Royal Commission recommended Harter-style legislation and this was echoed in 1918 by the Imperial War Conference. Accordingly, in 1920 an Imperial Shipping Committee was appointed, and a Report was issued in February 1921.[11] This recommended that 'there should be uniform legislation throughout the Empire on the lines of the existing Acts dealing with shipowners' liability, but based more precisely on the Canadian Water Carriage of Goods Act 1910'.[12] This recommendation was accepted by the Imperial Conference in 1921. **15.05**

ILA Maritime Law Committee (1921)   A set of uniform rules[13] were drafted under the auspices of the Maritime Law Committee of the International Law Association[14] at its meeting held in London in May 1921. Much of the draft was based on the Canadian Act. At its next conference, held at The Hague from 30 August to 3 September 1921,[15] the members attending agreed on the text of what was to become known as the Hague Rules. However, it was intended that these Rules should be voluntarily incorporated into bills of lading by reference and this met with a storm of protest from cargo interests.[16] **15.06**

Further consideration   The text of the Hague Rules as drafted was discussed by the International Chamber of Commerce (ICC) at its inaugural meeting held in London in June 1921. It appointed a Bill of Lading Committee under the auspices of Charles S Haight,[17] who later turned out to be one of the most ardent supporters of the Hague Rules and argued ceaselessly for their adoption.[18] The proposals were also discussed by the CMI at its conference in Antwerp in July 1921. In November 1921 the proposals were discussed at the World Shipping Conference and again by the CMI at its conference in London in October 1922. Within days of this conference the first Diplomatic Conference **15.07**

---

9 Sturley (1990), vol 1, 144. See also David C Frederick, 'Political Participation and Legal Reform in the International Maritime Rulemaking Process: From the Hague Rules to the Hamburg Rules' (1991) 22 JMLC 86.
10 See paras 14.11–14.13.
11 See Sturley (1998), 23. For the text of the Report, see Sturley (1990), vol 2, 127.
12 Reproduced in Sturley (1990), vol 2, 138.
13 Sturley (1990), vol 1, 101.
14 See Sturley (1998), 25.
15 At 28.
16 Knauth (1953), 126.
17 See as to Haight, Joseph Sweeney, 'The Prism of COGSA' (1999) 30 JMLC 543, 556 n 88.
18 Knauth (1953), 125.

on Maritime Law opened in Brussels. Because few of the delegates attending had had time since the end of the CMI conference just days before, it had not proved possible for them to receive instructions from their governments and so they were not in a position to commit their governments to the final text.[19] Accordingly, the delegates left the conference on the understanding that the exact terms of the Rules should be 'decided by a future meeting of the conference, or through the usual diplomatic channels'.[20] In the event the next consideration of the Rules took place in October 1923 at a meeting of an expanded subcommittee[21] on bills of lading, held in Brussels.[22] Most importantly, at this meeting the decision was taken to make the £100 limitation amount sound in 'gold value', with contracting states being permitted to translate that amount 'into terms of their own monetary system in round figures'.[23]

15.08 **The Brussels Convention signed**   The Hague Rules were considered at a diplomatic conference which was specially convened by the Belgian government at Brussels in August 1924 and were signed as the International Convention for the Unification of Certain Rules of Law Relating to Bills of Lading on 25 August 1924. The Protocol of signature provided that:

> At the time of signing the International Convention for the Unification of Certain Rules of Law relating to Bills of Lading the Plenipotentiaries whose signatures appear below have adopted this Protocol, which will have the same force and the same value as if its provisions were inserted in the text of the Convention to which it relates.

> The High Contracting Parties may give effect to this Convention either by giving it the force of law or by including in their national legislation in a form appropriate to that legislation the rules adopted under this Convention

15.09 **Implementation: Great Britain**   The UK was in the forefront of countries which adopted the Hague Rules. Thus, in 1923, even before the diplomatic conference, the Carriage of Goods by Sea Bill, was introduced in the House of Lords.[24] Although there was widespread support for it, the Bill also attracted significant opposition. For this reason, the House of Lords and House of Commons appointed a joint committee under the chairmanship of Lord Sterndale, the then Master of the Rolls. The Joint Committee conducted hearings and, significantly, heard strong opposition by Scrutton LJ, probably the leading commercial judge of his time and then member of one of the strongest appellate benches in England,[25] and his then pupil, FD MacKinnon, the co-author of Scrutton's famous treatise on *Charterparties and Bills of Lading*. Scrutton's principal objection was that the Rules were unclear and would lead to increased litigation.[26] In response, Sir Norman Hill was able to

---

[19] This point is made in CR Dunlop, 'The Hague Rules 1921' (1923) 5 JCLIL 258, 259.

[20] Sturley (1998), 37.

[21] Or sous-commission.

[22] For the text, see Sturley (1990), vol 1, 417.

[23] At 464. As we shall see later, this proved to be problematic after the enactment of the Rules: see para 29.08.

[24] 13 Geo 5, Bill No 26 (26 March 1923).

[25] Together with Atkin LJ and Bankes LJ.

[26] See Report from the Joint Committee on the Carriage of Goods by Sea Bill (HL) (16 July 1923), 86. See too Raymond E Negus: 'If the Rules are reduced to statutory form it is to be hoped that the doubts above suggested will at least receive attention. Any ambiguity in a Sea-Carriage of Goods Act will render such an Act more harmful then helpful' ((1922) 38 LQR 317, 338).

assuage these doubts and others and the Committee noted that ambiguous drafting 'was to be expected when it represented compromises and concessions necessarily made in order to secure an agreement'.[27] In due course, a new Carriage of Goods by Sea Bill was introduced. This occurred in February 1924.[28] There were few major differences between this Bill and the earlier Bill introduced in 1923. However, the latest version of the Hague Rules was attached to the Schedule of the Bill. On this occasion there was little opposition. Thus, on 20 March, the Bill was read a second time. The third reading took place on 8 April and, a day later, was moved to the House of Commons. The second reading in the Commons took place on 5 June and the third reading on 11 July.[29] The Carriage of Goods by Sea Act 1924[30] received the royal assent on 1 August 1924, which was some three weeks before the final diplomatic conference, and came into force on 1 January 1925.[31] Even well into the 1950s 'the Rules were . . . regarded with a mixture of pride, affection, and even slight awe as a largely English innovation and one that had achieved remarkable success'.[32]

Other enacting countries   Other countries, particularly those in the British Empire, were   **15.10**
quick to follow the lead taken in the UK.[33] Notably, however, many of these enactments were by countries which did not formally ratify or accede to the Brussels Convention. First off the mark was Australia, which enacted its Sea-Carriage of Goods Act (Cth) in 1924.[34] India followed a year later[35] and Singapore[36] a year after that. Canada,[37] New Zealand,[38] and South Africa[39] enacted national legislation many years later. Perhaps most significantly of all, the Hague Rules were sufficiently controversial for the United States to take 12 years before enacting them in 1936.[40] Outside the common law world, enactment of the Hague Rules initially proceeded at a much slower pace and this was a matter of considerable concern.[41] Thus, although Belgium[42] was relatively quick to do so, the pace did not really accelerate until after the United States enacted the Carriage of Goods by Sea Act 1936. France did not formally ratify the Hague Rules until a year after that,[43] largely, it is said, because of

---

[27] At xi.

[28] Carriage of Goods by Sea Bill, 14 Geo 5, Bill No 19 (22 February 1924).

[29] See the legislative timetable as set out in Cole (1924), 32.

[30] 14 & 15 Geo 5, c 22.

[31] See s 6(3) and an Order in Council of 9 October 1924.

[32] See Anthony Diamond QC, 'The Hague–Visby Rules' [1978] LMCLQ 225, 226.

[33] As to the different methods of adoption and the problems that this can cause, see Athanasios N Yiannopoulos, 'Uniform Rules Governing Bills of Lading: The Brussels Convention of 1924 in the Light of National Legislation' (1961) 10 AJCL 374.

[34] Sea-Carriage of Goods Act 1924, No 22. This Act received the royal assent on 17 September 1924 and commenced on 1 January 1925. See Temperley and Vaughan (1932), 111. Australia formally acceded to the Rules on 4 July 1955.

[35] Indian Carriage of Goods by Sea Act 1925, No 26. See Temperley and Vaughan (1932), 113.

[36] See The Carriage of Goods by Sea Ordinance 1927.

[37] Carriage of Goods by Water Act 1936, RSC 1985, c C-27. See Gold, Chircop and Kindred (2003), 433.

[38] Sea Carriage of Goods Act 1940.

[39] Merchant Shipping Act 1951.

[40] Carriage of Goods by Sea Act 1936 (COGSA). For the process leading to enactment, see Sturley (1998), 42.

[41] See, eg, HC Gutteridge, 'The unification of the law of the sea' (1934) 16 JCLIL 246, 248.

[42] Belgium ratified the Rules in 1930. The Netherlands permitted bills of lading to be subject to the Hague Rules, but did not actually ratify the Rules until 1956. See Appendix IIIA.

[43] 4 January 1937: see Appendix IIIA.

the intransigence of shippers, especially the Algerians, who wanted even stricter controls over shipowners.[44]

15.11 **Freedom of contract** Although much of the debate in the lead up to the enactment of the Hague Rules focused on the need to impose some restrictions on the almost complete freedom of contract hitherto subsisting, it is clear that the Rules were never intended to cover all the areas on which the parties might eventually contract. Thus, Devlin J in *Chandris v Isbrandtsen-Moller Co Inc* has stated that

> the Act is not untended as a code. It is not meant altogether to supplant the contract of carriage, but only to control on certain topics the freedom of contract which the parties would otherwise have. I see no reason why it should not be silent on such topics as the consequences of shipping cargo with the consent of the master, leaving the matter to be regulated by the parties themselves. On the contrary, I see good reason why silence might be thought desirable . . .[45]

15.12 **Signatories: a note** At various stages there have been up to 100 signatories to the Hague Rules.[46] This is a significant number of countries and represents an achievement of conspicuous success, albeit one which is referable to the time when the Rules were passed.

15.13 **Problems** The principal aim of the Hague Rules was to achieve a better balance between two main interest groups in international trading by sea, namely shipowners and cargo owners. Thus, the Rules set out to regulate the rights, duties, and immunities of the carrier under a contract of carriage by sea covered by a bill of lading, in relation to the shipper, the consignee named in the bill of lading, and the endorsee of the bill of lading. Compromises were made on both sides and this meant that clarity was sometimes sacrificed.[47] Thus, it has been said that:

> [T]his was not the first time, nor of course the last, that a kind of bewildered fascination has bemused those who have the task of interpreting an international convention. Due to the series of trade-offs and compromises involved in producing a multilateral contract between opposing political and commercial interests, it is not surprising that clarity and consistency of purpose tend to be sacrificed at times for the sake of producing agreement.[48]

A number of difficulties surfaced remarkably soon after the Brussels Conference in 1924. Perhaps the most important of these was the limit of liability per package or unit which had been fixed at £100 sterling gold value. As early as 1925, however, sterling had lost its convertibility into gold and each contracting state thereafter converted the £100 into its own currency.[49] The net effect of this difficulty was that the amount of limitation of liability per unit had rapidly deteriorated such that it was almost impossible for shipowners and their insurers to predict with accuracy what the total amount of exposure would be following a disaster to ship and cargo. The next principal difficulty, which arose several decades after

---

[44] Clarke (1976), 5.

[45] [1951] 1 KB 240, 247.

[46] See Appendix IIIA.

[47] They have also been described as 'unsystematic and even haphazard': Joseph Sweeney, 'The Prism of COGSA' (1999) 30 JMLC 536, 558.

[48] Anthony Diamond QC, 'The Hague–Visby Rules' [1978] LMCLQ 226, 228.

[49] For discussion, see para 29.08.

the enactment of the Rules, was the major technological innovation of containers,[50] which rapidly took hold in cargo transportation in the late 1960s and early 1970s. The Rules were not — and could not have been — designed with containers in mind. A third problem, which also became an acute one at an early stage, was documentary coverage: the Rules are only intended to cover bills of lading 'or similar documents of title'.[51]

D. Visby Protocol

Origins   We have already noted that certain difficulties were encountered with the Hague   **15.14**
Rules, some of them at a relatively early stage after their enactment. Some further difficulties may be highlighted at this point. One of the difficulties, which was to become even more advanced in the 1960s, was a rapidly changing political situation worldwide, particularly with the development of the UN system and the increasing numbers of former colonies which were becoming politically independent. No less significant were the interpretations of the Hague Rules by different national courts.[52] Two decisions of the English courts had caused particular consternation, the first being the decision by the Privy Council in *Vita Food Products v Unus Shipping Co*,[53] and the second a decision of the House of Lords in *Riverstone Meat Co Pty Ltd v Lancashire Shipping Co Ltd (The Muncaster Castle)*[54] on article III, rule 1 of the Rules.[55]

CMI Rijeka Conference   The first stage in the transformation of the Hague Rules   **15.15**
occurred when the CMI met in conference at Rijeka in 1959.[56] It was recognized that one of the most pressing areas for reform was the limitation provisions of the Hague Rules, but the CMI's International Sub-Committee on Conflicts of Law was also invited to consider whether other changes should be made.[57] A Sub-Committee on Bill of Lading Clauses was formed and this new subcommittee actively circulated member organizations. In 1962 it issued a Report making seven important recommendations: (1) clarifying that the carrier was not liable for negligent loading, stowage, or discharge of goods if those activities were carried out by the shipper or consignee; (2) clarifying that the failure to give notice of non-apparent loss or damage during the three-day period in article 3(6) created a presumption of proper delivery, but did not otherwise affect relations between the parties; (3) the addition of a two year limitation period to govern claims for wrongful delivery to persons not entitled to receive them; (4) replacement of the £100 package limitation and the gold

---

[50] See para 1.11. For discussion of the wider legal implications, see W David Angus, 'Legal Implications of "The Container Revolution" in International Carriage of Goods' (1968) 14 McGill LJ 395; Edward Schmeltzer and Robert A Peavy, 'Prospects and Problems of the Container Revolution' (1969–1970) JMLC 203; S Mankabady, 'Some legal aspects of the carriage of goods by container' (1974) 23 ICLQ 317.

[51] Article I(b). See para 19.19.

[52] This problem is developed at length in Michael F Sturley, 'International Uniform Laws in National Courts: The Influence of Domestic Law in Conflicts of Interpretation' (1986–1987) Virginia JIL 729, 735.

[53] [1939] AC 277 (PC). See para 18.05.

[54] [1961] AC 807. See para 26.21.

[55] Discussed at para 26.17.

[56] See Berlingieri (1997), 56.

[57] See Sturley (1998), 54.

clause with a 10,000 Poincaré franc package limitation provision; (5) adding a new provision to the Hague Rules to address the problem of Himalaya clauses;[58] (6) adding a new provision to govern nuclear damage; (7) urging the United States to adopt the same rules 'as the rest of the maritime world' as to collisions and thus solving the problem of the both-to-blame clause. Interestingly, no recommendation was made on a proposal to overrule *The Muncaster Castle*.[59]

15.16 **CMI Stockholm Conference** The next CMI conference was held in Stockholm in 1963 and the work of the Sub-Committee was considered at some length at the initial plenary session before being remitted back to it for further consideration. It now rejected recommendations one and two, substantially modified the third, accepted the fourth and fifth, with changes, accepted the sixth unchanged, and did not address the seventh. Subsequently, in plenary session, a number of other proposals were considered, including one which overruled *The Muncaster Castle*.[60] In due course, at the conclusion of its business, the draft protocol was signed at Visby (or Wisby),[61] the ancient capital of Gotland in Sweden.

15.17 **Brussels Conference** A diplomatic conference, again hosted by the Belgian government, was hosted in two sessions in Brussels in May 1967 and later in February 1968. Surprisingly, perhaps, *The Muncaster Castle* proposal was defeated,[62] but there was more conspicuous success with some of the other proposals. Thus, both the Himalaya proposal[63] and the nuclear damage[64] proposal were accepted at the 1967 Conference. At the February 1968 Conference, the delegations had to grapple with one vital problem, limitation of liability, at which no agreement had been reached in 1967. The most important innovations which came out of the 1968 Conference were the alternative weight basis for limitation,[65] the introduction of a container clause,[66] and a provision for breaking limitation in the event of intentional or reckless misconduct.[67] Although there had been a proposal that the Rules should be applied both inbound and outbound, this was abandoned in favour of a proposal which closed the so-called *Vita Food*[68] gap.

15.18 **Signature** At the conclusion of the second Brussels Conference, the delegations attending the Conference adopted the 'Protocol to Amend the International Convention for the

---

[58] See the discussion of Himalaya clauses at para 9.23.

[59] [1961] AC 807. See para 26.23.

[60] ibid.

[61] The Laws of Wisby were adopted c1350. Similar to (possibly derived from) the Rôles of Oléron, they gained wide authority in surrounding Baltic towns of the Hanseatic League and were based on the Rhodian sea laws of the Middle Ages. See Sanborn (1930), 76; Leon E Trakman, 'The Evolution of the Law Merchant: Our Commercial Heritage' (1980) 12 JMLC 1, 5; Anthony Diamond QC, 'The Hague–Visby Rules' [1978] LMCLQ 226, n1.

[62] See para 26.23.

[63] ie recommendation (5) of the Sub-Committee on Bill of Lading Clauses.

[64] Recommendation (6) of the Sub-Committee.

[65] Article IV, r 5(a). See para 29.07.

[66] Article IV, r 5(c). See para 29.19.

[67] Article IV, r 5(e). See para 29.28.

[68] ie the problem created by the decision in *Vita Food Products v Unus Shipping Co* [1939] AC 277 (PC). See para 18.05.

Unification of Certain Rules of Law Relating to Bills of Lading', known as the Brussels Protocol (or the Visby Rules) and this was signed on 23 February 1968. The Protocol came into force on 23 June 1977.

Hague–Visby Rules The 1924 Brussels Convention and the 1968 Brussels Protocol are intended to be read and interpreted as a single instrument,[69] and the original and amending Rules form a single set of rules known as the Hague–Visby Rules. **15.19**

Principles The Brussels Protocol has not radically altered the risk allocation regime set out in the Brussels Convention. While the Protocol expanded the scope of application of the Hague Rules, it did not radically alter the compromise between the demands of carriers on the one hand and cargo interests on the other. As we have seen, the Protocol was intended to amend those provisions of the Hague Rules which were universally acknowledged as causing problems. Thus, on one view, the Protocol provided no more than a facelift to the Hague Rules, given that the form and structure of the original Rules remained substantially unchanged. **15.20**

Signatories The Hague–Visby Rules were given statutory effect in the United Kingdom by the Carriage of Goods by Sea Act 1971[70] which came into force on 23 June 1977. The Hague–Visby Rules have effect by force of law under this Act.[71] Australia,[72] Canada,[73] Singapore,[74] and South Africa[75] are all examples of states which originally enacted legislation applying the Hague–Visby Rules, although not contracting states to the Protocol.[76] New Zealand brought into force both the Visby Protocol and the SDR Protocol in 1994.[77] Apart from those countries which apply the rules domestically, some 38 countries have ratified the Brussels Protocol. The most notable exception is the United States which has never ratified the Visby Protocol.[78] A further point, however, is that significantly fewer Hague countries have also ratified the Visby Protocol.[79] **15.21**

---

[69] Protocol, art 6.

[70] c 19.

[71] See section 1(2).

[72] Carriage of Goods by Sea Act 1991 (Cth). This Act was later amended: see the discussion at para 17.04.

[73] See the Carriage of Goods by Water Act, SC 1993, c 21 (since replaced by the Marine Liability Act, SC 2001, c 6). This statute enacted two sets of Rules: Schedule I, which contains the Hague–Visby Rules, and came into force when the Act received the royal assent, and Schedule II, which allows the Hamburg Rules to be brought into force at a later date, by Order-in-Council on the recommendation of the Minister of Transport. A report must be made by the Minister of Transport every five years. See Hugh Kindred, 'Goodbye to the Hague Rules: Will the new Carriage of Goods by Water Act make a Difference?' (1994–95) 24 Canadian BLJ 404; Gold, Chircop & Kindred (2003), 434.

[74] Carriage of Goods by Sea Act, cap 33 (in force on 16 January 1978). For discussion, see Tan Lee Meng, 'The Carriage of Goods by Sea Act 1972 and the Hamburg Rules' (1980) 22 Malaya LR 199; Tan Lee Meng (1994) 313.

[75] Carriage of Goods by Sea Act 1986, No 1. See Hilton Staniland, 'The new Carriage of Goods by Sea Act in South Africa' [1987] LMCLQ 305.

[76] Australia acceded to the Protocol on 16 July 1993. On the other hand, Canada, Singapore, and South Africa have never done so.

[77] The Maritime Transport Act 1994 (NZ) received the Royal Assent on 17 November 1994 and came into force on 20 March 1995. This gave effect to both the Visby Protocol and the SDR Protocol. See Paul Myburgh, 'Maritime Transport and Marine Pollution: Law Reform in New Zealand' [1995] LMCLQ 167; CC Nicoll, 'Significant Carriage of Goods by Sea Reform in New Zealand' (1995) 26 JMLC 443.

[78] See Allan I Mendelsohn, 'Why the US did not ratify the Visby Amendments' (1992) 23 JMLC 29.

[79] This can be seen from a comparison between those countries which have ratified the Brussels Convention and the Protocol: see Appendix III.

E. The SDR Protocol

15.22 **Origins** We have already noted that one of the achievements of the Brussels Protocol was to reform the package limitation provisions of the Hague Rules, problems with which had emerged within a year of the adoption of those Rules. In an effort to reform this serious problem, the limitation framework under the Brussels Protocol in 1968 was determined by reference to the Poincaré franc, with the amount set as 30 Poincaré francs per kilogramme and 10,000 Poincaré francs per package. In a repeat performance of what had happened following the adoption of the Hague Rules, the Poincaré system collapsed very soon after the Brussels Conference. This time, the main reason for the collapse was inflation.[80]

15.23 **Reform** In a renewed effort to promote some sort of uniformity, the CMI in 1977 appointed an International Sub-Committee to prepare proposals for reform, based on the new SDR[81] unit of account defined by the International Monetary Fund (IMF).[82] The draft proposals were once again submitted to the Belgian government, which agreed to call a new diplomatic conference in December 1979. The Conference adopted, without amendment, the SDR Protocol to the Visby Protocol on 21 December 1979. This replaced the Poincaré franc with the SDR and came into force on 14 February 1984.

15.24 **Signatories** Compared with the Brussels Convention and the Visby Protocol, there are a relatively small number of contracting states to the SDR Protocol. However, these include the United Kingdom. [83] As is the case with the 1968 Protocol, a number of states have implemented the SDR Protocol into domestic legislation.[84]

---

[80] See further para 29.11.
[81] Special Drawing Right.
[82] See para 29.12.
[83] By the Merchant Shipping Act 1981, s 2(4) (itself since repealed).
[84] See, eg, South Africa. The Shipping General Amendment Act 1997 No 23, s 48 inserts s 2A into the Carriage of Goods by Sea Act 1986 and amends art IV, r 5(a) of the Hague–Visby Rules.

16

THE MOVEMENT TO THE HAMBURG RULES

A. Introduction

Overview   We have now seen how the Hague–Visby Rules expanded the scope of   **16.01**
application of the Hague Rules, yet did not radically alter the Hague Rules compromise
between the demands of carriers on the one hand and cargo interests on the other. In this
chapter we examine the factors which led to the enactment of the Hamburg Rules.

B. Background

New political realities   In some circles, in particular developing (or 'third world') countries,   **16.02**
the Hague Rules together with the Protocols of 1968 and 1979 were seen as no more than
an attempt to pre-empt more fundamental changes to the existing international regime
applicable to the carriage of goods by sea.[1] Underpinning feelings of dissatisfaction was a
concern that the existing regime on the carriage of goods by sea did not ensure equal
treatment between developing nations, which by and large represented cargo interests, and
the developed nations which represented the shipowners.[2] There is some force in this as the
Hague–Visby Rules were effectively drafted by major industrialized countries and the
representatives at the meetings which led to the Hague and Hague–Visby Rules were
predominantly commercially-minded men (carriers, cargo owners, bankers, and insurers)
who worked out compromises which reflected commercial, rather than political, realities.

---

[1] There is an extensive literature on the Hamburg Rules. As a starting point, the series of five articles by
Professor Joseph C Sweeney should be consulted: 'The UNCITRAL Draft Convention on Carriage of Goods
by Sea' (1975–1976) 7 JMLC 69; (1975–1976) 7 JMLC 327; (1975–1976) 7 JMLC 487; (1975–1976)
7 JMLC 615; (1976–1977) 8 JMLC 167. Professor Sweeney was one of the United States' representatives at
the Hamburg Conference.

[2] This point is made by TK Thommen, 'Carriage of Goods by Sea: The Hague Rules and Hamburg Rules'
(1990) 32 JILI 285, 288.

16.03 **The pressure for change in UNCTAD** Political pressure for a change to the existing international regime was initially channelled through the United Nations Conference on Trade and Development (UNCTAD).[3] This organ of the UN was set up in 1964 to formulate policies on international trade and economic development, with particular reference to the problems of developing countries.[4] Developing countries distrusted the network which had been established by traditional maritime powers and reference to the UN reflected confidence in the United Nations as an organ dedicated to international problem solving. At its First Conference, held at Geneva from 23 March to 16 June 1964, the United Arab Republic raised the issue of international shipping legislation. The Western response to this was that UNCTAD was not technically qualified, but a proposal to entrust this matter to UNCITRAL, which was in the process of formation, was rejected by the developing countries, who had by now joined together as the so-called 'Group of 77'. Special Principal XII was agreed at this Conference:

> All countries should cooperate in devising measures to help developing countries build up maritime and other means of transport for their economic development, to ensure the unhindered use of international transport facilities, the improvement of terms of freight and insurance for the developing countries, and to promote tourism in these countries in order to increase their earnings and reduce their expenditure on invisible trade.

Under the influence of the Group of 77 countries, the Trade and Development Board of UNCTAD appointed a Committee on Shipping to consider a range of shipping issues concerning trade relations between developed and developing countries. A Second UNCTAD Conference met at New Delhi (India) from 1 February to 29 March 1968. It had before it a Report prepared by Dr TK Thommen.[5] It adopted ten resolutions relating to shipping, and most especially proposed the creation of an UNCTAD Working Group. By this time the considerable enmity towards UNCTAD's activities in the maritime law field by developed states had begun to make headway against the opposition of the Group of 77 countries.

16.04 **UNCITRAL** Following the creation of the United Nations Commission on International Trade Law (UNCITRAL)[6] by unanimous resolution of the General Assembly on 17 December 1966, legal questions relating to bills of lading were shifted to that forum while UNCTAD concentrated its energies on economic issues.[7] At the time, developing countries accounted for 64.7 per cent, in terms of weight, of all maritime shipments, but actually owned only 7.6 percent of the world's maritime fleet. UNCITRAL, which now comprises 60 states elected by the General Assembly for six years, was set up specifically to 'further the progressive harmonisation and unification of the law of international trade'. UNCITRAL set up a Working Group on International Legislation in Shipping.

---

[3] See now <www.unctad.org>.

[4] There are currently 192 members.

[5] *International Legislation on Shipping* (1968).

[6] See now <www.uncitral.org>. See Clive Schmitthoff, 'The Unification of the Law of International Trade' [1968] JBL 105.

[7] See E Allan Farnsworth, 'UNCITRAL — Why? What? How? When?' (1972) 20 AJCL 314; Gabriel M Wilner, 'Survey of the Activities of UNCTAD and UNCITRAL in the Field of International Legislation on Shipping' (1971–1972) 3 JMLC 129.

This comprised 21 states, representing each world region and legal system. The Working Group held six substantive sessions between 1971 and 1975.[8] At its first session in 1971, UNCITRAL resolved 'that within the priority topic of international legislation on shipping, the subject for consideration for the time being shall be bills of lading'.[9]

Draft Convention   UNCITRAL prepared a Draft Convention on Carriage of Goods by   **16.05**
Sea in 1975.[10] This Draft had the following six aims:[11] (1) to clarify the scope of its own application; (2) to shed or reduce the carrier's exceptions with a view to balancing the equities vis-à-vis shippers; (3) to permit cargo interests to pursue legal claims at destination where most if not all cargo claims arise; (4) to sustain carrier liability according to the provisions of the Convention notwithstanding transhipment and through shipment; (5) to prevent carriers from including invalid clauses in their bills of lading; (6) to raise unit limitation of liability nearer present day monetary values. The Draft Convention was submitted to all governments and interested international organizations for their comments, with a deadline of 27 January 1976.[12] A Plenary Meeting of UNCITRAL convened in 1976 and the Draft Convention was approved by UNCTAD in July 1976. Thereafter it was debated and endorsed by the General Assembly of the United Nations which resolved on 16 December 1976 to convene a Conference of Plenipotentiaries to consider it.

C. The Hamburg Conference

Introduction   The United Nations Conference on the Carriage of Goods by Sea met at   **16.06**
Hamburg from 6 to 31 March 1978, and was hosted by the then Federal Republic of Germany. Altogether, some 78 States were represented at the Conference, together with an observer from Guatemala and representatives of various NGOs,[13] specialized agencies,[14] and UN organs.[15] The President of the Conference was Rolf Herber[16] and he directed proceedings at all meetings of the General Committee of the Conference.

Committees   Three committees debated the issues before the Conference: (1) the First   **16.07**
Committee, which dealt with matters of substance, sat under the chairmanship of

---

[8] The proceedings of each of the sessions appear in the various *UNCITRAL Yearbooks*.

[9] *Report of the Working Group* (UNCITRAL, 1972).

[10] A/CN.9/105, annex, reproduced in *UNCITRAL Yearbook 1975*, 246.

[11] MJ Shah, 'The revision of the Hague Rules on bills of lading within the UN system: key issues' in Mankabady (1978), 11.

[12] UNCITRAL prepared a Report of these comments, with an analysis: A/CN.9/100, reproduced in *UNCITRAL Yearbook 1976*, vol 7, 263.

[13] Such as the Intergovernmental Maritime Consultative Organisation (IMCO), the predecessor of the International Maritime Organisation (IMO), BIMCO (the Baltic and International Maritime Conference), ICC (International Chamber of Commerce), International Chamber of Shipping, International Shipowners Association, CMI, etc.

[14] Such as the IMF.

[15] Notably UNCTAD.

[16] Later Director of the Institut für Seerecht und Seehandelsrecht at the University of Hamburg: <www2.jura.uni-hamburg.de/issr>. See 'The Hamburg Rules: Origin and Need for the New Liability System' in Kegels (1994), 33.

Professor Mohsen Chafik of Egypt; (2) the Second Committee, concerned with technical provisions regarding entry into force, the relationship between the new Convention and the Hague–Visby Rules, and future revisions, was chaired by Mr Dimitar Popov of the Foreign Ministry of Bulgaria; (3) a Drafting Committee, under the chairmanship of Mr DK Dixit of India.

16.08 **Main principles**   The draft proposal presented to the Hamburg Conference, which was the product of several years' work, heralded a marked difference of approach to that embodied in the Hague Rules. The Rules are nothing like a mere adaptation of the Hague Rules in the way that the Hague–Visby Rules and the United States Carriage of Goods by Sea Act 1936 were. Many of the main principles will be referred to in the chapters which follow, but for now the following general points may be noted. The Conference did not tamper with many of the basic provisions of the negotiating document, which was the result of six drafting sessions. The Hamburg Rules differ from the Hague and Hague–Visby Rules in that they apply both inward and outward[17] and extend over 'any contract whereby the carrier undertakes against payment of freight to carry goods by sea from one port to another'.[18] However, the most fundamental provision concerns carrier liability: the carrier is presumed to be at fault unless he proves that he, his servants, or agents, took all measures that could reasonably be required to avoid the occurrence and its consequences.[19] The obligation to exercise due diligence to make the ship seaworthy[20] is no longer expressly articulated and, most troubling for shipowning interests, the list of defences,[21] which is such a vital part of the Hague and Hague–Visby Rules, has been removed completely. The Rules make specific provision for delay in delivery[22] and extend the limitation period for instituting proceedings to two years.[23]

16.09 **Tensions**   There was a fundamental tension between two main groups of delegates at the Conference, many of whom were diplomats and not skilled experts in the area of carriage of goods by sea. The negotiations took on a distinctly political hue and there was much hard negotiation and 'horse trading'. On the one hand there were those who were determined to defend the principles on which Hamburg was predicated; on the other were a majority who were equally determined to slay what they regarded as a dragon. The different shades of meaning of the various words and phrases were fiercely debated, as was noted by one of the US delegates:

> The trading was so hard that when agreement was reached no one dared even touch a comma for the fear that the whole deal would be upset. This is the explanation for certain oddities and inconsistencies to be found in the drafting.[24]

---

[17] Article 2(1). The Hague and Hague–Visby Rules only apply outward: see art X.
[18] Article 1(6). The Hague and Hague–Visby Rules apply only to bills of lading and similar documents of title: see art I(b).
[19] Article 5(1).
[20] As in art III, r 1 of the Hague and Hague–Visby Rules.
[21] See art IV, r 2 of the Hague and Hague–Visby Rules.
[22] See art 5(1).
[23] Article 20(1). Cf art III, r 6 of the Hague and Hague–Visby Rules, where the period is 12 months.
[24] John C Moore, as noted in the Annual Report of the Committee on Bills of Lading of the US Maritime Law Association: Document No 615, p 6872 (5 May 1978).

At the end of the day, the majority view held sway, not without fierce opposition As Lord Roskill, the then Chairman of the British Association of Average Adjusters, said:

> Those who propose [the Hamburg Rules] do not, with all respect, seem to me to be asking the only relevant question — Is this change necessary to a better working result in practice? One begins to suspect, rightly or wrongly, that other influences were at work and that these proposals emanate from some who have no practical experience in how well the Hague Rules have worked over the last fifty years. Once again I venture to repeat, has anyone counted the cost of these changes if they are made?[25]

Signature   The text of the final act of the Conference was signed on 31 March 1978, **16.10** following its approval by a vote of 67 in favour, 0 against, and 4 abstentions (those of Canada, Greece, Liberia, and Switzerland).

Critique   The Hamburg Rules have been the subject of extensive and detailed critique **16.11** and comparison.[26] It has been said many times that the absence at Hamburg of official commercial delegates, other than those asked to represent their countries,[27] led to political compromises rather than economic bargaining and that this is reflected in the use of rather ambiguous language. Professor Joseph Sweeney, one of the US representatives in Hamburg, has commented that:

> I wish I could say that after all the time and money spent on the Hamburg Rules that they are perfect. They are not, but I believe that whenever conflicting economic interests must be compromised, the resulting structure must be inelegant and shaky. I do not see how the results could be noticeably improved in the foreseeable future by another conference. Sometime after the Hamburg Rules have come into force, it may be possible to revise some of the more infelicitous provisions in a new spirit of compromise.[28]

---

[25] Address on 11 May 1978. Cited by John C Moore, 'The Hamburg Rules' (1978) JMLC 1, 5.

[26] Warren Moseley, 'UNCITRAL attacks the ocean carrier bill of lading' (1972–1973) 17 St Louis ULJ 355; John D Kimball, 'Shipowner's Liability and the Proposed Revision of the Hague Rules' (1975–1976) 7 JMLC 217; Mankabady (1978); John C Moore, 'The Hamburg Rules' (1978–1979) 10 JMLC 1; James J Donovan, 'The Hamburg Rules: Why a new convention on Carriage of Goods by Sea' (1979) 4 Maritime Lawyer 1; William Tetley, 'The Hamburg Rules — A Commentary' [1979] LMCLQ 1; Erling Selvig, 'The Hamburg Rules, the Hague Rules and Marine Insurance Practice' (1980–1981) 12 JMLC 299; Benjamin W Yancey, 'The Carriage of Goods: Hague, COGSA, Visby, and Hamburg' (1982–1983) 57 Tulane LR 1238; George F Chandler III, 'A Comparison of "COGSA", the Hague/Visby Rules, and the Hamburg Rules' (1984) 15 JMLC 233; Joseph C Sweeney, 'UNCITRAL and the Hamburg Rules — The Risk Allocation Problem in Maritime Transport of Goods' (1991) 22 JMLC 511; AJ Waldron, 'The Hamburg Rules — A Boondoggle for Lawyers' [1991] JBL 305; Douglas A Werth, 'The Hamburg Rules Revisited — A Look at U.S. Options' (1991) 22 JMLC 59; R Glenn Bauer, 'Conflicting Liability Regimes: Hague–Visby v. Hamburg Rules — A Case by Case Analysis' (1993) 24 JMLC 53; CWH Goldie, 'Effect of the Hamburg Rules on Shipowners' Liability Insurance' (1993) 24 JMLC 111; John O Honnold, 'Ocean Carriers and Cargo; Clarity and Fairness — Hague or Hamburg?' (1993) 24 JMLC 75; Kegels (1994); Robert Force, 'A Comparison of the Hague, Hague–Visby, and Hamburg Rules: Much Ado About (?)' (1995–1996) 70 Tulane LR 2051; Samuel Robert Mandelbaum, 'Creating Uniform Worldwide Liability Standards for Sea Carriage of Goods Under the Hague, COGSA, Visby and Hamburg Conventions' (1995–1996) 23 Transportation LJ 471; Eun Sup Lee, 'The Changing Liability System of Sea Carriers and Maritime Insurance: Focusing on the Enforcement of the Hamburg Rules' (2002) 15 Transnational LJ 241.

[27] Such as Professor Joseph C Sweeney, Professor JO Honnold (USA), and Professor E Selvig (Sweden).

[28] Joseph C Sweeney, 'UNCITRAL and the Hamburg Rules — The risk allocation problem in the maritime transport of goods' (1991) 22 JMLC 511, 529–530.

16.12 **Coming into force**   The Hamburg Rules came into force on 1 November 1992, after the expiration of one year from the date of deposit of the twentieth instrument of ratification, acceptance, approval, or accession.[29] Although 31 countries have now ratified the Convention,[30] it has not been formally ratified by any major maritime nation.[31] Having said that, however, there are a number of countries which have enacted domestic legislation which draws in some respects on provisions of the Hamburg Rules. In the next chapter we look at some of these hybrid systems and their impact on current moves towards a new international instrument.

---

[29] Article 31.
[30] See Appendix IIID.
[31] With the notable exception of Chile.

17

HYBRID CARRIAGE REGIMES AND INTERNATIONAL UNIFORMITY

A. Introduction

Overview   In the previous chapters we have examined the principal movements which **17.01** led to the enactment of the Hague, Hague–Visby, and Hamburg Rules. In this chapter we consider the move away from international uniformity, the increasing trend towards national solutions,[1] and finally the current impetus to produce a new international convention.

B. The Move to Domestic Solutions

Hamburg holding legislation   After the coming into force of the Hamburg Rules in **17.02** 1992, a number of countries began actively to consider their implementation. Indeed, both Canada and Australia at one time had holding legislation making provision for the eventual enactment of the Hamburg Rules. The Canadian Carriage of Goods by Water Act[2] enacted two sets of Rules. Schedule I contained the Hague–Visby Rules and came into force when the Act received the royal assent. It covered bills of lading or similar documents of title entered into after 6 May 1993. Schedule II allowed the Hamburg Rules to be brought into force at a later date, by Order in Council on the recommendation of the Canadian Minister of Transport. The latter was required to lay a report before Parliament by 31 December 1999 and every 5 years thereafter, until the Schedule was implemented.[3] This has not, so far, occurred.

---

[1] See Paul Myburgh, 'Uniformity or Unilateralism in the Law of Carriage of Goods by Sea?' (2000) 31 Victoria UWLR 355.

[2] SC 1993, c 21. Since replaced by the Marine Liability Act SC 2001, c 6.

[3] See Hugh Kindred, 'Goodbye to the Hague Rules: Will the new Carriage of Goods by Water Act make a Difference?' (1994–95) 24 Canadian Business LJ, 404; Gold, Chircop & Kindred (2003), 434.

In the case of Australia, the Australian Carriage of Goods by Sea Act 1991 (Cth)[4] gave the force of law to the Hague–Visby Rules.[5] However, Section 2 of the Act provided that the Hamburg Rules would come into force automatically at midnight on 19 October 1997, unless both Houses of the Commonwealth Parliament resolved before then that they should be repealed or that consideration of their repeal should be postponed for a further three years, until 2000. They would actually have come into force on 31 October 1994, but Parliament resolved to wait for a further three years.[6] Parliament then pre-empted the Hamburg Rules from coming into force by passing the Carriage of Goods by Sea Amendment Act 1997 (Cth).[7] As we shall see in due course, the current position in Australia has been modified further.[8]

17.03   **The United States**   At one time it was thought that the catalyst for wider adoption of the Hamburg Rules might be their adoption by the USA. However, that possibility has always been extremely unlikely. A more pressing question has nevertheless been what steps should be taken there to amend the US Carriage of Goods by Sea Act 1936. In 1992 the US Maritime Law Association[9] set up an ad hoc Committee to prepare a draft Bill updating the 1936 Act and work continued on that for a number of years. Perhaps more so than any other national action, the draft Bill[10] led to polarized positions being taken on its respective merits and deficiencies in legal journals[11] and in the shipping press,[12] both within[13] and outside the United States,[14] although not by the CMI.[15] Though it was hoped that the

---

[4] Act No 160.

[5] Part 2 and Sch 1.

[6] See Martin Davies, 'Australian maritime law decisions 1994' [1995] LMCLQ 384.

[7] 15 September 1997. The Hamburg Rules were not removed from the Act altogether: see Davies and Dickey (2004), 174.

[8] See para 17.04.

[9] See <www.mlaus.org>. See Michael F Sturley, 'Revising the US Carriage of Goods by Sea Act: The work of the ad hoc liability rules study group' [1994] Il Diritto Marittimo 685; Michael F Sturley, 'Proposed Amendments to the Carriage of Goods by Sea Act' (1996) 18 Houston JIL 609

[10] The last version (24 September 1999) was the sixth draft.

[11] Regina Asariotis and Michael N Tsimplis, 'The proposed US Carriage of Goods by Sea Act' [1999] LMCLQ 126; Michael Sturley, 'Proposed Amendments to the US Carriage of Goods by Sea Act: A Response to English Criticisms' [1999] LMCLQ 519; Regina Asariotis and Michael N Tsimplis, 'Proposed amendments to the US Carriage of Goods by Sea Act: a reply to Professor Sturley's response' [1999] LMCLQ 530; Howard M McCormack, 'Uniformity of Maritime Law, History, and Perspective from the US Point of View' (1999) 30 JMLC 1481; William Tetley, 'The Proposed New United States Senate COGSA: The Disintegration of Uniform International Carriage of Goods by Sea' (1999) 30 JMLC 595.

[12] See, for example, Michael Ryan, 'US proposals still leading to comment', *Lloyd's List*, 30 December 1997; Andrea Felsted, 'Row over planned changes to US Cogsa', *Lloyd's List*, 5 May 1998; 'Fears over US carriage of goods plans', *Lloyd's List*, 7 May 1998; Vincent De Orchis, 'The new United States COGSA proposal: facts and fallacies', *The Maritime Advocate*, February 2000, 38.

[13] For dissenting views within the US, see the statement by Michael Marks Cohen (Burlingham Underwood LLP, New York), US MLA Document No 723, 10875; US MLA Document No 724, 86.

[14] See William Tetley, 'Law Conventions Trampled: US COGSA Sails its Own Quirky Course', Fairplay, 15 October 1998; Jan Ramberg, 'The Proposed US COGSA — An Outsider's View': <www.forwarderlaw.com/feature/ramart.htm>.

[15] It has stated that 'the CMI respects the right of the MLA to promote a compromise solution to the problems that have arisen in the United States after adoption of the Visby Protocol proved politically impossible'. See 'Intermodal Liability: Statement by the Comité Maritime International', 14 January 1999, *CMI Yearbook 1999*, 328.

1999 draft Bill would be placed before Congress, a Presidential election in 2000 and mounting opposition within the United States severely hampered the likelihood of its enactment, at least in its current form.[16] In any event, there were new and important developments on the international front and US plans were temporarily shelved in expectation of developments in that arena.

Hybrids: Australia   We have referred previously to steps taken in Australia to implement the Hamburg Rules. We now pick up the story.[17] We have noted already that an Act was passed in 1997 to forestall any further implementation of the Hamburg Rules in Australia. However, the Australian Department of Transport and Regional Services had initiated a comprehensive review of the existing cargo liability regime as early as 1995, with the aim of producing amendments to the existing Hague–Visby Rules. Following extensive consultations with a wide range of industry groups, the Carriage of Goods by Sea Regulations 1998 (Cth) were enacted and came into force on 1 July 1998. The effect of these Regulations is to amend the Carriage of Goods by Sea Act 1991 (Cth).[18] The changes effected by the Regulations are far from insubstantial and generally only apply to cargoes which are outward bound from Australia.[19] However, the new system will apply inward where the contract would not otherwise be governed 'by agreement or by law' by the Hague, Hague–Visby, or Hamburg Rules 'or a modification [thereof] by the law of a Contracting State'.[20] Included in the amended Act is enhanced documentary coverage to cover a much wider range of sea carriage documents.[21] There is also extended application of the Rules; thus, the traditional Hague and Hague–Visby 'tackle-to-tackle' period is extended to include any period before loading or after discharge when the goods are in the carrier's charge.[22] Finally, there is now express provision for delay.[23]

17.04

Hybrids: New Zealand   New Zealand[24] enacted its Maritime Transport Act[25] in 1994. Although it is probably not strictly correct to describe this legislation as 'hybrid', we may note that, while the Act gives effect to the Visby Protocol and the SDR Protocol,[26] it also extends their application to international carriage under a non-negotiable document

17.05

---

[16] See Michael F Sturley, 'The Proposed Amendments to the Carriage of Goods by Sea Act: An Update' (2000/2001) 13 USFMLJ 1.

[17] Considered authoritatively in Davies and Dickey (2004), 171. See also Ian Davis, 'COGSA 98: The Australian Carriage of Goods by Sea Act' (1998) 5 IML 223; Stuart Hetherington, 'Australian hybrid cargo liability regime' [1999] LMCLQ 12; Frances Hannah, 'Carriage of Goods by Sea' in White (2000), ch 3; Kate Lewins, 'Are the 1998 amendments to COGSA holding water?' (2000) 28 ABLR 422.

[18] Act No 160.

[19] Article 10(1).

[20] See art 10(2).

[21] Defined as meaning '(i) a bill of lading; (ii) or a negotiable document of title that is similar to a bill of lading and that contains or evidences a contract of carriage of goods by sea; or (iii) a bill of lading that, by law, is not negotiable; or (iv) a non-negotiable document (including a consignment note and a document of the kind known as a sea waybill or the kind known as a ship's delivery order) that either contains or evidences a contract of carriage of goods by sea': art I(1)(g).

[22] See art 1(2) & (3).

[23] Article 4A.

[24] See, generally, Paul Myburgh,'New Zealand' in Huybrechts Vol 2 (2002), ch 7.

[25] Act No 104 (NZ).

[26] It also repeals the Sea Carriage of Goods Act 1940 (s 212(1)).

which is not a bill of lading or similar document of title, where that document contains a paramount clause which states that the Hague–Visby Rules and SDR Protocol govern the carriage as if the document were a bill of lading.[27]

17.06 **Civilian hybrids** A number of hybrid domestic regimes have meanwhile been implemented or canvassed in civil law countries. Indeed this has multiplied during the last decade, a matter of real concern to the CMI.[28] A few examples must suffice here. In the case of China, the Maritime Law of the PRC of 1992[29] contains provisions on carriage of goods by sea which are drawn from the Visby Protocol and the Hamburg Rules.[30] Korea has adopted a similar approach.[31] In the case of the Nordic countries,[32] there has been a long tradition of co-operation in maritime matters and no less on carriage of goods legislation. Thus, following the coming into force of the Hamburg Rules, a number of important changes were made. Although maintaining the Hague–Visby Rules internationally, the various codes provide that the Hamburg Rules are to apply to the extent these are not in conflict with the Hague–Visby Rules. This has been implemented in the national laws of each Nordic member state.[33]

17.07 **Reactions** All these developments were viewed with considerable dismay in the international maritime community.[34] Given the advancing trend towards national approaches, which are the very antithesis of uniformity, the CMI and UNCITRAL, in particular,[35] were galvanized into action. In the next section we examine what action has been taken.

C. New Movements towards Uniformity

17.08 **The work of the CMI** During the period of national initiatives noted above, the CMI's role at the vanguard of unifying instruments, in this and other areas of maritime law has,

---

[27] See s 209(2).

[28] Patrick Griggs expressed the hope that '. . . the prospect (though distant) of a unifying instrument might discourage unilateral action': CMI News Letter 3/1999, 8.

[29] In force 1 July 1993. For a translation, see KX Li and CWM Ingram, *Maritime Law and Policy in China* (2002). For commentary, see L Li, 'The Maritime Code of the People's Republic of China' [1993] LMCLQ 204; Zhu Zengjie, 'The Maritime Code of the People's Republic of China' 1993 Il Diritto Marittimo 176; Zhang Lixing, 'Recent Maritime Legislation and Practice in the People's Republic of China' (1994) 6 USFMLJ 273.

[30] See ch IV of the Maritime Law of the PRC.

[31] See Rok Sang Yu and Jongkwan Peck, 'The Revised Maritime Section of the Korean Commercial Code' [1993] LMCLQ 403.

[32] ie Denmark, Finland, Iceland, Norway, and Sweden.

[33] See Hugo Tiberg and Anders Beijer, *The Swedish Maritime Code* 2nd edn (Stockholm, Axel Ax:son Johnson Institute of Maritime and Transport Law, 2001). Supplements are published at <www.juridicum.su.se/transport/Main/eframep.htm>. For commentary, see Hugo Tiberg, 'The Nordic Maritime Code' [1995] LMCLQ 527; Honka (1997), 15.

[34] See David Michael Collins, 'Admiralty — International Uniformity and the Carriage of Goods by Sea' (1985) 60 Tulane LR 165; Michael F Sturley, 'Uniformity in the Law Governing the Carriage of Goods by Sea' (1995) 26 JMLC 553; Patrick Griggs, 'Uniformity of Maritime Law — An International Perspective' (1999) 73 Tulane LR 1551; Erling Selvig, 'The International Shipping Law of the Twentieth Century under Pressure' (2000) 7 IML 190; William Tetley, 'Uniformity of International Private Maritime Law — The Pros, Cons, and Alternatives to International Conventions — How to Adopt an International Convention' (2000) 34 Tulane MLJ 775.

[35] See Niall McGovern, 'The role of Inter-Governmental Organisations in the Development of Private International Maritime Law' in Von Ziegler and Burckhardt (1993), 159.

been under threat.[36] It undertook much work on the subject of uniformity of carriage regimes, in particular at its Paris Conference in 1990[37] and in the period leading up to the Antwerp Centenary Conference in 1997, pursuant to the work of an International Subcommittee (ISC) on Uniformity of the Law of Carriage of Goods by Sea established under Professor Francesco Berlingieri, the CMI's President *ad honorem*, in 1995. The subject was one of the topics discussed at the Antwerp Conference[38] and the work concluded, after Antwerp, in a final Report[39] which was unanimously adopted by the CMI Assembly in 1999.[40]

Other interest groups   Outside the CMI, other interest groups were also at work, notably **17.09** the OECD's Directorate for Science, Technology and Industry (Maritime Transport Committee) which in January 2001 prepared a Report on Cargo Liability Regimes[41] and held a workshop on this subject in Paris on 25–26 January 2001, under the chairmanship of Alfred Popp. The OECD's aim was not to promote a further proliferation of cargo regimes, but to 'encourage a convergence of views to further harmonise international practices'.[42] Finally, work on the wider subject of intermodal liability[43] by the European Commission's Directorate-General VII has also contributed to the debate.

Co-operation   At the time of the CMI's Antwerp Conference in 1997,[44] UNCITRAL, as **17.10** part of its ongoing work on electronic commerce, invited the CMI to co-operate with it on work on the functions of bills of lading.[45] The CMI Executive Council established a Steering Committee, chaired by Patrick Griggs, and, in due course, an International Working Group (IWG) on Issues of Transport Law[46] was constituted under the chairmanship of Stuart Beare. A questionnaire[47] was sent to the CMI member associations at the end of April 1999.[48] Pursuant to the UNCITRAL brief to the CMI to obtain broadly-based information and involve the relevant international organizations, two 'round table' meetings were held in London in 1998 and again in 1999.[49] The CMI then established an

---

[36] See Paul Myburgh, 'Uniformity or Unilateralism in the Law of Carriage of Goods by Sea?' (2000) 31 Victoria UWLR 355; Erling Selvig, 'The International Shipping Law of the Twentieth Century under Pressure' (2000) 7 IML 190.

[37] A draft document, 'Uniformity of the Law of the Carriage of Goods by Sea in the Nineteen Nineties', was presented and discussed at the Conference. It was approved as a basis for further work. See *CMI Yearbook 1990*, 103.

[38] See *CMI Yearbook 1997: Antwerp II*, 288; *CMI Yearbook 1998*, 163.

[39] See Francesco Berlingieri, 'Uniformity of the Law of the Carriage of Goods by Sea — Report on the Work of the International Sub-Committee': CMI News Letter 2/1999, 1 (reprinted in *CMI Yearbook 1999*, 105).

[40] Minutes of the CMI Assembly, 8 May 1999: CMI News Letter 3/1999, 5.

[41] The Report was prepared by Roger Clarke and published in January 2001. See <www.oecd.org/dataoecd/38/5/2751633.pdf>.

[42] See the Outcome Summary on the OECD website.

[43] Through its Task Force: Intermodality (DG VII of the European Commission). See <www.cordis.lu/transport/src/ taskforce>.

[44] Minutes of the CMI Assembly, 14 June 1997: CMI News Letter 3/1997, 14.

[45] See UNCITRAL: Report of the Working Group on Electronic Data Interchange (EDI) on the Work of its Thirtieth Session (26 February–8 March 1996), A/CN.9/421, paras 104–108.

[46] See Minutes of the CMI Assembly, 15 May 1998: CMI News Letter 2/1998, 3.

[47] For the text, see *CMI Yearbook 1998*, 132.

[48] See *CMI Yearbook 1999*, 132.

[49] See Report of the United Nations Commission on International Trade Law on the Work of its Thirty-second Session (17 May–4 June 1999) A/54/17, paras 410–417.

International Sub-Committee (ISC) which met on four occasions during the course of 2000.[50] On 31 March 2000, the Secretary-General of UNCITRAL published a Report on possible future work on Transport Law.[51] A draft instrument was circulated in advance of the CMI's Singapore Conference in 2001 and this provided an important framework for the discussions at the Conference.[52] By December that year the CMI presented to UNCITRAL its Final Draft Instrument on Transport Law.[53] In short, by the end of 2001, an enormous amount of hard work and effort had already been expended on the preparation of a draft instrument, to be taken up in due course by UNCITRAL. There was no doubt, however, that it was the United States draft which proved to be the final catalyst for this initiative.[54]

D. The UNCITRAL Draft Convention

17.11 **Working Group**   Following the work undertaken by the CMI, the baton of responsibility for future work on a new international convention passed firmly to UNCITRAL. Early in 2002 UNCITRAL 'converted' the CMI's Final Draft into its own instrument, the 'Preliminary draft instrument on the carriage of goods by sea'.[55] The Preliminary Draft was referred to a revitalized UNCITRAL Working Group III (Transport Law).[56] Each year since April 2002 the Working Group has met twice, in New York and then in Vienna to discuss various aspects of the Draft.[57] A second version of the Preliminary Draft was issued in 2003, the 'Draft Instrument on the Carriage of Goods [Wholly or Partly] [By Sea]'.[58] In 2005 the 'Draft Convention on the carriage of goods [wholly or partly] [by sea]' was published.[59] Both the Draft Instrument and the Draft Convention have been under constant consideration by the Working Group, which has so far met six times at New York and Vienna[60] to examine it. A further session was held at Vienna in November 2006.[61]

---

[50] On 27 & 28 January; 6 & 7 April; 7 & 8 July; 12 & 13 October. The Reports of these meetings are published, in full, in *CMI Yearbook 2000: Singapore I*, 176.

[51] A/CN.9/476.

[52] See Stephen Girvin, 'The 37th Comité Maritime International Conference: a report' [2001] LMCLQ 406.

[53] For the text, see *CMI Yearbook 2001*, 182.

[54] As hoped for by the doyen of US maritime lawyers, Nicholas Healy, who, in endorsing the work done by the MLA Ad Hoc Liability Rules Study Group in 1996, said that: 'I think if the contents of the proposed bill are approved by the Association, it should be submitted to the CMI as a draft convention. Then let the CMI work over it and take what they want, disregard what they don't want, and come up with a convention that we can recommend for ratification by our government'. See US MLA document No 723, 10885.

[55] A/CN.9/WG.III/WP.21 (8 January 2002).

[56] See <www.uncitral.org/uncitral/en/commission/working_groups/3Transport.html>.

[57] For its work in the first two years, see particularly Michael F Sturley, 'The United Nations Commission on International Trade Law's Transport Law Project: An Interim View of a Work in Progress' (2003–2004) Texas ILJ 65.

[58] UNCITRAL Doc A/CN.9/WG.III/WP.32 (4 September 2003).

[59] UNCITRAL Doc A/CN.9/WG.III/WP56 (8 September 2005).

[60] New York: 17th Session (3–13 April 2006), 15th Session (18–28 April 2005), 13th Session (3–14 May 2004). Vienna: 12th Session (6–17 October 2003), 14th Session (29 November–10 December 2004), 16th Session (28 November–9 December 2005).

[61] 6–17 November 2006.

Scope   The current working version of the Draft Convention[62] is still under considera-   **17.12**
tion by Working Group III. It consists at present of 21 chapters and 105 sections. If eventually enacted it will be the most comprehensive and detailed convention ever drafted.
It will at once be clear that this new Draft Convention covers many areas which have not
formed a part of previous carriage conventions. Unlike many previous international instruments the Draft Convention tries to leave almost nothing to chance. The division of the
various chapters is as follows: Chapter 1 — General provisions; Chapter 2 — Electronic
communication; Chapter 3 — Scope of application; Chapter 4 — Period of responsibility;
Chapter 5 — Obligations of carrier; Chapter 6 — Liability of the carrier for loss, damage or
delay; Chapter 7 — Additional provisions relating to particular stages of carriage; Chapter 8 —
Obligations of the shipper; Chapter 9 — Transport documents and electronic transport records;
Chapter 10 — Delivery to the consignee; Chapter 11 — Right of control; Chapter 12 —
Transfer of rights; Chapter 13 — Limitation of liability; Chapter 14 — Rights of suit;
Chapter 15 — Time for suit; Chapter 16 — Jurisdiction; Chapter 17 — Arbitration;
Chapter 18 — General average; Chapter 19 — Other conventions; Chapter 20 — Validity of
contractual stipulations; Chapter 21 — Final Clauses.

Contents   Even a cursory survey of the chapter division of the Draft Convention gives   **17.13**
some indication of the additional areas which will be covered in this new instrument.
A major issue, still not fully resolved, is the scope of the instrument. Thus, the issue is the
extent to which the new Convention should apply on a 'door-to-door' basis or 'port-
to-port'.[63] This dilemma is reflected in the title to the Convention which is still '. . . [wholly
or partly] [by sea]' and in the fact that many provisions of the Draft contain variant
(or alternative) provisions.[64] Among the new areas covered in the Draft Convention are
detailed provision on electronic communications, rights of control, and transfer of rights.

Prospects   There can be no question that, if this Convention proceeds to a diplomatic   **17.14**
conference, or even if it is enacted by UNICTRAL without such a conference, this
Convention will have a profound impact on the existing international regime for the carriage of goods by sea. It is submitted, however, that there are a number of formidable difficulties ahead. On the one side there is the hope that, in the name of uniformity, the
Convention will prove popular and attract sufficient ratifications to make it viable. On the
other hand, its very comprehensiveness may yet prove to be its undoing.[65] Thus, the fact
that the Convention attempts, within the scope of one instrument, to cover such a multitude of issues may not make it very attractive to countries which have already enacted their

---

[62] ie that of 8 September 2005.

[63] See Francesco Berlingieri, 'A New Convention on the Carriage of Goods by Sea: Port-to-Port or Door-to-Door?' (2003) 8 Uniform LR 265.

[64] See, eg, arts 8 (general scope of application), 12 (transport beyond the contract of carriage), 15 (goods that may become a danger), 20(4) (liability of maritime performing parties), 24 (notice of loss, damage, or delay), 25 (deviation during sea carriage), 31 (basis of shipper's liability), 32 (material misstatement by ship-per), 43 (prima facie and conclusive evidence), 45 (freight prepaid), 55 (variations to the contract of carriage), 57 (carrier's execution of instruction), 64 (basis of limitation of liability), etc.

[65] Indeed, it is this which has already attracted criticism. See, eg, William Tetley, 'Reform of Carriage of Goods — The UNCITRAL Draft and Senate COGSA '99' (2003–2004) 28 Tulane MLJ 1.

own domestic modifications to existing international regimes. The other difficulty may well be in encouraging governments to enact the Convention. The acid test, as always with international conventions, is whether major world players, such as the United States, and emerging powerful economies, such as China and India, will take steps to enact it. For now, however, the landscape is still changing, and it remains difficult to predict the final form that the Convention will take. Finally, whatever final form the Convention takes, the extremely detailed drafting style is likely to cause many problems for courts faced with interpreting it.

18

THE LEGAL EFFECT AND INTERPRETATION OF THE HAGUE AND HAGUE–VISBY RULES

A. Introduction

Overview   We have looked in previous chapters at the events leading to the enactment of   **18.01**
the Hague and Hague–Visby Rules. In this chapter we are concerned with two principal
issues, namely the legal effect of the Rules and the approach of the English courts to
interpreting the Rules.[1]

B. The Legal Effect of the Hague Rules

Hague Rules   Article X[2] of the Hague Rules provides that: **18.02**

> The provisions of this convention shall apply to all bills of lading issued in any of the con-
> tracting States.

As has been noted by one distinguished commentator, the wording of article X 'is as simple
as the discussion to which it has given rise is complex'.[3] This must be read also with the
Protocol of Signature to the Rules, which provides that:

> The High Contracting Parties may give effect to this convention either by giving it the force
> of law or by including in their national legislation in a form appropriate to that legislation the
> rules adopted under this convention.

---

[1] See, generally, Scrutton (1996), section XX; Cooke (2001), ch 85; Carver (2005), ch 9.
[2] Berlingieri (1997), 684.
[3] Clarke (1976), 11. See too Yiannopoulos (1962), 36.

This provision was inserted because in some civil law countries the existence of an international convention which has been ratified diplomatically brings that convention into effect as a matter of domestic law.[4] However, this is not the case in the United Kingdom, where a further step is usually needed, the passing of an Act of Parliament. Thus the Carriage of Goods by Sea Act 1924 states

> ... whereas it is expedient that the [Hague] rules ... as set out with modifications in the Schedule to this Act ... should, subject to the provisions of this Act, be given the force of law with a view to establishing the responsibilities, liabilities, rights and immunities attaching to carriers under bills of lading

> Be it therefore enacted ... as follows:—

18.03 **Implementation in the UK** So as to give effect to article X, there are two material provisions in the 1924 Act:[5]

> 1. Subject to the provisions of this Act, the Rules shall have effect in relation to and in connection with the carriage of goods by sea in ships carrying goods from any port in Great Britain or Northern Ireland to any other port whether in or outside Great Britain or Northern Ireland.

> 2. Every bill of lading, or similar document of title, issued in Great Britain or Northern Ireland which contains or is evidence of any contract to which the Rules apply shall contain an express statement that it is to have effect subject to the provisions of the said Rules as applied by this Act.

18.04 **Analysis** A number of points should be made about these two sections of the Act. We may note that section 1 of the Act was only applicable 'in relation to and in connection with' the shipment of goods from ports in Great Britain to ports in or outside Great Britain. The port of destination was immaterial for the purposes of the Act. Thus, section 1 was narrower than was intended by article X.[6] The effect of section 1 was that it could not be relied upon to secure the application of the Rules by the courts of another country, unless the law of England was under the relevant conflict of law rules also the law governing the contract of carriage.[7] One way of dealing with the apparently restricted scope of section 1 was section 3 of the Act, which required a 'paramount clause'[8] to be inserted into a bill of lading to make the Rules applicable to the contract. It was believed that this would compel foreign courts confronted with bills of lading issued in the United Kingdom to apply the 1924 Act as part of the terms of the contract.[9] However, the sanction for failure to include a paramount clause was not stipulated and indeed section 3 was not, in reality, any more effective than section 1 in this respect.

---

[4] cf for the 1976 Limitation Convention, Griggs, Williams and Farr (2005). For discussion of that Convention, see para 29.37.

[5] See Clarke (1976), ch 3.

[6] Article X was not reproduced in the Schedule to the 1924 Act.

[7] It is worth remembering, however, that many commonwealth and other countries enacted measures which corresponded to the 1924 Act. See, eg s 4(1) and s 6 of the Australian Sea-Carriage of Goods Act 1924. See too para 15.10.

[8] See the discussion of paramount clauses at para 19.51.

[9] Clarke (1976), 19.

Vita Food   The difficulties of drafting in the 1924 Act arose directly for consideration in   **18.05**
the controversial case of *Vita Food Products v Unus Shipping Co*,[10] which many commentators regard as wrongly decided. Indeed, it has not been followed subsequently in other
cases. Here bills of lading were issued in Newfoundland, at that time not part of Canada,[11]
for the carriage of a cargo of fish between Newfoundland and New York. Newfoundland
had adopted the Hague Rules by statute in 1932 for all shipments within and outbound
from Newfoundland. Section 3 of the Newfoundland Carriage of Goods by Sea Act, which
corresponded to the 1924 UK Act, provided that every bill of lading 'shall contain an
express statement that it is to have effect subject' to the Hague Rules. But the bills of lading
in question contained no such statement and were expressly stated as being subject to
English law which, of course, could not apply the Rules unless the shipment was from the
UK. The ship in question, the *Hurry On*, stranded because of negligence in navigation and
the cargo was damaged. An action was brought in Nova Scotia, part of Canada, against the
shipowners in respect of this damage. Were the shipowners entitled to rely on the exceptions (negligence in navigation) in the bills of lading? At first instance, Chisholm CJ[12] held
that the absence of an express statement (a clause paramount) did not invalidate the bills of
lading. The 1932 Act applied and the rights of the parties therefore had to be decided by
reference to that Act. The Supreme Court of Nova Scotia[13] reversed this decision, however,
and held that the English law applied, thus ignoring the mandatory provisions of the Hague
Rules. The claimant could not, therefore, plead that the contract was illegal, because the Rules
did not apply. On further appeal to the Privy Council, the decision of the Nova Scotia Supreme
Court was upheld, namely, that the shipowners were entitled to rely on the bill of lading exceptions. Lord Wright noted that had the bills of lading been governed by Newfoundland law, they
would have been subject to the Hague Rules by virtue of section 1 of the Newfoundland Act.[14]
Further, the bills of lading were not illegal by Newfoundland law, or by any other relevant law,
and, though not subject to the Hague Rules, they were enforceable according to their own
terms. Finally, even had the bills of lading been illegal in Newfoundland, they would have been
enforceable, according to their terms, in Nova Scotia.[15]

Analysis   In essence what the Privy Council did was to apply the conflict of laws principle   **18.06**
of the express choice of the parties.[16] They ignored the compulsory nature of the Hague Rules,
as expressed in section 1 of the Act. It could be argued also that the clause which invoked
English law was also invalid in the sense that it relieved or lessened the carrier's responsibility
under the Hague Rules.[17] The effect of the case was to highlight a gap in the international
application of the Hague Rules and this came to be known as the '*Vita Food* gap'.[18]

---

[10] [1939] AC 277 (PC). See too *The Torni* [1932] P 78 (CA); *The St Joseph* [1933] P 119.
[11] England's oldest colony.
[12] [1938] 2 DLR 372.
[13] ibid.
[14] ie, the equivalent of s 1 of the Carriage of Goods by Sea Act 1924.
[15] [1939] AC 277 (PC), 296 (Lord Wright).
[16] See JHC Morris, 'The scope of the Carriage of Goods by Sea Act 1971' (1979) 95 LQR 59.
[17] ie, under art III, r 8. See the discussion at para 19.39.
[18] See too *PS Chellaram & Co Ltd v China Ocean Shipping Co (The Zhi Jiang Kou)* [1989] 1 Lloyd's Rep
413; *Pacific Electric Wire & Cable Co Ltd v Neptune Orient Lines Ltd* [1993] 3 SLR 60.

C. The Legal Effect of the Hague–Visby Rules

18.07 **Introduction**   One of the issues which had to be addressed in the lead up to the enactment of the Visby Protocol was the '*Vita Food* gap'; indeed this attracted early attention at the CMI's Rijeka Conference and in all the subsequent debates leading to the signing of the Visby Protocol.[19] Article V of the Protocol contains the new article X and deletes and replaces article X of the Hague Rules.[20]

18.08 **1971 Act**   Article X of the Hague–Visby Rules led to the employment of a different technique for their implementation in the United Kingdom. Thus, the Carriage of Goods by Sea Act 1971 expressly incorporates the Hague–Visby Rules and provides in section 1(2) as follows:

> The provisions of the Rules, as set out in the Schedule to this Act, shall have the force of law.

18.09 **Meaning of 'force of law'**   It is now a standard technique for international conventions to be given the 'force of law' in United Kingdom legislation.[21] This phrase is considered to be stronger than the wording which was used in section 1 of the 1924 Act.[22] Under article 7(2)[23] of the Rome Convention on the Law Applicable to Contractual Obligations,[24] the use of the wording 'force of law' has the effect of making the application of the Rules mandatory and, as such, the law of the forum must be applied, no matter what the governing law of the contract is. This is further reinforced by article X, the last part of which states '... whatever may be the nationality of the ship, the carrier, the shipper, the consignee, or any other interested person'.

18.10 *The Hollandia*   The leading English case on the meaning of 'force of law' is *The Hollandia*.[25] In this case a road-finishing machine, weighing 9,906kg, was shipped from Leith bound for Bonaire in the Netherlands Antilles. The carriers issued a through bill of lading[26] providing for transhipment at Amsterdam and this contained a Dutch choice of law clause and a further provision that the Court of Amsterdam should have exclusive jurisdiction in any dispute. The machine was damaged during unloading at Bonaire as a result of the negligence of the servants of the carrying vessel, the *Morviken*, which was under the Norwegian flag. The shippers commenced proceedings in the Admiralty Court in London in 1980 by means of an action *in rem*[27] against the *Hollandia*, a sister ship[28] of the *Morviken*.

---

[19] For discussion, see Berlingieri (1997), 687. See too para 15.17.

[20] See Clarke (1976) 105.

[21] Thus, the 1996 Protocol on Limitation of Liability has the force of law: see s 185(1) of the Merchant Shipping Act 1995, c 19. See para 29.60.

[22] One writer has stated that there 'is a world of difference' between the 1924 Act formulation and that in the 1971 Act: Tan Lee Meng (1994), 331.

[23] This provides as follows: 'Nothing in this Convention shall restrict the application of the rules of the law of the forum in a situation where they are mandatory irrespective of the law otherwise applicable to the contract'.

[24] See <www.rome-convention.org>. The Convention has been Implemented in the United Kingdom in the Contracts (Applicable) Law Act 1990, c 36.

[25] (sub nom *The Morviken*) [1983] 1 AC 565.

[26] Generally, as to through bills of lading, see para 3.21.

[27] See para 35.15.

[28] See para 35.47.

The carrier sought a stay of the proceedings on the basis of the jurisdiction clause in the bill of lading. At the time of the proceedings there were different limitation of liability provisions in the two jurisdictions. Thus, the Hague Rules were still in operation in the Netherlands,[29] and consequently the liability of the carrier would have been limited to approximately £250 (under the package or unit formula). However, under the Hague–Visby Rules in force in the UK, the shipper would have been entitled to a higher sum, calculated on the gross weight[30] of the damaged cargo and this would have amounted to £11,500. At first instance[31] the action was stayed but this was reversed by the Court of Appeal.[32] Lord Denning MR stated that:

> In my opinion [force of law] means that, in all Courts of the United Kingdom, the provisions of the rules are to be given the coercive force of law. So much so that, in every case properly brought before the Courts of the United Kingdom, the rules are to be given supremacy over every other provision of the bill of lading. If there is anything elsewhere in the bill of lading which is inconsistent with the rules or which derogates from the effect of them, it is to be rejected. There is to be no contracting-out of the Rules.[33]

The House of Lords likewise concluded that the Hague–Visby Rules were clearly applicable to the bills of lading in question, falling within both paragraphs (a) and (b) of article X.[34] Further, to give effect to the choice of law clause in the bill of lading in Lord Diplock's view would amount to a contravention of article III, rule 8 of the Rules, which renders void any attempt to lessen the carrier's liability as enshrined in the Rules.[35] According to Lord Diplock to reach any other conclusion

> would leave it open to any shipowner to evade the provisions of art III, r 8 by the simple device of inserting in his bill of lading issued in, or for carriage from a port in, any contracting state a clause in standard form providing as the exclusive forum for resolution of disputes what might aptly be described as a court of convenience, viz. one situated in a country which did not apply the Hague–Visby Rules.[36]

This decision has not been universally welcomed by critics, some of whom have argued that the phrase 'force of law' means that effect should be given to the intentions of the parties as expressed in their choice of law clause.[37] Notwithstanding these criticisms, the view of the House of Lords has been cited with approval and followed.[38] It should, however, be noted that the decision will only be relevant where the application of the Rules is mandatory, which is to say where the Rules apply by virtue of article X.

---

[29] The Netherlands acceded to the Visby protocol on 26 April 1982 (with entry into force on 26 July 1982): see Appendix IIIB.

[30] See art IV, r 5(a) and the discussion at para 29.07.

[31] [1981] 2 Lloyd's Rep 61.

[32] [1982] QB 872 (CA). See JG Collier, 'Conflict of Laws' (1982) CLJ 253.

[33] At 883.

[34] For discussion of these provisions of the Rules, see para 19.14.

[35] See the discussion at para 19.39.

[36] [1983] 1 AC 565, 574.

[37] See, eg, FA Mann, 'The Hague–Visby Rules and the "force of law"' (1987) 103 LQR 523, 526–527.

[38] See, eg, *RA Lister & Co v EG Thomson (Shipping Ltd) (The Benarty)(No 2)* [1983] 2 Lloyd's Rep 50; *The Epar* [1984] SLR 409; *Sidmar NV v Fednav International Ltd* (Federal Court of Canada, 11 October 1996). The case was also cited with approval by the US Supreme Court in *Vimar Seguros y Reaseguros SA v M/V Sky Reefer* 515 US 528 (1995), 540.

18.11 **Rules not applicable** Where the Rules are not mandatorily applicable, the courts will not be prepared to interpret a choice of English law as indicating an intention to incorporate the Rules into the contract of carriage within the meaning of article X. In *Hellenic Steel Co v Svolamar Shipping Co (The Komninos S)*[39] a cargo of steel coils were shipped from Thessaloniki to Ravenna under bills of lading which provided that any disputes arising under the contract of carriage were 'to be referred to British courts'. The Court of Appeal regarded this as an implied choice of law by the parties. In response to a claim for cargo damage, the shipowner sought to rely on exclusion clauses in the contract which would be rendered null and void by the Hague–Visby Rules, if the latter were applicable. However, as Greece was not then a contracting state,[40] the Hague–Visby Rules were not mandatorily applicable since shipment was not from a port in a contracting state, nor had the bill of lading been issued in a contracting state. The Rules would thus only be relevant if it was the intention of the parties that they should be incorporated into the contract of carriage within the meaning of article X(c). The Court of Appeal refused to infer such an intention merely from the inclusion in the contract of a choice of forum clause and the shipowner was able to invoke the protection of the contractual exceptions:

> Interpreting art X(c) as best I can, I find it impossible to conclude that 'All dispute(s) to be referred to British Courts' amounted to a provision that the legislation of the United Kingdom giving effect to the Rules should govern the contract.

> The consequence of concluding . . . that the Hague–Visby Rules were not incorporated is that the exemption clauses in the bills of lading protect the shipowners and the cargo-owners are unable to recover. The fact is that the cargo-owners contracted on terms which expressly relieved the shipowners, their master and crew, of responsibility for any act, error, neglect or default in the management, stowage, navigation or preparation of the vessel or otherwise. This judgment gives effect, for better or worse, to what the parties expressly agreed.[41]

D. Contractual Freedom

18.12 **Other documents?** We have looked so far at the meaning of the phrase 'force of law' in the Hague–Visby Rules. In the next chapter we shall see that the mandatory coverage of the Rules only extends to bills of lading or 'similar documents of title'.[42] However, apart from under the Rules, the Carriage of Goods by Sea Act[43] specifies that the parties are free expressly to incorporate the Hague–Visby Rules into a bill of lading or other negotiable

---

[39] [1991] 1 Lloyd's Rep 370 (CA). See FMB Reynolds, '*Vita Food* resurgent' (1992) 108 LQR 395.

[40] This has since changed. By Law 2107/29.12.1992, Greece ratified the Brussels Convention of 1924, together with the 1968 and 1979 Protocols. The provisions of the Convention and the Protocols came into force on 23 June 1993. See George Economou, 'Law applicable in Greece on the contracts of carriage of goods by sea' (1995) 2 IML 155.

[41] [1991] 1 Lloyd's Rep 370 (CA), 377 (Bingham LJ).

[42] See para 19.19.

[43] There was no such provision in the Carriage of Goods by Sea Act 1924.

instrument in situations where the Rules would not otherwise apply. This follows because of the terms of section 1(6)[44] which provides that:

Without prejudice to Article X(c) of the Rules, the Rules shall have the force of law in relation to:

(a) any bill of lading if the contract contained in or evidenced by it expressly provides that the Rules shall govern the contract,

and

(b) any receipt which is a non-negotiable document marked as such if the contract contained in or evidenced by it is a contract for the carriage of goods by sea which expressly provides that the Rules are to govern the contract as if the receipt were a bill of lading,

but subject, where paragraph (b) applies, to any necessary modifications and in particular with the omission in Article III of the Rules of the second sentence of paragraph 4 and of paragraph 7.

Rules 'shall govern the contract'   We may note that, in relation to section 1(6)(a), it is **18.13** provided that the Rules will have the force of law in relation to a bill of lading if the contract 'contained in or evidenced by it' expressly provides that the Rules shall govern the contract. This provision was not strictly necessary, for several reasons. In the first place, as we shall see, article X already provides that it will apply mandatorily to 'every bill of lading'. Indeed, section 1(6) expressly states that it is 'without prejudice' to article X(c), which provides that the Rules shall apply to 'the contract contained in or evidenced by the bill of lading' and 'provided that these Rules or legislation of any State giving effect to them are to govern the contract'.[45] As we have already seen, it is not necessary for a bill of lading under the Hague–Visby Rules to include a paramount clause incorporating the Rules.[46]

Non-negotiable receipts   Section 1(6)(b) is an important provision of the 1971 Act **18.14** because it permits the extension of the Rules to non-negotiable documents. The Rules will, however, only have the 'force of law' where the document expressly provides that the Rules are to govern the contract 'as if the receipt were a bill of lading'. This provision is potentially of great importance for those trades where shipments are habitually carried without bills of lading. Thus, roll-on/roll-off ferry shipments will be covered where the cargo is carried under non-negotiable receipts,[47] sea waybills,[48] or consignment notes. If a non-negotiable receipt is issued in this way, however, two provisions of the Rules are omitted, namely the second sentence of article III, rule 4, and article III, rule 7.

Conflicts   One problem which may occur is a conflict between the provisions of the Rules **18.15** and express terms of the non-negotiable receipt. There are two cases, both of which concerned

---

[44] There are similar provisions in the Singapore Carriage of Goods by Sea Act 1972 (see s 3(4)) and in the South African Carriage of Goods by Sea Act 1986 (s 1(1)(c)).

[45] See para 19.16.

[46] Contrasted with the position under the Hague Rules: see para 18.04.

[47] 'It is the invariable practice of all English cross channel operators not to issue bills of lading for the cross channel Ro-Ro ferry trade. Instead, they issue commercial non-negotiable receipts': *Browner International Ltd v Monarch Shipping Co Ltd (The European Enterprise)* [1989] 2 Lloyd's Rep 185, 187 (Steyn J); *The Rafaela S* [2003] EWCA Civ 556; [2004] QB 702, at [85] (Rix LJ).

[48] See also para 19.20.

the application of the Rules, but with different limits of liability. In the earlier case, *McCarren & Co Ltd v Humber International Transport Ltd (The Vechscroon)*,⁴⁹ 293 sides of pork were shipped on a ro-ro ferry between Poole and Cherbourg. The consignment note for the goods incorporated the Hague–Visby Rules but imposed a lower limit of liability than that defined in the Rules.⁵⁰ During the voyage to Cherbourg the refrigeration vehicle containing the pork overturned and the refrigeration equipment was switched off to minimize the risk of fire. Upon arrival at Cherbourg the goods were condemned. It was argued for the defendant carriers that there was a distinction to be drawn between a consignment note which said 'this non-negotiable receipt shall be governed by the Hague–Visby Rules' and a document which said 'this non-negotiable receipt shall be governed by the Hague–Visby Rules as if it were a bill of lading'.⁵¹ Lloyd J could

> think of no sensible reason why Parliament should have intended to draw any distinction between a document which says 'this non-negotiable receipt shall be governed by the Hague–Visby Rules' and a document which says 'this non-negotiable receipt shall be governed by the Hague–Visby Rules as if it were a bill of lading' . . . It seems to me that the purpose of the words is . . . quite simply to equate non-negotiable receipts, which are expressly governed by the rules, with bills of lading which are expressly governed by the rules.⁵²

On this reasoning the limitation clause could not be relied upon as it contravened the provision in the Hague–Visby Rules as to limitation.⁵³

18.16 *The European Enterprise*   *The Vechscroon* may be contrasted with the decision in *Browner International Ltd v Monarch Shipping Co Ltd (The European Enterprise)*.⁵⁴ Here a consignment of meat, packed in a refrigerated tractor trailer unit, was shipped from Dover to Calais, also under a non-negotiable consignment note. The consignment note expressly incorporated the Hague–Visby Rules subject to a number of provisos, including a limitation of liability provision which was 'substantially less generous'⁵⁵ than that contained in article IV, rule 5 of the Rules. When the goods were damaged in transit, the cargo owner argued that the lower contractual limit was rendered null and void by section 1(6)(b). However, Steyn J pointed out that, as the Rules themselves were not mandatorily applicable to non-negotiable receipts, the parties had freedom to negotiate their own terms and decide whether or not to incorporate the Rules, in whole or in part, into their contract. In his opinion

> it would be curious if a voluntary paramount clause, which reflected only a partial incorporation of the Rules, had a result that a statutory binding character was given to *all* the Rules, even where there was no primary contractual bond. It must be right that in enacting s 1(6)(b)

---

⁴⁹ [1982] 1 Lloyd's Rep 301.

⁵⁰ 'The sea-carriers' liability is limited to F2000 per package or unit whether or not any value in excess of these sums be stated in the document or otherwise declared to the sea-carrier . . .'.

⁵¹ There is no logical reason for the omission of the words 'or similar document of title', as in art I(b) of the Rules.

⁵² [1982] 1 Lloyd's Rep 301, 304–305.

⁵³ At this time (before the SDR Protocol) art IV, r 5(a) specified '10,000 francs per package or unit or 30 francs per kilo of gross weight'. See para 29.11.

⁵⁴ [1989] 2 Lloyd's Rep 185.

⁵⁵ At 187 (Steyn J).

the legislation did not intend to override the agreement of the parties when the parties had freedom of choice whether or not to incorporate the rules into their contract.[56]

Assessment   It is submitted that the decision in *The European Enterprise* is probably   **18.17** sounder in law than *The Vechscroon*. The Rules are not compulsorily applicable to non-negotiable receipts and only become applicable when the parties contract to make them applicable. Thus, while it is possible for the Rules to apply statutorily to waybills or non-negotiable consignment notes they only do apply if the consignment note complies in all respects with section 1(6)(b) of the Carriage of Goods by Sea Act 1971.

E. Interpretation of the Hague and Hague–Visby Rules

International Convention   As we have now seen, the Hague Rules as contained in the   **18.18** Carriage of Goods by Sea Act 1924, and the Hague–Visby Rules, as contained in the Carriage of Goods by Sea Act 1971, are the product of an international convention. The question which then arises is how such an international convention is to be interpreted when it has been enacted into English law.[57]

Earlier guidance   In *Stag Line Ltd v Foscolo, Mango & Co Ltd*[58] Lord Macmillan stated that: **18.19**

> As these rules must come under the consideration of foreign Courts it is desirable in the interests of uniformity that their interpretation should not be rigidly controlled by domestic precedents of antecedent date, but rather that the language of the rules be construed on broad principles of general acceptance.[59]

Lord Atkin likewise said that:

> In approaching the construction of these rules it appears to me to be important to bear in mind that one has to give the words as used their plain meaning, and not to colour one's interpretation by considering whether a meaning otherwise plain should be avoided if it alters the previous law .... For the purpose of uniformity it is, therefore, important that the Courts should apply themselves to the consideration only of the words used without any predilection for the former law ...[60]

Approach followed   The basic guidance given in the *Stag Line* case has been consistently   **18.20** followed by later courts. Thus, in *The Hollandia*,[61] Lord Diplock confirmed that:

> [The Rules] should be given a purposive rather than a narrow literalistic construction, particularly wherever the adoption of a literalistic construction would enable the stated purpose

---

[56] At 191 (emphasis in the original).

[57] See Charles Debattista, 'Carriage Conventions and their interpretation in English courts' [1997] JBL 130.

[58] [1932] AC 328.

[59] At 350. See *Tilbury v International Oil Pollution Compensation Fund* [2003] EWCA Civ 65; [2003] 1 Lloyd's Rep 327, at [16]; [21] (Mance LJ); *Shipping Corp of India Ltd v Gamlen Chemical Co (A/Asia) Pty Ltd* (1980) 147 CLR 142, 159 (Mason & Wilson JJ); *Anglo-Irish Beef Processors International v Federated Stevedores Geelong* [1997] 2 VR 676, 696 (Phillips JA).

[60] At 342–343. See too *William Holyman & Sons Pty Ltd v Foy & Gibson Pty Ltd* (1945) 73 CLR 622, where Dixon J said that 'the case law, English, Australian and American, dealing with other legislation thought to be in pari materia cannot be applied to the Hague Rules, except with great care and discrimination' (at 633).

[61] [1983] 1 AC 565.

of the international convention, viz. the unification of domestic laws of the contracting States relating to bills of lading, to be evaded by the use of colourable devices that, not being expressly referred to in the Rules, are not specifically prohibited.[62]

18.21 **Absence of clear wording in the Rules** In the absence of clear wording in the Rules, what approach should be followed? The answer again is provided in *Stag Line Ltd v Foscolo, Mango & Co Ltd*[63] where the House of Lords insisted, in relation to the effects of a deviation, that the courts should follow the domestic rule which pre-dated the Hague Rules position. Thus Lord Russell said that:

> It was well settled before the Act that an unjustifiable deviation deprived a ship of the protection of exceptions. They only applied to the contract voyage. If it had been the intention of the legislature to make so drastic a change in the law relating to contracts of carriage of goods by sea, the change should and would have been enacted in clear terms.[64]

In *Gosse Millerd Ltd v Canadian Government Merchant Marine Ltd*,[65] the House of Lords was asked to consider the scope of the exclusion in article IV, rule 2(a), namely, 'the management of the ship'.[66] In earlier, pre-Hague, cases this phrase was used in bill of lading exclusion clauses and was interpreted as excluding liability for bad stowage.[67] In concluding that the Rules did not alter the position, Viscount Sumner said that:

> When the legislature gave effect in 1924 to the labours of the International Conferences on Maritime Law of 1922 and 1923, it must be taken to have been aware of the English decisions, which from *The Ferro* in 1893 onwards had construed the words reproduced in art IV, r 2, and as that line of decisions had covered some thirty years and the clause had remained in general use in bills of lading, I think it must be taken that the legislature intended to confirm the construction thus judicially arrived at, except in so far as, by introducing variations into the language used, it clearly made a change.
>
> By forbearing to define 'management of the ship' ... the Legislature has, in my opinion, shown a clear intention to continue and enforce the old clause as it was previously understood and regularly construed by the Courts of law.[68]

18.22 **Use of *travaux préparatoires*** Article 32 of the Vienna Convention on the Law of Treaties[69] provides that:

> Recourse may be had to supplementary means of interpretation, including the preparatory work of the treaty and the circumstances of its conclusion, in order to confirm the meaning resulting from the application of article 31,[70] or to determine the meaning when the interpretation according to article 31:
>
> (a)   leaves the meaning ambiguous or obscure; or
> (b)   leads to a result which is manifestly absurd or unreasonable.

---

[62] At 572–573.
[63] [1932] AC 328.
[64] At 347.
[65] [1929] AC 223.
[66] See the discussion of this defence at para 28.07.
[67] See *The Ferro* [1893] P 38, discussed in the speech of Lord Hailsham LC: [1929] AC 223, 231.
[68] At 236–237.
[69] 1969 and in force 27 January 1980. The United Kingdom ratified the Convention on 25 June 1971: see Treaty Series No 058 (1980): Cmnd 7964.
[70] Article 31 lays down general rules of interpretation of treaties.

Further guidance on the use of *travaux préparatoires* was given in the leading case of *Fothergill v Monarch Airlines Ltd*,[71] where Lord Wilberforce stated that

> I think that it would be proper for us . . . to recognise that there may be cases where such travaux préparatoires can profitably be used. These cases should be rare, and only where two conditions are fulfilled, first, that the material involved is public and accessible, and secondly, that the travaux préparatoires clearly and indisputably point to a definite legislative intention.[72]

In the case of the Hague and Hague–Visby Rules, the *travaux préparatoires* are now widely available[73] and one might therefore expect to see greater use being made of them. However, as others have noted,[74] the debates leading to the Hague Rules and Hague–Visby Rules do not always throw up clear answers; indeed, at best, they may do no more than help expose a variety of different viewpoints or are of no assistance whatever.[75] After an exhaustive survey of them in relation to straight bills of lading,[76] Rix LJ has commented that 'as often occurs, the *travaux préparatoires* are rich in ambiguity'.[77]

Foreign language sources   In *James Buchanan & Co Ltd v Babco Forwarding and Shipping*   **18.23**
(UK) Ltd[78] important guidance was given on the use of foreign language sources by Lord Wilberforce:

> Conventions, when made part of English law, may be expressed in language texts in various ways. There may be only an English statutory text which is based upon the convention, the convention itself not being incorporated in the statute. There may be an English convention text which is incorporated in the statute. There may be a French (or other language) convention text with an English translation adopted by the English statute; there may be convention texts in two languages with or without a provision that one shall prevail in case of doubt . . . Different principles of interpretation may apply to each of these cases. Moreover, it is perfectly legitimate in my opinion to look for assistance, if assistance is needed, to the French text. This is often put in the form that resort may be had to the foreign text if (and only if) the English text is ambiguous, but I think this states the rule too technically.[79]

This guidance was followed more recently by the House of Lords in *The Rafaela S* where Lord Rodger[80] drew attention to the French text of the Hague Rules[81] in determining whether straight bills of lading were intended to be within their scope.[82]

Absence of uniformity of interpretation   There has not been nearly complete uniformity   **18.24**
of interpretation of the Hague and Hague–Visby Rules, notwithstanding *Riverstone Meat*

---

[71] [1981] AC 251.
[72] At 278. Cited with approval in *Jindal Iron & Steel Co Ltd v Islamic Solidarity Shipping Co Jordan Inc (The Jordan II)* [2004] UKHL 49; [2005] 1 WLR 1363, at [20] (Lord Steyn).
[73] Thanks to the work of Sturley (1990) and Berlingieri (1997).
[74] Carver (2005), para 9-098.
[75] See *Effort Shipping Co Ltd v Linden Management SA (The Giannis NK)* [1998] AC 605, 615 (Lord Lloyd). See too para 22.16.
[76] Discussed at para 19.21.
[77] *JI MacWilliam Co Inc v Mediterranean Shipping Co SA (The Rafaela S)* [2003] EWCA Civ 556; [2004] QB 702, at [59].
[78] [1978] AC 141. This was a case on the CMR.
[79] At 152. See also *Fothergill v Monarch Airlines Ltd* [1981] AC 251.
[80] [2005] UKHL 11; [2005] 2 AC 423, at [55].
[81] Which, of course, was the version actually signed at Brussels.
[82] See, generally, para 19.21.

Co Pty Ltd v Lancashire Shipping Co Ltd (The Muncaster Castle), where Viscount Simonds stated that: 'I think it is very important in commercial interests that there should be uniformity of construction adopted by the courts in dealing with words in statutes dealing with the same subject-matter'.[83] As was succinctly put by McHugh J of the High Court of Australia in its controversial decision, *The Bunga Seroja*:[84]

> International treaties should be interpreted uniformly by the Contracting States, especially in the case of treaties such as the Hague Rules whose aim is to harmonize and unify the law in cases where differing rules previously applied in the Contracting States. So far, however, uniformity of interpretation has not been a feature of the Hague Rules.[85]

---

[83] [1916] AC 807, 840. See the discussion of this case at para 26.21.

[84] See para 28.22.

[85] *Great China Metal Industries Co Ltd v Malaysian International Shipping Corporation Berhad (The Bunga Seroja)* [1999] 1 Lloyd's Rep 512, at [71].

19

THE SCOPE AND APPLICATION OF THE HAGUE AND HAGUE–VISBY RULES

A. Introduction

Overview   In this chapter we begin our examination of the substantive provisions of the **19.01** Hague and Hague–Visby Rules.[1] This preliminary examination is concerned with matters relating to the overall scope and application of the Rules or, putting this another way, we are concerned with the general question as to the circumstances in which the Rules will be applicable.

B. General Scope of Coverage

Introduction   As we have noted previously,[2] the Hague Rules and the Hague–Visby Rules **19.02** have applied at various times in the United Kingdom, although the Hague Rules regime,

---

[1] See, generally, Scrutton (1996), section XX; Cooke (2001), ch 85; Carver (2005), ch 9.
[2] At paras 15.09 and15.21.

as enacted by the Carriage of Goods by Sea Act 1924, was repealed[3] when the Carriage of Goods by Sea Act 1971 was passed. The Schedule to the 1971 Act contains the text of the Hague–Visby Rules, in much the same way as the Schedule to the 1924 Act contained the text of the Hague Rules.

19.03 **Brevity** A feature of both the Hague and Hague–Visby Rules is that the substantive rules are contained within a relatively short compass. This may be contrasted with later international conventions, such as the Hamburg Rules, which consists of 34 articles, and the proposed UNCITRAL Draft Convention, which contains 105 articles, but is of much wider coverage.

C. Operational Coverage

19.04 **Article II** Article II[4] of both the Hague and Hague–Visby Rules, provides that:

> Subject to the provisions of Article VI,[5] under every contract of carriage of goods by sea the carrier, in relation to the loading, handling, stowage, carriage, custody, care and discharge of such goods, shall be subject to the responsibilities and liabilities and entitled to the rights and immunities hereinafter set forth.[6]

This is an important provision of the Rules as this effectively sets out what has sometimes been termed the 'temporal' range of coverage of the Rules. In particular, we may note that the relationship between the carrier and the shipper of the goods is spelt out, and in particular the carrier's responsibilities and liabilities[7] and his entitlement to certain rights and immunities.[8] This provision also points to the fact that the Rules are intended to be a complete and self-contained code. Thus, it is the Rules which constitute the complete basis on which the contracting parties contract with each other. The Rules attach to the 'contract of carriage'[9] and will apply when such a contract falls within the ambit of the Rules, namely when the carriage relates to carriage of goods by sea.[10]

19.05 **Article VI** Article VI of the Rules is concerned with the shipment of particular goods and we shall return to that shortly.[11]

19.06 **'Contract of carriage'** The significance of the reference to the Rules covering the 'contract of carriage' relates back to one of the definitions provisions in the Rules, article I (b) to which we will return shortly.[12]

---

[3] Section 6(3)(a).
[4] See Berlingieri (1997), 142.
[5] See the discussion below at para 19.36.
[6] See *The Arawa* [1977] 2 Lloyd's Rep 416, 424–425 (Brandon J).
[7] These are largely contained in art III of the Rules. See ch 26.
[8] See art IV.
[9] See para 19.06.
[10] See art I(b); *Cia Compania Portorafti Commerciale SA v Ultramar Panama Inc (The Captain Gregos)* [1990] 1 Lloyd's Rep 310 (CA), 317–318 (Bingham LJ).
[11] See para 19.36.
[12] See para 19.19.

'Carrier' This is again a reference to one of the definitions in the Rules, article I(a), and   **19.07**
will be considered in due course.[13]

Operations falling within the Rules Although article II refers to a range of operations, ie   **19.08**
'loading, handling, stowage, carriage, custody, care and discharge', the question whether
these functions are part of the 'contract of carriage' is a matter of contractual agreement
between the parties. Devlin J has said that the object of the Rules

> is to define not the scope of the contract service but the terms on which that service is to be
> performed. On this view the whole contract of carriage is subject to the rules, but the extent
> to which loading and discharging are brought within the carrier's obligations is left to the
> parties themselves to decide.[14]

Thus, under this provision of the Rules, it is possible for the parties, by contract, to make
provision for the expense of the operations covered. However, this does not affect the risk
of those operations, which still falls on the carrier.[15] We shall return again to this issue when
we consider the scope of article III, rule 2 of the Rules.[16]

'Discharge' We may note that article II refers to the discharge of the goods. This may be   **19.09**
contrasted with article III, rule 6 (the limitation period)[17] which refers to 'delivery' of the
goods by the carrier. It should be pointed out, however, that the two operations are not
necessarily coextensive. On one distinguished interpretation, the word 'discharge' is
used because the period of responsibility during which the Rules applies ends when the
operations devolving upon the ship come to an end.[18]

D. Period of Coverage

Article I(e) While the issue of a bill of lading will ensure the operation of the Rules, the   **19.10**
Rules will still only apply during the period of the contract relating to sea transport. This
relates to the definition of 'contract of carriage' in article I(e),[19] viz 'the period from the time
when the goods are loaded on to the time they are discharged from the ship'.

Tackle-to-tackle This period covered is sometimes referred to as the 'tackle-to-tackle'   **19.11**
period. It is therefore said that the operative period is the time when the ship's tackle is
hooked onto the cargo at the port of loading until the hook of the tackle is released at the
port of discharge. The liability of the carrier will therefore not only extend during the course
of the voyage but will also be applicable during loading and discharging. The Rules will not,

---

[13] Paragraph 19.17.
[14] *Pyrene Co Ltd v Scindia Navigation Co Ltd* [1954] 2 QB 402, 418; *GH Renton & Co Ltd v Palmyra Trading Corporation of Panama* [1957] AC 149, 170 (Lord Morton), 174 (Lord Somervell); *The Arawa* [1977] 2 Lloyd's Rep 416, 424–425 (Brandon J); *Jindal Iron & Steel Co Ltd v Islamic Solidarity Shipping Co Jordan Inc (The Jordan II)* [2004] UKHL 49; [2005] 1 WLR 1363.
[15] *The Arawa* [1977] 2 Lloyd's Rep 416, 424–425 (Brandon J).
[16] See para 26.35.
[17] See para 34.04.
[18] See *Gosse Millerd v Canadian Government Merchant Marine Ltd* [1927] 2 KB 432, 434 (Wright J).
[19] Berlingieri (1997), 136.

however, apply during any additional time during which the goods are under the control of the carrier outside the tackle-to-tackle period. Article VII specifically provides that:

> Nothing herein contained shall prevent a carrier or a shipper from entering into any agreement, stipulation, condition, reservation or exemption as to the responsibility and liability of the carrier or the ship for the loss or damage to, or in connection with, the custody and care and handling of goods prior to the loading on, and subsequent to the discharge from, the ship on which the goods are carried by sea.

19.12 **Through bills of lading** What is the situation where goods are shipped on a through bill of lading or a combined transport document? Article I(b) specifically provides for contracts of carriage covered by bills of lading 'in so far as such document relates to the carriage of goods by sea'. Thus, it seems that the Rules will not be applicable to any segment of the through transport which involves carriage by air or road. In the case of *Captain v Far Eastern Steamship Co*[20] certain goods were shipped from Madras to Vancouver under a contract which envisaged that the cargo would be transhipped at some point on the route. The bill of lading contained a term providing that the responsibility of the carrier should be limited to that part of the transport performed by him on vessels under his management. When the cargo was transhipped at Singapore the container vans were stored in the open for three weeks during which they suffered rainwater damage amounting to $32,000. The Canadian court held that the carrier was entitled to rely on the contractual clause excluding liability during this period since the Hague Rules did not apply to that period during which the goods were stored on the dock:

> ... [T]hat part of the contract relating to holding the goods on the dock at Singapore awaiting loading upon the second vessel is not within the rules because it does not relate to 'the carriage of goods by water'.[21]

19.13 *Mayhew Foods* In *Mayhew Foods v Overseas Containers Ltd (OCL)*[22] there was an oral contract for the carriage by OCL of a refrigerated container of Mayhew's products, consisting of a quantity of chicken and turkey portions, from Uckfield to Jeddah. In order to maintain their quality it was essential that they be kept deep frozen at -18°C and it was therefore envisaged that they be carried aboard the *Benalder*. The goods were taken from Uckfield to Shoreham aboard a refrigerated container lorry and then transported from Shoreham to Le Havre aboard the *Voline*. The container was discharged and remained at Le Havre for approximately six days before it was shipped to Jeddah aboard the *Benalder*. On arrival in Jeddah, permission to discharge the container was refused as the contents had decayed; the temperature control on the container had been set at 2°C and the goods had therefore been subject to some heating while in the container. The bill of lading which was eventually issued provided for the carrier to accept liability for loss or damage to the goods from the time of receipt in Sussex to the time of delivery in Jeddah, although liability was limited to US$2 per kilo of the gross weight of the goods. On the basis that the damage occurred while the goods were at Le Havre, the carrier contended, on the basis of *Captain v Far Eastern Steamship Co* that the Rules were not applicable during this period and that

---

[20] [1979] 1 Lloyd's Rep 595 (SC of British Columbia) (MacDonald J).
[21] At 601–602.
[22] [1984] 1 Lloyd's Rep 317.

he could therefore limit his liability to the contractual figure of US $2 per kilo. Bingham J stated that

> ... the contract here clearly provided for shipment at a United Kingdom port, intended to be Southampton but in the event Shoreham, and from the time of that shipment, the Act and the Rules plainly applied.[23]

Thus, he declined to accept the argument that the Rules did not apply while the goods were stored at Le Havre and distinguished *Captain v Far Eastern Steamship Co* on the basis that:

> ... the shipper there was told when the contract was made that there would be transhipment and there were separate bills of lading for the two legs of the journey. The present case is factually different ... If, during [the] carriage, OCL chose to avail themselves of their contractual right to discharge, store and tranship, those were, in my judgment, operations 'in relation to and in connection with the carriage of goods by sea in ships', to use the language of the Act [section 1(3)], or were 'within the contractual carriage', to use the language of cl 21(2) of the bill of lading conditions. It would, I think, be surprising if OCL could, by carrying the goods to Le Havre and there storing the goods before transhipment, rid themselves of liabilities to which they would have been subject had they, as contemplated, shipped the goods at Southampton and carried them direct to Jeddah, the more so since Mayhew had no knowledge of any voyage to Le Havre. My conclusion is that the rules, having applied on shipment at Shoreham, remained continuously in force until discharge at Jeddah.[24]

Thus, this case is authority for the proposition that, whenever goods are shipped from a contracting state under a bill of lading which covers the entire seacarriage through to the ultimate destination then, despite any intermediate transhipment, the requirements of article X will be satisfied and the Rules will control the operation throughout.

E. Voyages Covered

Article X Article X[25] of the Hague–Visby Rules[26] provides as follows: **19.14**

> The provisions of these Rules shall apply to every bill of lading relating to the carriage of goods between ports in two different States if:
>
> (a) the bill of lading is issued in a contracting State, or
> (b) the carriage is from a port in a contracting State, or
> (c) the contract contained in or evidenced by the bill of lading provides that these Rules or legislation of any State giving effect to them are to govern the contract,
>
> whatever may be the nationality of the ship, the carrier, the shipper, the consignee, or any other interested person.

We may note various points. The first is that one of the principal criteria for the operation of the Rules is outward shipment from a contracting State.[27] The second point is that the

---

[23] At 320.
[24] ibid.
[25] Berlingieri (1997), 687.
[26] Note that there was no equivalent provision in the Hague Rules.
[27] ie a signatory to the Visby Protocol and the Brussels Convention. Under s 2(1) of the Carriage of Goods by Sea Act 1971, an Order in Council may certify that a state specified in the Order is a contracting state, or that a place or territory forms part of a contracting state.

Rules are designed to apply irrespective of 'the nationality of the ship, the carrier, the shipper, the consignee, or any other interested person'. The third, no less important criterion, is that the Rules apply to international voyages — 'in two different states' — but that the destination port need not be in a contracting state. Finally, the Rules apply also by virtue of the fact that a 'bill of lading'[28] is issued in a contracting state or 'the contract contained or evidenced by' the bill of lading provides that the Rules or the legislation of a contracting state is to govern the contract.

19.15   Coastal voyages   Section 1(3) of the Carriage of Goods by Sea Act 1971 provides that[29]

> . . . where the port of shipment is a port[30] in the United Kingdom, whether or not the carriage is between ports in two different states . . .

This provision extends the ambit of the Hague–Visby Rules to cover also domestic coastal voyages.[31]

19.16   Summary   As we have now seen, the Carriage of Goods by Sea Act 1971 applies, by force of law,[32] to the following voyages: (1) any voyage from a port in one state to a port in another state, where the bill of lading is issued in a contracting state (article X(a)); (2) any voyage from a port in a contracting state to a port in another state (article X(b)); (3) any voyage from a port in one state to a port in another state where the contract contained in or evidenced by the bill of lading provides that the Hague–Visby Rules or legislation of any state giving effect to them are to govern the contract (article X(c)); (4) all coastal voyages in the United Kingdom (section 1(3)). As we shall see in due course, there are also other situations when the Rules will apply, particularly in relation to other types of sea carriage documents.

F. Carriers

19.17   Article I(a)   Article I(a)[33] of the Rules provides that, for its operation,

> carrier includes the owner or the charterer who enters into a contract of carriage with a shipper.

There are a number of points to be made about this definition. In reverse sequence, we may note first that there is no definition anywhere of the term 'shipper'. One may therefore assume that this is intended to refer to all those persons who may be the shippers of the goods, including the c.i.f. seller. However, the definition begins by saying that the term carrier 'includes the owner'. This is an express indication of the well-known fact that the carrier is very often the registered shipowner. However, the word 'includes' opens up the

---

[28] See the discussion at para 19.20.
[29] cf also s 1 of the Carriage of Goods by Sea Act 1924.
[30] ie Great Britain and Northern Ireland. See the Interpretation Act 1978, s 5, Sch I.
[31] Other jurisdictions have similar provisions. See, eg, the Carriage of Goods by Sea Act 1986 (South Africa), s 1(1)(a); Carriage of Goods by Sea Act 1972 (Singapore), s 3(2); Carriage of Goods by Sea Regulations 1998 (Cth), art 10(4).
[32] ie compulsorily: see s 1(2); for discussion, see para 18.09.
[33] Berlingieri (1997), 87.

possibility that other parties functioning as the owner are also intended to be included. This would clearly include the situation where a freight forwarder is acting as carrier.[34] It will also cover the situation where the vessel is under bareboat charter.[35] Article I(a) also includes charterers, without distinction. Thus, in principle, the Rules apply to all types of charterer.[36] However, it should be noted that other provisions in the Rules exclude the application of the Rules to charterparties, save where a bill of lading is issued which 'regulates the relations between a carrier and a holder of the same'.[37] Thus, although the Rules apply to charterers in their capacity as carriers, the scheme of liabilities and immunities in the Rules does not apply to charterparties, at least until the issue of a bill of lading. As we shall see, however, the Rules may also be incorporated into a charterparty by means of a paramount clause.

G. Vessels

Definitions The Rules provide a definition in article I(d) of the term 'ship', which is said **19.18** to 'mean any vessel used for the carriage of goods by water'. This should also include a passenger vessel on which cargo is carried. As there is no restrictive wording, such as is found in the Merchant Shipping At 1995,[38] the definition is clearly not limited to vessels which are used in navigation.

H. Documents

Article I(b) Article I(b)[39] provides that the Rules will apply **19.19**

only to contracts of carriage covered by a bill of lading or any similar document of title in so far as such document relates to the carriage of goods by sea . . .

Article I(b) is reinforced by section 1(4) of the Carriage of Goods by Sea Act 1971 which provides that:

Subject to subsection (6) below, nothing in this section shall be taken as applying anything in the Rules to any contract for the carriage of goods by sea, unless the contract expressly or by implication provides for the issue of a bill of lading or any similar document of title.

We will now examine this problematic provision in more detail.

Bill of lading The Rules provide no definition of a bill of lading other than linking it to **19.20** 'any similar document of title' by the word 'or'. At first sight this might seem to indicate that it was the intention of the drafters of the Rules that only the traditional order (or ocean) bill of lading was contemplated. Another possibility is that it was intended that

---

[34] See the earlier discussion on the role of freight forwarders: paras 1.23; 3.13.
[35] See para 1.41. See also *Samuel v West Hartlepool Co* (1906) 11 Com Cas 115.
[36] See para 1.35 and chs 30 (voyage charterparties) and 32 (time charterparties).
[37] Article I(b). See also art V.
[38] See s 313 of that Act. See para 35.55.
[39] Berlingieri (1997), 89.

received for shipment bills of lading[40] and through bills of lading should be covered.[41] Although a received bill is not a document of title in the strict sense,[42] such bills of lading can be 'converted' into shipped bills of lading by stamping them as 'shipped'. It is undecided whether such bills of lading would be bills of lading for the purposes of the Rules.[43] Although there is Australian authority for the proposition that the words will extend also to consignment notes[44] it is very much an open question whether other sea carriage documents, such as sea waybills and ship's delivery orders, were intended to be covered. In the view of Lord Rodger in *The Rafaela S*:

> [The words 'or similar document of title'] ... were not included in order to cut down the range of contracts to which the Rules apply by narrowing the class of 'bills of lading' as understood in commercial circles; they were intended, rather, to extend that range by including contracts covered by any document of title that is similar to a bill of lading.[45]

19.21   **Straight bills of lading**   It is still undecided whether a straight bill of lading is a document of title at common law.[46] Most older authorities suggest that this is not so,[47] but in *JI MacWilliam Co Inc v Mediterranean Shipping Co SA (The Rafaela S)* Rix LJ appeared to suggest that a straight bill of lading was a document of title, even in the absence of any express provision in the bill of lading which required that it should be presented to obtain delivery of the goods.[48] However, that point was not taken up subsequently by the House of Lords.[49] The more fundamental question, whether article I(b) extends to straight bills of lading, was one of the main points which arose in *The Rafaela S*. It arose previously in *Parsons Corp v CV Scheepvaartonderneming Happy Ranger (The Happy Ranger)*,[50] where it was suggested obiter[51] that the term 'bill of lading' in article I(b) of the Rules should not be interpreted as including straight bills of lading.[52] *The Rafaela S* case arose out of the carriage of a cargo of containers of printing machinery shipped initially on the *Rosemary* from Durban to Felixstowe and then on-carried by the *Rafaela S* from Felixstowe to Boston. The machinery was out-turned badly damaged at Boston. The principal issue in the proceedings arose on appeal from an arbitration and was concerned with the preliminary issue whether the

---

[40] As a matter of domestic law, such bills of lading are within the documents covered by the Carriage of Goods by Sea Act 1992: see s 1(2)(b).

[41] See, eg, Temperley and Vaughan (1932) 7, n (h).

[42] See *Diamond Alkali Export Corp v Fl Bourgeois* [1921] 3 KB 443.

[43] cf the definition of 'sea-carriage document' in the Australian Carriage of Goods by Sea Regulations 1998 (Cth), art 1(1)(g).

[44] *Comalco Aluminium Ltd v Mogal Freight Services Ltd* (1993) 113 ALR 677, 700 (Sheppard J). See now art 1(1)(g) of the Carriage of Goods by Sea Regulations 1998 (Cth).

[45] [2005] UKHL 11; [2005] 2 AC 423, at [57].

[46] See paras 3.08; 8.02.

[47] See *Kum v Wah Tat Bank* [1971] 1 Lloyd's Rep 439 (PC), 446 (Lord Devlin).

[48] [2003] EWCA Civ 556; [2004] QB 702, at [145]. See too *APL Co Pte Ltd v Voss Peer* [2002] 2 Lloyd's Rep 707 and GH Treitel, 'The legal status of straight bills of lading' (2003) 119 LQR 608.

[49] Except very indirectly: [2005] UKHL 11; [2005] 2 AC 423, at [24] (Lord Bingham); at [51] (Lord Steyn). See Stephen Girvin, 'Straight bills of lading in international trade: principles and practice' [2006] JBL 86.

[50] [2001] 2 Lloyd's Rep 530.

[51] Although reversing the decision at first instance, the Court of Appeal reserved their opinion on this point: [2002] EWCA Civ 694; [2002] 2 Lloyd's Rep 357.

[52] [2001] 2 Lloyd's Rep 530, 539 (Tomlinson J).

contract of carriage contained in or evidenced by the bills of lading prescribed a package limitation under the Hague Rules, the Hague–Visby Rules, or the US Carriage of Goods by Sea Act 1936.[53] This required a close consideration of the bills of lading issued in Durban,[54] which was the only contractual document actually issued, and turned on whether the Carriage of Goods by Sea Act 1971 when read with article I(b) applied to the second leg of the voyage between Felixstowe and Boston. If it did, the relevant financial limitation provisions were those prescribed in article IV, rule 5(a)[55] of the Hague–Visby Rules. If it did not, the claim fell within the scheme of the US Act[56] and the damages recoverable would be limited to US$2,000.[57] In the arbitration there were two live issues, the first being whether the shipment from Durban to Boston was governed by one contract or two and the second being whether the bill of lading, which was a straight bill of lading, was within the 1971 Act. The award decided that there was one contract governing the shipment from Durban to Boston. In relation to the second issue, the arbitrators decided that the straight bill of lading was not within the 1971 Act. On appeal to the commercial court, Langley J[58] upheld the arbitrators' answer on the second issue and dismissed the appeal.[59] The buyers were given leave to appeal to the Court of Appeal on the same two grounds. A strong Court of Appeal[60] reversed the first instance decision[61] and held that a straight bill of lading was a bill of lading within the meaning of article I(b) of the Hague–Visby Rules. On appeal to the House of Lords, this was the only live question. They unanimously upheld the view taken also by the Court of Appeal.

Reasoning   The conclusion in *The Rafaela S* has finally settled the question, at least for   **19.22**
English law,[62] on whether a straight bill of lading should fall within the scope of the Hague–Visby Rules. Lord Steyn emphasized the 'contextual significance' that straight bills of lading were in use before the Hague Rules were adopted.[63] For this reason, the words in article I(b) were to be read as 'words of expansion as opposed to restriction'.[64] To do otherwise was to distort the language used; moreover, this would reveal 'a preoccupation with notions of domestic law regarding documents of title which ought not to govern the

---

[53] ie 46 USCA §§ 1300–1312.

[54] In substance the form was the same as that in *El Greco (Australia) Pty Ltd v Mediterranean Shipping Co SA* [2004] FCAFC 448; [2004] 2 Lloyd's Rep 537, 593.

[55] In the case of the UK the limits are 666.67 SDRs per package or 2 SDRs per unit. See para 29.12.

[56] Limitation is US$500 per package: see s 4(5) (46 USCA §1304). For discussion see Schoenbaum (2004), §10-34.

[57] Compared with US$150,000 under the Hague–Visby Rules.

[58] [2002] EWCH 593 (Comm); [2002] 2 Lloyd's Rep 403.

[59] On the first question, he held that there were two separate contracts, not one.

[60] [2003] EWCA Civ 556; [2004] QB 702.

[61] It agreed with Langley J that there was a separate contract of carriage in respect of the voyage from Felixstowe to Boston which entitled the shipper to demand a bill of lading.

[62] It is also in conformity with decisions of other courts in Continental Europe: see *The Duke of Yare* (ARR-RechtB Rotterdam, 10 April 1997); *The MSC Magallanes* (2002) 631 DMF 952 (Court of Appeal, Rennes), referred to in the judgment of the House of Lords in *The Rafaela S*: [2005] UKHL 11; [2005] 2 AC 423, at [21], (Lord Bingham).

[63] Although he also recognized that the *travaux préparatoires* were 'inconclusive': [2005] UKHL 11; [2005] 2 AC 423, at [43]. See too the speech of Lord Bingham: at [16].

[64] At [44].

interpretation of an international maritime convention'.[65] Lord Steyn also emphasized the lack of any cogent policy reason for excluding straight bills of lading from the ambit of the Rules:

> ... no policy reason has been advanced by the carrier why the draftsmen of the Hague Rules would have wanted to distinguish between a named consignee who receives an order bill of lading and a named consignee who receives a straight bill of lading. There is simply no sensible commercial reason why the draftsmen would have wished to deny the CIF buyer named in a straight bill of lading the minimum standard of protection afforded to the CIF buyer named in an order bill of lading. The importance of this consideration is heightened by the fact that straight bills of lading fulfil a useful role in international trade provided that they are governed by the Hague–Visby Rules, since they are sometimes preferred to order bills of lading on the basis that there is a lesser risk of falsification of documentation.[66]

A third strand in Lord Steyn's speech was his emphasis on commercial reality. Thus, in rejecting the interpretation argued for by the carrier, Lord Steyn considered that these arguments depended on 'fine and technical distinctions and arguments' which were antipathetic to traders, bankers, and insurers who would be inclined to take 'a more commercial view of straight bills of lading'.[67] Lord Bingham largely agreed with Lord Steyn but also emphasized the task of the court, when determining the true nature and effect of a legal document, not to be bound by any label which the parties had chosen to apply to it.[68] As the document in question called itself a bill of lading the court should be slow to reject the description which it bore, particularly where the document had been issued by the party seeking to reject the description.[69] However, Lord Bingham likewise accepted that it was not sufficient to resolve the question at large simply by reference to the document alone. Like Lord Steyn, he emphasized the fact that the Hague–Visby Rules were the product of international conferences and that recognition of this had to govern the court's approach to their interpretation. In particular, effect had to be given, so far as possible, to the international consensus expressed in the Rules and not to any divergent or inconsistent rules of domestic law.[70] For Lord Rodger the fact of the negotiability or transferability was simply an irrelevant consideration in determining whether article I(b) of the Rules was applicable to straight bills of lading.[71] There was, in his view, no rational reason for giving the protection of the Rules to a consignee under a transferable bill of lading but not to a consignee under a straight bill.[72]

19.23   **Other documents**   It now remains to be seen whether other documents will, in due course, be placed before the courts as falling within the scheme of the Rules. The requirement in article I(b) of 'bill of lading or similar document of title' probably excludes documents such as liner booking notes, tally clerk's receipts, mate's receipts, and ship's delivery orders.

---

[65] ibid.
[66] At [47].
[67] At [48].
[68] At [5].
[69] ibid.
[70] At [7]. Citing with approval *Stag Line Limited v Foscolo, Mango & Co Ltd* [1932] AC 328, 350; *Fothergill v Monarch Airlines Ltd* [1981] AC 251.
[71] At [70].
[72] ibid. See too [2003] EWCA Civ 556; [2004] QB 702, at [153] (Jacob J).

Nevertheless, some passages in Lord Rodger's speech[73] in *The Rafaela S* hold open the possibility that those documents issued for through transport and multimodal transport, might come within the mandatory application of the Rules,[74] although whether this could be the case for those legs which do not involve the sea is doubtful.[75]

Avoidance of the Rules   As we have now seen, article X of the Rules specifies that outward   **19.24**
shipment from a contracting state or shipment within the UK acts as one of the principal triggers for the operation of the Rules. However, the outward voyage is also linked to the issue of a bill of lading 'or similar document of title'. Accordingly, it would be possible for the carrier to avoid the application of the Rules by issuing some other document in place of a bill of lading.[76]

Intention to contract with a bill of lading   What happens when the parties intend that   **19.25**
their contract will be embodied in a bill of lading, but no such document is issued? The leading case, *Pyrene Co Ltd v Scindia Navigation Co*,[77] establishes that the Rules will indeed take effect in such an event. A consignment of fire tenders had been delivered alongside the *Jal-Azad* for shipment but, while one of them was being lifted aboard by the ship's own tackle, it fell onto the dockside and was badly damaged. The other tenders were lifted aboard safely. The bill of lading, when issued, made no reference to the damaged fire tender. The plaintiffs (the f.o.b. shippers of the tenders) sought to recover £966, the cost of repairing the tender. The carrier sought to limit his liability to £200 under the Hague Rules,[78] but the shipper argued that the damaged tender was not 'covered by a bill of lading'. Devlin J held that the important factor was whether the parties, when contracting, had envisaged the issue of a bill of lading and not whether one was in fact issued:

> The use of the word 'covered' [in article I(b) of the Hague Rules] recognises the fact that the contract of carriage is always concluded before the bill of lading, which evidences its terms, is actually issued. When parties enter into a contract of carriage in the expectation that a bill of lading will be issued to cover it, they enter into it upon those terms which they know or expect the bill of lading to contain. Those terms must be in force from the inception of the contract; if it were otherwise the bill of lading would not evidence the contract but would be a variation of it. Moreover, it would be absurd to suppose that the parties intend the terms of the contract to be changed when the bill of lading is issued: for the issue of the bill of lading does not necessarily mark any stage in the development of the contract; often it is not issued till after the ship has sailed . . . In my judgment, whenever a contract of carriage is concluded, and it is contemplated that a bill of lading will, in due course, be issued in respect of it, that contract is from its creation 'covered' by a bill of lading, and is therefore from its inception a contract of carriage within the meaning of the rules and to which the rules apply.[79]

---

[73] At [75].
[74] Some standard forms contain contractual terms incorporating provisions from the Hague–Visby Rules: see, eg, cl 11 of Combiconbill; cl 11 of Multidoc.
[75] See art I(b) and art I(e).
[76] Although art III, r 3 of the Rules confers a right on the shipper to demand the issue of a bill of lading (see para 26.04), he may only do so if the Rules are already in operation.
[77] [1954] 2 QB 402.
[78] Article IV, r 5.
[79] [1954] 2 QB 402, 419–420.

In the subsequent case of *Parsons Corp v CV Scheepvaartonderneming Happy Ranger (The Happy Ranger)* Tuckey LJ confirmed this:[80]

> It does not seem to me that the rules are concerned with whether the bill of lading contains terms which have been previously agreed or not. It is the fact that it is issued or that its issue is contemplated which matters. As it was put in one of the cases, 'the bill of lading is the bedrock on which the mandatory code is founded'.[81] If a bill of lading is or is to be issued the contract is 'covered' by it or 'provides for its issue' within the definitions of art. I(b) and s. 1(4) of the 1971 Act.[82]

I. Charterparties and the Rules

19.26 **Article V** Article V[83] of the Rules provides that

> the provisions of these Rules shall not be applicable to charterparties, but if bills of lading are issued in the case of a ship under a charterparty they shall comply with the terms of these Rules.

This provision of the Rules make it clear that the Rules are not intended to apply where the only document of carriage is a charterparty for the hire of a ship.[84] A bill of lading issued pursuant to such a charterparty merely acts as a receipt for shipment.[85] It is generally thought that this provision is intended to apply when bills of lading are issued to a shipper who is also the charterer. However, once the bills of lading are transferred to a third party, article I(b) provides that the Rules operate

> from the moment at which such bill of lading or similar document of title regulates the relations between a carrier and a holder of the same.

This provision of the Rules causes some difficulty in interpretation. Thus, there will be no contract of carriage for the purpose of the Rules so long as the charterer is the shipper. Once the charterer endorses the bills of lading, however, there is a question as to whether the Rules then relate back to the time of loading. It is generally thought that this must be the case given that the Rules apply 'in so far as such document relates to the carriage of goods by sea'.[86]

J. Cargoes Excluded

19.27 **Article I(c)** Article I(c) [87] of the Rules provides that:

> 'Goods' includes goods, wares, merchandise, and articles of every kind whatsoever except live animals and cargo which by the contract of carriage is stated as being carried on deck and is so carried.

---

[80] [2002] EWCA Civ 694; [2002] 2 Lloyd's Rep 357, reversing the first instance decision: [2001] 2 Lloyd's Rep 530.

[81] ie *Compania Portorafti Commerciale SA v Ultramar Panama Inc (The Captain Gregos)* [1990] 1 Lloyd's Rep 310 (CA), 317 (Bingham LJ).

[82] [2002] EWCA Civ 694; [2002] 2 Lloyd's Rep 357, 362.

[83] See Berlingieri (1997), 638.

[84] It is, however, not uncommon for some or all of the provisions of the 1971 Act to be incorporated into a charterparty by means of a 'clause paramount': see para19.51.

[85] See the earlier discussion at para 12.03.

[86] Article I(b).

[87] See Berlingieri (1997), 1331.

Deck cargoes   Deck cargoes are excluded from the operation of the Rules because of the **19.28** additional risks to which such cargoes must necessarily be exposed, such as exposure to sea water in rough seas. However, in order to avoid the operation of the Rules in respect of deck cargo, the cargo must actually be stowed on deck and this must be clearly stated on the bill of lading. Unless both these requirements can be met, the contract of carriage will be within the Rules. It may well be difficult to satisfy the requirement that a statement should appear on the bill of lading but the test would appear to be whether an innocent transferee could determine from scrutiny of the bill of lading whether the cargo had been stowed on deck.

Liberty to carry on deck   In *Svenska Traktor Aktiebolaget v Maritime Agencies (Southampton)* **19.29** *Ltd*[88] bills of lading stated that the carrier had liberty to stow part of a cargo of tractors (16 out of the total consignment of 50) on the deck of the *Glory*:

> Steamer has liberty to carry goods on deck and shipowners will not be responsible for any loss, damage, or claim arising therefrom.

One of the tractors was washed overboard during the voyage and the shipowner, who was the charterer of the vessel, sought to rely on a clause in the bill excluding liability for loss or damage to deck cargo. Pilcher J held that he was unable to do so because

> a mere general liberty to carry goods on deck is not, in my view a statement in the contract of carriage that the goods are in fact being carried on deck.[89]

The result was that the contract was governed by the Rules and the carrier was then held liable for a breach of article III, rule 2 in failing to look after the cargo properly and carefully during transit.

'Unless the ships objects'   The requirements for avoiding the application of the Rules in **19.30** the case of deck cargoes would also not be met by a clause in a bill providing that the carrier is entitled to carry the cargo on deck unless the shipper objects. This is because the transferee of a bill would not know whether or not the shipper has lodged an objection. In *Encyclopaedia Britannica v Hong Kong Producer*[90] a consignment of encyclopaedias was shipped in containers under a bill which authorized the carrier to stow the cargo on deck

> unless shipper informs carrier in writing before the delivery of goods to carrier that he requires under deck stowage.

An additional clause in the bill excluded the carrier from all liability for loss or damage to the goods during transit. When the goods arrived at their destination damaged by sea water, the carrier sought to rely on the exclusion clause. Anderson J held that article I(c) was not applicable since

> the bill of lading (short form and long form combined) nowhere states that the cargo is *being carried on deck*. Clause 13 says *it may be* so carried but not that it is being so carried. No consignee or assignee could tell from the bill whether it was below deck or on deck cargo. To hold otherwise would in my view do violence to the ordinary meaning of the words of Art. I(c) of the Act.[91]

---

[88] [1953] 2 Lloyd's Rep 124.
[89] At 130.
[90] [1969] 2 Lloyd's Rep 536.
[91] At 542 (emphasis in the original).

Accordingly, the Rules applied. To conclude, if the carrier wishes to avoid the applicability of the Rules, it would be essential to state on the bill of lading that the goods are being carried on deck.

19.31 **Effect of breach by the carrier**   We turn now to the effect of the carrier deciding to stow cargo on deck without first obtaining the consent of the shipper. Traditionally, such conduct would have amounted to a fundamental breach of contract, but that changed following two decisions of the House of Lords.[92] Following *Kenya Railways v Antares Co Ltd (The Antares)*,[93] it has been held that the unauthorized carriage of cargo on deck, while constituting a breach of the contract of carriage, will not prevent a carrier from relying for protection against a cargo claim on the Rules time limitation. In this case certain machinery had been shipped at Antwerp for carriage to Mombasa under bills of lading which were subject to the Hague or Hague–Visby Rules and which also contained arbitration clauses. On discharge at Mombasa it was found that part of the machinery had been loaded on deck and had been seriously damaged in the course of the voyage. MSC had chartered the vessel from the owners and the plaintiff consignees of the machinery mistakenly claimed against them. One year and two days after the final discharge of the cargo at Mombasa, MSC's solicitors informed the plaintiffs' solicitors that they were not the owners of the vessel. When a claim was made against the owners of the vessel they asserted that the claim was time barred. The plaintiffs sought a declaration that the owners were in fundamental breach of contract by stowing the goods on deck and that this precluded the owners from relying on the one year time bar contained in article III, rule 6 of the Hague–Visby Rules.[94] Lloyd LJ reiterated that the doctrine of fundamental breach of contract, which displaced exception clauses altogether, no longer existed.

19.32 **Reliance on exceptions**   Although it was clear, following *The Antares*, that a breach by the carrier would not affect his right to limit his liability, does the same hold true of exceptions clauses? This was considered in *Wibau Maschinenfabric Hartman SA v Mackinnon Mackenzie & Co (The Chanda)*.[95] WMH were the sellers of asphalt drying and mixing plant to certain f.o.b. buyers in Saudi Arabia. Because this equipment was so large it was necessary to transport it in parts. Part of the equipment, which included the cabin, was shipped aboard the *Chanda* from Bremen to Jeddah. In all, 35 packages out of 51 were loaded on deck, with the control cabin (which contained electronic equipment, thus constituting the cabin 90 per cent of the total value of the equipment) stowed on the No 1 hatch.[96] The bill of lading contained a clause paramount providing that the Hague Rules, as incorporated in West Germany, were to apply to the contract. The carrier's liability was accordingly limited to DM 1,250 per package. During her passage through the Bay of Biscay, the *Chanda* encountered severe weather. When she arrived in Jeddah, it was found that the control

---

[92] *Suisse Atlantique Société d'Armement Maritime SA v Rotterdamsche Kolen Centrale* [1967] AC 361; *Photo Production Ltd v Securicor Transport* [1980] AC 827.

[93] [1987] 1 Lloyd's Rep 424 (CA).

[94] As to art III, r 6, see para 34.04.

[95] [1989] 2 Lloyd's Rep 494.

[96] ie the hatch nearest the bow of the vessel and hence the most exposed to the sea.

cabin had been so badly damaged, both internally and externally, that the port authorities forbade its discharge. The main issue for Hirst J was whether the unauthorized carriage of the control cabin and its equipment on deck disentitled the defendants from relying on any exceptions or limitations contained in the Hague Rules. He found that

> ... the whole trouble here stemmed from the initial decision, for which the defendants are manifestly responsible, to carry this delicate piece of equipment on deck rather than under deck, and in a position (on top of the forward hatch) where it was subjected to the maximum exposure to the elements.

> ... [C]lauses which are clearly intended to protect the shipowner provided he honours his contractual obligation to stow goods under deck do not apply if he is in breach of [his] obligation. I am satisfied that the package limitation clause falls fairly and squarely within this category, since it can hardly have been intended to protect the shipowner who, as a result of the breach, exposed the cargo in question to such palpable risk of damage. Otherwise the main purpose of the shipowners' obligation to stow below deck would be seriously undermined.[97]

The Chanda overruled   The decision in *The Chanda* attracted considerable criticism, **19.33** although it was followed in New Zealand.[98] The point was revisited, however, in *Daewoo Heavy Industries Ltd v Klipriver Shipping Ltd (The Kapitan Petko Voivoda)*.[99] In this case, Longmore LJ expressly overruled the earlier authorities:

> I respectfully agree [with Lloyd LJ in *The Antares*].

> It seems to me ... that the cargo-owners can derive no benefit from the supposed principle stated in the deviation cases or, indeed, the warehouse cases. The duty of the Court is merely to construe the contract which the parties have made.[100]

Thus, following this case, the question as to whether the carrier may rely on any provisions of the Rules is one of construction of its terms.

Shipper's consent   In order to avoid a breach of contract by the carrier, the shipper must **19.34** have consented, either expressly or impliedly, to the stowage of his cargo on deck. The inclusion of a general liberty clause might suffice — even a clause to the effect that 'carrier permitted to stow on deck unless shipper objects' — provided that the shipper has sufficient notice of the clause at the time of shipment. In the *Svenska Traktor* case, the Court of Appeal, while refusing to permit the carrier to exclude the provision of the Hague Rules in the absence of a statement in the bill that the goods had been shipped on deck, held that, in view of the inclusion of a liberty clause in the bill of lading, deck stowage did not amount to a breach of the contract of carriage. The Court of Appeal was prepared to allow the carrier to take advantage of the defences provided by the Rules. Consent would normally be implied where it was customary in the trade to ship certain types of goods on deck, for example timber or containers on a specially designed container vessel. In such a case, it would not be necessary to clause the bill of lading indicating deck carriage.

---

[97] [1989] 2 Lloyds Rep 494, 500; 505.
[98] *Nelson Pine Industries Ltd v Seatrans New Zealand Ltd (The Pembroke)* [1995] 2 Lloyd's Rep 290.
[99] [2003] EWCA Civ 451; [2003] 2 Lloyd's Rep 1, upholding [2002] EWHC 1306 (Comm); [2002] 2 All ER (Comm) 560.
[100] At [14]–[15].

K. Shipment of Particular Goods

19.35   **Article VI**   Article VI[101] of the Hague and Hague–Visby Rules provides that:

> Notwithstanding the provisions of the preceding articles, a carrier, master or agent of the carrier and a shipper shall in regard to any particular goods be at liberty to enter into any agreement in any terms as to the responsibility and liability of the carrier for such goods, and as to the rights and immunities of the carrier in respect of such goods, or his obligation as to seaworthiness, so far as this stipulation is not contrary to public policy, or the care or diligence of his servants or agents in regard to the loading, handling, stowage, carriage, custody, care and discharge of the goods carried by sea, provided that in this case no bill of lading has been or shall be issued and that the terms agreed shall be embodied in a receipt which shall be a non-negotiable document and shall be marked as such.
>
> An agreement so entered into shall have full legal effect.
>
> Provided that this article shall not apply to ordinary commercial shipments made in the ordinary course of trade, but only to other shipments where the character or condition of the property to be carried or the circumstances, terms and conditions under which the carriage is to be performed are such as reasonably to justify a special agreement.

19.36   **Meaning**   This provision of the Rules is unusual in that it permits the carrier to make any agreement that he wishes in relation to 'particular goods'. If he does so, then article VI says that he is not bound by the Hague or Hague–Visby Rules provided that it is not an ordinary commercial shipment made in the ordinary course of trade, but is required 'where the character or condition of the property to be carried or the circumstances, terms and conditions under which the carriage is to be performed are such as reasonably to justify a special agreement'. An additional restriction, however, is that no bill of lading is or shall be issued and that the terms should be embodied in a non-negotiable receipt and marked as such. As we have seen, there is a provision of the Rules which excludes the application of the Rules to 'live animals' and goods carried on deck.

L. Additional Responsibilities

19.37   **Freedom of contract**   The Hague and Hague–Visby Rules set out a mandatory framework of contractual clauses for incorporation in a contract of carriage. However, the parties still have the freedom to negotiate their own additional terms. Thus, the first paragraph of article V[102] states that:

> A carrier shall be at liberty to surrender in whole or in part all or any of his rights and immunities or to increase any of his responsibilities and obligations under these Rules, provided such surrender or increase shall be embodied in the bill of lading issued to the shipper.

19.38   **Purpose**   The intention behind this provision is to enable a shipper to obtain better terms than those he might obtain under the compulsory provisions of the Rules. However, he could not surrender the rights given to him by the Rules. Likewise, the carrier could not seek to derogate from his responsibilities under the Rules.

---

[101] Berlingieri (1997), 647.
[102] Berlingieri (1997), 633.

M. No Derogation from the Rules

Article III, rule 8   Article III, rule8[103] of the Hague and Hague–Visby Rules provides that: **19.39**

Any clause, covenant, or agreement in a contract of carriage relieving the carrier or the ship from liability for loss or damage to, or in connection with, goods arising from negligence, fault, or failure in the duties and obligations provided in this article or lessening such liability otherwise than as provided in these Rules, shall be null and void and of no effect. A benefit of insurance in favour of the carrier or similar clause shall be deemed to be a clause relieving the carrier from liability.

Importance   This clause is potentially significant in a number of different ways and was   **19.40** clearly included in the Rules to emphasize the importance of not permitting carriers to avoid or reduce their main duties and obligations under the Rules. Any blatant attempt to do so will be nullified.[104] However, it is important to note that the clause will not be operative where the contract of carriage falls within art VII.

Time for adjudging null and void   One question which quickly arises in relation to this   **19.41** provision of the Rules is the time for judging whether the clause does or does not have the effect of lessening the carrier's liability. It has been held in *RA Lister & Co Ltd v EG Thomson (Shipping) Ltd (The Benarty)*[105] that the relevant time is when the party seeking to rely on the clause takes steps to define and state that reliance, and not the date of the contract or the date of the claim form.[106] We now need to examine the provision in more detail.

'Any clause, covenant or agreement …'   The types of provision which are prohibited   **19.42** are, in principle, widely defined. If only part of a clause offended against article III, rule 8, would the whole clause be rendered null and void? A literal interpretation of the words used would certainly lead to this result,[107] but a number of cases have permitted the offending parts of clauses to be severed. Thus in *Svenska Traktor Aktiebolaget v Maritime Agencies (Southampton) Ltd*[108] the judge severed an offending part of a clause from a non-offending part. This approach has been consistently followed in a number of decisions.[109]

Clauses nullified   There have been several cases which have already considered the scope   **19.43** of article III, rule 8 within the context of specific clauses. The obvious example is clauses which seek to nullify the carrier's obligation for loss or damage resulting from unseaworthiness. Thus, an attempt to provide that a survey certificate amounts to conclusive evidence of the exercise by the carrier of his obligation of due diligence in providing a seaworthy ship

---

[103] Berlingieri (1997), 350.
[104] See, eg, *The Hollandia* [1983] AC 565.
[105] [1985] QB 325 (CA).
[106] At 348 (Dunn LJ).
[107] As was suggested in *GH Renton & Co v Palmyra Trading Corp of Panama (The Caspiana)* [1955] 3 WLR 535, 547 (McNair J). The decision was later reversed in the Court of Appeal ([1956] 1 QB 462), with which the House of Lords agreed: see [1957] AC 149.
[108] [1953] 2 Lloyd's Rep 124. See the discussion of the case at para 19.29.
[109] See *Holland Colombo Trading Society Ltd v Alawdeen (Segu Mohamed Khaja)* [1954] 2 Lloyd's Rep 45 (PC); *British Imex Industries v Midland Bank Ltd* [1958] 1 QB 542; *Unicoopjapan & Marubeni-Iida Co v Ion Shipping Co (The Ion)* [1971] 1 Lloyd's Rep 541.

will fail.[110] Similarly, a clause which provided that the carrier could avoid liability for incorrect delivery if certain packing requirements, not required under the Rules, were not observed, was also held to infringe article III, rule 8.[111]

19.44 **Clauses not nullified**   Of course, there are also reported cases which have held that certain other types of clauses are not void. Chief among these are clauses which limit the scope of the carrier's duties but not the terms by which the carrier must perform the duties imposed by the Rules. The leading statement on this is in the judgment of Devlin J in *Pyrene Co Ltd v Scindia Navigation Co*[112] where he said that:

> [The] object [of the Rules] as it is put, I think, correctly in *Carver's Carriage of Goods by Sea*, 9th ed (1952), p 186, is to define not the scope of the contract service but the terms on which that service is to be performed.[113]

Likewise, a clause which gives a vessel a liberty to deviate will not infringe the Rules.[114] Neither, it seems, will a clause which gives the vessel liberty to have cargo transhipped on terms which are reasonable and consistent with the proper carriage of the goods[115] or a clause which gives the carrier a liberty to carry on deck.[116]

19.45 **Limitation provisions**   One obvious area which would attract the operation of article III, rule 8, is clauses which seek to impose lower limits of liability which are self-evidently not in conformity with those laid down in the Rules.[117] However, the cases have sometimes drawn some very fine distinctions and are not always easy to rationalize. Thus, it has been held that a clause agreeing a value of goods per package unless a higher value is declared, is valid,[118] but not one which purports to exempt liability in excess of a particular sum per package.[119] In *The Rosa S*,[120] a clause which purported to agree the £100 package limit in the Carriage of Goods by Sea Act 1924 as '£100 sterling' was invalid because £100 under the Act was Gold Value and not currency value.[121]

19.46 **Himalaya clauses**   In *Homburg Houtimport BV v Agrosin Private Ltd (The Starsin)*[122] the Hague Rules were incorporated by contract into the relevant bills of lading.[123] One of the issues which their Lordships had to consider was whether the terms of a Himalaya clause[124]

---

[110] See *Studebaker Distributors Ltd v Charlton Steamship Co Ltd* [1938] 1 KB 459; *The Australia Star* (1940) 67 Ll LR 110.

[111] *British Imex Industries v Midland Bank Ltd* [1958] 1 QB 542.

[112] [1954] 2 QB 402.

[113] At 418. Cited with approval in *Jindal Iron & Steel Co Ltd v Islamic Solidarity Shipping Co Jordan Inc (The Jordan II)* [2004] UKHL 49; [2005] 1 WLR 1363, at [11] (Lord Steyn).

[114] See *GH Renton & Co Ltd v Palmyra Trading Corporation of Panama* [1957] AC 149.

[115] See *Marcelino Gonzalez y Campania S En C v James Nourse Ltd* [1936] 1 KB 565.

[116] *Svenska Traktor Aktiebolaget v Maritime Agencies (Southampton) Ltd* [1953] 2 Lloyd's Rep 124. See para 19.29.

[117] See, eg, *Shun Cheong Steam Navigation Co Ltd v Wo Fong Trading Co* [1979] 2 MLJ 254.

[118] *Anthony Hordern & Sons v Commonwealth & Dominion Line* [1917] 2 KB 420.

[119] *Studebaker Distributors Ltd v Charlton Steamship Co Ltd* [1938] 1 KB 459.

[120] [1989] QB 419.

[121] See the further discussion at para 29.08.

[122] [2003] UKHL 12; [2004] 1 AC 715. See the discussion of other aspects of this case at paras 9.29 and 12.13.

[123] Clause 2.

[124] See, generally, on Himalaya clauses, para 9.23.

provided complete exemption from any liability for the shipowner or whether the clause was subject to article III, rule 8. The submission as to exemption was described by Lord Hobhouse as 'remarkable' because it sought to carry the reach of the Himalaya clause 'far further than any previous decision'.[125] Accordingly, he and a majority of their Lordships concluded that article III, rule 8 had the effect of circumscribing the protection which clause 5 sought to extend to the shipowners and the protection afforded had to be limited by that which was available under the Hague Rules. Thus, though the shipowner was not subject to the positive obligations laid upon the carrier in article III, rule 1 and article III, rule 2 of the Hague Rules, it would, in the words of Lord Bingham, have been anomalous to take no account of article III, rule 8 while giving the shipowner the benefit of clause 5.[126] Lord Steyn, who dissented,[127] took the view that as article III, rule 8 referred to a clause 'in a contract of carriage', this was to be taken as contemplating a contract with the 'usual incidents and executory obligations of a contract of carriage' and, focusing on article III, rule 8 the exemption in clause 5, the Himalaya clause, was not contained in a contract of carriage.[128]

Periods and activities beyond the Rules   We have already noted that the Rules apply tackle-to-tackle.[129] One question which may therefore arise is whether contractual stipulations which purport to exclude or restrict the carrier's liability for losses falling outside the scope of the Rules amount to a breach. Logically, they should not and this has been confirmed by the Court of Appeal of New South Wales in *PS Chellaram v China Ocean Shipping Co (The Zhi Jiang Kou)*.[130] However, in the case of the incorporation of the Rules into a charterparty by means of a paramount clause,[131] this question may be less easy to resolve, given that it will be necessary to ascertain to which obligations under the charterparty the Rules are intended to apply.[132]   **19.47**

Time for suit   As we shall see in a later chapter, the Rules prescribe a period of 12 months as the limit for the bringing of claims.[133] Clauses which seek to modify this period by reducing it will clearly be in breach of article III, rule 8,[134] but not clauses extending the period of time. Thus in *Unicoopjapan & Marubeni-Iida Co v Ion Shipping Co (The Ion)*[135] a cargo of fishmeal shipped to Kobe arrived short. Discharge was completed on 20 August 1969 and the cargo owners submitted their claim on 24 October. However, it was only on 21 July 1970, after the shipowners failed to appoint their own arbitrator, that the cargo owners   **19.48**

---

125 [2003] UKHL 12; [2004] 1 AC 715, at [140].
126 At [34]. See also Lord Hobhouse, at [157] and [160].
127 He did so 'in the spirit of accepting that one must not be too confident that one is right' (at [63]).
128 At [59].
129 See para 19.11.
130 [1991] 1 Lloyd's Rep 493; (1990) 28 NSWLR 354.
131 See para 19.51.
132 See, eg, *Seven Seas Transportation Ltd v Pacifico Union Marina Corp (The Satya Kailash and The Oceanic Amity)* [1984] 1 Lloyd's Rep 588 (CA).
133 See para 34.15.
134 As will clauses which require that claims be notified within a certain time of the vessel's arrival at the discharge port: see *Australasian United Steam Navigation Co v Hunt* [1921] 2 AC 351.
135 [1971] 1 Lloyd's Rep 541.

appointed their own arbitrator as sole arbitrator. The shipowners claimed that the claim was time barred by the Centrocon arbitration clause in the bills of lading which stated that the claimant's arbitrator must be appointed within three months, failing which the claim would be waived and absolutely barred. Brandon J held that this part of the Centrocon clause conflicted with the Hague Rules and, to that extent, declared it null and void. It should be noted, however, that a clause which gives the parties to the contract the right to elect for arbitration as opposed to litigation within a period of less than one year after discharge[136] would not be void; indeed it has been said that article III, rule 8 should be given a 'purposive construction'.[137]

19.49 Jurisdiction clauses   As we have already seen,[138] one potential area of difficulty is foreign jurisdiction clauses which require the parties to settle their disputes in countries which have lower limits. It was established in *The Hollandia*[139] that this amounted to an infringement of article III, rule 8,[140] at least where the Rules were mandatorily applicable by 'force of law' under the Carriage of Goods by Sea Act 1971.[141]

19.50 Tonnage limitation   The position is, however, different when looking at contracts which seek to apply tonnage limits of liability[142] which are less than the package limits in the Rules. This is partly because of article VIII[143] of the Rules which states that:

> The provisions of these Rules shall not affect the rights and obligations of the carrier under any statute for the time being in force relating to the limitation of the liability of owners of vessels.

In *RA Lister & Co Ltd v EG Thomson (Shipping) Ltd (The Benarty)*[144] bills of lading provided for the settlement of cargo disputes in Indonesia. In Indonesia the carriers were entitled to rely on section 410 of the Indonesian Commercial Code, which meant that they were entitled to limit their overall liability to a sum which was less than that under the Hague–Visby Rules. When action was commenced in England, the cargo owners sought to rely on *The Hollandia*[145] as authority for not staying the proceedings. However, the Court of Appeal stayed the proceedings because it took the view that the fact of reliance on a foreign limitation statute, if the dispute was settled in the place named in the bill of lading, was not a good reason to stay the English action.

N. Paramount Clauses

19.51 Introduction   Although, as we have seen, the Hague and Hague–Visby Rules do not apply to charterparties,[146] they are commonly incorporated in charterparties, both voyage

---

136 See *Government of Sierra Leone v Marmaro Shipping Co Ltd (The Amazona and the Yayamaria)* [1989] 2 Lloyd's Rep 130 (CA).
137 At 135 (Parker LJ). See too *The Hollandia* [1983] 1 AC 565, 572 (Lord Diplock).
138 See para 18.10.
139 [1983] 1 AC 565.
140 See too *The Epar* [1984] SLR 409.
141 ie under s 1(2). See para 18.09.
142 See para 29.29.
143 See Berlingieri (1997), 675.
144 [1985] QB 325 (CA).
145 [1983] 1 AC 565.

and time,[147] and also in some standard form bills of lading, such as Congerbill 2000. The clause which incorporates the Rules is usually known as a paramount clause.[148] The Congerbill 2000 clause provides as follows:

2. General Paramount Clause

The Hague Rules contained in the International Convention for the Unification of certain rules relating to Bills of Lading, dated Brussels the 25th August 1924 as enacted in the country of shipment shall apply to this contract. When no such enactment is in force in the country of shipment, the corresponding legislation of the country of destination shall apply, but in respect of shipments to which no such enactments are compulsorily applicable, the terms of the said Convention shall apply.

Trades where Hague–Visby Rules apply

In trades where the International Brussels Convention 1924 as amended by the Protocol signed at Brussels on February 23rd 1968 —The Hague–Visby Rules — apply compulsorily, the provision of the respective legislation shall be considered incorporated in this Bill of Lading. The Carrier takes all reservations possible under such applicable legislation, relating to the period before loading and after discharging and while the goods are in the charge of another Carrier, and to deck cargo and live animals.

Simple form of incorporation   The form that the paramount clause takes can vary.   **19.52**
In *The Agios Lazaros*[149] the relevant clause provided that:

31. New Jason clause, both to blame collision clause, P & I bunkering clause and Chamber of Shipping War Risks clauses Nos. 1 and 2 and also Paramount clause are deemed to be incorporated in this Charter Party.

The Court of Appeal explained that such a 'simple' clause should be interpreted in such a way as to give effect to it, rather than rendering it meaningless. Lord Denning MR then went on to answer what was meant by the phrase:

What does 'paramount clause' or 'clause paramount' mean to shipping men? Primarily it applies to bills of lading. In that context its meaning is, I think, clear beyond question. It means a clause by which the Hague Rules are incorporated into the contract evidenced by the bill of lading and which overrides any express exemption or condition that is inconsistent with it.

It seems to me that when the 'paramount clause' is incorporated, without any words of qualification, it means that all the Hague Rules are incorporated. If the parties intend only to incorporate part of the rules (for example art. IV), or only so far as compulsorily applicable, they say so. In the absence of any such qualification, it seems to me that a 'clause paramount' is a clause which incorporates all the Hague Rules. I mean, of course, the accepted Hague Rules, not the Hague–Visby Rules, which are of later date.[150]

Extended meaning: Hague–Visby   At the time of *The Agios Lazaros* case, the   **19.53**
Hague–Visby Rules were not yet in force. Does a simple paramount clause now invoke the

---

[146] See para 19.26.
[147] eg Asbatankvoy, cl 20(i); NYPE 93, cl 31(a), lines 318–328. There is no paramount clause in the Gencon (1994) charterparty.
[148] See too the discussion at para 18.04 in relation to the Carriage of Goods by Sea Act 1924.
[149] [1976] 2 Lloyd's Rep 47.
[150] At 50–51. See also *Mauritius Oil Refineries Ltd v Stolt-Nielsen Nederlands BV (The Stolt Sydness)* [1997] 1 Lloyd's Rep 273; *Lauritzen Reefers v Ocean Reef Transport Ltd SA (The Bukhta Russkaya)* [1997] 2 Lloyd's Rep 744.

Hague–Visby Rules or the Hague Rules? In *Seabridge Shipping AB v AC Orsleff's EFTS's A/S (The M/V Fjellvang)*[151] Thomas J confirmed that the bringing into force of the Hague–Visby Rules in the United Kingdom brought about the consequence that a paramount clause in a charterparty governed by English law incorporated the Hague–Visby Rules. However, he went on to say that this could 'only be a factor in determining what shipping men intended'.[152] Thus, if the charterparty is governed by English law, it would seem that this is a strong indication of incorporation of the Hague–Visby Rules.

19.54 **Reference to national statute** One particularly difficult variation of the simple type of paramount clause occurs when the relevant clause refers to a national statute. The main difficulty is that there are differences between the various national statutes. In *Adamastos Shipping Co v Anglo-Saxon Petroleum (The Saxon Star)*[153] the clause referred to the US Carriage of Goods by Sea Act:

> This bill of lading shall have effect subject to the provisions of the Carriage of Goods by Sea Act of the United States, approved April 16th, 1936, which shall be deemed to be incorporated herein, and nothing herein contained shall be deemed a surrender by the carrier of any of its rights or immunities or an increase of any of its responsibilities or liabilities under said Act. If any term of this bill of lading be repugnant to said Act to any extent, such term shall be void to that extent, but no further.

Lord Keith, after noting that the words 'this bill of lading' must be read as 'this charterparty', confirmed that such an incorporation amounted to a contractual incorporation of the US Act.[154] The effect of so holding is that the words of the statute so incorporated are construed by reference to the proper law of the contract and not according to the law of the state in which the statute was passed. Thus, in *Lauritzen Reefers v Ocean Reef Transport Ltd SA (The Bukhta Russkaya)*[155] there was a provision which provided for the application of the 'Canadian clause paramount':

> In trades between Canadian ports and ports other than US ports, the Canadian clause paramount to apply in lieu of the USA clause paramount, in trades involving neither US nor Canadian ports, the general paramount clause to apply in lieu of the USA clause paramount.

Thomas J explained that the effect of this clause was that, if the Hague Rules were enacted in the country of shipment, then they applied as enacted but that if the Hague Rules were not enacted in the country of shipment, the corresponding legislation of the country of destination applied. If there was no such legislation, the terms of the Convention containing the Hague Rules applied. Finally, if the Hague–Visby Rules were compulsorily applicable to the trade in question, then the legislation enacting those rules applied.[156] Applying the terms of the clause to the circumstances of the case, it was clear what was the applicable legislation at the ports of shipment and destination and that the Hague Rules should apply.[157]

---

151 [1999] 2 Lloyd's Rep 685.
152 At 689.
153 [1959] AC 133.
154 At 178.
155 [1997] 2 Lloyd's Rep 744.
156 At 746.
157 At 747. It was therefore not necessary to consider the charterers' argument that the overriding regime of the Hague–Visby Rules would have applied (in the absence of there being such a clause) on the basis that the charterparty was governed by English law.

Partial incorporation   Further difficulty is sometimes caused when a paramount clause   **19.55**
only incorporates part of the Rules and not the Rules in their entirety. Whether the Rules
are in fact given paramountcy in clear words will always be a question of interpretation.[158]

Effect of incorporation into a charterparty   We have begun to see that there can be diffi-   **19.56**
culties if a paramount clause is used. We now consider the effect of an incorporation of the
Rules into a charterparty. This question arises because of the different nature of a charterparty and the contracts to which the Rules are applicable. Charterparties, as we have
seen,[159] are contracts which are entered into between shipowners and charterers, with their
terms designed to regulate this relationship. The Hague and Hague–Visby Rules, on the
other hand, are designed to regulate the relations between carriers and shippers. Potentially,
the incorporation of the Rules may have the effect of giving them a wider application than
was intended.[160] In *Adamastos Shipping Co v Anglo-Saxon Petroleum (The Saxon Star)*[161] the
effect of a paramount clause was explained as follows by Viscount Simonds:

> [T]he parties to a charter-party often wish to incorporate the Hague Rules in their agree-
> ment: and by that I do not mean, nor do they mean, that they wish to incorporate the *ipsis-*
> *sima verba*[162] of those Rules. They wish to import into the contractual relation between
> owners and charterers the same standard of obligation, liability, right and immunity as under
> the Rules subsists between carrier and shipper: in other words they agree to impose upon the
> owners, in regard, for instance, to the seaworthiness of the chartered vessel, an obligation to
> use due diligence in place of the absolute obligation which would otherwise lie upon
> them.[163]

Thus, the effect of incorporation is that the Rules are treated as if they are set out in full, but
rejecting those provisions which make no sense in a charterparty context.[164]

---

[158] See *Marifortuna Naviera SA v Government of Ceylon (The Mariasmi)* [1970] 1 Lloyd's Rep 247 (cl 29 of
the charterparty held to be a limited provision); *Sabah Flour & Feedmills Sdn Bhd v Comfez Ltd* [1988] 2
Lloyd's Rep 18 (CA).

[159] Set out in broad terms at para 1.35.

[160] See, eg, *Seven Seas Transportation Ltd v Pacifico Union Marina Corp (The Satya Kailash and The Oceanic
Amity)* [1984] 1 Lloyd's Rep 588 (CA); *Grimaldi Compania di Navigazione SpA v Sekihyo Lines Ltd (The Seki
Rolette)* [1998] 2 Lloyd's Rep 638.

[161] [1959] AC 133.

[162] ie 'the exact words'.

[163] [1959] AC 133, 154.

[164] See *Compania Sud American Vapores v MS ER Hamburg Schiffahrtsgesellschaft MbH & Co KG* [2006]
EWHC 483 (Comm); [2006] 2 Lloyd's Rep 66.

PART IV

THE RESPONSIBILITIES OF THE SHIPPER

20

SHIPPER'S COMMON LAW OBLIGATIONS

A. Introduction

Overview   In this chapter we turn our attention to a consideration of the responsibilities **20.01** of the shipper. We focus here on the shipper's obligations at common law and principally those which will always be implied in the absence of some express provision in the contract of carriage. In the following chapters we will examine the obligation to pay freight and the shipper's obligations under the Hague and Hague–Visby Rules. We begin, however, with an outline of those obligations implied in law for both shippers and shipowners.

B. Obligations at Common Law

The general rule   Contracts, whether they are general contracts or contracts of affreight- **20.02** ment, contain express terms and may also contain implied terms.[1] Such implied terms may be implied by statute or custom. However, the court will only imply into a contract those terms as are necessary to give business efficacy to the contract, such as must have been intended by both parties. The court will not, however, make contracts for the parties. This was put as follows by Bowen LJ in one of the leading cases, *The Moorcock*:

> Now, an implied warranty ... as distinguished from an express contract or express warranty, really is in all cases founded on the presumed intention of the parties, and upon reason. The implication which the law draws from what must obviously have been the intention of the parties, the law draws with the object of giving efficacy to the transaction and preventing such a failure of consideration as cannot have been within the contemplation of either side; ... if one were to take all the cases ... of implied warranties or covenants in law, it will be found that in all of them the law is raising an implication from the presumed intention of the

---

[1] Generally as to implied terms, see Treitel (2003), 201; Scrutton (1996), art 45.

parties with the object of giving to the transaction such efficacy as both parties must have intended that at all events it should have. In business transactions such as this, what the law desires to effect by the implication is to give such business efficacy to the transaction as must have been intended at all events by both parties who are business men; not to impose on one side all the perils of the transaction, or to emancipate one side from all the chances of failure, but to make each party promise in law as much, at all events, as it must have been in the contemplation of both parties that he should be responsible for in respect of those perils or chances.[2]

20.03 **Contracts of affreightment** A contract of affreightment,[3] whether in the form of a bill of lading or a charterparty, will contain express provisions which have been agreed to by the parties to the contract. But in addition to these express clauses, which are negotiated against a background of custom and commercial usage, certain obligations are implied by law. These implied obligations will be incorporated into the contract in the absence of agreement to the contrary. Indeed, in the case of the implied obligations about to be referred to, it has been said that they have 'stood for many years, ... it must be rarely necessary for any further implication to be made'.[4]

20.04 **Voyage charterparties and bills of lading** In these two types of contract of affreightment the charterer or shipper impliedly undertakes not to ship dangerous goods.[5] On the other hand, the shipowner impliedly undertakes that the ship is seaworthy;[6] that the ship will proceed with reasonable despatch;[7] and that the ship will proceed without unjustifiable deviation.[8]

20.05 **Time charterparties** In time charterparties the charterer impliedly undertakes that he will use the vessel only between good and safe ports[9] and that he will not ship dangerous goods.[10] The shipowner impliedly undertakes that the vessel is seaworthy at the commencement of the period of hiring.[11]

C. Dangerous Cargoes

20.06 **Introduction** The description of the cargo for shipment invariably forms an important component of the negotiations between the parties to any shipping contract. This requirement becomes especially germane when it has been estimated that more than 50 percent of the cargoes transported by sea today may be regarded as dangerous, hazardous, and/or

---

2 (1889) 14 PD 64 (CA), 68. See also *Shirlaw v Southern Foundries Ltd* [1939] 2 KB 206 (CA), 227 (Mackinnon LJ).
3 See para 1.32.
4 *Compagnie Algerienne de Meunerie v Katana Societa di Navigazione Marittima SpA (The Nizeti)* [1960] 1 Lloyd's Rep 132 (CA), 138 (Hodgson LJ).
5 See para 20.06.
6 See below para 23.02.
7 Below para 25.02.
8 Below ch. 24.
9 See para 20.21.
10 See para 20.06.
11 See para 23.23.

harmful and which need to be handled with special care.[12] Although there is no list of cargoes which may be dangerous,[13] hazardous, or harmful to the carrier's ship or other cargoes aboard the ship, various statutes recognize that the shipper has certain obligations to the carrier with regard to cargo which is 'fraught with danger or risk; perilous, hazardous, unsafe; injurious'.

Definitions in the Merchant Shipping Acts   Section 446 of the Merchant Shipping Act **20.07** 1894, which imposed a fine for failure to ship dangerous goods not properly marked, interpreted 'dangerous' goods as 'aquafortis, vitriol, naphtha, benzine, gunpowder, lucifermatches, nitro-glycerine, petroleum, any explosive within the meaning of the Explosives Act 1875, and any other goods of a dangerous nature'.[14] This part of the 1894 Act was repealed by the Merchant Shipping Act 1993[15] with effect from 1 May 1994,[16] because its provisions had been superseded by safety regulations made pursuant to what is now section 85(1) of the Merchant Shipping Act 1995.[17] In addition, section 87(1) of the 1995 Act provides that where dangerous goods have been sent or carried, or attempted to be sent or carried, on board any ship, whether or not a United Kingdom ship, then any court that has Admiralty jurisdiction may declare the goods to be forfeited. The circumstances in which the court may do so include: (a) where the goods are not marked as required by safety regulations, (b) where no notice has been given as required by safety regulations, (c) where the goods are falsely described, or (d) where there is a false description of their sender or carrier. Dangerous goods are defined in section 87(5) as 'goods designated as dangerous goods by safety regulations'.

Regulations   The extant safety regulations are the Merchant Shipping (Dangerous **20.08** Goods and Marine Pollutants) Regulations 1997 which came into force on 1 November 1997.[18] 'Dangerous goods' are defined here as meaning:

> goods classified in the IMDG Code or in any other IMO publication referred to in these Regulations as dangerous for carriage by sea, and any other substance or article that the shipper has reasonable cause to believe might meet the criteria for such classification;
>
> This expression also includes —

(i) residues in empty receptacles, empty tanks or cargo holds which have been used previously for the carriage of dangerous goods unless such receptacles, empty tanks or cargo holds have been cleaned and dried, purged, gas freed or ventilated as appropriate or, in the case of radioactive materials, have been both cleaned and adequately closed; and
(ii) goods labelled, marked or declared as dangerous goods.

---

[12] See AFM de Biévre, 'Liability and Compensation for Damage in Connection With the Carriage of Hazardous and Noxious Substances by Sea' (1986) 17 JMLC 61.

[13] See Stephen D Girvin, 'Shippers' Liability for the Carriage of Dangerous Cargoes by Sea' [1996] LMCLQ 487; FD Rose, 'Cargo Risks: "Dangerous" goods' (1996) 55 CLJ 601.

[14] See also ss 447–450.

[15] 1993, c 22. Schedule 4, para 11(1).

[16] Merchant Shipping (Registration) Act 1993 (Commencement No 1 and Transitional Provisions) Order, 1993, SI 1993/3137.

[17] c 21. Previously s 21(1) of the Merchant Shipping Act 1979, c 39.

[18] SI 1997/2357, revoking the earlier Regulations, Merchant Shipping (Dangerous Goods and Marine Pollutants) Regulations 1990, SI 1990/2605.

The expression shall not include goods forming part of the equipment or stores of the ship in which they are carried.[19]

These Regulations apply to United Kingdom ships wherever they may be and to other ships while they are within the United Kingdom waters.[20] Part II of the Regulations lays down detailed requirements as to the carriage of packaged goods.

20.09 **IMDG Code** All-important for the purposes of the above Regulations and the provisions of the Merchant Shipping Act 1995 is the International Maritime Dangerous Goods Code (the IMDG Code).[21] The Code details nine classes of dangerous goods[22] and specifies the marking, identification and consignment procedures, labelling and placarding, documentation, and packing of these goods. The Code has always been very influential[23] and its importance was emphasized when it became part of the SOLAS Convention[24] and mandatory for all signatory states as from 1 January 2004.

20.10 **Details required from the shipper** The precise details which must be specified by the shipper, both in the negotiations and eventually in the written contract itself, will ultimately depend upon the type of cargo to be transported. If, for example, the carrier agrees to the carriage of one type of cargo, perhaps a bulk cargo such as ore, grain, or coal, then he will be contractually obliged to transport that cargo. But should the contract be for the transportation of cargoes which are recognized as inherently dangerous, such as oil-based products, gases, or chemicals, the carrier will be contractually obliged only to transport the goods as specified. Should the charterers or shippers purport to load goods which are outside the contract description or specifically excluded from the contract, this will constitute a breach of contract and the master of a ship could refuse to load the cargo.[25] Thus Devlin J stated in *GW Grace & Co Ltd v General Steam Navigation Co Ltd (The Sussex Oak)* that he could not think 'that the clause in the time charter-party which puts the master under the orders of the charterers as regards employment is to be construed as compelling him to obey orders which the charterer has no power to give'.[26]

20.11 **Standard forms: charterparties** It is not very common to find dangerous cargo clauses in the standard voyage charterparty forms, such as Gencon, possibly because it is in the nature of this charterparty that the cargo for shipment on the voyage will be expressly agreed between the contracting parties.[27] This may be contrasted with most time charterparty forms, where the charterer has a greater discretion as to the cargo to be shipped and where

---

[19] Regulation 2(1).

[20] Regulation 5(2).

[21] The current edition dates from 2004. Amendment 32-04 (2004 edition of the Code) became mandatory on 1 January 2006.

[22] For the basic division, see Reg 7(2).

[23] See H Wardleman, 'The Safe Transport of Dangerous, Hazardous and Harmful Cargoes by Sea' (1990) 35 ETL 747.

[24] 1974. See Part VII of SOLAS.

[25] If the master accepts the cargo tendered for shipment by the shipper, it may still be possible for the carrier to claim an enhanced rate of freight under an implied contract arising from the tender and acceptance of the goods: *Steven v Bromley* [1919] 2 KB 722.

[26] [1950] 2 KB 383, 396.

[27] See Gencon 1994, box 12 (cl 1).

it is more usual to find a clause expressly prohibiting the shipment of certain goods. The NYPE 1946 charterparty provided at lines 24–25 that the vessel was to be employed 'in carrying lawful merchandise, including petroleum and its products, in proper containers, excluding …'[28] but did not expressly specify that the shipper was prohibited from loading dangerous goods. This possible deficiency was rectified in the 1993 version of the charterparty, clause 4(a) of which provides that the vessel may only be employed

> in carrying lawful merchandise excluding any goods of a dangerous, injurious, flammable or corrosive nature unless carried in accordance with the requirements or recommendations of the competent authorities of the country of the Vessel's registry and of ports of shipment and discharge …. Without prejudice to the generality of the foregoing, in addition the following are specifically excluded: livestock of any description, arms, ammunition, explosives, nuclear and radioactive materials, …[29]

There are similar, but less detailed, provisions in certain of the more specialized time charterparty forms, such as Shelltime 4.[30] That none of the forms purport to be explicit in defining precisely what is meant by 'dangerous' is advantageous for carriers (and the converse for shippers) because it clearly brings within the ambit of the shipper's obligations the duty to account for a potentially wider category of cargoes.

Standard forms: bills of lading   Bill of lading standard forms commonly do contain dangerous goods clauses, either expressly, or by means of a paramount clause which purports to incorporate the Hague or Hague–Visby Rules.[31] Those forms which do have specific clauses concerning the carriage of dangerous goods are frequently drafted in a way which is markedly similar to article IV, rule 6 of the Hague and Hague–Visby Rules.[32] One example is the bill of lading for combined transport issued by the Ellerman Harrison Container Line Ltd which specifies: (i) that the shipper should obtain the express consent of the carrier where he proposes the carriage of goods which are 'or may become dangerous, inflammable or damaging including radio-active material(s); (ii) that these goods shall be distinctly marked; and (iii) that if the requisite consent has not been obtained or the goods properly marked and the goods are liable to become 'dangerous', then they may at 'any time be destroyed, disposed of, abandoned, or rendered harmless without compensation to the Merchant and without prejudice to the Carrier's right to Freight'.[33] The potential category of goods falling within such clauses in bills of lading is, at least in theory, unlimited: none of the forms purport to be explicit in defining precisely what is meant by 'dangerous'.   **20.12**

Effect of a breach   Where the shipment of an excluded cargo is so serious as to go to the root of the contract, the owners might be able to treat the contract as having been discharged. This aspect was considered in the case of *Chandris v Isbrandtsen-Möller Co Inc*,[34]   **20.13**

---

[28] cf Baltime 1939, lines 21–22. This expressly prohibits the carriage of 'dangerous goods' and then goes on to specify 'acids, explosives, calcium carbide, ferro silicon, naphtha, motor spirit, tar, or any of their products'. See Baltime 1939 (2001 rev), cl 2.

[29] Lines 49–54.

[30] Clause 28.

[31] See para 19.51.

[32] See para 22.12.

[33] Clause 19(1).

[34] [1951] 1 KB 240. This case was decided prior to the demise of the fundamental breach doctrine in contract.

where the charterparty expressly prohibited the carriage of 'acids, explosives, arms, ammunition or other dangerous cargo' and the charterers loaded a cargo of 1,540 tons of turpentine, with the knowledge of the master, causing a delay of sixteen days in discharge. The question for the court was whether this delay entitled the owners to damages for detention beyond the liquidated damages (demurrage) clause.[35] Alternatively, had they by their act of affirming the contract (by treating the dangerous cargo as coming within the contract description) restricted themselves to damages within the terms of the charterparty? Devlin J, although finding that the charterers were in breach of a 'fundamental term' of the charterparty, nevertheless held that the shipowners, in affirming the contract, would only be entitled to damages at the demurrage rate, notwithstanding that this rate was set rather low in the charterparty.[36]

20.14   **Liability at common law**   The courts, in implying an obligation on the shipper to notify the carrier of the dangerous character of his cargo, were initially much preoccupied with the question whether the shipper's liability for the shipment of dangerous goods was strict. The reason for implying such an obligation is clearly to give the carrier the opportunity either to refuse to carry the goods or to take the necessary precautions to protect his ship and the cargo of other shippers on board the ship. The shipper's liability at common law will only arise, however, when the carrier does not know, or ought not reasonably to know, of the dangerous character of the goods.[37] Once the shipper has given notice, his obligation to the carrier will be discharged. Likewise, once the carrier is aware of the character of the goods, or where he contracts to carry goods of a specified description,[38] the shipper will not be under any further obligation to give notice. A further issue is whether the obligation is an implied term of the contract or whether the cause of action exists in tort.

20.15   **Early principles**   In the first edition of his pioneering *Treatise of the Law Relative to Ships and Seamen*, published in 1802, Charles Abbott, speaking of the general duties of the merchant, stated two general principles: (i) that the hirer of any thing was required to use it in a lawful manner, and according to the purpose for which it was let; (ii) that 'the merchant must lade no prohibited or uncustomed goods, by which the ship may be subjected to detention or forfeiture'.[39] He cited no direct English authorities for either of these propositions, as there were clearly none, and referred to Justinian's *Digest* 19.2.61.1[40] and 'French Ordinance, liv 3, tit 3, Fret art 9'.[41] In the same year as the publication of Abbot's *Treatise*, the case of *Williams v The East India Company*[42] was argued in King's Bench. The plaintiffs had chartered their vessel, the *Princess Amelia*, to the East India Company and, on one of the voyages, a package of flammable oil/varnish was received aboard the vessel by the chief

---

[35] See *Moorsom v Bell* (1811) 2 Camp 616; 170 ER 1270.

[36] [1951] 1 KB 240, 250–251. See also Tiberg (1995), 562; para 31.56.

[37] In *Brass v Maitland* (1856) 6 El&Bl 470; 119 ER 940, Campbell CJ noted that the carrier 'has no right to expect any communication respecting the nature of the goods when he himself may easily discover it' (482). See also *Shaw Savill & Albion Co Ltd v Electric Reduction Sales Co Ltd (The Mahia)* [1955] 1 Lloyd's Rep 264.

[38] A point made by Mustill J in *The Athanasia Comninos* [1990] 1 Lloyd's Rep 277, 284.

[39] See the 5th edn (London, 1901), 270.

[40] A passage of Scaevola (*Digest*, book 7).

[41] ie the *Ordonnance sur la Marine*, 1681.

[42] (1802) 3 East 192; 102 ER 571.

mate, since deceased, allegedly with no declaration of its dangerous qualities. Had notice of the dangerous character of the goods been given to the owners? Lord Ellenborough CJ held that in order to make the putting on board wrongful, the defendant shippers had to be 'conusant of the dangerous quality of the article put on board; and if being so, they yet gave no notice, considering the probable danger thereby occasioned to the lives of those on board, ... for which [the defendants] were criminally liable, and punishable as for misdemeanours at least'.[43] Thus this case clearly limited the shipper's liability to those instances where he had knowledge of the dangerous nature of the goods.

Brass v Maitland[44]   The leading case of *Brass v Maitland*, which was argued before the   **20.16**
Queen's Bench, cited both Abbott and *Williams* with approval[45] but also went further on the standard of the shipper's liability. In this case a consignment of bleaching powder, which consisted largely of chloride of lime, was shipped aboard the plaintiff's 'general' ship, the *Regina*, in casks. During the voyage, the chloride of lime corroded, bursting the casks and mixing with and damaging other cargo. The majority of the court, Lord Campbell CJ and Wightman J, held that *ex contractu* the shippers should be strictly liable to the carriers. They had an obligation not to ship goods of such a dangerous character or so dangerously packed that (1) the carrier could not by reasonable knowledge and diligence be aware of their dangerous character, and (2) the carrier had not been so notified by the shipper or charterer.[46] Lord Campbell CJ held to this view even though the shippers were unaware of the dangerous nature of the goods, having shipped the casks immediately after receiving delivery from a third party, without opportunity for inspection. In his opinion ' ... ignorance ... can be no excuse for putting on board without notice the dangerous goods insufficiently packed'.[47] The underlying basis for this reasoning was expressed as follows:

> If the plaintiffs and those employed by them did not know and had no means of knowing the dangerous quality of the goods which caused the calamity, it seems most unjust and inexpedient to say that they have no remedy against those who might easily have prevented it ... [I]t seems much more just and expedient that, although they were ignorant of the dangerous qualities of the goods, or the insufficiency of the packing, the loss occasioned by the dangerous quality of the goods and the insufficient packing should be cast upon the shippers than upon the shipowners.[48]

The dissenting judge, Crompton J, strongly disagreed with this approach, principally because he reasoned, correctly, that there was no decisive authority to support an absolute obligation on the part of the shipper. He was not prepared to go any further than to say that a duty would be implied on the part of the shipper that he would take proper care and diligence to give notice of the shipment of goods of a dangerous nature.[49] In his view, it was 'very difficult to hold that the shipper can be liable for not communicating what he does not know'.[50]

---

[43] At 200.
[44] (1856) 6 El & Bl 470; 119 ER 940.
[45] At 484–485.
[46] At 481.
[47] At 486.
[48] At 483.
[49] At 493.
[50] At 491.

20.17 **Reaction**[51]   The dissenting opinion of Crompton J found support in certain first instance decisions. In *Hutchison v Guion*,[52] where salt cake caused damage to a vessel called the *Australia*, Willes J although finding for the shipowners, who did not know that saltcake was capable of corrosion and destruction, applied the reasoning of Crompton J. Chief Justice Erle also did so, taking the principle in *Brass v Maitland* 'in the narrowest and most limited way', in *Farrant v Barnes*.[53] Atkin J (as he then was) also applied the reasoning of Crompton J in *Mitchell, Cotts & Co v Steel Brothers & Co Ltd*,[54] although this was not a case of goods which were physically dangerous. In may decided cases, Lord Campbell's judgment has been strongly endorsed both at first instance and in the Court of Appeal. It received guarded support from Bramwell LJ in *Acatos v Burns*,[55] although it was not directly in point because that case concerned the carriage of a cargo of maize. The majority judges (Fletcher Moulton LJ and Farwell LJ) in *Bamfield & Goole v Sheffield Transport Co Ltd*[56] both accepted the existence of an absolute obligation in a case in which ferro-silicon, carried in casks, had given off the poisonous gases which killed the plaintiff's husband. Scrutton LJ endorsed this majority view in *Great Northern Railway Co v LEP Transport & Depositary*.[57]

20.18 **Modern case law**   Two reported decisions in recent years have endorsed the existence of an absolute obligation by the shipper. In *The Athanasia Comninos & Georges Chr Lemos*,[58] a case heard on 21 December 1979 but only actually reported in 1990, Mustill J concluded that the weight of authority supported the absolute obligation.[59] This view was also supported, obiter,[60] by the House of Lords in its decision in *Effort Shipping Co Ltd v Linden Management SA (The Giannis NK)*.[61] Lord Lloyd confirmed that:

> The dispute between the shippers and the carriers on this point is a dispute which has been rumbling on for well over a century. It is time for your Lordships to make a decision one way or the other. In the end that decision depends mainly on whether the majority decision in *Brass v Maitland*, which has stood for 140 years, should now be overruled. I am of the opinion, that it should not. I agree with the majority in that case and would hold that the liability of a shipper for shipping dangerous goods at common law, when it arises, does not depend on his knowledge or means of knowledge that the goods are dangerous.[62]

20.19 **Physically and non-physically dangerous goods**   Aside from those cases which involve the carriage of goods which are later found to be physically dangerous, the courts have included within the category of 'dangerous' two further types of case: (a) where the danger

---

[51] See, for example, the 14th edn (1901) of Abbott's *Treatise*, 644.

[52] (1858) 5 CB (NS) 149; 141 ER 59.

[53] (1862) 11 CB (NS) 553, 563; 142 ER 912, 916.

[54] [1916] 2 KB 610, 614.

[55] (1878) 3 Ex D 282 (CA), 288.

[56] [1910] 2 KB 94 (CA). cf Vaughan Williams LJ at 105–106.

[57] [1922] 2 KB 742 (CA), 764.

[58] [1990] 1 Lloyd's Rep 277.

[59] At 282.

[60] The case did not concern the common law obligation, but the obligation under art IV, r 6 of the Hague Rules. See further para 22.16.

[61] [1998] AC 605.

[62] At 619. See also Lord Steyn at 625 and the judgment of the Court of Appeal: [1996] 1 Lloyd's Rep 577 (CA), 587–588 (Hirst LJ). The absolute obligation has received support in Canada, citing the English authorities: see *Les Industries Perlite Inc v The Owners of the Marina Di Alimuri* [1996] LMLN 425.

is to be found in the surrounding circumstances rather than in the inherently dangerous nature of the goods themselves and (b) where the goods themselves are not physically dangerous to the vessel or other cargo. In *Micada Compania Naviera SA v Texim (The Agios Nicholas)*[63] a clause of the charter of the *Agios Nicolas* provided that 'no live stock nor injurious, inflammable or dangerous goods (such as acids, explosives, calcium carbide, ferro silicon, naphtha, motor spirit, tar, or any of their products) to be shipped'. Although the vessel was chartered for the carriage of iron ore, iron ore concentrate was loaded, the moisture content of which was such that it required the fitting of shifting boards. These were not fitted. Donaldson J, finding that the charterers were liable, held that the iron ore concentrate was dangerous: 'The danger consisted in the fact that the cargo was not what it seemed to be. In a word what [the master] was being offered was a wet wolf in a dry sheep's clothing and there was nothing to put him on notice that the cargo was radically and fundamentally different from that which it appeared to be'.[64] In the later case, *The Athanasia Cominos*,[65] two vessels were damaged by explosions caused by the ignition of a mixture of air and methane gas emitted by a cargo of coal after loading. Mustill J reasoned that, while it was impossible to categorize coal as either inherently dangerous or safe, it was common knowledge that it had a propensity to emit methane gas which might result in an explosion in certain conditions. In approaching such cases it was important to remember, when trying to find a test which would identify those cargoes whose shipment would be a breach of contract in the absence of specific warning as to their characteristics, that 'we are here concerned, not with the labelling in the abstract of goods as "dangerous" or "safe" but with the distribution of risk for the consequences of a dangerous situation arising during the voyage'.[66] Mustill J found against the carrier because, in contracting to carry goods of a specified description, he had assented to the presence on his ship of goods which possessed the attributes of the goods as described, including the capacity to create dangers which the accepted methods were not always sufficient to overcome.[67] He relied to some extent on the earlier case of *Atlantic Oil Carriers Ltd v British Petroleum Co Ltd (The Atlantic Duchess)*[68] where Pearson J had held that a cargo of butanized crude oil was not outside the contractual description of the charterparty.[69] *The Athanasia Comninos* was relied upon by Evans J in *General Feeds Inc v Burnham Shipping Corporation (The Amphion)*.[70] The *Amphion* was chartered to General Feeds on the Gencon form for the carriage of bagged fishmeal to China and this cargo ignited during unloading. Bagged fishmeal is known to be hazardous because of the potential for heat build-up and is listed as such under Class 9 of the IMDG Code. The hazard could be reduced, though not eliminated, by anti-oxidant treatment and the cargo was expressly described in the charterparty as 'anti-oxidant treated bagged fishmeal'. Evans J confirmed the finding of the arbitrators that while the shipowners might have accepted the risk of overheating occurring in 'properly treated cargo', properly handled,

---

[63] [1968] 2 Lloyd's Rep 57.
[64] At 62.
[65] [1990] 1 Lloyd's Rep 277.
[66] At 282. See too Michael Mustill QC, 'Carriers' liabilities and insurance' in Grönfors (1978), 77.
[67] At 284.
[68] [1957] 2 Lloyd's Rep 55.
[69] ie 'crude oil or fuel oil and/or diesel oil and/or gas oil and/or distillate of petroleum'.
[70] [1991] 2 Lloyd's Rep 101.

they had not accepted the risk from fishmeal 'not properly treated'.[71] The charterers were therefore held to be in breach of contract. Finally, in the case of *Mitchell, Cotts & Co v Steel Bros & Co Ltd*[72] the court extended the obligation to cases where the goods themselves were in no way physically dangerous. The charterers loaded a cargo of rice on board the *Kaijo Maru* and sent her to a port in Piraeus, knowing that the cargo could not be discharged there without the permission of the British authorities. The arbitrator found that at the time Piraeus was fixed as the port of delivery the charterers had not communicated the permission requirement to the shipowners; further, they had not obtained the requisite permission. The shipowners therefore did not know and could not have reasonably known that permission was needed to discharge the cargo of rice at Piraeus and damages were awarded against the charterers for the delay caused. In the view of Atkin J, the loading of unlawful cargo which might involve the vessel in the risk of seizure or delay was 'precisely analogous to the shipment of dangerous cargo which might cause the destruction of the ship'.[73]

20.20 **An artificial distinction?**   That there should be any distinction between the shipment of goods which are physically dangerous and those which are not physically dangerous, might seem, at first sight, to be an artificial limitation of the types of situations originally formulated as being within the class of cargo requiring disclosure of its 'dangerous' qualities. The courts have paid short shrift to attempts to restrict the absolute character of the obligation but it is submitted that the better approach might be that argued by Mustill J. If this shift in emphasis from 'dangerous' to 'injurious' were to take hold, then there might also be some justification for cutting down the scope of absolute liability.

D. The Obligation to Nominate a Safe Port

20.21 **The fundamental obligation**   Whenever a charterer has the right to nominate a port, whether under a time or voyage charter, he is under an implied obligation to nominate a safe port. In *Unitramp v Garnac Grain Co Inc (The Hermine)*[74] Roskill LJ (as he then was) explained that:

> The concept whether a particular port or berth is safe or unsafe is or at least should be simple, for the main purpose of such a warranty of safety in a charter-party is to ensure that a charterer, who has an otherwise unfettered right to nominate a port or berth, does not do so in such a way as to imperil the shipowners' ship, or, it may be, the lives of the shipowners' servants, by putting that ship or those lives in danger and thereby impose upon the shipowner the risk of financial loss. This limitation upon the charterer's right of nomination is of crucial importance to the shipowner because, by the terms of the contract of affreightment, whether it be a charter-party for time or for voyage, the shipowner has contracted with the charterer that his servants, that is, the master, officers and crew, will comply with the charterer's orders, so long as those orders are within the terms of the charter-party. As I say, this concept should be

---

[71] At 105.

[72] [1916] 2 KB 610.

[73] At 614. See also *Transoceanica Societa Italiana di Navigazione v HS Shipton & Sons* [1923] 1 KB 31; *Owners of Spanish SS Sebastian v De Vizcaya* [1920] 1 KB 332, 335 (Bailhache J). In *The Domald* [1920] P 56, Duke J, though following the reasoning of *Mitchell*, found that on the facts the cargo owners had not concealed any material facts which they ought to have disclosed.

[74] [1979] 1 Lloyd's Rep 212 (CA).

simple, but unfortunately its very simplicity has led to a multitude of decisions which at one time raised considerable doubt as to the exact meaning and extent of the warranty of safety.[75]

Implied obligation   There have been relatively few cases where a court has been asked to   **20.22**
imply a safe port obligation, because the obligation is usually reinforced by an express
clause in the charterparty. The court in *Vardinoyannis v Egyptian General Petroleum Corp*
(*The Evaggelos Th*)[76] was prepared to imply a term as to safety. *The Evaggelos Th*, a tanker,
was time chartered in November 1968 for trade in the Red Sea and elsewhere. At the material time this was a war zone and the charterers agreed to contribute to the cost of the ship's
war risks insurance. The charterparty did not, however, contain an express term as to the
safety of ports to which the ship might be ordered; it merely provided that

> 12. The Cargo or Cargoes shall be laden and discharged in any dock or at any wharf or place
> the Charterers may direct, where the vessel can always lie safely afloat.

The tanker was ordered to proceed to Suez at a time when there was a cease fire. However,
when the vessel arrived, hostilities erupted and the vessel became a constructive total loss as
a result of shell fire. Donaldson J held that the phrase 'always lie safely afloat' was

> concerned exclusively with the marine characteristics of the discharging place, and requires
> that the vessel shall at all times be water-borne and shall be able to remain there without risk
> of loss or damage from wind, weather or other craft which are being properly navigated. Thus
> a place which dries out or one in which the vessel can only lie to an anchor in fair weather or
> one in which the vessel might in certain winds or tides lie across the fairway would not be
> within the requirements of the clause. The position in which the vessel lay was not however,
> open to any such objection.[77]

He went on to hold that

> [an] implied term [as to a safe port] should in my judgment be limited to a warranty that the
> nominated port of discharge is safe at the time of nomination and may be expected to remain
> safe from the moment of the vessel's arrival until her departure. This is what the shipowner
> applies his mind to, if he is asked to include a named port in the charter. If, despite the fact that
> the nomination meets these requirements, the port is unsafe when the vessel arrives, no breach
> of contract is committed by the charterer, but the ship is not obliged to enter the port.[78]

Since Suez was not unsafe at the time of nomination, nor at that time expected to become
so, the charterers were not in breach of the implied term as to safety.

Business efficacy   The Court of Appeal were loath to imply such a clause in *Atkins*   **20.23**
International HA v Islamic Republic of Iran Shipping Lines (The APJ Pritt) because it was not
necessary to give business efficacy to the charterparty. Bingham LJ said:

> There is no ground for implying a warranty that the port declared was prospectively safe
> because the omission of an express warranty may well have been deliberate, because such an
> implied term is not necessary for the business efficacy of the charter and because such an
> implied term would at best lie uneasily beside the express terms of the charter.[79]

---

[75] At 214.
[76] [1971] 2 Lloyd's Rep 200.
[77] At 204.
[78] At 205.
[79] [1987] 2 Lloyd's Rep 37 (CA), 42.

The owners were in any case adequately protected by war clauses.

20.24 **Bills of lading**   The court was equally loath to imply such a clause in *Aegean Sea Traders Corporation v Repsol Petroleo SA (The Aegean Sea)*,[80] Thomas J stating that:

> ... [I]t does not follow that such a term should be implied into this bill of lading, assuming that the other party has the right to nominate. Although it would be necessary to imply a term that the port nominated be one at which it was possible for the vessel to discharge the cargo she had loaded, the implication of a term as to safety of that port would create a very onerous liability on those who became subjected to the liabilities under the bill of lading. The bill of lading does not specify that the port is to be safe and given the potentially onerous liabilities, it is difficult to see how an officious bystander would say 'of course' if the term were proposed. The position of the charterer is very different as he is in direct contractual relationship with the shipowner and will often insure his liabilities under a charterer's liability policy. In the case of a bill of lading that liability as to safety will be passed to the lawful holder who takes or demands delivery at the end of the chain; it would not necessarily be certain that in the case of this bill of lading that would be Repsol and it would be unlikely that they would ever contemplate insurance against such liabilities as the holders of a bill of lading, assuming such insurance was available. In my view if it had been intended that the onerous obligations as to safety were imposed under the bill of lading, the bill of lading would have made this express.[81]

20.25 **Voyage charterparties**   Safe port clauses are not commonly found in voyage charterparties because such charterparties tend to be drafted with a voyage between named ports in mind. As Lord Roskill said in *Kodros Shipping v Empresa Cubana de Fletes (The Evia (No 2))*:[82]

> But in considering whether there is any residual or remaining obligation after nomination it is necessary to have in mind one fundamental distinction between a time charterer and a voyage charterer. In the former case, the time charterer is in complete control of the employment of the ship. It is in his power by appropriate orders timeously given to change the ship's employment so as to prevent her proceeding to or remaining at a port initially safe which has since it was nominated become unsafe. But a voyage charterer may not have the same power. If there is a single loading or discharging port named in the voyage charterparty then, unless the charterparty specifically otherwise provides, a voyage charterer may not be able to order that ship elsewhere. If there is a range of loading or discharging ports named, once the voyage charterer has selected the contractual port or ports of loading or discharge, the voyage charterparty usually operates as if that port or those ports had originally been written into the charterparty, and the charterer then has no further right of nomination or renomination.[83]

There is no 'safe port' clause in the 1976 Gencon standard form, nor in the revised 1994 Gencon standard form.

---

[80] [1998] 2 Lloyd's Rep 39.
[81] At 68.
[82] [1983] 1 AC 736.
[83] At 763.

Tanker voyage charterparties There is usually a safe port/berth requirement in certain **20.26** tanker voyage charterparties. Shellvoy 5, clause 4 provides that:

> Charterers shall exercise due diligence to order the vessel only to ports and berths which are safe for the vessel and to ensure that transhipment operations conform to standards not less than those set out in the latest edition of ICS/OCIMF Ship-to-Ship Transfer Guide (Petroleum). Notwithstanding anything contained in this charter, Charterers do not warrant the safety of any port, berth or transhipment operation and Charterers shall not be liable for loss or damage arising from any unsafety if they can prove that due diligence was exercised in the giving of the order.[84]

Time charterparties Safe port clauses are almost universally found in time charterparties. **20.27** An example is clause 2 of Baltime 1939:

> **2. Trade**
> The vessel to be employed in lawful trades for the carriage of lawful merchandise only between good and safe ports or places where she can safely lie always afloat.

NYPE 93 provides:

> **5. Trading Limits**
> The Vessel shall be employed in such lawful trades between safe ports and safe places within … excluding … as the Charterers shall direct.

What is a 'safe port'? The classic definition is that of Sellers LJ in *Leeds Shipping Co Ltd* **20.28** *v Société Française Bunge (The Eastern City)*:

> If it were said that a port will not be safe unless, in the relevant period of time, the particular ship can reach it and return from it without, in the absence of some abnormal occurrence, being exposed to danger which cannot be avoided by good navigation and seamanship, it would probably meet all circumstances as a broad statement of the law.[85]

In this case a voyage charterparty contained a clause which stated that the vessel was to proceed from 'one or two safe ports in Morocco' to Japan. The charterer directed her to Mogador and she arrived and anchored there on 26 December. At Mogador there was a lack of shelter and a liability during the winter to the sudden onset of southerly gales, which could not be predicted, and which might quickly cause an anchor to drag. The port was very near some rocks and the anchorage was restricted. On 28 December the weather deteriorated and the master, fearing that his anchor was dragging, tried to put to sea. The *Eastern City* was caught by a strong gust of wind and driven onto the rocks adjacent to the anchorage. Upholding the judgment below of Pearson J,[86] the Court of Appeal agreed that the port was unsafe. Sellers LJ concluded that:

> The vital factors of unsafety in the present case, however, were the lack of reliable holding capacity for an anchor in the anchorage area, the lack of shelter and the liability to the

---

[84] See also Asbatankvoy cl 9. In *Palm Shipping Inc v Vitol SA (The Universal Monarch)* [1989] 2 Lloyd's Rep 483, Gatehouse J concluded that once the arbitrators had found that, on a vessel's arrival a port (Lisbon) was not safe in the absence of the tugs, the proper approach should have led them to conclude that the charterers were in breach of the safe port warranty and that the cost of obtaining tugs, from a distance represented by 16 hours' steaming time in order to remedy their breach and render the port safe was for the charterers to bear: at 485.
[85] [1958] 2 Lloyd's Rep 127 (CA), 131.
[86] [1957] 2 Lloyd's Rep 153.

sudden onset of high wind which could not be predicted and which might quickly cause an anchor to drag, and, in the circumstances, the restricted area of the anchorage and its close proximity to the rocks and shallows with a high wind or gale from the south or somewhere to the west of south.[87]

20.29 **The period of time** The period of time contemplated clearly covers the entire period during which the vessel is using the port from the moment of entry to the time of departure. Sometimes this may be extended to include risks encountered on approach to the port or dangers encountered on the open sea. Thus in *GW Grace & Co Ltd v General Steam Navigation Co Ltd (The Sussex Oak)*[88] the *Sussex Oak* was time chartered to proceed to Hamburg. During the course of her passage up the Elbe, ice was encountered. The pilot nevertheless considered it safe to proceed. Further on the *Sussex Oak* was halted by a large ice floe and as it was not then possible for her to turn or any way proceed — other than ahead — the vessel forced her way through the ice, sustaining damage. Devlin J said that:

> In my judgment there is a breach of clause 2 [of the Baltime charterparty] if the vessel is employed upon a voyage to a port which she cannot safely reach. It is immaterial in point of law where the danger is located, though it is obvious in point of fact that the more remote it is from the port the less likely it is to interfere with the safety of the voyage. The charterer does not guarantee that the most direct route or any particular route to the port is safe, but the voyage he orders must be one which an ordinarily prudent and skilful master can find a way of making in safety.[89]

20.30 **Unsafety factors** A port will be unsafe if the approach is such that the port cannot be reached without dismantling part of the ship's structure, or if the ship has to lighten her cargo to enter the port. The case of *K/S Penta Shipping A/S v Ethiopian Shipping Line Corp (The Saga Cob)*[90] has considered the effect of risk of a hostile seizure or attack and so-called 'political unsafety'. The charterparty was on the Shelltime 3 form[91] which provided that the vessel was to be employed in the Red Sea, the Gulf of Aden, and east Africa and was to carry petroleum products. The vessel called about 20 times at Massawa between January and August 1988 without risk. On 26 August the vessel was ordered to proceed to Massawa yet again. However, on 7 September 1988, the vessel was about 4–5 miles north east of the harbour entrance and was attacked by Eritrean guerillas. The master was wounded and there was substantial damage to the *Saga Cob*. The owners brought an action against the charterers on the basis that they were in breach of clause 3 of the charter which provided that:

> Charterers shall exercise due diligence to ensure that the vessel is only employed between and at safe ports ... where she can always lie safely afloat but ... Charterers shall not be deemed to warrant the safety of any port ... and shall be under no liability in respect thereof save for loss of damage caused by their failure to exercise due diligence ...

The Court of Appeal allowed the appeal because, in the words of Parker LJ,

> [a port] will not, in circumstances such as the present, be regarded as unsafe unless the 'political' risk is sufficient for a reasonable shipowner or master to decline to send or sail his vessel there.

---

[87] [1958] 2 Lloyd's Rep 127 (CA), 136.
[88] [1950] 2 KB 383.
[89] At 391.
[90] [1992] 2 Lloyd's Rep 545 (CA). See too *Ullises Shipping Corp v Fal Shipping Co Ltd (The Greek Fighter)* [2006] EWHC 1729.
[91] See now Shelltime 5.

There is no evidence in the present case that this was so and subsequent history shows that Massawa was on 26 August, 1988 and for a long time thereafter not regarded as presenting any such risk.[92]

Leaving in safety   Once loading or discharging has been completed, the vessel must be able to leave the port in safety. Thus in *The Sussex Oak*[93] the vessel was further damaged on her departure from Hamburg and the charterers were held liable for this damage also. The most frequently encountered danger in an unsafe port will be the risk of physical damage to the vessel, for example from an insufficient depth of water caused by the presence of ice or periodic silting.[94] However, other risks might include the imposition of a blockade or the outbreak of hostilities. **20.31**

Scope of the undertaking   What precisely is the scope of the undertaking given by the charterer? It seems to be clear that the undertaking refers to the safety of the port at the time that it is to be used, rather than to its safety at the time of nomination. In other words, the port must be prospectively safe, in the sense that its characteristics, both permanent and temporary, must be such that in the absence of some unexpected and abnormal event it will be safe for the ship at the time when she actually arrives there. The leading case is *Kodros Shipping Corp v Empresa Cubana de Fletes (The Evia (No 2))*.[95] In this case the *Evia* had been chartered on a Baltime form, although it was substantially amended and contained a number of typed clauses. The charterparty included the express words that 'The vessel to be employed . . . between good and safe ports . . .' In March 1980 the *Evia* was ordered by the charterers to load a cargo of cement in Cuba for passage to Basrah. At this time there was no reason to believe that Basrah was unsafe or indeed was likely to become unsafe in the foreseeable future. The *Evia* arrived in the Shatt-al-Arab waterway on 1 July 1980 but owing to congestion had to wait until 20 August before a berth was available in Basrah. Discharge of her cargo was not completed until 22 September, the day on which navigation in the Shatt-al-Arab ceased due to the outbreak of hostilities in the Iran–Iraq war. An arbitrator held that the charterer had not breached clause 2 of the charterparty and that it was frustrated as from 4 October. Robert Goff J[96] held that there had been a breach of clause 2. However, he also agreed with the umpire that apart from that breach the charterparty would have been frustrated but held that the charterers were debarred from relying on frustration as a defence to the shipowners' claim for hire because it was self-induced. The Court of Appeal allowed an appeal by the charterers,[97] holding that there had been no breach of clause 2 of the charterparty, and restored the arbitrator's award in that respect. The court also held, in agreement with the umpire and Robert Goff J, that clause 21 of the charterparty, relating to war risks, was not effective to exclude the operation of the doctrine of frustration. The shipowners appealed on the ground that any frustration was self-induced **20.32**

---

[92] [1992] 2 Lloyd's Rep 545 (CA), 551.

[93] [1950] 2 KB 383.

[94] In *Prekookeanska Plovidba v Felstar Shipping Corp (The Carnival)* [1994] 2 Lloyd's Rep 14 (CA), an underwater fender which penetrated a ship's hull was held to render a berth unsafe. See also *Maintop Shipping Co Ltd v Bulkindo Lines Pte Ltd (The Marinicki)* [2003] EWHC 1894; [2003] 2 Lloyd's Rep 655.

[95] [1983] 1 AC 736.

[96] [1981] 2 Lloyd's Rep 613.

[97] [1982] 1 Lloyd's Rep 334 (CA), by a majority, Lord Denning MR and Sir Sebag Shaw, Ackner LJ dissenting.

given that it had resulted from a breach of an express undertaking to nominate a safe port. The House of Lords rejected the shipowners' argument and upheld the decision of the Court of Appeal. They were unanimously of the view that the warranty as to a safe port did not amount to a continuing guarantee of the port's safety but referred only to the prospective safety of the port at the time of nomination. Since Basrah was prospectively safe at the time of nomination, and since the unsafety arose after the *Evia's* arrival and was due to an unexpected and abnormal event, there was no breach of clause 2 by the respondents.[98] Lord Diplock stated that:

> It is with the prospective safety of the port at the time when the vessel will be there for the loading or unloading operation that the contractual promise is concerned, and the contractual promise is given at the time when the charterer gives the order to the master or other agent of the shipowner to proceed to the loading or unloading port.[99]

Lord Roskill said that:

> In order to consider the scope of the contractual promise which these eight words impose upon a charterer, it must be determined how a charterer would exercise his undoubted right to require the shipowner to perform his contractual obligations to render services with his ship, his master, officers and crew, the consideration for the performance of their obligation being the charterer's regular payment of time charter hire. The answer must be that a charterer will exercise that undoubted contractual right by giving the shipowner orders to go to a particular port or place of loading or discharge. It is clearly at that point of time when that order is given that that contractual promise to the charterer regarding the safety of that intended port or place must be fulfilled. But that contractual promise cannot mean that that port or place must be safe when that order is given, for were that so, a charterer could not legitimately give orders to go to an ice-bound port which he and the owner both knew in all human probability would be ice-free by the time that vessel reached it. Nor, were that the nature of the promise, could a charterer order the ship to a port or place the approaches to which were at the time of the order blocked as a result of a collision or by some submerged wreck or other obstacles even though such obstacles would in all human probability be out of the way before the ship required to enter. The charterer's contractual promise must, I think, relate to the characteristics of the port or place in question and in my view means that when the order is given that port or place is prospectively safe for the ship to get to, stay at, so far as necessary, and in due course, leave. But if those characteristics are such as to make that port or place prospectively safe in this way, I cannot think that if, in spite of them, some unexpected and abnormal event thereafter suddenly occurs which creates conditions of unsafety where conditions of safety had previously existed and as a result the ship is delayed, damaged or destroyed, that contractual promise extends to making the charterer liable for any resulting loss or damage, physical or financial. So to hold would make the charterer the insurer of such unexpected and abnormal risks which in my view should properly fall upon the ship's insurers under the policies of insurance the effecting of which is the owner's responsibility under clause 3 unless, of course, the owner chooses to be his own insurer in these respects.
>
> My Lords, it will be seen that in this analysis I have stressed the point of time at which the order is given as the moment when the relevant obligation of the charterer arises, for it is then

---

[98] For a related case cf *Uni-Ocean Lines Pte Ltd v C-Trade SA (The Lucille)* [1984] 1 Lloyd's Rep 244. Here Basrah was held to be an unsafe port.

[99] [1983] 1 AC 736, 749. The House of Lords here approved the view of Donaldson J in V*ardinoyannis v Egyptian General Petroleum Corp (The Evaggelos Th)* [1971] 2 Lloyd's Rep 200, 205.

that the relevant employment of the ship will begin. I venture to think this is plain as a matter of construction. But when one looks at the authorities one sees that they strongly support the view which I have just expressed.[100]

The House of Lords also rejected the idea that the nature of the charterer's undertaking was in effect to provide a continuing guarantee of the safety of the port during the period it was to be used,[101] subject to rules of causation and remoteness.

Port becoming unsafe   What then would happen should the port become actually or prospectively unsafe to the knowledge of the charterer while the vessel was sailing towards the port, or perhaps after it was already berthed? The House of Lords took the view that the charterer would then have a secondary obligation (under a time charter) to cancel the original nomination and order the ship out of danger. And, if the vessel was originally in the port (as with the *Evia* herself), the obligation would only arise where it was still possible for the vessel to leave the port. Lord Roskill stated that: **20.33**

> In my opinion, while the primary obligation of a time charterer under clause 2 of this charterparty is that which I have already stated, namely, to order the ship to go only to a port which, at the time when the order is given, is prospectively safe for her, there may be circumstances in which, by reason of a port, which was prospectively safe when the order to go to it was given, subsequently becoming unsafe, clause 2, on its true construction, imposes a further and secondary obligation on the charterer.[102]

In relation to this Lord Roskill suggested that there were two possible situations requiring consideration. The first situation was where, after the time charterer had performed his primary obligation — to a port prospectively safe — and while the ship was still proceeding towards such a port, new circumstances arose which rendered the port unsafe. He concluded that

> ... [C]lause 2, on its true construction (unless the cause of the new unsafety be purely temporary in character), imposes on the time charterer a further and secondary obligation to cancel his original order and, assuming that he wishes to continue to trade the ship, to order her to go to another port which, at the time when such fresh order is given, is prospectively safe for her. This is because clause 2 should be construed as requiring the time charterer to do all that he can effectively do to protect the ship from the new danger in the port which has arisen since his original order for her to go to it was given.[103]

The second situation was where, after the time charterer had performed his primary obligation by ordering the ship to go to a port which was, at the time of such order, prospectively safe for her, and she had proceeded to and entered such port in compliance with such order, new circumstances arose which rendered the port unsafe.[104] Here Lord Roskill concluded that:

> ... the question ... will depend on whether, having regard to the nature and consequences of the new danger in the port which has arisen, it is possible for the ship to avoid such danger by

---

[100] At 757.
[101] A view propounded in a long line of cases. See *Transoceanic Carriers v Cook Industries (The Mary Lou)* [1981] 2 Lloyd's Rep 272, 290–291.
[102] [1983] 1 AC 736, 764.
[103] ibid.
[104] ibid.

leaving the port. If, on the one hand, it is not possible for the ship so to leave, then no further and secondary obligation is imposed on the time charterer. This is because clause 2 should not be construed as requiring the time charterer to give orders with which it is not possible for the ship to comply, and which would for that reason be ineffective. If, on the other hand, it is possible for the ship to avoid the new danger in the port which has arisen by leaving, then a further and secondary obligation is imposed on the time charterer to order the ship to leave the port forthwith, whether she has completed loading or discharging or not, and, assuming that he wishes to continue to trade the ship, to order her to go to another port which, at the time when such fresh order is given, is prospectively safe for her. This is again because clause 2 should be construed as requiring the time charterer to do all that he can effectively do to protect the ship from the new danger in the port which has arisen since his original order for her to go to it was given.[105]

It is undecided whether the charterer's secondary obligation to nominate a fresh port if the original choice becomes unsafe applies where the contract in question is a voyage charter.[106] A further unanswered difficulty arising out of the case is how diligent a charterer is expected to be in discovering any subsequent unexpected threat to the safety of the nominated port after nomination of a prospectively safe port.

20.34 **The nature of the risks covered**   Whether or not a port is safe will be a question of fact depending on the circumstances of each individual case and, in determining this, regard will be had to the type of vessel involved, the work to be done, and the conditions in the port at the relevant time. The fact that it is safe to enter the port will not be enough if the port may become unsafe for the ship to remain at it. In *Islander Shipping Enterprises SA v Empresa Maritima del Estado SA (The Khian Sea)*[107] a vessel was ordered to a berth in Valparaiso. She tied up at Baron Wharf, which was exposed to a heavy swell during adverse conditions. The Court of Appeal held that the berth was unsafe because, although the master had obtained adequate warning of an approaching storm, he was unable to leave the berth because of the presence of two other vessels anchored close by and the vessel suffered damage. Lord Denning MR proceeded to state the requirements which had to be satisfied under a safe port warranty:

> First there must be an adequate weather forecasting system. Second, there must be an adequate availability of pilots and tugs. Thirdly, there must be adequate sea room to manoeuvre. And fourthly, there must be an adequate system for ensuring that sea room and room for manoeuvre is always available.[108]

He therefore concluded that:

> In this case the first and second requirements were satisfied. The weather forecasting was adequate. The pilot and tug got there in time. But the third and fourth were not satisfied. There was not enough room to manoeuvre at the crucial time on that morning of May 19. That was the reason why the vessel could not get away from the berth. There was not an adequate system of ensuring that there was enough sea room. These two vessels anchored far too close to the Khian Sea that evening.[109]

---

105 At 764–765.
106 Lord Roskill was reluctant to explore this point: [1983] 1 AC 736, 765.
107 [1979] 1 Lloyd's Rep 545.
108 At 547.
109 ibid.

Good navigation   A port will not be rendered unsafe by the presence of risks which can   **20.35**
be avoided by good navigation and competent seamanship. In *Leeds Shipping Co Ltd v
Société Française Bunge (The Eastern City)* Sellers LJ said that:

> Most, if not all, navigable rivers, channels, ports, harbours and berths have some dangers from
> tides, currents, swells, banks, bars or revetments. Such dangers are frequently minimised by
> lights, buoys, signals, warnings and other aids to navigation and can normally be met and over-
> come by proper navigation and handling of a vessel in accordance with good seamanship.[110]

But if more than ordinary skill is required to avoid dangers, the port will be unsafe. Thus in
Kristiandsands Tankrederi A/S v Standard Tankers (Bahamas) Ltd (The Polyglory)[111] a tanker,
the *Polyglory*, was ordered to Port-La-Nouvelle (on the French Mediterranean coast). While
taking on ballast, the master and the port pilot decided to leave the berth because of increasing wind. Difficulties were encountered, however, mainly because the vessel was still light,
and one of her anchors dragged which caused damage to an underwater pipeline. The owners settled the claim in respeat of the damaged pipeline and sought to recover this in turn
from the charterers on the ground that the port was unsafe. The arbitrator had held that the
port was unsafe and, though the pipeline was damaged as a result of the pilot's negligence,
this did not break the chain of causation between the order to proceed to the port and the
damage. Parker J upheld the arbitrator's award. The principle to be applied was that

> … the port will be safe if an ordinarily prudent and skilful master can find a way of reaching
> it in safety. This means that when considering the question whether an order to proceed to a
> port is a breach of the safe port clause one relevant consideration is 'could an ordinarily
> prudent and skilful master get there in safety?'. If the answer is yes then at any rate as regards
> its approaches the port will be safe. Thus an assumption has to be made that ordinary care
> and skill will be used when the question of safety is being determined.

> … [I]f the only dangers to which a properly manned and equipped vessel of the size and type
> in question will be exposed are dangers which can be avoided by the exercise of ordinary
> reasonable care and skill that port is not, as a matter of law, unsafe and the order to proceed
> to it is not therefore a breach.[112]

Parker J held that the arbitrator was justified in finding the port unsafe because the dangers
could only be avoided by very high standards of navigation and seamanship. Further, he
also agreed that the pilot's negligence did not break the chain of causation.

Temporary obstacles   A temporary danger or obstacle, such as a neap tide,[113] will not   **20.36**
render a port unsafe. To render the port unsafe, the danger or obstacle would have to be
operative for a period which, having regard to the nature of the adventure and of the
contract, would be sufficient to frustrate the commercial object of the adventure. In
Unitramp v Garnac Grain Co Inc (The Hermine)[114] a vessel chartered on the Baltimore C
grain form was required to proceed to

> … one (1)/two (2) safe berths, one (1) safe port US Gulf … understood New Orleans,
> Destrehan, Ama, Myrtle Grove Reserve, count as one (1) port.

---

[110] [1958] 2 Lloyd's Rep 127, 131.
[111] [1977] 2 Lloyd's Rep 353.
[112] At 362–363.
[113] Tides at a certain time of the month when there is the least difference between high and low water.
[114] [1978] 2 Lloyd's Rep 37.

The *Hermine* was prevented from leaving Destrehan, a port on the Mississippi, owing to a lowering of the draught in the river 115 miles downriver due to continuing accretion of silt from floods originating upstream. There was a risk of delay of uncertain duration which in fact lasted 37 days. At first instance, Donaldson J held that Destrehan was not a safe port; he noted that:

> The point of the [safe port] warranty is that it speaks from the date of nomination, but it speaks about the anticipated state of the port when the vessel arrives. The charterer's sole right under a contract in the terms of this charter-party is to nominate a safe port and, in nominating a port under the charter-party, he impliedly warrants that it is a safe port. The charterer undertakes that, in the absence of some abnormal occurrence, the vessel will be able, at the relevant times, to reach, use and leave the port without being exposed to dangers which cannot be avoided by good navigation and seamanship. The warranty is absolute, but contains within itself the qualification in relation to abnormal occurrences.[115]

The Court of Appeal disagreed.[116] Roskill LJ stated that:

> How do you judge whether a particular delay is commercially unacceptable? It may be perfectly acceptable commercially to the charterer if he is in no hurry for his cargo and if he does not have to pay the shipowner for the delay. These matters cannot be judged unilaterally in the interests of one party only. There are two parties to the contract and their mutual rights and obligations have to be determined by reference to that upon which they have expressly or impliedly agreed in their contract.

> I see no reason why one should apply a different test, in the circumstances with which we are concerned, from that which has been enunciated in the various classes of case in the authorities ... Therefore, with very great respect to the learned Judge, I think he was wrong in the conclusion which he reached. I think that the arbitrators properly interpreted the authorities and, on those authorities, I think they were right in reaching the conclusion that Destrehan was not an unsafe port.[117]

20.37 **Remedies** A shipowner can refuse a nomination of a port by the charterer if he is aware that the port is inherently unsafe.[118] Thus in *Abu Dhabi National Tanker Co v Product Star Shipping Ltd (The Product Star)(No 2)*[119] there was a six-month time charterparty on the Beepeetime 2 form in terms of which a vessel was to be delivered at one safe port Fujairah and redelivered at one safe port Arabian Gulf/India range inclusive. Four such voyages were performed between Ruwais and Chittagong, Bangladesh. The charterers then telexed the master instructing him to proceed once again to Ruwais. Prior to her arrival, the owners telexed the charterers stating that entry to this port was now considered dangerous and requesting a different nomination. The charterers insisted that the vessel should proceed to Ruwais and an impasse was reached. The charterers then purported to accept the conduct of the owners as repudiatory. Leggatt LJ pointed out that:

> Where A and B contract with each other to confer a discretion on A, that does not render B subject to A's uninhibited whim. In my judgment, the authorities show that not only must the discretion be exercised honestly and in good faith, but, having regard to the provisions of

[115] At 47.
[116] [1979] 1 Lloyd's Rep 212 (CA).
[117] At 219.
[118] See *Tillmanns & Co v SS Knutsford Ltd* [1908] 2 KB 385 (CA), 406 (Farwell LJ).
[119] [1993] 1 Lloyd's Rep 397 (CA).

the contract by which it is conferred, it must not be exercised arbitrarily, capriciously or unreasonably. That entails a proper consideration of the matter after making any necessary inquiries. To these principles, little is added by the concept of fairness: it does no more than describe the result achieved by their application.[120]

It emerged that the owners had made no attempt to consult the master; indeed their refusal was made at short notice for no attack had been made at any material time on shipping trading either to or from the United Arab Emirates (UAE). Leggatt LJ stated that:

[I]n appraising the validity of owners' refusal several factors are pertinent. The owners had made no attempt to consult the master, who without demur was expecting to go to Ruwais; the refusal was made at short notice, attributing it inexplicably to 'the most recent development in waters adjacent to Ruwais'; no attack had been made at any material time on a ship trading to or from the UAE; and no explanation has ever been offered why the three directors of IMI, the managers of the vessel, should have suffered to trade in the Gulf between Sept. 15 and 25, 1987 a vessel called the *East Star*, which they also managed through IMI. The same three directors were also directors of the two one-ship companies which respectively owned *Product Star* and *East Star*. In my judgment, this factor is of such moment as to undermine, if not invalidate, the owners' reasons for declining to proceed. That in turn calls in question the owners' good faith, and in any event strongly suggests that their refusal was arbitrary.[121]

Waiver   In certain circumstances the owners will be regarded as having waived their right   **20.38**
to refuse a nomination by their conduct. This issue was considered by the House of Lords in *Motor Oil Hellas (Corinth) Refineries SA v Shipping Corporation of India (The Kanchenjunga)*.[122] The *Kanchenjunga* was chartered on the Exxonvoy form for loading in safe ports in the Arabian Gulf, excluding Fao and Abadan. This was just before the outbreak of the Iran–Iraq war. She was ordered to load at Kharg Island in Iran and upon arrival gave notice of readiness to load. She then waited for a week, but, following an attack on the terminal by Iraqi bombers, the master put out to sea. The owners called upon the charterers to nominate a safe port, but they insisted on maintaining their nomination of Kharg Island. Lord Goff explained the situation as follows:

This is a case in which the owners have complied with the charterers' orders to the extent that the vessel has proceeded to the unsafe port and given notice of readiness there, but then the master, having tasted at first hand the danger inherent in port's unsafety, has persuaded them not to persist in loading there but to sail away. Here the crucial question is whether, before the vessel sailed away, the owners had, by their words or conduct, precluded themselves from rejecting the charterers' nomination as not complying with the contract . . .

The present case is concerned not so much with repudiation as with an uncontractual tender of performance. Even so, the same principles apply. The other party is entitled to reject the tender of performance as uncontractual; and, subject to the terms of the contract he can then, if he wishes, call for a fresh tender of performance in its place. But if, with knowledge of the facts giving rise to his right to reject, he nevertheless unequivocally elects not to do so, his election will be final and binding upon him and he will have waived his right to reject the tender as uncontractual.[123]

---

120 At 404.
121 At 405.
122 [1990] 1 Lloyd's Rep 391 (HL).
123 At 391; 399.

He concluded that

> [O]n arrival at Kharg Island the master proceeded to serve notice of readiness. Thereafter ...
> the owners were asserting that the vessel was available to load; they were also calling upon the
> charterers to arrange priority berthing, and referring to the fact that laytime was running.
> In these circumstances, the owners were asserting a right inconsistent with their right to
> reject the charterers' orders.[124]

20.39 *Novus actus interveniens*   If a shipowner ignores obvious danger and enters a nominated
port, his conduct may well amount to a *novus actus interveniens* and this would prevent him
recovering compensation for any damage subsequently suffered by his vessel. In the majority of cases the master, on receiving the nomination, will be unaware of potential danger
and would be entitled to presume that the charterer is fulfilling his obligation by nominating a safe port. On arrival at the port if the master discovers a potential hazard he may refuse
to enter. Would the charterer then be able to make an alternative nomination? The answer
to this seems to depend on the nature of the contract of affreightment; thus in the case of a
time charter this would appear to be possible (because the owner has undertaken to carry
out the charterer's instructions) but not with a voyage charter.

20.40 **Causation**   Claims for breach of the safe port undertaking will be limited by rules of
causation and remoteness of damage. Normally a claim would consist of compensation for
the physical damage caused to the vessel. However, if no physical damage has resulted, the
shipowner may seek to recover the cost of avoiding the danger, for example, by engaging
tugs or lightening the vessel. Finally, where the vessel is trapped in a port because of the
outbreak of hostilities or silting for an inordinate period of time, then the claim will be for
damages for detention. The delay must be such as to frustrate the object of the contract in
such a case.

---

[124] At 400.

21

FREIGHT

A. Introduction

Overview   We have so far considered the shipper's obligation under the common law. **21.01** In this chapter we consider another central obligation of the shipper of the goods, namely his obligation to pay the freight for the carriage of his goods.

B. The Basic Obligation

Introduction   Freight is the consideration which is payable to the carrier for the carriage **21.02** and arrival of the goods in a merchantable condition, ready to be delivered at the port of discharge. Freight is payable under a voyage charterparty or under a bill of lading issued by the shipowner (in some cases also the charterer). Lord Donaldson MR explained this in *Compania Naviera General SA v Kerametal Ltd (The Lorna I)*:

> Freight is the consideration payable for the carriage of goods to and their delivery at the destination. In the absence of special contractual provisions, it is earned only upon the delivery of the goods at their destination.[1]

---

[1] [1983] 1 Lloyd's Rep 373 (CA), 374.

In the unlikely event that no amount has been agreed by the parties, it would be possible to determine a 'reasonable sum' as remuneration from the state of the freight market.[2] Such information is to be derived from many sources, for example the shipping press such as *Lloyd's List* and *Fairplay*. Both these publications regularly publish reported fixtures of ships and cargoes as well as market summaries. It is therefore relatively easy to determine the current rates for the shipment of goods on the trade routes in question at the time of shipment.

21.03 **Baltic Exchange** In addition to the published sources a great deal of information is passed informally between brokers and brokering companies, aided by the operation of the Baltic Exchange,[3] which has been in existence since the seventeenth century. The Baltic (as it is known) is the only self-regulated shipping exchange in the world whose members, currently more than 600 companies and over 1,500 individual members, are bound by a code of business ethics, reflected in its motto, 'Our Word Our Bond'. About half of the world's dry bulk and oil chartering tends to be handled by Baltic members. It is axiomatic to the subject of freight markets that: (1) owners will seek to employ their vessels at the highest possible rate of freight; (2) charterers will seek vessels which will carry cargo at the most competitive freight, compatible with the safe arrival of the cargo. An important element of the Baltic's work today is the Freight Futures Market (BIFFEX), the aim of which is to provide protection to the shipping and cargo industries against adverse price movements. It is based upon two highly respected indices: the Baltic Freight Index (for dry cargo) and the Baltic Tanker Index (for oil). The Freight Index is based on a 'basket' of thirteen frequently settled and fixed worldwide voyages, weighted to provide a balance of relative importance and representative of market shares of reported spot fixing. Likewise, the Tanker Index is based upon a 'basket' of nine trade routes for medium-sized tankers (not VLCCs or ULCCs).

21.04 **Factors** Factors which will influence the charterer's choice in seeking a fixture will include: (1) the relative age of the vessel; (2) the speed and bunker consumption of the vessel; (3) his cargo requirements,[4] some cargoes being less attractive for carriers than others, because of their corrosive properties (for example sulphur), or because they are 'dirty' (for example raw petroleum coke, a solid black residue obtained from petrol refining), or because of their potential for causing damage to the ship's structure (for example scrap metal); (4) speed of loading or discharging; (5) the area of trade (for example to a war risk part of the globe). The determination of the costs involved in transporting cargoes will be undertaken by specialized brokers, many of whom will have passed the examinations operated by the Institute of Chartered Shipbrokers.[5] The skilled task of working out costs, by both owners' and charterers' brokers, is known as voyage estimating.[6]

---

[2] For a technical account, see Kendall and Buckley (2001), ch. 13.
[3] See Farthing and Brownrigg (1997), 25–27.
[4] See Packard (1996).
[5] See Farthing and Brownrigg (1997), 35–36.
[6] See Packard (1981).

C. Freight at Common Law

Presumption   At common law the presumption is that freight is payable only on delivery   **21.05**
of the goods to the consignee at the port of discharge, on presentation of a bill of lading or
letter of indemnity. The carrier may not demand payment of freight unless he is willing and
able to deliver the goods at the place agreed. The payment of freight and the delivery of the
cargo at the port of discharge are therefore concurrent conditions. Theoretically this means
that the freight is due ton by ton as the cargo is delivered, a matter of some importance in
the carrier's ability to exercise a possessory lien over the goods on non-payment. If the
freight were to be payable after discharge or on completion of discharge, it would be difficult to sustain any right of lien. This point was made clear in the case of *Black v Rose* in the
Supreme Court of Ceylon and affirmed by the Privy Council.[7] Creasy CJ stated that:

> As a general principle, when there is no express stipulation as to the time and manner of pay-
> ment of freight, the Master is not bound to part with the goods until his freight is paid. We
> think it clear, that on . . . delivery [by the Master] and receipt [by the Merchant] the Master
> ceased to be responsible for the goods, and also ceased to have any lien on the goods. It is clear
> on all authority and common sense that he had a right to be paid before he gave up his lien.[8]

The leading case on freight is *Dakin v Oxley*.[9] The case was an action by a shipowner against a
charterer for the recovery of freight for a cargo of coal carried from Newport to Nassau
(Bahamas). Was the charterer whose cargo had been damaged by the fault of the master and
crew, so much so that at the port of discharge it was worth less than the freight, entitled to excuse
himself from payment of freight by abandoning the cargo to the shipowner? Willes CJ held that:

> . . . [T]he true test of the right to freight is . . . whether the service in respect of which the
> freight was contracted to be paid has been substantially performed; and, according to the law
> of England, as a rule, freight is earned by the carriage and arrival of the goods ready to be
> delivered to the merchant, though they be in a damaged state when they arrive. If the
> shipowner fails to carry the goods for the merchant to the destined port, the freight is not
> earned. If he carry part, but not the whole, no freight is payable in respect of the part not
> carried, and freight is payable in respect of the part carried unless the charterparty make the
> carriage of the whole a condition precedent to the earning of any freight . . .[10]

Freight and destination   At common law, no freight will be payable unless the cargo   **21.06**
reaches the agreed destination. Equally, no freight will be payable if the shipowner cannot
deliver the goods because they have been lost or destroyed; it does not matter how (or even
why) the goods are lost or destroyed, even if they destroy themselves through inherent vice.
No freight is payable where the loss occurs without fault on the part of the shipowner and
even if the cause of the loss is an excepted peril. Excepted perils may prevent the shipowner
being sued for losing or damaging the cargo, but they do not normally give a right to
freight. In *Metcalfe v Britannia Ironworks Co*[11] a cargo of railway bars was shipped under a

---

[7] (1864) 2 Moore PC (ns) 277; 16 ER 906.
[8] At 284; 16 ER 909. Confirmed by Bovill CJ in *Paynter v James* (1867) LR 2 CP 348.
[9] (1864) 15 CB (ns) 646; 143 ER 938.
[10] At 664–665; 143 ER 946.
[11] (1876) 1 QB 613.

charterparty from a port in England to Taganrog in the Sea of Azov or so near thereto as the ship could safely get. When the ship arrived at Kertch in the straits leading from the Black Sea into the Sea of Azov, it was found that the Sea of Azov was blocked with ice until the ensuing spring, and the cargo was unloaded at Kertch. Kertch was 300 miles from Taganrog. At first instance, Cockburn CJ said that:

> . . . [T]he plaintiff is not entitled to recover the full freight. [It is well] established that when a charterparty speaks of a vessel, bound to a particular port, discharging 'as near as she can get' to such port, this must be taken to mean some place 'within the ambit' of the port; and Kertch cannot be said to be within the ambit of the port of Taganrog.[12]

This was expressly upheld by the Court of Appeal.[13] Full freight will be payable where failure to reach the port of discharge is solely due to some act or default on the part of the cargo owner.

D. Calculation of Freight

21.07 **Generally** Freight will be payable according to the express stipulations of the charter or bill of lading and, failing them, according to the custom of the trade or port. Under a voyage charter, freight will be payable in accordance with the express provisions of the charter, thus: a certain proportion of the freight, or a certain lump sum on sailing; remainder on delivery, either by cash or by specified bills. If the charter is a round charter, or there are loading and discharging expenses which are incurred during the course of the voyage, the charter may require such disbursements to be advanced against the freight by the charterers or agents. Gencon 94 provides for the rate of freight to be inserted in Box 13 and provides in clause 4 that payment may either be 'prepaid' or paid 'on delivery'. Shellvoy 5, one of the leading oil voyage charterparty forms, provides that:

> 5. Freight shall be earned concurrently with delivery of cargo at the nominated discharge port or ports and shall be paid by Charterers to Owners without any deductions in United States dollars at the rate(s) specified in Part 1(G) on the gross Bill of Lading quantity as furnished by the shipper (subject to Clauses 8 and 40), upon receipt by Charterers of notice of completion of final discharge of cargo, provided that no freight shall be payable on any quantity in excess of the maximum quantity consistent with the International Load Line Convention for the time being in force.

> If the vessel is ordered to proceed on a voyage for which a fixed differential is provided in Worldscale, such fixed differential shall be payable without applying the percentage referred to in Part 1(G).

> If the cargo is carried between ports and/or by a route for which no freight rate is expressly quoted in Worldscale, then the parties shall, in the absence of agreement as to the appropriate freight rate, apply to Worldscale Association (London) Ltd, or Worldscale Association (NYC) Inc, for the determination of an appropriate Worldscale freight rate.

> Save in respect of the time when freight is earned, the location of any transhipment at sea pursuant to Clause 26(2) shall not be an additional nominated port for the purposes of this charter (including this Clause 5) and the freight rate for the voyage shall be the same as if such transhipment had not taken place.

---

[12] At 618.
[13] (1877) 2 QB 423 (CA), 426 (Lord Coleridge CJ).

Dry commodities   In the case of dry commodities and packages, the unit of freight may   **21.08**
be specified by weight, package, or cubic measurement. Where freight is payable on goods
according to their weight or measurement, and owing to swelling, expansion after
hydraulic pressure, or shrinkage, the same goods are larger or smaller at the port of destination than when loaded, freight will be payable, in the absence of express stipulation or
usage, on the amount shipped and not on the amount delivered. This may be illustrated by
the case of *Shell International Petroleum Ltd v Seabridge Shipping Ltd (The Metula).*[14] Shell
International chartered the *Metula* to Seabridge Shipping on the Exxonvoy 69 form. The
charter provided that the vessel should load a full and complete cargo of petroleum and/or
its products in bulk. The freight clause was as follows:

> 2. *Freight.* Freight shall be at the rate stipulated ... and shall be computed on intake quantity ...
> Payment of freight shall be made by Charterer without discount upon delivery of cargo at
> destination ... No deduction shall be made for water and/or sediment contained in the cargo.[15]

The vessel loaded a cargo of 190,415 tons of Arabian light oil at Ras Tanura (Saudi Arabia)
for carriage to Chile but stranded in the Magellan Straits and part of the cargo was lost. The
vessel only delivered 138,195.3 tons. The charterers paid the freight on the delivered quantity plus 5 per cent but the owners claimed a further sum of £178,602.38 on the basis that
freight was payable on the intaken quantity. At first instance Donaldson J found for the
owners, holding that the freight was to be calculated upon the intaken quantity and was
payable 'upon delivery of the cargo at destination', and the full freight became payable
when any of the intake quantity of cargo beyond a minimal amount was delivered. This was
upheld on appeal, where Lord Denning MR said:

> It seems to me the very purpose of having the computation being made on the intake quan-
> tity is that freight should be ascertained then, although payable later when the ship gets to its
> destination. There is no provision whatsoever for subsequent adjustment or calculations
> being made at the port of destination.
>
> ... [I]n my opinion on the true construction of this clause, although this is not a lump sum
> freight properly so-called, it has the characteristics of a lump sum in that the freight is com-
> puted on the intake quantity. When the cargo is delivered, it is to be paid on that intake quan-
> tity. Even though there is a shortage, that full freight has to be paid.[16]

Where, therefore, the cargo is likely to increase in weight owing to absorption of moisture,
it would be more prudent to assess the freight on the quantity shipped.[17]

Tankers   The assessment of rates of freight in the case of tankers is commonly fixed by   **21.09**
reference to the deadweight capacity of the ship. Indeed freight rates are commonly fixed by
reference to published rates for a notional tanker of deadweight capacity of 75,000 metric
tonnes, known as Worldscale 100 (so-called 'flat rates'). W100 is the rate per tonne which
gives a standard vessel of 75,000 dwt earnings of $12,000 per day on a stipulated voyage.
Worldscale, the Worldwide Tanker Nominal Freight Scale,[18] is published by the

---

[14] [1978] 2 Lloyd's Rep 5 (CA).
[15] See now cl 2 of Asbatankvoy.
[16] [1978] 2 Lloyd's Rep 5 (CA), 7.
[17] *Gibson v Sturge* (1855) 10 Exch 622; 156 ER 588.
[18] See Williams (1999), 35–36.

Worldscale Association (London) Ltd and Worldwide Association (NYC) Inc of New York. The system has operated, under various names, since the late 1940s and is intended to provide a set of rates for worldwide fixtures. Worldscale aims to create a schedule which will yield about the same rate of return for owners for each voyage that the tanker will perform. The aim of the Worldscale Association is expressed as follows:

> This Schedule of nominal freight rates is intended solely as a standard of reference, by means of which rates for all voyages and market levels can be compared and readily judged. It is the custom to express market levels of freight in terms of a percentage of the WORLD-SCALE nominal freight rate. Thus WORLDSCALE 100 (or WORLDSCALE FLAT which is sometimes used) means the rate as calculated and published by the Associations, while WORLDSCALE 175, for example, means 175 per cent of the published rate and WORLDSCALE 75 means 75 per cent of that rate.
>
> It is desired to make it completely clear that the responsibility of the two Associations is limited to providing subscribers with a schedule of comparative rates. The Associations do not and cannot accept any responsibility for the application of the rates. Should parties wish to depart from the basis of 'WORLDSCALE as at the date of commencement of loading' this should be clearly specified.[19]

The system established by Worldscale is important because it saves time (and money) in arranging fixtures involving a wide range of port options. The actual income for a tanker on the Worldscale rate will depend upon its size, performance and type and this will be reflected in the percentage of Worldscale at which the fixture is made. For the purpose of fixing these rates, the Worldscale organization pays close attention to the prices of bunker fuel, port charges, and shipping services. Such information is published by Lloyd's of London Press Ltd (inter alia in *Lloyd's List*) and Fairplay Ltd and is increasingly available on the internet, usually by subscription. Worldscale rates are amended annually but, in the event of critical market changes can be amended by circulars. Unless agreed otherwise between the parties, a reference to Worldscale in a charterparty would mean the rates in force at the date of the contract. Thus Shellvoy 5 states at Part I(G) that:

> Freight Rate At . . . % of the rate for the voyage as provided for in the Worldwide Tanker Nominal Freight Scale current at the date of commencement of loading (hereinafter referred to as 'Worldscale') per ton (2240lbs)/tonne (1000Kg).

Given that the Worldscale rates can change, it is important for the charterparty to be very clear as to when the rates are to apply, a matter that becomes crucial in the case of consecutive voyage charters.

E. Deductions from Freight

21.10 **Cargo damaged** If cargo arrives at its destination in a damaged state, or is short delivered, the agreed freight will still be payable in full by the cargo owner or receiver. There is no general right of set-off in English law — unless this right is expressly incorporated into the contract of carriage — even though the deterioration is so great that the cargo delivered is no longer worth the freight.[20] This proposition was emphatically endorsed by

---

[19] Ventris (1986), 277.
[20] See JC Sheppard, 'The rule against deduction from freight reconsidered' [2006] JBL 1.

Lord Wilberforce in the leading case of *Aries Tanker Corp v Total Transport Ltd (The Aries)*.[21] In this case there was a voyage charter on the BP form from the owners (Aries Tankers), a Liberian corporation, to Total Transport, a Bermuda company. The vessel was chartered to proceed to a port or ports in the Arabian Gulf and there to load a full and complete cargo of petroleum for carriage to a port or ports in the UK or Europe. Freight was payable upon the intaken quantity of cargo (clause 6) and was payable after completion of discharge in cash without discount (clause 7). Articles III, IV, and VIII of the Hague Rules were expressly incorporated into the charterparty by clause 30. Rotterdam was nominated by the charterers and on discharge of the cargo of regular and premium gasoline it was found that there was a short delivery of each product. The appellants paid the amount due for freight with a deduction of $30,000. The respondents refused to accept the deduction. After holding that the time limit of 12 months under the Hague Rules[22] was not merely procedural but had the effect of extinguishing the claim, Lord Wilberforce went on to consider the question of set-off:

> That a claim in respect of cargo cannot be asserted by way of deduction from the freight, is a long established rule in English law. As a rule it has never been judicially doubted or questioned or criticised; it has received the approval of authoritative textbooks.
>
> It is said to be an arbitrary rule — and so it may be, in the sense that no very clear justification for it has ever been stated and perhaps also in the sense that the law might just, or almost, as well have settled for a rule to the opposite effect. But this does not affect its status in law. In commercial matters it is all the more important that established rules, unless clearly wrong, should not be disturbed by the Courts.
>
> The rule against deduction in cases of carriage by sea is, in fact, as well settled as any common law rule can be.
>
> But beyond all this there is a decisive reason here why this House should not alter the rule . . . That is that the parties in this case have, I think beyond doubt, contracted upon the basis and against the background that the established rule is against deduction. Such a case as this, in fact, marks out very decisively the possible limits of judicial intervention: for it would be undesirable in this, or in any other case where the same question arose, for the Courts to declare that a rule, clearly shown to exist, and shown to be the basis of the contract before the Court, ought to be replaced by a different rule which would have to operate on the contract in question.
>
> I am therefore firmly of the opinion that the rule against deduction has to be applied to this charterparty so that the charterers' claim for short delivery cannot be relied on by way of defence. On any view, therefore, of the time bar, and even assuming the latter to be only procedural, it must defeat the claim . . .[23]

Counsel for the charterers also sought to argue that his clients might have a claim by way of equitable set-off in the event that the right of deduction was not upheld. But Lord Wilberforce paid short shrift to this too:

> One thing is certainly clear about the doctrine of equitable set-off — complicated though it may have become from its involvement with procedural matters — namely, that for it to

---

[21] [1977] 1 WLR 185 (HL). Upholding *Henriksens Rederi A/S v THZ Rolimpex (The Brede)* [1974] 1 QB 233 (CA).

[22] See art III, r 6, discussed further at para 34.04.

[23] [1997] 1 WLR 185 (HL), 189–191.

apply, there must be some equity, some ground for equitable intervention, other than the mere existence of a cross claim. But in this case Counsel could not suggest, and I cannot detect, any such equity sufficient to operate the mechanism, so as, in effect, to override a clear rule of the common law on the basis of which the parties contracted.[24]

21.11 **Counterclaim for damage**   The shipper will have a separate cause of action or counter-claim for the damage, unless caused solely by excepted perils or by the vice of the goods themselves. The question is whether the substance delivered is identical commercially with the substance loaded, though it may have deteriorated in quality. This principle was expressly approved by the Court of Appeal in *Henriksens Rederi A/S v THZ Rolimpex (The Brede)*,[25] itself followed in *The Aries*. The *Brede* was chartered on the Gencon form to carry a cargo of rice from Rangoon to Gdynia. The charterers' cargo was discharged at Gdynia but they withheld £3,000 from the balance of the freight because of short delivery and damage by water caused by unseaworthiness. The owners denied liability because suit had not been brought within a year under article III, rule 6 of the Hague Rules. Both the arbi-trator and Mocatta J[26] held that the owners' claim to the balance of the freight (£2,476) succeeded and that the charterers' claim for damages to cargo failed because that should have been brought within a year. This was upheld by the Court of Appeal, notwithstand-ing vigorous argument by counsel for the charterers to the contrary. Roskill LJ stated that:

> There are at least two . . . reasons for not disturbing the existing position, even if we are free so to do. First, the law has been as we have held it to have been for at least a century and a half. That of itself is good reason not to change it. Secondly . . . to alter the existing law would or at least might disturb the present distribution of risk between the shipowners' freight under-writers and their Protection and Indemnity Association. At present on the footing that there is no defence to a claim for freight, any liability of shipowners to cargo owners falls on the Protection and Indemnity Association. If there were a defence to a claim for freight it is at least arguable that there would then be a loss of freight which would or might fall on the own-ers' freight underwriters and not on the Protection and Indemnity Association. It has often been said that in relation to suggested changes in commercial law, the courts should not lightly alter the law from what it has hitherto been thought to be when to do so would be to disturb existing contractual arrangements entered into on the basis of long-established and existing legal principles. Further, the special position of voyage charterparty and bill of lading freight, as distinct from time-charter hire was recognised by Parliament as recently as 30 years ago in the Law Reform (Frustrated Contracts) Act 1943. I do not think that it would be right even if we were free so to do to disturb the law from what it has been for at least 150 years.[27]

21.12 **Goods unmerchantable**   No freight will be payable where the goods are so badly dam-aged on their arrival that they are unmerchantable in the sense that they no longer answer their commercial description. In *Asfar & Co v Blundell & another*[28] certain dates were shipped aboard the *Govino* under bills of lading which made freight payable to the plain-tiffs on right delivery in London. The total freight due under the bills of lading was £4,690. The *Govino* collided with another vessel in the Thames and sank. She was raised but the dates were then found to be unfit for human consumption owing to the dates having

---

[24] At 191.
[25] [1974] 1 QB 233 (CA).
[26] [1972] 2 Lloyd's Rep 511.
[27] [1974] 1 QB 233, 263–264.
[28] [1896] 1 QB 123 (CA).

become saturated with sewage and fermenting. The trial court found that the dates were unmerchantable as dates although a proportion were still recognizable and the cargo was still valuable and was sold for £2,400 for export for distillation. The trial court held that no freight was payable and this was endorsed in the Court of Appeal by Lord Esher MR:

> There is a perfectly well known test which has for many years been applied to such cases as the present — that test is whether, as a matter of business, the nature of the thing has been altered. The nature of a thing is not necessarily altered because the thing itself has been damaged; wheat or rice may be damaged, but may still remain the things dealt with as wheat or rice in business. But if the nature of the thing is altered, and it becomes for business purposes something else, so that it is not dealt with by business people as the thing which it originally was, the question for determination is whether the thing insured, the original article of commerce, has become a total loss. If it is so changed in its nature by the perils of the sea as to become an unmerchantable thing, which no buyer would buy and no honest seller would sell, then there is a total loss.[29]

Asfar **doubted** The correctness of the *Asfar* decision has been doubted on the basis that **21.13** the consignees actually took delivery of the goods and sold them commercially.[30] This point was dealt with in *Montedison SpA v Icroma SpA (The Caspian Sea)*.[31] The *Caspian Sea* was chartered to carry a part cargo of crude oil and/or dirty petroleum products from Punta Cardón (Venezuela) to Genoa. Freight was payable 'upon delivery of the cargo'. The oil shipped was 'Bachaquero crude', a Venezuelan crude free of paraffin and suitable for the production of lubricating oils of high quality. The charterers alleged that, on discharge, the oil contained paraffinic products derived from the residues of a previous cargo of low sulphur fuel oil which was not removed from the vessel's tanks prior to loading. Accordingly, they claimed that the owners had no immediate right to freight because what was eventually delivered was not merchantable as 'Bachaquero crude' or, alternatively, was not commercially identical with the crude loaded. Further, there was no right to freight now or at any other time because there was no 'delivery of the cargo' and freight had not been earned. Donaldson J stated that:

> The mere fact that the oil as delivered was not identical commercially with the cargo loaded does not, in my judgment, deprive the owners of their right to freight. Undamaged or uncontaminated goods can rarely be considered to be identical commercially with damaged or contaminated goods, but it is well settled that damage or contamination is not, as such, a bar to the right to freight.

> The owners will be entitled to freight if what they delivered could in commercial terms, bear a description which sensibly and accurately included the words 'Bachaquero Crude', e.g. 'Bachaquero Crude contaminated with paraffin or low sulphur oil residues'. The question is whether an honest merchant would be forced to qualify the description applicable to the goods on shipment to such an extent as to destroy it. If the qualification destroys the description, no freight has been earned because 'the cargo' has been delivered, albeit damaged or as the case may be contaminated. This, in my judgment, is what Lord Esher [in *Asfar*] meant by the test of merchantability or of the nature of the goods being so altered as to become for business purposes something else.[32]

---

[29] At 127.
[30] See Glanville Williams, 'Language and the Law' (1945) 61 LQR 296.
[31] [1980] 1 Lloyd's Rep 91.
[32] At 95–96.

21.14 **The effect of deviation** If there is an unjustifiable deviation,[33] and this amounts to a breach of the contract of carriage, freight due under the contract on delivery of the goods would no longer be payable. However there are dicta to the effect that, should the cargo be delivered safely to its destination, the carrier would be able to claim a reasonable sum for freight based on *quantum meruit*.[34] The leading case here is *Hain Steamship Co v Tate & Lyle*,[35] admitted by Scrutton LJ in the Court of Appeal to be one which raised 'troublesome questions of law and fact'.[36] The *Tregenna* was chartered to proceed to Cuba and load a cargo of sugar at two ports (Casilda and Santiago) and one port in San Domingo to be nominated by the charterer. The charterer made the required nominations but, owing to a failure of communication by the owners' agents, the master was not informed of the nominated port in San Domingo, San Pedro de Macoris. Consequently, once the cargoes had been loaded at the two Cuban ports, the master proceeded to Queenstown to await further instructions. Upon discovering the error, the master was ordered back to San Domingo to load the remaining cargo. On leaving the port in San Domingo, the *Tregenna* ran aground and part of the cargo was lost, the remainder being transhipped on another vessel (the *Baron Dalmeny*) for completion of the voyage to the United Kingdom. Shortly before the vessel arrived at its destination the bills of lading covering the cargo were endorsed to Tate & Lyle who took delivery of the cargo in ignorance of the deviation. The charterers had, with full knowledge of the facts, waived the breach by ordering the vessel back to San Domingo. In these circumstances the shipowners, in the event of any claim being made by the charterers, would be entitled to rely for protection on the charter exception of perils of the sea. But the position for the holders of the bill of lading was different; they were not bound by any waiver on the part of the charterers. Accordingly, the shipowners were unable to rely on the bill of lading exceptions as a defence to any cargo claim brought by the consignees. But on the freight point, Lord Atkin found that:

> On the ship's claim for the balance of freight in respect of the San Domingo sugar I have come to the conclusion that it must fail. An amendment to claim a *quantum meruit* was, however, allowed and this has occasioned me some difficulty. . . . [T]he balance of freight under the charter-party and therefore under the bill of lading was to be paid in New York after advice of right delivery and ascertainment of weight. . . . [T]he charterer remained and remains still liable for that freight. . . . I am not satisfied that conditions existed under which a promise should be implied whereby the shippers undertook to give to the ship a further and a different right to receive some part of what would be a reasonable remuneration for the carriage. I think, therefore, that the claim for freight fails.[37]

F. Advance Freight

21.15 **Introduction** It is possible for the parties to provide that the whole or part of the freight is to be payable in advance. However, given the strong presumption that freight is only payable on delivery of the goods at their destination, any provision specifying the payment

---

[33] As to deviation, see ch 24.

[34] See the judgment of Brandon J that 'for that service the reasonable remuneration on a quantum meruit is, in my opinion, 13s 6d per ton': (1936) 55 Ll LR 159, 168. But cf the judgment of Scrutton LJ (1934) 49 Ll LR 123 (CA), 131.

[35] (1936) 55 Ll LR 159 (HL).

[36] (1934) 49 Ll LR 123 (CA), 125.

[37] At 175.

of freight in advance would have to be clearly expressed to this effect. Indeed many dry cargo forms specify in some way that the freight, or at least a large portion of it, be prepaid in this way. Gencon 1994 allows the parties to determine whether the freight should be pre-paid or payable on delivery: see Box 13 and clause 4. The original commercial reasoning behind such clauses was explained by Brett J in the case of *William Allison v Bristol Marine Insurance Co Ltd*.[38] In this case the *Merchant Prince* was chartered to carry a cargo of coal from Greenock in Scotland to Bombay. The freight rate was 42s a ton, to be paid

> one half in cash on signing bills of lading . . . less 5 per cent for insurance . . . and the remainder on right delivery of the cargo.

Half the freight was paid in London and the shipowner then insured the freight, expecting to be reimbursed on delivery of the full cargo. The owner of the cargo insured the cargo for a sum inclusive of the value of the freight he had prepaid. The ship was then wrecked on a reef near Bombay. Half the cargo was saved and landed, but the cargo owner then declined to pay any further freight. The shipowner then claimed on his insurance policy asserting that he had suffered a total loss of half the freight not paid in advance. Brett J, called in to assist the House of Lords, explained:

> . . . I have drawn attention to all the cases, in order to shew how uniform the view has been as to what construction is to be put upon shipping documents in the form of the present charterparty, and as to the uniform, though perhaps anomalous rule, that the money to be paid in advance of freight must be paid, though the goods are before payment lost by perils of the sea. Although I have said that this course of business may in theory be anomalous, I think its origin and existence are capable of a reasonable explanation. It arose in the case of the long Indian voyages. The length of voyage would keep the shipowner for too long a time out of money; and freight is much more difficult to pledge, as a security to third persons, than goods represented by a bill of lading. Therefore the shipper agreed to make the advance on which he would ultimately have to pay, and, for a consideration, took the risk in order to obviate a repayment, which disarranges business transactions.

> It seems to me, and I submit that, on a review of all the cases, the true construction of the charterparty in this case is, that the 2,000, which were to be paid and were paid in advance, constituted a prepayment of the freight payable under the charterparty, and no part of it could be recovered back by the charterer from the shipowner, and that the stipulation as to deduction for insurance did not alter this right of the shipowner.[39]

The House of Lords unanimously found in favour of the shipowner.

Terms   Exactly when the freight is payable in advance may be expressed as 'on signing bills of lading', 'on sailing of vessel' or within a specified period following the occurrence of such an event, for example 'within five days of signing bills of lading'. The freight becomes due at the time indicated. If not paid, it remains due, even should the goods be lost in transit and not reach their destination. However, if the cargo is lost or the contract frustrated in some way before payment, the obligation to make payment will be discharged.   **21.16**

Freight recoverable   If freight has been paid in advance it will not be recoverable by the shipper when the cargo is lost during the voyage provided that the loss is covered by one of   **21.17**

---

[38] (1876) 1 App Cas 209.
[39] At 226.

the excepted perils. If the loss is not covered by an exception, the cargo owner can recover damages for non-delivery which will include any advance freight paid on the goods, together with the relevant insurance premium. Frequently there is an express clause in the contract of carriage which is to the effect that freight is not refundable 'ship and/or cargo lost or not lost'. This will place the risk on the charterer.

21.18 **Freight not recoverable** Advance freight will not be recoverable where the contract of carriage is frustrated before the cargo reaches its destination. This principle that freight is not refundable is unique to English law and was confirmed by Cockburn CJ in the case of *Byrne v Schiller*, though with reluctance:

> It is settled by the authorities . . . that by the law of England a payment made in advance on account of freight cannot be recovered back in the event of the goods being lost, and the freight therefore not becoming payable. I regret that the law is so.[40]

21.19 **Freight non-returnable** In *Compania Naviera General SA v Kerametal Ltd (The Lorna I)*,[41] a voyage charterparty provided for the carriage of iron or nickel from Durrësi (Albania) to various ports. The freight contract provided that:

> 16. Freight non-returnable cargo and/or vessel lost or not lost to be paid . . . to the Owners . . . as follows: 75% . . . within 5 . . . days after Master signed Bills of Lading and the balance after right and true delivery of the cargo and receipt of documents from discharging ports.

The *Lorna I* proceeded on a voyage through the Bosporus but after entering the Black Sea she ran into very heavy weather and was lost with all hands. Bills of lading in respect of her cargo had been signed on 6 December 1977; the contract was frustrated by the sinking before 23.59 on 11 December 1977. The issue was whether the 75 per cent instalment of freight was due before the date when the contract was frustrated. The Court of Appeal inter alia emphasized that freight was the consideration which was payable for the carriage of goods to, and their delivery at, their destination. Further, in the absence of special contractual provisions, it was due on the delivery of the goods at their destination and clause 16 of the contract contained no words appropriate to produce the result that any part of the freight was earned or deemed to be earned upon shipment or on signing bills of lading. Lord Donaldson MR said that:

> . . . [A] liability to pay advance freight does not *per se* affect the time when freight is earned. It is simply an obligation to make a payment on account of freight at a time when it has not yet been earned. However that obligation is subject to a customary incident, capable of being varied or confirmed by express stipulation, that advance freight paid pursuant to the contract is not returnable or recoverable should the contract be frustrated before the freight be earned.[42]

He concluded that:

> . . . [O]n the true construction of clause 16, there was no obligation to make any payment of or on account of freight until the expiration of the five-day period and before that occurred the contractual basis of the obligation had been undermined by the loss of the cargo

---

[40] (1871) LR 5 Ex 319, 325. See too *Fibrosa Spolka Akcyjna v Fairbairn Lawson Combe Barbour Ltd* [1943] AC 32.

[41] [1983] 1 Lloyd's Rep 373 (CA).

[42] At 374.

and of the vessel and the frustration of the contract. The ordinary meaning of the words is that advance freight, if paid, is non-returnable whether or not the cargo and/or vessel is subsequently lost, thereby confirming the customary incident of a contract for the payment of advance freight. To achieve any other construction would require much clearer words . . .[43]

On signing bills of lading   In *Oriental Steamship Co v Tylor*[44] the freight clause stated that: **21.20**

> The freight to be paid as follows — one-third on signing bills of lading, less 3 per cent for interest, insurance &c, and remainder, on unloading, in cash.

Bills of lading were to be signed by the captain or his agents as presented to him within 24 hours of loading. The *Fidele Primavesi* left the quay at Cardiff but sank — within 24 hours of loading — before reaching the dock gates. She had holed her side by fouling her anchor. The charterers refused to present bills of lading or pay any freight. Pollock B had found in their favour and the shipowners appealed. Bowen LJ allowed the appeal:

> . . . [W]e see that the signing of the bills of lading determines the time when certain rights arise and when certain rights cease. It is inconceivable that the rights which are given to the shipowner on signing bills of lading can be delayed by the act of the charterers in not presenting bills of lading for signature. . . . It is obvious that there must be an implied term in the charterparty, in order to make the contract effectual, that the charterers should present bills of lading to the captain or agent for signature within a reasonable time, so as to give effect to the rights of the shipowner.

> . . . Here there is a right, conditional, no doubt, on the signing of bills of lading, but, subject to that, an absolute right, to be paid advance freight, which is never lost so long as the bills of lading can be presented for signature and signed. The loss of the ship did not prevent the bills of lading being presented and signed. The charterers have broken the implied contract to present bills of lading, and, though the advance freight cannot be recovered as such, the measure of damages for breach of that contract is in this case the amount of advance freight.[45]

Express provision   In order to vary the rule that freight is earned only on delivery, the   **21.21** charterparty must expressly provide otherwise. In *Vagres Compania Maritima SA v Nissho-Iwai American Corporation (The Karin Vatis)*[46] the *Karin Vatis* sank shortly after passing Suez. The vessel was on a voyage from Liverpool to India with a cargo of shredded scrap and the contract was embodied in the Gencon 1976 form to which the following addendum had been added: (i) for a lump sum freight of $715,000; (ii) freight to be deemed earned as the cargo is loaded; (iii) 95 per cent of the freight to be paid within three banking days after completion of loading; and (iv) the balance of 5 per cent to be settled within 20 days after completion of discharge. The first tranche of freight had been paid by the charterers and they now argued that they were not obliged to pay the remaining 5 per cent, because the time for payment had never arisen. Arbitrators found in their favour and this was upheld at first instance by Leggatt J. However, the Court of Appeal took a different view. Lloyd LJ held that:

> The provision that freight is deemed to be earned as cargo is loaded is, to my mind, the paramount or controlling provision. It is well understood by commercial men. It casts the risk in

---

[43] At 375.
[44] [1893] 2 QB 518 (CA).
[45] At 527–528.
[46] [1988] 2 Lloyd's Rep 330 (CA).

relation to freight on the charterers. It excludes the ordinary rule of construction, whereby freight is only earned and therefore only payable on delivery.

... [T]he concluding part of the clause is dealing with the manner of payment, not the obligation to pay. It provides a formula for ascertaining the date of payment, and for insuring that loading and discharging port demurrage or despatch, as the case may be, and the balance of freight are all settled at the same time.[47]

21.22   *The Dominique*   In *Bank of Boston Connecticut v European Grain & Shipping Ltd (The Dominique)*[48] the freight clause stated that:

16. Freight shall be pre-paid within five days of signing and surrender of final Bills of Lading, full freight deemed to be earned on signing Bills of Lading, discountless and non-returnable, vessel and or cargo lost or not lost ...

The owners of *The Dominique* had assigned all her earnings to Colonial Bank. The owners got into serious financial difficulties because their P & I club cover was about to be cancelled and, during the performance of the voyage charter from Kakinada (India) to Northern Europe via Colombo for bunkers, the vessel was arrested by a creditor who had on an earlier occasion supplied such bunkers. The bank had meanwhile served notice of the assignment to the charterers. The owners indicated that they were either unwilling or unable to continue the voyage. European Grain & Shipping Ltd (the charterers) treated the failure of the owners to secure the release of the vessel as a repudiatory breach of contract. Subsequently, while the vessel was still under arrest, the charterers discharged the cargo and arranged for it to be transhipped to its destination. They did not pay the freight due ($223,676). The charterers were held liable for freight since, although they had been given a five-day period in which to pay, freight was deemed to have been earned on the signing of bills of lading. At first instance, Hobhouse J took the view that:

[L]iability for freight is ... correctly described as *debitum in praesenti, solvendum in futuro*. There is thus a liability for freight as an existing debt owed by the charterer to the shipowner but the time at which that debt or liability must be discharged is postponed. The debt existed from the moment the bills of lading were signed ...[49]

He also said that:

Advance freight is not adjustable according to what subsequently occurs, it is not repayable in whole or in part even if the voyage is never completed. It is not treated as a contractual obligation to which the rules of failure of consideration, or partial failure, apply in the same way as in other branches of the law of contract. Once earned, advance freight is at the risk of the charterer and the subsequent incidents and misfortunes of the voyage do not entitle him to transfer any of that risk back to the shipowner.[50]

The award of Hobhouse J was overturned by the Court of Appeal[51] and the bank (the assignee) appealed to the House of Lords. Lord Brandon concluded that:

... the contention for the bank is to be preferred to that for the charterers. The reason why I take that view is that the contention for the charterers gives no effect to the second phrase

[47] At 332.
[48] [1989] AC 1056.
[49] [1987] 1 Lloyd's Rep 239, 245.
[50] At 246.
[51] [1988] 1 Lloyd's Rep 215 (CA).

of clause 16 'full freight deemed to be earned on signing bills of lading', whereas the contention for the bank does. This conclusion accords with the decision of the Court of Appeal on a different but comparable clause in a charterparty in *Vagres Compania Maritima SA v Nissho-Iwai American Corporation* . . . I would therefore [say] that the owners' right to freight accrued before the termination of the charterparty.[52]

What was the effect of the termination of the contract? Lord Brandon concluded that:

> The circumstance that, by reason of the first phrase of clause 16, the charterers' obligation to pay the freight was postponed until after the termination of the charterparty does not, in my view, mean that the owners' prior acquisition of the right to the freight was conditional only. The postponement of payment was an incident attaching to the right acquired, but it was not a condition of its acquisition. It follows that, in accordance with the principles of law referred to above, the owners' right to the freight, having been unconditionally acquired before the termination of the charterparty, was not divested or discharged by such termination.[53]

Thus once liability for freight has accrued, either by the arrival of the date fixed for payment or as a result of freight being deemed to have been earned, it is treated as a liability in debt. The freight risk is then transferred to the charterer and he must insure the risk.

Freight or loan?   A further issue is whether payment made at the port of loading is on account of freight or merely a loan to the shipowner to cover ship's disbursements and current expenses. This must be determined by reference to the terms of the contract: what was the intention of the parties? The shipowner must establish that the payment was intended as advance freight. A loan would otherwise be recoverable. Usually this can be resolved by enquiring which party was responsible for insuring the advance payment. If it is the shipper, the payment must be intended as advance freight. A loan would be at the owners' risk. Thus a stipulation that freight shall be paid 'subject to the insurance' or 'less insurance' will indicate that the payment is an advance of freight.   **21.23**

Part payment   Where part of the freight is payable in advance, this is regarded as part payment of the whole sum due on delivery. Consequently, if any cargo is lost in transit, the merchant will only be liable for any balance if the overall freight due on the actual cargo delivered exceeds the amount paid in advance. *Ellis Shipping Corporation v Voest Alpine Intertrading (The Lefthero)*[54] was one of the cases arising out of the Iran–Iraq War. A voyage charterparty for the *Lefthero* on the Gencon 1976 form was agreed for a voyage between Lübeck and Hamburg to Bandar Khomeini. The cargo was about 25,000 tons of steel products. The charterparty stated: **21.24**

> 19. Freight to be paid into Owners' account 90% within 5 banking days after signing and releasing of marked 'freight prepaid' Bills of Lading less commissions. Balance payable after right and true delivery of the cargo ... Freight deemed earned on signing Bills of Lading non-returnable ship and/or cargo lost or not lost ...

When the vessel arrived at Bandar Abbas there was a convoy system in operation. On 6 August 1983 the vessel joined a convoy to go to Bushire where the next available

---

[52] [1989] AC 1056, 1098.
[53] At 1099.
[54] [1991] 2 Lloyd's Rep 599.

convoy for Bandar Khomeini was assembled. By 10 August, the pilot had turned back on the ground that the *Lefthero* was not able to make sufficient speed. If the vessel had proceeded on this voyage, she would have arrived there on 12 August, with eight laydays in hand.[55] A further attempt was made on 22 August but for the same reasons the pilot had to turn back. In due course it was agreed that the vessel's cargo should be discharged at Bushire. Discharge was eventually completed on 3 February 1984. Ninety per cent of the freight was paid but the charterers denied their liability for the remaining 10 per cent because there had not been a right and true delivery of the cargo, because that involved delivery at Bandar Khomeini (not Bushire). The owners claimed the balance of freight contending that the balance was earned when the bills of lading were signed and became payable after discharge was completed at Bushire. Evans J (as he then was) noted that the decision of the House of Lords in *The Dominique* showed 'that the later time for payment does not prevent the whole from becoming "earned" at the outset'.[56] This being so, he could

> see no justification for limiting the 'freight earned' provision to the 90 per cent, payable early in the voyage (within five banking days after signing and releasing of bills of lading). Both parts became payable later than the freight was earned, and so the different times for payment do not provide a basis for including one but excluding the other from the 'freight earned' provision.

> While I have, if I may say so, considerable sympathy with the charterers' submissions, the present case is not one which, in my judgment, can properly be distinguished from *The Karin Vatis*. It would not be useful to draw fine distinctions between 'completion of discharge' (*The Karin Vatis*) and 'right and true delivery' (here). If the parties intended the 'freight earned' provisions not to apply to the balance of freight, they could easily have said so, e.g. 'freight (save for the balance) deemed earned', etc. For these reasons, I hold that shipowners' claim is entitled to succeed.[57]

This may be contrasted with *Antclizo Shipping Corporation v Food Corporation of India (The Antclizo)(No 2)*.[58] Here there was an agreement for a charterparty voyage from the USA to Bombay. The freight clause read as follows:

> 29. ... Ninety percent freight to be paid within seven days of signing bills of lading ... The balance freight will be paid after completion of discharge and settlement of demurrage/despatch ...

The vessel arrived at the Bombay Floating Light (BFL) on 30 December 1973 and tendered NOR on 31 December. So far as the demurrage claim by the owners was concerned, the charterers had contended that the arbitrator had been wrong in finding that the vessel had customs clearance within the meaning of clause 34 once the prior entry procedure (one of three stages) had been completed. The issue of customs clearance was in part governed by the Indian Customs Act 1962. Parker LJ confirmed the finding of the arbitrator that the vessel was entered at the Bombay Customs House at the time notice of readiness

---

[55] The laytime point (but not the freight point) was subsequently overturned by the Court of Appeal: [1992] 2 Lloyd's Rep 109.

[56] [1991] 2 Lloyd's Rep 599, 609.

[57] At 609–610.

[58] [1992] 1 Lloyd's Rep 558 (CA).

was given. Accordingly, the notice of readiness was valid. On the freight point, Sir John Megaw stated:

> The parties have expressly agreed that the date when the balance of freight shall become payable by the owners shall be the date of the settlement of the demurrage/despatch account, and no other or earlier date. The fact that interest on the balance of the demurrage/despatch account may properly be awarded from an earlier date than the date of settlement . . . is wholly irrelevant. It cannot alter the contractual date of payment for the balance of freight from an earlier date than that which the parties have expressly agreed shall be the date of payment of that balance (*not* the date of payment of the demurrage/discharge balance).[59]

G. Lump Sum Freight

The principle   A lump sum freight is not tied directly to the quantity of cargo actually **21.25** carried. It is a definite sum agreed to be paid for the hire of a ship for a specified voyage. In *Williams & Co v Canton Insurance Office Ltd* Lord Lindley said that:

> A lump sum freight is a definite sum agreed to be paid for the hire of a ship for a specified voyage; and although only payable on the right and true delivery of the cargo, those words are not taken literally, but are understood to mean right and true delivery, having regard to and excluding the excepted perils. In other words, the cargo, in this clause of the charterparty, does not mean the cargo shipped, but the cargo which the shipowner undertakes to deliver. The non-delivery of some of that affords no defence to a claim for the lump sum freight . . .[60]

Right and true delivery   Where freight is made payable on the 'right and true delivery' of **21.26** the cargo at destination, it is not necessary for the whole of the cargo to be delivered before the carrier is entitled to payment of the lump sum freight. In *Williams & Co v Canton Insurance Office Ltd* the Brankelow Steamship Co Ltd chartered the *Ramleh* to Williams & Co for a voyage from Buenos Aires to Liverpool for a lump sum of £3,000, payable on the right and true delivery of the cargo, in cash. The charterers' liability was to cease on shipment of cargo, provided that the cargo was worth the freight, dead freight, and demurrage on arrival. The vessel was to have a lien on the cargo for the recovery of all freight, dead freight, demurrage, and all other charges. The owners and charterers jointly insured the lump freight 'chartered or as if chartered valued' at the lump sum 'on board or not on board'. The charterers then proceeded to load the ship with a general cargo. The master signed bills of lading in terms of which the goods mentioned in each bill were made deliverable on payment of the bill of lading freight payable in respect of those goods. The aggregate of the bill of lading freight exceeded the charter freight. In the course of her voyage to Liverpool the vessel ran aground and a portion of the cargo was lost by jettison. However, the vessel arrived in Liverpool with the balance of her cargo, which was on arrival worth the freight, dead freight, and demurrage. The bill of lading freight payable on the cargo was less than the chartered freight. The owners and charterers then brought an action jointly to recover the difference from their insurers. The House of Lords held that the owner was entitled to recover the full lump sum freight on delivery of the remaining goods at Liverpool. In *Skibs A/S Trolla & Skibs A/S Tautra v United Enterprises & Shipping (Pte) Ltd*

---

[59] At 569. See also Parker LJ at 567.
[60] [1901] AC 462, 473.

(The Tarva),[61] a case argued before the High Court of Singapore, the owners of the *Tarva* chartered her to the defendants for a voyage from Singapore and/or Port Swettenham to Lourenço Marques and Durban with a full and complete cargo of sawn bundle timber for a lump sum freight of £19,000. The charterparty inter alia provided that:

> 4. The freight . . . to be paid in 80% in 5 working days after signing Bills of Lading at mean rate of exchange ruling on day or days of payment, balance on right and true delivery of cargo at ports of discharge.

Eighty per cent of the freight was paid and the vessel delivered her cargo at Lourenço Marques and Durban. The plaintiffs then claimed the balance of the freight but the defendants contended that the balance was not payable until the plaintiffs had shown that there was 'right and true delivery' within the meaning of clause 4 of the charterparty of the whole of the cargo originally shipped. Chua J held that the words 'right and true delivery' in clause 4 did not mean right and true delivery of the whole of the cargo shipped, and consequently the lump sum freight became due when the cargo which had arrived at the ports of discharge had been completely delivered:

> The authorities . . . do not support the contention of the defendants. In my view the time at which the balance of the lump freight in this case became due from the defendants was when the cargo which had arrived at the ports of discharge had been completely delivered.[62]

It would seem that full freight would be payable even where a failure to deliver all the cargo shipped was attributable to fault on the part of the shipowner. Here the general rule against deductions would operate and any cargo claim would have to take the form of a separate action.

21.27 **Cargo delivered on a different ship** The carrier is still entitled to claim the lump sum freight even though the cargo, or that proportion of it which reached the port of discharge, did not arrive in the original ship. He is entitled to tranship the cargo if the vessel in which it was shipped becomes incapable of completing the voyage. He may also be able to recover where the cargo has been collected by the crew after being washed ashore from a stranded vessel. In *William Thomas & Sons v Harrowing Steamship Co*[63] the plaintiffs had chartered their steamship, the *Ethelwalda*, to the defendants for the carriage of pit props from Finland to Port Talbot (Wales) for a specified lump sum freight (£1,600). This became payable on unloading and right delivery of the cargo. The vessel arrived at Port Talbot but, owing to heavy weather, was driven against the breakwater and became a total loss. Two-thirds of the cargo was washed ashore and collected by the crew and delivered to the defendants. The plaintiffs now brought an action to recover the lump sum freight. The Court of Appeal and House of Lords found in their favour. In the Court of Appeal,[64] Kennedy LJ affirmed the statement of Coleridge LJ in *Merchant Shipping Co v Armitage*[65] that:

> If it were a matter entirely free from authority there might be some ground for saying that 'entire discharge and right delivery of cargo' meant the entire discharge and right delivery of

---

[61] [1973] 2 Lloyd's Rep 385 (Singapore HC).
[62] At 387.
[63] [1915] AC 58.
[64] [1913] 2 KB 171 (CA).
[65] (1873) LR 9 QB 99, 107.

the cargo originally put on board. But the fair and reasonable construction of it, regard being had to the contract being for a lump sum, seems to me to be that which the Courts have already put upon similar contracts — that the cargo is entirely discharged and rightly delivered, if the whole of it not covered by any of the exceptions in the contract itself is delivered. Now in this case that which was not delivered and which was not discharged was not so delivered and was not so discharged by reason of perils within the exceptions of the very contract itself; and therefore, according to these authorities, and according to the reason of the thing, it appears to me that the contract was complied with, and that the lump sum was earned, and that what has not been paid of the lump sum ought to be paid.

H. Pro Rata Freight

The general rule   At common law the general rule is that, in the absence of agreement to the contrary, no freight is payable unless the cargo is delivered at the agreed destination. The carrier will not be entitled to claim freight proportional to the amount of the voyage completed even though he may be excused from carrying the goods to the port of discharge by the intervention of an excepted peril. In *Hunter v Prinsep*[66] the *Young Nicholas* was chartered to carry a cargo of timber from Honduras Bay (Central America) to London. Freight was payable at agreed rates on or after a right and true delivery of the cargo. The ship and cargo were captured by a French privateer, recaptured by an English sloop but then wrecked at St Kitt's, where the Vice-Admiralty Court ordered a sale of the cargo on the master's application. The shipowner claimed to be entitled to freight *pro rata itineris*. This was denied on the basis that freight was only earned by delivery of the cargo at the agreed destination and that the master, by putting the goods up for sale in St Kitt's, had clearly indicated that he had no intention of completing the journey. Lord Ellenborough explained that: **21.28**

> The principles which appear to govern the present action are these: the ship owners undertake that they will carry the goods to the place of destination, unless prevented by the dangers of the seas, or other unavoidable casualties: and the freighter undertakes that if the goods be delivered at the place of their destination, that he, the freighter, engages to pay any thing. If the ship be disabled from completing her voyage, the ship-owner may still entitle himself to the whole freight, by forwarding the goods by some other means to the place of destination; but he has no right to any freight if they be not so forwarded; unless the forwarding them be dispensed with, or unless there be some new bargain upon this subject. If the ship-owner will not forward them, the freighter is entitled to them without paying anything. One party, therefore, if he forward them, or be prevented or discharged from so doing, is entitled to his whole freight; and the other, if there be a refusal to forward them, is entitled to have them without paying any freight at all. The general property in the goods is in the freighter; the ship-owner has no right to withhold the possession from him, unless he has either earned his freight, or is going on to earn it. If no freight be earned, and he decline proceeding to pay any, the freighter has a right to possession. The captain's conduct in obtaining an order for selling the goods, and selling them accordingly, which was unnecessary, and which disabled him from forwarding the goods, was in effect declining to proceed to earn any freight, and therefore entitled the plaintiff to the entire produce of his goods, without any allowance for freight. The postea must therefore be delivered to the plaintiff.[67]

---

[66] (1808) 10 East 378; 103 ER 818.
[67] At 394–395; 103 ER 825.

21.29 **Contractual provision** The contract may expressly provide for the payment of a proportion of the freight in specified circumstances. This position was explained by Brett J in *Hopper v Burness*:

> What, then, is the principle governing the question whether such freight is payable? It is only payable when there is a mutual agreement between the charterer or shipper and the captain or shipowner, whereby the latter being able and willing to carry on the cargo to the port of destination, but the former desiring to have the goods delivered to him at some intermediate port, it is agreed that they shall be so delivered, and the law then implies a contract to pay freight pro rata itineris.[68]

21.30 **Fault of the cargo owner** The carrier may have a claim for pro rata freight where the failure to deliver the cargo at destination results from the fault of the cargo owner. An obligation to pay pro rata freight may be implied where the cargo owner takes delivery of the goods short of destination and this raises the inference that the carrier need not carry them any further. This was explained by Park B in *Vlierboom v Chapman*:

> ... [T]o justify a claim for pro rata freight, there must be a voluntary acceptance of the goods at an intermediate port, in such a mode as to raise a fair inference, that the further carriage of goods was intentionally dispensed with.[69]

The inference will not be drawn from a mere acceptance of the cargo short of destination unless the shipowner is able and willing to complete the carriage.

I. Back Freight

21.31 **The principle** Should the carrier be prevented from delivering cargo at the agreed destination for some reason outside his control (for example outbreak of war or failure of the cargo owner to take delivery), he may deal with the cargo in the interest of the owner and at the owner's expense. This may take the form of landing and warehousing the goods, transhipment, carriage to another port, or return to the loading port. It depends on what action is appropriate in the circumstances. He may then claim the expenses incurred as back freight. The leading case is *Cargo ex Argos*.[70] Here the defendant shipped petroleum on the plaintiff's vessel for carriage from London to Le Havre. The bill of lading provided that the petroleum was to be taken out by the defendant within 24 hours of arrival. The vessel arrived at Le Havre but was ordered to leave the following day by the authorities owing to the presence of munitions in the port. The master then attempted to land the cargo at Honfleur and Trouville but was unsuccessful. He returned to Le Havre and was given permission to discharge the petroleum temporarily into a lighter in the outer harbour where it remained under his control. After a further four days, the *Argos* had discharged the remainder of her cargo and was ready to sail. As no request for delivery had been made, the master re-shipped the petroleum to London. Sir Montague Smith stated that:

> It is well established that, if the ship has waited a reasonable time to deliver goods from her side, the master may land and warehouse them at the charge of the merchant; and it cannot

---

[68] (1876) 1 CPD 137, 140.
[69] (1844) 13 M&W 230, 238; 153 ER 96, 99.
[70] (1873) LR 5 PC 134.

be doubted that it would be his duty to do so rather than to throw them overboard. In a case like the present, where the goods could neither be landed nor remain where they were, it seems to be a legitimate extension of the implied agency of the master to hold that, in the absence of all advices, he had authority to carry or send them on to such other place as in his judgment, prudently exercised, appeared to be most convenient for their owner; and if so, it will follow from established principles that the expenses properly incurred may be charged to him.[71]

J. Dead Freight

Full and complete cargo   Where the charterer fails in his obligation to provide a 'full and   **21.32** complete cargo', the shipowner is entitled to damages for breach of contract, known as 'dead freight'. The shipowner is under a duty to mitigate his loss and is expected to take reasonable steps to procure alternative cargo. He is entitled to the cost of taking such action together with the value of any freight still outstanding.

The Storviken   In *Wallems Rederi A/S v WH Muller & Co, Batavia (The Storviken)*[72] the   **21.33** charterers agreed to load a full and complete cargo at the *Storviken's* ports of loading in Java but failed to do so. At Alexandria, an intermediate port at which the ship called in order to discharge a portion of her cargo, the shipowners, without asking for or receiving the assent of the charterers, loaded additional cargo and minimized the damages for which the charterers would otherwise have been liable. The plaintiffs then claimed dead freight from the defendants for their breach of the charterparty contract in not loading 1,250 tons of sugar. The charterers argued that the delay (of five days) in loading the alternative cargo amounted to a deviation. MacKinnon J held, however, that, inasmuch as the shipowners had an implied right to minimize the damages caused by the charterers' default and load additional cargo to fill up the space in the ship left vacant by the charterers, the delay occasioned to the voyage by loading that cargo was impliedly authorized by the charterparty. Accordingly, there was no deviation and the plaintiffs were entitled to dead freight:

> . . . I think that it is an implied term of this and every other charter that if the charterer fails to fulfil his duty in shipping the cargo that he is bound to ship, the shipowner is at liberty to fill up the space in the ship which the charterer has left vacant, if in doing so he is acting reasonably. The best test of the reasonableness of such action by the shipowner is, if to do so will diminish his pecuniary loss arising from the fault of the charterer and so diminish the damages that the charterer will be liable for. If therefore a shipowner, acting reasonably, has implied liberty to take in other cargo to fill up the space in the ship left vacant by the charterer, then he must also have implied liberty to delay the charter voyage by the period of time reasonably and necessarily occupied in taking that substituted cargo.[73]

Calculation   How is dead freight to be calculated? This may be stipulated in the voyage   **21.34** charter in the form of a clause for liquidated damages. However it now seems that such a clause does not necessarily limit the extent of damages recoverable for the breach. The shipowner may also be able to claim for the loss of demurrage for a failure to load the

---

[71] At 165.
[72] [1927] 2 KB 99.
[73] At 107.

minimum agreed cargo. In *Total Transport Corp v Amoco Trading Co (The Altus)*[74] there was a tanker voyage charterparty using the Exxonvoy 69 standard form. The owners let the *Altus* to the charterers for the carriage of a cargo of crude oil. The vessel was to proceed to a range of ports in North Africa and load a minimum of 40,000 tons of crude oil for carriage to a range of ports in Italy. The owners inter alia claimed damages of $19,980.88 for the charterers' breach of their obligation to load a minimum of 40,000 tons of crude oil. Webster J held that:

> [W]here a charterer commits any breach, even if it is only one breach, of his obligation either to provide the minimum contractual load or to detain the vessel for no longer than the stipulated period, the owner is entitled not only to the liquidated damages directly recoverable for the breach of the obligation to load (dead freight) or for the breach of the obligation with regard to detention (demurrage), but also, in the first case, to the damages flowing indirectly or consequentially from any detention of the vessel (if it occurs) and, in the second case, to damages flowing indirectly or consequentially from any failure to load a complete cargo if there is such failure.

> [I]t follows that the plaintiffs are entitled, in addition to the deadfreight which they have already received, to the difference between the demurrage rates as damages for the loss of demurrage consequent upon the defendants' failure to load the minimum agreed cargo.[75]

In the absence of a liquidated damages clause, the amount due to the shipowners will be calculated on the basis of the freight appropriate to the amount of unutilized cargo space less the expenses, if any, which the shipowner would normally have incurred in earning this freight.

K. Payment of Freight

21.35 **Party from whom freight due**   The party who normally has responsibility for freight is the charterer in the case of a voyage charterparty or the shipper in the case of a bill of lading contract, but this general position may be modified by contract such that it becomes some other individual's responsibility.

21.36 **Charterparty freight**   In the case of a charterparty, it is the charterer who has the primary responsibility for the payment of freight. At least this will be the case under a voyage charterparty and likewise if he sub-charters the vessel or issues bills of lading to third parties. However, where the charterer has no substantial interest in the contract once the cargo has been shipped the charterparty might include a cesser clause which provides that the liability of the charterer for freight and other transport charges shall cease once the cargo has been loaded on the chartered vessel.[76]

21.37 **Bill of Lading freight**   The shipper, who is often the seller of the goods, will usually be responsible for freight under a bill of lading. He may, of course, merely be acting as agent on behalf of another party.

21.38 **Payment: shipper**   The position is that the responsibility of the shipper for payment of freight survives any subsequent endorsement to a consignee or other endorsee.

---

[74] [1985] 1 Lloyd's Rep 423.
[75] At 435–436.
[76] See para 27.27.

Although the consignee or endorsee became personally liable for payment of freight under the Bills of Lading Act 1855, section 2 of that Act expressly reserved the carrier's right of recourse against the shipper.[77] Under the 1992 Act the responsibility of the shipper for payment remains, despite endorsement of the bill of lading to a consignee or endorsee. Section 3(3) provides that, even where a subsequent consignee or endorsee becomes liable to pay freight, this will be without prejudice to the continuing liability of the shipper, as the original party to the contract of carriage.[78]

Payment: consignees and endorsees   The 1855 Act provided the carrier with a statutory right to recover freight from any consignee or endorsee of a bill of lading to whom property in the goods had passed as a result of its endorsement. There were two difficulties with this: where the Act was not applicable[79] and where the consignee or endorsee was liable for outstanding advance freight at the time delivery was taken of the goods. However, under the 1992 Act the consignee or endorsee who obtains title to sue under the 1992 Act will not automatically become subject to the obligations under the contract (including payment of freight). These will only attach when he seeks to enforce the contract, either by taking or demanding delivery of the goods from the carrier, making a claim under the contract of carriage, or having taken or demanded delivery of the goods before acquiring title to sue.[80] With respect to liability for advance freight, the Act provides that a subsequent endorsee or consignee shall become subject to the same liabilities under that contract as if he had been a party to that 'contract'.[81] **21.39**

Payment to whom: shipowner   The shipowner will normally be entitled to the payment of voyage charter freight and, in the absence of any charterparty, to freight due under a bill of lading contract.[82] However, under a demise charterparty this would be payable to the demise charterer. Payment may also be made to the loading broker,[83] the owners' agent, or some other specified party, such as the master[84] who may be authorized to collect freight as the shipowners' agent. **21.40**

Payment to whom: charterer   In the case of a demise charter, freight will be payable, both by sub-charter and under bills of lading, to the demise charterer. In the case of a voyage charter, entitlement to bill of lading freights will be a question of fact although in the normal course of events the bills of lading will be the shipowner's own. Even though issued by the charterers, they will signed by the master or other agent on the shipowner's behalf. Where this happens, the shipowner is entitled to appoint an agent to collect the freight on the bills at the port of discharge. After deducting any outstanding charter freight, the agent must account for the balance to the charterer. If the bills of lading are signed by the master or other agent on behalf of the charterer, they are treated as charterers' bills of **21.41**

---

[77] The Act was replaced by the Carriage of Goods by Sea Act 1992: see para 8.16.
[78] See para 8.26. See *Fox v Nott* (1861) 6 H&N 630; 158 ER 260.
[79] See para 8.13.
[80] section 3(1). See the discussion of this section at para 8.24.
[81] ibid.
[82] See, eg, *Smith v Plummer* (1818) 1 B&A 575, 581; 106 ER 212, 214 (Lord Ellenborough CJ).
[83] See para 1.24.
[84] See para 1.28. The master may be able to sue in person for freight: see Scrutton (1996), 342.

lading and the charterer will be entitled to payment of any freight due under the contract of carriage.[85]

21.42 **Entitlement of a ship purchaser**   The sale of a vessel normally carries with it entitlement to freight being earned at the time of sale and which is payable to the shipowner.

21.43 **Entitlement of the mortgagee of a ship**   The mortgage of a ship does not normally include any entitlement to freight. This will not arise until the mortgagee has taken either actual or constructive possession of the vessel.[86] However, once the mortgagee takes possession of the vessel, on an event of default by the mortgagor, the mortgagee is entitled to freight being currently earned but not to advance freight already paid to the shipowner.[87] He is also not entitled to freight which has accrued before he took possession or, in the case of charters, to unpaid freight on previous voyages. If there is more than one mortgage, priority for entitlement to freight will be determined by reference to the date of registration of the mortgage.

21.44 **Entitlement of an assignee**   It is possible to assign freight independently of the vessel, provided the requirements for statutory assignment are complied with and subject to equities.[88] The payer of freight is entitled to pay the first assignee giving him notice in the case of successive assignments. Assignments of freight take priority over subsequent sale or mortgage of the vessel unless, at the time of the mortgage, the mortgagee had no notice of the assignment. The assignment will not have precedence over a prior sale of the vessel because, as we have just seen,[89] this carries with it the right to any accruing freight. Given, however, that the mortgagee does not gain entitlement to freight until he takes possession, a subsequent assignee will have priority for freight which has already accrued.

---

[85] As to some of the problems which can be thrown up by this, see ch 12.
[86] See *Keith v Burrows* (1877) 2 App Cas 636.
[87] *Shillito v Biggart* [1903] 1 KB 683.
[88] Law of Property Act 1925, s 136(1).
[89] See para 21.42.

22

SHIPPER'S OBLIGATIONS AND IMMUNITIES UNDER THE HAGUE AND HAGUE–VISBY RULES

A. Introduction

Overview   In previous chapters we examined the shipper's obligations of common law **22.01** and his obligation to pay freight. In this chapter we consider the shipper's obligations under the various international conventions which have been the subject of our attention. We shall examine these obligations first from the perspective of both the Hague and Hague–Visby Rules.

B. Shipper's Guarantee of Particulars

Introduction   We have looked previously at the function of the bill of lading as a receipt **22.02** for the goods at common law.[1] We now return to this function, but in the context of the Hague and Hague–Visby Rules and the duty cast on the shipper.

Article III, rule 5   Article III, rule 5[2] of the Hague and Hague–Visby Rules provides as **22.03** follows:

> The shipper shall be deemed to have guaranteed to the carrier the accuracy at the time of shipment of the marks, number, quantity and weight, as furnished by him, and the shipper shall indemnify the carrier against all loss, damages and expenses arising or resulting from inaccuracies in such particulars. The right of the carrier to such indemnity shall in no way limit his responsibility and liability under the contract of carriage to any person other than the shipper.

---

[1] See ch 6.
[2] Berlingieri (1997), 263.

22.04 **Accuracy of particulars** There are a number of points to note concerning the matters guaranteed by the shipper. The first point to note is that the provision applies to 'marks, number, quantity and weight' only. There is no guarantee of the nature of the goods, nor indeed is there any warranty on the part of the shipper as to the condition of the goods. The second point to note is that article III, rule 5 only refers to the relation between the shipper and the carrier and therefore does not seem to cover the position where bills of lading are endorsed to a consignee. It should be noted, further, that though the Carriage of Goods by Sea Act 1992 refers to subsequent holders becoming subject to the same liabilities as if they were a 'party' to the contract,[3] there is nothing which says that they will be treated as 'shipper'.

22.05 **Consequences** The chief consequence of a failure to guarantee the matters referred to in article III, rule 5 is that the shipper 'shall indemnify the carrier against all loss, damages and expenses arising or resulting from inaccuracies'. On the part of the carrier, it should be noted, however, that in certain circumstances he may also be able to rely on certain of his immunities in article IV, rule 2, in particular that in article IV, rule 2(i) — for 'act of the shipper' — and article IV, rule 2(o) — 'insufficiency or inadequacy of marks' — in answer to any claim passed on to him by a receiver.[4] These defences might be particularly useful to the carrier in the event that a claim is made against him by the consignee or endorsee of the bill of lading.

22.06 **Reliance** Although it is not specified that there must have been reliance on the particulars given by the shipper, it is submitted that this should be the case, because otherwise there would not be the necessary causal link between the losses 'arising or resulting' from them.[5]

22.07 **Claim as against the charterer?** An issue which may arise in the context of a paramount clause, is whether the owner would have a right of recourse against a charterer. In *Paros Shipping Corp v Nafta (GB) Ltd (The Paros)* Hobhouse J thought that such a claim would lie,[6] but in *Boukadoura Maritime Corp v Societe Anonyme Marocaine de l'Industrie et du Raffinage (The Boukadoura)*[7] Evans J held, obiter, that there was no right to an indemnity unless there was an express provision in the charterparty to that effect.[8] It is submitted that the better view is the former one because there is no logical reason for excluding such a claim in the context of the incorporation of the Rules into a charterparty.

C. Notice of Loss or Damage

22.08 **Article III, rule 6** Article III, rule 6[9] of the Hague and Hague–Visby Rules provides that:

> Unless notice of loss or damage and the general nature of such loss or damage be given in writing to the carrier or his agent at the port of discharge before or at the time of the removal of the goods into the custody of the person entitled to delivery thereof under the contract of

---

3 Section 3(1).
4 See the discussion of these defences at paras 28.33; 28.41.
5 See Cooke (2001), para 85.150.
6 [1987] 2 Lloyd's Rep 269, 274.
7 [1989] 1 Lloyd's Rep 393.
8 At 400. He relied on *Miramar Maritime Corp v Holborn Oil Trading (The Miramar)* [1984] AC 676.
9 Berlingieri (1997), 267.

carriage, or, if the loss or damage be not apparent, within three days, such removal shall be *prima facie* evidence of the delivery by the carrier of the goods as described in the bill of lading.[10]

The notice in writing need not be given if the state of the goods has at the time of their receipt been the subject of joint survey or inspection.[11]

In the case of any actual or apprehended loss or damage the carrier and the receiver shall give all reasonable facilities to each other for inspecting and tallying the goods.

Interpretation   This provision of the Rules would seem, at first glance, to have potentially **22.09** important consequences for the shipper. On one view, there seems to be some ambiguity in what is said.[12] On another view, it seems that the effect of what is said amounts to no more than is the case at common law. Thus, it is clear that the rule is not dealing with the right to claim for loss or damage but with the question of evidence. In the case of a claim for loss or damage to goods, the onus of proof will lie upon the person who makes the claim.[13] Accordingly any claim may be made, on proof of it, and article III, rule 6 simply provides that removal without notice will be prima facie evidence of delivery of the goods as described in the bill of lading. In the case of non-apparent damage a three day period is specified.

'Actual or apprehended loss'   The meaning of this sub-paragraph of article III, rule 6 is **22.10** reasonably straightforward and is intended to formalize an obligation on the carrier and the receiver of the goods to permit the giving of 'all reasonable facilities . . . for inspecting and tallying the goods'. Of course, what this does not do is indicate what the consequences are of a failure to comply. Thus, it is a provision without teeth.

D. Shipment of Dangerous Cargoes

Introduction   In Chapter 20 we examined at some length the obligation on the shipper, **22.11** at common law, not to ship goods which are 'dangerous'.[14] We now examine the scope of the obligation under the Hague and Hague–Visby Rules.

Article IV, rule 6   Article IV, rule 6[15] of the Hague and Hague–Visby Rules[16] provides that: **22.12**

Goods of an inflammable, explosive or dangerous nature to the shipment whereof the carrier, master or agent of the carrier has not consented, with knowledge of their nature and character, may at any time before discharge be landed at any place or destroyed or rendered innocuous by the carrier without compensation, and the shipper of such goods shall be liable for all damages and expenses directly or indirectly arising out of or resulting from such shipment.

If any such goods shipped with such knowledge and consent shall become a danger to the ship or cargo, they may in like manner be landed at any place or destroyed or rendered innocuous by the carrier without liability on the part of the carrier except to general average, if any.

---

[10] Note that the Hague Rules contain the additional sentence: 'If the loss or damage is not apparent, the notice must be given within three days of the delivery of the goods.'

[11] At this point the part of article III, rule 6 dealing with the time bar is omitted. It is discussed fully at para 34.03.

[12] See, eg, Scrutton (1996), 434.

[13] See too article IV, rule 1, discussed at para 26.29.

[14] See para 20.06.

[15] Berlingieri (1997), 591.

[16] The provision is in the same terms in both the Hague and Hague–Visby Rules.

22.13 **No definition of 'dangerous'** As is the case at common law, the Rules do not provide any definition of what is meant by the use of the term 'dangerous'.

22.14 **Scope of the provision** There are two main elements in this provision of the Rules. The first is that, if goods of an 'inflammable, explosive or dangerous nature'[17] are shipped without the knowledge or consent of the carrier or his agents, then they may 'at any time' before discharge be landed, destroyed, or even rendered innocuous by the carrier without compensation to the shipper. In such circumstances, the shipper 'shall be liable for all damages and expenses directly or indirectly arising out of or resulting from such shipment'. The second main element in the definition is if any goods are shipped with the shipper's knowledge and consent and subsequently become a danger to the ship or cargo, then they too may be landed, destroyed, or rendered innocuous. These acts are expressed to be without any liability on the part of the carrier except in general average, if any.

22.15 **Physically dangerous only?** It has sometimes been assumed that the Rules apply only to goods which are physically dangerous and not to those situations where liability has been held to lie at common law for non-physically dangerous goods[18] but this is no longer good law following the decision in *Effort Shipping Co Ltd v Linden Management SA (The Giannis NK).*[19]

22.16 *The Giannis NK* The *Giannis NK*[20] loaded a cargo of groundnut extraction meal pellets into one of her holds at Dakar and these were fumigated after loading. Other holds contained bulk wheat pellets. Some of the pellets were offloaded at a Puerto Rican port before the *Giannis NK* proceeded to the Dominican Republic to offload the remainder. The vessel was quarantined on arrival because inspectors found evidence of Khapra beetle in the cargo. Repeated fumigations of the vessel's holds were to no avail and she was ordered to leave Rio Haina. Notice was served on the owners by the US Department of Agriculture to either return the cargo to its country of origin or dump it at sea. The owners chose the latter course. In their action against the shippers of the groundnut pellets, the owners claimed damages for the shipment of dangerous cargo, arguing that this constituted a physical danger to the ship by reason of the Khapra beetle infestation. They therefore claimed that they could recover from the shippers pursuant to article IV, rule 6 of the Hague Rules, which had been incorporated into the bills of lading. At first instance,[21] Longmore J found that the Khapra beetle had come aboard the *Giannis NK* with the cargo of groundnuts. He concluded that, if the Hague Rules did not deal with non-physically dangerous cargo, one could not determine the rights of the parties in relation to such cargo by reference to these Rules.[22] However, he said, the dumping of the cargo (which included the wheat pellets) was a direct result of the Khapra beetle and this cargo was therefore 'dangerous' in the sense of being liable to give rise to loss of other cargo shipped in the same vessel. Thus, for the

---

[17] The term 'dangerous' in this context should not be read *ejusdem generis* with 'inflammable, explosive': *Chandris v Isbrandtsen-Möller Co Inc* [1951] 1 KB 240, 246 (Devlin J). See too *Effort Shipping Co Ltd v Linden Management SA (The Giannis NK)* [1998] AC 605, 620 (Lord Steyn).
[18] See Scrutton (1996), 457.
[19] [1998] AC 605. See FD Rose, 'Liability for dangerous goods' [1998] LMCLQ 480.
[20] ibid.
[21] [1994] 2 Lloyd's Rep 171.
[22] At 180.

purpose of the Rules, the groundnuts were 'goods of a dangerous nature' and accordingly the shippers were strictly liable to the owners of the *Giannis NK*. The shippers then appealed against this finding[23] but Hirst LJ[24] upheld the judgment of Longmore J. In the further appeal to the House of Lords, their Lordships agreed, Lord Lloyd stating that he was in complete agreement with their reasoning.[25] Lord Steyn, likewise, emphasized that:

> … [I]t would be wrong to apply the *ejusdem generis* rule to the words 'goods of an inflammable, explosive or dangerous nature'. These are disparate categories of goods. Each word must be given its natural meaning, and 'dangerous' ought not to be restrictively interpreted by reason of the preceding words. Secondly, it would be wrong to detract from the generality and width of the expression 'goods of … [a] dangerous nature' by importing the suggested restriction that the goods must by themselves, or by reason of their inherent properties, pose a danger to the ship or other cargo. For my part I would resist any temptation to substitute for the ordinary and non-technical expression 'goods … of a dangerous nature' any other formulation.[26]

Article IV, rule 6 and due diligence The relationship between article IV, rule 6 and the carrier's duty before and at the beginning of the voyage to exercise 'due diligence' under article III, rule 1[27] was considered by the Court of Appeal in *Mediterranean Freight Services Ltd v BP Oil International Ltd (The Fiona)*.[28] Prior to discharge of a cargo of fuel oil at an offshore platform, a surveyor boarded the *Fiona* to take ullage and temperature soundings. Unfortunately, he used an unearthed electronic temperature probe and this caused an explosion which resulted in severe damage to the vessel and his own death by drowning. The owners claimed damages on the ground that the fuel oil cargo was dangerous cargo. It was said that the fuel oil had a propensity, known to BP but not the owners, to produce hydrocarbon vapour. BP contended that, even if the cargo was dangerous, the explosion and loss was caused by the failure of the owners to exercise due diligence to make the vessel seaworthy in that they had failed properly to remove residues of previous fuel cargo. At first instance,[29] Judge Diamond QC held that the owners' failure to remove condensate residues from the vessel, and in particular their failure to carry out a proper line and duct wash before loading commenced, constituted a breach by the owners of their duty under article III, rule 1 to exercise due diligence to make the ship seaworthy. The dominant cause of the explosion was the breach by the owners of their obligation under article III, rule 1 and they could not, therefore, claim their indemnity under article IV, rule 6 because one of the causes of the explosion was their breach of article III, rule 1. This reasoning was expressly endorsed in the Court of Appeal by Hirst LJ[30] and the appeal of the owners was dismissed.[31]

22.17

Apportionment The decision at first instance in *The Giannis NK*[32] opened up the interesting question whether there could, or should, be apportionment (under the Law Reform

22.18

---

[23] [1996] 1 Lloyd's Rep 577.
[24] Morritt and Ward LJJ agreed.
[25] [1998] AC 605, 613.
[26] At 620.
[27] See the discussion of this obligation at para 26.20.
[28] [1994] 2 Lloyd's Rep 506 (CA).
[29] [1993] 1 Lloyd's Rep 257.
[30] [1994] 2 Lloyd's Rep 506 (CA), 519.
[31] Hoffmann and Nourse LJJ agreed.
[32] [1994] 2 Lloyd's Rep 171.

(Contributory Negligence) Act 1945)[33] between the carrier's breach of his due diligence obligation under article III, rule 1 and the shipper's breach of his obligation not to ship dangerous goods under article IV, rule 6.[34] Section 1 of the 1945 Act permits damages to be reduced where any person suffers damage as the result partly of his own fault and partly that of other persons. While the carrier's breach of his obligation might well amount to 'fault' for the purposes of apportionment, this would be much more difficult in the case of the shipper's breach of article IV, rule 6, which is not limited to fault.

22.19 **Article IV, rule 6 and its relationship with Article IV, rule 3** One further issue which has received some consideration has been the relationship between article IV, rule 6 and article IV, rule 3. This provision of the Rules provides that the shipper shall not be responsible for loss or damage sustained by the carrier or the ship arising or resulting from any cause without the act, fault, or neglect of the shipper, his agents or his servants. Does this reduce the shipper's liability under article IV, rule 6 from an absolute obligation to indemnify the carrier to a qualified obligation to indemnify him where the shipper can be shown to have been at fault? Some writers have doubted whether the 'absolute' nature of the common law warranty is preserved under the Hague–Visby Rules in view of article IV, rule 3, while others have argued that article IV, rule 6 is a specific provision dealing with dangerous goods which should be seen as an exception to the provision in article IV, rule 3.[35] The matter was touched on briefly, albeit obiter, by Mustill J in *The Athanasia Comninos*.[36] Counsel for the plaintiffs in that case had sought to rely on two cases from the United States District Court for New York[37] and one from the Exchequer Court of Canada,[38] all three of which had decided that article IV, rule 3 (or, rather, its equivalent in the US Carriage of Goods by Sea Act 1936[39]) did indeed reduce the shipper's undertaking from that of an absolute warranty to something akin to the qualified warranty at common law. Mustill J hesitated to answer the question in the same way, but left it open: it made no difference to the outcome of the action before him and so this issue and the other questions asked in relation to the Rules by the plaintiffs were 'academic'.[40] Judge Diamond QC considered the same issue in his judgment in *The Fiona* but concluded that article IV, rule 3 was not relevant to the right of the carrier to claim an indemnity under article IV, rule 6.[41] The point was fully considered by the Court of Appeal in *The Giannis NK*.[42] Counsel for the appellants called upon Hirst LJ to follow three US authorities[43] which supported the contention that article IV, rule 6 should be given a qualified construction in view of article IV, rule 3. Hirst LJ refused to accede to

---

[33] For a thorough consideration of whether the Act should apply to contractual claims, see the Law Commission's Report, *Contributory Negligence as a Defence in Contract* (No 219) (1993), para 4.10.

[34] For discussion, see Cooke (2001), 794.

[35] See Tetley (1988), 467.

[36] [1990] 1 Lloyd's Rep 277.

[37] *Serraino v United States Lines* 1965 AMC 1038; *General SA General Trades Enterprises and Agencies v Consorcio Pesquerio Del Peru* 1974 AMC 2342.

[38] *Heath Steel Lines Ltd v The Erwin Schröder* [1969] 1 Lloyd's Rep 370.

[39] 46 USCA §§1300–1315.

[40] [1990] 1 Lloyd's Rep 277, 285. See also Pearson J in *Atlantic Oil Carriers v British Petroleum Co* [1957] 2 Lloyd's Rep 55.

[41] [1993] 1 Lloyd's Rep 257, 269.

[42] [1996] 1 Lloyd's Rep 577 (CA).

[43] The two cases cited in *The Athanasia Comninos*, as well as *The Stylianos Restis* 1974 AMC 2342.

this because, in his view, the clear words of rule 6, taken by themselves, were not capable of bearing such a qualified construction.[44] In the House of Lords, Lord Lloyd agreed:

> Article IV, rule 6 is a free standing provision[45] dealing with a specific subject matter. It is neither expressly, nor by implication, subject to Article IV, rule 3. It imposes strict liability on shippers in relation to the shipment of dangerous goods, irrespective of fault or neglect on their part.[46]

Lord Steyn took the same view as Lord Lloyd, though he also took due cognizance of the purpose of the Hague Rules:

> This much we know about the broad objective of the Hague Rules: it was intended to reign in [sic] the unbridled freedom of contract of owners to impose terms which were 'so unreasonable and unjust in their terms as to exempt from almost every conceivable risk and responsibility' ((1992) 108 LQR 501, at p. 502); it aimed to achieve this by a pragmatic compromise between interests of owners and shippers; and the Hague Rules were designed to achieve a part harmonization of the diverse laws of trading nations at least in the areas which the convention covered. But these general aims tell us nothing about the meaning of Article IV, rule 3 or Article IV, rule 6. One is therefore remitted to the language of the relevant parts of the Hague Rules as the authoritative guide to the intention of the framers of the Hague Rules.[47]

The Rules and the common law   The question whether article IV, rule 6 of the Rules is **22.20** intended to be a complete code covering dangerous goods and whether the shipper might, notwithstanding his absence of liability under the Rules, nevertheless be liable at common law, has now been considered in several cases. In *The Athanasia Comninos*,[48] Mustill J doubted whether the provision in the Rules formed a complete code, but as with the question whether article IV, rule 3 operated to reduce the absolute liability under article IV, rule 6, he declined to express a firm opinion on the matter.[49] Judge Diamond QC took a different view in *The Fiona*.[50] He thought that it was incorrect, when rules applied by statute, to consider the common law position relating to the obligation of the shipper as regards shipping dangerous goods. In his opinion the owners' exclusive remedy was to seek their indemnity under article IV, rule 6.[51] At first instance in *The Giannis NK*,[52] counsel for the shippers argued that 'goods of a dangerous nature' in article IV, rule 6 of the Rules could only refer to physically dangerous goods and that the shipowner would not have a remedy in relation to goods which caused delay but which were not themselves physically dangerous. Longmore J referred in this context to the statement of Devlin J in *Chandris v Isbrandtsen-Möller Co Inc* that the US Carriage of Goods by Sea Act 1936 was not intended as a code; it was 'not meant altogether to supplant the contract of carriage but only to control on certain topics the freedom of contract which the parties would otherwise have.'[53] Longmore J held

---

44 [1996] 1 Lloyd's Rep 577 (CA), 582.
45 But see on this Lord Cooke: [1998] AC 605, 627.
46 At 615.
47 At 621–622.
48 [1990] 1 Lloyd's Rep 277.
49 At 285.
50 [1993] 1 Lloyd's Rep 257.
51 At 268.
52 [1994] 2 Lloyd's Rep 171.
53 [1951] 1 KB 240, 247.

that if the Hague Rules were to be construed as relating to physically dangerous cargo, then they were not intended to control the parties' freedom of contract on the topic of non-physically dangerous cargo. In his view, 'if the parties have made no express provisions, the provisions implied by the law governing the contract of carriage will govern the rights of the parties'.[54] The question was not considered by the Court of Appeal or the House of Lords.

22.21 **Article IV, rule 6 and the Bills of Lading Act 1855**   One of the more surprising issues to emerge in *The Giannis NK*[55] was the question of the shipper's liability for dangerous goods under the Bills of Lading Act 1855.[56] The shippers had endorsed the bill of lading to their immediate purchasers and so the property in the cargo of groundnuts had passed to those purchasers under section 1 of the 1855 Act. Were the shippers divested of their liability for the carriage of dangerous goods by virtue of the endorsement to the purchasers of the groundnuts? Counsel for the shippers argued that this was the effect of the words '… and subject to the same liabilities in respect of such goods …' in section 1 of the 1855 Act but this was rejected by Longmore J who relied expressly[57] on the obiter statement of Mustill J in *The Athanasia Comninos*:

> It may well be that in the main a transfer of the document, satisfying the requirements of the Act, operates to transfer away many of the shipper's contractual obligations, but the Act cannot in my judgment have been intended to divest the shipper of responsibility for the consequences of loss, arising from the act of shipment itself.[58]

In the appeal,[59] Hirst LJ noted that at common law the shipper would have remained liable, notwithstanding endorsement of the bill of lading. He also emphasized that section 3(3) of the Carriage of Goods by Sea Act 1992 had made this point explicit:[60]

> In my judgment it would require very clear words indeed to divest the owner of his rights against the shipper (with whom he is in contractual relationship) and leave him with his sole remedy against a complete stranger who happens to be the consignee of the goods or the endorsee of the bill of lading, of whose whereabouts and financial stability he knows nothing, and who may be a man (or enterprise) of straw. … I am satisfied that the shippers were not divested of liability by virtue of section 1 of the 1855 Act.[61]

This reasoning was also followed in the House of Lords by both Lord Lloyd[62] and Lord Steyn.[63]

---

[54] [1994] 2 Lloyd's Rep 171, 179–180.

[55] The cause of action arose during the course of 1990 and so the Bills of Lading Act 1855, in so far as it was relevant, was applicable to the case.

[56] Now repealed by s 6(2) of the Carriage of Goods by Sea Act 1992: see para 8.15.

[57] He also drew support from *Fox v Nott* (1861) 6 H&N 630; 158 ER 260.

[58] [1990] 1 Lloyd's Rep 277, 281.

[59] [1996] 1 Lloyd's Rep 577 (CA).

[60] In endorsing the view taken by Longmore J, Hirst LJ drew upon the same authorities.

[61] [1996] 1 Lloyd's Rep 577 (CA), 586.

[62] [1998] AC 605, 618.

[63] At 626.

PART V

THE OBLIGATIONS OF THE CARRIER

23

SEAWORTHINESS

A. Introduction

Overview   In previous chapters we have considered various obligations which are placed **23.01**
on the shipper, both at common law and under the Hague and Hague–Visby Rules. In this
chapter we begin our consideration of the carrier's obligations, commencing with one of the
most fundamental of these, his obligation to provide a ship which is seaworthy.[1] In a later
chapter we shall consider this obligation in the context of the Hague and Hague–Visby Rules.[2]

B. The Common Law Obligation

An implied undertaking   In every contract of affreightment,[3] except where the Carriage of **23.02**
Goods by Sea Act 1971 applies,[4] there is an implied undertaking on the part of the shipowner,[5]
in the absence of an express undertaking, to provide a seaworthy vessel. In one of the leading cases[6]

---

[1] See, generally, Carver (2005), para 9-013; Scrutton (1996), art 51.
[2] See para 26.15.
[3] See para 1.32.
[4] See para 26.16.
[5] *Kopitoff v Wilson* (1876) 1 QBD 377, 380 (Field J).
[6] The case is also a leading case for the development of contract law. See FMB Reynolds, 'Maritime matters and the common law', Inaugural Ebsworth and Ebsworth Lecture (7 September 1992); 'Maritime and other influences on the common law' [2002] LMCLQ 182.

on the carrier's undertaking of seaworthiness, *Hongkong Fir Shipping Co Ltd v Kawasaki Kisen Kaisha*, Diplock LJ explained that:

> ... [T]he shipowners' undertaking to tender a seaworthy ship has, as a result of numerous decisions as to what can amount to 'unseaworthiness', become one of the most complex of contractual undertakings. It embraces obligations with respect to every part of the hull and machinery, stores and equipment and the crew itself. It can be broken by the presence of trivial defects easily and rapidly remediable as well as by defects which must inevitably result in a total loss of the vessel.[7]

C. Meaning of Seaworthiness

23.03 Introduction   What is meant by the shipowner's obligation to provide a seaworthy ship has been referred to in very many cases. Thus, in one of the leading cases it is said that a seaworthy vessel is one which is 'fit to meet and undergo the perils of sea and other incidental risks to which of necessity she must be exposed in the course of a voyage'.[8]

23.04 Objective test   The test for determining seaworthiness is an objective one and was stated as follows by Channell J in *McFadden v Blue Star Line*:

> A vessel must have that degree of fitness which an ordinary careful and prudent owner would require his vessel to have at the commencement of her voyage, having regard to all the probable circumstances of it. To that extent the shipowner, as we have seen, undertakes absolutely that she is fit, and ignorance is no excuse. If the defect existed, the question to be put is: Would a prudent owner have required that it should be made good before sending his ship to sea had he known of it? If he would, the ship was not seaworthy within the meaning of the undertaking.[9]

In this case certain bales of cotton were shipped aboard the *Tolosa* from Wilmington to Bremen. The bills of lading stated that the charterer would not be liable for perils of the sea or accidents of navigation even when occurring because of negligence. During loading of the cargo, a ballast tank was filled with water after which a failed attempt was made to close the relevant seacock. However, the seacock was defective in some way and consequently water got through a sluice door which had not been properly closed and thence into the hold where the plaintiff's cargo was located. Channell J held that there had been a breach of the warranty as to the fitness of the vessel to receive the cargo. What is required from the shipowner relates to the knowledge of the relevant standards at the applicable time. In *FC Bradley & Sons Ltd v Federal Steam Navigation Co Ltd*, Viscount Sumner expressed this as follows:

> In the law of carriage by sea neither seaworthiness nor due diligence is absolute. Both are relative, among other things, to the state of knowledge and the standards prevailing at the material time.[10]

---

[7] [1962] 2 QB 26 (CA), 71. See too *Smith Hogg & Co Ltd v Black Sea & Baltic General Insurance Co Ltd* [1940] AC 997, 1005 (Lord Wright).

[8] *Kopitoff v Wilson* (1876) 1 QBD 377, 380 (Field J); *Steel v State Line Steamship Co* (1877) 3 App Cas 72, 77 (Lord Cairns LC); *Virginia Carolina Chemical Co v Norfolk and North American Steam Shipping Co* [1912] 1 KB 229 (CA), 243–244 (Kennedy LJ).

[9] [1905] 1 KB 697, 706. See also *Alfred C Toepfer Schiffahrtsgesellschaft GmbH v Tossa Marine Co Ltd (The Derby)* [1985] 2 Lloyd's Rep 325 (CA), 332 (Kerr LJ).

[10] (1927) 27 Ll LR 395 (HL), 396.

D. Nature of the Obligation

Structural fitness   The seaworthiness obligation extends first to the structural fitness of   **23.05**
the vessel for the intended voyage.[11] Thus in *Steel v State Line*[12] the plaintiffs were the consignees of a bill of lading in respect of wheat shipped at New York on *The State of Virginia*
for carriage to London. One of the deck port holes was insufficiently fastened and during
the voyage water entered through the port and damaged the cargo of wheat. The court
found that the vessel was unseaworthy.[13] Other instances of structural unfitness leading
to unseaworthiness would include a fracture to the shell plating of a vessel[14] and leaking
rivets.[15]

Manning and equipment   A vessel must not only be structurally sound, but must also   **23.06**
have aboard her sufficient manning and equipment for the intended voyage. The requirement as to manning would extend to the competence of the vessel's crew, including her
master.[16] This was explained as follows by Lord Atkinson in the case of *Standard Oil Co of
New York v Clan Line Steamers Ltd*:

> It is not disputed, I think, that a ship may be rendered unseaworthy by the inefficiency of the
> master who commands her. Does not that principle apply where the master's inefficiency
> consists, whatever his general efficiency may be, in his ignorance as to how his ship may,
> owing to the peculiarities of her structure, behave in circumstances likely to be met with on
> an ordinary ocean voyage? There cannot be any difference in principle, I think, between dis-
> abling want of skill and disabling want of knowledge. Each equally renders the master unfit
> and unqualified to command, and therefore makes the ship he commands unseaworthy. And
> the owner who withholds from the master the necessary information should, in all reason, be
> as responsible for the result of the master's ignorance as if he deprived the latter of the general
> skill and efficiency he presumably possessed.[17]

A similar point arose in the case of *Hongkong Fir Shipping Co Ltd v Kawasaki Kisen Kaisha
Ltd*[18] where the court found that though certain of the vessel's machinery was in a reasonably good condition '. . . by reason of its age, it needed to be maintained by an experienced,
competent, careful and adequate engine room staff.' Salmon J said that:

> The test is: would a reasonably prudent owner, knowing the relevant facts, have allowed
> this vessel to put to sea with this engine room staff? . . . I have no doubt that the true
> answer to this question is 'No'. It is obvious from the owners' associated company's letter . . .
> to the owners' Hongkong agents that the owners were informed that as the engines were very

---

[11] Thus, a vessel was unseaworthy when she was unable to cope with stormy weather and rough seas:
Malayan Motor & General Underwriters (Pte) Ltd v MH Almojil [1982] 2 MLJ 2. See too *Zuellig (Gold Coin
Mills) v MV Autoly (The MV Katang)* [1970] SLR 427.

[12] (1877) 3 App Cas 72.

[13] See particularly at 90–91 (Lord Blackburn). See too *Gilroy, Sons & Co v WR Price & Co*
[1893] AC 56.

[14] *The Toledo* [1995] 1 Lloyd's Rep 40.

[15] *Charles Brown & Co v Nitrate Producers Steamship Co* (1937) 58 Ll LR 188 (although in this case
the owners were able to rely on a defence of latent defect under the Canadian Water Carriage of Goods Act
1910 — see too para 14.13).

[16] See Roger White, 'The human factor in unseaworthiness claims' [1995] LMCLQ 221.

[17] [1924] AC 100, 120–121.

[18] [1962] 2 QB 26.

old it was necessary to engage an engine room staff 'of exceptional ability, experience and dependability'.[19]

Although it is a requirement that the master and the crew must be competent there is no requirement that they must be perfect.[20] The requirement as to seaworthy equipment would extend to the provision of adequate bunkers for the intended voyage,[21] to cases where insufficient power caused serious fluctuations in temperature leading to 'shocked bananas',[22] and to cases where there is sludge present in the vessel's lubricating oil.[23] Also within the ambit of the vessel's equipment would be any cranes on board the vessel which are used for loading and offloading cargo.[24]

23.07 **Overloading and bad stowage** In some circumstances a vessel which is overloaded, or whose cargo has been improperly stowed, might be rendered unseaworthy. But not all cases of bad stowage will necessarily amount to unseaworthiness. Lord Sumner explained this in *Elder Dempster & Co Ltd v Paterson, Zachonis & Co Ltd*:

> Bad stowage, which endangers the safety of the ship, may amount to unseaworthiness, of course, but bad stowage, which affects nothing but the cargo damaged by it, is bad stowage and nothing more, and still leaves the ship seaworthy for the adventure, even though the adventure be the carrying of that cargo.[25]

In *The Thorsa*,[26] a cargo of cases of chocolate was stowed near gorgonzola cheese and became tainted by it. The Court of Appeal held that, as the vessel was fit to carry the chocolate when it was put on board, the damage caused to the chocolate was attributable to bad stowage and the shipowner was entitled to rely on an exception for bad stowage.[27] Swinfen Eady LJ explained that:

> The contention put forward really amounts to this, that if two parcels of cargo are so stowed that one can injure the other during the course of the voyage, the ship is unseaworthy. I am not prepared to accept that. It would be an extension of the meaning of 'unseaworthiness' going far beyond any reported case.[28]

In *Smith, Hogg & Co Ltd v Black Sea and Baltic General Insurance Co Ltd*[29] certain timber was shipped from Soroka aboard the *Lilburn* for delivery at Garston. The charterparty provided that the shipowner should not be liable for loss resulting from unseaworthiness, unless

[19] At 34. See the judgment also of Sellers LJ (at 56) and *The Makedonia* [1962] 1 Lloyd's Rep 316; *Robin Hood Flour Mills Ltd v NM Paterson & Sons Ltd (The Farrandoc)* [1967] 2 Lloyd's Rep 276; *Papera Traders Co Ltd v Hyundai Merchant Marine Co Ltd (The Eurasian Dream)* [2002] EWHC 118 (Comm); [2002] 1 Lloyd's Rep 719.
[20] *Rio Tinto Co Ltd v Seed Shipping Co* (1926) 42 TLR 381; *State Trading Corp of India v Doyle Carriers Inc (The Jute Express)* [1991] 2 Lloyd's Rep 55.
[21] *McIver v Tate Steamers* [1903] 1 KB 362; *Fiumana Societa di Navigazione v Bunge & Co Ltd* [1930] 2 KB 47.
[22] *Rey Banano del Pacifico CA v Transportes Navieros Ecuatorianos (The Isla Fernandina)* [2000] 2 Lloyd's Rep 15.
[23] *The Kriti Rex* [1996] 2 Lloyd's Rep 171.
[24] See *Parsons Corp v CV Scheepvaartonderneming (The Happy Ranger)* [2006] EWHC 122; [2006] 1 Lloyd's Rep 649.
[25] [1924] AC 522, 561–562. Followed in *A Meredith Jones & Co Ltd v Vangemar Shipping Co Ltd (The Apostolis) (No1)* [1997] 2 Lloyd's Rep 241 (CA). See also *Kish v Taylor* [1912] AC 604.
[26] [1916] P 257 (CA).
[27] See also *Bond, Connolly & Co v Federal Steam Navigation Co* (1906) 22 TLR 685.
[28] [1916] P 257 (CA), 262.
[29] [1940] AC 997.

caused by want of due diligence on the part of the shipowner to make his ship seaworthy, and act, neglect, or default of the master in the navigation or management of the ship. At the time of loading of the wood (known as 'St Petersburg standards'), which was to be carried on the deck of the *Lilburn*, the master had excluded 900 standards because the vessel was unstable and had listed five degrees to port. Within five days of sailing certain of the deck cargo had to be restowed because the list increased further. When the *Lilburn* put into Stornoway to take on additional bunkers she had to be beached and her deck cargo discharged. The House of Lords found that the shipowners had failed to make the ship seaworthy and so were liable for any loss or damage to the cargo of timber.

Relevant documentation   It will be a breach of the shipowner's seaworthiness obligation if   **23.08**
relevant documentation, charts, or navigational aids are not provided.[30] This requirement can be quite extensive and would extend to not getting a necessary health certificate from a port health authority, not being ISM compliant,[31] or not carrying a valid ISSC[32] certificate. Thus, in *Cheikh Boutros Selim El-Khoury v Ceylon Shipping Lines Ltd (The Madeleine)*, the ship did not possess a deratisation certificate[33] or an exemption certificate. Roskill J stated that:

> There was here an express warranty of seaworthiness and unless the ship was timeously delivered in a seaworthy condition, including the necessary certificate from the port health authority, the charterers had the right to cancel. That right, in my judgment, they possessed, and I think that the umpire was wrong in holding that they did not possess it.[34]

Cargoworthiness   In order to be seaworthy, it is further established that the vessel must   **23.09**
also be cargoworthy. The meaning of this requirement was set out by Brett J in the case of *Stanton v Richardson*:[35]

> It is found that the cargo offered was a reasonable cargo, and that the ship was not fit to carry a reasonable cargo . . . What then is the effect of these findings, considered with regard to the

---

[30] See, eg, *Papera Traders Co Ltd v Hyundai Merchant Marine Co Ltd (The Eurasian Dream)* [2002] EWHC 118 (Comm); [2002] 1 Lloyd's Rep 719.

[31] ie under the International Safety Management Code. At the time of the incident in *The Eurasian Dream* [2002] EWHC 118 (Comm); [2002] 1 Lloyd's Rep 719, the ISM Code was not mandatory for phase 2 ships, although it became mandatory with effect from 1 July 2002. On the evidence as presented in the case it is difficult to see that, even if she had held the relevant documentation, the *Eurasian Dream* would have passed muster as a seaworthy vessel. It would be a breach of the carrier's marine insurance cover not to have such certification: see, eg, the International Hull Clauses (1/11/03), cl 13.1.4 and 13.1.5.

[32] ie an International Ship Security Certificate, issued under the International Ship and Port Facility Security Code (ISPS Code). For full discussion of the ISPS Code, see Stephen Girvin, 'Commercial Implications of the ISPS Code' (2005) 330 Marius 307.

[33] ie a certificate confirming that the ship is free of rats. See the website of the Association of Port Heath Authorities in the United Kingdom which provides a list of the ports worldwide which require the relevant certificates: <www.apha.org.uk/pdiaotihr.html>.

[34] [1967] 2 Lloyd's Rep 224, 241. See *Toepfer v Tossa Marine (The Derby)* [1985] 2 Lloyd's Rep 325 (CA) where line 22 of the NYPE charter provided that 'vessel on her delivery to be ready to receive cargo . . . and in every way fitted for the service . . . (and with a full complement of officers, seamen . . .)'. The vessel was delayed at Leixoes (Portugal) when the ITF found that the vessel did not have and was not qualified for an ITF 'blue card' because the crew were not being paid at European rates of pay. Kerr LJ held that there was no scope for including an ITF blue card within the scope of the words in line 22. See too *Papera Traders Co Ltd v Hyundai Merchant Marine Co Ltd (The Eurasian Dream)* [2002] EWHC 118 (Comm); [2002] 1 Lloyd's Rep 719.

[35] (1872) LR 7 CP 421. Affirmed by the Exchequer Chamber: (1874) LR 9 CP 390. See also *Tattersall v The National Steamship Co Ltd* (1884) 12 QBD 297, 300 (Day J).

reciprocal duties arising between the charterer and shipowner from the mere fact of their having entered into an ordinary charterparty? It seems to me that the obligation of the shipowner is to supply a ship that is seaworthy in relation to the cargo which he has undertaken to carry.[36]

In this case the vessel was engaged to carry a cargo of sugar in bags but when wet sugar was loaded this gave off such a quantity of molasses in the hold that the vessel was rendered unseaworthy when the moisture could not be drained. Other cases have been concerned with refrigerated cargos. Thus, in the case of cargo which needs to be refrigerated, the equipment must be adequate.[37] Likewise, in the case of a vessel which has to carry live animals, the vessel must be free of disease.[38] Finally, it may be noted that, in order to be cargoworthy, the vessel must be able to discharge and deliver the cargo safely at its destination. This arose in *Empresa Cubana Importada de Alimentos Alimport v Iasmos Shipping Co SA (The Good Friend)* where a cargo of soyabean meal could not be offloaded because of infestation with insects. Staughton J stated that:

> The undertaking of seaworthiness at common law in my opinion includes, under the heading of what is sometimes called cargoworthiness, an undertaking that the ship shall be reasonably fit to receive and carry the cargo and deliver it at the specified destination. If the ship's condition is such that she is not reasonably fit for those tasks, the undertaking has been broken, even if the cargo suffers no physical damage and it is only the adventure that is lost.[39]

E. Extent of the Obligation

23.10 **Strict duty** At common law, the obligation of the shipowner to provide a seaworthy ship is an unconditional one and he will be absolutely liable, irrespective of fault, for any breach of the undertaking. Though sometimes described as an absolute 'warranty', this is somewhat misleading[40] in the modern context because the obligation is not an absolute promise or guarantee. In the context of a breach the obligation to provide a seaworthy vessel is neither a warranty nor a condition. Lord Blackburn in *Steel v State Line* described the seaworthiness obligation as amounting to an undertaking 'not merely that they [the owners] should do their best to make the ship fit, but that the ship should really be fit'.[41] In *McFadden Brothers & Co v Blue Star Line Ltd* Channell J stated that:

> [The] warranty is an absolute warranty; that is to say, if the ship is in fact unfit at the time when the warranty begins, it does not matter that its unfitness is due to some latent defect which the shipowner does not know of, and it is no excuse for the existence of such a defect

---

[36] At 435.

[37] See *Owners of Cargo on the Maori King v Hughes* [1895] 2 QB 550 (CA).

[38] See *Tattersall v National Steamship Co Ltd* (1884) 12 QBD 297; *Sleigh v Tyser* [1900] 2 QB 333.

[39] [1984] 2 Lloyd's Rep 586, 592. See also *Ciampa v British India Steam Navigation Co Ltd* [1915] 2 KB 774, 780 (Rowlatt J).

[40] See *Hongkong Fir Shipping Co Ltd v Kawasaki Kisen Kaisha Ltd* [1962] 2 QB 26 (CA). See also Treitel (2002), ch 3. Warranty has a very different meaning in the marine insurance context: see s 33(3) of the Marine Insurance Act 1906.

[41] (1877) 3 App Cas 72, 86.

that he used his best endeavours to make the ship as good as it could be made. And there is also another matter which seems to me to be equally clear — that the warranty of seaworthiness in the ordinary sense of that term, the warranty, that is, that the ship is fit to encounter the ordinary perils of the voyage, is a warranty only as to the condition of the vessel at a particular time, namely, the time of sailing; it is not a continuing warranty, in the sense of a warranty that she shall continue fit during the voyage.[42]

Time when obligation attaches   The absolute obligation of seaworthiness at common law **23.11** attaches at two points. It attaches at the commencement of loading when the ship must be fit to receive her cargo and fit as a ship for the ordinary perils of lying afloat in harbour while receiving her cargo.[43] Secondly, the ship must be fit in design, structure, condition, and equipment to encounter the ordinary perils of the voyage.[44] In *The Rona* Sir James Hannen stated that:

> . . . [T]he voyage must be considered to have commenced from the time when the ship started from whatever were her moorings, with her cargo on board, for the purpose of proceeding down the New York harbour and out to sea, and that therefore the warranty of seaworthiness had been fulfilled.[45]

These two requirements were encapsulated in *Virginia Carolina Chemical Co v Norfolk & North American Steam Shipping Co* when Kennedy LJ stated that:

> There is . . . in every contract with regard to the carriage of goods by sea an absolute warranty that the carrying vessel must, at the time sailing with the goods,[46] have that degree of fitness as regards both the safety of the ship and also the safe carriage of the cargo in the ship which an ordinary careful and prudent owner would require his vessel to have at the commencement of the voyage, having regard to the probable circumstances of that voyage and its nature.[47]

Not a continuing obligation   At common law the obligation which attaches at the com- **23.12** mencement of the voyage is not a continuing one. Thus, in *McFadden v Blue Star Line* Channell J stated that:

> The warranty . . . is a warranty only as to the condition of a vessel at a particular time, namely, the time of sailing; it is not a continuing warranty in the sense of a warranty that she shall continue fit during the voyage. If anything happens whereby the goods are damaged during the voyage, the shipowner is liable because he is an insurer, except in the event of the damage happening from some cause in respect of which he is protected by the exceptions . . .[48]

Standard expected   The standard of seaworthiness required is relative to the nature of the **23.13** ship, the voyage contracted for, and the particular stages of the voyage. Other considerations

---

[42] [1905] 1 KB 697, 703. See also *Virginia Carolina Chemical Co v Norfolk & North American Steam Shipping Co* [1912] 1 KB 229 (CA), 243 (Kennedy LJ).
[43] There is no implied obligation that the ship must be seaworthy on the approach voyage to the port: see *Compagnie Algerienne de Meunerie v Katana Societa di Navigazione Marittima SpA (The Nizeti)* [1960] 1 Lloyd's Rep 132 (CA), 137 (Hodson LJ).
[44] *Stanton v Richardson* (1872) LR 7 CP 421; *McFadden v Blue Star Line* [1905] 1 KB 697, 703–704 (Channell J).
[45] (1884) 51 LT 28, 30–31. This would also embrace the requirement that the vessel must have adequate bunker fuel on board for the voyage. See, eg, *McIver & Co Ltd v Tate Steamers Ltd* [1903] 1 KB 362 (CA), 366 (Mathew LJ).
[46] Note that this is not the case in respect of time charterparties. See para 23.23.
[47] [1912] 1 KB 229 (CA), 243–244.
[48] [1905] 1 KB 697, 703.

include whether the voyage is in summer or winter waters, while loading in harbour and when sailing. Seaworthiness may also vary with the particular cargo to be carried. Thus, in *President of India v West Coast Steamship Co (The Portland Trader)* Kilkenny DJ stated that:

> Although the duty to furnish a seaworthy ship is absolute and is a species of liability without fault, limited neither by concepts of negligence nor by those which might be contractual in nature . . . the obligation does not require the owner to furnish a ship or gear beyond that which is reasonably fit for the use intended. In other words, the standard is not an accident-free ship, nor an obligation to provide a ship or gear which might withstand all conceivable hazards. In the last analysis, the obligation, although absolute, means nothing more or less than the duty to furnish a ship and equipment reasonably suitable for the intended use or service.[49]

23.14 **Voyages in stages** In many instances voyages occur in stages and, in the case of the liner business, ships call at a series of ports in regular rotation.[50] However, stages may also occur naturally, as when the vessel has to sail along a river to reach the high seas.[51] In the latter type of case (and possibly in the former)[52] the common law requires that the vessel must be seaworthy at the beginning of each stage.[53] In the case of bunkering stops, the position is that the vessel must take on sufficient fuel to reach 'a particular convenient or usual bunkering port on the way'.[54] In such a case it is relatively clear that the ship must be seaworthy at the beginning of each stage. In *The Vortigern* AL Smith JA stated that:

> The only way in which this warranty can be complied with is for the shipowners to extend the existing warranty to the commencement of each stage, and I can see no reason why such a warranty should not be implied, and I have no difficulty in making the implication, for it is the only way in which the clear intention of the parties can be carried out, and the undoubted and admitted warranty complied with.[55]

In this case a vessel on a voyage from the Philippines to Liverpool was to call at Colombo and Suez. At Colombo she took on insufficient fuel to get her to Suez and her cargo of copra (dried coconut kernels) had to be burned as fuel. The Court of Appeal held that the shipowner was in breach of his obligation to provide a seaworthy vessel because she was not seaworthy at the beginning of the Colombo to Suez stage of the voyage.

F. Burden of Proof and Causation

23.15 **Burden of proof** The common law rule is that the burden of proving unseaworthiness lies on the claimant.[56] In some circumstances this burden of proof will be assisted if there

---

[49] [1963] 2 Lloyd's Rep 278, 280–281 (Dist Ct, Oregon).
[50] See para 1.03.
[51] See *Northumbrian Shipping Co Ltd v E Timm & Son Ltd* [1939] AC 397, 403–404 (Lord Wright).
[52] See *Maxine Footwear Co Ltd v Canadian Government Merchant Marine Ltd* [1959] AC 589 (PC), 604 (Lord Somervell): 'The doctrine of stages had its anomalies and some important matters were never elucidated by authority'.
[53] See *Biccard v Shepherd* (1861) 14 Moo PC 471; 15 ER 383; *Dixon v Sadler* (1839) 5 M&W 405; 151 ER 172; *Thin v Richards & Co* [1892] 2 QB 141 (CA).
[54] *Northumbrian Shipping Co Ltd v E Timm & Son Ltd* [1939] AC 397, 404 (Lord Wright).
[55] [1899] P 140, 155 (CA). See also Collins LJ at 159–160 and *McFadden Brothers & Co v Blue Star Line Ltd* [1905] 1 KB 697, 704 (Channell J). The obligation is the same with respect to consecutive voyage charters: see *Adamastos Shipping Co Ltd v Anglo-Saxon Petroleum Co Ltd* [1959] AC 133.
[56] See *Uni-Ocean Lines Pte Ltd v Kamal Sood (The Reunion)* [1983] 2 MLJ 189.

are facts which might give rise to an inference of unseaworthiness. Thus, in *Pickup v Thames & Mersey Insurance Co Ltd,* Cockburn CJ stated that:

> If a vessel very shortly after leaving port founders, or becomes unable to prosecute her voyage, in the absence of any external circumstances to account for such disaster or inability the irresistible inference arises, that her misfortune has been due to inherent defects existing at the time at which the risk attached. But this is not by reason of any legal presumption or shifting of the burden of proof, but simply as matter of reason and common sense brought to bear upon the question as one of fact, inasmuch as in the absence of every other possible cause the only conclusion, which can be arrived at, is that inherent unseaworthiness must have occasioned the result.[57]

Causation In order to succeed in a claim based on the unseaworthiness of the vessel, the **23.16** claimant must show that the unseaworthiness caused the loss. Thus, in *The Europa,* Bucknill J stated that:

> It appears to us, therefore, that whenever a cargo-owner has claimed damages from a shipowner for loss occasioned to his goods on the voyage, and the ship was in fact unseaworthy at the material time, the cargo-owner has had to prove that the loss was occasioned through or in consequence of the unseaworthiness, and it has not been sufficient to say merely that the ship was unseaworthy, and therefore that he was entitled to recover the loss, although there was no relation between the unseaworthiness and the damage.[58]

ISM Code A series of incidents involving roll-on/roll-off vessels in the 1980s and early **23.17** 1990s provide the background to the International Safety Management (ISM) Code. This was adopted by the International Maritime Organisation (IMO)[59] in 1995 and subsequently added to the SOLAS Convention as Chapter IX, 'Management for the safe operation of ships'.[60] The Code lays down detailed requirements for shipping companies which are required to develop, implement, and maintain a Safety Management System (SMS). Following an audit process the company will be issued with a Document of Compliance (DOC) and this must be kept on board the ship so that it can be produced for verification. Further, a Safety Management Certificate (SMC) will be issued to every ship which has verified that its shipboard management operates in accordance with the system.[61] The importance of this Code in seaworthiness cases should not be underestimated and it may well assist a claimant in proof of unseaworthiness, or absence of due diligence to provide a seaworthy ship,[62] if he can show a failure to comply with the Code or the absence of any relevant documentation.[63]

---

[57] (1878) 3 QBD 594 (CA), 597. See too *Lindsay v Klein (The Tatjana)* [1911] AC 194, 205 (Lord Shaw of Dunfermline).

[58] [1908] P 84, 97–98. See also *International Packers London Ltd v Ocean Steamship Co Ltd* [1955] 2 Lloyd's Rep 218.

[59] See <www.imo.org>.

[60] This entered into force on 1 July 1998 and was implemented in the United Kingdom in the Merchant Shipping (International Safety Management (ISM) Code) Regulations 1998, SI 1998/1561.

[61] Regulation 4(1),(2) & (3) of SOLAS ch 9.

[62] ie under the Hague and Hague–Visby Rules, article III, rule 1. See para 26.17.

[63] See, eg, *The Torepo* [2002] EWHC 1481 (Admlty); [2002] 2 Lloyd's Rep 535; *Papera Traders Co Ltd v Hyundai Merchant Marine Co Ltd (The Eurasian Dream)* [2002] EWHC 118 (Comm); [2002] 1 Lloyd's Rep 719.

G. Effect of Unseaworthiness

23.18 **Breach of an innominate term**   A breach of the implied obligation of unseaworthiness was confirmed as the breach of an innominate (or intermediate) term by the Court of Appeal in *Hongkong Fir Shipping Co v Kawasaki*.[64] While damages will always be available for a breach of the undertaking,[65] a charterer should only be allowed to repudiate his obligations under the charterparty where the breach deprived him 'of substantially the whole benefit which it was the intention of the parties they should obtain from further use of the vessel . . .'.[66] Everything would depend on the effects of the breach in each individual case and the test as to whether a party had been deprived of substantially the whole benefit of the contract should be the same whether it resulted from breach of contract by the charterer or from the operation of the doctrine of frustration.

23.19 **Breach before performance**   A distinction must also be drawn between the situation where the breach is discovered before performance of the charterparty has commenced and where the breach only comes to light once the vessel has sailed. In *Stanton v Richardson*,[67] bilge pumping equipment on the *Isle of Wight* was inadequate to deal with surplus water from a cargo of wet sugar. This affected the safety of the ship on the voyage and consequently her cargo was immediately discharged. The charterer was held entitled to repudiate the contract when it was established that new pumps could not be installed within a reasonable time. The owner was therefore liable to the charterer for failing to provide a vessel which was fit for the carriage of wet sugar.

23.20 **Breach after sailing**   What is the position where the unseaworthiness of the vessel is discovered after she sails on the contract voyage? This will usually be more relevant in the case of a time charterparty, but the position is that acceptance of the vessel does not amount to a waiver of the charterer's right to damages. Neither will it be a waiver of the charterer's right to repudiate the charterparty, provided that the breach is serious.

23.21 **Damages**   It will be clear that, if the effects of breach are less severe, the claimant will usually be restricted to a remedy sounding in damages. The consequences for the shipowner may also be more serious if the vessel is under charter. Thus, a relatively short delay may frustrate a voyage charterparty, but not a time charterparty. Consequently in *Hongkong Fir Shipping Co v Kawasaki*[68] the absence of a vessel for a period of five months while undergoing repairs did not frustrate a time charterparty, the duration of which was 24 months.

---

[64] [1962] 2 QB 26 (CA). See Brian Davenport, 'Some Thoughts on the Classification of Contract Terms' in Rose (2000), ch 1.

[65] This will be the invariable remedy when the goods are carried under a bill of lading.

[66] [1962] 2 QB 26 (CA), 73.

[67] (1872) LR 7 CP 421. Affirmed by the Exchequer Chamber: (1874) LR 9 CP 390.

[68] [1962] 2 QB 26 (CA).

H. Express Seaworthiness Clauses

Voyage charterparties Most voyage charterparties contain express provisions regarding   **23.22**
seaworthiness. In the Gencon (1994) form,[69] the first part of clause 2[70] provides that:

> The Owners are to be responsible for loss of or damage to the goods or for delay in delivery
> of the goods only in case the loss, damage or delay has been caused by personal want of due
> diligence on the part of the Owners or their Manager to make the Vessel in all respects sea-
> worthy and to secure that she is properly manned, equipped and supplied, or by the personal
> act or default of the Owners or their Manager.[71]

The main point to notice about this contractual obligation to provide a seaworthy ship is
that the clause operates in place of the implied obligation. The other particular point to
notice about the clause is that the obligation to provide a seaworthy ship and to ensure that
she is 'properly manned, equipped and supplied' is one of due diligence.[72] This is the same
as under the Hague and Hague–Visby Rules[73] and means that the obligation is not an
absolute one, as it would be at common law.[74]

Time charterparties Most time charterparties, like their voyage charterparty counter-   **23.23**
parts, invariably contain an express seaworthiness clause. However, unlike the position
under voyage charterparties and bills of lading, in a time charterparty the obligation at common law attaches at the commencement of hiring. In the case of *Giertsen v Turnbull & Co*[75]
Lord Ardwall stated that

> the implied warranty of seaworthiness was complied with when the vessel was handed over to
> the charterers in a seaworthy condition at the commencement of the period of hiring . . .[76]

Express clauses NYPE 93, clause 2 requires that the vessel 'on her delivery' should be   **23.24**
'tight, staunch and strong and in every way fitted for ordinary cargo service'.[77] The Baltime
form likewise provides that the vessel is warranted as 'being in every way fitted for cargo service'.[78] Each of these clauses imposes an express obligation of seaworthiness on the shipowner
and, as is the position with the voyage charterparty forms, the absolute obligation, which
would otherwise be implied at common law, falls away. It may be noted, however, that the
obligation is not one of 'due diligence' although that may be read into the charterparty if
there is a paramount clause.[79] In *Hongkong Fir Shipping Co Ltd v Kawasaki Kisen Kaisha*[80]

---

[69] See Appendix II.
[70] For full discussion of this clause, see Cooke (2001), ch 11.
[71] Lines 15–21. See *Eridania SpA v Rudolf A Oetker (The Fjord Wind)* [2000] 2 Lloyd's Rep 191 (CA),
which concerned the construction of a similar clause.
[72] As is the clause in Asbatankvoy: see cl 1.
[73] See the discussion at para 26.20.
[74] See para 23.10.
[75] 1908 SC 1101.
[76] At 1110.
[77] Lines 33–35. See Wilford (2003), para 8.4.
[78] Clause 2, lines 25–26. See too Shelltime 4, cl 1.
[79] See, eg, *The Torepo* [2002] EWHC 1481 (Admlty); [2002] 2 Lloyd's Rep 535. As to paramount clauses,
see para 19.51.
[80] [1962] 2 QB 26 (CA).

the words 'she being in every way fitted for cargo service' in clause 1 of a Baltime 1939 time charter were treated as forming part of an express warranty that the vessel was seaworthy and it was held that the warranty required the provision of a sufficient and competent crew to operate the vessel for the purposes of the charter service. In this case the *Hongkong Fir* had been chartered for a period of 24 months. On a voyage between Liverpool and Osaka she was at sea for over eight weeks, off-hire for about five weeks, and had £21,400 spent on her for various repairs. At Osaka a further 15 weeks and £37,000 were required to make her fit for her next voyage. Not unexpectedly, the charterers repudiated their charter contract and claimed damages for breach of contract. It had emerged that the complement of engine room staff was inadequate and that the chief engineer was addicted to drink and repeatedly neglected his duties.

23.25 **Continuing obligation**   Most time charterparties contain an additional clause which is not present in voyage charterparties, namely an ongoing obligation to provide a seaworthy vessel. This is provided as follows in the NYPE 93 form, at clause 6:

> The Owners . . . shall maintain the Vessel's class and keep her in a thoroughly efficient state in hull, machinery and equipment for and during the service, and have a full complement of officers and crew.[81]

In *Tyndale Steam Shipping Co Ltd v Anglo-Soviet Shipping Co Ltd* a similar clause was interpreted as follows by Lord Roche:

> . . . [I]t is sufficient to say that in my judgment there is no doubt that this stipulation . . . does not constitute an absolute engagement or warranty that the shipowners will succeed in so maintaining her whatever perils or causes may intervene to cause her to be inefficient for the purpose of her services.[82]

I. Exempting Clauses

23.26 **General principle**   Shipowners will often seek to contract out of their absolute obligation to provide a seaworthy ship. If so, the words used are fundamental. Thus, in *Sleigh v Tyser*, Bigham J stated that 'to exclude the implied warranty of seaworthiness the words used must be express, pertinent, and apposite'.[83] The underlying reason for this principle was further explained by Lord Sumner in *Atlantic Shipping and Trading Co Ltd v Louis Dreyfus & Co (The Quantock)*:

> Underlying the whole contract of affreightment there is an implied condition upon the operation of the usual exceptions from liability — namely, that the shipowners shall have provided a seaworthy ship. If they have, the exceptions apply and relieve them; if they have not, and damage results in consequence of the unseaworthiness, the exceptions are construed as not being applicable for the shipowners' protection in such a case.[84]

---

[81] Lines 81–82. See also Baltime (1939) cl 3, lines 40–41; Shelltime 4, cl 3. For discussion, see Wilford (2003), para 11.4.

[82] (1936) 54 Ll LR 341 (CA), 344–345. If appropriate words are used, the obligation may well be an absolute one. See Scrutton (1996), 363.

[83] [1900] 2 QB 333, 337–338. Citing *Quebec Marine Insurance Co v Commercial Bank of Canada* (1870) LR 3 PC 234, 242 (Lord Penzance).

[84] [1922] 2 AC 250, 260. See also *The Rossetti* [1972] 2 Lloyd's Rep 116, 118 (Brandon J).

Thus, we can see that underlying this statement of principle there is a requirement at common law that the absolute obligation may not be interfered with.[85]

Negligence exceptions   An exception clause which refers to negligence will likewise not   **23.27**
apply where loss or damage which is caused by unseaworthiness results from negligence.
Thus, in *Ingram and Royle Ltd v Services Maritimes du Tréport*[86] a clause provided that the
shipowners were absolved for:

> ... [A]ny act, neglect, or default whatsoever of the master, officers, crew, stevedores, servants,
> or agents of the owners ... in the management, loading, stowing ... or otherwise ...

Scrutton J emphasized that these exceptions would only apply if the ship was seaworthy.[87]

Exempting clauses and express undertakings   The discussion so far has focused on   **23.28**
exempting clauses and the implied obligation of seaworthiness. However, as we have now
seen, many charterparties commonly contain an express obligation as to seaworthiness. In
such a case the clause in question may be more narrow in scope than the common law obligation and it may then be possible for the shipowner to rely on an exception where the loss
or damage has resulted from unseaworthiness but where he has complied with the requirements of the express obligation. In *Cosmopolitan Shipping Co Inc v Hatton & Cookson (The
Rostellan)* Scrutton J explained that:

> ... [I]f the contract does limit the implied warranty of seaworthiness, that limitation must be
> given effect to; and if the shipowner proves himself within the limited warranty, the fact that
> he has not proved compliance with the unlimited warranty does not, in my opinion, destroy
> the limited warranty. If the implied warranty would be of A and B, and there is an express
> clause in the contract that the shipowner shall not be liable if B does not exist provided he
> complies with A, I cannot see how he can be liable for B.[88]

The Irbenskiy Proliv   A number of points discussed so far were considered in *Mitsubishi*   **23.29**
Corp v Eastwind Transport Ltd (The Irbenskiy Proliv).[89] The exemption clause this time
appeared on the reverse of a bill of lading and read as follows:

> 4. Carrier's exemption clause. Subject to clause 1 hereof the Carrier shall not be responsible
> for loss or damage to or in connection with the Goods of any kind whatsoever ... however
> caused (whether by unseaworthiness or unfitness of the vessel or any other vessel, tender,
> lighter or craft or any other mode of conveyance whatsoever or by faults, errors or negligence,
> or otherwise howsoever).
>
> In particular and without prejudice to the generality of the foregoing
>
> A. The Carrier shall be under no such responsibility:
>
> (i) at any time prior to the loading of the Goods on to and subsequent to the discharge of the
> Goods or part thereof from the vessel when but for the provisions of this clause such goods

---

[85] See *Nelson Line (Liverpool) Ltd v James Nelson & Sons Ltd* [1908] AC 16; *Sunlight Mercantile Pte Ltd v Ever Lucky Shipping Co Ltd* [2004] 1 SLR 171. See too Stephen Girvin, 'Exempting clauses and the obligation to provide a seaworthy vessel at common law' [2004] LMCLQ 297.
[86] [1913] 1 KB 538. Reversed on appeal on another point: see [1914] 1 KB 541 (CA).
[87] At 1 KB 538, 545, citing *The Glenfruin* (1885) LR10 PD 103 'and numerous other cases'.
[88] (1929) 35 Ll LR 117 (CA), 121. See also *Cargo ex Laertes* (1887) LR 12 PD 187.
[89] [2004] EWHC 2924; [2005] 1 Lloyd's Rep 383.

would be the responsibility of the Carrier and (ii) in the case of live animals or of cargo which in this Bill of Lading is stated as being carried on deck and is so carried none of which is subject to the Convention or legislation referred to in Clause 1 hereof at any time when, but for the provisions of this clause such goods would be the responsibility of the carrier.

The cargo claimant alleged that 109,344 cartons of frozen chicken parts were delivered in a damaged state because the vessel's refrigeration systems were not working and/or the vessel was unseaworthy and/or uncargoworthy. A preliminary issue now arose as to whether clause 4 exempted the shipowner from any potential liability. The shipowner argued that, in commercial matters, where risks were normally borne by insurers, the parties should be free to apportion risks as they thought fit. The cargo owner argued, contra, that the clause was so wide as to be repugnant to the whole purpose of the contract and should be rejected in its entirety.[90] The court was not, however, sympathetic to these arguments and considered that the clause did not operate to relieve the carrier of liability for any and every breach of contract but bore a restricted meaning. In particular Ian Glick QC[91] held that:

> [T]he principle that, in cases of doubt a contractual provision will be construed against the person who produced it, and for whose benefit it operates, does not extend to construing a contractual provision as widely as possible so as to render it repugnant to the main object of the contract read as a whole when it can be given a meaning consistent with that object.

This case is an important reminder that not all exemption clauses, wide though they may be, will necessarily be construed against the shipowner, particularly where there is no absolute obligation of seaworthiness.

---

[90] Relying on *Glynn v Margetson & Co* [1893] AC 351.
[91] Sitting as a Deputy High Court judge.

24

DEVIATION

A. Introduction

Overview   In this chapter we move on to a consideration of a further significant obliga- **24.01**
tion which falls on the shipowner, namely the obligation not to deviate.[1] Once described as
a 'long-standing feature of English maritime law'[2] we shall see that its origins are indeed
ancient but that its continuing importance is a matter of some criticism given a number of
contemporary developments.[3]

B. Meaning

Origins   The origins of the doctrine of deviation[4] have recently been shown authorita- **24.02**
tively to have existed, at least in maritime law texts, as early as the seventeenth century.[5]

---

[1] See, generally, Carver (2005), para 9-036; Scrutton (1996), art 127. This topic has attracted a significant
and important body of academic commentary. See Coote (1964), ch 6 and 'Deviation and the Ordinary Law'
in Rose (2000), ch 2; Steven F Friedell, 'The Deviating Ship' (1980–1981) Hastings LJ 1535; CP Mills, 'The
future of deviation in the law of the carriage of goods' [1983] LMCLQ 587; Charles Debattista,
'Fundamental Breach and Deviation in the Carriage of Goods by Sea' [1989] JBL 22; John Livermore,
'Deviation, Deck Cargo and Fundamental Breach' (1990) 2 JCL 241; Simon Baughen, 'Does deviation still
matter?' [1991] LMCLQ 70; FMB Reynolds, 'The Implementation of Private Law Conventions in English
Law: The Example of the Hague Rules' in Markesinis (1992), 1.

[2] Martin Dockray, 'Deviation: a doctrine all at sea?' [2000] LMCLQ 76.

[3] Even in 1940 one commentator stated that 'there is probably no example . . . of a salutary and necessary
principle being pushed to such absurd lengths as this': RST Chorley, 'Liberal trends in present-day commercial law' (1940) 3 MLR 272, 286. See too *Farr v Hain Steamship Co (The Tregenna)* 121 F 2d 940, 944 (1941)
(Learned Hand CJ).

[4] The word is said to derive from the Latin *de via* or 'from the way'. See 'Deviation in the law of shipping —
The United States, United Kingdom and Australia, a comparative study' (1976–1977) JILE 147, 148.

[5] William Welwod, *Abridgement of all Sea-Lawes* (1613).

It is, however, customary to trace its origins, in English law, to the case of *Davis v Garratt* where Chief Justice Tindal stated that

> ... the law does imply a duty in the owner of a vessel, whether a general ship or hired for the special purpose of the voyage, to proceed without unnecessary deviation in the usual and customary course.[6]

It is generally thought that the origins of the doctrine lie in marine insurance. When the ship deviates from the insured route the position used to be that she was from then on uninsured.[7] The problem today is less acute than this for two reasons. The first reason is that marine insurance policies contain so-called 'held-covered' clauses whereby the assured will be covered in the event of a deviation, on payment of an additional premium.[8] The second reason is that P & I insurers, although routinely excluding cover for liabilities, costs, and expenses arising out of deviation[9] will offer cover for certain additional risks, including deviation.[10]

24.03 **Usual and customary course** As we have seen, the obligation at common law is that the owner of a vessel impliedly undertakes to proceed in that ship by 'the usual and customary course'.[11] A deviation is therefore a deliberate and unjustifiable departure from whatever is the usual and customary course which the vessel must follow in getting from its loading port to the discharge port. In the absence of a standard form charterparty, which would make express provision for the route to be followed, it is usually said that the usual and proper route is the direct geographical route. In *Reardon Smith Line v Black Sea and Baltic General Insurance*[12] Lord Porter summarized the law on the route to be followed:

> It is the duty of a ship, at any rate when sailing upon an ocean voyage from one port to another, to take the usual route between those two ports. If no evidence be given, that route is presumed to be the direct geographical route but it may be modified in many cases, for navigational or other reasons, and evidence may always be given to show what the usual route is, unless a specific route be prescribed by the charterparty or bill of lading.
>
> It is not the geographical route but the usual route which has to be followed, though in many cases the one may be the same as the other. But the inquiry must always be, what is the usual route, and a route may become a usual route in the case of a particular line though that line is accustomed to follow a course which is not that adopted by the vessels belonging to other lines or to other individuals. It is sufficient if there is a well known practice of that line to call at a particular port.[13]

---

6 (1830) 6 Bing 716, 725; 130 ER 1456, 1460.
7 See *Rendall v Arcos* (1937) 43 Com Cas 1 (HL), 15 (Lord Wright); *Hain Steamship Co v Tate & Lyle* (1936) 55 Ll LR 159 (HL), 173 (Lord Atkin). For the marine insurance background, see Bennett (2006), para 18.34.
8 See *State Trading Corp of India Ltd v M Golodetz Ltd* [1989] 2 Lloyd's Rep 277 (CA), 289 (Lloyd LJ).
9 See, eg, Britannia P & I Club, Rule 19(ii); Gard Club, Rule 34.1(x); Standard Club, Rule 20.20 (and 20.21)(iv).
10 See, eg, Gard Club, Appendix I, r 2.
11 *Davis v Garratt* (1830) 6 Bing 716, 725; 130 ER 1456, 1460.
12 (1939) 64 Ll LR 229.
13 At 241.

As the dicta in this case indicates, the direct geographical route is the benchmark, but it will be open to the shipowner to show that a different route is the customary one.[14] In practice the course sailed between two ports may vary considerably for navigational reasons, such as the need to avoid inclement weather conditions or even the draught restrictions for a particular vessel. In the case of a voyage charterparty the vessel is not likely to have to call at any intermediate port, except perhaps for the purpose of bunkering.[15] In the case, however, of a vessel which is operating a liner trade, there will necessarily be calls at intermediate ports.[16] If a vessel deviates from the route because of negligence this will not be a deviation[17] and the shipowner would be able to raise the defence of negligence in navigation.[18]

Bunkers   A departure from the direct route in order to take on bunkers may be justified. **24.04** Thus, in *Reardon Smith Line v Black Sea and Baltic General Insurance*[19] the *Indian City* was chartered to proceed from a Black Sea port (either Nicolaieff or Poti, as ordered) to Sparrow Point in the USA with a cargo of ore. After departure from Poti, the vessel deviated from the direct geographical route in order to bunker in Constanza (an extra distance of 193 miles), where cheap supplies of oil fuel were available. The *Indian City* grounded in Constanza. On proof that vessels engaged in that trade invariably put into Constanza and that 25 per cent of ocean-going oil-burning vessels passing through the Bosphorous followed a similar practice, the House of Lords held that there had been no deviation from the normal route.[20]

Special clauses   As we have now seen, there can be difficulties with an obligation which **24.05** is linked to performance of a voyage via the most direct geographical route. For this reason, it is not uncommon for the contract of carriage to specify that the shipowner can follow a route other than the most direct one between two ports. An example of such a clause is clause 5 of Conlinebill 2000,[21] which reads as follows:

The Scope of Carriage
The intended carriage shall not be limited to the direct route but shall be deemed to include any proceeding or returning to or stopping or slowing down at or off any ports or places for any reasonable purpose connected with the carriage including bunkering, loading, discharging, or other cargo operations and maintenance of Vessel and crew.

C. Justifiable Deviations

Introduction   In certain circumstances at common law, departure from the proper route **24.06** is permissible. The two main situations are deviating to save human life and for the purpose of avoiding danger to the ship or cargo. We shall look at each of these in turn.

---

[14] See too *Achille Lauro Fu Gioacchino & Co v Total Societa Italiana Per Azioni* [1969] 2 Lloyd's Rep 65 (CA), 67–68 (Lord Denning MR).

[15] See para 24.04.

[16] See *James Morrison & Co Ltd v Shaw, Savill & Albion Co Ltd* [1916] 2 KB 783 (CA), 797 (Phillimore LJ); *Frenkel v MacAndrews & Co Ltd* [1929] AC 545.

[17] See *Rio Tinto Co Ltd v Seed Shipping Co Ltd* (1926) 24 Ll LR 316.

[18] See, eg, Hague and Hague–Visby Rules, art IV, r 2(a). See para 28.07.

[19] (1939) 64 Ll LR 229.

[20] But cf *Thiess Bros (Queensland) Pty Ltd v Australian Steamships Pty Ltd* [1955] 1 Lloyd's Rep 459.

[21] See Appendix II.

24.07 **Saving human life**   It has long been recognized that there will be no deviation where a decision is made to assist others in peril on the seas. The leading case is *Scaramanga v Stamp* where Cockburn CJ said that:

> Deviation for the purpose of saving life is protected and involves neither forfeiture of insurance nor liability to the goods' owner in respect of loss which would otherwise be within the exceptions of 'perils of the seas'. And, as a necessary consequence of the foregoing, deviation for the purposes of communicating with a ship in distress is allowable, inasmuch as the state of the vessel in distress may involve danger to life. On the other hand, deviation for the sole purpose of saving property is not thus privileged, but entails all the usual consequences of deviation.
>
> If, therefore, the lives of the persons on board a disabled ship can be saved without saving the ship, as by taking them off, deviation for the purpose of saving the ship will carry with it all the consequences of an unauthorised deviation.[22]

In this case, the *Olympias*, which had been chartered to carry a cargo of wheat from Cronstadt to Gibraltar, deviated to save another, the *Arion*, which was in distress following a breakdown in her machinery. However, instead of only attempting to save the crew, the *Olympias* also tried to earn salvage by towing the *Arion* into the port of Texel. While attempting the towage, the *Olympias* herself grounded and was lost with all her cargo. In these circumstances, the Court of Appeal found that the deviation was unjustifiable, and that the claimant charterers were entitled to recover the value of the cargo against the defendants as owners of the ship.

24.08 **Statutory duty**   Many countries now impose a statutory obligation to save life at sea, particularly in situations of distress. In the UK, section 93(1) of the Merchant Shipping Act 1995 provides that:

> The master of a ship, on receiving at sea a signal of distress or information from any source that a ship or aircraft is in distress, shall proceed with all speed to the assistance of the persons in distress (informing them if possible that he is doing so) unless he is unable, or in the special circumstances of the case considers it unreasonable or unnecessary, to do so, or unless he is released from this duty under subsection (4) or (5) below.[23]

The duty in section 93 is imposed on the masters of United Kingdom ships and on the masters of foreign ships when in United Kingdom waters.[24] The consequences for a breach of the obligation can include, for a summary conviction, imprisonment for a term not exceeding six months, or a fine not exceeding the statutory miniumum, 'or both'. For a conviction on indictment, the penalty is imprisonment for a term not exceeding two years, or a fine, 'or both'.[25] The ambit of this statutory obligation and its consequences is, however, limited as it does not extend to events occurring on the high seas, outside the territorial sea.

---

[22] (1880) 5 CPD 295 (CA), 304.
[23] ie if he is informed by the persons in distress, or by the master of any ship that has reached the persons in distress, that assistance is no longer required.
[24] Section 93(3).
[25] Section 93(6).

Avoiding danger to ship or cargo   The master of a vessel may justifiably deviate from the   **24.09**
proper course in order to ensure the safety of the vessel and its cargo. The dangers to the
vessel may result from natural causes, such as storms, ice, or fog, or political factors, such as
the outbreak of war[26] or the fear of capture by hostile forces. The danger must, however, be
of a reasonably permanent nature. Thus, in an old Pennsylvania case, *Hand v Baynes*,[27]
Rogers J stated that:

> The Court are . . . of the opinion, that the clause in the receipt, 'the dangers of the
> navigation', does not apply to dangers caused by the canal's being, by inevitable accident,
> rendered impassable. Occasional interruptions of trade, arising from breaches in
> canals, or other accidents, are inconveniences, but in no sense can they be considered
> as dangers of the navigation, coming within the exception. The contract excepts the
> dangers by the navigation on the route of the canal, and when there may be such a danger
> as is provided for, it will be time enough to decide when it arises. By an alteration
> of the voyage, the shipper was exposed to risks which he would not have voluntarily
> encountered.

Kish v Taylor   The case of *Kish v Taylor*[28] is an illustration of a case where a vessel, for   **24.10**
safety reasons, put into port for repairs to damage sustained on the voyage occasioned
by unseaworthiness. The *Wearside* was chartered to load a full and complete cargo of
timber at Mobile or Pensacola. The charterers failed to provide a full cargo[29] so the
master sought to mitigate the owners' loss by obtaining additional cargo. The *Wearside*
became overloaded with deck cargo but left the port. On encountering bad weather
she had to take refuge in Halifax for repairs and restowage of her cargo. The respondent's portion of the cargo arrived undamaged at Liverpool, the contractual port of
discharge. The shipowners claimed a lien on the cargo for dead freight[30] in respect of
the charterers' failure to provide a full cargo but the cargo owners disputed the existence
of the lien, arguing that the deviation to Halifax was unjustifiable.[31] Lord Atkinson
stated that:

> On the whole, I am of opinion that a master, whose ship is, from whatever cause, in a perilous
> position, does right in making such a deviation from his voyage as is necessary to save his ship
> and the lives of his crew, and that while the right to recover damages from all breaches of con-
> tract, and all wrongful acts committed either by himself or by the owners of his ship, is pre-
> served to those who are thereby wronged or injured, the contract of affreightment is not put
> at an end to by such a deviation . . .[32]

Risk to cargo alone   It seems to be reasonably clear that a deviation may be justified where   **24.11**
the risk to be avoided affects the ship and not the cargo. If the effects are to the cargo alone,
the law is rather less certain.[33]

---

[26] See *Duncan v Köster (The Teutonia)* (1872) LR 4 PC 171.
[27] (1839) 4 Wharton 204.
[28] [1912] AC 604.
[29] See para 30.28.
[30] See para 21.32.
[31] For the consequences of a deviation, see para 24.16.
[32] [1912] AC 604, 618. See too *James Phelps & Co v Hill* [1891] 1 QB 605 (CA).
[33] There is no requirement for the master to deviate for the sole purpose of saving a part of the cargo: see
Notara v Henderson (1870) LR 5 QB 346.

D. Liberty Clauses

24.12 **Introduction** Departure from an ascertained route may be justified by express clauses, known as 'liberty' or 'deviation' clauses. A typical example of such a clause is clause 3 of the Gencon 1994 form:

> The Vessel has liberty to call at any port or ports in any order, for any purpose, to sail without pilots, to tow and/or assist Vessels in all situations, and also to deviate for the purpose of saving life and/or property.[34]

It is well established that such liberty clauses must be interpreted so as to be consistent with the contemplated voyage. In the case of *Frenkel v MacAndrews & Co Ltd*[35] Viscount Sumner said that

> the principle [is] that these two parts of the bill of lading, the described voyage and the liberty to deviate, must be read together and reconciled, and that a liberty, however generally worded, could not frustrate but must be subordinate to the described voyage.[36]

The reason for this type of approach is clear; such a clause, were it literally applied, could have far-reaching effects for the charterer or the holder of a bill of lading.

24.13 *Glynn v Margetson* In *Glynn v Margetson & Co*[37] a cargo of oranges was shipped on the *Zena* under a bill of lading on a printed form which showed that the vessel was lying in the port of Malaga, bound for Liverpool. The printed form provided that she had

> liberty to proceed to and stay at any ports in any rotation in the Mediterranean, Levant, Black Sea or Adriatic, or on the coasts of Africa, Spain, Portugal, France, Great Britain and Ireland, for the purpose of delivering coals, cargo or passengers, or for any other purpose whatsoever.[38]

On leaving Malaga the *Zena* did not sail towards Liverpool but sailed first to Burriana, about 350 miles from Malaga on the east coast of Spain.[39] The oranges arrived damaged at Liverpool because of the delay. The House of Lords found that the main object and intent of the contract was the carriage of perishable cargo from Malaga to Liverpool. Since the general words in the printed form would defeat the main purpose of the contract if given full effect, the words were to be given a more limited construction or, if this was not possible, the general words were to be rejected. On the facts, the general words only entitled the owners to call (for the purposes stated) at ports in which in a business sense could be said to be on the voyage between Malaga and Liverpool. Lord Herschell LC explained that:

> . . . [I]f the meaning to be given to those words is that the vessel may take those ports in any order she pleases in a reasonable sense, nevertheless the ports referred to must still, in my

---

[34] Lines 28–31. For other charterparty clauses, see eg Asbatankvoy, cl 20(vii); NYPE 93, cl 22; Shelltime 4, cl 27(b). See Appendix II.

[35] [1929] AC 545.

[36] At 562.

[37] [1893] AC 351 (HL).

[38] The last clause of the bill of lading ran thus: 'Notice — In accepting this bill of lading the shipper or other agent of the owner of the property carried expressly accepts and agrees to all its stipulations, exceptions and conditions, whether written or printed.'

[39] ie in the opposite direction to the voyage to Liverpool.

opinion, be ports lying between Malaga and the port of destination, Liverpool, even although there might be a justification for her not touching at any particular one of those ports, or more than one of them, in the exact order in which they would come in the voyage between those two places. It is not necessary to decide what effect should be given to those words 'in any rotation'; but even giving to them the fullest possible effect they do not seem to me to enlarge the number of ports at which it would be justifiable for this vessel to touch during the course of her voyage.[40]

Special clauses   The effect of the decision in the above case may be negated by the   **24.14** presence of a clause which makes it clear that the shipowner is not restricted to ports in their geographical routing. Thus in *Connolly Shaw Ltd v A/S Det Nordenfjeldske D/S* [41] a contract for the carriage of a cargo of lemons from Palermo to London provided that the vessel had liberty

> either before or after proceeding towards the port of delivery of the said goods, to proceed to or return to and stay at any ports or places whatsoever (although in a contrary direction to or out of or beyond the route of the said port of delivery) once or oftener in any order, backwards or forwards, for loading or discharging cargo . . .

The *Ragnvald Jarl* proceeded first to Valencia to load potatoes and then direct to Hull to discharge them, before finally steaming for London to discharge the cargo of lemons. Branson J held that the clause gave the ship liberty to call at any port or ports, whether beyond the route of the port of delivery or not, which she could call at in the course of her voyage without frustrating the object of the voyage, namely the safe carriage of a perishable cargo.[42]

Other special liberties   As no two charterparties or bills of lading are the same, it is possi-   **24.15** ble in a liberty clause to make provision for any number of eventualities, including the possibility of strikes. Thus, in *GH Renton & Co Ltd v Palmyra Trading Corp of Panama (the Caspiana)*[43] a cargo of timber was shipped from Nanaimo in British Columbia under bills of lading stipulating carriage to 'London or Hull or so near thereunto as the vessel may safely get . . .'.[44] The direct contractual route was not specified. A liberty clause in the bill of lading (clause 14(c)) provided that

> should it appear that . . . strikes . . . would prevent the vessel from . . . entering the port of discharge or there discharging in the usual manner and leaving again . . . safely and without delay, the Master may discharge the cargo at port of loading or any safe and convenient port . . .

During the course of the voyage, strikes broke out both at the port of London and at Hull and the shipowners therefore ordered the vessel to proceed to Hamburg and discharge the cargo of timber there. The plaintiffs (who were endorsees of the bill of lading) claimed

---

[40] [1893] AC 351 (HL), 356. See too *Leduc v Ward* (1888) 20 QBD 475 (CA), discussed further at para 7.11.

[41] (1934) 49 Ll LR 183.

[42] At 191. See too *Evans, Sons & Co v Cunard Steamship Company Ltd* (1902) 18 TLR 374; *Hadji Ali Akbar & Sons Ltd v Anglo-Arabian and Persian Steamship Company Ltd* (1906) 11 Com Cas 219; *Frenkel v MacAndrews & Co Ltd* [1929] AC 545.

[43] [1956] 1 QB 462 (CA).

[44] This is a typical 'near' clause, which is found in many voyage charterparties: see para 30.20.

damages for breach of contract. Jenkins LJ distinguished clause 14(c) from *Glynn v Margetson*[45] as follows:

> It seems to me that there is a material difference between a deviation clause purporting to enable the shipowners to delay indefinitely the performance of the contract voyage simply because they choose to do so, and provisions such as those contained in cl 14(c) . . . which are applicable and operative only in emergencies. The distinction is between a power given to one of the parties which, if construed literally, would in effect enable that party to nullify the contract at will, and a special provision stating what the rights and obligations of the parties are to be in the event of obstacles beyond the control of either arising to prevent or impede the performance of the contract in accordance with its primary aim.

As to which ports may be 'substantially on the course of a voyage' or 'in a business sense on the way' there may clearly be some debate.[46]

E. Effect of Unjustifiable Deviation

24.16   **Damages**   At its most basic, an unjustified deviation will attract an award of damages in favour of the party who has suffered loss thereby. In *Koufos v C Czarnikow Ltd (The Heron II)*,[47] the leading case on remoteness of damage in contract,[48] there was a deviation under a charterparty. The terms of the charterparty provided that after loading sugar at Constanza the *Heron II* was to proceed with all convenient speed to Basrah. The ship called at several ports en route to Basrah, taking nine days longer to arrive than it would have done had she sailed directly to Basrah. During this period the price of sugar fell, such that the respondents' sugar was sold for less than it would have been had it arrived promptly. Although the appellant did not know that the respondents intended to sell the sugar promptly on arrival, it admitted that the delay was in breach of the charterparty. The House of Lords held that the appellant ought to have foreseen that delay would involve a serious possibility of a real danger that the price of sugar would decline and awarded damages, being the difference between the price which the sugar ought to have fetched if it had arrived on time and the price which it in fact fetched.

24.17   **Other consequences**   The further consequences which follow from an unjustified deviation are much more difficult to rationalize. In summary, these may include: (1) a displacement of the contract, such that the shipowner loses the benefit of all the clauses in the contract which are for his benefit; (2) a discharge of the contract by breach. We shall now look at each of these possibilities in turn.

24.18   **Displacement of the contract**   There is a very long line of cases which are to the effect that, from the moment that the ship departs from the contract route, the shipowner loses the benefit of clauses which exempt him from liability. Thus, in *James Morrison v Shaw, Savill & Albion*[49] a shipowner was held unable to rely on the exception of King's enemies[50]

---

[45] [1893] AC 351 (HL). See para 24.13.
[46] See, eg, *James Morrison v Shaw, Savill & Albion* [1916] 1 KB 783 (CA).
[47] [1969] 1 AC 350.
[48] See, eg, Treitel (2003), 966.
[49] [1916] 1 KB 783 (CA).
[50] See now art IV, r 2(f) of the Hague and Hague–Visby Rules: para 28.26.

after having been sunk by an enemy submarine during World War I. This occurred when the *Tokomaru* deviated 107 miles on a 12,000 mile journey to deliver other cargo. Thus, the sinking occurred while the vessel was in the 'act' of deviating. However, it seems that the displacement consequences follow even after the deviation has finished.

Joseph Thorley In *Joseph Thorley Ltd v Orchis Steamship Co Ltd*[51] 897 tons of locust beans **24.19** were shipped aboard the *Orchis* from Limassol to the Port of London. The bills of lading contained an exception clause which exempted the shipowners from liability for loss arising from:

> Any act, neglect, or default whatsoever of the pilot, master, officers, engineers, crew, stevedores, servants, or agents of the owners, in the management, loading, stowing, discharging, or navigation of the ship, or otherwise.

After loading the cargo, the *Orchis* proceeded to London via Asia Minor, Palestine, and Malta. When the beans were unloaded in London it was found that they had been damaged owing to contact with poisonous earth known as terra umber which was stowed elsewhere on the ship and that this had occurred at discharge. The court held that the shipowners were liable in damages and that their deviation had displaced the contract such that they could not rely on the exemption clause. Lord Collins MR stated that:

> The principle . . . seems to be that the undertaking not to deviate has the effect of a condition, or a warranty in the sense in which the word is used in speaking of the warranty of seaworthiness, and, if that condition is not complied with, the failure to comply with it displaces the contract. It goes to the root of the contract . . . [The] shipowner cannot set up the exception clause in the bill of lading contract, which only exists for his benefit, if he has not performed a condition precedent upon which his right to rely on that contract depends.[52]

The outcome in this case produces extreme consequences for the shipowner and the reasoning in it is generally thought to be unsatisfactory, by modern standards, and should be rejected.[53] It has never been overruled.

Wider displacement consequences The authorities discussed so far embody the princi- **24.20** ple that, from the moment of the deviation, the contract is displaced such that the shipowner loses the protection of clauses which are in his favour. This was taken to an even further extreme, however, in the case of *US Shipping Board v Bunge y Born*[54] where it was held that a right to demurrage at the port of discharge was lost because this had occurred after the deviation.[55] Other consequences, such as the question as to whether freight is payable,[56] were not resolved by this group of cases.

Discharge by breach In *Hain Steamship Co v Tate & Lyle*[57] the House of Lords formally **24.21** considered the deviation doctrine for the first time. A vessel called the *Tregenna* was

---

[51] [1907] 1 KB 660 (CA). See the detailed analysis of this case by FMB Reynolds in Markesinis (1992), 34.
[52] At 667–668. Relying on the poorly reported case of *Balian v Joly, Victoria & Co* (1890) 6 TLR 345.
[53] Carver (2005), para 9-053.
[54] (1925) 42 TLR 174.
[55] Demurrage earned at the port of loading was not lost, because this was earned before the deviation occurred. Generally as to demurrage, see para 31.56.
[56] ie assuming that the contract of carriage provides for the payment of freight in a lump sum on delivery of the cargo. See para 21.25.
[57] (1936) 55 Ll LR 159 (HL).

chartered to proceed to the West Indies and load a cargo of sugar at two ports in Cuba (Casilda and Santiago) and also one port in San Domingo to be nominated by the charterer. The charterer made the required nominations but, owing to a failure of communication by the owners' agents, the master was not informed of the nominated port in San Domingo, San Pedro de Macoris. Consequently, once the cargoes had been loaded at the two Cuban ports, the master proceeded to Queenstown to await further instructions. Shipowners and charterers soon discovered the error and the master was ordered back to San Domingo to load the remaining cargo. On leaving the port in San Domingo, the vessel ran aground and part of the cargo was lost, the remainder being transhipped on the *Baron Dalmeny* for completion of the voyage to the United Kingdom. Shortly before the vessel arrived at its destination the bills of lading covering the cargo were endorsed to Tate & Lyle who took delivery of the cargo in apparent ignorance of the deviation. The House of Lords decided that the deviation constituted a 'fundamental breach of contract' entitling the cargo owners to treat the contract as repudiated. Lord Atkin stated that:

> I venture to think that the true view is that the departure from the voyage contracted to be made is a breach by the shipowner of his contract, a breach of such a serious character that, however slight the deviation, the other party to the contract is entitled to treat it as going to the root of the contract, and to declare himself as no longer bound by any of the contract terms.
>
> If this view be correct, then the breach by deviation does not automatically cancel the express contract, otherwise the shipowner by his own wrong can get rid of his own contract.[58]

Thus, on this view, the consequences of an unjustifiable deviation were markedly different from those espoused in *Joseph Thorley Ltd v Orchis Steamship Co Ltd*.[59] In particular the innocent party would have an election as to whether he was to be bound by the contract. He could, if he desired, treat himself as no longer bound or he could elect to maintain the contract, reserving his right to damages.[60]

24.22   **The effects of waiver**   The charterers in *Hain Steamship Co v Tate & Lyle*[61] had, with full knowledge of the facts, elected to waive the breach. They had affirmed the contract by ordering the vessel back to San Domingo. As the aggrieved party, said Lord Atkin 'the cargo owner can elect to treat the contract as subsisting; and if he does this with full knowledge of his rights, he must in accordance with the general law of contract be held bound'.[62] In these circumstances the shipowners, in the event of any claim being made by the charterers, would be entitled to rely for protection on any exception clauses, including for perils of the sea.[63] But on the facts of the case, the bills of lading had been endorsed to the claimants. The House of Lords held that they were not bound by any waiver on the part of the charterers and, for this reason, the shipowners were unable to rely on the bill of lading exceptions as a defence to any cargo claim brought by the consignees. A further issue in the

---

[58] At 173–174.

[59] [1907] 1 KB 660 (CA). See para 24.19.

[60] See too the judgment of Lord Wright: (1936) 55 Ll LR 159 (HL), 178.

[61] (1936) 55 Ll LR 159 (HL).

[62] At 174.

[63] For perils of the sea, see now art IV, r 2(c) of the Hague and Hague–Visby Rules and the discussion at para 28.18.

case concerned the entitlement of the shipowners to freight, but that has already been discussed elsewhere.[64]

Hain summarized   The effect of this decision may be summarized thus. A shipowner whose ship deviates unjustifiably breaches a 'fundamental' condition of the contract arising from a breach of the contract in a way not contemplated by the contract. The innocent party could either treat the breach as a repudiation bringing the contract to an end or he could elect to waive the deviation and treat the contract as still subsisting, reserving his right to damages. In the latter case, all the terms of the contract would still remain in force and the shipowner would be able both to enforce any rights arising out of the contract and rely on any exception clause which may be applicable to a casualty occurring before or after the deviation, and would be liable only for damages resulting from the deviation itself.   **24.23**

'Fundamental' breach reasoning   The matter cannot be left there because *Hain Steamship Co v Tate & Lyle*[65] and the doctrine of breach of a fundamental obligation there espoused was later developed by the courts in the context of cases falling within the general law of contract.[66] The main impetus for the development of the so-called 'substantive doctrine' of fundamental breach was judicial concern that injustices were being caused by standard written terms used by traders. However, it has been shown that the early cases did not involve a constructive analysis of the exempting clauses[67] and hence, applied to commercial transactions, the doctrine was bound to upset what was a reasonable allocation of contractual risks. If the breach was considered 'fundamental' then any exemptions in the contract were irrelevant, whether or not they actually covered the breach. There were a number of difficulties with this doctrine, however. In the first place, it was founded on the destruction of the contract *ab initio* from the moment that the breach of contract occurred — and, as one writer has pointed out, this was a contradiction of general contract theory.[68] The second, more fundamental, objection was the issue of whether the doctrine was a substantive rule of law, which applies regardless of the original intentions of the parties to the contract, or a rule of construction. This was squarely addressed in *Suisse Atlantique Société d'Armement Maritime SA v NV Rotterdamsche Kolen Centrale*[69] where the House of Lords considered that the correct approach to fundamental breach was constructive and that exempting clauses were to be viewed in the context of the entire contract. This position was reiterated in *Photo Production Ltd v Securicor (Transport)*[70] where Lord Wilberforce indicated that, since the passage of the Unfair Contract Terms Act 1977 (UCTA), the doctrine of fundamental breach of contract had been rendered superfluous. Thus, for the general law of contract, exemption clauses stand or fall on their construction, considering all the circumstances of the contract.[71]   **24.24**

---

[64] See para 21.14.

[65] (1936) 55 Ll LR 159 (HL).

[66] Treitel (2003), 225.

[67] See CP Mills, 'The future of deviation in the law of the carriage of goods' [1983] LMCLQ 587.

[68] See Brian Coote, 'The Second Rise and Fall of Fundamental Breach' (1981) ALJ 788.

[69] [1967] 1 AC 361.

[70] [1980] AC 827. Described as the case in which the fundamental breach doctrine was given its 'formal burial': *Daewoo Heavy Industries Ltd v Klipriver Shipping Ltd (The Kapitan Petko Voivoda)* [2003] EWCA Civ 451; [2003] 2 Lloyd's Rep 1, at [10] (Longmore LJ).

[71] See too *Thomas National Transport v May & Baker* (1966) 115 CLR 353, 376 (Windeyer J).

24.25 **A special rule for deviation?**   However, what the House of Lords did not do in the above two cases was to cast doubt on, inter alia, the deviation cases. Lord Wilberforce in *Photo Production Ltd v Securicor (Transport)*[72] was merely of the opinion that the deviation cases should be 'considered as a body of authority sui generis with special rules derived from historical and commercial reasons'.[73]

24.26 **Quasi deviations**   There is a growing body of case law, much more widely developed in the USA, which equates other types of breaches by the shipowner as amounting to a deviation.[74] Of particular interest for English law has been a number of decisions concerned with deck carriage.[75] Deck carriage has, since the advent of containerization,[76] become an increasingly common phenomenon. On one view the carriage of such cargoes on deck presents a modern-day argument for the retention of the special arguments which are made for deviation in the sense that carriage on deck,[77] especially in breach of an agreement to the contrary, does expose cargo to the risk of exposure to the elements, particularly sea water. However, it is difficult to suggest that there should be an extension of the English doctrine of deviation. Although it is established that deck carriage amounts to a breach of contract[78] it is undecided whether the carriage of containers on deck will always amount to a breach of contract. In most cases, the shipowner is likely to be protected by an express clause, such as clause 16(b) of Conlinebill 2000:

> The Carrier shall have the right to carry containers, trailers, transportable tanks and covered flats, whether stowed by the Carrier or received by him in a stowed condition from the Merchant, on or under deck without notice to the Merchant.

24.27 **The current law**   There have been no new cases on deviation in English law which have begun to resolve the difficulties hinted at earlier. However, two quasi-deviation[79] cases have suggested that the deviation cases have not survived the demise of the fundamental breach doctrine. The first of these was *Kenya Railways v Antares Co Pte Ltd (The Antares Nos 1 & 2)*.[80] Certain machinery was shipped on deck for carriage from Antwerp to Mombasa and was seriously damaged in the course of the voyage. The bills of lading included a demise clause[81] but the claimants instituted their claim against the charterers, MSC. When a claim was eventually brought against the owners of the vessel they asserted that the claim was time barred. The claimants sought a declaration that the owners were in fundamental breach of contract by stowing the goods on deck and that this precluded the owners from relying on the one year time bar in the Hague–Visby Rules.[82] Lloyd LJ reiterated that the doctrine of

---

[72] [1980] AC 827.

[73] At 845. See too *State Trading Corp of India Ltd v M Golodetz Ltd* [1989] 2 Lloyd's Rep 277, 287 (Kerr LJ).

[74] See Schoenbaum (2004), 714. See too Theodora Nikaki, 'The Quasi-Deviation Doctrine' (2004) 35 JMLC 45.

[75] See James B Wooder, 'Deck Cargo: Old Vices and New Law' (1991) 22 JMLC 131.

[76] See para 1.14.

[77] Cargo carried on deck may not be subject to the Hague and Hague–Visby Rules as well. See para 19.28.

[78] See *Royal Exchange Shipping Co v WJ Dixon & Co* (1886) 12 App Cas 11.

[79] ie cases which did not concern a deviation from the geographical route.

[80] [1987] 1 Lloyd's Rep 424 (CA).

[81] As to demise clauses, see para 12.12.

[82] Article III, r 6. See para 34.04.

fundamental breach of contract, which displaced exception clauses altogether, no longer existed. Turning to the question of whether deviation cases may have survived those decisions of the House of Lords, Lloyd LJ said the following:

> Whatever may be the position with regard to the deviation cases strictly so called (I would myself favour the view that they should now be assimilated into the ordinary law of contract), I can see no reason for regarding the unauthorised loading of deck cargo as a special case . . . The sole question therefore is whether, on its true construction, art III, r 6 applies. It is clear that it does. It provides that the carrier shall in any event be discharged from all liability whatsoever unless suit is brought within one year.[83]

Subsequently, in a package limitation case,[84] *Daewoo Heavy Industries Ltd v Klipriver Shipping Ltd (The Kapitan Petko Voivoda),*[85] this suggestion was accepted in the Court of Appeal by Longmore LJ.[86] Thus the strong suggestion being made by distinguished judges in these two cases is that, were the deviation doctrine to be reconsidered by the House of Lords, it would not survive as an independent legal concept.

Conclusions   If, as has been suggested, the existing rules in English law as to the effects of **24.28** a deviation were unified with those under the general law of contract, the consequences would be as follows. An unjustified deviation would constitute a breach of contract by the shipowner and the right to treat the contract as having been discharged would still arise. However, the discharge would only take effect at the time that the option to discharge was exercised and not retrospectively. In the case of a breach causing loss, there would still be a right to a claim in damages.[87]

Other causes of action   Aside from contract, a further possible right of recourse for a **24.29** claimant, following a deviation, might lie in bailment.[88] Under the law of bailment, the bailee who stores goods other than in the place contemplated may find that he is liable for all loss which occurs while the goods are so stored unless he can prove that the loss would anyway have occurred, even if they had been stored in the agreed place.[89]

---

[83] [1987] 1 Lloyd's Rep 424 (CA), 430.
[84] And hence also a quasi-deviation case.
[85] [2003] EWCA Civ 451; [2003] 2 Lloyd's Rep 1. Discussed further at para 29.27.
[86] At [14].
[87] See FMB Reynolds in Markesinis (1992), 46.
[88] See para 9.14.
[89] See, eg, *Lilley v Doubleday* (1881) 7 QBD 510, 511 (Grove J).

25

REASONABLE DESPATCH

A. Introduction

Overview In this chapter we consider the last of the important implied obligations **25.01** imposed on the shipowner, the obligation of reasonable despatch.[1] As we shall in due course see, the implied obligation has rarely been articulated in case law in modern times. The principal is, nevertheless, an old one, but its contemporary relevance is owed to express clauses which are frequently to be found in voyage and time charterparties.

B. Common Law

Implied term The shipowner in all contracts of carriage impliedly undertakes that his **25.02** vessel shall be ready to commence the voyage agreed on and to load the cargo to be carried, and shall proceed upon and complete the voyage agreed upon, with all reasonable despatch. The 'utmost despatch' clause was described by Lord Sumner in *Suzuki & Co Ltd v T Benyon & Co Ltd*[2] as a merchants' clause with the object of giving effect to the mercantile policy of saving time. Thus, if no time is specified for a particular obligation there is an implied obligation to complete the performance within a reasonable time. In *Hick v Raymond* Lord Watson stated that:

> When the language of the contract does not expressly, or by necessary implication, fix any time for the performance of a contractual obligation, the law implied that it shall be performed within a reasonable time. In the case of other contracts the condition of reasonable time has been frequently interpreted; and has invariably been held to mean that the party upon whom it is incumbent duly fulfils his obligations notwithstanding protracted delay, so

---

[1] Or 'dispatch'. See, generally, Carver (2005), para 9-033; Scrutton (1996), art 52. See too David Chong Gek Sian, 'Reasonable despatch in voyage charterparties' [1993] SJLS 401.

[2] (1926) 24 ULR 49 (HL), 54.

long as such delay is attributable to causes beyond his control, and he has neither acted negligently nor unreasonably.[3]

25.03 **Effect of breach** What is the effect of a breach of this implied condition? As with the implied condition of seaworthiness,[4] this undertaking is an innominate term of the contract and the claimant's primary remedy will be in damages.[5] He would not be able to refuse to load a cargo.[6] Whether the breach is so important as to enable the innocent party to avoid the contract will depend on the effects of the relevant breach; repudiation of the contract will only be permitted if the delay is such as to frustrate the object of the contract. In *Freeman v Taylor*[7] a vessel had been chartered to take cargo to Cape Town and, having discharged it, to proceed with all convenient speed to Bombay in order to load the charterer's cargo of cotton. In Cape Town the master on his own account took on board a cargo of mules and cattle for carriage to Mauritius en route to Bombay. As a result of this diversion, the vessel was six weeks later in arriving in Bombay than she would have been if she had proceeded direct. The charterer refused to load in Bombay and the court found in his favour; the delay was sufficiently long to frustrate the object of the charter.

C. Express Clauses

25.04 **Voyage charterparties** Express despatch clauses are commonly found in voyage charterparty forms. Sometimes this is in the form of an undertaking that the vessel is 'expected ready to load'[8] but in several forms, the words 'reasonable despatch'[9] are actually used. Examples which may be referred to include the Asbatankvoy form, where clause 1 provides that the vessel 'shall with all convenient dispatch, proceed as ordered to Loading Port(s)'.[10]

25.05 **Time charterparties** Despatch clauses are not only to be found in voyage charterparties. Thus, the performance clause in the NYPE 93 charterparty, clause 8, states that 'the captain shall prosecute his voyages with the utmost despatch'.[11] Under the Shelltime 4 charterparty, the shipowner likewise undertakes that he will 'prosecute all voyages with the utmost despatch'.[12] The NYPE clause was under consideration in the case of *Whistler International Ltd v Kawasaki Kisen Kaisha Ltd (The Hill Harmony)*.[13] Thus, Lord Bingham stated that:

> The starting point in the present case is, in my opinion, the master's obligation to prosecute his voyages with the utmost dispatch. Irrespective of any express orders by the charterer, that

---

[3] [1893] AC 22, 32. See too *WP & R M'Andrew v Adams* (1834) 1 Bing NC 29, 38; 131 ER 1028, 1031 (Tindal CJ); *MacAndrew v Chapple* (1866) LR 1 CP 643.

[4] See para 23.18.

[5] See, eg, *Medeiros v Hill* (1832) 8 Bing 232; 131 ER 390; *Monarch Steamship Co Ltd v Karlshamns Oljefabriker A/B* [1949] AC 196.

[6] See *Clipsham v Vertue* (1843) 5 QB 265; 114 ER 1249.

[7] (1831) 8 Bing 124; 131 ER 348. See too *Evera SA Comercial v North Shipping Co Ltd* [1956] 2 Lloyd's Rep 367.

[8] As in Gencon (1994), cl 1 (line 4); see para 34.14.

[9] Or 'dispatch'.

[10] At line 2. Such clauses may also be found in towage contracts: see, eg, *Ease Faith Ltd v Leonis Marine Management Ltd* [2006] EWHC 232; [2006] 1 CLC 345.

[11] At line 100. See also cl 9 of Baltime 1939 (lines 119–120).

[12] Clause 2(b)(i), line 69.

[13] [2001] 1 AC 638. See too *Mitsui OSK Lines Ltd v Garnac Grain Co Inc (The Myrtos)* [1984] 2 Lloyd's Rep 449.

would ordinarily require him to take the route which is shortest and therefore quickest, unless there is some other route which is usual or there is some other maritime reason for not taking the shortest and quickest route.[14]

The *Hill Harmony* was under sub-sub time charter by her disponent owners for a trip between Vancouver and Shiogama in Japan on amended versions of the NYPE form. Hire was deducted on the grounds that the master had refused to proceed from Canada to Japan using the northern great circle route, which had been recommended by the charterer's weather routing service, but instead insisted on proceeding by the more southerly rhumb line route, which took longer and used more bunkers. Although much of the decision went to the question of the master's duty to obey orders as to employment of the vessel,[15] Lord Hobhouse also held that:

> As a matter of this mercantile policy and, indeed, as a matter of the use of English a voyage will not have been prosecuted with the utmost dispatch if the owners or the master unnecessarily chooses a longer route which will cause the vessel's arrival at her destination to be delayed. If the charterer has sub-voyage-chartered the vessel to another or has caused bills of lading to be issued, the charterer will be under a legal obligation to ensure that the voyage be prosecuted without undue delay and without unjustifiable deviation. The charterer is entitled to look to the owner of the carrying vessel to perform this obligation and that is one of the reasons why the 'utmost dispatch' clause is included in the usual forms of time charter.[16]

---

[14] At 641.
[15] See para 32.81.
[16] At 653.

26

THE CARRIER'S OBLIGATIONS UNDER THE HAGUE AND HAGUE–VISBY RULES

A. Introduction

Overview   In the preceding chapters we have considered various important duties which **26.01** fall on the carriers at common law and by means of contractual terms in bills of lading and charterparties. In this chapter we return to our consideration of the Hague and Hague–Visby Rules and consider the obligations which fall on the carrier under these Rules.[1] For the main part, this involves a consideration of those provisions falling within article III of the Rules.

B. Issue of Bills of Lading

Introduction   We have previously looked at the function of the bill of lading as a receipt **26.02** for the goods.[2] We now examine various provisions in the Rules associated with the carrier's obligations in this respect.[3]

Article III, rule 3   Article III, rule 3[4] of the Hague and Hague–Visby Rules provides as **26.03** follows:

> After receiving the goods into his charge the carrier or the master or agent of the carrier shall, on demand of the shipper, issue to the shipper a bill of lading showing among other things —

---

[1] See the earlier discussion of the other substantive provisions of the Hague and Hague–Visby Rules in chs 18 and 19.

[2] See ch 6.

[3] See, generally, Scrutton (1996), section XX; Cooke (2001), para 85.121; Carver (2005), para 9-149.

[4] See Berlingieri (1997), 187.

(a) The leading marks necessary for identification of the goods as the same are furnished in writing by the shipper before the loading of such goods starts, provided such marks are stamped or otherwise shown clearly upon the goods if uncovered, or on the cases or covering in which such goods are contained, in such a manner as should ordinarily remain legible until the end of the voyage.

(b) Either the number of packages or pieces, or the quantity, or weight, as the case may be as furnished in writing by the shipper.

(c) The apparent order and condition of the goods.

26.04 **'Demand'**   It will be noted that article III, rule 3 provides that the shipper can demand that the carrier issue a bill showing certain information. However, there is no obligation on the part of the carrier to issue such a bill of lading unless requested to do so by the shipper. If there is a demand the carrier is bound to issue a bill of lading which satisfies the other requirements of article III, rule 3. It may be noted that there is no requirement that a particular type of bill of lading must be issued. Thus, it would seem that the carrier may issue a shipped or a received for shipment bill of lading in response to a demand.[5]

26.05 **'Showing among other things . . .'**   The bill of lading which is issued must show certain information specified in article III, rule 3. However, there is no obligation on the carrier to 'show' only the required information.[6] He may elect to 'show' other information as well, although there may not be any advantage to him in doing so.

26.06 **Leading marks**   By article III, rule 3(a) the carrier is obliged to show 'the leading marks necessary for identification of the goods as the same are furnished in writing by the shipper before the loading of such goods'.[7] If bills of lading are presented for signature and these refer to goods which bear particular marks but which the master has not had an opportunity to check it would seem that the carrier will be entitled to an indemnity for any liability.[8]

26.07 **'Number . . . quantity . . . weight'**   In addition to showing the relevant leading marks, under article III, rule 3(b) the carrier must show 'either the number of packages or pieces, or the quantity, or weight, as the case may be . . .'.[9] The choice as to which method he uses to quantify the cargo will lie with the carrier. As the rule makes plain, he is not obliged to acknowledge more than one and can disclaim all knowledge of the others.

26.08 **'Apparent order and condition'**   We have previously looked at this type of representation in the context of the common law.[10] Thus a bill of lading which is issued following a demand by the shipper must show the apparent, external, condition of the goods.[11] Further, however, such a statement must be an accurate statement of fact. It has been

---

[5] Although see art III, r 7; para 26.14.

[6] See *Noble Resources Ltd v Cavalier Shipping Corporation (The Atlas)* [1996] 1 Lloyd's Rep 642, 646 (Longmore J); *Agrosin Pte Ltd v Highway Shipping Co Ltd (The Mata K)* [1998] 2 Lloyd's Rep 614, 618 (Clarke J). See too para 26.13.

[7] See the earlier discussion of leading marks at para 6.20.

[8] This arises both at common law (see *Elder Dempster v Dunn* (1909) 15 Com Cas 49) and under article III, rule 5. For discussion of article III, rule 5, see para 22.03.

[9] See the earlier discussion of quantity at para 6.04.

[10] See para 6.15.

[11] See, eg, *The Peter der Grosse* (1875) 1 PD 414, 420 (Sir Robert Phillimore).

described as an absolute contractual undertaking and not merely a duty to take reasonable care, except that, where the making of the statement requires some skill, the duty is cast as one to take reasonable care.[12]

Reservations   Article III, rule 3 contains an important proviso, which runs as follows: **26.09**

> Provided that no carrier, master or agent of the carrier shall be bound to state or show in the bill of lading any marks, number, quantity, or weight which he has reasonable ground for suspecting not accurately to represent the goods actually received or which he has had no reasonable means of checking.

Thus, it seems that under the Hague and Hague–Visby Rules it is possible for the master to insert reservations into the bill of lading.[13] As we have seen, these reservations can include the phrases 'weight and quantity unknown',[14] and 'said to contain'.[15] The reservations so inserted only qualify the matters referred to and will not affect the status of other statements made in the bills of lading.[16] Also, it is important to note that, in respect of statements as to condition specified in article III, rule 3(c), no reservation may be made.

'Said to weigh'   In *Oricon Waren-Handelgesellschaft MbH v Intergraan NV*[17] a bill of lading   **26.10** to which the Hague Rules applied[18] acknowledged receipt of 2,000 packages containing copra cakes.[19] A clause stated:

> Contents and condition of contents, specification, measurement, weight, gauge, brand, countermark, quality or value unknown, any reference in this Bill of Lading to these particulars is for the purpose of calculating freight only …

The bill also stated under the heading *Description of Goods*: 'Said to Weigh Gross, 105 000 kgs …'. During the voyage from Semarang to Amsterdam aboard the *Suva Breeze*, the copra cake was stowed in the Nos 4 and 5 'tween decks.[20] A fire broke out in the No 4 hold and considerable quantities of water were used to extinguish the fire, flooding the hold. The court held:

> It is … as plain as plain can be that, while … the bills of lading being Hague Rules bills of lading acknowledged the numbers of packages shipped and are *prima facie* evidence of those numbers, neither bill of lading is any evidence whatever of the weight of the goods shipped.[21]

Accordingly, the burden of proof vested in the consignee to establish the weight of cargo shipped before he could succeed in an action for short delivery.

---

[12] See *Trade Star Line Corp v Mitsui & Co Ltd* [1996] 2 Lloyd's Rep 449 (CA), 458 (Evans LJ); *Oceanfocus Shipping Ltd v Hyundai Merchant Marine Co Ltd (The Hawk)* [1999] 1 Lloyd's Rep 176, 185 (Judge Diamond QC).

[13] For the position at common law, see para 6.10.

[14] See para 6.11.

[15] See para 6.12.

[16] See, eg, *Pendle & Rivet Ltd v Ellerman Lines* (1928) 33 Com Cas 70, 77; *Attorney-General of Ceylon v Scindia Steam Navigation Co Ltd* [1962] AC 60 (PC), 74 (Lord Morris).

[17] [1967] 2 Lloyd's Rep 82.

[18] The provisions of art III, r 3 are the same in both the Hague and Hague–Visby Rules.

[19] Copra is the dried meat, or kernel, of the coconut.

[20] As to the meaning of this, see para 1.13.

[21] [1967] 2 Lloyd's Rep 82, 90 (Roskill J). As to evidence, see art III, r 4 and the discussion at para 26.12.

26.11 **Reservations and article III, rule 8** We have already examined the scope of article III, rule 8 which, it will be recalled, essentially provides that the carrier may not derogate from his responsibilities under the Rules.[22] The Privy Council in *Canada & Dominion Sugar Co Ltd v Canadian National (West Indies) Steamships Ltd*[23] was prepared to countenance a qualification of liability on the part of the shipowner even though it was argued that the provisions of the Hague Rules rendered the qualification 'signed under guarantee to produce ship's clean receipt' void. Lord Wright stated that the Rules only applied

> if the shipper demands a bill of lading showing the apparent order and condition of the goods. There is no evidence that the shipper here made such a demand: indeed, no demand of this nature is alleged. The condition of the rule is thus not fulfilled.[24]

A reservation inserted in a bill of lading which is subject to the application of the Hague or Hague–Visby Rules therefore will not infringe article III, rule 8.[25]

26.12 **Evidentiary value** Article III, rule 4[26] provides that:

> Such a bill of lading shall be prima facie evidence of the receipt by the carrier of the goods as therein described in accordance with paragraphs 3(a), (b) and (c). However, proof to the contrary shall not be admissible when the bill of lading has been transferred to a third party acting in good faith.

Thus, article III, rule 4, like the common law, regards the bill in the hands of the shipper as prima facie evidence of the amount of cargo shipped.[27] The Hague–Visby Rules,[28] but not the Hague Rules, differ from the common law in so far as third parties are concerned, however, because, in such a case, the bill of lading is stated to be conclusive evidence. A qualified statement as to the matters in article III, rule 3 will not, however, be prima facie evidence, as is illustrated by the next case, *Noble Resources Ltd v Cavalier Shipping Corporation (The Atlas)*.[29]

26.13 *The Atlas* In *Noble Resources Ltd v Cavalier Shipping Corporation (The Atlas)*[30] bills of lading recorded the shipment of hot rolled square steel billets loaded at Nakhodka and stated that there were 1,380 bundles with a net weight of 12,038 tonnes. Noble Resources, the voyage sub-charterers, sold the steel billets on to receivers in Taiwan and, as shippers, caused a second set of bills of lading to be issued because they did not wish the Taiwanese cargo receivers to know the identity of their Russian suppliers. The Congenbill bills of lading[31] stated that 'weight . . . quantity . . . unknown'. The cargo receivers at Kaohsiung (Taiwan) alleged shortfall of 32 bundles or 1,281 tonnes. It was argued that, although the Russian bills of lading did not evidence a contract of carriage, nevertheless they could be

---

[22] If he does so, such a provision will be 'null and void and of no effect': see para 19.39.
[23] [1947] AC 46 (PC). See the discussion of this case at para 6.19.
[24] At 57.
[25] See too *Noble Resources Ltd v Cavalier Shipping Corporation (The Atlas)* [1996] 1 Lloyd's Rep 642, 646 (Longmore J); *Agrosin Pte Ltd v Highway Shipping Co Ltd (The Mata K)* [1998] 2 Lloyd's Rep 614, 619 (Clarke J).
[26] See Berlingieri (1997), 221; Cooke (2001), para 85.134; Carver (2005), para 9–171.
[27] See the discussion as to evidential value at paras 6.04, 6.17.
[28] See Berlingieri (1997), 259.
[29] [1996] 1 Lloyd's Rep 642.
[30] ibid. This case is also discussed in relation to the issue of 'switch' bills of lading: see para 11.14.
[31] See Appendix II.

relied on as receipts and that since they and the switch bills contained only a 'weight unknown' clause, they could be relied upon as prima facie evidence of the quantity shipped. However, this was rejected by Longmore J:

> ... [I]t is impossible to imagine that the *New Chinese Antimony* case would have been decided differently if the bill in that case had said merely 'weight unknown'; one has to construe the bill of lading to determine whether it is an unqualified assertion or representation of the shipment of a particular quantity of goods. If the bill of lading provides that the weight is unknown it cannot be an assertion or representation of the weight in fact shipped. [Counsel] said the typed figures prevail over the printed 'weight unknown' but, if the Russian bills are construed as a whole, they must be held to mean that the shipowners are not committing themselves, one way or the other, as to the weight of cargo shipped.[32]

Accordingly, the claimant receivers had not proved that any particular number of bundles or any particular weight of cargo was discharged from the ship. Further, they had not proved that the shipowner landed or discharged on the quay a lesser quantity than was shipped. [33]

Issue of a shipped bill of lading   Article III, rule 7[34] provides that: **26.14**

> After the goods are loaded the bill of lading to be issued by the carrier, master or agent of the carrier, to the shipper shall, if the shipper so demands, be a 'shipped' bill of lading, provided that if the shipper shall have previously taken up any document of title to such goods, he shall surrender the same as against the issue of the 'shipped' bill of lading, but at the option of the carrier such document of title may be noted at the port of shipment by the carrier, master, or agent with the name or names of the ship or ships upon which the goods have been shipped and the date or dates of shipment, and when so noted the same shall for the purpose of this Article be deemed to constitute a 'shipped' bill of lading.

As we have previously noted, article III, rule 3 does not specify whether the bill of lading which the carrier is required to issue is a shipped or received for shipment bill of lading.[35] Article III, rule 7 seems to contemplate the scenario that a received for shipment bill of lading was issued originally and, under it, it seems that the shipper can 'demand' a 'shipped' bill of lading, against surrender of the 'received' bill of lading.[36]

C. Seaworthiness

Background   We have, in a previous chapter, looked at the scope of the carrier's obliga-   **26.15**
tion to provide a seaworthy vessel.[37] We turn now to examine this same obligation in the context of the Hague and Hague–Visby Rules.[38]

---

[32] [1996] 1 Lloyd's Rep 642, 646.

[33] See too *Agrosin Pte Ltd v Highway Shipping Co Ltd (The Mata K)* [1998] 2 Lloyd's Rep 614.

[34] See Berlingieri (1997), 325.

[35] See para 26.03.

[36] This is a potentially important qualification because it ensures that two sets of bills of lading are not in circulation.

[37] See ch 23.

[38] See, generally, Scrutton (1996), section XX; Cooke (2001), para 85.82; Carver (2005), para 9-133; Clarke in Rose (2000), ch 6.

26.16 **Common law absolute undertaking not applicable** Where the Hague–Visby Rules apply to the contract of carriage,[39] the absolute undertaking of seaworthiness[40] is replaced by an undertaking that the shipowner will before and at the beginning of the voyage exercise due diligence to make the ship seaworthy. Section 3 of the Carriage of Goods by Sea Act 1971 states that:

> There shall not be implied in any contract for the carriage of goods by sea to which the Rules apply by virtue of this Act any absolute undertaking by the carrier of the goods to provide a seaworthy ship.

It is, however, important to note, as one distinguished commentator has, that it is not the common law of seaworthiness which is abolished, but 'common law *level* seaworthiness'.[41]

26.17 **Article III, rule 1** This provision[42] of the Hague and Hague–Visby Rules provides that:

> The carrier shall be bound before and at the beginning of the voyage to exercise due diligence to
>
> (a) Make the ship seaworthy.
>
> (b) Properly man, equip and supply the ship.
>
> (c) Make the holds, refrigerating and cool chambers, and all other parts of the ship in which goods are carried, fit and safe for their reception, carriage and preservation.

26.18 **Extent of the seaworthiness obligation** It is widely recognized that the obligation in article III, rule 1 embraces the distinct aspects of seaworthiness recognized at common law. Thus, in *Empresa Cubana Importada de Alimentos Alimport v Iasmos Shipping Co SA (The Good Friend)* it was stated that

> the word 'seaworthy' in The Hague Rules is used in its ordinary meaning, and not in any extended or unnatural meaning. It means that the vessel — with her master and crew — is herself fit to encounter the perils of the voyage and also that she is fit to carry the cargo safely on that voyage.[43]

26.19 **Duration** The Rules refer to the provision of a seaworthy ship 'before and at the beginning of the voyage'. The meaning of this principle was considered in the famous case of *Maxine Footwear Co Ltd v Canadian Government Merchant Marine Ltd*.[44] The appellants were the consignees of a cargo of shoe leather loaded aboard the *Maurienne* at Halifax in Nova Scotia for carriage to Kingston, Jamaica. The contract was subject to the Canadian Water Carriage of Goods Act 1936.[45] Shortly before the vessel was due to sail, an attempt was made to thaw frozen scupper pipes with an acetylene torch. The ship's officer in charge used a shore-based firm from Halifax for the task. A fire was started in cork insulation

---

[39] The Carriage of Goods by Sea Act 1924 contained a similar provision: see s 2 (para 18.03).

[40] As to the meaning of this, see para 23.10.

[41] Clarke (1976), 231. See too *W Angliss and Co (Australia) Pty Ltd v Peninsular and Oriental Steam Navigation Co* [1927] 2 KB 456, 460 (Wright J).

[42] See Berlingieri (1997), 145.

[43] [1984] 2 Lloyd's Rep 586, 592 (Staughton J); *Actis Steamship Co Ltd v The Sanko Steamship Co Ltd (The Aquacharm)* [1982] 1 WLR 119 (CA); *The Gang Cheng* (1998) 6 MLJ 488; *Great China Metal Industries Co Ltd v Malaysian International Shipping Corp Berhad (The Bunga Seroja)* [1999] 1 Lloyd's Rep 512, at [86] (McHugh J).

[44] [1959] AC 589 (PC).

[45] As to this Act, see para 15.10.

around the pipe and this eventually forced the master to scuttle the ship. The appellant's cargo was lost and it was admitted that the officer who had ordered and supervised the thawing was negligent. It was argued that article III, rule 1 only obliged the carrier to exercise due diligence to make the ship seaworthy at the beginning of the loading and the beginning of the voyage. Lord Somervell of Harrow who delivered the judgment of the Privy Council said that:

> In their Lordships' opinion 'before and at the beginning of the voyage' means the period from at least the beginning of the loading until the vessel starts on her voyage. The word 'before' cannot in their opinion be read as meaning 'at the commencement of the loading'.

> On that view the obligation to exercise due diligence to make the ship seaworthy continued over the whole of the period from the beginning of loading until the ship sank. There was a failure to exercise due diligence during that period. As a result the ship became unseaworthy and this unseaworthiness caused the damage to and loss of the appellant's goods. The appellants are therefore entitled to succeed.[46]

Meaning of due diligence   It has often been said that this phrase derives from the US   **26.20**
Harter Act of 1893.[47] However, this is not strictly correct as the Liverpool Conference Form of 1882[48] contains a reference to the 'want of due diligence by the Owners of the Ship'.[49] Although not without its difficulties,[50] the concept has been interpreted by the courts as being roughly equivalent to the common law duty of reasonable care[51] and this was confirmed in *Papera Traders Co Ltd v Hyundai Merchant Marine Co Ltd (The Eurasian Dream)* by Cresswell J when he said that 'the exercise of due diligence is equivalent to the exercise of reasonable care and skill . . . lack of due diligence is negligence . . .'.[52]

Obligation non-delegable   The obligation in article III, rule 1 has been interpreted as   **26.21**
being personal and not delegable.[53] The leading English case is *Riverstone Meat Co Pty Ltd v Lancashire Shipping Co Ltd (The Muncaster Castle)*.[54] Cases of canned ox tongue were shipped aboard *The Muncaster Castle* from Sydney to London under bills of lading which were subject to the Australian Sea-Carriage of Goods Act 1924.[55] When the goods were discharged, most of the cases were found damaged by sea water which had entered the hold through defective inspection covers to storm valves. Shortly before the start of the voyage,

---

[46] [1959] AC 589 (PC), 602.

[47] See para 14.05. Section 2 states: 'It shall not be lawful for any vessel transporting merchandise or property from or between ports of the United States of America and foreign ports, her owner, master, agent, or manager, to insert in any bill of lading or shipping document any covenant or agreement whereby the obligations of the owner or owners of said vessel to exercise due diligence [to] properly equip, man, provision, and outfit said vessel, and to make said vessel seaworthy and capable of performing her intended voyage, or whereby the obligations of the master, officers, agents, or servants to carefully handle and stow her cargo and to care for and properly deliver same, shall in any wise be lessened, weakened or avoided.'

[48] See para 14.04.

[49] See Sturley (1990), vol 2, 62.

[50] Largely because of the decision of the House of Lords in *Riverstone Meat Co Pty Ltd v Lancashire Shipping Co Ltd (The Muncaster Castle)* [1961] AC 807. See Clarke (1976), 203.

[51] See *Riverstone Meat Co Pty Ltd v Lancashire Shipping Co Ltd (The Muncaster Castle)* [1960] 1 QB 536 (CA), 581 (Willmer LJ).

[52] [2002] EWHC 118 (Comm); [2002] 1 Lloyd's Rep 719.

[53] See Sir Stephen Tomlinson in Rose (2000), ch 8. See also Clarke (1976), ch 17.

[54] [1961] AC 807.

[55] This Act embodied the Hague Rules: see para 15.10.

the inspection covers had been removed during the survey of the vessel under the supervision of a Lloyd's surveyor. Following completion of the inspection, the task of replacing the inspection covers on the storm valves was delegated to a fitter employed by the ship repairers. He was negligent in tightening the nuts holding the covers and they loosened during the voyage. Both McNair J[56] and the Court of Appeal[57] held that, although the vessel was unseaworthy, the shipowners had exercised due diligence and were not liable for the damage to the cargo. But the House of Lords overruled these decisions and held that the carrier was liable for breach of the obligation to exercise due diligence. Viscount Simonds said that

> no other solution is possible than to say that the shipowners' obligation of due diligence demands due diligence in the work of repair by whomsoever it may be done.[58]

In the course of his speech Lord Keith said the following:

> It would, however, be a most sweeping change if [the Hague Rules] had the result of providing carriers with a simple escape from their new obligation to exercise due diligence to make a ship seaworthy. If this were the plain effect of the statute, cadit quaestio.[59] But in dubio the courts should, in a change of the suggested dimensions, lean to the other way. The language of the Hague Rules does not, I think, lead to the result contended for by the respondents. The carrier will have some relief which, weighed in the scales, is not inconsiderable when contrasted with his previous common law position.[60]

26.22 **Effect** The *Muncaster Castle*[61] decision is therefore to the effect that if particular responsibilities are delegated to independent contractors or Lloyd's surveyors, and those persons are negligent, the carrier remains liable.[62] It is no defence for him to argue that he engaged reliable experts or indeed that he himself lacked the necessary expertise to check their work.[63]

26.23 **Reform** The decision in the case caused some consternation internationally and in the UK and this was one of the issues for revision considered by the CMI at its Conference at Rijeka in 1959 and at its Stockholm Conference in 1963.[64] The British delegation was vocal in proposing change[65] and its amendment was duly adopted by a majority. However, at the later Diplomatic Conference at Brussels in 1967 and 1968, the amendment was rejected because: (i) it was believed to be contrary to fundamental legal principles in some countries, (ii) it disturbed the balance achieved in 1924 between the various interests, and (iii) it made it difficult for cargo interests or their insurers to recover against independent contractors at fault.[66]

26.24 **Carrier responsible only when he controls the vessel** It is established that the carrier will not be responsible for the seaworthy condition of a vessel until it comes under his control

---

[56] [1959] 1 QB 74.
[57] [1960] 1 QB 536.
[58] [1961] AC 807, 844.
[59] ie 'the question falls' — the matter is resolved.
[60] [1961] AC 807, 872.
[61] [1961] AC 807.
[62] See too *Eridania SpA v Rudolf A Oetker (The Fjord Wind)* [2000] 2 Lloyd's Rep 191 (CA), 199 (Clarke LJ).
[63] He may be able to cover himself by claiming an indemnity from the independent contractor involved.
[64] See Berlingieri (1997), 148.
[65] At 150.
[66] See Clarke (1976), 253.

or his ambit. Thus, if the carrier commissions the building of a new vessel,[67] or charters or purchases a ship from someone else, he will not be liable for existing defects rendering the vessel unseaworthy unless these were reasonably discoverable by the exercise of due diligence at the time of takeover. If the defect could have been apparent on a reasonable inspection of the vessel at the time that he took the vessel over, the carrier cannot in that event rely for protection even on the certificate of a Lloyd's surveyor or any other classification society. These issues arose recently in the case of *Parsons Corp v CV Scheepvaartonderneming Happy Ranger (The Happy Ranger)*.[68] The claimants sued the shipowners for damage caused to a process vessel required for a gas plant which fell from a crane while being loaded onto the *Happy Ranger*, which was on her maiden voyage. The process vessel was being lifted from a low loader on the quay by means of the ship's two cranes when one of the double ramshorn hooks on the aft crane broke and the process vessel fell to the ground. The hook had failed at its shank as a result of a brittle fracture because it suffered from casting defects. It emerged that the hook had never been tested to its safe working load. The shipowners, however, contended that they could not be liable for the negligence of the manufacturers of the ship, crane, or hook prior to the delivery of the ship by the shipbuilders. The court agreed that the ship had not come 'within the shipowner's orbit' until delivery and accordingly it was not responsible for any negligence prior to the delivery.[69] However, the court went on to find that the shipowners had failed to discharge the burden of showing that they exercised due diligence to make the ship seaworthy after taking delivery.[70] In particular, they failed to appreciate on and after handover that there had been no adequate proof testing of the hooks. After delivery of the ship a special exemption had been obtained from the classification society for the purposes of lifting the process vessel. Accordingly, the shipowner had not exercised due diligence in relation to obtaining that exemption and the classification society, for whose failings it was responsible, had not carried out its function of granting the exemption with due diligence.[71]

Latent defects   The carrier might be assisted in avoiding a claim under article III, rule 1 **26.25** if he can show that there was a latent defect[72] arising from the construction of the vessel and if he can produce evidence to show that no defect was discovered during inspections carried out by surveyors. A leading case on this point is *Union of India v NV Reederij Amsterdam*.[73] The claimants sought damages under a contract to carry 11,400 tons of wheat in bulk from Portland, Oregon to Bombay. The wheat was shipped under a bill of lading which incorporated the US Carriage of Goods by Sea Act 1936.[74] In the course of the voyage the vessel sustained engine breakdown due to failure of her reduction gear. She had to be towed to Honolulu and later to Kobe for repairs and the cargo was delivered to the plaintiffs at Kobe who alleged that the defendants had failed to exercise due diligence to make the

---

[67] See *W Angliss and Co (Australia) Pty Ltd v Peninsular and Oriental Steam Navigation Co* [1927] 2 KB 456; *Riverstone Meat Co Pty Ltd v Lancashire Shipping Co Ltd (The Muncaster Castle)* [1961] AC 807.
[68] [2006] EWHC 122 (Comm); [2006] 1 Lloyd's Rep 649.
[69] At [37] (Gloster J).
[70] At [45].
[71] At [62].
[72] Generally for latent defects as a defence, see art IV, r 2(p). See para 28.42
[73] [1963] 2 Lloyd's Rep 223 (HL).
[74] See as to the US Carriage of Goods by Sea Act 1936, para 15.10.

ship seaworthy. The vessel had been built in 1922 but was acquired by the defendant in 1956 following an inspection by a Lloyd's surveyor. Lord Reid stated that

> if the appellants are to escape from liability they must prove that due diligence had been exercised not only by themselves and their servants, but by the Lloyd's Register of Shipping surveyor who surveyed this [reduction] gear but failed to discover the crack [in the after helix tyre of the main gear drum].[75]

On the facts of the case, the House of Lords held that the Lloyd's surveyor had taken reasonable care in conducting the survey, thus discharging the burden of proof on the carrier that due diligence had been exercised.

26.26 *The Fjord Wind* In *Eridania SpA v Rudolf A Oetker (The Fjord Wind)*[76] Moore-Bick J gave judgment against the disponent owners and shipowners in respect of loss and damage to the cargo caused by the unseaworthiness of the vessel which manifested itself when the No 6 crankpin bearing on her main engine failed while she was proceeding down the River Paraná. On appeal[77] the focus centred on two clauses in the voyage charterparty, which were properly incorporated into the relevant bills of lading. Clause 1 provided that 'the said vessel, being tight, staunch and strong and in every way fit for the voyage, shall with all convenient speed proceed to [the river Plate] . . . and there load . . .' Clause 35 provided that:

> Owners shall be bound before and at the beginning of the voyage to exercise due diligence to make the ship seaworthy and to have her properly manned, equipped and supplied and neither the vessel nor the Master or Owners shall be or shall be held liable for any loss of or damage or delay to the cargo for causes excepted by the US Carriage of Goods by Sea Act 1936 or the Canadian Water Carriage of Goods Act 1936.

Clarke LJ concluded that the obligation as to seaworthiness was to exercise due diligence to make the ship seaworthy[78] and held that the vessel was unseaworthy when she left Rosario because there was present a defect which the owners should have rectified, had they known that it was present.[79] The evidence confirmed that a thorough investigation was called for and that the owners had failed to demonstrate that a proper investigation was carried out.[80]

26.27 **Later defects** Provided that the carrier has exercised due diligence to make the ship seaworthy in all respects before she sails on her voyage he will not breach article III, rule 1 if defects develop on the voyage[81] or arise during a call at an intermediate port. 'Voyage' is construed as covering the entire voyage covered by the bill of lading, irrespective of calls at intermediate ports. Thus, there is no doctrine of stages under the Hague and Hague–Visby Rules.[82]

---

[75] [1963] 2 Lloyd's Rep 223 (H2), 229.

[76] [1999] 1 Lloyd's Rep 307.

[77] [2000] 2 Lloyd's Rep 191 (CA).

[78] At 197.

[79] At 199.

[80] At 204.

[81] Unless it can be shown that these defects have occurred soon after the commencement of the voyage and that this raises an inference of unseaworthiness: see, eg, *Phillips Petroleum Co v Cabaneli Naviera SA (The Theodegmon)* [1990] 1 Lloyd's Rep 52.

[82] See *Leesh River Tea Co Ltd v British India Steam Navigation Co Ltd* [1967] 2 QB 250 (CA); *Owners of Cargo Lately Laden on Board the Makedonia v Owners of the Makedonia (The Makedonia)* [1962] P 190; *Sellers Fabrics Pty Ltd v Hapag-Lloyd AG* [1998] NSWSC 646.

Proof of unseaworthiness   Article IV, rule 1[83] provides that: **26.28**

Neither the carrier nor the ship shall be liable for loss or damage arising or resulting from unseaworthiness unless caused by want of due diligence on the part of the carrier to make the ship seaworthy, and to secure that the ship is properly manned, equipped and supplied, and to make the holds, refrigerating and cool chambers and all other parts of the ship in which goods are carried fit and safe for their reception, carriage and preservation in accordance with the provisions of paragraph 1 of Article III. Whenever loss or damage has resulted from unseaworthiness the burden of proving the exercise of due diligence shall be on the carrier or other person claiming exemption under this article.

Meaning   It will be seen that this lengthy provision reiterates much of the duty to exercise   **26.29** due diligence to provide a seaworthy ship in article III, rule 1. On a literal interpretation, there is no liability for unseaworthiness 'unless caused by want of due diligence on the part of the carrier . . .' and the burden of proving that due diligence has been exercised 'shall be on the carrier'. This would appear to indicate that there is a positive obligation on the carrier to prove that he has exercised due diligence.[84] However, as we shall see, the practice is somewhat different from this literal interpretation. Indeed, what has come to be accepted over a long period of time is the transposition of the common law scheme of proof to the Convention.[85]

Prima facie case   It is established, both at common law and under the Rules, that the first   **26.30** stage in the claims process is for the claimant to establish a prima facie case against the carrier. This is usually achieved by showing that he is the person with the right of suit under the contract of carriage and also proof of the nature and the amount of his loss. He must furthermore show that it is the defendant carrier who is prima facie liable for his loss because the goods which have been entrusted to him in good order and condition have not arrived at all, or have arrived in a damaged condition.[86]

Carrier's response   The carrier will now seek to meet the prima facie allegation head-on   **26.31** by pleading and proving an exception,[87] such as a peril of the seas or one or more of the other exceptions available to him under article IV, rule 2.[88] He is not bound to prove that he has provided a seaworthy ship. Thus, in *The Hellenic Dolphin*,[89] a cargo of asbestos was found, on discharge, to have been damaged by sea water. It was established later that the sea water had gained access to the hold through a four foot long indent in the ship's plating, of which the shipowner had previously been unaware. There was no available evidence as

---

[83] See Berlingieri (1997), 364 and, more generally, Clarke (1976), ch 12; Scrutton (1996) section XX; Cooke (2001), para 85.237; Carver (2005), para 9-203. See too Chinyere Ezeoke, 'Allocating onus of proof in sea cargo claims: The contest of conflicting principles' [2001] LMCLQ 261.

[84] This is the view taken by one very distinguished academic commentator: see Tetley (1988), 376.

[85] See *Minister of Food v Reardon Smith Line Ltd* [1951] 2 Lloyd's Rep 265, 271–272 (McNair J).

[86] See, eg, *Albacora SRL v Westcott & Laurance Line Ltd* [1966] 2 Lloyd's Rep 53 (HL), 63 (Lord Pearson); *Robin Hood Flour Mills Ltd v NM Paterson & Sons Ltd (The Farrandoc)* [1967] 2 Lloyd's Rep 276, 284 (Noel J); *The Hellenic Dolphin* [1978] 2 Lloyd's Rep 336, 339 (Lloyd J); *Phillips Petroleum Co v Cabaneli Naviera SA (The Theodegmon)* [1990] 1 Lloyd's Rep 52, 54 (Phillips J); *Great China Metal Industries Co Ltd v Malaysian International Shipping Corp Berhad (The Bunga Seroja)* [1999] 1 Lloyd's Rep 512, at [87] (McHugh J).

[87] See, eg, *Robin Hood Flour Mills Ltd v NM Paterson & Sons Ltd (The Farrandoc)* [1967] 2 Lloyd's Rep 276, 284 (Noel J); *The Hellenic Dolphin* [1978] 2 Lloyd's Rep 336, 339 (Lloyd J); *Phillips Petroleum Co v Cabaneli Naviera SA (The Theodegmon)* [1990] 1 Lloyd's Rep 52, 54 (Phillips J).

[88] For the exception of perils of the seas, see art IV, r 2(c), discussed at para 28.18.

[89] [1978] 2 Lloyd's Rep 336.

to whether the damage to the vessel was inflicted before or after the cargo had been loaded. Lloyd J allowed the shipowner to rely on the exception of perils of the sea since, in his opinion and in the absence of evidence to the contrary 'the incursion of seawater through an undetected defect in the ship's basic plating is a classic case of damage by perils of the sea'.[90]

26.32 **Displacement of the carrier's defence**   The next phase in the claims process is for the claimant to cast some doubt on the defence(s) raised by the carrier. If he cannot do this and accepts that the defence pleaded was the immediate cause of the loss or damage, then he must try to attack the defence by showing that behind the excepted peril there was some breach of the carrier's obligation of due diligence.[91] In effect, what he must do is to prove that the ship was unseaworthy before and at the beginning of the voyage and that this defect was responsible for causing the loss or damage complained of. This may be a difficult route for the claimant, simply because as receiver of the cargo he will face difficulties in getting evidence about the state of the ship and the crew at this early stage of the voyage.[92] However, he may be assisted by proof of damage by sea water as affording prima facie evidence of damage caused by unseaworthiness.[93]

26.33 **Carrier's further defence**   In answer to the allegations thrown up by the claimant it is necessary for the carrier to prove that the defect proved by the claimant came about despite the exercise of due diligence by him, as required under article III, rule 1.[94]

26.34 **Overriding effect of article III, rule 1**   The cargo claimant will be assisted by a further aspect of the interpretation of article III, rule 1, namely that the obligation there stated is an overriding one, such that the carrier could not raise any defences in article IV, rule 2 if he has breached it. This was stated as follows by Lord Somervell in the case of *Maxine Footwear Co Ltd v Canadian Government Merchant Marine Ltd*:[95]

> Article III, rule 1, is an overriding obligation. If it is not fulfilled and the nonfulfilment causes the damage the immunities of article IV cannot be relied on. This is the natural construction apart from the opening words of article III, rule 2. The fact that that rule is made subject to the provisions of article IV and rule 1 is not so conditioned makes the point clear beyond argument.[96]

The exact reason for this interpretation is hard to pin down, but it should be noted that this reasoning is not necessarily followed in all jurisdictions.[97] There are, however, some

---

[90] At 339.

[91] *The Hellenic Dolphin* [1978] 2 Lloyd's Rep 336, 339 (Lloyd J); *Phillips Petroleum Co v Cabaneli Naviera SA (The Theodegmon)* [1990] 1 Lloyd's Rep 52, 54 (Phillips J); *Great China Metal Industries Co Ltd v Malaysian International Shipping Corp Berhad (The Bunga Seroja)* [1999] 1 Lloyd's Rep 512, at [87] (McHugh J).

[92] Although inference may help.

[93] See *Commonwealth v Burns Philp & Co Ltd* (1946) 46 SR (NSW) 307, 312; *BHP Trading Asia Ltd v Oceaname Shipping Ltd* (1996) 67 FCR 211, 229 (Hill J).

[94] *The Hellenic Dolphin* [1978] 2 Lloyd's Rep 336, 339 (Lloyd J); *Phillips Petroleum Co v Cabaneli Naviera SA (The Theodegmon)* [1990] 1 Lloyd's Rep 52, 54 (Phillips J); *The Polessk and Akademik Iosif Orbeli* [1996] 2 Lloyd's Rep 40, 45 (Clarke J); *Great China Metal Industries Co Ltd v Malaysian International Shipping Corp Berhad (The Bunga Seroja)* [1999] 1 Lloyd's Rep 512, at [87] (McHugh J).

[95] [1959] AC 589 (PC), 602–603; *The Gang Cheng* (1998) 6 MLJ 468, 490 (Kamalanathan Ratnam J).

[96] Cited with approval in *Great China Metal Industries Co Ltd v Malaysian International Shipping Corp Berhad (The Bunga Seroja)* [1999] 1 Lloyd's Rep 512, at [143] (Kirby J). See too *Shipping Corp of India Ltd v Gamlen Chemical Co (A/Asia) Pty Ltd* (1980) 147 CLR 142, 152.

[97] See Clarke (1976), ch 12 (comparing the position in the UK and France). For the USA, see Schoenbaum (2004), §10–25.

plausible reasons, such as that article III, rule 1 is not made subject to article IV.[98] This interpretation of article III, rule 1 has been generally accepted and applied in some situations arising under the Rules.[99] It has however, been held that a breach by the carrier of article III, rule 1 will not deprive him of his right to limit his liability under the Rules.[100]

D. Due Care

Care of cargo   Article III, rule 2[101] provides that: **26.35**

Subject to the provisions of Article IV, the carrier shall properly and carefully load, handle, stow, carry, keep, care for and discharge the goods delivered.

Importance   This provision of the Rules is of central importance, in much the same way   **26.36**
as it would be unthinkable to talk about the carrier's obligations and omit any consideration of article III, rule 1. If there is no issue as to the unseaworthiness of the vessel, but the goods have arrived in a damaged condition or have been short delivered, it will form the central plank of the claimant's case. Indeed, in such an event, there will be a prima facie breach of article III, rule 2 and the carrier will be liable unless he can establish a defence under article IV, rule 2.[102] In many cases it is not unusual to find that the claimant pleads article III, rule 1 and article III, rule 2 as alternative bases of claim.[103]

The proviso   We may note, as a preliminary point, that article III, rule 2 is expressly made   **26.37**
subject to the provisions of article IV,[104] which would include the carrier's defences in art IV, rule 2 and his right to limit his liability under article IV, rule 5.[105] On one view the fact that article III, rule 2 is made subject to article IV, may indicate that this provision is not intended to have overriding status in the way that article III, rule 1 is.[106]

'Properly and carefully'   It will be noted that the carrier's obligation under article III, rule 2   **26.38**
must be exercised 'properly and carefully'. The meaning of these words was considered by the House of Lords in *Albacora v Westcott and Laurance Line*.[107] In this case the owners of the *Maltasian*, an unrefrigerated vessel, were sued by the appellants, merchants of Genoa,

---

[98] cf article III, rule 2. See para 26.35.

[99] See, eg, *Mediterranean Freight Services Ltd v BP Oil International Ltd (The Fiona)* [1994] 2 Lloyd's Rep 506 (CA), 513–514, where the exceptions in article IV, rule 6 were held to be subject to the carrier's overriding obligation in article III, rule 1 (Hirst LJ). For article IV, rule 6, see the discussion at para 22.12.

[100] See *National Jaya (Pte) Ltd v Hong Tat Marine Shipping Pte Ltd* [1978] SLR 416; *Parsons Corp v CV Scheepvaartonderneming Happy Ranger (The Happy Ranger)* [2002] EWCA Civ 694; [2002] 2 Lloyd's Rep 357 (CA), 364 (Tuckey LJ).

[101] See Berlingieri (1997), 185 and, more generally, Scrutton (1996), section XX; Cooke (2001), para 85.100; Carver (2005), para 9-143.

[102] *Albacora SRL v Westcott & Laurance Line Ltd* [1965] 2 Lloyd's Rep 37, 46 (Lord Cameron); *Marbig Rexel Pty Ltd v ABC Container Line NV (The TNT Express)* [1992] 2 Lloyd's Rep 636, 642–643 (Carruthers J); *The Polessk and Akademik Iosif Orbeli* [1996] 2 Lloyd's Rep 40, 45 (Clarke J).

[103] See, eg, *Parsons Corp v CV Scheepvaartonderneming Happy Ranger (The Happy Ranger)* [2006] EWHC 122 (Comm); [2006] 1 Lloyd's Rep 649, 663 (Gloster J).

[104] *Shipping Corp of India Ltd v Gamlen Chemical Co (A/Asia) Pty Ltd* (1980) 147 CLR 142, 162 (Mason and Wilson JJ).

[105] See para 29.07.

[106] See para 26.34.

[107] [1966] 2 Lloyd's Rep 53 (HL).

for £8,180 as damages for deterioration in a consignment of 1,200 cases of wet salted ling fillets during a voyage from Glasgow to Genoa. At first instance before the Court of Session,[108] the court found for the appellants and awarded £1,157 damages. The fish harboured halophilic bacteria and these caused no harm provided the fish were kept at temperatures below 41°F. No special instructions were given by the consignor, other than that the cases were marked: 'Keep away from engines and boilers'. When the cargo arrived in Genoa the fish had deteriorated substantially in quality as a result of the work of the bacteria. Had the cargo been carried 'properly' within the meaning of article III, rule 2? Lord Reid said that

> . . . here 'properly' means in accordance with a sound system and that may mean rather more than carrying the goods carefully . . . In my opinion the obligation is to adopt a system which is sound in the light of all the knowledge which the carrier has or ought to have about the nature of the goods. And if that is right, then the respondents did adopt a sound system. They had no reason to suppose that the goods required any different treatment from that which the goods in fact received.[109]

Lord Pearce agreed:

> The word 'properly' presumably adds something to the word 'carefully'. A sound system does not mean a system suited to all the weaknesses and idiosyncrasies of a particular cargo, but a sound system under all the circumstances in relation to the general practice of carriage of goods by sea. It is tantamount, I think, to efficiency. To accept the pursuer's contention would be to import into the Hague Rules a revolutionary departure from the scheme of the common law.[110]

In the absence of any breach of duty under article III rule 2, the carrier was allowed to rely on the defence of inherent vice under article IV, rule 2(m).[111] This view of the meaning of 'properly' has been applied elsewhere[112] and has been approved in many cases.[113]

26.39 'Load, handle . . .' The wording of article III, rule 2 seems to require that the carrier take full responsibility from the commencement of loading to the completion of discharge. However, as we have seen, it is possible for the parties to the contract of carriage to agree that these duties be the responsibility of the shipper or consignee. Devlin J said that the object of the Rules

> is to define not the scope of the contract service but the terms on which that service is to be performed. On this view the whole contract of carriage is subject to the rules, but the extent to which loading and discharging are brought within the carrier's obligations is left to the parties themselves to decide.[114]

---

[108] 1965 SLT 3.

[109] [1966] 2 Lloyd's Rep 53 (HL), 58.

[110] At 62.

[111] See the discussion of this defence at para 28.39.

[112] See, eg, *Caltex Refining Co Pty Ltd v BHP Transport Ltd (The Iron Gippsland)* [1994] 1 Lloyd's Rep 335, 337 (Carruthers J); *Great China Metal Industries Co Ltd v Malaysian International Shipping Corp Berhad (The Bunga Seroja)* [1999] 1 Lloyd's Rep 512, at [143] (Kirby J).

[113] See most recently, *Parsons Corp v CV Scheepvaartonderneming Happy Ranger (The Happy Ranger)* [2006] EWHC 122 (Comm); [2006] 1 Lloyd's Rep 649, discussed at para 26.24 (in relation to art III, r 1).

[114] *Pyrene Co Ltd v Scindia Navigation Co Ltd* [1954] 2 QB 402, 418. This view was recently characterized by Lord Steyn as 'principled and reasonable': *Jindal Iron & Steel Co Ltd v Islamic Solidarity Shipping Co Jordan Inc (The Jordan II)* [2004] UKHL 49; [2005] 1 WLR 1363, at [19]. See also para 19.08.

Thus, under article III, rule 2, the English view is that the carrier may contract out of the obligations listed.[115] However, if he undertakes any of the specified obligations then he is obliged to ensure that he does so 'properly and carefully'. This view of the Rules is accepted in other jurisdictions[116] but there is contrary authority in Australia,[117] South Africa,[118] and the United States,[119] which may be more in accord with the intentions of those who drafted the Rules.[120]

FIOS clauses   It is open to the parties to contract FIO (free in and out), FIOS (free in and   **26.40** out, stowed), or FIOST (free in and out, stowed and trimmed). In essence, these terms are introduced into the contract of carriage to specify that it is the cargo owner who is to perform some or all of the obligations of loading, stowing, trimming, and discharging of the goods. In effect, the carrier contracts out of responsibility for the performance of these obligations.[121] As we have just seen, he may do so as a matter of English law, a view confirmed recently by the House of Lords in *Jindal Iron & Steel Co Ltd v Islamic Solidarity Shipping Co Jordan Inc (The Jordan II)*.[122]

The Jordan II   In *Jindal Iron & Steel Co Ltd v Islamic Solidarity Shipping Co Jordan Inc*   **26.41** *(The Jordan II)*[123] the *Jordan II* was voyage chartered for the carriage of a cargo of steel coils from India to Spain. The shipper alleged that the cargo was damaged by defective loading, stowage, lashing, securing, dunnaging, separation, and discharge of the cargo. The charterer sued under the terms of the charterparty, while the shipper and the receivers of the cargo sued under the bills of lading. The charterparty terms included clause 3, which stated that freight was payable 'FIOST lashed/ secured/ dunnaged' and clause 17, which provided:

> Shipper/Charterers/Receivers to put the cargo on board, trim and discharge cargo free of expense to the vessel. Trimming is understood to mean levelling off the top of the pile and any additional trimming required by the Master is to be for Owners' account.

The claimants argued that the effect of these clauses relieved the shipowners from their duties under article III, rule 2 of the Rules and were void and of no effect pursuant to

---

[115] See also *GH Renton & Co Ltd v Palmyra Trading Corporation of Panama* [1957] AC 149, 170 (Lord Morton), 174 (Lord Somervell); *The Arawa* [1977] 2 Lloyd's Rep 416, 424–425 (Brandon J); *Jindal Iron & Steel Co Ltd v Islamic Solidarity Shipping Co Jordan Inc (The Jordan II)* [2004] UKHL 49; [2005] 1 WLR 1363.

[116] Australia: *Shipping Corporation of India v Gamlen Chemical Co (A/Asia) Pty Ltd* (1980) 147 CLR 142; *Hunter Grain Pty Ltd v Hyundai Merchant Marine Co Ltd* (1993) 117 ALR 507. New Zealand: *International Ore & Fertilizer Corp v East Coast Fertilizer Co Ltd* [1987] 1 NZLR 9. India: *The New India Assurance Co Ltd v M/S Splosna Plovba* (1986) AIR Ker 176. Pakistan: *East & West Steamship Co v Houssain Brothers* (1968) 20 PLD SC 15.

[117] *Nikolay Malakhov Shipping Co Ltd v SEAS Sapfor Ltd* (1998) 44 NSWLR 371, 387–388 (Sheller JA).

[118] *The MV Sea Joy* (1998) 1 SA 487 (C).

[119] *Associated Metals and Minerals Corp v M/V The Arktis Sky* 978 F 2d 47 (2nd Cir 1992); *Tubacex Inc v M/V Risan* 45 F 3rd 951 (5th Cir 1995). Cf also *Sumitomo Corp of America v M/V Sie Kim* 632 F Supp 824 (SDNY 1985); *Atlas Assurance Co v Harper, Robinson Shipping Co* 508 F 2d 1381 (9th Cir, 1975). See too Schoenbaum (2004), §10-26.

[120] See Martin Davies, 'Two views of FIOS clauses in bills of lading' (1994) 22 ABLR 198.

[121] Se, eg, *Balli Trading Ltd v Afalona Shipping Ltd (The Coral)* [1993] 1 Lloyd's Rep 1 (CA); *Jindal Iron & Steel Co Ltd v Islamic Solidarity Shipping Co Jordan Inc (The Jordan II)* [2004] UKHL 49; [2005] 1 WLR 1363.

[122] [2004] UKHL 49; [2005] 1 WLR 1363. See Sarah Derrington, 'The Hague Rules — a lost opportunity' (2005) 121 LQR 209.

[123] ibid.

article III, rule 8. At first instance, the judge concluded that the authority on this point[124] bound the court to the effect that article III, rule 2 did not oblige the carrier to load, stow, carry, and discharge the goods properly and carefully, but only obliged the carrier to do so if it had agreed to perform those functions.[125] The Court of Appeal confirmed this.[126] Accordingly, as the shipowners were under no liability for damage caused by loading, stowage, dunnage, securing, or discharging, article III, rule 8 did not render the charter-party clauses null and void. The House of Lords agreed,[127] declining to overrule the previous authorities, and noting that the weight of opinion in foreign jurisdictions was fairly evenly divided.[128] Further, shipowners, charterers, shippers, and consignees had acted on the basis that the earlier cases correctly stated the law[129] and, even if persuaded that the cargo owners' interpretation of the Rules was correct, the case against departing from them was overwhelming.[130] Thus, the real difficulty for the claimants were the authorities of nearly fifty years' standing, by respected English commercial judges, and the principle of certainty in commercial transactions, represented as follows by Lord Mansfield in *Vallejo v Wheeler*:

> In all mercantile transactions the great object should be certainty: and therefore, it is of more consequence that a rule should be certain, than whether the rule is established one way or the other. Because speculators in trade then know what ground to go upon.[131]

26.42 **Non-delegable** As is the case with article III, rule 1, it would seem that the obligations cast on the carrier under article III, rule 2 are personal. Thus, while responsibility may be delegated to the servants or agents of the carrier, liability for proper and careful performance remains with him.[132] Nevertheless, he may prove the operation of one or more of the exceptions since, as we have seen, article III, rule 2 is expressly made subject to article IV.[133]

26.43 **Proof** Once the cargo owner has proved that the goods have been lost or damaged in transit, the onus shifts to the carrier to bring the cause of damage within one of the exceptions listed in article IV, rule 2 (a)-(p). If he is unable to do so, he will be held liable unless he can prove that the damage or loss occurred 'without the actual fault or privity of the carrier, or without the fault or neglect of the agents or servants of the carrier'.[134] If he can succeed in bringing the loss within an exception, the carrier will escape liability unless the

---

124 ie, *Pyrene Co Ltd v Scindia Steam Navigation Co Ltd* [1954] 2 QB 402; *GH Renton & Co Ltd v Palmyra Trading Corp* [1957] AC 149.
125 [2002] EWHC 1268 (Comm); [2002] 2 All ER (Comm) 364.
126 [2003] EWCA Civ 144; [2003] 2 Lloyd's Rep 87.
127 [2004] UKHL 49; [2005] 1 WLR 1363.
128 At [24].
129 At [28].
130 At [29].
131 (1774) 1 Cowp 143, 153; 98 ER 1012, 1017. Cited with approval by their Lordships: at [16]. See too *Homburg Houtimport BV v Agrosin Private Ltd (The Starsin)* [2003] UKHL 12; [2004] 1 AC 715, at [13], (Lord Bingham).
132 See *W Angliss & Co (Australia) Pty Ltd v Peninsular and Oriental Steam Navigation Company* [1927] 2 KB 456, 462 (Wright J); *International Packers London Ltd v Ocean Steam Ship Co Ltd* [1955] 2 Lloyd's Rep 218, 236 (McNair J); *Riverstone Meat Co Pty Ltd v Lancashire Shipping Co Ltd (The Muncaster Castle)* [1961] AC 807, 856 (Lord Merriman); *Leesh River Tea Co v British India Steam Navigation Co (The Chyebassa)* [1966] 1 Lloyd's Rep 450.
133 See para 26.37.
134 Article IV, rule 2(q). See para 28.46.

cargo owner can establish a breach of the carrier's duty of care within article III, rule 2. This view of the burden of proof was applied in *The Glendarroch* by Lopes LJ:[135]

> The question raised on this appeal is as to the onus of proof; as a general rule, it may be said that the burden of proof lies on the person who affirms a particular thing … [I]t appears to me in this case that the burden of proving that the loss which has happened is attributable to an excepted cause lies on the person who is setting it up. That in this case would be the defendants, the shipowners. If, however, the excepted cause by itself is sufficient to account for the loss, it appears to me that the burden of showing that there is something else which deprives the party of the power of relying on the excepted cause lies on the person who sets up that contention.[136]

E. Deviation

Article IV, rule 4   Article IV, rule 4[137] provides that: **26.44**

> Any deviation in saving or attempting to save life or property at sea, or any reasonable deviation shall not be deemed to be an infringement or breach of these Rules or of the contract of carriage, and the carrier shall not be liable for any loss or damage resulting therefrom.

Rules and common law   This provision does not disturb the existing common law prin-   **26.45** ciples on deviation.[138] Indeed, the provision recognizes the well-known liberty of 'saving or attempting to save life'. However, extended protection is given to shipowners in the form of deviations to save property and reasonable deviations. These extensions are potentially of great significance.

'Reasonable deviation'   The main difficulty which arises in article IV, rule 4 lies in inter-   **26.46** preting the phrase 'any reasonable deviation'. One of the leading cases is *Stag Line v Foscolo, Mango & Co Ltd*.[139] Here the appellants were the owners of a steamship, the *Ixia*, which was chartered to Foscolo to carry a cargo of coal from Swansea to Constantinople. The ship was fitted with a heating apparatus designed to make use of the heat otherwise wasted as steam. As this was not working satisfactorily, the owners arranged for engineers to undertake certain tests during the voyage. However, owing to excessive drinking by those on board the night before,[140] the necessary head of steam was not reached for the test to be made and the ship was obliged to make a detour to St Ives to land the engineers. Following this procedure the ship followed the coast of Cornwall too closely and ran aground on the Vyneck rock. Both the vessel and her cargo were totally lost. The charterers sought to recover damages for the loss of their cargo on the ground that there had been an unlawful deviation. The owners

---

135 Although this was not, of course, a case decided under the Rules.
136 [1894] P 226 (CA), 234–235. For an alternative, bailment, basis, see *Gosse Millard v Canadian Government Merchant Marine Ltd* [1927] KB 432, 434–435 (Wright J). This view was applied in *Successors of Moine Comte & Co Ltd v East Asiatic Co Ltd & Singapore Harbour Board* [1954] 1 MLJ 113, 115; *Yeo Goon Nyoh v Ocean Steamship Co Ltd* [1966] SLR 401, 403; *The Gang Cheng* (1998) 6 MLJ 468, 489.
137 See Berlingieri (1997), 433 and, more generally, Scrutton (1996), section XX; Cooke (2001), para 85.343; Carver (2005), para 9-239.
138 Discussed in detail at ch 24.
139 [1932] AC 328.
140 Lord Buckmaster explained that 'the firemen on board the ship were not in possession of their full energies' (at 332).

argued that the accident was a peril of the sea and that the deviation was reasonable and so was not an infringement of the contract of carriage. On the deviation point, Lord Atkin said that:

> A deviation may, and often will, be caused by fortuitous circumstances never contemplated by the original parties to the contract; and may be reasonable, though it is made solely in the interests of the ship or solely in the interests of the cargo, or indeed in the direct interest of neither: as for instance where the presence of a passenger or of a member of the ship or crew was urgently required after the voyage had begun on a matter of national importance; or where some person on board was a fugitive from justice, and there were urgent reasons for his immediate appearance. The true test seems to be what departure from the contract voyage might a prudent person controlling the voyage at the time make and maintain, having in mind all the relevant circumstances existing at the time, including the terms of the contract and the interests of all parties concerned, but without obligation to consider the interests of any one as conclusive.[141]

Applying the test set out above, Lord Atkin concluded that after the *Ixia* left St Ives the course set by the master was not the correct course which would ordinarily be set in those circumstances. It was obvious that the small extra risk to ship and cargo caused by the deviation to St Ives was vastly increased by the subsequent course and so the appeal was dismissed.[142]

26.47   **Concept successfully invoked**   There are a small number of cases where the concept 'reasonable deviation' has been successfully invoked. One of the most important, *Lyric Shipping Inc v Intermetals Ltd (The Al Taha)*, concerned a planned bunkering stop.[143] The owners of the *Al Taha* time chartered their vessel to charterers who in turn sub-chartered the vessel for a time charter voyage via United States ports to Izmit. Both charters incorporated the Hague Rules. In January 1982, following loading at Portsmouth, the *Al Taha* was ordered to Boston to take on bunkers and to have one of the derricks, which had been damaged in heavy weather, repaired. On completion of the bunkering and repairs, the docking pilot took the *Al Taha* out of her berth too soon while the tide was still rising and she grounded and sustained damage, the effects of which became apparent when the ship was at sea the following day. This necessitated a return to Boston as a port of refuge and the expenses thereby incurred formed the basis of the action in the case. One of the issues in the case was whether there had been a deviation from the contractual voyage. Phillips J found that the decision to bunker at Boston after loading was reasonable[144] as this was not merely a usual bunkering port for such a vessel but it was the usual bunkering port:

> ... to bunker at Portsmouth after loading, rather than call at Boston for bunkering and repairs before loading, was the only reasonable decision to make once the fact and implications of the heavy weather damage were appreciated.[145]

---

[141] At 343–344.

[142] At 344. See also *Thiess Bros (Queensland) Pty Ltd v Australian Steamships Pty Ltd* [1955] 1 Lloyd's Rep 459.

[143] [1990] 2 Lloyd's Rep 117.

[144] For bunkering cases at common law, see *Reardon Smith Line v Black Sea and Baltic General Insurance* (1939) 64 Ll LR 229 and the discussion at para 24.04.

[145] [1990] 2 Lloyd's Rep 117, 127.

Considering the effect of article IV, rule 4 of the Hague Rules, he found that a 'reasonable deviation' could be a deviation planned before the voyage had begun or the bills of lading had been signed:

> In the present case the No 6 boom was necessary if *Al Taha* was to be reasonably fit to discharge her cargo at her destination. The boom was not necessary to render the vessel seaworthy at the commencement of the voyage. It was reasonable to plan to deviate to collect the boom en route rather than to wait for the weather conditions to permit delivery at Portsmouth. This mode of performance was, in my judgment, within the liberty afforded by article IV, rule 4.[146]

As the deviation was not unlawful, the owners were able to rely on article IV, rule 2(a)[147] which exempted them from liability for negligent navigation. Further, an act of negligent navigation in the course of carrying out a reasonable deviation would not render the deviation itself unreasonable.[148]

Express liberties   The provision in article IV, rule 4 does not have an effect on other **26.48** contractual terms which give the carrier the liberty to perform his contractual obligations, such as calling at substitute ports.[149] It would seem that these clauses amount to performance of the contract of carriage and will not be caught by article III, rule 8.[150]

Effect of an unreasonable deviation   Article IV, rule 4 does not spell out what the conse- **26.49** quences of an unlawful deviation will be. It is thought that the result is probably the same as at common law,[151] though this is still undecided.

---

[146] At 128.
[147] For discussion of this exemption, see para 28.07.
[148] [1990] 2 Lloyd's Rep 117, 129.
[149] See *GH Renton & Co Ltd v Palmyra Trading Corporation of Panama (The Caspiana)* [1956] 1 QB 462 (CA). See the discussion of this case at para 24.15.
[150] For discussion of art III, r 8, see para 19.39.
[151] See Cooke (2001), para 85.350.

PART VI

THE RIGHTS AND IMMUNITIES
OF THE CARRIER

27

LIENS

A. Introduction

Overview   In this chapter we consider one of the carrier's most important remedies, **27.01** namely his right to exercise a lien over the cargo of others. We shall consider first the different types of lien, before considering liens at common law and contractual liens which, in practice, are the most important. Lastly, we consider the status of cesser clauses, which are usually said to be dependent on the existence of a lien.

B. Types of Lien

Definition   The classic definition of a 'lien' is that of Grose J in the case of *Hammonds v* **27.02** *Barclay* that '. . . a lien is a right in one man to retain that which is in his possession belonging to another, till certain demands of him the person in possession are satisfied'.[1] This definition, however, provides an introduction to only one type of lien, the common law (or possessory) lien, which is one species in which we are interested.

Main types   There are, in fact, four main types of lien in English law: (i) the common law **27.03** (possessory) lien just mentioned; (ii) the statutory lien, such as the unpaid seller's lien under the Sale of Goods Act 1979, sections 41–43; (iii) the equitable lien, such as that in favour of the unpaid vendor of land; (iv) maritime liens.[2]

---

[1] (1802) 2 East 227, 235; 102 ER 356, 359.
[2] See para 35.17.

27.04 **Possessory (shipowners') liens** A shipowner may have a lien on goods carried for charges incurred in carrying them at common law or by express contractual agreement. At common law the shipowner will have a lien for (i) freight; (ii) general average contributions; and (iii) expenses incurred by the shipowner or master in protecting and preserving the goods. We shall look at each of these in turn.

C. Liens at Common Law

27.05 **Introduction** In the carriage context, a shipowner's possessory lien is one which is dependent on his possession of the cargo. It arises only in the following three situations: (i) for the recovery of a general average contribution due from cargo; (ii) for expenses incurred by the shipowner in protecting the cargo; (iii) to recover freight due on delivery of the cargo.

27.06 **The lien for freight** The common law lien for freight is only enforceable so long as the shipowner retains the cargo. The right is lost once the cargo has been handed over to the charterer or the consignee at the port of discharge and it will only exist where freight is payable on delivery of the cargo.[3]

27.07 **Lien restricted to the particular cargo** The right to exercise the possessory lien on cargo is restricted to the consignment of cargo on which the freight is due and may be exercised over the entire consignment, even where only part of the freight is still outstanding.[4] The lien may not, however, be exercised over goods on different voyages covered by different contracts of carriage.

27.08 **Freight in advance** Difficulties sometimes arise where freight is expressed to be paid in advance.[5] However, the normal rule is that freight paid in advance is not subject to the common law possessory lien.[6] Nor can the lien be exercised where the freight is payable after delivery of the cargo or where it is not due when the cargo is claimed.[7]

27.09 **Right to possession** A further point to notice is that, unlike a maritime lien,[8] the shipowners' lien for freight merely gives a right of possession of the goods. There is no right of sale of the goods, even where expense has been incurred in retaining the cargo in lieu of payment, unless the goods have been abandoned.[9]

---

[3] See *Tamvaco v Simpson* (1866) LR CP 363; *William Allison v Bristol Marine Insurance Co Ltd* (1876) 1 App Cas 209, 225 (Brett J).

[4] See *Perez v Alsop* (1862) 3 F&F 188; 176 ER 85.

[5] See para 21.15.

[6] See, eg, *Kirchner v Venus* (1859) 12 Moore PC 361; 14 ER 948; *Gardner & Sons v Trechmann* (1884) 15 QBD 154 (CA). Similarly for dead freight: see *Phillips v Rodie* (1812) 15 East 547; 104 ER 950.

[7] See, eg, *Foster v Colby* (1853) 3 H&N 705; 157 ER 651. In *Canadian Pacific (Bermuda) Ltd v Lagon Maritime Overseas (The Fort Kipp)* [1985] 2 Lloyd's Rep 168, a stipulation that freight was payable after the completion of discharge had the effect of precluding the exercise of a contractual lien for freight for cargo still on board a vessel.

[8] See para 35.17.

[9] See, eg, *Enimont Overseas AG v Ro Jugotanker Zadar (The Olib)* [1991] 2 Lloyd's Rep 108, 115 (Webster J).

The lien for general average   The topic of general average does not fall within the scheme **27.10** of this book but arises when there has been some sort of act which has necessitated the jettison of cargo, the towage of a disabled vessel, expenses and repairs in a port of refuge, or on-carriage of cargo.[10] The costs of such an act on the part of the master are apportioned among all those participating in the voyage, including the shipowner and the cargo owners, and the claim for general average contribution is secured by a lien over the property, usually the cargo. Release of the cargo is usually obtained by the cargo owner executing an Average Bond, under which his cargo will be released in return for agreeing to pay the amount adjudged to him by an average adjuster.

Expenses incurred by the shipowner   So far as the final category of lien at common law **27.11** is concerned, the master of a ship has authority to take whatever steps are necessary to protect the cargo owner's interest during the course of the voyage.[11]

D. Express Contractual Liens over Cargo

Introduction   It is very common for the parties to a contract of carriage to make express **27.12** provision for a lien, whether under a bill of lading or a charterparty.

Specific clauses   The Gencon clause provides that 'Owners shall have a lien on the cargo **27.13** for freight, dead freight, demurrage and damages for detention'. The NYPE 1946 charter provides:

> 18. That the Owners shall have a lien upon all cargoes, and all sub-freights for any amounts due under this Charter, including General Average contributions, and the Charterers to have a lien on the Ship for all monies paid in advance and not earned, and any overpaid hire or excess deposit to be returned at once. Charterers will not suffer, nor permit to be continued, any lien or encumbrance incurred by them or their agents, which might have priority over the title and interest of the owners of the vessel.[12]

This may be contrasted with the clause in the NYPE 93 charterparty:

> 23. **Liens**
>
> The Owners shall have a lien upon all cargoes and all sub-freights and/or sub-hire for any amounts due under this Charter Party, including general average contributions, and the Charterers shall have a lien on the Vessel for all monies paid in advance and not earned, and any overpaid hire or excess deposit to be returned at once.
>
> The Charterers will not directly or indirectly suffer, nor permit to be continued, any lien or encumbrance, which might have priority over the title and interest of the Owners in the Vessel. The Charterers undertake that during the period of this Charter Party, they will not procure any supplies or necessaries or services, including any port expenses and bunkers, on the credit of the Owners or in the Owners' time.[13]

Characteristics   Contractual liens, like common law liens, are possessory in character and **27.14** create rights of lien between the parties to the contract in which they are contained.

---

[10] See Scrutton (1996), art 134; Rose (2005).
[11] See *Hingston v Wendt* (1876) 1 QBD 367.
[12] Lines 110–113.
[13] Lines 259–267.

No rights of lien are created as against third party bill of lading holders.[14] In *Turner v Haji Goolam Mahomed Azam*[15] the *Bombay* was chartered for a period of six months with an option to sub-let and was sub-chartered for a round voyage. The head charter provided that bills of lading were to be signed at any rate of freight the charterers or their agents might direct without prejudice to the charter. The charter also provided that the owners were to have a lien 'upon all cargoes for freight or charter money due under this charter'. Bills of lading were duly issued to the sub-charterers and the owners then purported to exercise a lien on the sub-charterers' cargo for time charter hire. The Privy Council held that the owners had no right of lien on the sub-charterer's cargo. Lord Lindley said:

> ... [A]s regards ... giving a lien upon all cargoes for freight or charter money due under that charter. This is a stipulation binding on the time charterer, and gives the shipowner a more extensive lien than he would have for freight payable in advance. But this clause does not override or limit the power of the captain to issue bills of lading at different rates of freight, or entitle the shipowners to a lien on the goods of persons who have come under no contract with them conferring a lien for the freight payable under the time charter. A right to seize one person's goods for another person's debt must be clearly and distinctly conferred before a court of justice can be expected to recognise it.[16]

27.15 **Exercise against a consignee** A contractual lien may be exercised against a third party where the bill of lading contains a clause which incorporates the charterparty clause. This point was made by Mocatta J in *Santiren Shipping Ltd v Unimarine SA (The Chrysovalandou Dyo)*:[17]

> ... [I]f the lien was on the facts properly exercised, it applied to the cargo here by reason of the incorporating clause in the bill of lading ...[18]

27.16 **The NYPE 93 clause** Clause 23 of the NYPE 93 charterparty[19] provides that the shipowner has a 'lien upon all cargoes and all sub-freights for any amounts due under this charter'. This raises the issue whether the shipowner can detain cargo not owned by the time charterers. There are conflicting decisions on this point. In *Steelwood Carriers Inc of Monrovia, Liberia v Evimeria Compania Naviera SA of Panama (The Agios Giorgis)*[20] the charterparty, which was on the NYPE 1946 form, contained just such a clause. The charterparty was for the carriage of cargo aboard the *Agios Giorgis* from Korea to Charleston (South Carolina) and Norfolk (Virginia). One of the main issues for consideration by Mocatta J was the ability of the charterers to deduct from a hire instalment an amount of $19,860 for an alleged speed deficiency. The owners had taken the view that there was no entitlement to deduct this amount and they duly instructed the master not to allow discharge of the cargo at Norfolk. The cargo was detained for a period of two days until the charterers agreed to pay the balance of the hire. Mocatta J held that there was no automatic right to deduct hire. So far as the exercise of the lien was concerned, he said that:

> The difficulty ... for the owners is that they are relying upon a contractual lien, not one given at common law, as against the cargo owners, who were not parties to the time charter ... I am

---

[14] Although see para 27.15.
[15] [1904] AC 826 (PC).
[16] At 837.
[17] [1981] 1 Lloyd's Rep 159.
[18] At 165.
[19] See para 27.13.
[20] [1976] 2 Lloyd's Rep 192.

unable to see how cl 18 can give the owners the right to detain cargo not belonging to the charterers and on which no freight was owing to the owners. There is no finding that the bills of lading contained any clause rendering the cargo shipped under them subject to this charterparty lien.[21]

A different view was, however, taken by Donaldson J in *Aegnoussiotis Shipping Corp of Monrovia v Kristian Jebsens Rederi of Bergen (The Aegnoussiotis)*,[22] though he knew of the earlier decision of Mocatta J. The case was also concerned with a charterparty entered into on the NYPE 1946 form, this time for a round voyage in the St Lawrence Seaway. The dispute over the exercise of the contractual lien under the charterparty again arose in connection with the payment of hire. While the vessel was in the course of discharging cargo a dispute arose as to whether any and, if so, how much hire was due by the charterers during the period when discharge of the cargo had been suspended. After threatening to halt discharge of the consignee's cargo unless hire was paid by a certain time, the owners gave instructions to the master of the *Aegnoussiotis* after the time had passed and no hire was forthcoming. So far as the lien was concerned, however, Donaldson J took the view that clause 18 was to be construed as meaning what it said:

> . . . namely, that the time charterers agree that the owners shall have a lien upon all cargoes. In so far as such cargoes are owned by third parties, the time charterers accept an obligation to procure the creation of a contractual lien in favour of the owners. If they do not do so and the owners assert a lien over such cargo, the third parties have a cause of action against the owners. But the time charterers themselves are in a different position. They cannot assert and take advantage of their own breach of contract. As against them, the purported exercise of the lien is valid.[23]

If this view is correct, it seems that the time charterer will be obliged to secure a lien in favour of the shipowner from the cargo owner. Usually, this will be done by means of a charterparty incorporation clause in the bill of lading.[24]

Time of exercise   If the shipowner has the right to exercise a lien over cargo, this cannot **27.17** be exercised by halting the laden ship en route to the port of discharge. In *International Bulk Carriers (Beirut) SARL v Evlogia Shipping Co SA (The Milhalios Xilas)*[25] the owners had let their vessel on the Baltime form and this provided that hire was payable monthly in advance, with a right of withdrawal on default of payment. It also provided that the charterers were to deposit a further 30 days hire, a so-called 'escrow hire payment'. The vessel was delivered at Marseilles but neither the advance hire nor the escrow hire were paid by the charterers. The vessel was ordered to Casablanca and the master, on the instructions of the owners, refused to load until the advance hire had been paid. The vessel then called at Augusta to load bunkers but as the escrow hire payment was still outstanding the owners instructed the master not to sail. The vessel eventually sailed and completed discharge of cargo at Constanza, Sulina, and Brila. At Brila the vessel was withdrawn for non-payment

---

[21] At 204.

[22] [1977] 1 Lloyd's Rep 268.

[23] At 276.

[24] As *Santiren Shipping Ltd v Unimarine SA (The Chrysovalandou Dyo)* [1981] 1 Lloyd's Rep 161. See para 27.15.

[25] [1978] 2 Lloyd's Rep 186.

of hire. One of the issues for Donaldson J was whether the owners could exercise a lien on the cargo at Augusta by refusing to carry it further. He said that:

> ... I do not think that a shipowner can usually be said to be exercising a lien on cargo by refusing to carry it further. The essence of the exercise of a lien is the denial of possession of the cargo to someone who wants it. No one wanted the cargo in Augusta and the owners were not denying possession of it to anyone. It may be possible to exercise a lien by refusing to complete the carrying voyage, but I think that this can only be done when, owing to special circumstances, it is impossible to exercise a lien at the port of destination and any further carriage will lead to loss of possession of the cargo following the arrival at that port. In such circumstances a refusal to carry further can be said to be a denial of the receiver's right to possession. There was no finding that this was the case in the present instance.[26]

27.18 **Place of exercise** It would seem that it is usually sufficient for the ship to have anchored off the declared port of discharge for the lien to be exercised, as to require otherwise 'might involve unnecessary expense and in certain cases cause congestion in the port . . . [which] would seriously limit the commercial value of a lien on cargo granted by a clause in a charter'.[27]

E. Liens over Sub-Freights

27.19 **Introduction** We have already noted that the NYPE 93 charterparty provides that the contractual lien under the charterparty extends to 'sub-freights'.[28] This reference to sub-freights includes any remuneration earned by the charterers from the employment of the ship, whether payable by the shipper under a bill of lading or by a sub-charterer under a voyage sub-charter. Under the NYPE clause, the shipowner merely has the right to intercept such payments made to the charterer, by demanding payment to it rather than to the time charterer. There is no right to follow the sub-freights once these have been paid. In *Tagart, Beaton & Co v James Fisher & Sons* Lord Alverstone stated that:[29]

> A lien such as this on a sub-freight means a right to receive it as freight and to stop that freight at any time before it has been paid to the time charterer or his agent; but such a lien does not confer the right to follow the money paid for freight into the pockets of the person receiving it simply because that money has been received in respect of a debt which was due for freight.[30]

27.20 **Owners' bills of lading** If the owners are parties to the bill of lading contract,[31] the shipowners will not have to rely on any right of lien over sub-freights because they, rather

---

[26] At 191–192.
[27] *Santiren Shipping Ltd v Unimarine (The Chrysovalandou Dyo)* [1981] 1 Lloyd's Rep 159, 165 (Mocatta J).
[28] Line 260. See para 27.13. See too NYPE (1946), cl 18, line 110.
[29] [1903] KB 391 (CA).
[30] At 395. See too *Ellerman Lines Ltd v Lancaster Maritime Co Ltd (The Lancaster)* [1980] 2 Lloyd's Rep 497, 501 (Robert Goff J).
[31] See generally as to this point, para 12.09.

than the charterers, will be entitled to receive the freight. Greer J made this point in *Molthes Rederi A/S v Ellerman's Wilson Line Ltd*:[32]

> ... the bill of lading contract is a contract between the shipowners and the shipper, and not a contract between the charterers and the shipper. If this be so, the legal right to the freight is in the owner and not in the charterer, and the former can intervene at any time before the agent has received the freight and say to him: 'I am no longer content that the charterer should collect the freight. If you collect it at all, you must collect it for me.' If the agent then collects the freight, it follows that the shipowner can sue for it as money had and received.[33]

Payment of freight to charterers   Where a ship is under a time charterparty, bill of lading   **27.21** freight will usually be paid to the charterers' agents, even though the cargo is actually shipped under bill of lading contracts to which the shipowners are a party. If the shipowners notify the charterers' agents of their claim to the bill of lading freight before the agents receive the freight the agents may be obliged to then collect it for them rather than for the charterers. If the shipowners give notice after the freight has been received by the agents it would seem that the agents will remain obliged to hand over the freight to the owners.[34]

In *Molthes Rederi A/S v Ellerman's Wilson Line Ltd*[35] the *Sproit* was time chartered on the Baltic and White Sea Time Charter form, 1912, and then sub-chartered for a voyage between Riga and Hull. Agents were appointed at the port of discharge by the time charterers to attend to discharge and to collect freight due under the bill of lading. However, before any freight was paid, representatives of the shipowners required the agents to collect the freight as agents for the owners because a considerable amount of hire was still outstanding on the time charter. Greer J held that, although the agents were agents for the time charterers, the shipowners were perfectly entitled to call upon them to collect the freight on their behalf when they were parties to the bill of lading contracts.[36]

Payment of hire   So far we have considered the situation where the lien on sub-freights   **27.22** under the charterparty relates to outstanding freight. Where, however, the shipowner purports to use the lien to collect any outstanding charter hire, this can only be exercised in respect of the hire which has already accrued before the sub-freight came into the hands of an agent and not for hire which accrues after that date, even though the relevant funds are still held by the agent. In *Wehner v Dene Shipping Co*[37] the *Ferndene* was on time charter and was also sub-time chartered for a trip. The sub-time charterers were appointed as agents to collect the bill of lading freight. They received the freight from the consignee on 15 December and, one day later, the shipowners notified the agents of their claim for the freight collected. At this time, part of the hire due under the head charter was still owed. A further hire payment was due some days later. Channell J held that since the bill of lading contract was with the owners, they were entitled to the bill of lading freight. He further

---

[32] [1927] 1 KB 710.
[33] At 715–716.
[34] See *Wehner v Dene* [1905] 2 KB 92.
[35] [1927] 1 KB 710.
[36] The court also held that the agents would not be entitled to deduct from the freight any disbursements incurred by them in their capacity as agents for the charterers: at 718 (Greer J).
[37] [1905] 2 KB 92.

held that the owners were entitled to the freight received by the agents on 15 December but were bound to account for it to the sub-time charterers, deducting only the amount due to the owners at the date of receipt. Finally, the owners were not entitled to deduct the amount of hire which only became due on 23 December.

27.23 **Sub-hire**   In *Itex Itagrani Export v Care Shipping Corp (The Cebu)(No 2)*[38] the owners of the *Cebu* let her on a time charter trip on the NYPE 1946 form. She was in turn sub-chartered to Lamsco, who themselves sub-chartered her to Itex, a sub-sub-charterer. During September 1981 at least a month's hire was due and notice was sent that under the terms of clause 18 of the charter there was a 'lien upon all cargoes and all sub-freights'. The hire instalment was paid to Lamsco. Had the shipowners exercised their rights under their contractual lien on sub-freights under clause 18 in respect of hire due under a sub-sub-time charter? In effect Itex was asking the court whether the lien on 'all sub-freights' covered time charter hire and covered sub-sub hire? Steyn J referred first in some detail to the judgment of Lloyd J in the earlier dispute of *Care Shipping v Latin American Shipping Co (The Cebu)(No 1)*.[39] Lloyd J had said here that:

> In the 20th Century there has been a progressive tendency to assimilate, so far as possible, the rules relating to voyage charters and time charters. This seems to me a sensible approach, particularly since the advent and rapid growth of the time charter trip. No doubt the time charter trip has many advantages over the voyage charter. For one thing it avoids the hideous complexities of demurrage. But it would be an odd consequence of the charterers opting to enter into a sub-time charter trip that the owners should inadvertently be deprived of their security on sub-freights. I would hold that the lien on sub-freights conferred by cl18 includes a lien on any remuneration earned by the charterers from the employment of the vessel, whether by way of voyage freight or time chartered hire.[40]

This view was not accepted by Steyn J, who concluded that

> . . . at all material times the ordinary meaning of freight, in the shipping trade, included only bill of lading freight and freight payable under a voyage charterparty. . . . I find nothing in either the printed NYPE [1946] form nor in the typed conditions to justify the stretching of the ordinary meaning of freight to cover hire. On the contrary, the consistent use of the word 'hire' in both parts of the charters points the other way. . . . I am satisfied that properly construed 'sub-freights' in cl.18 does not include sub-time charter hire.[41]

Accordingly, the owners' claim against the sub-sub-time charterers of the vessel was not within the scope of the lien on sub-freights and so it followed that the claim failed. The matter is now made clear in the NYPE 93 charterparty which provides that there is a lien for 'sub-hire'.[42]

27.24 **Registration of charges**   If the time charterers are a company incorporated in England or Wales, the owners' lien on sub-freights will be void against any liquidator or creditor of the time charterers unless the particulars of the lien are registered as a charge under the Companies Act 1985, section 395 or section 410 within 21 days of the charge

---

[38] [1993] QB 1.
[39] [1983] 1 Lloyd's Rep 302.
[40] At 305.
[41] [1993] 1 QB 1 13-15.
[42] Clause 23, line 260. See para 27.13.

being created. This issue arose in *Re Welsh Irish Ferries Ltd (The Ugland Trailer)*.[43] Here Welsh Irish Ferries Ltd operated a ferry service between Barry and Cork. In 1983, a Norwegian company chartered one of their vessels, the *Ugland Trailer*, to Welsh Irish Ferries, on the NYPE 1946 form. The charterparty was not registered under what was then the Companies Act 1948, section 95. During the charterparty the company executed a debenture in favour of Lloyd's Bank charging with the payment of all moneys and liabilities agreed to be thereby secured 'all book debts both present and future due or owing to the company and the benefit of all rights relating thereto'. The charge was registered as a first fixed charge under the Companies Act 1948, section 95. Following a default on the hire by Welsh Irish Ferries, the owners terminated the charterparty and notified all known shippers, requiring them to pay all outstanding sums due by way of freight or hire to them. Following the winding up of the company, the bank sought a court order for direction whether to pay the sums collected from various shippers in respect of freight to the owners or to the bank. Nourse J held that the lien on sub-freights in the charter created an equitable charge on the company's book debts, including the sub-freights. On the clear wording of section 95 of the Companies Act 1948, such a lien was registrable under that section and, since the lien was unregistered, the bank's fixed charge took priority. Nourse J so held reluctantly because such a finding '. . . will come as something of a shock to those who deal with matters of this kind'.[44]

Companies Act 1989   An attempt was made to dispel the effect of this case in section 93   **27.25**
of the Companies Act 1989. It was intended that the new section 396(2) of the Companies Act 1985 would state that:

> (g) a shipowners' lien on sub-freights shall not be treated as a charge on book debts for the purposes of paragraph (c)(iii) or as a floating charge for the purposes of the paragraph (e).

However, this part of the Companies Act 1989 never come into force.[45]

Freight prepaid   There can be further problems where bills of lading are issued which   **27.26**
provide that freight is to be 'prepaid'. In such an instance the lien on sub-freights will be lost, much as that for advance freight would be lost.[46] The master cannot refuse to sign freight prepaid bills of lading if these are required by the charterers. In *The Shillito*[47] the owners of the *Shillito* time chartered her to Ercole Conti. Clauses in the charterparty provided that:

> 10. The captain shall sign bills of lading at any rate of freight the charterer or his agents may choose, without prejudice to the stipulations of this charterparty, and the charterer hereby agrees to indemnify the owners from any consequences that may arise . . .

> 14. The owner shall have a lien upon all cargoes and on all sub-freights for freight and hire due under this charter, and charterer to have a lien on the ship for all moneys paid in advance and not earned.

The charterers sub-chartered the *Shillito* for a voyage between Barletta and the River Plate. At the loading port bills of lading were presented to the master for signature, showing

---

[43] [1986] Ch 471.
[44] At 480.
[45] See now cl 1864 (7) of the Companies Bill 2005–06.
[46] See para 27.08.
[47] (1897) 3 Com Cas 44.

that all the freight had been paid in advance. The bills of lading contained no reference to the charterparty. In due course the charterer defaulted on payment of hire. The owners sought to prevent the cargo being unloaded at the ports of discharge but were unable to and they now brought a claim in negligence against the master for signing the bills of lading in such a way that they could not enforce their lien. Barnes J held that:

> The charterer has a right to present any bills he chooses, and although there is a lien clause, it is inoperative, because the bills of lading contain no reference to the charterparty, and there is no freight on which a lien can be exercised.[48]

F. Cesser Clauses

27.27 **Introduction** In the case of goods which are delivered under a bill of lading, or bills of lading which are issued pursuant to a charterparty, the consignee is the party generally responsible for any charges incidental to the transport of the goods, in particular the payment of freight. But where bills of lading are issued under a charterparty it is usual for the charterer to remain liable for demurrage, damages for detention, and dead freight. In those instances, where the charterer does not wish to remain responsible for performance of the contract after the goods are loaded, he may insert in the charterparty a so-called 'cesser clause' whereby his liability for transport charges is to cease once the cargo has been shipped. The effect of such clauses was considered in *Kish v Cory*.[49] In this case the charterparty provided that cargo was to be loaded in thirteen working days and discharged at not less than 30 tons per working day. An additional period of ten days demurrage was to be allowed. The court was required to consider the effect of the clause which stated:

> Charterer's liability to cease when the ship is loaded, the captain or owner having a lien on cargo for freight and demurrage.[50]

The Court of Exchequer Chamber held that the charterer upon loading the cargo was discharged from liability for demurrage incurred at the port of loading. The important thing about this particular clause was that it expressly stated that liability was to cease on loading. From the point of view of the shipowner, ultimately cesser clauses are far from ideal because, instead of the charterer whom he knows, he is referred to a person unknown to him, often in an unfamiliar port, where collection of claims may not be easy. The receiver may, of course, not pay the freight as he should. These difficulties are avoided by the Gencon 1994 clause:

8. Lien Clause

The Owners shall have a lien on the cargo and on all sub-freights payable in respect of the cargo, for freight, deadfreight, demurrage, claims for damages and for all other amounts due under this Charter Party including costs of recovering same.[51]

---

[48] At 49. See too *Federal Commerce & Navigation Co v Molena Alpha Inc (The Nanfri, The Benfri, The Lorfri)* [1978] QB 927 (CA).

[49] (1875) 10 QB 553.

[50] For other examples of cesser clauses, see Gencon (1976), cl 8.

[51] Lines 132–136.

General approach of the courts   The general approach to cesser clauses was considered   **27.28**
by Donaldson J in *Overseas Transportation Co v Mineralimportexport (The Sinoe)*.[52]
Here the plaintiffs (the shipowners) had chartered the *Sinoe* to the charterers for the
carriage of a cargo of cement between Constanza and Chittagong. The charterparty was
on the Gencon form and contained the following clauses:

> 27. Charterers' liability shall cease as soon as the cargo is on board. Owners having an
> absolute lien on the cargo for freight, dead freight, demurrage and average.

> 32. . . . Charterers to remain ultimately responsible for freight, dead freight and demurrage
> at loading port.

At Chittagong (Bangladesh) the laydays were exceeded owing to the slowness and incompetence
of the stevedores. It was, however, impossible to exercise the lien for demurrage under clause 27
for practical reasons. The owners claimed demurrage or damages for detention because the charterers were in breach of contract in regard to the engagement and employment of the stevedores.
However, the charterers maintained that the cargo had been loaded and the owners had a lien
for demurrage and, therefore, under clause 27 they (the charterers) had no further liability.
Further, clauses 26 (demurrage) and 32 relieved them from liability in respect of demurrage
at the port of discharge. During the course of his judgment, Donaldson J said:

> Cesser clauses are curious animals because it is now well established that they do not mean
> what they appear to say, namely that the charterers' liability shall cease as soon as the cargo is
> on board. Instead, in the absence of special wording which is not present in this charter,
> they mean that the charterers' liability shall cease if and to the extent that the owners have an
> alternative remedy by way of lien on the cargo.[53]

On the facts, he held that clause 27 could not be relied on by the charterers, for it only came
into force if the owners had an effective right to a lien on the cargo. On the evidence, the
right was not effective. The umpire in arbitration proceedings had found that the
combined effect of local law and practice in Chittagong was such that no lien for demurrage
could be exercised by or on behalf of the owners either on shore or on board the ship. Thus
the cesser clause was of no avail to the charterers.[54]

The shipowners' lien   The charterer will only be released from liability under the charter   **27.29**
to the extent that the shipowner is given a lien on the cargo. In *Fidelitas Shipping Co Ltd v
V/O Exportchleb (The Sophia)*[55] the owners of the *Sophia* chartered her to respondents on a
voyage for the carriage of grain between Zhdanov on the Black Sea to Basrah on the Persian
Gulf. When the vessel arrived at Zhdanov she gave notice of readiness to load but nothing
actually happened for another five days when it was agreed that the charterparty should be
cancelled. A new charterparty was entered into (dated 6 October) with contract destinations
of Avonmouth and Manchester. The question before the Court of Appeal concerned the
effect of a clause in the charterparty:

> 27. The Charterers' liability on this charter to cease when the cargo is shipped, . . . the Owner
> or his Agent having a lien on the cargo for freight, dead freight, demurrage, lighterage at
> port of discharge and average.

---

[52] [1971] 1 Lloyd's Rep 514.
[53] At 516.
[54] See also the decision of the Court of Appeal: [1972] 1 Lloyd's Rep 201 (CA).
[55] [1963] 2 Lloyd's Rep 113 (CA).

Did this clause absolve the charterers from liability for delay in loading? The matter was complicated by bills of lading which provided that 'all terms and conditions as per Charter Party' and further contained a clause stating that the carrier was to have a lien upon the goods for and until payment of freight and all other charges and expenses due under the contract of carriage. Harman LJ accepted that cesser clauses would only avail the charterers to the extent to which they could show that they did provide the owners with a proper lien on the freight. The Court of Appeal found that, on the facts, the clause in the charterparty was operative and that the charterers were not liable for port of loading demurrage. So far as the bill of lading clause was concerned, this too covered loading port demurrage. Even if the lien given by the bill of lading did not cover port of loading demurrage, that could be imported from the charterparty without inconsistency between the two documents. The Court of Appeal accordingly dismissed the appeal from the judgment of Megaw J. Pearson LJ stated that:

> On shipment of the goods the lien comes into existence and the charterer is relieved of his personal liability, even if he is and remains the owner of the goods: in such a case the shipowner must rely on his lien, and, if he loses his lien by parting with the goods without receiving payment, he cannot successfully sue the charterers. Thus the lien arises in the first instance under the charterparty. Usually, however, there is a bill of lading, and it comes into the hands of some person other than the charterer, and such person is conveniently known as the receiver of the goods. Then the bill of lading will regulate the contractual relations between the shipowner and the receiver of the goods. A lien for demurrage exists only under contract. Consequently the shipowner will not have a lien for demurrage as against the receiver of the goods under the bill of lading unless the bill of lading provides for it either by a lien clause of its own or by incorporation in the charterparty.[56]

Thus, it is essential for charterparty liens to be effectively incorporated into the relevant bills of lading.

27.30 **Wording of the clause**   The wording of the clause must be adequate to cover the relevant charge. Thus, a clause which provides for a lien for demurrage will not extend to a claim for damages for detention. In *Clink v Radford*[57] a cesser clause provided for the charterer's liability to cease on the cargo being loaded, the owners having a lien on the cargo for freight and demurrage. The charter provided for laytime and demurrage at the discharge port, but at the load port the charter envisaged customary laytime with detention thereafter. Although the ship was delayed unreasonably at the load port, the charterers denied liability for detention on the basis of the cesser clause. This was rejected by Lord Esher MR:

> . . . the main rule to be derived from the cases as to the interpretation of the cesser clause in a char-terparty, is that the court will construe it as inapplicable to the particular breach complained of, if by construing it otherwise the shipowner would be left unprotected in respect of that particu-lar breach, unless the cesser clause is expressed in terms that prohibit such a conclusion . . .[58]

27.31 **Effective exercise**   The granting of the lien must be capable of being effectively exercised by the shipowner. If, therefore, the contract of carriage itself provides that demurrage is not payable until a week after the date fixed for discharge of the cargo, the lien could not

---

[56] At 122–123.
[57] [1891] 1 QB 625 (CA).
[58] At 627.

be effectively exercised. In *Bravo Maritime (Chartering) Est v Alsayed Abdullah (The Athinoula)*[59] Mocatta J had to consider a charter which not only had a cesser/lien clause which provided for the charterers to remain liable for discharge port demurrage in so far as the owners were unable to obtain payment by exercising their lien, but also had a further clause which required the owners to submit time sheets and statements of fact which they were unable to do until discharge was complete — by which time the possibility of exercising their lien would have vanished. Mocatta J therefore concluded that the two clauses could not be reconciled and that since the clause requiring presentation of the time sheets was an additional clause, that had to prevail.

Lien incapable of exercise The lien may not be capable of enforcement where a foreign   **27.32** government does not allow the lien to be exercised at the port of discharge. Thus, in *Action SA v Britannic Shipping Corp Ltd (The Aegis Britannic)*[60] the *Aegis Britannic* was chartered to carry a cargo of rice from a United States Gulf port to Basrah in Iraq. A clause in the charterparty provided that:

> 35. Charterers liability under the charterparty to cease upon cargo being shipped except as regards payment of freight, dead freight and demurrage incurred at both ends.

During discharge by stevedores at Basrah the cargo was partially damaged. The receivers claimed against the owners in the Administrative Court of Basrah and obtained judgment against them. In arbitration proceedings the owners claimed against the charterers the amount which they had to pay and a declaration of indemnity as to the balance. The arbitrator had found that the charterers were responsible for the damage by the stevedores and that therefore the charterers were responsible as between them and the owners. A quantity of 73 of the bags of rice were also wet on shipment and the arbitrator held that the charterers were not responsible for that damage. The charterers appealed on the basis that under clause 35 their liability had ceased since this was not a claim for freight, dead freight, or demurrage. Staughton J held that there was a long line of authority which showed that cesser clauses had a special and limited meaning: to relieve the charterers from liability where no effective lien was provided there would have to be special wording which made that point clear beyond any doubt. Here there was no special wording and the charterers were accordingly not relieved from liability. The Court of Appeal upheld this reasoning. Lloyd LJ stressed that

> . . . a charterparty should not be construed as imposing a liability on charterers and taking away that same liability in the same breath, unless the Court is driven to that conclusion. Accordingly, the cesser clause has usually been construed as applying only where the charterparty provides the owners with an alternative remedy, a remedy which is not only effective in theory but also effective in practice.

> Here the alternative remedy is to be found in cl 5 which provides that the cargo is to be discharged at the expense and risk of the receivers/charterers. If the remedy against the receivers under cl 5 is ineffective for whatever reason, other than the fault of the owners, then applying the reasoning underlying all the cesser clause cases, I would hold that the cesser clause is to that extent cut down.[61]

---

[59] [1980] 2 Lloyd's Rep 481.
[60] [1987] 1 Lloyd's Rep 119 (CA).
[61] At 123.

28

EXCLUSION OF LIABILITY UNDER THE HAGUE AND HAGUE–VISBY RULES

A. Introduction

Overview   We have referred previously to the common law position on exclusion clauses.[1]   **28.01** We have seen that it was the presence of exclusion clauses which prompted domestic and international movement towards new cargo liability reforms. In this chapter, our concern is the provisions in the Hague and Hague–Visby Rules which potentially exclude the carrier from liability.[2]

B. Exemptions in the Carrier's Favour

Background   The list (or catalogue) of exemptions in article IV, rule 2 was   **28.02** included primarily as one of the balancing factors in the Rules. As Sir Norman Hill explained:

> It would have been absolutely impossible to secure agreement to the Rules without an Article setting out in detail the exceptions to which the shipowners and cargo owners are accustomed. They would never have acted on an assurance that the Law Courts would construe any form of general words as covering those, and only those, exceptions.[3]

Thus, while the Rules impose on the carrier the obligations in article III, rule 1, in return the carrier may rely on the provisions of article IV, such as article IV, rule 2 and various

---

[1] See para 14.02.

[2] See, generally, Scrutton (1996), section XX; Cooke (2001), para 85.244; Carver (2005), para 9-205.

[3] Evidence given before the Sterndale Committee: Report from the Joint Committee on the Carriage of Goods by Sea Bill (HL) (16 July 1923), 133. See too para 15.09.

cognate provisions, such as article IV, rule 5 (limitation of liability). Article IV, rule 2 sets out the catalogue of exceptions from liability which are available to the carrier. These may be surrendered in part[4] but may not be added to.[5]

28.03 **Article IV, rule 2** Article IV, rule 2[6] as a whole reads as follows:

Neither the carrier nor the ship shall be responsible for loss or damage arising or resulting from

(a) act, neglect, or default of the master, mariner, pilot or the servants of the carrier in the navigation or in the management of the ship;

(b) fire, unless caused by the actual fault or privity of the carrier;

(c) perils, dangers and accidents of the sea or other navigable waters;

(d) act of God;

(e) act of war;

(f) act of public enemies;

(g) arrest or restraint of princes, rulers or people, or seizure under legal process;

(h) quarantine restrictions;

(i) act or omission of the shipper or owner of the goods, his agent or representative;

(j) strikes or lockouts or stoppage or restraint of labour from whatever cause, whether partial or general;

(k) riots and civil commotions;

(l) saving or attempting to save life or property at sea;

(m) wastage in bulk or weight or any other loss or damage arising from inherent defect, quality or vice of the goods;

(n) insufficiency of packing;

(o) insufficiency or inadequacy of marks;

(p) latent defects not discoverable by due diligence;

(q) any other cause arising without the actual fault and privity of the carrier, or without the fault or neglect of the agents or servants of the carrier, but the burden of proof shall be on the person claiming the benefit of this exception to show that neither the actual fault or privity of the carrier nor the fault or neglect of the agents or servants of the carrier contributed to the loss or damage.

28.04 **'Carrier'** This is a reference back to the definition in article I(a), which provides that the term 'carrier' includes 'the owner or the charterer who enters into a contract of carriage with the shipper'.[7]

28.05 **'Ship'** This reference to ship is partly a reference back to article I(d)[8] but it is also, like certain other references to ship in the Rules,[9] an opaque reference to the fact that in admiralty claims it is possible to bring proceedings *in rem* as well as *in personam*.[10]

28.06 **'Loss or damage'** This refers to the fact that claims under the Rules lie for loss or damage to goods. However, it should be noted that the loss or damage referred to is not confined to physical loss of or damage to the goods themselves and may include other

---

[4] Article V.

[5] Article III, r 8.

[6] See Berlingieri (1997), 370.

[7] See the discussion at para 19.17.

[8] See para 19.18.

[9] See, eg, art III, r 6, discussed at para 34.04.

[10] See ch 35.

losses in connection with the goods. Thus, although the Rules do not expressly refer to liability for delay,[11] it may nevertheless be possible to recover for losses caused by delay or misdelivery.[12]

'Act, neglect, or default ... in the navigation or in the management of the ship'[13] This **28.07** provision of the Rules can be traced to the Harter Act 1893, which contained a provision which exempted owners from 'faults or errors in navigation, or in the management of the said vessel'.[14] However, the origins also go back further than this and there would be no difficulty in finding similar wording in earlier bills of lading,[15] particularly those which notoriously contained so many exemptions that they were said to have 'surpassed all bounds of reason and fairness'.[16] Historically, this 'nautical fault' exception was justified on the basis that shipowners lacked the means to communicate with their ships on long voyages and so masters had to act in their own judgement. Modern communications have defeated this underlying rationale but shipowners still want to claim the benefit of the exception. Thus, notwithstanding its long existence, the exemption is still controversial.[17]

Persons covered   Article IV, rule 2(a) is quite explicit as to the persons for whom the **28.08** carrier is not responsible. These are the 'master, mariner, pilot, or other servants of the carrier . . .'. Stevedores are not included.[18] Further, if a loss is caused by the combined negligence of someone within the list and someone outside, for example the master and a stevedore, this will not fall within the exemption.[19]

'Navigation . . . of the ship'   The meaning of 'navigation' was considered in the time **28.09** charterparty case, *Whistler International Ltd v Kawasaki Kisen Kaisha Ltd (The Hill Harmony)*,[20] where their Lordships held that, as a matter of construction, the exception would not apply to a decision by the master to follow different routing instructions from those given by the charterer.[21] They held that any error which the master made was not an error in the navigation or management of the vessel as it did not concern any matter of seamanship. Accordingly, the owners had failed to discharge the burden of proof which lay upon them to bring themselves within the exception. Thus, it would seem that 'navigation' when used here would not refer to the commercial, economic, or legal aspects of the operation of the ship. An error

---

[11] cf art 5(1) of the Hamburg Rules.
[12] See, eg, *Anglo-Saxon Petroleum Co v Adamastos Shipping Co* [1957] 2 QB 233, 253 (Devlin J), approved by the House of Lords: [1957] AC 149, 157 (Viscount Simonds); 186 (Lord Somervell).
[13] Article IV, r 2(a). See Berlingieri (1997), 391.
[14] See s 3. See too the Conference Form 1882. For the text, see Sturley (1990), vol 2, 61.
[15] See, eg, *Hayn, Roman & Co v Culliford* (1879) LR 4 CP 182 (CA); *The Ferro* [1893] P 38.
[16] Knauth (1953), 120. See the earlier discussion at para 14.03.
[17] See Leslie Tomasino Weitz, 'The Nautical Fault Debate (the Hamburg Rules, the US COGSA 95, the STCW 95, and the ISM Code' (1997–1998) 22 Tulane MLJ 581; Eun Sup Lee and Seon Ok Kim, 'A Carrier's Liability for Commercial Default and Default in Navigation or Management of the Vessel' (2000) 27 Transportation LJ 205.
[18] See, eg, *Hayn, Roman & Co v Culliford* (1879) LR 4 CP 182 (CA); *The Ferro* [1893] P 38.
[19] *Minister of Food v Reardon Smith Line Ltd* [1951] 2 Lloyd's Rep 265, 270.
[20] [2001] 1 AC 638. Overruling the Court of Appeal: see [2000] 1 QB 241 (CA).
[21] The case arose in the context of the employment clause in a time charterparty: see para 32.81. See too *Suzuki & Co Ltd v T Benyon & Co Ltd* (1926) 24 Ll LR 49 (HL).

by the master in proceeding to the wrong port, because he had misinterpreted the terms of a contract as to ice-bound ports, would not be sufficiently connected with navigation.[22] On the other hand, steering a wrong course would be an error in navigation.[23]

28.10 '. . . **Management of the ship**' In this context, 'management' is a reference to the management of the ship, not the management of the cargo. Thus, if the management relates to the ship, the carrier will be able to bring himself within the defence. If, on the other hand, the management relates in some way to the care of cargo alone,[24] this will not be covered and the carrier will be responsible under article III, rule 2. The leading opinion on the matter is the dissenting judgment of Greer LJ in the Court of Appeal in *Gosse Millerd v Canadian Government Merchant Marine*.[25] The facts were that boxes of tin plates were shipped at Swansea for carriage to Vancouver aboard the *Canadian Highlander*. En route to Vancouver a quantity of lumber was unloaded at Liverpool where the vessel docked to discharge some of the cargo. During discharge there was heavy rain and the vessel collided with a pier and damaged her stern. The repairmen who entered to repair the tail shaft took off tarpaulins used to cover the cargo and the rain then wetted the unprotected cargo. Greer LJ stated that:

> If the cause of the damage is solely, or even primarily, a neglect to take reasonable care of the cargo, the ship is liable, but if the cause of the damage is a neglect to take reasonable care of the ship, or some part of it as distinct from the cargo, the ship is relieved from liability; for if the negligence is not negligence towards the ship, but only negligent failure to use the apparatus of the ship for protection of the cargo, the ship is not so relieved.[26]

The House of Lords[27] upheld this dissenting judgment, declaring that the error was in the management of the cargo because the act, although made by persons directing their attention to the ship, was one which affected cargo alone.

28.11 **Negligent stowage** Negligent stowage, including improper handling of cargo would be regarded as conduct primarily directed towards cargo care and any resultant damage would not be covered by the exception.[28]

28.12 **Safety of the vessel** If the primary objective is the safety of the vessel, it will be immaterial that the negligent conduct also affects the cargo. Thus, in the Canadian case of *Kalamazoo Paper Co v CPR Co*[29] the SS *Nootka* was seriously damaged after hitting a rock on a voyage from Port Alice to Vancouver. She was beached at Quatsino in order to prevent her sinking and the cargo insurers claimed damages for the alleged negligence of the master and crew in failing to use all available pumping facilities in order to keep the water level down after the vessel had grounded. Rand J held that the use of the pumping machinery affected the

---

[22] See, eg, *SS Knutsford Ltd v Tillmanns & Co* [1908] AC 406.
[23] See *Seven Seas Transportation Ltd v Pacifico Union Marina Corp (The Satya Kailash & Oceanic Amity)* [1982] 2 Lloyd's Rep 465.
[24] Pilferage by stevedores will not fall within the exception. First, stevedores are not covered, and secondly, the pilferage relates to the cargo alone. See *Hourani v T & J Harrison* (1927) 28 Ll LR 120 (CA).
[25] [1928] 1 KB 717 (CA).
[26] At 749.
[27] [1929] AC 223. See too *Compania Sud American Vapores v MS ER Hamburg Schiffahrtsgesellsclaft mbH & Co KG* [2006] EWHC 483 (Comm); [2006] 2 Lloyd's Rep 66.
[28] See, eg, *The Ferro* [1893] P 38.
[29] [1950] DLR 369.

general safety of the ship and that therefore the actions of the crew fell within the 'management of ship' exception:

> The further question is whether an act or omission in management is within the exception when at the same time and in the same mode it is an act or omission in relation to the care of cargo. It may be that duty to a ship as a whole takes precedence over duty to a portion of the cargo; but, without examining that question, the necessary effect of the language of art III, r 2 'subject to the provisions of Art IV' seems to me to be that once it is shown that the omission is in the course of management, the exception applies, notwithstanding that it may also be an omission in relation to cargo. To construe it otherwise would be to add to the language of clause (a) the words 'and not being a neglect in the care of the goods'.[30]

However, if the default in machinery which caused the loss or damage related only to the cargo and not the ship, then this would not be covered within the exception.[31] This will even include hatch covers for the reason that these are provided so as to keep sea water and other elements away from the cargo.[32]

'Fire, unless caused by the actual fault or privity of the carrier'[33]   In *Papera Traders Co*   **28.13**
Ltd v Hyundai Merchant Marine Co Ltd (The Eurasian Dream) Cresswell J stated that:

> Fire is one of the greatest threats to ships at sea. The ship's fire fighting ability and, therefore, its seaworthiness is crucially dependent upon the competence of its crew as the fire-fighters and, in particular, the master as their leader.[34]

What is covered is actual fire and this means that there must be ignition or flame involved. Thus, heat alone is not enough, but damage by heat will be included if flame is present.[35] Also included would be cargo damage from reasonable efforts to extinguish the fire, such as the use of water.[36]

Fire and due diligence   It is clear that fire which results from failure to exercise due   **28.14**
diligence to make the vessel seaworthy before and at the beginning of the voyage would not be covered by the exception.[37] But the mere fact that a ship has caught fire will not mean that the carrier is liable for a want of due diligence. In *A Meredith Jones & Co Ltd v Vangemar Shipping Co Ltd (The Apostolis)* Leggatt LJ stated that:

> To show breach of art III, r 1 [the claimant] must show that the carriers failed to make the ship seaworthy and that their loss or damage was caused by the breach, or in other words that the fire was caused by unseaworthiness. [They] have to contend that the unseaworthiness consisted in exposure of the cargo to the risk of fire from a spark entering the hold. But even

---

[30] At 378.
[31] See, eg, *Caltex Refining Co Pty Ltd v BHP Transport Ltd (The Iron Gippsland)* [1994] 1 Lloyd's Rep 335, 358: '[T]he purpose of the inert gas system is primarily to manage the cargo, not only for the protection of the cargo but for the ultimate protection of the vessel from adverse consequences associated with that cargo' (Carruthers J). See also *Foreman & Ellams Ltd v Federal Steam Navigation Co Ltd* [1928] 2 KB 424; *Chubu Asahi Cotton Spinning Co Ltd v The Ship Tenos* (1968) 12 FLR 291.
[32] See, eg, *Gosse Millerd v Canadian Government Merchant Marine* [1929] AC 223.
[33] Article IV, r 2(b). See Berlingieri (1997), 398.
[34] [2002] EWHC 118 (Comm); [2002] 1 Lloyd's Rep 719, 739.
[35] See *Tempus Shipping Co Ltd v Louis Dreyfus & Co* [1930] 1 KB 699.
[36] *The Diamond* [1906] P 282.
[37] See *Maxine Footwear Co Ltd v Canadian Government Merchant Marine Ltd* [1959] AC 589 (PC), discussed at para 26.19.

if that is what occurred, it was not unseaworthiness which caused the fire, but the fire which rendered the vessel unseaworthy. Nothing about the state of the ship rendered her unseaworthy. The owners were not in breach of art III, r 1 merely because welding exposed the cargo to an ephemeral risk of ignition. The holds themselves were not intrinsically unsafe. Here the ship only became [unseaworthy] on account of the fire in the cargo.[38]

Thus, if the fire is not due to unseaworthiness then it would fall within the exception, unless 'caused by the actual fault or privity of the carrier'.[39]

28.15 **Onus** It is not clear from article IV, rule 2(b) whether the carrier must prove that he was not guilty of 'actual fault or privity' or whether the cargo claimant must show this. It would appear to be the case, however, that the onus is on the cargo owner.[40]

28.16 **Merchant Shipping Act** Article IV, rule 2(b) must be read with section 186 of the Merchant Shipping Act 1995,[41] the relevant part of which reads as follows:

(1) Subject to subsection (3) below, the owner of a United Kingdom ship shall not be liable for any loss or damage in the following cases, namely—
   (a) where any property on board the ship is lost or damaged by reason of fire on board the ship . . .

(3) This section does not exclude the liability of any person for any loss or damage resulting from any such personal act or omission of his as is mentioned in Article 4 of the [Convention on Limitation of Liability for Maritime Claims 1976] set out in Part I of Schedule 7.

Thus, under the Act, the burden of proof is shifted to the cargo owner and in order to recover his loss, he will have to establish that the fire resulted from '. . . any such personal act or omission of [the carrier] as is mentioned in Article 4 of the [Convention on Limitation of Liability for Maritime Claims 1976] set out in Part I of Schedule 7'.[42]

28.17 **Differences** Article IV, rule 2(b) appears to have two clear advantages for claimants over the Merchant Shipping Act 1995. Thus, article IV, rule 2(b) applies to 'carriers' as defined in the Rules,[43] while the cover in the 1995 Act extends only to 'the owner of a United Kingdom ship'.[44] The second advantage of the Rules is that the exception in article IV, rule 2(a) applies throughout the period of coverage of the Rules.[45] The relief under the 1995 Act can only be relied on in respect of cargo damage resulting from fire 'on board the ship'.[46]

---

[38] [1997] 2 Lloyd's Rep 241 (CA), 244–245.
[39] For older cases on the meaning of 'actual fault or privity', see *Lennard's Carrying Co v Asiatic Petroleum Co Ltd* [1915] AC 705; *Arthur Guinness, Son & Co (Dublin) Ltd v Owners of Motor Vessel Freshfield (The Lady Gwendolyn)* [1965] 1 Lloyd's Rep 335 (CA); *Grand Champion Tankers Ltd v Norpipe A/S (The Marion)* [1984] AC 563.
[40] There is US authority for this: see the discussion in Schoenbaum (2004), §10-28.
[41] Previously s 502(i) of the Merchant Shipping Act 1894.
[42] For discussion of this, see para 29.52
[43] ie in art I(a): see para 19.17.
[44] Merchant Shipping Act 1995, s 186(1).
[45] See art I(e).
[46] Section 186(1)(a).

'Perils, dangers and accidents of the sea'[47]   In *P Samuel & Co v Dumas*, Scrutton LJ **28.18**
indicated that in order to rely on perils of the sea

> there must be a peril, an unforeseen and evitable accident, not a contemplated and inevitable
> result; and it must be of the seas, not merely on the seas. The ordinary action of the winds and
> waves is 'of the seas', but not a 'peril'.[48]

Though a clause exempting the carrier from 'perils of the sea' was included in the
Conference form of 1882,[49] the history of such clauses can be traced at least to the reign of
Henry VIII[50] and, with greater certainty, to the reign of Charles I.[51] Aside from the carriage
of goods context, marine policies of insurance have, since the revision of the Lloyd's SG
Policy in 1779, exempted the carrier from liability for loss arising from perils of the sea.
It has repeatedly been held that 'perils of the sea' means the same in bills of lading as it does
in marine insurance policies,[52] but a note of caution has been sounded in *Great China
Metal Industries Co Ltd v Malaysian International Shipping Corp Berhad (The Bunga Seroja)*
where it was said that 'care and discrimination' must be shown in applying decisions about
marine insurance to the Rules.[53]

Common law authorities   The traditional principle at common law is that for a loss to   **28.19**
fall within the exception, whether in marine insurance or carriage of goods cases, the peril
must be 'of the sea' and not merely on the seas.[54] In *Canada Rice Mills Ltd v Union and
General Marine Insurance Co*, Lord Wright stated that 'rain is not a peril of the sea, but at
most a peril on the sea'.[55] In the leading English case, *The Xantho*,[56] the endorsees of cargo
shipped on the *Xantho* brought a claim for non-delivery against the carrier. This claim arose
out of the loss of the *Xantho* after a collision with the *Valuta* in fog. The bills of lading
contained exceptions for dangers and accidents of the sea and the House of Lords, reversing
the Court of Appeal,[57] upheld this defence. Lord Herschell stated that the term 'perils of the
sea' would not cover every accident or casualty of which the sea was the immediate cause
covered by these words. The words would not protect

> against that natural and inevitable action of the wind and waves which results in what may
> be described as wear and tear. There must be some casualty, something which could not be
> foreseen as one of the necessary incidents of the adventure.[58]

---

[47] Article IV, r 2(c). See Berlingieri (1997), 404. See Stephen Girvin, ' "Perils of the Sea" under the Hague
(and Hague–Visby) Rules' (1999) 4 S & TLI 18.
[48] [1923] 1 KB 592 (CA), 618. In this case the issues arose out of a policy of marine insurance.
[49] See Sturley (1990), vol 2, 62.
[50] See *Thorne v Vincent (The St Michael)* (1541).
[51] See, for example, *Pickering v Barkley* (1648) Style 132; 82 ER 587, cited in *Hamilton, Fraser & Co v
Pandorf & Co* (1886) 17 QBD 670 (CA), 684.
[52] See *The Freedom* (1871) LR 3 PC 594, 601-602 (Sir Robert Phillimore); *The Xantho* (1887) 12 App Cas
503, 514 (Lord Bramwell); *Skandia Insurance Co Ltd v Skoljarev* (1979) 142 CLR 375.
[53] [1999] 1 Lloyd's Rep 512, at [17].
[54] See *Cullen v Butler* (1816) 5 M & S 461; 105 ER 1119, 1121 (Lord Ellenborough CJ); *The Xantho* (1887)
12 App Cas 503, 509 (Lord Herschell); *P Samuel & Co v Dumas* [1923] 1 KB 592 (CA), 618 (Scrutton LJ).
[55] [1941] AC 55, 64.
[56] (1887) 12 App Cas 503.
[57] (1886) 11 PD 170.
[58] (1887) 12 App Cas 503, 509.

In *Hamilton, Fraser & Co v Pandorf & Co*[59] the defendants shipped rice aboard the *Inchrhona* from Sittwe (Burma) to Bremerhaven. During the voyage, however, rats ate a hole in a leaden pipe thus allowing sea water into the ship and damaging her cargo of rice. It was held that this was a peril of the sea, although it would not have been if the water had entered through a leaky hull because of ordinary deterioration. Lord Bramwell stated that:

> In the present case the sea has damaged the goods. That it might do so was a peril that the ship encountered. It is true that rats made a hole through which the water got in, and if the question were whether rats making a hole was a peril of the sea, I should say certainly not . . . The damage was caused by the sea in the course of navigation with no default in any one. I am, therefore, of opinion that the damage was caused by peril of the sea within the meaning of the bill of lading . . .[60]

Other successful cases have included: damage caused to a cargo of sugar by the entry of sea water arising out of the negligence of the shipowner or his servants;[61] damage resulting from a collision occurring at sea without fault on the part of the master;[62] loss caused by piracy;[63] where overheating had caused damage to cargo as the result of lack of ventilation brought about by the necessity of closing ventilators during a storm of exceptional severity and duration;[64] where a ship grounded in a harbour by reason of a heavy swell;[65] where a ship took in sea water while being towed in heavy seas;[66] where a ship listed while loading a deck cargo timber, causing loss of a portion of the cargo;[67] where a ship sank in smooth water shortly after leaving port;[68] where a ship ran aground.[69] On the other hand, the following cases have been unsuccessful: where damage was occasioned by imperfect insulation causing sea water to disable a transatlantic telegraph cable;[70] when a ship ran aground after the tide ebbed;[71] when a vessel was lost by deliberate scuttling.[72] At common law the carrier could not raise the defence of perils of the sea if his negligence caused the loss.[73]

28.20 **Cases arising under the Rules** Cases in England on the defence under the Rules have frequently been concerned with the question whether there has been a breach by the carrier of his obligations under article III. Thus, in *The Friso*,[74] the vessel developed a list of 40–45 degrees in heavy weather and the master gave the order to abandon ship. Though the

---

[59] (1887) App Cas 518.
[60] At 527.
[61] *Blackburn v Liverpool, Brazil and River Plate Steam Navigation Co* [1902] 1 KB 290.
[62] *Buller v Fisher* (1799) 3 Esp 67; 170 ER 540; *Martin v Crokatt* (1810) 14 East 465; 104 ER 679; *The Xantho* (1887) 12 App Cas 503.
[63] *Pickering v Barkley* (1648) Style 132; 82 ER 587.
[64] *The Thrunscoe* [1897] P 301; *Canada Rice Mills Ltd v Union Marine and General Insurance Co* [1941] AC 55.
[65] *Fletcher v Inglis* (1819) 2 B & Ald 315;106 ER 382.
[66] *Hagedorn v Whitmore* (1816) 1 Stark 157; 171 ER 432.
[67] *The Stranna* [1938] P 69.
[68] *Skandia Insurance Co Ltd v Skoljarev* (1979) 142 CLR 375.
[69] *The Zinovia* [1984] 2 Lloyd's Rep 264.
[70] *Paterson v Harris* (1861) 1 B & S 336; 121 ER 740.
[71] *Magnus v Buttemer* (1852) 11 CB 876; 138 ER 720.
[72] *P Samuel & Co Ltd v Dunas* [1924] AC 431.
[73] See *Paterson Steamships Ltd v Canadian Co-operative Wheat Producers Ltd* [1934] AC 538, 545 (Lord Wright); *Smith, Hogg & Co v Black Sea and Baltic Insurance Co* [1940] AC 997, 1004 (Lord Wright).
[74] [1980] 1 Lloyd's Rep 469.

vessel was later recovered, the deck cargo had had to be jettisoned in order to reduce the list. Sheen J held that the carrier could not rely on article IV, rule 2(c), because he found that the vessel was not seaworthy at the beginning of the voyage and that, accordingly, there was a breach of the carrier's obligation to exercise due diligence.[75] In *The Tilia Gorthon*,[76] where deck cargo of packaged lumber was washed overboard in force 10 conditions, Sheen J concluded that:

> It seems highly probably that none of the deck cargo would have been lost but for the evidence of the storm. But the evidence as to the weather has not satisfied me that the conditions encountered were such as could not and should not have been contemplated by the shipowners. Fortunately for the mariners, winds of 48–55 knots (Beaufort Force 10) are encountered infrequently. But they are by no means so exceptional in the North Atlantic in the autumn and winter that the possibility of encountering them can be ignored. A ship embarking on a voyage across the Atlantic ocean at that time of the year ought to be in a condition to weather such a storm.[77]

Thus, on the facts he was not prepared to find in favour of the carrier seeking to rely on perils of the sea as a defence.

Differences of approach   There are differences of approach to the exception in different jurisdictions. In *Shipping Corporation of India Ltd v Gamlen Chemical Co (A/Asia) Pty Ltd*,[78] Mason and Wilson JJ noted that there was a difference between the Anglo–Australian conception of 'perils of the sea' and the United States–Canadian conception. So far as the latter is concerned, 'perils of the sea' will only apply to losses peculiar to the sea which are 'of an extraordinary nature or arise from irresistible force or overwhelming power, and which cannot be guarded against by the ordinary exertions of human skill and prudence' or 'something so catastrophic as to triumph over those safeguards by which skilful and vigilant seamen usually bring ship and cargo to port in safety'.[79]   **28.21**

The Bunga Seroja   In *Great China Metal Industries Co Ltd v Malaysian International Shipping Corp Berhad (The Bunga Seroja)*[80] a consignment of 40 cases of aluminium can body stock in coils was contracted for carriage between Sydney and Keelung. The coils were stowed on pallets in containers and placed aboard the *Bunga Seroja*. The containers were stowed in forward hold No 5 aboard the ship. While en route from Burnie to Fremantle in Western Australia, crossing the Great Australian Bight, the *Bunga Seroja* encountered weather conditions which included winds of force 11 on the Beaufort Scale. During the course of this weather eight containers were washed overboard. Other containers were damaged, including those belonging to the claimants. The carrier sought to rely on the   **28.22**

---

[75] Other cases where the carrier has been held to be in breach of his obligation to exercise due diligence under art III include *The Bulknes* [1979] 2 Lloyd's Rep 39; *The Torenia* [1983] 2 Lloyd's Rep 210.

[76] [1985] 1 Lloyd's Rep 552.

[77] At 555.

[78] (1980) 147 CLR 142.

[79] *The Giulia* 218 F 744, 746 (2nd Cir 1914) (Rogers CJ); *The Rosalia* 264 F 285, 288 (2nd Cir 1920). See the discussion in Schoenbaum (2004), §10-29. See too *Kruger Inc v Baltic Shipping Co* [1988] 1 FC 262, 278–279 (Pinard J); *Goodfellow Lumber Sales Ltd v Verreault* [1971] 1 Lloyd's Rep 185, 189 (Ritchie J); *Zim Israel Navigation Ltd v The Israeli Phoenix Assurance Co Ltd (The Zim-Marseilles)* (1999) 502 LMLN 3.

[80] [1999] 1 Lloyd's Rep 512. For criticism of the decision, see Martin Davies, 'Application of the Hague Rules' "Perils of the Sea" Defence in Australia: *The Bunga Seroja*' (1999) 23 Tulane MLJ 449.

exception of perils of the sea in article IV, rule 2(c). At first instance,[81] Carruthers J noted that, for the carrier to succeed, the court would have to be satisfied, on a balance of probabilities, that the proximate cause of the damage to the cargo was a specific fortuitous accident or casualty of the seas rather than some other cause such as the ordinary action of the wind and waves and wear and tear. The shippers argued that the defendants were in breach of article III, rule 1 of the Hague Rules because they failed to carry out the master's instructions on load planning. Carruthers J found that there was no failure from proper standards of seamanship and no breach of either article III, rule 1 or article III, rule 2. In Carruthers J's view the defendant had established to the requisite degree that the damage to the subject cargo was occasioned by perils of the sea.[82] It was clear 'on the highest authority' that the mere fact that damage to cargo was occasioned by a storm which was 'expectable' did not, of itself, exclude a finding that the damage was occasioned by perils of the sea.[83] The case then went to the Court of Appeal of New South Wales, who dismissed the appeal with costs.[84] In a lengthy judgment, the High Court[85] dismissed the appeal. Kirby J concluded that:

> No error has been shown either in the approach of the Court of Appeal or of Carruthers J on [the perils of the sea] point. None of the judges below treated the intensity of the weather conditions, or the fact that gales had been forecast, as irrelevant. Neither did they treat them as determinative in the way that [Great China Metals] urged. Instead, they adopted the correct course of examining all the facts and circumstances. They concentrated attention upon whether the hazards encountered were such as could, and should, have been prevented by the carrier's properly and carefully conducting itself with this particular vessel in this place and these circumstances. They asked whether the loss or damage shown arose, or resulted from, the sea hazard or from a want of proper and careful conduct on the part of the carrier. Not only was the approach taken by their Honours clearly open to them. In my view, it was correct. The conclusion reached was inevitable.[86]

28.23 'Act of God'[87] The exception 'Act of God' denotes natural accidents, such as lightning, earthquake, and storm, or a freak wave that swamps a ship.[88] In *Nugent v Smith*,[89] James LJ said that:

> Act of God is a mere short way of expressing this proposition: A common carrier is not liable for any accident as to which he can show that it is due to natural causes, directly and exclusively without human intervention, and that it could not have been prevented by any amount of foresight and pains and care reasonably to be expected from him.[90]

28.24 **Damage foreseen** The carrier would not be able to rely on 'Act of God' if the damage could have been foreseen and reasonable steps could have been taken to prevent it or where

---

81 [1994] 1 Lloyd's Rep 455, 462–463.
82 At 469.
83 At 470.
84 (1995) 39 NSWLR 683.
85 [1999] 1 Lloyd's Rep 512.
86 At [148].
87 Article IV, r 2(d). See Berlingieri (1997), 406.
88 See *Turgel Fur Co Ltd v Northumberland Ferries Ltd* (1966) 59 DLR (2d) 1 (NSSC).
89 (1876) 1 CPD 423 (CA).
90 At 444.

there is any human participation in the occurrence which causes the loss. In *Liver Akali v Johnson*[91] a barge ran aground as a result of fog and salt cake was damaged. At first instance, the jury found that the owner of the barge was not negligent. However, the accident was a peril of navigation and was in no sense an Act of God. This was affirmed by the Court of Exchequer. In *Siordet v Hall*[92] goods were shipped under a bill of lading which purported to exempt the shipowner for 'acts of God'. On the night before she was due to sail the ship's boiler was filled, as was the normal practice. However, owing to frost, a pipe connected with the boiler burst, damaging the goods. The court held that although frost was an 'act of God', negligence in filling the boiler overnight excluded the exception.

'Act of war'[93] Whether or not there is an act of war will be a question of fact which **28.25** does not require a formal declaration of war, nor even the severing of diplomatic relations between governments.[94] The 'ordinary business meaning' of the term is what is important.[95] It is thought that the term would include civil war,[96] as it does in the insurance context.[97]

'Act of public enemies'[98] In English law the old formulation of this defence used to be **28.26** 'Queen's enemies' or 'King's enemies'. The defence in the Rules relates to acts done by enemies in an actual state of war at any time during the carriage of the goods.[99] It will not include thieves, rioters, robbers on land, or hijackers, but is said to include pirates[100] and rebels in insurrection against their own governments, including terrorists.

'Arrest or restraint of princes...'[101] This first part of the exception has an early history **28.27** and may be found in many nineteenth century bills of lading. The final words used, 'or seizure under legal process', expand the common law concept and would cover the forcible taking of either the ship or cargo or part of them by judicial process.[102] This exception applies to forcible interferences by a state or the government of a country taking possession of goods and examples include blockades,[103] embargoes,[104] or prohibitions on the import

---

[91] (1874) LR 9 Ex 338.

[92] (1828) 4 Bing 607;130 ER 902.

[93] Article IV, r 2(e). See Berlingieri (1997), 407.

[94] See *Kawasaki Kisen Kabushiki Kaisha v Belships Co Ltd (The Belpareil)* (1939) 63 Ll LR 175; *Kawasaki Kisen Kaisha v Bantham Steamship Co* [1939] 2 KB 544.

[95] *National Oil Co of Zimbabwe v Sturge* [1991] 2 Lloyd's Rep 281.

[96] See *Curtis & Sons v Mathews* [1919] 1 KB 425.

[97] See *Pesquerias Y Secaderos de Bacalao de Espana SA v Beer* [1949] 1 All ER 845.

[98] Article IV, r 2(f). See Berlingieri (1997), 408.

[99] See *Russell v Niemann* (1864) 17 CB (ns) 163; 141 ER 66.

[100] Seagoing pirates have been held to be a 'peril of the seas': see *Pickering v Barkley* (1648) Sty 132; 82 ER 587. In marine insurance terms, piracy can take place near to the shore as well as within the territorial waters of a state: *Athens Maritime Enterprises Corp v Hellenic Mutual War Risks Association (Bermuda) Ltd (The Andreas Lemos)* [1983] QB 647; *Bayswater Carriers Pte Ltd v QBE Insurance (International) Pte Ltd* [2005] SGHC 185; [2006] 1 SLR 69.

[101] Article IV, r 2(g). See Berlingieri (1997), 409.

[102] eg, such as the arrest of the ship *in rem*. See further, ch 35.

[103] See *Geipel v Smith* (1872) LR 7 QB 704.

[104] See *Aubert v Gray* (1861) 3 B & S 163; 122 ER 62; *Seabridge Shipping Ltd v Antco Shipping Ltd (The Furness Bridge)* [1977] 2 Lloyd's Rep 367.

and export of goods.[105] Thus, any forcible interference, or threat of force,[106] with government or quasi-governmental authority backing it, would suffice. The scope of the exception will not apply to mobs, rebels, or guerrillas, ie non-governmental authorities.[107]

28.28 **Imminent threat** Actual forcible interference is not essential; what is required is an imminent threat of force being applied. In *Rickards v Forestal Land, Timber & Railways Co*[108] the owner of a German ship complied with the orders of the German government at the outbreak of World War II by scuttling his ship, the *Minden*, off the Faroe Islands in order to avoid capture by a British warship. The shipowner was entitled to rely on the exception, for in the words of Lord Wright

> ... there may be a restraint, though the physical force of the state concerned is not immediately present. It is enough, I think, that there is an order of the state, addressed to a subject of that state, acting with compelling force on him, decisively exacting his obedience and requiring him to do the act which effectively restrains the goods. Thus the seizure or restraint effected in obedience to that order becomes, in a case like the present, the belligerent act of the German government though it is committed by the master of a German merchantman, on the high seas or in neutral territory.[109]

Further, it would be enough for the restraint to operate on the person of the shipowner or the ship's officers, provided those persons are subject to the jurisdiction of the enforcing state, such as being physically present there or being subjects of it.[110]

28.29 **Timing** It is possible for shipowners to rely on the exception to cover any loss which may result from taking avoiding action when faced with the imminent threat of state intervention. However, it will not apply where the restraint is merely apprehended, even if natural and real. In *Watts, Watts & Co Ltd v Mitsui & Co Ltd*[111] a steamship was chartered to ship a cargo of sulphate of ammonia from the port of Marioupol in the Sea of Azov to Japan. The owners subsequently declined to name a vessel for the voyage because they feared that the Turkish authorities were on the point of closing the Dardenelles and that this would result in their vessel becoming trapped in the Black Sea. This in fact happened 25 days later (on 26 September 1914). However, the House of Lords were of the opinion that, though the shipowners' apprehension was reasonable, it was not covered by the exception. Earl Loreburn said that:

> In my opinion there was no restraint of princes on 1 September when the shipowners declared their intention of not carrying out their contract. There was an available force at hand in the Dardenelles, and if the situation had been so menacing that a man of sound judgment would think it foolhardiness to proceed with the voyage I should have regarded that as in fact a restraint of princes. It is true that mere apprehension will not suffice, but on the other hand it has never been held that a ship must continue her voyage till physical force is actually exercised.[112]

---

[105] It would not apply to the judgment of any court: see *Finlay v Liverpool & Great Western Steamship Co Ltd* (1870) 23 LT 251, 254.
[106] Even if the powers are not used: see *British & Foreign Marine Insurance Co v Samuel Sanday & Co* [1916] 1 AC 650.
[107] See *Nesbitt v Lushington* (1792) 4 TR 783; 100 ER 1300.
[108] [1942] AC 50.
[109] At 81–82.
[110] See *Furness, Withy & Co v Rederiaktiebolaget Banco* [1917] 2 KB 873.
[111] [1917] AC 227.
[112] At 236. cf *Phosphate Mining Co v Rankin* (1915) 21 Com Cas 248.

Knowledge of risk   May the exception be relied upon when the contracting parties know **28.30** about the risk of state intervention at the time of contracting? In *Ciampa v British India Steam Navigation Co Ltd*[113] certain lemons belonging to the plaintiffs were loaded aboard the *Matiana* at Naples for carriage to London. The vessel had previously been on a voyage from Mombasa. On leaving Naples the *Matiana* proceeded to Marseilles and there she was subjected to deratisation, whereby sulphur was pumped into her holds. The French authorities had decreed Mombasa a plague contaminated port. The lemons arrived in London in a damaged state, 'not only spoilt in flavour, but were affected in substance also, being to a certain extent rotted'.[114] The shipowners had known at the time of contracting that the French port authorities would subject their vessel to this cleansing process.[115] Rowlatt J declined to allow the shipowners to invoke the exception:

> I am not deciding that the application of the ordinary law of a country may not in some circumstances constitute a 'restraint of princes', but I think the facts which bring that law into operation must be facts which have supervened after the ship has started on the voyage in question. When facts exist which show conclusively that the ship was inevitably doomed before the commencement of the voyage to become subject to restraint, I do not think that there is a restraint of princes.[116]

Risks unknown   The situation may be different where the risks were unknown to the **28.31** parties at the time of contracting. In *Steamship Induna Co Ltd v British Phosphate Commissioners*[117] Sellers J permitted a charterer to rely on a laytime exception covering 'intervention of constituted authorities' when the time of loading was circumscribed by local labour regulations. Unknown to the contracting parties this prohibited stevedores from working between 9 pm and 6 am. The judge commented that:

> [I]f the circumstances were unknown to the parties, it seems to me that they could be relied on if they existed and caused delay when the vessel arrived for loading and discharge.[118]

It would be unlikely that a case on similar facts would be decided this way today, given the ready availability of information as to working practices in ports worldwide.

'Quarantine restrictions'[119]   This exception attracted little attention in the discussions **28.32** which led to the enactment of the Rules. The wording is fairly self-explanatory, but it is likely that a carrier could rely on the 'restraint of princes' exception in many cases. It should be noted that this exception will not be available where the carrier or his servants carelessly or deliberately exposed the vessel or cargo to conditions that resulted in quarantine restraints.[120]

'Act or omission of the shipper or owner of the goods . . .'[121]   Again, this exception seems **28.33** fairly self-explanatory and there are few examples of it being raised. If the shipper or the

---

[113] [1915] 2 KB 774.
[114] At 780.
[115] Similarly, where a party is careless, he will not be able to rely on 'restraint of princes': see *Dunn v Bucknall Bros* [1902] 2 KB 614.
[116] [1915] 2 KB 774, 779.
[117] [1949] 2 KB 430.
[118] At 438.
[119] Article IV, r 2(h). See Berlingieri (1997), 410.
[120] See *Dunn v Bucknall Bros* [1902] 2 KB 614.
[121] Article IV, r 2(i). See Berlingieri (1997), 412.

owner of the goods were to give advice as to the stowage, carriage, and discharge of goods and this were relied upon by the shipowner such that the cargo is damaged, there ought to be no difficulty for the shipowner in relying on this defence.[122]

28.34 **'Strikes or lockouts or stoppage or restraint of labour'** . . .[123]   This provision of the Rules is widely framed to include strikes, lockouts, stoppages, and restraints of labour 'from whatever cause'. In *Williams Bros (Hull) Ltd v Naamlooze Vennootschap WH Berghuys Kolenhandel*[124] Sankey J defined a strike as 'a general concerted refusal by workmen to work in consequence of an alleged grievance'. In *J Vermaas' Scheepvaartbedrijf NV v Association Technique de L'Importation Charbonnière (The Laga)*[125] McNair J said that:

> [T]he word strike is a perfectly good, appropriate word to use to cover a sympathetic strike and a general strike and there is no need today to have any ingredient of grievance between those who are refusing to work and their employers . . .[126]

In *Tramp Shipping Corp v Greenwich Marine Inc (The New Horizon)*[127] a vessel was chartered for a voyage to St Nazaire with a fixed time for discharge. Clause 8 of the charterparty provided that:

> If the cargo cannot be discharged by reason of riots, civil commotions, or of a strike or lock-out of any class of workmen essential to the discharge, the time for loading or discharging as the case may be, shall not count during the continuance of such causes . . .[128]

The normal practice at the berth in question was for crane drivers to work 24 hour periods, with the periods divided into three shifts. When the *New Horizon* was ready to discharge, however, drivers were only working for eight hours, in an attempt to improve their working conditions. The Court of Appeal held that there had been a 'strike'. Lord Denning MR said that:

> I think a strike is a concerted stoppage of work by men done with a view to improving their wages or conditions, or giving vent to a grievance or making a protest about something or other, or supporting or sympathising with other workmen in such endeavour. It is distinct from a stoppage which is brought about by an external event such as a bomb scare or by apprehension of danger.[129]

In the modern context, no distinction would likely be made between industrial and political strikes.[130] Furthermore, a stoppage of work because of a bomb scare or even the fear of contracting a disease would likely be covered by the exception.

---

122 See, eg, *Ismail v Polish Ocean Lines (The Ciechocinek)* [1976] QB 893 (CA), 903 (Lord Denning MR).
123 Article IV, r 2(j). See Berlingieri (1997), 413.
124 (1915) 21 Com Cas 253, 257.
125 [1966] 1 Lloyd's Rep 582.
126 At 591.
127 [1975] 2 Lloyd's Rep 314 (CA).
128 Most modern charter forms specifically provide for the eventuality of strikes or lockouts. See, for example, the Gencon 1994 general strike clause (cl 16). A recent case involving the construction of a charterparty strike clause was *Frontier International Shipping Corp v Swissmarine Corp Inc (The Cape Equinox)* [2004] EWHC 8 (Comm); [2005] 1 Lloyd's Rep 390.
129 [1975] 2 Lloyd's Rep 314 (CA), 317. See *Cero Navigation Corp v Jean Lion & Cie (The Solon)* [2000] 1 Lloyd's Rep 292, a recent voyage charterparty case concerned with the application of a strike clause in the Sugar Charterparty 1969 form.
130 See *Candelwood Navigation Corp Ltd v Mitsui OSK Lines Ltd* [1986] 1 AC 1.

No limits on persons   There is no limitation on the persons whose stoppage or strike **28.35** action is contemplated. Thus, stoppages by crews, stevedores, lightermen, tug operators, customs, and sanitary officers would all seem to be included.[131]

'Riots and civil commotions'[132]   This exception should be understood as complementing **28.36** the earlier exception of 'Act of war'.[133] In domestic law, the meaning of a riot has a specific meaning in the criminal law, as described by Phillimore LJ in the case of *Field v Metropolitan Police Receiver*:

> We deduce that there are five necessary elements of a riot — (1) number of persons, three at least; (2) common purpose; (3) execution or inception of the common purpose; (4) an intent to help one another by force if necessary against any person who may oppose them in the execution of their common purpose; (5) force or violence not merely used in demolishing, but displayed in such a manner as to alarm at least one person of reasonable firmness and courage.[134]

This meaning has been accepted in the insurance context[135] and it is thought would apply with equal force in the context of the Rules.

Civil commotions   Lord Mansfield interpreted this term in *Langdale v Mason* as: **28.37**

> An insurrection of the people for general purposes, though it may not amount to a rebellion, where there is a usurped power.[136]

More recently, Luxmoore LJ interpreted the phrase as follows in *Levy v Assicurazioni Generali*:

> This phrase is used to indicate a stage between a riot and civil war. It has been defined to mean an insurrection of the people for general purposes, though not amounting to rebellion; but it is probably not capable of any very precise definition. The element of turbulence or tumult is essential; an organised conspiracy to commit criminal acts, where there is no tumult or disturbance until after the acts, does not amount to civil commotion.[137]

'Saving or attempting to save life at sea'[138]   This provision links with article IV, rule 4   **28.38** (deviation), which has already been discussed.[139]

'Wastage in bulk or weight . . . from inherent defect, quality or vice . . .'[140]   The defence   **28.39** of inherent vice of the goods has had a long history in the context of the carriage of goods by sea. Thus, the strict liability of the bailee would be excluded for such risks.[141] As Willes J explained in *Blower v Great Western Railway*:

> By the expression 'vice', I . . . mean . . . that sort of vice which by its internal development tends to the destruction or the injury of the animal or thing to be carried, and which is likely to lead

---

[131] See *The Alne Holme* [1893] P 173 where a strike by timber workers at Gloucester docks was held included in the equivalent bill of lading exception.

[132] Article IV, r 2(k). See Berlingieri (1997), 416.

[133] See *Republic of Bolivia v Indemnity Mutual Marine Assurance Co* [1909] 1 KB 785, 801 (Farwell LJ).

[134] [1907] 2 KB 853, 860.

[135] See *London & Lancashire Fire Insurance Co Ltd v Bolands Ltd* [1924] AC 836.

[136] (1780) 2 Parke on Ins 965.

[137] [1940] AC 791 (PC), 800. See too *Spinney's (1948) Ltd v Royal Insurance Co Ltd* [1980] 1 Lloyd's Rep 406, 438 (Mustill J).

[138] Article IV, r 2(l). See Berlingieri (1997), 418.

[139] See para 26.44.

[140] Article IV, r 2(m). See Berlingieri (1997), 421.

[141] See too the Marine Insurance Act 1906, s 55(2).

to such a result. If such a cause of destruction exists and produces that result in the course of the journey, the liability of the carrier is necessarily excluded from the contract between the parties.[142]

A more recent definition is that inherent vice is:

> The risk of deterioration of the goods shipped as a result of their natural ordinary behaviour in the ordinary course of the contemplated voyage without the intervention of any fortuitous external accident or casualty.[143]

The policy underlying the defence seems to be that it is the shipper rather than the carrier who should know about the inherent characteristics of the goods shipped and so should bear responsibility for them.[144] The carrier will not be able to rely on the exception where the cause of the damage was a breach of his obligation under article III, rule 1 or article III, rule 2.[145]

28.40 **'Insufficiency of packing'**[146]   This exception, which is usually treated as an example of inherent vice,[147] covers the situation where goods are so packed that they will not withstand the ordinary hazards which are likely to be encountered during transit. Packaging in this context clearly refers to the external packing of the goods. Thus, if it is obvious at the time of receipt for shipment that the packing is deficient in some respect, it would be prudent for the carrier to note the details on the bill of lading. As we have previously noted,[148] there can be problems for the carrier who issues an unclaused bill of lading and then subsequently seeks the protection of the exception. Thus, in *Silver v Ocean Steamship Co Ltd*,[149] which concerned damage to a shipment of Chinese eggs, the carrier was estopped from invoking the exception in article IV, rule 2(n) against a consignee who had relied in good faith on the clean bill of lading. Slesser LJ said that:

> Now I think there may well be cases where the insufficiency of the packing is not apparent; but in this case, where the insufficiency, if any, was obvious, the shipowners were nevertheless prepared to take the goods without complaint and give a clean bill that the goods were shipped in good order and condition. I think that the capacity of the goods safely to travel was part of their order and condition; and so, being apparent on the face of it, I cannot see how the shipowners can now say that the goods were insufficiently packed.[150]

One of the ways in which the carrier can establish this defence is by showing that the method of packing which the shipper has employed has fallen short in some way of the normal practice for these type of goods for this particular type of voyage.[151]

---

[142] (1872) LR 7 CP 655, 662–663. See too *The Barcore* [1896] P 294, 297 (Gorell Barnes J).

[143] *Soya GmbH Mainz KG v White* [1983] 1 Lloyd's Rep 122 (HL), 125 (Lord Diplock).

[144] See Schoenbaum (2004), 704.

[145] See *Colonial Sugar Refining Co Ltd v British India Steam Navigation Co Ltd* (1931) 32 SR (NSW) 425, where the defence was unsuccessful because it was established that the damage was caused by condensation from the hull of the ship and not from the goods themselves.

[146] Article IV, r 2(n).

[147] See para 28.39.

[148] See para 6.16.

[149] [1930] 1 KB 416 (CA).

[150] At 440–441. See *Successors of Moine Comte & Co Ltd v East Asiatic Co Ltd & Singapore Harbour Board* [1954] 1 MLJ 113, 115, where the court held that 'apparent good order and condition' could not possibly cover 'inherent defect' or a defect not apparent to careful visual examination (Knight J).

[151] See, eg, *Great China Metal Industries Co Ltd v Malaysian International Shipping Corp Berhad (The Bunga Seroja)* [1994] 1 Lloyd's Rep 455, 456, where the containerized packing of aluminium can body stock was described as being in accordance with 'normal, well-established practice for world-wide voyages' (Carruthers J).

'Insufficiency or inadequacy of marks'[152]   This exception is intended to be read with   **28.41**
article III, rule 3 of the Rules and concerns the non-delivery or misdelivery of goods which
is due to inadequate marking as to their destination or ownership.[153] In particular, it would
be possible for the carrier to rely on this exception when the goods have become mixed with
other goods, such that they cannot any longer be distinguished.[154]

'Latent defects not discoverable by due diligence'[155]   In practice, this defence is potentially   **28.42**
important because, if successful, the carrier will be absolved from liability for loss or damage
resulting from a latent defect which is not discoverable by the exercise of due diligence.
It should be noted that a latent defect in this context relates to the ship, not the goods; in
the latter case, it would be open to the carrier to raise the defence of inherent vice.[156]

Meaning of 'latent'   In *Charles Brown & Co Ltd v Nitrate Producers' Steamship Co Ltd*   **28.43**
Porter J explained that

> 'latent defect' does not mean latent to the eye. It means latent to the senses, that is, it may be
> hammer-tested, or there may be any other test. The only question is whether by 'latent' it
> means that you have to use every possible method to discover whether it exists, or whether
> you must use reasonable methods. I cannot myself believe that in every case it is obligatory
> upon a ship's officer on the commencement of a voyage to go and tap every rivet to find if it
> has a defect or not. If that were so, ships would be held up in port for a very long time while
> the rivets were being tapped and eyes used to determine whether a defect existed or not.
> I think it means such an examination as a reasonably careful man skilled in that matter would
> make, and I think that such an examination as that was in fact made.[157]

Difficulty of proof   One of the major difficulties with the exception, however, is the   **28.44**
difficulty of proof. This may be illustrated by the decision of the Court of Appeal in
The Antigoni.[158] The *Antigoni* was built by a German firm in 1977 and she was powered by
an engine built by Alpha Diesel A/S. The crankshaft of the engine had 10 counterweights
attached to it whose function was to balance the crankshaft and so prevent or counteract
vibration. It was necessary as a matter of routine maintenance to inspect the bolts holding
the counterweights in place; Alpha Diesel recommended that they be checked and
tightened every 5,000 engine hours. During the course of a voyage off the cost of Africa,
the vessel's engine sustained a major breakdown and the vessel was immobilized. She was
obliged to accept towage under LOF[159] and was taken to Las Palmas. It was discovered that
the cause of the engine seizure was one of the counterweights, which had struck the
connecting rod of the crankshaft and broken through the engine. The owners of the cargo
contended that the owner's employees had negligently failed to carry out the recommended
steps for servicing and that the owners had therefore failed to exercise due diligence to make
the vessel seaworthy as required by article IV, rule 1 of the Hague–Visby Rules. At first

---

[152] Article IV, r 2(o). See Berlingieri (1997), 422.
[153] See para 6.20.
[154] As to mixing of cargoes generally, see the discussion at para 30.41.
[155] Article IV, r 2(p). See Berlingieri (1997), 423.
[156] See the discussion at para 28.39.
[157] (1937) 58 Ll LR 188, 191–192.
[158] [1991] 1 Lloyd's Rep 209 (CA).
[159] ie Lloyds Open Form, the widely used salvage contract.

instance,[160] Judge Diamond QC found the owners liable but they appealed contending that the unseaworthiness of the vessel was caused by a latent defect not discoverable by due diligence (article IV, rule 2(p)). Staughton LJ found that the most that could be said on the evidence was that there was a theoretical possibility that the bolts holding the counter-weights had a propensity to work loose after less than 5,000 running hours. Accordingly, the owners were not able to show that the cause of the loss was a latent defect.

28.45 **Overlap with the duty to exercise due diligence**   We have noted previously that the carrier's 'overriding' duty under the Rules is to exercise due diligence to provide a seaworthy vessel[161] but that a carrier might, at least, potentially be aided by the presence of a latent defect.[162] It is worth making the point that the exception will only really assist the carrier where there are defects not discoverable by due diligence during the voyage, given the carrier's obligation to exercise due diligence 'before and at the beginning' of that voyage.[163]

28.46 **'Any other cause . . .'** [164]   The final clause in the catalogue of exceptions contained in article IV provides:

> Any other cause arising without the actual fault or privity of the carrier, or [165] without the fault or neglect of the agents or servants of the carrier, but the burden of proof shall be on the person claiming the benefit of this exception to show that neither the actual fault or privity of the carrier nor the fault or neglect of the agents or servants of the carrier contributed to the loss or damage.

This 'catch-all' exception[166] provides a further right of recourse for the carrier in defending cargo claims, assuming that he has been unsuccessful in raising one or more of the other exceptions. The carrier will be able to avoid liability for any damage or loss not falling within the named exceptions provided that he can establish that this occurred without his own fault or privity and that it did not result from any fault or neglect on the part of his servants or agents. In *Goodwin, Ferreira & Co v Lamport & Holt Ltd* [167] bales of cotton yarn discharged into a lighter sustained damage because other machinery was dropped into the lighter and broke open and holed it, permitting sea water to damage the yarn to some 80 per cent of its value. The shipowners were able to satisfy the court that this occurred owing to the other cargo being insecurely nailed before shipment and that it broke open without the fault or neglect of their servants or agents.[168]

---

[160] [1990] 1 Lloyd's Rep 45.

[161] See para 26.34.

[162] See para 26.25.

[163] See para 26.19. See *Parsons Corp v CV Scheepvaartonderneming Happy Ranger (The Happy Ranger)* [2006] EWHC 122 (Comm); [2006] 1 Lloyd's Rep 649, where there was a latent defect, but the carrier was nevertheless in breach of his obligation under art III, r 1 and art III, r 2. See para 26.24.

[164] Article IV, r 2(q). See Berlingieri (1997), 425.

[165] This has been interpreted by the courts as meaning 'and': see *Hourani v T & J Harrison* (1927) 28 Ll LR 120 (CA), 125 (Bankes LJ); *Paterson Steamships Ltd v Canadian Co-operative Wheat Producers Ltd* [1934] AC 538 (PC), 549 (Lord Wright).

[166] Or, as it is less favourably put, 'the last resort of the rogue': see Richardson (1994), 39.

[167] (1929) 34 Ll LR 192.

[168] At 196 (Roche J).

Pilferage and theft   The consequences of pilferage and theft are not specifically dealt   **28.47**
with in the Rules and the question remains whether the carrier would be able to bring such
activities within article IV, rule 2(q). There is some authority for the proposition that
the carrier could not invoke article IV, rule 2(q) where there had been a theft of cargo by the
carrier's servants or even by employees of a firm of stevedores engaged by the carrier to
discharge the cargo.[169] In *Leesh River Tea Co v British India Steam Navigation Co
(The Chyebassa)*[170] the brass cover plate of a storm valve was pilfered at an intermediate
port, Port Sudan, by a stevedore or stevedores and this led to sea water entering the
Chyebassa and damaging the remaining cargo of tea. The Court of Appeal held that the
shipowners were protected by article IV, rule 2(q) because the stevedores were not agents
or servants of the shipowners when they stole the plate and the theft was an act unconnected
with the cargo and so outside the course of their employment. Sellers LJ said that

> in the present case the act of the thief ought, I think, to be regarded as the act of a stranger.
> The thief in interfering with the ship and making her, as a consequence, unseaworthy, was per-
> forming no duty for the shipowner at all, neither negligently, nor deliberately, nor dishonestly.
> He was not in fact their servant . . . The appellants were only liable for his acts when he, as a
> servant of the stevedores, was acting on behalf of the appellants in the fulfilment of the work
> for which the stevedores had been engaged.[171]

However, where the thief is regarded as a 'confederate' of the carrier's servants, the exception
would not apply.[172]

C. Servants and Agents

Introduction   In the past there was little or no scope for the protection of servants   **28.48**
or agents of the carrier because such parties were not privy to the contract of carriage.[173]
Unless the parties to the contract of carriage included a clause, such as a Himalaya clause,[174]
extending the defences and limits of liability to these third parties, they often went
unprotected.

Article IV bis[175]   Article IV bis, rule 2 provides that: **28.49**

> If such an action is brought against a servant or agent of the carrier (such servant or agent not
> being an independent contractor), such servant or agent shall be entitled to avail himself of
> the defences and limits of liability which the carrier is entitled to invoke under these Rules.

The purpose of this provision is to extend the protection of the statutory exceptions in the
Rules to those persons other than the carrier. The major qualification in this rule is that it
is not extended to independent contractors, such as stevedores. Potentially, however, the
provision may exclude other classes of individuals who are independent contractors.

---

[169] See *Hourani v T & J Harrison* (1927) 28 Ll LR 120 (CA). Neither could art IV, r 2(a) be invoked.
[170] [1967] 2 QB 250 (CA).
[171] At 272.
[172] See *Heyn v Ocean Steamship Co* (1927) 27 Ll LR 334.
[173] See, eg, *Adler v Dickson* [1955] 1 QB 158 (CA).
[174] See para 9.23.
[175] See Berlingieri (1997), 595.

28.50 Limits on the amounts recoverable Article IV bis, rule 3 provides that:

> The aggregate of the amounts recoverable from the carrier, and such servants and agents, shall in no case exceed the limit provided for in these Rules.

This provision is self-explanatory.

28.51 No recovery Article IV bis, rule 4 provides that:

> Nevertheless, a servant or agent of the carrier shall not be entitled to avail himself of the provisions of this Article, if it is proved that the damage resulted from an act or omission of the servant or agent done with intent to cause damage or recklessly and with knowledge that damage would probably result.

This provision is similar to that in article IV, rule 5(e),[176] but is more extensive in that it deprives the servant of the carrier not only of his right to limit his liability, but also all his statutory defences (ie under article IV, rule 2).

---

[176] See para 29.28.

29

LIMITATION OF LIABILITY

A. Introduction

Overview   In this chapter we consider the shipowner's right to limit his liability. We **29.01** consider first the underlying principles before moving to the carrier's package limitation under the Hague and Hague–Visby Rules. We conclude with an examination of the Limitation Convention 1976 and the shipowner's right to limit his liability globally.

B. Background to Limitation

Historical background   One of the distinctive features of shipping law is that shipowners **29.02** may limit their liability.[1] Scholars[2] have traced the idea of limitation to its development in Italy and in Spain[3] some time in the middle ages[4] and the traditional justification, which

---

[1] See Gaskell (1986); Griggs, Williams and Farr (2005).

[2] See James J Donovan, 'The Origins and Development of Limitation of Shipowners' Liability' (1978–1979) 53 Tulane LR 999, 1000–1005; George C Sprague, 'Limitation of Ship Owners' Liability' (1934–1935) 12 NYULQ 568.

[3] See, eg, the *Consolato del Mare* (c 1494); Sanborn (1930), 118.

[4] There is, for example, evidence of limitation in the writing of Roman–Dutch civilian writers, such as Hugo Grotius: see *De Jure Belli ac Pacis* (1625), I.2.11.13; *The Dundee* (1823) 1 Hag 109, 121; 66 ER 39, 44 (Lord Stowell).

achieved critical momentum in the eighteenth century, was that, as a matter of policy,[5] limitation was needed in shipping in order to encourage investment and to serve the needs of commerce.[6] It is also said that limitation of liability protects the carrier from risks associated with cargoes of high undisclosed value and encourages the shipowner to offer uniform and cheaper freight rates. Lord Denning MR once famously opined that 'limitation of liability is not a matter of justice . . . [but] a rule of public policy which has its origin in history and its justification in convenience'.[7]

29.03 **Regulation**   Given the danger that the shipowner might seek to limit his liability to amounts which are derisory, such limits and the terms on which limitation is offered are prescribed by international conventions, including the Hague, Hague–Visby, and Hamburg Rules. Additionally, limitation is available under maritime oil pollution conventions,[8] and under two general (or tonnage) limitation conventions, the 1957 Limitation Convention,[9] and the 1976 'London' Convention on the Limitation of Liability for Marine Claims.[10]

29.04 **Types of limitation**   The type of limitation of liability which arises under the carriage of goods conventions is known as 'package' limitation which is restricted to individual and separate claims made under a contract of carriage whereas the type of limitation given to the shipowner under the general maritime conventions is known as 'global' limitation. This is calculated by reference to the tonnage[11] or other particulars of the vessel and, unlike 'package' limitation, applies to all claims arising out of the same occurrence by all claimants. In other words, this type of limitation is applicable to claims not only in connection with the carriage of goods but also the other forms of claim which may arise, for example hull and property damage and personal injury arising out of a collision between ships. Provided that the carrier can satisfy the requirements imposed by any of the categories of limitation, there is nothing to prevent him from relying on that category which gives him the greater protection.[12]

29.05 **Critique and appraisal**   Although it is undoubtedly true that the commercial structure of maritime trade is built upon the foundation of limited liability, it has sometimes been questioned whether the policy of encouraging shipping, set against the equally compelling policy

---

[5] See, eg, Dr Lushington in *Cail v Papayanni (The Amalia)* (1863) 1 Moo PC (ns) 471, 473; 15 ER 778, 779: 'The principle of limited liability is, that full indemnity, the natural right of justice, shall be abridged for political reasons'.
[6] See, eg, *Gale v Laurie* (1826) B & C 156, 163–164; 108 ER 58, 61 (Abbott CJ); *British Columbia Telephone Co v Marpole Towing Ltd* [1971] SCR 321, 338 (Ritchie J); *Browner International Ltd v Monarch Shipping Co Ltd (The European Enterprise)* [1989] 2 Lloyd's Rep 185, 191 (Steyn J). For a robust defence, see also David Steel, 'Ships are different: the case for limitation of liability' [1995] LMCLQ 77.
[7] *Alexandra Towing Co Ltd v Millet and Egret (The Bramley Moore)* [1964] P 200 (CA), 220. See also *Polish Steam Ship Co v Atlantic Maritime Co (The Garden City (No 2))* [1984] 2 Lloyd's Rep 37 (CA), 44 (Griffiths LJ).
[8] In particular, the International Conventions on Civil Liability for Oil Pollution Damage 1969 (CLC 1969) and 1992 (CLC 1992). For discussion, see de la Rue and Anderson (1998), 100.
[9] ie, the Brussels International Convention Relating to the Limitation of the Liability of Sea-going Ships 1957.
[10] See para 29.37.
[11] Pursuant to the International Convention on Tonnage Measurement of Ships 1969.
[12] This right is expressly reserved to the carrier by art VIII of the Hague and Hague–Visby Rules and art 25(1) of the Hamburg Rules.

of compensating victims,[13] is always morally persuasive.[14] There have been cases where limitation of liability has sometimes produced decidedly unsavoury results, at least in the eyes of the general public. Thus, the owners of the *Titanic* were able to limit their liability in respect of those killed in what is probably the world's best-known maritime disaster.[15] Another illustration is the incident in which the *Bowbelle* ran over the *Marchioness* in the River Thames in London in 1989 and in which the owner of the *Bowbelle* was held entitled to limit his liability.[16] In such circumstances, where limitation protects the shipowners' insurer at the expense of the victims of the disaster, underlying policy justifications can seem less convincing in general terms.[17] However, these arguments have to be set against others, which reject moralist arguments as missing the point and emphasize the fact that limitation exists to create certainty in commercial relations. Thus, the argument runs that under a known scheme of limitation of liability both the carrier and the cargo owner know the limits of their respective exposure and can insure themselves accordingly.[18]

C. Package Limitation

Introduction   As we have seen previously,[19] the Hague Rules of 1924 regulate the rights, **29.06** duties, and immunities of the carrier under a contract of carriage by sea covered by a bill of lading. The carrier's right under the Rules to limit his liability is contained in article IV, rule 5[20] and this right, as much as any of the other provisions, underlines the desire of those involved in drafting the Rules of ameliorating the commercial unfairness of many existing contracts of carriage. The provision in the Hague Rules is quite different in several respects to what now appears in the Hague–Visby Rules; nevertheless, there are still a number of points of similarity and these will be dealt with in the analysis which follows there. This part of the discussion focuses on those provisions which are unique to the Hague Rules.

The provision   Article IV, rule 5 of the Hague Rules contains four paragraphs setting out **29.07** the essential terms on limitation, as follows:

> Neither the carrier nor the ship shall in any event be or become liable for any loss or damage to or in connexion with goods in an amount exceeding 100 pounds sterling per package or unit, or the equivalent of that sum in other currency unless the nature and value of such goods have been declared by the shipper before shipment and inserted in the bill of lading.

---

[13] See *Noferi v Smithers* [2002] NSWSC 508, at [5].

[14] For criticism of the principle, see Lord Mustill, 'Ships are different — or are they?' [1993] LMCLQ 490; Gotthard Gauci, 'Limitation of liability in maritime law: an anachronism?' (1995) 19 Marine Policy 65.

[15] See *Oceanic Steam Navigation Co v Mellor (The Titanic)* 233 US 718 (1914). See too *The Princess Victoria* [1953] 2 Lloyd's Rep 619, where a ship sank, despite the unwillingness of the master to sail her (she was unseaworthy), and the shipowner was still held entitled to limit his liability for the deaths of 133 people on board her.

[16] See *The Bowbelle* [1990] 1 Lloyd's Rep 532.

[17] See *Schlederer v The Ship Red Fin* [1979] 1 NSWLR 258, 273 (Sheppard J).

[18] CWH Goldie, 'Effect of the Hamburg Rules on Shipowners' Liability Insurance' (1993) 24 JMLC 111, 112–113.

[19] See para 15.13.

[20] See Berlingieri (1997), 445. The provision broadly follows s 8 of the Canadian Water Carriage of Goods Act 1910. See para 14.13.

This declaration if embodied in the bill of lading shall be *prima facie* evidence, but shall not be binding or conclusive on the carrier.

By agreement between the carrier, master or agent of the carrier and the shipper another maximum amount than that mentioned in this paragraph may be fixed, provided that such maximum shall not be less than the figure above named.

Neither the carrier nor the ship shall be responsible in any event for loss or damage to, or in connexion with, goods if the nature or value thereof has been knowingly misstated by the shipper in the bill of lading.

29.08 **Limitation amounts**   The limitation sum of £100[21] was arrived at after considerable discussion[22] in the deliberations leading to the Hague Rules.[23] At the time this represented a fair figure[24] for the average value of a package shipped.[25] The reference to this sum has to be read with article 9, which provides that the monetary units in the Rules are to be taken to be 'gold value' and further provides that 'those contracting States in which the pound sterling is not a monetary unit reserve to themselves the right of translating the sums indicated in this Convention in terms of pound sterling into terms of their own monetary system in round figures'.[26] The gold value in question has to be ascertained, at least for English law, by reference to the Coinage Act 1971,[27] and means the currency value of £100 of gold taken at the date of the breach.[28] On this basis, the currency value of £100 gold in two of the reported cases was, respectively, Kenyan £6,491.25 and A$32,221.33 per package.[29] English law apart, however, it is clear that there soon grew up widely divergent limits worldwide. Indeed, as one commentator remarked, these provisions did not succeed in achieving certainty, uniformity, stability, and the maximum degree of protection against currency inflation, which are objectives which should be achieved in an international convention.[30]

29.09 **Gold Clause Agreement**   The UK version of article 9, appended to the Carriage of Goods by Sea Act 1924, provided that 'the monetary units mentioned in these Rules are taken to

---

[21] The official French text of the Rules refers to '100 livres sterling' (100 pounds sterling).

[22] See Berlingieri (1997), 263–271; 279–307.

[23] It has not been adopted in the United States Carriage of Goods by Sea Act 1936, which provides for a limit of '$500 per package lawful money of the United States': 40 USCA §1304.

[24] Some writers have suggested that the limitation amounts agreed upon represented a major improvement for cargo interests: see, eg, F Cyril James, 'Carriage of Goods by Sea — The Hague Rules' (1925–26) 74 U of Pennsylvania LR 672, 688.

[25] Lord Diplock has explained that 'the economic purpose of the [Hague Rules] limitation was to enable the shipowner, on the basis of knowing that his liability was limited to that figure, to offer standard freight rates for all ordinary cargo without the delay and cost to himself and to the cargo-owner which would be incurred by inquiring into the value of the particular consignment and by adjusting the freight rate accordingly': 'Conventions and Morals — Limitation Clauses in International Maritime Conventions' (1969–1970) 1 JMLC 525, 529.

[26] See *The Rosa S* [1989] QB 419, 425 (Hobhouse J); *Pyrene Co v Scindia Navigation Co* [1954] 2 QB 402, 413; *Brown Boveri (Australia) Pty Ltd v Baltic Shipping Co (The Nadezhda Krupskaya)* [1989] 1 Lloyd's Rep 518. But cf *The Vishva Pratibha* [1980–1981] SLR 319, 324, which was not followed in *The Thomaseverett* [1992] 2 SLR 1068.

[27] c 24. See too the previous Coinage Act 1870, 33 & 34 Vict, c 10 (as amended).

[28] See, eg, *The Thomaseverett* [1992] 2 SLR 1068, 1082 (Chao Hick Tin J).

[29] *The Rosa S* [1989] QB 419, 432; *Brown Boveri (Australia) Pty Ltd v Baltic Shipping Co (The Nadezhda Krupskaya)* [1989] 1 Lloyd's Rep 518, 520 (upholding (1989) 93 ALR 171, Yeldham J). See too Francesco Berlingieri, 'Conversion of the gold monetary unit into money of payment' [1991] LMCLQ 97.

[30] Anthony Diamond QC, 'The Hague–Visby Rules' [1978] LMCLQ 226, 237.

be gold value'.[31] However, the amount of limitation of liability per unit under the Hague Rules quickly deteriorated to such an extent that it became almost impossible for shipowners and their insurers to predict with accuracy what the total amount of exposure would be following a disaster to ship and cargo. A study undertaken by the British Maritime Law Association therefore emphasized that it was 'manifestly desirable both to resolve these problems and to achieve, as far as possible, uniformity in the manner in which the limit of liability is applied in practice'.[32] This study resulted in the so-called 'Gold Clause Agreement' which was adopted by a combination of shipowners' associations, P & I Clubs, cargo owners' associations, and underwriting associations[33] and this set a limit of £200[34] 'Sterling lawful money of the United Kingdom per package or unit of cargo . . . notwithstanding that some other monetary unit is laid down by the legislation to which the contract of carriage is subject'.[35] The Agreement did not infringe article III, rule 8 of the Rules because it was not part of a 'contract of carriage'.[36] The Privy Council has subsequently held, on appeal from the Court of Appeal of New Zealand,[37] that a term of a contract stipulating that limitation was to be 'deemed to be £100 Sterling, lawful money of the United Kingdom per package or unit . . .' was a reference to £100 sterling in ordinary or paper currency.[38]

CMI Stockholm Conference 1963   One of several issues under consideration at the **29.10** CMI's Stockholm Conference was the revision of the limitation provisions of the Hague Rules. The CMI's Bill of Lading Sub-Committee noted, with remarkable understatement, that 'a system which allows the limitation figures to depreciate and to vary in various countries seems due for overhaul'[39] and recommended, in order to achieve uniformity, the use of the Poincaré franc.[40] This was duly accepted, after much debate, at the Diplomatic Conferences held in 1967 and 1968.[41] An additional innovation thrashed out by the delegations at the Diplomatic Conferences was an alternative weight basis of limitation[42] as well as provision for containerized cargo.[43]

---

[31] At the time that the Act came into force (1 January 1925) the UK was not on the gold standard and although it subsequently resumed it for a period of years this was abandoned on 21 September 1931.

[32] *Shipowners' Liability for Loss of or Damage to Cargo under the Hague Rules* (British Maritime Law Association, 26 July 1950), 1.

[33] Dated London, Liverpool, and Glasgow, 1 August 1950 and to remain in force 'for a period of five years . . .' (cl 7).

[34] This was subsequently revised to £400.

[35] Clause 2 of the Agreement.

[36] Although a term in a contract of carriage limiting liability to '£100 sterling' would be rendered null and void by art III, r 8: see *The Rosa S* [1989] QB 419, 422 (Hobhouse J).

[37] [2002] 3 NZLR 353, reversing [2002] 1 NZLR 265; [2001] 2 Lloyd's Rep 665.

[38] *Dairy Containers Ltd v Tasman Orient Line CV* [2004] UKPC 22; [2004] 2 Lloyd's Rep 647, 652.

[39] Berlingieri (1997), 514.

[40] Named after the French prime minister under whose government the gold value of the franc was set at 65.5 milligrams of gold of millesimal fineness nine hundred: see TMC Asser, 'Golden Limitations of Liability in International Transport Conventions and the Currency Crisis' (1973–1974) 5 JMLC 645.

[41] See Berlingieri (1997), 509–585.

[42] See para 29.23.

[43] See para 29.19.

29.11 **Limitation amounts: Poincaré francs**   The limit fixed at Visby was 10,000 gold francs[44] per package or unit or 30 gold francs per kilo of gross weight of the goods lost or damaged.[45] The Protocol defined a franc as meaning 'a unit consisting of 65.5 milligrammes of gold of millesimal fineness 900' and further provided that the date of conversion of the sum awarded into national currencies should be governed by the law of the court seized of the case.[46] Unfortunately, the Poincaré franc system collapsed very soon after the Brussels Conference, largely because of the ravages of inflation.[47] The main issue for contracting states quickly became whether the number of gold francs was convertible into national currency on the basis of the market value of gold and this unsatisfactory state of affairs continued until measures were taken by the Belgian government two years after the coming into force of the Visby Protocol.

29.12 **Limitation amounts: SDRs**   In an effort to promote some sort of uniformity, the Belgian government called a new diplomatic conference in 1979 with a view to resolving the difficulties associated with the Poincaré franc. The result was the 1979 SDR Protocol to the Hague Rules.[48] The Protocol replaced the Poincaré franc with the Special Drawing Right (SDR), an artificial unit of the International Monetary Fund (IMF).[49] This Protocol was duly ratified by the United Kingdom and implemented by legislation in 1981[50] and the amended article IV, rule 5(d) now provides that:

> The unit of account mentioned in this Article is the Special Drawing Right as defined by the International Monetary Fund. The amounts mentioned in sub-paragraph (a) of this paragraph shall be converted into national currency on the basis of the value of that currency on a date to be determined by the law of the Court seized of the case.[51]

29.13 **Declaration of value**   Apart from containing certain limitation amounts 'per package or unit', article IV, rule 5(a), is subject to the proviso that 'unless the nature and value of such goods have been declared by the shipper before shipment and inserted in the bill of lading...'. The effect of this proviso is to permit a declaration of higher valued cargoes but, in order to displace the rest of article IV, rule 5, such a declaration must be stated in the bill of lading.[52] Further, it should be noted that Article IV, rule 5(f) provides that:

---

[44] At the time estimated to be worth £235 or $662: see Anthony Diamond QC, 'The Hague–Visby Rules' [1978] LMCLQ 226, 229.

[45] Article IV, r 5(a).

[46] Article IV, r 5(d). For the UK, s 1(5) of the enabling Act, the Carriage of Goods by Sea Act 1971, enabled the sterling equivalent of the specified quantity of gold francs to be fixed by statutory instrument: see, eg, the Carriage of Goods by Sea (Sterling Equivalents) Order 1977, SI 1977/1044.

[47] For fuller analysis, see Allan I Mendelsohn, 'The Value of the Poincaré Franc in Limitation of Liability Conventions' (1973–1974) 5 JMLC 125; Diamond [1978] LMCLQ 226, 348.

[48] Not all countries which are party to the Visby Protocol have ratified the SDR Protocol. See Appendix III.

[49] The basket of currencies on which the SDR is based is currently the euro, the Japanese yen, pound sterling, and the US dollar. See <www.imf.org>.

[50] By the Merchant Shipping Act 1981, s 2(4) (itself since repealed).

[51] For the UK provisions as to conversion, see s 1A of the Carriage of Goods by Sea Act 1971 (as added by the Merchant Shipping Act 1995, s 314 and Sch 13, para 45).

[52] In the United States, the courts have read into this provision the so-called 'fair opportunity' requirement whereby the carrier must permit the shipper a fair opportunity to declare a higher value. See the seminal articles by Michael Sturley, 'The Fair Opportunity Requirement under COGSA Section 4(5): A Case Study in the Misinterpretation of the Carriage of Goods by Sea Act' (1988) 19 JMLC 1; 157. See too Schoenbaum (2004), §10-36.

The declaration mentioned in sub-paragraph (a) of this paragraph, if embodied in the bill of lading, shall be *prima facie* evidence, but shall not be binding or conclusive on the carrier.

Higher but not lower limits   It is possible for the carrier and the shipper to agree higher, but not lower, limits of liability[53] under the Rules. Article IV, rule 5(g) accordingly provides that: **29.14**

> By agreement between the carrier, master or agent of the carrier and the shipper other maximum amounts than those mentioned in sub-paragraph (a) of this paragraph may be fixed, provided that no maximum amount so fixed shall be less than the appropriate maximum mentioned in that sub-paragraph.

Misstatements by the shipper   Article IV, rule 5(h) provides that: **29.15**

> Neither the carrier nor the ship shall be responsible in any event for loss or damage to, or in connection with, goods if the nature or value thereof has been knowingly mis-stated by the shipper in the bill of lading.

'... neither the carrier nor the ship ...'   Article IV, rule 5(a) and rule 5(h) provide that it   **29.16**
is 'neither the carrier nor the ship' which is entitled to the benefit of its limitation provisions. As we shall see later in connection with proceedings *in rem* against a ship,[54] this provision was likely included to make it clear that it was the ship against which such claims were made, although this 'personification' theory[55] has now been rejected by the House of Lords.[56]

'Package': generally   The centrepiece of article IV, rule 5 of both the Hague and the   **29.17**
Hague–Visby Rules is that limitation is available to the carrier 'per package or unit ... whichever is the higher'.[57] The notion of a 'package' is not a novel one, at least in so far as English domestic law is concerned, because of the existence of an earlier statute, the Carriers Act 1830,[58] which excluded the liability of common carriers by land for loss or damage 'contained in any parcel or package' when the value of the goods exceeded £10.[59] However, the concept is not defined in the Rules. A dictionary definition sometimes resorted to by the courts is that a package is 'a bundle of things packed up, whether in a box or other receptacle, or merely compactly tied up'.[60] In *Studebaker Distributors Ltd v Charlton Steam Shipping Co Ltd* Goddard J stated that:

> 'Package' must indicate something packed. It is obvious that this clause cannot refer to all cargoes that may be shipped under the bill of lading; for instance, on a shipment of grain it could apply to grain shipped in sacks, but could not, in my opinion, possibly apply to shipment in bulk. If the shipowners desire that it should refer to any individual piece of cargo, it would not be difficult to use appropriate words, as for instance 'package or unit', to use the language of the Hague Rules.[61]

---

53 Lower limits of liability would infringe art III, r 8. See para 19.39.
54 See para 35.15.
55 See eg Holmes (1881), 24; Gilmore and Black (1975), 589.
56 See *Republic of India v India Steamship Co Ltd (The Indian Grace)(No 2)* [1998] AC 878. See para 35.20.
57 See para 29.21.
58 11 Geo 4 & 1 Will 4, c 68.
59 Section 1. See *Whaite v Lancashire & Yorkshire Ry Co* (1874) LR 9 Ex 67.
60 *Oxford English Dictionary.*
61 [1938] 1 KB 459, 467.

In a number of decided cases, courts throughout the commonwealth have held that the following constitute packages: a tractor and a generating set;[62] a motor cruiser stored on the deck on top of containers;[63] crates of plywood;[64] bundles of timber.[65] Although no general principle can readily be drawn from these cases, it may reasonably be concluded that each case will be decided on its own facts.

29.18 **'Package': containers under Hague**   The Hague Rules were developed and drafted at a time when no one could have forecast the technological advances in shipping which would occur in the latter half of the twentieth century. In the 1920s most cargoes were shipped 'break-bulk' in cartons or other types of packaging[66] but such carriage is now a very small part of the liner trade. Accordingly, courts throughout the common law world have had to grapple with the meaning of 'package' in the light of containerization and the importance of bulk cargo carriage since World War II.[67] In the container context, the issue is whether the container is the package or whether the individual contents carried in the container constitute packages for the purpose of limitation. Much, though not all, of the case law on this issue has been generated in the United States,[68] principally because that country has not adopted the Visby Protocol.[69] The leading English case is *River Gurara v Nigerian National Shipping Line Ltd*[70] and the principal issue to be resolved was whether, in the circumstances of the case, the packages on which the limits of liability were to be calculated were the containers or the individual items within them. At first instance, Colman J held that it was the number of items described in the bill of lading as being within the containers, rather than the number of containers themselves, that was the basis for calculation of the limit.[71] The Court of Appeal agreed only to the extent that parcels loaded in containers would constitute the relevant packages, drawing attention to similar decisions in the USA, Canada, Australia,[72] France, Holland, Italy, and Sweden.[73] However, Phillips LJ[74] went on to say that the basis of limitation under the Hague Rules did not depend upon the agreement of the parties as to what constituted the relevant 'packages' as represented by the

---

[62] *Falconbridge Nickel Mines Ltd v Chimo Shipping Ltd* [1973] 2 Lloyd's Rep 469.

[63] *Chapman Marine Pty Ltd v Wilhelmsen Lines A/S* [1999] FCA 178, where it was suggested that the notion of a 'package' involves wrapping: at [40]–[44]. See too *Orient Overseas Container Line (UK) Ltd v Sea-Land Service Inc (The Sealand Quality)* (2000) 122 F Supp 2d 481 (SDNY).

[64] *The Nea Tyhi* [1982] 1 Lloyd's Rep 606.

[65] *Bekol BV v Terracina Shipping Corp*, unreported, 13 July 1988 (cited in *River Gurara v Nigerian National Shipping Line Ltd* [1998] QB 610, 617).

[66] See para 1.03.

[67] See Stopford (1997), 15.

[68] For comprehensive coverage, see Schoenbaum (2004), §10-34; Craig Still, 'Thinking outside the box — the application of COGSA's $500 per-package limitation to shipping containers' (2001–2002) 24 Houston JIL 81.

[69] For one account of why the USA did not do so, see Allan I Mendelsohn, 'Why the US did not ratify the Visby Amendments' (1992) 23 JMLC 29.

[70] [1998] QB 610 (CA). This was not, however, the first case: see *Bekol BV v Terracina Shipping Corporation* (LEXIS, 13 July 1988), referred to in the instant case.

[71] [1996] 2 Lloyd's Rep 53, 62.

[72] See *PS Chellaram & Co Ltd v China Ocean Shipping Co* [1989] 1 Lloyd's Rep 413 (SC, NSW).

[73] [1998] QB 610 (CA), 618 (Phillips LJ).

[74] Mummery LJ concurred.

description of the cargo on the face of the bill of lading.[75] Rather, this fell to be calculated on the number of packages proved to have been loaded in the containers, not the number of containers.[76] In effect, he expressly declined to treat the Hague Rules as having the same effect as the 1968 Protocol.[77] Finally, it was necessary to interpret a clause of the bill of lading which purported to provide that the container was the package or unit where not packed or filled by the carrier.[78] The Court of Appeal had no hesitation in determining that such a clause was void as contrary to article III, rule 8.

Package: Containers under Visby[79]   During the decade in which the Visby Protocol was   **29.19** under serious consideration, the development of containerization as a serious transportation model was still in its infancy.[80] Nevertheless, those responsible for preparing the Visby Protocol were already keenly aware of the difficulties raised by the issue. It is notable that in the deliberations leading to the enactment of the Visby Protocol the Chairman of a Working Party on the proposed Protocol concluded that 'the best basis of limitation was "package or unit", and that no general definition of these words could cover every possible case'.[81] Nevertheless, in response to the issues thrown up in connection with the similar provisions of the Hague Rules, the following provision was eventually adopted in relation to containers in Article IV, rule 5(c), following work done in a drafting committee under the leadership of Diplock LJ (as he then was):[82]

> Where a container, pallet or similar article of transport is used to consolidate goods, the number of packages or units enumerated in the Bill of Lading as packed in such article of transport shall be deemed the number of packages or units for the purpose of this paragraph as far as these packages or units are concerned. Except as aforesaid such article of transport shall be considered the package or unit.

This provision makes it clear that what is enumerated on the face of the bill of lading is deemed the number of packages or units for the purposes of limitation.[83] One leading Australian authority has suggested that there is no reason to read into the word 'enumeration' any requirement that the enumeration must be contractually agreed to be binding.[84] Thus, an enumeration means the setting out of numbers (in words or numbers) on the face of the bill. Accordingly, if a bill of lading states '1 container, containing 10 packages of goods', there will have been an enumeration of 10 packages. Conversely, if there is no enumeration of the contents of the container, such as '1 container containing machinery', then there is no enumeration and the container is the package. Similarly, an enumeration on the

---

[75] [1998] QB 610 (CA), 624. Following *The Aegis Spirit* [1977] 1 Lloyd's Rep 93 (DC, Seattle), also reported as *Matsushita Electric Corp v SS Aegis Spirit* 414 F Supp 894.

[76] At 627.

[77] cf the dissenting judgment of Hirst LJ on this point: at 627.

[78] Clause 9(B).

[79] See the discussion in Diamond [1978] LMCLQ 226, 242–244.

[80] See Hayuth (1987).

[81] See Berlingieri (1997), 524.

[82] At 561.

[83] See too, for recent authority giving primacy to the face of the bill, *Homburg Houtimport BV v Agrosin Private Ltd (The Starsin)* [2003] UKHL 12; [2004] 1 AC 715; para 12.13.

[84] *El Greco (Australia) Pty Ltd v Mediterranean Shipping Co SA* [2004] FCAFC 202; [2004] 2 Lloyd's Rep 537, 583.

face of the bill of lading showing a number of pieces of cargo that could be packed in a variety of ways and not showing the packages (or units) as packed, will not constitute an enumeration called for by Article IV, rule 5(c).[85]

29.20 'Unit' Both the Hague and the Hague–Visby Rules allow for limitation also by 'units'. There is, however, a considerable lack of clarity as to the meaning of this term[86] and it has been the subject of much debate. The starting point must be the context of the Rules themselves which, as we have seen, refers to 'package or unit'. The appearance of the alternative for 'package' in the Hague Rules was introduced at a rather late stage in the proceedings[87] of the International Law Association's Maritime Law Committee[88] in 1921.[89] This clearly emphasizes a different meaning for 'unit' and is further reinforced by the provision in article III rule 3(b), which refers to 'packages or pieces'.[90] As to the meaning of unit, two possibilities have been presented. The first is that the reference to unit is a reference to 'freight unit', being the unit of measurement applied to calculate the freight. However, this approach has been generally rejected.[91] The second possibility is a reference to the 'shipping unit', being the physical unit which the shipper hands over to the carrier. There has been support for this in a number of cases.[92] Thus, it would seem that a motor vehicle shipped without any form of packaging is a unit,[93] as is an unpacked tractor,[94] a log of wood or a bar of metal,[95] but not bulk cargoes, such as grain or liquids in bulk.[96] One eminent commentator has suggested that 'unit' should be construed as referring to an individual article or piece of goods which is not a package.[97] It may be noted that in the United States, the Carriage of Goods by Sea Act 1936 uses the words 'per customary freight unit',[98] in effect providing a limit for bulk cargoes, but this has also led to difficulties.[99]

29.21 **'Units' and containers: *El Greco*** One of the difficulties with the limitation provisions in general, and the 'container' provision in particular, is the use of the word 'unit'.[100] The difficulty arises because smaller items can be packed into a container. How is 'unit' to

---

[85] At 586.

[86] Notwithstanding the view taken *inter alia* at the CMI's 1963 Stockholm Conference that 'no serious problems have arisen regarding the construction of the words "package or unit". . .': Berlingieri (1997), 516.

[87] On the fourth day of the proceedings.

[88] This Committee was an offshoot of the British Maritime Law Association and, in effect, drafted the Hague Rules. See, eg, Dor (1960), 19.

[89] See the statement by Sir Henry Duke, the Chairman of the Conference: Sturley (1990), vol 1, 322.

[90] See para 26.07.

[91] See *Anticosti Shipping Co v Viateur St-Amand* [1959] 1 Lloyd's Rep 352. It has not been considered as such in England.

[92] See *Studebaker Distributors Ltd v Charlton Steamship Co Ltd* [1938] 1 KB 459.

[93] ibid.

[94] *Falconbridge Nickel Mines Ltd v Chimo Shipping Ltd* [1973] 2 Lloyd's Rep 469.

[95] See Temperley & Vaughan (1932), 81.

[96] Recently affirmed in *El Greco (Australia) Pty Ltd v Mediterranean Shipping Co SA* [2004] FCAFC 202; [2004] 2 Lloyd's Rep 537, 585.

[97] Diamond [1978] LMCLQ 22, 241.

[98] Section 4(5); 46 USCA §1304.

[99] See H Edwin Anderson III and Jason P Waguespack, 'Assessing the Customary Freight Unit: A COGSA Quagmire' (1996–97) USFMLJ 173; Schoenbaum (2004), §10-35.

[100] See, eg, *El Greco (Australia) Pty Ltd v Mediterranean Shipping Co SA* [2004] FCAFC 202; [2004] 2 Lloyd's Rep 537, 585.

be defined in this context? This was one of the issues in the leading case of *El Greco (Australia) Pty Ltd v Mediterranean Shipping Co SA*.[101] Bills of lading in respect of a container of prints and posters for carriage from Australia to Greece via Antwerp provided '1 x 20ft FCL/FCL general purpose container said to contain 200945 pieces posters and prints'[102] and 'shippers load stow and count'. When the goods arrived at their destination they were discovered to have been damaged by sea water and, in due course, one of the issues for resolution by a full bench of the Federal Court of Australia was whether the single posters and prints were the 'units' for the purposes of article IV, rule 5(a) or whether the container was. In the view of Allsop J,[103] for the word unit to be operative in such a context, the enumeration in the bill of lading must manifest how the units are made up for transport and how they are packed into the container. If not, the 'default' rule would apply and the container would rank as the package:

> If it is not clear from the face of the bill what numbers of packages or units are packed as such by some words (perhaps by the natural meaning of the language describing the item) such that one cannot tell how many packages or units were packed as such in the container or other article of transport, there will only be one package or unit — the container or other article of transport. An enumeration on the face of the bill of a number of pieces of cargo that could be packed in a variety of ways and thereby not showing the packages or units as packed — that is, how or in what number they are packed, will not be an enumeration called for by art IV, r 5(c).
>
> If numbers are used, and from the words used in the bill, including the description of the cargo, it is not clear whether the articles or pieces of cargo are packed in the container as such, then there will be one package: the container.[104]

Applying this reasoning to the facts, Allsop J[105] concluded that the container was the package for the purposes of the Rules:

> The statement on the face of the bill was to the effect that according to the shipper there were present in the container over 200,000 pieces of paper or cardboard. The bill did not make clear what number of packages or units as packed there were. The nature of the cargo was such as to be obvious that the bill did not disclose how and in what number such goods had been made up for transport *as packed* in the container. This was only confirmed by the balance of the face of the bill which tended against any conclusion that the items had been packed as packages or units. Accordingly, there was no enumeration in the document for the purposes of art 4, r 5(c) of the Amended Rules.[106]

Although this decision is, it is submitted, the correct one on the particular facts, it remains yet to be seen whether the more general principles developed in the judgment of Allsop J will readily transmit to other similar decisions in the future. It is likely that any future decision will still have to grapple with the meaning of 'unit' in the context of small items or items which are of too low value and not a part of a bulk cargo.

---

[101] [2004] FCAFC 202; [2004] 2 Lloyd's Rep 537. See FMB Reynolds 'The package or unit limitation and the Visby Rules' [2005] LMCLQ 1; S Derrington 'A piece — neither a package nor a unit' (2005) 68 MLR 111.

[102] Additional complicating factors were that the total figure was overstated by about 70,000 and that the posters were in fact made up into 2,000 packages.

[103] Black CJ concurring.

[104] [2004] FCAFC 202; [2004] 2 Lloyd's Rep 537, 586.

[105] Beaumont J dissenting.

[106] At 590–591.

29.22 **Effect of a reservation in the bill of lading**   The next point which has to be dealt with is the effect of a reservation in the bill of lading. As we have previously seen,[107] such a reservation might include the commonly used words 'said to contain' or 'STC'. It is submitted, however, that there is nothing inconsistent with such a statement and the carrier's right to rely on the limitation provisions.

29.23 **Weight limitation**   The Hague–Visby Rules, unlike the Hague Rules, provide for an alternative weight limitation intended to provide for the case of bulk cargoes which could not accurately be described as a 'package' (or a 'unit'). This alternative was arrived at after protracted discussion in the deliberations leading to the Visby Protocol and was suggested by the Norwegian delegation.[108] Thus, article IV, rule 5(a) provides that '. . . or units of account per kilo of gross weight of the goods lost or damaged, whichever is the higher'. The weight limit, as currently reflected, is 2 SDRs per kilogram.[109]

29.24 **The amount recoverable**   Article IV, rule 5(b) of the Rules provides that:

> The total amount recoverable shall be calculated by reference to the value of such goods at the place and time at which the goods are discharged from the ship in accordance with the contract or should have been so discharged.

> The value of the goods shall be fixed according to the commodity exchange price or, if there be no such price, according to the current market price, or, if there be no commodity exchange price or current market price, by reference to the normal value of goods of the same kind and quality.

There has been relatively little authority[110] on the meaning of these words[111] and there exists some uncertainty as to the reasons for inserting the provision. Nevertheless, it may be conjectured that the likely reason was to exclude from limitation any claims for consequential losses.[112]

29.25 **Breaches of the Rules: earlier authorities**   Article IV, rule 5(a) of the Rules provides that the limits of liability prescribed are applicable 'in any event' and section 1(2) of the Carriage of Goods by Sea Act 1971 provides that the Rules 'shall have the force of law'. The generally held view is that, read together, the Rules are applicable irrespective of any fundamental breach of the contract of carriage. *Kenya Railways v Antares Co Ltd (The Antares)*[113] concerned the time limitation provisions of the Rules.[114] Machinery shipped at Antwerp for carriage to Mombasa was subject to the Hague or Hague–Visby Rules. On discharge at Mombasa it was found that part of the machinery had been loaded on deck and was seriously damaged during the course of the voyage. One of the issues on appeal was whether the owners' fundamental breach of contract in stowing the goods on deck precluded them from relying on the time bar contained in article III, rule 6 of the Rules. The Court of

---

[107] See para 6.12.

[108] See Berlingieri (1997), 551.

[109] Under the unamended Hague–Visby Rules the amount was 30 francs per kilo.

[110] See now the judgment of Beaumont J in *El Greco (Australia) Pty Ltd v Mediterranean Shipping Co SA* [2004] FCAFC 202; [2004] 2 Lloyd's Rep 537.

[111] There is no equivalent in the Hague Rules.

[112] The normal rule being that carriers can be liable in respect of losses within their contemplation. See *Hadley v Baxendale* (1854) 9 Ex 341; 156 ER 145.

[113] [1987] 1 Lloyd's Rep 424.

[114] Generally as to the time bar in the Rules, see para 35.04.

Appeal concluded that the time bar was applicable; there was no fundamental breach of contract and the plaintiffs were therefore not entitled to a declaration that the defendants were barred from relying on article III, rule 6.

Breaches: *The Chanda*   More directly in point was *Wibau Maschinenfabric Hartman SA v*   **29.26**
Mackinnon Mackenzie & Co (The Chanda).[115] In this case the sellers of asphalt drying and mixing plant sold f. o. b. to buyers in Saudi Arabia. Part of the equipment was shipped aboard the *Chanda* with some 35 packages out of 51 loaded on deck. The control cabin which contained electronic equipment, thus constituting the cabin 90 per cent of the total value of the equipment, was stowed on the No 1 hatch.[116] During her passage the *Chanda* encountered severe weather and, on arrival, it was found that the control cabin had been so badly damaged, both internally and externally, that the port authorities forbade its discharge. The main issue for Hirst J was whether the unauthorized carriage of the control cabin of the equipment on deck disentitled the defendants from relying on any exceptions or limitations contained in the Hague Rules. He concluded that clauses which were intended to protect the shipowner, provided he honoured his contractual obligation to stow under deck, did not apply if he was in breach of that obligation. The package limitation clause fell also within this category and, accordingly, the package limitation clause 'being repugnant to and inconsistent with the obligation to stow below deck, was inapplicable'.[117] He accepted that if he was wrong, and the question had to be settled by a construction within the four walls of the bill of lading itself, clause 10 of the bill of lading laid down a complete and comprehensive code for transportation on deck.[118]

Breaches: the modern authorities   Tuckey LJ took a different view in *Parsons Corp v CV*   **29.27**
Scheepvaartonderneming Happy Ranger (The Happy Ranger):[119]

> I think the words 'in any event' [in article IV, rule 5(a)] mean what they say. They are unlimited in scope and I can see no reason for giving them anything other than their natural meaning. A limitation of liability is different in character from an exception. The words 'in any event' do not appear in any of the other Art IV exemptions including r 6 and as a matter of construction I do not think they were intended to refer only to those events which give rise to the Art IV exemptions. I do not attach significance to the fact that the only other place where they appear is in Art III where it is accepted that the time bar provisions apply both to Art III, rr 1 and 2 claims.

This case was applied in *Daewoo Heavy Industries Ltd v Klipriver Shipping Ltd (The Kapitan Petko Voivoda)*.[120] The case arose following the partial loss and damage of a consignment of 34 excavators carried from Korea to Turkey. Some 26 excavators were subsequently discharged

---

[115] [1989] 2 Lloyd's Rep 494. See *Nelson Pine Industries Ltd v Seatrans New Zealand Ltd (The Pembroke)* [1995] 2 Lloyd's Rep 290 (NZHC).

[116] This is the hatch nearest the bow of the vessel and hence the most exposed.

[117] [1989] 2 Lloyd's Rep 494, 505.

[118] See Brian Davenport QC, 'Limits on the Hague Rules' (1989) 105 LQR 521.

[119] [2002] EWCA Civ 694; [2002] 2 Lloyd's Rep 357, 364. Reversing the first instance decision: [2001] 2 Lloyd's Rep 530.

[120] [2003] EWCA Civ 451; [2003] 2 Lloyd's Rep 1, overruling *Wibau Maschinenfabric Hartman SA v Mackinnon Mackenzie & Co (The Chanda)* [1989] 2 Lloyd's Rep 494 and declining to follow *Nelson Pine Industries Ltd v Seatrans New Zealand Ltd (The Pembroke)* [1995] 2 Lloyd's Rep 290 (NZHC).

and restowed on deck en route although no notice of the restowage was given to the cargo owners. Subsequently, eight of the excavators were lost overboard in heavy seas and the others suffered minor damage. It was accepted that the loss was caused by 'perils of the sea', pursuant to article IV, rule 2(c) of the Hague Rules, by inadequate lashing, by carriage of the excavators on deck, and by insufficiency of packaging of the excavators which remained on board. At first instance[121] it was held that although there was a breach of contract the carrier was entitled to rely on the limitation provisions of article IV, rule 5 but not on the exemptions of article IV, rule 2 which, properly construed, only applied to carriage under deck. There was no logic or reason for interpreting the words 'in any event' in article IV, rule 5 as meaning anything less than what those words said. On appeal the sole issue was whether the carrier was precluded from relying on the limitation provisions of article IV, rule 5. Following the reasoning of Tuckey LJ in *Parsons Corp v CV Scheepvaartonderneming (The Happy Ranger)*[122] and treating the matter as one of construction, the words 'in any event' meant 'in every case'. Thus, although it was argued that the package limitation clause was repugnant to and inconsistent with the obligation to stow below deck, once one took account of the words 'in any event' there was no such repugnancy. Longmore LJ thought that reasoning derived from the deviation cases was very far from 'being a principle of general acceptation' and no support could be derived from it. Furthermore, he upheld the obiter view of Lloyd LJ in *The Antares*[123] that the unauthorized loading of deck cargo could not be regarded as a special case.[124]

29.28 **Misconduct** The Hague–Visby Rules prescribe certain types of misconduct which will deprive the carrier of the protection of the limitation provisions. article IV, rule 5(e) provides that:

> Neither the carrier nor the ship shall be entitled to the benefit of the limitation of liability provided for in this paragraph if it is proved that the damage resulted from an act or omission of the carrier done with intent to cause damage or recklessly and with knowledge that damage would probably result.

As we shall see, this provision, which 'breaks' limitation, is similar to that in the 1976 Limitation Convention.[125] It may be noted too that similar conduct by a servant or agent of the carrier will deprive him personally of the benefit of the limitation provisions and the other defences provided for in the Rules. Thus article IV bis, rule 4 provides that:

> Nevertheless, a servant or agent of the carrier shall not be entitled to avail himself of the provisions of this article, if it is proved that the damage resulted from an act or omission of the servant or agent done with intent to cause damage or recklessly and with knowledge that damage would probably result.[126]

---

[121] [2002] EWHC 1306 (Comm); [2002] 2 All ER (Comm) 560.

[122] [2002] EWCA Civ 694; [2002] 2 Lloyd's Rep 357.

[123] [1987] 1 Lloyd's Rep 424, 430.

[124] This outcome also reinforces the gap between the US authorities and the UK. In the US it is settled that art IV, r 5 is inapplicable in the case of on-deck carriage. See *St Johns Shipping Corp v SA Companhia Geral Commercial Do Rio De Janeiro* (1923) 263 US 119; *Jones v The Flying Clipper* (1953) 116 F Supp 386.

[125] For discussion, see para 29.52.

[126] ibid.

D. Global Limitation

Two systems   There have historically been two systems of limitation of liability. The earlier **29.29** of the two was based on the principle that the shipowner's liability should be limited to the value of his vessel together with the current freight to be paid on completion of the voyage.[127] An alternative formula,[128] based on the tonnage of the vessel,[129] and in use in the United Kingdom since 1854,[130] has been adopted internationally.

Early British background[131]   The distinctive British history of limitation may be traced to **29.30** 1733 and the outcome in *Boucher v Lawson*[132] where a shipowner was held liable for the loss of a cargo of bullion taken on board in Portugal and subsequently stolen by the master. A number of London shipowners thereupon petitioned Parliament, 'greatly alarmed', and complaining that 'when they became Owners of Ships [they] did not apprehend themselves exposed to such Hazard, or liable as Owners to any greater Loss than that of the ships and Freight'.[133] Unless provision were made for their relief, they argued that trade and navigation would be greatly discouraged, 'since Owners of Ships find themselves, without any Fault on their Part, exposed to ruin, from which their greatest Circumspection cannot secure them, through their Malversation of the Masters, or Mariners, who they are obliged to employ'.[134] This petition was sympathetically received and the Responsibility of Shipowners Act[135] was passed in 1734, limiting a shipowner's liability for loss of cargo by theft by the master or crew to the value of the ship and freight, recognizing that, not to do so, merchants and others would be 'greatly discouraged from adventuring their fortunes, as owners of ships or vessels, which will necessarily tend to the prejudice of the trade and navigation of this Kingdom'.[136]

Further statutory development   That the 1734 Act was extremely limited was under- **29.31** lined by the case of *Sutton v Mitchell*.[137] A ship moored on the Thames was forcibly plundered during the night by a gang of thieves acting on information supplied by one of the seamen aboard the vessel. It was only this latter fact which enabled the shipowner to limit his liability for, had the thieves acted otherwise than in collusion with one of the men aboard the vessel, the owner's liability would have been unlimited. Buller J stated that:

> This Act is as strong as possible, and was meant to protect the owner against all treachery in the master or mariners, as appears from the clause in question as well as the preamble of the Act. It meant to relieve the owners of ships from hardships, and to encourage them; at the

---

[127] ie the system still in use in the USA, known as the 'abandonment' approach. For analysis of American Law, see Gilmore & Black (1975), ch 10; Schoenbaum (2004), ch 11.

[128] The 'price-per-ton' system.

[129] As to tonnage measurement generally, see the International Convention on the Tonnage Measurement of Ships 1969.

[130] In the Merchant Shipping Act 1854, 17 & 18 Vict, c 104.

[131] See Abbott, Part III, ch 5; *Aegean Sea Traders Corporation v Repsol Petroleo SA (The Aegean Sea)* [1998] 2 Lloyd's Rep 39, 44; *CMA CGM SA v Classica Shipping Co Ltd* [2003] EWHC 641 (Comm); [2003] 2 Lloyd's Rep 50, at [14]–[17].

[132] (1734) Cas TH 85; 95 ER 53.

[133] See Michael Thomas, 'British Concepts of Limitation of Liability' (1978–1979) 53 Tulane LR 1205–1206.

[134] ibid.

[135] 7 Geo 2, c 15.

[136] Preamble.

[137] (1785) 1 TR 18; 99 ER 948.

same time saying, that so far as you have trusted the master and mariners yourself, so far you shall be answerable; which is to the value of the ship and freight.[138]

The Responsibility of Shipowners Act 1786[139] was subsequently passed to fill this lacuna. Later statutes extended the benefit of limitation to loss or damage arising from collision,[140] and to cases involving loss of life and personal injury.[141] The Merchant Shipping (Amendment) Act 1862[142] was subsequently passed to settle the question as to ascertainment of the value of the ship and freight.

29.32 **Merchant Shipping Act 1894**[143] This Act although, in general terms, a major consolidating statute,[144] re-enacted the substance of the provisions previously passed as to limitation of liability. The main provision was section 503, but this was subsequently amended on a number of occasions.[145]

29.33 **Merchant Shipping Act 1995** The current law on limitation of liability in the United Kingdom is contained in section 185 of the Act and implements the provisions of the 1976 Limitation Convention.[146]

E. Earlier International Conventions

29.34 **1924 Convention** There have been two Brussels Limitation Conventions, both implemented under the guidance of the Comité Maritime International (CMI). The first of these was the International Convention for the Unification of Certain Rules Relating to the Limitation of the liability of Owners of Sea-going Vessels 1924, agreed to in August of that year and which entered into force on 2 June 1931.[147] The United Kingdom was never a party to this Convention.

29.35 **1957 Convention** The 1957 Brussels International Convention relating to the Limitation of the liability of Owners of Sea-going Ships,[148] which was intended to replace the 1926 Convention, came into force on 31 May 1968. This has been ratified or acceded to by fifty-one

---

[138] At 20; 99 ER 949.

[139] 26 Geo 3, c 86.

[140] Responsibility of Shipowners Act 1813, 53 Geo 3, c 159.

[141] Merchant Shipping Act 1854, 17 & 18 Vict, c 104.

[142] 25 & 26 Vict, c 63.

[143] 57 & 58 Vict, c 60.

[144] Comprehensively analysed in successive editions of Temperley on the Merchant Shipping Acts. See, most recently, Thomas and Steel (1976).

[145] See the Merchant Shipping (Liability of Shipowners) Act 1898, 61 & 62 Vict, c 14; the Merchant Shipping (Liability of Shipowners and Others) Act 1900, 63 & 64 Vict, c 32; the Merchant Shipping Act 1906, 6 Edw 7, c 48; the Merchant Shipping Act 1921, 11 & 12 Geo 5, c 28; the Merchant Shipping (Liability of Shipowners and Others) Act 1958, 6 & 7 Eliz 2, c 62.

[146] See para 29.38.

[147] This Convention was not widely supported, with only 15 ratifications or accessions. It has been pointed out that, despite the fact that there have been two further Conventions, nine of those original 15 states have not denounced the 1924 Convention, even though some of them have also ratified or acceded to the 1957 or the 1976 Convention (or both). As one commentator has stated: 'This, of course, is calculated to cause delicious confusion . . .': Patrick JS Griggs, 'Obstacles to Uniformity of Maritime Law: The Nicholas J Healy Lecture' (2003) 34 JMLC 191, 195.

[148] In force from 31 May 1968 (see <www.comitemaritime.org>).

states, including the United Kingdom,[149] and still applies in a number of important trading countries.[150]

Conduct barring the right to limit   Under the 1957 Limitation Convention[151] limitation **29.36** is not available where 'the occurrence giving rise to the claim resulted from the actual fault or privity of the owner'. Whether the claim is the result of the owner's actual fault or privity is a question of fact and has been the subject of much litigation, much of it relating to the question as to who is 'owner' where the liable party is a company. At common law, companies have a separate personality and must therefore act through human agents. There are particular problems in treating a company as being capable of forming the intention necessary for a particular act and generally in attributing 'fault' to an artificial person which has no mind of its own and so the courts have been prepared to regard the acts and thoughts of certain agents of a company as the acts and thoughts of the company itself.[152] The principal difficulty with this theory is discovering who will be identified with a company. Many of the leading cases on the interpretation of the wording 'actual fault or privity' arose in the context of section 502 of the Merchant Shipping Act 1894, which was to the effect that the owner of a British seagoing ship would not be liable to make good to any extent whatever 'any loss or damage happening without his actual fault or privity' where any goods or merchandise taken in or put on board his ship are lost or damaged by reason of fire on board the ship. In this context, company directors' acts were attributed to the company,[153] as were those of the head of a traffic department of a brewing company.[154] However, in more recent years, a different test has been propounded by the Privy Council, namely one of construction of the relevant statute. As explained by Lord Hoffmann:

> It is a question of construction in each case as to whether the particular rule requires that the knowledge that an act has been done, or the state of mind with which it was done, should be attributed to the company.[155]

F. The International Convention on Limitation of Liability for Maritime Claims 1976 (LLMC)

Introduction   The main feature[156] of the new Convention is that it made available a sig- **29.37** nificantly enhanced fund at what was then perceived to be the maximum insurable level[157]

---

149 Which enacted the Convention in the form of the Merchant Shipping (Liability of Shipowners and Others) Act 1958, 6 & 7 Eliz 2, c 62, later criticized by Lord Denning MR as not being a 'piece of English . . . [but] a collection of word-symbols': *The Putbus* [1969] P 136 (CA), 149.

150 Including, until recently, Singapore (see the (Singapore) Merchant Shipping Act 1995, cap 179, Part VIII).

151 Article 1(1). See too s 503 of the Merchant Shipping Act 1894.

152 Known as the 'identification' theory or 'alter ego' theory. See, eg, *Lennard's Carrying Co Ltd v Asiatic Petroleum Co Ltd* [1915] AC 705, 713–714.

153 *Lennard's Carrying Co Ltd v Asiatic Petroleum Co Ltd* [1915] AC 705; *Grand Champion Tankers Ltd v Norpipe A/S (The Marion)* [1984] AC 563.

154 But not those acts of employees of the company or even of junior management: *Browner International Ltd v Monarch Shipping Co Ltd (The European Enterprise)* [1989] 2 Lloyd's Rep 185 (though this in the context of art IV, r 5 of the Hague–Visby Rules).

155 *Meridian Global Funds v Securities Commission (NZ)* [1995] 2 AC 500 (PC), 511.

156 See Erling Selvig, 'An Introduction to the 1976 Convention' in Gaskell (1986), ch 1.

157 See *CMA CGM SA v Classica Shipping Co Ltd* [2003] EWHC 641 (Comm); [2003] 2 Lloyd's Rep 50, at [25].

and in return for making it more difficult to 'break' the limits.[158] Subsequent events showed that the limitation amounts adopted were unrealistic and, in 1996, a Protocol to the Convention was passed. After a lengthy delay in obtaining the requisite number of ratifications,[159] the Protocol entered into force on 13 May 2004.[160] The Protocol and the Convention are to be read as one instrument[161] and the Protocol will apply to claims 'arising out of occurrences which take place after the entry into force for each State of this Protocol'.[162]

29.38   **Implementation in the UK**   The relevant provisions of the Merchant Shipping Act 1894 were repealed by the Merchant Shipping Act 1979[163] as from 1 December 1986,[164] giving the force of law[165] to the 1976 Convention.[166] Following the consolidation of the Merchant Shipping Act in 1995,[167] the text of the Convention is to be found at Schedule 7.[168] Section 185(1) provides that the Convention is to have the force of law in the United Kingdom, while section 185(2) provides that Part II of Schedule 7 of the Merchant Shipping Act 1995 'shall have effect in connection with the Convention, and subsection (1) above shall have effect subject to the provisions of that Part'.

29.39   **Persons entitled to limit**   Article 1(1) entitles shipowners and salvors to limit their liability under the Convention. The term 'shipowner' is defined by article 1(2) as including 'the owner, charterer,[169] manager or operator of a seagoing vessel'.[170] Article 1(4) extends the protection of the Convention to 'any person for whose act, neglect or default the shipowner is responsible', should such a person be sued directly. Although the shipowner may not be personally liable on a claim, article 1(5) provides that, for limitation purposes, 'the liability of the shipowner shall include liability in an action brought against the vessel herself'. Article 1(6) provides that an insurer of liability for claims subject to limitation (such as a P & I Club) is entitled to the benefits of the Convention to the same extent as the assured himself.

29.40   **Owners**   While this has not been expressly decided under the Convention, it has been held as a matter of English law that the term would include an equitable or registered owner[171] and

---

[158] As to which, see art 4 of the Convention. See para 29.52.

[159] Article 11 (1) of the Protocol provided that it should enter into force 'ninety days following the date on which ten States have expressed their consent to be bound by it'.

[160] Following the accession by Malta. See IMO Press Release, 17/02/04, 'Maritime claims: liability limits increase after Malta signs up to 1996 Protocol'.

[161] See art 9(1) of the Protocol.

[162] See art 9(3) of the Protocol.

[163] c 39. See Steven Hazelwood, 'The United Kingdom and the Limitation Convention' in Gaskell (1986), ch 19.

[164] Merchant Shipping Act 1979 (Commencement No 10) Order 1986, SI 1986/1052.

[165] section 17.

[166] The 1976 Limitation Convention has been ratified by more than 34 states: see <www.imo.org>.

[167] c 21.

[168] This contains the text of the 1976 Convention, but with some omissions as the United Kingdom has not ratified all the provisions. The UK instrument of accession stated that the United Kingdom was 'Reserving the right, in accordance with article 18, paragraph 1, of the Convention, on its own behalf and on behalf of the above mentioned territories, to exclude the application of article 2, paragraph 1(d); and to exclude the application of article 2, paragraph 1(e) with regard to Gibraltar only'.

[169] It is not settled whether a slot charterer would fall within this definition: see *CMA CGM SA v Classica Shipping Co Ltd* [2004] EWCA Civ 114; [2004] 1 Lloyd's Rep 460, at [18] (Longmore LJ).

[170] ie, this includes parent companies: see *The Amoco Cadiz* [1984] 2 Lloyd's Rep 304, 336–337.

[171] See *The Spirit of the Ocean* (1865) Br & L 336; 167 ER 388. Generally as to ownership, see *Ownership and Control of Ships* (Paris, OECD, 2003).

a demise[172] charterer.[173] Although subsequently repealed, the English Merchant Shipping Act 1906[174] expressly provided that the expression 'owner' should be deemed to include any charterer to whom the ship was demised.[175] It has been held that that 'owner or operator of a ship' in article 1(2) of the 1976 Convention should be interpreted to include a demise charterer.[176]

Salvors   One of the most important changes introduced by the 1976 Convention is the   **29.41** inclusion of salvors, a concession made in response to pressure from international salvage interests. Article 1(3) defines 'salvor' as 'any person rendering services in direct connection with salvage operations'. Previously, under the 1957 Convention, salvors could not limit their liability for claims arising from acts or omissions of persons either not on board the tug or not involved in its management. In *Tojo Maru (Owners) v NV Bureau Wijsmuller (The Tojo Maru)*[177] salvors rendered salvage services to a tanker, *The Tojo Maru*, and were successful in salving the tanker as well as most of her cargo of oil. During the course of the salvage operations the salvor's chief diver descended into the water from their tug (he was not a permanent crew member) and, contrary to orders, fired a bolt from a Cox bolt gun through the shell plating of the vessel. The bolt entered a gas-filled cargo tank and caused an explosion resulting in substantial damage to the ship. The House of Lords held that the salvors were not entitled to limit their liability as the negligent act of their diver was not done either in the 'management of' or 'on board' the tug.

Charterers   There has been no reported English decision which has considered the extent   **29.42** of the term 'charterer' for the purposes of article 1(4). While it is unarguable that charterer must certainly mean voyage charterer or time charterer,[178] it has not been expressly considered[179] whether the right to limit would extend to someone who merely had a right to use a specified part of the cargo carrying capacity of a vessel, as under a slot charter where space, usually a fixed number or percentage of container slots on voyages, is chartered.[180] Although historically only the person who had an interest in the whole ship was entitled to limit his liability,[181] it is at least open to doubt whether this is a requirement under the Convention. It is therefore an open question whether a slot charterer would be an 'owner' or 'operator' of a 'seagoing ship' but it is submitted that there is no good reason for concluding that a slot charterer should not be allowed to limit his liability.

---

172   *The Guiseppe di Vittorio* [1998] 1 Lloyds', Rep 136(CA), 156–157 (Evans LJ).
173   See *MSC Mediterranean Shipping Co SA v Delumar BVBA (The MSC Rosa M)* [2000] 2 Lloyd's Rep 399, 401 (David Steel J); *Sir John Jackson Ltd v Owners of the Steamship Blanche (The Hopper No 66)* [1908] AC 127, 130 (Lord Loreburn LC).
174   6 Edw 7, c 48.
175   See s 71.
176   See *MSC Mediterranean Shipping Co SA v Delumar BVBA (The MSC Rosa M)* [2000] 2 Lloyd's Rep 399, 401 (David Steel J).
177   [1972] AC 242.
178   An attempt under the New Zealand legislation (The Maritime Transport Act 1994, s 85), to read down 'owner' as excluding time charterers and sub-time charterers, was refused by the New Zealand High Court: see *The Tasman Pioneer* [2003] 2 Lloyd's Rep 713, 718 (Williams J).
179   Longmore LJ declined to be drawn on this is in *CMA CGM SA v Classica Shipping Co Ltd* [2004] EWCA Civ 114; [2004] 1 Lloyd's Rep 460, at [18].
180   See (in the context of the 1952 Arrest Convention) *The Tychy* [1999] 2 Lloyd's Rep 11 (CA), 21 (Clarke LJ).
181   See the Responsibility of Shipowners Act 1734, 7 Geo 2, c 15.

29.43 **Claims between owners and charterers**   Until *Aegean Sea Traders Corporation v Repsol Petroleo SA (The Aegean Sea)*[182] there was no reported case[183] which had considered whether a charterer might be able to limit his liability under the 1976 Convention, following a claim which had already been settled by the ship's owners and which they sought to recoup from the charterers. The charterers claim to limitation was rejected by Thomas J who confirmed that the benefit of limitation available to the charterer was the same as that available to the shipowner but that this did not entitle the charterers to limit their liability for claims such as those brought against them by the owners.[184] The matter was revisited by Steel J and the Court of Appeal in *CMA CGM SA v Classica Shipping Co Ltd* which arose pursuant to a charterparty on the NYPE form and was brought to the fore in a claim by owners against charterers in respect of their exposure to cargo claims and general average following an explosion and fire on board the *CMA Djakarta*. At first instance, Steel J followed the view of Thomas J in the earlier case and concluded that the term 'shipowner' could only include those who, if they had no beneficial or possessory interest in the vessel, were nevertheless in a real sense directly concerned in the operation of the vessel and had incurred liability as such.[185] In an important ruling, the Court of Appeal has held that the word 'charterer' in article 1 has to be given its ordinary meaning and not the restrictive meaning previously suggested by Steel J and Thomas J.[186]

29.44 **Claims: loss of life, personal injury, or loss or damage to property**   It is not enough to establish that a particular claimant falls within the scope of the Convention. The claimant has to establish that his claim is one which falls within article 2 of the Convention, subject to the exclusions in article 3.[187] Article 2(1)(a) provides that claims for loss of life[188] or personal injury or loss of or damage to property (including damage to harbour walls, basins, and waterways, and aids to navigation) are subject to limitation. Such claims, which extend also to consequential loss, must occur on board[189] or 'in direct connection'[190] with the operation of the ship[191]

---

182 [1998] 2 Lloyd's Rep 39. This case arose out of the disastrous founding on the Torres de Hercules Rocks at La Coruña of the oil tanker, *Aegean Sea*. See, for proceedings involving the IOPC Fund, *IOPC Annual Report 2003* (London, IOPC, 2003) 48. More generally, see Gaskell, 'Pollution, Limitation and Carriage in *The Aegean Sea*' in Rose (2000), ch 5.

183 It should be noted, in passing, that the case also considered several other important issues, including the question of whether a port was safe (see para 20.21), and whether there was any entitlement to an indemnity (see para 32.86).

184 [1998] 2 Lloyd's Rep 39, 49–50.

185 [2003] EWHC 641 (Comm); [2003] 2 Lloyd's Rep 50, at [31].

186 [2004] EWCA Civ 114; [2004] 1 Lloyd's Rep 460, at [18]; [20].

187 See para 29.48.

188 A widely reported example of limitation in respect of loss of life occurred following a disastrous collision between the *Bowbelle* and the *Marchioness* on the river Thames: see *The Bowbelle* [1990] 1 Lloyd's Rep 532. An inquiry carried out by the Marine Accident Investigation Branch (MAIB) of the Department for Transport (see <www.dft.gov.uk>) established that the immediate cause of the casualty was a failure of lookout in each vessel.

189 This does not include loss of or damage to the ship itself: see *Aegean Sea Traders Corporation v Repsol Petroleo SA (The Aegean Sea)* [1998] 2 Lloyd's Rep 39; *CMA CGM SA v Classica Shipping Co Ltd* [2004] EWCA Civ 114; [2004] 1 Lloyd's Rep 460, at [22] (Longmore LJ).

190 Said to cater for cases of collision with another ship: *CMA* ibid, at [23].

191 Not available in *CMA* op cit where containers loaded by the charterers, containing bleaching powder, exploded. It was held that art 2(1)(a) did not extend the right to limit to a claim for damage to the vessel by reference to the tonnage of which limitation was to be calculated: at [26].

or with salvage operations.[192] Claims for bunkers would fall within the provision,[193] as would pollution claims,[194] but not loss of freight,[195] amounts for salvage remuneration,[196] general average claims,[197] or those arising under a knock-for-knock agreement, such as under the BIMCO Towhire agreement.[198]

Other claims   The other claims covered by article 2 include: those resulting from delay in   **29.45** the carriage of cargo or passengers by sea;[199] those in respect of other loss resulting from the infringement of rights other than contractual rights;[200] those in respect of the raising, removal, or destruction of wreck;[201] those in respect of the removal, destruction, or the rendering harmless of the cargo of the ship;[202] and third party claims in respect of measures taken to minimize the loss caused by the defendant.[203] Claims under the last head would include those for salvage award which the owners of the cargo aboard a ship were obliged to pay and which they now sought to recover from the shipowner.[204]

Claims: not limited to damages or contract   Under the 1957 Convention regime, it was   **29.46** mandatory for all claims to sound in damages.[205] Under the 1976 Convention, however, limitation will apply to all such claims whatever the basis of liability may be, and even if brought by way of recourse or for indemnity under a contract or otherwise.[206] Thus, limitation would be available under the 1976 Convention whether sounding in debt or damages and whether the cause of action is tortious or contractual.

Cargo claims   In cases where there is loss of or damage to cargo being carried on the ship,   **29.47** the shipowner will be entitled to limit his liability to cargo owners under article IV, rule 5 of the Hague–Visby Rules.[207] He would also be entitled to limit his liability for cargo damage under article 2(1)(a) of the 1976 Convention, even if he is also entitled to some protection

---

[192] An argument in *Bouygues Offshore SA v Caspian Shipping Co* [1998] 2 Lloyd's Rep 461 (CA), that the claims must be in respect of loss of life or personal injury or loss of or damage to property and the claims must be in direct connection with the operation of the ship, was expressly rejected by Sir John Knox (following the court below [1997] 2 Lloyd's Rep 507): at 473–474.
[193] *Aegean Sea Traders Corporation v Repsol Petroleo SA (The Aegean Sea)* [1998] 2 Lloyd's Rep 39, 51. See too *Caspian Basin Specialised Emergency Salvage Administration v Bouygues Offshore SA* [1997] 2 Lloyd's Rep 507, 522.
[194] ibid.
[195] ibid. It was held that such claims would also not fall with art 2(1)(c).
[196] *CMA CGM SA v Classica Shipping Co Ltd* [2004] EWCA Civ 114; [2004] 1 Lloyd's Rep 460, at [29] (Longmore LJ).
[197] At [30].
[198] See *Smit International (Deutschland) GmbH v Josef Mobius Baugesellschaft GmbH & Co* [2001] 2 All ER (Comm) 265; [2001] CLC 1545.
[199] Article 2(1)(b).
[200] Article 2(1)(c).
[201] Article 2(1)(d). This would include claims for pollution caused by cargo or by bunkers: see *Aegean Sea Traders Corporation v Repsol Petroleo SA (The Aegean Sea)* [1998] 2 Lloyd's Rep 39.
[202] Article 2(1)(e). This would include claims for pollution caused by cargo or by bunkers: see *Aegean Sea Traders Corporation v Repsol Petroleo SA (The Aegean Sea)* [1998] 2 Lloyd's Rep 39.
[203] Article 2(1)(f).
[204] See *The Breydon Merchant* [1992] 1 Lloyd's Rep 373.
[205] See art 1. In *The Stonedale No 1* [1956] AC 1 it was held that an owner could not limit his liability for wreck removal expenses payable under statute since such expenses were in the nature of a debt rather than damages.
[206] See art 2(2).
[207] As to which, see para 29.17.

under the Hague–Visby Rules. In practice, however, the shipowner will rely on the Hague–Visby limits per package or kilogram if the total of the separate limits for the cargo lost or damaged is less than the global limit under the 1976 Convention, but will rely on the 1976 Convention if the total of the separate Hague–Visby limits per package or kilogram is higher.

29.48 **Claims excluded** Certain types of claim are expressly excluded from the ambit of the 1976 Convention. These include claims for salvage, including, if applicable, any claim for special compensation under article 14 of the Salvage Convention 1989 or contribution in general average;[208] claims for oil pollution damage under the International Convention on Civil Liability for Oil Pollution Damage;[209] claims subject to any international convention or national legislation governing nuclear damage;[210] claims against the shipowner of a nuclear ship for nuclear damage;[211] and claims for loss of life, personal injury or property damage caused by crew members whose contracts of service are governed by UK law.[212]

29.49 **Salvage and general average** Article 3(a), as amended, provides that claims for salvage including, if applicable, any claim for special compensation under article 14 of the Salvage Convention 1989[213] or contribution in general average are excluded. This exclusion of salvage claims relates solely to claims by a salvor against the owner of the salved property and does not extend to claims between other parties relating to salvage payments, which are subject to limitation. In *The Breydon Merchant* Sheen J explained that:

> There are good reasons why limitation of liability should not apply to claims for salvage … First, any limitation upon the amount of the salvage reward would discourage salvors. It is public policy to encourage mariners to go to the assistance of persons and property in peril at sea. Secondly, it would be anomalous if shipowners could limit their liability for salvage, whereas cargo-owners are not afforded that privilege. Such reasons do not have any relevance when considering the question: upon whom does the burden ultimately fall?[214]

Prior to the amendment by the Protocol, it was clear that a shipowner could not limit his liability for claims under article 13 of the Salvage Convention 1989. What was not clear was whether article 14 claims were similarly restricted. Schedule 7 of the Merchant Shipping Act 1995 originally contained at paragraph 4(1) of Part II the following provision:

> The claims excluded from the Convention by paragraph (a) of article 3 include claims under article 14 of the International Convention on Salvage, 1989 as set out in Part I of Schedule 11 and corresponding claims under a contract.[215]

---

208 Article 3(a), as amended by art 2 of the 1996 Protocol.

209 Article 3(b). The reference in the 1976 Convention is to the CLC 1969 'or of any amendment or Protocol thereto which is in force'.

210 Article 3(c).

211 Article 3(d).

212 Article 3(e). See now as to this *Todd v Adams and Chope (T/A Trelawney Fishing Co) (The Maragetha Maria)* [2002] 2 Lloyd's Rep 293 (CA).

213 As to art 14, see *Semco Salvage & Marine Pte Ltd v Lancer Navigation Co Ltd (The Nagasaki Spirit)* [1997] AC 455. See Stephen Girvin, 'Special Compensation under the Salvage Convention 1989: A fair rate?' [1997] LMCLQ 321.

214 [1992] 1 Lloyd's Rep 373, 375. See too *Aegean Sea Traders Corporation v Repsol Petroleo SA (The Aegean Sea)* [1998] 2 Lloyd's Rep 39, 55 (Thomas J).

215 Inserted by the Merchant Shipping (Salvage and Pollution) Act 1994, c 28.

This provision is no longer in the Act and has, instead, been replaced by one which excludes claims for damage within the International Convention[216] on Liability and Compensation for Damage in Connection with the Carriage of Hazardous and Noxious Substances by Sea 1996.[217] For those states which do not ratify the Protocol or which have not made express provision for the exclusion of article 14 claims, it is to be doubted whether such claims would be excluded because such claims are not, strictly speaking, 'salvage', though they derive from the Salvage Convention 1989.[218]

Oil pollution claims   Article 3(b) provides that claims for oil pollution damage within   **29.50** the meaning of the International Convention on Civil Liability for Oil Pollution Damage dated 29 November 1969 (CLC) or of any amendment or Protocol thereto which is in force are excluded. This provision was included because of the necessity of avoiding any overlap with the CLC limitation provisions[219] which are much greater than the limits of the 1976 Protocol. Also explicitly excluded are the Protocols to the CLC, including the 1992 Protocol. A further issue for consideration is whether article 3(b) has a wider effect than under the CLC, given that it excludes claims 'within the meaning of' the CLC. On one view, this would appear to exclude not only liabilities incurred under the CLC, but all claims for oil pollution damage within the CLC, even if liability arises for it outside the CLC regime and outside its limitation provisions. Given that only the owner of a ship can incur liability under the CLC, the effect of a wider reading of the 1976 Convention is that neither the CLC nor the 1976 Convention provides any right of limitation in such circumstances. However, in *Aegean Sea Traders Corporation v Repsol Petroleo SA (The Aegean Sea)*, Thomas J took the view that

> what is excluded by art 3(b) is only a claim against the person seeking the right to limit that is actually made under the CLC. The words of art 3(b) have, in my view, to be read in that way, for otherwise a party other than the shipowner would face unlimited liability for pollution claims. That can never have been intended . . . . The language in art 3(b) 'claims for oil pollution damage within the meaning of the [CLC]' should be read as claims within 'the meaning of' in the sense of claims that can 'be brought under'.[220]

This issue been dealt with in the UK in paragraph 4(2) of Part II of Schedule 7 to the Merchant Shipping Act 1995 which provides that:

> The claims excluded from the Convention by paragraph (b) of Article 3 are claims in respect of any liability incurred under section 153 of this Act.

Another interesting variation is the case of claims for pollution by bunkers from vessels other than tankers. Article 1 of the CLC makes it clear that pollution damage applies only

---

[216] Known as the HNS Convention. This Convention is still not in force; see, however, the website of the IMO Correspondence Group on Implementation: <http://folk.uio.no/erikro/WWW/HNS/hns.html#impl>. Generally, see Rosalie Balkin, 'The Hazardous and Noxious Substances Convention: Travail or Travaux — The Making of an International Convention' (1999) 20 AYIL 1; Gavin Little, 'The Hazardous and Noxious Substances Convention: a new horizon in the regulation of marine pollution' [1998] LMCLQ 554.

[217] Inserted as Sch 5A of the Merchant Shipping Act 1995, by the Merchant Shipping and Maritime Security Act 1997, c 28, Sch 3.

[218] It is arguable that such claims would fall under art 2(1)(d) and/or (e) of the 1976 Convention.

[219] See art V of the CLC 1992 (and the CLC 1969).

[220] [1998] 2 Lloyd's Rep 39, 54.

to a 'ship' within the meaning of the CLC — ie a tanker. Accordingly, a dry cargo ship would not be a 'ship' for the purposes of the CLC and bunker oil pollution is not 'oil pollution damage' for the purpose of the CLC. Liability for such damage would therefore not be excluded by article 3(b) of the 1976 Convention. However, it would then be necessary for the defendant under the 1976 Convention to prove that his claim falls under article 2 of that Convention. This has specifically been assisted in the UK by section 168 of the Merchant Shipping Act 1995, the effect of which is that bunker spill liabilities are deemed to be liability for property damage for the purposes of article 2(1)(a) of the 1976 Convention.[221]

29.51   **Crew members**   Article 3(e) provides that the Convention does not apply to claims by servants of the shipowner or salvor whose duties are connected with the ship or salvage operations, including claims of their heirs, dependants or other persons entitled to make such claims, if under the law governing the contract of service between the shipowner and salvor and such servants the shipowner or salvor is not entitled to limit his liability in respect of such claims, or if he is by such law only permitted to limit his liability to an amount greater than that provided for in article 6. In essence this subsection provides that the limits set out in the Convention shall not be available in respect of claims arising under certain contracts of service where the law governing the particular contract of service imposes a higher financial limit than those which are set out in the Convention or provides that there shall be no right to limit.

29.52   **Conduct barring the right to limit**   It is possible for a claimant to break the limits set by the 1976 Convention. Article 4 provides, however, that in order to do so the claimant must prove that the loss or damage resulted from a personal act or omission of the party liable, 'committed with the intent to cause such loss or recklessly and with knowledge that such loss would probably result'. As will be evident from this standard, the higher limits prescribed under the Convention are balanced by a test which makes the likelihood of breaking the limits extremely difficult.[222] Not only must the loss result from a personal act or omission of the party liable, but it must be established that the party liable either intended such loss or was reckless as to the consequences of his act or omission in the sense that he realized that such a loss would probably result.[223] Knowledge means actual, not constructive knowledge[224] and merely 'turning a blind eye' would not constitute actual knowledge.[225]

29.53   *The MSC Rosa M*   *MSC Mediterranean Shipping Co SA v Delumar BVBA (The MSC Rosa M)*,[226] was a limitation action which arose out of an incident that occurred when the *MSC Rosa M*, a container ship under demise charter to MSC, nearly capsized. The crew abandoned the ship and the vessel was subsequently taken in tow, beached, and salved under an

---

221 This is done by way of cross-referral to s 154.

222 See, for example, *MSC Mediterranean Shipping Co SA v Delumar BVBA (The MSC Rosa M)* [2000] 2 Lloyd's Rep 399, 401 (David Steel J).

223 See, for a case involving art 25 of the Warsaw Convention (which uses the same words as art 4), *Goldman v Thai Airways International Ltd* [1983] 1 WLR 1186 (CA). See too Neil R McGilchrist, 'Art 25: an English approach to recklessness' [1983] LMCLQ 488.

224 At 1194 (Eveleigh LJ); *MSC Mediterranean Shipping Co SA v Delumar BVBA (The MSC Rosa M)* [2000] 2 Lloyd's Rep 399.

225 *MSC Mediterranean Shipping Co SA v Delumar BVBA (The MSC Rosa M)* [2000] 2 Lloyd's Rep 399, at [15] (David Steel J).

226 ibid.

LOF salvage agreement. Steel J, while noting that the shipowners (ie the demise charterers) had established that their claim fell within article 2 of the Convention,[227] next had to consider whether the defendants had established a defence under article 4. Steel J noted that, to do so, they must plead and prove on the facts that (i) the capsize was caused by the personal act or omission of the demise charterers; (ii) the personal acts or omissions were committed recklessly; and (iii) at the time of those acts or omissions, that the alter ego of the demise charterers actually knew that a capsize would probably result.[228] On the facts, he concluded that the defendants' case reflected an unsuccessful attempt to disguise a plea of actual fault or privity for the purposes of the 1957 Limitation Convention as a plea of reckless conduct, with knowledge of the probable consequences, in the context of the 1976 Convention and struck out the defence.[229]

The limits of liability   At the time of the making of the 1976 Convention, one of the   **29.54**
main features was a substantial increase in the liability limits, especially for small ships, based on gross tonnage.[230] With the passage of time, however, those limits did not prove to have kept pace with developments in the market place and hence the need for a Protocol amending the limits. The limitation unit of account is the Special Drawing Right (SDR) of the International Monetary Fund (IMF),[231] derived from the currencies of members having the largest exports of goods and services[232] and the basis of many modern international maritime conventions.[233] For those countries which do not ratify to the Protocol, the general limits are set out in article 6.[234] There are separate and distinct limits for claims arising from loss of life and personal injury (article 6(1)(a)), as opposed to claims which result from cargo damage or other losses (article 6(1)(b)). The limits under article 6(1)(a) are 333,333 SDRs for a ship with a tonnage not exceeding 500 tons. For ships in excess of 500 tons, the following additional amounts must be added: (i) for each ton from 501 to 3,000 tons, 500 SDRs; (ii) for each ton from 3,001 to 30,000 tons, 333 SDRs; (iii) for each ton from 30,001 to 70,000 tons, 250 SDRs; and (iv) for each ton in excess of 70,000 tons, 167 SDRs. The limits under article 6(1)(b) are 167,000 SDRs for ships with a tonnage not exceeding 500 tons. Again, for ships in excess of 500 tons, the following amounts must be added: (i) for each ton from 501 to 30,000 tons, 167 SDRs; (ii) for each ton from 30,001 to 70,000 tons, 125 SDRs; and (iii) for each ton in excess of 70,000 tons, 83 SDRs. Where an event gives rise to both death and/or personal injury claims and property claims and the fund calculated under article 6(1)(a) is not sufficient to satisfy such claims in full, then the fund calculated under article 6(1)(b) is available to meet the unsatisfied balance of the loss of life/personal injury claims.[235] Putting this another way, once the fund for personal injury

---

[227] ibid.
[228] [2000] 2 Lloyd's Rep 399, 403.
[229] At 405. See too *The Tasman Pioneer* [2003] 2 Lloyd's Rep 713.
[230] Calculated in accordance with the measurement rules contained in Annex I of the International Convention on Tonnage Measurement of Ships 1969: art 6(5). This Convention came into force in 1982, for ships built after 17 July 1982, and for 'all existing ships' as of 18 July 1994.
[231] Article 8. See <www.imf.org>.
[232] The euro, pound sterling, Japanese yen, and US dollar.
[233] See the 1979 SDR Protocol to the Hague–Visby Rules, the Hamburg Rules, etc.
[234] The limits for passenger claims, which fall outside the scope of this chapter, are set out in art 7.
[235] Article 6(2).

claims is exhausted, outstanding personal injury claims rank *pari passu*[236] with claims for property damage or other losses. One final point to notice about the limits is that, for a salvor not operating from any ship, or for any salvor operating solely on the ship to, or in respect of, which he is rendering salvage services, the limits are to be calculated according to a tonnage of 1,500 tons.

29.55 **Limitation without constitution of a limitation fund** Article 10(1) of the Convention provides that, in order to invoke limitation of liability, it is not necessary to constitute a limitation fund, unless this is required by national law. It is not necessary to do so under English law and this is because article 10(3) provides that any questions of procedure may be decided in accordance with the national law of the state party in which the action is brought. There are clear financial advantages, however, in constituting a fund because of the fact that the limitation amounts are linked to the value of the SDR which, being based on a basket of currencies, fluctuates in value. The Convention provides that the applicable value of the SDR is that prevailing at the date that the fund is actually constituted.[237]

29.56 **Constitution of the fund** Article 11(1) of the Convention provides that a person liable may constitute a fund with the court or other competent authority in any state party in which legal proceedings[238] are instituted. The fund may either consist of a deposit of the sum, or by producing a guarantee, subject to the legislation of the state party where the fund is constituted.[239] Once constituted, this fund is only available for the payment of claims in respect of which limitation can be invoked. In England the mechanics of constituting the fund are regulated by the Civil Procedure Rules (CPR).[240]

29.57 **Distribution of the fund** Article 12(1) provides that the limitation fund will be distributed among the claimants in proportion to their established claims against the fund. Article 12(2) then goes on to provide that if, before the fund is distributed, the person liable or his insurer has settled any claim against the fund, such a person will, up to the amount he has paid, acquire by subrogation the rights which the person so compensated would have enjoyed under the Convention. Article 12(4) provides, finally, that an appropriate portion of a fund can be set aside for use at a future time to cope with claims for which the person liable (or his insurer) knows he will have a liability but which have not yet been presented or proved against him.

29.58 **Bars to other actions** Article 13(1) of the Convention provides that, if a fund has been constituted, no other assets of a person liable are to be further exposed to legal action. In other words, any claimant's rights may only be exercised against the constituted fund. Thus, in *The Bowbelle*,[241] the owners had constituted a limitation fund under article 11 but various claimants against those owners sought security for their claims by arresting surrogate

---

[236] ie equally; proportionately.
[237] Article 8(1).
[238] This is not limited to court proceedings and can include proceedings by way of arbitration: see *ICL Shipping Ltd v Chin Tai Steel Enterprise Co Ltd (The ICL Vikraman)* [2003] EWHC 2320 (Comm); [2004] 1 Lloyd's Rep 21.
[239] Article 11(2).
[240] See, in particular, CPR part 61.11(18).
[241] [1990] 1 Lloyd's Rep 532.

(or 'sister') ships,[242] notwithstanding article 13. Her owners accordingly filed a praecipe against arrest with the Admiralty Registrar, requesting that a caveat against the arrest of fourteen named ships be entered into the caveat book, but this was refused by the Registrar. In allowing the appeal and permitting an entry to be made in the caveat book, Sheen J concluded that Art 13 'was drafted with the intention of . . . ensuring that shipowners would only be compelled to provide one limitation fund, in respect of any one incident giving rise to claims'.[243] Article 13(2) then provides that, once a limitation fund has been constituted, any ship or other property belonging to a person on behalf of whom the fund has been constituted, which has been arrested or attached, may be released. However, under article 13(3) both these provisions only apply if the claimant can bring a claim against the limitation fund before the court administering that fund and the fund is actually available and freely transferable in respect of that claim. This provision was in issue in *Bouygues Offshore SA v Caspian Shipping Co*.[244] Although counsel sought to argue that the court had no jurisdiction to grant a limitation decree before liability was established by admission or finding, the court disagreed.[245]

Governing law   Article 14 of the Convention provides that the rules relating to the constitution and distribution of the limitation fund and all rules of procedure are to be governed by the law of the state party in which the fund is constituted. In the case of the United Kingdom, this is dealt with in the Civil Procedure Rules (CPR).[246]   **29.59**

G. The 1996 Protocol to the Convention

Introduction   The 1996 Protocol[247] was drafted during the course of the deliberations in London between 15 April and 3 May 1996 which led to the drafting of the Hazardous and Noxious Substances (HNS) Convention. During the debate on the HNS Convention there was considerable discussion on the minimum tonnage which would apply in calculating the limitation fund of an HNS-carrying vessel and it was agreed that the minimum tonnage should be 2,000 gross tons.   **29.60**

Entry into force   Article 11(1) to the 1996 Protocol provided that it would enter into force 90 days following the date on which 10 states have agreed to be bound by it. Although it was anticipated that there would be enough support for the increased limits of liability to see the Protocol being in force within a period of five years, this was not, in fact, the case and the Protocol only came into force on 13 May 2004.   **29.61**

Implementation: the UK   In a move signifying early acceptance of the Protocol, section 15 of the Merchant Shipping Maritime and Security Act 1997[248] made changes to the   **29.62**

---

[242] As to which, see para 35.47.
[243] [1990] 1 Lloyd's Rep 532, 535–536.
[244] [1998] 2 Lloyd's Rep 461 (CA).
[245] At 473 (Sir John Knox), upholding the judgment of Rix J: [1997] 2 Lloyd's Rep 507.
[246] CPR Part 61.11 and its associated Practice Direction.
[247] See Patrick Griggs, 'LLMC Protocol 1996: Limits of Liability' [1996] IJOSL 322; Nicholas Gaskell, 'New limits for passengers and others in the United Kingdom' [1998] LMCLQ 312; B Soyer, '1996 Protocol to the 1976 Limitation Convention: A More Satisfactory Global Limitation Regime for the New Millennium' [2000] JBL 153.
[248] c 28.

Merchant Shipping Act 1995, such that modifications to the relevant provisions of that Act could be made following the coming into force of the Protocol. Statutory instruments in 1998[249] and 2004[250] made the relevant changes.

29.63 **The limits of liability** The minimum tonnage figure identified for the HNS Convention has been carried over into the 1996 Protocol. As was the case also under the parent Convention, the Protocol has produced a dramatic increase in the limits for small vessels in an attempt to restore the purchasing power of the amounts fixed in 1976. The limits under article 3(1)(a)[251] are 2 million SDRs for a ship with a tonnage not exceeding 2,000 tons. For ships in excess of 2,000 tons, the following additional amounts must be added: (i) for each ton from 2,001 to 30,000 tons, 800 SDRs; (ii) for each ton from 30,001 to 70,000 tons, 600 SDRs; and (iii) for each ton in excess of 70,000 tons, 400 SDRs. The limits under article 3(1)(b)[252] are 1 million SDRs for ships with a tonnage not exceeding 2,000 tons. Again, for ships in excess of 2,000 tons, the following amounts must be added: (i) for each ton from 2,001 to 30,000 tons, 400 SDRs; (ii) for each ton from 30,001 to 70,000 tons, 300 SDRs; and (iii) for each ton in excess of 70,000 tons, 200 SDRs.

29.64 **Other changes** Apart from the increases in limits, the 1996 Protocol makes various other substantive changes to the 1976 Convention. As already noted, art 2 of the Protocol amends article 3(a) of the 1976 Convention so as to exclude from the right of limitation any claim for special compensation under article 14 of the Salvage Convention.[253] A further feature of the Protocol is article 8 which introduces a revised system for the amendment of the limitation amounts. This so-called 'quick amendment' procedure has been introduced in order that it will be possible in future to amend limitation figures more quickly in line with inflation.

H. Conflicts between Jurisdictions

29.65 **The clash of conventions** In limitation cases, difficulties can often arise because a substantial number of countries continue to apply the 1957 Convention rather than the 1976 Convention. Since the coming into force of the 1996 Protocol this will be magnified because a number of countries will not ratify the Protocol. The temptation for shipowners will be to 'forum shop', so as to bring limitation proceedings in countries where the most favourable Convention is in force.[254] The potential for forum shopping may be further exacerbated because countries also ratify new conventions without denouncing older ones. As an illustration,[255] Poland appears to have ratified and implemented all three of the international

---

[249] Merchant Shipping (Convention on Limitation of Liability for Maritime Claims) (Amendment) Order 1998, SI 1998/1258.

[250] Merchant Shipping (Convention on Limitation of Liability for Maritime Claims) (Amendment) Order 2004, SI 2004/1273.

[251] ie for claims arising from loss of life and personal injury.

[252] ie those claims resulting from cargo damage or other losses.

[253] See para 29.49.

[254] And likewise for the claimant who has suffered the loss.

[255] See Patrick JS Griggs, 'Obstacles to Uniformity of Maritime Law: The Nicholas J Healy Lecture' (2003) 34 JMLC 191, 195; 207.

conventions, but not to have denounced the 1924 and 1957 ones. Thus, were there a collision between a Polish ship and a Turkish ship[256] and the limitation proceedings come before a Polish court, that court would be obliged to permit the Turkish ship to apply the 1924 Convention. This is because the Vienna Convention of Treaties provides that states must apply the 'treaty to which both States are parties'. [257]

The advantageous forum As there is some mileage in selecting a forum where the right to **29.66** limit is most advantageous, each side is as likely to want to challenge the other as to jurisdiction by applying for a stay (or dismissal) of jurisdiction. The English courts were initially sympathetic to arguments in favour of English jurisdiction. In *Caltex Singapore Ptd Ltd v BP Shipping Ltd* [258] the court had to decide whether Singapore or England was the appropriate forum and whether the action before the English Admiralty Court should be stayed. In respect of limitation in Singapore, Clarke J concluded that the ends of justice would best be served if the claimants were permitted to proceed in England:

> It is true that many countries have not ratified the 1976 Convention. It is however the policy of IMO that they should. It has been recognised by countries which have 43 per cent of the world's tonnage. It is desirable that as many countries as possible should apply the same standards, partly because that is desirable in itself and partly because it avoids problems such as have arisen in this case. It seems to me to be proper to regard the 1976 Convention as representing a widely accepted development from the regime which existed under the 1957 Convention.[259]

1976 forum not determinative The earlier English view was expressly disapproved of by **29.67** the Court of Appeal in *The Herceg Novi and Ming Galaxy*.[260] That case arose following a collision between the *Herceg Novi* and *Ming Galaxy* within the traffic separation scheme in the straits of Singapore. The *Herceg Novi* sank as a result of the collision and the owners of each vessel now criticized the navigation of the other. The limit of liability of *Ming Galaxy* was about US$5,800,000 in England, but only US$2,900,000 in Singapore. In granting an unconditional stay of the English proceedings,[261] the Court of Appeal applied the principle set out by Lord Goff in the landmark House of Lords decision, *The Spiliada*,[262] to the effect that the court's duty was to consider where a case might be tried 'suitably for the interests of all the parties and for the ends of justice' and that the existence in a particular forum of a legitimate personal juridical advantage for one party should not deter the court from granting a stay if it was satisfied that substantial justice would be done in an alternative, more appropriate forum. The Court of Appeal held that it was appropriate to grant a stay for three reasons: (i) the 1976 Convention had not received universal acceptance but has merely been adopted by some states; (ii) the IMO which has commended the 1976 Convention to the international maritime community is not a legislature and the adoption

---

[256] Turkey is a signatory to the 1924 Convention.

[257] 1969: see art 30(4)(b).

[258] [1996] 1 Lloyd's Rep 286.

[259] At 298–299. See too *The Vishva Abha* [1990] 2 Lloyd's Rep 312.

[260] [1998] 2 Lloyd's Rep 454 (CA).

[261] But cf *The Kapitan Shvetsov* [1998] 1 Lloyd's Rep 199 where the Hong Kong Court of Appeal refused to stay the proceedings on the grounds that the jurisdiction of the court had been properly invoked.

[262] *Spiliada Maritime Corp v Cansulex Ltd* [1987] AC 460.

of its views should not be used to deprive sovereign states of their rights to operate a different regime; (iii) it would be wrong to say that substantive justice was not available in Singapore.[263]

29.68 **Substantive or procedural right** The question may well arise as to whether a right to limit liability on the part of the shipowner is a substantive or a procedural right. This issue was addressed by Clarke J in *Caltex Singapore Ptd Ltd v BP Shipping Ltd*.[264] While in Singapore waters the *British Skill* collided with Caltex Singapore's jetty causing considerable damage. The total claim was estimated at US $10.5 million. BP had admitted liability for the collision in limitation proceedings which it had commenced in Singapore. However, the limits of liability in Singapore were then less than the limits of liability in England[265] and so the defendants (BP) applied for a stay of the action on the ground that the plaintiffs' claims should be heard and determined in Singapore. Clarke J stated that:

> I have reached the conclusion that the right conferred by [the Merchant Shipping Act] is procedural, or at least that it is not part of the substantive law for the purposes of the conflict of laws. It further follows that if the plaintiffs' claim is litigated in England the English Court will not apply the Singapore limit. What the correct approach would be in the event that BP obtained a limitation decree in Singapore is not something which it is necessary to examine at present. [266]

This analysis of the law was subsequently approved in *The Happy Fellow* by Longmore J:

> I respectfully agree with Mr. Justice Clarke that a shipowner's right to limit . . . does not attach to or qualify the substantive right of the claimant but, rather, limits the extent to which that right can be enforced against a particular fund. I also agree that the position under the 1976 Convention . . . is no different from that under earlier legislation such as the 1894 Act.[267]

---

[263] [1998] 2 Lloyd's Rep 454 (CA), 460. Reversing the decision of Clarke J below: [1998] 1 Lloyd's Rep 167. See too *Bouygues Offshore SA v Caspian Shipping Co* [1998] 2 Lloyd's Rep 461 (CA), 470 (Sir John Knox); *Evergreen International SA v Volkswagen Group Singapore Pte Ltd* [2004] 2 SLR 457.

[264] [1996] 1 Lloyd's Rep 286.

[265] From 1 May 2005 this would no longer be the case as Singapore has now ratified the 1976 Convention. See the Merchant Shipping (Amendment) Act 2004, No 56.

[266] [1996] 1 Lloyd's Rep 286, 296.

[267] [1997] 1 Lloyd's Rep 130, 135.

PART VII

CHARTERPARTIES

30

VOYAGE CHARTERPARTIES

A. Introduction

Overview   In this chapter we begin our consideration of one of the most important **30.01** charterparty types, the voyage charterparty.[1] We begin with an outline of the Gencon 1994 charterparty, which is one of the most important standard forms in common usage.[2] We then look in outline at the Asbatankvoy charterparty, which is one of the most important of the liquid bulk forms. The main part of this chapter then examines each of the four main stages in the performance of a voyage charterparty. The crucially important subject of laytime and demurrage is considered separately in the next chapter.[3]

B. The Gencon 1994 Charterparty

Introduction   The Gencon 1994 charterparty,[4] is one of the standard forms recommended **30.02** for use by BIMCO.[5] As with most standard voyage charterparty contracts, it consists of two main parts, Part I, which contains 26 boxes for the provision of information by the shipowner and voyage charterer, and Part II, which contains 19 detailed clauses, some (but not all) of which relate specifically to the boxes in Part I.

---

[1] See too the earlier discussion at para 1.37. For detailed coverage of the entire topic, see especially Cooke (2001); Williams (1999), ch 1.

[2] See Appendix II.

[3] See ch 31.

[4] Revised 1922, 1976, and 1994. Gencon (1976), the earlier version of the form, is still used.

[5] See <www.bimco.dk>.

30.03 **Introductory clauses**   Part I inter alia contains boxes which specify the contracting parties, the vessel, and the agreed voyage. Gencon 1994 makes this explicit in Boxes 3–5 and 10–11. For the charterer it will be crucial to know the cargo capacity of the vessel and this is normally expressed as deadweight tonnage.[6] Box 7 of the Gencon 1994 charterparty provides for 'DWT all told on summer load line in metric tons (abt)'. This will not be an absolute guarantee because much will depend on the stowage factor of the cargo and hence the qualifying phrase 'abt' (about). In respect of the voyage, the charter may specifically identify the ports of loading and discharge (for example Gencon 1994, Boxes 10–11) or, alternatively, the charterer may have the right to nominate such ports.

30.04 **Cargo clauses**   When a vessel is chartered by a seller for the delivery of an export order, generally speaking the description of the type and quantity of cargo will be specific, for example 40,000 metric tonnes of sugar. Alternatively, the charterer may be able to select one or more from a specified range of cargoes, such as 'meat and/or maize and/or rye'. The charterer will usually be required to ship 'a full and complete cargo', ie the maximum amount of that particular cargo which the ship can carry, qualified by a permitted allowance. If the charterer then fails to supply the required quantity, he will be required to pay compensation for the shortfall in the form of dead freight.[7]

30.05 **Freight clauses**   The charterparty normally specifies the agreed rate of freight, the unit of measurement of cargo to which this applies, and the time and place of payment.[8] In particular, it will be important to indicate whether the assessment of freight is to be made on the quantity of the cargo shipped or on the quantity discharged especially as there may be differences caused by defects in weighing machinery or by natural factors. Gencon (1976) provides that whether freight is payable on delivered or intaken quantity should be stated (see Box 12). Gencon 1994 now provides in clause 4(a) that 'the freight at the rate stated in Box 13 shall be paid in cash calculated on the intaken quantity of cargo'. But note that clause 4(c) provides in respect of freight paid 'On delivery' that charterers are to have an option 'of paying the freight on delivered weight/quantity . . .'. Provision will usually be made in the standard form indicating whether the freight is payable in advance on signing bills of lading, or only on delivery of the goods at their destination. Gencon (1976), clause 4 provides:

> The freight to be paid in the manner prescribed in Box 14 in cash without discount on delivery of the cargo at mean rate of exchange ruling on day or days of payment, the receivers of the cargo being bound to pay freight on account during delivery, if required by Captain or Owners.

But note that in Gencon 1994, Box 13 requires that a statement should be made as to whether freight is prepaid or payable on delivery. This relates specifically to clause 4(b) and (c) of Part II of the charter. In respect of a delivery clause, it will be usual to protect the interests of the shipowner by including a clause granting him a lien on the cargo until the freight is paid (see Gencon 1994, clause 8). It is not uncommon for there to be a

---

[6] ie the weight of cargo the vessel is capable of carrying when loaded to its maximum draught, the latter being the depth of water which a ship requires to float her.

[7] See para 21.32.

[8] See the discussion of freight generally at ch 21.

requirement that part of the freight be paid in advance and the balance on delivery of the cargo. Additional clauses make provision for the currency in which the freight is to be paid and this can be significant where there are fluctuating exchange rates or where the expenses of the voyage will be incurred in a different currency (see Gencon 1994, Box 14 and clause 4).

Other clauses   In addition to the above clauses specifically discussed there will be various   **30.06** additional provisions concerning, inter alia, the shipowners' responsibility for the care of cargo, deviation (for example Gencon 1994, clause 3), and the effect on performance of the contract of such matters as ice (Gencon 1994, clause 18), war (Gencon 1994, clause 17), or strikes (Gencon 1994, clause 16).

C. The Asbatankvoy Charterparty

Introduction   The Asbatankvoy charterparty (1977) is issued by the Association of   **30.07** Shipbrokers and Agents (USA) Inc[9] and is a leading voyage form for usage in the oil trade. The Asbatankvoy form consists of a Preamble and two parts. The Preamble expressly states that 'in the event of a conflict, the provisions of Part I will prevail over those contained in Part II'. Part I, consisting of Parts A to M, consists of spaces for the provision of information relating to the voyage by the shipowner and the voyage charterer. Part II contains 26 written clauses.

Contents   Much of the same basic clauses noted above in relation to the Gencon charter-   **30.08** party are to be found in this charterparty. The main differences relate to clauses which are unique to the oil trade. There are, for example, special clauses which deal with the allocation of responsibility for pumping oil on to and off the vessel (clause 10) and the provision of hoses for mooring at sea terminals (clause 11). In addition to these clauses there are special clauses relating to the cargo (clause 13), for the cleaning of the 'tanks, pipes and pumps' of the vessel (clause 18), and for oil pollution (clause 26).

D. Performance Clauses

Four stages   There are four stages in the performance of a voyage charterparty: the   **30.09** preliminary voyage to the place which is specified as the loading point in the charterparty; the loading operation, which covers both loading and stowage; the carrying voyage to the place specified for delivery of the cargo; and the discharging operation.[10] Responsibility for stages 1 and 3 falls on the shipowner. The remaining stages, ie 2 and 4, will be joint responsibilities, although it is normally the case that the primary obligation falls on the charterer. It may then become crucial to determine on whom falls any risk of loss which results from delay in performance which is beyond the control of either party.

---

[9] See <www.asba.org/>.
[10] *EL Oldendorff & Co GmbH v Tradax Export SA (The Johanna Oldendorff)* [1974] AC 479, 556 (Lord Diplock).

Voyage charters are susceptible, more than other charters, to such incidents as bad weather, engine trouble, adverse tides, strikes, or the unavailability of berths at the designated port of discharge. Subject, of course, to the specific terms of the charter, the general rule is that the risk of accidental delay is to be carried by the party who is responsible for the performance of the particular stage during which delay occurs. The difficulty arises in establishing with some precision at which point one stage begins and another commences. This is less complex when it concerns loading and discharge, but the courts have struggled to find a formula for determining the point when the respective voyage stages are completed and laytime begins to run.

E. The Preliminary Voyage

30.10 **Nomination of the port of loading**   The port of loading may be specified in the charter-party as a fixed berth ('berth 2 at Lagos'), a fixed port ('1 safe berth Dunedin'), a fixed area ('1 safe port/1 safe berth Korea'), or several ports ('berth 2 at Lagos and 1 safe berth Singapore').[11] The charterer may have the right to nominate a port, for example from a given geographical area ('Bordeaux/Hamburg range') or from a list of named ports ('Amsterdam/Rotterdam/ Antwerp'). Where the port is specifically identified, the shipowner will be under an absolute obligation to go there; there will then be no implied warranty by the charterer as to the safety of the port.[12]

30.11 **Charterer's nomination**   Where the charterer has an obligation to nominate a port, he is not obliged to consider either the convenience of the owner or the expense of complying with the nomination. It will usually be advisable for the parties to insist on a clause fixing the latest time at which the charterer can nominate the port. An example would be:

> Discharging port to be nominated by Charterers latest at commencement of loading.

A charterer who has the right to nominate a port(s) must exercise his election within the time specified or otherwise within a reasonable time. If he fails to do so, the shipowner is not permitted to withdraw his vessel but must wait for instructions unless the delay is so prolonged as to result in frustration of the charterparty.[13] The charterer will be liable for any loss to the shipowner resulting from the delay in giving the necessary instructions. In *Zim Israel Navigation Co Ltd v Tradax Export SA (The Timna)*[14] the charterers were held liable in damages from the time when the order for the port of discharge should have been given to the time when it was in fact given. In *Reardon Smith Line Ltd v Ministry of Agriculture, Fisheries and Food* Willmer LJ stated that:

> Subject . . . to an implied obligation not to nominate an utterly impossible port . . . the principle is well established that where a charterparty provides a choice of named places for loading or discharge, the charterer is free to exercise his option as he chooses, and in doing so is in no way bound to consult the convenience of the shipowners . . .[15]

---

[11] Gencon 1994, cl 1, lines 7–8 + Box 10; Asbatankvoy, cl 1 + cl 4 + Part C.
[12] As to the safe port obligation, see para 20.21.
[13] For a general discussion of frustration, see ch 33.
[14] [1971] 2 Lloyd's Rep 91 (CA).
[15] [1962] 1 QB 42 (CA), 110. See also [1963] AC 691.

In this case the charterers nominated the port of Vancouver where a strike of elevator men was already in progress. Even though loading of a cargo of wheat was prevented for six weeks, the court held that the delay was not so unreasonable as to frustrate the charter. Furthermore, the charterers could invoke a strike exception in the charter to avoid liability for demurrage accruing during the waiting period.

Unfettered choice   But does this mean that the charterer necessarily has an unfettered **30.12** choice as to the choice of port? In *Pilgrim Shipping v State Trading Corporation of India (The Hadjitsakos)*[16] a vessel was chartered for a voyage from British Columbia to 'one or two safe ports in India'. She proceeded via Singapore and the charterers nominated Bombay and Calcutta as the discharging ports in that order. The court held that the charterer was not entitled to nominate them other than in their geographical order. For this reason, it is not uncommon for a clause to specify that the ports are to be called at 'in geographical rotation'.

Entitlement to change the nomination   Where the charterer is required to nominate a **30.13** port, the effect of his nomination once made is that it cannot be altered. In *Anglo-Danubian Transport Co Ltd v Ministry of Food*, Devlin J stated that:

> The first point [counsel] has taken is that the charterer is not debarred from changing his mind after he has nominated the vessel's berth, but that he can nominate another berth at any time before the ship begins to discharge, or, at any rate, before she becomes an arrived ship. It is clearly settled by the authorities that where there is an express reservation in the charterparty to the charterer to nominate the port or berth, that port or berth, when nominated, is to be treated as if it had been written into the charterparty. That being so, the position seems to me to be that when the charterers nominated New Hibernia Wharf, it was to be treated as if it was written into the charter-party as the place of discharge, and it follows from that that it cannot be altered by the charterers. To permit the charterers to alter it would be to permit a unilateral alteration of the contract.[17]

A safe port   Where the charterparty requires the charterer to nominate a safe port or **30.14** place, his obligation is to nominate a port or place which is prospectively safe for the vessel to reach, use, and return from. Where he fails so to do, the damages recoverable will extend to cover such items as actual physical injury to the vessel, losses resulting from any delay, and the additional expenses incurred in discharging the cargo at an alternative port.[18]

The voyage to the loading port   Generally speaking, it will be necessary for the chartered **30.15** vessel to undertake a preliminary voyage to the agreed port of loading. The charterer will obviously wish to know with some degree of precision when the vessel is expected to arrive in order that the necessary arrangements can be made in respect of the cargo. He will not wish to incur needless storage costs or indeed demurrage costs (ie because the cargo arrived too late). The shipowner, likewise, will not wish to be too specific because he will wish to

---

[16] [1975] 1 Lloyd's Rep 356 (CA).
[17] (1950) 83 Ll LR 137, 139. See *Bulk Shipping AG v Ipco Trading SA (The Jasmine B)* [1992] 1 Lloyd's Rep 39 where clause M1A expressly permitted the charterer to change his nomination.
[18] As to safe ports generally, see para 20.21.

avoid liability for breach of contract should the vessel be delayed. In *Evera SA Comercial v North Shipping Co Ltd*, Diplock J explained this as follows:

> A charterer manifestly wants, if he can get it, a fixed date for the arrival of the ship at the port of loading. He has to make arrangements to bring down the cargo and to have it ready to load when the ship arrives and he wants to know as near as he can what that date is going to be. On the other hand, it is to the interest of the shipowner, if he can have it, to have the date as flexible as possible because of the inevitable delays due to bad weather or other circumstances that there might be in the course of a voyage. He can never be sure that he can arrive at a port on a fixed and certain day. Therefore, in order to accommodate these two views as far as possible it has been the general practice for a long time past to have a clause under which the shipowner, without pledging himself to a fixed day, gives a date in the charterparty of expected readiness, that is the date when he expects that he will be ready to load.[19]

30.16 **Expected ready** Most standard form charterparties require the position of the vessel to be stated with some degree of accuracy; see, for example, Gencon (1976) and (1994) Boxes 8 ('present position') and 9 ('expected ready to load' — ERL), pursuant to clause 1.[20] The meaning and effect of the words 'expected ready' or 'expected ready to load' (ERL) has been considered in a number of cases. Edmund-Davies LJ stated in *Maredelanto Compania Naviera SA v Bergbau-Handel GmbH (The Mihalis Angelos)* that

> ... these words mean that, in the light of the facts known to the owner at the time of making the contract, he honestly expected the vessel would be ready as stated and, further, that such expectation was based on reasonable grounds.[21]

The *Mihalis Angelos*, a steamer, was chartered for a voyage from Haiphong (North Vietnam) to load a cargo of ore for carriage to Hamburg or another North European port. The vessel was described as 'now trading and expected ready to load under this charter about July 1, 1965'. The cancelling date under the charter was 20 July 1965. There were two difficulties for the contracting parties: (1) it was likely that the vessel would only arrive in Haiphong on 13 or 14 July; (2) owing to the bombing of a railway line, there was no ore available for loading by the charterers at Haiphong. The charterers purported to cancel the charterparty on the grounds of *force majeure* on 17 July 1965 and this was accepted by the owners as a repudiation of the contract. One of the questions which was considered in the Court of Appeal was whether the 'expected ready to load clause' was a condition of the contract. Lord Denning MR pointed out that

> if the owner of a ship or his agent states in a charter that she 'is expected ready to load about 1 July 1965', he is making a representation as to his own state of mind; that is, of what he himself expects: and, what is more, he puts it in the contract as a term of it, binding himself to its truth. If he or his agent breaks that term by making the statement without any honest belief in its truth or without any reasonable grounds for it, he must take the consequences. It is at lowest a misrepresentation which entitles the other party to rescind; and at highest a breach of contract which goes to the root of the matter. The charterer who is misled by the statement is entitled, on discovering its falsity, to throw up the charter. It may, therefore, properly be described as a 'condition'.[22]

---

[19] [1956] 2 Lloyd's Rep 367, 370.
[20] See too Asbatankvoy, clause 1, line 3 + Part A.
[21] [1971] 1 QB 164 (CA), 197. Expressly approved by Neill LJ in *Geogas SA v Trammo Gas Ltd (The Baleares)* [1993] 1 Lloyd's Rep 215 (CA), 225. See para 30.19.
[22] At 194.

The Court of Appeal held that the charterers were entitled to rescind the contract on 17 July 1965, three days before the formal cancelling date.

Substantial errors   The courts attach great importance to the accuracy of ERL statements **30.17** in charterparties and substantial errors will amount to a breach of condition entitling the charterer to repudiate and seek damages, if desired. In the old case of *Behn v Burness*[23] it was agreed that Behn, the owner of the *Martaban*, 'now in the port of Amsterdam', would 'with all possible dispatch' send her to Newport (Wales). The defendant was there to load her with a full cargo of coal for carriage to Hong Kong. At the time the charterparty was made, the *Martaban* was not in port, owing to strong gales which meant that she could not discharge at Amsterdam until four days after this charterparty was made. The charterer refused to load her at Newport. What was the effect of this statement in the charterparty that the *Martaban* was 'now in the port of Amsterdam'? In the Court of Exchequer Chamber, Williams J, reading the judgment of the court said:

> Now the place of the ship at the date of the contract, where the ship is in foreign parts and is chartered to come to England, may be the only datum on which the charterer can found his calculations of the time of the ship's arriving at the port of load. For most charters, considering winds, markets and dependent contracts, the time of the ship's arrival to load is an essential fact, for the interest of the charterer. [I]f the statement of the place of the ship is a substantive part of the contract, it seems to us that we ought to hold it to be a condition . . . unless we can find in the contract itself or the surrounding circumstances reason for thinking that the parties did not so intend. If it was a condition and not performed, it follows that the obligation of the charterer dependent thereon, ceased at his option and considerations either of the damage to him or of proximity to performance on the part of the shipowner are irrelevant.[24]

The Court of Exchequer Chamber therefore reversed the decision of the Queen's Bench Division.[25] As we have seen, the common law also implies an obligation to proceed to the loading port with reasonable despatch, though this may of course be varied by express agreement in the charter.

The lay/can   Many charter forms require the shipowner to indicate a date at which the **30.18** vessel is expected to be ready to load and to couple this with a clause — the so-called lay/can — entitling the charterer to cancel the charter should the vessel not have arrived by a specified later date.[26] Once the date for cancellation has been reached, the charterer can make other arrangements for the shipment of his cargo. He cannot repudiate the charterparty when he knows that the chartered vessel cannot arrive in time. The cancelling clause does not entitle the charterer to claim damages for delay. These will be possible only if the shipowner has breached his obligation to proceed with reasonable despatch. The shipowner must continue to proceed to the loading port with reasonable despatch until the option to cancel has been exercised.

---

[23] (1863) 3 B&S 751; 122 ER 281. Confirmed in *Geogas SA v Trammo Gas Ltd (The Baleares)* [1993] 1 Lloyd's Rep 215 (CA), 225.
[24] At 759; 122 ER 284.
[25] (1862) 1 B&S 877; 121 ER 939.
[26] See Gencon 1994, cl 9 (lines 137–153); Asbatankvoy, cl 5 + Part B. For a case involving a sophisticated cancelling clause, see *Universal Bulk Carriers Ltd v Andre et Cie SA* [2000] 1 Lloyd's Rep 459.

30.19 **Breach of contract** A statement by the shipowner as to the date of readiness to load does not amount to an undertaking on his part that the vessel will be ready to load at that date. Late arrival does not per se amount to breach of contract; the charterer would only be able to repudiate the contract if the delay was such as to frustrate the object of the enterprise. If the shipowner makes a prediction of arrival knowing full well that it will not be possible for the ship to reach the loading port by that date, he then commits a breach of a condition and the charterer may repudiate. Some of the issues raised above were considered by the Court of Appeal in *Geogas SA v Trammo Gas Ltd (The Baleares)*.[27] In January 1987 the *Baleares* was chartered by Trammo from Geogas to proceed to one safe berth Bethioua and there load 30,000 tonnes LPG. The charter was on the Asbatankvoy form and described the vessel as 'Now trading' and 'Expected ready 31st January 1987' with 'Laydays Commencing 30th January 1987. Cancelling 5th February 1987'. On 20 January, Geogas purported to substitute *Stena Oceanica* for the *Baleares* and notified Trammo, informing them also that the substitute would be unable to meet the cancelling date. Trammo protested immediately and informed Geogas that the late arrival would cause damage in respect of which they would seek compensation. By 6 February neither of the vessels had arrived at Bethioua and Trammo cancelled the charterparty without prejudice to their claim for damages. The dispute was referred to arbitration, was then appealed to the Queens Bench Division and thence to the Court of Appeal. The charterers argued inter alia that the breach of the owners was the cause of a rise of US$50 per metric tonne in the price between 20 and 31 January. The Court of Appeal emphasized that the expected readiness clause was a condition of the charter and once it had been breached, the charterers could repudiate the contract. However, they had not sought to do so until the operation of the cancellation clause. Neill LJ refused to find that a charterer was obliged to wait until the vessel left the last discharge point before he could treat the owners as being in breach. Further, considering *The Mihalis Angelos*,[28] the Court of Appeal found that a right to treat a charterparty as having been repudiated by the owners might arise before a contractual right to cancel where it was clear that there was no reasonable prospect of the vessel being able to perform the contemplated voyage. Accordingly, Neill LJ endorsed the view of the arbitrators that 'the owners were in breach of the obligation to proceed . . . throughout the period during which the increase in price was gradually taking effect'[29] and rejected the argument of the owners that the obligation to proceed with all reasonable despatch had not commenced until 31 January. Finally, Neill LJ held that the combination of the ETA provision and the undertaking to proceed with all reasonable despatch resulted in an obligation to 'start in time' and the breach thereof caused the loss.

30.20 **The near clause** When added after the name of the port of discharge, a clause stating that '. . . or as near to as she may safely get[30] and always lie afloat'[31] is intended to protect the owner against hindrances which arise after the negotiation of the fixture. The effect,

---

27 [1993] 1 Lloyd's Rep 215 (CA).
28 [1971] 1 QB 164 (CA). See para 30.16.
29 [1993] 1 Lloyd's Rep 215 (CA), 226.
30 The word 'safely' in the clause refers to the safety of the ship and not to the safety of the cargo.
31 See Gencon 1994, cl 1 (lines 8–9); Asbatankvoy, cl 1, lines 3–4.

therefore, of the clause is to limit what would otherwise be an absolute obligation on the shipowner to enter the port named in spite of sand, bars, ice, blockade, etc. If successfully invoked, the contractual voyage is complete on the ship's arrival at the alternative port and the shipowner is then entitled to claim freight. The consignee bears the cost of transporting the goods to the original destination. The governing principle was expressed as follows by Brett LJ in *Nelson v Dahl*:

> . . . [L]ay days do not begin to run, either for the purpose of loading or unloading, until the shipowner has brought his ship to the primary destination named in the charterparty, so as to be ready, so far as the ship is concerned, to receive or deliver there, unless he is prevented from getting his ship to that destination by some obstruction or disability of such a character that it cannot be overcome by the shipowner by any reasonable means, except within such a time as, having regard to the object of the adventure of both the shipowner and charterer, is as a matter of business wholly unreasonable.[32]

Length of time   As to the length of time spent waiting, Scrutton LJ put this as follows in **30.21** *Fornyade Rederiaktiebolaget Commercial v Blake & Co*:

> When you are chartered to go to a discharging place and cannot get there, first of all you are bound to wait a reasonable time before having recourse to the clause 'or so near thereunto as she may safely get'. You cannot arrive, and when you find you cannot get in at the exact minute, or on the exact day you desire, you immediately go off to a place which you describe as 'so near thereunto as she may safely get'. When a reasonable time has elapsed, and when there is no chance of your getting in to your discharging place within a reasonable time, the ship is at liberty to go to a reasonable discharging place . . .[33]

Permanent obstacles   The near clause will only relate to permanent obstacles, not those **30.22** contemplated as ordinary incidents of the voyage. A temporary obstacle, such as an unfavourable state of the tide or insufficient water to enable the ship to get into dock, will not make the place unsafe so as to discharge the shipowner from liability to unload there, unless the terms of the contract indicate otherwise. In the case of ice, if the situation could have been reasonably anticipated when the charterparty was concluded, then the vessel may be obliged to wait. In *Metcalfe v Britannia Ironworks Co*[34] delivery was to be made at Taganrog, on the Sea of Azov. The charterparty stipulated that the ship should go 'to Taganrog, or as near as she could safely get and deliver the cargo afloat'. The vessel arrived at Kertch (300 miles by sea from Taganrog) in December when the Sea of Azov was closed by ice; it was unlikely that passage to Taganrog would be available until the next April (ie 4 months). The court held that the shipowner was not entitled to freight by delivering as near as he could get at Kertch. The question whether an obstacle was temporary or permanent was not so much one of length of time as of what might be regarded as contemplated incidents of the voyage. The court took the view that the shipowner should have been aware of conditions in the Sea of Azov at that time of the year. Lord Coleridge CJ said that:

> It is not necessary to say more than that the obstruction was only temporary, and is such as must be incident to every contract for voyage to a frozen sea, and it cannot be said that in

---

[32] (1879) 12 Ch D 568 (CA), 593–594.
[33] (1931) 39 Ll LR 205 (CA), 207.
[34] (1877) 2 QBD 423 (CA).

all these contracts the words 'at that time' or 'then and there', are to be inserted after the words 'as near thereto as the ship can safely get'.[35]

In *Athamas SS (Owners) v Dig Vijay Cement Co Ltd (The Athamas)*[36] the terms of the charterparty were that the *Athamas* was to discharge her cargo at Phnom Penh or 'so near thereto as she may safely get'. She could not get to Phnom Penh and had to discharge her cargo at Saigon, 250 miles away. The Pilotage Authority refused to take her to Phnom Penh on the ground that the depth of water was insufficient to enable the lightly laden ship to navigate in safety. The ship would have had to wait five months before the depth of water was sufficient to allow her to proceed. The court held that the shipowners were entitled to discharge the whole of the cargo at Saigon and to recover the full freight for two-port discharge. Pearson LJ said that the parties should be deemed to have general maritime knowledge and therefore to know that that part of the world was sparsely provided with ports, so that there might well be a long distance between the named port and any possible substitute. Sellers LJ stated that:

> . . . [The court or tribunal] should apply the conception of reasonableness in relation to distance. The distance might be so great in relation to the contemplated length, duration and nature of the adventure that notwithstanding that it was the nearest safe port or place the substituted place of discharge could not be assumed to be within the contemplation of the parties as fair and reasonable men.[37]

30.23 Ambit test There will clearly be a conflict between the interests of the consignee and the shipowner when it comes to the choice of an alternative discharging port. The consignee will wish to minimize additional transport costs while the shipowner will only be attracted by the nearest safe port if it has adequate facilities for discharging the cargo. The courts in such circumstances have imposed the so-called 'ambit test', which requires that the alternative port must be within an area or zone in close proximity to the original port. In *Athamas SS (Owners) v Dig Vijay Cement Co Ltd (The Athamas)* Pearson LJ stated that:

> [My] examination of the authorities has not yielded any precise definition of the range of proximity or vicinity within which the substitute destination must lie in order to be, in relation to the named destination for the ship, 'as near thereto as she may safely get'. I do, however, derive from these authorities an impression that the range is fairly narrow, and that in an ordinary case a substitute destination 250 miles by water from the named destination would be outside the range of proximity. This, however, is an extraordinary case in that Saigon, though 250 miles by water away from Phnom Penh, is nevertheless the nearest port to Phnom Penh, at any rate for the purpose of unloading the cargo concerned . . . The question is largely one of degree and to be decided mainly on a basis of commercial knowledge and experience.[38]

30.24 'Always afloat' Finally, the addition of the words 'always afloat' protects the shipowner from possible damage to the vessel by grounding and entitles him to unload at the nearest safe port if unreasonable delay would otherwise result.

---

[35] At 426.
[36] [1963] 1 Lloyd's Rep 287 (CA).
[37] At 296.
[38] [1963] 1 Lloyd's Rep 287 (CA), 302.

F. The Loading Operation

Division of responsibility At the port of loading, the rights of the shipowner and the **30.25** obligations of the charterer as regards loading the cargo would depend on the following being done by the owner: (i) the ship being at the place where she was bound to be ready for cargo or, if there is such a provision in the charter, 'so near thereto as she can safely get'; (ii) the ship being ready to load; (iii) the charterer having notice of the above information.

Charterer's obligations All things being equal, the charterer must: (i) procure a cargo; **30.26** (ii) bring it alongside the vessel; (iii) load a full and complete cargo; (iv) load in the time stipulated. In most contexts the 'alongside rule' operates, namely that the charterer must assume responsibility for bringing the cargo within reach of the vessel's tackle and the shipowner has the responsibility for loading it. The loading operation may be undertaken by shore-based stevedores. The charterparty may provide that the goods are carried FIO,[39] in which case the charterer must pay the costs of loading and discharging. Gencon (1976), clause 5(a) states that:

> The cargo to be brought alongside in such a manner as to enable vessel to take the goods with her own tackle . . . Charterers to procure and pay the necessary men on shore or on board the lighters to do the work there, vessel only heaving the cargo on board.

This clause has been somewhat expanded in the Gencon 1994 form. If the charterparty does not do so, the common law will imply the 'alongside rule' and the charterer will not have to bear the cost of loading which will fall for the shipowner's account.

Provision of cargo The charterer will be under an absolute duty to provide the cargo **30.27** and arrangements for procuring it will not normally fall within the scope of the contract with the shipowner. It will not be sufficient that all reasonable diligence has been exercised to obtain the cargo. In this respect, the leading case is *Sociedad Financiera de Bienes Raices v Agrimpex (The Aello)*.[40] The facts here were that the *Aello* was chartered to provide a cargo of wheat and/or maize and/or rye at ports in the Parana and to complete loading at Buenos Aires. The charterers wished to load maize but vessels loading maize had to wait 22 miles away until they had been awarded a 'giro' (a permit) by the customs authorities. This would not be issued until the shippers had obtained a certificate from the grain board and had available a cargo for loading. The ship reached the anchorage on 12 October but the shippers did not have a cargo of maize available for loading until 29 October and the consequence was that the vessel was delayed until then in reaching the loading area of the port. Lord Radcliffe stated that:

> where the completion of the ship's voyage is entirely dependent upon the availability of the cargo, I think it is only natural that the law should throw the burden of any delay that occurs upon the charterer's side. I am sure that . . . the charterers did everything that was reasonable to do to procure the completion cargo, the cargo certificates and the giro; but that in itself seems to me an insufficient reason for throwing the consequences of their failure on to the owners of the ship.[41]

---

[39] 'Free in and out'. See para 26.40.
[40] [1961] AC 135. The dicta in this case on the 'arrived ship' are no longer good, following the decision in *The Johanna Oldendorff*. See the discussion at para 31.09.
[41] At 177.

30.28 **Full and complete cargo** Normally the cargo to be provided by the charterer will be specifically stated in the charterparty, for example 10,000 tonnes of sugar. There usually is an obligation to load 'a full and complete cargo' to the full extent of the vessel's capacity.[42] What is the consequence of failure to do so? In *Hunter v Fry*[43] the charterparty provided that the charterer should 'immediately receive on board from the agents or correspondents of the freighters, a full and complete cargo of coffee, in bags and casks'. The agents did not supply a full and complete cargo, loading 288 tons of sugar and 28 tons of coffee (the *Hunter* could have taken 340 tons of coffee in bags and 40 tons in casks). The defendants only paid freight for the actual cargo shipped and the plaintiff owners then claimed an additional sum. The court found for the owners. Best J said that

> the stipulation in the charterparty is not that the owner should receive, and the freighter put on board, a cargo equivalent to the tonnage described in the charter-party; but that the one should receive a full and complete cargo, not exceeding what the ship was capable of receiving with safety, and that the other should put such a cargo on board. [I]t seems to me that the defendant, who has covenanted to load a full and complete cargo, is . . . liable in damages, for not having laden such a cargo as the ship could safely carry.[44]

30.29 **Alternatives** The following formulation is also possible:

> . . . a full and complete cargo of wheat in bulk . . . and/or barley in bulk and/or flour in sacks as below . . . Charterer has the option of loading up to one third cargo of barley in bulk . . . Charterer has the option of loading up to one third flour in bags . . .[45]

Generally speaking the charterer will have a free choice in such a case, even though the respective freight rates might vary. But he will be under an obligation to load a full cargo from the range open to his selection. The reason for this is that, if a full cargo is not loaded, the shipowner would lose freight on account of some part of the ship's carrying capacity not being utilized. The owner would then be entitled to recover damages in the form known as 'dead freight'.[46]

30.30 **Mutuality of obligations** It has been recognized that there are mutual obligations on the charterer and the shipowner when it comes to the loading of a full and complete cargo. In *China Offshore Oil (Singapore) International Pte Ltd* v *Giant Shipping Ltd (The Posidon)*[47] the voyage charterer undertook to load 'a full and complete cargo of petroleum and/or its products in bulk'. At Xijiang, loading took place from a Floating Production Storage and Offloading (FPSO) unit. The vessel arrived at Xijiang and, though the weather was already bad and was expected to deteriorate further, the *Posidon* was permitted to moor and commenced loading. By the following morning loading operations had to be stopped and, by this time, 400,000 barrels of oil (out of a maximum of 600,000 barrels) had been loaded. No further instructions to re-moor were given because the weather remained too bad and the charterers ordered the vessel to the discharging port. The charterers paid a lump sum freight of US$181,332 (instead of US$307,500), contending that

---

[42] Gencon 1994, cl 1; Asbatankvoy, cl 1.
[43] (1819) 2 B&Ald 421; 106 ER 420.
[44] At 426–427; 106 ER 422.
[45] *Reardon Smith Line Ltd v Ministry of Agriculture, Fisheries and Food* [1963] AC 691.
[46] See the discussion of dead freight at para 21.32.
[47] [2001] 1 Lloyd's Rep 697.

they were entitled to prorate the freight to reflect the amount of cargo actually loaded. The owners contended that they were entitled to the balance of the agreed lump sum freight. The charterers argued that the vessel had been ordered off the FPSO unit because of various other defects as much as the weather conditions. They contended that the *Posidon* was unable to re-berth as she was not allowed to return to her mooring because of various defects which the terminal regarded as compromising the safety of the loading operation. The arbitrators awarded the owners the balance of the lump sum freight and dismissed the charterers' counterclaim for damages, holding that there had been no breach of contract by the owners. The issue on appeal to the High Court was whether the charterers were in breach of the 'full and complete cargo' provision. Tomlinson J held that there were obligations on the charterers to load and on the shipowners to receive the cargo:

> . . . Cl 1 imposes a mutual obligation upon the owners to receive on board and upon the charterers to supply a full and complete cargo. The parties from whom the vessel receives the cargo are deemed to be 'factors' or agents of the charterers. The mutual obligation to load a full and complete cargo requires the charterers to ship the cargo on board and the owners to receive it on board. There is no absolute obligation on the owners to load — their obligation is contingent upon and cannot be performed without performance by the charterers of their obligation to ship or to tender for shipment a full and complete cargo.[48]

He rejected the argument of the charterers that there had been a breach by the shipowners:

> The short point is therefore that the vessel did not load a full and complete cargo because the charterers did not provide one and instead ordered the vessel to sail for the discharge port when only two thirds full. There was no breach of contract by the owners in failing to load cargo which was not tendered to them for shipment. If there was no failure by the owners in performing their part of the bargain contained in cl 1 of the charter-party and if, as the arbitrators also found, the owners remained ready and willing to complete loading if and when the vessel was permitted to remoor when the weather abated, there is in my judgment simply no basis on which it can be asserted that the circumstance that the vessel did not load a full and complete cargo renders the owners in breach of contract.[49]

Reasonable time   Where the charterer is prevented from loading his original choice of **30.31** cargo, he will be entitled to a reasonable time in which to make alternative arrangements. Thus in *South African Dispatch Line v Owners of the Panamanian SS Niki*[50] a single voyage charterparty for a lump sum freight of $185,000 provided for shipment to four districts

> in Coos Bay/British Columbia Range . . . as ordered by charterers, loading rotation to be North/South or South/North at charterer's option, with charterer's option of commencing loading on the Columbia River or Coos Bay, then British Columbia, thence South to Columbia River to complete.

Shipment was of a cargo of lumber and/or timber and/or wheat in bulk and/or lawful merchandise, excluding dangerous cargo. A further clause provided that:

> 4. . . . Charterers shall not be responsible for any delay if the cargo intended for shipment under this charterparty cannot be provided, delivered, loaded or discharged by reason of . . . strikes . . . connected in any way with, or essential to the providing, delivery, loading or discharging of the cargo . . .

---

[48] At 701–702.
[49] At 702.
[50] [1960] 1 QB 518 (CA).

The charterers had booked a cargo of lumber at Victoria (BC) but a strike broke out which prevented loading of lumber at all BC ports. As the strike was still in process ten days later, the charterers proposed a variation in the rotation and the loading of an alternative cargo of wheat if it proved impossible to load the lumber because of the strike. The ship then sailed to Vancouver where she loaded wheat before proceeding to Portland (Oregon) where she completed loading. The owners refused to compensate the charterers for the cost of loading the alternative cargo and rearranging the rotation as they contended that, if the *Niki* had gone to Victoria to load lumber as planned, the laydays would have begun to run irrespective of the strike. The Court of Appeal held that the exception clause did not exempt the charterers from seeking an alternative cargo when the cargo of lumber became unavailable; it merely excused delay in loading for such a time as was reasonably required to obtain the alternative cargo. In these circumstances the charterers were not entitled to send the vessel to Victoria and to count as laytime an indefinite period of waiting until a cargo of lumber became available. The shipowners were therefore entitled to succeed in the sum of $11,000, the amount which had been withheld by the charterers. Hodson LJ stated that:

> The charterers' duty would be to make preliminary arrangements . . . before they sent the ship to Victoria if there was a reasonable likelihood of the strike continuing when the vessel arrived, and to make definite arrangements as soon as it was clear that it would continue. I agree . . . that they would then be entitled to a reasonable time to make those arrangements.[51]

30.32   **Exception clauses**   What is the position where a failure to load cargo is directly related to an exception clause in the charterparty? If a failure to load a particular cargo is covered by an exception, the charterer will not be relieved from his obligation to load an alternative cargo. In *Reardon Smith Line Ltd v Ministry of Agriculture, Fisheries and Food*, Viscount Radcliffe stated that:

> If a shipper has undertaken to ship a full and complete cargo made up of alternative commodities, as in the terms 'wheat and/or maize and/or rye', his obligation is to have ready at the port of shipment a complete cargo within the range of those alternatives. Consequently the fact that he is prevented from loading one of the possible types of cargo by a cause within the exception clause, even though that is the type he has himself selected and provided for, is not an answer to a claim for demurrage.[52]

Many charters will include exceptions which cover a delay in loading but there is a strong presumption that these apply only to the actual process of loading the cargo when ready and not to a delay in providing the cargo. In *Grant & Co v Coverdale, Todd & Co*[53] a ship was chartered to

> proceed to Cardiff East Bute Dock and there load iron in the customary manner . . . cargo to be supplied as fast as steamer can receive . . . time to commence from the vessel's being ready to load, excepting in case of hands striking work, or frost, or floods, or any other unavoidable accidents preventing the loading.

---

[51] At 530.
[52] [1963] 1 Lloyd's Rep 12 (HL), 28.
[53] (1884) 9 App Cas 470.

The charterer's agent had his own iron at a wharf in a canal outside the dock, but there were other agents with wharves in the dock, and it was possible, though expensive, to bring the iron from the wharf to the dock by land. Frost stopped the transit of the iron by canal to the dock, though it would not have stopped the loading if the cargo had been in the dock. The court held that the charterers were liable for the delay, as the frost did not prevent the loading, but only the transit of the cargo to the place of loading by one of the ways usual at the port. In *Brightman & Co v Bunge y Born Limitada Sociedad* [54] the charterparty provided that the charterers were to load a 'cargo of wheat and/or maize and/or rye' at a specified rate for carriage between Rosario and the Continent. The clause then continued that

> if the cargo cannot be loaded . . . by reason of obstruction . . . beyond the control of the charterers on the railways . . . the time for loading . . . shall not count during the continuance of such causes.

The loading of the *Castlemoor* was not completed on time and continued for a period of 10 days and 19 hours beyond the agreed laytime. The owners claimed demurrage for this period. The charterers had resolved to load a cargo of wheat but this was not available at the port when the *Castlemoor* arrived and it had to be shipped from the interior of Argentina. The charterers were making use of the Central Argentine Railway when that company was in the midst of a 'go slow' or 'ca canny' movement. During this period the Argentine government issued a prohibition on the export of wheat and the charterers had to cease loading wheat. They commenced loading maize instead of wheat some days after the prohibition came into effect. In response to the owners, the charterers responded that they were excused demurrage by virtue of the 'ca canny' movement on the Central Argentine Railway; this was an 'obstruction' within the meaning of the exception clause in the charterparty. At first instance, Bailhache J held that, where a charterer undertook to load a mixed cargo of various named kinds, the fact that he was prevented from loading one ingredient of the cargo did not excuse him from loading the other ingredients which he was not prevented from loading. The Court of Appeal held that the 'ca canny' movement and the consequent obstruction to the charterer's loading programme did not come within the exception clause of the charterparty and upheld the finding of the arbitrator on this point. Bankes LJ took the view that the scheme of the railway company's employees did not on the facts amount to an obstruction. Atkin LJ pointed out that:

> It is found that there is a very considerable warehouse accommodation at Rosario; it is not found that the whole or part of the cargo is of necessity or even customarily loaded from rail, though that is one of the modes of loading; and there is an express finding — although in this there may lurk an ambiguity — that there was no reason why the respondents should not have had a full cargo ready for the *Castlemoor* on her arrival. [55]

Thus on this view, though the 'go slow' movement was an obstruction, the exception was *prima facie* limited to one which prevented the cargo from being loaded, as distinguished from one which prevented it from coming forward. The scheme of the employees here did not prevent the cargo from being loaded because the wheat might have been shipped by one of the other railways or it might have been stored ready in the warehouses and

---

[54] [1924] KB 619 (CA).
[55] At 636.

therefore have been independent of the railways altogether. The obstruction was therefore not an 'obstruction on the railways' within the clause for it had to be read as referring to the railways in the port itself directly connected with the process of loading. So far as the demurrage was concerned, although the prohibition against the export of wheat bound the charterers to load maize or rye, they were not bound to load it immediately, but were entitled to a reasonable time to see whether the prohibition would be removed and to make arrangements for loading the substituted cargo, and to the extent of that reasonable time they were excused from paying demurrage.[56]

30.33 **Shipowners' decisions**   Sometimes the charterparty will state that the amount of cargo to be loaded is to be decided by the shipowners, for example '10,000 tons or 2,240 lbs., 10% more or less at owner's option'. Alternatively, the phrase may be qualified by terms such as 'about' or 'thereabouts' and the courts have interpreted these as permitting an allowance of from 3–5 per cent either way. In *Louis Dreyfus & Cie v Parnaso Cia Naviera SA*[57] the charterparty provided that the *SS Dominator* was to proceed to La Pallice '. . . and there load a full and complete cargo of not more than 10,450 tons and not less than 8,550 tons wheat in bulk, quantity in owner's option, to be declared by the master in writing on commencement of loading . . .' The master overestimated the capacity of the vessel by 331 long tons and the charterers incurred expenses which they now sought to recover from the shipowners. The Court of Appeal found that a deficiency of 331 tons in a cargo of 10,400 tons (ie just over 3 per cent) fulfilled the obligation to ship 'about 10,400 tons' and was a reasonable commercial margin. Sellers LJ said that:

> . . . [O]nce the declaration [by the master] was properly made the quantity stated therein became substituted for the wide range of maximum and minimum quantities stipulated in the charterparty and established the quantity to be loaded. I doubt whether it is right or necessary to say that such a quantity is deemed to be a full and complete cargo, although that might often be the effect. It becomes the maximum which the shipper is required to load, but I am inclined to think that, in this case and with this declaration, if the vessel had not been fully laden with 10,400 tons, the charterers could have required the acceptance of a similar margin, say 3 per cent, above that quantity, relying on the provision that she was to take a full and complete cargo limited only by the declared quantity; that is, the shipowners could not have relied on the minimum quantity of his declaration.[58]

30.34 **Failure to provide cargo**   If there is a failure on the part of the charterer to provide cargo on arrival of the vessel at the port of loading, the shipowner must wait for laytime to expire. But even then he may not withdraw his ship until it is either clear that the charterer has no intention of loading a cargo or if the delay is such as to frustrate the object of the charterparty. This emerged in the case of *Universal Cargo Carriers v Citati*.[59] The *Catherine D Goulandris* was chartered to load a quantity of scrap iron for carriage from Basrah to Buenos Aires (Argentina). When the vessel arrived at Basrah the charterer failed to nominate an effective shipper and waited off the port. Three days before the expiry date for laytime, when no cargo had yet been provided, the owners cancelled the charterparty

---

[56] See also *Triton Navigation Ltd v Vitol SA (The Nikmary)* [2003] EWCA Civ 1715; [2004] 1 Lloyd's Rep 55.
[57] [1960] 2 QB 49 (CA).
[58] At 57.
[59] [1957] 2 QB 401.

and re-chartered the vessel. The owners claimed damages for breach of contract on the grounds of the charterers' breach of a condition of the contract (to provide cargo) and hence that their conduct amounted to a repudiation of the charterparty. Devlin J first pointed out that the obligation to nominate a berth, or shipper, and to provide a cargo, were obligations preliminary to loading the cargo. Loading had to be completed within the laydays and the charterer would be in breach of contract if he failed to do so. It followed that the nomination of the berth and the provision of cargo had to be made in sufficient time to enable the vessel to be completely loaded within the laydays. Devlin J found that the breaches by the charterer were of a warranty, not a condition of the charterparty. Accordingly, there was no right to rescind, but only a claim in damages in the form of demurrage. But what about the effect of a prolonged delay? Was this a frustration of the charterparty? Devlin J stated that:

> On the facts, it seems plain that by July 18 the charterer had got no cargo to ship, and indeed no shipper, and that he was in the position of having within three days of the expiry of the laydays to begin a search for a shipper of a cargo of a commodity which was not easy to find. It can be argued that a contract under which a ship is expected to go and hang about while the charterer negotiates for a cargo is, commercially speaking, a quite different venture from that which the ordinary charterparty contemplates. I do not find it possible to say that the facts are so strong that the inference of frustration is the only one that can properly be drawn from them.[60]

Was the conduct of the charterer nevertheless a repudiation of the charterparty? Devlin J spoke at some length on repudiation evinced by a renunciation (either by words or by conduct) of one of the parties to a contract to discharge his responsibilities under it. An injured party could anticipate an inevitable breach; an anticipatory breach meant simply that a party was in breach from the moment when his actual breach became inevitable: 'The reason for the rule is that a party is allowed to anticipate an inevitable event and is not obliged to wait till it happens, it must follow that the breach which he anticipates is of just the same character as the breach which would actually have occurred if he had waited.'[61] If the owner could establish that the charterer had on July 18 'become wholly and finally disabled' from finding a cargo and loading it before delay frustrated the venture, then he was entitled to succeed.

Anticipatory breach   If the charterer expressly refuses to load, the shipowner may treat **30.35** this as an anticipatory breach of contract and withdraw the vessel before expiration of laytime. He must then take reasonable steps to mitigate his loss. Refusal to accept non-compliance with the undertaking to load will mean that the contract continues; the shipowner then has no claim if the charterer loads subsequently or a supervening event frustrates performance of the contract.

G. The Carrying Voyage

Shipowner's obligation   Once loading has been completed, responsibility for the **30.36** continuing performance of the charterparty will pass to the shipowner. As we have already

---

[60] At 435.
[61] At 438.

seen, at common law he has an implied obligation to proceed with reasonable despatch and to convey the cargo to its destination.[62]

H. The Discharging Operation

30.37 **Obligations** The obligations of shipowner and shipper are much the same as those at the port of loading, though obviously the operation is conducted in reverse. Laytime will run as soon as the vessel arrives at the port of discharge and is ready to unload. The responsibility for discharge will be shared between the shipowner and the consignee, although this may be modified by the custom of a particular port or the express terms of the charterparty.[63] The shipowner should move the cargo to the ship's side and the consignee must then make the necessary arrangements to transport it from the quay. Contractually, the shipowner is obliged to deliver the cargo to an identified person, namely the person named as the consignee in the bill of lading, but it could also be the the person to whom the bill of lading has been endorsed. In *Erichsen v Barkworth* Baron Bramwell stated that:

> The holder of the bill of lading is entitled to have the goods delivered to him direct from the ship. Assuming that in this case the holders were entitled to the lay days, they were not entitled to more; and within a reasonable time after the arrival of the ship they were bound to unload.[64]

30.38 **Failure of the consignee to accept delivery** The shipowner's contractual obligation is to make personal delivery of the cargo and so the master is not permitted merely to unload the goods onto the wharf. He will be required to allow the consignee a reasonable time in which to collect the cargo and only once this has elapsed, may he land and warehouse the cargo at the consignee's expense. In *Bourne v Gatliff*[65] the shipowner was held responsible for the loss of goods which he had landed in London, without waiting a reasonable time.

30.39 **Custom of the port** The requirement of personal delivery may be excused by the custom of the port or by an express provision to that effect in the charterparty. In *Chartered Bank of India, Australia and China v British India Steam Navigation Co*[66] certain goods were shipped to Penang to be delivered there 'to order or assigns' under bills of lading which contained the condition that

> in all cases and under all circumstances liability of the Company shall absolutely cease when the goods are free of the ship's tackle, and thereupon the goods shall be at the risk for all purposes and in every respect of the shipper or consignee.

The employees of the landing agents appointed by the defendants fraudulently delivered the goods which had arrived aboard the *Teesta* to persons other than the consignees. The House of Lords held that although there had been no delivery

> . . . their Lordships cannot think that there is any ambiguity in the clause providing for cesser of liability. It seems to be perfectly clear. There is no reason why it should not be held

---

[62] As to this, see ch 25.
[63] Gencon 1994, cl 1, lines 12–14 + Box 11 + cl 5(a), lines 50–59; Asbatankvoy, cl 1 + Part D + cl 10.
[64] (1858) 3 H&N 601, 616; 157 ER 608, 615. See the previous discussion on the shipowners' contractual obligation to deliver only on presentation of a bill of lading: ch 10.
[65] (1844) 11 C&F 45; 8 ER 1019.
[66] [1909] AC 369.

operative and effectual in the present case. They agree with the learned Chief Justice that it affords complete protection to the respondent company.[67]

Statute Shipowners were formerly protected, other than at common law, by the Merchant **30.40** Shipping Act 1894, Part VII,[68] but this was repealed by the Statute Law (Repeals) Act 1993.[69] It has not been reproduced in the Merchant Shipping Act 1995, a consolidating statute, on the assumption that delivery tends now to be regulated by the parties in their terms of contract.

Delivery of mixed or unidentifiable cargo The obligation of the shipowner is to deliver **30.41** to the consignee at the port of discharge the quantity of goods shipped and in the condition in which they were shipped. Where goods have become mixed and unidentifiable, it is possible to distinguish between two classes: where these result from excepted perils and where the cause of the peril is not an excepted peril.

Excepted perils The shipowner will avoid liability in such a situation, and the consignees **30.42** become tenants in common of the mixed goods in proportion to their respective interests and the shipowner must deliver to them proportionately. The effect of this is that if A's 60,000 tonnes of oil are mixed with B's 40,000, they share the 100,000 tonnes resulting in the ratio 3:2 and any shrinkage arising from the fault of neither is shared in the same proportion. The leading case is *Spence v Union Marine Insurance Co Ltd.*[70] Here cotton belonging to different owners was shipped from Mobile to Liverpool in specially marked bales. On her voyage the vessel was wrecked, all the cotton was more or less damaged, some of it was lost, and some was so damaged that it had to be sold at an intermediate port. The rest was sent on to Liverpool. As a result of the wreck, the marks on all but a portion of that sent on to Liverpool were obliterated. The plaintiff was the holder of a bill of lading for 43 bales. Of these two only were identifiable in Liverpool and were sent on to him. The case involved an action by him against the underwriters for his total loss, ie 41 bales. The unidentifiable part of the cargo had all been sold and the proceeds divided among the owners who had not received their goods, in proportion to the number of bales short delivered. Bovill J rejected the plaintiff's argument and formulated the principle as follows:

> . . . [W]hen goods of different owners become by accident so mixed together as to be undis-tinguishable, the owners of the goods so mixed become tenants in common of the whole in the proportions which they have severally contributed to it . . . It has long been settled in our law, that, where goods are mixed so as to become undistinguishable, by the wrongful act or default of one owner, he cannot recover, and will not be entitled to his proportion, or any part of the property, from the other owner: but no authority has been cited to shew that any such principle has ever been applied, nor indeed could it be applied, to the case of an accidental mixing of the goods of two owners; and there is no authority nor sound reason for saying that the goods of several persons which are accidentally mixed together thereby absolutely cease to be the property of their several owners, and become *bona vacantia*.[71]

In a similar case, *Indian Oil Corporation Ltd v Greenstone Shipping SA Panama (The Ypatianna)*[72] there was an admixture of a consignment of 75,000 tons of Russian crude oil

---

[67] At 375–376 (Lord Macnaghten).
[68] 57 & 58 Vict, c 60, ss 492–498.
[69] c 50: Sch I, Part XV.
[70] (1868) LR 3 CP 427.
[71] At 437–438.
[72] [1987] 2 Lloyd's Rep 286.

on a tanker bound for India. Already aboard was a quantity of 9,545 barrels of Iranian crude left over from an earlier voyage. When the consignees of the Russian oil claimed to be entitled to the Iranian oil on the ground of the carrier's wrongful mixture, Staughton J held, applying *Spence*, that the total was owned in common between the consignees and the shipowner and so the consignees were not entitled to the residue remaining after their cargo had been pumped out:

> . . . [W]here B wrongfully mixes the goods of A with goods of his own, which are substantially of the same nature and quality, and they cannot in practice be separated, the mixture is held in common and A is entitled to receive out of it a quantity equal to that of his goods which went into the mixture, any doubt as to that quantity being resolved in favour of A. He is also entitled to claim damages from B in respect of any loss he may have suffered, in respect of quality or otherwise, by reason of the admixture.[73]

30.43 **Absence of an excepted peril**   Where the cause of the mishap is not an excepted peril, the shipowner will be in breach of his obligation to deliver the specified goods to the consignee and will not be able to reduce his liability by requiring the consignee to accept an appropriate proportion of the mixed goods. The leading case is *Sandeman (FS) & Sons v Tyzack and Branfoot Shipping Co* which came on appeal to the House of Lords from the Court of Session of Scotland.[74] Here a quantity of barrels of jute were shipped aboard the *Fulwell* to various consignees under bills of lading which recorded the relevant identification marks. The bales were specifically marked, but the shipowner was exempted from liability for 'obliteration or absence of marks'. When the cargo was unloaded, 14 bales were missing and 11 others could not be identified as belonging to any particular consignment. The plaintiff consignee claimed a short delivery of six bales from his consignment. The shipowner argued that the consignee should be required to accept an appropriate proportion of the 11 unidentifiable bales in mitigation of his loss. The House of Lords rejected the shipowner's argument; he was only entitled to succeed if he could prove that the plaintiff's missing bales were to be found among the 11 unidentifiable bales. Only then would he be able to rely on the exception in the bill of lading covering 'obliteration or absence of marks'. Lord Moulton said that

> . . . in the present case there is not the slightest proof that any of the goods shipped under the bills of lading issued to the defenders are to be found in the unidentifiable bales. Everything, indeed, points the other way, because they are of a wholly different quality to any of the jute purported to be shipped by the defenders . . . It follows, therefore, that . . . the doctrines as to the effect of a confusion of goods . . . afford no ground for requiring the defenders to accept the position of co-owners of the unidentifiable bales.

> The [shipowners'] duty is to deliver the goods entrusted to them for carriage, and they do not perform that duty if all that the consignee obtains is a right to claim as tenant in common a mixture of those goods with the goods of other people.[75]

Where goods are shipped in bulk under different bills of lading covering undivided portions of the bulk, and the cargo is damaged on the voyage, the shipowner is not under any obligation to apportion the loss, or the damaged goods, between the various holders. He is entitled to make complete delivery of sound goods to the first consignee on delivery.

---

[73] At 298.
[74] [1913] AC 680.
[75] At 696–697.

31

LAYTIME AND DEMURRAGE

A. Introduction

Overview   In the previous chapter we looked at some of the main substantive provisions **31.01** which are commonly found in voyage charterparties. In this chapter we turn our attention to the subject of laytime and demurrage,[1] which is an integral part of the law relating to voyage charterparties. A crucial clause in any charterparty is that specifying the period of time which is available for the loading and unloading of cargo, the laydays. The laydays are usually free of charge to the charterer who is usually regarded as having paid for them in the freight. If the laydays are exceeded, the charterer has to pay compensation to the shipowner either in the form of agreed damages (demurrage) or liquidated damages (damages for detention). There are essentially two competing interests, those of the charterer and those of the shipowner. The former will wish to secure an adequate number of laydays to cover any unexpected contingencies which may arise during the process of loading or discharge of the cargo, while the latter would wish to have his ship available for sailing elsewhere in pursuance of further employment.[2]

---

[1] See too the earlier discussion at para 1.37. For detailed coverage of the entire topic, see especially Williams (1999), ch 1; Cooke (2001); Schofield (2005).

[2] For an example of laytime provisions in a charterparty, see in particular Gencon 1994, Box 16 and cl 6; Asbatankvoy, cl 7.

B. Commencement of Laytime

31.02 **Introduction** The first difficulty is to determine when laytime commences.[3] The usual formula requires two conditions, the first of these being that the vessel must become an 'arrived ship' by reaching the point of destination specified in the charter and the second being that a valid notice of readiness must have been given. It may happen that congestion prevents a vessel from reaching its agreed destination (ie it cannot then become an 'arrived ship') and consequently the risk of the resulting delay falls on the shipowner unless he has inserted a clause in the charterparty providing that time waiting for a berth is to count as laytime. Once the ship is an 'arrived ship', laytime begins to run within a specified period of the shipowner giving notice of readiness to load, for example:

> Laytime for loading and discharging shall commence at 13.00 hours, if notice of readiness is given up to and including 12.00 hours, and at 06.00 hours next working day if notice given during office hours after 12.00 hours. Notice of readiness at loading port to be given to the Shippers named in Box 17 or if not named, to the Charterers or their agents named in Box 18. Notice of readiness at the discharging port to be given to the Receivers or, if not known, to the Charterers or their agents named in Box 19.[4]

Laytime runs against the charterer as from that time and it is therefore essential that the charter give a reasonably accurate indication of the time at which the vessel is likely to reach the loading port, in order that he may ensure that the cargo is available. The normal procedure is for the charter to name a date at which the vessel is expected to be ready to load at the loading port and to couple it with a cancelling date after which the charterer has an option of terminating the charter if the vessel has still not arrived. Again there is a conflict between the interests of the shipowner on the one hand and that of the charterer on the other. The former will wish to have as long a period as possible between the two dates whereas the latter would wish to seek to secure the shortest possible time in order to minimize the costs to him of storage at the loading port.[5]

31.03 **Voylayrules** The *Voyage Charterparty Laytime Interpretation Rules 1993* (*Voylayrules 93*) are issued jointly by the Baltic and International Maritime Council (BIMCO), Copenhagen, Comité Maritime International (CMI), Antwerp, the Federation of National Associations of Ship Brokers and Agents (FONASBA), London, and INTERCARGO, London.[6] The definitions contained in the *Voylayrules 93* are not binding on any court of law, nor on anyone else, unless the parties agree to an additional clause in the charterparty, such as one to the effect that:

> The words or phrases used in this charterparty shall be interpreted in accordance with the *Voylayrules 93* in so far as any dispute in connection with laytime/demurrage is concerned.

This is also expressly provided for in the preamble to the *Voylayrules 93*:

> The interpretations of words and phrases used in a charterparty, as set out below, and the corresponding initials if customarily used, shall apply when expressly incorporated in the

---

[3] See for specialist treatment, Davies (2006).
[4] Gencon 1994, cl 6(c), lines 101–108.
[5] For discussion of this lay/can period, see para 30.18.
[6] The predecessor of these rules was the *Charterparty Laytime Definitions 1980*.

charterparty, wholly or partly, save only to the extent that they are inconsistent with any express provision of it.

The Baltic Code 2000   The Baltic Code 2000 also includes charterparty laytime   **31.04** terminology and definitions.

C. The Arrived Ship

Types of charter   Voyage charters are essentially of three types, depending on whether   **31.05** the loading (or discharging) point has been specified as a berth, a dock, or a port.[7]

Berth charters   The *Voylayrules 93* define a 'berth' in the following terms: **31.06**

2. 'Berth' — shall mean the specific place within the port where the vessel is to load or discharge. If the word 'berth' is not used, but the specific place is (or is to be) identified by its name, this definition shall still apply.[8]

Thus a berth is an individual loading point on a jetty, wharf or in a dock, usually referred to by number, such as 'No 1 berth', 'No 2 berth'. In the case of a berth charterparty the specified destination is reached when the vessel is in that berth. Thus, in *North River Freighters Ltd v President of India*, Jenkins LJ stated that:

. . . [I]n the case of a berth charter (that is to say, a charter which requires the vessel to proceed for loading to a particular berth either specified in the charter or by the express terms of the charter to be specified by the charterer) lay days do not begin to run until the vessel has arrived at the particular berth, is ready to load, and has given notice to the charterer in manner prescribed by the charter of her readiness to load.[9]

The risk of delay in reaching the specified berth has to be borne by the shipowner, unless there is some clause in the charterparty which transfers the risk to the charterer.

Dock/wharf   A dock is usually defined as 'an artificial basin excavated round with   **31.07** masonry and fitted with flood gates, into which ships are received for purposes of loading and unloading or for repair'.[10] As is the case with a berth charterparty, the ship only becomes an 'arrived ship' when it enters the specified dock. The risk of delay in reaching the specified dock will be borne by the shipowner, unless the risk is transferred to the charterer.

Port charterparties   The major difficulty is in formulating the test for an 'arrived ship' in the   **31.08** case of a port charterparty. This is because a port may be defined in legal, administrative, fiscal, geographical, or commercial terms. The *Voylayrules 93* provide the following definition:

1. 'Port' — shall mean an area, within which vessels load or discharge cargo whether at berths, anchorages, buoys or the like, and shall also include the usual places where ships wait for their turn or are ordered or obliged to wait for their turn no matter the distance from that area.

---

[7] Gencon 1994, cl 1 (lines 8–9) requires the vessel to 'proceed to the loading port(s) or place(s) stated in Box 10 . . .'.

[8] cf cl 2 of the Baltic Code.

[9] [1955] 2 Lloyd's Rep 668 (CA), 679.

[10] *Shorter Oxford Dictionary*. See *Bastifell v Lloyd* (1862) 1 H & C 388; 158 ER 936.

If the word 'port' is not used, but the port is (or is to be) identified by its name, this definition shall still apply.[11]

31.09   *The Johanna Oldendorff*   The leading case is *EL Oldendorff & Co GmbH v Tradax Export SA (The Johanna Oldendorff)*.[12] The *Johanna Oldendorff* was chartered to carry grain to one of six ports at the charterer's option. The charterer ordered her to discharge her cargo at Liverpool/Birkenhead. On 3 January 1972 she anchored at the Mersey Bar anchorage on the instructions of the port authority and waited for a berth to become available. Her anchorage was some 17 miles from the dock area but within the administrative limits of the port. It was the usual waiting place for grain ships discharging at the port. The *Johanna Oldendorff* did not berth until 21 January. Was she an 'arrived ship' when she arrived at the Mersey Bar or when she took up her berth 16 days later? The House of Lords extended the area within which a ship may be 'arrived' to include not merely 'that part of the port where a ship can be loaded when a berth is available'[13] but the whole area of the port 'in its commercial sense', ie as understood by shippers, charterers, and shipowners. Accordingly, the *Johanna Oldendorff* was an 'arrived ship' when she reached the anchorage, for she was then at the immediate and effective disposition of the charterer. The House of Lords recognized that anchorage might or might not coincide with the legal area of the port. The area within which the port authority exercised powers regulating the movements and conduct of ships might be an indication, although powers over matters such as pilotage were sometimes exercised far beyond the limits of the port in its commercial sense. Lord Reid expressed his test in these terms:

> I would therefore state what I would hope to be the true legal position in this way. Before a ship can be said to have arrived at a port she must, if she cannot proceed immediately to a berth, have reached a position within the port where she is at the immediate and effective disposition of the charterer. If she is at a place where waiting ships usually lie, she will be in such a position unless in some extraordinary circumstances, proof of which would lie in the charterer. For as Mr Justice Donaldson [1971] 2 Lloyd's LR 96, at p.100, points out:
>
> > . . . 'In this context a delay of two or three hours between the nomination of a berth and the ship reaching it is wholly immaterial because there will be at least this much notice before the berth becomes free . . .'
>
> If the ship is waiting at some other place in the port then it will be for the owner to prove that she is as fully at the disposition of the charterer as she would have been if in the vicinity of the berth for loading or discharge.[14]

Lord Reid therefore lays down two conditions: (i) that the ship should be within the port and (ii) that she should be at the immediate and effective disposition of the charterers. It is generally recognized that the main difficulty with this reasoning is the first stipulation that the vessel must be 'within the port' in order to be an arrived ship. Many ports do not have coherently defined legal limits and there have been some notable examples of difficulty, most of which have been settled in arbitration.

---

[11] See cl 1 of the Baltic Code 2000.

[12] [1974] AC 479.

[13] This was the test suggested by Parker LJ in *Agrimpex Hungarian Co for Agricultural Products v Sociedad Financiera De Bienes Raices (The Aello)* [1961] AC 135.

[14] [1974] AC 479, 535–536.

Further cases   The matter arose for consideration once again by the House of Lords in   **31.10**
Federal Commerce and Navigation Co Ltd v Tradax Export SA (The Maratha Envoy).[15] Here an
unsuccessful attempt was made to widen the guidelines set out in *The Johanna Oldendorff*[16]
so that a vessel anchored at the usual waiting place would always be considered an 'arrived
ship' under a port charterparty, regardless of whether the waiting place was inside or outside
the port limits. The *Maratha Envoy*, a grain-carrying vessel, anchored at the Weser Light vessel on 8 December 1970 while awaiting a berth at the port of Brake. On that day she made an
excursion to Brake, turned there, and went back to the Weser Light vessel. She did the same
on 12 December. This manoeuvre was described by Lord Diplock as 'showing her chimney',
'a charade', and 'a voyage of convenience'.[17] Had the *Maratha Envoy* become an 'arrived ship'
by anchoring at the Weser Lightship? At first instance,[18] Donaldson J held that the *Maratha
Envoy* was not an 'arrived ship' either on 8 or 12 December 1970; her voyage had not ended
for she had merely been on a trip to Brake and back to the Light vessel. It was immaterial that
she was in the port of Brake in a commercial and legal sense when she was off the quay. She
could not validly tender notice of readiness. The House of Lords endorsed the earlier decision
of *The Johanna Oldendorff* in holding that the *Maratha Envoy* had not become an 'arrived
ship' by anchoring at the Weser Lightship. The anchorage was outside the mouth of the river
Weser and was outside the legal, fiscal, and administrative limits of Brake which was 25 miles
away. Further, charterers, shippers, and shipowners who used the Weser ports did not regard
the waiting area at the Lightship as forming part of any of the ports. Lord Diplock said that:

> Where charterers and shipowners as part of their bargain have desired to alter the allocation
> of the risk of delay from congestion at the named port which would otherwise follow from
> the basic nature of their contract, they have not sought to do so by undermining whatever
> legal certainty had been attained as to when a voyage stage ends. Instead they have achieved
> the same result without altering the basic nature of the contract, by inserting additional
> clauses to provide that time should begin to run for the purposes of laytime or demurrage if,
> although the voyage stage is not yet ended, the ship is compelled to wait at some place
> outside the named port of destination until a berth falls vacant in port.[19]

D. Charterparty Provisions Shifting the Risk of Delay

Introduction   We have now considered the position at common law where no provision   **31.11**
is made for covering delay resulting from congestion in the port. But congestion is such a
frequent occurrence that typically there will be a clause which shifts the risk of loss arising
from congestion from the shipowner to the charterer, before the ship is technically an
'arrived ship'. These clauses can take various forms and we shall consider four.

Clauses designed for specific ports   Where certain ports are commonly congested or   **31.12**
where the normal waiting place is outside the port limits, a typical clause will provide that
laytime is to run from the time when a ship reaches a specific point but cannot proceed

---

[15] [1978] AC 1.
[16] [1974] AC 479.
[17] [1978] AC 1, 12.
[18] [1975] 1 WLR 1372.
[19] [1978] AC 1, 14.

because of a shortage of berths or other obstruction. An example is *Compania Naviera Termar SA v Tradax Export SA (The Ante Tropic)*.[20] The *Ante Tropic* was chartered for the carriage of a cargo of corn from the US to London or Hull and was in fact ordered to discharge at Hull. Clause 17 of the charter provided that:

> In the event of the vessel being ordered to Hull and being unable to berth immediately upon arrival on account of congestion, time to count from next working period after vessel's arrival at Spurnhead anchorage but time used in shifting from anchorage to discharging berth in Hull not to count as laytime.

No berth was available on the vessel's arrival at Hull and she anchored at Spurn Head. When a berth became available she was unable to move upriver because of insufficient water and there was a delay of four days before she could do so. The charterers argued that this time should be excluded as being part of the time used in shifting. The owners argued that only the actual time of moving should not count. The House of Lords followed the view propounded by one of the majority judges in the Court of Appeal that the plain meaning of the words in the clause was that time used in shifting started when the vessel weighed anchor:

> Why should not the words be given their ordinary meaning? I do not think that one solves this problem by arguing whether the *Ante Tropic* was an 'arrived' ship or not when she reached Spurn Head, or whether she had completed her contract voyage, or whether the risks of delay on voyage are normally accepted by owners, and of delay in discharge by charterers, or on any principle that once laytime begins to run it does not cease to do so unless some express term in the contract applies or further delay is caused by default of the owner. To give the words their ordinary meaning seems to me in this case to make business sense.[21]

The House of Lords found for the shipowners and the four days fell for the charterers' account.

31.13 **Berth 'reachable on arrival'** Some charterparties include a clause requiring the charterer to nominate a 'reachable berth' on the arrival of the ship at her destination. An example is clause 9 of the Asbatankvoy charterparty:

> 9. The vessel shall load and discharge at any safe place or wharf, or alongside vessels or lighters reachable on her arrival, which shall be designated and procured by the Charterer, provided the vessel can proceed thereto, lie at, and depart therefrom always safely afloat, any lighterage being at the expense, risk and peril of the Charterer. The Charterer shall have the right of shifting the Vessel at ports of loading and/or discharge from one safe berth to another on payment of all towage and pilotage shifting to next berth, charges for running lines on arrival at and leaving that berth, additional agency charges and expense, customs overtime and fees, and any other extra port charges or port expenses incurred by reason of using more than one berth. Time consumed on account of shifting shall count as laytime except as otherwise provided in Clause 15.

The *Voylayrules 93* provide that:

> 3. 'Reachable on her arrival' or 'Always accessible' shall mean that the charterer undertakes that an available loading or discharging berth be provided to the vessel on her arrival at the port which she can reach safely without delay in the absence of an abnormal occurrence.[22]

---

20 [1966] 1 Lloyd's Rep 566 (HL).
21 [1965] 2 Lloyd's Rep 79 (CA), 85.
22 cf cl 3 of the Baltic Code 2000.

The courts have considered the effect of such clauses in a number of cases, many of which have concerned tankers.[23] The net effect of these cases is that the cause of unreachability is immaterial and no distinction is to be drawn between commercial congestions and navigational obstacles. The charterer will be in breach of contract if he nominates a berth that cannot be reached by the ship when it arrives at the port.

'Arrival'   In the context of this clause, arrival does not have the same meaning as the   **31.14**
requirement that the vessel has to be an 'arrived ship' for the laytime to start. Thus, the charterer will be in breach of the clause even if the vessel is forced to wait for the nominated berth outside the fiscal and legal limits of the port.

Physical obstruction and congestion   *In Inca Compania Naviera SA and Commercial and*   **31.15**
Maritime Enterprises Evanghelos P Nomikos SA v Mofinol Inc (The President Brand)[24] the port of discharge was Lourenço Marques. On arrival there the *President Brand* was unable to cross the bar to enter the port for four days because of her draught. When there was sufficient water for her to cross the bar, she did so, anchoring within the port to await a berth as another vessel was occupying the relevant berth. A berth became available later the same day, but the vessel was unable to shift until the following day on the afternoon high tide. On arrival at the second anchorage within the port she gave a valid notice of readiness. On the meaning of 'reachable', Roskill J said:

> 'Reachable' as a matter of grammar means 'able to be reached'. There may be many reasons why a particular berth or discharging place cannot be reached. It may be because another ship is occupying it; it may be because there is an obstruction between where the ship is and where she wishes to go; it may be because there is not a sufficiency of water to enable her to get there. The existence of any of these obstacles can prevent a particular berth or dock being reachable and in my judgment a particular berth or dock is just as much not reachable if there is not enough water to enable the vessel to traverse the distance from where she is to that place as if there were a ship occupying that place at the material time. Accordingly, in my judgment, the charterer's obligation was to nominate a berth which the vessel could reach on arrival and they are in breach of that obligation if they are unable so to do.[25]

Accordingly, it was the charterers who had to bear the risk of the delays caused by the vessel's inability to move into the port because of the bar and because of the congestion when she was able to enter the port.

Congestion alone   One of the leading cases is *Nereide SpA di Navigazione v Bulk Oil*   **31.16**
International Ltd (The Laura Prima).[26] The vessel was chartered on the Exxonvoy (1969) form,[27] which contained clauses similar to clause 9 of the Asbatankvoy form, to the effect that, on arrival at the port of loading, notice of readiness to load could be given 'berth or no berth' and laytime would commence either 6 hours later or when the vessel arrived at her berth if that occurred earlier. The clause concluded that 'where delay is caused to vessel getting into berth after giving notice of readiness for any reason over which the Charterer

---

23 See, eg, *Sociedad Carga Oceanica SA v Idolinoele Vertreibsgesellschaft mbH* [1964] 2 Lloyd's Rep 28.
24 [1967] 2 Lloyd's Rep 338.
25 At 348.
26 [1982] 1 Lloyd's Rep 1 (HL).
27 This form was the predecessor of the Asbatankvoy form.

has no control, such delay shall not count as used laytime'. The *Laura Prima* was required to load at one safe berth Marsa El Hariga (Libya) where she duly arrived and tendered notice of readiness (NOR). However, she could not berth because no berth was available owing to congestion, something over which the charterers had no control. When the owners claimed demurrage, the charterers claimed protection under clause 6 of the charterparty, alleging that the reason for the congestion was something over which they had no control. The House of Lords held that, although the time spent waiting for a berth was beyond the control of the charterers, laytime ran during the period of delay because the charterers could not rely on their own failure to designate and procure a berth which was reachable on arrival. 'Reachable on arrival' meant immediately reachable on arrival and clause 6 only protected the charterers once they had designated a loading place which actually was so reachable. It was only thereafter if some intervening event occurred causing delay over which the charterers had no control that the last sentence of the clause applied:

> 'Reachable on arrival' is a well-known phrase and means precisely what it says. If a berth cannot be reachable on arrival, the warranty is broken unless there is some relevant protecting exception . . . The berth is required to have two characteristics; it has to be safe and it also has to be reachable on arrival.[28]

Accordingly, the owners succeeded in their claim for demurrage.

31.17 ***The Fjordaas*** In *K/S Arnt J Moerland v Kuwait Petroleum Corporation (The Fjordaas)* [29] the vessel was chartered on the Asbatankvoy form for the carriage of crude oil from Mina al Ahmadi (Kuwait) to Mohammedia (Morocco). The dispute concerned the discharge of the oil at Mohammedia. The *Fjordaas* tendered NOR at 00.45 on 8 April but was unable to proceed to her berth because the port authorities prohibited night navigation. Attempts to berth the vessel during the next week had to be abandoned because of bad weather. Once the bad weather abated, there was a strike by tug officers. The vessel eventually berthed at 14.45 on 18 April. Were the owners entitled to claim demurrage? Steyn J found that the arbitrators, in finding in favour of the charterers, had failed to give the words 'reachable on arrival' their ordinary meaning. He stated that

> . . . the distinction between physical causes of obstruction and non-physical causes rendering a designated place unreachable is not supported by the language of the contract or common sense; it is in conflict with the reasoning in *The Laura Prima*; and it is insupportable on the interpretation given to that provision in *The President Brand*. . . . I believe it to be wrong.[30]

The owners accordingly succeeded.

31.18 **Bad weather** In *Palm Shipping Inc v Kuwait Petroleum Corp (The Sea Queen)*[31] the charterparty also included a clause similar to clause 9 of the Asbatankvoy charterparty. The *Sea Queen* had been ordered to load at Mina al Ahmadi (Kuwait) and had arrived off that port at 06.55 on 1 January 1985. She then tendered NOR. There was a delay until 14.00 owing to the unavailability of tugs and from then until 22.15 on 3 January bad

[28] [1982] 1 Lloyd's Rep 1 (HL), 6 (Lord Roskill).
[29] [1988] 1 Lloyd's Rep 336.
[30] At 342.
[31] [1988] 1 Lloyd's Rep 500. See too *Sale Corp of Monrovia v Turkish Cargo Lines General Manager (The Amiral Fahri Engin)* [1993] 1 Lloyd's Rep 75.

weather prevented the *Sea Queen* berthing. She finally berthed on 4 January. Saville J applied *The Laura Prima* [32] and held that the charterers had warranted in clear and simple words that there would be a berth which the vessel would be able to reach on her arrival so that if there was not, for whatever reason, the charterers had failed to perform their part of the bargain.[33] It would therefore seem that where there is a 'reachable on arrival' clause the ship does not have to be an 'arrived ship' in the technical sense for the charterer to incur liability. All that is required is that the ship should have reached a point either inside or outside the port; the charterer will bear the risk of delay in the form of liability for damages for breach of contract.

Double recovery We have seen that the meaning of arrival here is not the same as in the technical meaning of 'arrived ship'. If the vessel is also an 'arrived ship', with laytime commencing to run, would the charterer be required to pay twice for the same time? The Court of Appeal considered this issue in *Shipping Developments Corporation SA v V/O Sojuznefexport (The Delian Spirit)*.[34] The *Delian Spirit* arrived off the port of Tuapse (a Russian port on the Black Sea) to load a cargo of crude oil, but because of congestion no berth was available. The vessel anchored in the roads[35] and gave notice of readiness. She lay in the roads for five days before the berth became available. The Court of Appeal followed the reasoning of Roskill J in *The President Brand*:[36]

31.19

> . . . [I]t is said the charterers are liable in damages . . . and are also liable to demurrage after the laytime expired. [Donaldson J] accepted that submission, but I cannot agree with it. It would be most unjust that the charterers should be made liable twice over. The answer is given by a long line of cases which establish that where the charterers have been guilty of a breach causing delay, they are entitled to apply their laytime so as to diminish or extinguish any claim for the delay, leaving the shipowners to claim for demurrage at the agreed rate for any extra delay over and above the laytime. The reason is because they have bought their laytime and paid for it in the freight, and are entitled to use it in the way which suits them best, and in particular to use it so as to wipe out or lessen any delay for which they would otherwise be responsible. It seems to me that the charterers are entitled to their full laytime from Feb 19, 1964, when notice of readiness was given. After using up that time, they are liable for demurrage at the agreed rate . . . [37]

Fenton Atkinson LJ concurred:

> While in certain circumstances which I do not think it is necessary to attempt to define on the facts of this case you can have an arrival of a ship . . . before that ship becomes technically an arrived ship for laytime purposes, and therefore the charterer who has failed to provide a berth at the time of such arrival will become liable for damages for detention, once the ship becomes an arrived ship in the technical sense the position is different, and in my judgment the charterer gets the advantage of the laytime provided by the charterparty . . .[38]

---

[32] [1982] 1 Lloyd's Rep 1 (HL).

[33] [1988] 1 Lloyd's Rep 500, 502.

[34] [1972] 1 QB 103 (CA). Note that this case was decided before *The Johanna Oldendorff* (1973).

[35] The reference to the 'roads' is to a sheltered piece of water near the shore where vessels can lie at anchor in safety. This will often (but not always) lie within the port limits.

[36] [1967] 2 Lloyd's Rep 338.

[37] [1972] 1 QB 103 (CA), 123 (Lord Denning MR).

[38] At 124–125.

31.20   **'Time lost waiting for a berth to count as laytime'**   This clause is found in Gencon 1994, (lines 109–120):

> 6 (c) If the loading/discharging berth is not available on the Vessel's arrival at or off the port of loading/discharging, the Vessel shall be entitled to give notice of readiness within ordinary office hours on arrival there, whether in free pratique or not, whether customs cleared or not. Laytime or time on demurrage shall then count as if she were in berth and in all respects ready for loading/discharging provided that the Master warrants that she is in fact ready in all respects. Time used in moving from the place of waiting to the loading/discharging berth shall not count as laytime.
>
> If, after inspection, the Vessel is found not to be ready in all respects to load/discharge time lost after the discovery thereof until the Vessel is again ready to load/discharge shall not count as laytime.

The *Voylayrules* 93 provide:

> 21. 'Time lost waiting for berth to count as loading or discharging time' or 'as laytime' — shall mean that if no loading or discharging berth is available and the vessel is unable to tender notice of readiness at the waiting place then any time lost to the vessel shall count as if laytime were running, or as time on demurrage if laytime has expired. Such time shall cease to count once the berth becomes available. When the vessel reaches a place where she is able to tender notice of readiness laytime or time on demurrage shall resume after such tender and, in respect of laytime, on expiry of any notice time provided in the charterparty.[39]

31.21   **Purpose**   The aim of this clause is to shift the risk before the vessel becomes an arrived ship. In the case of a berth charter, it will cover the period while the vessel is waiting in port until a berth is available. In the case of a port charter, it will apply while the vessel is waiting inside the port in circumstances where it is not immediately and effectively at the disposal of the charterer. The crucial question is whether the reason for the delay is the unavailability of a berth due to congestion and not whether the vessel is forced to wait by weather or other causes.

31.22   *The Darrah*   In the leading case, *Aldebaran Compania Maritima SA Panama v Aussenhandel AG Zürich*, Lord Diplock gave the following explanation of the commercial reasoning behind the introduction of the clause:

> In a berth charter the effect of the clauses is to put the shipowner in the same position financially as he would have been if, instead of being compelled to wait, his vessel had been able to go straight to her berth and the obligations of the charterer to carry out the loading or discharging operation had started then. In a port charter the clauses are superfluous so far as concerns time spent in waiting in turn within the limits of the port. This counts as laytime anyway; it is laytime. The clauses would, however, have the same effect as in a berth charter in respect of ports like Hull or Glasgow where the usual waiting place is outside the limits of the port.[40]

The *Darrah* was chartered on the Gencon (1976) form to carry a cargo of cement from Novorossisk (a Russian port on the Black Sea) to Tripoli (Libya). The carrying voyage was completed on the vessel reaching a usual waiting place within the port limits of Tripoli. She therefore became an 'arrived ship' and gave notice of readiness on 2 January. Under the

---

[39] cf cl 23 of the Baltic Code 2000.
[40] [1977] AC 157, 166.

normal rules time had commenced to run and the question was whether periods of adverse weather and holidays/weekends, which would normally be excluded from laytime,[41] should be excluded from waiting time. The *Darrah* was unable to berth until 9 January owing to port congestion. The shipowners claimed that the 7 days and 6 hours spent waiting for a berth counted against the time allowed for discharge (which was 8 days and 7 hours) and that therefore just under 14 days' demurrage was due to them (worth about $10,000). But both the Court of Appeal and the House of Lords found in favour of the charterers. Where a ship was an 'arrived ship', waiting for a berth, the laytime provisions prevailed over the 'time lost waiting for a berth to count as laytime' clause. In the computation of time lost in waiting for a berth, the laytime exceptions had to be applied just as if the vessel had actually been in berth and laytime was running:

> 'Time lost in waiting for berth' in the context of the adventure contemplated by a voyage charter, as it seems to me, must mean the period during which the vessel would have been in berth and at the disposition of the charterer for carrying out the loading or discharging operation, if she had not been prevented by congestion at the port from reaching a berth at which the operation could be carried out.[42]

It is generally thought that the House of Lords reached the right conclusion in *The Darrah*. They defeated the rather startling position which had arisen whereby an owner was enriched simply because the absence of a berth prevented the charterer from using some of the exceptions which would otherwise have been available to him. The improved position is therefore that one would make a calculation as if the vessel had not been prevented from berthing because of congestion at the port and had moved into a loading or discharging berth immediately.

'Time to count whether in berth or not' (WIBON)   The WIBON clause is designed   **31.23** to deal with the problem of a ship, chartered under a berth charterparty, arriving at her destination and finding no berth available to her. When this occurs, such a clause allows the shipowner to give a valid notice of readiness to load as soon as the vessel arrives in port, provided that the other conditions for a valid notice are satisfied. In effect, such a clause converts a 'berth' charterparty, but only if the vessel is within the legal, fiscal, and administrative limits of the port. The *Voylayrules 93* provide that:

> 22. 'Whether in berth or not' (WIBON) or 'berth or no berth' shall mean that if no loading or discharging berth is available on her arrival the vessel, on reaching any usual waiting-place at or off the port, shall be entitled to tender Notice of Readiness from it and laytime shall commence in accordance with the charterparty. Laytime or time on demurrage shall cease to count once the berth becomes available and shall resume when the vessel is ready to load or discharge at berth.[43]

The Kyzikos   In *Bulk Transport Group Shipping Co Ltd v Seacrystal Shipping Co*[44]   **31.24** clauses 5 and 6 of the Gencon (1976) charterparty, concerning loading and discharging respectively, both provided that

---

41 ie laytime would be suspended during these periods.
42 [1977] AC 157, 165.
43 cf cl 24 of the Baltic Code 2000.
44 [1989] AC 1264.

time lost in waiting for berth to count as loading/discharging time. Time to count as per Clause 5 WIPON/WIBON/WIFPON/WCCON [whether in port or not; whether in berth or not; whether in free pratique or not; and whether Customs cleared or not] . . .

The dispute here concerned the liability of the charterers for demurrage of $30,435.72 at the port of discharge, Houston. On arrival at Houston the master had given NOR but at the time when notice of readiness was tendered the *Kyzikos* could not proceed to her eventual berth because of fog. Did laytime for discharging count during the period when the ship was prevented from proceeding to her berth by reason of fog? Lord Brandon stated that the phrase 'whether in berth or not' had over a very long period been treated as shorthand for what, if set out in longhand, would be 'whether in berth (a berth being available) or not in berth (a berth not being available)'.[45] He continued that:

> Two views have been advanced, at each stage of the proceedings, with regard to the meaning of the phrase 'whether in berth or not' in a berth charterparty. One view, put forward by the charterers and accepted by Mr Justice Webster[46] is that the phrase covers cases where the reason for the ship not being in berth is that no berth is available, but does not cover cases where a berth is available and the only reason why the ship cannot proceed to it is that she is prevented by bad weather such as fog. The other view, put forward by the owners and accepted by the arbitrator and the Court of Appeal,[47] is that the phrase covers cases where the ship is unable to proceed to a berth either because none is available or because, although a berth is available, the ship is prevented by bad weather such as fog from proceeding to it.
>
> . . . I am of opinion, having regard to the authorities . . . and the context in which the acronym 'wibon' is to be found in the charterparty here concerned, that the phrase 'whether in berth or not' should be interpreted as applying only to cases where a berth is not available and not also to cases where a berth is available but is unreachable by reason of bad weather.[48]

Thus the charterers won their case here; the NOR given on 17 December was not validly given and the clause only applied to congestion, not bad weather.[49]

E. Readiness to Load or Discharge

31.25 **Introduction**   Before laytime commences to run, the vessel must be both an 'arrived ship' at the designated port of loading and the shipowner must have given the prescribed notice of readiness to load. Further, the vessel must be ready to load.

31.26 **Purpose**   The *Voylayrules 93* provide:

> 19. 'Notice of Readiness' (NOR) — shall mean the notice to the charterer, shipper, receiver or other person as required by the charterparty that the vessel has arrived at the port or berth, as the case may be, and is ready to load or discharge.[50]

---

[45] At 1276.
[46] [1987] 1 Lloyd's Rep 48.
[47] [1987] 2 Lloyd's Rep 122 (CA).
[48] [1989] AC 1264, 1274; 1278–1279.
[49] This may be contrasted with the stricter approach of the courts in interpreting 'reachable on arrival' clauses. See para 31.13.
[50] See cl 21 of the Baltic Code 2000.

The purpose of the notice is to inform the charterer that loading may commence and this provides a starting point for the operation of laytime.

Form of the notice   At common law, notice of readiness may be given either orally or   **31.27** in writing, or, if no notice is given, the shipowner must show that the charterer was aware that the vessel was ready to load, having reached her specified destination at the first load port. Notice need not be given, in the absence of specific requirements to the contrary, at subsequent load ports or at discharge ports. However, it is usual for the charterparty to stipulate the form[51] in which notice of readiness must be given, to whom it is to be given,[52] and when.[53] If the vessel is not ready to load the notice will be ineffective and laytime will not commence to run. Before laytime can begin, it would be necessary to tender a fresh, accurate notice of readiness when the ship is actually ready to load or discharge.[54]

Place of notice   In *TA Shipping Ltd v Comet Shipping Ltd (The Agamemnon)*,[55] Thomas J   **31.28** considered the effect of a notice of readiness which was given at a time when the vessel was ready but for the fact that she had not arrived at the place required under the charter. The *Agamemnon* had been chartered for a voyage carrying uncoated steel pipes from one good and safe berth Baton Rouge to Brisbane. Clause 19 stated that the ship was at the South West Pass at the mouth of the Mississippi 'ready to proceed to loading port, weather permitting'. A further clause provided that

> 32. *Waiting for berth*
>
> If the loading/discharging berth is not available on vessel's arrival at or off the port of loading/discharging or so near thereto as she may be permitted to approach, the vessel shall be entitled to give notice of readiness on arrival there with the effect that laytime counts as if she were in berth and in all respects ready for loading/discharging, provided that the Master warrants that she is in fact ready in all respects . . .

Though the *Agamemnon* was indeed at the South West Pass, a customary waiting area for vessels about to enter the Mississippi, she had to sail from her anchorage due to severe weather warnings and the onset of Hurricane Opal. She subsequently returned to the South West Pass where NOR was given on 5 October at 23.00. However, the *Agamemnon* only arrived at the port at 10.25 on 7 October, where her designated berth was occupied. The court had to consider the effect of a NOR which was given at a time when the vessel was ready but for the fact that she had not arrived at the place required under the charterparty. Thomas J concluded that:

> When the notice of readiness was given at the South West Pass, the vessel had not, on the findings of fact made by the arbitrators, reached a point as close to the loading berth as she might be permitted to approach; she only reached that point when she arrived at the Baton Rouge anchorage at 1025 on Oct 7. Thus at the time the notice was given, the owners

---

51 See Gencon 1994, cl 6(c); Asbatankvoy, cl 6.

52 Such as to the charterer's load port agents or the loading terminal.

53 eg, whether at any time or only in office hours.

54 See *Galaxy Energy International Ltd v Novorossiysk Shipping Co (The Petr Schmidt)* [1997] 1 Lloyd's Rep 284, 285 (Longmore J): 'This is commercially sensible since the charterer cannot be expected to keep checking whether the ship is ready or not.'

55 [1998] 1 Lloyd's Rep 675.

had not complied with the terms of the charterparty for the giving of notice. It was not a valid notice and could not operate as the event to trigger the commencement of laytime.[56]

Thus, on the facts, the laytime only commenced on loading, not when the vessel reached the Baton Rouge anchorage.

31.29 **Time of notice** In *Galaxy Energy International Ltd v Novorossiysk Shipping Co (The Petr Schmidt)*[57] a charterparty on the Asbatankvoy form provided that:

> 30. *Notice of Readiness Clause*
>
> Vessel not to tender notice of readiness at loading port prior to laydays unless charterers give their consent to do so. Notice of readiness at loading and discharging port is to be tendered within 06.00 and 17.00 local time.

NOR was, in each case, given outside the hours stipulated in the charterparty. The charterers contended that the notices were invalid and of no effect, having been tendered outside the period specified in clause 30. They submitted that, in each case, laytime commenced no earlier than when the loading or discharging operation began. At first instance, Longmore J[58] concluded that

> the ship was ready when the notices of readiness were given. They were notices which stated the truth viz. that the vessel was ready to load or discharge as the case may be. The only thing wrong about the notices was the time that they were tendered, which was outside the contractual hours as specified in the contract. To say that such notices were invalid and must therefore be nullities begs the question. They were accurate but non-contractual in the sense that they were tendered outside the contractual hours. To my mind that does not make them invalid notices in the sense of being nullities.

The charterers subsequently appealed to the Court of Appeal,[59] submitting that a NOR was invalid and a nullity if it was tendered outside the period stated in clause 30. The shipowners submitted that the notices were 'tendered' when office hours began at 06.00 on the morning after the telex or fax messages were sent and Evans LJ agreed with this argument.[60] The charterers also submitted that the notices were invalid because the statements in them related not to the time of tender but to the earlier time when the messages were sent. Evans LJ accepted that a notice was invalid if statements made in the notice were in fact incorrect when the notice was tendered, received, or given. But it did not follow from this that the notices could not relate to the time when they were made. The primary requirement was always that they should be statements of existing fact. He accepted the charterers' suggestion that there was an implied representation that the statements were accurate at the moment when the notice was tendered. However, this did not mean that a notice given earlier was invalid because the statements (of present readiness) were made at some earlier time. In such a case, the implied representation was that the statement remained accurate when the notice was tendered.[61]

---

56 At 679.
57 [1998] 2 Lloyd's Rep 1 (CA).
58 [1997] 1 Lloyd's Rep 284, 287.
59 [1998] 2 Lloyd's Rep 1 (CA).
60 At 5.
61 Ibid. See now *Tidebrook Maritime Corp v Vitol SA (The Front Commander)* [2006] EWCA Civ 944; [2006] 2 Lloyd's Rep 251.

Waiver We have so far looked at the circumstances required for the giving of a valid   **31.30**
NOR. If the notice is invalid, a fresh notice should be given. In *Transgrain Shipping BV v
Global Transporte Oceanico SA (The Mexico I)*[62] the Court of Appeal considered whether
the giving of a fresh notice might be waived. Here a charterparty was for the carriage of
5,000 tonnes of bagged maize and contained the following laytime clause:

> 24. At loading and discharging ports Notice of Readiness shall be delivered . . . at the office
> of the shippers/receivers . . . Time to commence to count next working day 08 00 hours a.m.
> whether in berth or not.

The *Mexico I* was also carrying a second cargo of alubia beans for the charterers under a separate agreement and both cargoes were partially overstowed with beans and other cargo for
the owners' account. At Luanda, notice of readiness (NOR) was given on 20 January. The
maize cargo was not accessible for the purposes of discharge until 6 February (at which time
no further notice of readiness was tendered) and the cargo of beans was not available to the
charterers until 19 February. The owners claimed demurrage. On appeal the issues were
whether laytime for the maize commenced on 6 February or only on 19 February when discharge of the cargo of beans commenced. A further point was whether the contractual
arrangements for the cargo of beans meant that laytime for the discharging of the beans and
maize began only on 19 February, when the whole of the cargo was accessible. At first
instance, Evans J had stated that, when the charter required that a NOR be given, the charterer was entitled to insist that the laytime could not begin until the notice had been given.
The arbitrators had stated that by commencing discharge the charterers had waived any entitlement they might have had to a fresh notice of readiness. Mustill LJ, who gave the principal
judgment, confessed to 'some difficulty in finding the necessary elements of a waiver in the
bare fact that a discharge was carried out'[63] but he did not pursue this point. He stated that:

> To my mind the contract stated with absolute clarity what step must be taken to start the
> laytime, and I find it impossible to say that the taking of this wrong step is somehow to
> be deemed as the taking of the right step. Moreover, I would find it very odd if the contract
> had contemplated any such result.
>
> I would therefore agree with [Evans J] in his rejection of the argument that the notice
> [of readiness] was a delayed action device, effective to start the laytime automatically
> when, at a later date, the ship became ready to discharge the contractual cargo: and also the
> linked argument that time began when the charterers knew or ought to have known of
> the readiness.[64]

The Court of Appeal therefore held that laytime for the discharge commenced at the time
when the discharge itself commenced.

Waiver accepted In *Glencore Grain Ltd v Flacker Shipping Ltd (The Happy Day)*[65] the   **31.31**
Court of Appeal revisited the waiver point. The *Happy Day* was chartered for the carriage
of wheat and a clause (clause 28) provided that, if there was congestion, the master could

---

[62] [1990] 1 Lloyd's Rep 507 (CA).
[63] At 510.
[64] At 513.
[65] [2002] EWCA Civ 1068; [2002] 2 Lloyd's Rep 487. See too *Glencore Grain Ltd v Goldbeam Shipping
Inc (The Mass Glory)* [2002] EWHC 27; [2002] 2 Lloyd's Rep 244.

tender NOR 'whether in berth or not, whether in port or not'. Another clause, clause 30, provided that notice was to be given to the receivers or their agents 'during normal local office hours and laytime to start counting at 8 am next working day whether in berth or not, whether in port or not'. At the discharge port, Cochin, the *Happy Day* was unable to berth immediately because she had missed the tide. The master purported to give NOR immediately, although the next available tide was the next morning. The *Happy Day* berthed at 13.15 on 26 September. Given that the charter was a berth charter and there was no congestion, the NOR given outside the berth was an invalid notice. In fact, no NOR was ever given and discharge was only completed on 25 December. The owners argued that, notwithstanding clause 30, the laytime had commenced because the charter was a port charter and because the NOR was marked 'accepted' when tendered. The charterers contended that no valid NOR was ever given and claimed despatch. The arbitrators held that the charterparty was a berth charterparty and concluded that the laytime commenced at 08.00 on 29 September, the first occasion on which it could have commenced under clause 30 had a valid notice been given in accordance with that clause. Langley J allowed the charterer's appeal[66] but this was reversed by the Court of Appeal. In an appropriate commercial context, silence in response to the receipt of an invalid notice in the sense of a failure to intimate rejection of it, could, at least in combination with some other step taken or assented to under the contract, amount to a waiver of the invalidity, or could amount to acceptance of the notice as complying with the contract. However, on an objective construction, although the charterers were not under a contractual duty to indicate rejection of the owner's NOR, by their failure to do so, coupled with their assent to the commencement of discharging operations, they intimated, and the reasonable shipowner would have concluded, that they thereby waived reliance on any invalidity in the NOR and any requirement for further notice. Laytime could commence when no valid NOR had been served in circumstances where (i) NOR valid in form was served upon the charterers or receivers as required under the charterparty prior to the arrival of the vessel, (ii) the vessel thereafter arrived and was, or was accepted to be, ready to discharge to the knowledge of the charterers, (iii) discharge commenced to the order to the charterers or receivers without either having given any intimation of rejection or reservation in respect of the NOR previously served or any indication that further NOR was required before laytime commenced. Where this occurred the charterers would be deemed to have waived reliance upon the invalidity of the original notice as from the time of commencement of discharge and laytime would commence as if a valid NOR had been served at that time. Accordingly, laytime had commenced on 29 September 1998. Potter LJ stated that:

> In my view the circumstances of the case and the demands of commercial good sense are such that the Court should be reluctant to apply or adopt doubts expressed in *obiter dicta* (even from so distinguished a source as Lord Justice Mustill) so as to arrive at a result whereby, despite the fact that the vessel has arrived, NOR has been tendered and the unloading operation commenced without any reservation expressed in respect of it, the charterers are free of any constraints upon the time which they take in unloading and, despite delays for which they would otherwise be liable for demurrage, they are in fact entitled to despatch.[67]

---

[66] [2001] 1 Lloyd's Rep 754.
[67] [2002] EWCA Civ 1068; [2002] 2 Lloyd's Rep 487, at [77].

The Court of Appeal clearly took to heart the argument by the owners that the earlier outcome was 'legally misguided [and] produced a commercially absurd result'[68] where a charterer, aware of the readiness of the vessel, had taken three months to discharge the cargo and only later disputed the validity of the NOR. The Court of Appeal's decision must mean that charterers, if they object to the issue of a NOR, should communicate this to the owners. Failure to do so on the part of charterers may, in the light of this case, mean that they will be deemed to have waived the need for a second, valid, NOR. From the owners' point of view, it will undoubtedly be wise to send repeated NORs in any case where there is a doubt about the validity of an earlier NOR.

Actual readiness to load   Whether or not a vessel is in fact ready to load will depend on: **31.32** her position; her physical ability to receive the cargo; whether she has complied with all the port health and other documentary requirements.

Physical position   Notice of readiness to load may be given even though it is impossible **31.33** to commence the loading operation because the vessel is not in berth, for example, where the charter contains a WIBON clause. So far as physical condition is concerned, a ship would not be ready to load unless 'she is discharged and ready in all her holds so as to give the charterer complete control of every portion of the ship available for cargo, except so much as is reasonably required for ballast to keep her upright'.[69] The charterer is entitled to have access to all the cargo space. The ship will not be ready to load so long as even the smallest proportion of the previous cargo remains to be discharged, or ready to unload if overstowed cargo has to be removed before access can be gained to the charterer's cargo.

Overstowed cargo   The problem of overstowed cargo has resulted in several cases. **31.34** In *Government of Ceylon v Société Franco-Tunisienne d'Armement-Tunis (The Massalia) (No 2)*[70] a vessel was chartered with a part cargo of flour from Antwerp and Bordeaux to Colombo. The owners were given liberty to complete with other cargo and they did so, overstowing their flour loaded at Port Said in most of the holds. The laytime commencement clause at the discharge port provided that:

6. Time to commence at 2 pm if notice of readiness to discharge is given before noon, and at 8 am next working day if notice given during office hours after noon. Time lost in waiting for berth to count as discharging time.

On the day of arrival (18 October 1956) the *Massalia* gave notice at 9 am. Six days later (24 October) the vessel entered the port, discharge of the flour and overstowed cargo began. However, all the flour cargo was only accessible three days after that (27 October). Diplock J (as he then was) said that it was only then that laytime commenced because the notice referred to in the laytime commencement clause was a notice of readiness to discharge the charterer's flour.

Cargoworthiness   A further aspect of physical readiness is cargoworthiness, or the ability **31.35** of the ship to receive the contract cargo. This would embrace the holds being clear

---

[68] At [31].
[69] *Lyderhorn Sailing Ship Co Ltd v Duncan, Fox & Co* [1909] 2 KB 929 (CA), 938 (Cozens-Hardy MR).
[70] [1960] 2 Lloyd's Rep 352.

and free from any contamination, as well as the readiness of the required loading gear or special equipment required for particular cargoes. The contamination issue was explored in *Compania de Naviera Nedelka SA v Tradax Internacional SA (The Tres Flores)*.[71] Roskill LJ said:

> . . . [I]t has long been accepted in this branch of the law that a vessel which presents herself at a loading port must be in a position to give the charterer unrestricted access to all her cargo spaces before she can give a valid notice of readiness. This state of readiness must be unqualified. It is not open to the shipowner to say: 'Here is my ship; she is not quite ready yet but I confidently expect to be able to make her ready by such time as I consider it likely that you will in fact need her'. The charterer has contracted for the exclusive and unrestricted use of the whole of the vessel's available cargo space, and he is entitled to expect that that space will be placed at his disposal before he can be called upon to accept the vessel as having arrived and thereafter being at his risk and expense as regards time.[72]

In this case the vessel was chartered to load grain in Varnia, Bulgaria. The charterparty provided that notice of readiness could be given from the Roads at Barna and this happened because no berth was available. The vessel's holds were inspected by the port authorities prior to the loading of a cargo of maize and were found to be infested. As a result, the port authorities ordered the fumigation of the vessel and it was not until this was completed that the courts held that she was ready. In *Sofial SA v Ove Skou Rederi (The Helle Skou)*[73] a vessel was chartered for the carriage of skimmed milk in bags, the previous cargo having been fishmeal in bags. One of the charter clauses required the vessel to be presented with her holds clean and dry as well as being free from smell. The charterers accepted the vessel without verifying the state of the holds and commenced loading. The vessel was not in fact free from smell and eventually it became necessary to discharge the cargo of skimmed milk in order that the holds might be properly cleaned. Four days were lost doing so. The owners, though they admitted that notice of readiness should not have been given, denied that the charterers were entitled, as they contended, to reject the notice of readiness since they had begun loading. Donaldson J upheld the claim of the owners.

31.36 **Readiness of cargo loading gear** The issue of the readiness of the vessel's loading gear was considered in *Noemijulia Steamship Co Ltd v Minister of Food (The San George)*; Tucker LJ explained this as follows:

> It seems to me that there is a real distinction to be drawn between the cargo space and the gear. The charterer is entitled to the control of the whole of the cargo space from the outset of the voyage . . .

> The loading gear had not got to be placed at his disposal and he had no rights with regard thereto save in so far as it was necessary to enable the shipowner to perform his contractual obligations under the charterparty. Providing the shipowner was able, when required, to load any cargo which the charterer was entitled to tender to him alongside, it was a matter for him to decide by what means he would carry out his contractual obligations.[74]

The *San George* was chartered to load grain in Argentina and, if she was to be loaded from lighters rather than in berth, she would have to use her own cargo handling equipment.

---

[71] [1974] QB 264 (CA).
[72] At 276.
[73] [1976] 2 Lloyd's Rep 205.
[74] [1951] 1 KB 223 (CA), 235.

Her notice of readiness was rejected when she arrived because her derricks were not rigged and the charterparty was cancelled. The umpire in the arbitration proceedings found that there was no evidence whether the vessel was to be loaded at berth or from lighters, nor whether the derricks could be rigged without delay, if required. The Court of Appeal held that the charterer was not entitled to cancel the charterparty. It has been held that an 'arrived ship' under a port charter can give notice of readiness even though the hatches had not been removed or the discharging gear rigged, provided that such work could be completed by the time the vessel berthed.[75]

Legal readiness   The final aspect of readiness is legal readiness, which entails compliance   **31.37**
with port regulations, such as health requirements and the obtaining of the necessary documentation from the Customs, Immigration, and Health authorities. Customs may wish to inspect the ship's certificate of registry, the cargo manifest, the official log book, list of dutiable stores, crew list, and ship's articles. Individual ports and countries often add considerably to this list.

Free pratique   Shipowners have been allowed to give notice of readiness even though   **31.38**
they have not received free pratique, permission or licence granted by the port medical authorities upon arrival from a foreign port for her crew to go ashore and for local people to go aboard, or a police permit to move upriver. Thus Lord Denning MR stated in *Shipping Developments Corporation SA v V/O Sojuznefteexport (The Delian Spirit)* that:

> I can understand that, if a ship is known to be infected by a disease such as to prevent her getting her pratique, she would not be ready to load or discharge. But if she has apparently a clean bill of health such that there is no reason to fear delay, then even though she has not been given her pratique, she is entitled to give notice of readiness, and laytime will begin to run.[76]

The *Voylayrules 93* provide that:

> 23. 'Vessel being in free pratique' and/or 'having been entered at the custom house' shall mean that the completion of these formalities shall not be a condition precedent to tendering notice of readiness, but any time lost by reason of delay in the vessel's completion of either of these formalities shall not count as laytime or time on demurrage.[77]

The Linardos   In *Cobelfret NV v Cyclades Shipping Co Ltd (The Linardos)*[78] the *Linardos*   **31.39**
was chartered for the carriage of a cargo of coal from Richards Bay (South Africa) to Antwerp. Clause 4 of the charterparty provided that:

> 4. Time commencing . . . 18 hours after Notice of Readiness has been given by the Master, certifying that the vessel has arrived and is in all respects ready to load whether in berth or not . . .

> Any time lost subsequently by vessels not fulfilling requirements for Free Pratique or readiness to load in all respects, including Marine Surveyor's Certificate . . . or for any other

---

[75] See *Armement Adolf Deppe v Robinson* [1917] 2 KB 204.
[76] [1972] 1 QB 103 (CA).
[77] See cl 25 of the Baltic Code 2000.
[78] [1994] 1 Lloyd's Rep 28.

reason for which the vessel is responsible, shall NOT count as notice time, or as the time allowed for loading.

A typescript clause provided that:

> 25. In the event of vessel having to wait for berth at load/discharge port due to congestion then Notice of Readiness may be tendered by cable or telex or off the port whether in berth or not, whether in port or not, whether in free pratique, whether customs cleared or not.

NOR to load was given at 16.50 on 4 October 1991 but at this time a loading berth was not then available. The ship eventually berthed on the morning of 7 October but a marine surveyor failed her for loading because of water and rust in her hatches. The owners contended that a valid NOR was given on 4 October and that laytime ran as from 10.50 on 5 October. They argued that they were due $40,227.77 in respect of demurrage. The charterers argued that the NOR only became effective at 06.30 on 8 October, when the hatches were accepted as sufficiently clean. The arbitrator had found in favour of the owners. Colman J, in upholding the finding of the arbitrator, pointed out that in approaching the construction of the clauses of the charterparty

> . . . one must not lose sight of the fact that, although in general a valid notice of readiness cannot be given unless and until the vessel is in truth ready to load, it is always open to the parties to ameliorate the black or white effect of this principle by express provisions to the contrary . . .
>
> In my view, the words of cl 4 contemplate that subsequently to the giving of notice of readiness the loading of the vessel will be delayed. They further contemplate that the causes of such delay may be failure to obtain free pratique or unreadiness to load in all respects or other reasons for which the vessel is responsible . . . the effect of cl 4 is to contract out of the normal rule requiring that the vessel must be ready at the time of the giving of notice.[79]

31.40 *The Antclizo* *Antclizo Shipping Corporation v Food Corporation of India (The Antclizo) (No 2)*[80] involved a charterparty voyage from the USA to Bombay. Clause 34 provided that:

> At first or sole discharging port or place, time to count from 24 hours after receipt of Master's written Notice of Readiness to discharge given to Charterers or their Agents during ordinary office hours on a weekday before 4pm (similarly before noon if on a Saturday), vessel also having been entered at Custom House and in free pratique whether in berth or not.

The vessel arrived at the Bombay Floating Light (BFL) on 30 December 1973 and tendered NOR on 31 December. One of the issues in the case was a claim for demurrage by the owners. The charterers contended that the arbitrator had been wrong in finding that the vessel had customs clearance within the meaning of clause 34 once the prior entry procedure (one of three stages) had been completed. The issue of customs clearance was in part governed by the Indian Customs Act 1962. Parker LJ confirmed the finding of the arbitrator that the vessel was entered at the Bombay Customs House at the time notice of readiness was given. Accordingly the notice of readiness was valid and the appeal of the charterers failed.

---

79 At 31–32.
80 [1992] 1 Lloyd's Rep 558 (CA).

F. Calculation of Laytime

Introduction   We have so far in this chapter looked at the factors which will be needed   **31.41**
to start the laytime. In this section we look at some of the essential principles of laytime.
The *Voylayrules 93* define laytime as follows:

> 4. 'Laytime' shall mean the period of time agreed between the parties during which the
> owner will make and keep the vessel available for loading or discharging without payment
> additional to the freight.[81]

Laytime is therefore the period of time in which the loading or discharging operation is
to be completed. The cost of laytime is usually included in the freight payable and so
laytime will be at the free disposal of the charterer. In *Shipping Developments Corporation
SA v V/O Soujuzneftexport (The Delian Spirit)* Lord Denning MR observed that '. . . [the
charterers] have bought their laytime and paid for it in the freight, and are entitled to use it
in the way which suits them best and in particular to use it so as to wipe out or lessen any
delay for which they would otherwise be responsible'.[82]

Penalties   If the charterer exceeds the period of laytime then he will be required to pay   **31.42**
demurrage (compensation) or damages for detention to the shipowner. Devlin J said in
Compania de Navegación Zita SA v Louis Dreyfus & Cie:

> The shipowner's desire is to achieve a quick turn-around; time is money for him. The object
> of fixing lay days and providing for demurrage and despatch money is to penalise dilatoriness
> in loading and to reward promptitude.[83]

Customary laytime   Voyage charters may be divided into two types, depending on the   **31.43**
provisions for laytime which they contain. Where there is a customary laytime charter,
the laytime allowed will be the length of time which is reasonable in the circumstances
in the particular port with the particular ship at the time of loading or discharging. In
Lyle Shipping Co v Corporation of Cardiff, Romer LJ said:

> The first question we have to consider is as to the meaning of the not uncommon provision
> in a charterparty as to the ship being discharged 'with all dispatch as customary'. I think it
> is now settled that such a provision means that the discharge shall take place with all reason-
> able dispatch, and that in considering what is reasonable you must have regard, not to a
> hypothetical state of things (that is, to what would be reasonable in an ordinary state of
> circumstances), but to the actual state of things at the time of discharge and in particular
> to the customs of the port of discharge.[84]

Since this time will vary from ship to ship and time to time, it is not normally possible to
determine the time in advance. If the parties do not specify how much laytime is allowed,
customary laytime will be implied by law.

Fixed laytime   The other, more usual, type of laytime is fixed laytime. As the name   **31.44**
implies, laytime will be of fixed duration and may be described in terms of days or hours,
a variation thereof, or as a rate of working cargo. We will now examine the meaning of
these terms when used in the context of a laytime clause.

---

[81] See too cl 4 of the Baltic Code 2000.
[82] [1972] 1 QB 103 (CA), 123.
[83] [1953] 1 WLR 1399, 1401–1402.
[84] (1900) 5 Com Cas 397, 406.

31.45 Days The *Voylayrules 93* define 'day' as follows:

> 7. 'Day' shall mean a period of twenty-four consecutive hours running from 0000 hours to 2400 hours. Any part of a day shall be counted pro rata.[85]

In respect of days, the alternative to counting days from midnight to midnight (calendar days) is the conventional day where time runs in periods of 24 hours, starting from the time when the notice of readiness expired. The term 'running days' came into being towards the end of the nineteenth century as a means of distinguishing 'days' from 'working days' and includes Sundays and holidays. Thus the *Voylayrules 93* provide:

> 11. 'Running days' or 'Consecutive days' shall mean days which follow one immediately after the other.[86]

Similarly:

> 8. 'Clear days' shall mean consecutive days commencing at 0000 hours on the day following that on which a notice is given and ending at 2400 hours on the last of the number of days stipulated.[87]

The sequence of days can be interrupted by specific exceptions in the charterparty or by the proof of custom excluding certain days at the particular port. A working day is a day in the normal sense, in that it has 24 hours, and is used to describe those days at the port in question when work can normally be expected to take place. The *Voylayrules 93* provide:

> 10. 'Working days' (WD) shall mean days not expressly excluded from laytime.[88]

Originally the 'working day' may have been used specifically to exclude Sundays and holidays. In *Cochran v Retberg*, Lord Eldon held, with regard to what was then customary in the Port of London that . . . 'the fourteen days mentioned in the bill of lading means working days, that is a construction which excludes Sundays and holidays . . .'.[89] 'Working days' also excludes the local equivalent of Sunday in non-Christian countries. Thus in *Reardon Smith Line Ltd v Ministry of Agriculture*, Lord Devlin said: 'But there may, of course, be days in some ports, such as the Mohammedan Friday, which are not working days and yet cannot well be described as Sundays or holidays'.[90]

31.46 Weather working days This type of working day is one in which the weather allows the particular ship in question to load or discharge cargo of the type intended to be loaded or discharged, if she is then at a place or position where the parties intend her to so load or discharge. The *Voylayrules 93* provide:

> 12. 'Weather working day' (WWD) or 'Weather working day of 24 hours' or 'Weather working day of 24 consecutive hours' shall mean a working day of 24 consecutive hours except for any time when weather prevents the loading or discharging of the vessel or would have prevented it, had work been in progress.[91]

---

[85] See too cl 7 of the Baltic Code 2000.
[86] See also cl 11 of the Baltic Code 2000.
[87] See also cl 8 of the Baltic Code 2000.
[88] See also cl 10 of the Baltic Code 2000.
[89] (1800) 3 Esp 121,123; 170 ER 560.
[90] [1963] 1 Lloyd's Rep 12, 39.
[91] See also cl 12 of the Baltic Code 2000.

A leading case on 'weather working days' is *Compania Naviera Azuero SA v British Oil & Cake Mills Ltd*.[92] In this case a charterparty provided that a certain number of 'weather working days' should be allowed for discharge. There was in fact rain on several occasions during discharge, but this had not delayed discharge because work was not actively in progress at the time. Pearson J gave his own definition of the phrase:

> In my view, a correct definition of a 'weather working day' is a day on which the weather permits the relevant work to be done, whether or not any person avails himself of that permission; in other words, so far as the weather is concerned, it is a working day.

> In my view also, the converse proposition must be on the same basis. A day is not a weather working day, it fails to be a weather working day, in so far as the weather on that day does not permit the relevant work to be done, and it is not material to inquire whether any person has intended or planned or prepared to do any relevant work on that day. The status of a day as being a weather working day, wholly or in part or not at all, is determined solely by its own weather, and not by extraneous factors, such as the actions, intentions and plans of any person.[93]

Bad weather when the vessel is an arrived ship   It may sometimes occur that the weather **31.47** prevents a vessel getting into berth or when it is in berth may force it to leave. In the former case, provided the vessel has become an 'arrived ship', laytime will begin to run. In *Compania Crystal de Vapores v Herman & Mohatta (India) Ltd*[94] the *Maria G* was ordered to move off the berth to buoys by the harbourmaster because a 'bore tide' was expected and he feared possible damage to the jetty and the vessel. Devlin J held that the expression 'weather working days' could not be construed so widely so as to cover the circumstances of the case, in that if the effect of weather was not to interfere with the operation of loading but to render the berth unsafe the time so lost was not what the parties contemplated when they referred to weather working days. In *Dow Chemical (Nederland) BV v BP Tanker Co Ltd (The Vorras)*[95] the *Vorras* was chartered to load a cargo under the Beepeevoy 2 charter form. On arrival at the nominated loading port of Skikda (Algeria) the loading berth was occupied by another vessel. When that vessel left, the port had to be closed because of bad weather. After this, another vessel occupied the loading berth. Her loading was also interrupted by bad weather and, after she had left, the port had to again be closed. Even when the *Vorras* eventually got into the berth, her loading was continuously interrupted by the weather. The charterers argued that the effect of the bad weather was to postpone the expiry of the laytime. Clause 15 of the charterparty stated that laytime was '72 running hours, weather permitting'. Donaldson MR found that there was no case directly in point and that, therefore, he had to construe the words used in their natural meaning and, accordingly held that this meant '72 hours when the weather was of such a nature as to permit loading'.

Rates of loading and discharge   Modern charterparties sometimes base the calculation **31.48** of laytime on a specified daily rate of loading or discharging of the cargo.[96] In *William*

---

[92] [1957] 1 Lloyd's Rep 312.
[93] At 329.
[94] [1958] 1 Lloyd's Rep 616.
[95] [1983] 1 Lloyd's Rep 579 (CA).
[96] eg, 'The steamer shall be loaded at the rate of . . . tons per running day and at destination cargo to be received at . . . tons per weather working day'.

Alexander & Sons v Aktieselskabet Dampskibet Hansa[97] the vessel was chartered to carry a cargo of timber from Archangel to Ayr. The charterparty provided that the cargo was to be loaded and discharged 'at the rate of not less than 100 standards per day . . . whether berth available or not, always provided the steamer can load and discharge at this rate'. Discharge was not, however, carried out at the stipulated rate because of a shortage of labour and the shipowner claimed demurrage for seven days. Viscount Findlay in his speech pointed out that

> . . . if the charterer has agreed to load or unload within a fixed period of time . . . he is answerable for the non-performance of that engagement, whatever the nature of the impediments, unless they are covered by exceptions in the charterparty or arise through the fault of the shipowner or those for whom he is responsible.

> With regard to the construction [of the words 'always provided the steamer can load and discharge at this rate'] . . . such words should be read as referring merely to the physical capacity of the ship for discharging, and that where the inability to discharge was due to want of labour without fault on the part of the shipowner or of his servants, the charterer would not be protected by such words.[98]

31.49 **Working hatch** A working hatch is one from which on a particular day cargo is being worked and, once the hold served by that hatch is empty or full, the hatch ceases to be a working hatch. It is only after the completion of loading, when the precise quantities loaded are known, that the exact amount of laytime can be calculated. The leading case on this type of clause is *The Sandgate*.[99] Here a charter on the Welsh Coal Charter 1896 form provided for the carriage of a cargo of coal from Cardiff to San Rosario. The charter provided for an 'average rate of discharge of 125 tons per working hatch per day . . . .' The ship had four hatches and the shipowners argued that this meant a discharge rate of 500 tons per day. The charterers argued that this ignored the fact that once a hold became empty, it could no longer be described as a working hatch and they contended that the total discharging rate should be proportionately reduced as each hold became empty, without affecting the rate per hatch. The latter view prevailed both at first instance and subsequently on appeal. Thus Scrutton LJ, in rejecting the shipowners' argument, stated that:

> I come to the conclusion that . . . [the phrase cannot be read] as a roundabout way of saying what might have been said quite simply: 'I will discharge 500 tons per day out of four cargo hatches, 125 tons for each hatch'. What it does mean is to assume that the amount may vary per day, according as there is a working hatch — a hatch which can be worked because there is coal in it. Whether it was a reasonable agreement to make or not, it is not for me to say.[100]

In the case of *Lodza Compania de Navigacione SA v Government of Ceylon (The Theraios)*[101] a charterparty for the carriage of 4,500 metric tons of lentils from Lattakia to Colombo (Sri Lanka) provided:

> 17. The cargo is to be loaded . . . at the average rate of 120 metric tons per hatch per weather working day . . . cargo is to be discharged at the average rate of 120 metric tons per hatch per working day.

97 [1920] AC 88.
98 At 94–95. Lord Wrenbury dissented (at 101).
99 [1930] P 30 (CA).
100 At 34.
101 [1971] 1 Lloyd's Rep 209.

21. Vessel has 5 (five) hatches which shall be at all times available for loading and discharging.

The arbitrators held that an 'average rate per hatch per day' meant simply what it said and that to find the total daily rate all that was necessary was to multiply the rate by the number of hatches. If the total quantity loaded was then divided by this figure, this produced the allowed laytime. This view was upheld by Salmon and Widgery LJJ in the Court of Appeal. In particular, Salmon LJ said that the term 'working hatch' was used

> to denote a hatch which can be worked either because under it there is a hold into which cargo can be loaded or a hold out of which cargo can be discharged. Once the hatch has been loaded or discharged its hatch ceases to be a working hatch . . . Therefore the average daily quantity to be loaded into or discharged from the ship cannot be ascertained until the loading or discharging operations have begun, and may vary as those operations proceed.

> Since this vessel has five hatches, the clause seems to me to be a round about way of saying that the vessel shall be loaded and discharged at an average rate of 600 tons per day, that is to say five hatches at 120 tons per hatch . . . . The average rate . . . is only a rough average daily rate, negotiated no doubt after taking into consideration all foreseeable contingencies and in the light of all the relevant facts, including the size of the various holds.[102]

Some of these issues were considered further in *President of India v Jebsens (UK) Ltd (The General Capinpin, Proteus, and Free Wave)*[103] where the owners had let four of their vessels (including the *General Capinpin*) to the charterers for the carriage of cargo to India. The cargo discharging clause provided that:

14. (a) Cargo to be discharged by consignee's stevedores free of risk and expense to vessel at the average rate of 1000 metric tonnes basis 5 or more available workable hatches, pro rata if less number of hatches per weather working day . . .

What exactly was the effect of these words? The owners argued that the clause provided for an overall rate for the ship, 1,000 tonnes per weather working day, and that the added words qualified the clause as follows: (1) if, when the vessel commenced discharging, less than five workable hatches were available, the overall rate would be discharged pro rata; (2) if, in the course of discharging, any of the vessel's hatches were temporarily unavailable, the relevant period (to the extent that it had an impact upon the laytime) would not count towards the laytime used. The mere fact that the discharging of a particular hatch was completed did not of itself effect the computation of laytime, because the rate of discharging was not a rate per hatch, but an overall rate for the vessel. This approach was accepted by the arbitrators. The majority of the House of Lords upheld the approach of the arbitrators (and the Court of Appeal) in the following speech of Lord Goff:

> It is plain . . . that the clause did indeed provide for an overall rate of discharge, and did not expressly provide for a rate per hatch, despite the existence of well-known authorities dealing with clauses which so provided. [The arbitrators] were simply not prepared to ignore the express provision for the overall rate; they preferred to treat the reference to 'available workable hatches' not as substituting a rate per hatch for the expressly provided overall rate for the ship, but rather as imposing a qualification upon it.[104]

---

[102] At 211–212.
[103] [1991] 1 Lloyd's Rep 1 (HL).
[104] At 9.

G. Suspension of Laytime

31.50 **The principle** In respect of laytime which is not fixed (customary laytime), any obstruction which interrupts loading will excuse the charterer, provided that this is outside his control and that he has otherwise conducted the operation with reasonable despatch. Where the agreed laytime is specified (fixed laytime) in the charterparty, the charterer will be under a strict obligation to load/discharge within the prescribed time limit and will bear the risk of any obstructions unless they are specifically covered by exceptions in the charterparty or arise through the fault of the shipowner. Charterers have in the past been required to pay for time lost as a result of port congestion, strikes of stevedores employed by the shipowner, and the need to take on ballast to keep the ship upright during loading.

31.51 **Shipowners' fault** The charterer will not be required to pay if the delay is attributable to the fault of the shipowner. An example of this is *Gem Shipping Co of Monrovia v Babanaft (Lebanon) SARL (The Fontevivo)*.[105] The *Fontevivo* was a small tanker running under the Somali flag. She was chartered to carry gasoline from Turkey to Lattakia in Syria. Discharge of her cargo began but was not completed as the vessel sailed away claiming that the port was not safe owing to war risks. Three days later she was persuaded to return and completed the discharge of cargo. The question was whether absence from her berth counted as part of the laytime. Donaldson J pointed out that ' . . . the mere fact that the shipowner by some act of his prevents the continuous loading or discharging of the vessel is not enough to interrupt the running of the laydays; it is necessary to show also that there was some fault on the part of the shipowner . . . '.[106] He found that in this case there was no doubt as to the shipowner's responsibility for the actions of the master of the vessel who had decided to leave the discharging berth. Consequently time did not run against laytime during the period of the vessel's absence from Lattakia.

31.52 **Exceptions** Charterparties often include exceptions providing for the suspension of laytime and these usually relate to port congestion, strikes,[107] bad weather, delay,[108] civil commotion, and even 'any other cause beyond the control of the charterers', as was the case in *Induna SS Co Ltd v British Phosphate Commissioners*.[109]

31.53 **Breakdown in equipment** The case of *Portolana Compania Naviera Ltd v Vitol SA Inc (The Afrapearl)*[110] highlighted the effect of an exception clause relating to machinery. The *Afrapearl* was chartered for a voyage from two loading ports US Gulf to Dakar, Senegal and Gibraltar. The charterparty, which was on the Asbatankvoy form (with amendments), allowed 84 hours' laytime. The other pertinent clauses in the charterparty included clause 6, the notice of readiness (NOR) clause, which provided that, 'where delay is caused to the vessel after notice of readiness for any reason over which Charterer has no control, such

---

105 [1975] 1 Lloyd's Rep 339. See too *Stolt Tankers Inc v Landmark Chemicals SA* [2002] 1 Lloyd's Rep 786.
106 At 342.
107 For a recent example of such a strike clause, see *Frontier International Shipping Corp v Swissmarine Corp Inc (The Cape Equinox)* [2004] EWHC 8 (Comm); [2005] 1 Lloyd's Rep 390.
108 See *Triton Navigation Ltd v Vitol SA (The Nikmary)* [2003] EWCA Civ 1715; [2004] 1 Lloyd's Rep 55.
109 [1949] 2 KB 430.
110 [2004] EWCA Civ 864; [2004] 1 WLR 3111.

delay shall not count as used laytime or demurrage'. Clause 7 provided that time consumed in moving from the discharge port anchorage to her discharging berth was not to 'count as used laytime or time on demurrage'. The demurrage clause (clause 8) provided that:

> If, however, delays occur and/or demurrage shall be incurred at ports of loading and/or discharge by reason of . . . breakdown of machinery or equipment in or about the plant of the Charterer . . . or consignee of the cargo, such delays shall count as half laytime or, if on demurrage, the rate of demurrage shall be reduced one half of the amount stated in Part II . . .

At Dakar the *Afrapearl* tendered NOR on 10 July. The decision was made to discharge first at the M'bao sealine and, in due course, a pilot came aboard to assist in manoeuvring the vessel to this sealine, with the assistance of two tugs. Discharge was soon suspended as oil was observed coming to the surface. Although the *Afrapearl* remained at the sealine, on two occasions she left to await further developments at the anchorage. Discharge was eventually completed, but at a reduced speed. The shipowner sought demurrage (in the sum of US$455,851.44) as well as additional agency fees and expenses but the charterer relied on the exceptions clauses as excluding the running of laytime. At first instance[111] the court held that the shipowner was entitled to recover demurrage and additional agency fees and expenses. The charterers appealed, on the basis that the delays were caused by a 'breakdown of . . . equipment in or about the plant of the . . . consignee of the cargo'. The Court of Appeal allowed the appeal on the basis that once it was recognized that the pipe or sealine was 'equipment' and that there was a 'breakdown of equipment' if the equipment malfunctioned, whatever the cause of the malfunction it was difficult to conclude that there was no 'breakdown in equipment' within the meaning of clause 8.[112] It was plain that, in ordinary parlance, the breakdown caused the delay and that the evidential burden was on the charterers to show that there was a break in the chain of causation. Accordingly, the owners were entitled only to half-demurrage in the relevant period. Thus, following this case, just because a defect pre-dates a fixture or has occurred intermittently in the past does not mean that there has not been a breakdown.

Completion of loading We have already seen that laytime is for the benefit of the **31.54**
charterers. The shipowner cannot therefore complain if work does not commence immediately the ship is in position to load or discharge cargo or if there are delays during the running of laytime caused by the charterer's inactivity. In *Novorossisk Shipping Co v Neopetro Ltd (The Ulyanovsk)*[113] charterers, anticipating a fall in the market price of the cargo they intended to buy, ordered the vessel only to tender notice of readiness at the load port to themselves and not to berth and commence loading until so instructed by the charterers. Contrary to these instructions, the master tendered notice to the refinery and shippers, berthed, and commenced loading shortly after arrival. The purchase price of the cargo was linked to the date of the bill of lading, after which the market continued to fall resulting in a substantial loss to the charterers. The owners sought to resist a claim for damages resulting from the loss and argued that the charterers were not entitled to

---

111 [2003] EWHC 1904 (Comm); [2003] 2 Lloyd's Rep 671.

112 The Court of Appeal took a broad approach in line with the guidance given by Robert Goff J in his unreported judgment in *Olbena SA v Psara Maritime Inc (The Thanassis A)* 22 March 1982: see [2004] EWCA Civ 864; [2004] 1 WLR 3111, at [12]–[13].

113 [1990] 1 Lloyd's Rep 425.

delay loading since this would have meant the allowed laytime would have been exceeded. Steyn J said that:

> In terms of the charterparty the charterers were given a total laytime of 72 running hours. They bought that laytime and paid for it in the freight. They are entitled to use that laytime as they wish. Even if they can load in less than the stipulated laytime, they may keep the ship for the whole of the laytime. Their right to the whole of the laytime is not to be abridged by requiring them to commence loading at any particular time.[114]

31.55 Detention beyond the loading Can charterers detain the vessel once loading/discharging has been completed? This was considered in *Margaronis Navigation Agency Ltd v Henry W Peabody & Co of London Ltd*.[115] Here a ship (the *Vrontados*) was chartered to load maize at Cape Town. By the end of work on 29 December (Friday), virtually all the cargo had been loaded. The charterers then insisted on keeping the vessel over the holiday weekend and loading the remaining few tons the following Tuesday. This was in order that January bills of lading could be issued. On the question as to how and for what the permitted laytime should be used, Roskill J (at first instance) said that:

> A charterer is entitled to have that time to load, but once he has loaded, he must not use that time for some other purpose. But, so long as he has not completed loading, that time is his, and he is under no obligation to accelerate that rate of loading so as to shorten the time to which he is otherwise entitled.[116]

Accordingly the charterers were entitled to detain the vessel until the balance of the agreed cargo was loaded. However, this case should be compared with *Owners of the Steamship Molisement v Bunge y Born*. Loading was completed 19 days before the expiration of laytime but there was a delay of a further three days before the charterers presented bills of lading to the master of the vessel. The reason for this was that they had not made up their minds about where the ship should be discharged. In the Court of Appeal, Swinfen Eady LJ said that

> . . . if all the lay days are consumed in loading, there is no breach for which the charterer is liable; but in a charterparty in this form, where the ship is loaded at an accelerated rate, the charterer has no right to say that, as he might have taken more time to load the ship, he can detain her for the rest of the period which he might have occupied in loading without being liable in damages for detention.[117]

Accordingly, the charterers were held liable for damages for two days' detention. On completion of the loading stage of the operation, the risk of any subsequent delay passes to the shipowner.

H. Demurrage

31.56 A definition The *Voylayrules 93* define demurrage as follows:

> 24. 'Demurrage' shall mean an agreed amount payable to the owner in respect of delay to the vessel beyond the laytime, for which the owner is not responsible. Demurrage shall not be subject to laytime exceptions.[118]

---

[114] At 431.
[115] [1965] 2 QB 430 (CA).
[116] [1964] 1 Lloyd's Rep 173,186.
[117] [1917] 1 KB 160, 170.
[118] See too cl 26 of the Baltic Code 2000.

Devlin J in *Chandris v Isbrandtsen-Moller Co Inc* stated that:

> A demurrage clause is merely a clause providing for liquidated damages for a certain type of breach. It is presumably the parties' estimate of the loss of prospective freight which the owner is likely to suffer if his ship is detained beyond the lay days. The demurrage rate in this case appears to have been a good deal lower than the freight market rate; and I suppose I need not shut my eyes to the fact that a sum produced by demurrage is generally less than damages for detention, which are presumably assessed by reference to the market rate of freight at the time of the breach. To this extent a demurrage clause may be in practice a concession to the charterer. But I am not, and I do not think I could be, invited to consider it as different in its nature from an ordinary liquidated damage clause.[119]

The charterer will be in breach of contract if he exceeds the specified number of laydays. However most charterparties include a clause which states that the charterer may retain the vessel for a specified number of additional days in order to complete loading or discharging. Strictly speaking, demurrage is the *money* payable for time in excess of the allowed laytime, but the term is also often used to describe the *period* during which such money is payable. Gencon (1976) states of lines 101–104:

> 7. Ten running days on demurrage at the rate stated in Box 18 per day or pro rata for any part of a day, payable day by day, to be allowed Merchants altogether at ports of loading and discharging.[120]

Gencon 1994 has extended this. Lines 122–136 state:

> 7. Demurrage at the loading and discharging port is payable by the Charterers at the rate stated in Box 20 in the manner stated in Box 20 per day or pro rata for any part of a day. Demurrage shall fall due day by day and shall be payable upon receipt of the Owner's invoice.
>
> In the event the demurrage is not paid in accordance with the above, the Owners shall give the charterers 96 running hours written to rectify the failure. If the demurrage is not paid at the expiration of this time limit and if the vessel is in or at the loading port, the Owners are entitled at any time to terminate the Charter Party and claim damages for any losses caused thereby.

Rescission If the charterparty contains a demurrage provision, the shipowner may only **31.57** rescind the contract if the failure of the charterer amounts to a repudiation of the contract or the delay is so substantial as to amount to frustration. This will be the case whether the charterparty provides for a specific duration for demurrage or merely provides a demurrage rate, leaving the period unspecified. A demurrage clause, in effect, provides for agreed damages for detention of the vessel once the lay days are exceeded. The sum stipulated will be recoverable by the shipowner without the necessity of proving damage and will cover loss of freight arising under subsequent charterparties affected by the delay or a reduction of voyages possible under a consecutive voyage charterparty.

Court interference Demurrage clauses may be struck down by the courts if the rate **31.58** fixed is so high as to be extravagant and unconscionable in comparison with the greatest possible loss which could flow from the breach.[121] But the courts will not usually interfere

---

[119] [1951] 1 KB 240, 249.

[120] This clause was invariably altered because it was only during the specified period of 'ten days' that damages for delay in loading/discharging were liquidated at the rate stipulated in the charterparty.

[121] *Dunlop v New Garage* [1975] AC 79, 86 (Lord Dunedin).

where the rate of demurrage is low. One of the leading cases is *Suisse Atlantique Société d'Armement Maritime SA v NV Rotterdamsche Kolen Centrale*.[122] A charterparty was entered into by the owners of the *General Guisan* for the carriage of coal from the US to Europe for a two-year period. Eight voyages were performed during this time. Demurrage was incurred on each occasion of loading and discharge apart from the first. Had loading and discharge been completed on time, additional voyages could have been undertaken and the profit earned would have exceeded the demurrage paid on the reduced number of voyages. The charterparty did not provide that any minimum number of voyages should be undertaken during the two-year period. One of the reasons why so few voyages were performed was because the freight rate agreed for the whole period was relatively high and the demurrage rate did not reflect the high freight rates which could be earned at the start of the charterparty. After the freight rates had dropped, the owners claimed that the charterers had deliberately kept the number of voyages low because of this. All three courts who heard the case (Mocatta J in the Queens Bench Division, the Court of Appeal, and the House of Lords) rejected the shipowners' claim to recover the losses they said they had incurred. In the Court of Appeal, Sellers LJ said:

> It cannot, I think, be said that any breach of contract has been established except the failure on all but the first occasion to load and discharge within the laytime. I can find no other contractual obligation expressed or to be implied. That means that there was delay only and that the vessel was detained. The remedy for that delay is the liquidated damages which had been agreed and fixed by the demurrage rate.[123]

31.59 **Rate and payment of demurrage** As to the rate and payment of demurrage, Lord Diplock said in *Dias Compania Naviera SA v Louis Dreyfus Corporation (The Dias)* that:

> It is the almost invariable practice nowadays for these damages to be fixed by the charterparty at a liquidated sum[124] per day and *pro rata* for part of a day (demurrage) which accrues throughout the period of time for which the breach continues.[125]

He also said that:

> If laytime ends before the charterer has completed the discharging operation he breaks his contract. The breach is a continuing one; it goes on until discharge is completed and the ship is once more available to the shipowner to use for other voyages. But unless the delay in what is often, though incorrectly, called redelivery of the ship to the shipowners, is so prolonged as to amount to a frustration of the adventure, the breach by the charterer sounds in damages only. The charterer remains entitled to continue to complete the discharge of the cargo, while remaining liable in damages for the loss sustained during the period for which he is being wrongfully deprived of the opportunity of making profitable use of his ship.[126]

31.60 **Whole day's demurrage** Unless the charter provides for portions of a day, prima facie the shipowner is entitled to a whole day's demurrage if any time is used. Thus in *South Australian Voluntary Wheat Pool v Owners of the Riol*[127] a 31½ hour delay resulted in two

---

[122] [1966] 1 Lloyd's Rep 529 (HL).
[123] [1965] 1 Lloyd's Rep 533 (CA), 538.
[124] ie a specified sum expressed in pounds and pence.
[125] [1978] 1 WLR 261, 263.
[126] ibid.
[127] (1926) 24 Ll LR 363.

days' demurrage. The entitlement to demurrage will accrue usually on a day-by-day basis and payment will normally be made on completion of the voyage after the vessel has departed for her next fixture.

Laytime exceptions   Are laytime exceptions applicable to demurrage clauses? The answer   **31.61**
to this is that they are not unless specifically worded to this effect. Lord Reid, approving the statement of Lord Justice Scrutton, stated in *Compania Naviera Aeolus SA v Union of India* that:

> When once a vessel is on demurrage no exceptions will operate to prevent demurrage continuing to be payable unless the exceptions clause is clearly worded so as to have that effect.[128]

This issue arose for consideration in *Ellis Shipping Corp v Voest Alpine Intertrading (The Lefthero)*.[129] Here there was a charterparty on the Gencon (1976) form for a voyage between Lübeck and Hamburg to Bandar Khomeini. The cargo was about 25,000 tons of steel products. The charterparty provided that:

> 6.   . . . Time lost in waiting for berth to count as discharging laytime, whether in berth or not . . . *Time to count from arrival pilot station Bandar Abbass until passing pilot station Bandar Abbass, except for actual steaming time to and from Bandar Khomeini which to be excluded from time counting.*[130]
>
> 28.   Neither the vessel nor the Owners' nor Master nor the Charterers/Shippers/Receivers shall be responsible for any loss or damage or delay or failure in performing hereunder, arising or resulting from . . . restraint of princes . . .

The charterparty voyage took place during the Iran–Iraq War, so when the vessel arrived at Bandar Abbas there was a convoy system in operation. On 6 August 1983 the vessel joined a convoy to go to Bushire where the next available convoy for Bandar Khomeini was assembled. By 10 August, the pilot had turned back on the ground that the *Lefthero* was not able to make sufficient speed. If the vessel had proceeded on this voyage, she would have arrived there on 12 August, with eight laydays in hand. A further attempt was made on 22 August, but for the same reasons the pilot had to turn back. In due course it was agreed that the vessel's cargo should be discharged at Bushire. Discharge was eventually completed on 3 February 1984. Lloyd LJ found that, on the face of it, the words of clause 28 were wide enough to cover delay by the charterers in discharging the vessel. However, he emphasized that, in order to protect a charterer against liability for demurrage, the language of the exceptions clause had to be clearly worded to that effect. Further, the general rule that 'once on demurrage, always on demurrage' was applicable here even though the vessel was not already on demurrage when the peril ('restraint of princes') operated. He went on to say that:

> The typed addition to cl.6, under which time was to count from arrival at Bandar Abbas, shows that the underlying objective of the parties was to compensate the owners for any delay due to the operation of the convoy system. Of course, it would have been possible for an exception to override that objective. But it would take very clear words indeed.[131]

---

[128] [1964] AC 868, 879.
[129] [1992] 2 Lloyd's Rep 109 (CA).
[130] These words were added in typescript to the printed form.
[131] [1992] 2 Lloyd's Rep 109 (CA), 113.

Accordingly, he allowed the appeal by the owners and remitted the case to the arbitrators to calculate the demurrage to be awarded.

31.62 **Fault of the shipowner** Demurrage will not normally be payable where delay is caused by the fault of the shipowner or results from any action which he has taken for his own convenience. Demurrage will, however, accrue where the delay is accidental and not due to the fault of either shipowner or charterer. Some charterparties specify that demurrage is to be at half the normal rate for occurrences which are beyond the control of the charterer.

I. Damages for Detention

31.63 **The principle** A shipowner will be able to sue for damages for detention[132] if the laydays have expired and demurrage has not been provided for; or the time for loading or discharge is not agreed, and a reasonable time for loading or discharge has expired; or demurrage is only to be paid for an agreed number of days and a further delay takes place. In relation to the first two of these, the damages will be assessed by the court in relation to the actual loss suffered by the shipowner. In relation to the third, the court will assess the damages at a figure corresponding to the agreed demurrage rate. It would be open to either party to prove that such a rate does not represent the actual loss suffered by the shipowner. In *Moorsom v Bell* the charterparty allowed 50 days for loading and unloading with a further 10 days on demurrage at 8 guineas per day. The vessel was in fact detained for a further 65 days. Lord Ellenborough said that:

> If a ship is detained beyond her days of demurrage, *prima facie* the sum allowed as demurrage shall be taken as the measure of compensation. This is a rule both of convenience and justice. But it is open to the shipowner to show, that more damage has been sustained; and to the freighter to show, there has been less than would thus be compensated . . .[133]

In *Associated Bulk Carriers Ltd v Shell International Petroleum Co Ltd (The Nordic Navigator)*[134] the *Nordic Navigator* undertook a voyage between Newcastle (New South Wales) and Mitzushima (Japan) carrying a cargo of coking coal. After discharge of the cargo and cleaning of the holds, the vessel was let to the charterers for the carriage of a cargo of light crude oil from Seria (Brunei) to Kanokawa (Japan). When the *Nordic Navigator* was discharging her cargo at Kanokawa it was found that there was a small quantity of coal among the oil which had been discharged. It was another three weeks before any further oil was discharged, but this attempt was aborted because of insufficient available space in the shore tank. The *Nordic Navigator* then sailed for Owase where the local refinery refused the cargo. It was eventually discharged at Yokohama. The owners claimed demurrage for 30 days and freight for the voyages to Owase and Yokohama respectively. The charterers disputed their liability on the ground of the owners' failure to clean the holds or tanks. Neil J found, however, on the facts that the owners were not in breach of the charterparty; the owners had indeed exercised due diligence to ensure that the tanks were fit to receive

---

[132] See Robert Gay, 'Damages in addition to demurrage' [2004] LMCLQ 72.
[133] (1811) 2 Camp 616; 170 ER 1270.
[134] [1984] 2 Lloyd's Rep 182.

the cargo. Neill J refused to accede to the claim for additional freight as the two voyages to Owase and Yokohama had been ordered by the consignees of the cargo (Mitsubishi). However, he held that the owners were entitled to demurrage in the sum of US $188,044.67.

J. Despatch Money

Generally   Despatch is the money which a shipowner is sometimes required under a **31.64** charter to pay to the charterer for completing loading or discharging in less than the allowed laytime. The *Voylayrules 93* state:

> 25. 'Despatch money' or 'Despatch' shall mean an agreed amount payable by the owner if the vessel completes loading or discharging before the laytime has expired.

Entitlement   At common law the owner is not entitled to such an award but, as an incen- **31.65** tive to the charterer, such clauses are often to be found in standard form dry-cargo voyage charterparties. It is not provided for in the Gencon (1976) or Gencon 1994 forms. However, the Multiform charterparty provides:

> 9. If the vessel is longer detained in loading/discharging, demurrage is to be paid by Charterers to Owners at the rate of . . . per day or pro rata.
>
> For laytime saved in loading/discharging, Owners are to pay Charterers despatch money at the rate of half the demurrage rate per day or pro rata.

Rate of despatch   Where despatch is payable, the rate of despatch is commonly half **31.66** the demurrage rate. It is often difficult to determine precisely the time which has been saved. The most common interpretation given to such clauses is to say that the clause provides for the shipowner to pay for all time saved to the ship, calculated in the way in which demurrage would be calculated, ie. without taking account of the laytime excep- tions, unless the clause specifically so provided. In *Mawson Shipping Co Ltd v Beyer,*[135] the terms of a charterparty stated that the cargo of 5,142 units was to be loaded at the average rate of 500 units per running day of 24 consecutive hours (Sundays and non-working holidays excepted). If the *Thirlwall* was detained for longer, then demurrage was to be paid. The charterparty also stated that: 'Owners agree to pay charterers £10 per day for all time saved in loading'. The question for the court was whether despatch money was payable only in respect of laydays saved or in respect of all time saved to the ship. Was despatch the same as demurrage? The contention of the owners was that they were not obliged to pay despatch for a Sunday, because if it were a layday it would not have counted. Bailhache J reached the following conclusions from the authorities he surveyed:

> 1. *Prima facie* the presumption is that the object and intention of these despatch clauses is that the shipowner shall pay to the charterers for all time saved to the ship, calculated in the way in which, in the converse case, demurrage would be calculated; that is, taking account of the lay day exceptions.

---

[135] [1914] 1 KB 304.

2. This *prima facie* presumption may be displaced, and is displaced, where either (i) lay days and time saved by despatch are dealt with in the same clause and demurrage in another clause (ii) lay days, time saved by despatch, and demurrage are dealt with in the same clause, but upon the construction of that clause the Court is of opinion, from the colloca-tion of the words, or other reason, that the days saved are referable to and used in the same sense as the lay days as described in the clause, and are not referable or used in the same sense as days lost by demurrage.[136]

Bailhache J found in favour of the charterers as his first case (2(i)) applied; Sunday was to be counted among despatch days although Sundays were excluded from the lay days. In *Themistocles (Owners) v Compagnie Intercontinentale de l'Hyperphosphate, Tangier*[137] the *Themistocles* was chartered for a voyage from Sfax (Tunisia) and Casablanca (Morocco) to one or two safe ports in Finland, carrying a cargo of phosphate in bags. The despatch clause provided that 'on all time saved at port of loading, owners to pay to shippers despatch money at half of demurrage rate per day (portions of a day pro rata)'. The question for the court concerned the amount of despatch payable and, in particular, what was meant by 'all time saved at port of loading'. The owners contended that despatch should be calculated by reference to actual loading time saved, whereas the charterers contended that it should be calculated by reference to the difference between the allowable loading time and the time during which the shippers could, without paying demurrage, have kept the ship in port for the purpose of loading. Morris J expressly approved the approach taken by Bailhache J in *The Thirlwall* and emphasized that the court had to approach such clauses by construing them in the context of their use in a particular contract. He upheld the charterers' contention that they were entitled to claim despatch money in respect of the total saving out of the total time that the ship might have stayed in port. In *Thomasson Shipping Co Ltd v Henry W Peabody & Co of London Ltd*[138] the despatch clause in a charter-party stated that:

11. Dispatch money (which is to be paid to charterers in London), shall be payable for all working time saved in loading and discharging at the rate of £100 per day, or *pro rata* for part of a day saved.

The dispute in this case turned on the word 'day' used in clause 11. The shipowners contended that 'time saved' meant hours saved and that 'day' meant a period of 24 hours; a period of 76 hours 10 minutes had to be divided by 24 to find the number of days to which the rate of £100 per day was to be applied. The charterers contended that 'per day' meant 'per working day of 8 hours 40 minutes' and that they were therefore entitled to £100 for each working day saved, ie:

$$\frac{76 \text{ hours } 10 \text{ minutes}}{\text{'8 hours 40 minutes'}} \times £100$$

McNair J found that ' . . . as a simple matter of construction [the true effect of this clause] is that dispatch money is payable at the rate of £100 per day and *pro rata* for each day

---

[136] At 312.
[137] (1949) 82 Ll LR 232.
[138] [1959] 2 Lloyd's Rep 296.

upon which working time is saved'.[139] He concluded that 'day', unqualified, meant a calendar day of 24 hours and not merely a period of 24 hours and therefore found in favour of the charterers. Despatch clauses often require separate calculations for loading and discharging. However, where there is more than one load or discharge port, the time taken at all the load ports or all the discharge ports must first be added together. Separate calculations are not normally made for each port, although, where each port has a different loading (or discharging) rate, this may not be so.

---

[139] At 304.

32

TIME CHARTERPARTIES

A. Introduction

Overview   The essence of the straight time charterparty is that it is a contract between **32.01** a shipowner and a charterer for the hire of a manned ship, for an agreed period of time. In this chapter we consider the scope of time charterparties in detail.[1] A considerable part of the world shipping fleet sails on the time charter basis, typically because large oil companies are accustomed to adding to their own fleets without the necessity of incurring the risks and burdens of ship ownership and operation in the long term. A further reason for their comparative popularity compared with voyage charterparties is that time charterparties are sometimes coupled with rather sophisticated hire provisions for financing the purchase and operation of ships. Then, there is also the fact that many first shipping ventures are based on speculative short-term time charters. It is suggested that this is because shipowners are familiar with the devices which may have to be utilized by a charterer in

---

[1] See too the earlier discussion at para 1.36. For detailed coverage of the entire topic, see especially Wilford (2003); Williams (1999), ch 3.

default of hire payment, perhaps because he has been undone by an unexpected freight market movement against him. We begin with an outline of the NYPE 93 charterparty and the Shelltime 4 charterparty.[2]

B. The NYPE 93 Charterparty

32.02 **Introduction** The NYPE 93 charterparty[3] is one of the standard forms recommended for use by BIMCO.[4] The first 22 lines are for the provision of information by the shipowner and the time charterer. Then follows 45 detailed clauses.

32.03 **Typical provisions** The following provisions are typically found in time charterparties:

  (i) The shipowner agrees to provide a vessel for a period of time and states her size, speed, fuel consumption, and amount of fuel on board (NYPE, clauses 1 & 9 and lines 10–20).

  (ii) The port of delivery and the time of delivery of the vessel to the charterer (NYPE, clause 2).

  (iii) The charterer agrees to engage only in lawful trades and between safe ports and safe places (NYPE, clauses 4 & 5).

  (iv) The shipowner agrees to pay for the crew's wages, for the vessel's insurance and her provisions, and promises to maintain her in a 'thoroughly efficient state' (NYPE, clause 6).

  (v) The charterer agrees to provide and pay for bunkers, to pay port charges, and arrange and pay for loading and discharge (NYPE, clause 7).

  (vi) The charterer agrees to pay a named sum for the hire of the vessel (NYPE, clauses 10 & 11).

  (vii) A clause concerning the redelivery of the vessel (NYPE, clause 10).

  (viii) Certain events will be stated on the occurrence of which hire will cease to be payable (NYPE, clause 17).

  (ix) The master is to be under the orders of the charterer (NYPE, clause 8).

  (x) A list of 'excepted perils' (NYPE, clause 21).

  (xi) The charterer agrees to indemnify the shipowner for loss or damage to the vessel by careless loading or discharge by stevedores (NYPE, clause 35).

  (xii) A delivery/cancelling clause (NYPE, clause 16).

  (xiii) A clause incorporating the York–Antwerp Rules 1974 (as amended) relating to general average (NYPE, clause 25).

  (xiv) An arbitration clause (NYPE, clause 45).

  (xv) Protective clauses, especially a 'clause paramount' and a 'war clause' (NYPE, clause 31 (a) & (e)).

---

[2] See Appendix II.
[3] Amended 1921, 1931, 1946. The 1946 version of the form is still heavily used.
[4] See <www.bimco.dk>.

C. The Shelltime 4 Charterparty

Introduction The Shelltime 4 charterparty[5] is issued by one of the leading worldwide oil **32.04** companies, Shell.[6] This form is a leading time form for usage in the oil trade. The Shelltime 4 form consists of five lines for the provision of basic information by the shipowner and time charterer and is followed by 48 clauses.

Contents Much of the same basic clauses noted above in relation to the NYPE 93 **32.05** charterparty are to be found in this charterparty. As is the case with the Asbatankvoy charterparty, the main differences relate to clauses which are unique to the oil trade.

D. Description of the Vessel

Importance The clauses describing the vessel are of crucial importance in a time charter- **32.06** party because the charterer is obliged to pay a fixed rate (called hire) for the vessel.[7] The details setting out the vessel's speed, her fuel consumption, and cargo capacity are all issues which will affect the profits that the charterer can expect to make during the period of the charter. Thus a relatively minor discrepancy between the vessel's stated capacity and her actual performance can all too readily have a pronounced effect on profitability. A difference of even one knot between the ship's actual cruising speed and that stated in the charterparty affects the time it takes to complete a voyage and has a knock-on effect on the number of voyages that the ship can be expected to complete over a period of time.

Name Usually, there is a detailed description of the vessel relating to name and flag, **32.07** her ownership, her class, gross and net registered tonnage, cargo capacity, speed, and fuel consumption. So far as the statement as to name is concerned, this is required to be stated at line 10 of NYPE 93 and has the status of a condition of the contract. The charterers cannot be compelled to accept delivery of another ship under the charterparty, even if it has identical characteristics. In *Société Navale de L'Ouest v RWJ Sutherland & Co*, the plaintiff claimed damages for breach of contract, against the claim of Sutherland & Co, who argued that they could put forward a substitute vessel whether or not the contracted vessel (the *John Knox*) was lost or not. Bailhache J stated that:

> The contract being for the *John Knox*, and Messrs R W J Sutherland & Co not being in a position to put forward the *John Knox*, the charter was broken in a fundamental point which went to the whole root of the Charter-party, and, in my judgment, the French Company were quite right when they found that out to treat it as a complete breach of the whole of the Charter-party. . . . Messrs. R W J Sutherland & Co . . . were not right in tendering these other ships.[8]

This case therefore is authority for the proposition that delivery of a vessel which does not meet the specification indicated in the charterparty normally gives the charterer the right

---

[5] Issued 1984, revised December 2003.
[6] <www.shell.com>. Other oil companies issue their own forms.
[7] NYPE 93, lines 10–20; Shelltime 4, cl 1, lines 6–24.
[8] (1920) 4 Ll LR 58, 59.

to terminate the contract, unless the charterparty expressly gives the owner the right to deliver a substitute vessel. In *SA Maritime et Commerciale v Anglo-Iranian Oil Co Ltd* a vessel called the *Driade* had been chartered for a series of voyages — hence under a consecutive voyage charterparty — and a clause of the charterparty stated:

> 38. Owners have the liberty of substituting a coiled vessel of similar size and position at any time before or during this charterparty and owners undertake to give charterers reasonable notice of such intention.

The owners purported to substitute the *Nayade*, subsequently re-substituting the *Driade* at a later date. The charterers claimed that there could only be one substitution, but this argument was not accepted by the Court of Appeal:

> [T]hese words are capable of meaning that at any time before or at any time during the charter-party the owners may have the liberty of substituting for the first, second or other voyage another vessel, provided she is of similar size. I think that is their natural meaning in this contract. . . . This being a charter-party under which the vessel originally named is to perform successive voyages, or as many as she can, and the owners are given liberty to substitute, I think the natural meaning is that they can do so whenever it may become convenient.[9]

In a further case, *Niarchos (London) Ltd v Shell Tankers Ltd*,[10] a case concerned with the provision of tanker tonnage by Shell over a period of years, a transportation agreement between the parties stated that:

> 5. Owners reserve the right to substitute vessels of larger deadweight tonnage during the period of the new building charters than the ones mentioned in paragraph 2 above, such substitutions, however, to be subject to charterers' approval as regards dimensions and draft.

Following the loss of a tanker called the *World Sky* (20,200 tons), Niarchos claimed to be able to fix or cause to be fixed to the charterers (a) a vessel called the *World Glen* (20,514 tons); or alternatively (b) a vessel called the *World Integrity* (41,384 tons) (i) in substitution for the *World Sea* or (ii) in substitution for the *World Sea* and the *World Sky*. McNair J held that the effect of this was that

> . . . on the true construction of Clause 5 of the agreement, Niarchos are not entitled to substitute a larger vessel for a vessel or vessels under time-charter under Clause 4; nor, since the right of substitution is only given as respects larger vessels, are Niarchos entitled to substitute another vessel of a similar or smaller deadweight.[11]

32.08 **Nationality**   A vessel's flag (and also registry) is usually determined according to grounds other than purely commercial ones. An important consideration will be the restrictions imposed by financial or the fiscal authorities. A statement concerning the ship's flag in a charterparty[12] will usually be regarded as an intermediate term of the contract. Where, however, the flag of the ship has a vital bearing on the ship's safety or on her trading opportunities — as in the case of Kuwaiti oil tankers re-flagged as American ships in order

---

9 [1954] 1 Lloyd's Rep 1(CA), 4 (Somervell LJ).
10 [1961] 2 Lloyd's Rep 496.
11 At 504.
12 See NYPE 93, line 10.

to protect them from attack in the Iran–Iraq war — then the statement as to flag will be treated as a condition and any breach will permit the charterers to treat the contract as discharged.

Class on the register   A statement in a charterparty as to the ship's class on the register,[13] **32.09** for example '100 A1 at Lloyds', will be regarded as a condition.[14] Classification societies,[15] such as Lloyd's Register (LR),[16] are independent, non-profit making associations directed by committees representing shipowners and builders and insurance underwriters. Their purpose is to ensure that ships are properly constructed and maintained in a seaworthy and safe condition. Most importantly, they arrange and carry out surveys during the building of a ship and throughout the vessel's subsequent trading life. Although it is not mandatory for a shipowner to enter his vessel with a classification society, it would in practice otherwise be impossible to trade. This is because many charterparties stipulate that a vessel be of the 'highest class' of the classification society in which she is entered. Most flag states, including the UK, make use of the services of surveyors from classification societies for flag surveys required by statute. So far as class is concerned, all vessels built or maintained in accordance with the Class Rules and Regulations of a particular classification society will be assigned a class status which will be conditional on compliance with the society's rules in respect of hull and machinery. A failure to maintain the required standards may result in a withdrawal of class by the society which will lead to great difficulties in trading for the shipowner. A leading case on class is *French v Newgass*.[17] The charterparty stated that:

> A 1 Record of American and Foreign Shipping Book. London, 4 Sept., 1876. Charterparty. It is mutually agreed between the owners of the ship *William Jackson*, newly classed as above . . . and B. Newgass & Co., merchants, of Liverpool, &c.

After her arrival at the port of loading the ship was found to be unseaworthy and her class was cancelled by the American and Foreign Shipping Association. The defendant declined to load her with his cargo. Bramwell LJ held that

> . . . the shipowner warrants that the American and Foreign Shipping Association, having satisfied themselves by such means as they thought fit as to the condition of the ship, have put her on the register, and that she is there as such, but the shipowner does not say that they will not change their minds, and rightly or wrongly take her off. It seems to me impossible to hold that there is an undertaking on the part of the shipowner that the vessel shall continue on the register . . .[18]

Thus a statement as to class in a charterparty does not amount to a promise that the vessel is properly so classed, nor that she will be so classed at the time of delivery to the charterer,

---

[13] See NYPE 93, line 12; Shelltime 4, cl 1(a), line 7.
[14] See *Ollive v Booker* (1847) 1 Ex 416, 424; 154 ER 177, 180 (Parke B).
[15] See *Marc Rich & Co AG v Bishop Rock Marine Co Ltd (The Nicholas H)* [1996] 1 AC 211; Hannu Honka, 'The Classification System and its Problems with Special Reference to the Liability of Classification Societies' (1994) 19 Tulane MLJ 1.
[16] Other well-known examples include American Bureau of Shipping(ABS), Bureau Veritas (BV), Germanischer Lloyd (GL), and Det Norske Veritas (DNV). All of these are leading members of the International Association of Classification Societies (IACS). See <www.iacs.org.uk>.
[17] (1878) 3 CPD 163.
[18] At 165.

nor that she will continue in that classification throughout the charter period.[19] To require that the shipowner should keep the chartered ship at the same classification after the making of the contract would make it responsible for the subsequent actions of a classification society, over which it has no control.[20] However, if the ship does lose its classification during the course of the charter period, the shipowner may still be liable for a breach of his obligation to maintain the ship in a seaworthy condition. Any breach of the classification clause entitles the charterer to terminate the contract for breach and to damages for the cost of finding another ship of the agreed classification.[21]

32.10   **Speed and fuel consumption**   Litigation in time charterparties often centres on the ship's speed,[22] and fuel consumption. This is because these details will ultimately affect any profits that the charterer will make during the period of the charter. Even a minor difference between the ship's stated capacity (whether as to speed or carrying capacity)[23] may have a major effect on the overall profitability of the enterprise. Any difference in speed, for example, would have a direct impact on the period that it would take to complete any given voyage and impact on the number of voyages that could be undertaken during the period of the charter. Statements in the charterparty as to speed and consumption of bunkers[24] will usually be an intermediate term of the contract. A lack of speed (or an excess of bunker consumption) will generally be compensated by damages. Where there is a serious discrepancy then the charterer will be able to treat the contract as at an end. Where the term is preceded by the word 'about', then a margin either side of the stated speed will be allowed and the extent of the margin will be a matter of fact, not of law. The leading case is *Arab Maritime Petroleum Transport Co v Luxor Trading Corporation (The Al Bida)*.[25] In this case the clause stated that:

> Vessel to be capable of maintaining under normal working conditions an average sea speed of about 15.5. knots in moderate weather . . . on an average consumption of 53 metric tons IFO 1500 fully laden and 50 metric tonnes in ballast . . . per 24 hours . . .

It was argued that there were only two possible margins that could be allowed for the word 'about', half a knot or 5 per cent. Parker LJ rejected this argument, agreeing with the arbitrators that

> the margin imported in the word 'about' cannot be fixed as a matter of law. The margin must, as the arbitrators rightly held, 'be tailored to the ship's configuration, size, draft and trim, etc'.[26]

---

[19] This point was expressly accepted by Atkinson J in *Lorentzen v White Shipping Co Ltd* (1942) 74 Ll LR 161.

[20] See *Cosmos Bulk Transport Inc v China National Foreign Trade Transportation Corp (The Apollonius)* [1978] 1 Lloyd's Rep 53, 62 (Mocatta J).

[21] See *Routh v MacMillan* (1863) 2 H & C 749; 159 ER 310.

[22] See Cedric Barclay, 'Why do ships fail to maintain their warranted speed?' [1974] LMCLQ 13.

[23] The Plimsoll line (or mark) is painted on the side of vessels, showing the various draught levels to which the ship may be loaded, usually including tropical fresh water, fresh water, tropical sea water, summer sea water, and winter sea water.

[24] See NYPE 93, lines 18–20; Shelltime 4, cl 24, lines 450–514.

[25] [1987] 1 Lloyd's Rep 124 (CA).

[26] At 129.

Parker LJ expressed little surprise that both speed and consumption were expressed as averages and the speed 'about' 15.5 knots:

> The averages, in my view, do no more than recognise that both normal working conditions and moderate weather may so vary that, from day to day, the consumption and sea speed may (indeed inevitably will) move either side of the specified figures, and that the only fair thing to do is to take a running average over a reasonable period.[27]

'In good weather conditions'   The proviso 'in good weather conditions', enables arbitrators   **32.11** to ignore checks made on days when prevailing winds range above force 4 or 5 on the Beaufort Scale. 'Good weather conditions' signifies weather conditions which do not significantly impede the vessel's forward progress. The way in which a vessel is affected by meteorological conditions will be affected by a range of factors, including most notably her size. Thus a large cargo vessel or tanker with good engines might be expected to be only relatively marginally affected by winds up to Beaufort Scale 6. Whether a particular vessel will be adversely affected could be determined by reference to the vessel's log. The Beaufort Scale describes wind forces in numbers (from 1–17), ranging from calm to violent storm and hurricane conditions. The scale provides specifications for each wind force, both at sea and on land. Speed equivalents are then given in knots, statute miles per hour, and metres per second. Thus Beaufort Scale 4 is described as follows: 'Wind (Moderate breeze); Sea (Small waves, becoming longer; fairly frequent white horses); Land (Raises dust and loose paper; small branches are moved); Knots (7–10); Miles (8–12)'.

Legal effect   What is the precise legal effect of statements as to speed in a charterparty?   **32.12** The earlier case of *Lorentzen v White Shipping Co Ltd*[28] appeared to suggest, but only obiter, that the speed-and-consumption term was an undertaking that the ship was capable of making the named speed at the time when the contract was made. Having referred to *French v Newgass*,[29] which confirmed that a statement as to class applied at the time the charterparty was made, Atkinson J ruled that

> . . . if that is true as to classification it must be equally true as to the description of the capacity of the ship. After all, the classification is not a condition, and the description of the capacity of a ship merely amounts to a warranty that at the date of the charter-party the ship was of that capacity . . .[30]

This has subsequently been modified in *Cosmos Bulk Transport Incorporated v China National Foreign Trade Transportation Co (The Apollonius)*.[31] In this case the *Apollonius* was time chartered for a trip on the Baltime form and described as

> . . . when fully loaded capable of steaming about 14 1/2 knots in good weather and smooth water on a consumption of about 38 tons of oil fuel.

The time charter was entered into on 28 August and the ship was to be delivered not before 25 September, the cancelling date being 15 October, later extended to 31 October. An additional clause stated that 'owners have the option of dry-docking vessel prior

---

[27] ibid.
[28] (1943) 74 Ll LR 161.
[29] (1878) 3 CPD 163.
[30] (1943) 74 Ll LR 161, 163.
[31] [1978] 1 Lloyd's Rep 53.

to delivery'. Between 7 September and 26 October the ship was discharging at Whampoa, a Cantonese port on the River Pearl in Southern China, and her bottom was badly fouled by molluscs. She was then able to average only 10.61 knots on the charter voyage, which was from Fukuyame in Japan to Ensanada in Argentina. The owners did not dispute that upon delivery the ship was not capable of the warranted speed, but they argued that their obligation related not to the time of delivery but only to the time the charter was made. But Mocatta J was not sympathetic to this argument:

> ... [I]t seems to be clear that the whole purpose of the description of the vessel containing a speed warranty is that when the vessel enters on her service, she will be capable of the speed in question, subject of course to any protection which her owners may obtain if there has been some casualty between the date of the charter and the date of delivery affecting her speed which, under an exceptions clause, protects them from liability in relation to a failure to comply with the warranty. From the charterer's point of view, the speed warranty is clearly of very great importance in relation to his calculations as to the time which the ship would take to complete the one trip voyage for which this time charter engaged the *Apollonius*. For the business point of view, I think it is clear that commercial considerations require this description as to the vessel's speed to be applicable as at the date of her delivery whether or not it is applicable at the date of the charter.[32]

He therefore concluded that there were 'overwhelming commercial considerations' favouring the charterer's contention that the obligation as to speed applied at the time of delivery. He left open whether it might also apply at any earlier or later date. He took a similar view in respect of representations as to fuel consumption and cargo capacity.

32.13 **Continuing obligation**   Two recent cases have considered the effect of clauses imposing a continuing obligation to maintain the warranted speed. In *Dolphin Hellas Shipping SA v Itemslot Ltd (The Aegean Dolphin)*[33] the charterers were an English company which proposed to organize and market cruises from the east coast of Australia on a basis which they believed would be attractive to potential customers as well as profitable. They chartered the *Aegean Dolphin* for a period of three years from 1 October 1988 to 14 December 1991. The charterparty provided that:

> 5.(e) ... Timetables for all itineraries ... shall be based on the speed of 18 knots in good weather conditions.

The charterers subsequently wrote to the owners on 26 May 1988 accepting the vessel as delivered to them in accordance with the charterparty and noting that 'we have your assurance that ... the ship will cruise at 18 knots in good weather ...'. Relations between the parties deteriorated, however, and each held the other to be in repudiation of the charter. The matter then went to arbitration and the majority found that the lack of speed of the vessel went to the root of the charter; the charterers had been deprived of what they had bargained for. Hobhouse J agreed that the charter had a clear and contemplated commercial objective which was appreciated by both parties and was the basis on which their contract was drawn. However, he found that, although the charterers were not precluded

---

[32] At 64.
[33] [1992] 2 Lloyd's Rep 178.

from subsequently suing for breaches of the charterparty, they were precluded from rejecting the vessel:

> If the charterers are not satisfied that the vessel is satisfactory in its entirety for the performance of its obligations under the charter, then they are at liberty to say so . . . In the present case having accepted the vessel in May, the charterers in August, without any intervening change of circumstances, sought to reject the vessel and terminate the charterparty. That was not a course which was open to them in the light of their earlier acceptance and it would follow from this that their termination of the charterparty was accordingly a wrongful repudiation on their part.[34]

In *Exmar NV v BP Shipping Ltd (The Gas Enterprise)*[35] the plaintiffs argued that the *Gas Enterprise* was not capable of performing in accordance with the contract description as to speed. The charterparty, on the Gas Form C, provided that:

> 5. (2) Owners undertake that the maximum average speed of the vessel during the period of this Charter shall be 16.0 knots in respect of laden and ballast passages and at such speed the maximum average bunker consumption shall be 62 tonnes of fuel oil/8 tonnes of diesel oil.
>
>   (3) The vessel is capable of steaming at a minimum average speed of 13.5 knots in a laden condition and at such speeds the average bunker consumption shall be 41 tonnes of fuel oil/ 8 tonnes of diesel oil.
>
>   Should Charterer instruct the vessel to proceed at an average speed or average bunker consumption between those set out above the vessel shall be capable of achieving, on sea passages, the average speeds and average bunkering consumption set out in the table hereunder . . .
>
>   (4) For the purpose of assessing the performance of the vessel, the average speed and bunker consumption of the vessel shall be calculated upon the distance made, the time taken and the quantity of bunkers consumed by the vessel on each sea passage as ordered to be performed by Charterers, but inclusive of any deviation from, or change in, the passage as actually carried out by the vessel, from Pilot Station to Pilot Station up to and including Beaufort Force 4 wind and wave.

The charterers claimed that the speed warranty applied throughout the vessel's service under the charterparty, but the owners counter-claimed that the warranty only applied during those times when wind and wave were force 4 or less on the Beaufort Scale. They were claiming the sum of $329,584 (ie, the sum due under the charterparty or alternatively as damages). Lloyd LJ found that it was

> common ground that sub-cl. (4) provides what [His Honour Judge Diamond QC] called a contractual yardstick for measuring the extent of the vessel's capacity to perform. That being so I can see no reason for confining the application of the yardstick to periods when the weather was force 4 or less. The warranty set out in sub-cll. (1)–(3) is expressed to apply generally in respect of all sea passages, whether laden or in ballast. Prima facie the charterers are entitled to be compensated for any breach of that warranty. A vessel which cannot comply with her contract speed or consumption in good weather, is unlikely to be able to comply with the contract when the weather is bad.[36]

---

[34] At 186.
[35] [1993] 2 Lloyd's Rep 352 (CA).
[36] At 365–366.

Roch LJ noted that it was clear that

> the method of assessing the performance of the vessel is to calculate the average speed and
> bunker consumption of the vessel on each sea passage that the vessel makes on the orders of
> the charterers. The average speed and bunker consumption of the vessel has to be calculated
> on the distance made, the time taken and the quantities of bunkers consumed by the vessel
> on that sea passage, subject to the exclusion of those periods already stated. If the owners had
> intended to warrant the ship's performance only in good weather conditions, then they could
> and should have stated that expressly or at the very least included in clear language among the
> periods to be disregarded when making calculations under sub-cl.(4) those periods when the
> weather conditions were above force 4 on the Beaufort Scale.[37]

The court therefore dismissed the appeal and found in favour of the charterers.

32.14 **Burden of proof** The burden of proving that there has been a failure to comply with the
speed specification rests on the charterer. This is not an easy burden to discharge. Breach
might give the charterer the right to throw up the charter but in practice his right will
normally be restricted to one of compensation. The appropriate measure in damages would
be the difference between the market rate for hire of the vessel on the stated specifications
and those with the vessel actually delivered. In some instances, for example *The Apollonius*,
the court will permit the charterer to treat the vessel as off-hire for the extra time taken on
the relevant voyage. Other remedies for errors in description may occasionally be derived
from other clauses in the charterparty, such as the obligation to prosecute 'all voyages
with reasonable despatch'. In *Ocean Glory Compania Naviera SA v A/S PV Christensen
(The Ioanna)*[38] the charterparty stated that the vessel was capable of steaming 'about
13 knots fully loaded'. Furthermore:

> 51. (305) In the event of loss of time either in port or at sea . . . caused by . . . damages
> or lack of maintenance to hull . . . machinery or equipment . . . or by any other cause
> whatsoever preventing the full working of the vessel the payment of hire . . . shall cease for
> the time thereby lost until the vessel is again ready and in an efficient state to resume her
> service . . . and all extra expenses are to be for owners' account and may be deducted
> from hire.

> (316) . . . and if upon the voyage the speed be reduced by defect in . . . any part of her
> hull machinery or equipment the time so lost and the cost of any extra fuel consumed
> . . . and all extra expenses are to be for owners' account and may be deducted from
> the hire.

The charterers lost 7.2 days by way of extra time taken to complete the voyages undertaken
during the charter period because the *Ioanna* commenced the chartered service with her
bottom fouled. The charterers therefore brought an action against the owner to recover the
7.2 days' hire as well as 1.5 tonnes of marine diesel oil consumed on each of these extra days.
The owners claimed that they could set off against this the 50 tonnes of oil saved by the
slower performance of the vessel. The charterers rejected this; in Staughton J's words they
wanted 'the plums but not the duff'.[39] He found that though the fouling constituted

---

[37] At 367–369.
[38] [1985] 2 Lloyd's Rep 164.
[39] At 166–167.

a defect in the vessel's hull the charterers were entitled to recover the net cost of extra fuel and diesel taken together:

> If, as in this case, there has been extra consumption of diesel oil but a saving in fuel oil, it is only the net balance, if any, which is recoverable by the charterers . . . . [I]t seems to me that the losing of time and the proceeding at a slower speed were one and the same event which continued throughout the charter-party. Just as that one and the same event caused an extra consumption of diesel oil, so it saved consumption of fuel oil. So only the net amount can in my judgment be claimed under cl.51.[40]

Cargo capacity   The statements in a charterparty describing a vessel's carrying capacity   **32.15** are of great importance to the charterer. This is usually referred to as her deadweight capacity, the actual cargo carrying capacity of the vessel, when she is fully loaded with cargo, so that the hull is immersed in water up to her Plimsoll marks. To this must be added the weight of fresh water and bunkers, these variables together constituting the vessel's deadweight tonnage.[41] Some charterparties also provide for a statement as to the cubic capacity of the vessel in respect of 'grain' and 'bale space'.[42] This is because any given commodity will occupy a certain space, measured in cubic feet per metric tonne. The actual space required will vary, depending on the commodity. A tonne of corn might occupy, for example, 50 cubic feet of space, while iron ore requires less 'space' for the same weight, perhaps 15 cubic feet. When one refers to the stowage factor of cargo, one is speaking of the average cubic space occupied by 1 tonne weight of cargo as stowed aboard the ship. The stowage factor is usually expressed as cubic feet per metric tonne. Where the deadweight cargo capacity is preceded by the word 'about' then this allows the owners a margin of accuracy. What the margin is will depend on the accuracy with which the deadweight can reasonably be measured and also what margin would be regarded as reasonable in a particular trade.

Nature of the obligation   A statement as to the cargo capacity of the chartered ship   **32.16** creates an intermediate obligation. This view of the matter was confirmed by the court in the time charterparty case *Compagnie Generale Maritime v Diakan Spirit SA (The Ymnos)*.[43] Here the charterparty stated that the owners 'guaranteed' the loading of containers onto the chartered ship according to an agreed stowage plan:

> . . . owners guarantee the loading of the containers in the stowage plan without any stability problem.

Considerable stability problems were in fact encountered, both at loading and discharging, and the charterers sought to discharge the contract either on the grounds that the shipowners had breached a condition of the charterparty, or on the grounds that the shipowners' breach of the cargo capacity term was one which went to the root of the contract. Robert Goff J sought guidance in the leading case of *Hongkong Fir Shipping Co Ltd v Kawasaki*

---

[40] At 167–168.
[41] NYPE 93, lines 13–15.
[42] NYPE 93, line 16.
[43] [1982] 2 Lloyd's Rep 574.

Kisen Kaisha Ltd.[44] After noting that the Court of Appeal in that case had declined to classify a shipowners' obligation to tender a seaworthy ship as a condition, he stated that:

> When I turn to consider the so-called container guarantee clause in the present case, I am satisfied that it cannot properly be classified as a condition. It is preceded by the sentence which specifies the number of containers which can be stowed on the ship; and the function of the container guarantee clause is to provide an undertaking by the owners that such containers can be loaded, and presumably discharged, without any stability problem. But it is obvious from the facts of this case that the effect of a breach of this clause can be slight or serious. . . . [I]n my judgment the use of the word 'guarantee' in the clause under consideration means no more than that any stability problem during loading of the contractual number of containers will result in a breach of contract by the owners. I cannot derive from these words the conclusion that the provision is one which should be construed as a condition; and having regard to the nature and content of the obligation, I decline to construe it as such.[45]

32.17 **Carrying capacity**   The carrying capacity of a vessel can be expressed in terms of volume or weight but in the case of container ships this will be by reference to the number of shipping containers the vessel can carry. This container capacity is usually expressed as the number of twenty-foot units (or TEUs). Such containers are usually 8 ft 6 ins high, 8 ft wide, and either 20 ft (1 TEU) or 40 ft long (2 TEUs). The volumetric capacity of the ship, whether for containers or the size of the holds of the ship, will be well known and is readily verifiable. Owner's brokers advertising the services of the ship for chartering will often specify what the carrying capacity of the ship will be. The vessel's deadweight capacity will often vary during the course of a calendar year, owing to her load line markings specified by a classification society. The vessel's maximum draught will vary between summer and winter and also whether the vessel is travelling in fresh water, salt water, tropical water, and temperate water. Much will also depend upon the density of the cargo being carried; thus, even though the vessel's holds may be full, the cargo may be of low density and it will be necessary to take on ballast to ensure the ship's stability during the voyage. Where the deadweight capacity of the vessel is given with reference to an agreed cargo then this will describe the ship's ability to carry that agreed amount of cargo. This is not generally the case, however. In *W Millar & Co Ltd v Owners of SS Freden*[46] a clause provided that:

> The owners guarantee the ship's deadweight capacity to be 3200 tons and freight to be paid on this quantity.

Bankes LJ held that

> the expression 'the ship's dead-weight capacity' . . . has reference primarily to the vessel's lifting or weight-carrying capacity in the abstract, and I find nothing either in the position in which the words are used in this charterparty or in any other of the provisions of the charterparty itself to displace that primary meaning and lead to the conclusion that [a] secondary meaning ought to be adopted here as contended for by the appellants.[47]

---

44 [1962] 2 QB 26 (CA). See the discussion at para 23.18.
45 [1982] 2 Lloyd's Rep 574, 584.
46 [1918] KB 611 (CA).
47 At 613–614 (upholding Rowlatt J at first instance: [1917] 2 KB 657).

In *Re Thomson & Co & Brocklebank Ltd*[48] Devlin J likewise held that

> if the shipowners place at the disposal of the charterers a ship having a capacity to carry 5600 tons of cargo they have satisfied their contract, and in the present case they have done it. The matter is made quite plain in this case by the reference in the guarantee to the cubical capacity, which is to be gauged by reference to the builders' plan. What is meant in these circumstances is that there is 300,000 cubic feet bale space, which the charterers can see by looking at the plan, which is available for carrying cargo, and that space, even if they like to fill it up with dunnage, will be there.[49]

Accuracy   So long as the general carrying capacity of the ship is accurately described, the   **32.18**
charterer has no action against the shipowner if the ship cannot carry the agreed amount of some particular cargo. In *Cargo Ships El-Yam Ltd v Invoer-En Transport Onderneming Invotra NV*[50] a charterparty for the *Tel Aviv* provided that she was

> of about 478,000 cubic feet bale capacity including one and three deep tanks which understood to be of total 27,000 cubic feet.

The charterers purported to repudiate the charterparty on the basis that the bale capacity of the ship was actually 484,000 cubic feet (a difference of 1.2 per cent). Devlin J explained the difference between 'bale capacity' and 'grain capacity' as follows:

> They are both measurements of the space in the ship that is available for cargo, but whereas if cargo is loaded in bulk, such as grain cargo, it can fill, so to speak, every nook and cranny of the hold, cargo that is loaded in bales cannot do that, and, therefore, the cubic space available cannot be used as economically. It is for this reason that there are these two measurements of capacity.[51]

He continued that

> no one has suggested, and no one can suggest, that an excess of some 6,000 cubic feet of bale capacity — I repeat 'excess' — can have any effect upon this contract at all. It must be quite immaterial to the charterer, provided he can carry all the cargo he wants, whether he has some excess capacity left in the deep tanks or not, and no one has suggested otherwise.[52]

The *Tel Aviv* was rather unusual because she was built with wartime conditions in mind and was therefore fitted with deep tanks for use as ballast or for extra bunkering. However, the ballast tanks were also available for cargo, although not for coal (the subject of the current charterparty). So far as differences between the actual deep tank space and the space notified to the charterers were concerned, Devlin J again stated that this was not a basis for the charterers being able to rescind.[53] In *Louis Dreyfus & Cie v Parnaso Cia Naviera SA*[54] the master calculated the quantity of cargo which the vessel could load on the basis of her summer load line marks, rather than her winter marks. The charterparty, on the Gencon form, stated that 'the approximative [sic] cargo to the holds will be . . . Total 10,400 tons'.

---

[48] [1918] 1 KB 655.
[49] At 661.
[50] [1958] 1 Lloyd's Rep 39.
[51] At 45.
[52] At 52–53.
[53] At 53.
[54] [1960] 2 QB 49 (CA). Discussed previously in the voyage charterparty context requiring the provision of a 'full and complete cargo': see para 30.28.

The *SS Dominator* was unable to load 10,400 tons, being 331 long tons short and in respect of this incurred expenses agreed at £155 8s 2d. Devlin J at first instance permitted the charterers to recover that sum from the owners. Sellers LJ held that 'approximative' was the same as 'about' and that

> 331 tons deficiency in a cargo of 10,400 tons, a deficiency of just over 3 per cent, [fulfilled] the obligation to ship about 10,400 tons. In the absence of any trade evidence on the matter, it is, in my opinion, within a reasonable commercial margin in respect of such a cargo.[55]

This case therefore confirms that some margin of error will be permitted in describing the carrying capacity of a vessel, usually by reference to reasonable commercial expectations.

32.19　**Effect of breach**　Because the cargo capacity clause is regarded as an intermediate obligation, any breach will give rise to a claim in damages. Such damages will be assessed in the time charterparty context as the difference between the hire paid for a ship of the specified cargo capacity and the hire that would be payable for a ship of the actual capacity of the one chartered. This rule was stated in the case of *Tibermede v Graham* where the vessel's deadweight capacity was greater than that stated and her cubic capacity less. In upholding the contention argued by the charterer, Shearman J stated that:

> The contract was entered into on the basis that the charterers wanted a ship of the size guaranteed. There is no question that in the case of a sale the measure of damages is perfectly clear. If you buy a ship of a certain cubic capacity, and one of less cubic capacity is tendered, you can deduct the difference in value from the price. I am unable to see that there is a difference in the case of hiring.[56]

E.　Delivery

32.20　**Introduction**　In a time charterparty, it is usual to find a provision in the charterparty dealing with the period within which delivery of the vessel should be made to the charterer. However, in *Cheikh Boutros Selim El-Khoury v Ceylon Shipping Lines Ltd (The Madeleine)* Roskill J pointed out that:

> It is, of course, axiomatic that in a time charter . . . delivery does not import any transfer of possession. An owner delivers a ship to a time charterer under this form of charterparty by placing her at the charterers' disposal and by placing the services of her master, officers and crew at the charterers' disposal, so that the charterers may thenceforth give orders (within the terms of the charter-party) as to the employment of the vessel to the master, officers and crew, which orders the owners contract that their servants shall obey.[57]

32.21　**Time for delivery**　The shipowner will not usually be in a position to state precisely when a chartered ship will be available for delivery to the charterer under a time charterparty. The vessel chartered will usually be completing voyages under other contracts at the time that it is fixed ahead on charter. The precise moment of the vessel's availability will depend upon the completion of her prior obligations. Most standard form time charterparties

---

[55] At 55.
[56] (1921) 7 Ll LR 250, 251.
[57] [1967] 2 Lloyd's Rep 224, 238.

make provision for a period within which the shipowner must deliver the ship to the charterer.[58] The effect of the period is that the charterparty provides a date before which the charterer is not obliged to accept delivery and a date on which the charterer is entitled to cancel. Although laytime and demurrage are not relevant considerations in a time charterparty, this period in time charterparties is still usually referred to as the 'lay/can'.

Breach of contract The shipowner will not necessarily be in breach of contract if the   **32.22** vessel has not been delivered by the cancelling date. This was one of the matters considered by Roskill J in *Cheikh Boutros Selim El-Khoury v Ceylon Shipping Lines Ltd (The Madeleine).*[59] Here the relevant clauses were as follows:

1. The Owners let, and the Charterers hire the Vessel for a period of three calendar months (15 days more or less in Charterer's option) from the time (not a Sunday or a legal Holiday unless taken over) the Vessel is delivered and placed at the disposal of the Charterers between 9 a.m. and 6 p.m., or between 9 a.m. and 2 p.m. if on Saturday, at Calcutta in such available berth where she can safely lie always afloat, she being in every way fitted for ordinary cargo service.

22. Should the Vessel not be delivered by the 2nd day of May 1957 the Charterers to have the option of cancelling.

   If the Vessel cannot be delivered by the cancelling date, the Charterers, if required, to declare within 48 hours after receiving notice thereof whether they cancel or will take delivery of the Vessel.

The cancellation date in clause 22 was later extended to 10 May 1957, but the vessel was in any event refused a de-ratting exemption certificate on 9 May. Fumigation was not completed until midnight on 10 May. The charterers purported to cancel at 8 am (and again at 8.48 pm) on 10 May. Had the charterers wrongfully repudiated the charterparty, as claimed by the owners? After noting that it was well established that clauses could not be construed in isolation from each other, Roskill J continued that:

It is important to emphasise that that which the charterers are claiming to exercise is an express contractual right given by Clause 22. Their right to cancel does not in any way depend upon any breach of the charter-party by the owners. Entitlement to cancel under Clause 22 depends not on any breach by the owners but upon whether the owners have timeously complied with obligations under Clause 1. If they have, there is no right to cancel. If they have not, there is a right to cancel.[60]

Disagreeing with the arbitrator, he found that there

was here an express warranty of seaworthiness [in Clause 1] and unless the ship was timeously delivered in a seaworthy condition, including the necessary certificate from the port health authority, the charterers had the right to cancel. That right in my judgment they possessed . . . .[61]

As to the time of cancellation, Roskill J stated that:

In my judgment, both as a matter of construction of the charter-party and as a matter of authority, it is clear law that there is no contractual right to rescind a charter-party under the

---

[58] See NYPE 93, cl 2, lines 29–38; Shelltime 4, cl 5, lines 145–147.
[59] [1967] 2 Lloyd's Rep 224.
[60] At 239.
[61] At 241.

cancelling clause unless and until the date specified in that clause has been reached. In other words . . . there is no anticipatory right to cancel under the clause . . . Of course, the fact that there is no contractual right to cancel in advance does not prevent a charterer seeking to claim the right to rescind in advance of the cancelling date, as the learned authors of *Scrutton* put it 'at common law'.

. . . [I]n my judgment there is under the cancelling clause no anticipatory right to cancel in advance of the specified cancelling date.[62]

On this basis the cancellation at 8 am was premature, but not that given at 8.48 pm.

32.23 Obligation not absolute   The obligation to deliver before the cancelling date under the charterparty is not absolute, however; if the shipowner has used reasonable diligence to deliver the vessel by that date, he is not in breach. In *Marbienes Compania Naviera v Ferrostal AG (The Democritos)*[63] one of the clauses stated that:

If required by Charterers, time not to commence before 1st December 1969, and should vessel not have given written notice of readiness on or before 20th December, 1969, but not later than 4pm. Charterers or their agents to have the option of cancelling this charter any time not later than the best notice of the vessel's readiness . . .

The *Democritos* arrived in Durban on 16 December 1969 whereupon it was found that her 'tween deck in the No 2 hold had collapsed. Loading of 9,230 long tons of steel began on 18 December 1969. The charterers claimed that the owners were under an absolute obligation to deliver the vessel by the cancelling date in a fit condition as required by the charter, but that the owners were in breach. Lord Denning MR stated that:

. . . [T]here is nothing in this charter which binds the owners positively to deliver by Dec. 20, 1969. The only clue to any time of delivery is to be found in the cancelling clause. There is, of course, an implied term that the owners will use reasonable diligence to deliver the ship in a fit condition by Dec. 20, 1969. But that is not an absolute obligation. So long as they have used reasonable diligence, they are not in breach. In this case it is found that reasonable diligence was used, so there is no breach by them of that implied obligation.

. . . [A]s long as the owner uses reasonable diligence, he is not in breach, but the charterer is entitled to cancel if the vessel is not delivered by the cancelling date.[64]

32.24 Cancellation for non-delivery   Although the charterer will be entitled to cancel the charterparty for non-delivery, he cannot also recover damages for breach of contract. In the *Democritos*, Lord Denning MR relied on the US case of *United States Gypsum Transport Co v Dampskibs Aktiselskabet Karmoy*.[65] Here Campbell DJ stated that:

The most that can be required of the owner . . . where no delivery date is provided in the charter, is to tender with reasonable dispatch, and the burden of proof is on the [charterer] to show that the owner has not used reasonable dispatch in tendering the ship.

The charter . . . did not by its terms promise that the vessel would be delivered by any specified date, nor did it by reason of any of its provisions imply a promise by the owner to deliver the vessel on or before any specified day . . . but the most that was implied . . . was that the owner would use reasonable dispatch in tendering the vessel.[66]

---

[62] At 244–245.
[63] [1976] 2 Lloyd's Rep 149 (CA).
[64] At 152.
[65] (1930) 48 Fed Rep (2nd) 376 (District Court, New York).
[66] At 377–378.

Breach   If the late delivery does also constitute a breach because of the shipowner's failure   **32.25**
to make a reasonable effort to deliver the ship on time, the charterer is entitled to cancel and
to recover damages, unless the charterparty contains an exclusion clause protecting the
shipowner from the consequences of the breach.[67] The measure of damages will be the
charterer's additional expenditure in finding an alternative ship of the same description as
that in the charterparty. This matter was considered in *Blackgold Trading Ltd of Monrovia v
Almare SpA di Navigazione of Genoa (The Almare Seconda and Almare Quinta).*[68] The owners
chartered the *Almare Seconda* or the *Almare Quinta* to the charterers for the carriage of
a cargo of gas oil from the Caribbean to Europe. The vessel was stated to be 'now trading and
expected ready about 20th August, 1978 basis Punta Cardon', cancelling 3 September 1978.
A clause provided that:

> 5. Should the vessel not be ready to load by 4.00 o'clock p.m. on the cancelling date
>   . . . the charterers shall have the option of cancelling this charter by giving the
>   Owners notice of such cancellation . . . otherwise this charter to remain in full force
>   and effect.

The charterers had meanwhile committed themselves to purchase two cargoes of gas oil,
one f.o.b. Amuay Bay, Venezuela, and the other f.o.b. Punta Cardon. The cargoes were in
turn sold c.i.f. to purchasers in Norway. On 15 August the owners elected to substitute
Almare Quinta for *Almare Seconda*, but on 21 August they informed the charterers that the
best estimated time of arrival for the vessel at Punta Cardon was 5 or 6 September. This was
later altered again to 10 September. The charterers meanwhile made alternative arrangements
for the shipment of the cargoes. However, they did not immediately cancel the charter as the
market rate had by this time risen. They were unsuccessful in finding alternative employment
for the *Almare Quinta* and cancelled the charter on 4 September. They claimed
$123,597.11, the extra cost of shipping the two cargoes. The arbitrators found in their
favour and this was confirmed by Robert Goff J:

> . . . [I]n the present case, the situation is very simple. There was a breach of contract. That
> breach caused damage, in the form of the extra cost of the alternative arrangements which the
> charterers had to make for their intended cargo. The charterers did not determine their
> contract with the owners, but kept it alive in an effort to mitigate their damage. Their efforts
> were unsuccessful; and they then exercised their right to cancel under the cancelling clause.
> It is difficult to see what else the charterers could have done in the circumstances; and I do
> not see why, on ordinary principles, they should not be entitled to recover the damages which
> the arbitrators have awarded them.

> Let it not be forgotten that, by cancelling the charter when they did (as the owners were
> in effect pressing them to do), they released *Almare Quinta* to the owners when the market
> had risen; the owners then had the opportunity to take advantage of that market and, if they
> did so successfully, their profit could, for all I know, have contributed to or even extinguished
> the damages which they have been held liable to pay to the charterers. It is hard to see
> how, in those circumstances, there is any injustice of which the owners can legitimately
> complain.[69]

---

[67] But cf *Christie & Vesey Ltd v Maatschappij tot Exploitatie van Schepen en Anderer Zaken (The Helvetia-S)*
[1960] 1 Lloyd's Rep 540, 548–549 (Pearson J).

[68] [1981] 2 Lloyd's Rep 433.

[69] At 437.

32.26 **Timing of cancellation** The charterer will not be entitled to cancel the charterparty before the cancelling date, but if he purports to do so, and the cancellation is accepted by the shipowner, the charter will be brought to an end by agreement. This point was considered in *Christie & Vesey Ltd v Maatschappij Tot Explotatie van Schepen en Andere Zaken (The Helvetia-S)*.[70] Clause 22 provided that:

> Should the Vessel not be delivered by the 15th day of July, 1956, the Charterers to have the option of cancelling.

> If the Vessel cannot be delivered by the cancelling date, the Charterers, if required, to declare within 48 hours after receiving notice thereof whether they cancel or will take delivery of the Vessel.

The case arose over a dispute as to the shipowners' liability to pay brokers' commission. The *Helvetia-S* was at the time of fixture still in the process of being built, and this is where the difficulties for the charterparty really began, because there were a number of protracted delays. The ship was in fact delivered to the owners in October, rather than 30 June. On 15 June the charterers' brokers wrote to the owners' agents exercising their option to cancel the charter. Had the owners accepted the cancellation? Pearson J stated that:

> . . . [I]t is now quite plain that the owners were in breach by not delivering by the specified date. It is quite plain, also, that they would have been unable to deliver by the cancellation date, which was July 15 . . . . [I]n my view, there was a breach by the owners under this charter and that breach was the cause of the full hire not being paid.[71]

As to whether there could be a prospective cancellation, Pearson J held that

> the prospective notice of cancellation which the charterers gave in this case was not validly given under Clause 22. Perhaps it was, in the first instance, intended to be so, but I am inclined to think that a short time after, at any rate, the charterers did not feel sure that they had given a valid notice under Clause 22 because they wrote asking whether the owners would accept it as a cancellation. The owners, most unequivocally, later on accepted it as a cancellation.

> . . . I come to the conclusion here that there was cancellation by agreement.[72]

The charterer can waive his right to cancel the charterparty for late delivery by unequivocally accepting delivery after the cancelling date.

32.27 **Place and moment of delivery** Standard form charterparties frequently provide for a range of ports or places within which delivery must be made. Clause 2 of the NYPE 93 charterparty leaves it open for the parties to specify a range of places or a particular place.[73] There are advantages for both parties in providing a range of places; the charterer may at the time of fixture be uncertain where the first cargo will become available for loading, while the owner may not be clear where the chartered ship will become available because of the vessel's previous engagements. The usual practice is for the owner to have the right to nominate the

---

[70] [1960] 1 Lloyd's Rep 540.
[71] At 551.
[72] At 552.
[73] See lines 30–33.

delivery port and the charterer the redelivery port. In *Segovia Compagnia Naviera SA v R Pagnan & Fratelli (The Aragon)*[74] the trading limits were defined as

> . . . (always within Institute Warranty Limits) East Coast Canada, U.S.A. East of Panama Canal, U.K. Continent Gibralter – Hamburg Range, Mediterranean . . .

Were the charterers entitled to order the Aragon to New Orleans (in the Gulf)? At first instance, Donaldson J held that the trading limits were wide enough to enable going down the east side of the USA.[75] This was upheld by Lord Denning MR:

> I have never known of a case where trading limits are defined by a meridian of longitude or a parallel of latitude. The limits are always defined by reference to geographical areas, ports or capes . . . . The brokers on the Baltic Exchange know perfectly well that the phrase 'U.S.A. east of Panama Canal' means a port in the U.S.A. but the vessel must not go through the Panama Canal.

> The result is that, having found no cargo available at Port Cartier, the charterers were entitled to send the vessel down to New Orleans and load a cargo of grain there.[76]

If the charterparty provides for delivery at a port, then it seems that, by analogy with the 'arrived ship' cases, valid delivery will take place when the chartered ship arrives at a place within the legal, fiscal, and administrative limits of the port where she is at the immediate and effective disposition of the charterer. Another possibility is for delivery to take place at a berth within a port, as in clause 1 of the Baltime 1939 charterparty which provides for delivery of the chartered ship at the nominated port 'in such available berth where she can safely lie always afloat'. The party who nominates a port under such a clause impliedly promises that a berth will be available on arrival. If the obligation falls on the charterer and he fails to comply with it he must pay the owner damages at the charterparty rate for the period of waiting for a berth. Thus in *Anders Utkilens Rederi A/S v Compagnie Tunisienne de Navigation of Tunis (The Golfstraum)*[77] the question for Mocatta J was whether if the vessel could not be delivered owing to congestion in the port named for delivery, the time lost was for the owners' or charterers' account. Mocatta J relied upon the following dictum of Lord Esher MR in *Harris & Dixon v Marcus Jacobs & Co*:[78]

> In order to determine this case one must see whether the charterers would be liable if they were in the position of these defendants. That would depend on the construction of the charterparty, and in whose favour the word 'ready' which is an express word, was inserted there before the words 'quay berth as ordered by charterers'. It seems to me that the stipulation that the vessel should proceed 'to such quay berth as ordered by the charterers', was one which would be in favour of the charterers, and that when the word 'ready' was inserted before 'quay berth', that must be in favour of the shipowners, in order that the ship should not be kept waiting until a quay berth was ready. The meaning of the charterparty is, I think, that the charterers undertake to order the ship to go to such dock and to such quay berth there as they may wish, all of which is for their benefit, but with this stipulation in favour of the shipowners, that it shall be to a quay berth which is ready. That being so

---

[74] [1977] 1 Lloyd's Rep 343 (CA).
[75] [1975] 2 Lloyd's Rep 216.
[76] [1977] 1 Lloyd's Rep 343 (CA), 345.
[77] [1976] 2 Lloyd's Rep 97.
[78] (1885) 15 QB 247.

the charterers would be bound to name a quay berth which was ready, and there was a default on their part in the present case as the quay berth was not ready for the vessel.[79]

The dispute in the *Golfstraum* was whether the charterers were in breach of the charterparty in failing to order the vessel to an available berth on her arrival at Sfax. The owners were claiming damages of $6,400. Mocatta J held that:

> If I am right in thinking that the charterers must give their directions as to a berth before or on the arrival of the vessel, I think it follows that they impliedly warrant that a berth will be available on the vessel's arrival at any time between Mar. 8 and 12. . . . I have reached the conclusion that the context of the time charter as a whole as well as the authority last cited bring the scales down in favour of the owners, so that upon its true construction the answer to the question of law is in the affirmative.[80]

The parties in a time charterparty can avoid difficulties by providing that delivery is 'on dropping outward pilot' at the nominated port.

32.28   **The North Sea**   In *Georgian Maritime Corporation plc v Sealand Industries (Bermuda) Ltd (The North Sea)*[81] the relevant delivery clause provided that:

> Vessel shall be placed at the disposal of the Charterers at Charterers' berth Hong Kong or dlosp [dropping last outward sea pilot] Hong Kong in Charterers' option any time day/night . . . Acceptance of delivery of the vessel by Charterers shall not constitute a waiver of Charterers' rights under this Charter Party.

The charterparty also contained a cancellation clause (clause 14). The owners gave the charterers successive notices that the vessel would be delivered at 10.00 and requests were made to the charterers enquiring where they wanted the vessel delivered but no instructions were forthcoming. The vessel was at an anchorage in Hong Kong and remained there but did not proceed to either the charterers' berth nor to the outward bound pilot station. Once the cancellation deadline passed, the charterers purported to exercise their right of cancellation, on the ground that the *North Sea* was at neither of the two spots mentioned in the charterparty nor ready. The arbitrator rejected the charterers' ground of cancellation on the basis that the owners' obligation to go to one or other of the places specified required the co-operation of the charterers which had not been provided. At first instance,[82] Mance J held that the charterers' omission to exercise their option as to the place in Hong Kong where delivery should be made debarred them from availing themselves of the right to cancel. Accordingly, he found in favour of the owners on this point. On appeal, Hobhouse LJ agreed and said that:

> One of the striking features of this particular charterparty is that the vessel was already in Hong Kong . . . It can be strongly argued that if the Charterers do not exercise their option to direct the vessel to one or other place within Hong Kong delivery in Hong Kong suffices. They have waived their right to require the vessel to proceed (for their own benefit) to one or other of the two places first, or have precluded themselves from insisting that the vessel do so. This is not a point of general principle: it is simply a conclusion which is capable of being supported on the particular terms and circumstances of this charter.[83]

---

79   At 250.
80   [1976] 2 Lloyd's Rep 97,102.
81   [1999] 1 Lloyd's Rep 21 (CA).
82   [1997] 2 Lloyd's Rep 324.
83   [1999] 1 Lloyd's Rep 21 (CA), 26.

Bunkers on delivery   The term 'bunkers'[84] can include both the tanks or holds in **32.29** which a vessel's fuel oil is stored as well as the actual fuel. The term comes from the shipbuilding term 'coal bunker', which described the space where coal is stored on the vessel, but is now used to refer to the viscous liquid marine fuel oil. It has been suggested that the number of disputes over bunkers has grown in number in recent years for a number of reasons. The first is that bunker prices were until the mid-1970s relatively stable, but that there was subsequently a dramatic rise in cost (nearly a tenfold increase up to 1986). Bunkers therefore constitute a key element in calculating the overall profitability of an owner's or charterer's trade. A second factor relates to the quality of bunkers; cost considerations have played a role in the dropping of quality standards. A third factor has been the proliferation of smaller suppliers operating in the bunker supply market. Less scrupulous suppliers make use of questionable stock, or blend stock to supply bunkers at more competitive prices and to enhance profit margins.[85]

Cost of bunkering   Time charterparties usually provide expressly who is to bear **32.30** the cost of bunkering the vessel during the duration of the charterparty.[86] This is because in time (or demise) charters, but not voyage charters, it is the charterer who is responsible for the provision and payment for fuel. It has been estimated that nearly 80 per cent of the present day provision of ship's bunkers worldwide is to order by charterers rather than owners.[87] Should the charterparty not specify a price at which the fuel must be bought, the charterer is obliged to pay the market price at the delivery port, whether or not that bears any relation to the price paid by the shipowner for those bunkers. This was one of the matters before the Court of Appeal in *Harmon Shipping Co SA v Saudi-Europe Line Ltd (The Good Helmsman)*.[88] The main issue in the case was whether the charterparty was genuine and intended to create legal relations between the parties or whether it was a mere sham signed by the defendants solely in order to help the plaintiffs with the mortgaging of the *Good Helmsman* to their bank. A cross-appeal concerned payment for bunkers. On this point, Ackner LJ stated that:

> The basis for the accepted obligation by the shipowners to pay for the bunkers on board on redelivery, and indeed for the charterers to pay for them on delivery, is that neither the charterers immediately prior to redelivery nor the owners immediately prior to redelivery are to be expected to empty the fuel tanks. Moreover it can, as a broad generalisation, be confidently assumed that it is to the charterer's advantage to have fuel on board when they take over the ship and equally for the owners to have bunkers on board when the vessel is redelivered. Both the charterers on delivery and the owners on redelivery take over for their own use property which they would usually otherwise have to buy on the open market.

---

84 See generally, Fisher and Lux (1994).
85 Fisher and Lux (1994), 79–80.
86 See NYPE 93, cl 9, lines 109–124. See too Shelltime 4, cl 15, lines 287–296.
87 Fisher and Lux (1994), 98.
88 [1981] 1 Lloyd's Rep 377; 405 (CA).

In such circumstances it seems to me to be clear that the law implies an obligation to pay a reasonable price for that property, that is, the market price.[89]

When the purchase price for the bunker fuel is fixed at the time of the contract, the parties will usually specify the means of calculating the amount of fuel to be purchased, by agreeing that the bunkers be surveyed by an independent surveyor on delivery and redelivery.[90]

32.31   **Bunker estimate**   If the shipowner makes an estimate in the charterparty of the fuel that will be in the ship's bunkers on delivery, the estimate will be regarded as an intermediate term of the contract. This will impose an obligation upon the shipowner to make an estimate which is both honest and based on reasonable grounds. Breach will usually be covered by damages, unless the breach is such as to go to the root of the contract. Thus in *Effploia Shipping Corp Ltd v Canadian Transport Co Ltd (The Pantanassa)*[91] the charterparty stated:

> 3. That the charterers, at the port of delivery, and the owners, at the port of redelivery, shall take over and pay for all fuel remaining on board the vessel, the vessel to be delivered with bunkers as aboard at the current Moji price, plus barging (expected about 6/700 tons) and to be redelivered with bunkers as aboard, but not more than 300 tons at the current price at the port of redelivery.

The owners of the *Pantanassa* brought an action against the charterers for £ 804 11s, said by them to be due for fuel oil contained in the vessel at the time that she was delivered. Prior to the commencement of the fixture the master notified the owners' agents that he estimated that the amount of bunkers left on board would be 658 tons. When the vessel was delivered there were in fact 936 tons of fuel aboard. The result of the underestimate was that the shipowners claimed the Moji price of 176 s per ton on a larger quantity of fuel than was anticipated. The charterers objected and paid a lesser sum. Who was to suffer for the master's error? Diplock J held that the shipowners, while they made the estimate perfectly honestly, did not do so on reasonable grounds.[92] As to the consequences of the shipowners' breach, he continued that:

> It seems to me that when the vessel is delivered with bunkers as aboard, it is the obligation of the charterers to take over and pay for all the fuel remaining on board the vessel. They are left with their remedy in damages for any breach by the shipowners of the warranty on their part which I have held is contained in the words 'expected about 6/700 tons'.

> I think, therefore, that the plaintiffs, in claiming the £804 11s, are justified in doing so. But I do not think that the defendants have lost their right to claim damages for the breach of warranty merely because they accepted the vessel or took over the vessel with the full quantity, the 936 tons, on board as I think they were bound to do. I think, therefore, that the plaintiffs succeed on their claim, but the defendants have established the counterclaim. . . . It follows, therefore, that the plaintiffs are entitled to recover on the claim £804 11s and the defendants are entitled to recover on the counterclaim £804 11s.[93]

---

[89] At 418–419.
[90] See NYPE 93, cl 3, lines 39–47.
[91] [1958] 2 Lloyd's Rep 449.
[92] At 456–457.
[93] At 458–459.

F. Period of Hire

Introduction   One of the crucial provisions in a time charterparty is that concerned with   **32.32**
the period of hire. Fluctuating freight rates often mean that this is the area of time charterparties not infrequently in dispute and hence before arbitrators. One of the clauses in the
charterparty will typically state the length of the charter period. Thus, indicating its status
as a clause of the first importance in time charterparties, the NYPE 93 charterparty
provides for duration at the beginning.[94]

The period stated   The time may be stated in years or by a combination of days and years.   **32.33**
A further variation is for the period to be measured by the duration of a certain voyage
instead of a stated number of months or days. Some examples include: 'about 12 months',
'12 months, 45 days more or less', '12 months minimum, 14 months maximum'.
In *Marbienes Compania Naviera v Ferrostal AG (The Democritos)*[95] the duration of a charter
on the NYPE 1946 form was expressed as follows:

> The Owners agree to let and the Charterers agree to hire the said vessel from the time of delivery
> for about a trip via port or ports via the Pacific, duration about 4 to 6 months . . .

One of the issues in the case concerned the late redelivery of the vessel — she was redelivered
35 days later than the prescribed time. The charterers sought to argue that the redelivery
clause was drafted in such a way as to make the contract a hybrid between a voyage and time
charter, so that the owners could not, on ordinary principles, claim damages for overrun
beyond the six months. But this was rejected by the Court of Appeal who held that the
contract was still clearly a time charter. Lord Denning MR stated that

> . . . it seems to me that those words are far too indefinite to indicate any specific voyage at all.
> They do little more than state the trading limits within which the vessel is to trade during the
> time charter. They only show that the vessel has to call in at the Pacific during its course of
> operations. But that cannot affect the duration period which is specified in the charter itself.
> It was to my mind clearly a time charter.[96]

Express overlap/underlap clauses   One of the difficulties with time charters is that the final   **32.34**
voyage may fall short of the time limit (underlap) or exceed it (overlap). This point was made
as follows by Lord Mustill in *Torvald Klaveness A/S v Arni Maritime Corporation (The Gregos)*:

> [The agreed] distribution of risk[s] holds good for most of the chartered service. As the time for
> redelivery approaches things become more complicated. (The word 'redelivery' is inaccurate,[97]
> but it is convenient, and I will use it). If the market is rising, the charterer wants to have the

---

[94] Lines 23–28. Shelltime 4, cl 4, lines 110–144. For an interpretation of the Shelltime 4 clause, see
*Marimpex Mineraloel Handelsgesellschaft mbH & Co v Compagnie de Gestion et D'Exploitation Ltd (The Ambor
and the Once)* [2001] 1 All ER (Comm) 182. For the Shelltime 3 clause, see *Chiswell Shipping Ltd v National
Iranian Tanker Co (The World Symphony and World Renown)* [1991] 2 Lloyd's Rep 251 (CA); *Petroleo Brasileiro
SA v Kriti Akti Shipping Co SA (The Kriti Akti)* [2004] EWCA Civ 116; [2004] 1 Lloyd's Rep 712.

[95] [1976] 2 Lloyd's Rep 149 (CA).

[96] At 153.

[97] For an explanation as to why this is so, see the judgment of Donaldson J in *The Berge Tasta* [1975] 1
Lloyd's Rep 423, 424.

use of the vessel at the chartered rate for as long as possible. Conversely, the shipowner must think ahead to the next employment, and if as is common he had made a forward fixture he will be in difficulties if the vessel is retained by the charterer longer than had been foreseen. This conflict of interest becomes particularly acute when there is time left for only one more voyage before the expiry of the charter, and disputes may arise if the charterer orders the ship to perform a service which the shipowner believes will extend beyond the date fixed for redelivery.[98]

32.35 **Clauses for a simple period**   Where the charter is for a simple stated period, for example 'six months' or 'three years', the court will imply a reasonable margin or allowance 'to allow for the exigencies of maritime commerce'.[99] This approach recognizes that it is often not commercially practicable for the charterers when planning a voyage to calculate exactly the day on which the final voyage will end and the ship be ready for redelivery. Thus where the vessel does exceed the stated period and the market rate has risen, the charterer will only be bound to pay the charter rate until the vessel is actually redelivered. In *The Democritos*, the charterers argued that they were only bound to pay at the charter rate of hire ($1,450 per day) for the overrun, but the owners countered that they should pay the market rate, which had risen to $3,000 per day. As to what amounts to an acceptable margin of error, this will usually be determined by reference to questions of commercial convenience. In this case the arbitrators allowed a margin of five days (for six months), but this issue did not arise before the court at first instance or the Court of Appeal.[100] Kerr J at first instance said that the effect of the addition of the word 'about' before the charter period was that this would be taken as an express incorporation of the otherwise implied reasonable allowance.[101]

32.36 **No margin**   Where the parties provide by express words or implication that there is to be no margin or allowance, the charterer must ensure that the vessel is redelivered within the stated period. If he does not do so and the market rate rises, he will be bound to pay the higher rate for the period after the charter period ends. Thus in *Watson Steamship Co v Merryweather & Co*[102] the charter provided:

> 5. The charterers shall pay for the use and hire of the said vessel . . . per calendar month, commencing on and from the date of her delivery as aforesaid, and at and after the same rate for any part of a month; hire to continue from the time specified for terminating the charter until her redelivery to owners (unless lost) between 15 and 31 October 1912.

The charterers despatched the *Hugin* to St Petersburg knowing full well that it would not be possible for her to be redelivered to the owners at an east coast port by 31 October 1912. The court held that failure to deliver by 31 October 1912 was a breach of contract. Atkin J said that:

> . . . I think the proper inference to draw is that [the parties] expressly intended to negative the right to continue the contract beyond October 31; in other words, they used these words for

---

[98] [1995] 1 Lloyd's Rep 1 (HL), 4.
[99] See *Watson Steamship Co v Merryweather & Co* (1913) 18 Com Cas 294, 300 (Atkin J); *Hyundai Merchant Marine Co Ltd v Gesuri Chartering Co Ltd (The Peonia)* [1991] 1 Lloyd's Rep 100, 107 (Bingham LJ).
[100] [1976] 2 Lloyd's Rep 149, 153 (Lord Denning MR).
[101] [1975] 1 Lloyd's Rep 386.
[102] (1913) 18 Com Cas 294.

the express purpose of making the time mentioned in the charterparty as of the essence of the contract, so that the hire should terminate on October 31, and that the ship should be delivered by that date.[103]

Minimum and maximum   Where the parties have expressed the charter period as being **32.37** between a certain minimum and a certain maximum, the court will not usually imply an additional margin beyond the stated maximum and a charterer who redelivers the vessel outside these limits will be regarded as being in breach of contract and liable to pay hire at the market rate, if higher. Thus, in *Arta Shipping v Thai Europe Tapioca Shipping Service (The Johnny)*,[104] the *Johnny* was chartered for 'minimum 11/maximum 13 calendar months' under the Baltime 1939 form. In addition a clause of the charterparty provided:

> 7.   Should the vessel be ordered on a voyage by which the Charter period will be exceeded, the Charterers to have the use of the vessel to enable them to complete the voyage, provided . . . but for any time exceeding the termination date of the Charter the charterers to pay the market rate if higher than the rate stipulated herein.

The maximum 13 months was due to expire on 7 November 1974. On 19 September the charterers fixed the ship for a voyage from the UK/Continent to Karachi. She loaded at Rotterdam between 2 and 18 October and was redelivered to Karachi on 7 December, ie, 29 days late. It was therefore clear that the charterers had exceeded the terms of the charterparty as to hire. What was the appropriate market rate payable under clause 7? The arbitrators held that the 'market rate' denoted the rate for a time charter trip from UK/Continent to Karachi. At first instance Donaldson J disagreed and held that when the ship was off the coast of Southern Africa on her way to Karachi, the rate applicable would be that contained in the charterparty, the owners being responsible for bunkers and port charges, and that for the remainder of the voyage the rate payable would be a daily rate calculated from the provisions of the assumed new charter and on the same basis as to bunkers and port charges.[105] The majority of the Court of Appeal upheld this.[106] Sir David Cairns stated that:

> 'Market rate' must in my judgment be ascertained by postulating a charter-party which corresponds as closely as possible with the actual charter-party under which the voyage is performed, except of course that the hypothetical charter-party must be supposed to be entered into at the time from which the market rate is to be assessed.
>
> . . . I am satisfied that what cl 7 required is a comparison of like with like. The use of the words 'if higher than the rate stipulated herein' point to a comparison between time charter rates at different times and not to a comparison between the stipulated rate and the rate for a single voyage on time charter terms. The rate to be ascertained is one appropriate to the time for which the charterers are to have the use of the vessel after the primary delivery date: it is not a rate for a voyage but for the time taken over part of a voyage.[107]

More or less   Where the parties provide an express margin in their definition of the charter **32.38** period, for example, by adding to the basic period '20 days more or less', the leading case is

---

103 At 301.
104 [1977] 2 Lloyd's Rep 1.
105 [1977] 1 Lloyd's Rep 257.
106 Lord Denning MR dissenting.
107 [1977] 2 Lloyd's Rep 1, 4.

Alma Shipping Corporation v Mantovani (The Dione).[108] The *Dione* was time chartered on the Baltime 1939 form and the charter provided that:

1. The Owners let and the Charterers hire the vessel for a period of 6 (six) months time charter 20 days more or less in Charterers' option from the time the Vessel is delivered and placed at the disposal of the Charterers when/where ready Savannah . . .

The period of six months from the date of delivery ended on 8 September 1970, and 20 days more than six months on 28 September. On 24 July, while the ship was discharging at Ancona, the charterers proposed to send her on a further voyage to the River Plate (about 73 days duration). The ship was not then redelivered to the owners until 7 October and they claimed damages of £6,050. The arbitrators found that if a margin was to be allowed over six months and 20 days, the actual overlap of 8.4 days was reasonable. But the Court of Appeal held by a majority[109] that: (1) the clause expressly defined the margin as '20 days more or less' and left no room for any implied margin beyond this; (2) the charter expired on 28 September and the orders given by the charterers to the ship to sail to the River Plate on 2 August were illegitimate as it was then inevitable that the voyage would not be completed within the charter period; (3) the charterers were liable to pay the higher market rate of hire for the ship from 28 September to 7 October. Browne LJ stated that:

. . . [O]n the ordinary principles governing the implication of terms in a contract, I should have thought it clear . . . that where the parties have expressly agreed on a period of tolerance, as they did in this charter-party by the words '20 days more or less in Charterer's option', it would be impossible to imply a term that there should be any further tolerance.

. . . I should, therefore, hold that in the present case the charterers' express obligation was to redeliver the ship at latest on Sept 28; that it is impossible to imply any further tolerance; that they were in breach of contract in failing to do so; and that the owners were entitled to succeed.[110]

The Court of Appeal followed this in *Hyundai Merchant Marine Co Ltd v Gesuri Chartering Co Ltd (The Peonia)*.[111] Here the charterparty provided that:

. . . [T]he said Owners agree to let, and the said Charterers agree to hire the said vessel, from the time of delivery, for about minimum 10 months maximum 12 months time charter. Exact duration in Charterers option. Charterers have further option to complete last voyage within below mentioned trading limits.[112]

The *Peonia* was delivered to the charterers on 11 June 1987 and on 16 May 1988 they concluded a sub-charter to carry soya beans from the River Plate to Singapore and Butterworth; this would have meant that the vessel would be redelivered no earlier than 19 July 1988 (the expiry date being 11 June 1988). The owners protested on two occasions on hearing of this but the charterers refused to accede and the vessel was withdrawn. On the period point, Bingham LJ stated that:

It would seem to me . . . that every time charter must have a final terminal date, that is a date by which (in the absence of an exonerating clause) the charterer is contractually obliged to

---

[108] [1975] 1 Lloyd's Rep 115.
[109] Orr LJ dissenting.
[110] [1975] 1 Lloyd's Rep 115, 121. See also Lord Denning MR at 118 and *Jadranska Slobodna Plovidba v Gulf Shipping Line Ltd (The Matija Gubec)* [1983] 1 Lloyd's Rep 24, 27.
[111] [1991] 1 Lloyd's Rep 100 (CA), 107.
[112] Lines 13–15.

redeliver the vessel. Where the law implies a margin or tolerance beyond an expiry date stipulated in the charter-party, the final terminal date comes at the end of such implied extension. When the parties have agreed in the charter-party on the margin or tolerance to be allowed, the final terminal date comes at the end of such agreed period. But the nature of a time charter is that the charter is for a finite period of time and when the final terminal date arrives the charterer is contractually bound (in the absence of an exonerating clause) to redeliver the vessel to the owner.[113]

The Court of Appeal held that the inclusion of the word 'about' before the express period of 'minimum 10 months, maximum 12 months' was effective to provide an additional margin of reasonable tolerance outside the stipulated range. However, on the facts, even this additional margin could not cover the five-week period between 11 June and 19 July (which was when the vessel would have at the earliest been redelivered).

Option to renew   Where the charterer is given an option to renew a charterparty on **32.39** the same terms for the same period, the question may arise whether an express overlap or underlap period is to be allowed once or twice. In *Gulf Shipping Lines Ltd v Compania Naviera Alanje SA (The Aspa Maria)*[114] the charterparty provided that

> . . . the said Owners agree to let, and the said Charterers agree to hire the said vessel, from the time of delivery, for 6 months 30 days more or less at Charterers' option.
>
> 13. That the Charterers shall have the option of continuing this Charter for a further period of further 6 months 30 days more or less at Charterers' option declarable at the end of fourth month.

After exercising their option to renew, the charterers contended that they were entitled to use the chartered ship for a total period of 12 months and 60 days. The shipowners argued that the maximum charter period was only 12 months and 30 days. The Court of Appeal found in their favour. The phrase '30 days more or less' did not constitute an extension of the charter period, but was merely a period of tolerance in redelivery. Orr LJ stated that:

> On the basis . . . that 30 days more or less represents tolerance period as respects the date of redelivery, the learned Judge [Mocatta J][115] was, in my view, entirely right in holding that it can hardly have been the intention of the parties that the charterers in the circumstances of this case should have the benefit of two tolerance periods in respect of only one delivery.[116]

Underlap   Where the vessel is returned to the owner before the expiry of the stated mini- **32.40** mum period of hire it seems that the charterer is not entitled to a refund but will be required to pay the full hire for the agreed period.[117] If this in itself is regarded as a breach of contract, it would then be arguable that the owner is under a duty to mitigate his loss by rehiring the vessel, provided that this is commercially possible within the balance of the charter period.

Late redelivery   The liability of the charterer for late redelivery will depend on whether or **32.41** not he is in breach of contract. If redelivery of the vessel is made within the express period

---

[113] [1991] 1 Lloyd's Rep 100 (CA), 107.
[114] [1976] 2 Lloyd's Rep 643 (CA).
[115] [1976] 1 Lloyd's Rep 542.
[116] [1976] 2 Lloyd's Rep 643 (CA), 645.
[117] As to the quantum of damages for an early repudiation, in anticipation of the second Gulf War, see now *Golden Strait Corp v Nippon Yusen Kubishika Kaisha* [2005] EWCA Civ 1190; [2006] 1 WLR 533.

of tolerance the extra time will be paid for at the normal charter rate. However, where redelivery is made outside the period of tolerance, whether express or implied, damages will be assessed in relation to the current market rate of hire. The courts apply the 'legitimate last voyage' test in determining whether a charterer is in breach of contract. Thus the last voyage is 'legitimate' if there is a reasonable expectation that it will be completed before the 'final terminal date' — ie, before the end of any overlap period, express and/or implied.[118] In *The Peonia* Bingham LJ explained that

> in the . . . case of the legitimate last voyage the charterer gives orders for the employment of the vessel which can reasonably be expected to be performed by the final terminal date. These are orders which the charterer is entitled to give, and so legitimate. If the parties' reasonable expectations are fulfilled and the voyage is performed by the final terminal date no difficulty of course arises.[119]

32.42 **Illegitimate voyages** An illegitimate voyage is one which cannot be completed within the charter period. Again, as Bingham LJ explained:

> [The charterer] is seeking to avail himself of the services of the vessel at a time when the owner had never agreed to render such services. It is accordingly an order which the charterer is not entitled to give . . . and in giving it the charterer commits a breach of contract (perhaps a repudiatory breach but that we need not decide).[120]

In *The Peonia* the owners had let her

> . . . from the time of delivery, for about minimum 10 months maximum 12 months time charter. Exact duration in Charterers option. Charterers have further option to complete last voyage within below mentioned trading limits.

The arbitrators declared that the charterers were entitled to order the vessel to undertake a last voyage that started before the latest time for redelivery (11 June 1988) as extended by the word 'about'. But at first instance, Saville J[121] held that the charterers were not entitled to order the vessel to perform a voyage which could not be completed before about 11 June 1988 and the owners were entitled to refuse to accede to such an order. The charterers appealed to the Court of Appeal who confirmed that the charterer was bound to redeliver by the final terminal date, even where the orders for the last voyage were legitimate. Where the charterer gave an order such that the vessel could not be redelivered by the final terminal date, this was illegitimate and he committed a breach of contract. If the owner of the vessel complied with an illegitimate order

> . . . although not bound to do so . . . he is entitled to the payment of hire at the charterparty rate until the redelivery of the vessel and (provided he does not waive the charterer's breach) to damages (being the difference between the charter rate and the market rate if the market rate is higher than the charter rate) for the period between the final terminal date and redelivery.[122]

Further, with regard to the 'further option' in the clause, Bingham LJ said that:

> What the charterers are really claiming is not an option to complete, since no one doubts that a voyage once begun must in any ordinary circumstances be completed. What they are really

---

[118] *The Peonia* [1991] 1 Lloyd's Rep 100, 107 (Bingham LJ).
[119] At 108.
[120] At 107–108.
[121] [1991] 1 Lloyd's Rep 100.
[122] At 108.

claiming is a right to require the owners not to complete but to embark upon an illegitimate last voyage. That is by definition a voyage which is not under the charterparty but outside it.[123]

The Gregos These matters were taken a step further in *Torvald Klaveness A/S v Arni* **32.43** *Maritime Corporation (The Gregos).*[124] In this case, a charterparty on the NYPE 1946 form, the charterers let the *Gregos* for a period of 'about 50 to maximum 70 days Time charter in Charterers' option'.[125] Clause 4 provided that 'Hire . . . to continue until the hour of the day of her redelivery.' The vessel performed two voyages in South America between Trobetas (Brazil) and Matanzas (Venezuela) carrying a cargo of bauxite but, before completion of the second, was ordered on 9 February 1988 to proceed from Matanzas to a nearby Venezuelan port, Palua, to load a cargo of iron ore for carriage to Fos in Italy. This became impossible by 25 February as another vessel had grounded in the River Orinoco preventing passage from Matanzas to Palua. When the vessel gave notice of readiness to load at Palua on 25 February the owners contended that the orders to proceed to Fos were illegitimate and threatened to treat the charterers as being in repudiatory breach and to withdraw the vessel. While this disagreement was in process, the owners negotiated a replacement fixture with another concern for a higher rate of freight than under the existing charter. The parties entered into a without prejudice agreement, however, and the vessel duly performed her final voyage. She was redelivered on 26 March, eight days late.

The operative date issue In *The Gregos*[126] the charterers contended that the date for **32.44** determining the lawfulness or otherwise of an order for a final voyage had to be tested at the date when it was given. Not surprisingly, the owners argued that the operative date was when compliance with the order was required. Lord Mustill considered that the debate about the operative date issue had 'been led astray by concentrating too much on the final order and not sufficiently on the shipowners' promise to provide the vessel, which is what the contract is about'.[127] He concluded that, as a matter of common sense, the time for such measurement was, primarily at least, the time when performance fell due. However, if circumstances changed, so that compliance with the order would call for a service which in the original contract the shipowner never undertook, the obligation to comply fell away.[128] Accordingly, concentrating on the charterparty, he held that the correct date for the assessment of the operative date was 25 February, the day when an order originally permissible had become illegitimate.

The repudiation issue In *The Gregos*[129] Lord Mustill adopted a fresh approach to the **32.45** repudiation issue as he considered that the House was 'free to approach the matter from first principles'.[130] Lord Mustill preferred to see an invalid final voyage order as a special

---

[123] At 116.
[124] [1995] 1 Lloyd's Rep 1 (HL). See too Stephen Girvin, 'Time Charter Overlap: Determining Legitimacy and the Operation of Repudiatory Breach of Contract' [1995] JBL 200; Chan Leng Sun, 'Last orders and late redelivery' [1995] LMCLQ 318.
[125] Line 14.
[126] [1995] 1 Lloyd's Rep 1 (HL).
[127] At 7.
[128] ibid.
[129] [1995] 1 Lloyd's Rep 1 (HL).
[130] [1995] 1 Lloyd's Rep 1 (HL), 10. See also Lord Mustill's lecture, 'Anticipatory Breach of Contract: The Common Law at Work', *Butterworth Lectures 1989–90* (1990) 1.

case of an order issued for the performance of a service which lay outside the scope of the shipowners' promise. On this analysis, he canvassed three different grounds upon which it could be said that the charterer had called upon the shipowner to perform an extra-contractual service such that the latter would be entitled to treat himself as discharged from the contract. First, giving an illegitimate order for the employment of the ship was in its nature a repudiatory breach. Secondly, redelivery after the final date would be a breach of condition and would entitle the shipowner to treat himself as discharged (and it followed that an order for an illegitimate final voyage would be a repudiatory breach). Thirdly, the charterer's persistence in giving an illegitimate order would be conduct 'evidencing an intention no longer to be bound' by the contract. Taking these grounds in order, Lord Mustill accepted that an order which was illegitimate would itself be a breach of contract. He was not, however, persuaded of a commercial necessity to hold that an invalid order would automatically entitle the shipowner to terminate the charter. On the second ground, Lord Mustill hesitated to express a firm view although he accepted that the obligation to redeliver was an 'innominate' obligation.[131] On the third ground, Lord Mustill held that, although the illegitimate order did not itself constitute a repudiation, the charterers' persistence in it after it had become invalid showed that they did not intend to perform their obligations under the charter.[132] Once the charterers refused to give a valid order, they had evinced an intention no longer to be bound by the charterparty, and this was an anticipatory breach of contract. It therefore followed that the owners were entitled to treat the contract as at an end. The charterers were under a continuing obligation to give a valid order.[133]

32.46 **The damages award** In *The Gregos*[134] the arbitrator assessed the damages on the basis that the owners would, but for the without prejudice agreement, have been able to withdraw the vessel for wrongful repudiation on 25 February and re-charter her at the prevailing higher rate. In the Court of Appeal, Hirst LJ was sympathetic to the charterers' concern that the owners' case on repudiation would enable them 'to recover from the charterers windfall damages'.[135] Though Lord Mustill saw force in the point that a comparatively minor breach by the charterers might seem out of proportion to their ability to sub-charter the vessel, he thought that this was insufficient to 'overcome the contractual logic'. In a volatile freight market, the contract breaker (the charterer) might well find that the consequences of his breach were 'multiplied to a surprising degree by adventitious factors'.[136] As the charterers were mistaken in standing their ground as they had done, they would have to

---

[131] In the Court of Appeal, Hirst LJ had made the point that the law had always regarded the redelivery obligation as prima facie flexible and subject to a margin of tolerance in certain circumstances, having regard to the exigencies of maritime commerce: [1993] 2 Lloyd's Rep 335 (CA), 344.

[132] [1995] 1 Lloyd's Rep 1 (HL), 10.

[133] ibid.

[134] [1995] 1 Lloyd's Rep 1 (HL).

[135] [1993] 2 Lloyd's Rep 335 (CA), 348.

[136] [1995] 1 Lloyd's Rep 1 (HL), 10.

'suffer the consequences, harsh as they may seem'.[137] The owners were in effect being remunerated for performing a voyage from which they would otherwise have been free.[138]

G. Payment for Hire

Introduction   In a time charterparty one of the express clauses will state the time, place, **32.47** and frequency of payments of hire. The currency for payment will normally be specified as well.[139]

Payment in cash   Time charters invariably specify that payment for hire is to be in cash. **32.48** In *Tenax Steamship Co v Brimnes (The Owners)*[138A] clause 5 provided that:

> Payment of said hire to be made in New York in cash in United States Currency to Morgan Guaranty Trust Co of New York, 23 Wall Street, New York, for the credit of the account for Reinante Transoceanica Navegacion SA of Panama re ms 'Brimnes' monthly in advance.

Brandon J said of the requirement that payment be 'in cash' that:

> In my view these words must be interpreted against the background of modern commercial practice. So interpreted it seems to me that they cannot mean payment in dollar bills or other legal tender of the US. They must, as the shipowners contend, have a wider meaning, comprehending any commercially-recognised method of transferring funds, the result of which is to give the transferee the unconditional right to the immediate use of the funds transferred.[140]

It has been accepted that banker's drafts and payment slips are valid tender, as is payment by transfer of funds from one account to another, provided that the money is immediately available to the shipowner on transfer.

Payment orders   There is some uncertainty about a 'payment order' under the London **32.49** Currency Settlement Scheme. This question arose in *Mardorf Peach & Co Ltd v Attica Sea Carriers Corp (The Laconia)*[140A] where clause 52 provided that:

> Hire to be paid to owners Messrs Attica Sea Carriers Corporation of Liberia into their account with First National City Bank of New York, 34, Moorgate, London, EC2 to the credit of OFC Account No 705586.

Lord Salmon explained the system in the London Currency Settlement Scheme, as follows:

> [The Scheme] . . . is used by the banks in London who are parties to it, solely for the purpose of transferring USA and Canadian dollars as requested by their customers. The transfers are made by payment orders from the issuing bank crediting the recipient bank with an amount in favour of a named customer of the recipient bank. This system has the advantage of saving the time and money which would otherwise be spent in sending telegraphic and mail transfers and drafts between members banks in London and involving their respective correspondents

---

[137] ibid.
[138] ibid.
[138A] [1972] 2 Lloyd's Rep 465.
[139] NYPE 93, cl 11, lines 140–158; Shelltime 4, cl 9, lines 179–205.
[140] At 476.
[140A] [1977] AC 850.

in the USA and Canada. As debit and credit balances build up between participating banks in relation to payment orders passing between them, settlements are made between them at their convenience. Payment orders are regarded in the banking world as the equivalent of cash. When a payment order is received by a bank in favour of one of its customers a certain amount of paper work or processing, usually taking about 24 hours, is required until the amount of the payment order is credited to the customer's account.[141]

Although the case was disposed of on other grounds, two members of the House of Lords (Lords Salmon and Russell)[142] expressed obiter views that payment would be effective upon delivery of such a 'payment order' to the owner's bank. Although Lord Fraser disagreed,[143] the better view is probably that such orders should be accepted in the interests of reasonable commercial certainty.

32.50 **Telex transfers** By analogy, a telex transfer of funds from one bank to another would also constitute 'payment in cash'. The difficulty with telexes is that the owner's right to the immediate use of the funds transferred is required to be 'unconditional'. In *A/S Awilco v Fulvia SpA di Navigazione (The Chikuma)*[144] a vessel was chartered on the NYPE 1946 form with payment to 'Barclays Bank Ltd, 54 Lombard Street'. Clause 5 of the charterparty provided that:

> Payment of said hire to be made in London in cash in United States Currency monthly in advance . . . otherwise failing the punctual and regular payment of the hire . . . the Owners shall be at liberty to withdraw the vessel from the service of the Charterers . . .

Following the sale of the *Chikuma* to new owners, a novation took place, Addendum 4 to the charterparty providing that freights were to be payable to the new owners' bank in Genoa:

> [All freights to be paid to the owners' agents] . . . care of Instituto Bancario San Paolo di Torino — Sede di Genova ['the owners' bank'].

A monthly payment of hire (due on 22 January 1976) was paid to the bank on the due date but the paying bank included in its telex transfer a 'value date', for interest, four days after this (26 January). The effect of this stipulation in Italy was that the owners could have withdrawn the funds from their bank at once but may then have been obliged to pay interest on the funds from then until the 'value date'. The owners withdrew their ship on 24 January 1976 and this right was upheld by the House of Lords. Payment did not amount to 'cash' because the liability to pay interest on the funds transferred prevented the owners from having an 'unconditional' right to their immediate use. Lord Bridge stated that:

> The book entry made by the owners' bank on January 22 in the owners' account was clearly not the equivalent of cash, nor was there any reason why the owners should have been prepared to treat it as the equivalent of cash. It could not be used to earn interest, eg, by immediate transfer to a deposit account. It could only be drawn subject to a (probable) liability to pay interest. In substance it was the equivalent of an overdraft facility which the bank was bound to make available . . .[145]

---

[141] At 879.
[142] At 888.
[143] At 884–885.
[144] [1981] 1 Lloyd's Rep 371.
[145] At 376.

Payment in advance A further refinement of the payment clause is that payment may be   **32.51**
required to be paid 'in advance'.[146] This means that payment must be made before performance and may be made on or before the due date. It is strictly construed. If the due date
is Sunday, payment must be made on the previous banking day and breach of this will mean
that the charterer is in default. In *Afovos Shipping Co SA v R Pagnan & F Lli (The Afovos)*[147]
a clause of the charterparty provided that:

> 5. Payment of said hire to be made in London, to the FIRST NATIONAL BANK OF
>   CHICAGO . . . London EC3P 3DR, for the credit of ANGELICOUSSIS SHIPHOLD-
>   ING GROUP, LIMITED . . . in cash in United States Currency, semi-monthly in advance
>   . . . otherwise failing the punctual and regular payment of the hire . . . the Owners shall be
>   at liberty to withdraw the vessel from the service of the Charterers . . .

The issue before the House of Lords involved a consideration of this clause in conjunction
with a so-called 'anti-technicality clause' (clause 31) in the charterparty. Payment was due
by the charterers on 14 June 1979 and on 11 June the charterers gave instruction for
payment by their bank to FNBC. The charterers' bank (Credito Italiano) purported to
telex a transfer of funds on 13 June. The telex never arrived since it was sent by mistake to
a firm in Reigate, Surrey. The owners withdrew the vessel on 18 June. Lord Hailsham LC
stated that

> in principle, only one answer is possible, namely at midnight on the last day available to them
> for the due and punctual payment of the hire, ie June 14. I take it to be a general principle of
> law not requiring authority that where a person under an obligation to do a particular act has
> to do it on or before a particular date he has the whole of that day to perform his duty.
> No doubt as the hours pass it becomes less and less probable that he will be able to do it.
> That is the risk he runs. But he is not actually in default until the time arrives.[148]

Payment will not be dependent on banking hours.

Overpayment of hire The case of *Pan Ocean Shipping Co Ltd v Creditcorp Ltd (The Trident*   **32.52**
Beauty)[149] considered the issue whether hire overpaid by the charterer might be recovered
from an assignee of freight receivables. Pan Ocean chartered the mv *Trident Beauty* from the
disponent owners, Trident Shipping Co Ltd, on the NYPE 1946 form. The charter was for
a single time charter trip, at the rate of $6,400 per day, payable as follows:

> 5. Payment of said hire to be made in London in cash in United States currency in advance,
>   and for the last half month or part of same the approximate amount of hire, but always
>   subject to clause 29 [charterers' right to deduct from last hire payments any fines and
>   owners' disbursements . . .]
>
> 16. That should the vessel be lost, money paid in advance and not earned … shall be
>   returned to the charterers at once . . .

In order to finance its activities Trident had arranged finance facilities with Creditcorp.
At the same time as executing the charterparty, Trident 'irrevocably and exclusively'
assigned to investors 'free of all encumbrances and third party interests' its right title and

---

146 NYPE 93, cl 11(a), line 147; Shelltime 4, cl 9, line 185.
147 [1983] 1 Lloyd's Rep 335 (HL).
148 At 340.
149 [1994] 1 WLR 161 (HL).

interest in and to freight receivables, including such sums as were payable to them for the charter of the *Trident Beauty*. Following notification to them of the assignment, the charterers made a third payment in advance to Creditcorp ($93,600, to cover the period 31 May to 15 June 1991). But at the time of this third payment the ship was off-hire and about to undergo repairs in a Singaporean shipyard. She remained off-hire throughout the period of the third hire payment. On 12 June 1991 the charterers were informed that the vessel had been withdrawn from Trident by the head owners. Although repairs had been completed, the vessel could not resume service because Trident had failed to pay the ship repair yard. On 10 July the charterers accepted Trident's conduct as amounting to a repudiation of the charterparty. By this time Trident was no longer worth suing and the charterers sought to recover from Creditcorp the advance payment made on 31 May. There was no direct authority on the point. The House of Lords, upholding the Court of Appeal, declined to permit the charterers to recover from Creditcorp. Lord Woolf (as he then was) gave the following reasons:

> It is one thing to require the other party to the contract to repay if he does not provide the consideration which under the contract he was under obligation to supply, it is another to make the assignee, who was never intended to be under any obligation to supply the consideration liable to make the repayment. It is conceded that there is no right to trace monies which are paid to an assignee and there is never any question of there being any restriction on the assignee preventing him dealing with the money as his own. There is no justification for subjecting an assignee, because he has received a payment in advance, to an obligation to make a repayment because of the non-performance of an event for which he has no responsibility.[150]

H. The Off-Hire Clause

32.53 **Introduction** All standard form time charterparties will contain a clause specifying that hire will not be payable by the charterer during any period when the full use of the vessel is not available because of some accident or deficiency which falls on the shipowner. The clause in effect operates as an exception to the charterer's primary obligation to pay hire continuously throughout the charter period. With certain exceptions, off-hire clauses tend to be drafted at some length, probably because the burden is on the charterer to prove that hire has been suspended.[151]

32.54 **Main principles** Some of the main principles were neatly articulated by Kerr J in *Mareva Navigation Co Ltd v Canaria Armadora SA (The Mareva AS)*:

> It is settled law that prima facie hire is payable continuously and that it is for the charterers to bring themselves clearly within an off-hire clause if they contend that hire ceases. This clause undoubtedly presents difficulties of construction and may well contain some tautology, eg in the reference to damage to hull, machinery or equipment followed by 'average accidents to ship'. But I think that the object is clear. The owners provide the ship and the crew to work her. So long as these are fully efficient and able to render to the charterers the service then required, hire is payable continuously. But if the ship is for any reason not in full working

---

[150] At 170–171.
[151] See NYPE 93, cl 17, lines 219–236; Shelltime 4, cl 21, lines 339–398.

order to render the service then required from her, and the charterers suffer loss of time in consequence, then hire is not payable for the time so lost.[152]

Burden on the charterer   Standard off-hire clauses will be triggered by the occurrence **32.55** of one of the specified events, irrespective of the fault of the shipowner. The burden will be on the charterer to show that the off-hire clause operates in the relevant circumstances. Bucknill LJ said in *Royal Greek Government v Minister of Transport (The Ilissos)* that:

> ... [T]he cardinal rule in interpreting such a charter-party as this, is that the charterer must pay hire for the use of the ship unless he can bring himself clearly within the exceptions. If there is a doubt as to what the words mean, then I think those words must be read in favour of the owners because the charterer is attempting to cut down the owners' right to hire. In that connexion, I attach considerable importance to the words ... .[153]

The case clearly establishes that any ambiguity in the off-hire clause will be resolved in favour of the owner.

Similar causes   Standard clauses sometimes conclude with the phrase 'or by any other **32.56** [similar] cause preventing the full working of the vessel'.[154] Such 'other similar causes' are usually restricted to those which directly affect the running of the vessel and exclude external events which do not relate to the physical condition of the vessel or of its crew. In *Mareva Navigation Co Ltd v Canaria Armadora SA (The Mareva AS)* one of the issues for consideration by Kerr J was the interpretation of the off-hire clause:

> 15.   That in the event of the loss of time from deficiency of men or stores, fire, breakdown or damages to hull, machinery or equipment, grounding, detention by average accidents to ship or cargo, dry-docking for the purpose of examination or painting bottom, or by any other cause preventing the full working of the vessel, the payment of hire shall cease for the time thereby lost.

The charter required delivery to be made on the vessel 'passing outwards Shatt el Arab' and hire was set at $4,000 per day, until redelivery. The charterers sub-chartered the *Mareva AS* for a voyage from one port in the Texas–US Gulf Range to one or two ports in Algeria with a cargo of wheat in bulk. There was a discharging demurrage rate of $5,000 per day. One of the factors causing eventual delay of the vessel was wetting of the cargo, mainly because, in breach of the owners' seaworthiness obligations, the hatch covers were not sound. This caused delay in discharging in Algeria and, eventually, late redelivery under the head charterparty. The arbitrators found that the charterers were paid demurrage by the sub-charterers for some or all of the time during which the cargo could either not be discharged or could only be discharged at a slower rate. While the owners were prepared to accept that they should refund hire to the charterers at the rate of $7,000 for the period of 15 days' delay, they argued that, in so far as the charterers had received demurrage at the rate of $5,000 under the sub-charter for the same period, they were entitled to credit for this. Kerr J denied the owners any recovery by way of credit:

> ... [I]n one way or another the charterers have clearly paid for the right to demurrage as part of their bargain. The owners, as wrong-doers, cannot be entitled to lessen their liability by

---

[152] [1977] 1 Lloyd's Rep 368, 381–382.
[153] [1949] 1 KB 525 (CA), 529.
[154] See NYPE 93, cl 17, line 225; Shelltime 4, cl 21(a)(i), line 345.

claiming credit for one benefit which accrued to the charterers from this bargain, ignoring whatever the charterers may have had to concede in order to obtain this benefit.[155]

The charterers sought to argue that there was a loss of time under clause 15. Further they claimed that 'detention' under the clause meant no more than delay and that the words 'or by any other cause preventing the full working of the vessel' were mere sweeping-up words, not qualifying the earlier incidents mentioned in the clause. In response to this Kerr J held that:

> The word 'other' in the phrase 'or by any other cause preventing the full working of the vessel' in my view shows that the various events referred to in the foregoing provisions were also only intended to take effect if the full working of the vessel in the sense just described was thereby prevented and the time lost in consequence. But if, for instance, the cargo is damaged as a result of an accident, but the vessel's ability to work fully is not thereby prevented or impaired, because the vessel in herself remains fully efficient in all respects, then I do not think that the charterers bring themselves within the clause. On this analysis . . . I . . . consider that the vessel was not off-hire.[156]

The general view seems to be that the phrase 'any other cause' must be interpreted *ejusdem generis* and hence confined to other causes related to the physical condition of the ship or crew.[157] However, it seems that the *ejusdem generis* rule will be excluded where the word 'whatsoever' is inserted in the off-hire clause after 'any other cause'.[158]

32.57 *The Laconian Confidence* The case of *Andre & Cie SA v Orient Shipping (Rotterdam) BV (The Laconian Confidence)*[159] had to consider the effect of the phrase 'any other cause' in the context of a refusal by the Bangladesh port authorities at Chittagong to allow the *Laconian Confidence* to proceed because of the presence on board of residue sweepings. The interference by the authorities resulted in a delay of 18 days until the *Laconian Confidence* was permitted to dump these residues and sail. Was the ship off-hire during this period? The arbitrators found against the charterers and they appealed to Rix J. Rix J found that:

> [I]t is well established that [the words 'any other cause'], in the absence of 'whatsoever', should be construed either ejusdem generis or at any rate in some limited way reflecting the general context of the charter and clause . . . A consideration of the named clauses indicates that they all relate to the physical condition or efficiency of either vessel (including its crew) or, in one instance, cargo. . . . In such circumstances it is to my mind natural to conclude that the unamended words 'any other cause' do not cover an entirely extraneous cause, . . . or the interference of authorities unjustified by the condition (or reasonably suspected condition) of ship or cargo. Prima facie it does not seem to me that it can be intended by a standard off-hire clause that an owner takes the risk of delay due to the interference of authorities, at any rate where that interference is something beyond the natural or reasonably foreseeable consequence of some named cause. Where, however, the clause is amended to include the word 'whatsoever', I do not see why the interference of authorities which prevents the vessel performing its intended service should not be regarded as falling within the clause, and I would be inclined to say that that remains so whether or not that interference can be related to some underlying cause internal to the ship, or is merely capricious.

---

155 [1977] 1 Lloyd's Rep 368, 380.
156 At 382.
157 See *Actis Co Ltd v Sanko Steamship Co Ltd (The Aquacharm)* [1982] 1 Lloyd's Rep 237, 239 (Lloyd J).
158 See *Sidermar SpA v Apollo Corporation (The Apollo)* [1978] 1 Lloyd's Rep 200, 205 (Mocatta J).
159 [1997] 1 Lloyd's Rep 139.

In the absence of the word 'whatsoever', the unexpected and unforeseeable interference by the authorities at Chittagong at the conclusion of what was found to be a normal discharge was a totally extraneous cause . . . unconnected with, because too remote from, the merely background circumstance of the cargo residues of 15.75 tonnes. There was no accident to cargo, and there was nothing about the vessel herself, her condition or efficiency, nor even anything about the cargo, which led naturally or in the normal course of events to any delay. If the authorities had not prevented the vessel from working, she would have been perfectly capable of discharging the residues or of sailing and dumping them without any abnormal delay. In such circumstances I reject [counsel's] submission that the action of the authorities was in any sense ejusdem generis any of the named causes within the clause.[160]

Seizure or detention   In *Nippon Yusen Kaisha Ltd v Scindia Steam Navigation Co Ltd*   **32.58**
(The Jalagouri)[161] the Court of Appeal considered an off-hire clause (clause 53) which referred to 'the vessel [being] seized or detained or arrested or delayed by any authority . . .'. The *Jalagouri* had collided with a breakwater, causing an ingress of water which damaged car components stored in her hold. At the discharge port the authorities ordered the vessel to berth at the port's inner anchorage and refused permission to discharge the damaged cargo without a financial guarantee for the costs of storing the damaged parts or of clearing them from the port area. The charterers provided such a guarantee and then purported to deduct US$67,872.87 from hire, on the basis that the vessel was off-hire under the charterparty. The Court of Appeal held that the vessel was indeed off-hire.[162]

Security detention   The case of *Hyundai Merchant Marine Co Ltd v Furness Withy*   **32.59**
(Australia) Pty (The Doric Pride)[163] has focused attention, for the first time, on the consequences of a vessel falling foul of a sovereign state's port security measures.[164] The *Doric Pride* was time chartered for

> . . . one time charter trip via safe anchorage(s), safe berth(s), safe ports always afloat, always Institute Warranty Limits from US Gulf to South Korea with bulk grain, duration of about 65–75 days without guarantee . . .

The vessel was ordered to New Orleans to load a cargo of soya beans and, after arriving at the South West Passage, the master was notified by telex from the US Coastguard that the *Doric Pride* had been targeted as a 'High Interest Vessel', was prohibited from entering the lower Mississippi, and was directed to a waiting position pending inspection by a US Coastguard boarding team. The *Doric Pride* arrived at the designated waiting position on 20 February 2004, but, following a collision which closed the South West Passage, she was directed to await inspection there. Inspection of the *Doric Pride* was subsequently delayed until 26 February when it was successfully completed. Clause 85 of the charterparty

---

160 At 150–151.

161 [2000] 1 Lloyd's Rep 515 (CA). See Stephen Girvin, '"Detention" and the NYPE Off-Hire Clause' [2001] LMCLQ 186.

162 At 519 (Tuckey LJ). cf *Ocean Marine Navigation Ltd v Koch Carbon Inc (The Dynamic)* [2003] EWHC 1936 (Comm); [2003] 2 Lloyd's Rep 693, where an off-hire clause did not apply to arrests during the currency of the charter.

163 [2006] EWCA Civ 599;[2006] 2 Lloyd's Rep 175.

164 See Stephen Girvin, 'Commercial Implications of the ISPS Code' (2005) 330 Marlus 307; Baris Soyer and Richard Williams, 'Potential legal ramifications of the International Ship and Port Facility Security (ISPS) Code on maritime law' [2005] LMCLQ 515.

provided for the suspension of hire following 'capture, seizure, arrest'.[165] The charterer argued that the vessel was 'detained' and off-hire from 20 February to 26 February. The court at first instance so found on the basis that the detention was the result of regulations and legal powers under which the US Coastguard operated throughout the US.[166] The Court of Appeal agreed that responsibility for the detention had to lie with the shipowners, although Rix LJ went on to say that it was possible to view the reasoning of the judge

> that the vessel would be likely to receive the same treatment whichever port in the US Gulf she was sent to by the charterers, as a reflection of the underlying fact that the real problem lay in the vessel's status and not in the charterers' trading.[167]

32.60 **Independent of breach** The off-hire clause operates independently of any common law breach of contract by the owners. If the charterers are able to invoke the clause because of one of the off-hire events, then their rights will be spelt out in the off-hire clause and any question of damages arising out of the off-hire event will have to be determined at common law. In *Ocean Glory Compania Naviera SA v A/S PV Christensen (The Ioanna)*, Staughton J stated that:

> Off-hire events are not necessarily a breach of contract at all. So one should not be surprised if one finds that [the off-hire clause] leads to a different answer than would ensue in the case of a claim for damages for breach of contract.[168]

32.61 **Period of off-hire** Generally speaking the charterer will be unable to rely on an off-hire clause unless he is deprived of the use of the vessel by the occurrence of one of the specified events. The happening of one of the listed incidents, such as a breakdown of machinery, does not result in an automatic interruption of hire unless it can be shown that time was lost to the charterers. The ship may well be off-hire because of a breakdown of propulsion machinery while she is required to be at sea but she will be on-hire immediately the machinery is no longer relevant to the particular service which the charterers next require. In *Hogarth v Miller*[169] an off-hire clause provided that:

> In the event of loss of time from deficiency of men or stores, break-down of machinery, want of repairs, or damage, whereby the working of the vessel is stopped for more than forty-eight consecutive working hours, the payment of hire shall cease until she be again in an efficient state to resume her service.

On a voyage between Africa and Harburg, the *Westfalia's* high-pressure engine broke down requiring her to put into Las Palmas. Repairs could not be effected there and the vessel had to be towed to Harburg with some assistance being given by her low-pressure engine. At Harburg the cargo was offloaded using the ship's steam winches and cargo machinery which were in efficient working order. The question for the House of Lords was whether or not the *Westfalia* was off-hire during the towage voyage between Las Palmas

---

[165] The court found that the clause was a 'period' off-hire clause, rather than a 'net loss of time' clause. See para 32.62.
[166] [2005] EWHC 945 (Comm); [2005] 2 Lloyd's Rep 470.
[167] [2006] EWCA Civ 599; [2006] 2 Lloyd's Rep 175, at [49].
[168] [1985] 2 Lloyd's Rep 164, 167.
[169] [1891] AC 48.

and Harburg. The House of Lords held that the ship was off-hire for although the cargo was carried to its destination she was not fully efficient during the tow because she could not proceed without the aid of the tug. But once discharge of the cargo had commenced, the *Westfalia* came on hire again as she was efficient for what was then required of her. Lord Halsbury LC stated that:

I should read the contract as meaning this, . . . that she should be efficient to do what she was required to do when she was called upon to do it; and accordingly, at each period, if what was required of her was to lie at anchor, if it was to lie alongside the wharf, upon each of these occasions, if she was efficient to do it at that time she would then become, in the language of the contract, to my mind 'efficient', reading with it the other words, 'for the working of the vessel'.[170]

Another illustration of this point is the case of *Sig Bergesen DY & Co v Mobil Shipping & Transportation Co (The Berge Sund)*.[171] In this case, the off-hire clause provided that:

8(a) In the event that a loss time, not caused by Charterer's fault, shall continue, (i) due to repairs, breakdown, accident or damage to the vessel, collision, stranding, fire, interference by authorities or any other cause preventing the efficient working of the vessel, for more than twenty-four (24) consecutive hours . . . then hire shall cease for all time so lost until the vessel is again in an efficient state to resume her service and has regained a point of progress equivalent to that when hire ceased hereunder.

The charterers ordered the *Berge Sund* to load and carry a cargo of butane (which has a high sulphur content) from Chiba (Japan) to Terneuzen in The Netherlands. Following discharge of the butane, the vessel was sub-chartered to P & O, delivery off Fujairah or on passing Quoin Island inbound. The voyage from Terneuzen was a ballast voyage during the course of which some tank cleaning was undertaken. When surveyors, appointed by the charterers, conducted tests on the vessel's tanks it was found that they were contaminated. Was the *Berge Sund* off-hire during the ballast voyage to the Gulf? Both the arbitrators and Steyn J found that she was off-hire, but this was overturned by the Court of Appeal. Staughton LJ's reasoning was as follows:

. . . [C]leaning is in the ordinary way an activity required by a time charterer. It is his choice what cargoes are loaded, and consequently when and what cleaning is required. If in a particular case the charterer declines to load until there has been further or extraordinary cleaning, the service required is that cleaning. . . .

. . . I can see no ground for distinguishing between ordinary cleaning and extraordinary or unusual cleaning. If either is required by the charterer, it is the service which for the time being the vessel must be efficient to perform, and time spent on it is not time lost.[172]

Types of clause   Off-hire clauses are usually distinguished as being 'net loss of time' **32.62** or 'period' clauses but it is always a matter of construction as to what clause is in question. Robert Goff J provided the following useful explanation of the two types of clause in *Western Sealanes Corporation v Unimarine SA (The Pythia)*:[173]

Historically some time charters have contained period clauses under which in certain specified circumstances the ship goes off-hire for a certain period. However there are also . . . net

170 At 56–57.
171 [1993] 2 Lloyd's Rep 453 (CA).
172 At 461. See also Sir Roger Parker at 463.
173 [1982] 1 Lloyd's Rep 160, 168.

loss of time clauses, under which the ship is only put off-hire for the 'time lost thereby', so that the time charterers cannot escape all liability for hire in respect of time for which they have at least some use of the vessel for the services immediately required of her.[174]

32.63 **Period clauses** Period clauses designate the start and end of any period for which hire is suspended; the clause will state that hire ceases to be due from the off-hire event until the vessel is again in an efficient state to resume service. Efficiency is the crucial consideration in such clauses and partial inefficiency has the same effect as total inefficiency. In either case, the ship will be off-hire with no allowance being made for the partial working of the ship. In *Tyndale SS Co Ltd v Anglo-Soviet Shipping Co Ltd*[175] the 'period' off-hire clause provided:

> 10. In the event of loss of time . . . time so lost and expenses incurred shall be for charterers' account, even if caused through fault or want of due diligence by owners' servants.

While en route from Archangel (Russia) to Liverpool the *Hordern* encountered heavy weather which caused damage to her mast. In Liverpool the vessel could only discharge half of her cargo of timber at a time. The forward part of the ship could not be discharged and the charterers had to hire lighter craft to carry out discharge at the port. Lord Roche relied directly on the reasoning of Lord Halsbury LC in *Hogarth v Miller*, a case which also contained a 'period' off-hire clause.[176] The wording of the clause established a clear-cut 'period' of off-hire:

> Now, converting that into the language necessary for the present purpose, you are to consider in the matter of discharge what means of discharge were contemplated. Answer: the winches and the derricks. Were those means of discharge available? Answer: No, half of them were not. It seems to me that it follows from that reasoning that the vessel was not fit or able to work for the services required and stipulated for by the initial words of the charter-party, and under those circumstances two results follow. Under Clause 2 it was the duty of the owners then to put her back into an efficient state in hull and machinery for that purpose. Under Clause 10 events had happened which put into operation the cesser of hire clause.
>
> . . . [U]pon the true construction of the charter and upon the facts as here found, that is to say, found in the case, the shipowners' right to be paid hire ceased in respect of the time occupied in discharge, that is to say, they could get no further hire during the continuance of that period.[177]

32.64 **Net loss** The 'net loss of time clause' provides that hire is not payable for time lost as the result of the occurrence of one of the specified events.[178] Efficiency, as such, is not relevant. What matters is how much time has been lost as a result of the off-hire event. This clause makes it clear that full hire again becomes payable after the resumption of (full) efficiency. Hire would be deductible in the case of partial efficiency only if and to the extent that time is actually lost by reason of the partial inefficiency. One of the leading cases on the 'net loss'

---

174 It has been said that the distinction between 'period' and 'net loss' clauses is a 'sorry little complexity [which] does little credit to the law or lawyers': Williams (1999), 89.

175 (1936) 54 Ll LR 341 (CA).

176 [1891] AC 48.

177 (1936) 54 Ll LR 341, 347–348.

178 The NYPE 93 clause is such a clause: see cl 17, lines 219–236. See *Vogemann v Zanzibar Steamship Co Ltd* (1902) 7 Com Cas 254, 257 (Collins MR).

clause is *Eastern Mediterranean Maritime (Liechtenstein) Ltd v Unimarine SA (The Marika M)*.[179] The *Marika M* was chartered on the NYPE 1946 form for a time charter trip and was due to berth at Bahrain on 18 July. However she grounded on 17 July, was not refloated until 27 July, and had to wait for berth until 6 August. The charterers contended that the period of off-hire continued beyond 27 July (when she was again fully efficient) until 6 August since this period was also time lost as a result of the grounding. The owners denied that the ship was off-hire after she refloated and was again in full working order. Parker J upheld the arbitrator's award in favour of the owners and emphasized the difficulty of assessing any consequential loss of time and the fact that the interpretation contended for by the owners had been accepted for many years:

> But running through [all the authorities], and I do not trouble to give their references, is a clear approach by the Courts to cl 15 [of NYPE 1946] that it is intended to deal with periods during which the full working of the vessel is prevented and no further.[180]

It would, of course, be possible for express provision to be made for precisely the sort of contingency which occurred in *The Marika M*.[181] However, in *Forestships International Ltd v Armonia Shipping & Finance Corp (The Ira)*[182] the relevant clause provided that:

> 15. . . . In the event of loss of time from drydocking preventing the full working of the vessel the payment of hire shall cease for the time thereby lost.

In this case there was a dispute concerning the amount of time lost from drydocking. The parties to the charterparty of the *Ira* had mutually agreed that she would drydock at Piraeus (Greece) while en route from Ravenna in Italy to Novorossisysk in the Black Sea. The charterers argued that the time lost by the drydocking was from dropping the outward pilot at Ravenna – ie for the duration of the voyage from Ravenna to Piraeus. The owners argued the time spent in sailing to Piraeus was not lost to the charterers because that voyage was en route to Novorossisysk. The arbitrator upheld the owners' argument and the charterers then appealed to Tuckey J, sitting in the Commercial Court of the Queen's Bench Division. He pointed out that:

> A net time clause, such as this clause is, required the charterer to prove the happening and the duration of the off-hire event, and that time has been lost to him thereby. So it is a two-stage operation and it does not follow merely by proof of the off-hire event and its duration that he is able to establish a loss of time to him. That must depend upon the circumstances of the particular case.[183]

The arbitrator, in interpreting the clause in the charterparty, had considered the 'time lost to the charterers' and found that:

> If the vessel had been fixed to load at Novorossiysk before she had completed discharge at Ravenna, I think it is impossible to say that the time spent sailing to Piraeus, apart from the deviation period, had been lost to the charterers because it was on the way to the loading port. I cannot see why the position is different because the voyage charter was not made until the vessel had nearly completed drydocking in Piraeus. In both cases, the voyage to Piraeus is

---

[179] [1981] 2 Lloyd's Rep 622.
[180] At 625.
[181] See Intertanktime 80 form, cl 20; Shelltime 3, cl 21; Texacotime 2, cl 9.
[182] [1995] 1 Lloyd's Rep 103.
[183] At 104.

en route to the loading port. The position would of course have been different had the vessel been fixed to load, say, at a port west of Ravenna, but the Respondents chose to fix to load at Novorossisyk and so had the benefit of the voyage to Piraeus.[184]

Tuckey J agreed with this approach, refusing to countenance the argument put by counsel for the charterers that whether the vessel was operating on the orders of the owners or charterers affected the calculation of what time was actually lost to the charterers as a result of the off-hire event. He went on to say that:

> Were this a period off-hire clause, then that approach would be perfectly proper. One could count the time, minute by minute, without regard to the consequences; but that is not the case here. Here the tribunal must obviously count the time and count the duration of the off-hire event but it must then go on to see what causative effect that has had upon the charterers in the particular circumstances of the case.

> It is obvious that in certain circumstances it is not possible to determine what loss of time has occurred until the end of the off-hire event. If one asks the question at that stage in this case . . . there can only really, in my judgment, be one answer. [The charterers] have not lost the time that it has taken for the vessel to sail from Ravenna to Piraeus, apart from the small amount of time involved in the deviation into that port for the purpose of drydocking.[185]

32.65 **Effect of the operation of the off-hire clause** Off-hire clauses sometimes include a *de minimus* provision whereby the clause will not be activated until the lapse of 24 or 48 hours from the occurrence of the event.[186] Once the clause is operative, however, all time lost counts, including the initial period of 24 or 48 hours. If there is not provision to the contrary, the charterer will still have to maintain his other obligations under the charterparty.

I. Deductions from Hire

32.66 **Introduction** In certain circumstances the time charterer may be entitled to an overall adjustment for hire. The charterers may deduct from payments of hire those amounts specifically permitted by the terms of the charter, such as advances for ship's disbursements under the NYPE 93 form,[187] or failure to proceed at any guaranteed speed in the Shelltime 4 form.[188] Other charterparty forms make similar express provision for the charterer to make deductions from future payments of hire for disbursements made on the owners' behalf or for periods of off-hire.

32.67 **Self-help** Where there is no express right to deduct given in the charter, the courts were formerly reluctant to allow the charterer a self-help remedy. Thus in *Seven Seas Transportation Ltd v Atlantic Shipping Co SA (The Satya Kamal)*[189] Donaldson J held that there was no general equitable right of set-off for time lost under an off-hire clause:

> I have come to the conclusion that hire must be treated in the same way as freight, and that to do so is not an extension of the established exception. Finally there is the practical consideration

---

184 At 105.
185 At 105–106.
186 See *Compania Sud Americana de Vapores v Shipmair BV (The Teno)* [1977] 2 Lloyd's Rep 289.
187 Clause 11(d), lines 175–178.
188 Clause 21(b), lines 369–377. See also NYPE 93, cl 17, lines 233–236.
189 [1975] 2 Lloyd's Rep 188.

that if any alleged claim for breach of a time-charter can, if subsequently proved, be set off against hire, there will be total confusion as to when hire is overdue and a vessel can be withdrawn.[190]

A very different approach was advocated in *Compania Sud Americana de Vapores v Shipmair BV (The Teno)*.[191] In this case the charterers raised a defence to a claim by the owners for hire, arising out of the failure of the ship to load a full cargo. Parker J expressed the view that 'it would be grossly unjust to allow an owner to recover hire in respect of a period during which he had, in breach of contract, failed to provide that for which the hire was payable'.[192] He therefore favoured the existence of an equitable right of set-off under which the charterer was entitled to make deductions from future payments of hire to cover disbursements made on the owner's behalf and to cover periods while the vessel was off-hire due to a breakdown of machinery. This right would extend to a partial withdrawal of the ship as well.[193]

These views were considered by Lord Denning MR in *Federal Commerce & Navigacion Co Ltd v Molena Alpha Inc (The Nanfri, The Benfri, The Lorfri)*.[194] In 1975 the *Nanfri* had suffered engine breakdown on a voyage from Antwerp to Durban and had to put into a port of refuge for repairs on two occasions. She was off-hire during the period of the repairs. Deductions were made and agreed for this. However, after breakdown, the vessel's speed was reduced below normal and the charterers now purported to deduct $47,122.43 from the hire due on 1 October 1977. Having considered the line of cases ending with *The Teno*,[195] Lord Denning MR said:

> This line of cases is so convincing that I would hold that, when the shipowner is guilty of a breach of contract which deprives the time charterer of part of the consideration for which the hire has been paid in advance, the charterer can deduct an equivalent amount out of the hire falling due for the next month.

> I would as at present advised limit the right to deduct to cases when the shipowner has wrongly deprived the charterer of the use of the vessel or has prejudiced him in the use of it. I would not extend it to other breaches or default of the shipowner, such as damage to cargo arising from the negligence of the crew.

> In my opinion therefore in a time charter, if the shipowner wrongly and in breach of contract deprives the charterer for a time of the use of the vessel, the charterer can deduct a sum equivalent to the hire for the time so lost.[196]

This part of the decision was not reviewed in the appeal to the House of Lords[197] but its philosophy received support at first instance in *Century Textiles & Industry Ltd v Tomoe Shipping (Singapore) Pte Ltd (The Aditya Vaibhav)*.[198] The question for Saville J was whether equitable set-off in relation to a claim for hire allowed the charterer to deduct from the

190 At 191.
191 [1977] 2 Lloyd's Rep 289.
192 At 296.
193 At 297.
194 [1978] QB 927 (CA).
195 [1977] 2 Lloyd's Rep 289.
196 [1978] QB 927 (CA), 976–977.
197 [1978] AC 1.
198 [1991] 1 Lloyd's Rep 573.

claim all recoverable losses and expenses sustained through the owner's failure to provide the services for which the hire was payable, or whether (as submitted for the owners) the charterers could only make such deductions up to the amount of hire otherwise payable for the period during which such services were not provided. In finding for the owners, Saville J stated that:

> What is needed is something so closely connected with the owners' claim for hire that it would offend justice to require the charterers to pay hire and then pursue their own claims.
>
> To my mind that close connection exists in relation to a claim for hire which in effect is a claim in respect of a period during which the owners, in breach of the charter, have failed to provide the very thing for which that hire was payable. . . . To allow such a claim would indeed be manifestly unjust. However in respect of other periods when the owners are providing that for which hire is payable, such manifest injustice does not appear. The reason for this is that a claim for hire in respect of such periods cannot be impeached by saying that owners are in any sense asking to be paid for a service which they have not provided. In other words, the cross-claim has no connection with the period when the vessel is at the service of the charterers other than it arises out of the same transaction.[199]

J. Right to Withdraw for Non-Payment of Hire

32.68 **Introduction** Time is not of the essence at common law and, for this reason, a shipowner will be unable to repudiate the charterparty and withdraw his vessel for late payment of an instalment for hire unless the circumstances are such that there is clear evidence of an intention on the part of the charterer not to perform. Examples of such an intention would include an express repudiation or repeated non-payment. Typically, charterparties will contain an express contractual right of withdrawal. [200]

32.69 **Anti-technicality clauses** The NYPE 93 charterparty contains a much more sophisticated withdrawal provision and,[201] in particular, contains a so-called 'anti-technicality' clause, which provides a grace period during which late payment, provided it is made within the number of days specified in the charterparty, will be a 'regular and punctual' payment for the purposes of the charter. The reason for the redrafting of the withdrawal clause may be sought in the very nature of such clauses, designed almost to compensate the owner for the working habits of bankers and accountants and possible time differences for the moving of funds between banks in different countries. In the decades before the 1993 revision of NYPE the number of cases involving withdrawals had increased significantly, because of marked fluctuations in the freight markets. In a rising freight market the shipowner tends to eye the slightest of opportunities to withdraw his ship in order to take advantage of increased freight rates. In a falling freight market, on the other hand, the shipowner is more willing to overlook late payment of hire but the charterer will prefer to take advantage of the falling freight rates and escape his existing charterparty obligations in favour of the

---

[199] At 574.
[200] See NYPE (1946), cl 6. Clause 5 makes provision for self-help on the part of the shipowner 'failing the regular and punctual payment of hire'.
[201] See cl 11.

more favourable rates secured from other owners. Little wonder that Lord Denning MR described time charterparties as the 'sport of the shipping markets'.[202] In *Tropwood AG of Zug v Jade Enterprises Ltd (The Tropwind No 2)* he said that:

> When market rates are rising, the shipowners keep close watch on payments of hire. If the charterer makes a slip of any kind—a few minutes too late or a few dollars too little—the shipowners jump on him like a ton of bricks. They give notice of withdrawal and demand thenceforward full payment of hire at the top market rate. Very rarely is the vessel actually withdrawn. Arrangements are made by which she continues in the service of the charterer just as if nothing had happened. Then there is a contest before the arbitrators or in the courts. It is as to whether the notice of withdrawal was justified or not. In the ensuing discussion, . . . the merits have become submerged in a sea of technicalities. They have deteriorated into a game of wits which is played out between shipowners and charterers, backed up by lawyers, and banks.[203]

Interpretation   In *Italmare Shipping Co v Ocean Tanker Co Inc (The Rio Sun)* Lord **32.70** Denning MR said that:

> These clauses . . . give the charterers an opportunity of remedying the breach before they are exposed to forfeiture of their charter . . . It serves to bring the charterers to their senses.[204]

In *Afovos Shipping Co SA v R Pagnan & F Lli (The Afovos)*[205] the charter for the *Afovos* was on the NYPE 1946 form with an added anti-technicality clause, clause 31. Hire was due on 14 June. The charterers' bank in Italy intended to remit the funds in good time by telex transfer to the owners' bank in London, but the transfer did not reach the owners' bank. At 16.40 on 14 June, the owners' agents telexed the charterers: 'Owners have instructed us that in case we do not receive the hire which is due today, to give charterers notice as per the clause of the charterparty for withdrawal of the vessel from their service'. The Court of Appeal held that (1) there was no default in payment of hire by the charterers until after midnight on the due date; (2) on a true construction of the clause, the 48-hour notice could not be given until after the last moment for payment; (3) in any event, the notice was not a good notice because it was conditional in terms. The reasons for the strict adherence to such clauses were explained by Griffiths LJ:

> . . . [P]ayments of [hire] are normally made by telex through a number of banks and it may well be that, through some slip up, the money does not arrive in the owner's account as quickly as the charterer has a right to expect. Once the charterer has instructed his bank to pay he has no further control over the payment which is now in the banking chain. . . . I therefore accept that charterers do require to be told by the owners that payment has not been received. There is little point in telling the charterer that payment has not been received until the time for payment has expired; if the charterer is told that payment has not been received before the time for payment has expired, he may not realise the urgency of the matter and continue to expect that the payment will be credited in time. On the other hand, if he is told after the time for payment has expired, he will realise that he is in breach and has only 48 hours in which to save himself.[206]

---

[202] *Federal Commerce & Navigacion Co Ltd v Molena Alpha Inc (The Nanfri, The Benfri, The Lorfri)* [1978] QB 927 (CA), 965.

[203] [1982] 1 Lloyd's Rep 232, 234. See also *Federal Commerce & Navigacion Co Ltd v Molena Alpha Inc (The Nanfri, The Benfri, The Lorfri)* [1978] QB 927 (CA), 965.

[204] [1981] 2 Lloyd's Rep 489 (CA), 496.

[205] [1982] 1 Lloyd's Rep 562 (CA); affirmed [1983] 1 Lloyd's Rep 335 (HL).

[206] At 567.

32.71 **Notice under the anti-technicality clause**   In *Schelde Delta Shipping BV v Astarte Shipping Ltd (The Pamela)*[207] the question was whether a notice given under an anti-technicality clause was validly given. Clause 27 of the charterparty provided that:

> If hire is due and not received, the Owners, before exercising the option of withdrawing the vessel will give Charterers forty-eight (48) hours notice, Saturday, Sunday and Holidays excluded, and will not withdraw the vessel if the hire is paid within these 48 hours.

The eighth instalment was due on 2 December 1994 but was not punctually paid. By telex timed at 23.41 the owners' brokers informed the charterers that they were in breach of contract and that the vessel was being withdrawn. The charterers contended that the withdrawal was unlawful. The arbitrators found that the notice was not received by the charterers until the opening of business on Monday 5 December and was therefore not premature or invalid. This was upheld by the judge. What should the notice have said? Gatehouse J held that:

> . . . I have come to the conclusion that it is not enough to enquire whether the particular charterers must have known, from the surrounding circumstances, what the notice was impliedly saying. In my view, authority has laid down, as a matter of law, the minimum requirements of an anti-technicality clause in the present form. In addition to the notification that hire is overdue, the notice itself must clearly tell the charterers that the owners require them to remedy their default within 48 hours or risk losing the vessel.

> The bare message 'please notify charterers of withdrawal of the vessel' is not sufficient. . . . [I]n my view the law prescribes that every such notice must be in the form of a clear and unambiguous ultimatum; it is not enough to establish that, as a matter of fact, the particular charterer ought to have realised the significance of a cryptic message.[208]

The owners had therefore unlawfully withdrawn the *Pamela*.

32.72 **Requirements for exercise of right of withdrawal**   The charterer must be in default by failing to pay an instalment of hire, or failing to pay it on time. There will be default if only part payment is made on the due date. This was clear from *China National Foreign Trade Transportation Corp v Evlogia Shipping Co Ltd (The Mihalios Xilas)*.[209] The *Mihalios Xilas* was chartered on the Baltime 1939 form. One day before the nine months payment the charterers paid rather less than a full month's hire. They made deductions in respect of certain advances and estimated bunkers and disbursements on redelivery, showing that they regarded this hire payment as the last under the charter. At first instance, Kerr J held that the owners were entitled to withdraw. The main issue for the court, however — and it was on this that the case went to the House of Lords[210] — was whether the owners had subsequently waived their right to withdraw.[211]

32.73 **Timing**   Payments will not satisfy the requirements of being 'punctual' or 'made in advance' unless they are effected on or before the specified date. Thus where an instalment

---

207 [1995] 2 Lloyd's Rep 249.
208 At 253–254. See too *Western Bulk Carriers K/S v Li Hai Maritime Inc (The Li Hai)* [2005] EWHC 735 (Comm); [2005] 2 Lloyd's Rep 389.
209 [1979] 2 Lloyd's Rep 303 (HL).
210 See para 32.75.
211 See, for waiver, para 32.74.

falls due on a day when the banks are not open, payment must normally be made before close of trading on the immediately preceding day of business. Such requirements are construed strictly when disputes come before the courts. This was made clear by Lord Uthwatt in *Tankexpress A/S v Compagnie Financière Belge des Pètroles SA (The Petrofina)*:[212]

> A stipulation for payment on a fixed day or for punctual payment on a fixed day (unless controlled as to meaning by other provisions of the document) means exactly what is said. Payment is not made on the fixed day if it is made later. Parties are at liberty to make such bargains as to dates as appeal to them, and full effect must be given to such bargains however unreasonable it may appear that the exact terms should be insisted upon. Courts of equity, indeed, in appropriate cases relieve against failure to pay on a stipulated day, but, in so doing, they do not affect to modify the terms of the bargain, though they alter the result of failure to comply with them.

Clear notice of withdrawal by the shipowner is required to be given to the charterers or their agents and notice to the master of the chartered vessel will not be acceptable.

Waiver of right to withdraw   In certain circumstances the shipowner may lose his right   **32.74** to withdrawal because he has waived the charterer's breach. In order for this to be the case, however, his conduct must amount to a clear and unequivocal act such might reasonably cause the charterer to believe that it had been accepted.[213] In *Mardorf Peach & Co Ltd v Attica Sea Carriers Corp (The Laconia)*, Lord Wilberforce stated that:

> Although the word 'waiver' like 'estoppel', covers a variety of situations different in their legal nature, and tends to be indiscriminately used by the courts as a means of relieving parties from bargains or the consequences of bargains which are thought to be harsh or deserving of relief, in the present context what is relied on is clear enough. The charterers had failed to make a punctual payment but it was open to the owners to accept a late payment as if it were punctual, with the consequence that they could not thereafter rely on the default as entitling them to withdraw. All that is needed to establish waiver, in this sense, of the committed breach of contract, is evidence, clear and unequivocal, that such acceptance has taken place, or, after the late payment has been tendered, such a delay in refusing it as might reasonably cause the charterers to believe that it has been accepted.[214]

Receipt of a late payment by an agent will not amount to waiver unless the agent has express (actual) authority to take such decisions on behalf of the shipowner. Thus in this case, which we have already encountered under the London Currency Settlement Scheme,[215] the bankers took delivery of the payment order over the counter but, on subsequently informing the shipowners of its receipt, were instructed to refuse the money and return it to the charterer's bank. The House of Lords held that the shipowners were still entitled to withdraw the vessel as their bankers were in the position of agents. Lord Salmon said that:

> There is nothing to suggest that the bank was familiar with the terms of the charter or knew whether or not the charterers were in default. Certainly it was not within the bankers' express or implied authority to make commercial decisions on behalf of their customers by accepting

---

[212] [1949] AC 76, 100.
[213] See *More Og Romsdal Fylkesbatar AS v The Demise Charterers of the Ship Jotunheim* [2004] EWHC 671 (Comm); [2005] 1 Lloyd's Rep 181, where the court found no waiver because the owners had, in an ultimatum, effectively made time of the essence for the purpose of the withdrawal clause.
[214] [1977] AC 850, 871.
[215] See para 32.49.

or rejecting late payments of hire without taking instructions. They did take instructions and were told to reject the payment. They did so and returned it to the charterers on the following day which in any view must have been within a reasonable time. If the bank had kept the payment for an unreasonable time, the charterers might well have been led to believe that the owners had accepted payment. This would have amounted to a waiver of their right to withdraw the vessel. But nothing of the kind happened in the present case.[216]

32.75   **Acceptance of part of the hire due**   The acceptance of part of the hire on or before the date due does not amount to a waiver of the owner's right to withdraw the vessel if the balance of the hire is not paid by midnight on the due date. The owners will normally be entitled to hold the insufficient payment and to wait and see whether the charterers pay the balance in time. In *China National Foreign Trade Transportation Corp v Evlogia Shipping Co Ltd (The Mihalios Xilas)*,[217] although the shipowners had objected to the proposed deductions, they had not instructed their bankers to refuse payment of the balance of the hire when this was made on 21 March. When they purported to withdraw the vessel on 26 March, the charterers claimed damages for wrongful withdrawal on the basis that the owners, by accepting the payment tendered on 21 March, had waived their right to withdraw the vessel. The House of Lords held that acceptance of part of the hire on 21 March did not amount to a waiver since, as the charterer had at least until the end of trading on 22 March in which to make payment, there was no default of payment for the owner to waive at that stage. As to the delay of four days before withdrawing the vessel, Lord Diplock took the view that:

> Waiver requires knowledge, and I agree . . . that the owners were entitled to a reasonable time to make enquiries of the charterers and of the master of the vessel (as they did) with a view to ascertaining whether [the right to withdraw the vessel under clause 7 had accrued] before electing whether to withdraw or not. That being so, his finding that from March 21 to noon on March 26 was a reasonable time to do so is one of fact which cannot be disturbed.
>
> . . . [T]he owners were entitled to a reasonable time to ascertain whether the amounts comprising the deduction were correct, before deciding to exercise a right of withdrawal which would accrue to them only if the deductions were wrong.[218]

Neither did the retention of the advance payment of hire during this period amount to an unequivocal act of waiver.[219]

32.76   **Grace periods**   Subsequent cases have suggested that a delay of from four to five days after the failure to make payment on the due date is not unreasonable and will not constitute waiver of the breach. In the view of Lloyd J in *Scandanavian Trading Tanker Co AB v Flota Petrolera Ecuatoriana (The Scaptrade)*:

> What is the shortest time reasonably necessary will still depend upon all the circumstances of the case. In some cases it will be reasonable for the owners to take time to consider their position, as withdrawal under a time charter is a serious step not lightly to be undertaken. In other cases it may be reasonable for owners to seek legal advice . . . it would be quite wrong

---

[216] [1977] AC 850, 880.
[217] [1979] 2 Lloyd's Rep 303 (HL).
[218] At 307.
[219] At 307. See also Lord Salmon at 310.

in cases of this kind to require owners to grasp at the first opportunity to withdraw or to hold that they act at their peril by giving charterers two or three days grace.[220]

Possible bars to exercise of the right of withdrawal   The owners may not withdraw where **32.77** the lateness of the payment has arisen from the use by the charterers of a particular method of making payment which has, with the owners' approval, been used for the previous instalments in substitution for strict compliance with the requirements of the charter — unless and until reasonable notice has been given to the charterers that strict compliance will in future be required. The leading case is *Tankexpress A/S v Compagnie Financière Belge des Pétroles (The Petrofina)*.[221] The *Petrofina* was time chartered by her Norwegian owners to Belgian charterers for seven years from 1937. Clause 11 of the charter stated that:

> Payment of the said hire to be as follows: in cash monthly in advance in London. In default of such payment the owners shall have the faculty of withdrawing the said vessel from the service of the charterers.

In practice the charterers posted a cheque for the relevant amount from Brussels to Hambros Bank in London, at the same time advising the owners in Oslo and their brokers in Paris that they were doing so. The cheques were posted two days before the hire was due to allow for postal delays. This had become the 'accepted method between the parties'. Payment in late September 1939 was a day late owing to the outbreak of war and the owners withdrew their ship. The House of Lords held that they were not entitled to do so. Lord Porter said:

> No doubt the owners could at any time have insisted upon a strict performance of the contract after due notice, but they were not, in my view, entitled suddenly to vary the accepted mode of performance without first notifying the charterers in time to enable them to perform the contract in strict conformity with the terms of the charterparty. I think, therefore, that payment was duly made in accordance with the practice adopted and accepted between the parties and in the way and at the time stipulated.[222]

Previous late payments   The mere fact that on previous occasions payments of hire **32.78** have been made late and accepted without protest is unlikely to prevent the owners from withdrawing in the face of another failure by the charterers to pay on time. Thus in *Scandanavian Trading Tanker Co AB v Flota Petrolera Ecuatoriana (The Scaptrade)* Goff LJ, upholding the decision at first instance of Lloyd J, said that:

> . . . [I]t is not at all easy to infer, from the mere fact that late payments had been accepted in the past by the owners without protest, an unequivocal representation by them not to exercise their strict legal right of withdrawal in the event of late payment by the charterers of a subsequent instalment of hire — if only because the circumstances prevailing at the time when the earlier payments were accepted may not be the same as those prevailing in the future. Of course, if for example the charterers chose regularly to use a particular route for payment which involved the consequence that payments were always received by the owners, say, two days late, and the owners knowingly acquiesced in this course of conduct, the court might be able (depending on the circumstances) to infer a sufficient representation from the owners' conduct; but such a case is very far from the present.[223]

---

[220] [1981] 2 Lloyd's Rep 425, 429–430.
[221] [1949] AC 76.
[222] At 93.
[223] [1983] 1 QB 529 (CA), 535.

Thus it is possible for conduct by the owners, in the face of late payments of hire, to amount to a clear representation to the charterers that the right to withdraw will not be exercised in respect of late payment of subsequent instalments. If the owners then unexpectedly purport to exercise that right in respect of such lateness, they will be prevented from doing so if the court is willing in all the circumstances to invoke the principle of equitable estoppel.

32.79 **Equitable relief** Clearly the owners' right to withdraw may operate very harshly against the charterers, who may lose a valuable charter and suffer heavy losses in consequence of a small error on their part or that of their bankers. Some judges, taking their cue from Lord Simon in *Mardorf Peach & Co Ltd v Attica Sea Carriers Corp (The Laconia)*,[224] considered invoking the equitable power to grant relief against forfeiture (withdrawal). But the House of Lords in *Scandanavian Trading Tanker Co AB v Flota Petrolera Ecuatoriana (The Scaptrade)*,[225] affirming the Court of Appeal, held that there was no jurisdiction to grant equitable relief in cases of withdrawal under time charters.[226] Lord Diplock confirmed that:

> . . . [Q]uite apart from the juristic difficulties in the way of recognising a jurisdiction in the court to grant relief against the operation of a withdrawal clause in a time charter there are practical reasons of legal policy for declining to create any such new jurisdiction out of sympathy for charterers. The freight market is notoriously volatile. If it rises rapidly during the period of a time charter, the charterer is the beneficiary of the windfall which he can realise if he wants to by sub-chartering at the then market rates. What withdrawal of the vessel does is to transfer the benefit of the windfall from charterer to shipowner.[227]

32.80 **Effect of exercise of right to withdraw** Following a valid withdrawal by the owner, the charter comes to an end and the contract is terminated from that point. The owner cannot temporarily withdraw the vessel in an attempt to pressure the charterer into paying the hire — unless there is an express term to that effect.[228] Such an act by the owner would amount to a breach of contract for which damages are recoverable. The owner would also not be entitled to withdraw the charterer's contractual authority to sign bills of lading or instruct the master not to sign prepaid bills of lading.

K. Employment and Agency Clause

32.81 **Employment of the ship** Most time charters contain a clause entitling the charterer to have full use of the vessel during the charter and undertaking that the master will comply with the charterer's instructions.[229] Time charterparties are entered into so that the time charterer can enter into contracts of carriage of goods by sea with third parties, either by means of the issue of a bill of lading or the sub-chartering of the ship. In *Hyundai Merchant Marine Co Ltd v Gesuri Chartering Co Ltd (The Peonia)* Bingham LJ explained that:

> A time charterparty such as this is a contract by which the shipowner agrees with the time charterer that during a certain named period he will render services by his servants and crew

---

[224] [1977] AC 850, 873.
[225] [1983] 2 AC 694.
[226] [1983] 1 QB 529 (CA), 539; 541.
[227] [1983] 1 AC 694, 703. See too [1983] QB 529 (CA), 540–541 (Robert Goff LJ).
[228] See *Lauritzencool AB v Lady Navigation Inc* [2004] EWHC 2607 (Comm); [2005] 1 Lloyd's Rep 260.
[229] See NYPE 93, cl 8(a), lines 99–105; Shelltime 4, cl 13, lines 225–282.

to carry the goods which are put on board his ship by the time charterer . . . It is for the time charterer to decide, within the terms of the charter-party, what use he will make of the vessel.[230]

Effect   The effect of such clauses is that the charterer may give the master orders relating   **32.82** to the employment of the ship,[231] but not the employment of the master and crew. In *Larrinaga SS Co Ltd v The King (The Ramon de Larrinaga)*[232] Lord Wright explained that:

'Employment' means employment of the ship to carry out the purposes for which the charterers wish to use her. . . . This opinion, based on the words, seems to me to be confirmed by looking at the structure and scheme of the charterparty as a whole. . . . I think the word 'employment' . . . means the services which the ship is ordered to perform, such as the voyages to or from particular ports, with particular cargoes or in ballast.[233]

Master's duty   The master's duty on receiving orders from the time charterer is to act   **32.83** reasonably; he is not required to obey them immediately. This was one of the central issues in *Midwest Shipping Co Ltd Inc v DI Henry (Jute) Ltd (The Anastasia)*.[234] After loading a cargo of jute at Chalna (a port in Bangladesh) and setting sail for Europe, the master received orders from the charterers to put back to port. He did not comply at once because, on the charterers' instructions, he had lied to the port authorities about his destination — stating that this was Singapore — and he was also concerned as to whether there would be sufficient water to cross the bar at the port of Chalna. In concluding that the master's actions were justified, Donaldson J stated that:

. . . [I]t is important to remember that the master of a merchant ship occupies a civilian post. He is not the captain of a naval vessel who might well be expected to comply instantly with an order and seek verification or reconsideration afterwards. Furthermore, he is not receiving the instruction from somebody who is his professional superior, as would be the case in the services. He is the representative of his owners and also to some extent of the charterers. He occupies a post of very great responsibility, and he occupies that post by virtue of long training and experience. If he was the type of man who would immediately act upon any order from charterers without further consideration, he would probably be unfitted for that post. It seems to me that against that background it must be the duty of the master to act reasonably upon receipt of orders. Some orders are of their nature such that they would, if the master were to act reasonably, require immediate compliance. Others would require a great deal of thought and consideration before a reasonable master would comply with them.[235]

It has been suggested, in the context of orders for a final voyage, that it would be legitimate to treat silence on the owners' part after the expiry of a reasonable interval for consideration as connoting consent to the order.[236]

Potential peril   In general the master may reasonably delay obeying, or may refuse to obey,   **32.84** an order that threatens to expose the ship and cargo to potential peril. That much was

---

[230] [1991] 1 Lloyd's Rep 100 (CA), 107. See too *Kuwait Maritime Transport Co v Rickmers Linie KG (The Danah)* [1993] 1 Lloyd's Rep 351, 353

[231] Including the giving of orders to proceed to a warm water port: see *Action Navigation Inc v Bottigliere di Navigazione SpA (The Kitsa)* [2005] EWHC 177 (Comm); [2005] 1 Lloyd's Rep 432.

[232] [1945] AC 246.

[233] At 254–255.

[234] [1971] 1 Lloyd's Rep 375.

[235] At 379.

[236] *Torvald Klaveness A/S v Arni Maritime Corporation (The Gregos)* [1993] 2 Lloyd's Rep 335 (CA), 346 (Hirst LJ).

recognized by Phillips J in *Kuwait Petroleum Corpn v I & D Oil Carriers Ltd (The Houda)*.[237] In this case, the *Houda*, a tanker, was lying at Mina' Al Ahmadi, about to load a cargo of crude oil, when Iraq invaded Kuwait. After loading a part cargo of 151,000 tonnes the charterers issued orders that the vessel should proceed to the Red Sea there to discharge her cargo at Ain Sukhna. The vessel had by then proceeded to an anchorage off Fujairah. The owners refused to proceed until they had taken legal advice as to who now had authority to give orders on behalf of the charterers. Following the Iraqi invasion the charterers had moved their offices to London. The charterers had also meanwhile sent instructions for a survey of the cargo aboard the *Houda* but the owners declined to allow the survey until they were satisfied that the charterers' London offices had authority to act for the charterers. The owners refused to allow the discharge of the cargo at Ain Sukhna without bills of lading (which had been lost). Was their act reasonable? Or were they in breach of contract in refusing to obey the charterers' lawful orders? Phillips J at first instance found in the charterers' favour[238] but this was reversed on appeal. Millett LJ noted that

> ... the authorities establish two propositions of general application: (1) the master's obligation on receipt of an order is not one of instant obedience but of reasonable conduct; and (2) not every delay constitutes a refusal to obey an order; only an unreasonable delay does so.[239]

Neill LJ stated that it was

> necessary to take a broad and comprehensive view of the duties and responsibilities of the owners and master and to ask . . . 'How would a man of reasonable prudence have acted in the circumstances?'. . . It is not of course for this Court to decide whether on the facts the owners had reasonable grounds to pause, but I am satisfied that in a war situation there may well be circumstances where right, and indeed the duty, to pause in order to seek further information about the source of and the validity of any orders which may be received is capable of arising even if there may be no immediate physical threat to the cargo or the ship. . . . [I]t seems to me that it is at least possible that where a country has been invaded prudent owners may be entitled to guard against the risk that their orders may have come from the 'wrong' side.[240]

32.85 **Voyage orders**   In *Whistler International Ltd v Kawasaki Kisen Kaisha Ltd (The Hill Harmony)*,[241] the House of Lords had to determine whether the master of the *Hill Harmony* was in breach of his obligation to follow charterers' orders as to employment. The charterers deducted hire on the grounds that the master had refused to proceed from Canada to Japan using the so-called 'northern great circle route', which had been recommended by the charterers' weather routing service (Ocean Routes), but instead insisted on proceeding by the more southerly so-called 'rhumb line route', which took longer and used more bunkers. The majority arbitrators found that the orders given were orders as to employment and that the master was bound to follow them unless he could justify his refusal so to do. The evidence had failed to demonstrate that the master had acted reasonably having regard to all the relevant circumstances in rejecting the charterers' orders on the relevant voyages. Clarke J overturned this decision and held that the orders or directions of the charterers to follow the great circle route were not orders or directions as to employment within

---

[237] [1993] 1 Lloyd's Rep 333, 345.
[238] At 343.
[239] [1994] 2 Lloyd's Rep 541 (CA), 555.
[240] At 549.
[241] [2001] 1 AC 638.

the meaning of clause 8 of the NYPE charterparty.[242] The Court of Appeal dismissed the appeal.[243] The House of Lords reinstated the conclusion of the arbitrators. Lord Hobhouse noted that 'employment' embraced the exploitation of the earning potential of the vessel, whereas 'navigation' embraced matters of seamanship. However, to use the word 'navigation' as if it included everything which involved the vessel proceeding through the water was both mistaken and unhelpful. Thus, where seamanship was in question, choices as to the speed or steering of the vessel would be matters of navigation, as would be the exercise of laying off a course on a chart.[244] Lord Bingham concluded that, in the absence of evidence that the rhumb line route was the usual route or a usual route, and in the absence of any satisfactory navigational or other reason for taking a longer and slower route, the master's obligation of utmost despatch[245] required him to take the shortest and quickest route. Lord Bingham said that, subject to safety considerations and the specific terms of the charter, the charterers could not only order a vessel to sail from A to B but might also direct the route to be followed between the two.[246] The majority arbitrators were therefore right to hold that the orders to take the great circle route on both the disputed voyages were orders which the charterers were entitled to give and with which the owners were bound to comply.

The indemnity principle   If the shipowner suffers loss as a result of the master obeying   **32.86** any order about employment or agency, he will be entitled to an indemnity from the charterer. This obligation is made explicit in some charterparties.[247] Although neither the NYPE 1946 nor the NYPE 93 form provide an express obligation to indemnify the owner, such an obligation will usually be implied, although not automatically.[248] This point was also considered by Staughton LJ in *Sig Bergesen DY & Co v Mobil Shipping & Transportation Co (The Berge Sund)*:[249]

> It is accepted that, even without an express term, a time charter contains an implied under-taking by the charterers to indemnify the owners against the consequences of complying with their orders.... [I] take the view that the application of that term [is] excluded in the present case because (i) the charter-party ha[s] a specific clause dealing with off-hire, and (ii) furthermore that clause contain[s] the exception of charterers' fault. That in my opinion excludes any implied term that the charterers will indemnify the owners against loss of hire under the clause caused by compliance with the charterers' orders, if there has not been charterers' fault.[250]

Extent of the indemnity   Whether express (as in most charterparties), or implied, the   **32.87** indemnity will not be limited to the consequences of the master signing bills of lading

---

[242] [1999] QB 72. See Brian Davenport, 'Rhumb line or great circle? — That is a question of navigation' [1998] LMCLQ 502.
[243] [2000] QB 241 (CA), strongly criticized by Donald Davies, 'Right to Routes' [1999] LMCLQ 461.
[244] *Suzuki & Co Ltd v T Benyon & Co Ltd* (1925) 24 Ll LR 4.
[245] See the discussion of this issue at para 25.05.
[246] [2001] 1 AC 638, 646–647.
[247] See cl 9 of Baltime 1939, lines 123–128; Shelltime 4, cl 13(a), lines 228–234.
[248] See *Naviera Magor SA v Société Metallurgique de Normandie (The Nogar Marin)* [1988] 1 Lloyd's Rep 412 (CA), 422: 'It seems to us plain and the authorities leave us in no doubt that the implication of an obligation to indemnify is not automatic. It must always depend on the facts of the individual case, and on the terms of any underlying contractual relationship' (Mustill LJ).
[249] [1993] 2 Lloyd's Rep 453 (CA).
[250] At 462.

presented by the charterer; it covers all matters relating to employment and agency of the ship, and may overlap with other clauses of the charterparty, such as the off-hire clause. This was the case in *Royal Greek Government v Minister of Transport (The Ann Stathatos)*[251] where clause 9 of the charterparty provided:

> The master to prosecute all voyages with the utmost dispatch and to render customary assistance with the vessel's crew. The master to be under the orders of the charterer as regards employment, agency or other arrangements. The charterer to indemnify the owners against all consequences or liabilities, arising from the master, officers or agents signing bills of lading or other documents or otherwise complying with such orders, as well as from any irregularity in the vessel's papers or for over-carrying goods . . .

In this case there was a series of explosions aboard the *Ann Stathatos*, as a result of which she had to undergo repairs. The cause of the explosions was the starting of a flame or spark in the gas emanating from a cargo of coal ordered to be loaded on the instructions of the charterers. The owners contended that the *Ann Stathatos* was not off-hire during the repairs necessitated by the explosion. Further, they contended that they were entitled to be indemnified by the charterers under clause 9. Devlin J held that 'an order to load a particular cargo is an order as to employment of the ship . . . and that the consequences of complying with such an order are within the scope of the indemnity provided by Clause 9'.[252] In the earlier case of *Portsmouth SS Co Ltd v Liverpool and Glasgow Salvage Association*,[253] the *Hillcroft*, chartered to the Liverpool & Glasgow Salvage Association, sustained considerable damage from semi-congealed or wholly congealed palm oil, mahogany logs, and crude oil taken on from the *West Heseltine*. The owners argued that the indemnity clause applied to the dispute and that the shipowners were entitled to be indemnified for the consequences of following the charterers' instructions. Roche J held that the

> clause bears the meaning contended for by the plaintiffs, and that it covers the shipowners in respect of consequences that arise directly from the charterers' instructions. I say 'directly' because if some act of negligence intervenes or some marine casualty intervenes then I think the chain of causation is broken and the indemnity does not operate.[254]

The owners were held entitled to compensation for the damage caused by the palm oil and the logs but not the leakage of fuel oil from the forepeak tank of the *Hillcroft*. The leak was due to a supervening marine casualty for which the charterers were not responsible.

32.88 **Implied indemnities** The shipowner will have an implied right to be indemnified against the consequences of complying with any order that the charterer gives for the employment of the ship, even if the charterer was entitled by the terms of the charterparty to give the order, and the shipowner was bound to obey it. This was the issue which arose for consideration in *Triad Shipping Co v Stellar Chartering & Brokerage Inc (The Island Archon)*.[255] The *Island Archon*, chartered on the NYPE 1946 form in 1979, was, in the course of her employment, ordered on a voyage from European ports to Iraq. Cargo claims

---

[251] (1949) 83 Ll LR 228.
[252] At 235. See also *The Athanasia Comninos* [1990] 1 Lloyd's Rep 277.
[253] (1929) 34 Ll LR 459.
[254] At 462.
[255] [1994] 2 Lloyd's Rep 227 (CA).

were asserted by certain Iraqi receivers and the shipowners were required to provide security to the State Enterprise for Maritime Agency (SEMA) before the ship was allowed to leave Basrah, giving rise to delay. Were the shipowners entitled, in the absence of an express indemnity, to an implied indemnity against their losses from the time charterers? At first instance, Cresswell J held that they were entitled to succeed.[256] The judge had relied on the statement of Mustill J in *The Athanasia Cominos* that:

> It has long been established that a provision in this [NYPE] form impliedly requires the charterer to indemnify the shipowner against the consequences of complying with an order as to the employment of the ship.[257]

Evans LJ upheld this statement of the law as being correct. Thus, the shipowners were held entitled to an implied indemnity against the consequences of complying with the time charterers' orders. Such an implication was justified

> first by 'business efficacy' in the sense that if the charterer requires to have the vessel at his disposal, and to be free to choose voyages and cargoes and bill of lading terms also, then the owner must be expected to grant such freedom only if he is entitled to be indemnified against loss and liability resulting from it, subject always to the express terms of the charter-party contract . . .[258]

Types of claims indemnified   The charterer must indemnify the shipowner if the chartered   **32.89** ship is damaged as a result of loading a particular cargo pursuant to the charterer's orders.[259] He must also indemnify the shipowner if the chartered ship is delayed at a port to which it has been ordered by the charterer, even if it is the harbour authority which directs the ship to the loading or discharging place within that port. This was the issue that arose in *New A Line v Erechthion Shipping Co SA (The Erechthion)*.[260] By a time charter trip, the *Erechthion* was ordered from Flushing to West Africa, where she was instructed to discharge her general cargo at Port Harcourt on the Bonny River in Nigeria. Traffic in the river was controlled by the Port Harcourt harbour authority. After embarking a pilot, and because of her draught, it was decided that she would lighten in the river, at the Dawes Island anchorage. She grounded and struck a submerged object, which caused flooding to the engine room. Were the charterers obliged to indemnify the owners against the consequences of compliance with their orders? The arbitrators so found and the matter was then appealed to the Commercial Court before Staughton J. Both parties accepted that there was an implied obligation to indemnify the owners against consequences caused by compliance with the charterers' orders as to employment of the vessel. Staughton J noted that

> a charterer . . . is only bound to indemnify the owner against the consequences of orders as to employment, and not of orders as to navigation. . . . Seeing that the manifest intention was for

---

256 [1993] 2 Lloyd's Rep 407. See *Action Navigation Inc v Bottigliere di Navigazione SpA (The Kitsa)* [2005] EWHC 177 (Comm); [2005] 1 Lloyd's Rep 432, where it was held the owners' expenses of de-fouling the bottom of the vessel were outside the scope of the implied indemnity provided by the charterparty.

257 [1990] 1 Lloyd's Rep 277, 290.

258 [1994] 2 Lloyd's Rep 227(CA), 237.

259 See *Royal Greek Government v Minister of Transport* (1949) 83 Ll LR 228; *The Athanasia Cominos & Georges Chr Lemos* [1990] 1 Lloyd's Rep 277; *Deutsche Ost-Afrika-Linie GmbH v Legent Maritime Co Ltd (The Marie H)* [1998] 2 Lloyd's Rep 71.

260 [1987] 2 Lloyd's Rep 180.

the vessel to lighten [at the Dawes Island anchorage] by discharging part of her cargo, I am of opinion that it was plainly an order as to employment.[261]

This case therefore makes it clear that the charterer is not ordinarily bound to indemnify the shipowner against the consequences of orders as to navigation, because navigational matters remain the shipowners' responsibility.

32.90 **Direct consequences** The charterer will only be obliged to indemnify the shipowner against the direct consequences of the master obeying its orders regarding employment or agency. The indemnity will not operate where the chain of causation has been broken (for example by a member of the crew). The shipowner must prove an unbroken chain of causation between the instructions of the charterers and the loss suffered. In *A/B Helsingfors SS Co Ltd v Rederiaktiebolaget Rex*[262] the *White Rose* was ordered to load grain at Duluth (Minnesota). The charterers, in accordance with their obligations, appointed as loading stevedores a firm of average competence by local standards. One of the stevedores fell through an unfenced part of a deck hatch. He sued the owners for damages and they claimed to be indemnified by the charterers. This was rejected by Donaldson J because the accident, and thus the owners' loss, had been caused by the lack of fencing (for which the charterers were not responsible) and the negligence of the injured man himself, and not by their compliance with the charterers' orders to load grain at Duluth or the selection by the charterers of incompetent stevedores.[263]

32.91 **Vicarious liability** Although the master is obliged to follow the charterer's orders regarding employment or agency, the shipowner remains vicariously liable for any negligence of the master in the execution of those orders.

32.92 **Agency** References in charterparty clauses to 'agency' are a reference to the fact that the charterer will be entitled to appoint agents to act on behalf of the ship at its various ports of call, and must pay them. In *A/S Hansen-Tangens Rederi III v Total Transport Corp (The Sagona)*[264] Staughton J explained the position and functions of a ship's agent as follows:

> When a merchant ship calls at any port it is the common if not invariable practice for some shore-based person or firm to be appointed as the ship's agent. He will be responsible for dealing with the port health, immigration and customs authorities; for securing the services of tugs and pilots; for arranging a place at which the ship may load or discharge; and for attending to the needs of the master in respect of provisions and stores, fuel, repatriation and replacement of crew, and repairs. . . . What is greatly disputed is whether the agent is also under a duty to check the bill of lading, and to inform the master who it is that appears to be entitled to take delivery of the cargo; and if so, whether that duty is one which he performs on behalf of the owner or the charterer.[265]

If the shipowner is responsible under the charterparty for loading and discharging the cargo, the agency clause will not entitle the charterer or his agents to hire loading and discharging tackle at the shipowner's expense. Agents appointed and paid for by the charterer are, in the words of Staughton J, 'as between the owners and charterers to be considered

---

[261] At 185.
[262] [1969] 2 Lloyd's Rep 52.
[263] At 59.
[264] [1984] 1 Lloyd's Rep 194.
[265] At 198.

the agents of the charterers for all the ordinary business of a ship in port'.[266] He went on to say that

> there may be some business which, as between the owners and the charterers, the master ought to do himself, and not delegate to the agents. If the master does nevertheless entrust such a task to the agents, then it may be that the agent's omission to perform it would be an omission on behalf of the owners and not on behalf of the charterers.[267]

Issuing and signing bills of lading At this point we consider the effect of the separate   **32.93**
obligation of the master to sign bills of lading at the charterers' behest. This was addressed
by Lord Wilberforce in *Federal Commerce & Navigation Co Ltd v Molena Alpha Inc
(The Nanfri, The Benfri, The Lorfri)*:

> It is important in this connection to have in mind that the present charters are time charters, the nature and purpose of which is to enable the charterers to use the vessels during the period of the charters for trading in whatever manner they think fit. The issue of bills of lading in a particular form may be vital for the charterers' trade, and indeed in relation to this trade, which involves cif or c & f contracts the issue of freight pre-paid bills of lading is essential if the trade is to be maintained. Furthermore, clause 9 [of the Baltime 1939 form], as is usual in time charters, contains an indemnity clause against all consequences or liabilities arising from the master signing bills of lading. This underlines the power of the charterers, in the course of exploiting the vessel, to decide what bills of lading are appropriate for their trade and to instruct the masters to issue such bills, the owners being protected by the indemnity clause.[268]

Thus, because it is the charterer who deals with third parties shipping goods aboard the ship, it is the charterer who prepares and issues bills of lading in accordance with the particulars provided by those third party shippers. Once the bills of lading have been drawn up, the charterer either presents them to the master for signature, or signs them itself on behalf of the master if it has been authorized to do so under the terms of the charterparty.[269] An indemnity will usually be implied, assuming that the charterparty does not expressly provide an indemnity.[270]

Inconsistencies If there is any inconsistency between the terms of the bill of lading   **32.94**
presented by the charterer and signed by the master, and the terms agreed by the shipowner
under the charterparty, the charterer must indemnify the shipowner for any loss it suffers
as a result. These matters arose before the House of Lords in *Kruger & Co Ltd v Moel Tryvan
Ship Co Ltd*.[271] In this case the charterparty for the *Invermore* contained a clause that
exempted the shipowner from liability for stranding and other accidents of navigation,
even where occasioned by the negligence of the master. The master was required to sign
clean bills of lading without prejudice to the charter. The ship was chartered to proceed
to Rangoon (Burma) and there load a cargo of rice before proceeding to Rio de Janeiro.
The bill of lading in respect of this cargo did not contain the charterparty exemption.
The cargo was in fact lost through the negligence of the master and this compelled the owners

---

[266] At 199.
[267] ibid.
[268] [1979] AC 757, 777.
[269] See NYPE 93, cl 30(a), lines 307–310.
[270] Shelltime 4, cl 13(a), lines 228–234. See NYPE 93, cl 30(b), lines 311–314.
[271] [1907] AC 272.

to pay the value of the cargo in an action brought by the endorsees of the bills of lading. They now brought an action against the charterers under an indemnity and this was successful.[272]

32.95 **Indemnity where clean bills of lading signed**   The charterer is not obliged to indemnify the shipowner against any liability the latter may incur as a result of the master signing a clean bill of lading presented by the charterer when the goods were, in fact, not in good order and condition on shipment. This arose for consideration in *Naviera Mogor SA v Société Metallurgique de Normandie (The Nogar Marin)*.[273] The *Nogar Marin* sailed from Caen in France to Tampa (Florida) laden with a cargo of wire rods in coils. Some of the coils were rusty when shipped, but the ship's agents signed clean bills of lading. The rust was discovered on arrival and the receivers of the cargo had the ship arrested. The owners settled their claim of $86,462 and now sought reimbursement from the charterers for the sum paid, together with $28,173, being the cost of resisting and settling the claim. One of the questions of law for the Court of Appeal was whether an implied indemnity arose through the delivery of the mate's receipt for signature by the master. Mustill LJ held that it did not:

> ... [T]he master should at least have recognised enough of the true facts to require the bill to be qualified. The making of a proper inspection is not just a matter between the master and his owners; it affects the transferees as well. We see no reason to imply a term which takes the ultimate responsibility for this task, away from the master's employers and places it on the shoulders of the charterer.
>
> Everyone in the shipping trade knows that the master need not sign a clean bill just because one is tendered; everyone knows that it is the master's task to verify the condition of the goods before he signs. . . . [T]he claim for an indemnity must fail.[274]

L. Liability for Loss or Damage to Cargo

32.96 **Introduction**   It is clear that in most time charterparties the cargo carried aboard the chartered ship is not that belonging to the charterer, but third parties who have contracted under bills of lading or voyage sub-charterparties for their goods to be carried on the ship. Should the third party shipper's cargo be lost or damaged, he must decide whether to sue the time charterer or the shipowner. We shall not examine that particular problem here.[275] A separate question arises for the charterer and shipowner as to whom must ultimately bear any loss resulting from the damage or loss of the cargo carried on the ship.[276]

32.97 **Cargo handling**   Most charterparties make specific provision for responsibility for the physical processes of cargo handling.[277] The common law position was

---

[272] At 276 (Lord Loreburn LC).

[273] [1988] 1 Lloyd's Rep 412 (CA). See too para 6.27.

[274] At 421–422.

[275] See para 12.08.

[276] See, eg, *Stargas SpA v Petredec Ltd (The Sargasso)* [1994] 1 Lloyd's Rep 412.

[277] This can lead also to the allocation of liability for injuries sustained during loading and discharging: see *CV Scheepvaartonderneming Flintermar v Sea Malta Co Ltd (The Flintermar)* [2005] EWCA Civ 17; [2005] 1 Lloyd's Rep 409.

explained by Donaldson MR in *Filikos Shipping Corp of Monrovia v Shimpair BV (The Filikos)*:

> [T]he task of loading from ship's rail, stowing and discharging overside is the sole responsibility of the shipowner. However, either or both of the duties of (a) arranging for these processes to be carried out and (b) paying for them to be carried out may be transferred to the charterers. So too can liability for breach of the duty of care in these processes, whether or not either or both the duties of arranging for their performance have been so transferred.[278]

Usually time charterparties transfer this responsibility to the time charterer as well as any liability as between shipowner and charterer for any failure to perform these processes properly. Thus the NYPE 93 charterparty provides that:

> [T]he Charterers shall perform all cargo handling, including but not limited to loading, stowing, trimming, lashing, securing, dunnaging, unlashing, discharging, and tallying, at their risk and expense, under the supervision of the Master.[279]

The effect of the clause is that it transfers the responsibility for all the named processes. If the cargo is damaged by stevedores during loading or unloading, or bad stowing or trimming, then it will be the charterer, not the shipowner, who bears the loss. If the shipowner must compensate the cargo owner in a claim made under a bill of lading, then the charterer must indemnify the shipowner. Likewise, if the shipowner himself suffers such losses, then again the charterer must indemnify him. In the case of *Canadian Transport Co Ltd v Court Line Ltd*[280] Lord Wright explained that the

> words ['under the supervision of the master'] expressly give the master a right which I think he must in any case have, to supervise the operations of the charterers in loading and stowing. The master is responsible for the seaworthiness of the ship and also for ensuring that the cargo will not be so loaded as to be subject to damage, by absence of dunnage and separation, by being placed near to other goods or parts of the ship which are liable to cause damage, or in other ways. ... But I think this right is expressly stipulated not only for the sake of accuracy, but specifically as a limitation of the charterers' rights to control the stowage. It follows that to the extent that the master exercises supervision and limits the charterers' control of the stowage, the charterers' liability will be limited in a corresponding degree.[281]

These issues were considered further in the case of *AB Marintrans v Comet Shipping Co (The Shinjitsu Maru No 5)*.[282] The *Shinjitsu Maru No 5*, a vessel designed primarily as a log carrier, was let for a time charter trip from New Zealand to West Africa on the NYPE 1946 form. Clause 8 inter alia provided that:

> ... Charterers are to load, stow, trim and discharge the cargo at their expense under the supervision *and responsibility* of the captain ...

The *Shinjitsu Maru No 5* was to carry a cargo of palletized milk powder, although she was not ideally suited to do so. Much boxing with wood was necessary in order that fork lift trucks could stow the cargo. However, some of the pallets were loaded before the woodwork

---

[278] [1983] 1 Lloyd's Rep 9 (CA), 11.
[279] Clause 8(a), lines 103–105.
[280] [1940] AC 834.
[281] At 943. See too *Compania Sud American Vapores v MS ER Hamburg Schiffahrtsgesellschaft mbH & Co KG* [2006] EWHC 483 (Comm); [2006] 2 Lloyd's Rep 66.
[282] [1985] 1 Lloyd's Rep 568.

was complete. The master of the ship put to sea notwithstanding that he was not happy about the manner in which the cargo had had to be stowed. On encountering bad weather, the cargo shifted, so much so that the vessel took on a list of 25 degrees. The crucial question for Neill LJ, sitting in the Commercial Court, was the effect of the typed words 'and responsibility'. He decided that

> the correct approach is to construe the words 'and responsibility' as effecting a prima facie transfer of liability for bad stowage to the owners, but that if it can be shown in any particular case that the charterers by, for example, giving some instructions in the course of the stowage, have *caused* the relevant loss or damage the owners will be able to escape liability to that extent.

> If this analysis is correct, the added words 'and responsibility' will place the *primary* duty on the master and owners but with the possibility that their liability will be affected by some intervention by the charterers.[283]

He came to the conclusion on the facts that the charterers were not estopped by any act or conduct for which they were responsible from making a claim against the owners. Further, taking into account the master's responsibility for ensuring that the vessel was seaworthy, the dominant and effective cause of the losses was the negligence of the master. The charterers were entitled to succeed in full in their claim against the owners.[284]

32.98 **Limits of clauses** It will be noted that the NYPE 93 clause only allocates responsibility in respect of cargo handling at the ports of loading and discharge. It does not cover such losses during the voyage, which must be borne by the shipowner and it applies even if the time charterparty incorporates the Hague or Hague–Visby Rules by reference.

32.99 **Deck cargoes** A further potential complication concerns deck cargo. Clause 30(c) of the NYPE 93 charterparty provides that:

> (c) Bills of lading covering deck cargo shall be claused: 'Shipped on deck at Charterers', Shippers' and Receivers' risk, expense and responsibility, without liability on the part of the Vessel, or her Owners for any loss, damage, expense or delay howsoever caused.'[285]

The effect of this clause is that it will negative the shipowners' assumption of responsibility for damage or loss caused by cargo handling in so far as it relates to deck cargo. If the owner of deck cargo successfully claims against the shipowner under a bill of lading, the shipowner will be entitled to an indemnity from the charterer.[286]

M. The Inter-Club Agreement

32.100 **Introductory** Although the legal principles governing the allocation of responsibility between the shipowner and time charterer under the NYPE 93 form are as set out in clause 8, the application of clause 8 can sometimes give rise to legal difficulties on the given facts.

---

[283] At 575 (emphasis in original).
[284] See too *Macieo Shipping Ltd v Clipper Shipping Lines Ltd (The Clipper Sao Luis)* [2000] 1 Lloyd's Rep 645.
[285] Lines 315–317.
[286] See *Transocean Liners Reederei GmbH v Euxine Shipping Co Ltd (The Imvros)* [1999] 1 Lloyd's Rep 848. See too Simon Baughen, 'Problems with deck cargo' [2000] LMCLQ 295.

Some of these difficulties were explained by Kerr LJ in *D/S A/S Idaho v Peninsula & Oriental Steam Navigation Co (The Strathnewton)*.[287] Noting that clause 8 was of a type designed to allocate the functions of loading, stowing, trimming, and discharging to the charterers, he continued that the words 'under the supervision of the Captain' had given rise to considerable difficulty — in particular there might be issues as to the extent to which the master had exercised a controlling supervision. Was the master's supervision to be active or 'passive' supervision? If the master actively intervened in the stowage was his active intervention the sole and only cause of the damage to the cargo? There might also be issues as to whether the damage to the cargo was due to improper loading or trimming on the one hand or to improper stowage on the other. Even were the Hague Rules incorporated into the charterparty by means of a clause paramount, this would not preclude the parties from agreeing that certain functions set out in article III, rule 2 were to be transferred to the shipper or receiver of cargo.[288]

Origins   The Inter-Club Agreement[289] was first concluded in 1969 and came into force with effect from 20 February 1970. A revised Agreement was issued by the Clubs in 1984 — the Inter-Club Agreement (revised 1984) — and this has been revised again in 1996 as the Inter-Club New York Produce Exchange Agreement 1996. The 1996 Agreement, dated 1 September 1996, replaces the 1984 Agreement and applies to any charterparty which is entered into after this date on the NYPE (1946) form, NYPE 93 form, or Asbatime Form 1981.[290]   **32.101**

The scheme of the Agreement   The Inter-Club Agreement 1996 is essentially an agreement between the various P & I Clubs which apportions, in a purely mechanical way, liability for claims under the NYPE forms. The purpose of the agreement is to eliminate disputes, in so far as this is possible. A cargo claim for the purpose of the Agreement is any claim for loss, damage, shortage (including slackage, ullage, or pilferage), over-carriage of or delay to cargo including customs dues or fines in respect of such loss, damage, shortage, over-carriage, or delay and includes: any legal costs claimed by the original person making any such claim; any interest claimed by the original person making any such claim; all legal costs incurred in defending or settling a claim, but not costs incurred in making a claim under the Agreement or in seeking an indemnity under a charterparty.[291] In practice, the allocation of responsibility under the Agreement amounts to an allocation of losses between the P & I Clubs because both the owner and the time charterer will usually insure against their third party liability with one of these P & I Clubs. This was confirmed in *Ben Line Steamers Ltd v Pacific Steam Navigation Co (The Benlawers)*[292] by Hobhouse J: **32.102**

> The argument is that it is unjust to the shipowners if there was no fault on their part under the charterparty, and if there was nothing wrong with the ship under the terms of the charterparty, and if they were not negligent in any way. It is said: 'Why should they pay?'

---

[287] [1983] 1 Lloyd's Rep 219 (CA), 222–223.
[288] See para 26.35.
[289] This part of the chapter is based on my earlier article, 'The NYPE Interclub Agreement' [1999] Il Diritto Marittimo 1096.
[290] Clause (1).
[291] Clause (3).
[292] [1989] 2 Lloyd's Rep 51.

The answer is, that there is an agreement which is primarily for the benefit of the respective parties' insurers that is of the character of a knock-for-knock agreement. It has advantages and disadvantages for the shipowners, but is intended to work in that way: it solves insurance problems and it is not concerned with such considerations as hardship or lack of moral culpability.[293]

32.103 **Claims under the Agreement** The 1996 Agreement specifies that a claim may be made where the claim occurs under a contract of carriage 'whatever its form' and the cargo responsibility clauses in the charterparty have not been materially amended, and the claim has been properly settled or compromised.[294] In respect of the latter it would appear that, without any formal judgment on liability, any properly settled claim between one or other of the shipowner and charterer with the third party claimant would have to be an amicable, compromised, settlement. On one view of this requirement, the Agreement would have little hope of eliminating or minimizing disputes unless each P & I Club which is a party to the Agreement placed trust in the way the other party handled the third-party claim with the primary claimant. Further, the Agreement is stated to apply regardless of legal forum or the place of arbitration specified in the charterparty and regardless of any incorporation of the Hague, Hague–Visby, or Hamburg Rules.[295]

32.104 **Applicability** The basic formula for apportionment is in clause (7) and clause (8) of the (1996) Agreement, but this only becomes relevant once it has been determined that the Agreement applies to the dispute. These matters are specified in clause (4).[296] In particular, the claims formula will only apply where the cargo responsibility clauses — ie., those in clauses 8 and 26 of the NYPE form — have not been materially amended.[297] A 'material' amendment is then stated to be one which makes responsibility for cargo claims clear as between the parties where before it was uncertain. It is then expressly stated that the addition of the words 'and responsibility' in clause 8 of the NYPE form would not constitute a 'material' amendment.[298] However, if the words 'cargo claims' were to be inserted in the second sentence of clause 26 of the NYPE 93 (and NYPE 1946) forms, apportionment under the Agreement shall not be applied.[299]

32.105 **Apportionment** The scheme of apportionment provided in clause (8) in essence attributes claims arising from unseaworthiness 100 per cent to the owners, with claims arising out of loading, stowage, lashing, discharge, storage, or other handling of the cargo 100 per cent for the charterers' account. If the words 'and responsibility' are added to clause 8 of the NYPE form then such claims are settled equally (ie, 50 per cent each) by the owners and the Charterers.[300] However, were the charterers to prove that the failure properly to load, stow, lash, discharge, or handle the cargo was caused by the unseaworthiness of the vessel, then

---

[293] At 60. See too *Transpacific Discovery SA v Cargill International SA (The Elpa)* [2001] 2 Lloyd's Rep 596.
[294] Clause (4). There is a similar provision in the 1984 Agreement: see clause (1)(i).
[295] Clause (5).
[296] In the 1984 version this falls under the clause headed 'Application and Interpretation of the Agreement': cl (1).
[297] Clause (4)(b).
[298] Clause (4)(b)(i). Note, this is a change from the 1984 Agreement: see cl (1)(ii)(b).
[299] Clause 4(b)(ii).
[300] See *Macieo Shipping Ltd v Clipper Shipping Lines Ltd (The Clipper Sao Luis)* [2000] 1 Lloyd's Rep 645.

any claim would have to be met as to 100 percent by the owners. The above is the scheme set out in clause (8)(a) and (b). Subject to this, claims for shortage or over-carriage are settled equally, unless there is clear and irrefutable evidence that the claim arose out of pilferage or act or neglect by one or the other (including their servants or subcontractors — such as stevedores), in which case that party would have to bear 100 per cent of the claim.[301] All other cargo claims 'whatsoever', including claims for delay to cargo, are shared equally, unless there is clear and irrefutable evidence that the claim arose out of the act or neglect of the one or the other (including their servants or subcontractors), in which case that party must bear 100 per cent of the claim.[302]

Legal character   The signatories to the Agreement are all P & I Clubs[303] and the Agreement   **32.106** binds the Clubs in so far as the Clubs agree to recommend to their members that they should accept the terms of the Agreement.[304] It is increasingly common for the terms of the Agreement to be incorporated into the NYPE (1946) form as a rider; it appears expressly as a term of the NYPE 93 form (clause 27). As such, the Agreement is a contractual provision of the form and so can be subject to judicial or arbitral interpretation in the context of the charterparty as a whole.

Time bars and the relationship with the Hague Rules   In *D/S A/S Idaho v Peninsula &*   **32.107** *Oriental Steam Navigation Co (The Strathnewton)*[305] the owners let the *Strathnewton* to the charterers (D/S A/S Idaho) for a time charter trip. The NYPE (1946) charterparty contained a clause incorporating a US clause paramount[306] and provided that cargo claims were to be settled under the Inter-Club Agreement. The *Strathnewton* had loaded general cargo at a number of ports in the United States under a large number of bills of lading and discharged the cargo at various Persian Gulf ports. There were several claims by the receivers of the cargo against the charterers under these bills of lading. The charterers settled 72 claims by the holders of the bills of lading but failed to bring any suit against the owners for settlement of any cargo claims pursuant to clause 55 of the charterparty within one year of the delivery. The owners therefore alleged that the charterers' claims were time barred by Section 3(6) of the US Carriage of Goods by Sea Act 1936. Against this the charterers pointed to the provision of the Agreement which provided that claims pursued under it should be notified 'within two years from the date of discharge or the date when the goods should have been discharged'.[307] In response to the question, 'What connection can the parties have intended between a settlement under the Inter-Club Agreement pursuant to clause 55 and the Hague Rules in relation to such settlement?' Kerr LJ noted that there was no connection:

> The scheme of the Inter-Club Agreement lies precisely in the opposite direction. It cuts right across any allocation of functions and responsibilities based on the Hague Rules; indeed, the

---

301 Clause (8)(c).
302 Clause (8)(d).
303 See the list at the end of the 1996 version and compare this more extensive list of P & I Clubs with that in the 1984 version.
304 See the preface to the 1996 Agreement.
305 [1983] 1 Lloyd's Rep 219 (CA).
306 As to this, see para 19.51.
307 See clause (3)(iv) of the 1984 Agreement and clause (6) of the 1996 Agreement.

avoidance of such allocation is the very objective of the Inter-Club Agreement. In this connection it is common ground that cl 55 must itself prevail notwithstanding art III(8) of the Hague Rules, which invalidates any agreement which relieves the carrier to any extent 'from liability for loss or damage to or in connection with the goods . . .' The Inter-Club Agreement . . . provides a more or less mechanical apportionment of financial liability which is wholly independent of [Hague Rules] standards of obligation. The agreed apportionment has nothing to do with the Hague Rules, and is in fact designed to overcome many of the difficulties which would result from their application. It seems to me that in these circumstances art III(6) has no place in a settlement between owners and charterers under the Inter-Club Agreement.[308]

32.108 **Seaworthiness and the Agreement**   In *Ben Line Steamers Ltd v Pacific Steam Navigation Co (The Benlawers)*[309] certain owners let their ship, the *Benlawers*, to the charterers for one round voyage from the United Kingdom to the west coast of South America. An addendum to the charterparty later extended it to cover a second round voyage. The NYPE (1946) form provided that:

> 47. Cargo claims under this Charter Party to be settled between Owners and Charterers under the inter club New York Produce Exchange Agreement.

> 48. . . . the Charterer agrees to indemnify the Owners in respect of any cargo claims which under the terms of this Charter Party are due.

During the course of the first round voyage, there were no difficulties, but on the second voyage the *Benlawers* loaded a part cargo of 4,000 tons of onions in Chile. The bills of lading in respect of this cargo incorporated the Hague Rules. When the cargo was out-turned at Avonmouth, a discharge survey was carried out. Before discharge the onions revealed evidence of sprouting; after discharge several onions were of wasted and soft condition. The receivers commenced proceedings against the owners and charterers for damages for breach of contract and/or duty and/or negligence in and about the stowage, custody, and care of the onions. The owners paid the receivers the sum of £159,073.70 and sought to recover this sum from the charterers by way of a claim for an indemnity. The arbitrators had held that the shipowners were not entitled to any such indemnity. Before Hobhouse J the shipowners now sought to claim against the charterers by way of an implied indemnity[310] and, secondly, by way of an express indemnity in clause 48 of the charterparty. Further the owners claimed either a full or 50 per cent indemnity under the Inter-Club Agreement which was incorporated into the charterparty by clause 47. Clause 8 of the charterparty was the typical NYPE (1946) clause 8 whereby the charterers were expressed to be under the 'supervision and responsibility of the captain' with respect to loading, stowage, trimming, and discharge of the cargo. Hobhouse J concluded that the dispute was governed by clause 47 of the charterparty and the Inter-Club Agreement. The arbitrators had concluded that the true cause of the damage to the onions was that the vessel was not fitted with a ventilation system which could supply adequate ventilation for safe carriage of the cargo — the vessel was not cargoworthy. Accordingly under clause (1)(ii)(c) of the (1984) Agreement the owners had to bear 100 percent of the financial loss for the damage to the onions.

---

308 [1983] 1 Lloyd's Rep 219 (CA), 225–226.
309 [1989] 2 Lloyd's Rep 51.
310 By analogy with *The Athansia Comninos & Georges Chr Lemos* [1990] 1 Lloyd's Rep 277.

Before Hobhouse J the owners sought to argue that any warranty as to 'cargoworthiness' was not included within the use of the word 'seaworthiness' in the Agreement. Hobhouse J did not accept this argument — 'unseaworthiness' had to be used in its natural and broader sense.[311] Hobhouse J therefore concluded that the arbitrators were right to come to the conclusion which they had. On the facts the owners were not entitled to any indemnity from the charterers in respect of the claim. Accordingly, under clause (1)(ii)(c) the owners' liability was 100 percent.

Documents and the Agreement In *A/S Iverans Rederi v KG MS Holstencruiser Seeschiffartsgesellschaft mbH & Co (The Holstencruiser)*[312] the main issues concerned the scope of the Inter-Club Agreement as incorporated into various time charterparties and also what criteria had to be satisfied in order to make it applicable to any given cargo claim and the effect of the Agreement once it had been decided that it applied. The following clause was contained in the charterparty: **32.109**

39. Any liability to third parties for cargo claims to be borne by Owners/Time charterers in accordance with the Inter-Club NYPE Agreement (1970/1972) . . .

The claims in question concerned the impact of pilferage and of shortage in the context of container transport. The owners argued that such problems, in so far as they arose out of container transport and which were not demonstrated to have occurred during the sea transit fell outside the scope of the transit. The charterers argued that they came within the scope of the Agreement and fell to be divided between the owners and charterers 50:50 unless the proviso to clause (2) (of the Agreement) applied. So far as the question as to what transactions might fall within clause 39 was concerned, Hobhouse J held that these must be claims under bills of lading which conformed to the provisions of the time charter. The charterers had to be prepared to prove that the relevant bills of lading were 'properly issued' under the time charterparty — that is to say was issued for goods which it could be proved had passed into the possession of the owners. A related point concerned the scope, or extent, of the contract contained in or evidenced by the bill of lading. In the case of the *Holstensailor*, the container containing the goods was packed and shipped at Keelung (in Taiwan) and shipped on a vessel called the *Ming Pleasure*. The bill of lading in respect of the container was signed on behalf of the owners of the *Ming Pleasure* by the charterers' agents and named the discharge port as Buenos Aires. On the charterers' instructions the goods were in fact discharged at Savannah and from there transhipped onto the *Holstensailor* which then carried them to Buenos Aires. In respect of such a bill of lading, Hobhouse J concluded that if the charterers sought to rely on it for the purpose of mounting a claim under the Inter-Club Agreement, then it had to be a bill of lading which related to those services. A transhipment or a through bill of lading would not have that character because it did not relate either wholly or in part to service to be provided for others.[313] Accordingly

---

[311] He referred in particular to *The Good Friend* [1984] 2 Lloyd's Rep 586. See also *Kamilla Hans-Peter Eckhoff AG v AC Oerssleff's EFTF A/B (The Kamilla)* [2006] EWHC 509 (Comm); [2006] 2 Lloyd's Rep 238.

[312] [1992] 2 Lloyd's Rep 378.

[313] At 386.

wherever there has been a transhipment it will not suffice for the charterers to show that there
has been a claim under a bill of lading purportedly issued on behalf of the owners and invoke
cl. 39 and the inter-club agreement. The charterers will have to prove that the loss or damage
in respect of which there was a liability to the bill of lading holder occurred, or was caused,
during the carriage of the container on the owners' vessel.[314]

Hobhouse J therefore concluded that the issue of a through bill of lading or a transhipment
bill on behalf of another carrier would not suffice for the purposes of the Inter-Club
Agreement. Indeed it was expressly excluded from the Agreement.

32.110   *The Hawk*   In *Oceanfocus Shipping Ltd v Hyundai Merchant Marine Co Ltd (The Hawk)*[315]
the dispute concerned the sum of $23,920.85 but involved the proper construction of the
NYPE Agreement and, in particular, a term of the 1972 version. The charterparty contained
the following two critical clauses:

> 8. That the Captain Master shall prosecute his voyages with the utmost despatch, and shall
> render all customary assistance with the ship's crew and boats. The Captain (although
> appointed by the Owners) shall be under the orders and directions of the Charterers as
> regards employment and agency; and Charterers are to load stow *tally, lash, unlash,
> secure and discharge* and trim the cargo at their expense under the supervision of the
> Captain, who is to sign Bills of Lading *if requested to do so by Charterers* for cargo as
> presented in conformity with Mate's or Tally Clerk's receipts.

> 50. Charterers and/or their Agents are hereby authorised by Owners to sign on Master's
> and/or on Owners behalf Bill of Lading as presented in accordance with Mate's or Tally
> Clerk's receipts without prejudice to this Charter Party.

The *Hawk* performed a time charter trip from the Far East to various ports in the
United States between August and November 1990. The cargo carried included plywood and
steel products. Various claims under the relevant bills of lading for this cargo were settled
by the charterers who now claimed their right to be indemnified under the Agreement.
The claims settled by the charterers were in respect of shortage, condensation damage, and
sea water damage. The owners had raised three defences to the charterers' claims when the
matter went to arbitration: that in respect of some of the claims no mate's receipts had been
produced by the charterers; that the bills of lading had not been signed in strict accordance
with the mate's receipts; that the charterers had failed to comply with clause 63 of the charterparty in that supporting documents had not been submitted to the owners 'as soon as
possible'. The main argument which was advanced before Judge Diamond QC was
concerned with the question whether it was a condition precedent to recovery under the
Inter-Club Agreement that the bill of lading under which a claim had been brought must
have been authorized by the charterparty. This was in relation to clause 1(1) of the
Agreement which provided that:

> It shall be a condition precedent to settlement under the Agreement that . . . the cargo (was)
> carried under a bill or bills authorised by the charterparty . . .[316]

---

[314] At 387.

[315] [1999] 1 Lloyd's Rep 176.

[316] cf cl (1)(i) of the Inter-Club Agreement 1984; cl (4)(a) of the NYPE Agreement 1996, neither of which
contains these words.

The owners contended that under both clause 8 and clause 50 of the charterparty, a bill of lading which was not in conformity with the mate's receipts would be unauthorized and not in compliance with the terms of the charter. However, the charterers contended that clause 50 merely conferred a general authority on the charterers to issue bills of lading and that additional reference to the bills being 'in accordance with Mate's or Tally Clerk's receipts' gave rise to a separate undertaking by the charterers. On this issue, agreeing with *The Holstencruiser*,[317] the judge said that:

> Looking at the matter in the round I see little escape from the conclusion that it is to be implied in cl.1(1) of the inter-club agreement, as incorporated in the charter-party, that to qualify for settlement under the agreement, the bill of lading under which the claim is brought must have been authorised by the charter-party. To my mind, however, it is important that this test be applied broadly and flexibly so as to give effect to the commercial purpose of the inter-club agreement and so as not reduce its effectiveness as a means of settling the incidence of liability for cargo claims as between owners and charterers.[318]

In construing clause 8 and clause 50 of the charterparty, Judge Diamond thought that it was important to have regard to the factual matrix in which they appeared. Accordingly

> Having regard to the diverse nature of the representations to be found in mate's receipts and the wide spectrum of importance of the failure to include in the bills notations appearing in the mate's receipts, ranging from serious misrepresentations to trivial or justified omissions, I would be reluctant to hold that charterers' authority to issue bills of lading on behalf of shipowners is delimited by the requirement that the bills must precisely and exactly conform to mate's or tally clerk's receipts. I would construe cll. 8 and 50 as conferring a general authority on charterers to sign any bill which the master was authorised to sign . . . and as containing an independent undertaking that bills so signed will conform to mate's or tally clerk's receipts.[319]

Judge Diamond agreed with the arbitrators that it would be 'uncommercial' to construe clause 1(1) of the Inter-Club Agreement and clauses 8 and 50 of the charterparty so as to make it a condition precedent to the right to rely on the Inter-Club Agreement that the bills of lading issued by the charterers must have complied in every respect with mate's or tally clerk's receipts. He concluded that there was nothing to justify the owners' contentions that the absence of a mate's receipt was a bar to recovery, whatever the cause of the loss. Where there was a shortage claim and the question arose as to whether the relevant goods were ever delivered into the possession of the owners or their agents at the port of loading, then it would be for the charterers to prove that the bill of lading was authorized in the sense that it was a bill which the master would have had the authority of the owners to sign. Where there was no such issue, then prima facie the bills would be 'authorized' bills and any omission in the bills of notations to be found in the receipts would not, of itself, constitute a bar to recovery under the Inter-Club Agreement. Where, however, there was a causal connection between the cargo claims in respect of which indemnity was sought and the discrepancy between mate's receipts and the relevant bill of lading, the owners may be able to recover damages for breach of clauses such as clauses 8 and 50 and such damages would either reduce or extinguish the contribution due to the charterers under the

---

[317] [1992] 2 Lloyd's Rep 378.
[318] [1999] 1 Lloyd's Rep 176,185.
[319] At 187.

Inter-Club Agreement.[320] Accordingly, Judge Diamond QC dismissed the owners' appeal and upheld the award of the arbitrators.

32.111 **Legal costs and the Agreement** This point was also addressed in *A/S Iverans Rederi v KG MS Holstencruiser Seeschiffartsgesellschaft mbH & Co (The Holstencruiser).*[321] The first point concerned the meaning of the phrase 'the cargo claim, including any legal costs incurred thereon' used in clause (1)(i). Hobhouse J considered that this meant the legal costs of the (third party) claimant which the claimant would be entitled to have paid along with the settlement of his claim. There was no right of the charterers to recover any costs they might have incurred from the owners. In respect of the *Savannah*, the charterers had had to pay certain customs fines to the authorities at Santos, Brazil. They were seeking to recover 50 per cent of these fines from the owners. Hobhouse J held that they were not entitled to do so — they were outside the scope of the Agreement.

32.112 **Short delivery claims** In *A/S Iverans Rederi v KG MS Holstencruiser Seeschiffartsgesellschaft mbH & Co (The Holstencruiser)*[322] the owners sought to give a restrictive interpretation to the phrase 'short delivery claims' as used in clause (2). Hobhouse J considered that the phrase had to be given its ordinary meaning — ie claims by the owner of the goods that all the goods he delivered to the carrier have not been redelivered to him. However, he went on to say that:

> . . . I have in effect accepted that there is a break-off point for the liability of the owners to contribute to losses occurring at the discharge port. I have also accepted that a liability that arises from some estoppel created by the bill of lading issued by the charterers (on behalf of the owners) will not come within the scope of the agreement as incorporated and thus cannot give rise to a short delivery claim for the purposes of cl (2).[323]

32.113 **Condensation damage** In *A/S Iverans Rederi v KG MS Holstencruiser Seeschiffartsgesellschaft mbH & Co (The Holstencruiser)*[324] the goods owners claimed for condensation damage. Hobhouse J noted that such damage fell within the express words of clause (2) — and that such a claim would be apportioned 50:50 between the owners and charterers unless the proviso to clause (2) applied. The fact that a container in question was stored on deck did not alter this conclusion because the terms of carriage were either the Hague (or Hague–Visby) Rules or 'terms no less favourable' (clause (1)(i)). Both the time charterparty and the bills of lading contemplated and permitted carriage on deck. In respect of the proviso to clause (2) of the Agreement, Hobhouse J noted that the mere fact that the owners might subsequently be able to prove that there can have been no condensation damage did not prove that the damage was 'due solely to bad stowage' which was the only basis under the proviso to clause (2) for imposing 100 per cent liability on the charterers.

32.114 **Differences between versions** Because of various difficulties with the 1984 version of the Agreement which had to be addressed by the courts, the Agreement was redrafted in 1996. The points which have been addressed include: an accurate definition of legal costs; to what carriage documents the Agreement should apply; what does 'cargo claims' include. As we

---

[320] At 187–188.
[321] [1992] 2 Lloyd's Rep 378.
[322] Ibid.
[323] 388.
[324] Ibid.

have seen,[325] in *A/S Iverans Rederi v KG MS Holstencruiser Seeschiffartsgesellschaft mbH & Co (The Holstencruiser)*[326] Hobhouse J had concluded that a through transport document or combined transport document fell outside the scope of the Agreement. Clause (4)(a) of the 1996 Agreement now provides that it applies to any contract of carriage 'whatever its form'. Thus waybills, voyage charters, traditional bills of lading, or through transport documents are all documents to which the Agreement may apply if a cargo claim arises. But in respect of through transport or combined transport, the loss, damage, shortage, over-carriage, or delay must have occurred between the commencement of loading and the completion of discharge.[327] So far as cargo claims are concerned, clause (3) reverses *A/S Iverans Rederi v KG MS Holstencruiser Seeschiffartsgesellschaft mbH & Co (The Holstencruiser)*[328] and provides that customs dues or fines in respect of the loss are included. However, *The Holstencruiser* is endorsed in the 1996 Agreement to the extent that legal expenses are defined as those which are incurred in the defence of or settlement of the third party (primary) cargo claim (including Club correspondents' and experts' costs) and not legal costs incurred in the consequential claim as between owner and charterer in attempting to resolve any dispute about the correct apportionment of costs.[329]

Properly settled claims A further matter which has been settled under the 1996   **32.115**
Agreement concerns what must be proved to justify its claim under the Agreement — ie what constitutes a 'properly settled or compromised and paid' claim for the purposes of clause (4)(c) of the Agreement. Clause (7) provides that the amount of any cargo claim to be apportioned shall be the amount 'in fact' borne by the party to the charterparty seeking apportionment, regardless of whether that claim may be or has been apportioned by application of this Agreement to another charterparty.

Time bars The question of the time bar under the Agreement is addressed in clause (6).   **32.116**
The Agreement now provides a two-tier system. Thus it recognizes the existence of the coming into force of the Hamburg Rules and provides for a 36 month period for notification in writing of an indemnity claim — but only where the Hamburg Rules are compulsorily applicable to the primary claim by operation of law. Otherwise, the time bar is stated to be 24 months.

N. Redelivery of the Vessel

The general principle Usually the charter will require redelivery of the vessel to its owner at   **32.117**
a specified port or ports 'in like good order and condition, ordinary wear and tear excepted'.[330]

Redelivery ports It will usually be the case that a range of redelivery ports is specified   **32.118**
rather than a particular port. Even where the parties have agreed to a range for redelivery, it can be important to determine around which particular ports that range is centred.

---

[325] See para 32.109.
[326] [1992] 2 Lloyd's Rep 378.
[327] Clause (4)(a)(iii).
[328] [1992] 2 Lloyd's Rep 378.
[329] Clause 3.
[330] NYPE 93, cl 10, lines 130–136; Shelltime 4, cl 16(b), lines 308–310.

In *Reardon Smith Line Ltd v Sank Steamship Co Ltd (The Sanko Honour)*[331] the charterparty provided that:

> The vessel shall be delivered by Owners as a new building unused at or off Builders' Shipyard Japan at Owner's option and redelivered to Owners at a port or point at sea worldwide within Institute warranty limits but not further in distance than Persian Gulf is from Japan at Charterer's option.

The *Sanko Honour* was redelivered at Honolulu but the owners contended that Honolulu was not a legitimate place to redeliver the vessel because it was further from the Persian Gulf than Japan was. Hobhouse J held that the phrase 'not further in distance than Persian Gulf is from Japan' was

> completely clear. It is a clause which provides that the distance is from Japan, as it says.

> It follows . . . that the correct construction of this charter-party is that the distance is a distance from Japan, as the clause says, and, therefore, that Honolulu is within the redelivery range which is laid down by this charter-party and, therefore, the award that the arbitrator has made must be set aside.[332]

32.119 **Breach** A redelivery outside the agreed range will amount to a breach of contract by the charterer. The usual rule in damages is that the charterer must pay to the shipowner the full charterparty hire for the shortest, quickest voyage that would take the ship from the actual redelivery port to the agreed redelivery range, less whatever sums the ship could reasonably be expected to earn in that period.[333] This was one of the issues that arose in the case of *Santa Martha Baay Scheepvaart & Handelsmaatschappij NV v Scanbulk A/S (The Rijn)*.[334] The owners of the ship had let her for one time charter trip via South Africa to the USA and thence a return cargo to the Far East. The charterparty provided:

> 4. That the Charterers shall pay for the use and hire of the said vessel . . . commencing on and from the day of her delivery . . . hire to continue until the hour of her redelivery in like good order and condition ordinary wear and tear excepted, to the Owners . . . at a safe port SOUTH JAPAN (not north of TOKYO BAY)/SINGAPORE RANGE . . .

The *Rijn* was delivered to the charterers at Kobe (Japan) and while on passage to Baltimore and Wilmington had to call at Cape Town for removal of some of the fouling of the hull incurred at the intermediate port of Lorenço Marques. This marine growth on the hull affected her speed and was likely to continue to affect her speed. The charterers then nominated Galveston as the port of loading for the final voyage. They terminated the charterparty at Galveston 'as is, where is'. Had the charterers repudiated the contract? Mustill J held that:

> . . . [W]here the ship is tendered at a port which is not within the redelivery range, . . . there is no question of the charterer breaking a collateral obligation attaching at the moment of redelivery, nor is it the owner's sole complaint that the ship has been returned to him in the wrong place. He has a contractual right to have the ship kept in employment at the charter

National final voyage (?)

---

[331] [1985] 1 Lloyd's Rep 418.
[332] At 420–421.
[333] See *Malaysian International Shipping Corp v Embresa Cubana de Fletes (The Bunga Kenanga)* [1981] 2 Lloyd's Rep 518.
[334] [1981] 2 Lloyd's Rep 267.

rate of hire until the service is completed. This does not happen until the ship reaches the redelivery range, and the voyage to that range forms part of the chartered service. In a case such as the present, therefore, the tender is not only in the wrong place but also at the wrong time; and full compensation for the breach requires the charterer to restore to the owner the hire which he would have earned if the voyage had in fact been performed.

I therefore consider that the arbitrators were right in basing their award of damages on the cost of a notional final voyage to Japan . . . . This was a voyage to the nearest safe port within the redelivery range, namely, Yokohama; and it would have been a voyage in ballast, because this would have saved time which would otherwise have been occupied in loading and discharge.[335]

This case therefore confirms that the calculation of damages is worked out on the basis of a notional voyage in ballast to the nearest port within the agreed range.

Obligation to redeliver The charterer's obligation to redeliver 'in like good order' is   **32.120** separate from the obligation to redeliver the vessel. Thus, redelivery at the right place at the right time is a proper redelivery and this brings to an end the charterer's obligation to pay hire, even if the ship has been redelivered in poor condition. In *Attica Sea Carriers Corporation v Ferrostaal (The Puerto Buitrago)*[336] the *Puerto Buitrago* was demise chartered for 17 months. The ship was to be redelivered

> to the Owner in the same good order and condition as on delivery, having been maintained in accordance with Clause 10A, ordinary wear and tear excepted and in class without recommendations. At the redelivery survey, surveyors . . . shall determine and state the repairs or work necessary to place the vessel in the condition and class required in this paragraph . . . Charterer before redelivery, shall make all such repairs and do all such work so found to be necessary at its expense and time.

After only six months on hire, the Puerto Buitrago developed engine trouble and had to be towed from Rio de Janeiro (Brazil) to Gdynia in Poland where her cargo of soya bean meal was unloaded. She was then towed to Kiel for repairs. The charterers admitted liability for $400,000 of the repairs and redelivered the vessel, terminating the charterparty. The shipowners refused to accept redelivery contending that under the charterparty the charterers were bound to repair the vessel whatever the cost and to pay the charter hire until the vessel was repaired. At first instance Mocatta J held that the charterers were bound to repair the vessel before redelivery and that the owners were entitled to hire until the charterers repaired the vessel. The Court of Appeal disagreed and held that after the end of the charter period the charterers might make a good redelivery of the ship in badly damaged condition, subject to the owner's claim for damages. Lord Denning MR stated that

> . . . when the charterers tendered redelivery at the end of the period of the charter — in breach of the contract to repair — the shipowners ought in all reason to have accepted it. They cannot sue for specific performance — either of the promise to pay the charter hire, or of the promise to do the repairs — because damages are an adequate remedy for the breach.[337]

The damage here was such that the necessary repairs, which were estimated at $2 million, would have greatly exceeded her value ($1 million) when repaired.

---

[335] At 270.
[336] [1976] 1 Lloyd's Rep 250.
[337] At 255.

32.121   Assessment of damages   The case of *Channel Island Ferries Ltd v Cenargo Navigation Ltd (The Rozel)*[338] concerned the assessment of damages following the alleged breach of the following charterparty clause:

> 13. The Vessel shall be re-delivered to the owners in the same or as good structure, state, condition and class as that in which she was delivered fair wear and tear not affecting class excepted . . .

The *Rozel*, a passenger ferry, was redelivered by the charterers to the owners in February 1992, the entablature of the port inner auxiliary generator having been damaged and repaired by the charterers in the course of the charter. The owners now contended that the condition of the entablature and the effect that this condition had on the classification of the vessel constituted breaches of the charterers' redelivery obligations and claimed as damages the notional cost of replacing the entablature. The arbitrator found against the charterers in the sum of £87,500. The charterers now appealed, contending that the arbitrator had applied the wrong test in law to the assessment of damages. Phillips J held that:

> Where a contract makes specific provision for the condition or attributes of a vessel upon delivery or redelivery to her owners, the owners will not necessarily be able to recover as damages the cost of remedying a failure to comply with the provision. Such cost will only be recoverable if this represents reasonable expenditure, and this will be judged on the basis of the commercial implications of the breach of contract. . . . [I]n a commercial context a plaintiff will not recover damages on a 'cost of cure' basis if that cost is disproportionate to the financial consequences of the deficiency.[339]

He accordingly held that the arbitrator had not applied the correct approach to the assessment of damages and remitted the award to the arbitrator so that he could apply the correct legal approach to the assessment of damages. This case therefore emphasizes that it is important to understand that the obligation to redeliver is not absolute and that it must be read in the context of the charterparty as a whole. The shipowner will usually be required to keep the ship in good order throughout the charter period.

32.122   No damages for shipowners' defective maintenance   The charterer will not be liable for damage caused by the shipowners' own defective maintenance. He will only be liable for damage caused by his own default. This matter was considered by the Court of Appeal in *Limerick Steamship Co Ltd v WH Stott & Co Ltd (The Innisboffin)*.[340] In this case, the plaintiffs chartered their ship, the *Innisboffin* for a Baltic round voyage to the defendants. The charterers ordered her to Åbo in Finland and in the course of the voyage she was damaged by ice. The port of Åbo was kept open all year by ice-breakers and so the judge at first instance found that it was not an ice-bound port.[341] The vessel had in fact tried to ram her way through ice some 200 miles from Åbo. Her forepeak tank was found to be leaking as a result of this. Were the charterers liable for this damage? The Court of Appeal found that they were not. Scrutton LJ held that:

> What the master will do when he meets thick ice seems to be a matter of his navigation. The charterer does not give him orders as to this situation or 'oblige' him to do anything, and

---

[338] [1994] 2 Lloyd's Rep 161.
[339] At 167.
[340] [1921] 2 KB 613 (CA).
[341] [1921] 1 KB 508 (Bailhache J).

he will not prejudice his owners' hire by waiting till he can get through. He is not 'obliged to force ice'. In this particular case by sending for the ice-breaker he could have got through without damaging himself. I am unable to see what breach of charter the charterers have committed in this case; the damage seems to have resulted from the captain's decision to take a course of action which by the charter he was relieved from the obligation to take. Some damage is supposed to have resulted from storms blowing the steamer on the thick ice at the edge of the ice-breaker's channel. This does not seem to be the charterers' affair.[342]

Ancillary costs Although the charterer will be liable for the cost of repair if the ship is 32.123 redelivered in a damaged condition, he will not be liable for any ancillary costs of ensuring that the ship is repaired immediately after redelivery. In *Somelas Corp v A/S Gerrards Rederi (The Pantelis A Lemos)*[343] the parties had provided that the owners were to take redelivery of the vessel with damages unrepaired and that each party was to appoint a surveyor at the redelivery port with instructions to make a joint survey of all the damages. The charterparty addendum containing this agreement was added just before the time arrived for the redelivery of the vessel in Spring 1978. The addendum stated that:

3. The . . . two surveyors are to estimate the cost of repair of each item of damage and to agree between themselves on each item cost . . .

5. The surveyors are to clarify in the total list of damages what is fair wear and tear and what is stevedore damage. Damages affecting Class or cargo to be repaired before redelivery.

6. Charterers will not concede and Owners shall not seek any compensation for theoretical time consumed by those repairs agreed to be for Charterers' option.

7. Charterers to pay Owners the above agreed repairing cost within one month of receipt of list.

Following survey at Rotterdam, it was estimated that the costs for carrying out repairs would be Dfls 349,880. In order to effect the repairs, it was also necessary to clean and gas her fuel oil double bottom tanks at an additional cost of Dfls 102,800. The charterers declined to pay this second sum. Were the owners entitled to it? Robert Goff J stated that:

It is common knowledge, of course, that when the question of such matters as stevedore damage occur and these matters arise, as they frequently do, on redelivery at the end of a time charter, then although the items of damage will be listed for the purposes of dealing with the final hire account under the time charter nevertheless the owners will not necessarily carry out the repairs straightaway.

. . . [O]ne gets the clearest possible indication in this document that the intention was that the ship should sail on her next commitment as soon as she was free to do so apart from the carrying out of repairs of damage affecting class or cargo operation. There is nothing to suggest that any of the stevedore damage listed in this survey report fell into that category and, therefore, this agreement contemplates that the repair of this damage would not be carried out straightaway.

As I read it the intention is that when it was provided that the surveyors were to agree between themselves on each item's cost, that was looking to the actual cost of repair of each item. It was not intended to include any theoretical loss of time while they were repaired, and on the words used it could not include the costs involved in maintaining the ship during repairs, while they were being repaired.[344]

---

[342] [1921] 2 KB 613 (CA), 621.
[343] [1980] 2 Lloyd's Rep 102.
[344] At 105–106.

CARGO CLAIMS

33

FRUSTRATION

A. Introduction

Overview   The doctrine of frustration (or *force majeure*) is one of considerable complexity.[1] **33.01**
It is a doctrine of general contract law, but many of the leading cases have been shipping
cases. In this chapter we look at these cases and the importance of the doctrine in contracts
for the carriage of goods by sea.

B. Frustration and Contracts of Carriage of Goods by Sea

Introduction   In certain circumstances the contract of carriage of goods by sea might **33.02**
be brought to an end because it has become frustrated. Lord Radcliffe in the leading
case, *Davis Contractors Ltd v Fareham Urban District Council*, described the concept as
follows:

> Frustration occurs whenever the law recognises that without default of either party a
> contractual obligation has become incapable of being performed because the circumstances
> in which performance is called for would render it a thing radically different from that
> which was undertaken by the contract. *Non haec in foedora veni* — it was not this that
> I promised to do.[2]

---

[1] See, eg, Scrutton (1996), art 14; Cooke (2001), ch 22; Treitel (2004).
[2] [1956] AC 696, 729.

The doctrine evolved to mitigate the rigour of the common law's insistence of the literal performance of absolute promises.[3] As Bingham LJ explained:

> The object of the doctrine was to give effect to the demands of justice, to achieve a just and reasonable result, to do what was reasonable and fair, as an expedient to escape from injustice where such would result from enforcement of a contract in its literal terms after a significant change in circumstances.[4]

33.03   **Nature**   The decision as to whether or not the contract has been frustrated is a question of law but 'that conclusion is almost completely determined by what is ascertained as the mercantile usage and the understanding of commercial men'.[5]

C. Types of Frustration

33.04   **Impossibility of performance**   One of the most common kinds of frustration occurs when performance becomes impossible owing to the actual loss or the constructive total loss of the ship.[6] Some time charters, such as NYPE 93, provide expressly that, in the event of hire having being paid in advance, this will be returned in such an event should it not have been earned:

> **20. *Total Loss***
>
> Should the Vessel be lost, money paid in advance and not earned (reckoning from the date of loss or being last heard of) shall be returned to the Charterers at once.

An illustration of constructive total loss is the case of *Blane Steamships v Ministry of Transport (The Empire Gladstone)*.[7] Here the *Empire Gladstone* was demise chartered from the Minister of Transport for a period of five years. As is typical with such charters, the charterers were to bear all risks and were responsible for insuring her. Clause 11 stated that the charterers had the option to purchase the ship, to be exercised 'not later than three months before the expiration of the charterparty'. In September 1950 the ship was on a voyage from Sydney to Adelaide when she stranded. The charterers duly gave notice of abandonment to the underwriters and a day later purported to exercise their option to purchase. The owners refused to accept for the reason that the ship was about to become a constructive total loss. This actually occurred approximately two weeks later. The plaintiffs contended that the option to purchase had been validly exercised. However, the Court of Appeal unanimously found that, at the time they purported to exercise their option, the charterers no longer enjoyed the right to exercise it.

33.05   **Supervening illegality**   A contract of affreightment will be frustrated should a change in the law (regardless of whether this is of the UK, or the country where the contract is to be

---

[3] *Hirji Mulji v Cheong Yue Steamship Co Ltd* [1926] AC 497 (PC), 510 (Lord Sumner); *Denny Mott & Dickson Ltd v James B Fraser & Co Ltd* [1944] AC 265, 275 (Lord Wright); *Joseph Constantine Steamship Line Ltd v Imperial Smelting Corp Ltd* [1942] AC 154, 171 (Viscount Maugham). As to the latter case, see para 33.18.

[4] *J Lauritzen AS v Wijsmuller BV (The Super Servant Two)* [1990] 1 Lloyd's Rep 1 (CA). See para 33.17.

[5] *BTP Tioxide Ltd v Pioneer Shipping Ltd (The Nema)* [1982] AC 724, 752 (Lord Roskill).

[6] A marine insurance term, defined in s 60 of the Marine Insurance Act 1906. See Bennett (2006), para 21.53.

[7] [1951] KB 965.

performed) render performance under the contract illegal. This will commonly occur where an outbreak of war renders further performance illegal. In *Fibrosa Spolka Akcyjna v Fairbairn Lawson Combe Barbour Ltd*[8] the respondents had contracted to deliver certain flax-hackling machines at a sum of £4,800 c.i.f. (cost, insurance, freight) Gdynia. The contract provided that if the despatch was hindered in any way by any cause outside the vendors' reasonable control (such as war) a reasonable extension of time should be given. Further, one third of the purchase price was to be paid at the time of the giving of the order. The appellants paid marginally less than the one third at the outbreak of war in September 1939. It was contended that, notwithstanding the express clause in the contract, the contract had been frustrated by the German occupation of Poland. Further the appellants asserted that the amount already paid (£1,000) should be repaid to them. On appeal to the House of Lords, Lord Atkin stated that:

> I have no doubt that the contract in this case came to an end before the time for complete performance had arrived by reason of the arising state of war which caused an indefinite delay not contemplated by the parties, and eventually on account of the legal impossibility of delivering the goods at a port occupied by the enemy. In other words . . . the commercial adventure was frustrated.[9]

The appellants were held entitled to a return of the £1,000 which they had paid in advance because this was money paid upon a consideration which failed.

Delay If there is a delay in performance of a contractual obligation, then the contract **33.06** may be frustrated, although this will depend on whether the delay is so prolonged as to defeat the commercial object of the adventure. This would have to be decided on the facts of each case, although the test will usually be an objective one and there may well be differences for time and voyage charterparties.[10] The test was explained as follows by Bailhache J in *Anglo-Northern Trading Co Ltd v Emlyn Jones & Williams*:

> The parties must have the right to claim that the charterparty is determined by frustration as soon as the event upon which the claim is based happens. The question will then be what estimate would a reasonable man of business take of the probable length of withdrawal of the vessel from such service with such materials as are before him, including, of course, the cause of the withdrawal and it will be immaterial whether his anticipation is justified or falsified by the event.[11]

Delay in voyage charterparties *Jackson v The Union Marine Insurance Co Ltd*[12] involved **33.07** a voyage charterparty between Newport and San Francisco. 'All and every the dangers and accidents of the seas' were excepted. While on the voyage to the loading port the *Spirit of the Dawn* ran onto rocks in Carnarvon Bay. She was so badly damaged that the charterers gave the owner notice rejecting the charterparty and chartered another ship to carry their cargo. The majority of the Court of Exchequer Chamber held[13] that a condition had

---

8 [1943] AC 32.
9 At 130.
10 See, as to be basic differences between the two types, paras 1.38–1.39. Delay is regarded as an ordinary incident of salvage operations: *Edwinton Commercial Corp v Tsarliris Russ Ltd* (The Sea Angel) [2006] EWHC 1713.
11 [1917] 2 KB 78, 84. The judgment was affirmed on appeal, reported as *Countess of Warwick Steamship Co v Le Nickel SA* [1918] 1 KB 372 (CA).
12 (1874) LR 10 CP 125.
13 Cleasby B dissenting.

to be implied into the charterparty that the ship should arrive at Newport at a reasonable time in order to commence the voyage to San Francisco. As this obligation was not fulfilled, the charterers' obligation to load the vessel was discharged and further, as the delay was caused by an excepted peril of the sea, no action lay against the charterers for recovery of any freight.

33.08 **Delay in time charterparties** The case of *Nitrate Corp of Chile Ltd v Pansuiza Compania de Navigacion SA (The Hermosa)*[14] involved a sub-time charter to Nitrates for a period of two years. The charterparty was on the NYPE form. During her first voyage from Chile to Terneuzen carrying a cargo of nitrates and iodine, it was found that the cargo had been badly damaged by seawater. Following the discharge of the damaged cargo, the vessel went into dry dock at Dunkirk and Nitrates relet her in order to provide a return cargo for her journey to Chile. Nitrates lost the fixture while the vessel was in dry dock and the vessel had to undertake the return journey in ballast to Chile. During this ballast voyage the *Hermosa* collided with another vessel and sustained damage to her bows. She was sent to Curaçao for repairs and Nitrates eventually repudiated the sub-charter. Some months later the head charterers accepted Nitrates' refusal to take the vessel back into service as a repudiation of the sub-charter. One of the issues in the case was whether the charterparty had been frustrated. After reviewing the authorities, Mustill J emphasized that what was essential was that it was the consequences of the events, not their origins, which mattered:

> At the very least, one can feel sympathy for the inconvenience and hardship suffered by Nitrates . . . However . . . this is not enough. There must be such a change in the significance of the obligation that the thing undertaken would, if performed, be a different thing from that contracted for, or . . . something which went to the root of the contract as depriving the charterers of substantially the whole benefit of the contract. I cannot find that anything of the kind existed in the present case.[15]

33.09 **Delay and strike clauses** In *The Penelope*[16] a clause in a time charterparty provided that, in the event of any stoppage arising from 'strikes, lockouts . . .'[17] continuing for a period of six running days from the time of the vessel being ready to load, the charter should, provided that, no cargo had been shipped on board the vessel previous to such stoppage, become null and void. During the course of 1926 there was a general coal strike which prevented the vessel loading coal from the named ports. The ship then performed two voyages with the assent of the claimants and one to which they did not assent. At the end of December 1926, the claimants ordered the vessel to the Mumbles Roads to await further orders. The defendants refused on the ground that the strike had frustrated the commercial object of the adventure. Lord Merrivale, taking into account the words of Viscount Sumner in *Bank Line Ltd v Arthur Capel & Co*,[18] came to the conclusion that 'there was an unforeseen compulsory change of circumstances not contemplated by the parties,' and that as soon as it manifestly prevented performance of the charter according to its true intent

---

14 [1980] 1 Lloyd's Rep 638.
15 At 649. See also *Ullises Shipping Corp v Fal Shipping Co Ltd (the Greek Fighter)* [2006] EWHC 1729.
16 [1928] P 180.
17 See too the discussion at para 28.32.
18 *Bank Line Ltd v Arthur Capel & Co* [1919] AC 435. See too para 33.10.

'the time had arrived at which the fate of the contract falls to be decided'.[19] He further found that the charterparty as varied by two substituted voyages was not further varied or prolonged by the third voyage. The strike provisions in the charter contemplated an interruption of work due to a local withdrawal of labour and not the total impossibility of any export of coal for as long as the case had been. It was this change of circumstances which prevented performance of the charterparty and so the action for breach of contract by the charterers of the *Penelope* failed.

Pioneer Shipping Ltd v BTP Tioxide Ltd also involved a strike clause.[20] The *Nema* was chartered for seven consecutive voyages between Sorel and Calais or Hartlepool in 1979. Cl 5 provided that time lost in strikes was not to be computed in the loading or discharging time. Following the first round trip, there was a strike and the parties, after an interval of three weeks, agreed an addendum in which the owners were permitted to take the *Nema* for an intermediate transatlantic voyage before returning to load at Sorel and extending the charterparty for a further seven voyages during 1980. When the strike continued into July 1979, a third addendum to the charter was made in which the charterers agreed to pay the owners compensation at the rate of $2,000 a day until the strike ended or the *Nema* obtained an intermediate voyage. She was released to the owners and sailed on an intermediate voyage to Glasgow in August 1979. The charterers then wished her to return to Sorel, but the owners had meanwhile fixed her for a further intermediate voyage. At an arbitration hearing, the arbitrator found that the whole of the charterparty contract was frustrated. He did not give any consideration to the seven consecutive voyages which had been arranged for 1980. Robert Goff J[21] reversed the arbitrator on this point but this was overturned by the Court of Appeal.[22] The House of Lords took the view that the charterparty voyages for the 1979 and 1980 seasons were separate, distinct, and independent adventures.[23] Much of the ground on this issue of the appeal was considered in the speech of Lord Roskill who concluded that there was

> no reason in principle why a strike should not be capable of causing frustration of an adventure by delay ... It is not the nature of the cause of delay which matters so much as the effect of that cause upon the performance of the obligations which the parties have assumed one towards the other.[24]

Effect of war   In *FA Tamplin Steamship Co Ltd v Anglo-Mexican Petroleum Products Co Ltd*[25]   **33.10** the *FA Tamplin* was time chartered for a period of 60 months for the carriage of oil. However following the outbreak of the First World War, when the charterparty had still another three years to run, the vessel was requisitioned and certain alterations made to enable her to carry troops. The majority of the House of Lords found that the charterparty did not come to an end when the steamer was requisitioned and consequently this did not suspend the charterparty or indeed affect the rights of the owners or charterers under it.

---

19 [1928] P 180, 197.
20 [1982] AC 724.
21 [1980] 2 Lloyd's Rep 83.
22 [1980] QB 547 (CA).
23 [1982] AC 724, 751.
24 At 754.
25 [1916] 2 AC 397.

This case may be contrasted with *Bank Line Ltd v Arthur Capel & Co*.[26] The defendant owners had let the *Quito* for a period of 12 months from the time that the vessel could be delivered and placed at the disposal of the charterers at a coal port in the UK. Loss or damage arising from restraint of princes was excepted.[27] Although the *Quito* was not delivered by the express cancelling date, the charterers did not exercise their right to cancel. Following her requisition, the question was whether the charterers were entitled to damages for non-delivery. The House of Lords so held, Lord Porter concluding that 'the requisitioning of the *Quito* destroyed the identity of the chartered service and made the charter as a matter of business a totally different thing. It hung up the performance for a time, which was wholly indefinite and probably long.'[28]

33.11 **Iran–Iraq war** Other cases which have involved frustration through delay occurred during the course of the Iran–Iraq war.[29] In *International Sea Tankers Inc v Hemisphere Shipping Co Ltd (The Wenjiang)*[30] a time charterparty was negotiated for a period of 12 months, commencing in April 1980. In September 1980, the charterers ordered the *Wenjiang* to proceed to Basrah. After the completion of loading, hostilities between Iran and Iraq erupted and it was not possible for the *Wenjiang* to leave the Shatt-el-Arab waterway. Eventually 60 vessels were trapped in the waterway. The arbitrator fixed the date of frustration as 24 November 1980 for the reason that there was the possibility that the vessel might be released before that date. A different arbitrator in the case concerning the *Evia*,[31] had found that that charterparty was frustrated on 4 October. Fox LJ stated that

> the provisional conclusion which I reach is that the arbitrator was not right in deciding upon 24 November as the date of frustration. His findings of fact, in my view, suggest that the proper date was early October by which time there was a 'high probability' that the duration of the war might be lengthy.[32]

In the circumstances, the judge was, in the view of the Court of Appeal, right in giving leave to appeal on the question of the date of frustration. This point was dealt with by Lord Denning MR:

> [The] present case . . . is not a singular case. It is one of 60 ships trapped in the Shatt. If each award by each arbitrator — as to the date of frustration — were considered *in isolation* — with no knowledge of the others — there would seem to be no good ground for interfering with it. It is of great importance to the trade that there should be uniformity of decision. When the question of frustration arises on 60 ships in a like situation, on like evidence, each decision should be the same as the other. . . . I am quite clear that the Judge was right to give leave to appeal in both cases — so that he, or the Court of Appeal, could consider — and decide — what is the correct date to take as the date of frustration.[33]

---

26 [1919] AC 435.
27 See para 28.25.
28 [1919] AC 435, 460.
29 See Bernard J Hibbits, 'The Impact of the Iran-Iraq Cases on the Law of Frustration of Charterparties' (1985) 16 JMLC 441.
30 [1982] 1 Lloyd's Rep 128.
31 See *Kodros Shipping Corp of Monrovia v Empresa Cubana de Fletes (The Evia) (No 2)* [1983] 1 AC 736, which went to the House of Lords on the safe port point: see para 20.32.
32 [1982] 1 Lloyd's Rep 128, 135.
33 At 131 (emphasis in the orginal).

D. Factors

Introduction   The innocent party who wishes to rely on frustration will be responsible   **33.12**
for proving it.[34] In considering the matter, the court may be guided by a number of potential factors which we now consider. However, as always in frustration cases, it is difficult to
lay down any general principles and the examples discussed are just that. Much will ultimately depend on the facts.

Frustration of the commercial object   One of the important factors which the court will   **33.13**
look at is whether performance has been rendered either impossible or so radically different that it would be unjust to hold the parties bound to the terms of the contract. In
Tsakiroglou & Co Ltd v Noblee Thorl GmbH[35] there was written contract by which the sellers
of Sudanese groundnuts agreed to ship them c.i.f. Hamburg in November/December 1956.
However, owing to the Suez crisis, the Suez Canal was closed to navigation on 2 November
and the only possible route was therefore around the Cape of Good Hope. This route was
more than twice as long and would have incurred enhanced freight charges. The sellers did
not ship the goods and when the matter went to arbitration it was held that the performance
of the contract by shipping the goods on a vessel routed by the Cape of Good Hope was
not commercially or indeed fundamentally different from performance of the contract via
Suez. The House of Lords agreed. In the course of his speech, Lord Reid pointed out that

> . . . all commercial contracts ought to be interpreted in light of commercial considerations.
> I cannot imagine a commercial case where it would be proper to hold that performance is
> fundamentally different in a legal though not in a commercial sense. Whichever way one
> takes it the ultimate question is whether the new method of performance is fundamentally
> different and that is a question of law.[36]

The issue arose again in *Ocean Tramp Tankers Corp v V/O Sovfracht (The Eugenia)*.[37] The
Eugenia was let to the charterers for a 'trip out to India via Black Sea' and it was intended
that the risk of any prolongation of the voyage, such as the closure of the Suez Canal, should
fall on the charterers.[38] Cl 21 of the charterparty provided that the vessel, unless with the
consent of the owners, was not to be ordered nor to continue to any place which would
bring her within a zone which was dangerous as a result of any actual or threatened act of
war, war hostilities, or warlike operations. The vessel was delivered at Genoa and then
embarked on a voyage from Odessa via Suez for India. When the *Eugenia* arrived at
Port Said, Suez was 'dangerous' within the meaning of cl 21 but the *Eugenia* nevertheless
proceeded on her journey and was eventually prevented from proceeding south. She was
ultimately able to return to Alexandria in January 1957. The charterers meanwhile claimed
that the charterparty was frustrated by the blocking of the canal. The owners denied frustration. The Court of Appeal found that the charterers were in breach of cl 21 in ordering
the vessel to enter the Suez Canal. Further, they held, applying Lord Radcliffe in *Davis*

---

[34] See para 33.18.
[35] [1962] AC 93.
[36] At 119.
[37] [1964] 2 QB 226 (CA).
[38] As to such 'trip' charterparties, see para 1.40.

Contractors Ltd v Fareham Urban District Council,[39] that the blocking of the Suez Canal had not brought about so fundamentally a different situation as to frustrate the venture.

33.14 **Contract transformed by some radical event** If there is some radical event which transforms the obligations of the parties in a way not contemplated by them when they entered into the contract, it may be regarded as having been frustrated. Thus in *WJ Tatem Ltd v Gamboa*[40] the claimants chartered the *Molton*, to the defendant for the evacuation of the civil population from northern Spain. Following delivery at Santander the *Molton* was seized by a Nationalist ship inside territorial waters off Santander and then taken to Bilbao. Following her release the *Molton* sailed for Bordeaux where she was redelivered to the plaintiffs. The defendant had paid in advance for the hire of the *Molton* but thereafter declined to pay on the basis of frustration of the venture. Goddard J found that the foundation of the contract was destroyed as soon as the *Molton* was seized:

> If the foundation of the contract goes, it goes whether or not the parties have made a provision for it . . . It seems to me, therefore, that when one uses the expression 'unforeseen circumstances' in relation to the frustration of the performance of a contract one is really dealing with circumstances which are unprovided [sic] for, circumstances for which (and in the case of a written contract one only has to look at the document) the contract makes no provision.[41]

33.15 **Contractual provision** As the discussion in the above case indicates, it would be possible for the parties to make express provision in their contract for the occurrence of a particular event as frustrating the contract. If this is the case, the provision would be strictly construed by the courts. An example is *Jackson v The Union Marine Insurance Co Ltd*[42] where, as we have already seen,[43] the phrase 'all and every the dangers and accidents of the seas excepted' was insufficient to cover the fundamental alteration in the nature of the contract. A similar point was made in *Bank Line Ltd v Arthur Capel & Co*[44] where Lord Haldane LC stated that

> . . . what is clear is that, where people enter into a contract which is dependent for the possibility of its performance on the continued availability of the subject-matter, and that availability comes to an unforeseen end by reason of circumstances over which its owner had no control, the owner is not bound unless it is quite plain that he has contracted to be so.[45]

33.16 **Self-induced frustration** The normal rule is that frustration must not arise through the default of either party.[46] In *Maritime National Fish Ltd v Ocean Trawlers Ltd*[47] appellants chartered the *St Cuthbert* for a period of 12 months, subject to a right of three months termination from either party. The vessel was equipped with an otter trawl. The charterparty was renewed for a further period of 12 months and, at this time, the parties knew that legislation made it a punishable offence to leave a Canadian port with intent to fish with a vessel using an otter trawl—unless a licence for the purpose had been granted. The charterers

---

[39] [1956] AC 696. See para 33.02.
[40] [1939] 1 KB 132.
[41] At 138.
[42] (1874) LR 10 CP 125.
[43] Para 33.07.
[44] [1919] AC 435.
[45] At 445.
[46] In *Bank Line Ltd v Arthur Capel & Co*, Lord Sumner stated that 'reliance cannot be placed on self-induced frustration': [1919] AC 435, 452.
[47] [1935] AC 524 (PC).

applied for licences for five vessels which they were operating, but only three were granted. No licence was granted to the *St Cuthbert* because she was not named by the charterers. They then tried to claim that they were no longer bound by the charterparty and in an action for charter hire by the owners claimed that the charterparty had become frustrated. The Supreme Court of Nova Scotia[48] found that the contract had not been frustrated because the frustration was due to the act of the charterers who had failed to nominate the *St Cuthbert* for one of the three licences granted. In agreeing with this on appeal to the Privy Council, Lord Wright made the following points:

> The essence of 'frustration' is that it should not be due to the act or election of the party. If it be assumed that the performance of the contract was dependent on a licence being granted, it was that election which prevented performance, and on that assumption it was the appellants' own default which frustrated the adventure: the appellants cannot rely on their own default to excuse them from liability under the contract.[49]

The Super Servant Two   The issue was considered again by the Court of Appeal in **33.17** *J Lauritzen AS v Wijsmuller BV (The Super Servant Two)*.[50] The defendants had contracted to carry a drilling rig, the *Dan King*, from Japan to Rotterdam. Carriage was to be effected by a 'transportation unit', *Super Servant One* or *Super Servant Two*. The owners of these specialist vessels had the right to cancel the contract in the event of *force majeure* and to substitute the transportation unit by other means of transport. In January 1981, the *Super Servant Two* sank and a month later the owners informed Lauritzen that they would not carry out the transportation of the drilling rig. *Super Servant One* was the subject of another fixture and hence not available for the purpose of performing the carriers' contract with the plaintiff. Despite these events, the parties entered into a 'without prejudice' agreement and the rig was transported to Rotterdam on a large barge towed by tug. The issues were whether the defendant owners were entitled to cancel the contract and whether the contract was frustrated (i) if the loss of *Super Servant Two* occurred without the negligence of the defendants or (ii) if the loss was caused by the negligence of the defendants. In respect of the first point, the Court of Appeal upheld the finding of Hobhouse J at first instance[51] that there had been no breach of duty by the owners to the charterer because the time for performance of the contract had not arisen at the time of the sinking of the transportation unit. On the second point, Bingham LJ accepted the argument that the present case did not fall within the very limited class of cases in which the law would relieve one party from an absolute promise he had chosen to make. In his view, the real question was whether the frustrating event relied upon was truly an outside event or extraneous change of situation or whether it was an event which the party seeking to rely on it had the means and opportunity to prevent but nevertheless caused or permitted to come about. Dillon LJ pointed out that under the contract the owners could have satisfied their obligation by using *Super Servant One* after *Super Servant Two* had sunk but that they had elected not to do so. In the end, the Court of Appeal dismissed the appeal, taking the view that the contract was not

---

48 [1934] 4 DLR 288.
49 [1935] AC 524 (PC), 530–31.
50 [1990] 1 Lloyd's Rep 1 (CA). See Ewan McKendrick, 'The construction of *force majeure* clauses and self-induced frustration' [1990] LMCLQ 153.
51 [1989] 1 Lloyd's Rep 148.

frustrated since it was open to the defendants to perform the contract with *Super Servant One*. The fact that they chose not to do so, even though that choice was made under pressure of unforeseen events, led to the conclusion that the frustration was self-induced. Further, if the loss of *Super Servant Two* had been brought about by the negligence of the defendants (or their servants) they would have been prevented from relying upon frustration on that ground also, because an event brought about by a person's negligence could not be said to be outside his control.

E. Burden of proof

33.18 **On the party making the allegation**   It seems that the burden of proving that the breach is self-induced will fall on the party who makes the allegation. So, if the owners were to establish that *prima facie* the charter had been frustrated, the burden would be on the charterers to prove that this situation had been induced by the owners. This was one of the issues which was considered by the House of Lords in *Joseph Constantine Steamship Line Ltd v Imperial Smelting Corp Ltd*.[52] The owners of the *Kingswood* chartered her for a voyage with a cargo of ores and concentrates from Port Pirie in South Australia to Europe. Before she became an 'arrived ship',[53] there was an explosion in the vessel's boiler room and this caused such damage to the vessel that she could not perform the charterparty. The charterers claimed damages, alleging that the owners had broken the charterparty by their failure to load a cargo. The owners set up the defence that the contract was frustrated by the destruction of the *Kingswood* following the explosion. The House of Lords emphasized that when frustration of a contract occurs, the contract comes to an end and the charterer would only be able to succeed in an action for damages for the subsequent non-performance of the charter by the owner if he proved that the end of the contract was caused by the owner's default. Where a contract was frustrated by the supervening destruction of essential subject matter of the contract, the owner who relied on the frustration was not bound to prove affirmatively that the destruction was not brought about by his neglect or default. It was for the charterer who sought to avoid the legal result of the frustration to establish that the destruction was due to the neglect or default of the owner (was self-induced). The House of Lords therefore concluded that the shipowners, having established that the explosion had frustrated the commercial object of the adventure, were not bound to prove further that the explosion was not due to their neglect or default. Accordingly, the defence of frustration by the owners succeeded.

F. Effect of Frustration

33.19 **Common law**   At common law, once the charter has been frustrated the parties to it are excused further performance under it but the contract remains valid and effective up until the moment that the frustration occurs. In *Hirji Mulji v Cheong Yue Steamship Co Ltd*,[54]

---

[52] [1942] AC 154.
[53] As to this, see para 31.07.
[54] [1926] AC 497 (PC).

the *Singaporean* was chartered to Hirji Mulji on terms that all disputes should be settled by arbitration in Hong Kong. The ship was requisitioned by the Hong Kong government and was not released until February 1919. Hirji Mulji then refused to take delivery and an arbitrator awarded the owners damages for breach of contract. The Privy Council found that the frustration of the charterparty in 1917 brought the whole contract to an end, including the submission to arbitration, and accordingly the arbitrator did not have jurisdiction to hear the case. Lord Sumner explained that

> . . . whatever the consequences of the frustration may be upon the conduct of the parties, its legal effect does not depend on their intention or their opinions, or even knowledge, as to the event, which has brought this about, but on its occurrence in such circumstances as show it to be inconsistent with further prosecution of the adventure . . .

> An arbitration clause is not a phoenix, that can be raised again by one of the parties from the dead ashes of its former self. By its very terms, as well as by the fact that it was only one part of the indivisible charter, it had come to an end also . . .[55]

Effect on freight and hire   The general principle is that any freight or hire due under the   **33.20** charter, or damages for breach accruing before frustration, will remain enforceable, despite the frustration. However, sums due after the frustration would no longer be payable; and where the effect of the frustration is such that the consideration for a payment already made or due has wholly failed, that payment would be recoverable or, if not paid, would cease to be payable. This point arose in *Fibrosa Spolka Akcyna v Fairbairn Lawson Combe Barbour Ltd*,[56] a case we have already considered.[57]

Effect on advance freight   It seems that freight payable in advance[58] is not recoverable   **33.21** following a frustration even though the goods were not delivered at the contract destination. However, freight payable on completion of the voyage would not be payable unless the cargo was delivered to the consignee at the destination.

The Law Reform (Frustrated Contracts) Act   In a strangely bi-focal approach for the   **33.22** consequences of frustration, the common law rules apply in the case of voyage charterparties and bills of lading. However, s 2(5)(a) of the Law Reform (Frustrated Contracts) Act 1943[59] provides that the provisions of that Act apply to time and demise charterparties. Section 1(2) provides that all sums paid or payable before the frustrating event shall, if paid, be recoverable and, if not paid, shall cease to be payable. Under the proviso to s 1(2) a court has a discretionary power to grant compensation for expenses which are incurred before the frustrating event. Furthermore, where one party receives a valuable benefit, before frustration, s 1(3) provides that the court can order that a suitable payment be made to the other party.

---

[55] At 509, 510–11. See also *Maritime National Fish Ltd* v *Ocean Trawlers Ltd* [1935] AC 524 (PC), 527 (Lord Wright), discussed at para 33.16.

[56] [1943] AC 32.

[57] See para 33.05.

[58] See para 21.15.

[59] c 40.

34

LIMITATION PERIODS

A. Introduction

Overview   In this chapter we consider those rules of the general law and under the Hague **34.01**
and Hague–Visby Rules as to limitation of time.[1] In practice this factor becomes the most
powerful weapon in the hands of the carrier — and the most dangerous defence which the
cargo claimant will face. It has been said that the reason in the carriage context for the time
bar, is that it 'meets an obvious commercial need, namely, to allow shipowners, after that
period, to clear their books'.[2]

B. Domestic Law Provisions

Limitation Act   Domestic law invariably prescribes time limits within which actions have **34.02**
to be brought for the recovery of compensation. In the UK, the Limitation Act 1980 prohibits the initiation of a contractual or tortious claim after the expiration of six years from
the time when the goods were delivered or should have been delivered. Section 2, which
deals with tort actions, provides that 'an action founded on tort shall not be brought after
the expiration of six years from the date on which the cause of action accrued'. Section 5,
for contract actions, provides that 'an action founded on simple contract shall not be
brought after the expiration of six years from the date on which the cause of action accrued'.
This Act will be relevant in those cases which are not subject to the time-bar provisions of
the Hague or Hague–Visby Rules.

---

[1] See Scrutton (1996), section XX; Cooke (2001), para 85.160; Carver (2005), para 9-178.
[2] *Aries Tanker Corporation v Total Transport (The Aries)* [1977] 1 WLR 185 (HL), 188 (Lord Wilberforce);
Port Jackson Stevedoring Pty Ltd v Salmond & Spraggon (Aust) Pty Ltd (1978) 139 CLR 231, 238 (Barwick CJ);
Cia Portorafti Commerciale SA v Ultramar Panama Inc (The Captain Gregos) (No 1) [1990] 1 Lloyd's Rep 310
(CA), 315 (Bingham LJ).

C. Under the Hague and Hague–Visby Rules

34.03 **Introduction**   We have so far looked at a host of provisions regulating the relationship between carriers and shippers under the Rules. The provisions as to time bar are to be found in part of article III, rule 6 of the Hague and Hague–Visby Rules, but it should be noted at the outset that there are some changes in the Hague–Visby Rules.

34.04 **Article III, rule 6 of the Hague Rules**   The relevant part of Article III, rule 6[3] of the Hague Rules provides that:

> ✗ In any event the carrier and the ship shall be discharged from all liability in respect of loss or damage unless suit is brought within one year after delivery of the goods or the date when the goods should have been delivered.

Article III, rule 6   The relevant part of the Hague–Visby Rules[4] provision reads as follows:

> ✓ Subject to paragraph 6 bis the carrier and the ship shall *in any event* be discharged from all liability *whatsoever* in respect of *the goods*, unless suit is brought within one year of their delivery or of the date when they should have been delivered. *This period may, however, be extended if the parties so agree after the cause of action has arisen.*[5]

34.05 **'Subject to paragraph 6 bis'**   This proviso to the Hague–Visby Rules is added to take account of article III, rule 6 bis, which was added to the Rules at Visby and concerns actions for an indemnity. It is discussed in due course.[6]

34.06 **'Discharged from all liability'**   The meaning of this phrase was interpreted by the House of Lords in the case of *Aries Tanker Corporation v Total Transport (The Aries)*.[7] The *Aries*, a tanker, was voyage chartered for the carriage of petroleum from the Arabian Gulf to Rotterdam. Clause 30 provided as follows:

> The provisions of Articles III (other than Rule 8), IV and VIII of the Schedule to the Carriage of Goods by Sea Act 1924,[8] of the United Kingdom shall apply to this Charter and shall be deemed to be inserted *in extenso* herein.[9]

On discharge of the cargo in May 1973 there was short delivery of the cargo and the charterers withheld $30,000 from the sum due in respect of the freight. In October 1974 the owners, who did not accept the validity of the deduction,[10] issued a writ claiming payment of the unpaid amount of freight. In February 1975 the charterers claimed by their defence that they were entitled to set off the loss against the freight and counterclaimed for $30,000. Donaldson J, whose decision was upheld by the Court of Appeal,[11] gave judgment for the owners. The House of Lords held that the charterers' defence was inadmissible because any

---

[3] See Berlingieri (1997), 299.
[4] At 307.
[5] The highlighted parts of the Rule indicate a change from the position under the Hague Rules.
[6] See para 34.21.
[7] [1977] 1 WLR 185 (HL).
[8] As to this Act, see para 15.09.
[9] ie this was a partial paramount clause. See para 19.51.
[10] As to this point in the case, see para 21.10.
[11] [1976] 2 Lloyd's Rep 256 (CA).

right on which it might have been based was extinguished by the lapse of time. Lord Wilberforce stated that:

> My Lords, if this case is to be decided on the terms of the contract, it would appear to me to be a comparatively simple one. There is an obligation to pay freight, calculated upon the amount of cargo intaken, which obligation arises upon discharge. The contract contemplates the possibility of a cross-claim by the charterers in respect of loss or damage to the cargo and it expressly provides by incorporation of article III, rule 6 of the Hague Rules that the carrier and the ship *shall be discharged* unless suit is brought within one year after the date of delivery or the date when delivery should have been made. This amounts to a time bar created by contract. But, and I do not think that sufficient recognition to this has been given in the courts below, it is a time bar of a special kind, viz. one which extinguishes the claim . . . not one which bars the remedy while leaving the claim itself in existence. The charterer's claim, after May 1974 and before the date of the writ, had not merely become unenforceable by action, it had simply ceased to exist . . .[12]

Thus the House of Lords confirmed in this case that the provision in the Rules barred the remedy and extinguished the right to claim.[13]

Carrier's fault as a defence   Although, as we have now seen, the cargo claimant's claim is   **34.07** extinguished under the time-bar provisions of article III, rule 6 if he does not bring his claim within 12 months, this does not mean that he also loses the right to raise the carrier's fault as a defence to a claim by the carrier.[14] This point was confirmed in *Goulandris Brothers Ltd v B Goldman & Sons Ltd* by Pearson J:

> Now I have to consider what effect, if any, the third paragraph of article III, rule 6, of the Hague Rules has had upon the legal position. Has it destroyed the respondents' equitable defence, and has it destroyed their cross-claim? In my view clearly it has not destroyed the equitable defence because it brings about only a discharge of liabilities and not a barring of defences. Therefore, if I am right in my conclusion that the equitable defence is one of the 'remedies' preserved by . . . the York–Antwerp Rules, that defence is unaffected by the third paragraph of article III, rule 6, of the Hague Rules, and defeats the claimants' claim.[15]

'In any event . . . whatsoever'   The addition of these words to the provision in the   **34.08** Hague–Visby Rules has the effect of making emphatic the preceding phrase 'all liability'.[16] In particular, the words make it clear that the time limit will apply even where the carrier has breached some other obligation, such as committing a deviation,[17] or if he has recklessly acted or omitted to act, with knowledge that the damage would probably result.[18] It has

---

[12] [1977] 1 WLR 185 (HL), 188 (emphasis in the original).

[13] See too *Consolidated Investment & Contracting Co v Saponaria Shipping Co (The Virgo)* [1978] 1 WLR 986 (CA); *The Kusu Island* [1989] SLR 119, 130; *Mediterranean Freight Services Ltd v BP Oil International Ltd (The Fiona)* [1994] 2 Lloyd's Rep 506 (CA), 520 (Hirst LJ).

[14] This is based on the equitable principle that a person cannot recover from any other person in respect of the consequences of his own wrong: see *Goulandris Brothers Ltd v B Goldman & Sons Ltd* [1958] 1 QB 74, 98 (Pearson J).

[15] [1958] 1 QB 74, 104; *Mediterranean Freight Services Ltd v BP Oil International Ltd (The Fiona)* [1994] 2 Lloyd's Rep 506 (CA), 520 (Hirst LJ).

[16] The operation of the *ejusdem generis* rule is excluded: see *Sidermar SpA v Apollo Corp (The Apollo)* [1978] 1 Lloyd's Rep 200.

[17] See art IV, r 4 and the discussion at para 26.44. See too *Kenya Railways v Antares Co Pte Ltd (The Antares No 1 & 2)* [1986] 2 Lloyd's Rep 633, discussed at para 24.27.

[18] ie has acted intentionally. See *Cia Portorafti Commerciale SA v Ultramar Panama Inc (The Captain Gregos) (No 1)* [1990] 1 Lloyd's Rep 310 (CA), 316 (Bingham LJ).

now been held in *Daewoo Heavy Industries Ltd v Klipriver Shipping Ltd (The Kapitan Petko Voivoda)*[19] that, as a matter of interpretation, the package or unit limitation in article IV, rule 5 will apply in the case of goods wrongfully stowed on deck. This reasoning is also intended to apply to the time bar, although it was obiter on the facts.[20]

34.09 **'In respect of [loss or damage][the goods]'**   In the Hague Rules, part of article III, rule 6 read 'in respect of loss or damage', now substituted in the Hague–Visby Rules by the wider words 'in respect of the goods'. The case of *Cargill International SA v CPN Tankers (Bermuda) Ltd (The Ot Sonja)*[21] considered the interpretation to be given to the similar words in section 3(6) of the US Carriage of Goods by Sea Act 1936, which had been incorporated into the charterparty. The owners of the *Ot Sonja* chartered her for the carriage of a cargo of vegetable oils from ports in the Hamburg–Rotterdam range to China. The charterers claimed losses amounting to $143,000 owing to dirty tanks which required cleaning and allegedly caused them financial loss; furthermore, they alleged that the cargo had been contaminated. The question for the court was whether the words 'loss or damage' in section 3(6) referred only to physical loss of or damage to the goods or whether they extended to loss or damage related to the goods. If the latter, the further question was whether the time limit operated where the goods to which the loss or damage related had never been loaded on the vessel. Saville J held that the claims were for loss or damage within section 3(6) of Carriage of Goods by Sea Act 1936 and were claims that related to the goods and hence that the time limit did apply. This was followed by the Court of Appeal. Hirst LJ held that:

> There are no express words to provide a subject-matter for the 'loss or damage', and there are no express words to identify 'the goods'. But in my view, there is an implied reference to the cargo-owner's goods. The liability of the carrier and the ship must be a liability to the cargo-owner, who is the other party to the contract of carriage, and the loss or damage for which the carrier or the ship is initially liable must be loss or damage arising out of the contract for the carriage of the cargo-owner's goods, and the goods of which the date of delivery or non-delivery is significant for the cargo-owner must be his goods. In my view the loss or damage referred to must be loss or damage which is related to the cargo-owner's goods, and the delivery of the goods must mean the delivery of his goods.

> I am satisfied, and I hold, that the . . . words 'loss or damage' in the limitation clause extend to loss or damage which is related to the goods.[22]

Thus, apart from delay, there is case law which suggests that the wording would apply to claims in tort[23] and, it is submitted, that the Hague–Visby wording would cover both types of claim as well.

34.10 **'Unless suit is brought': the earlier view**   This phrase appears in both the Hague and Hague–Visby formulation of article III, rule 6. It was interpreted narrowly in *Compania Colombiana de Seguros v Pacific Steam Navigation Co*[24] where it was held that the suit must

---

19 [2003] EWCA Civ 451; [2003] 2 Lloyd's Rep 1. Discussed further at para 29.27.
20 At [17] (Longmore LJ).
21 [1993] 2 Lloyd's Rep 435 (CA).
22 At 439; 444. See too *Goulandris Brothers Ltd v B Goldman & Sons Ltd* [1958] 1 QB 74, 105 (Pearson J).
23 See, eg, *Port Jackson Stevedoring Pty v Salmond & Spraggon (Australia) Pty (The New York Star)* [1981] 1 WLR 138 (PC). See the earlier discussion of this case at para 9.26.
24 [1965] 1 QB 101.

be brought within the relevant jurisdiction during this period. Bills of lading provided for disputes to be referred to the exclusive jurisdiction of the English courts. The claimant, who at the time did not have title to sue, initiated proceedings against the shipowners in the Supreme Court of New York. The action was dismissed for the reason that that court had no jurisdiction, although the proceedings were not a nullity. Approximately four months later, during which time the limitation period had expired, the correct claimants commenced proceedings in London. The shipowners sought to rely upon article III, rule 6 and the plaintiffs countered that suit had been brought in time, albeit in New York. Roskill J stated that:

> I think the true proposition in English law is that where in an action in the English courts the plaintiff seeks relief and the defendant pleads limitation, the issue which an English court had to determine is whether the action before the court, and not some other action, has been instituted within the relevant limitation period. In the end the question is this: Does 'unless suit is brought within one year' mean 'unless suit is brought *anywhere* within one year', or does it mean 'unless the suit *before the court* is brought within one year'? Applying the ordinary canons of construction to the rule I think that it must mean 'unless the suit *before the court* is brought within one year'.[25]

Wider view   The general principle established in *Compania Colombiana de Seguros v Pacific*   **34.11**
Steam Navigation Co[26] was modified by the Court of Appeal in *Hispanica de Petroleos SA v Vencedora Oceanica Navegación SA (The Kapetan Markos).*[27] Parker LJ said:

> Although we accept the correctness of Roskill J's decision for the present purposes, we should however not be taken to have approved the proposition stated as being of universal application. It appears to us to at least be arguable that in certain circumstances a defence under art III rule 6 might be defeated by the fact that another suit had been brought elsewhere. If . . . a shipowner wishes to rely on the r 6 discharge from liability he must establish first that the goods were carried under a contract of carriage by sea, next that suit to establish liability under the rules in respect of loss of or damage to the goods carried under contract has not been brought within a year.[28]

In this case the claimant cargo owners brought suit within the time limit, claiming breach of the contract of carriage. After the time limit had expired they sought to make various amendments to their claim. The Court of Appeal held that the defendants could not rely successfully on article III, rule 6. The claimants had set up a contract of carriage under a bill of lading incorporating the Hague Rules and to hold that suit had not been brought within a year would be an abuse of language.[29]

Suit and actions *in rem*   It is also established that the bringing of proceedings *in personam*   **34.12**
in one jurisdiction would not bar the bringing of proceedings *in rem* in another jurisdiction, at least for the purposes of the time-bar provisions in the Rules.[30] In *The Nordglimt*[31]

---

[25] At 126.
[26] [1965] 1 QB 101.
[27] [1986] 1 Lloyd's Rep 211 (CA).
[28] At 231.
[29] But cf *Continental Fertilizer Co Ltd v Pionier Shipping CV (The Pionier)* [1995] 1 Lloyd's Rep 223.
[30] There are, however, potentially other difficulties. See *Republic of India v India Steamship Co Ltd (The Indian Grace)(No 2)* [1998] AC 878, discussed at para 35.20.
[31] [1988] QB 183 (CA).

a vessel, the *Nordkap*, was chartered for the carriage of barley between Antwerp and Jeddah. The cargo receivers alleged damage and shortage and commenced their action *in personam* before the Court of Commerce of Antwerp in January 1985. However, in April 1987 they commenced an action *in rem* before the English Admiralty Court and issued a warrant for the arrest of the *Nordglimt*, a sister ship of the *Nordkap*, claiming damages. The *Nordglimt* was arrested and released on payment of security. The shipowners sought to have the action *in rem* struck out on the basis that their liability to the plaintiffs had been discharged under article III, rule 6 of the Hague–Visby Rules as the proceedings had not been brought within a year of the date of delivery of the goods. Hobhouse J concluded that:

> The proceedings in Belgium were competent and brought in time by a party with title to sue. The carrier was accordingly not discharged from liability. The liability which is the subject matter of the present action in England accordingly continues to exist upon the true construction of the bill of lading and the legislation to which it is subject. The carrier is thus unable to assert the fact, namely that suit has not been brought within the relevant period, which is necessary to support his allegation that he has been discharged from liability.[32]

The shipowners' application for the arrest of the ship to be set aside also failed.

34.13 **'Suit': a summary**   For the purposes of article III, rule 6, suit will mean suit being brought before a competent court by a person who has title to sue.[33] In relation to bringing suit before a 'competent' court, although not defined, competence would appear to require that the court must have jurisdiction under its own rules or there must have been a submission to the jurisdiction of the English courts. Thus, suit would not be competent if the parties have contractually agreed to the exclusive jurisdiction of a court in a different country. If a bill of lading contained an exclusive Norwegian jurisdiction clause, instituting an action before the English courts would not constitute the bringing of suit for the purpose of article III, rule 6.[34] Similarly, bringing suit before the courts in New York in breach of a London arbitration clause would not be sufficient to constitute 'suit' for the purpose of article III, rule 6.[35] Further, the suit must be actively in existence and not in breach of any rules of court.[36] Accordingly, a claim form validly issued, but not served, may trigger the operation of the time bar.[37]

34.14 **Commencement of arbitrations**   'Suit' was interpreted in *The Merak*[38] as including both litigation and arbitration proceedings. Thus, where the contract contains an arbitration

---

[32] At 193.

[33] As to this requirement, see *Central Insurance Co Ltd v Seacalf Shipping Corp (The Aiolos)* [1983] 2 Lloyd's Rep 25 (CA), 30 (Oliver LJ); *Transworld Oil (USA) Inc v Minos Compania Naviera SAL (The Leni)* [1992] 2 Lloyd's Rep 48.

[34] See *The Havhelt* [1993] 1 Lloyd's Rep 523; *Fort Sterling Ltd v South Atlantic Cargo Shipping NV (The Finnrose)* [1994] 1 Lloyd's Rep 559.

[35] See *Thyssen Inc v Calypso Shipping Corp SA* [2000] 2 Lloyd's Rep 243. See too *Government of Sierra Leone v Marmaro Shipping Co Ltd (The Amazona and Yayamaria)* [1989] 2 Lloyd's Rep 130 (CA).

[36] See *Thye Lam v The Eastern Shipping Corp Ltd* [1960] 1 MLJ 235 where letters admitting liability were given by the defendants but no steps were taken to enforce the claim. It was, said Rigby J, '... the clear duty of the plaintiffs, as prudent persons, to enforce their threat of legal proceedings and protect their right of action by issuing a Writ of Summons' (at 238). See too *Fort Sterling Ltd v South Atlantic Cargo Shipping NV (The Finnrose)* [1994] 1 Lloyd's Rep 559.

[37] An argument that the issue of a writ *in rem* without service would constitute suit has been described as 'breathtaking': see *Thyssen Inc v Calypso Shipping Corp SA* [2000] 2 Lloyd's Rep 243, 248 (David Steel J).

[38] [1965] P 223.

clause and the parties agree to arbitrate their dispute there will be 'suit' for the purpose of article III, rule 6.[39] In this context it would be sufficient if one party notified their choice of arbitrator to the other side, even if this subsequently proved ineffective.[40]

'Within one year' The period specified for the bringing of suit under the Rules is 'one year'. **34.15** This period is not defined in the Rules, but it has been suggested that this should be a calendar year.[41] Thus, by way of illustration, if delivery is (or should have been) effected on 1 June 2005, time started to run on 2 June 2005 and terminated at the end of 1 June 2006. It was established in *The Clifford Maersk*[42] that, where the final day of the limitation period fell on a Sunday or other day on which the office of the Supreme Court was closed, suit would be brought in time if the writ was issued on the next day on which the office was open.[43]

'Delivery or . . . date when they should have been delivered' The 12-month period is **34.16** stated to run from the time when the goods were delivered or should have been delivered. It should be noted that this provision of the Rules places an emphasis on 'delivery', which is concerned with that time in the contract when actual or constructive possession passes. It may be recalled that article I(e) of the Rules refers to 'discharge'[44] — in the context of the so-called tackle-to-tackle period — but this is a physical act and the notion of 'discharge' is not synonymous with 'delivery'.[45] Time starts to run under the Rules by reference to 'delivery'.[46] The question which therefore needs to be addressed is when delivery is validly effected under this provision.

Delivery of the agreed quantity It is clear that if the agreed quantity of goods is delivered **34.17** to the holder of a bill of lading at the port of discharge, then, for the purposes of this Rule, time will start to run. This should be the case even if the goods delivered are, in fact, damaged.

No delivery Where no delivery is made at all, the starting point must be the provision of **34.18** article III, rule 6, namely the 'date when they should have been delivered'. Assuming that all the parties have performed their obligations, it should then be possible to find out when the goods ought to have been delivered.[47] It may, however, be less easy to establish this in cases where goods are delivered late, or where some of the goods are delivered and the remainder lost, or where the vessel discharges the cargo at a port or place other than that agreed.[48]

---

[39] See *Anglo-Irish Beef Processors International v Federated Stevedores Geelong* [1997] 2 VR 676, 695–696 (Phillips JA).

[40] See *Transpetrol Ltd v Ekali Shipping Co Ltd (The Aghia Marina)* [1989] 1 Lloyd's Rep 62.

[41] See Cooke (2001), para 85.188.

[42] [1982] 2 Lloyd's Rep 251.

[43] See too CPR Part 2.8(4).

[44] See para 19.11.

[45] See *Pacific Milk Industries (M) Bhd v Koninklinjke Jaya (Royal Interocean Lines)(The Straat Cumberland)* [1973] 2 Lloyd's Rep 492, 494; *PS Chellaram & Co Ltd v China Ocean Shipping Co (The Zhi Jiang Kou)* [1991] 1 Lloyd's Rep 493, 499 (Gleeson CJ); *Borealis AB v Stargas Ltd (The Berge Sisar)* [2002] 2 AC 205, at [36] (Lord Hobhouse).

[46] But cf *Denny Mott & Dickson Ltd v Lynn Shipping Co Ltd* [1963] 1 Lloyd's Rep 339.

[47] See *Cargill International SA v CPN Tankers (Bermuda) Ltd (The Ot Sonja)* [1993] 2 Lloyd's Rep 435 (CA).

[48] Perhaps because of the presence of a 'near' clause in a charterparty incorporated into the bills of lading: see para 30.20.

34.19 Wrongful delivery   If the goods are wrongfully delivered, such as against a letter of indemnity or because they were stolen before delivery was possible, then the delivery date is 'when the consignment ought to have been delivered by the appellant to the respondent'.[49]

34.20 Extension   The period of a year may be extended under article III, rule 6 'if the parties so agree after the cause of action has arisen'. The period of one year may not be reduced, however, as this will be void under article III, rule 8.[50]

34.21 Article III, rule 6 bis   Article III, rule 6 bis[51] of the Hague–Visby Rules provides that:

> An action for indemnity against a third person may be brought even after the expiration of the year provided for in the preceding paragraph if brought within the time allowed by the law of the Court seized of the case. However, the time allowed shall not be less than three months, commencing from the day when the person bringing such action for indemnity has settled the claim or has been served with process in the action against himself.

In *China Ocean Shipping Co v Andros (The Xingcheng and Andros)* Lord Brandon explained that

> r 6 *bis* of art III creates a special exception to the generality of r 6. Rule 6 *bis*, must, therefore, in a case to which it applies, have a separate effect of its own independently of r 6. The case to which r 6 *bis* applies is a case where shipowner A, being under actual or potential liability to cargo-owner B, claims an indemnity by way of damages against ship or shipowner C. If that claim by shipowner A against ship or shipowner C is made under a contract of carriage to which the Hague–Visby Rules apply, then the time allowed for bringing it is that prescribed by r 6 *bis* and not that prescribed by r 6. There is no express requirement in r 6 *bis* that the liability to cargo-owner B in respect of which shipowner A claims an indemnity against ship or shipowner C must also arise under a contract of carriage to which the Hague–Visby Rules apply. Nor do their Lordships see any good reason why, when such a requirement is not expressed, it should be implied.[52]

---

[49] See *Port Jackson Stevedoring Pty Ltd v Salmond & Spraggon (Aust) Pty Ltd* (1978) 139 CLR 231, 238 (Barwick CJ); *PS Chellaram & Co Ltd v China Ocean Shipping Co (The Zhi Jiang Kou)* [1991] 1 Lloyd's Rep 493, 499 (Gleeson CJ).

[50] As to art III, r 8, see para 19.39.

[51] See Berlingieri (1997), 321.

[52] [1987] 1 WLR 1213 (PC).

35

ADMIRALTY CLAIMS

A. Introduction

Overview   In this chapter we consider the principal mechanism for dispute settlement   **35.01**
available to the cargo claimant. Many claims will be settled by cargo insurers working with
the shipowners' P & I insurers. However, in many instances this settlement mechanism will
not prove sufficient to meet the claim and, in any event, the insurer might wish to recover
for its loss. Many cargo claims, particularly charterparty claims, will be settled in arbitration. In some cases, it may be prudent to consider an Admiralty claim. In this chapter we
consider the nature of such claims.[1]

B. Historical Background

Early history   For a long time the administration of Admiralty business in England rested   **35.02**
in the hands of maritime courts sitting on the seashore from tide to tide.[2] The earliest
references to the High Court of Admiralty may be found in the mid-fourteenth century;[3] by

---

[1] For detailed consideration see Meeson (2003); Jackson (2005).
[2] For detailed consideration of the history, see Lionel H Laing, 'Historical Origins of Admiralty
Jurisdiction in England' (1946–1947) 45 Michigan LR 163; Hutchison (1987); Edward F Ryan, 'Admiralty
Jurisdiction and the Maritime Lien: An Historical Perspective' (1968) 7 Western Ontario LR 173; CW
O'Hare, 'Admiralty Jurisdiction' (1979–1980) 6 Monash LR 91; Charles S Cumming, 'The English High
Court of Admiralty' (1992–1993) 17 Tulane MLJ 209.
[3] 'The origin of the Admiralty court can be traced with tolerable certainty to the period between the years
1340 and 1357. It was instituted in consequence of the difficulty which had been experienced in dealing with
piracy or "spoil" claims made by and against foreign sovereigns': Marsden (1894), xiv.

the time of Richard II (1377–1400) the admiral and his deputy, the vice-admiral, were transacting enough judicial business, both criminal and civil, to move Parliament to limit their jurisdiction by statute to 'a thing done upon the sea':

> A great and common clamour and complaint hath been often times made before this time and yet is, for that the Admirals and their deputies hold their sessions within divers places within this realm, as well within franchise as without, accroaching to them greater authority than belongeth to their office. The admirals and their deputies shall not meddle from henceforth with anything done within the realm, but only of a thing done upon the sea, as it hath been used in the time of King Edward, grandfather of our Lord the King that is now.[4]

A further statute decreed that:

> Of all manner of contracts, pleas, and quarrels, and all other things rising within the bodies of the counties (*infra corpus comitatus*), as well as by land as by water, and also of wreck of the sea, the Admiral's court shall have no manner of cognizance, power nor jurisdiction. Nevertheless, of the death of a man, and of a mayhem done in great ships, being and hovering in the main stream of the great rivers, only beneath the bridges of the same rivers nigh to the sea (*infra primos pontes*), and in none other places of the same rivers, the Admiral shall have cognizance.[5]

The reason for these statutes may be found in the great increase of Admiralty business being undertaken.

35.03 Jurisdictional conflict The history of the jurisdiction of the Admiralty court is marked by repeated jurisdictional battles between it and the common law courts. In the Tudor period, the Admiralty court became particularly active and developed its jurisdiction in both mercantile and maritime causes. As Marsden puts it:

> It was, probably, the rapid increase of business in the Admiralty Court connected generally with shipping and foreign trade that first aroused the professional jealousy of the practitioners of the common law. All contracts made abroad, bills of exchange (which at this period were for the most part drawn or payable abroad), commercial agencies abroad, charter-parties, insurance, average, freight, non-delivery of, or damage to, cargo, negligent navigation by masters, mariners, or pilots, breach of warranty of seaworthiness, and other provisions contained in charter-parties; in short, every kind of shipping business was dealt with by the Admiralty Court.[6]

Indeed, the Admiralty judges were watched with considerable suspicion and jealousy by the common law judges who issued writs of prohibition[7] against proceedings in admiralty except within narrow limits. One of the reasons was undoubtedly that the Admiralty court was presided over by a judge who was a member of Doctor's Commons, an ancient Inn of Court which required a doctorate in civil law of the University of Cambridge or of the University of Oxford. The law applied by the Court was based on the *ius gentium*, the universal law of the sea, derived from early compilations of sea law, such as that of Rhodes (the Rhodian sea law)[8] and the Rolls of Oléron.[9] In the early case of *Pilk v Venor* (1350) the

---

[4] 13 Richard II, c 5 (1389).
[5] 15 Richard II, c 3 (1391).
[6] (1894) lxvii.
[7] See, eg, *Smith v Brown* (1871) LR 6 QB 729.
[8] See Ashburner (1909).
[9] See Timothy J Runyan, 'The Rolls of Oleron and Admiralty Court in Fourteenth Century England' (1975) 19 American JLH 95.

'Laws of Olèron' were cited by both parties.[10] This continued to be the case even during the purges of admiralty jurisdiction in the sixteenth century; in the *Charter Party of the 'George'* (1538) reference is made to the fact that a merchant 'shall have his juste parte [of any prize pirches flotezon or lagason or any other casueltie] accordyng to the lawe of Oleron'.[11] Likewise, reference was made to the Laws of Olèron in the case of *Tye v Spryngham* (1561).[12]

Jurisdiction at a low ebb In 1536 the criminal jurisdiction was turned over to the common law by statute. By 1600 the jurisdiction of the court was at a low ebb; according to the Elizabethan judges, the Court of Admiralty could not try causes arising on land beyond the seas, but only causes arising on the sea; and the sea for this purpose ended at low water mark, except when the tide was in.[13] This excluded charterparties and foreign maritime contracts; the common law had taken these over by means of fictions. The Admiralty was left to deal with seamen's wages earned at sea, collision, and salvage and prize.[14] In 1633 the Privy Council directed a settlement of the dispute between the Court of Admiralty and the common law courts under which the Court of Admiralty was to be allowed actions for freight and actions to enforce charterparties relating to overseas voyages and maritime contracts made on foreign soil. During the course of the debate on the authority and jurisdiction of the court, Sir Henry Martin, judge of the Admiralty Court, stated that 'the judge (of the Admiralty) is a common law judge since he judgeth by the common law and ancient customs of the sea and admiralty, and only used civill law when the common law and customs fayle'.[15]

35.04

Common law victory The settlement brokered by the Privy Council did not last and by the end of the century the common law courts had succeeded in depressing the Court of Admiralty to such an extent that it never really revived, apart from a brief surge during the Napoleonic wars. But, despite these difficulties, by the beginning of the nineteenth century[16] the instance (civil) jurisdiction of the Admiralty Court ranged over the following legal issues: (1) droits, which were property rights in wreck at sea; (2) salvage; (3) contract; (4) hypothecation (ie mortgage, especially of a ship, perhaps via a bottomry bond); (5) freights (and in particular the enforcement of the master's possessory lien for freights); (6) wages; (7) torts; (8) possession and restraint. By the time of the judgeship of Sir William Scott (later Lord Stowell), from 1798 to 1827,[17] actions *in rem* had already begun to outweigh in importance actions *in personam* in Admiralty. The proceeding *in rem* was frequently employed in suits in seamen's wages, on hypothecation, of possession, and in cases of collision.

35.05

---

[10] Matthew Hale, *A Disquisition Touching the Jurisdiction of the Common Law and Courts of Admiralty in Relation to Things Done Upon or Beyond the Sea, and Touching Maritime and Merchants Contracts* (c 1675). See Pritchard and Yale (1993), 33.

[11] Marsden (1894), 82.

[12] Marsden (1897),122.

[13] *Constable's Case* (1601) 5 Co Rep 106; 77 ER 218. See too George F Steckley, 'Merchants and the Admiralty Court During the English Revolution' (1978) 22 American JLH 137.

[14] Prize (from the French, *prendre*) is the right to share in the proceeds of enemy ships and cargoes seized at sea.

[15] Cited in Kiralfy (1958), 186.

[16] See Wiswall (1970).

[17] See Wiswall (1970), ch 1; Bourguignon (1987).

35.06 **Nineteenth century** The Admiralty Court Acts of 1840[18] and 1861[19] confirmed and extended the general jurisdiction of the Admiralty Court, in effect abolishing the restrictions which had been imposed during the time of Richard II. [20] New jurisdiction conferred by the Act of 1840 included cognizance taken of mortgages on ships incidental to actions *in rem*, questions of legal title, any 'claims in the nature of salvage for services and necessaries',[21] and claims for towage. Since this time, the jurisdiction of the Court has been consolidated three times by statute, in the Supreme Court of Judicature (Consolidation) Act 1925,[22] the Administration of Justice Act 1956[23], and finally, the Supreme Court Act 1981.[24] The latter two statutes were passed to give effect in the UK[25] to the 1952 Arrest Convention.[26]

35.07 **Twentieth century** Admiralty jurisdiction is currently regulated by the Supreme Court Act 1981, sections 19–27[27] and these provisions must be read with the current version of the Civil Procedure Rules (CPR).[28] There is still an Admiralty Judge, presently Mr Justice David Steel,[29] and Admiralty business is conducted out of a separate registry, the Admiralty and Commercial Registry.[30]

C. Statutory Framework

35.08 **Introduction** The Admiralty claims framework is primarily to be found in the Supreme Court Act 1981 and the provisions there consist of an enabling provision (section 20(1)), a list of claims within the jurisdiction (section 20(2)), and the mechanism for exercising the jurisdiction, either *in personam* (section 21(1)) or *in rem* (section 21(2) or (4)), or by virtue of a maritime lien (s 21(3)). We shall now consider these aspects of the Act in more detail.

35.09 **The enabling provision** Section 20(1) of the Act provides as follows:

The Admiralty jurisdiction of the High Court shall be as follows, that is to say—

(a) jurisdiction to hear and determine any of the questions and claims mentioned in subsection (2);

---

[18] 3 & 4 Vict, c 65.

[19] 24 & 25 Vict, c 10.

[20] See para 35.02.

[21] Admiralty Court Act, ss 3, 4 and 6.

[22] 15 & 16 Geo 5, c 49.

[23] 4 & 5 Eliz 2, c 46.

[24] c 54.

[25] See, eg, *The Jade (The Eschersheim)* [1976] 1 WLR 430, 434.

[26] International Convention for the Unification of Certain Rules Relating to the Arrest of Sea-going Ships (Brussels, 1952). For the list of current signatories, see the Belgian Ministry of Foreign Affairs, Foreign Trade and Development Cooperation (<www.diplobel.fgov.be/en/>). See especially Berlingieri (2000).

[27] See *Centro Latino Americano de Commercio Exterior SA v Owners of the Kommunar (The Kommunar) (No 2)* [1997] 1 Lloyd's Rep 8, 20 (Colman J), as to the interpretation of this Act in the light of the 1952 Convention.

[28] CPR, Pt 61 is concerned with Admiralty claims (available at <www.dca.gov.uk/civil/procrules_fin/index.htm>). See Michael Tsimplis and Nicholas Gaskell, 'Admiralty Claims and the new CPR Part 61' [2002] LMCLQ 520.

[29] Admiralty matters now fall within the jurisdiction of the Queen's Bench Division.

[30] The postal address is: Room E200, Royal Courts of Justice, The Strand, London WC2A 2LL. See <www.hmcourts-service.gov.uk/infoabout/admiralcomm/index.htm>.

(b) jurisdiction in relation to any of the proceedings mentioned in subsection (3);

(c) any other Admiralty jurisdiction which it had immediately before the commencement of this Act; and

(d) any jurisdiction connected with ships or aircraft which is vested in the High Court apart from this section and is for the time being by rules of court made or coming into force after the commencement of this Act assigned to the Queen's Bench Division and directed by the rules to be exercised by the Admiralty Court.

Jurisdiction for claims in section 20(2)   Section 20(1)(a) provides that the High Court **35.10** in the exercise of its jurisdiction is vested to hear the list of Admiralty claims set out in section 20(2).

Jurisdiction for claims in section 20(3)   Section 20(1)(b) cross-refers to section 20(3), **35.11** which provides that the court has jurisdiction in relation to any application to the High Court under the Merchant Shipping Act 1995 (section 20(3)(a)), jurisdiction in collision matters (section 20(3)(b)), and limitation actions (section 20(3)(c)).

Any other jurisdiction   Section 20(1)(c) is a curious provision which, in effect, extends **35.12** the jurisdiction to include matters over which the court may have had jurisdiction under previous Acts. The paragraph incorporates the 'sweeping up' provisions of section 1(1) of the Administration of Justice Act 1956, which provided:

> together with any other jurisdiction which either was vested in the High Court of Admiralty immediately before the date of commencement of the Supreme Court of Judicature Act 1873 (that is to say, the first day of November 1875) or is conferred by or under an Act which came into operation on or after that date on the High Court as being a court with Admiralty Jurisdiction.

In effect, this means that the 1875 jurisdiction of the High Court of Admiralty is preserved, together with any additional jurisdiction granted between 1875 and 1956. The jurisdiction of the High Court of Admiralty on 1 November 1875 was derived from three sources: the inherent jurisdiction of the High Court of Admiralty, the Admiralty Act of 1840,[31] and the Admiralty Act 1861.[32]

The list of claims   A specific list of claims admissible in the English Admiralty Court is **35.13** found in section 20(2), at paras (a)–(s). These claims cover the whole range of potential Admiralty claims, including a number of heads of claim which are likely to be of interest for the carriage of goods by sea. We shall only be referring to these particular heads of claim.

Exercise of jurisdiction   Section 21 provides four main heads for the exercise of the **35.14** Admiralty jurisdiction of the High Court. The first of these, section 21(1) provides for the exercise of the jurisdiction *in personam*, 'in all cases'. The second, section 21(2) provides for the exercise of the jurisdiction *in rem*, but only in respect of four specified heads of claim enumerated in section 20(2). The third, section 21(3), provides for the exercise of the jurisdiction *in rem*, where there is a maritime lien 'or other charge on any ship . . .'. Finally, section 21(4) provides for the exercise of the jurisdiction *in rem*, in the case of most heads of claim

---

[31] 3 & 4 Vict, c 65.
[32] 24 & 25 Vict, c 10

enumerated in section 20(2), subject to fulfilment of the specific criteria enumerated in that rule. We shall, in due course, look in more detail at each of these methods of exercising the court's jurisdiction,[33] with a particular focus on those methods which are likely to be important in carriage cases.

35.15 **Actions *in rem*** In English law the availability of an action *in rem* is restricted to those claims specified by the Act, namely those claims set out in section 20(2)(a)–(c) and (e) – (s),[34] any maritime lien,[35] and any claim enforceable thereby in the past or future.[36] The Act does not provide an action *in rem* in respect of one of the heads of claim in section 20(2), namely for 'damage received by a ship'.[37] Various juridical bases have been suggested for the action *in rem*. The first, the 'personification' theory, is based on the notion that the ship is the judicial entity against whom the action is brought. As one distinguished law lord explained, 'admiralty practitioners and judges used the concept that the ship is a defendant in an action *in rem* as a means of defending and extending the jurisdiction of the High Court of Admiralty'.[38] The second theory, the so-called 'procedural' theory, identified the ship as the means to compel her owner to appear in court to defend the claim against her.[39] Thus Marsden has explained that:

> The fact that goods and ships that had no connection with the cause of action, except as belonging to the defendant, were subject to arrest, points to the conclusion that arrest was merely procedure, and that its only object was to obtain security that the judgment should be satisfied.[40]

A third theory was the so-called 'conflict' theory, where the action *in rem* could be explained as an attempt to found jurisdiction in admiralty during a time when any attempt to assume jurisdiction *in personam* was prohibited by the common law courts.[41] Of all these theories, however, the procedural theory has come to dominate, at least in England.[42] Lord Steyn explained in *Republic of India v India Steamship Co Ltd (The Indian Grace) (No 2)*[43] that:

> The idea that a ship can be a defendant in legal proceedings was always a fiction. But before the Judicature Acts this fiction helped to defend and enlarge Admiralty jurisdiction in the form of an action *in rem*. With the passing of the Judicature Acts that purpose was effectively spent. That made possible the procedural changes which I have described. The fiction was discarded.[44]

---

[33] See para 35.34.

[34] section 21(4).

[35] section 21(3).

[36] section 20(1)(c) (past); s 20(1)(d) (future).

[37] section 20(2)(d).

[38] *Republic of India v India Steamship Co Ltd (The Indian Grace)(No 2)* [1998] AC 878, 907 (Lord Steyn). See Holmes (1881), 24; Gilmore and Black (1975), 589; Martin Davies, 'In Defence of Unpopular Virtues: Personification and Ratification' (2000–2001) 75 Tulane LR 337.

[39] See the detailed examination of this 'theory' in *The Dictator* [1892] P 304, 309 (Jeune J); *The Burns* [1907] P 137, 148–150.

[40] (1894), lxxi.

[41] *The Beldis* [1936] P 51, 73-74 (Lord Merriman).

[42] But see also two Singapore cases: *The Kusu Island* [1982-1983] SLR 502, 508 (Lai Kew Chai J); *Dauphin Offshore Engineering & Trading Pte Ltd Inc v The Capricorn* [1999] 2 SLR 390, 394 (S Rajendran J).

[43] [1998] AC 878.

[44] At 913.

Actions *in personam* The action *in personam* is simply the process for enforcing a claim **35.16** which would apply in England, regardless of the nature of the claim.[45] The aim of such an action is to seek a remedy against the defendant. Section 21(1) provides that any claim within Admiralty may be enforced by an action *in personam*. This is, however, subject to section 22 of the Act, which imposes restrictions on the action *in personam* in respect of any claim for damage, loss of life, or personal injury arising out of collision.

Maritime liens In section 21(3), the Act provides for the enforcement of maritime lien **35.17** claims. A maritime lien is just one kind of lien[46] but its main characteristics are that it is non-possessory in nature[47] and attaches to the property at the moment when the particular cause of action arises. It remains attached, travelling with the property through changes of ownership.[48] From the moment of attachment, the maritime lien is inchoate unless and until it is enforced by means of an action *in rem*.[49] In *The Ripon City*, Gorell Barnes J described a maritime lien in the following terms:

> . . . [A] lien is a privileged claim upon a vessel in respect of service done to it, or injury caused by it, to be carried into effect by legal process. It is a right acquired by one over a thing belonging to another — a *jus in re aliena*. It is, so to speak, a subtraction from the absolute property of the owner in the thing.[50]

Once enforced by an action *in rem*, the vessel can be arrested and, if no security is forthcoming, sold to realize its value.[51] The importance of the maritime lien is reflected also in its place in priority over other claims, including ship mortgages.[52]

Maritime lien claims The claims which qualify as maritime liens are not stated explicitly **35.18** in the Act and so one has to look for these in judicial development and earlier statutory provisions. Claims which attract a maritime lien are included within the Admiralty jurisdiction of the Supreme Court in section 20(2) but they feature as 'claims' and not specifically as 'maritime lien' claims. It is now accepted that maritime liens attach to the following claims: salvage; damage done by a ship;[53] seamen's wages;[54] masters' wages;[55] master's disbursements;[56]

---

[45] See the CPR, Pt 61.
[46] See para 27.02.
[47] *Harmer v Bell (The Bold Buccleugh)* (1851) 7 Moo 267, 284–285; 13 ER 884, 890–891 (Sir John Jervis).
[48] Ibid. See too *The Tolten* [1946] P 135 (CA), 149–150 (Scott LJ).
[49] Ibid.
[50] [1897] P 226, 242.
[51] *The Tervaete* [1922] P 259 (CA), 273 (Atkin LJ).
[52] *The Tolten* [1946] P 135 (CA), 149–150 (Scott LJ). In *The Royal Arch* (1857) Swa 269, 282; 166 ER 1131, 1139, Dr Lushington stated that: 'Where money is advanced on mortgage of a ship, the mortgagee must always be aware that he takes his security subject to all legal liens, and if he suffers therefrom his only remedy must be against the owners.'
[53] *Harmer v Bell (The Bold Buccleugh)* (1851) 7 Moo 267; 13 ER 884; *The Veritas* [1901] P 304, 314; *Currie v M'Knight* [1897] AC 97.
[54] See *The Sydney Cove* (1815) 2 Dods 11, 13; 165 ER 1399, 1400 (Lord Stowell); *The Minerva* (1825) 1 Hagg 347, 355; 166 ER 123, 126 (Lord Stowell).
[55] The lien for wages and for master's wages rank *pari passu*: *The Royal Wells* [1985] QB 86, 91–92 (Sheen J).
[56] *The Mary Ann* (1865) LR 1 A&E 8, later overruled by *The Sara* (1889) 14 App Cas 209. The decision in the latter caused such great consternation that the legislature intervened and nullified its effect by conferring upon the master an express statutory maritime lien for disbursements in s 1 of the Merchant Shipping Act 1889. See now s 41 of the Merchant Shipping Act 1995.

bottomry;[57] and respondentia.[58] All the above, with the exception of respondentia, also appear in section 20(2) and may be enforced as maritime lien claims under section 21(3) or under section 21(4).

35.19 **Actions *in rem* are different to actions *in personam*** The traditional view is that there is a difference between the two types of action in Admiralty. Thus, in *The Burns*, Collins MR stated that there 'is a real, and not a mere technical, distinction between an action *in rem* and an action *in personam*'.[59] In the same case, Fletcher Moulton LJ said:

> I am of opinion that this view cannot be supported . . . . [T]he fundamental proposition of the argument of the appellant's counsel fails, and that the action *in rem* is an action against the ship itself. It is an action in which the owners may take part, if they think proper, in defence of their property, but whether or not they will do so is a matter for them to decide, and if they do not decide to make themselves parties to the suit in order to defend their property, no personal liability can be established against them in that action. It is perfectly true that the action indirectly affects them. So it would if it were an action against a person whom they had indemnified . . . I do not think that we are entitled to suppose that there has been a change in the nature of the action *in rem* merely because the modern language of the writ by which it is now commenced is unsuitable to that which I think the authorities establish to be its real nature.[60]

35.20 ***The Indian Grace*** The traditional view has been brought into question following the House of Lords decision in *Republic of India v India Steamship Co Ltd (The Indian Grace)(No 2)*.[61] The case arose out of section 34 of the Civil Jurisdiction and Judgments Act 1982 which provides that:

> No proceedings may be brought by a person in England and Wales . . . on a cause of action in respect of which a judgment has been given in his favour in proceedings between the same parties, or their privies . . . in a court of an overseas country, unless that judgment is not enforceable or entitled to recognition in England and Wales . . .[62]

The *Indian Grace* loaded a cargo of munitions in Sweden for carriage to Cochin in India, for delivery to the Indian government. A few days after sailing a fire broke out in the No 3 hold of the ship. The master and crew managed to extinguish it and also jettisoned various artillery shells and charges. After calling at Cherbourg in France the ship proceeded to Cochin and discharged the cargo. The Indian government brought a claim for damages in respect of the shells and charges in Cochin and the judge gave judgment in their favour in the equivalent of £7,200. Before judgment in this trial the Indian government issued a writ *in rem* in the Admiralty Court in England against the *Indian Endurance*, a sister ship of the *Indian Grace*. The *Indian Endurance* was permitted to sail against a letter of undertaking by the Steamship Mutual P & I Club. The statement of claim was in respect of all the damage

---

[57] *The Atlas* (1827) 2 Hag Adm 48, 53–54; 166 ER 162, 164 (Lord Stowell).

[58] Respondentia does not appear in the Act but involves the hypothecation of the ship's cargo by the master while away from the vessel's home port, as security for a loan to pay for goods or services needed to preserve the ship or complete the voyage.

[59] [1907] P 137, 147.

[60] At 148–150.

[61] [1998] AC 878.

[62] The Act incorporates directly into English law the provisions of the EC Jurisdiction and Judgments Convention of 1968 (as amended).

to the cargo in the No 3 hold. Sheen J held that the cause of action was the same as that on which the plaintiffs had relied in India and that accordingly section 34 was an absolute bar to the English proceedings. This was upheld by the Court of Appeal.[63] In the House of Lords[64] the plaintiffs sought to raise, for the first time, the argument that the judgment of the Court in Cochin was not a judgment between the parties because it was a judgment *in personam*, whereas the action in London was an Admiralty action *in rem*. This was remitted to the Admiralty judge, Clarke J, and reported as *The Indian Grace (No 2)*.[65] His decision was unanimously overturned in the Court of Appeal[66] and was taken to the House of Lords for the second time. The first issue which Lord Steyn had to consider was whether the English action *in rem* was 'between the same parties, or their privies' within the meaning of section 34 as the action in which the plaintiffs obtained judgment in Cochin. Lord Steyn noted that the head of claim on which the plaintiff relied was section 20(2)(g) and (h).[67] He concluded that the action *in rem* was an action against the owner of the ship. On section 34 he stated that:

> The function of s 34 was to overcome the anomaly created by the fact the doctrine of merger did not apply in the case of foreign, i.e. non-English, judgments . . . The rationale of the bar against proceedings caught by s 34 is that it is unjust to permit the same issue to be litigated afresh between the same parties . . . Given this legislative objective, it would in my view be wrong to permit an action *in rem* to proceed despite a foreign judgment *in personam* obtained on the same cause of action. The purpose of s 34 militates in favour of the bar created by it applying to the action *in rem*.

Lord Steyn accordingly dismissed the appeal.

An action *in rem* becomes also an action *in personam* if and when the issue or service of the writ is acknowledged   In *The Tatry*,[68] the Court of Appeal held that after acknowledgement of service in an Admiralty action *in rem* the action does not lose its *in rem* character, but proceeds as a kind of hybrid, being both *in rem* and *in personam*, even though the *res* may have been released by the court. This was further amplified by the Court of Appeal in *The Broadmayne* by Bankes LJ: **35.21**

> In my opinion an action which has been commenced as an action *in rem* continues until its termination as an action *in rem* unless it undergoes some alteration in its character by amendment, by order of the Court, or under the rules of the Court. It is, in my opinion, a mistake to say that the action changes its character and ceases to be an action *in rem* and becomes an action *in personam* when the owner appears and gives bail. It is no doubt true that when this is done the action, so far as its special characteristic as an action *in rem* is concerned, has served its purpose, or possibly its chief purpose, when the owner of the *res* has been induced, by reason of the arrest or fear of the arrest of his vessel, to enter an appearance and to give bail in order to obtain the release, or avoid the seizure, of his vessel. It also true that when once the owner of the *res* has appeared the plaintiff has the advantage of being able in the case of necessity to take his property in satisfaction of the judgment in addition to the bail. These consequences,

---

[63] [1992] 1 Lloyd's Rep 124 (CA).
[64] [1993] AC 410.
[65] [1994] 2 Lloyd's Rep 331.
[66] [1996] 1 Lloyd's Rep 12 (CA).
[67] [1998] AC 878. As to s 20(2)(g) and (h), see paras 35.26 and 35.27.
[68] [1992] 2 Lloyd's Rep 552 (CA).

however, are, in my opinion, incidents which only arise in the course of the action *in rem*, which add to its value but which in no way later on deprive it of its special character.

> ... The advantage of the action being an action *in rem* still remains in the sense that, should the exceptional occasion arise, the Court in a proper case would no doubt still have jurisdiction to order the arrest of the vessel.[69]

35.22 **Judgment in an action *in rem* a bar to subsequent action *in personam*?** It has hitherto been well established that though a judgment has already been obtained *in rem*, a litigant may bring an action *in personam* in respect of the same claim, unless the proceeds of sale are sufficient to cover the damages. The converse is also true in that judgment and execution *in personam* would not preclude a subsequent action *in rem*. This was stated by Sir Henry Duke, President of the Probate, Admiralty & Divorce Division of the High Court in *The Joannis Vatis (No 2)*:

> An action *in rem* carried to its conclusion did not preclude a subsequent action *in personam*, and a previous action *in personam* with judgment and execution would not have precluded a subsequent action *in rem*.[70]

But this would now have to be read subject to *Republic of India v India Steamship Co Ltd (The Indian Grace)(No 2)*[71] where, at least for the purposes of section 34 of the Civil Jurisdiction and Judgments Act 1982, the House of Lords set its face against permitting an action *in rem* to be brought in respect of a cause of action already commenced *in personam* in another jurisdiction (India). On one view, the House of Lords has simply sought to employ a 'sensible and purposive approach' to statutory construction. It has, consequently, been argued that the approach needs to be applied within the framework of the existing law, thus recognizing the continuing existence of the limited range of maritime liens as the basis for an action *in rem*.[72] Another, more critical, response is that the reasons advanced by the House of Lords for a reappraisal of the nature of the Admiralty action *in rem* do not support that reappraisal and that, further, much uncertainty will be introduced in this area of law.[73]

35.23 **An Admiralty action *in rem* may be brought to enforce a foreign judgment *in rem*** An Admiralty action *in rem* may be brought in England to enforce the judgment of a foreign court where such a judgment has been given in an action *in rem*.[74] No such action may be brought to enforce a foreign judgment *in personam*.

D. Subject Matter

35.24 **Introduction** We now look at a number of the heads of claim in section 20(2) which are likely to be of greatest use in carriage of goods cases.[75]

---

[69] [1916] P 64 (CA), 76–77.
[70] [1922] P 213, 221.
[71] [1998] AC 878.
[72] See FD Rose, 'The Nature of Admiralty Proceedings: *The Indian Grace (No 2)*' [1998] LMCLQ 27.
[73] See Nigel Teare, 'The Admiralty action *in rem* and the House of Lords' [1998] LMCLQ 33.
[74] *The City of Mecca* (1879) 5 PD, 28, 30; 32–33 (Phillimore J).
[75] For the remaining claims, see especially Meeson (2003), ch 2.

Claims for 'damage done by a ship'   This head of claim is listed in section 20(2)(e).[76]   **35.25**
Admiralty jurisdiction under section 20(2)(e) also extends to any claim in respect of oil pollution liability incurred under Chapter III of Part VI of the Merchant Shipping Act 1995
and to any claim in respect of liability falling under the International Oil Pollution
Compensation Fund under Chapter IV of Part VI of the Merchant Shipping Act 1995, by
virtue of section 20(5)(a) and (b) of the Act. In *The Jade (The Eschersheim)*, Lord Diplock
said that:

> The figurative phrase 'damage done by a ship' is a term of art in maritime law whose mean-
> ing is well settled by authority . . . To fall within the phrase not only must the damage be the
> direct result or natural consequence of something done [or omitted to be done] by those
> engaged in the navigation of the ship, but the ship itself must be the actual instrument by
> which the damage was done. The commonest case is that of collision . . . but physical contact
> between the ship and whatever object sustains the damage is not essential — a ship may neg-
> ligently cause a wash by which some other vessel or some property on shore is damaged.[77]

There is authority that this head of claim will include causes of action for: damage done by
a ship colliding with another ship;[78] damage done by a ship to another ship, but not arising
from a collision;[79] damage done by a ship to some other structure;[80] damage done by a ship
to individuals on board another ship, causing them personal injury;[81] any other damage
done by a ship, where this is the direct result or natural consequence of a breach of duty in
the navigation of a ship.[82] The potential importance in a carriage of goods case is that a
claim will lie for damage done by a ship to cargo, baggage and personal effects carried on
board another ship,[83] but not damage to cargo on board the carrying ship.[84]

Claims for 'loss of or damage to goods carried in a ship'   This head of claim, listed in sec-   **35.26**
tion 20(2)(g),[85] is not limited to any particular legal basis of claim. Originally, it was
restricted to claims by consignees or assignees of any bill of lading or owners of goods carried into any port in England and Wales on ships owned by persons domiciled outside
England and Wales for damage done to such goods.[86] However, these limitations were
removed by the time the Administration of Justice Act 1956 was enacted. The 'ship'
referred to is the carrying ship and the provision was designed to cover the claim of a cargo
owner against the ship to which he has entrusted his cargo.[87] In *The Tesaba*[88] certain salvors
strove to include in the provision a claim based upon LOF.[89] They alleged failure of the

---

[76] Introduced by s 7 of the Admiralty Court Act 1861.
[77] [1976] 1 WLR 430 (HL), 438.
[78] See *The Warkworth* (1884) 9 PD 20.
[79] See, eg, *The Industrie* (1871) LR 3 A&E 303.
[80] See *The Tolten* [1946] P 135, where damage was caused to a wharf.
[81] See *The Vera Cruz (No 2)* [1884] 9 PD 96.
[82] *The Industrie* (1871) LR 3 A&E 303.
[83] See *The Jade (The Eschersheim)* [1976] 1 WLR 430 (HL).
[84] See *Berliner Bank AG v C Czarnikow Sugar Ltd (The Rama)* [1996] 2 Lloyd's Rep 281.
[85] Introduced by s 6 of the Admiralty Court Act 1861.
[86] Goods now includes baggage: see s 24(1) of the Act.
[87] *The Jade (The Eschersheim)* [1976] 1 Lloyd's Rep 81 (CA), 93 (Sir Gordon Willmer). cf claims for damage done by a ship, at para 35.25.
[88] [1982] 1 Lloyd's Rep 397.
[89] ie Lloyds Open Form.

shipowners to use their best endeavours to ensure that the cargo owners provide security before release of their cargo. Sheen J held that, giving the words in section 20(2)(g) 'their ordinary and natural meaning', they did not describe the claim before him as there was no loss or damage to goods.[90]

35.27 **Claims 'arising out of any agreement relating to the carriage of goods in a ship or the use or hire of a ship'**   The language of this head of claim, in section 20(2)(h),[91] is such that it is wide enough to cover claims, whether in contract or in tort, arising out of any agreement relating to the carriage of goods in a vessel.[92] Accordingly, in practice this is likely to be the most important head of claim for the carriage of goods by sea. Clearly falling within the scope of the provision include the following: claims for loss of or damage to cargo; bill of lading claims,[93] including antedating of bills of lading;[94] breaches of charterparties,[95] including claims for demurrage and freight;[96] wrongful detention of goods;[97] claims for wrongful refusal to carry agreed cargo;[98] claims arising out of slot charters;[99] indemnity claims arising from contracts of carriage;[100] breaches of towage contracts.[101] Matters not covered[102] include breaches of salvage agreements,[103] contracts of insurance,[104] and contracts for the international sale of goods.[105]

35.28 **Meaning of 'arising out of'**   It would not be necessary that the claim in question be directly connected with some agreement for the carriage of goods in a ship or for the use or hire of a ship or that the agreement be one made between the two parties to the action. These issues were considered by the House of Lords in *Samick Lines Co Ltd v Owners of The Antonis P Lemos (The Antonis P Lemos)*.[106] Samick Lines was a sub-charterer of the *Antonis P Lemos* for a time charter trip and was permitted to sub-sub-charter the vessel. They did so for a voyage charter for the carriage of a full cargo of heavy grains and/or sorghums and/or soya beans from a North American port to Alexandria or Port Said. The charter contained an express guarantee that the vessel's maximum draught on arrival at the port of discharge

---

[90] [1982] 1 Lloyd's Rep 397, 400.

[91] The origins of this provision lie in the County Court Admiralty Jurisdiction Amendment Act 1869, 32 & 33 Vict, c 51, subsequently extended to the High Court by s 5(1) of the Administration of Justice Act 1920, 10 & 11 Geo V, c 81.

[92] *Schwarz & Co (Grain) v St Elefterio ex Arion (The St Elefterio)* [1957] P 179, 183 (Willmer J). The ship must be specifically identified: see *The Lloyd Pacifico* [1995] 1 Lloyd's Rep 54, 57 (Clarke J).

[93] *The Rona* (1882) 7 PD 247; *Pugsley v Ropkins* [1892] 2 QB 184 (CA), 194–195.

[94] *Schwarz & Co (Grain) v St Elefterio ex Arion (The St Elefterio)* [1957] P 179; *The Sennar* [1983] 1 Lloyd's Rep 295.

[95] *The Alina* (1880) 5 Ex D 227 (CA).

[96] *Cargo ex Argos* (1873) LR 5 PC 134.

[97] *The Gina* [1980] 1 Lloyd's Rep 398.

[98] *The Alina* (1880) 5 Ex D 227 (CA).

[99] See *MSC Mediterranean Shipping Co SA v The Tychy* [1999] 2 Lloyd's Rep 11 (CA).

[100] *The Hamburg Star* [1994] 1 Lloyd's Rep 399, 406.

[101] *The Conoco Britannia* [1972] 2 QB 543; *The Isca* (1886) 12 PD 34.

[102] See Meeson (2003), para 2.76.

[103] *The Tesaba* [1982] 1 Lloyd's Rep 397, 401 (Sheen J).

[104] *Gatoil International Inc v Arkwright-Boston Manufacturers Mutual Insurance Co (The Sandrina)* [1985] AC 255.

[105] *Petrofina SA v AOT Ltd (The Maersk Nimrod)* [1992] QB 571.

[106] [1985] AC 711.

would not exceed 32 feet in salt water. When the ship arrived at Alexandria, as nominated, her draught exceeded 32 feet and she had to discharge some of her cargo onto lighters before she could berth. The respondents incurred the costs of lightening and certain other costs. They then brought an action *in rem* against the vessel in the Admiralty Court. The owners sought an order releasing the vessel on the ground that the Admiralty Court had no such jurisdiction. Sheen J found in their favour at first instance.[107] The Court of Appeal allowed the appeal[108] and gave leave to appeal to the House of Lords. The sole question for the House of Lords was whether the claim of the respondents came with section 20(2)(h). Lord Brandon held, dismissing the appeal, that the language of section 20(2)(h) was wide enough to cover claims whether in contract or in tort arising out of any agreement relating to the carriage of goods in a ship, and that for such an agreement to come within paragraph (h) it was not necessary that the claim in question be directly connected with some agreement of the kinds referred to in it or that the agreement be one made between the two parties to the action themselves. In particular, Lord Brandon said that the phrase 'arising out of' had, in this context, to be given the broader meaning of 'connected with' and not the narrower meaning of 'arising under'.[109]

Meaning of 'relating to' In *Gatoil International Inc v Arkwright-Boston Manufacturers Mutual Insurance Co (The Sandrina)* Lord Keith explained that: **35.29**

> It is necessary to attribute due significance to the circumstance that the words of the relevant paragraphs speak of an agreement 'in relation to' not 'for' the carriage of goods in a ship and the use or hire of a ship. The meaning must be wider than would be conveyed by the particle 'for'. It would, on the other hand, be unreasonable to infer from the expression actually used, 'in relation to', that it is intended to be sufficient that the agreement in issue should be in some way connected, however remotely, with the carriage of goods in a ship or with the use or hire of a ship . . . There must, in my opinion, be some reasonably direct connection with such activities. An agreement for the cancellation of a contract for the carriage of goods in a ship or for the use or hire of a ship would, I think, show a sufficiently direct connection.[110]

Any claim in respect of 'goods or materials supplied to a ship for her operation or main-   **35.30**
tenance' This head of claim in section 20(2)(m)[111] covers not only claims which are made directly by the supplier of goods or materials, but also claims by other persons making advances to enable the purchase of goods or materials.[112] It is an essential ingredient of claims under this paragraph that they relate to a particular identified ship. This aspect was considered in *The River Rima*.[113] Here the owners of the *River Rima*, a 'Combo' vessel equipped to carry containers as well as general cargo, were the Nigerian National Shipping Line (NNSL). NNSL leased containers from the plaintiffs. The claimants issued a writ

---

[107] [1983] 2 Lloyd's Rep 310.
[108] [1984] 2 WLR 825 (CA).
[109] [1985] AC 711, 731. See too *The Indriani* [1996] 1 SLR 305.
[110] [1985] AC 255, 270–271.
[111] This jurisdiction was given to the Admiralty Court in s 6 of the Admiralty Court Act 1840 and extended further by s 5 of the Admiralty Court 1861.
[112] Originally the claim was for 'necessaries': see *The Fairport (No 5)* [1967] 2 Lloyd's Rep 162, 163 (Brandon J).
[113] [1988] 1 WLR 758 (HL).

in rem claiming damages in the tort of conversion for certain containers it had leased to the NNSL and for also failing to maintain the containers in a good state of repair in breach of NNSL's contractual obligations. Did such claims fall within section 20(2)(m)? At first instance Sheen J held that the court did have *in rem* jurisdiction as containers were goods supplied to the ship for her operation. The Court of Appeal allowed the defendant's appeal. The House of Lords concluded that the contracts for the lease of the containers were made with the shipowner, but not with reference to a particular ship. It was an essential ingredient that section 20(2)(m) contemplated claims relating to necessaries supplied to a particular ship. As the plaintiffs did not know what ship their containers were eventually carried on, the required specific identity was missing. Section 20(2)(m) was therefore irrelevant. Lord Brandon stated that:

> There are two main kinds of contract pursuant to which goods or materials required for the operation of a ship may reach her. The first kind of contract is one which expressly provides that the goods or materials are required for the use of a particular ship, the identity of which is specified in the contract or will be specified by the time when the contract comes to be performed. The second kind of contract is one which contains no reference to a particular ship for the use of which the goods or materials are required, leaving the shipowner to make his own decision about that later. The first kind of contract is, in my opinion, a contract under which goods or materials are 'supplied to a ship' within the meaning of para (m) [of section 20(2)]. The second kind of contract, however, is in my opinion, not a contract for goods or materials to be 'supplied to a ship' within the meaning of para (m). It is no more than a contract for the supply of goods and materials to a shipowner and as such does not come within para (m).[114]

Claims which have been held to fall within this head of jurisdiction include food, drink, and other consumables supplied for the use of the officers and crew; food, drink, stationery, and other consumables supplied for the use or consumption by passengers on the vessel; the provision of services, in particular the provision of officers and crew of suitable calibre for the operation and manning of the vessel; equipment supplied to the vessel.[115]

35.31 **Any claim 'in respect of the construction, repair or equipment of a ship or in respect of dock charges or dues'**   This head of jurisdiction, in section 20(2)(n),[116] was considered in *Secony Bunker Oil Co Ltd v Owners of the Steamship D'Vora*.[117] The court made a distinction between 'equip' and 'supply' and held that a claim for bunkers supplied to a ship did not come within the predecessor of this head under the 1925 Act. The plaintiffs had supplied bunkers to the *D'Vora* in Haifa and were now claiming the purchase price. Willmer J held that:

> In my judgment, there is an important difference between 'equip' and 'supply', 'supply' being a word which is appropriate for use in connection with consumable stores such as fuel oil, whereas 'equip', to my mind, connotes something of a more permanent nature than consumable stores. I can well understand that anchors, cables, hawsers, sails, ropes and such things,

---

[114] At 763. See too *Centro Latino Americano de Commercio Exterior SA v Owners of the ship 'Kommunar' (The Kommunar)* [1997] 1 Lloyd's Rep 8.

[115] *The Edinburgh Castle* [1999] 2 Lloyd's Rep 362. See too *The Nore Challenger and The Nore Commander* [2001] 1 Lloyd's Rep 103.

[116] Jurisdiction for this head existed under s 4 of the Admiralty Court Act 1861, with the caveat that, at the time proceedings were brought, the ship or its proceeds must be under the arrest of the court. This restriction does not exist in the modern jurisdiction.

[117] [1953] 1 WLR 34.

may be said to be part of a ship's equipment, and that, none the less, though they may have to be renewed from time to time; but such things as fuel oil, coal, boiler water and food — consumable stores — seem to me to be in quite a different category.[118]

Any 'claim by a master, shipper, charterer or agent in respect of disbursements made on **35.32**
account of a ship' This head is to be found in section 20(2)(p)[119] and gives rise to a maritime lien. It has tended to be viewed broadly. Thus, in *The Feronia* Sir Robert Phillimore considered it to have been the intention of the legislature in conferring jurisdiction on the court to entertain claims for disbursements to include 'all proper expenditure made by the master upon the ship, whether the particular articles, the subject of this expenditure, were obtained by immediate or by promised payment'.[120] In *The Orienta*, Lord Esher MR observed that:

> The real meaning of the word 'disbursements' in Admiralty practice is disbursement by the master, which he makes himself liable for in respect of necessary things for the ship, for the purpose of navigation, which he, as master of the ship, is there to carry out — necessary in the sense that they must be had immediately — and when the owner is not there, able to give the order, and he is not so near to the master that the master can ask for his authority, and the master is therefore obliged, necessarily, to render himself liable in order to carry out his duty as master.[121]

While bunkers clearly would be included, a marine insurance premium is not.[122]

Any 'claim arising out of an act which is or is claimed to be a general average act' It may **35.33**
well happen that there is a general average claim. As such claims are often made in relation to cargo there is a head of jurisdiction for this in section 20(2)(q).[123] A 'general average act' is defined by section 66(2) of the Marine Insurance Act 1906 as follows:

> There is a general average act where any extraordinary sacrifice or expenditure is voluntarily and reasonably made or incurred in time of peril for the purpose of preserving the property imperilled in the common adventure.

Where the York–Antwerp Rules 2004 have been incorporated into the contract, the definition contained in Rule A would be applicable as follows:

> 1) There is a general average act when, and only when, an extraordinary sacrifice or expenditure is intentionally and reasonably made or incurred for the common safety for the purpose of preserving from peril the property involved in a common maritime adventure.

> 2) General average sacrifices and expenditures shall be borne by the different contributing interests on the basis hereinafter provided.

Although there is no maritime lien in respect of a claim for general average, the shipowner would, at common law, have a possessory lien over the cargo for cargo owners' proportion of general average which is enforceable against the consignee of the cargo even though the consignee is under no personal liability to contribute in general average, not being the owner of the cargo when the general average act occurred.

---

[118] At 35–36.
[119] The origins are to be found in s 10 of the Admiralty Court Act 1861.
[120] (1868) LR 2 A&E 65, 75.
[121] [1895] P 49 (CA), 55.
[122] See *The Sea Friends* [1991] 2 Lloyd's Rep 322 (CA).
[123] This head of claim was introduced by s 47(2)(g) of the Administration of Justice Act 1956.

E. The Exercise of Admiralty Jurisdiction

35.34 **Introduction**   Having considered the heads of claim under which most carriage of goods claims are likely to fall, we move finally to a consideration of exercising the jurisdiction. All of the claims so far referred to can be enforced (i) *in personam*[124] or (ii) *in rem*. In relation to the latter method of enforcement, the claims may either be enforced under section 21(3), because they are maritime lien claims, or under section 21(4), because they are claims which fall within section 20(2)(e)–(r) of the Act. We shall look first at the requirements for proceeding under section 21(4) before considering section 21(3).

35.35 **The action *in rem***   The essence of the action *in rem* is that it is an action against a thing, rather than against a person. The principal advantage is that, by proceeding against a *res*, the plaintiff will obtain security for his claim. The *res* may be arrested by the court and sold to satisfy a judgment *in rem* against it. It is possible to bring an action *in rem* provided that the *res* is within the jurisdiction of the court. By contrast, it would not be possible to bring such an action *in personam* against foreign owners of that same property unless there were grounds permitting leave to serve a claim form *in personam* out of the jurisdiction.

35.36 **The action *in rem* in relation to the claims within section 20(2)(e)–(r)**   Section 21(4) of the Act provides that:

> In the case of any such claim as is mentioned in section 20(2)(e) to (r), where —
>
> (a) the claim arises in connection with a ship; and
>
> (b) the person who would be liable on the claim in an action *in personam* ('the relevant person') was, when the cause of action arose, the owner or charterer of, or in possession or in control of, the ship,
>
> an action *in rem* may (whether or not the claim gives rise to maritime lien on that ship) be brought in the High Court against —
>
> (i) that ship, if at the time when the action is brought the relevant person is either the beneficial owner of that ship as respects all the shares in it or the charterer of it under a charter by demise; or
>
> (ii) any other ship of which, at the time when the action is brought, the relevant person is the beneficial owner as respects all the shares in it.

The draftsman of the Act introduced an important change in the wording from that in the Administration of Justice Act 1956 by adding the words 'or the charterer of it under a charter by demise' in section 21(4)(i).

35.37 **The 'one claim, one ship' principle**   A claimant proceeding *in rem* under section 21(4) is not permitted to proceed against 'the ship' and against 'any other ship' in respect of the same cause of action. In *Monte Ulia v The Banco*, Lord Denning MR stated that:

> The important word in that subsection is the word 'or'. It is used to express an alternative as in the phrase 'one *or* the other'. It means that the Admiralty jurisdiction *in rem* may be invoked *either* against the offending ship *or* against any other ship in the same ownership, but

---

[124] See s 21(1).

not against both. This is the natural meaning of the word 'or' in this context. It is the meaning which carries into effect the International Convention.[125]

This is further emphasized in section 21(8) of the Act:

> Where, as regards any such claim as is mentioned in section 20(2)(e) to (r), a ship has been served with a writ or arrested in an action *in rem* brought to enforce that claim, no other ship may be served with a writ or arrested in that or any other action *in rem* brought to enforce that claim; but this subsection does not prevent the issue, in respect of any one such claim, of a writ naming more than one ship or of two or more writs each naming a different ship.[126]

This issue arose in *Centro Latino Americano de Commercio Exterior SA v Owners of the ship 'Kommunar' (The Kommunar)(No 2)*.[127] The defendant (AOL) submitted that proceedings *in rem* had been commenced against a sister ship in South Africa before the arrest of the *Kommunar* and that by the South African proceedings the plaintiffs claimed in respect of the same disbursements as in these proceedings. Service of a writ was, accordingly, in breach of section 21(8). The plaintiffs countered this with argument that section 21(8) only applied to multiple proceedings confined to England and did not apply to international multiple proceedings. Colman J so held:

> Section 21(8) makes no express reference to proceedings outside this jurisdiction. Moreover, it is located at the end of s 21 which in all its other sub-sections deals with English Admiralty jurisdiction *in personam* and *in rem* without referring to overseas proceedings.... The description of the earlier proceedings against the ship as 'a ship has been served with a writ or arrested in an action *in rem*' strongly suggest proceedings in this country rather than in any overseas jurisdiction. The reference to a writ or action *in rem* appears to be too specifically related to English Admiralty procedure to be intended to have wider application.

> If Parliament had intended s 21(8) to have wider application than to proceedings in the Courts of this country I feel sure that it would not have been worded in the way in which one finds it. Express reference would have been made to prior foreign as well as English proceedings.

> I conclude, therefore, that s 21(8) of the 1981 Act applies only to proceedings *in rem* or to a prior arrest in this country and that accordingly, the proceedings in South Africa are not a bar to these present proceedings.[128]

'... arises in connection with a ship'   In order to bring an action *in rem* the claim must first **35.38** arise 'in connection with a ship' (section 21(4)(a)). This restricts the jurisdiction of the Admiralty Court to 'ship' claims, and excludes 'other property', such as cargo or freight, which are referred to in section 21(2) and section 21(3). The reference to 'ship' means the same ship as that referred to in section 20(2)(e)–(r). In *The Jade (The Eschersheim)*, Lord Diplock explained that:

> It is clear that to be liable to arrest a ship must not only be the property of the defendant to the action but must also be identifiable as the ship in connection with which the claim made in the action arose (or a sister ship of that ship). The nature of the 'connection' between the ship and the claim must have been intended to be the same as is expressed in the corresponding phrase in the convention 'the particular ship in respect of which the maritime claim arose'.

---

125 [1971] P 137 (CA), 512.
126 *The Banco* [1971] 1 Lloyd's Rep 49 (CA).
127 [1997] 1 Lloyd's Rep 8.
128 At 20–21.

One must therefore look at the description of each of the maritime claims included in the list in order to identify the particular ship in respect of which a claim of that description could arise.[129]

35.39   '... the person who would be liable on the claim in an action *in personam* ...'   This is a reference to the 'relevant' person who would be liable in an action *in personam*. In *Schwarz & Co (Grain) v St Elefterio ex Arion (The St Elefterio)* Willmer J explained that:

> In my judgment the purpose of the words relied upon by [counsel], that is to say, the words 'the person who would be liable on the claim in an action *in personam*' is to identify the person or persons whose ship or ships may be arrested in relation to this new right, (if I may so express it) of arresting a sister ship. The words used, it will be observed, are 'the person who would be liable' not 'the person who is liable', and it seems to me, bearing in mind the purpose of the Act that the natural construction of those quite simple words is that they mean the person who would be liable on the assumption that the action succeeds.[130] This action might or might not succeed if it were brought *in personam* ...[131]

This must be read with section 21(7) which provides that:

> In determining for the purposes of subsections (4) and (5) whether a person would be liable on a claim in an action in personam it shall be assumed that he has his habitual residence or a place of business within England or Wales.

The claimant's obligation at this point is merely to show that he has a good arguable case.[132]

35.40   'When the cause of action arose ...'   The reference in section 21(4)(a) to 'cause of action' would be widely interpreted to mean a cause of action sounding in tort or contract. It would include payments under a contract[133] and probably also indemnity claims.[134]

35.41   '... [the relevant person was] the owner ... of the ship'   In *The Evpo Agnic*[135] Donaldson MR considered that the reference to 'owner' in section 21(4)(a) meant 'registered owner' and not a beneficial owner[136] who was not a registered owner. This has, however, been doubted in other jurisdictions.[137]

---

[129] [1976] 1 WLR 430 (HL), 436–437. See too *The Lloyd Pacifico* [1995] 1 Lloyd's Rep 54, 57 (Clarke J).

[130] In *The Yuta Bondarovskaya* [1998] 2 Lloyd's Rep 357 the claim failed because the person who would be liable for a bunker claim under a time charterparty was the time charterer. See too *The Tychy (No 2)* [2001] EWCA Civ 1198; [2001] 2 Lloyd's Rep 403.

[131] [1957] P 179, 185. See also *The Moschanthy* [1971] 1 Lloyd's Rep 37, 42 (Brandon J), cited with approval by the High Court of Australia in *Iran Amanat v KMP Coastal Oil Ptd Ltd* (1999) 196 CLR 130.

[132] See *The Opal 3* [1992] 2 SLR 585, 590 (Selvam JC); *The AA V* [2001] 1 SLR 207, 215 (Judith Prakash J); *The Rainbow Spring* [2003] 3 SLR 362 (CA), at [15] (Judith Prakash J).

[133] See, eg, *Techno Maritime Ltèe v Deep Diving Systems Ltd* [1980] 2 FC 766.

[134] *The Salina* [1999] 1 SLR 486, 494 (Karthigesu JA).

[135] [1988] 1 WLR 1090 (CA).

[136] As to 'beneficial owner', see para 35.45.

[137] *The Ohm Mariana ex Peony* [1993] 2 SLR 698, 710 (LP Thean J); *Tisand (Pty) Ltd v Owners of the MV Cape Moreton (ex Freya)* [2005] FCAFC 68; (2005) 143 FCR 43. In the latter case, the Federal Court of Australia said that, in determining the meaning to be given to 'owner' (in s 17 of the Admiralty Act 1988), the question to be asked was whether, in all the relevant circumstances, a person answered the description of 'the owner' in a proprietary sense (at [119]–[120]).

'... [the relevant person was the] charterer of ... the ship ...' The reference to 'char- **35.42**
terer'[138] has been widely interpreted and would include a time charterer, voyage charterer,
demise charterer,[139] and slot charterer.[140]

'or in possession or in control of, the ship ...' This would include salvors[141] and pur- **35.43**
chasers of ships under instalment payment agreements.

'That ship, if at the time when the action is brought ...' Section 21(4) provides that the **35.44**
claimant *in rem* may either proceed against 'that ship' or 'any other ship' and 'at the time
when the action is brought'. This is crucially important for the claimant. Provided he
issues a claim form, he may continue to take any steps necessary to prosecute his claim,
despite any subsequent change in ownership. In *The Monica S*, Brandon J stated that:

> ... [T]he conclusion at which I arrive from my examination of the authorities is that
> counsel ... has not made good his contention that, under the law in force before the Act of
> 1956, a change of ownership after issue of writ but before service or arrest defeated a statu-
> tory right of action *in rem*. I go further and state my view that, on the balance of authority,
> that contention is shown to be wrong.
>
> ... [T]he jurisdiction which is invoked by an action *in rem* ... is the jurisdiction to hear and
> determine the questions and claims listed in [section 20(2)]. I see no reason why, once a
> plaintiff has properly invoked that jurisdiction by bringing an action *in rem*[142] ... he should
> not, despite a subsequent change of ownership of the *res*, be able to prosecute it through all
> its stages, up to and including judgment against the *res*, and payment of the amount of the
> judgment out of the proceeds.[143]

'Beneficial owner' There has sometimes been controversy as to what is meant by the **35.45**
phrase 'beneficial owner'. However, in *I Congreso del Partido*,[144] Goff J held that the words
'beneficially owned', as they appeared in the corresponding provisions of the Administration
of Justice Act 1956, referred only to cases of equitable ownership, whether or not accompanied by legal ownership, and were not wide enough to include cases of possession or control
without ownership, however full and complete such possession might be and however
much control over the ship the person might have:

> In my judgment, the natural and ordinary meaning of these words ['beneficially owned'] is
> that they refer only to such ownership as is vested in a person who, whether or not he is the
> legal owner of the vessel, is in any case the equitable owner ... Furthermore, on the natural and
> ordinary meaning of the words, I do not consider them apt to apply to the case of a demise
> charter or indeed any other person who has only possession of the ship, however full and com-
> plete such possession may be, and however much control over the ship he may have.[145]

---

[138] The charter must actually be in existence; it is not sufficient that the liability arises out of having been
a charterer: see *The Faial* [2000] 1 Lloyd's Rep 47.
[139] *The Span Terza* [1982] 1 Lloyd's Rep 225 (CA), 227; *Medway Drydock & Engineering Co v The Andrea Ursula*
[1973] QB 265, 269–270 (Brandon J); *The Permina 108* [1978] 1 Lloyd's Rep 311, 314 (Wee Chong Jin CJ).
[140] *The Tychy* [1999] 2 Lloyd's Rep 11 (CA).
[141] See *The Evpo Agnic* [1988] 1 WLR 1090 (CA).
[142] ie, when the writ *in rem* is issued.
[143] [1968] P 741, 771; 773.
[144] [1978] QB 500. cf *Smith's Dock Co Ltd v The St Merriel* [1963] P 247.
[145] At 538.

He went on to say that:

> As I read [section 21(4)], the intention of Parliament in adding the word 'beneficial' before the word 'owner' in [section 21(4)] was simply to take account of the institution of the trust, thus ensuring that, if a ship was to be operated under the cloak of a trust, those interested in the ship would not thereby be able to avoid the arrest of the ship.[146]

There have been many cases which have raised the issue of beneficial ownership, particularly following the break-up of the Soviet Union.[147]

35.46 **'Lifting the veil'** In the case of a registered company, the rule in English law is that the company is a separate entity.[148] However, in some cases the courts will lift the veil of incorporation and look to the realities of the situation where there is a façade or sham or where there is fraud.[149] In *The Aventicum* there was a dispute as to the beneficial ownership of a vessel and Slynn J said that:

> Where damages are claimed by cargo owners and there is a dispute as to the beneficial ownership of the ship, the Court in all cases can and in some cases should look beyond the registered ownership to determine the true beneficial ownership.

> It is plain that . . . the Act intends that the Court shall not be limited to a consideration of who is the registered owner or who is the person having the legal ownership of the shares in the ship; the directions are to look at the beneficial ownership. Certainly where there is a suggestion of a trusteeship or nominee holding, there is no doubt that the Court can investigate it . . .[150]

The court will not, however, lift the veil simply because it is alleged that there is a one-ship[151] company. On the other hand, if there are allegations of a sham, the courts will be prepared to lift the veil.[152]

35.47 **'Any other ship . . .'** The right to arrest 'any other ship' — or 'sister ships' — was introduced in article 3(1) of the Arrest Convention 1952[153] and is to be found in section 21(4)(ii)

---

[146] At 542. See also *The Father Thames* [1979] 2 Lloyd's Rep 364, 367 (Sheen J). But cf *The Permina 3001* [1975–1977] SLR 252; *The Temasek Eagle* [1999] 4 SLR 250.

[147] See *The Nazym Khikmet* [1996] 2 Lloyd's Rep 362 (CA); *Sovrybflot v The Efim Gorbenko* [1996] 2 NZLR 727; *The Guiseppe di Vittorio* [1998] 1 Lloyd's Rep 136; *Centro Latino Americano de Commercio Exterior SA v Owners of the Kommunar (The Kommunar)(No 2)* [1997] 1 Lloyd's Rep 8; *The Ivanovo* [2002] 4 SLR 978. See D Rhidian Thomas, 'State reconstruction and ship arrest' [1998] IJOSL 236.

[148] *Salomon v Salomon & Co Ltd* [1897] AC 22.

[149] *Trustor AB v Smallbone (No 3)* [2001] 1 WLR 1177, 1185 (Morritt V-C).

[150] [1978] 1 Lloyd's Rep 184, 187; *The Evpo Agnic* [1988] 1 WLR 1090 (CA); *The Maritime Trader* [1981] 2 Lloyd's Rep 154, 157 (Sheen J); *The Ohm Mariana ex Peony* [1993] 2 SLR 698 (CA), 711 (LP Thean J); *The Opal 3* [1992] 2 SLR 585, 590 (Selvam JC).

[151] In *Bakri Bunker Trading Co Ltd v The Neptune* [1986] HKLR 345, Nazareth J noted that: 'It is not disputed that all the ships concerned were owned by one-ship companies. . . Again that by itself does not suggest fraud. Counsel in the *Maritime Trader* asked the rhetorical question "What is wrong with using the company structure to limit liability?" and said the answer must be "Nothing, unless it is a sham". Sheen J agreed. I share his view. One-ship companies, I was informed by counsel, are by no means uncommon, and as a legitimate means of limiting liability, in my opinion, do not of themselves raise any inference of fraud' (at 350). See too *The Skaw Prince* [1994] 2 SLR 379, 386 (Amerjeet Singh JC).

[152] See *The Saudi Prince* [1982] 2 Lloyd's Rep 255; *The Tjaskemolen* [1997] 2 Lloyd's Rep 465.

[153] Notwithstanding late attempts by the UK to introduce modifications based on the associated ship provisions of the South African Admiralty Jurisdiction Regulation Act 1983, the right to arrest a sister ship has been retained in the 1999 Arrest Convention (see art 3(2)).

of the Act. However, the action only lies as against a relevant person who is the beneficial owner as respects all the shares in it.[154]

Limitations on the action *in rem*   At this point it may be noted in passing that there are **35.48** likely to be three principal types of limitation on bringing an action *in rem*. The first of these concerns immunity for government ships where the action *in rem* is excluded.[155] The second concerns foreign sovereign immunity and is regulated by the State Immunity Act 1978.[156] Finally, where the owner of the ship (or other property) becomes insolvent, then there will be a conflict between those claimants asserting claims against the ship and other claimants who do not have an *in rem* claim. There are different priority rules in each case. While the normal insolvency rule is that claims rank *pari passu*, in Admiralty proceedings there are different rules of priority, which are not enshrined in statute,[157] essentially comprising an equitable jurisdiction, developed by the courts, and largely settled.[158]

The maritime lien or 'other charge'   We have now seen that it is possible to arrest a ship **35.49** *in rem* for the list of claims in section 20(2)(e)–(r). However, in such a case the requirements are laid down in section 21(4). We have in addition seen that certain claims also give rise to a maritime lien and such are enforceable *in rem* under section 21(3), as follows:

> In any case in which there is a maritime lien or other charge on any ship, aircraft or other property for the amount claimed, an action *in rem* may be brought in the High Court against that ship, aircraft or property.

The action *in rem* which enforces a claim as a maritime lien under section 21(3) is against the 'ship or other property' in which there is a maritime lien but not against 'any other ship'.

F. Property against which an Action *In Rem* May Be Brought

Introduction   Although an action *in rem* will commonly be brought against a ship, it is **35.50** also possible to bring such an action against other property in respect of certain claims, namely those which are enforceable under section 21(3) — maritime lien claims — and the limited jurisdictional head in section 21(2).[159]

Property on board a ship   In most cases claims against property will include the ship's **35.51** apparel, tackle, and stores (including her bunkers). In *The Silia*, Sheen J said that:

> I have no doubt that in the context of an action *in rem* the word 'ship' includes all property aboard the ship other than that which is owned by someone other than the owner of the ship.

---

[154] section 21(4)(ii) does not contain the words 'or the charterer of it under a charter by demise' — see s 21(4)(i) (for arrests of 'that ship'). See *The Maritime Trader* [1981] 2 Lloyd's Rep 154.

[155] See the Crown Proceedings Act 1947, 10 & 11 Geo 6, c 44, s 29(1); Supreme Court Act 1981, s 24(2). See Meeson (2003), para 3.58.

[156] c 33. See Meeson (2003), para 3.62.

[157] In some jurisdictions this is statutory: see, eg, the South African Admiralty Jurisdiction Regulation Act 1983, No 105, s 11.

[158] See, eg, *Patrick Stevedores No 2 Pty Ltd v Proceeds of the sale of the MV Skulptor Konenkov* (1997) 144 ALR 394, 397 (Sheppard J).

[159] For the enforcement of claims *in rem* in respect of s 20(2)(a), (c), or (s).

The advantage of an Admiralty action *in rem* is that it enables the plaintiff to detain property of the shipowner which has come within the territorial jurisdiction of the Court in order to secure a maritime claim. That advantage would be reduced if part of the property of the shipowner were exempt from attachment.[160]

35.52 **Cargo and freight** For those claims giving rise to a maritime lien, the cargo may be proceeded against where the cargo is salvaged or subject to bottomry or respondentia,[161] but not where the claim is for damage done by a ship.[162] This will also apply in relation to claims *in rem* for forfeiture or condemnation of cargo, restoration after seizure, or for droits of admiralty.[163] Freight may be seized if subject to a maritime lien, but this would depend on there being a maritime lien on the ship which earned the freight. In *The Castlegate*, Lord Watson said that:

> . . . the Admiralty Court has never recognised the possibility of there being a proper maritime lien upon freight which is not associated with or founded upon a right to proceed *in rem* against the ship. No process having for its sole object the attachment of cargo in order to enforce a maritime lien for freight can issue from that Court.[164]

It would not be possible to proceed *in rem* against freight separate from the ship and cargo, or ship or cargo, and it is also not possible to proceed *in rem* against the proceeds of freight already paid to the shipowners by the cargo owners or consignees. But where the freight has not yet been paid the cargo may be arrested in respect of the freight payable to the shipowner, even though there is no claim against the cargo itself.

35.53 **The ship** Section 24(1) of the Act provides that:

> 'Ship' includes every description of a vessel used in navigation and (except in the definition of 'port' in section 22(2) and in subsection 2(c) of this section) includes, subject to section 2(3) of the Hovercraft Act, a hovercraft.[165]

In *Ex parte Ferguson & Hutchinson* Blackburn J suggested:

> that every vessel that substantially goes to sea is a 'ship'. I do not mean to say that a little boat going out for a mile or two to sea would be a ship; but where it is its business really and substantially to go to sea, if it is not propelled by oars, it shall be considered a ship for the purpose of this Act. Whenever the vessel does go to sea, whether it be decked or not decked, or whether it goes to sea for the purposes of fishing or anything else, it would be a ship. I take it that this was what the justices thought. The facts stated are, that this vessel, though of small size (of only ten tons burthen, and only twenty-four feet long), yet goes out twenty or thirty miles to sea — does go there almost entirely with sails, does stay out many hours, as the affidavits state, and I think it is probable that it goes out for days and nights. This makes it impossible to say that it is not a sea-going vessel, and consequently a 'ship', coming within the Act without the aid of the interpretation clause.[166]

---

[160] [1981] 2 Lloyd's Rep 534, 537.
[161] Such claims are today thought to be obsolete.
[162] See s 20(2)(j), (r), and (e).
[163] See 20(2)(s).
[164] [1893] AC 38, 54.
[165] A ship is so defined also in the Merchant Shipping Act 1995, s 313.
[166] (1871) LR 6 QB 280, 291.

'Vessel' There is no statutory meaning of the term 'vessel'. In *Steedman v Scofield* Sheen J   **35.54**
said that:

> ... [A] vessel is usually a hollow receptacle for carrying goods or people. In common parlance
> 'vessel' is a word used to refer to craft larger than rowing boats and it includes every descrip-
> tion of watercraft used or capable of being used as a means of transportation on water.[167]

'Used in navigation' This seems to imply that the vessel must be capable of being used in   **35.55**
navigation and the waters upon which she is actually used must be navigable waters. In
Steedman v Scofield Sheen J considered what was meant by the phrase 'used in navigation'
and said:

> Navigation is the nautical art or science of conducting a ship from one place to another. The
> navigator must be able (1) to determine the ship's position and (2) to determine the future
> course or courses to be steered to reach the intended destination. The word 'navigation' is also
> used to describe the action of navigating or ordered movement of ships on water. Hence 'nav-
> igable waters' means waters on which ships can be navigated. To my mind the phrase 'used in
> navigation' conveys the concept of transporting persons or property by water to an intended
> destination. A fishing vessel may go to sea and return to the harbour from which she sailed,
> but that vessel will nevertheless be navigated to her fishing grounds and back again.
> 'Navigation' is not synonymous with movement on water. Navigation is planned or ordered
> movement from one place to another.[168]

On the facts of the case, which concerned a 'jet ski', Sheen J held that, though it may be possible to navigate a 'jet ski', this was not a vessel used in navigation:

> A jet ski is capable of movement on water at very high speed under its own power, but its pur-
> pose is not to go from one place to another.

> It may be possible to navigate a jet ski, but in my judgment it is not a 'vessel used in navigation'.[169]

Similarly, a gas float[170] and a pontoon carrying a crane[171] have also been held as not being
'used in navigation'. However, a mobile offshore drilling rig has been held to be within the
definition.[172]

---

[167] [1992] 2 Lloyd's Rep 163, 166.
[168] ibid.
[169] ibid. This has been confirmed by the Court of Appeal in *R v Goodwin* [2005] EWCA Crim 3184;
[2006] 1 WLR 546.
[170] See *Wells v Owners of the Gas Float Whitton (No 2)* [1897] AC 337.
[171] *Merchants Marine Insurance Co Ltd v North of England P & I Association* (1926) 26 Ll LR 201 (CA).
[172] *Global Marine Drilling Company Ltd v Triton Holdings Ltd (The Sovereign Explorer) (No 1)* (unreported,
Court of Session), available from <www.scotcourts.gov.uk>. There was an appeal, but this did not consider
this issue (reported at [2001] 1 Lloyd's Rep 60).

APPENDIX I

STATUTES

Carriage of Goods by Sea Act 1992 (c 50)

An Act to replace the Bills of Lading Act 1855 with new provision with respect to bills of lading and certain other shipping documents.

Be it enacted by the Queen's most Excellent Majesty, by and with the advice and consent of the Lords Spiritual and Temporal, and Commons, in this present Parliament assembled, and by the authority of the same, as follows:—

1. Shipping documents etc to which Act applies.

(1) This Act applies to the following documents, that is to say—

    (a) any bill of lading;

    (b) any sea waybill; and

    (c) any ship's delivery order.

(2) References in this Act to a bill of lading—

    (a) do not include references to a document which is incapable of transfer either by indorsement or, as a bearer bill, by delivery without indorsement; but

    (b) subject to that, do include references to a received for shipment bill of lading.

(3) References in this Act to a sea waybill are references to any document which is not a bill of lading but—

    (a) is such a receipt for goods as contains or evidences a contract for the carriage of goods by sea; and

    (b) identifies the person to whom delivery of the goods is to be made by the carrier in accordance with that contract.

(4) References in this Act to a ship's delivery order are references to any document which is neither a bill of lading nor a sea waybill but contains an undertaking which—

    (a) is given under or for the purposes of a contract for the carriage by sea of the goods to which the document relates, or of goods which include those goods; and

    (b) is an undertaking by the carrier to a person identified in the document to deliver the goods to which the document relates to that person.

(5) The Secretary of State may by regulations make provision for the application of this Act to cases where a telecommunication system or any other information technology is used for effecting transactions corresponding to—

    (a) the issue of a document to which this Act applies;

    (b) the indorsement, delivery or other transfer of such a document; or

    (c) the doing of anything else in relation to such a document.

(6) Regulations under subsection (5) above may—

    (a) make such modifications of the following provisions of this Act as the Secretary of State considers appropriate in connection with the application of this Act to any case mentioned in that subsection; and

    (b) contain supplemental, incidental, consequential and transitional provision;

and the power to make regulations under that subsection shall be exercisable by statutory instrument subject to annulment in pursuance of a resolution of either House of Parliament.

2. Rights under shipping documents

(1) Subject to the following provisions of this section, a person who becomes—

    (a) the lawful holder of a bill of lading;

(b) the person who (without being an original party to the contract of carriage) is the person to whom delivery of the goods to which a sea waybill relates is to be made by the carrier in accordance with that contract; or

(c) the person to whom delivery of the goods to which a ship's delivery order relates is to be made in accordance with the undertaking contained in the order,

shall (by virtue of becoming the holder of the bill or, as the case may be, the person to whom delivery is to be made) have transferred to and vested in him all rights of suit under the contract of carriage as if he had been a party to that contract.

(2) Where, when a person becomes the lawful holder of a bill of lading, possession of the bill no longer gives a right (as against the carrier) to possession of the goods to which the bill relates, that person shall not have any rights transferred to him by virtue of subsection (1) above unless he becomes the holder of the bill—

(a) by virtue of a transaction effected in pursuance of any contractual or other arrangements made before the time when such a right to possession ceased to attach to possession of the bill; or

(b) as a result of the rejection to that person by another person of goods or documents delivered to the other person in pursuance of any such arrangements.

(3) The rights vested in any person by virtue of the operation of subsection (1) above in relation to a ship's delivery order—

(a) shall be so vested subject to the terms of the order; and

(b) where the goods to which the order relates form a part only of the goods to which the contract of carriage relates, shall be confined to rights in respect of the goods to which the order relates.

(4) Where, in the case of any document to which this Act applies—

(a) a person with any interest or right in or in relation to goods to which the document relates sustains loss or damage in consequence of a breach of the contract of carriage; but

(b) subsection (1) above operates in relation to that document so that rights of suit in respect of that breach are vested in another person,

the other person shall be entitled to exercise those rights for the benefit of the person who sustained the loss or damage to the same extent as they could have been exercised if they had been vested in the person for whose benefit they are exercised.

(5) Where rights are transferred by virtue of the operation of subsection (1) above in relation to any document, the transfer for which that subsection provides shall extinguish any entitlement to those rights which derives—

(a) where that document is a bill of lading, from a person's having been an original party to the contract of carriage; or

(b) in the case of any document to which this Act applies, from the previous operation of that subsection in relation to that document;

but the operation of that subsection shall be without prejudice to any rights which derive from a person's having been an original party to the contract contained in, or evidenced by, a sea waybill and, in relation to a ship's delivery order, shall be without prejudice to any rights deriving otherwise than from the previous operation of that subsection in relation to that order.

3. Liabilities under shipping documents

(1) Where subsection (1) of section 2 of this Act operates in relation to any document to which this Act applies and the person in whom rights are vested by virtue of that subsection—

(a) takes or demands delivery from the carrier of any of the goods to which the document relates;

(b) makes a claim under the contract of carriage against the carrier in respect of any of those goods; or

(c) is a person who, at a time before those rights were vested in him, took or demanded delivery from the carrier of any of those goods, that person shall (by virtue of taking or demanding delivery or making the claim or, in a case falling within paragraph (c) above, of having the rights vested in him) become subject to the same liabilities under that contract as if he had been a party to that contract.

(2) Where the goods to which a ship's delivery order relates form a part only of the goods to which the contract of carriage relates, the liabilities to which any person is subject by virtue of the operation of this section in relation to that order shall exclude liabilities in respect of any goods to which the order does not relate.

(3) This section, so far as it imposes liabilities under any contract on any person, shall be without prejudice to the liabilities under the contract of any person as an original party to the contract.

4. Representations in bills of lading

A bill of lading which—

(a) represents goods to have been shipped on board a vessel or to have been received for shipment on board a vessel; and

(b) has been signed by the master of the vessel or by a person who was not the master but had the express, implied or apparent authority of the carrier to sign bills of lading,

shall, in favour of a person who has become the lawful holder of the bill, be conclusive evidence against the carrier of the shipment of the goods or, as the case may be, of their receipt for shipment.

5. Interpretation etc

(1) In this Act—

'bill of lading', 'sea waybill' and 'ship's delivery order' shall be construed in accordance with section 1 above;

'the contract of carriage'—

(a) in relation to a bill of lading or sea waybill, means the contract contained in or evidenced by that bill or waybill; and

(b) in relation to a ship's delivery order, means the contract under or for the purposes of which the undertaking contained in the order is given;

'holder', in relation to a bill of lading, shall be construed in accordance with subsection (2) below;

'information technology' includes any computer or other technology by means of which information or other matter may be recorded or communicated without being reduced to documentary form; and

'telecommunication system' has the same meaning as in the [1984 c 12] Telecommunications Act 1984.

(2) References in this Act to the holder of a bill of lading are references to any of the following persons, that is to say—

(a) a person with possession of the bill who, by virtue of being the person identified in the bill, is the consignee of the goods to which the bill relates;

(b) a person with possession of the bill as a result of the completion, by delivery of the bill, of any indorsement of the bill or, in the case of a bearer bill, of any other transfer of the bill;

(c) a person with possession of the bill as a result of any transaction by virtue of which he would have become a holder falling within paragraph (a) or (b) above had not the transaction been effected at a time when possession of the bill no longer gave a right (as against the carrier) to possession of the goods to which the bill relates;

and a person shall be regarded for the purposes of this Act as having become the lawful holder of a bill of lading wherever he has become the holder of the bill in good faith.

(3) References in this Act to a person's being identified in a document include references to his being identified by a description which allows for the identity of the person in question to be varied, in accordance with the terms of the document, after its issue; and the reference in section 1 (3)(b) of this Act to a document's identifying a person shall be construed accordingly.

(4) Without prejudice to sections 2(2) and 4 above, nothing in this Act shall preclude its operation in relation to a case where the goods to which a document relates—

(a) cease to exist after the issue of the document; or

(b) cannot be identified (whether because they are mixed with other goods or for any other reason);

and references in this Act to the goods to which a document relates shall be construed accordingly.

(5) The preceding provisions of this Act shall have effect without prejudice to the application, in relation to any case, of the rules (the Hague–Visby Rules) which for the time being have the force of law by virtue of section 1 of the [1971 c 19] Carriage of Goods by Sea Act 1971.

6. Short title, repeal, commencement and extent

(1) This Act may be cited as the Carriage of Goods by Sea Act 1992.

(2) The [1855 c 111] Bills of Lading Act 1855 is hereby repealed.

(3) This Act shall come into force at the end of the period of two months beginning with the day on which it is passed; but nothing in this Act shall have effect in relation to any document issued before the coming into force of this Act.

(4) This Act extends to Northern Ireland.

Carriage of Goods by Sea Act 1971 (c 19)

An Act to amend the law with respect to the carriage of goods by sea.

1. Application of Hague Rules as amended

(1) In this Act, 'the Rules' means the International Convention for the unification of certain rules of law relating to bills of lading signed at Brussels on 25th August 1924, as amended by the Protocol signed at Brussels on 23rd February 1968 [and by the Protocol signed at Brussels on 21st December 1979].

(2) The provisions of the Rules, as set out in the Schedule to this Act, shall have the force of law.

(3) Without prejudice to subsection (2) above, the said provisions shall have effect (and have the force of law) in relation to and in connection with the carriage of goods by sea in ships where the port of shipment is a port in the United Kingdom, whether or not the carriage is between ports in two different States within the meaning of Article X of the Rules.

(4) Subject to subsection (6) below, nothing in this section shall be taken as applying anything in the Rules to any contract for the carriage of goods by sea, unless the contract expressly or by implication provides for the use of a bill of lading or any similar document of title.

(5) ...

(6) Without prejudice to Article X (c) of the rules, the Rules shall have the force of law in relation to—

(a) any bill of lading if the contract contained in or evidenced by it expressly provides that the Rules shall govern the contract, and

(b) any receipt which is a non-negotiable document marked as such if the contract contained in or evidenced by it is a contract for the carriage of goods by sea which expressly provides that the Rules are to govern the contract as if the receipt were a bill of lading.

but subject, where paragraph (b) applies, to any necessary modifications and in particular with the omission in Article III of the Rules of the second sentence of paragraph 4 and of paragraph 7.

(7) If and so far as the contract contained in or evidenced by a bill of lading or receipt within paragraph (a) or (b) of subsection (6) above applies to deck cargo or live animals, the Rules as given the force of law by that subsection shall have effect as if Article I(c) did not exclude deck cargo and live animals.

In this subsection 'deck cargo' means cargo which by the contract of carriage is stated as being carried on deck and is so carried.

1A. Conversion of special drawing rights into sterling

(1) For the purposes of Article IV of the Rules the value on a particular day of one special drawing right shall be treated as equal to such a sum in sterling as the International Monetary Fund have fixed as being the equivalent of one special drawing right—

(a) for that day; or

(b) if no sum has been so fixed for that day, for the last day before that day for which a sum has been so fixed.

(2) A certificate given by or on behalf of the Treasury stating—

(a) that a particular sum in sterling has been fixed as aforesaid for a particular day; or

(b) that no sum has been so fixed for a particular day and that a particular sum in sterling has been so fixed for a day which is the last day for which a sum has been so fixed before the particular day,

shall be conclusive evidence of those matters for the purposes of subsection (1) above; and a document purporting to be such a certificate shall in any proceedings be received in evidence and, unless the contrary is proved, be deemed to be such a certificate.

(3) The Treasury may charge a reasonable fee for any certificate given in pursuance of subsection (2) above, and any fee received by the Treasury by virtue of this subsection shall be paid into the Consolidated Fund.

2. Contracting States, etc

(1) If Her Majesty by Order in Council certifies to the following effect, that is to say, that for the purposes of the Rules—

    (a) a State specified in the Order is a contracting State, or is a contracting State in respect of any place or territory so specified; or

    (b) any place or territory specified in the Order forms part of a State so specified (whether a contracting State or not),

the Order shall, except so far as it has been superseded by a subsequent Order, be conclusive evidence of the matters so certified.

(2) An Order in Council under this section may be varied or revoked by a subsequent Order in Council.

3. Absolute warranty of seaworthiness not to be implied in contracts to which Rules apply

There shall not be implied in any contract for the carriage of goods by sea to which the Rules apply by virtue of this Act any absolute undertaking by the carrier of the goods to provide a seaworthy ship.

4. Application of Act to British possessions, etc

(1) Her Majesty may by Order in Council direct that this Act shall extend, subject to such exceptions, adaptations and modifications as may be specified in the Order, to all or any of the following territories, that is—

    (a) any colony (not being a colony for whose external relations a country other than the United Kingdom is responsible),

    (b) any country outside Her Majesty's dominions in which Her Majesty has jurisdiction in right of Her Majesty's Government of the United Kingdom.

(2) An Order in Council under this section may contain such transitional and other consequential and incidental provisions as appear to Her Majesty to be expedient, including provisions amending or repealing any legislation about the carriage of goods by sea forming part of the law of any of the territories mentioned in paragraph (a) and (b) above.

(3) An Order in Council under this section may be varied or revoked by a subsequent Order in Council.

5. Extension of application of Rules to carriage from ports in British possessions, etc

(1) Her Majesty may by Order in Council provide that section 1(3) of this Act shall have effect as if the reference therein to the United Kingdom included a reference to all or any of the following territories, that is—

    (a) the Isle of Man;

    (b) any of the Channel Islands specified in the Order;

    (c) any colony specified in the Order (not being a colony for whose external relations a country other than the United Kingdom is responsible);

    (d) . . .

    (e) any country specified in the Order, being a country outside Her Majesty's dominions in which Her Majesty has jurisdiction in right of Her Majesty's Government of the United Kingdom.

(2) An Order in Council under this section may be varied or revoked by a subsequent Order in Council.

6. Supplemental

(1) This Act may be cited as the Carriage of Goods by Sea Act 1971.

(2) It is hereby declared that this Act extends to Northern Ireland.

(3) The following enactments shall be repealed, that is—

    (a) the Carriage of Goods by Sea Act 1924,

    (b) section 12(4)(a) of the Nuclear Installations Act 1965,

and without prejudice to section 38(1) of the Interpretation Act 1889, the reference to the said Act of 1924 in section 1(1)(i) (ii) of the Hovercraft Act 1968 shall include a reference to this Act.

(4) It is hereby declared that for the purposes of Article VIII of the Rules section 186 of the Merchant Shipping Act 1995 (which entirely exempts shipowners and others in certain circumstances for loss of, or damage to, goods) is a provision relating to limitation of liability.

(5) This Act shall come into force on such day as Her Majesty may by Order in Council appoint, and, for the purposes of the transition from the law in force immediately before the day appointed under this subsection to the provisions of this Act, the Order appointing the day may provide that those provisions shall have effect subject to such transitional provisions as may be contained in the Order.

Schedule (s 1)
The Hague Rules as Amended by the Brussels Protocol 1968

Article I

In these Rules the following words are employed, with the meanings set out below:—

(a) 'Carrier' includes the owner or the charterer who enters into a contract of carriage with a shipper.

(b) 'Contract of carriage' applies only to contracts of carriage covered by a bill of lading or any similar document of title, in so far as such document relates to the carriage of goods by sea, including any bill of lading or any similar document as aforesaid issued under or pursuant to a charterparty from the moment at which such bill of lading or similar document of title regulates the relations between a carrier and a holder of the same.

(c) 'Goods' includes goods, wares, merchandise, and articles of every kind whatsoever except live animals and cargo which by the contract of carriage is stated as being carried on deck and is so carried.

(d) 'Ship' means any vessel used for the carriage of goods by sea.

(e) 'Carriage of goods' covers the period from the time when the goods are loaded on to the time they are discharged from the ship.

Article II

Subject to the provisions of Article VI, under every contract of carriage of goods by sea the carrier, in relation to the loading, handling, stowage, carriage, custody, care and discharge of such goods, shall be subject to the responsibilities and liabilities, and entitled to the rights and immunities hereinafter set forth.

Article III

1. The carrier shall be bound before and at the beginning of the voyage to exercise due diligence to—

   (a) Make the ship seaworthy.
   (b) Properly man, equip and supply the ship.
   (c) Make the holds, refrigerating and cool chambers, and all other parts of the ship in which goods are carried, fit and safe for their reception, carriage and preservation.

2. Subject to the provisions of Article IV, the carrier shall properly and carefully load, handle, stow, carry, keep, care for, and discharge the goods carried.

3. After receiving the goods into his charge the carrier or the master or agent of the carrier shall, on demand of the shipper, issue to the shipper a bill of lading showing among other things—

   (a) The leading marks necessary for identification of the goods are the same are furnished in writing by the shipper before the loading of such goods starts, provided such marks are stamped or otherwise shown clearly upon the goods if uncovered, or on the cases or coverings in which such goods are contained, in such a manner as should ordinarily remain legible until the end of the voyage.

   (b) Either the number of packages or pieces, or the quantity, or weight, as the case may be, as furnished in writing by the shipper.

   (c) The apparent order and condition of the goods.

Provided that no carrier, master or agent of the carrier shall be bound to state or show in the bill of lading any marks, number, quantity, or weight which he has reasonable ground for suspecting not accurately to represent the goods actually received, or which he has had no reasonable means of checking.

4. Such a bill of lading shall be *prima facie* evidence of the receipt by the carrier of the goods as therein described in accordance with paragraph 3(a), (b) and (c). However, proof to the contrary shall not be admissible when the bill of lading has been transferred to a third party acting in good faith.

5. The shipper shall be deemed to have guaranteed to the carrier the accuracy at the time of shipment of the marks, number, quantity and weight, as furnished by him, and the shipper shall indemnify the carrier against all loss, damages and expenses arising or resulting from inaccuracies in such particulars. The right of the carrier to such indemnity shall in no way limit his responsibility and liability under the contract of carriage to any person other than the shipper.

6. Unless notice of loss or damage and the general nature of such loss or damage be given in writing to the carrier or his agent at the port of discharge before or at the time of the removal of the goods into the custody of the person entitled to delivery thereof under the contract of carriage, or, if the loss or damage be not apparent, within three days, such removal shall be *prima facie* evidence of the delivery by the carrier of the goods as described in the bill of lading.

The notice in writing need not be given if the state of the goods has, at the time of their receipt, been the subject of joint survey or inspection.

Subject to paragraph 6 bis the carrier and the ship shall in any event be discharged from all liability whatsoever in respect of the goods, unless suit is brought within one year of their delivery or of the date when they should have been delivered. This period may, however, be extended if the parties so agree after the cause of action has arisen.

In the case of any actual or apprehended loss or damage the carrier and the receiver shall give all reasonable facilities to each other for inspecting and tallying the goods.

6 bis. An action for indemnity against a third person may be brought even after the expiration of the year provided for in the preceding paragraph if brought within the time allowed by the law of the Court seized of the case. However, the time allowed shall be not less than three months, commencing from the day when the person bringing such action for indemnity has settled the claim or has been served with process in the action against himself.

7. After the goods are loaded the bill of lading to be issued by the carrier, master, or agent of the carrier, to the shipper shall, if the shipper so demands, be a 'shipped' bill of lading, provided that if the shipper shall have previously taken up any document of title to such goods, he shall surrender the same as against the issue of the 'shipped' bill of lading, but at the option of the carrier such document of title may be noted at the port of shipment by the carrier, master, or agent with the name or names of the ship or ships upon which the goods have been shipped and the date or dates of shipment, and when so noted, if it shows the particulars mentioned in paragraph 3 of Article III shall for the purposes of this article be deemed to constitute a 'shipped' bill of lading.

8. Any clause, covenant, or agreement in a contract of carriage relieving the carrier or the ship from liability for loss or damage to, or in connection with, goods arising from negligence, fault, or failure in the duties and obligations provided in this article or lessening such liability otherwise than as provided in these Rules, shall be null and void and of no effect. A benefit of insurance in favour of the carrier or similar clause shall be deemed to be a clause relieving the carrier from liability.

Article IV

1. Neither the carrier nor the ship shall be liable for loss or damage arising or resulting from unseaworthiness unless caused by want of due diligence on the part of the carrier to make the ship seaworthy, and to secure that the ship is properly manned, equipped and supplied, and to make the holds, refrigerating

and cool chambers and all other parts of the ship in which goods are carried fit and safe for their reception, carriage and preservation in accordance with the provisions of paragraph 1 of Article III. Whenever loss or damage has resulted from unseaworthiness the burden of proving the exercise of due diligence shall be on the carrier or other person claiming exemption under this article.

2. Neither the carrier nor the ship shall be responsible for loss or damage arising or resulting from—

   (a) Act, neglect, or default of the master, mariner, pilot, or the servants of the carrier in the navigation or in the management of the ship.
   (b) Fire, unless caused by the actual fault or privity of the carrier.
   (c) Perils, dangers and accidents of the sea or other navigable waters.
   (d) Act of God.
   (e) Act of war.
   (f) Act of public enemies.
   (g) Arrest or restraint of princes, rulers or people, or seizure under legal process.
   (h) Quarantine restrictions.
   (i) Act or omission of the shipper or owner of the goods, his agent or representative.
   (j) Strikes or lockouts or stoppage or restraint of labour from whatever cause, whether partial or general.
   (k) Riots and civil commotions.
   (l) Saving or attempting to save life or property at sea.
   (m) Wastage in bulk or weight or any other loss or damage arising from inherent defect, quality or vice of the goods.
   (n) Insufficiency of packing.
   (o) Insufficiency or inadequacy of marks.
   (p) Latent defects not discoverable by due diligence.
   (q) Any other cause arising without the actual fault or privity of the carrier, or without the fault or neglect of the agents or servants of the carrier, but the burden of proof shall be on the person claiming the benefit of this exception to show that neither the actual fault or privity of the carrier nor the fault or neglect of the agents or servants of the carrier contributed to the loss or damage.

3. The shipper shall not be responsible for loss or damage sustained by the carrier or the ship arising or resulting from any cause without the act, fault or neglect of the shipper, his agents or his servants.

4. Any deviation in saving or attempting to save life or property at sea or any reasonable deviation shall not be deemed to be an infringement or breach of these Rules or of the contract of carriage, and the carrier shall not be liable for any loss or damage resulting therefrom.

5. (a) Unless the nature and value of such goods have been declared by the shipper before shipment and inserted in the bill of lading, neither the carrier nor the ship shall in any event be or become liable for any loss or damage to or in connection with the goods in an amount exceeding 666.67 units of account per package or unit or 2 units of account per kilogramme of gross weight of the goods lost or damaged, whichever is the higher.

   (b) The total amount recoverable shall be calculated by reference to the value of such goods at the place and time at which the goods are discharged from the ship in accordance with the contract or should have been so discharged.
   The value of the goods shall be fixed according to the commodity exchange price, or, if there be no such price, according to the current market price, or, if there be no commodity exchange price or current market price, by reference to the normal value of goods of the same kind and quality.

   (c) Where a container, pallet or similar article of transport is used to consolidate goods, the number of packages or units enumerated in the bill of lading as packed in such article of transport shall be deemed the number of packages or units for the purpose of this paragraph as far as these packages or units are concerned. Except as aforesaid such article of transport shall be considered the package or unit.

   (d) The unit of account mentioned in this Article is the special drawing right as defined by the International Monetary Fund. The amounts mentioned in sub-paragraph (a) of this paragraph shall be converted into national currency on the basis of the value of that currency on a date to be determined by the law of the Court seized of the case.

    (e) Neither the carrier nor the ship shall be entitled to the benefit of the limitation of liability provided for in this paragraph if it is proved that the damage resulted from an act or omission of the carrier done with intent to cause damage, or recklessly and with knowledge that damage would probably result.

    (f) The declaration mentioned in sub-paragraph (a) of this paragraph, if embodied in the bill of lading, shall be *prima facie* evidence, but shall not be binding or conclusive on the carrier.

    (g) By agreement between the carrier, master or agent of the carrier and the shipper other maximum amounts than those mentioned in sub-paragraph (a) of this paragraph may be fixed, provided that no maximum amount so fixed shall be less than the appropriate maximum mentioned in that sub-paragraph.

    (h) Neither the carrier nor the ship shall be responsible in any event for loss or damage to, or in connection with, goods if the nature or value thereof has been knowingly mis-stated by the shipper in the bill of lading.

6. Goods of an inflammable, explosive or dangerous nature to the shipment whereof the carrier, master or agent of the carrier has not consented with knowledge of their nature and character, may at any time before discharge be landed at any place, or destroyed or rendered innocuous by the carrier without compensation and the shipper of such goods shall be liable for all damages and expenses directly or indirectly arising out of or resulting from such shipment. If any such goods shipped with such knowledge and consent shall become a danger to the ship or cargo, they may in like manner be landed at any place, or destroyed or rendered innocuous by the carrier without liability on the part of the carrier except to general average, if any.

Article IV bis

1. The defences and limits of liability provided for in these Rules shall apply in any action against the carrier in respect of loss or damage to goods covered by a contract of carriage whether the action be founded in contract or in tort.
2. If such an action is brought against a servant or agent of the carrier (such servant or agent not being an independent contractor), such servant or agent shall be entitled to avail himself of the defences and limits of liability which the carrier is entitled to invoke under these Rules.
3. The aggregate of the amounts recoverable from the carrier, and such servants and agents, shall in no case exceed the limit provided for in these Rules.
4. Nevertheless, a servant or agent of the carrier shall not be entitled to avail himself of the provisions of this article, if it is proved that the damage resulted from an act or omission of the servant or agent done with intent to cause damage or recklessly and with knowledge that damage would probably result.

Article V

A carrier shall be at liberty to surrender in whole or in part all or any of his rights and immunities or to increase any of his responsibilities and obligations under these Rules, provided such surrender or increase shall be embodied in the bill of lading issued to the shipper. The provisions of these Rules shall not be applicable to charter-parties, but if bills of lading are issued in the case of a ship under a charter-party they shall comply with the terms of these Rules. Nothing in these Rules shall be held to prevent the insertion in a bill of lading of any lawful provision regarding general average.

Article VI

Notwithstanding the provisions of the preceding articles, a carrier, master or agent of the carrier and a shipper shall in regard to any particular goods be at liberty to enter into any agreement in any terms as to the responsibility and liability of the carrier for such goods, and as to the rights and immunities of the carrier in respect of such goods, or his obligation as to seaworthiness, so far as this stipulation is not contrary to public policy, or the care or diligence of his servants or agents in regard to the loading, handling, stowage, carriage, custody, care and discharge of the goods carried by sea, provided that in this case no bill of lading has been or shall be issued and that the terms agreed shall be embodied in a receipt which shall be a non-negotiable document and shall be marked as such.

Any agreement so entered into shall have full legal effect.

Provided that this article shall not apply to ordinary commercial shipments made in the ordinary course of trade, but only to other shipments where the character or condition of the property to be carried or the circumstances, terms and conditions under which the carriage is to be performed are such as reasonably to justify a special agreement.

Article VII

Nothing herein contained shall prevent a carrier or a shipper from entering into any agreement, stipulation, condition, reservation or exemption as to the responsibility and liability of the carrier or the ship for the loss or damage to, or in connection with, the custody and care and handling of goods prior to the loading on, and subsequent to the discharge from, the ship on which the goods are carried by sea.

Article VIII

The provisions of these Rules shall not affect the rights and obligations of the carrier under any statute for the time being in force relating to the limitation of the liability of owners of sea-going vessels.

Article IX

These Rules shall not affect the provisions of any international Convention or national law governing liability for nuclear damage.

Article X

The provisions of these Rules shall apply to every bill of lading relating to the carriage of goods between ports in two different States if:

(a) the bill of lading is issued in a contracting State, or

(b) the carriage is from a port in a contracting State, or

(c) the contract contained in or evidenced by the bill of lading provides that these Rules or legislation of any State giving effect to them are to govern the contract,

whatever may be the nationality of the ship, the carrier, the shipper, the consignee, or any other interested person.

APPENDIX II

STANDARD FORMS

605

Page 1

<table>
<tr><td>Shipper (full style and address)</td><td colspan="2">**BIMCO LINER BILL OF LADING**
CODE NAME: 'CONLINEBILL 2000'

Amended January 1950; August 1952; January 1973;
July 1974; August 1976; January 1978; November 2000.</td></tr>
<tr><td rowspan="2">Consignee (full style and address) or Order</td><td>B/L No.</td><td>Reference No.</td></tr>
<tr><td colspan="2">Vessel</td></tr>
<tr><td rowspan="2">Notify Party (full style and address)</td><td colspan="2">Port of loading</td></tr>
<tr><td colspan="2">Port of discharge</td></tr>
</table>

PARTICULARS DECLARED BY THE SHIPPER BUT NOT ACKNOWLEDGED BY THE CARRIER

Container No./Seal No./Marks and Numbers	Number and kind of packages; description of cargo	Gross weight, kg	Measurement, m³

SHIPPED on board in apparent good order and condition (unless otherwise stated herein) the total number of Containers/Packages or Units indicated in the Box opposite entitled 'Total number of Containers/Packages or Units received by the Carrier' and the cargo as specified above, weight, measure, marks, numbers, quality, contents and value unknown, for carriage to the Port of discharge or so near thereunto as the vessel may safely get and lie always afloat, to be delivered in the like good order and condition at the Port of discharge unto the lawful holder of the Bill of Lading, on payment of freight as indicated to the right plus other charges incurred in accordance with the provisions contained in this Bill of Lading. In accepting this Bill of Lading the Merchant* expressly accepts and agrees to all its stipulations on both Page 1 and Page 2, whether written, printed, stamped or otherwise incorporated, as fully as if they were all signed by the Merchant. One original Bill of Lading must be surrendered duly endorsed in exchange for the cargo or delivery order, whereupon all other Bills of Lading to be void. IN WITNESS whereof the Carrier, Master or their Agent has signed the number of original Bills of Lading stated below right, all of this tenor and date.

Total number of Containers/Packages or Units received by the Carrier

Shipper's declared value	Declared value charge

Freight details and charges

Carrier's name/principal place of business	Date shipped on board	Place and date of issue
	Number of original Bills of Lading	
	Pre-carriage by**	

Signature	Place of receipt by pre-carrier**
.... Carrier or, for the Carrier .... as Master (Master's name/signature) .... as Agents (Agent's name/signature)	
	Place of delivery by on-carrier**

*As defined hereinafter (Cl. 1)
**Applicable only when pre-/on-carriage is arranged in accordance with Clause 8

Printed and sold by Fr. G. Knudtzons Bogtrykkeri A/S, Vallensbaekvej 61, DK-2625 Vallensbaek, Fax: +45 4366 0701
by authority of The Baltic and International Maritime Council (BIMCO), Copenhagen

BIMCO LINER BILL OF LADING

Code Name: 'CONLINEBILL 2000'

1. Definition.
'Merchant' includes the shipper, the receiver, the consignor, the consignee, the holder of the Bill of Lading, the owner of the cargo and any person entitled to possession of the cargo.

2. Notification.
Any mention in this Bill of Lading of parties to be notified of the arrival of the cargo is solely for the information of the Carrier and failure to give such notification shall not involve the Carrier in any liability nor relieve the Merchant of any obligation hereunder.

3. Liability for Carriage Between Port of Loading and Port of Discharge.
(a) The International Convention for the Unification of Certain Rules of Law relating to Bills of Lading signed at Brussels on 25 August 1924 ('the Hague Rules') as amended by the Protocol signed at Brussels on 23 February 1968 ('the Hague-Visby Rules') and as enacted in the country of shipment shall apply to this Contract. When the Hague-Visby Rules are not enacted in the country of shipment, the corresponding legislation of the country of destination shall apply, irrespective of whether such legislation may only regulate outbound shipments.
When there is no enactment of the Hague-Visby Rules in either the country of shipment or in the country of destination, the Hague-Visby Rules shall apply to this Contract save where the Hague Rules as enacted in the country of shipment or, if no such enactment is in place, the Hague Rules as enacted in the country of destination apply compulsorily to this Contract. The Protocol signed at Brussels on 21 December 1979 ("the SDR Protocol 1979") shall apply where the Hague-Visby Rules apply, whether mandatorily or by this Contract.
The Carrier shall in no case be responsible for loss of or damage to cargo arising prior to loading, after discharging, or with respect to deck cargo and live animals.
(b) If the Carrier is held liable in respect of delay, consequential loss or damage other than loss of or damage to the cargo, the liability of the Carrier shall be limited to the freight for the carriage covered by this Bill of Lading, or to the limitation amount as determined in sub-clause 3(a), whichever is the lesser.
(c) The aggregate liability of the Carrier and/or any of his servants, agents or independent contractors under this Contract shall, in no circumstances, exceed the limits of liability for the total loss of the cargo under sub-clause 3(a) or, if applicable, the Additional Clause.

4. Law and Jurisdiction.
Disputes arising out of or in connection with this Bill of Lading shall be exclusively determined by the courts and in accordance with the law of the place where the Carrier has his principal place of business, as stated on Page 1, except as provided elsewhere herein.

5. The Scope of Carriage.
The intended carriage shall not be limited to the direct route but shall be deemed to include any proceeding or returning to or stopping or slowing down at or off any ports or places for any reasonable purpose connected with the carriage including bunkering, loading, discharging, or other cargo operations and maintenance of Vessel and crew.

6. Substitution of Vessel.
The Carrier shall be at liberty to carry the cargo or part thereof to the Port of discharge by the said or other vessel or vessels either belonging to the Carrier or others, or by other means of transport, proceeding either directly or indirectly to such port.

7. Transhipment.
The Carrier shall be at liberty to tranship, lighter, land and store the cargo either on shore or afloat and reship and forward the same to the Port of discharge.

8. Liability for Pre- and On-Carriage.
When the Carrier arranges pre-carriage of the cargo from a place other than the Vessel's Port of loading or on-carriage of the cargo to a place other than the Vessel's Port of discharge, the Carrier shall contract as the Merchant's Agent only and the Carrier shall not be liable for any loss or damage arising during any part of the carriage other than between the Port of loading and the Port of discharge even though the freight for the whole carriage has been collected by him.

9. Loading and Discharging.
(a) Loading and discharging of the cargo shall be arranged by the Carrier or his Agent.
(b) The Merchant shall, at his risk and expense, handle and/or store the cargo before loading and after discharging.
(c) Loading and discharging may commence without prior notice.
(d) The Merchant or his Agent shall tender the cargo when the Vessel is ready to load and as fast as the Vessel can receive including, if required by the Carrier, outside ordinary working hours notwithstanding any custom of the port. If the Merchant or his Agent fails to tender the cargo when the Vessel is ready to load or fails to load as fast as the Vessel can receive the cargo, the Carrier shall be relieved of any obligation to load such cargo, the Vessel shall be entitled to leave the port without further notice and the Merchant shall be liable to the Carrier for deadfreight and/or any overtime charges, losses, costs and expenses incurred by the Carrier.
(e) The Merchant or his Agent shall take delivery of the cargo as fast as the Vessel can discharge including, if required by the Carrier, outside ordinary working hours notwithstanding

any custom of the port. If the Merchant or his Agent fails to take delivery of the cargo the Carrier's discharging of the cargo shall be deemed fulfilment of the contract of carriage. Should the cargo not be applied for within a reasonable time, the Carrier may sell the same privately or by auction. If the Merchant or his Agent fails to take delivery of the cargo as fast as the Vessel can discharge, the Merchant shall be liable to the Carrier for any overtime charges, losses, costs and expenses incurred by the Carrier.
(f) The Merchant shall accept his reasonable proportion of unidentified loose cargo.

10. Freight, Charges, Costs, Expenses, Duties, Taxes and Fines.
(a) Freight, whether paid or not, shall be considered as fully earned upon loading and non-returnable in any event. Unless otherwise specified, freight and/or charges under this Contract are payable by the Merchant to the Carrier on demand. Interest at Libor (or its successor) plus 2 per cent. shall run from fourteen days after the date when freight and charges are payable.
(b) The Merchant shall be liable for all costs and expenses of fumigation, gathering and sorting loose cargo and weighing onboard, repairing damage to and replacing packing due to excepted causes, and any extra handling of the cargo for any of the aforementioned reasons.
(c) The Merchant shall be liable for any dues, duties, taxes and charges which under any denomination may be levied, *inter alia*, on the basis of freight, weight of cargo or tonnage of the Vessel.
(d) The Merchant shall be liable for all fines, penalties, costs, expenses and losses which the Carrier, Vessel or cargo may incur through non-observance of Customs House and/or import or export regulations.
(e) The Carrier is entitled in case of incorrect declaration of contents, weights, measurements or value of the cargo to claim double the amount of freight which would have been due if such declaration had been correctly given. For the purpose of ascertaining the actual facts, the Carrier shall have the right to obtain from the Merchant the original invoice and to have the cargo inspected and its contents, weight, measurement or value verified.

11. Lien.
The Carrier shall have a lien on all cargo for any amount due under this contract and the costs of recovering the same and shall be entitled to sell the cargo privately or by auction to satisfy any such claims.

12. General Average and Salvage.
General Average shall be adjusted, stated and settled in London according to the York-Antwerp Rules 1994, or any modification thereof, in respect of all cargo, whether carried on or under deck. In the event of accident, danger, damage or disaster before or after commencement of the voyage resulting from any cause whatsoever, whether due to negligence or not, for which or for the consequence of which the Carrier is not responsible by statute, contract or otherwise, the Merchant shall contribute with the Carrier in General Average to the payment of any sacrifice, losses or expenses of a General Average nature that may be made or incurred, and shall pay salvage and special charges incurred in respect of the cargo. If a salving vessel is owned or operated by the Carrier, salvage shall be paid for as fully as if the salving vessel or vessels belonged to strangers.

13. Both-to-Blame Collision Clause.
If the Vessel comes into collision with another vessel as a result of the negligence of the other vessel and any act, negligence or default of the Master, Mariner, Pilot or the servants of the Carrier in the navigation or in the management of the Vessel, the Merchant will indemnify the Carrier against all loss or liability to the other or non-carrying vessel or her Owner in so far as such loss or liability represents loss of or damage to or any claim whatsoever of the owner of the cargo paid or payable by the other or non-carrying vessel or her Owner to the owner of the cargo and set-off, recouped or recovered by the other or non-carrying vessel or her Owner as part of his claim against the carrying vessel or Carrier. The foregoing provisions shall also apply where the Owner, operator or those in charge of any vessel or vessels or objects other than, or in addition to, the colliding vessels or objects are at fault in respect of a collision or contact.

14. Government directions, War, Epidemics, Ice, Strikes, etc.
(a) The Master and the Carrier shall have liberty to comply with any order or directions or recommendations in connection with the carriage under this Contract given by any Government or Authority, or anybody acting or purporting to act on behalf of such Government or Authority, or having under the terms of the insurance on the Vessel the right to give such orders or directions or recommendations.
(b) Should it appear that the performance of the carriage would expose the Vessel or any cargo onboard to risk of seizure, damage or delay, in consequence of war, warlike operations, blockade, riots, civil commotions or piracy, or any person onboard to risk of loss of life or freedom, or that any such risk has increased, the Master may discharge the cargo at the Port of loading or any other safe and convenient port.
(c) Should it appear that epidemics; quarantine; ice; labour troubles, labour obstructions, strikes, lockouts (whether

onboard or on shore); difficulties in loading or discharging would prevent the Vessel from leaving the Port of loading or reaching or entering the Port of discharge or there discharging in the usual manner and departing therefrom, all of which safely and without unreasonable delay, the Master may discharge the cargo at the Port of loading or any other safe and convenient port.
(d) The discharge, under the provisions of this Clause, of any cargo shall be deemed due fulfilment of the contract of carriage.
(e) If in connection with the exercise of any liberty under this Clause any extra expenses are incurred they shall be paid by the Merchant in addition to the freight, together with return freight, if any, and a reasonable compensation for any extra services rendered to the cargo.

15. Defences and Limits of Liability for the Carrier, Servants and Agents.
(a) It is hereby expressly agreed that no servant or agent of the Carrier (which for the purpose of this Clause includes every independent contractor from time to time employed by the Carrier) shall in any circumstances whatsoever be under any liability whatsoever to the Merchant under this Contract of carriage for any loss, damage or delay of whatsoever kind arising or resulting directly or indirectly from any act, neglect or default on his part while acting in the course of or in connection with his employment.
(b) Without prejudice to the generality of the foregoing provisions in this Clause, every exemption from liability, limitation, condition and liberty herein contained and every right, defence and immunity of whatsoever nature applicable to the Carrier or to which the Carrier is entitled, shall also be available and shall extend to protect every such servant and agent of the Carrier acting as aforesaid.
(c) The Merchant undertakes that no claim shall be made against any servant or agent of the Carrier and, if any claim should nevertheless be made, to indemnify the Carrier against all consequences thereof.
(d) For the purpose of all the foregoing provisions of this Clause the Carrier is or shall be deemed to be acting as agent or trustee on behalf of and for the benefit of all persons who might be his servants or agents from time to time and all such persons shall to this extent be or be deemed to be parties to this Contract of carriage.

16. Stowage.
(a) The Carrier shall have the right to stow cargo by means of containers, trailers, transportable tanks, flats, pallets, or similar articles of transport used to consolidate goods.
(b) The Carrier shall have the right to carry containers, trailers, transportable tanks and covered flats, whether stowed by the Carrier or received by him in a stowed condition from the Merchant, on or under deck without notice to the Merchant.

17. Shipper-Packed Containers, trailers, transportable tanks, flats and pallets.
(a) If a container has not been filled, packed or stowed by the Carrier, the Carrier shall not be liable for any loss of or damage to its contents and the Merchant shall cover any loss or expense incurred by the Carrier, if such loss, damage or expense has been caused by:
(i) negligent filling, packing or stowing of the container;
(ii) the contents being unsuitable for carriage in container; or
(iii) the unsuitability or defective condition of the container unless the container has been supplied by the Carrier and the unsuitability or defective condition would not have been apparent upon reasonable inspection at or prior to the time when the container was filled, packed or stowed.
(b) The provisions of sub-clause (i) of this Clause also apply with respect to trailers, transportable tanks, flats and pallets which have not been filled, packed or stowed by the Carrier.
(c) The Carrier does not accept liability for damage due to the unsuitability or defective condition of reefer equipment or trailers supplied by the Merchant.

18. Return of Containers.
(a) Containers, pallets or similar articles of transport supplied by or on behalf of the Carrier shall be returned to the Carrier in the same order and condition as handed over to the Merchant, normal wear and tear excepted, with interiors clean and within the time prescribed in the Carrier's tariff or elsewhere.
(b) The Merchant shall be liable to the Carrier for any loss, damage to, or delay, including demurrage and detention incurred by or sustained to containers, pallets or similar articles of transport during the period between handing over to the Merchant and return to the Carrier.

ADDITIONAL CLAUSE
U.S. Trade. Period of Responsibility.
(i) In case the Contract evidenced by this Bill of Lading is subject to the Carriage of Goods by Sea Act of the United States of America, 1936 (U.S. COGSA), then the provisions stated in said Act shall govern before loading and after discharge and throughout the entire time the cargo is in the Carrier's custody and in which event freight shall be payable on the cargo coming into the Carrier's custody.
(ii) If the U.S. COGSA applies, and unless the nature and value of the cargo has been declared by the shipper before the cargo has been handed over to the Carrier and inserted in this Bill of Lading, the Carrier shall in no event be or become liable for any loss or damage to the cargo in an amount exceeding USD 500 per package or customary freight unit.

CODE NAME: 'CONGENBILL'. EDITION 1994

Shipper

BILL OF LADING
TO BE USED WITH CHARTER-PARTIES

B/L No.

Page 2

Reference No.

Consignee

Notify address

Vessel	Port of loading

Port of discharge

Shipper's description of goods

Gross weight

(of which)

on deck at Shipper's risk; the Carrier not

being responsible for loss or damage howsoever arising)

Freight payable as per
CHARTER-PARTY dated

FREIGHT ADVANCE.
Received on account of freight:

Time used for loading   days   hours.

SHIPPED at the Port of Loading in apparent good order and condition on board the Vessel for carriage to the Port

of Discharge or so near thereto as she may safely get the goods specified above.

Weight, measure, quality, quantity, condition, contents and value unknown.

IN WITNESS whereof the Master or Agent of the said Vessel has signed the number of Bills of Lading indicated below all of this tenor and date, any one of which being accomplished the others shall be void.

FOR CONDITIONS OF CARRIAGE SEE OVERLEAF

Freight payable at	Place and date of issue
Number of original Bs/L	Signature

Printed by the BIMCO Charter Party Editor

BILL OF LADING

TO BE USED WITH CHARTER-PARTIES
CODE NAME: 'CONGENBILL'
EDITION 1994
ADOPTED BY
THE BALTIC AND INTERNATIONAL MARITIME COUNCIL (BIMCO)

Conditions of Carriage

(1) All terms and conditions, liberties and exceptions of the Charter Party, dated as overleaf, including the Law and Arbitration Clause, are herewith incorporated.

(2) **General Paramount Clause.**
(a) The Hague Rules contained in the International Convention for the Unification of certain rules relating to Bills of Lading, dated Brussels the 25th August 1924 as enacted in the country of shipment, shall apply to this Bill of Lading. When no such enactment is in force in the country of shipment, the corresponding legislation of the country of destination shall apply, but in respect of shipments to which no such enactments are compulsorily applicable, the terms of the said Convention shall apply.

(b) Trades where Hague-Visby Rules apply.
In trades where the International Brussels Convention 1924 as amended by the Protocol signed at Brussels on February 23rd 1968 - the Hague-Visby Rules - apply compulsorily, the provisions of the respective legislation shall apply to this Bill of Lading.

(c) The Carrier shall in no case be responsible for loss of or damage to the cargo, howsoever arising prior to loading into and after discharge from the Vessel or while the cargo is in the charge of another Carrier, nor in respect of deck cargo or live animals.

(3) **General Average.**
General Average shall be adjusted, stated and settled according to York-Antwerp Rules 1994, or any subsequent modification thereof, in London unless another place is agreed in the Charter Party.
Cargo's contribution to General Average shall be paid to the Carrier even when such average is the result of a fault, neglect or error of the Master, Pilot or Crew. The Charterers, Shippers and Consignees expressly renounce the Belgian Commercial Code, Part II, Art. 148.

(4) **New Jason Clause.**
In the event of accident, danger, damage or disaster before or after the commencement of the voyage, resulting from any cause whatsoever, whether due to negligence or not, for which, or for the consequence of which, the Carrier is not responsible, by statute, contract or otherwise, the cargo, shippers, consignees or the owners of the cargo shall contribute with the Carrier in General Average to the payment of any sacrifices, losses or expenses of a General Average nature that may be made or incurred and shall pay salvage and special charges incurred in respect of the cargo. If a salving vessel is owned or operated by the Carrier, salvage shall be paid for as fully as if the said salving vessel or vessels belonged to strangers. Such deposit as the Carrier, or his agents, may deem sufficient to cover the estimated contribution of the goods and any salvage and special charges thereon shall, if required, be made by the cargo, shippers, consignees or owners of the goods to the Carrier before delivery.

(5) **Both-to-Blame Collision Clause.**
If the Vessel comes into collision with another vessel as a result of the negligence of the other vessel and any act, neglect or default of the Master, Mariner, Pilot or the servants of the Carrier in the navigation or in the management of the Vessel, the owners of the cargo carried hereunder will indemnify the Carrier against all loss or liability to the other or non-carrying vessel or her owners in so far as such loss or liability represents loss of, or damage to, or any claim whatsoever of the owners of said cargo, paid or payable by the other or non-carrying vessel or her owners to the owners of said cargo and set-off, recouped or recovered by the other or non-carrying vessel or her owners as part of their claim against the carrying Vessel or the Carrier.
The foregoing provisions shall also apply where the owners, operators or those in charge of any vessel or vessels or objects other than, or in addition to, the colliding vessels or objects are at fault in respect of a collision or contact.

For particulars of cargo, freight,
destination, etc., see overleaf.

1. Shipbroker	RECOMMENDED **THE BALTIC AND INTERNATIONAL MARITIME COUNCIL** **UNIFORM GENERAL CHARTER (AS REVISED 1922, 1976 and 1994)** (To be used for trades for which no specially approved form is in force) **CODE NAME: 'GENCON'**
	Part I
	2. Place and date
3. Owners/Place of business (Cl. 1)	4. Charterers/Place of business (Cl. 1)
5. Vessel's name (Cl. 1)	6. GT/NT (Cl. 1)
7. DWT all told on summer load line in metric tons (abt.) (Cl. 1)	8. Present position (Cl. 1)
9. Expected ready to load (abt.) (Cl. 1)	
10. Loading port or place (Cl. 1)	11. Discharging port or place (Cl. 1)
12. Cargo (also state quantity and margin in Owners' option, if agreed; if full and complete cargo not agreed state "part cargo") (Cl. 1)	
13. Freight rate (also state whether freight prepaid or payable on delivery) (Cl. 4)	14. Freight payment (state currency and method of payment; also beneficiary and bank account) (Cl. 4)
15. State if vessel's cargo handling gear shall not be used (Cl. 5)	16. Laytime (if separate laytime for load. and disch. is agreed, fill in a) and b). If total laytime for load. and disch., fill in c) only) (Cl. 6)
17. Shippers/Place of business (Cl. 6)	a) Laytime for loading
18. Agents (loading) (Cl. 6)	b) Laytime for discharging
19. Agents (discharging) (Cl. 6)	c) Total laytime for loading and discharging
20. Demurrage rate and manner payable (loading and discharging) (Cl. 7)	21. Cancelling date (Cl. 9)
	22. General Average to be adjusted at (Cl. 12)
23. Freight Tax (state if for the Owners' account) (Cl. 13 (c))	24. Brokerage commission and to whom payable (Cl. 15)
25. Law and Arbitration (state 19 (a), 19 (b) or 19 (c) of Cl. 19; if 19 (c) agreed also state Place of Arbitration) (if not filled in 19 (a) shall apply) (Cl. 19)	
(a) State maximum amount for small claims/shortened arbitration (Cl. 19)	26. Additional clauses covering special provisions, if agreed

It is mutually agreed that this Contract shall be performed subject to the conditions contained in this Charter Party which shall include Part I as well as Part II. In the event of a conflict of conditions, the provisions of Part I shall prevail over those of Part II to the extent of such conflict.

Signature (Owners)	Signature (Charterers)

Printed by The BIMCO Charter Party Editor

PART II
'Gencon' Charter (As Revised 1922, 1976 and 1994)

1. It is agreed between the party mentioned in Box 3 as the Owners of the Vessel 1
named in Box 5, of the GT/NT indicated in Box 6 and carrying about the number 2
of metric tons of deadweight capacity all told on summer loadline stated in Box 3
7, now in position as stated in Box 8 and expected ready to load under this 4
Charter Party about the date indicated in Box 9, and the party mentioned as the 5
Charterers in Box 4 that: 6
The said Vessel shall, as soon as her prior commitments have been completed, 7
proceed to the loading port(s) or place(s) stated in Box 10 or so near thereto as 8
she may safely get and lie always afloat, and there load a full and complete 9
cargo (if shipment of deck cargo agreed same to be at the Charterers' risk and 10
responsibility) as stated in Box 12, which the Charterers bind themselves to 11
ship, and being so loaded the Vessel shall proceed to the discharging port(s) or 12
place(s) stated in Box 11 as ordered on signing Bills of Lading, or so near 13
thereto as she may safely get and lie always afloat, and there deliver the cargo. 14

2. Owners' Responsibility Clause
The Owners are to be responsible for loss of or damage to the goods or for 16
delay in delivery of the goods only in case the loss, damage or delay has been 17
caused by personal want of due diligence on the part of the Owners or their 18
Manager to make the Vessel in all respects seaworthy and to secure that she is 19
properly manned, equipped and supplied, or by the personal act or default of 20
the Owners or their Manager. 21
And the Owners are not responsible for loss, damage or delay arising from any 22
other cause whatsoever, even from the neglect or default of the Master or crew 23
or some other person employed by the Owners on board or ashore for whose 24
acts they would, but for this Clause, be responsible, or from unseaworthiness of 25
the Vessel on loading or commencement of the voyage or at any time 26
whatsoever. 27

3. Deviation Clause
The Vessel has liberty to call at any port or ports in any order, for any purpose, 29
to sail without pilots, to tow and/or assist Vessels in all situations, and also to 30
deviate for the purpose of saving life and/or property. 31

4. Payment of Freight
(a) The freight at the rate stated in Box 13 shall be paid in cash calculated on the 33
intaken quantity of cargo. 34
(b) *Prepaid.* If according to Box 13 freight is to be paid on shipment, it shall be 35
deemed earned and non-returnable, Vessel and/or cargo lost or not lost. 36
Neither the Owners nor their agents shall be required to sign or endorse bills of 37
lading showing freight prepaid unless the freight due to the Owners has 38
actually been paid. 39
(c) *On delivery.* If according to Box 13 freight, or part thereof, is payable at 40
destination it shall not be deemed earned until the cargo is thus delivered. 41
Notwithstanding the provisions under (a), if freight or part thereof is payable on 42
delivery of the cargo the Charterers shall have the option of paying the freight 43
on delivered weight/quantity provided such option is declared before breaking 44
bulk and the weight/quantity can be ascertained by official weighing machine, 45
joint draft survey or tally. 46
Cash for Vessel's ordinary disbursements at the port of loading to be advanced 47
by the Charterers, if required, at highest current rate of exchange, subject to 48
two (2) per cent to cover insurance and other expenses. 49

5. Loading/Discharging
(a) *Costs/Risks* 51
The cargo shall be brought into the holds, loaded, stowed and/or trimmed, 52
tallied, lashed and/or secured and taken from the holds and discharged by the 53
Charterers, free of any risk, liability and expense whatsoever to the Owners. 54
The Charterers shall provide and lay all dunnage material as required for the 55
proper stowage and protection of the cargo on board, the Owners allowing the 56
use of all dunnage available on board. The Charterers shall be responsible for 57
and pay the cost of removing their dunnage after discharge of the cargo under 58
this Charter Party and time to count until dunnage has been removed. 59
(b) *Cargo Handling Gear* 60
Unless the Vessel is gearless or unless it has been agreed between the parties 61
that the Vessel's gear shall not be used and stated as such in Box 15, the 62
Owners shall throughout the duration of loading/discharging give free use of 63
the Vessel's cargo handling gear and of sufficient motive power to operate all 64
such cargo handling gear. All such equipment to be in good working order. 65
Unless caused by negligence of the stevedores, time lost by breakdown of the 66
Vessel's cargo handling gear or motive power - pro rata the total number of 67
cranes/winches required at that time for the loading/discharging of cargo 68
under this Charter Party - shall not count as laytime or time on demurrage. 69
On request the Owners shall provide free of charge cranemen/winchmen from 70
the crew to operate the Vessel's cargo handling gear, unless local regulations 71
prohibit this, in which latter event shore labourers shall be for the account of the 72
Charterers. Cranemen/winchmen shall be under the Charterers' risk and 73
responsibility and as stevedores to be deemed as their servants but shall 74

always work under the supervision of the Master. 75
(c) *Stevedore Damage* 76
The Charterers shall be responsible for damage (beyond ordinary wear and 77
tear) to any part of the Vessel caused by Stevedores. Such damage shall be 78
notified as soon as reasonably possible by the Master to the Charterers or their 79
agents and to their Stevedores, failing which the Charterers shall not be held 80
responsible. The Master shall endeavour to obtain the Stevedores' written 81
acknowledgement of liability. 82
The Charterers are obliged to repair any stevedore damage prior to completion 83
of the voyage, but must repair stevedore damage affecting the Vessel's 84
seaworthiness or class before the Vessel sails from the port where such 85
damage was caused or found. All additional expenses incurred shall be for the 86
account of the Charterers and any time lost shall be for the account of and shall 87
be paid to the Owners by the Charterers at the demurrage rate. 88

6. Laytime
* *(a) Separate laytime for loading and discharging* 90
The cargo shall be loaded within the number of running days/hours as 91
indicated in Box 16, weather permitting, Sundays and holidays excepted, 92
unless used, in which event time used shall count. 93
The cargo shall be discharged within the number of running days/hours as 94
indicated in Box 16, weather permitting, Sundays and holidays excepted, 95
unless used, in which event time used shall count. 96
* *(b) Total laytime for loading and discharging* 97
The cargo shall be loaded and discharged within the number of total running 98
days/hours as indicated in Box 16, weather permitting, Sundays and holidays 99
excepted, unless used, in which event time used shall count. 100
(c) Commencement of laytime (loading and discharging) 101
Laytime for loading and discharging shall commence at 13.00 hours, if notice of 102
readiness is given up to and including 12.00 hours, and at 06.00 hours next 103
working day if notice given during office hours after 12.00 hours. Notice of 104
readiness at loading port to be given to the Shippers named in Box 17 or if not 105
named, to the Charterers or their agents named in Box 18. Notice of readiness 106
at the discharging port to be given to the Receivers or, if not known, to the 107
Charterers or their agents named in Box 19. 108
If the loading/discharging berth is not available on the Vessel's arrival at or off 109
the port of loading/discharging, the Vessel shall be entitled to give notice of 110
readiness within ordinary office hours on arrival there, whether in free pratique 111
or not, whether customs cleared or not. Laytime or time on demurrage shall 112
then count as if she were in berth and in all respects ready for loading/ 113
discharging provided that the Master warrants that she is in fact ready in all 114
respects. Time used in moving from the place of waiting to the loading/ 115
discharging berth shall not count as laytime. 116
If, after inspection, the Vessel is found not to be ready in all respects to load/ 117
discharge time lost after the discovery thereof until the Vessel is again ready to 118
load/discharge shall not count as laytime. 119
Time used before commencement of laytime shall count. 120
* Indicate alternative (a) or (b) as agreed, in Box 16. 121

7. Demurrage
Demurrage at the loading and discharging port is payable by the Charterers at 123
the rate stated in Box 20 in the manner stated in Box 20 per day or pro rata for 124
any part of a day. Demurrage shall fall due day by day and shall be payable 125
upon receipt of the Owners' invoice. 126
In the event the demurrage is not paid in accordance with the above, the 127
Owners shall give the Charterers 96 running hours written notice to rectify the 128
failure. If the demurrage is not paid at the expiration of this time limit and if the 129
vessel is in or at the loading port, the Owners are entitled at any time to 130
terminate the Charter Party and claim damages for any losses caused thereby. 131

8. Lien Clause
The Owners shall have a lien on the cargo and on all sub-freights payable in 133
respect of the cargo, for freight, deadfreight, demurrage, claims for damages 134
and for all other amounts due under this Charter Party including costs of 135
recovering same. 136

9. Cancelling Clause
(a) Should the Vessel not be ready to load (whether in berth or not) on the 138
cancelling date indicated in Box 21, the Charterers shall have the option of 139
cancelling this Charter Party. 140
(b) Should the Owners anticipate that, despite the exercise of due diligence, 141
the Vessel will not be ready to load by the cancelling date, they shall notify the 142
Charterers thereof without delay stating the expected date of the Vessel's 143
readiness to load and asking whether the Charterers will exercise their option 144
of cancelling the Charter Party, or agree to a new cancelling date. 145
Such option must be declared by the Charterers within 48 running hours after 146
the receipt of the Owners' notice. If the Charterers do not exercise their option 147
of cancelling, then this Charter Party shall be deemed to be amended such that 148

PART II
'Gencon' Charter (As Revised 1922, 1976 and 1994)

the seventh day after the new readiness date stated in the Owners' notification 149
to the Charterers shall be the new cancelling date. 150
The provisions of sub-clause (b) of this Clause shall operate only once, and in 151
case of the Vessel's further delay, the Charterers shall have the option of 152
cancelling the Charter Party as per sub-clause (a) of this Clause. 153

10. Bills of Lading 154
Bills of Lading shall be presented and signed by the Master as per the 155
'Congenbill' Bill of Lading form, Edition 1994, without prejudice to this Charter 156
Party, or by the Owners' agents provided written authority has been given by 157
Owners to the agents, a copy of which is to be furnished to the Charterers. The 158
Charterers shall indemnify the Owners against all consequences or liabilities 159
that may arise from the signing of bills of lading as presented to the extent that 160
the terms or contents of such bills of lading impose or result in the imposition of 161
more onerous liabilities upon the Owners than those assumed by the Owners 162
under this Charter Party. 163

11. Both-to-Blame Collision Clause 164
If the Vessel comes into collision with another vessel as a result of the 165
negligence the other vessel and any act, neglect or default of the Master, 166
Mariner, Pilot or the servants of the Owners in the navigation or in the 167
management of the Vessel, the owners of the cargo carried hereunder will 168
indemnify the Owners against all loss or liability to the other or non-carrying 169
vessel or her owners in so far as such loss or liability represents loss of, or 170
damage to, or any claim whatsoever of the owners of said cargo, paid or 171
payable by the other or non-carrying vessel or her owners to the owners of said 172
cargo and set-off, recouped or recovered by the other or non-carrying vessel 173
or her owners as part of their claim against the carrying Vessel or the Owners. 174
The foregoing provisions shall also apply where the owners, operators or those 175
in charge of any vessel or vessels or objects other than, or in addition to, the 176
colliding vessels or objects are at fault in respect of a collision or contact. 177

12. General Average and New Jason Clause 178
General Average shall be adjusted in London unless otherwise agreed in Box 179
22 according to York-Antwerp Rules 1994 and any subsequent modification 180
thereof. Proprietors of cargo to pay the cargo's share in the general expenses 181
even if same have been necessitated through neglect or default of the Owners' 182
servants (see Clause 2). 183
If General Average is to be adjusted in accordance with the law and practice of 184
the United States of America, the following Clause shall apply: "In the event of 185
accident, danger, damage or disaster before or after the commencement of the 186
voyage, resulting from any cause whatsoever, whether due to negligence or 187
not, for which, or for the consequence of which, the Owners are not 188
responsible, by statute, contract or otherwise, the cargo shippers, consignees 189
or the owners of the cargo shall contribute with the Owners in General Average 190
to the payment of any sacrifices, losses or expenses of a General Average 191
nature that may be made or incurred and shall pay salvage and special charges 192
incurred in respect of the cargo. If a salving vessel is owned or operated by the 193
Owners, salvage shall be paid for as fully as if the said salving vessel or vessels 194
belonged to strangers. Such deposit as the Owners, or their agents, may deem 195
sufficient to cover the estimated contribution of the goods and any salvage and 196
special charges thereon shall, if required, be made by the cargo, shippers, 197
consignees or owners of the goods to the Owners before delivery.". 198

13. Taxes and Dues Clause 199
(a) *On Vessel* -The Owners shall pay all dues, charges and taxes customarily 200
levied on the Vessel, howsoever the amount thereof may be assessed. 201
(b) *On cargo* -The Charterers shall pay all dues, charges, duties and taxes 202
customarily levied on the cargo, howsoever the amount thereof may be 203
assessed. 204
(c) *On freight* -Unless otherwise agreed in Box 23, taxes levied on the freight 205
shall be for the Charterers' account. 206

14. Agency 207
In every case the Owners shall appoint their own Agent both at the port of 208
loading and the port of discharge. 209

15. Brokerage 210
A brokerage commission at the rate stated in Box 24 on the freight, dead-freight 211
and demurrage earned is due to the party mentioned in Box 24. 212
In case of non-execution 1/3 of the brokerage on the estimated amount of 213
freight to be paid by the party responsible for such non-execution to the 214
Brokers as indemnity for the latter's expenses and work. In case of more 215
voyages the amount of indemnity to be agreed. 216

16. General Strike Clause 217
(a) If there is a strike or lock-out affecting or preventing the actual loading of the 218
cargo, or any part of it, when the Vessel is ready to proceed from her last port or 219

at any time during the voyage to the port or ports of loading or after her arrival 220
there, the Master or the Owners may ask the Charterers to declare, that they 221
agree to reckon the laydays as if there were no strike or lock-out. Unless the 222
Charterers have given such declaration in writing (by telegram, if necessary) 223
within 24 hours, the Owners shall have the option of cancelling this Charter 224
Party. If part cargo has already been loaded, the Owners must proceed with 225
same, (freight payable on loaded quantity only) having liberty to complete with 226
other cargo on the way for their own account. 227
(b) If there is a strike or lock-out affecting or preventing the actual discharging 228
of the cargo on or after the Vessel's arrival at or off port of discharge and same 229
has not been settled within 48 hours, the Charterers shall have the option of 230
keeping the Vessel waiting until such strike or lock-out is at an end against 231
paying half demurrage after expiration of the time provided for discharging 232
until the strike or lock-out terminates and thereafter full demurrage shall be 233
payable until the completion of discharging, or of ordering the Vessel to a safe 234
port where she can safely discharge without risk of being detained by strike or 235
lock-out. Such orders to be given within 48 hours after the Master or the 236
Owners have given notice to the Charterers of the strike or lock-out affecting 237
the discharge. On delivery of the cargo at such port, all conditions of this 238
Charter Party and of the Bill of Lading shall apply and the Vessel shall receive 239
the same freight as if she had discharged at the original port of destination, 240
except that if the distance to the substituted port exceeds 100 nautical miles, 241
the freight on the cargo delivered at the substituted port to be increased in 242
proportion. 243
(c) Except for the obligations described above, neither the Charterers nor the 244
Owners shall be responsible for the consequences of any strikes or lock-outs 245
preventing or affecting the actual loading or discharging of the cargo. 246

17. War Risks ('Voywar 1993') 247
(1) For the purpose of this Clause, the words: 248
(a) The 'Owners' shall include the shipowners, bareboat charterers, 249
disponent owners, managers or other operators who are charged with the 250
management of the Vessel, and the Master; and 251
(b) 'War Risks' shall include any war (whether actual or threatened), act of 252
war, civil war, hostilities, revolution, rebellion, civil commotion, warlike 253
operations, the laying of mines (whether actual or reported), acts of piracy, 254
acts of terrorists, acts of hostility or malicious damage, blockades 255
(whether imposed against all Vessels or imposed selectively against 256
Vessels of certain flags or ownership, or against certain cargoes or crews 257
or otherwise howsoever), by any person, body, terrorist or political group, 258
or the Government of any state whatsoever, which, in the reasonable 259
judgement of the Master and/or the Owners, may be dangerous or are 260
likely to be or to become dangerous to the Vessel, her cargo, crew or other 261
persons on board the Vessel. 262
(2) If at any time before the Vessel commences loading, it appears that, in the 263
reasonable judgement of the Master and/or the Owners, performance of 264
the Contract of Carriage, or any part of it, may expose, or is likely to expose, 265
the Vessel, her cargo, crew or other persons on board the Vessel to War 266
Risks, the Owners may give notice to the Charterers cancelling this 267
Contract of Carriage, or may refuse to perform such part of it as may 268
expose, may be likely to expose, the Vessel, her cargo, crew or other 269
persons on board the Vessel to War Risks; provided always that if this 270
Contract of Carriage provides that loading or discharging is to take place 271
within a range of ports, and at the port or ports nominated by the Charterers 272
the Vessel, her cargo, crew, or other persons onboard the Vessel may be 273
exposed, or may be likely to be exposed, to War Risks, the Owners shall 274
first require the Charterers to nominate any other safe port which lies 275
within the range for loading or discharging, and may only cancel this 276
Contract of Carriage if the Charterers shall not have nominated such safe 277
port or ports within 48 hours of receipt of notice of such requirement. 278
(3) The Owners shall not be required to continue to load cargo for any voyage, 279
or to sign Bills of Lading for any port or place, or to proceed or continue on 280
any voyage, or on any part thereof, or to proceed through any canal or 281
waterway, or to proceed to or remain at any port or place whatsoever, 282
where it appears, either after the loading of the cargo commences, or at 283
any stage of the voyage thereafter before the discharge of the cargo is 284
completed, that, in the reasonable judgement of the Master and/or the 285
Owners, the Vessel, her cargo (or any part thereof), crew or other persons 286
on board the Vessel (or any one or more of them) may be, or are likely to be, 287
exposed to War Risks. If it should so appear, the Owners may by notice 288
request the Charterers to nominate a safe port for the discharge of the 289
cargo or any part thereof, and if within 48 hours of the receipt of such 290
notice, the Charterers shall not have nominated such a port, the Owners 291
may discharge the cargo at any safe port of their choice (including the port 292
of loading) in complete fulfilment of the Contract of Carriage. The Owners 293
shall be entitled to recover from the Charterers the extra expenses of such 294
discharge and, if the discharge takes place at any port other than the 295
loading port, to receive the full freight as though the cargo had been 296

PART II
'Gencon' Charter (As Revised 1922, 1976 and 1994)

carried to the discharging port and if the extra distance exceeds 100 miles, 297
to additional freight which shall be the same percentage of the freight 298
contracted for as the percentage which the extra distance represents to 299
the distance of the normal and customary route, the Owners having a lien 300
on the cargo for such expenses and freight. 301
(4) If at any stage of the voyage after the loading of the cargo commences, it 302
appears that, in the reasonable judgement of the Master and/or the 303
Owners, the Vessel, her cargo, crew or other persons on board the Vessel 304
may be, or are likely to be, exposed to War Risks on any part of the route 305
(including any canal or waterway) which is normally and customarily used 306
in a voyage of the nature contracted for, and there is another longer route 307
to the discharging port, the Owners shall give notice to the Charterers that 308
this route will be taken. In this event the Owners shall be entitled, if the total 309
extra distance exceeds 100 miles, to additional freight which shall be the 310
same percentage of the freight contracted for as the percentage which the 311
extra distance represents to the distance of the normal and customary 312
route. 313
(5) The Vessel shall have liberty:- 314
(a) to comply with all orders, directions, recommendations or advice as to 315
departure, arrival, routes, sailing in convoy, ports of call, stoppages, 316
destinations, discharge of cargo, delivery or in any way whatsoever which 317
are given by the Government of the Nation under whose flag the Vessel 318
sails, or other Government to whose laws the Owners are subject, or any 319
other Government which so requires, or any body or group acting with the 320
power to compel compliance with their orders or directions; 321
(b) to comply with the orders, directions or recommendations of any war 322
risks underwriters who have the authority to give the same under the terms 323
of the war risks insurance; 324
(c) to comply with the terms of any resolution of the Security Council of the 325
United Nations, any directives of the European Community, the effective 326
orders of any other Supranational body which has the right to issue and 327
give the same, and with national laws aimed at enforcing the same to which 328
the Owners are subject, and to obey the orders and directions of those who 329
are charged with their enforcement; 330
(d) to discharge at any other port any cargo or part thereof which may 331
render the Vessel liable to confiscation as a contraband carrier; 332
(e) to call at any other port to change the crew or any part thereof or other 333
persons on board the Vessel when there is reason to believe that they may 334
be subject to internment, imprisonment or other sanctions; 335
(f) where cargo has not been loaded or has been discharged by the 336
Owners under any provisions of this Clause, to load other cargo for the 337
Owners' own benefit and carry it to any other port or ports whatsoever, 338
whether backwards or forwards or in a contrary direction to the ordinary or 339
customary route. 340
(6) If in compliance with any of the provisions of sub-clauses (2) to (5) of this 341
Clause anything is done or not done, such shall not be deemed to be a 342
deviation, but shall be considered as due fulfilment of the Contract of 343
Carriage. 344

18. General Ice Clause 345
Port of loading 346
(a) In the event of the loading port being inaccessible by reason of ice when the 347
Vessel is ready to proceed from her last port or at any time during the voyage or 348
on the Vessel's arrival or in case frost sets in after the Vessel's arrival, the 349
Master for fear of being frozen in is at liberty to leave without cargo, and this 350
Charter Party shall be null and void. 351
(b) If during loading the Master, for fear of the Vessel being frozen in, deems it 352
advisable to leave, he has liberty to do so with what cargo he has on board and 353
to proceed to any other port or ports with option of completing cargo for the 354
Owners' benefit for any port or ports including port of discharge. Any part 355
cargo thus loaded under this Charter Party to be forwarded to destination at the 356
Vessel's expense but against payment of freight, provided that no extra 357
expenses be thereby caused to the Charterers, freight being paid on quantity 358
delivered (in proportion if lumpsum), all other conditions as per this Charter 359
Party. 360
(c) In case of more than one loading port, and if one or more of the ports are 361
closed by ice, the Master or the Owners to be at liberty either to load the part 362
cargo at the open port and fill up elsewhere for their own account as under 363
section (b) or to declare the Charter Party null and void unless the Charterers 364
agree to load full cargo at the open port. 365

Port of discharge 366
(a) Should ice prevent the Vessel from reaching port of discharge the 367
Charterers shall have the option of keeping the Vessel waiting until the re- 368
opening of navigation and paying demurrage or of ordering the Vessel to a safe 369
and immediately accessible port where she can safely discharge without risk of 370
detention by ice. Such orders to be given within 48 hours after the Master or the 371
Owners have given notice to the Charterers of the impossibility of reaching port 372

of destination. 373
(b) If during discharging the Master for fear of the Vessel being frozen in deems 374
it advisable to leave, he has liberty to do so with what cargo he has on board and 375
to proceed to the nearest accessible port where she can safely discharge. 376
(c) On delivery of the cargo at such port, all conditions of the Bill of Lading shall 377
apply and the Vessel shall receive the same freight as if she had discharged at 378
the original port of destination, except that if the distance of the substituted port 379
exceeds 100 nautical miles, the freight on the cargo delivered at the substituted 380
port to be increased in proportion. 381

19. Law and Arbitration 382
* (a) This Charter Party shall be governed by and construed in accordance with 383
English law and any dispute arising out of this Charter Party shall be referred to 384
arbitration in London in accordance with the Arbitration Acts 1950 and 1979 or 385
any statutory modification or re-enactment thereof for the time being in force. 386
Unless the parties agree upon a sole arbitrator, one arbitrator shall be 387
appointed by each party and the arbitrators so appointed shall appoint a third 388
arbitrator, the decision of the three-man tribunal thus constituted or any two of 389
them, shall be final. On the receipt by one party of the nomination in writing of 390
the other party's arbitrator, that party shall appoint their arbitrator within 391
fourteen days, failing which the decision of the single arbitrator appointed shall 392
be final. 393
For disputes where the total amount claimed by either party does not exceed 394
the amount stated in Box 25** the arbitration shall be conducted in accordance 395
with the Small Claims Procedure of the London Maritime Arbitrators 396
Association. 397
* (b) This Charter Party shall be governed by and construed in accordance with 398
Title 9 of the United States Code and the Maritime Law of the United States and 399
should any dispute arise out of this Charter Party, the matter in dispute shall be 400
referred to three persons at New York, one to be appointed by each of the 401
parties hereto, and the third by the two so chosen; their decision or that of any 402
two of them shall be final, and for purpose of enforcing any award, this 403
agreement may be made a rule of the Court. The proceedings shall be 404
conducted in accordance with the rules of the Society of Maritime Arbitrators, 405
Inc.. 406
For disputes where the total amount claimed by either party does not exceed 407
the amount stated in Box 25** the arbitration shall be conducted in accordance 408
with the Shortened Arbitration Procedure of the Society of Maritime Arbitrators, 409
Inc.. 410
* (c) Any dispute arising out of this Charter Party shall be referred to arbitration at 411
the place indicated in Box 25, subject to the procedures applicable there. The 412
laws of the place indicated in Box 25 shall govern this Charter Party. 413
(d) If Box 25 in Part 1 is not filled in, sub-clause (a) of this Clause shall apply. 414
* (a), (b) and (c) are alternatives; indicate alternative agreed in Box 25. 415
** *Where no figure is supplied in Box 25 in Part 1, this provision only shall be void* 416
but the other provisions of this Clause shall have full force and remain in effect. 417

Code Name: 'NYPE 93'

Recommended by
The Baltic and International Maritime Council (BIMCO)
The Federation of National Associations of
Ship Brokers and Agents (FONASBA)

TIME CHARTER©

New York Produce Exchange Form

Issued by the Association of Ship Brokers and Agents (U.S.A.) Inc

November 6th, 1913 - Amended October 20th, 1921; August 6th, 1931; October 3rd, 1946.
Revised June 12th, 1961, September 14th 1993.

THIS CHARTER PARTY, made and concluded in	1
this day of 19	2
Between	3
	4
Owners of the Vessel described below, and	5
	6
	7
Charterers.	8
Description of Vessel	9
Name Flag Built (year).	10
Port and number of Registry	11
Classed in	12
Deadweight long*/metric* tons (cargo and bunkers, including freshwater and	13
stores not exceeding long*/metric* tons) on a salt water draft of	14
on summer freeboard.	15
Capacity cubic feet grain cubic feet bale space.	16
Tonnage GT/GRT.	17
Speed about knots, fully laden, in good weather conditions up to and including maximum	18
Force on the Beaufort wind scale, on a consumption of about long*/metric*	19
tons of	20
Delete as appropriate.	21
For further description see Appendix 'A' (if applicable)	22

1. Duration

The Owners agree to let and the Charterers agree to hire the Vessel from the time of delivery for a period	24
of	25
	26
	27
within below mentioned trading limits.	28

2. Delivery

The Vessel shall be placed at the disposal of the Charterers at	30
	31
	32
The Vessel on her delivery	33
shall be ready to receive cargo with clean-swept holds and tight, staunch, strong and in every way fitted	34
for ordinary cargo service, having water ballast and with sufficient power to operate all cargo-handling gear	35
simultaneously.	36
The Owners shall give the Charterers not less than days notice of expected date of	37

(line 23 **Duration**)

NYPE 93 Page 1

delivery. 38

3. On-Off Hire Survey 39

Prior to delivery and redelivery the parties shall, unless otherwise agreed, each appoint surveyors, for their 40
respective accounts, who shall not later than at first loading port/last discharging port respectively, conduct 41
joint on-hire/off-hire surveys, for the purpose of ascertaining quantity of bunkers on board and the condition 42
of the Vessel. A single report shall be prepared on each occasion and signed by each surveyor, without 43
prejudice to his right to file a separate report setting forth items upon which the surveyors cannot agree. 44
If either party fails to have a representative attend the survey and sign the joint survey report, such party 45
shall nevertheless be bound for all purposes by the findings in any report prepared by the other party. 46
On-hire survey shall be on Charterers' time and off-hire survey on Owners' time. 47

4. Dangerous Cargo/Cargo Exclusions 48

(a) The Vessel shall be employed in carrying lawful merchandise excluding any goods of a dangerous, 49
injurious, flammable or corrosive nature unless carried in accordance with the requirements or 50
recommendations of the competent authorities of the country of the Vessel's registry and of ports of 51
shipment and discharge and of any intermediate countries or ports through whose waters the Vessel must 52
pass. Without prejudice to the generality of the foregoing, in addition the following are specifically 53
excluded: livestock of any description, arms, ammunition, explosives, nuclear and radioactive materials, 54
55
56
57
58
59
60
61
62
63
64
(b) If IMO-classified cargo is agreed to be carried, the amount of such cargo shall be limited to 65
tons and the Charterers shall provide the Master with any evidence he may 66
reasonably require to show that the cargo is packaged, labelled, loaded and stowed in accordance with IMO 67
regulations, failing which the Master is entitled to refuse such cargo or, if already loaded, to unload it at 68
the Charterers' risk and expense. 69

5. Trading Limits 70

The Vessel shall be employed in such lawful trades between safe ports and safe places 71
within 72
excluding 73
74
75
as the Charterers shall direct. 76

6. Owners to Provide 77

The Owners shall provide and pay for the insurance of the Vessel, except as otherwise provided, and for 78
all provisions, cabin, deck, engine-room and other necessary stores, including boiler water; shall pay for 79
wages, consular shipping and discharging fees of the crew and charges for port services pertaining to the 80
crew; shall maintain the Vessel's class and keep her in a thoroughly efficient state in hull, machinery and 81
equipment for and during the service, and have a full complement of officers and crew. 82

7. Charterers to Provide 83

The Charterers, while the Vessel is on hire, shall provide and pay for all the bunkers except as otherwise 84
agreed; shall pay for port charges (including compulsory watchmen and cargo watchmen and compulsory 85
garbage disposal), all communication expenses pertaining to the Charterers' business at cost, pilotages, 86

NYPE 93 Page 2

towages, agencies, commissions, consular charges (except those pertaining to individual crew members 87
or flag of the Vessel), and all other usual expenses except those stated in Clause 6, but when the Vessel 88
puts into a port for causes for which the Vessel is responsible (other than by stress of weather), then all 89
such charges incurred shall be paid by the Owners. Fumigations ordered because of illness of the crew 90
shall be for the Owners' account. Fumigations ordered because of cargoes carried or ports visited while 91
the Vessel is employed under this Charter Party shall be for the Charterers' account. All other fumigations 92
shall be for the Charterers' account after the Vessel has been on charter for a continuous period of six 93
months or more. 94

The Charterers shall provide and pay for necessary dunnage and also any extra fittings requisite for a 95
special trade or unusual cargo, but the Owners shall allow them the use of any dunnage already aboard 96
the Vessel. Prior to redelivery the Charterers shall remove their dunnage and fittings at their cost and in 97
their time. 98

8. Performance of Voyages 99

(a) The Master shall perform the voyages with due despatch, and shall render all customary assistance 100
with the Vessel's crew. The Master shall be conversant with the English language and (although 101
appointed by the Owners) shall be under the orders and directions of the Charterers as regards 102
employment and agency; and the Charterers shall perform all cargo handling, including but not limited to 103
loading, stowing, trimming, lashing, securing, dunnaging, unlashing, discharging, and tallying, at their risk 104
and expense, under the supervision of the Master. 105

(b) If the Charterers shall have reasonable cause to be dissatisfied with the conduct of the Master or 106
officers, the Owners shall, on receiving particulars of the complaint, investigate the same, and, if 107
necessary, make a change in the appointments. 108

9. Bunkers 109

(a) The Charterers on delivery, and the Owners on redelivery, shall take over and pay for all fuel and 110
diesel oil remaining on board the Vessel. The Vessel shall be delivered with: 111
long*/metric* tons of fuel oil at the price of   per ton; 112
tons of diesel oil at the price of   per ton. The vessel shall 113
be redelivered with: tons of fuel oil at the price of   per ton; 114
tons of diesel oil at the price of   per ton. 115

* *Same tons apply throughout this clause.* 116

(b) The Charterers shall supply bunkers of a quality suitable for burning in the Vessel's engines 117
and auxiliaries and which conform to the specification(s) as set out in Appendix A. 118

The Owners reserve their right to make a claim against the Charterers for any damage to the main engines 119
or the auxiliaries caused by the use of unsuitable fuels or fuels not complying with the agreed 120
specification(s). Additionally, if bunker fuels supplied do not conform with the mutually agreed 121
specification(s) or otherwise prove unsuitable for burning in the Vessel's engines or auxiliaries, the Owners 122
shall not be held responsible for any reduction in the Vessel's speed performance and/or increased bunker 123
consumption, nor for any time lost and any other consequences. 124

10. Rate of Hire/Redelivery Areas and Notices 125
The Charterers shall pay for the use and hire of the said Vessel at the rate of $ 126
U.S. currency, daily, **or** $ U.S. currency per ton on the Vessel's total deadweight 127
carrying capacity, including bunkers and stores, on   summer freeboard, per 30 days, 128
commencing on and from the day of her delivery, as aforesaid, and at and after the same rate for any part 129
of a month; hire shall continue until the hour of the day of her redelivery in like good order and condition, 130
ordinary wear and tear excepted, to the Owners (unless Vessel lost) at 131
132
133
unless otherwise mutually agreed. 134

The Charterers shall give the Owners not less than   days notice of the Vessel's 135
expected date and probable port of redelivery. 136

For the purpose of hire calculations, the times of delivery, redelivery or termination of charter shall be 137
adjusted to GMT. 138

11. Hire Payment 139

(a) *Payment* 140

Payment of Hire shall be made so as to be received by the Owners or their designated payee in 141
                             , viz 142
 143
 144
                           in 145
           currency, or in United States Currency, in funds available to the 146
Owners on the due date, 15 days in advance, and for the last month or part of same the approximate 147
amount of hire, and should same not cover the actual time, hire shall be paid for the balance day by day 148
as it becomes due, if so required by the Owners. Failing the punctual and regular payment of the hire, 149
or on any fundamental breach whatsoever of this Charter Party, the Owners shall be at liberty to 150
withdraw the Vessel from the service of the Charterers without prejudice to any claims they (the Owners) 151
may otherwise have on the Charterers. 152

At any time after the expiry of the grace period provided in Sub-clause 11 (b) hereunder and while the 153
hire is outstanding, the Owners shall, without prejudice to the liberty to withdraw, be entitled to withhold 154
the performance of any and all of their obligations hereunder and shall have no responsibility whatsoever 155
for any consequences thereof, in respect of which the Charterers hereby indemnify the Owners, and hire 156
shall continue to accrue and any extra expenses resulting from such withholding shall be for the 157
Charterers' account. 158

(b) *Grace Period* 159

Where there is failure to make punctual and regular payment of hire due to oversight, negligence, errors 160
or omissions on the part of the Charterers or their bankers, the Charterers shall be given by the Owners 161
          clear banking days (as recognized at the agreed place of payment) written notice to rectify the 162
failure, and when so rectified within those   days following the Owners' notice, the payment shall 163
stand as regular and punctual. 164

Failure by the Charterers to pay the hire within   days of their receiving the Owners' notice as 165
provided herein, shall entitle the Owners to withdraw as set forth in Sub-clause 11 (a) above. 166

(c) *Last Hire Payment* 167

Should the Vessel be on her voyage towards port of redelivery at the time the last and/or the penultimate 168
payment of hire is/are due, said payment(s) is/are to be made for such length of time as the Owners and 169
the Charterers may agree upon as being the estimated time necessary to complete the voyage, and taking 170
into account bunkers actually on board, to be taken over by the Owners and estimated disbursements for 171
the Owners' account before redelivery. Should same not cover the actual time, hire is to be paid for the 172
balance, day by day, as it becomes due. When the Vessel has been redelivered, any difference is to be 173
refunded by the Owners or paid by the Charterers, as the case may be. 174

(d) *Cash Advances* 175

Cash for the Vessel's ordinary disbursements at any port may be advanced by the Charterers, as required 176
by the Owners, subject to 2½ percent commission and such advances shall be deducted from the hire. 177
The Charterers, however, shall in no way be responsible for the application of such advances. 178

12. Berths 179

The Vessel shall be loaded and discharged in any safe dock or at any safe berth or safe place that 180
Charterers or their agents may direct, provided the Vessel can safely enter, lie and depart always afloat 181
at any time of tide. 182

13. **Spaces Available** 183

(a) The whole reach of the Vessel's holds, decks, and other cargo spaces (not more than she can 184
reasonably and safely stow and carry), also accommodations for supercargo, if carried, shall be at the 185
Charterers' disposal, reserving only proper and sufficient space for the Vessel's officers, crew, tackle, 186
apparel, furniture, provisions, stores and fuel. 187

(b) In the event of deck cargo being carried, the Owners are to be and are hereby indemnified by the 188
Charterers for any loss and/or damage and/or liability of whatsoever nature caused to the Vessel as a 189
result of the carriage of deck cargo and which would not have arisen had deck cargo not been loaded. 190

14. **Supercargo and Meals** 191

The Charterers are entitled to appoint a supercargo, who shall accompany the Vessel at the Charterers' 192
risk and see that voyages are performed with due despatch. He is to be furnished with free 193
accommodation and same fare as provided for the Master's table, the Charterers paying at the rate of 194
per day. The Owners shall victual pilots and customs officers, and also, when 195
authorized by the Charterers or their agents, shall victual tally clerks, stevedore's foreman, etc., 196
Charterers paying at the rate of per meal for all such victualling. 197

15. **Sailing Orders and Logs** 198

The Charterers shall furnish the Master from time to time with all requisite instructions and sailing 199
directions, in writing, in the English language, and the Master shall keep full and correct deck and engine 200
logs of the voyage or voyages, which are to be patent to the Charterers or their agents, and furnish the 201
Charterers, their agents or supercargo, when required, with a true copy of such deck and engine logs, 202
showing the course of the Vessel, distance run and the consumption of bunkers. Any log extracts 203
required by the Charterers shall be in the English language. 204

16. **Delivery/Cancelling** 205

If required by the Charterers, time shall not commence before and should the 206
Vessel not be ready for delivery on or before but not later than hours, 207
the Charterers shall have the option of cancelling this Charter Party. 208

Extension of Cancelling 209

If the Owners warrant that, despite the exercise of due diligence by them, the Vessel will not be ready 210
for delivery by the cancelling date, and provided the Owners are able to state with reasonable certainty 211
the date on which the Vessel will be ready, they may, at the earliest seven days before the Vessel is 212
expected to sail for the port or place of delivery, require the Charterers to declare whether or not they will 213
cancel the Charter Party. Should the Charterers elect not to cancel, or should they fail to reply within two 214
days or by the cancelling date, whichever shall first occur, then the seventh day after the expected date 215
of readiness for delivery as notified by the Owners shall replace the original cancelling date. Should the 216
Vessel be further delayed, the Owners shall be entitled to require further declarations of the Charterers in 217
accordance with this Clause. 218

17. **Off Hire** 219

In the event of loss of time from deficiency and/or default and/or strike of officers or crew, or deficiency 220
of stores, fire, breakdown of, or damages to hull, machinery or equipment, grounding, detention by the 221
arrest of the Vessel, (unless such arrest is caused by events for which the Charterers, their servants, 222
agents or subcontractors are responsible), or detention by average accidents to the Vessel or cargo unless 223
resulting from inherent vice, quality or defect of the cargo, drydocking for the purpose of examination or 224
painting bottom, or by any other similar cause preventing the full working of the Vessel, the payment of 225

hire and overtime, if any, shall cease for the time thereby lost. Should the Vessel deviate or put back 226
during a voyage, contrary to the orders or directions of the Charterers, for any reason other than accident 227
to the cargo or where permitted in lines 257 to 258 hereunder, the hire is to be suspended from the time 228
of her deviating or putting back until she is again in the same or equidistant position from the destination 229
and the voyage resumed therefrom. All bunkers used by the Vessel while off hire shall be for the Owners' 230
account. In the event of the Vessel being driven into port or to anchorage through stress of weather, 231
trading to shallow harbors or to rivers or ports with bars, any detention of the Vessel and/or expenses 232
resulting from such detention shall be for the Charterers' account. If upon the voyage the speed be 233
reduced by defect in, or breakdown of, any part of her hull, machinery or equipment, the time so lost, and 234
the cost of any extra bunkers consumed in consequence thereof, and all extra proven expenses may be 235
deducted from the hire. 236

18. Sublet 237

Unless otherwise agreed, the Charterers shall have the liberty to sublet the Vessel for all or any part of 238
the time covered by this Charter Party, but the Charterers remain responsible for the fulfillment of this 239
Charter Party. 240

19. Drydocking 241

The Vessel was last drydocked 242

*(a) The Owners shall have the option to place the Vessel in drydock during the currency of this Charter 243
at a convenient time and place, to be mutually agreed upon between the Owners and the Charterers, for 244
bottom cleaning and painting and/or repair as required by class or dictated by circumstances. 245

*(b) Except in case of emergency no drydocking shall take place during the currency of this Charter 246
Party. 247

* Delete as appropriate 248

20. Total Loss 249

Should the Vessel be lost, money paid in advance and not earned (reckoning from the date of loss or 250
being last heard of) shall be returned to the Charterers at once. 251

21. Exceptions 252

The act of God, enemies, fire, restraint of princes, rulers and people, and all dangers and accidents of the 253
seas, rivers, machinery, boilers, and navigation, and errors of navigation throughout this Charter, always 254
mutually excepted. 255

22. Liberties 256

The Vessel shall have the liberty to sail with or without pilots, to tow and to be towed, to assist vessels 257
in distress, and to deviate for the purpose of saving life and property. 258

23. Liens 259

The Owners shall have a lien upon all cargoes and all sub-freights and/or sub-hire for any amounts due 260
under this Charter Party, including general average contributions, and the Charterers shall have a lien on 261
the Vessel for all monies paid in advance and not earned, and any overpaid hire or excess deposit to be 262
returned at once. 263

The Charterers will not directly or indirectly suffer, nor permit to be continued, any lien or encumbrance, 264
which might have priority over the title and interest of the Owners in the Vessel. The Charterers 265
undertake that during the period of this Charter Party, they will not procure any supplies or necessaries 266
or services, including any port expenses and bunkers, on the credit of the Owners or in the Owners' time. 267

24. **Salvage**   268

All derelicts and salvage shall be for the Owners' and the Charterers' equal benefit after deducting   269
Owners' and Charterers' expenses and crew's proportion.   270

25. **General Average**   271

General average shall be adjusted according to York-Antwerp Rules 1974, as amended 1990, or any   272
subsequent modification thereof, in   and settled in   273
currency.   274

The Charterers shall procure that all bills of lading issued during the currency of the Charter Party will   275
contain a provision to the effect that general average shall be adjusted according to York-Antwerp Rules   276
1974, as amended 1990, or any subsequent modification thereof and will include the 'New Jason   277
Clause' as per Clause 31.   278

Time charter hire shall not contribute to general average.   279

26. **Navigation**   280

Nothing herein stated is to be construed as a demise of the Vessel to the Time Charterers. The Owners   281
shall remain responsible for the navigation of the Vessel, acts of pilots and tug boats, insurance, crew,   282
and all other matters, same as when trading for their own account.   283

27. **Cargo Claims**   284

Cargo claims as between the Owners and the Charterers shall be settled in accordance with the Inter-Club   285
New York Produce Exchange Agreement of February 1970, as amended May, 1984, or any subsequent   286
modification or replacement thereof.   287

28. **Cargo Gear and Lights**   288

The Owners shall maintain the cargo handling gear of the Vessel which is as follows: 289
                                                                                                       290
                                                                                                       291
                                                                                                       292
providing gear (for all derricks or cranes) capable of lifting capacity as described. The Owners shall also   293
provide on the Vessel for night work lights as on board, but all additional lights over those on board shall   294
be at the Charterers' expense. The Charterers shall have the use of any gear on board the Vessel. If   295
required by the Charterers, the Vessel shall work night and day and all cargo handling gear shall be at the   296
Charterers' disposal during loading and discharging. In the event of disabled cargo handling gear, or   297
insufficient power to operate the same, the Vessel is to be considered to be off hire to the extent that   298
time is actually lost to the Charterers and the Owners to pay stevedore stand-by charges occasioned   299
thereby, unless such disablement or insufficiency of power is caused by the Charterers' stevedores. If   300
required by the Charterers, the Owners shall bear the cost of hiring shore gear in lieu thereof, in which   301
case the Vessel shall remain on hire.   302

29. **Crew Overtime**   303

In lieu of any overtime payments to officers and crew for work ordered by the Charterers or their agents,   304
the Charterers shall pay the Owners, concurrently with the hire   per month   305
or pro rata.   306

30. **Bills of Lading**   307

(a) The Master shall sign the bills of lading or waybills for cargo as presented in conformity with mates   308
or tally clerk's receipts. However, the Charterers may sign bills of lading or waybills on behalf of the   309
Master, with the Owner's prior written authority, always in conformity with mates or tally clerk's receipts.   310

(b) All bills of lading or waybills shall be without prejudice to this Charter Party and the Charterers shall 311
indemnify the Owners against all consequences or liabilities which may arise from any inconsistency 312
between this Charter Party and any bills of lading or waybills signed by the Charterers or by the Master 313
at their request. 314

(c) Bills of lading covering deck cargo shall be claused: 'Shipped on deck at Charterers', Shippers' and 315
Receivers' risk, expense and responsibility, without liability on the part of the Vessel, or her Owners for 316
any loss, damage, expense or delay howsoever caused.' 317

31. **Protective Clauses** 318

This Charter Party is subject to the following clauses all of which are also to be included in all bills of lading 319
or waybills issued hereunder: 320

(a) CLAUSE PARAMOUNT 321
'This bill of lading shall have effect subject to the provisions of the Carriage of Goods by Sea Act of the 322
United States, the Hague Rules, or the Hague-Visby Rules, as applicable, or such other similar national 323
legislation as may mandatorily apply by virtue of origin or destination of the bills of lading, which shall 324
be deemed to be incorporated herein and nothing herein contained shall be deemed a surrender by the 325
carrier of any of its rights or immunities or an increase of any of its responsibilities or liabilities under said 326
applicable Act. If any term of this bill of lading be repugnant to said applicable Act to any extent, such 327
term shall be void to that extent, but no further.' 328

and 329

(b) BOTH-TO-BLAME COLLISION CLAUSE 330
'If the ship comes into collision with another ship as a result of the negligence of the other ship and any 331
act, neglect or default of the master, mariner, pilot or the servants of the carrier in the navigation or in 332
the management of the ship, the owners of the goods carried hereunder will indemnify the carrier against 333
all loss or liability to the other or non-carrying ship or her owners insofar as such loss or liability represents 334
loss of, or damage to, or any claim whatsoever of the owners of said goods, paid or payable by the other 335
or non-carrying ship or her owners to the owners of said goods and set off, recouped or recovered by the 336
other or non-carrying ship or her owners as part of their claim against the carrying ship or carrier. 337

The foregoing provisions shall also apply where the owners, operators or those in charge of any ships or 338
objects other than, or in addition to, the colliding ships or objects are at fault in respect to a collision or 339
contact.' 340

and 341

(c) NEW JASON CLAUSE 342
'In the event of accident, danger, damage or disaster before or after the commencement of the voyage 343
resulting from any cause whatsoever, whether due to negligence or not, for which, or for the 344
consequences of which, the carrier is not responsible, by statute, contract, or otherwise, the goods, 345
shippers, consignees, or owners of the goods shall contribute with the carrier in general average to the 346
payment of any sacrifices, losses, or expenses of a general average nature that may be made or incurred, 347
and shall pay salvage and special charges incurred in respect of the goods. 348

If a salving ship is owned or operated by the carrier, salvage shall be paid for as fully as if salving ship 349
or ships belonged to strangers. Such deposit as the carrier or his agents may deem sufficient to cover 350
the estimated contribution of the goods and any salvage and special charges thereon shall, if required, 351
be made by the goods, shippers, consignees or owners of the goods to the carrier before delivery.' 352

and 353

(d) U.S. TRADE - DRUG CLAUSE 354
'In pursuance of the provisions of the U.S. Anti Drug Abuse Act 1986 or any re-enactment thereof, the 355
Charterers warrant to exercise the highest degree of care and diligence in preventing unmanifested 356
narcotic drugs and marijuana to be loaded or concealed on board the Vessel. 357

Non-compliance with the provisions of this clause shall amount to breach of warranty for consequences 358
of which the Charterers shall be liable and shall hold the Owners, the Master and the crew of the Vessel 359
harmless and shall keep them indemnified against all claims whatsoever which may arise and be made 360
against them individually or jointly. Furthermore, all time lost and all expenses incurred, including fines, 361
as a result of the Charterers' breach of the provisions of this clause shall be for the Charterer's account 362
and the Vessel shall remain on hire. 363

Should the Vessel be arrested as a result of the Charterers' non-compliance with the provisions of this 364
clause, the Charterers shall at their expense take all reasonable steps to secure that within a reasonable 365
time the Vessel is released and at their expense put up the bails to secure release of the Vessel. 366

The Owners shall remain responsible for all time lost and all expenses incurred, including fines, in the 367
event that unmanifested narcotic drugs and marijuana are found in the possession or effects of the 368
Vessel's personnel.' 369

and 370

(e) WAR CLAUSES 371
'(i) No contraband of war shall be shipped. The Vessel shall not be required, without the consent of the 372
Owners, which shall not be unreasonably withheld, to enter any port or zone which is involved in a state 373
of war, warlike operations, or hostilities, civil strife, insurrection or piracy whether there be a declaration 374
of war or not, where the Vessel, cargo or crew might reasonably be expected to be subject to capture, 375
seizure or arrest, or to a hostile act by a belligerent power (the term 'power' meaning any de jure or de 376
facto authority or any purported governmental organization maintaining naval, military or air forces). 377

(ii) If such consent is given by the Owners, the Charterers will pay the provable additional cost of insuring 378
the Vessel against hull war risks in an amount equal to the value under her ordinary hull policy but not 379
exceeding a valuation of   In addition, the Owners may purchase and the 380
Charterers will pay for war risk insurance on ancillary risks such as loss of hire, freight disbursements, 381
total loss, blocking and trapping, etc. If such insurance is not obtainable commercially or through a 382
government program, the Vessel shall not be required to enter or remain at any such port or zone. 383

(iii) In the event of the existence of the conditions described in (i) subsequent to the date of this Charter, 384
or while the Vessel is on hire under this Charter, the Charterers shall, in respect of voyages to any such 385
port or zone assume the provable additional cost of wages and insurance properly incurred in connection 386
with master, officers and crew as a consequence of such war, warlike operations or hostilities. 387

(iv) Any war bonus to officers and crew due to the Vessel's trading or cargo carried shall be for the 388
Charterers' account.' 389

32. War Cancellation 390

In the event of the outbreak of war (whether there be a declaration of war or not) between any two or 391
more of the following countries: 392
393
394
395

either the Owners or the Charterers may cancel this Charter Party. Whereupon, the Charterers shall 396
redeliver the Vessel to the Owners in accordance with Clause 10; if she has cargo on board, after 397
discharge thereof at destination, or, if debarred under this Clause from reaching or entering it, at a near 398
open and safe port as directed by the Owners; or, if she has no cargo on board, at the port at which she 399
then is; or, if at sea, at a near open and safe port as directed by the Owners. In all cases hire shall 400
continue to be paid in accordance with Clause 11 and except as aforesaid all other provisions of this 401
Charter Party shall apply until redelivery. 402

33. Ice 403

The Vessel shall not be required to enter or remain in any icebound port or area, nor any port or area 404

where lights or lightships have been or are about to be withdrawn by reason of ice, nor where there is 405
risk that in the ordinary course of things the Vessel will not be able on account of ice to safely enter and 406
remain in the port or area or to get out after having completed loading or discharging. Subject to the 407
Owners' prior approval the Vessel is to follow ice-breakers when reasonably required with regard to her 408
size, construction and ice class. 409

34. Requisition 410

Should the Vessel be requisitioned by the government of the Vessel's flag during the period of this Charter 411
Party, the Vessel shall be deemed to be off hire during the period of such requisition, and any hire paid 412
by the said government in respect of such requisition period shall be retained by the Owners. The period 413
during which the Vessel is on requisition to the said government shall count as part of the period provided 414
for in this Charter Party. 415
If the period of requisition exceeds   months, either party shall have the option 416
of cancelling this Charter Party and no consequential claim may be made by either party. 417

35. Stevedore Damage 418

Notwithstanding anything contained herein to the contrary, the Charterers shall pay for any and all 419
damage to the Vessel caused by stevedores provided the Master has notified the Charterers and/or their 420
agents in writing as soon as practical but not later than 48 hours after any damage is discovered. Such 421
notice to specify the damage in detail and to invite Charterers to appoint a surveyor to assess the extent 422
of such damage. 423

(a) In case of any and all damage(s) affecting the Vessel's seaworthiness and/or the safety of the crew 424
and/or affecting the trading capabilities of the Vessel, the Charterers shall immediately arrange for repairs 425
of such damage(s) at their expense and the Vessel is to remain on hire until such repairs are completed 426
and if required passed by the Vessel's classification society. 427

(b) Any and all damage(s) not described under point (a) above shall be repaired at the Charterers' option, 428
before or after redelivery concurrently with the Owners' work. In such case no hire and/or expenses will 429
be paid to the Owners except and insofar as the time and/or the expenses required for the repairs for 430
which the Charterers are responsible, exceed the time and/or expenses necessary to carry out the 431
Owners' work. 432

36. Cleaning of Holds 433

The Charterers shall provide and pay extra for sweeping and/or washing and/or cleaning of holds between 434
voyages and/or between cargoes provided such work can be undertaken by the crew and is permitted by 435
local regulations, at the rate of   per hold. 436

In connection with any such operation, the Owners shall not be responsible if the Vessel's holds are not 437
accepted or passed by the port or any other authority. The Charterers shall have the option to re-deliver 438
the Vessel with unclean/upswept holds against a lumpsum payment of   in lieu of cleaning. 439

37. Taxes 440

Charterers to pay all local, State, National taxes and/or dues assessed on the Vessel or the Owners 441
resulting from the Charterers' orders herein, whether assessed during or after the currency of this Charter 442
Party including any taxes and/or dues on cargo and/or freights and/or sub-freights and/or hire (excluding 443
taxes levied by the country of the flag of the Vessel or the Owners). 444

38. Charterers' Colors 445

The Charterers shall have the privilege of flying their own house flag and painting the Vessel with their 446
own markings. The Vessel shall be repainted in the Owners' colors before termination of the Charter 447
Party. Cost and time of painting, maintaining and repainting those changes effected by the Charterers 448
shall be for the Charterers' account. 449

39. **Laid up Returns** 450

The Charterers shall have the benefit of any return insurance premium receivable by the Owners from their 451
underwriters as and when received from underwriters by reason of the Vessel being in port for a minimum 452
period of 30 days if on full hire for this period or pro rata for the time actually on hire. 453

40. **Documentation** 454

The Owners shall provide any documentation relating to the Vessel that may be required to permit the 455
Vessel to trade within the agreed trade limits, including, but not limited to certificates of financial 456
responsibility for oil pollution, provided such oil pollution certificates are obtainable from the Owners' 457
P & I club, valid international tonnage certificate, Suez and Panama tonnage certificates, valid certificate 458
of registry and certificates relating to the strength and/or serviceability of the Vessel's gear. 459

41. **Stowaways** 460

(a) (i) The Charterers warrant to exercise due care and diligence in preventing stowaways in gaining 461
access to the Vessel by means of secreting away in the goods and/or containers shipped by the 462
Charterers. 463

(ii) If, despite the exercise of due care and diligence by the Charterers, stowaways have gained 464
access to the Vessel by means of secreting away in the goods and/or containers shipped by the 465
Charterers, this shall amount to breach of charter for the consequences of which the Charterers 466
shall be liable and shall hold the Owners harmless and shall keep them indemnified against all 467
claims whatsoever which may arise and be made against them. Furthermore, all time lost and all 468
expenses whatsoever and howsoever incurred, including fines, shall be for the Charterers' account 469
and the Vessel shall remain on hire. 470

(iii) Should the Vessel be arrested as a result of the Charterers' breach of charter according to 471
sub-clause (a)(ii) above, the Charterers shall take all reasonable steps to secure that, within a 472
reasonable time, the Vessel is released and at their expense put up bail to secure release of the 473
Vessel. 474

(b) (i) If, despite the exercise of due care and diligence by the Owners, stowaways have gained 475
access to the Vessel by means other than secreting away in the goods and/or containers shipped 476
by the Charterers, all time lost and all expenses whatsoever and howsoever incurred, including 477
fines, shall be for the Owners' account and the Vessel shall be off hire. 478

(ii) Should the Vessel be arrested as a result of stowaways having gained access to the Vessel 479
by means other than secreting away in the goods and/or containers shipped by the Charterers, 480
the Owners shall take all reasonable steps to secure that, within a reasonable time, the Vessel 481
is released and at their expense put up bail to secure release of the Vessel. 482

42. **Smuggling** 483

In the event of smuggling by the Master, Officers and/or crew, the Owners shall bear the cost of any 484
fines, taxes, or imposts levied and the Vessel shall be off hire for any time lost as a result thereof. 485

43. **Commissions** 486

A commission of   percent is payable by the Vessel and the Owners to 487
488
489
490
on hire earned and paid under this Charter, and also upon any continuation or extension of this Charter. 491

44. **Address Commission** 492

An address commission of   percent is payable to 493

	494
	495
on hire earned and paid under this Charter.	496

45. Arbitration
497

(a) NEW YORK

498

All disputes arising out of this contract shall be arbitrated at New York in the following manner, and subject to U.S. Law:
499
500

One Arbitrator is to be appointed by each of the parties hereto and a third by the two so chosen. Their decision or that of any two of them shall be final, and for the purpose of enforcing any award, this agreement may be made a rule of the court. The Arbitrators shall be commercial men, conversant with shipping matters. Such Arbitration is to be conducted in accordance with the rules of the Society of Maritime Arbitrators Inc.
501
502
503
504
505

For disputes where the total amount claimed by either party does not exceed US $ ** the arbitration shall be conducted in accordance with the Shortened Arbitration Procedure of the Society of Maritime Arbitrators Inc.
506
507
508

(b) LONDON

509

All disputes arising out of this contract shall be arbitrated at London and, unless the parties agree forthwith on a single Arbitrator, be referred to the final arbitrament of two Arbitrators carrying on business in London who shall be members of the Baltic Mercantile & Shipping Exchange and engaged in Shipping, one to be appointed by each of the parties, with power to such Arbitrators to appoint an Umpire. No award shall be questioned or invalidated on the ground that any of the Arbitrators is not qualified as above, unless objection to his action be taken before the award is made. Any dispute arising hereunder shall be governed by English Law.
510
511
512
513
514
515
516

For disputes where the total amount claimed by either party does not exceed US $ ** the arbitration shall be conducted in accordance with the Small Claims Procedure of the London Maritime Arbitrators Association.
517
518
519

*Delete para (a) or (b) as appropriate
520

** Where no figure is supplied in the blank space this provision only shall be void but the other provisions of this clause shall have full force and remain in effect.
521
522

If mutually agreed, clauses   to   , both inclusive, as attached hereto are fully incorporated in this Charter Party.
523
524

APPENDIX 'A'
525

To Charter Party dated
526

Between	Owners	527
and	Charterers	528
		529

Further details of the Vessel:
530

Inter-Club New York Produce Exchange Agreement 1996

This Agreement is made on the 1st of September 1996 between the P&I Clubs being members of The International Group of P&I Associations listed below (hereafter referred to as 'the Clubs').

This Agreement replaces the Inter-Club Agreement 1984 in respect of all charterparties specified in clause (1) hereof and shall continue in force until varied or terminated. Any variation to be effective must be approved in writing by all the Clubs but it is open to any Club to withdraw from the Agreement on giving to all the other Clubs not less than three months' written notice thereof, such withdrawal to take effect at the expiration of that period. After the expiry of such notice the Agreement shall neverthe-less continue as between all the Clubs, other than the Club giving such notice who shall remain bound by and be entitled to the benefit of this Agreement in respect of all Cargo Claims arising out of charter-parties commenced prior to the expiration of such notice.

The Clubs will recommend to their Members without qualification that their Members adopt this Agreement for the purpose of apportioning liability for claims in respect of cargo which arise under, out of or in connection with all charterparties on the New York Produce Exchange Form 1946 or 1993 or Asbatime Form 1981 (or any subsequent amendment of such Forms), whether or not this Agreement has been incorporated into such charterparties.

Scope of application

(1) This Agreement applies to any charterparty which is entered into after the date hereof on the New York Produce Exchange Form 1946 or 1993 or Asbatime Form 1981 (or any subsequent amend-ment of such Forms).

(2) The terms of this Agreement shall apply notwithstanding anything to the contrary in any other pro-vision of the charterparty; in particular the provisions of clause (6) (time bar) shall apply notwith-standing any provision of the charterparty or rule of law to the contrary.

(3) For the purposes of this Agreement, Cargo Claim(s) mean claims for loss, damage, shortage (includ-ing slackage, ullage or pilferage), overcarriage of or delay to cargo including customs dues or fines in respect of such loss, damage, shortage, overcarriage or delay and include:

   (a) any legal costs claimed by the original person making any such claim;
   (b) any interest claimed by the original person making any such claim;
   (c) all legal, Club correspondents' and experts' costs reasonably incurred in the defence of or in the settlement of the claim made by the original person, but shall not include any costs of whatso-ever nature incurred in making a claim under this Agreement or in seeking an indemnity under the charterparty.

(4) Apportionment under this Agreement shall only be applied to Cargo Claims where:

   (a) the claim was made under a contract of carriage, whatever its form,

     (i) which was authorised under the charterparty;
       or

    (ii) which would have been authorised under the charterparty but for the inclusion in that contract of carriage of Through Transport or Combined Transport provisions,

       provided that

   (iii) in the case of contracts of carriage containing Through Transport or Combined Transport pro-visions (whether falling within (i) or (ii) above) the loss, damage, shortage, overcarriage or delay occurred after commencement of the loading of the cargo on to the chartered vessel and prior to completion of its discharge from that vessel (the burden of proof being on the Charterer to establish that the loss, damage, shortage, overcarriage or delay did or did not so occur); and

   (iv) the contract of carriage (or that part of the transit that comprised carriage on the chartered vessel) incorporated terms no less favourable to the carrier than the Hague or Hague Visby

Rules, or, when compulsorily applicable by operation of law to the contract of carriage, the Hamburg Rules or any national law giving effect thereto; and

(b) the cargo responsibility clauses in the charterparty have not been materially amended. A material amendment is one which makes the liability, as between Owners and Charterers, for Cargo Claims clear. In particular, it is agreed solely for the purposes of this Agreement:

    (i) that the addition of the words 'and responsibility' in clause 8 of the New York Produce Exchange Form 1946 or 1993 or clause 8 of the Asbatime Form 1981, or any similar amendment of the charterparty making the Master responsible for cargo handling, is not a material amendment; and

    (ii) that if the words 'cargo claims' are added to the second sentence of clause 26 of the New York Produce Exchange Form 1946 or 1993 or clause 25 of the Asbatime Form 1981, apportionment under this Agreement shall not be applied under any circumstances even if the charterparty is made subject to the terms of this Agreement; and

(c) the claim has been properly settled or compromised and paid.

(5) This Agreement applies regardless of legal forum or place of arbitration specified in the charterparty and regardless of any incorporation of the Hague, Hague Visby Rules or Hamburg Rules therein.

Time bar

(6) Recovery under this Agreement by an Owner or Charterer shall be deemed to be waived and absolutely barred unless written notification of the Cargo Claim has been given to the other party to the charterparty within 24 months of the date of delivery of the cargo or the date the cargo should have been delivered, save that, where the Hamburg Rules or any national legislation giving effect thereto are compulsorily applicable by operation of law to the contract of carriage or to that part of the transit that comprised carriage on the chartered vessel, the period shall be 36 months. Such notification shall if possible include details of the contract of carriage, the nature of the claim and the amount claimed.

The apportionment

(7) The amount of any Cargo Claim to be apportioned under this Agreement shall be the amount in fact borne by the party to the charterparty seeking apportionment, regardless of whether that claim may be or has been apportioned by application of this Agreement to another charterparty.

(8) Cargo Claims shall be apportioned as follows:

(a) Claims in fact arising out of unseaworthiness and/or error or fault in navigation or management of the vessel:

100% Owners

Save where the Owner proves that the unseaworthiness was caused by the loading, stowage, lashing, discharge or other handling of the cargo, in which case the claim shall be apportioned under sub-clause (b).

(b) Claims in fact arising out of the loading, stowage, lashing, discharge, storage or other handling of cargo:

100% Charterers

unless the words 'and responsibility' are added in clause 8 or there is a similar amendment making the Master responsible for cargo handling in which case:

50% Charterers

50% Owners

save where the Charterer proves that the failure properly to load, stow, lash, discharge or handle the cargo was caused by the unseaworthiness of the vessel in which case:

100% Owners

(c) Subject to (a) and (b) above, claims for shortage or overcarriage:

50% Charterers

50% Owners

unless there is clear and irrefutable evidence that the claim arose out of pilferage or act or neglect by one or the other (including their servants or sub-contractors) in which case that party shall then bear 100% of the claim.

(d) All other cargo claims whatsoever (including claims for delay to cargo):

50% Charterers

50% Owners

unless there is clear and irrefutable evidence that the claim arose out of the act or neglect of the one or the other (including their servants or sub-contractors) in which case that party shall then bear 100% of the claim.

Governing law

(9) This Agreement shall be subject to English Law and Jurisdiction, unless it is incorporated into the charterparty (or the settlement of claims in respect of cargo under the charterparty is made subject to this Agreement), in which case it shall be subject to the law and jurisdiction provisions governing the charterparty.

American Steamship Owners Mutual Protection & Indemnity Association, Inc
Assuranceforeningen Gard
Assuranceforeningen Skuld
The Britannia Steam Ship Insurance Association Ltd
The Japan Ship Owners' Mutual Protection and Indemnity Association
Liverpool and London Steamship Protection and Indemnity Association Ltd
The London Steam-Ship Owners' Mutual Insurance Association Ltd
Newcastle Protection and Indemnity Association
The North of England Protecting and Indemnity Association Ltd
The Shipowners' Mutual Protection and Indemnity Association (Luxembourg)
Skuld Mutual Protection and Indemnity Association (Bermuda) Ltd
The Standard Steamship Owners' Protection & Indemnity Association Ltd
The Standard Steamship Owners Protection & Indemnity Association (Bermuda) Ltd
The Steamship Mutual Underwriting Association (Bermuda) Ltd
Sveriges Angfartygs Assurans Forening (The Swedish Club)
The United Kingdom Mutual Steam Ship Assurance Association (Bermuda) Ltd
The West of England Ship Owners Mutual Insurance Association (Luxembourg)

APPENDIX III

SIGNATORIES TO CONVENTIONS

International Convention for the Unification of Certain Rules Relating to Bills of Lading
[Hague Rules]
Brussels, 25 August 1924[1]

[In force 2 June 1931]

Article 11

After an interval of not more than two years from the day on which the Convention is signed, the Belgian Government shall place itself in communication with the Governments of the High Contracting Parties which have declared themselves prepared to ratify the Convention, with a view to deciding whether it shall be put into force. The ratifications shall be deposited at Brussels at a date to be fixed by agreement among the said Governments. The first deposit of ratifications shall be recorded in a *procès-verbal* signed by the representatives of the Powers which take part therein and by the Belgian Minister of Foreign Affairs.

The subsequent deposit of ratifications shall be made by means of a written notification, addressed to the Belgian Government and accompanied by the instrument of ratification.

A duly certified copy of the *procès-verbal* relating to the first deposit of ratifications, of the notifications referred to in the previous paragraph, and also of the instruments of ratification accompanying them, shall be immediately sent by the Belgian Government through the diplomatic channel to the Powers who have signed this Convention or who have acceded to it. In the cases contemplated in the preceding paragraph, the said Government shall inform them at the same time of the date on which it received the notification.

Article 12

Non-signatory States may accede to the present Convention whether or not they have been represented at the International Conference at Brussels.

A State which desires to accede shall notify its intention in writing to the Belgian Government, forwarding to it the document of accession, which shall be deposited in the archives of the said Government.

The Belgian Government shall immediately forward to all the States which have signed or acceded to the Convention a duly certified copy of the notification and of the act of accession, mentioning the date on which it received the notification.

Article 14

The present Convention shall take effect, in the case of the States which have taken part in the first deposit of ratifications, one year after the date of the protocol recording such deposit.

---

[1] Source: Belgian Ministry of Foreign Affairs, Foreign Trade and Development Cooperation <www.diplobel. fgov.be/en/>.

As respects the States which ratify subsequently or which accede, and also in cases in which the Convention is subsequently put into effect in accordance with Article 13, it shall take effect six months after the notifications specified in paragraph 2 of Article 11 and paragraph 2 of Article 12 have been received by the Belgian Government.

Algeria	13/04/1964(a)
Angola	2/02/1952(a)
Anguilla	2/12/1930(a)
Antigua and Barbuda	2/12/1930(a)
Argentina	19/04/1961(a)
Ascension	3/11/1931(a)
Australia	4/07/1955(a)
Bahamas	2/12/1930(a)
*Barbados	2/12/1930(a)[2]
Belgium	2/06/1930(r)
Belize	2/12/1930(a)
Bermuda	2/12/1930(a)
Bolivia	28/05/1982(a)
British Antartic Territory	2/12/1930(a)
British Virgin Islands	2/12/1930(a)
Brunei	2/12/1930(a)
*Cameroon	2/12/1930(a)[3]
Canada	2/12/1930(a)
Cape Verde Islands	2/02/1952(a)
Cayman Islands	2/12/1930(a)
Croatia	30/07/1992(a)
Cuba	25/07/1977(a)
Cyprus	2/12/1930(a)
Denmark	1/07/1938(a)
Dominican Republic	2/12/1930(a)
Ecuador	23/03/1977(a)
*Egypt	29/11/1943(a)[4]
Falkland Islands	2/12/1930(a)
Fiji	2/12/1930(a)
Finland	1/07/1939(a)
France	4/01/1937(r)
*Gambia	2/12/1930(a)[5]
Germany	1/07/1939(r)
Ghana	2/12/1930(a)
Gibraltar	2/12/1930(a)
Goa	2/02/1952(a)
Grenada	2/12/1930(a)
*Guinea Bissau	2/02/1952(a)[6]
Guyana	2/12/1930(a)
Hong Kong SAR	2/12/1930(a)
*Hungary	2/06/1930(r)[7]
Iran	26/04/1966(a)

---

[2] Barbados acceded to the Hamburg Rules on 2/02/1981, but it is not clear whether it has denounced the Hague Rules.
[3] Cameroon acceded to the Hamburg Rules on 2/10/1993, but it is not clear whether it has denounced the Hague Rules.
[4] Egypt denounced the Hague Rules on 1/11/1997, following its accession to the Hamburg Rules on 23/04/1979.
[5] Gambia acceded to the Hamburg Rules on 7/02/1996, but it is not clear whether it has denounced the Hague Rules.
[6] Guinea acceded to the Hamburg Rules on 23/01/1991, but it is not clear whether it has denounced the Hague Rules.
[7] Hungary acceded to the Hamburg Rules on 5/07/1984, but it is not clear whether it has denounced the Hague Rules.

Ireland	30/01/1962(a)
Israel	5/09/1959(a)
Italy	7/10/1938(r)
Ivory Coast	15/12/1961(a)
Jamaica	2/12/1930(a)
Japan	1/07/1957(r)
*Kenya	2/12/1930(a)[8]
Kiribati	2/12/1930(a)
Kuwait	25/07/1969(a)
Latvia	4/04/2002(a)
*Lebanon	19/07/1975(a)[9]
Lithuania	2/12/2003(a)
Macao SAR	2/02/1952(a)
Madagascar	13/07/1965(a)
Malaysia	2/12/1930(a)
Mauritius	24/08/1970(a)
Monaco	15/05/1931(a)
Montserrat	2/12/1930(a)
Mozambique	2/02/1952(a)
Nauru	4/07/1955(a)
Netherlands	18/08/1956(a)
*Nigeria	2/12/1930(a)[10]
North Borneo (Sabah)	2/12/1930(a)
Norway	1/07/1938(a)
Palestine	2/12/1930(a)
Papua New Guinea	4/07/1955(a)
*Paraguay	22/11/1967(a)
Peru	29/10/1964(a)
Poland	26/10/1936(r)
Portugal	24/12/1931(a)
*Romania	4/08/1937(r)[11]
St Helena	3/11/1931(a)
St Kitts and Nevis	2/12/1930(a)
St Lucia	2/12/1930(a)
*St Vincent & the Grenadines	2/12/1930(a)[12]
Sao Tome and Principe	2/02/1952(a)
Sarawak	2/12/1930(a)
*Senegal	14/02/1978(a)[13]
Seychelles	2/12/1930(a)
*Sierra Leone	2/12/1930(a)[14]
Singapore	2/12/1930(a)

---

[8] Kenya acceded to the Hamburg Rules on 31/07/1989, but it is not clear whether it has denounced the Hague Rules.

[9] Lebanon denounced the Hague Rules on 1/11/1997, following its accession to the Hamburg Rules on 4/04/1983.

[10] Nigeria acceded to the Hamburg Rules on 7/11/1988, but it is not clear whether it has denounced the Hague Rules.

[11] Romania denounced the Hague Rules on 21/03/2003, following its accession to the Hamburg Rules on 7/01/1982.

[12] St Vincent denounced the Hague Rules on 22/07/2003, following its accession to the Hamburg Rules on 12/09/2000.

[13] Senegal acceded to the Hamburg Rules on 17/03/1986, but it is not clear whether it has denounced the Hague Rules.

[14] Sierra Leona acceded to the Hamburg Rules on 7/10/1988, but it is not clear whether it has denounced the Hague Rules.

Slovenia	15/05/1996(a)
Solomon Islands	2/12/1930(a)
Somalia	2/12/1930(a)
Spain	2/06/1930(r)
Sri Lanka	2/12/1930(a)
Sweden	1/07/1938(a)
Switzerland	28/05/1954(a)
*Syrian Arab Republic	1/08/1974(a)[15]
*Tanzania	3/12/1962(a)[16]
Timor	2/02/1952(a)
Tonga	2/12/1930(a)
Trinidad & Tobago	2/12/1930(a)
Turkey	4/07/1955(a)
Turks & Caicos Islands	2/12/1930(a)
Tuvalu	2/12/1930(a)
United Kingdom	2/06/1930(r)
United States of America	29/06/1937(r)
Virgin Islands	2/12/1930(a)
Yugoslavia	17/04/1959(r)
Zaire	17/07/1967(a)

[15] Syria acceded to the Hamburg Rules on 16/10/2002, but it is not clear whether it has denounced the Hague Rules.
[16] Tanzania acceded to the Hamburg Rules on 24/07/1979, but it is not clear whether it has denounced the Hague Rules.
* These countries are now signatories to the Hamburg Rules.

Protocol to Amend the International Convention for the Unification of Certain Rules Relating to Bills of Lading [Visby Protocol]

Brussels, 23 February 1968[1]

[In force 23 June 1977]

Article 6

As between the Parties to this Protocol the Convention and the Protocol shall be read and interpreted together as one single instrument.

A Party to this Protocol shall have no duty to apply the provisions of this Protocol to Bills of Lading issued in a State which is a Party to the Convention but which is not a Party to this Protocol.

Article 12

Accession to this Protocol shall have the effect of accession to the Convention.

Article 13

(1) This Protocol shall come into force three months after the date of the deposit of ten instruments of ratification or accession, of which at least five shall have been deposited by States that have each a tonnage equal or superior to one million gross tons of tonnage.

(2) For each State which ratifies this Protocol or accedes thereto after the date of deposit of the instrument of ratification or accession determining the coming into force such as is stipulated in paragraph (1) of this Article, this Protocol shall come into force three months after the deposit of its instrument of ratification or accession.

Australia	16/07/1993(a)[2]
Belgium	6/09/1978(r)
Bermuda	1/11/1980(a)
British Antarctic Territories	20/10/1983(a)
Cayman Islands	20/10/1983(a)
Croatia	28/10/1998(a)
Denmark	20/11/1975(r)
Ecuador	23/03/1977(a)
Egypt	31/01/1983(r)
Falkland Islands	20/10/1983(a)
Finland	1/12/1984(r)
France	10/03/1977(r)
Georgia	20/02/1996(a)[3]
Germany	14/02/1979(a)
Gibraltar	22/09/1977(a)
Greece	23/03/1993(a)
Hong Kong SAR	1/11/1980(a)
Ireland	6/02/1997(a)
Isle of Man	1/10/1976(a)
Italy	22/08/1985(r)
Japan	1/03/1993(a)

---

[1] Source: Belgian Ministry of Foreign Affairs, Foreign Trade and Development Cooperation <www.diplobel.fgov.be/en/>.

[2] Carriage of Goods by Sea Act 1991 (Cwth), as amended by the Carriage of Goods by Sea Regulations 1998 (No 2).

[3] The Republic of Georgia has acceded to both the Hague–Visby Rules (on 20 February 1996) and the Hamburg Rules (on 21 March 1996).

Latvia	4/04/2002(a)
Lebanon	19/07/1975(a)
Lithuania	2/12/2003(a)
Mexico	20/05/1994(a)
Montserrat	20/10/1983(a)
Netherlands	26/04/1982(a)
New Zealand	20/12/1994(a)
Norway	19/03/1974(r)
Poland	12/02/1980(r)
Singapore	25/04/1972(a)
South Georgia	20/10/1983(a)
Spain	6/01/1982(a)
Sri Lanka	21/10/1981(a)
Sweden	9/12/1974(r)
Switzerland	11/12/1975(r)
Syrian Arab Republic	1/08/1974(a)
Tonga	13/06/1978(a)
United Kingdom	1/10/1976(r)
Virgin Islands	20/10/1983(a)

Protocol to Amend the International Convention for the Unification of Certain Rules Relating to Bills of Lading as modified by the Amending Protocol
[SDR Protocol]
Brussels, 21 December 1979[1]

[In force 14 February 1984]

Article VI

(1) This Protocol shall be ratified.

(2) Ratification of this Protocol by any State which is not a Party to the Convention shall have the effect of ratification of the Convention.

(3) The instruments of ratification shall be deposited with the Belgian Government.

Article VII

(1) States not referred to in Article V may accede to this Protocol.

(2) Accession to this Protocol shall have the effect of accession to the Convention.

(3) The instruments of accession shall be deposited with the Belgian Government.

Article VIII

(1) This Protocol shall come into force three months after the date of the deposit of five instruments of ratification or accession.

(2) For each State which ratifies this Protocol or accedes thereto after the fifth deposit, this Protocol shall come into force three months after the deposit of its instrument of ratification or accession.

Australia	30/11/1983(a)
Belgium	7/09/1983(r)
Croatia	28/10/1999(a)
Denmark	3/11/1983(a)
Finland	1/12/1984(r)
France	18/11/1986(r)
Greece	23/03/1993(a)
Italy	22/08/1985(r)
Japan	1/03/1993(r)
Latvia	4/04/2002(a)
Lithuania	2/12/2003(a)
Luxembourg	18/02/1991(a)
Mexico	20/05/1994(a)
Netherlands	18/02/1986(r)
New Zealand	20/12/1994(a)
Norway	1/12/1983(r)
Poland	6/07/1984(r)
Portugal	30/04/1982(r)
Russian Federation	29/04/1999(a)
Spain	14/05/1982(r)
Sweden	14/11/1983(r)
Switzerland	20/01/1988(r)
United Kingdom	2/03/1982(r)

[1] Source: Belgian Ministry of Foreign Affairs, Foreign Trade and Development Cooperation <www.diplobel.fgov.be/en/>.

United Nations Convention on the Carriage of Goods by Sea

[Hamburg Rules]

Hamburg, 31 March 1978[1]

[In force 1 November 1992]

Article 28

Signature, Ratification, Acceptance, Approval, Accession

1. This Convention is open for signature by all States until 30 April 1979 at the Headquarters of the United Nations, New York.
2. This Convention is subject to ratification, acceptance or approval by the signatory States.
3. After 30 April 1979, this Convention will be open for accession by all States which are not signatory States.
4. Instruments of ratification, acceptance, approval and accession are to be deposited with the Secretary-General of the United Nations.

Article 30

Entry into force

1. This Convention enters into force on the first day of the month following the expiration of one year from the date of deposit of the twentieth instrument of ratification, acceptance, approval or accession.
2. For each State which becomes a Contracting State to this Convention after the date of the deposit of the twentieth instrument of ratification, acceptance, approval or accession, this Convention enters into force on the first day of the month following the expiration of one year after the deposit of the appropriate instrument on behalf of that State.
3. Each Contracting State shall apply the provisions of this Convention to contracts of carriage by sea concluded on or after the date of the entry into force of this Convention in respect of that State.

Austria	29/07/1993(r)
Barbados	2/02/1981(a)
Botswana	16/02/1988(a)
Burkina Faso	14/08/1989(a)
Burundi	4/09/1998(a)
Cameroon	21/10/1993(a)
Chile	9/07/1982(r)
Czech Republic	23/06/1995(r)
Egypt	23/04/1979(r)
Gambia	7/02/1996(a)
Georgia	21/03/1996(a)
Guinea	23/01/1991(a)
Hungary	5/07/1984(r)
Jordan	10/05/2001(a)
Kenya	31/07/1989(a)
Lebanon	4/04/1983(a)
Lesotho	26/10/1989(a)
Liberia	16/09/2005(a)[2]

---

[1] In force from 1 November 1992. Source: <http://untreaty.un.org> (UN Treaty Collection).
[2] In force 1 October 2006.

Malawi	18/03/1991(a)
Morocco	12/06/1981(a)
Nigeria	7/11/1988(a)
Paraguay	19/07/2005(a)[3]
Romania	7/01/1982(a)
St Vincent & the Grenadines	12/09/2000(a)
Senegal	17/03/1986(a)
Sierra Leone	7/10/1988(a)
Syrian Arab Republic	6/10/2002(a)
Tanzania	24/07/1979(a)
Tunisia	15/09/1980(a)
Uganda	6/07/1979(a)
Zambia	7/10/1991(a)

[3] In force 1 August 2006.

INDEX